Nineteenth-Century Literature Criticism

Guide to Gale Literary Criticism Series

For criticism on	Consult these Gale series
Authors now living or who died after December 31, 1959	*CONTEMPORARY LITERARY CRITICISM (CLC)*
Authors who died between 1900 and 1959	*TWENTIETH-CENTURY LITERARY CRITICISM (TCLC)*
Authors who died between 1800 and 1899	*NINETEENTH-CENTURY LITERATURE CRITICISM (NCLC)*
Authors who died between 1400 and 1799	*LITERATURE CRITICISM FROM 1400 TO 1800 (LC)* *SHAKESPEAREAN CRITICISM (SC)*
Authors who died before 1400	*CLASSICAL AND MEDIEVAL LITERATURE CRITICISM (CMLC)*
Authors of books for children and young adults	*CHILDREN'S LITERATURE REVIEW (CLR)*
Dramatists	*DRAMA CRITICISM (DC)*
Poets	*POETRY CRITICISM (PC)*
Short story writers	*SHORT STORY CRITICISM (SSC)*
Black writers of the past two hundred years	*BLACK LITERATURE CRITICISM (BLC)*
Hispanic writers of the late nineteenth and twentieth centuries	*HISPANIC LITERATURE CRITICISM (HLC)*
Native North American writers and orators of the eighteenth, nineteenth, and twentieth centuries	*NATIVE NORTH AMERICAN LITERATURE (NNAL)*
Major authors from the Renaissance to the present	*WORLD LITERATURE CRITICISM, 1500 TO THE PRESENT (WLC)*

ISSN 0732-1864

Volume 81

Nineteenth-Century Literature Criticism

Excerpts from Criticism of the
Works of Novelists, Poets, Playwrights,
Short Story Writers, Philosophers, and Other
Creative Writers Who Died between 1800
and 1899, from the First Published Critical
Appraisals to Current Evaluations

Suzanne Dewsbury
Editor

GALE GROUP

Detroit
New York
San Francisco
London
Boston
Woodbridge, CT

This book is printed on acid-free paper that meets the minimum requirements of American National Standard for Information Sciences—Permanence Paper for Printed Library Materials, ANSI Z39.48-1984.

Library of Congress Catalog Card Number 84-643008
ISBN 0-7876-3152-3
ISSN 0732-1864
Printed in the United States of America

10 9 8 7 6 5 4 3 2 1

Contents

Preface vii

Acknowledgments xi

Preface

Since its inception in 1981, *Nineteenth-Century Literature Criticism* has been a valuable resource for students and librarians seeking critical commentary on writers of this transitional period in world history. Designated an "Outstanding Reference Source" by the American Library Association with the publication of its first volume, *NCLC* has since been purchased by over 6,000 school, public, and university libraries. The series has covered more than 300 authors representing 29 nationalities and over 17,000 titles. No other reference source has surveyed the critical reaction to nineteenth-century authors and literature as thoroughly as *NCLC*.

Scope of the Series

NCLC is designed to introduce students and advanced readers to the authors of the nineteenth century, and to the most significant interpretations of these authors' works. The great poets, novelists, short story writers, playwrights, and philosophers of this period are frequently studied in high school and college literature courses. By organizing and reprinting commentary written on these authors, *NCLC* helps students develop valuable insight into literary history, promotes a better understanding of the texts, and sparks ideas for papers and assignments. Each entry in *NCLC* presents a comprehensive survey of an author's career or an individual work of literature and provides the user with a multiplicity of interpretations and assessments. Such variety allows students to pursue their own interests; furthermore, it fosters an awareness that literature is dynamic and responsive to many different opinions.

Every fourth volume of *NCLC* is devoted to literary topics that cannot be covered under the author approach used in the rest of the series. Such topics include literary movements, prominent themes in nineteenth-century literature, literary reaction to political and historical events, significant eras in literary history, prominent literary anniversaries, and the literatures of cultures that are often overlooked by English-speaking readers.

NCLC continues the survey of criticism of world literature begun by Gale's *Contemporary Literary Criticism (CLC)* and *Twentieth-Century Literary Criticism (TCLC),* both of which excerpt and reprint commentary on authors of the twentieth century. For additional information about *TCLC, CLC,* and Gale's other criticism series, users should consult the Guide to Gale Literary Criticism Series preceding the title page in this volume.

Coverage

Each volume of *NCLC* is carefully compiled to present:

- criticism of authors, or literary topics, representing a variety of genres and nationalities
- both major and lesser-known writers and literary works of the period
- 4-8 authors or 4-6 topics per volume
- individual entries that survey critical response to an author's work or a topic in literary history, including early criticism to reflect initial reactions, later criticism to represent any rise or decline in reputation, and current retrospective analyses.

Organization

An author entry consists of the following elements: author heading, biographical and critical introduction, list of principal works, excerpts of criticism (each preceded by a bibliographic citation and an annotation), and a bibliography of further reading.

- The **Author Heading** consists of the name under which the author most commonly wrote, followed by birth and death dates. If an author wrote consistently under a pseudonym, the pseudonym will be listed in the author heading and the real name given in parentheses on the first line of the biographical and critical introduction. Also located at the beginning of the introduction to the author entry are any name variations under which an author wrote, including transliterated forms for an author whose language uses a nonroman alphabet.

- The **Biographical and Critical Introduction** outlines the author's life and career, as well as the critical issues surrounding his or her work. References are provided to past volumes of *NCLC* in which further information about the author may be found.

- Most *NCLC* entries include a **Portrait** of the author. Many entries also contain reproductions of materials pertinent to an author's career, including manuscript pages, title pages, dust jackets, letters, and drawings, as well as photographs of important people, places, and events in an author's life.

- The list of **Principal Works** is chronological by date of first publication and identifies the genre of each work. In the case of foreign authors with both foreign-language publications and English translations, the English-language version is given in brackets. Unless otherwise indicated, dramas are dated by first performance, not first publication.

- **Criticism** in each author entry is arranged chronologically to provide a perspective on changes in critical evaluation over the years. All titles of works by the author featured in the entry are printed in boldface type to enable the user to easily locate discussion of particular works. Also for purposes of easier identification, the critic's name and the publication date of the essay are given at the beginning of each piece of criticism. Unsigned criticism is preceded by the title of the journal in which it appeared. Publication information (such as publisher names and book prices) and some parenthetical numerical references (such as page and line references to specific editions of works) have been deleted at the editors' discretion to provide smoother reading of the text. Footnotes that appear with previously published pieces of criticism are reprinted at the end of each essay or excerpt. In the case of excerpted criticism, only those footnotes that pertain to the excerpted text are included.

- A complete **Bibliographic Citation** provides original publication information for each piece of criticism.

- Critical excerpts are prefaced by **Annotations** providing the reader with a summary of the critical intent of the piece. Also included, when appropriate, is information about the critic's reputation, individual approach to literary criticism, and particular expertise in an author's works, as well as information about the relative importance of the critical excerpt. In some cases, the annotations cross-reference excerpts by critics who discuss each other's commentary.

- An annotated list of **Further Reading** appearing at the end of each entry suggests secondary sources on the author. In some cases it includes essays for which the editors could not obtain reprint rights.

Cumulative Indexes

- Each volume of *NCLC* contains a cumulative **Author Index** listing all authors who have appeared in Gale's Literary Criticism Series, along with cross-references to such biographical series as *Contemporary Authors* and *Dictionary of Literary Biography*. Useful for locating authors within the various series, this index is particularly valuable for those authors who are identified with a certain period but who, because of their death dates, are placed in another, or for those authors whose careers span two periods. For example, Fyodor Dostoevsky is found in *NCLC*, yet Leo Tolstoy, another major nineteenth-century Russian novelist, is found in *TCLC* because he died after 1899.

- Each *NCLC* volume includes a cumulative **Nationality Index** which lists all authors who have appeared in *NCLC*, arranged alphabetically under their respective nationalities.

- Each new volume in Gale's Literary Criticism Series includes a cumulative **Topic Index**, which lists all literary topics treated in *NCLC, TCLC, LC 1400-1800*, and the *CLC* Yearbook.

- Each new volume of *NCLC*, with the exception of the Topics volumes, contains a **Title Index** listing the titles of all literary works discussed in the volume. In response to numerous suggestions from librarians, Gale has also produced a **Special Paperbound Edition** of the *NCLC* title index. This annual cumulation lists all titles discussed in the series since its inception. Additional copies of the index are available on request. Librarians and patrons have welcomed this separate index: it saves shelf space, is easy to use, and is recyclable upon receipt of the following year's cumulation. Titles discussed in the Topics volume entries are not included in the *NCLC* cumulative index.

Citing *Nineteenth-Century Literature Criticism*

When writing papers, students who quote directly from any volume in Gale's Literary Criticism Series may use the following general forms to footnote reprinted criticism. The first example pertains to material drawn from periodicals, the second to material reprinted from books:

[1]Kim McQuaid, "William Apes, Pequot: An Indian Reformer in the Jackson Era," *The New England Quarterly*, 50 (December 1977), 605-25; excerpted and reprinted in *Nineteenth-Century Literature Criticism,* Vol. 73, ed. Janet Witalec (Farmington Hills, Mich.: The Gale Group, 1999), pp. 3-4.

[2]Richard Harter Fogle, *The Imagery of Keats and Shelley: A Comparative Study* (Archon Books, 1949); excerpted and reprinted in *Nineteenth-Century Literary Criticism,* Vol. 73, ed. Janet Witalec (Farmington Hills, Mich.: The Gale Group, 1999), pp. 157-69.

Suggestions Are Welcome

In response to suggestions, several features have been added to *NCLC* since the series began, including annotations to excerpted criticism, a cumulative index to authors in all Gale literary criticism series, entries devoted to criticism on a single work by a major author, more illustrations, and a title index listing all literary works discussed in the series.

Readers who wish to suggest authors, single works, or topics to appear in future volumes, or who have other suggestions, are cordially invited to write: The Editors, *Nineteenth-Century Literature Criticism*, The Gale Group, 27500 Drake Rd., Farmington Hills, MI 48331-3535; call toll-free at 1-800-347-GALE.

Acknowledgments

The editors wish to thank the copyright holders of the excerpted criticism included in this volume and the permissions managers of many book and magazine publishing companies for assisting us in securing reproduction rights. We are also grateful to the staffs of the Detroit Public Library, the Library of Congress, the University of Detroit Mercy Library, Wayne State University Purdy/Kresge Library Complex, and the University of Michigan Libraries for making their resources available to us. Following is a list of the copyright holders who have granted us permission to reproduce material in this volume of *NCLC*. Every effort has been made to trace copyright, but if omissions have been made, please let us know.

COPYRIGHTED MATERIALS IN *NCLC*, VOLUME 81, WERE REPRODUCED FROM THE FOLLOWING PERIODICALS:

American Transcendental Quarterly, v. 2, March, 1988. Copyright 1988 by Kenneth Walter Cameron. Reproduced by permission.—*Books at Iowa*, n. 45, November, 1986. Copyright © 1986 The University of Iowa. Reproduced by permission.—*Bucknell Review*, v. 28, 1983. Copyright © Bucknell Review 1983. Reproduced by permission.—*Eighteenth-Century Fiction*, v. 4, January, 1992. Reproduced by permission.—*ELH*, v. 59, Summer, 1992. Copyright © 1992 by The Johns Hopkins University Press. All rights reserved. Reproduced by permission.—*The Germanic Review*, v. LII, January, 1977. Copyright © 1977 Helen Dwight Reid Educational Foundation. Reproduced with permission of the Helen Dwight Reid Educational Foundation, published by Heldref Publications, 1319 18th Street, NW, Washington, DC 20036-1802.—*Philological Quarterly*, v. 62, Spring, 1983 for "The 'Twilight of Probability': Uncertainty and Hope" by Claudia L. Johnson; v. 69, Fall, 1990 for "Jane Austen's 'Sense and Sensibility': The Politics of Point of View" by Barbara M. Benedict. Copyright © 1983, 1990 by The University of Iowa. Reproduced by permission of the respective authors.—*Renascence: Essays on Values in Literature*, v. XXXV, Summer, 1983. © copyright, 1983, Marquette University Press. Reproduced by permission.—*Seminar: A Journal of Germanic Studies*, v. III, June, 1972; v. X, November, 1974; v. XIV, November, 1978. © The Canadian Association of University Teachers of German 1972, 1974, 1978. All reproduced by permission of the publisher.—*South Atlantic Review*, v. 59, January, 1994. Copyright © 1994 by the South Atlantic Modern Language Association. Reproduced by permission.—*Symposium*, v. XXXII, Summer, 1978. Copyright © 1978 Helen Dwight Reid Educational Foundation. Reproduced with permission of the Helen Dwight Reid Educational Foundation, published by Heldref Publications, 1319 18th Street, NW, Washington, DC 20036-1802.—*Tulsa Studies in Women's Literature*, v. 7, Fall, 1988. © 1988, The University of Tulsa. Reproduced by permission.—*Women & Literature*, v. 3, 1983. Copyright © 1983 by Janet M. Todd. Reproduced by permission of Holmes & Meier.

COPYRIGHTED MATERIAL IN *NCLC*, VOLUME 81, WERE REPRODUCED FROM THE FOLLOWING BOOKS:

Brissenden, R. F. From "The Task of Telling Lies: Candor and Deception in 'Sense and Sensibility' " in *Greene Centennial Studies*. Edited by Paul J. Korshiin and Robert R. Allen. University Press of Virginia, 1984. Copyright © 1984 by the Rector and Visitors of the University of Virginia. Reproduced by permission.—Burkhard, Marianne. From *Conrad Ferdinand Meyer*. G. K. Hall & Company, 1978. Copyright © 1978 by G. K. Hall & Co. All rights reserved. Reproduced by permission

Physical Difference: Discourses of Disability. The University of Michigan Press, 1997. Copyright © by the University of Michigan 1997. All rights reserved.

Sense and Sensibility

Jane Austen

The following entry presents criticism of Austen's novel *Sense and Sensibility* (1811). For discussion of Austen's complete career, see *NCLC,* Volume 1; for discussion of the novel *Pride and Prejudice*, see *NCLC,* Volume 13; for discussion of the novel *Emma*, see *NCLC,* Volume 19; for discussion of the novel *Persuasion*, see *NCLC,* Volume 33; and for discussion of the novel *Northanger Abbey*, see *NCLC*, Volume 51.

INTRODUCTION

Sense and Sensibility was Jane Austen's first published novel. Although similar to her other novels in plot, tone, and type of characters, *Sense and Sensibility* differs from the others in its representation of the courtship of two sisters; rather than one heroine, there are two. Elinor, the subdued, quiet one, and Marianne, the emotional, outgoing one, are contrasting character types Austen would use alternately in later novels. In addition, *Sense and Sensibility* brings to the fore issues of property, patronage, and gender that were prominent in the years following the French Revolution. Like Austen's other novels, *Sense and Sensibility* is regarded as a classic and is still widely read.

Austen began writing the story in 1795 at the age of twenty-one. At that time it was probably in epistolary form, and was titled "Elinor and Marianne." Austen began to revise it two years later in third-person narrative form, and in 1809 and 1810 worked the story into what is now known as *Sense and Sensibility*.

After Austen finished the novel, one of her brothers served as an intermediary between her and her publisher, Thomas Egerton. Expecting that the book would cost more than it returned, Austen had saved some money to pay for the printing of the book. She retained copyright and the publisher received a commission for distributing the book. *Sense and Sensibility* was published in the fall of 1811, the title page stating only that the novel was "By A Lady." Because "authoresses" at that time were regarded with hostility and "proper" women did not appear as public characters, Austen insisted on anonymity. The first edition sold out in less than two years. Austen's next publication would be *Pride and Prejudice* (1813), again a revision of an earlier work and also well received. Although this subsequent novel was also published anonymously, Austen's authorship became known publicly.

Plot and Major Characters

Sense and Sensibility begins with the widowed Mrs. Dashwood and her three daughters—Elinor, Marianne, and Margaret—being ousted from their home when the new owner, John Dashwood and his wife, Fanny, move in. John Dashwood, Mr. Dashwood's eldest son from his first marriage, inherits his father's entire estate, under the laws of primogeniture. The Dashwood women are given a home, Barton Cottage, on the estate of Sir John Middleton, a distant relative. One visitor to the area, Colonel Brandon, is interested romantically in Marianne, but he does not fit her ideal of a romantic hero and she ignores him. However, another visitor to the area, Willoughby, matches her expectations and she falls in love with him. Meanwhile, Elinor becomes disappointed that the man in whom she is interested, Edward Ferrars (Fanny Dashwood's brother, a young clergyman), does not call on her as she had expected. Other guests at the Middletons' include the Palmers and the Misses Steele (who, like the Dashwood sisters, are dependent upon others to avoid slipping from gentility to poverty), the younger of whom, Lucy, reveals to Elinor that she is secretly engaged to Edward Ferrars. Although bitterly disappointed, Elinor promises to keep the secret and bears this news with fortitude. In London, Marianne discovers that Willoughby is going to marry for money and reject her entirely. When Lucy Steele reveals her secret engagement to Edward, he is disinherited in favor of his younger brother, Robert. Returning to Barton, Marianne falls ill at the Palmers' estate. Willoughby arrives, concerned about Marianne, and confesses to Elinor that he loves Marianne and must now suffer an unhappy marriage. At Barton, Marianne recovers and Elinor learns that Edward has been freed from his engagement. Upon learning of Edward's disinheritance, Lucy turns to his brother, Robert, as the better prospect. Edward, having accepted Colonel Brandon's offer of a position, proposes to Elinor, and Marianne comes to see the virtues of the colonel and marries him.

Major Themes

Critics agree that *Sense and Sensibility* reflects Austen's own experience in terms of her role as a woman in her family and in post-Revolutionary society. Austen's situation as a young woman mirrored that of the Dashwood sisters at the outset of the novel: after her father's death, Austen, along with her mother and sister, were forced to rely on the benevolence of relatives (in Austen's case, her brothers) for financial support. Although the novel is not autobiographical, Austen understood the position of women who were deprived of the means to earn an income but needed to maintain their social standing. This predicament was also reflected in the Steele sisters, who were without parents and were wards of their uncle, but who relied on coquetry and intrigue (considered vulgar in post-Revolutionary society) for social advancement. The worst of court culture (artificial politeness and social games) is demonstrated through the Dashwoods (John and Fanny) and old Mrs. Ferrars.

All of this accords with the post-Revolutionary society in which Austen lived. "Sensibility," the indulgence of personal absolutes regardless of social conventions and laws, was viewed widely as a major source of Revolutionary transgression; "sense" was often opposed to Revolutionary theory. The triumph of sense over sensibility in the novel establishes the value of conventional feminine virtues, a position also espoused by other writers in the aftermath of the Revolution. Elinor and Marianne's "sense" triumphs and suffering brings happiness in the end.

Critical Reception

Much critical commentary on *Sense and Sensibility* deals with the terms referred to in the title—"sense" versus "sensibility." Some critics have concluded that Austen advocated a woman's possessing "sense," not

"sensibility," while others have argued that Austen advocated possessing neither one nor the other, but a balance between the two. It is not surprising that a good deal of criticism on the novel revolved around comparisons of one type or another which harken back to the one Austen presents to readers in the title. Critics compare Elinor and Marianne, Willoughby and Edward Ferrars, and lesser characters such as Fanny Dashwood and Lucy Steele. One critic aligns the Dashwood sisters and Willoughby against the rest of the novel's characters. Commenting on other comparisons or "pairings," other critics note that Austen negotiates between actual and hypothetical language; private desire and public voice; epistolary and objective narration.

In addition, several critics have commented on the novel's position within feminist and gender studies. One critic finds the novel the most antifeminist of all Austen's books in its consideration of female authority and power, while another posits that feminist criticism is vital to evaluating *Sense and Sensibility* for the way in which it offers new ways of valuing the female experience. Yet another critic argues that Austen has created, through the character of Elinor, a female intellectual, signaling Austen's attempt to reshape ideas about gender through her novel.

Criticism

Marilyn Butler (essay date 1975)

SOURCE: *"Sense and Sensibility,"* in *Jane Austen and the War of Ideas,* Clarendon Press, 1987, pp. 182-237.

[*In the following essay, originally published in 1975, Butler discusses Austen's use of didactic comparison in* Sense and Sensibility, *focusing primarily on the Dashwood sisters, Willoughby, and Edward Ferrars.*]

Of the novels Jane Austen completed, ***Sense and Sensibility*** appears to be the earliest in conception. An uncertain family tradition suggests that its original letter-version, 'Elinor and Marianne', may have been written in 1795:[1] before the publication of Mrs. West's similar *Gossip's Story,* and in the same year as Maria Edgeworth's *Letters of Julia and Caroline.* The didactic novel which compares the beliefs and conduct of two protagonists—with the object of finding one invariably right and the other invariably wrong—seems to have been particularly fashionable during the years 1795-6. Most novelists, even the most purposeful, afterwards abandon it for a format using a single protagonist, whose experiences can be handled more flexibly and with much less repetition.[2] On the whole, therefore, all Jane Austen's other novels are more sophisticated in conception, and they are capable of more interesting treatment of the central character in relation to her world. But there is a caveat. Catherine in **Northanger Abbey** is dealt with, as we have seen, in an inhibited manner. A rather mindless character, of somewhat undefined good principles, she matures in a curiously oblique process that the reader does not quite witness. The format of the contrast-novel, with all its drawbacks, at least obliges Jane Austen to chart the mental processes of her heroines directly, and to locate the drama in their minds.

By its very nature **Sense and Sensibility** is unremittingly didactic. All the novelists who choose the contrast format do so in order to make an explicit ideological point. Essentially they are taking part in the old argument between 'nature' and 'nurture': which is the more virtuous man, the sophisticated, or schooled individual, or the natural one? Obviously there is a total division on the issue between the type of traditional Christian who takes a gloomy view of man's unredeemed nature, and the various schools of eighteenth-century optimists, whether Christian or not. Although a Catholic, Mrs. Inchbald is also a progressive: of the two brothers in her *Nature and Art,* the sophisticated one stands for greed, self-seeking, worldly corruption, the 'natural' one for primal simplicity, honesty, sympathy, and innate virtue.[3] Maria Edgeworth, although in a sense favouring 'nurture' in her *Letters of Julia and Caroline,* does so on idiosyncratic terms which take her out of rancorous current controversy. But Mrs. West, in preferring her disciplined, self-denying Louisa to her self-indulgent Marianne, is entirely relevant to the contemporary issue, and entirely conservative. So, too, is Jane Austen.[4]

Jane Austen conscientiously maintains the principle of a didactic comparison. Her novel advances on the assumption that what happens to one of the central characters must also happen to the other; at every turn the reader cannot avoid the appropriate conclusion. The motif of the first volume is the attitude of each girl towards the man she hopes to marry. When the novel opens Elinor already knows Edward Ferrars. Her views about him are developed in conversation with Mrs. Dashwood, and the reader is also given Marianne's rather qualified opinion. When Edward and Elinor have to separate, Mrs. Dashwood invites him to visit them at Barton, but Edward seems reluctant. Thereafter Elinor's endurance of uncertainty about Edward's feelings becomes a factor in her character, and in our response to her.

Shortly after the family's arrival at Barton Cottage, Marianne's lover, Willoughby, enters the novel. His dramatic arrival is in keeping with his more flamboyant character; his appearance, too, is contrasted with Edward's; but the manner in which the sequence of his courtship is developed shows Jane Austen's concern to enforce a similarity of situation in order to bring out a dissimilarity of character. Again, Mrs. Dashwood gives

her enthusiastic approval, while the other sister, in this case Elinor, expresses her reservations. When Willoughby leaves, Mrs. Dashwood once more issues her invitation, which is inexplicably not accepted, and Marianne, like Elinor, is left to a period of loneliness and anxiety.

When in the second volume the two heroines go to London they are placed, again, in a similar predicament. Both expect to meet the loved one there, both are obliged uneasily to wait; cards are left by each of the young men; each is lost, or seems lost, to a rival woman. In all the embarrassments and worries of the London visit, the reader's developing knowledge of the sisters is based on a substructure which demands that he adjudicate between them. And they leave London, as they entered it, still similarly placed, travelling towards the county, Somerset, where each believes her lover to be setting up house with his bride.

The parallels can be taken further, for example to the influence first of upbringing, later of idleness, on the characters of the two young men. The entire action is organized to represent Elinor and Marianne in terms of rival value-systems, which are seen directing their behaviour in the most crucial choices of their lives. It is an arrangement which necessarily directs the reader's attention not towards what they experience, but towards how they cope with experience, away from the experiential to the ethical.

In the two contrasted opening sequences the emphasis is on each girl's scale of values as she applies it to both young men. Edward Ferrars's attractions are not external. 'Edward Ferrars was not recommended to their good opinion by any peculiar graces of person or address. He was not handsome, and his manners required intimacy to make them pleasing.'[5] But even Marianne, who has reservations about Edward as a lover, has 'the highest opinion in the world of his goodness and sense. I think him everything that is worthy and aimiable.'[6] For Elinor, this is commendation so high that she does not know what more could be said. As for herself, she admits that she 'greatly esteems' and 'likes' him: words which define the state of her understanding rather than her feelings, and, as such, seem to Marianne inappropriate.

But Marianne hesitates because in addition to Edward's lack of physical grace (what we might call physical attractiveness), he does not act like a lover with Elinor. In Marianne's language, he wants fire and spirit. His passionless temperament is further illustrated in his attitude to literature and to matters of 'taste' generally. When set by Marianne to read Cowper, he was, as she complains to her mother, tame and spiritless:

> 'To hear those beautiful lines which have frequently almost driven me wild, pronounced with such impenetrable coldness, such dreadful indifference!——'

'He would certainly have done more justice to simple and elegant prose. I thought so at the time; but you *would* give him Cowper.'

'Nay, Mama, if he is not to be animated by Cowper!—but we must allow for difference of taste. Elinor has not my feelings, and therefore she may overlook it, and be happy with him. But it would have broke *my* heart had I loved him, to hear him read with so little sensibility!'[7]

Marianne's objection is that Edward does not give free rein to the intuitive side of his nature. She equates lack of 'taste' with lack of response, an inability to enter subjectively into the emotions of a writer, or to attempt *rapport* with the spirit of a landscape. Again, as in *Northanger Abbey,* the reader is certainly not supposed to draw a moral distinction between characters concerned with literature, and characters concerned with life: for Elinor likes books and drawing, and Edward, who has views about both, and about landscape too, would do justice to 'simple and elegant prose'. But he, like Elinor, approaches the arts differently from Marianne. He would be likely to concern himself more than she with the intellectual content; when he looks at a landscape, he considers questions of utility—such as whether the terrain would be good for farming—and practicality—such as whether a lane would be too muddy for walking.

Edward's tastes can be considered aesthetically, as Augustan and thus in terms of contemporary landscape art old-fashioned: he has more in common with Pope than would please Marianne. But, and this is more to the novel's purposes, they are also the tastes of a self-effacing man, who likes to apply objective criteria, independent of his own prejudices and the limitations of his knowledge. His objective approach to art resembles Elinor's way of evaluating him. She knows enough of his background to see beyond the defects of his manner to the enduring qualities of his mind and spirit, his 'sense' and 'goodness', and both these words imply that Edward's virtues are those of a given code of value, namely the Christian. Edward's character, Edward's aesthetic opinions, and Elinor's method of assessing Edward, all have this much in common—that they are based on prescribed standards, not on subjective impulse.

With all this Marianne's choice of Willoughby is carefully compared. His entrance, like that of the 'preserver' of the heroine in a romantic novel, at once gives him a superficial glamour. He is 'uncommonly handsome' and his manner 'frank and graceful', so that not merely Marianne, but Mrs. Dashwood and Elinor,[8] are struck with admiration on his first appearance. His beauty encourages an intuitive response from Marianne, and receives it. She reacts to Willoughby with the same whole-hearteded impulsiveness with which she reacts to

books, and indeed before long she is reacting to books and Willoughby together, in a style that suggests all feeling, little or no intellectual detachment:

The same books, the same passages were idolized by each—or, if any difference appeared, any objection arose, it lasted no longer than till the force of her arguments and the brightness of her eyes could be displayed. He acquiesced in all her decisions, caught all her enthusiasm; and long before his visit concluded, they conversed with the freedom of a long-established acquaintance.[9]

When Elinor teases Marianne for running so recklessly through the beauties of Cowper and Scott, Jane Austen clearly means no criticism of two poets who were among her own favourites. But she does mean to criticize, through Elinor, the way Willoughby and Marianne read, and to show that, when they abandon themselves to their reading together, the result is grossly self-indulgent. Everything they do follows the same pattern of shared selfishness. Wholly absorbed in one another and in their exclusive pursuits, they rudely ignore the rest of their social circle, and, on the day of the cancelled outing, drive off together to Allerton in Willoughby's phaeton. As it happens, Sir John Middleton and Mrs. Jennings cheerfully tolerate the lovers. They in their turn are less tolerant; indeed, their self-sufficiency has an unattractive arrogance about it, which is displayed when they mount their unreasonable joint attack on Colonel Brandon. Willoughby's irrationality is as apparent here—'he has threatened me with rain when I wanted it to be fine'[10]—as it is later, when he begs that no lateration be made to Barton Cottage because he has pleasant associations with it as it is.[11] That Marianne has gone far along the same subjective path is demonstrated after her visit to Allerton. Elinor argues that she has been guilty of serious impropriety in going there in Mrs. Smith's absence. Marianne relies on her usual criterion, intuition: '"If there had been any real impropriety in what I did, I should have been sensible of it at the time, for we always know when we are acting wrong, and with such a conviction I could have had no pleasure."'[12]

She believes in the innate moral sense; and, since man is naturally good, his actions when he acts on impulse are likely to be good also. Just as Marianne has no doubts about herself, so she can have none about her *alter ego,* Willoughby. Neither can Mrs. Dashwood, who, proceeding according to the same intuitional method as her second daughter, is wholly convinced of the goodness of Willoughby. When Elinor tries to argue with her, and to check instinct with the objective test of Willoughby's behaviour, her mother protests. She rightly sees that a broader question is at issue: Elinor's sense (stemming from the Christian tradition that man's nature is fallible) has come into conflict with the sentimentalist's tendency to idealize human nature. From Elinor's caution, Mrs. Dashwood draws a universal inference. 'You had rather take evil upon credit than good.'[13]

So far, then, the issue between the two contrasted sisters is presented according to the view of the na- ture-nurture dichotomy usually adopted by conserva- tives. The contrast, as always, is between two modes of perception. On the one hand, Marianne's way is subjective, intuitive, implying confidence in the natu- ral goodness of human nature when untrammelled by convention. Her view is corrected by the more cau- tious orthodoxy of Elinor, who mistrusts her own desires, and requires even her reason to seek the sup- port of objective evidence.

It is in keeping with Elinor's objectivity (and also typi- cal of the feminine variant of the anti-jacobin novel) that she should advocate a doctrine of civility in oppo- sition to Marianne's individualism. Elinor restrains her own sorrow in order to shield her mother and sister. By her politeness to Mrs. Jennings she steadily makes up what Marianne has carelessly omitted. She respects Colonel Brandon for his activity in helping his friends long before Mrs. Dashwood and Marianne have seen his virtues. Civility is a favourite anti-jacobin theme, which does not appear in *Northanger Abbey,* although it is present in Jane Austen's later novels. Its objec- tive correlative, the sketch given in *Sense and Sen- sibility* of society at large, is impoverished compared with the solid worlds of *Mansfield Park, Emma,* and *Persuasion:* the Middletons and Colonel Brandon, even supported by Mrs. Jennings, hardly stand in for a whole community. Yet this is a judgement arrived at by a comparison with Jane Austen's later work. If *Sense and Sensibility* is compared with other novels of the same genre, and originating at the same time, it can be seen to move in innumerable small ways towards fullness and naturalness. A conception of ci- vility illustrated by gratitude to Mrs. Jennings is more natural, for example, than portraying a similar con- cept in terms of prayers beside a dying father, or fidelity to the death-bed advice of an aunt.[14]

In fact, granted the rigidity imposed by the form, the second half of *Sense and Sensibility* is remarkably natural, flexible, and inventive. Both the sisters are presented as plausible individuals as well as profes- sors of two opposing creeds. Another contemporary novelist—Mrs. West, Mrs. Hamilton, or the young Maria Edgeworth—would almost certainly have had Marianne seduced and killed off, after the errors of which she has been guilty. For during the first half of the novel Marianne has stood for a doctrine of com- placency and self-sufficiency which Jane Austen as a Christian deplored:

> Teach us to understand the sinfulness of our own hearts, and bring to our knowledge every fault of

temper and every evil habit in which we have indulged to the discomfort of our fellow-creatures, and the danger of our own souls. . . . Incline us to ask our hearts these questions oh! God, and save us from deceiving ourselves by pride or vanity. . . .

> Incline us oh God! to think humbly of ourselves, to be severe only in the examination of our own conduct, to consider our fellow-creatures with kindness, and to judge of all they say and do with that charity which we would desire from them ourselves.[15]

After Allerton, Marianne failed to examine her own conduct at all. She had none of the Christian's under- standing of the sinfulness of her own heart; and she showed a notable lack of Christian charity towards Colonel Brandon, Mrs. Jennings, and the Middletons. Elinor alone had exercised the self-examination pre- scribed for the Christian, by questioning the state of her heart in relation to Edward, and, even more, her com- plex and disagreeable feelings about Lucy. Elinor never had the same certainty that Edward loved her which Marianne always felt about Willoughby. 'She was far from depending on that result of his preference of her, which her mother and sister still considered as certain.'[16]

The most interesting feature of the character of Elinor, and a real technical achievement of *Sense and Sen- sibility,* is that this crucial process of Christian self- examination is realized in literary terms. Elinor is the first character in an Austen novel consistently to reveal her inner life. The narrative mode of *Sense and Sen- sibility* is the first sustained example of 'free indirect speech', for the entire action is refracted through Elin- or's consciousness as *Northanger Abbey* could not be through the simple-minded Catherine's. Other techni- cal changes necessarily follow. Dialogue is far less important in *Sense and Sensibility,* since the heroine is not so much in doubt about the nature of external truth, as concerned with the knowledge of herself, her passions, and her duty. Judging by the narrative mode alone, *Sense and Sensibility* is, like *Mansfield Park* after it, an introspective novel. And yet it is clearly important to recognize that both are introspective only within closely defined limits. The inner life led by Elinor, and later by Fanny, is the dominant medium of the novel, but it is entirely distinct from the irrational and emotional states which the post-Romantic reader thinks of as 'consciousness'.

Technically, as well as intellectually, Elinor's scrupu- lous inner life has great importance in the novel, and Jane Austen brings it out by giving similar qualities to the two male characters who approach a moral ideal. Edward Ferrars and Colonel Brandon have the same wary scepticism about themselves. Rather to the detri- ment of their vitality, Jane Austen's characteristic word for both of them is 'diffident'. Diffidence helps to explain Edward's unwillingness to expatiate on matters of taste; and 'the epicurism, selfishness and conceit' of Mr. Palmer are contrasted with Edward's 'generous temper, simple tastes and diffident feelings'.[17] Robert Ferrar's complacent comparison of himself with his brother Edward enforces a similar point.[18] And diffidence, especially in relation to Marianne, is also the characteristic of Colonel Brandon as a lover.[19]

But it is Elinor alone who can be seen living through the moments of self-examination that are evidently typical of both men. The most interesting sequence in which she is shown doubting herself occurs after she has heard Willoughby's confession. Many modern critics interpret this passage as evidence that Jane Austen is qualifying her own case, in order to arrive at a compromise solution somewhere between 'Sense' and 'Sensibility'. According to Mr. Moler, for example, Elinor feels after she has heard Willoughby that her own 'Sense' has been inadequate: 'Elinor's rationality causes her to reach a less accurate estimate of Willoughby than Marianne and Mrs. Dashwood reach with their Sensibility.'[20]

Such interpretations are interesting as evidence of the difficulty the twentieth-century reader has with the notion of an objective morality. What happens in this episode is surely that Elinor is shaken by her feelings, for she finds both that she pities Willoughby and that she has a renewed sense of his 'grace', or personal attractiveness. Her judgment is assailed by involuntary sympathy: part of her wants to excuse his injuries to Marianne and Miss Smith. Yet the fact that Willoughby was tempted—by the two young women on the one hand, and by an education in worldliness on the other—does not in fact absolve the adult man, or not, at least, if one employs the objective ethical code rather than the relativist subjective one. The progressive supposedly sees the evil in individual men as social conditioning, the operation of impersonal forces which the individual cannot help. Elinor now considers Willoughby from this point of view—which is, of course, his own—and she finds it impossible to absolve him. 'Extravagance and vanity had made him coldhearted and selfish.'[21] This is not Jane Austen qualifying Elinor's sense with a dash of Marianne's sensibility. On the contrary, she shows Elinor's judgement reasserting itself, with some difficulty, after a most effective and deeply felt appeal has been made to her sympathies:

> . . . Willoughby, in spite of all his faults, excited a degree of commiseration for the sufferings produced by them, which made her think of him as now separated for ever from her family with a tenderness, a regret, rather in proportion, as she soon acknowledged within herself—to his wishes than to his merits. She felt that his influence over her mind was heightened by circumstances which ought not in reason to have weight; by that person of uncommon attraction, that open, affectionate and lively manner which it was no merit to possess; and

> by that still ardent love for Marianne, which it was not even innocent to indulge. But she felt that it was so long, long before she could feel his influence less.[22]

It is easy to mistake Elinor's sense for coldness. She is intended to be quite as loving and quite as accessible to 'feeling' as Marianne. The difference between them is one of ideology—Marianne optimistic, intuitive, unself-critical, and Elinor far more sceptical, always ready to study the evidence, to reopen a question, to doubt her own prior judgements. She can be ready to revise her opinion of Willoughby. She can admit her mistakes, as she does of her wrong estimate of Marianne's illness.[23] The point about both episodes is that Elinor was never intended to be infallible, but to typify an active, struggling Christian in a difficult world. Indeed, Jane Austen clearly argues that we do not find the right path through the cold, static correctness of a Lady Middleton, but through a struggle waged daily with our natural predisposition to err.

It is the role of Marianne Dashwood, who begins with the wrong ideology, to learn the right one. After her illness she applies her naturally strong feelings to objects outside herself, and her intelligence to thorough self-criticism in the Christian spirit. In what for her is the crisis of the book, her confession of her errors to Elinor,[24] Marianne resembles Jane Austen's other heroines Catherine, Elizabeth, and Emma, all of whom arrive at the same realization that (in the words of Jane Austen's prayer) 'pride' and 'vanity' have blinded them in relation both to themselves and to external reality.

It is quite false to assume that merely because Marianne is treated with relative gentleness, Jane Austen has no more than a qualified belief in the evils of sensibility. She spares Marianne, the individual, in order to have her recant from sensibility, the system. Even this is possible only because Marianne, with her naturally affectionate disposition and her intelligence, is never from the start a typical adherent of the doctrine of self: youth and impetuosity for a time blinded her, so that she acted against the real grain of her nature.[25] Because Marianne is not representative, other characters are needed, especially in the second half of the novel, to show the system of self in full-blooded action. Jane Austen provides them in the group of characters who fawn upon and virtually worship that false idol compounded of materialism, status-seeking and self-interest, Mrs. Ferrars.

The leading characters who take over from Marianne the role of illustrating what worship of the self really means are Lucy Steele and Fanny Dashwood. It is clear, of course, that neither Lucy nor Fanny is a 'feeling' person at all. Both are motivated by ruthless self-interest, Lucy in grimly keeping Edward to his engagement, Fanny in consistently working for her immediate family's financial advantage. But both Lucy and Fanny, though in reality as hard-headed as they could well be, clothe their mercenariness decently in the garments of sensibility. Lucy flatters Lady Middleton by pretending to love her children. She acts the lovelorn damsel to Elinor. Her letters are filled with professions of sensibility. Similarly, in the successive shocks inflicted by Lucy's insinuation of herself into the family, 'poor Fanny had suffered agonies of sensibility'.[26] It is no accident that at the end the marriages of the two model couples, Elinor and Marianne and their two diffident, withdrawing husbands, are contrasted with the establishments, far more glorious in worldly terms, of Lucy and Fanny and their complacent, mercenary husbands.[27] Lucy and Fanny may quarrel, but it is suitable that they should end the novel together, the joint favourites of old Mrs. Ferrars, and forever in one another's orbit. However it begins, the novel ends by comparing the moral ideal represented by Sense with a new interpretation of 'individualism'. The intellectual position, originally held in good faith by Marianne, is abandoned; what takes its place is selfishness with merely a fashionable cover of idealism—and, particularly, the pursuit of self-interest in the economic sense. Willoughby's crime proves after all not to have been rank villainy, but expensive self-indulgence so habitual that he must sacrifice everything, including domestic happiness, to it. Lucy's behaviour is equally consistent, and it, too, is crowned with worldly success:

> The whole of Lucy's behaviour in the affair, and the prosperity which crowned it, therefore, may be held forth as a most encouraging instance of what an earnest, an unceasing attention to self-interest . . . will do in securing every advantage of fortune, with no other sacrifice than that of time and conscience.

Jane Austen's version of 'sensibility'—that is, individualism, or the worship of self, in various familiar guises—is as harshly dealt with here as anywhere in the anti-jacobin tradition. Even without the melodramatic political subplot of many anti-jacobin novels, Mrs. Ferrars's London is recognizably a sketch of the anarchy that follows the loss of all values but self-indulgence. In the opening chapters especially, where Marianne is the target of criticism, 'sensibility' means sentimental (or revolutionary) idealism, which Elinor counters with her sceptical or pessimistic view of man's nature. Where the issue is the choice of a husband, Jane Austen's criteria prove to be much the same as Mrs. West's: both advocate dispassionate assessment of a future husband's qualities, discounting both physical attractiveness, and the *rapport* that comes from shared tastes, while stressing objective evidence. [29] Both reiterate the common conservative theme of the day, that a second attachment is likely to be more reliable than a first. [30] By all these characteristic tests, **Sense and Sensibility** is an anti-jacobin novel just as surely as is *A Gossip's Story*.

The sole element of unorthodoxy in **Sense and Sensibility** lies in the execution, and especially in the skilful adjustment of detail which makes its story more natural. **Sense and Sensibility** is not natural compared with Jane Austen's later novels. Any reader will notice the stiffness of some of the dialogue, particularly perhaps those speeches early in the novel where Elinor sums up the character of Edward.[31] And yet, especially in the second half of the novel, it is remarkable how the harsh outlines of the ideological scheme are softened. Often the changes are small ones, such as turning the jilted heroine's near-obligatory decline and death into a feverish cold caught, plausibly, from staying out to mope in the rain. Alternatively the difference may show in the born novelist's sense of occasion, her flair for a scene. Twice in the latter half of the novel, for example, there are theatrical entrances, consciously worked for: Edward's, when at last he calls on Elinor in London, only to find her with Lucy Steele; and Willoughby's, when he comes to Cleveland in response to the news that Marianne is dying. Developments like this do more than rub away some of the angularities of the old nature-nurture dichotomy. They begin to make so many inroads on it (particularly in relation to Marianne) that many readers have had the impression Jane Austen was trying to break it down altogether. Certainly there is plenty of evidence in the second half of the novel that Jane Austen was impatient with the rigidity of her framework; and yet all the modifications she makes are a matter of technique, not ideology. Lucy Steele resembles Isabella Thorpe and Mary Crawford, George Wickham, Henry Crawford, Frank Churchill, and William Walter Elliott in that she does not come, like some other authors' representations, vociferously advocating free love, or revolution, or the reading of German novels. She is a harbinger of anarchy for all that.

Compared with the common run of anti-jacobin novels it is a considerable achievement, and yet it has never been found quite good enough. **Sense and Sensibility** is the most obviously tendentious of Jane Austen's novels, and the least attractive. The trouble is not merely that, for all the author's artistic tact, the cumbrous framework and enforced contrasts of the inherited structure remain. It matters far more that the most deeply disturbing aspect of all anti-jacobin novels, their inhumanity, affects this novel more than Jane Austen's skilled mature work. In a way **Sense and Sensibility** is worse affected than many clumsy works by lesser writers, because it is written naturally, and with more insight into at least some aspects of the inner life. The reader has far too much real sympathy with Marianne in her sufferings to refrain from valuing her precisely on their account. There is plenty of evidence that Jane Austen, anticipating this reaction, tried to forestall it. As far as possible she tries to keep us out of Marianne's consciousness: Marianne's unwonted secrecy, after Willoughby has left Barton, and after her arrival in

London, functions quite as effectively in restricting the reader's sympathy as in restricting Elinor's. Merely to have Marianne's sufferings described after she has received Willoughby's letter is sufficient, however, to revive all the reader's will to identify himself with her. The effort to point up Elinor's feelings instead will not do: either we do not believe in them, and conclude her frigid, or the felt presence of suffering in the one sister helps us to supply imaginatively what we are not told about the inner life of the other. It is difficult, in short, to accept the way consciousness is presented in this novel. Marianne, and to some extent also Elinor, are drawn with strong feelings which the reader is accustomed to sympathize with, and actually to value for their own sake. But it is the argument of the novel that such feelings, like the individuals who experience them, are not innately good. Unfortunately, in flat opposition to the author's obvious intention, we tend to approach Marianne subjectively. Right or wrong, she has our sympathy: she, and our responses to her, are outside Jane Austen's control. The measure of Jane Austen's failure to get us to read her story with the necessary ethical detachment comes when she imposes her solution. What, innumerable critics have asked, if Marianne never brought herself to love Colonel Brandon? The fact that the question still occurs shows that in this most conscientiously didactic of all the novels the moral case remains unmade.

Notes

[1] W. Austen Leigh and R. A. Austen Leigh, *Jane Austen, her Life and Letters, A Family Record*, London, 1913, p. 80.

[2] Maria Edgeworth does not completely discard the contrast-novel, which recurs in one of the *Popular Tales, The Contrast,* 1804, and in *Patronage,* 1814. Jane Austen does not quite discard it either—for *Mansfield Park* is a contrast-novel, of the consecutive rather than the continuous type. . . .

[3] *Nature and Art* appears to borrow its format from Thomas Day's Rousseauistic *Sandford and Merton,* 1783-9, with its spoilt little aristocrat Tommy Merton, and its robust, simple farmer's son, Harry Sandford.

[4] The very terminology adopted by some of the titles is revealing. Mrs. Inchbald sees the issue in terms of 'nature' versus 'art', art in this context having the connotation of artificiality. 'Sense' gives nurture a very different bearing. By the mid-nineties sensibility is commonly a pejorative word. See E. Erämetsä, *A Study of the Word 'Sentimental'*, etc., Helsinki, 1951.

[5] *Sense and Sensibility*, ed. R. W. Chapman, Oxford, 1923, p. 15.

[6] Ibid., p. 20.

[7] Ibid., p. 18.

[8] *Sense and Sensibility*, p. 42. Elinor's involuntary admiration of Willoughby is important in the light of their last interview together. . . .

[9] Ibid., p. 47. Cf. the courtship in *A Gossip's Story*. . . .

[10] Ibid., p. 52.

[11] Ibid., p. 73.

[12] Ibid., p. 68.

[13] *Sense and Sensibility*, p. 78.

[14] Tests of the heroine's virtue in, respectively, Mrs. West's *Gossip's Story,* and Mrs. Hamilton's *Memoirs of Modern Philosophers.*

[15] Prayers composed by Jane Austen: *Minor Works,* ed. R. W. Chapman, Oxford, rev. ed., 1963, pp. 453-4 and 456.

[16] *Sense and Sensibility*, p. 22.

[17] *Sense and Sensibility*, p. 305.

[18] Ibid., pp. 250-1.

[19] Ibid., p. 338.

[20] *Jane Austen's Art of Allusion*, p. 70. For other expositions of the view that J A is 'ambivalent' between sense and sensibility, see Mary Lascelles, *Jane Austen and her Art,* p. 120; Andrew Wright, *Jane Austen's Novels: A Study in Structure,* pp. 30-1 and 92; and Lionel Trilling, 'A Portrait of Western Man', *The Listener,* 11 June 1953, 970.

[21] *Sense and Sensibility*, p. 331.

[22] *Sense and Sensibility*, p. 333.

[23] For Mr. Moler, Elinor's complacent first opinion, that Marianne will soon recover, is further evidence that J A meant to show the limits of sense, and to strike a balance with sensibility. *Jane Austen's Art of Allusion*, pp. 62-73.

[24] *Sense and Sensibility*, pp. 345 ff.

[25] Marianne's intelligence is of a kind which gives her moral stature within Jane Austen's system of belief. Although she begins the novel professing an erroneous system, it is always clear that she has the capacity for the searching self-analysis of the Christian. Simple, good characters like Mrs. Jennings are valued by Jane Austen, but she never leaves any doubt that individuals with active moral intelligence are a higher breed. . . .

²⁶ *Sense and Sensibility,* p. 371.

²⁷ Some critics have called Elinor's marriage 'romantic', Lucy's 'prudent', and the end another instance of J A's compromise between sense and sensibility. (Cf. Andrew Wright, *Jane Austen's Novels,* p. 92.) But this shows a continued misunderstanding of J A's interpretation of her two terms: her 'sense' approximates to the traditional Christian personal and social ethic, her 'sensibility' to a modern individualist ethic in two different manifestations, Marianne's and Lucy's.

²⁸ *Sense and Sensibility,* p. 376.

²⁹ See above, pp. 97-101.

³⁰ Marianne, Colonel Brandon, Edward Ferrars, the late Mr. Dashwood, and even perhaps Lucy Steele are better matched in their second choice than in their first.

³¹ *Sense and Sensibility,* p. 20.

Zelda Boyd (essay date 1983)

SOURCE: "The Language of Supposing: Modal Auxiliaries in *Sense and Sensibility*," in *Jane Austen: New Perspectives,* Vol. 3, edited by Janet Todd, Holmes & Meier, 1983, pp. 142-54.

[*In the following essay, Boyd presents evidence of a new pairing in* Sense and Sensibility—*that of the actual and the hypothetical.*]

Given Jane Austen's fondness for balanced verbal pairs—sense and sensibility, pride and prejudice—it is perhaps not inappropriate for me to propose another such set for discussion, namely, the actual and the hypothetical. The actual has to do with existing states of affairs, with the way the world in fact is as distinct from our wishes, desires, and suppositions. However much philosophers may argue about the external world, the actual is very real for Austen. Estates are unfairly entailed. Young men are engaged elsewhere. Uncles arrive unannounced to abort theatricals. Worse yet, uncles die (as in *Sense and Sensibility*) and leave their estates contrary to everyone's expectations. Every novel of hers turns at the beginning on a dislocation in the world, either a marriage or a death, an arrival or departure.

In addition, the books pulse with the small details of life. Think of the sides of pork and bushels of apples that go from Hartfield and Donwell Abbey to the Bateses. Think of the ribbons that are purchased, the wedding cake that is consumed. Consider Mrs. Allen's careful inventory of every new hat and gown that is to be seen in Bath, or Elizabeth Bennet's much remarked-

upon muddy skirts. The sense of the circumstantial is so strong that critics have been tempted to see Jane Austen very much as the careful recorder of particulars, the acute historian of a world she knew so well. Caroline Mercer, for example, in the "Afterword" to the Signet edition of *Sense and Sensibility,* quotes from the *Letters* to underscore Austen's devotion to detail and desire to ground her fiction in fact:

> If you could discover whether Northamptonshire is a country of Hedgerows, I should be glad again.¹

This view is not wrong. At the same time we know there is another Jane Austen, who is as much concerned with how people ought to behave as she is with hedgerows. Presumably this is the Austen that F. R. Leavis had in mind when he cited her as the progenetrix of the Great Tradition, because of her "intensely moral preoccupation."² Leavis, too, is right. Although he is maddeningly evasive about what a "moral preoccupation" would entail, we recognize intuitively what he means about Austen. The question is how to put it into words.

Maybe one way to begin is with the hypothetical, with the world of supposition and desire as opposed to the world of hedgerows and apples. In this world we find the comic figures—like Mr. Woodhouse or Mrs. Jennings or Sir John Middleton—who are comic precisely because they are always busily remaking the actual to suit their assumptions. For Mr. Woodhouse, Mrs. Weston is forever "poor Miss Taylor." Mrs. Jennings is forever assuming that possible engagements are real ones, and Sir John insists that events "must and shall" be as he wishes them. They are incorrigible. But even misguided heroines fall into the same temptation, and the happy endings present us not only with suitable marriages but with a presumably reformed Catherine Morland or Emma Woodhouse or Marianne Dashwood now prepared to deal with things as they are. Yet who has not harbored the suspicion that young girls, even heroines, are not so easily rehabilitated? And what of the multitude of other fiction-makers in the novels? Who can assume that human nature is so malleable, so easily subdued to the exigencies of the actual? Certainly not Jane Austen.

The picture of Jane Austen as the judgmental narrator who delivers the main characters from error, leaving the minor ones forever mired in their delusions, and then steps in to tell us in a magisterial way how people ought to behave is no more adequate than the picture of her as an ironic miniaturist, simply sketching human foibles for our amusement. Yet, as everyone has noticed, her language *is* the language of judgment. There is scarcely a page that doesn't abound with "musts," "oughts," "shoulds," "coulds"—in fact, the whole range of modals, that peculiar set we were taught to call "helping verbs" in grammar school.³

If we begin, then, with her language and specifically with her use of modal auxiliaries, perhaps we can arrive at a more subtle, more modulated view of Austen. The etymology of the word "modal" is itself unclear but provocative. It comes either from the Old English *mod* for "mind" or from the Latin *modus* meaning "manner," or conceivably from both. The Old English and the Latin are not so different as to pose difficulties, for one could easily regard modals as reflecting the manner of the mind. They are the language of what I have called "the hypothetical"—of reflection, supposition, deliberation, judgment, in contrast to matters of fact.

The first question to consider is who uses modals in Austen. And the answer to that is easy: everyone uses modals,[4] Mr. Knightley as well as Emma, Elinor Dashwood as well as Sir John. There is hardly a conversation anywhere in the novels that doesn't revolve around what someone believes might be, should be, must be. And conversely, there is surprisingly little talk of the actual, of what was or is,[5] except as a point of departure for speculation, and that of course brings us back to the realm of the hypothetical (the modal).

Consider, for instance, the conversation between Mr. and Mrs. Dashwood in Chapter 2 of *Sense and Sensibility.* The actuality here is that John promised at his father's deathbed to take care of his stepmother and half-sisters. Now, at leisure, with the dead buried, Mr. and Mrs. Dashwood consider whether three thousand pounds would constitute reasonable care. Mrs. Dashwood is an expert at hypothetical deliberations of this sort.

> How *could* he rob his child, and his only child, too, of so large a sum? And what possible claim *could* the Miss Dashwoods . . . have. . . . [6]

John's answer—that it was his father's wish—is easily countered by her. He could not have meant them to give away half their fortune (which, needless to say, it is not). Yes, concedes John,

> "Perhaps it *would* have been as well if he had left it wholly to myself. He *could* hardly suppose I *should* neglect them. But as he required the promise, I *could* not do less than give it: at least I thought so at the time. The promise . . . *must* be performed. Something *must* be done." . . .

Mrs. Dashwood seizes the opportunity to remind him that money, once gone,

> never *can* return. . . . Your sisters *will* marry . . . the time *may* come [when] it *would* be a very convenient addition.

"It *would*," John echoes.

The discussion goes on like this for five pages, full of "woulds," "coulds," and "mays" with which Mrs. Dashwood sketches various possible scenarios, all of which augur doom for them and prosperity for Marianne and Elinor, only to conclude with a series of "cans," "wills," and "musts" which assert a happy ending for all if they do nothing. John is easily turned around. He never needed much convincing—a paragraph would have sufficed to disinherit the women—but who could cut short such a delicious scene of self-interest masquerading as disinterested deliberation?

I have focused on this scene because it provides the clearest example of what modals can do—not to mention what people can do with modals. They allow us to talk about the nonliteral, for they constitute the world of possibility, in this particular case the unsavory world of self-justifying fictions. And we do find in Austen, in *Sense and Sensibility* and elsewhere, that the foolish, the selfish, the manipulative are those most prone to fall into modal language, since they are forever reshaping the facts to match their desires. Sir John Middleton, for example, while miles beyond the Dashwoods in generosity, is just as bent as they upon remaking the world to conform to his will. Consider his response when it appears that the trip to Whitwell must be canceled because of Colonel Brandon's sudden departure.

> "We *must* go," said Sir John. "It *shall* not be put off when we are so near it. You *cannot* go to town till to-morrow, Brandon, that is all."

Here modals serve for what we surely read as imperatives. But whereas imperatives are direct expressions of will, the modals simply report *that* an imperative exists. Thus Sir John's "cannots" and "shall nots" and "musts" tend to mask (although very thinly in this case) the crudely willful nature of his outburst. They transform subjective desire into objective grounds, "I want you to stay" into "It is absolutely necessary that you stay." When Colonel Brandon proves recalcitrant, Sir John reluctantly assents to his going. Indeed, he could hardly do otherwise. But lest we should think that he has learned any lessons in submission, Sir John immediately begins planning the colonel's return. "He *must* and *shall* come back," he declares.

The covert willfulness expressed by modal language is not exclusively the mark of comic characters, however. We find even Elinor sounding very much like Sir John when, in reply to her mother's question about Willoughby, "Do you suppose him really indifferent to her?" she says, "No, I *cannot* think that. He *must* and does love her. I am sure." The certainty of that "I am sure" is illusory. We can be sure that there are or are not hedgerows in Northamptonshire, but our inferences about other minds are not similarly verifiable. Mrs. Dashwood is righter than she knows in asking "Do you suppose," for that is precisely what they are doing. And Elinor's answer is curiously evasive, for all its positiveness. After all, "I cannot think that" does not mean that she doesn't, and "He must love her" doesn't mean that he does. Binding as they are, "can" and "must" apply only to what is possible or necessary in an ideal world; they do not ensure the actual—in this case, the condition of Willoughby's heart. Finally, Elinor is invoking a hypothetical (and just) order in which lovers love where they ought, and appearances are not deceiving. She is as prone as Sir John or her contemptible brother- and sister-in-law to fictionalizing, creating scenarios in which events match her wishes.

The sensible characters, it turns out, are not much more immune to the charms of the hypothetical than the most self-indulgent wishful thinkers. One finds surprisingly little difference in the use or the frequency of their modals. Elinor, Edward, and Colonel Brandon use as many as Marianne or Sir John or Mrs. Jennings does, and all of them use modals to invoke nonactual worlds (some more pleasing or plausible than others) which instantiate and objectify their desires. Evidently, the distinction between Elinor and Marianne, or, for that matter, between Edward, the supposed literalist, and Marianne, the emotionalist, is less sharp than the contrastive "and" of the title suggests, at least insofar as their language is concerned.

Elinor is presumably the model of sense. She does none of the foolish things Marianne does in the name of love—no passionate letters or secret visits to ancestral houses for her. She never abandons herself to her feelings when her lover fails her, and, unlike Marianne, she is never publicly distraught. Moreover, Elinor doesn't seek out occasions for self-dramatization. She abjures poetical farewells and picturesque vistas, all opportunities for modal language. In contrast, Marianne savors such moments. "Oh! happy house," she exclaims on leaving Norland,

> "*could* you know what I suffer . . . I *may* view you no more . . . but you *will* continue the same. No leaf *will* decay . . . although we *can* observe you no longer . . . but who *will* remain to enjoy you?"

Marianne's posturing here is closely akin to her love of the picturesque, as becomes clear in her exchange with Edward about the picturesqueness of Barton Valley.

> "Look up at it and be tranquil if you *can*."

> "It is a beautiful country," he replied; "but these bottoms *must* be dirty in winter."

> "How *can* you think of dirt with such objects before you?"

> "Because," replied he, smiling, "among the rest of the objects before me, I see a very dirty lane."

Although this exchange appears to set up a clear-cut opposition between the literal and the imaginative, there is something more subtle going on: Edward is revealed to be less wooden and more fallible than one might guess. He sees the dirty road only partly, as he claims, because it's there. In fact, he, too, selects, focusing on the dirt because Marianne doesn't, and because he is low in spirits and in no mood to be shown the splendors of anything. So he offers his own projection to counter hers. His answer that the bottoms "must" be dirty in winter is no more an account of the actual than is her poeticizing. It is, rather, another hypothetical version, as the inferential "must" indicates.

In a slightly less fractious mood, Edward continues:

> "I shall call hills steep which *ought* to be bold; surfaces strange and uncouth which *ought* to be irregular and rugged; and distant objects out of sight which *ought* to be indistinct."

It is clear that Edward sees the picturesque as connected with a series of modal prescriptions, and the "oughts" of Marianne's doctrine offend him. What is less clear is the way in which Edward himself is using those same modals to argue unfairly. His characterization—hills that *ought* to be bold and surfaces that *ought* to be irregular—places the obligation squarely on the natural scene to behave as Marianne wishes, and although there is surely some truth in this parody, the "oughts" are, after all, Edward's misrepresentation and not hers.

Elinor herself is, in private, less sensible than one might expect. She is all too willing to construct arguments to rationalize Edward's behavior, which she continually contrasts favorably with Willoughby's. Looked at from the outside, it seems open to question whether there is so sharp a division between the two men as Elinor makes. If Willoughby makes love to Marianne and then drops her for a provident marriage, Edward too engages Elinor's affections although he cannot hope to wed her. Nor is he discreet. In his quiet way he makes his preference as public as Willoughby does his, with the additional consideration that Edward is *engaged,* while Willoughby is at least free. Yet rarely does Elinor seriously blame Edward. Quite the contrary. At the beginning of Book II, having heard Lucy's astonishing secret, she is "at liberty to think and be wretched." And liberty she takes. She cannot doubt the truth of the engagement, "supported as it was . . . by such probabilities and proofs, and contradicted by nothing but her own wishes." Nevertheless, she manages to envision a state of affairs very different from that described by Lucy. In a long introspective flight, full of hypotheses about how "it might have been," "it ought to be," she persuades herself that his affection was all her own. She *could* not be deceived in that . . . the youthful infatuation of nineteen *would* naturally blind him . . . but the four succeeding years . . . *must* have opened his eyes. . . .

Although Elinor tries hard to separate the reality from her own "wishes," she manages, against all internal warnings about persuasion, to persuade herself of what she wants to believe.

It appears that all of us, even Elinor, live rather more than we admit in modal rather than actual worlds. And one lesson of *Sense and Sensibility,* like that of *Northanger Abbey* or *Emma,* seems to be that we must give up these imaginary realms to take up firmer residence in the here and now. But Austen's view is not so simple, nor are modals so avoidable. Modals can be used to serve the ends of false reason precisely because they are fundamentally the language of all reasoning. And the most important lesson to be learned from Austen is not that some people are deluded, or even that all people are deluded, but that hypothesis, inference, supposition are what John Searle calls ground-floor properties of the human mind.

Almost everyone in *Sense and Sensibility* at some point considers the question of what would constitute right reasoning, even those least likely to act on that knowledge. The most amazing people invoke rationality. Marianne judges her mother's decision that they remain in London "to be entirely wrong, formed on mistaken grounds," and when Elinor assures Willoughby that Marianne "has long forgiven you," he objects, "Then she has forgiven me before she ought. . . . But she shall forgive me again, and on more reasonable grounds." Elinor criticizes her mother and Marianne because "with them, to wish was to hope, and to hope was to expect," only to have her own cautious skepticism called into question by Mrs. Dashwood, who asks, quite reasonably, "Are no probabilities to be accepted merely because they are not certainties?"

Accurate or not, the hypothetical is an inescapable mode (and inescapably modal) in a world where there are many more probabilities than certainties, and in actual life thought and discourse turn less on empirically verifiable statements like "The cat is on the mat" than on modal ones about unobservable things like causes, reasons, states of mind. Even as the talk ranges from trifling subjects like Mrs. Dashwood's intended remodeling to serious discussions of Edward's future, or Marianne's possible engagement, it involves the same processes of supposing and speculating about what someone might do, will do, ought to do. If Mr. and Mrs. Dashwood's vision of their own poverty on several thousands a year and their relations' affluence on several hundred serves as an ironic instance, other conversations equally full of modals need to be taken seriously.

As an illustration, here is Colonel Brandon speculating about what Edward will do now that he has offered him a living. Brandon does not

> suppose it possible that the Delaford living *could* supply such an income as any body in his style of life *would* venture to settle on . . ."This little rectory *can* do no more than make Mr. Ferrars comfortable . . . it *cannot* enable him to be married. . . . What I am now doing . . . *can* advance him so little toward what *must* be his principal . . . object of happiness. His marriage *must* still be . . . distant . . . it cannot take place very soon."

Brandon's assessment of the situation is not inaccurate, as Edward and Elinor later confirm when considering whether the income will suffice for them. (It won't.) Unlike the Dashwoods, Brandon is neither self-interested nor rationalizing reluctance in saying he would do more if he could. About Edward's actual eagerness to marry, both the reader and the colonel may harbor some doubts. But Brandon is reasoning theoretically; his argument rests not on Edward's real feelings, but on a (not incorrect) supposition about what men of his class should feel and would do, what Edward himself would undoubtedly have done if Lucy had not conveniently defected. In other words, Brandon is not discussing what the facts are (for Edward could easily choose to ignore all of the supposed difficulties and marry); he is outlining what *must* be the case if Edward behaves as he ought.

David Hume argued earlier in the century that it is impossible to derive an "ought" from an "is," that "oughts" occupy a separate realm derived from non-empirical premises, and Austen, in describing the way we reason, supports this. What one *does* is very different from what one might do, could do, or even must do. Conversely, "can" asserts global possibility without entailing its enactment. "I can call you" doesn't mean that I do; nor does "I might call" mean that I will; not even "must" entails necessity in the actual world. "If that's the noon whistle, it must be twelve o'clock" is a reasonable supposition, although the whistle may have gone off at eleven-thirty. Only in the mental realm of pure deduction, which exists independent of the empirical world, do "musts" hold absolutely—two and two must be four because we have priorly defined them that way, but that a man who is engaged ought to be in love is true only if we assume as the major premise that men always engage themselves honorably. Of course, that premise is not only a supposition, but one open, especially in Austen, to the gravest doubts.

The hypothetical and the actual, then, do not simply exist side by side in discrete realms; although distinct, they intersect, and we are constantly being asked to consider the connection (and often the disconnection) between the two. While surmising that it must be twelve o'clock because the noon whistle went off is legitimate enough, we need also ask whether the whistle went off when it ought—that is, we need to check the "ought" against the empirical question of whether it did. Now, figures like Mrs. Bennet rarely move from their fictive worlds into the actual. She never gives way on the subject of the entail and is saved from her refusal to acknowledge it only through the kindly offices of the novelist, who provides the rich suitors Mrs. Bennet has no reasonable right to expect. No one is quite so recalcitrant in *Sense and Sensibility* but, on the other hand, everyone is caught to varying degrees within the circle of his or her suppositions.

Consider, for example, how everyone in *Sense and Sensibility* handles one of the central questions in the book: Is Marianne engaged to Willoughby? No one seems to find it legitimate to cut the Gordian knot by asking Marianne how things stand. Elinor believes it is her mother's place to ask; Mrs. Dashwood feels that to ask would be an intrusion; Mrs. Jennings and Sir John simply assume an engagement; and Colonel Brandon is far too tactful to inquire—although perhaps he prefers speculation to certain knowledge.

Elinor, for one, works hard to shape her limited bits of information into a reasonable hypothesis and is the first to suspect that Marianne is not assured of Willoughby. After Willoughby's public rebuff, Elinor ponders the affair.

> That some kind of engagement has subsisted . . . she *could* not doubt . . . however Marianne *might* still feed her own wishes she *could* not. . . . Nothing but a . . . change of sentiment *could* account for it . . . absence *might* have weakened his regard, and convenience *might* have . . . overcome it, but that such a regard had . . . existed she *could* not bring herself to doubt.

> As for Marianne on the pangs, which so unhappy a meeting must . . . have given her, and . . . on those . . . which *might* await her . . . she *could* not reflect without deepest concern.

Elinor is quite correct in her suppositions; a change has taken place, and Marianne's suffering is real enough. Nevertheless, Elinor clings to a mistaken assumption in order to judge her sister less harshly, and both her sympathy and her inferences are founded on a false premise—that there was an engagement—a premise she surely knows enough of her sister's impetuous nature to question. She doesn't because she is reasoning less about the real Marianne than about what ought to be the case, supposing Marianne's behavior to be justified.

Elinor is clever and, like Emma Woodhouse later, she reasons well, but reasoning well is not enough, as

Austen makes patently clear in *Emma* and suggests even in this earlier novel. At some point hypothetical constructs must touch base with the actual. If the literalness of the inexperienced Catherine Morland, who never speculates about anything until she is seduced by *Udolpho* and abused by the world, is no model for wisdom, neither is Emma's willful disregard of the actual lest it fail to confirm her scenarios. Elinor in contrast tries hard to avoid either of these extremes, and it is less her error than a mark of the fundamental fugitiveness of human knowledge that she too comes to imperfect assessments.

That reasonable sequences often turn out to be wrong is one of the great sources of irony in Austen's work, but it is important to understand that the irony derives less from faulty reasoning than from the collision between the smooth logic of hypothetical scenarios and the unpredictability of the actual world. For example, Miss Steele's account of Lucy and Edward's conversation realizes all of Colonel Brandon's earlier assumptions about money and marriage. Lucy has told Edward that "she *could* live with him upon a trifle and how little soever he *might* have she *should* be very glad . . ." They (Lucy and Edward) "talked for some time about what they *should* do and they agreed that he *should* take orders directly, and they *must* wait to be married. . . . " But of course none of this comes to pass, for Lucy is not about to wait or to be poor if she can help it.

Perhaps the highest comic dissonance between the hypothetical and the actual is achieved in those scenes where Lucy and Elinor play at being confidantes in a language filled with the politest and most tentative of modals, while each is very much aware of the other's real motives.[7] Elinor has surmised quite correctly that Lucy's revelations are directed at stinging her to jealousy while at the same time warning her to stay away from Edward. "What other reason for the disclosure . . . *could* there be but that Elinor *might* be informed . . . of Lucy's superior claims." Elinor on her part "*could* not deny herself the comfort of endeavoring to convince Lucy that her heart was unwounded." In a sequestered corner they chat. Lucy confesses that she feared she *might* have offended Elinor by her secret. "Offended me! How *could* you suppose so. . . . *Could* you have a motive for the trust that was not honourable and flattering to me?"—the answer to which, we all know, is yes, indeed, she can and does. Lucy proceeds to sketch a charming fictional version of her innocent and romantic attachment:

> I *could* give up every prospect . . . and *could* struggle with any poverty for him . . . we *must* wait, it *may* be for many years. With almost any other man . . . it *would* be an alarming prospect; but Edward's affection and constancy nothing *can* deprive me of, I know.

"That conviction *must* be everything to you" is Elinor's sweetly acid reply, while thinking to herself, "All this . . . is very pretty but it *can* impose on neither of us." The delicacy of these modals hardly needs to be demonstrated. If we substitute indicatives for the modals, we can see at once how the archness is lost as the insinuation becomes an assertion. We also see how dangerously confrontational the game becomes.

There is more than comedy to be gained by the modal language of supposition and more than wisdom about human reasoning to be learned. Society moves on these smoothly greased modal rails, and while hypothesis needs to be checked against the empirical world, acknowledging the actual too directly risks bringing the whole machine to a grinding halt. For instance, when Mrs. Jennings commits the ultimate gaucherie of openly referring to pregnancy, asking Colonel Brandon, "How does Charlotte do? I warrant you she is a fine size by this time," the colonel as a gentleman can only change the subject, hoping desperately, no doubt, that the size of a woman's belly is never again made the topic of polite conversation. With Elinor, too, the literal borders on the obscene when she defends Colonel Brandon against Marianne's charge of "infirmity." Taking the word in its literal, i.e., etymological sense, she assures Marianne that, aged as he "may appear . . . you can hardly deceive yourself as to his having the use of his limbs." These embarrassments of frankness only underscore the need for decorum and reticence, and among other things the indirect language of modals provides the very means of comfortable social intercourse.

The point is that modal language is neither the mark of the foolish and the willful nor strictly the sign of the self-reflective, although it certainly serves both of these functions. Beyond that, however, it is the language that binds human society together, the language that creates, both in the best and the worst sense, the fictions we live by. While reasoning rightly about others is at its best difficult, given our imperfect knowledge both of other minds and of our own, nevertheless, as Austen recognizes, human beings do (and probably must) make suppositions, perhaps even fictions, about the world in order to live in it, and that process, unideal yet inescapable, is reflected in the modal language of **Sense and Sensibility.** The gossip, the endless examination of trivia, the possible scenarios are all subcategories of deliberation. And deliberation is at the center of the novels—people reflecting on their own situations and those of others. Finally, it is the nature of thinking itself, hypothetical, suppositious, sometimes confusing desire with certainty, that we are being asked to consider, and I suspect this is what Leavis was responding to when he praised Austen's "intensely moral preoccupation," for her preoccupation is with the moral, not in the prescriptive sense of telling us (or her characters) what to believe or do, but in the wider sense of showing us how we come to decide these issues.

Notes

1 Jane Austen, *Sense and Sensibility,* with an afterword by Caroline G. Mercer (New York: New American Library, 1961), pp. 307ff.

2 F. R. Leavis, *The Great Tradition* (Garden City: Doubleday, 1954), p. 16.

3 Grammatically, modal auxiliaries constitute a finite syntactic set: "can"/"could," "may"/"might," "will"/"would," "shall"/"should," "must" and, with qualifications, "ought." These operate like the main auxiliaries, "be," "do," "have," in that the negative is attached directly to them and in the interrogative they are simply moved from the second to the first place in the sentence. But modals differ from the main auxiliaries (and are unique in English) because they are oddly morphologically defective. They don't inflect in the third person ("He eats," "He does eat," but not "He cans eat"); they have neither a present nor a past participle, nor a passive, nor an infinitive. Modals also form a semantic set, sharing the feature of what I have called the hypothetical, or nonactual. Where the other auxiliaries mark tense and/or aspect, modal auxiliaries mark certain nonindicative moods: possibility, necessity, obligation, permission. This is where philosophers pick up modals. Their concern is with conceptual notions like possibility or necessity, and while there are other ways of expressing these ideas (notably through adverbs—"maybe," "probably"—or through catenatives like "have to," or through subjective complements like "is possible" or "is a possibility"), the analysis of these concepts usually involves, especially in ordinary language philosophy, a discussion of the modal auxiliaries per se. Although one could certainly follow the philosophers and consider all kinds of modalized sentences, I have chosen to follow the traditional grammarians and consider specifically those sentences containing modal auxiliaries, partly as a convenient way of delimiting the topic, but, more important, because such sentences from so large a part of Austen's language.

4 Any writer who is much concerned with deliberation and possibility can be expected to use a highly modalized language. Henry James is an example. Conversely, the marked absence of modals also tells us something important about a writer's preoccupations. Hemingway, especially in the short stories, is in full flight from reflection and deliberation, and if we look at the places (there are not many of them) where modals do occur in his stories, we find that they are always connected with uncertainty and discomfort.

5 Notice that "will be" has been omitted from the temporal series, since the division hypothetical/actual places the future in the hypothetical domain. The etymology of the word "future"—from Latin "futurus," meaning roughly "the about to be"—serves to corroborate this

placement. Moreover, regarding the future as hypothetical is not only philosophically plausible it also allows us to avoid the difficulties in English between "shall" and "will," both of which are used for the future, sometimes to make predictions about what is to come, sometimes to make declarations of intention about bringing it about. The conceptual distinctions between "shall" and "will" are real enough, but for the purposes of this essay it is sufficient to see them both as expressions of the nonactual.

[6] All quotations are from Jane Austen, *The Novels of Jane Austen,* ed. R. W. Chapman, 5 vols., 3rd edition (London: Oxford University Press, 1932-34, 1966). The italics here and hereafter are mine unless otherwise indicated.

[7] It is hard these days to avoid the question of "women's language" when dealing with a woman writer. The fact that modals are sometimes used as politeness forms and/or to express tentativeness rather than assertion has invited speculation about whether modal language is not peculiarly feminine (if we think in terms of the traditional stereotypes). I do not think Austen offers support for this view. In the standard case, modals characterize not the language of reticence but the language of anyone concerned with reflection and deliberation, with what is possible or necessary. And this is certainly Austen's primary use of them. Moreover, her characters are, at their worst, more willful than polite; at their best, more deliberative than decorous. Not one of them exhibits "feminine" deference, either in language or behavior. In fact, unctuousness, the mark of fools like Mr. Elton or Mr. Collins or Miss Steele, is remarkably free from modals, not surprisingly, since the people never stop to think.

Claudia L. Johnson (essay date 1983)

SOURCE: "The 'Twilight of Probability': Uncertainty and Hope," *Philological Quarterly,* Vol. 62, No. 2, Spring, 1983, pp. 171-86.

[*In the following essay, Johnson discusses Austen's indebtedness to Samuel Johnson's "tradition of doubt" in* Sense and Sensibility.]

Sense and Sensibility is Jane Austen's least loved and least respected novel. One reason why is that most readers believe that *Sense and Sensibility* is about its title. Critics typically explain the moral theory relevant to the novel, survey Elinor's and Marianne's predecessors in late eighteenth-century fiction and then almost invariably conclude that neither "sense" nor "sensibility" alone is adequate to human experience.[1] The polarized abstractions in the novel's title, however, do not provide the most inclusive or penetrating terms for understanding *Sense and Sensibility,* and so critical preoccupation with them has produced readings that are simpler and more schematic than the novel itself.

A cursory review of the plot of *Sense and Sensibility* will disclose what this novel is really about. Marianne loves a man who has all the attributes of a devoted suitor but who is not, we later learn, a devoted suitor at all. He drops Marianne in favor of a more lucrative attachment, marries, but finally confesses that, to his own surprise, he had not been deceiving Marianne all along after all. Meanwhile, Elinor loves a man who is not demonstrative but who really is, we eventually discover, her ardent admirer. He likewise drops her because of another, mysterious attachment, and is on the brink of marriage, only to be unexpectedly released at the very last minute and left free to marry the woman he has always truly but almost covertly loved. Although the way each sister bears these utterly incalculable twists does reflect some of the competing claims of sense and sensibility, the logic that unifies and propels the plot does not depend on an opposition between sense and sensibility. Marvin Mudrick perceived this apparent discrepancy long ago: "Has it been Marianne's *sensibility* that was responsible for her mistake [about Willoughby]? Judgment, on the basis of partial evidence, is difficult for any one."[2] Precisely. But because Mudrick believes that Marianne's mistakes ought to be causally related to the governing theme of sensibility, he, like many readers, concludes that Austen is willfully unfair to Marianne.

The fact is that both Elinor and Marianne consistently err because they must judge, as Mudrick puts it, "on the basis of partial evidence." Because both are confronted with suitors who are, as Elinor says specifically of Willoughby, "unfathomable,"[3] both have difficulty in knowing what to believe and what to expect. *Sense and Sensibility* has as its starting point, then, epistemological problems—problems of knowing and assent—that baffle Elinor and Marianne alike. The characters themselves often formulate this problem explicitly. When Elinor argues with her mother about Willoughby's suspiciously abrupt departure and the possibility of his bad faith towards Marianne, Mrs. Dashwood, always anxious to make excuses, indignantly responds, "Are no probabilities to be accepted, merely because they are not certainties?" (pp. 78-79). This question pinpoints the problem the sisters face—though Marianne hardly suspects it—as they try to ascertain and anticipate the intentions of their extremely misunderstandable suitors.

The terms of Mrs. Dashwood's question, like so much else in this opaque and sceptical novel, place *Sense and Sensibility* in the eighteenth-century philosophical tradition, where the distinction between certainty and probability figures prominently. Locke, for example, argues that our understandings are so nar-row and the world so complex that our certainty is limited to very few kinds of propositions and that we live in the "twilight . . . of *probability*" with respect to just about everything.[4] Jane Austen's favorite moralist in prose, Dr. Johnson, shares many of Locke's philosophical assumptions, but insists even more strenuously and far more anxiously on "our ignorance of the most common objects and effects."[5] Although Johnson most frequently dwells on our uncertainty about the future, our inability to have certain knowledge about the present also pre-occupies him:

> Such is the uncertainty, in which we are always likely to remain with regard to questions, wherein we have the most interest, and which every day affords opportunity to examine: we may examine indeed, but we never can decide, because our faculties are unequal to the subject. (*Adventurer*, no. 107)

This tradition of doubt what we can know bears very forcefully on *Sense and Sensibility.* The stock terms of sensibility surface here only occasionally and somewhat vestigially. But, as I will show, terms such as "doubt," "belief," "conjecture," "certainty" and "probability" conspicuously dominate the novel as a whole. Such "philosophic words" testify to Austen's concern with the fallibility of our knowledge and serve to depict a dark and pervasive "twilight of probability."[6] As Austen's most saliently Johnsonian novel, *Sense and Sensibility* dramatizes the danger of accepting even the most compelling of probabili-ties as certainties, and urges the need to govern what we allow ourselves to hope and to believe; for error and delusion "with regard to questions, wherein we have the most interest," and Johnson puts it, can be crushing and, in Marianne's case, almost deadly.

At the beginning of the novel, Elinor is differenti-ated from her family not so much in terms of the power of her feelings as in terms of the powers of her understanding. Whereas Elinor is noted for her "coolness of judgment" and "strength of understand-ing," Marianne and Mrs. Dashwood share "clever-ness" and "eagerness of mind" (p. 6). "Judgment" here, of course, does not refer to a general sort of good sense, but to an ability to make distinctions and to discern differences and relations, an ability which, in Elinor's case, is cool and independent of her inclinations. "Eagerness of mind," on the other hand, suggests less measured, hastier and more pas-sional mental activity. Furthermore, while "clever-ness" signals adroit but not necessarily sound think-ing, Elinor's "strength of understanding" alerts the reader to her steady and reliable use of the mind. Terms such as these merit serious attention because they are more than clichés used to introduce the

characters. Indeed the ability to make distinctions soon becomes the very stuff of the plot.

Mrs. Dashwood and Marianne consistently fail to ex-ercise judgment:

> "Like him!" replied her [Elinor's] mother with a smile. "I can feel no sentiment of approbation inferior to love."

> "You may esteem him,"

> "I have never yet known what it was to separate esteem and love." (p. 16)

> Marianne was afraid of offending, and said no more on the subject; but the kind of approbation which Elinor described as excited in him [Edward] by the drawings of other people, was very far from that rapturous delight, which, in her opinion, could alone be called taste. (p. 19)

These passages unquestionably exhibit the warm sensi-bility of Marianne and her mother, but they also dem-onstrate an eager tendency to compress distinctions be-tween ideas, much as Marianne will later equate com-petence and wealth, or a touch of rheumatism with virtual decrepitude. In such cases, Marianne does not discriminate, and yet she believes her opinions so firmly that the discovery that they are not shared or borne out prompts her to exclaim ingenuously "How strange this is!" (p. 39)—as if the problem did not originate in her own hasty judgments. These are but small miscalcula-tions compared to her more serious and more plausible mistake of believing Willoughby.

Elinor, of course, does make distinctions and, unlike Marianne, does not cherish her determinations too con-fidently. Elinor's scepticism is a persistent source of tension in her family. Mrs. Dashwood charges that Elinor ungraciously "love[s] to doubt where [she] can" (p. 78), while Elinor in turn regrets that she cannot "inspire her [mother] with distrust" (p. 155) of Willoughby. In addi-tion to telling polite lies, Elinor's major activity through-out the novel is doubting—resisting eager or premature assent. She rarely by-passes distinctions for the sake of reaching attractive conclusions: proof of Willoughby's "affection," for example, must not be confounded with proof of his "engagement" (p. 78). Wary of misplaced credence, Elinor habitually distinguishes and deliberates.

By juxtaposing these differences between Elinor and Marianne, Austen examines the problem of making judg-ments. Though Austen has in many ways stacked the deck against Marianne, she still deals her a respectable hand. The same steep hill and sudden downpour that expose Marianne's absurd enthusiasm for nature also occasion an extravagant but nevertheless actual heroic rescue. Whatever the excesses of Marianne's sensibility, her opinions, about Willoughby in particular, are not deluded or far-fetched. If anything, they are excessively simple. To Marianne, the world is transparent and people are as they seem. If appearances are not partial or doubtful, then judgments can be formed every bit as confidently and conclusively as Marianne forms them. Thus Willoughby seems to be and therefore must be honorable and manly, and his manifest courtship of her unquestionably bespeaks an intention of marriage. In a similar way, Marianne infers from Mrs. Jennings' coarse humor that she has a callous heart, or from Colonel Brandon's reserve that he is dull and passionless. Because Marianne presumes that one can effortlessly know precisely whom one is dealing with, the painstaking discrimination Elinor routinely practices is simply superfluous, and the protectively decorous reserve she urges "a disgraceful subjection of reason to commonplace and mistaken notions" (p. 53) which needlessly complicates the whole business of knowing and dealing with others. Much more is at stake here than impetuous sensibility, for while Marianne is not altogether right, she is certainly not all wrong either. If she errs in inferring that Elinor is not in love because she is neither sleepless, antisocial nor starved, she is on the mark in observing Edward's coolness and in concluding it shamefully inappropriate for a suitor.[7]

The case of Willoughby proves that Austen is more interested in probing the fallibility of Marianne's judgments than in exposing the folly of her sensibility. Although Willoughby is everything Marianne's "fancy had delineated . . . as capable of attaching her" (p. 49), he is not a projection of her sensitive imagination. In fact, she has every apparent reason for believing in the sincerity of his suit because, as every one can attest, "his behaviour declared his wishes to be in that respect as earnest, as his abilities were strong" (p. 49). Only with the benefit of hindsight can anyone discover the discrepancy between behavior and wish, or learn that the wish itself changes. Confounding certainty with probability, Mrs. Dashwood believes that Willoughby and her family have "perfectly understood each other" (p. 80), that nothing "has passed to justify doubt" (pp. 80-81), and that nothing can challenge her "method of understanding" (p. 78) Willoughby's admittedly strange departure.

Elinor's is the only voice of cautionary dissent. She alone seems to recognize that all live in a "twilight of probability" and that judgments therefore must be formed tentatively. There is truth to Mrs. Dashwood's quip to Elinor, "If you were to see them [Marianne and Willoughby] at the altar, you would *suppose* they were going to be married" (p. 80, emphasis added), because Elinor rarely knows quite what to think. Indeed, when Mrs. Dashwood insists that Elinor declare exactly what she suspects of Willoughby, Elinor replies, "I can hardly tell you myself" (p. 79). Her doubts about Willoughby as well as about Edward spring from a recognition that she knows so little, that, for example, the elaborate

circumstances Mrs. Dashwood postulates to account for Willoughby's conduct quite simply "may, or may *not* have happened" (p. 78).

By subjecting what she perceives to be partial appearances to her judgment, Elinor avoids Marianne's stubbornness of opinion as well as her credulity. Elinor frequently practices the same kind of suspension of assent which Marianne wishes Willoughby had practiced when she supposes that a wicked woman has calumniated her name: "Whatever he might have heard against me—ought he not to have suspended his belief?" (p. 190). If Elinor candidly refuses to decide upon "imperfections so much in the mass" (51), she also declines to decide upon perfections in the mass. Alerted by Willoughby's inconsistency, Elinor suspends her belief in him, content instead to "acknowledge the probability of many, and hope for the justice of all" (p. 82) her mother's explanations. Elinor is just as wary about believing in Edward, though doubt and impartiality here require considerably more effort. Marianne and Mrs. Dashwood eagerly await her imminent marriage to Edward, but Elinor resists. She "required greater certainty of it to make Marianne's conviction of their attachment agreeable to her" (p. 21). Aware that Edward's affection for her is "doubtful" and not yet "fully known," Elinor resolves "to avoid any encouragement of [her] own partiality, by believing or calling it [Edward's regard] more than it is" (p. 21). Elinor's concern with the control of assent itself is made even more explicit when, after allowing Marianne to believe whatever she pleases about the extent of her own affection for Edward, she insists that Marianne refrain from deciding upon Edward's affection: " . . . farther than this you must *not* believe" (p. 21).

Yet for all Elinor's cautious discernment, she is just as error-prone as Marianne, and both often make mistakes which good judgment could hardly avoid. The pronouncement "Mrs. Dashwood could find explanations whenever she wanted them" (p. 84)—a statement which encapsulates so much of the drama in this novel—applies just as aptly to Elinor. Mrs. Jennings unwittingly articulates the central problem in *Sense and Sensibility* when, impatient with Elinor's denials that Marianne and Willoughby are engaged, she protests, "Did I not *see* them together in Devonshire every day, and all day long; and did I not *know* that your sister came to town with me on purpose to buy wedding clothes?" (p. 182, emphasis added). Mrs. Jennings may be vulgar, but she is not imperceptive, and her explanation for what she sees is all too credible. In *Sense and Sensibility,* however, there is a chasm between seeing and knowing that no one, not even the judicious Elinor, can bridge. While Mrs. Dashwood explains away Willoughby's inconsistency by supposing him dependent on a capricious aunt, Elinor rationalizes Edward's puzzling conduct by attributing it to "fettered inclination" (p. 102) in the form of parental tyranny, little suspecting that his inclination is fettered in quite another way. Similarly, when Elinor sees a lock of hair around Edward's finger, she is "instantaneously" (p. 98) satisfied, "beyond all doubt" (p. 99), that the hair is her own. But, needless to say, Elinor has no idea that a Lucy Steele exists, just as she and Marianne could not possibly have suspected anything about Willoughby's libertine past. By consistently striving to place her characters in the "twilight of probability," Austen dramatizes the fallibility of the inferential process itself—and she does not let the reader in on the irony, as she does in **Pride and Prejudice** and even in **Emma.**

If Elinor with all her scrupulous judgment is just as error-prone as Marianne with all her intrepid credulity, what then do the differences between them amount to and how are they consequential? Austen's concern with the management of the mind is not limited to judgment or assent in any dryly intellectual sense. She is also concerned with how beliefs are complicated by wishes, hopes or fears. Austen's subject matter is particularly well-suited to this set of psychological concerns, for the passivity and circumscription of women's lives give rise to intense situations of hope, fear or—later perhaps—regret. Because they do not have what Henry Tilney terms "the advantage of choice" (*NA,* p. 77), women can only wait for and conjecture about the possibility of proposals. They must observe their suitors' gestures, review their encouraging words, speculate about their intentions, and then wait. As bold and active as they are in every other respect, even Elizabeth Bennet and Emma Woodhouse must finally wait in doubtful suspense, and this is practically all that Fanny Price and Anne Elliot ever do.

Elinor and Marianne too do little else than wait for Edward and Willoughby to disclose their intentions. While they wait, however, hopeful and fearful anticipations operate on their understandings and their beliefs in very different and very telling ways. Austen carefully specifies these differences early in the novel:

> [Elinor] knew that what Marianne and her mother conjectured at one moment, they believed in the next—that with them, to wish was to hope, and to hope was to expect. (p. 21)

> [Marianne's] mother too, in whose mind not one speculative thought of their marriage had been raised, by his [Willoughby's] prospect of riches, was led before the end of a week to hope and expect it; and secretly to congratulate herself on having gained two such sons-in-law as Edward and Willoughby. (p. 49)

As usual, the judicious Elinor observes that conjecture is tenuous knowledge indeed, and that wishing, hoping and expecting are related but distinct activities which imply different degrees of assent. To wish is to express a desire, to hope is to desire with some confidence, and

to expect is to anticipate something as a virtual certainty. The way Marianne and her mother eagerly and carelessly pass from wishful speculation to cherished and certain conviction recalls Johnson's observation, "what men allow themselves to hope, they will soon believe" (*Rambler,* no. 8). This path towards delusion which Johnson so often delineates is difficult to avoid, for the "natural flights of the human mind" are and should be "from hope to hope" (*Rambler,* no. 2). At the same time, however, hopes tend to take violent and unshakable possession of the mind as they are admitted and believed in as actualities. The astronomer's madness, for instance, begins with no more than a wish. Austen's debt to Johnson is usually assessed stylistically or normatively.[8] But the most dynamic and suggestive aspect of Johnson's legacy to Austen is his distinctive conception of psychology, his emphasis on the operations of hope and anticipation or, conversely, regret and memory, and his conviction that these activities must be properly regulated.[9] While later novels such as **Mansfield Park** and **Emma** explore the need to regulate such mental activities as wit and memory within an explicitly moral context, **Sense and Sensibility** explores how the limitation of what we can know for certain requires us to regulate what we hope in the interest of preserving sanity. Austen's concern here is to show how the mind animated by hope is later shackled by expectation and finally despondently arrested by disappointment, and how any hope or sorrow can become what Johnson calls a "pertinacious adhesion" (*Idler,* no. 72).

Marianne is particularly reckless about the management of her mind. Willoughby's departure creates a vacuum in her life which she endeavors to fill first by recollection and then by anticipation, thus dramatizing Johnson's formula for the mind's behavior when the present is "unable to fill desire or imagination with immediate enjoyment" (*Rambler,* no. 203). Marianne indulges sorrowful recollections as a "duty" (p. 77). Such behavior is typical of countless heroines of sensibility, but the basis of Austen's critique of it can best be traced to Johnson, for whom the indulgence of sorrow is an invitation to obsession:

> [M]ournful ideas, first violently impressed and afterwards willingly received, so much engross the attention, as to predominate in every thought, to darken gayety, and perplex ratiocination. An habitual sadness seizes the soul, and the faculties are chained to a single object, which can never be contemplated but with hopeless uneasiness. (*Rambler,* no. 47)

Johnson also treats this process in the chapters devoted to Nekayah's grief in *Rasselas*. Like Marianne, Nekayah resists consolation, ritualizes her sorrow as a duty, feels ashamed when her thoughts stray elsewhere and exploits memory in order, as Johnson elsewhere puts it, to renovate "the impression which time is always wearing away, and which new images are striving to obliterate" (*Idler,* no. 72). By courting "the misery which a contrast between the past and present was certain of giving" (p. 83), both women attempt to arrest their minds. Austen explicitly presents Marianne's behavior not merely as an excess of sensibility, but more fundamentally as a misuse of the mind itself. Elinor can walk with Marianne in order to protect her from the dangers of seclusion, but she realizes that she cannot force Marianne to turn her thoughts elsewhere: "Marianne's *mind* could not be controuled" (p. 85, emphasis Austen's).

Marianne is just as careless about indulging anticipations, likewise in order to fix Willoughby in her mind. As she is walking with Elinor, focusing her inward attention on him alone, she and Elinor notice a gentleman in the distance galloping towards them—whereupon Marianne rapturously cries, "It is he; it is indeed;—I know it is! . . . I knew how soon he would come" (p. 86). An abrupt dis-illusionment follows. The gentleman is not Willoughby—"The person is not tall enough for him, and has not his air" (p. 86), as Elinor could discern—but rather Edward, whose unprepossessing appearance Austen has already contrasted with Willoughby's dashing air. Marianne's eager indulgence of hope has prompted her in an almost hallucinatory fashion to project her inward wish upon outward fact. Austen's attitude to the pathetically ardent hope that gives rise to Marianne's delusion is complex. Until learning of Willoughby's engagement, Marianne is in a persistent state of expectation, and Elinor, for one, views this "rapture of delightful expectation which fill[s] the whole soul and beam[s] in the eyes of Marianne" (p. 159) quite positively. Having just learned of Edward's engagement, Elinor, like Anne Elliot later, must live without having anything to look forward to, and so she envies Marianne for having an "animating object in view," a "possibility of hope," a "prospect" (p. 159).

The basis of Elinor's respect is again Johnsonian. Johnson's caution that the "understanding of a man, naturally sanguine, may, indeed, be easily vitiated by the luxurious indulgence of hope" must be balanced by his assertion that hope is "necessary to the production of every thing great or excellent" (*Rambler,* no. 2). Hope must be admitted as an animating incentive to purposeful action, a blessing happily holding forth the possibility of some future good, without which we could never bestir ourselves: "[I]t is necessary to hope, tho' hope should always be deluded, for hope itself is happiness, and its frustrations, however frequent, are yet less dreadful than its extinction" (*Idler,* no. 58).[10] Hope becomes vitiating to the mind when its demands, like those of any desire, become imperious, when "by long indulgence it becomes ascendent in the mind" (*Rambler,* no. 207).[11]

Austen dramatizes this process of ascendancy in the London episode, where Marianne's expectations become progressively more frantic, even manic. Here (again) Marianne's ecstatic conviction that Willoughby is approaching—"[I]t is Willoughby, indeed it is!" (p. 161)—is abruptly undercut, this time by Colonel Brandon's appearance. This reversal only reinforces Marianne's hope: the "disappointment of the evening before seemed forgotten in the expectation of what was to happen that day" (p. 164). Wherever Marianne goes, she expects to see him: "[H]er eyes were in constant inquiry . . . her mind was . . . abstracted from every thing actually before them" (p. 164). Because her thoughts are filled with the urgent anticipation of a future so unaccountably delayed, her present is crowded out and she passes her time between "the anxiety of expectation and the pain of disappointment" (p. 166), watching from the window and awaiting the "long-expected rap" (p. 166). When she eventually does see Willoughby, only to be chilled by his distant civility, she must "feed her own wishes" (p. 178). Finally, after receiving his letter, Marianne still must hope that he will write, rescue and reassure her of his enduring devotion. As Elinor observes, Marianne's "endeavours to acquit" Willoughby irritate her mind "more than a perfect conviction of his unworthiness" (p. 211) could, because these efforts maintain the punishing turbulence of hope and disappointment that has buffetted her ever since Willoughby left Barton.

Once Marianne's "mind [is] no longer supported by the fever of suspense" (p. 185), Marianne has a new torment to undergo: desolating sorrow about the past, this time suffered in earnest rather than voluntarily indulged as a matter of duty. For Marianne, to whom the faculty of memory had been so dear, recollection is now a source of anguish which calls her entire manner of judging and behaving, her "happy ardour of youth" (p. 159), into question. Once again, Johnson can illuminate Marianne's painful discovery:

> Hope will predominate in every mind, till it has been suppressed by frequent disappointments. The youth has not yet discovered how many evils are continually hovering about us . . . his care is rather to accumulate good, than to shun evil. (*Rambler,* no. 196)

Reproaching herself in particular for her "unguarded affection" (p. 345), Marianne acquires an awareness that the world abounds in hovering, incalculable evils and obstacles to which her sanguine and unsuspecting ardor render her especially vulnerable. Significantly, Marianne feels the "loss of Willoughby's character" more acutely than the "loss of his heart" (p. 212), because it obliges her to doubt everything she formerly believed in and depended upon so confidently. Oppressed by this disappointment, Marianne's mind "settle[s] in a gloomy dejection" (p. 212), and her immovable despondency is later reinforced by the "pain of continual self-reproach" which deprives her even of the "hope of amendment" (p. 279).

Elinor always guards herself against possible evils. Indeed Mrs. Dashwood charges that she would "rather take evil upon credit than good" (p. 78). The truth is that Elinor prefers to take nothing on credit at all. Consequently, she makes it a point to restrain speculative activity. When Colonel Brandon speaks too feelingly about a young lady much like Marianne, Elinor fancifully connects his present emotion with the recollection of a past love affair, but "attempted no more" (p. 57). Elinor extends this same restraint to her personal, but equally speculative, hopes. During Marianne's illness, for example, she begins "to fancy, to hope she could perceive a slight amendment in her sister's pulse" (p. 314). But Elinor "wait[s], watche[s], and examine[s]" before yielding to her hope. Once "hope had already entered," Elinor feels "all its anxious flutter" as intensely as Marianne herself would. But here and everywhere else, Elinor "con[s] over every injunction of distrust" (p. 314). Later, hearing the approach of a carriage, Elinor cannot believe that Colonel Brandon and her mother have arrived, even though she has wished for and envisioned their arrival all evening. Instead, she considers the "*almost* impossibility of their being already come." She opens a window "to be satisfied of the truth." And when she sees that the carriage is drawn by four horses, she at last has "some explanation" for "such rapidity" (p. 316). Of course, Elinor is wrong, despite all her efforts to be right. As she rushes into the drawing room to greet her eagerly awaited mother, she sees "only Willoughby" (p. 316). But what is significant here is that Elinor does not behave as Marianne does in identical situations. Elinor is not disposed to credit hopes with the status of actualities. Like everyone else, Elinor sees by "uncertain light" (p. 316). But she does not assume that everything she sees is what she wishes: she does not cry out in visionary rapture, "It is she! Indeed I knew how soon she would come!"

Unlike Marianne, then, Elinor respects the differences between wishing, hoping, and expecting just as judiciously as she distinguishes between wealth and competence. Not only does she refuse to call or believe Edward's affection more than it might really be, but she refuses as well to "depend[. . .] on that result of his preference of her, which her mother and sister still considered as certain" (p. 22). Having erroneously concluded that Mrs. Ferrars is the "general excuse for every thing strange" (p. 101) in Edward's behavior, Elinor sagely reflects on the age-old opposition of duty and will and even permits herself a fanciful Marianne-like vision of that felicitous time when all such conflict will cease. But if Elinor's judgment is helpless to keep her free from error, it can and does oblige her to turn away from these "vain wishes" (p. 102) about a future too uncertain to be expected or depended upon.

After Edward leaves Barton, Elinor aims to control her mind. Unlike Marianne, she does not "augment and fix her sorrow, by seeking silence, solitude and idleness" (p. 104). In *Rambler,* no. 85, Johnson, citing Locke, singles out idleness and solitude as two primary threats to the well-being of the understanding because an "empty and unoccupied" mind is more vulnerable to the incursions of "any wild wish or vain imagination." Anticipating the terms of Anne Elliot's debate with Captain Harville about the durability of women's affections, Johnson continues by arguing that the confined and undiversified quality of women's lives makes them more likely to be "cankered by the rust of their own thoughts" and therefore more in need of occupations which provide "security against the most dangerous ensnarers of the soul, by enabling them to exclude idleness from their solitary moments, and with idleness her attendant train of passions, fancies, and chimeras, fears, sorrows and desires." Elinor resorts to employment and social activity in order to avoid the snares Johnson describes, yet finds that her thoughts perforce return to Edward:

> Her mind was inevitably at liberty, her thoughts could not be chained elsewhere; and the past and the future, on a subject so interesting, must be before her, must force her attention, and engross her memory, her reflection, and her fancy. (p. 105)

The language of this passage is strikingly Johnsonian. The words "chained," "forced" and "engross" convey the irresistible power with which ideas can usurp the mind.[12] Austen's implicit point here is that Elinor endeavors to resist the kind of violent fixation Marianne actually invites.

Elinor is maintaining equipoise between hope and doubt when Lucy Steele presents her with a "body of evidence" consisting of "probabilities and proofs" that can be contradicted only by her own "wishes" (p. 139). Lucy's surprising disclosure about her engagement to Edward accomplishes "the extinction of all her [Elinor's] dearest hopes" (p. 141). But compared to Marianne's reflections on a similar occasion, Elinor's reflections are remarkable for what they do not include. She never wishes his engagement away, never fancies that he will fly to her feet and never gives way to sorrow. Johnson defines sorrow as

> that state of mind in which our desires are fixed upon the past, without looking forward to the future, an incessant wish that something were otherwise than it has been, a tormenting and harassing want of some enjoyment or possession which we have lost, and which no endeavours can possibly regain. (*Rambler,* no. 47)

Johnson's definition perfectly describes Marianne's paralyzing sense of irretrievable loss, but it never applies to Elinor. In fact, she seems implicitly to practice Johnson's "art of forgetting" as she puts aside "useless and afflictive" remembrances so that the "past may no longer encroach upon the present" (*Idler*, no. 72). Elinor avoids talking with Marianne about Edward's engagement "upon principle, as tending to fix still more upon her thoughts, by the too warm, too positive assurances of Marianne, that belief in Edward's continued affection for herself which she rather wished to do away" (p. 270). All of Elinor's exertions are aimed at achieving "composure of mind" (p. 264)—what Johnson calls "intellectual domination" (*Idler*, no. 72)—by resisting the predominance of painful ideas, vain wishes and possibly delusive expectations.

When the Dashwoods hear of Lucy Steele's marriage, everyone reasonably concludes what they expected, that is, that Edward and not Robert Ferrars is her husband. Only now does Elinor discover that "in spite of herself, she had always admitted a hope" (p. 357) that Edward would extricate himself. Now definitively deprived of her prospect, Elinor experiences an impatient need for "something to look forward to" (p. 358) and resolves to expect Colonel Brandon's informative visit, when Edward arrives instead to claim her hand.

Viewed in isolation, Lucy's marriage to Robert Ferrars seems mere literary sleight-of-hand which Austen employs only to bring her novel to a close. Its preposterousness even stumps Elinor:

> To her own heart it was a delightful affair, to her imagination it was even a ridiculous one, but to her reason, her judgment, it was completely a puzzle. (p. 364)

Lucy's marriage is a puzzle, but one which is of a piece with all the other unforeseeable twists in this novel that baffle the reason and judgment. The rationale for Austen's persistent use of surprise can be found earlier in the novel when, describing Mrs. John Dashwood's incivility to her sisters-in-law, Austen writes,

> But while the imaginations of other people will carry them away to form wrong judgments of our conduct, and to decide on it by slight appearances, one's happiness must in some measure be always at the mercy of chance. (p. 248)

Austen gets more specific by relating how a random visitor "allowed her fancy so far to outrun truth and probability" (p. 248) as to infer that the Dashwood sisters were staying with their brother. Of course, the visitor's inference is hardly implausible, and all this talk about outstripping truth and probability is ironic. But Austen's generalization nevertheless stands and points to the fallibility of even the most peripheral, modest and probable determinations in the novel. In an essay on chance, Johnson poses the problem this way:

> [Let the reader] enquire how he was placed in his present condition. He will find that of the good or

ill which he has experienced, a great part came unexpected, without any visible gradations of approach; that every event has been influenced by causes acting without his intervention, and that whenever he pretended to the prerogative of foresight, he was mortified with a new conviction of the shortness of his views. (*Rambler*, no. 184)

Chance plays an important role in Austen's fiction. But ***Sense and Sensibility*** is most patently a novel of surprises. Here, unobservable causes continually reverse expectations and unfold misleading prospects or doubtful retrospects in order to demonstrate the "shortness of our views" and what Lady Russell later calls "the uncertainty of all human events and calculations" (*P*, p. 159). Only when we recognize that the most reasonable judgments are eluded by the unseen and unforeseen can we evaluate the conduct of each sister. In her principled ardor, Marianne has allowed her hope for Willoughby to exceed a dearly desired wish and to become a radical dependency on something which, after all, might not be. Marianne may think she is devoting herself to the ideal of a single attachment, but she is actually cultivating a "pertinacious adhesion." Johnson aptly describes the monomania Marianne cultivates:

> We represent to ourselves the pleasures of some future possession, and suffer the thoughts to dwell attentively upon it, till it has wholly ingrossed the imagination, and permits us not to conceive any happiness but its attainment, or any misery but its loss. (*Rambler*, no. 17)

Austen chastizes Marianne's single-minded ardor not because it fosters unseemly emotionality, but because it is not the appropriate response to a world where "one's happiness must in some measure be always at the mercy of chance" (p. 248). It is the disappointment of an entirely plausible but obsessively cherished hope that debilitates and almost destroys Marianne.

The circumspect Elinor would seem to be the one who, in Johnson's words, "too scrupulously balances probabilities, and too perspicaciously foresees obstacles" (*Rambler*, no. 43) and so ventures nothing in order to lose nothing. Mrs. Dashwood senses this possibility when she censures Elinor's unwillingness to go to London: "[I]f Elinor would ever condescend to anticipate enjoyment, she would foresee it there from a variety of sources" (p. 157). But Elinor does not anticipate desolation either. When she must teach herself to expect Edward's marriage to Lucy, she still quietly and patiently admits a hope. In this respect Elinor resembles Johnson's wise man:

> He never considered things not yet existing as the proper objects of his attention; he never indulged dreams till he was deceived by their phantoms; nor ever realized non-entities into his mind. (*Rambler*, no. 29)

Elinor's "strength of understanding" (p. 6) keeps her from realizing "non-entities" into her mind. And given the mind's tendency to live obsessively "in idea"—as Johnson puts it in *Rambler,* no. 2—Elinor's effort to be animated but not deluded by hope is genuinely heroic. Knowing that hopes are only probable, she does not allow them to engross her mind, and instead cultivates a lucid readiness for any eventuality which enables her to go forward—the activity which Johnson insists is "the business of life" (*Idler,* no. 72).

Sense and Sensibility closes with a prospect of muted felicity: Elinor and Marianne will be happy principally because they and their husbands do not quarrel. The destinies of the other characters are described in similarly negative ways: Lucy and Robert Ferrars are granted "harmony" (p. 377) despite frequent eruptions of family bickering; Willoughby enjoys "no small degree of domestic felicity" because his wife is "not always out of humour, nor his home always uncomfortable" (p. 379). The anti-climactic quality of this conclusion is especially significant because Austen's aim has been not so much to expose the folly of intense feeling as to show the danger of hoping too intensely for so much, given a world that cannot be penetrated by our understandings, much less conjured by our wishes. Austen circumscribes her heroines' felicity, then, to show that this is the most which may safely be hoped for. And, ironically, it is only in comparison to the confidently high-wrought expectations that Marianne once nurtured that the prospect of an ordinary but everlastingly happy marriage seems like such a severe comedown. **Sense and Sensibility** is not as bleak as "The Vanity of Human Wishes." But it does express a concern to restrain wishes as well as the act of wishing itself, precisely in order to achieve one of the few salutary wishes Johnson allows for in that poem: "a healthful mind."[13]

Notes

[1] For the literary heritage of *Sense and Sensibility* see Alan McKillop, "The Context of *Sense and Sensibility,*" *Rice Institute Pamphlets,* 44 (April, 1957), 65-78; and relevant chapters in Kenneth Moler's *Jane Austen's Art of Allusions* (U. of Nebraska Press, 1957) and Henrietta Ten Harmsel's *Jane Austen: A Study in Fictional Conventions* (The Hague: Mouton, 1964). Studies stressing moral theory include Everett Zimmerman, "Admiring Pope No More Than Is Proper," in *Jane Austen: Bicentenary Essays,* ed. John Halperin (Cambridge U. Press, 1975), pp. 229-42; Ian Watt, "On *Sense and Sensibility,*" in *Sense and Sensibility,* ed. Ian Watt (New York: Harper, 1961), pp. 229-42; and Alistair Duckworth's chapter on this novel in *The Improvement of the Estate* (Johns Hopkins U. Press, 1971).

[2] *Jane Austen: Irony as Defense and Discovery* (Princeton U. Press, 1952), p. 82.

[3] *Sense and Sensibility,* ed. R. W. Chapman (London: Oxford U. Press, 1953), p. 199. Subsequent citations from Chapman's edition of Austen's novels will be noted parenthetically.

[4] *Essay Concerning Human Understanding,* ed. John W. Yolton (New York: Dutton, 1961), IV.xiv.2.

[5] *Idler,* no. 32 in *The Adventurer and the Idler,* ed. W. J. Bate, John M. Bullitt and L. F. Powell (Yale U. Press, 1963), p. 98. The numbers of Johnson's periodical essays cited subsequently are based on *The Yale Edition of the Works of Samuel Johnson* (Yale U. Press, 1958-). II-V, and will be noted parenthetically.

[6] Several critics have noted Locke's relevance to Austen's novels. Considering the matter generically, Sheridan Baker remarks that "how the mind will generate its cloudy expectations, and how the event will inevitably differ" is the "center of Jane Austen's comedy" and her "legacy from Locke by Sterne." See "The Idea of Romance in the Eighteenth-Century Novel," *Papers of the Michigan Academy of Science, Arts, and Letters,* 49 (1964), 519-20. In his introduction to the Penguin edition of *Pride and Prejudice,* Tony Tanner uses the works of Locke and Hume to illuminate Elizabeth Bennet's assent to first impressions. Tanner does not, however, allow for the bearing of these epistemologists on the problems of Elinor and Marianne; see *Sense and Sensibility,* ed. Tony Tanner (Baltimore: Penguin Press, 1969), p. 26. Lloyd Brown has discussed the pervasive importance of "reasoned assent" in Austen's fiction and has isolated the significance of Locke's *Essay,* IV.xiv.3-4; see *Bits of Ivory: Narrative Technique in Jane Austen's Fiction* (Louisiana State U. Press, 1973), pp. 40-41.

[7] In the best recent discussion of *Sense and Sensibility,* Stuart Tave argues that Marianne is excessively bound to the "rigid forms" of sensibility; see *Some Words of Jane Austen* (U. of Chicago Press, 1973), p. 80. Tave's point is well taken, but it is worth noting that Marianne bases her argument on an appeal to reason. Marianne's objections to concealment seem more compelling and less merely conventional when we consider them within the context of the problem of knowing. This is how the issue of concealment is canvassed in *Pride and Prejudice.*

[8] The best discussions of Austen's debt to Johnson's style include Mary Lascelles, *Jane Austen's Art* (London: Oxford U. Press, 1939), pp. 107-09; A. W. Litz, *Jane Austen: A Study of Her Artistic Development* (New York: Oxford U. Press, 1965), pp. 49-51; and Norman Page, *The Language of Jane Austen* (Oxford: Blackwell, 1972). Studies which argue that Johnson supplied Austen with moral norms often imply a Johnson more prescriptive, conservative and commonsensical than he really is. These include C. S. Lewis,

"A Note on Jane Austen," *Essays in Criticism,* 4 (October, 1954), 359-71; rpt. in *Jane Austen: A Collection of Critical Essays,* ed. Ian Watt (Englewood Cliffs, N. J.: Prentice-Hall, 1963); Frank W. Bradbrook, *Jane Austen and Her Predecessors* (Cambridge U. Press, 1966), pp. 12-15; and Robert Scholes, "Dr. Johnson and Jane Austen," *PQ,* 54 (1975), 380-90. More recently, Peter L. De Rose has claimed that Johnsonian norms of common sense, experience, reason and discipline govern Austen's novels; see *Jane Austen and Samuel Johnson* (Washington, D.C.: U. Press of America, 1980).

[9] See W. Jackson Bate's discussion of hoping, wishing and "the hunger of the imagination" in *The Achievement of Samuel Johnson* (New York: Oxford U. Press, 1955), pp. 63-91. In an excellent recent book on Austen, Susan Morgan also discusses such activities as waiting and remembering. But Morgan turns to the Romantic poets to illuminate Austen's treatment of the mind's existence in time, having previously asserted that Johnson and Locke are not relevant to Austen's work. See *In the Meantime: Character and Perception in Jane Austen's Novels* (U. of Chicago Press, 1980).

[10] The following description of Mrs. Dashwood shows how closely Jane Austen follows Johnson in her treatment of hope: "In seasons of cheerfulness, no temper could be more cheerful than hers, or possess, in a greater degree, that sanguine expectation of happiness which is happiness itself" (p. 8).

[11] See Johnson's development of this same view in *Boswell's Life of Johnson,* ed. George Birkbeck Hill, rev. L. F. Powell (Oxford: Clarendon Press, 1971), I. 368.

[12] W. Jackson Bate highlights Johnson's use of these metaphors: "The imagery of being dragged down and shackled or enchained is a recurring figurative expression of dread on Johnson's part when he is speaking of something he fears," in particular, the fear of losing the ability "to be a free agent." See *Samuel Johnson* (New York: Harcourt, c. 1977), pp. 386-87.

[13] "The Vanity of Human Wishes," line 359.

P. Gila Reinstein (essay date 1983)

SOURCE: "Moral Priorities in *Sense and Sensibility,*" in *Renascence: Essays on Values in Literature,* Vol. XXXV, No. 4, Summer, 1983, pp. 269-83.

[*In the following essay, Reinstein argues that in* Sense and Sensibility *Austen promotes moderation—"the mixture of prudence and decorum"—as the ideal quality to possess, not the strict extremes of sense and sensibility.*]

In *Sense and Sensibility* Jane Austen ostensibly opposes practicality and sensitivity, praising the former and censuring the latter. Further examination of the novel, however, reveals a subtler, more significant moral opposition between selfishness and unselfishness. Although the title of the novel suggests a simplistic approach to values, Austen's characters and moral discriminations are, in fact, complex, reflecting the complexity of life itself. The qualities of sense and sensibility are embodied by characters in the novel in many gradations and with different shades of definition. Neither consistent, unmitigated sense nor thoroughgoing sensibility is, finally, acceptable in the novel, for both tend to lead to selfish, even destructive behavior. Moderation, the mixture of prudence and decorum with warm emotions and aesthetic enthusiasm, seems to be the ideal presented in *Sense and Sensibility.*

Austen skillfully portrays the tensions between sense and sensibility, selfishness and selflessness through the characters she creates, both in their actions and in their patterns of speech and thought. Norman Page, in his excellent study, *The Language of Jane Austen,* suggests that this novel "evinces an alert interest in language as an aspect of social behavior,"[1] and establishes his point by analyzing the syntax of the chief characters, especially Elinor and Marianne. I would like to extend his study by utilizing the techniques of stylistic analysis to explore the language patterns of various significant characters both major and minor, and to relate the results to a thematic analysis in the tradition of what might be called the "morality school" of Austen criticism.[2]

The most important characters to consider are the heroines, Elinor and Marianne Dashwood. In the course of the novel, each grows to be less one-sided and more like her sister. On this point I disagree with Robert Garis, who asserts that *Sense and Sensibility* fails because Elinor neither learns nor changes, and is "emphatically praised for not needing to."[3] It seems to me that one of Austen's central points is that both sisters need to change, and the novel is a comedy because both are able to. When the novel opens, Elinor is prudent, judicious, and self-controlled to the point of stiffness, whereas Marianne abandons herself to quivering passions and irrational intuitive judgments. Elinor is conscious of her duties to family and society; Marianne rejects all outside claims and lives according to her own personal standards. Neither, to be sure, is a pure caricature of sense or sensibility, even initially. Austen clearly indicates that both possess good qualities of mind and feeling, but exercise them differently. When Austen first introduces the heroines, she tells us that Elinor has "strength of understanding and coolness of judgment," but also "an excellent heart;—her disposition was affectionate, and her feelings were strong; but she knew how to govern them."[4] Marianne, in turn, "was sensible [here meaning intelligent] and clever; but eager in everything; her sorrows, her joys, could have no moderation . . . she was everything but prudent" (p. 6).

At the beginning of the novel, the reader learns that each sister has constructed a self-image which she tries to realize completely and use as a standard in everyday affairs. Elinor determines to be judicious; Marianne, sensitive. The girls are innocent and inexperienced, and therefore believe that they will be able to control their lives and their reactions to the lives of those around them by merely choosing to do so. Marianne expresses their complacent sense of self control: "At my time of life opinions are tolerably fixed. It is not likely that I should see or hear anything to change them" (p. 93). Life, however, does get in the way. A self-image is very easy to preserve under circumstances that do not challenge it beyond its limits. Elinor and Marianne are taxed beyond their control and find themselves shaken by feelings and occurrences they cannot dominate. A similar set of events happens to them, and they are both educated and matured through their experiences. Both fall in love with a man who is not able or willing to get attached, but who, despite himself, reciprocates the affection. The young women suffer a trial of waiting while their lovers' worth is tested: the men have to uphold or break a previous decision. Both seem to have lost their loves and endure intense pain. Finally, all is explained, and Elinor triumphs by consummating her romantic attachment, while Marianne grows wiser, learning that love can have many manifestations. It is an ironic touch that prudent Elinor marries Edward, her first and only love, despite family opposition, on the verge of poverty, and then only by a quirk of fate—Lucy Steele's sudden shift. Marianne, on the other hand, is forced to retract her youthful, ignorant assertions about romantic first love. She makes a rational, practical match for esteem and comfort, with a man whom she learns to love slowly, in a mild and quiet way, altogether unlike her earlier images of what satisfactory love must be. At the end of the book, both young women are more mature and less one sided; Marianne makes a conscious effort toward self-control and propriety, and Elinor is so overwhelmed by emotions that she shows her feelings openly and spontaneously.

The plot gives some idea of the way in which the girls change, but language reveals far more. Austen's use of syntax is "a medium for communicating, by imitation rather than summary or analysis, the outline of a passage of experience, and the structure of the sentence forces upon the reader . . . a miming of the heroine's experience" (*Page,* 99). Consider Elinor. At the beginning of the book she speaks of her regard for Edward.

> "Of his sense and his goodness," continued Elinor, "no one can, I think, be in doubt, who has seen him often enough to engage him in unreserved conversation. The excellence of his understanding

and his principles can be concealed only by that shyness which too often keeps him silent. You know enough of him to do justice to his solid worth. But of his minuter propensities as you call them, you have from peculiar circumstances been kept more ignorant than myself." (p. 20)

Elinor's prose is balanced, and sentences frequently divide neatly into two equal parts joined by a coordinating conjunction. Her use of the formal sentence reflects her sense of the importance of self control, discipline, and duty. "Her syntax is thus an index of her temperament," according to Norman Page (*Page,* 94). Elinor's sentences are heavy with nouns and substantives (participles, gerunds, and infinitives used as nouns) such as "sense," "goodness," "conversation," "excellence," "to do justice" and so on, which give the sentences a weighted, static tone. Notice her concern for judging and evaluating, which here she expresses in terms of "solid worth." She seems deliberately hesitant to use adjectives and adverbs, and she avoids colorful phrasing. Her verbs are most often "state of being" words or passive voice or impersonal constructions or verbs of intellectual activity such as seeing, knowing, thinking. Instead of describing Edward in bold terms, Elinor uses limiting, qualifying words and negatives which repress emotional intensity and put a distance between Elinor and her own opinions: "*no one* can, *I think,* be *in doubt,* who has seen him *often enough,*" and so on. She seems to put her most private feelings and thoughts into the third person, as if that were the only way to justify them.

Contrast Marianne's "autumn leaves" speech, which also appears early in the book.

> "Oh!" cried Marianne, "with what transporting sensations have I formerly seen them fall! How have I delighted as I walked, to see them driven in showers about me by the wind! What feelings have they, the season, the air altogether inspired! Now there is no one to regard them. They are seen only as a nuisance, swept hastily off, and driven as much as possible from the sight." (pp. 87-88)

Her sentences are asymmetrical; instead of balancing clauses, Marianne piles up phrases of increasing intensity which come to a climax. Jane Austen uses a great variety of rhetorical devices to heighten Marianne's style. In the quoted passage, an interjection sets the tone of excitement. Marianne's speeches are typically graced with rhetorical questions, apostrophe, personification, and hyperbole. Elinor speaks in a static prose of nouns and colorless verbs; not so Marianne. Marianne's verbs are active, and her adjectives, participles, and adverbs evoke lively pictures: "walked," "driven," "have inspired," "hastily swept," and so on. By assigning such a style to Marianne, Austen brings to life, rather than merely tells about, a girl of strong feelings, susceptible to beauty in her environment and prone to exaggerated modes of expression. Elinor, in contrast, keeps in abeyance all those feelings not strictly permitted by the social code. She takes an amused, mildly critical view of Marianne's excesses. After the latter concludes her nostalgic outburst, Elinor dryly remarks, "It is not every one . . . who has your passion for dead leaves."

These are the heroines at the beginning of the novel, before life steps in to overturn their self images. When Elinor first learns she has lost Edward to Lucy Steele, she is still in relative control of herself, but her balance begins to break down, in speech as well as in behavior.

> "Engaged to Mr. Edward Ferrars!—I confess myself so totally surprised at what you tell me, that really— I beg your pardon; but surely there must be some mistake of person or name. We cannot mean the same Mr. Ferrars." (p. 131)

And yet, for all the dashes, and disjointed and fragmentary sentences, Elinor exerts herself to maintain politeness to Lucy, and by so doing, keeps herself from falling apart. She spares herself humiliation, and Lucy, triumph. Later, alone, she weeps more for Edward's mistake than for her own disappointment. Because her sense of duty sustains her—duty to Lucy's confidence and duty to spare her mother and sister unnecessary and premature suffering—she manages to conceal the painful information for months.

Marianne's reaction to the sudden collapse of her hopes is characteristically different. When Willoughby returns her letters and informs her that he is engaged to Miss Grey, Austen contrasts Elinor's long-suffering, unselfish control with Marianne's self-centered emotionalism.

> "Exert yourself, dear Marianne," she cried, "if you would not kill yourself and all who love you. Think of your mother; think of her misery while *you* suffer; for her sake you must exert yourself."

> "I cannot, I cannot," cried Marianne; "leave me, leave me, if I distress you; leave me, hate me, forget me! but do not torture me so. Oh! how easy for those who have no sorrow of their own to talk of exertion! Happy, happy Elinor, *you* cannot have an idea of what I suffer."

> "Do you call *me* happy, Marianne? Ah! if you knew!—And can you believe me to be so, while I see you so wretched?" (p. 185)

Elinor urges Marianne to fulfill her responsibility to those who love her. Her own sense of duty sustains her, but Marianne's is insufficient to the task. Marianne

bursts out with intense, illogical hyperboles and exclamations. Elinor, of course, has been rejected in the same way by her beloved—indeed, in a more irritating manner, by nasty Lucy Steele in person. Elinor here almost slips and reveals her own sorrow when Marianne accuses her of being happy, but quickly covers up her momentary lapse with a credible, if self-righteous excuse. Elinor's discipline is strong to a fault, for she denies herself the sympathy of those who love her and refuses them the chance to give, which is, after all, half of the act of loving. Both young women are suffering, both are deeply touched, but one selfishly wallows in misery while the other tries to carry on her life as usual.

Thus far, the self-images hold up rather well, with only minor deviations. When life becomes more complicated, however, the over-sensitive Marianne is chastened, while the self-negating Elinor loses control and pours out repressed feelings despite herself. Illness frightens Marianne and then allows her time to meditate. She recovers, a reformed young woman, and her speech pattern reflects her new attempt to control herself and observe decorum (*Page*, 196). For the first time she concerns herself with rational judgment, moral responsibility, and propriety. Of the Willoughby affair she says, "I *can* talk of it now, I hope, as I ought to do" (p. 344). Austen assigns to Marianne the stylistic quirks of Elinor, such as qualifying statements with apologetic phrases, to show us Marianne's newly reflective nature. Marianne, realizing the resemblance between her own and her sister's misfortunes, is doubly humbled when she compares their reactions to pain.

> "Do not, my dearest Elinor, let your kindness defend what I know your judgment must censure. My illness has made me think—it has given me leisure and calmness for serious recollection. Long before I was enough recovered to talk, I was perfectly able to reflect. I considered the past; I saw in my behaviour since the beginning of our acquaintance with him last autumn, nothing but a series of imprudence towards myself, and want of kindness to others." (p. 345)

Here her sentences are balanced and symmetrical, turning on carefully polished antitheses and parallels. Verbs are static or describe mental, rather than physical, action. The new pace of Marianne's sentences is slow and dignified, not impulsive and irregular as before. Marianne's maturation/reformation is reflected by her use of Elinor-like sentences.

Elinor has an opposite development. She, through long tension and disappointment, begins to let emotional, bitter words escape, as her carefully guarded propriety cracks. Under stress she occasionally repeats, accumulates phrases for emphasis, and conveys the breathless, impulsive tone originally characteristic of Marianne. Speaking of Lucy's engagement to Edward, she says,

"It was told me,—it was in a manner forced on me by the very person herself, whose prior engagement ruined all my prospects; and told me, as I thought, with triumph. . . . I have had her hopes and exultations to listen to again and again." (p. 263)

Although here Jane Austen opens Elinor's heart and has the character show some of the turmoil it contains, Elinor is still able to express herself verbally. There is one further step in her education to womanhood: she must be so deeply moved that she is speechless and unable to depend on the polite formulas with which society usually provides her. This final chastening experience happens when Edward suddenly returns after Elinor has, presumably, lost him forever. In this scene, she is at first able to make small talk, to "rejoice in the dryness of the season" (p. 359), but then is forced to put her head down in "a state of such agitation as made her hardly know where she was" (p. 360). When the truth of Lucy's marriage to Robert Ferrars comes out, Elinor completely loses control of herself, can no longer sit in her place, but dashes out of the room and bursts "into tears of joy, which at first she thought would never cease" (p. 360). Elinor is overcome by sensibility.

Why do Elinor and Marianne both need to change in the novel? What is it that each has that the other must learn? Is it simply that Marianne must correct her irresponsible freedom and adopt Elinor's stifling prudence? Are warmth and sensitivity frowned upon? Are practical concerns set above personal ones? It seems to be more complicated than that. Neither sense nor sensibility by itself is attacked; neither, unqualified, is sufficient. The focus of Austen's criticism seems to be elsewhere.

The true opposition in the novel is between selfishness and selflessness. Marianne's relationship with Willoughby errs, not in its warmth, but in its self-centeredness. In public they have words and glances only for each other. Their imprudent display of attachment, their lack of reserve in company and between themselves comes from belief in a personal morality which cuts them off from the rest of the world. Their relationship flourishes for their own pleasure, independent of the demands of society and family. Since they feel superior to everyone else in sensitivity and candor, they judge others without honest reflection and continually mock their friends. Their love is exclusive and smugly self-centered; when the relationship collapses, Marianne is left with the bitter residue of those feelings. In her suffering, she believes herself to be unique and inconsolable; instead of trying to pull herself out of misery, she remains "equally illdisposed to receive or communicate pleasure" (p. 171). The illness, which she cannot call up or dismiss by whim, cures her of her exclusive concern for her own pleasures and pains.

Elinor's relationship with Edward is something rather different. Although his family objects to a marriage between them, their friendship is acceptable to their society. Their behavior is decorous and inoffensive. In public they are active members of whatever group they find themselves in; to Elinor's immediate family, the friendship brings comfort and delight, because everyone is welcome to share in the affection of the couple. Their love, unlike Marianne and Willoughby's, turns outward.

Marianne is sensitive and absorbed in herself, while Elinor is practical and concerned primarily with her duty to others. Neither is a caricature of either extreme, and as the book develops, they grow toward a golden mean. To Jane Austen, neither sense nor sensibility is all-good or all-bad. Her judgment upon all the characters, including the heroines, depends on whether they use their sense or sensibility for selfish satisfaction or for the general comfort.

Austen seems to use Elinor as a voice for her own opinions, and is altogether less critical of her than of Marianne. Elinor, for example, is the ear into which Lucy, Colonel Brandon, Willoughby, and Marianne confess. Elinor advises and lectures the others how to behave properly under their difficult trials. For these reasons it seems as if Austen's principal approval lies on the side of sense rather than sensibility. This imbalance of emphasis is really caused by the fact that sensibility is inclined to individual satisfaction at the expense of general happiness, whereas sense tends toward the opposite.

As if to underscore this point, the novel includes several secondary characters who speak for greater extremes of sense or sensibility, with differing amounts of selfishness and unselfishness. The John and Fanny Dashwoods, for example, are prime instances of people abounding in hard, cold sense and very little else. Austen condemns them beautifully in the second chapter of the first volume, which contains the dicussion of John's promise to his dying father. Fanny, exercising brilliant logic and playing on selfish rationalizations, pares down the aid John is to give his sisters from three thousand pounds to nothing. Their language is almost a parody of Elinor's balanced, reflective, polished sentences.

"Well, then, *let* something be done for them; but *that* something need not be three thousand pounds. Consider," she added, "that when the money is once parted with, it never can return." (p. 9)

The repetition of phrases, the symmetry, and the careful concern for cause and effect, is the style of sense. Or again, consider this passage:

"Indeed, to say the truth, I am convinced within myself that your father had no idea of your giving them any money at all. The assistance he thought of, I dare say, was only such as might be reasonably expected of you." (p. 12)

Notice the apologetic, qualifying phrases that give a weighted, judicious tone to the inexcusably greedy sentiments. Austen lets us know that these people are practical, but laughably self-centered.

Mrs. Dashwood, the girls' mother, is at the opposite extreme. She, because she is older, is fully confirmed in her imprudent, impractical ways. To be sure, she is often able to comfort her daughters in the abundance of her warmth, but she is also able to inflict pain from her want of caution. She "valued and cherished" (p. 6) Marianne's excesses of sensibility. She persistently pushes Marianne and Willoughby, and Elinor and Edward together, by assuming and letting it be spoken of, that the couples are about to be engaged. Her injudicious, misplaced affection is an agent of unintentional destruction; her unguarded, hasty statements or guesses cause suffering precisely where she means to soothe and strengthen. Trusting feeling, rather than thought, she blinds herself to whatever does not suit her purposes. One notable instance is the letter she sends to Marianne praising Willoughby, which reaches London after Willoughby's engagement to Miss Grey has been announced. Her letter, instead of supporting Marianne and leading her to wise self-government, cuts her so deeply that she falls apart. After Marianne's illness, Mrs. Dashwood is somewhat more sympathetic to Elinor's pleas for prudence, but she has not really learned: she is, for example, carried away by Colonel Brandon's love for Marianne, and invents and exaggerates to suit her fancy. Her impractical, sensitive self-absorption is shown to be sometimes dangerous, always foolish.

Perhaps an ideal combination of sense and sensibility on a lower level of education and refinement than that of the heroines', is Mrs. Jennings. She is a mother-substitute for them during most of the story, and therefore can be contrasted reasonably with Mrs. Dashwood. Mrs. Jennings' speech is occasionally ungrammatical and coarse, and she is addicted to gossip and teasing. Norman Page notes that, "She is exceptional in Jane Austen's gallery in being given dubious linguistic habits which nevertheless carry no overtones of moral censure" (*Page,* 145). Despite her language, she functions properly in society, like Elinor, and communicates affection in her family circle, like Marianne. Most significantly, toward the end of the novel she evaluates situations more justly than any other adult.

Austen first introduces Mrs. Jennings in the role of a buffoon—fat, merry, loquacious, even boisterous and vulgar. She retains the character of a foolish jokester until the sisters accompany her to London. There, in her own home, Austen develops Mrs. Jennings into a truly worthy woman. She is genuinely kind and solici-

tous for the happiness of her guests, although surrounded by superficial, egotistical people. Unlike her daughter, Lady Middleton, Mrs. Jennings is not a snob. She is loyal to her "old city friends" (p. 168) who seem distastefully unfashionable to her elegant children. Her town house, her friends, her way of life are described as handsome and not at all insipid. Full of life, Mrs. Jennings is able to laugh at herself as well as at others, and her jokes are good-humored, without barbs. What is possibly the most impressive of Mrs. Jennings' qualities is that, while she knows the world and understands the call of money, she holds people and their feelings to be more important. Her nature is warm like Mrs. Dashwood's, but she is neither tremulously sensitive nor blind to the realities of society. Although her mind is acute, she is neither cold nor reserved. When all the adults suddenly turn against Edward, after his engagement to Lucy is made known, she defends him and his spirit. She approves of his loyalty and willingness to sacrifice material comfort for what is, as the reader must agree, a high and unselfish end. Mrs. Jennings delights in the youth and joy of the couple although there is no question of any personal gain for her. When events turn so that Elinor wins Edward, she does not become sour or resentful that her happy predictions were mistaken. It is enough for her generous heart that a bit of happiness is advanced in the world.

Mrs. Jennings' style of speech is an amusing mixture of controlled balance and effusive disorder. At some points she speaks evenly weighted prose with parenthetical expressions to slow the pace and formalize the tone. Her words are never ponderous, because her lively mind undercuts any heavy seriousness.

> "Upon my word I never saw a young woman so desperately in love in my life! *My* girls were nothing to her, and yet they used to be foolish enough; but as for Miss Marianne, she is quite an altered creature. I hope, from the bottom of my heart he won't keep her waiting much longer, for it is quite grievous to see her look so ill and forlorn. Pray, when are they to be married?" (p. 181)

This combination of logic (or semi-logic), of comparison and contrast, of affectionate catch phrases ("Upon my word," "from the bottom of my heart"), of unlabored, yet approximately symmetrical structure, is typical of Mrs. Jennings at her best. Much of her language, however, is fragmented, disjointed, and relatively chaotic in form. She overflows with the breathless wordiness of a fat, merry, middle-aged woman to whom meanness or hardness of any sort is foreign.

> "Poor soul!" cried Mrs. Jennings, as soon as she [Marianne] was gone, "how it grieves me to see her! And I declare if she is not gone away without finishing her wine! And the dried cherries too! Lord!

nothing seems to do her any good. I am sure if I knew of any thing she would like, I would send all over the town for it. Well, it is the oddest thing to me, that a man should use such a pretty girl so ill! But when there is plenty of money on one side, and next to none on the other, Lord bless you! they care no more about such things!—" (p. 194)

Although she sees the cruel pursuit of wealth and position around her, it does not corrupt her judgment of how things ought to be. Mrs. Jennings is free of what Jane Nardin calls "Ambition . . . the farthest extreme of mercenary 'sense' and it characterizes all the really bad people in the novel . . ."⁵ She may be an incorrigible chatterer, but she is also a faithful friend in all her attitudes and actions. She talks a lot, but she does more and does it gladly, without complaint. In a way, Jane Austen explains Mrs. Jennings by putting these words in her mouth: "And what good does talking ever do you know?" (p. 195). Her noisiness does little good, as she herself knows, but neither does it do any harm, for it is always light in tone. Her actions, her steady, honest giving of warmth, encouragement, and spirit, help Elinor through the hard days, and set an example of mingled good sense and sensibility, unmarred by selfishness.

Willoughby is another character whose actions demonstrate that neither sense nor sensibility is implicitly frowned upon, but that both are evil when selfishly applied: Willoughby acts both parts, but is always consummately self-centered. His life is guided solely by what will bring him maximum pleasure at minimum expense of wealth or emotional effort. He becomes involved with Marianne mostly because she is a convenient distraction to fill the idle time he must spend in the country with Mrs. Smith. Charmed by Marianne's beauty and vivacity, he falls into her pattern of self-indulged, exclusive sensitivity. That Willoughby follows Marianne's lead, Austen makes clear by her wry, after-thought inclusion of Willoughby's beliefs.

> But Marianne abhorred all concealment where no real disgrace could attend unreserve; and to aim at the restraint of sentiments which were not in themselves illaudable, appeared to her not merely an unnecessary effort, but a disgraceful subjection of reason to commonplace and mistaken notions. Willoughby thought the same. . . . (p. 53)

He is a weak, drifting character, willing to change himself, if the change will assist him in his pursuit of pleasure. "He acquiesced in all her decisions, caught all her enthusiasm" (p. 47). Typical of his flabby morality is the way in which he excuses himself for the dreadful affair with Eliza Williams, Colonel Brandon's ward; he lays the blame on her, calling her wild and ignorant, rather than castigating himself for taking advantage of her.

A comparison of Willoughby's actions and speeches with those of his fellow-suitor, Edward, brings to light some curious parallels. Willoughby, like Marianne, superficially represents the "sensible," and Edward, like Elinor, the "sense." As the book develops, however, Willoughby acts more for selfish, practical motives, and Edward for unselfish, emotional, even romantic ones. Both men have prior attachments when they meet the Dashwood sisters, and both want only an innocent friendship, without complications. Edward is so involved with Lucy that he feels himself safe from serious emotional attachment. Willoughby, deeply in debt, has prior plans of marrying a lady with a fortune, and uses Marianne as a means to remove the summer tedium, as well as to gratify his vanity by winning her affection. Both men, contrary to their intentions, fall in love and find themselves in a dilemma. Willoughby takes the cold, mercenary way out—he chooses the selfish "sense" of Fanny and John Dashwood, of Mrs. Ferrars, of Lucy Steele. Edward, on the other hand, determines to stand by his rash, youthful promise. He refuses to compromise his honor and cannot bring himself to inflict pain where he thinks he is trusted and long loved. Elinor's extreme reserve keeps him ignorant of her love, and he has no real sense of hurting her by his loyalty to Lucy. Willoughby makes a money match and regrets it; Edward stands by one love match until free to make a second, and is rewarded for his choice.

The language of the two men is as markedly different as that of the sisters. Most of the time Willoughby speaks wittily, twisting Elinor's logically structured sentences into clever jests by using anti-climax, surprise antithesis, and nonsensical pseudo-logic. Answering Elinor's defense of Colonel Brandon,

> "Miss Dashwood," cried Willoughby, "you are now using me unkindly. You are endeavouring to disarm me by reason, and to convince me against my will. But it will not do. You shall find me as stubborn as you can be artful. I have three unanswerable reasons for disliking Colonel Brandon: he has threatened me with rain when I wanted it to be fine; he has found fault with the hanging of my curricle, and I cannot persuade him to buy my brown mare." (pp. 51-52)

His flippant sentences balance, turn neatly on polished constructions, and have many of the other characteristics previously attributed to Elinor's more serious prose. He does occasionally speak in the language of enthusiasm borrowed from Marianne:

> "And yet this house you would spoil, Mrs. Dashwood? You would rob it of its simplicity by imaginary improvement! and this dear parlour . . . you would degrade to the condition of a common entrance, and everybody would be eager to pass through the room

which has hitherto contained within itself, more real accommodation and comfort than any other apartment of the handsomest dimensions in the world could possibly afford." (pp. 73-74)

The sentence structure rambles asymmetrically, accumulates phrases, uses extreme, hyperbolic words and superlatives altogether out of place with the normal amount of energy given to discussions of household improvement, and generally takes on the traits of "sensibility." Willoughby's language vacillates between the two styles, depending on whom he is with and what kind of impression he wants to make. His vacillation differs from Mrs. Jennings' in that he seems able to manipulate his style to curry favor: his fickle, insincere point of view matches his glib talk.

When he comes to confess to Elinor, that stormy night when Marianne lies deathly ill, he uses the vocabulary of a Lovelace. He scourges himself verbally, but in his melodrama, he seems as insincere as ever. He cannot simply admit to himself that he did wrong and caused pain. Instead, he must convince himself of his remorse by using high flown diction: "Oh God! what an hard-hearted rascal I was!" (p. 324); "*I* was a libertine" (p. 322); "Thunderbolts and daggers!" (p. 325), and so on.

Contrast this carrying on with Edward's more modest, but no less interesting, words. Throughout the novel, Edward's speeches are self-effacing, even mildly self-mocking. He has an excellent sense of humor, which is always directed against himself. Discussing the countryside around the Dashwood cottage, in response to Marianne's lyric excitement, he says:

> "You must not inquire too far, Marianne—remember I have no knowledge in the picturesque, and I shall offend you by my ignorance and want of taste if we come to particulars. I shall call hills steep, which ought to be bold; surfaces strange and couth, which ought to be irregular and rugged; and distant objects out of sight, which ought only to be indistinct through the soft medium of a hazy atmosphere. You must be satisfied with such admiration as I can honestly give." (pp. 96-97)

His prose is smooth and even, like Elinor's, and has a similarly slow, reflective pace, because Austen uses many of the same stylistic devices for both. He judges himself by strict standards, but is not self-righteous. He maintains the same style of speech, regardless of his audience: he is consistent, unlike the hypocritical Willoughby. Edward's sense of his own worth is very small; he does not believe that anything is owed to him because of his personal merits or birth. His under-estimation of his own worth leads to a certain amount of trouble, causing him to attach himself to Lucy originally, though he was worthy of far better. That is also how he failed to see Elinor's growing

love—someone who esteems himself so lightly and judges himself so sternly is unlikely to assume that a young woman is falling in love with him, especially without encouragement.

When he finally returns to Barton to explain his new freedom and express his love for Elinor, he chooses simple, characteristically modest phrases. After the few broken sentences which consititute the scene that dramatically reveals Lucy's duplicity, Edward comes back to make a full confession of his mistakes. Unlike Willoughby, he does not accuse himself of grand and dastardly deeds, but of a natural stupidity based on inexperience and insecurity. His words are halting, qualified by apologetic phrases: "I think," "what I thought at the time," "at least I thought so *then,* and I had seen so little of other women," and so on. The conclusion and climax of his speech are in negatives of reasonable self-censure, not at all hyperbolic or artificially intensified by diction or imbalanced structure—but the intensity, although suppressed, is evident:

> "Considering everything, therefore, I hope, foolish as our engagement was, foolish as it has since in every way been proved, it was not at the time an unnatural, or an inexcusable piece of folly." (pp. 362-63)

He concerns himself with judgment, with the standards of society, and does not exclude himself from humanity because of his guilt, as Willoughby tries to do. And yet, Edward's remorse and chagrin are clearly conveyed, and the passage is charged with restrained emotion of a more convincing sort than that professed by Willoughby.

Edward and Willoughby, Elinor and Marianne, more than extremes of sense and sensibility, represent extremes of ego-negation and ego-centrism. In the course of the novel, Edward's modesty wins him rewards after much suffering. Willoughby reveals himself to be pitifully cold and selfish under his facade of sensibility. The sisters grow to be refined, elegant young women, following the excellent moral example of Mrs. Jennings. Overwhelming sense is criticized in the persons of John and Fanny Dashwood; and overwhelming sensibility, in the character of Mrs. Dashwood. Both poles inflict pain by self-willed blindness to the feelings of others or to the consequences of their actions. *Sense and Sensibility* is a novel describing the education of two young women into the world of mature responsibility, the world in which compromises are necessary when circumstances get out of control. The sisters learn to look to others instead of being engrossed in themselves; they learn to accept the love and help of others instead of assuming that they can manage alone; they learn to combine warmth and intensity with prudence and judgment. Elinor and Marianne, when the novel closes, are prepared to add to the pleasure and happiness of those immediately around them as well as to their society in general. *Sense and Sensibility* presents a complicated and compelling morality through an excellent story.

Notes

[1] Norman Page, *The Language of Jane Austen* (New York: Harper and Row, 1972), p. 20, hereafter cited parenthetically in the text as *Page.*

[2] See, for examples, Gilbert Ryle's essay, "Jane Austen and the Moralists," in *Critical Essays on Jane Austen,* ed. B. C. Southam (New York: Barnes and Noble, 1968), pp. 106-22, and Jane Nardin's *Those Elegant Decorums: The Concept of Propriety* in *Jane Austen's Novels* (Albany: SUNY Press, 1973).

[3] Robert Garis, "Learning Experience and Change," in *Critical Essays on Jane Austen,* p. 61.

[4] *Sense and Sensibility,* ed. R.W. Chapman (London: 1953), p. 6. All quotations from the novel are cited in the text.

[5] Nardin, p. 37.

R. F. Brissenden (essay date 1984)

SOURCE: "The Task of Telling Lies: Candor and Deception in *Sense and Sensibility,*" in *Greene Centennial Studies,* edited by Paul J. Korshin and Robert R. Allen, University Press of Virginia, 1984, pp. 442-52.

[*In the following essay, Brissenden proposes that the characters of Willoughby and the Dashwood sisters stand in stark contrast to the novel's other characters who are rooted in artificial politeness and social games.*]

No one would wish to argue that *Sense and Sensibility* is Jane Austen's greatest novel. The title, however, is one of her most brilliant touches. Titles of this sort, in which two related, often antinomous, qualities or concepts are set together, were of course, popular at the time.[1] No other, I think, crystallizes so lightly and precisely such a large and significant subject. The debate concerning the relative merits of the head and the heart, the reason and the feelings, had been pursued widely and vigorously during the eighteenth century—to such a degree, indeed, that by the time Jane Austen put her novel into its final shape one could have been forgiven for assuming that the subject was exhausted. The freshness, vivacity, and openness with which she explores it, however, prove that in her hands at least it was not. Indeed, one of the strongest impressions which the novel leaves us with is the sense that the question is ultimately irresolvable and inexhaustible. Among the most surprising and admirable features of what in some ways is

very much a "first" book is the air of ambiguity and mystery with which in the end it is pervaded.

At one level it purports to resolve the question posed by the title in a simple and final way—and it is possible that Jane Austen thought that this was what she was doing. If we believe this we shall no doubt read *Sense and Sensibility* as little more than a *roman à thèse* and find it, as Marilyn Butler does, "the most obviously tendentious of Jane Austen's novels and the least attractive."[2] In this view the work is relatively uncomplicated, and what complexities do exist have arisen incidentally to what the author saw as her primary objective: "Marianne, and to some extent Elinor, are drawn with strong feelings which the reader is accustomed to sympathise with, and actually to value for their own sake. But it is the argument of the novel that such feelings, like the individuals who experience them, are not innately good. Unfortunately, in flat opposition to the author's obvious intentions, we tend to approach Marianne subjectively. Right or wrong, she has our sympathy: she, and our responses to her, are outside Jane Austen's control."[3] Quite apart from the very large assumptions made about the author's aims and purposes, such a reading of the novel strikes me as limited and unsatisfactory. It sets up a moral paradigm to which Jane Austen would no doubt have been happy to acknowledge allegiance—but it does not take adequately into account the extent to which as a human being and specifically as a creative writer she was aware of the incongruities—often painful, often amusing—that arise when one attempts to fit the lives of ordinary, fallible people to preordained moral patterns. It may well be that her consciousness of these incongruities grew as she was writing the book: like most first novels *Sense and Sensibility* is a work of self-discovery. As a result there is a degree of untidiness about the action which leaves us at the conclusion with some dissatisfaction: the neatness with which the two sisters, Marianne and Elinor, are disposed of does not fully accord with our sense of them as living, individual, and to a degree unpredictable people—a sense that has been able to develop only through the imaginative insight and vitality with which Jane Austen has envisaged them, and the dramatic freedom with which she has allowed them to move and grow. But this does not mean that they are out of her control or that, specifically, she does not appreciate the degree to which Marianne has engaged our sympathies. What it does suggest, I think, is that she came to realize in the course of writing and rewriting the novel that the questions it raised were incapable of any final solution—at least within the context of the situation with which she originally set herself to work. But the questions themselves have not been evaded. As Ian Watt observes, "Clearly no very simple verdicts are being invited in this early novel,"[4] and "there is every evidence that Jane Austen intended a complex and not a complacent response."[5] Although *Sense and Sensibility* may be a minor piece, it is the work of a major writer; and among its most striking qualities are the creative flexibility, imaginative insight, and human sympathy with which the author renders and reanimates a stereotyped situation.

Her originality displays itself most powerfully and also most subtly in her treatment of the "sensible" sister, Elinor. According to a well-established fictive convention, stories in which "sense" and "sensibility" characters were set against each other were designed to demonstrate the dangers of trusting entirely to the feelings and the merits of being reasonable, conventionally moral, and to a degree hard-headed. Although *Sense and Sensibility* in general conforms to this pattern, the triumph of sense is by no means clearcut: Elinor and Marianne act not only as foils to but as moderating influences upon each other.[6] By the end of the novel Elinor has learned to acknowledge and respect the power and value of spontaneous feeling just as much as Marianne has learned the necessity of prudence and self-control. But there is more to her spontaneity than this. The freshness, honesty, and strength of Marianne's feelings and the depth of her suffering (it almost brings about her death) arouse in us an unavoidable sense of loss: the price that is paid not merely by Marianne but by society in order to acquire prudence, restraint, and conventional wisdom is substantial. And it is a mistake to assume that Jane Austen is neither aware of nor troubled by this sacrifice. The felt and acknowledged complexity of her attitude is borne out not merely through the power with which Marianne's passion is delineated—to a degree this is what the formula demands—but also and more interestingly by the sympathetic yet at the same time ironic and probing manner in which Elinor's character and the moral and social attitudes she stands for are presented and examined.

In the end it is Elinor who engages most deeply not only our attention but also our feelings. Stuart M. Tave puts it well: "*Sense and Sensibility* is the story of Elinor Dashwood. The action of the novel is hers; it is not Marianne's and it is not equally divided between the sisters; it is Elinor's."[7] Although Marianne's grief and anguish are moving, in the process of the novel they eventually become significant not so much in themselves as in the effect they have on Elinor. The incident in London in which Willoughby publicly rejects Marianne provides a significant instance. Ostensibly, the main focus of our regard is directed toward Marianne: she has been deeply wounded, and it soon becomes clear from the intensity of her grief that hers is no merely sentimental or hysterical reaction. What guarantees the authenticity of her suffering, however, is Elinor's behavior: she also—but uncharacteristically—gives way "to a burst of tears . . . scarcely less violent than Marianne's."[8] And when she reads the letter in which Willoughby brutally breaks off the relationship her response in its own way is almost more angry and shocked than Marianne's:

She [could not] have supposed Willoughby capable of departing so far from the appearance of every honourable and delicate feeling—so far from the common decorum of a gentleman, as to send a letter so impudently cruel: a letter which, instead of bringing with his desire of a release of any profession of regret, acknowledged no breach of faith, denied all particular affection whatever—a letter of which every line was an insult, and which proclaimed its writer to be deep in hardened villany.

She paused over it for some time with indignant astonishment; then read it again and again; but every perusal only served to increase her abhorrence of the man, and so bitter were her feelings against him, that she dared not trust herself to speak. [p. 159]

On the evidence Elinor's attitude would not appear to be unreasonable, and her sister's loyalty to the Willoughby she thinks she knows seems sentimental and self-delusory. "'Elinor, I have been cruelly used, but not by Willoughby.' 'Dearest Marianne, who but himself? By whom can he have been instigated?' 'By all the world rather than by his own heart. I could rather believe every creature of my acquaintance leagued together to ruin me in his opinion, than believe his nature capable of such cruelty'" (p. 164). Later in the same conversation Marianne swings over to Elinor's position—"It is too much! Oh! Willoughby, Willoughby, could this be yours! Cruel, cruel—nothing can acquit you. Elinor, nothing can" (p. 165). But her first response is not completely unjustified: Willoughby's heart has not been entirely corrupted, and he has indeed been used. But we are not to learn this fact until later. The revelation comes in what is unquestionably the most powerful scene in the novel—a scene that for all its theatricality is one of the most powerful in the corpus of Jane Austen's fiction—the final confrontation between Elinor and Willoughby. The meeting, be it noted, is with Elinor not Marianne—although Marianne's near fatal illness is what has brought it about. But it is to say the least interesting that Elinor's relationship with Willoughby should in the end be the most significant in the novel—more significant than the relationship between Marianne and Willoughby and more significant than the relationship between Elinor and her own lover, the colorless Edward Ferrars.

The quality of the scene in which Elinor hears Willoughby's confession has been commented on by a number of critics—and this is not surprising.[9] What has not been brought out, however, is the extent to which its effectiveness and force derive from what has gone before, especially from what occurs in Volume I. The way in which the situation, the developing action, and above all the character of Elinor are here presented to the reader is of the greatest importance. The presentation is, one need hardly say, ironical—but the full range and subtlety of the irony are not perhaps immediately apparent, particularly in the case of Elinor. Probably the main reason for this is that the primary objects of Jane Austen's wit and satire stand out so clearly. Marianne's sentimental self-indulgence and her determination to see everything in romantic and literary terms are obvious targets; so too are the insensitive heartiness and oppressive sociability of the Middleton family and the sly hypocrisy of the Steele sisters. Jane Austen's touch in this first volume of her first novel is as delicate and assured as it is anywhere in her later work. She evokes a world which is full of noise, bustle, and people—Sir John Middleton's "prevailing anxiety was the dread of being alone" (p. 136)[10]—but which is, or at least appears to be, essentially empty. It is a world in which privacy seems to be impossible; and the incessant gossip and boisterous teasing, the unrelenting succession of hints, digs, and queries about beaux and lovers, soon induce an atmosphere of mounting claustrophobia. Austen gives this claustrophobia a disturbingly physical dimension in scenes such as the one in which the Middletons, Mrs. Jennings, and the Palmers practically burst in upon Elinor as she sits alone for a few moments in the cottage enjoying the luxury of being able to think about Edward. Sir John doesn't bother to knock at the door but steps across the turf, obliging her "to open the casement to speak to him, though the space was so short between the door and the window as to make it hardly possible to speak at one without being heard at the other" (p. 90); Mrs. Jennings also comes "hallooing to the window"; Lady Middleton and the two strangers walk in through the door; and Mrs. Dashwood and Margaret come down the stairs—everybody talking at once. One is left with the enduring impression that Barton Cottage is rather small and constricted while Barton Hall is excessively noisy.

Against this background Marianne's genuine (as distinct from her conventional) spontaneity of feeling, Willoughby's apparent directness and lack of stuffiness, and Elinor's sensitive and tactful awareness of other people stand out with refreshing sharpness and clarity. Willoughby, like the Dashwood sisters, brings a breath of clear air and good humor into the artificially polite and strenuously sociable world of Barton; and from his first conventionally gallant entrance onto the scene the aspect of his character that most impresses everybody—including the reader—is its pleasant candor. He is open and direct in his response to people while at the same time preserving an air of tact and friendliness. When he brings Marianne into the cottage after her fall we are told that "he apologized for his intrusion . . . in a manner so frank and so graceful, that his person, which was uncommonly handsome, received additional charms from his voice and expression" (p. 36). The next day, when he calls to inquire after her health, Marianne soon loses her shyness when she sees "that to the perfect good-breeding of the gentleman, he united frankness and vivacity" (p.

39). He has "good abilities, quick imagination, lively spirits, and open, affectionate manners"; and the only fault that Elinor can find in him is a propensity to say what he thinks "without attention to persons or circumstances." But in a world of Middletons, Palmers, Steeles, and John Dashwoods it seems a positive virtue rather than a fault to slight in this way "the forms of worldly propriety" (p. 41). Elinor's reservations about his social recklessness cannot in the end withstand his charm—or his genuine candor. The whole force of their final interview for Elinor lies in the reassurance it gives her that, at least in his feelings for Marianne, he had been honest and sincere—he had not been deliberately deceptive. His "disposition," she is able to tell herself, was "naturally open and honest," and he had "a feeling, affectionate temper." It was "the world [that] had made him extravagant and vain" (p. 290).[11]

Willoughby may be more of a fool than a knave, but it cannot be denied that he has acted badly. Nonetheless, the genuineness and spontaneity of his feelings set him apart from the cold, self-deluding, and hypocritical villains of the piece, John Dashwood and Robert Ferrars. These are damned completely because they have almost no feelings, no sensibility at all. Willoughby has feelings and, even though he eventually acts against them, he suffers for it. And it is because of this quality that he not only appears to be but is more interesting, a richer character than Edward. From the beginning Edward is set in contrast to Willoughby. Edward suffers from a "want of spirits, of openness, of consistency" (p. 87), and although he takes a much tougher line with Marianne's sentimental enthusiasms than anyone else does, he is not sufficiently confident of the validity of his *own* feelings to be emotionally honest with either Lucy or Elinor. Edward's coolly deflating comments on landscape and the picturesque somehow don't carry as much weight as Willoughby's frank avowal of his affection. And even though he behaves irresponsibly and eventually very cruelly, Willoughby does not in the end deny either his love for Marianne or the weakness and selfishness that have led him into his marriage. He may be a deceiver but he is not a hypocrite. And it is this honesty of feeling to which Elinor responds—almost like a thirsty woman reaching for a glass of water—in their final conversation. Willoughby may have been corrupted by "the world," but not without some sort of fight nor without some understanding of the cost. Edward Ferrars never openly says what he really thinks about his mother or his brother—Willoughby, on the other hand, is prepared to confess to Elinor that his wife's death would give him a "blessed chance at liberty," (p. 291), a chance to think of Marianne again. The thought is reprehensible, the dream is impossible—but the candor is refreshing; and even though Elinor reproves Willoughby for the thought, she cannot prevent herself from entertaining it, if only briefly, in the days after their meeting. "Willoughby, 'poor Willoughby' as she now allowed herself to call him, was constantly in her thoughts . . . She . . . doubted whether . . . [Marianne] could ever be happy with another; and for a moment wished Willoughby a widower. Then, remembering Colonel Brandon, reproved herself . . . and wished any thing rather than Mrs. Willoughby's death" (pp. 293-94). To admit openly to such feelings is not what "the world" would advise; and, despite all his faults, Willoughby, though defeated and corrupted by it, never belongs entirely to "the world." Indeed, in the opening sequences of the novel Willoughby's frankness and lack of cant serve as a means of criticizing the society of which he is a member. In this respect he shows most clearly his lineal connection to Richardson's Lovelace. Lovelace, of course, is a genuine and deliberate villain—but he is also a shrewd exposer of the hypocrisies and vanities of the world.

It is against "the world" that Jane Austen's irony is most obviously directed, especially in the first volume. And the contrast between those who clearly belong to the world and those who do not is so marked and so dramatically effective that our attention is drawn away from another level at which Jane Austen's irony is operating, and operating in a much more gentle and subtle manner. Because the Dashwood family—and to all appearances, Willoughby—are so different from the majority of the people with whom they have to mix, and because we see things for the most part from Elinor's point of view, we do not immediately realize that Elinor herself is also an object—indeed the most important object—of Jane Austen's ironic vision. *Vision* is the operative word: while the way in which Elinor sees herself and the world often coincides with the way in which Jane Austen sees these things and presents them—and thus with the "truth" or "reality" of the fictive world of the novel—there are occasions on which this coincidence is lacking. These occasions, as one would imagine, are of considerable significance; and one of the central elements in the process of the novel is the gradual clarification and realignment of Elinor's vision of herself and the world. By the end of the novel she has, like Emma, learned, though not so painfully, "to understand, thoroughly understand her own heart."[12]

The question of how people in general—not merely Elinor—see themselves is of central importance. Equally if not more important is the question of how people wish to be seen by the world, and consequently of how they present themselves to others. The contrast between appearance and reality and the fact that things are not always what they seem, that our eyes and ears can deceive us, is continually emphasized. Mistaken interpretations of character and situation function as one of the primary motive forces of the novel. And they range from things as complex as the assessment of Willoughby by the Dashwoods to things as simple and as broadly theatrical as Marianne's mistaking Edward Ferrars for

Willoughby, Elinor's assumption that the lock of hair Edward wears in his ring is from her own head, Mrs. Jennings's mistaking Colonel Brandon's conversation with Elinor for a proposal, and the conclusion that Lucy had married Edward and not Robert Ferrars—a conclusion drawn by the Dashwoods' servant who, significantly, does not see Lucy's husband clearly nor hear him speak: "I just see him leaning back in [the carriage], but he did not look up;—he never was a gentleman much for talking" (p. 311). It is indicative of the fundamental unity and coherence of *Sense and Sensibility* that this incident, the most blatant piece of stage machinery in the novel, should be so completely in harmony with its essential thematic preoccupations. Jane Austen is, of course, concerned throughout her fiction with the conflict between illusion or appearance and reality. But the emphasis given to this theme in *Sense and Sensibility,* particularly in Volume I, seems to be unusually pronounced. As new characters are brought on to the scene we are repeatedly shown how they "appear," what they "seem" to be, how their "address" or "manner" strikes people on first acquaintance. We are then invited—often within the space of a few sentences—to consider whether the "appearance" accurately reflects or expresses the reality. Thus when Sir John Middleton calls on his cousins in their new home we are told that "his countenance was thoroughly good-humoured; and his manners were as friendly as the style of his letter." Then the qualification is added: "Their arrival *seemed* to afford him *real* satisfaction, and their comfort to be an object of *real* solicitude to him (p. 25; my italics). With Lady Middleton the contrast is made even more sharply. After sending the Dashwoods a "very civil message" and receiving "an invitation equally polite," she calls at the cottage. "They were of course very anxious to see a person on whom so much of their comfort at Barton must depend; and the elegance of her appearance was favourable to their wishes. . . . her face was handsome, her figure tall and striking, and her address graceful. . . . But . . . her visit was long enough to detract something from their first admiration, by shewing that though perfectly well-bred, she was reserved, cold and had nothing to say for herself beyond the most common-place inquiry or remark" (pp. 25-26).

Throughout Volume I the theme is developed and explored. The Dashwood family, for instance, in their response to their acquaintance—and especially, in the end, to Willoughby—come back always to the question of genuineness and integrity. "You must think wretchedly indeed of Willoughby," says Mrs. Dashwood to Elinor, "if after all that has openly passed between them, you can doubt the nature of the terms on which they are together." The key word is "openly"—Willoughby *must be* what he has *appeared* to be. Then she goes on to ask (in expectation of being refuted) the basic question: "Has he been acting a part in his behaviour to your sister all this time?" Elinor's reply, of course, is "No, I cannot think that" (p. 69). But later, in a theoretical discussion of the whole business of assessing people she confesses that she sometimes makes mistakes: "I have frequently detected in myself . . . a total misapprehension of character . . . fancying people so much more gay and grave, or ingenious or stupid than they really are, and I can hardly tell why, or in what the deception originated" (p. 80). The reductio ad absurdum is reached when Elinor asks Mrs. Palmer whether they saw much of Willoughby at Cleveland and "whether they were intimately acquainted with him." "Oh! dear, yes," she replies, "I know him extremely well. . . . Not that I ever spoke to him indeed; but I have seen him for ever in town" (p. 98).

The climactic touch is achieved with the arrival of the Miss Steeles. Sir John enthusiastically commends them as "the sweetest girls in the world, and they are so "doatingly fond" of Lady Middleton's spoiled children that she declares them "to be very agreeable girls" (p. 102). "Agreeable" appears more than once in the account given of the Steele sisters—but Elinor's response is cool: "Their manners were particularly civil, and Elinor soon allowed them credit for some kind of sense, when she saw with what constant and judicious attentions they were making themselves agreeable to Lady Middleton" (p. 103). The way in which Lucy Steele and her sister sweetly suffer the Middleton brats is the occasion of some of the happiest comedy in the novel. But they serve as more than a mere source of amusement. They act, in a fairly obvious way, as foils to the two Dashwood sisters; and less obviously, perhaps, they provide a means by which the moral and social sensibilities of the two girls may be tested and compared.

Marianne's response is quick and positive to the point of rudeness. She "had never much toleration for anything like impertinence, vulgarity, inferiority of parts, or even difference of taste from herself"; and "the invariable coldness of her behaviour towards them" cannot be disguised (p. 109). Elinor, however, allows them "some kind of sense"—a significant allowance, surely, in view of the title and the theme of the novel— and although she has no illusions about the real nature of the Steele sisters, particularly Lucy, she is prepared to play the social game with them. She allows Lucy to involve her in long—and, ultimately, very painful—heart-to-heart discussions, even while admitting to herself that "she could have no lasting satisfaction in the company of a person who joined insincerity with ignorance, and who suffered from "a thorough want of delicacy, of rectitude, and integrity of mind" (p. 110). And when Marianne, who finds it "impossible . . . to say what she did not feel, however trivial the occasion," becomes so disgusted that she cannot even bring herself to take part in social small talk with the sisters, we are told that "upon Elinor therefore the whole task of telling lies when politeness required it, always fell" (p. 105).

"Telling lies"—the phrase is used lightly; and Jane Austen's wry insistence that absolute honesty in conversation would make ordinary social intercourse impossible is amusing rather than horrifying. But, as always, she is perfectly aware of what the words she is using mean. In order to be tactful and prudent Elinor has to tell lies—and the degree of her prevarication is heightened by the very falsity and hypocrisy of the society in which she moves. To compromise with people like Lucy Steele and Lady Middleton is to be corrupted: despite her own toughness and honesty Elinor is seduced into playing the game of polite lying to some degree on their terms. And she does it, of course, very well: in the two "confidential discourses" she has with Lucy about Edward, the honors may appear to be even, but there is no doubt as to who has the real mastery of the situation or the better understanding of it.

And yet it is Elinor's understanding—her "sense"— that at crucial points in the action, lets her down or leads her astray, even though in the end it may be her salvation. This is most obvious in her commitment to decorum. She assumes that, provided one knows what one is doing, provided one is prepared to call a lie a lie, it is often better to preserve the social priorities than to embarrass others through excessive frankness. This is a view that we may safely assume Jane Austen would have endorsed. Commenting on the passage, Tony Tanner observes that "the astringent realism of Jane Austen's vision is [here] clearly in evidence . . . for society is indeed maintained by necessary lies."[13] But it is maintained at a cost—and the way in which the limitations in Elinor's position are exposed and explored suggest very clearly what the cost may be. It is not that she undervalues candor—on the contrary. And her unwillingness to follow Marianne's example and attempt to speak the truth at all times no matter what the penalty may be is understandable and indeed commendable. But to begin with at least she is rather too ready to follow the apparently easier and wiser paths of polite prevarication. And at certain crucial points in the action this has a disproportionately significant effect. There are moments at which if Elinor had been prepared to say what she really thought and felt the outcome of events may have been rather different.

This is demonstrated most clearly in her response to the relationship between Marianne and Willoughby. Her intuitive assessment of the situation is basically sound. As she says to her mother, "I want no proof of their affections . . . but of their engagement I do" (p. 40). And she sensibly points out that the whole problem could be settled very simply: "Why do you not ask Marianne at once whether she is or is not engaged to Willoughby?" (p. 72). But when her mother refuses to do this for fear of hurting Marianne's feelings. Elinor allows herself to be persuaded against her better judgment to remain silent: "[She] urged the matter farther but in vain; common sense, common care, common prudence, were all sunk in Mrs. Dashwood's romantic delicacy" (p. 73). In one way this is a triumph of "sensibility" over "sense." But in another it is not. To begin with, Mrs. Dashwood's "delicacy" is a false delicacy: it is "romantic." And then Elinor's acquiescence exhibits "some kind of sense"—though not the highest kind. She refuses to commit the impropriety of going against the wishes of her mother. Thus decorum is preserved—as it is when Elinor sustains polite conversation with the Steeles—and Marianne's feelings are, for the moment, spared. And the convenient fiction—the lie—of Willoughby's engagement to Marianne remains unchallenged.

Elinor's greatest error—and it is one that Marianne to begin with, but only briefly, also falls into—occurs in her assessment of Mrs. Jennings. Although at first sight merely a comic buttress to the main action, Mrs. Jennings plays a most significant role in the novel—a role that is similar to and almost as important as that of Miss Bates in **Emma.** Elinor initially is repelled by Mrs. Jennings's apparent vulgarity, her insensitivity to the demands of decorum and propriety, and repelled to such a degree that when the old lady asks them to stay with her in London Elinor at first rejects the invitation not only on her own behalf but also—assuming a right she does not possess—on Marianne's. "Though I think very well of Mrs. Jennings' heart" she tells her mother primly, "she is not a woman whose society can afford us pleasure, or whose protection will give us consequence" (p. 134). She makes a similar and potentially much more disastrous mistake in her initial refusal to take Marianne's illness seriously. Mrs. Jennings, even though she enjoys the morbid drama of the situation, is the one who acts with real sense and prudence: it is she who insists that the apothecary be sent for, that Mrs. Palmer and the baby be got out of the house, and that she stay to help look after the patient—displaying in all this "a kindness of heart that made Elinor really love her" (p. 269). Kindness and common sense—these are what she invariably shows when the chips are down. When Marianne collapses after receiving Willoughby's dismissal, Mrs. Jennings shows "real concern" and "great compassion"—and a healthy feminine contempt for the perfidy of men: "a good-for-nothing fellow! I have no patience with him. . . . I wish with all my soul his wife may plague his heart out . . . if I ever meet him again, I'll give him such a dressing as he has not had this many a day" (p. 166). And once Willoughby is out of the way she immediately starts thinking of how this will improve Colonel Brandon's chances:

> Lord how he'll chuckle over this news! I hope he will come tonight. It will be all to one a better match for your sister. Two thousand a year without debt or drawback—except the little love-child, indeed; aye, I had forgot her; but she may be 'prenticed out at a small cost, and then what does it signify? Delaford is a nice place, I can tell you; exactly what I call a nice old fashioned place, full

of comforts and conveniences; quite shut in with great garden walls that are covered with the best fruit-trees in the country: and such a mulberry tree in one corner! Lord, how Charlotte and I did stuff the one time we were there! Then, there is a dovecote, some delightful stewponds, and a very pretty canal; and everything, in short, that one could wish for. [pp. 170-71]

No nonsense concerning flannel waistcoats and middle age here—this is the real world that Mrs. Jenning is talking about, and doing so with a warmth and concreteness that bring it vividly to life and give the whole novel a solidity and vitality that it would otherwise lack.

This is the world with which Elinor and Marianne and through them the reader have to come to terms. It is also true that they are forced by both social and literary conventions to come to terms with something less—with the accepted priorities and niceties of civilized behavior as the world in Jane Austen's day understood it. The concluding chapters of **Sense and Sensibility** are neat, banal, and to a degree unsatisfying—the characters are reduced to ciphers, and the whole task of telling lies that politeness demands is here deftly picked up by the author herself. But in a real sense this does not matter—we can easily accept the conclusion as a mere conventional formality that cannot and does not destroy the authenticity of what has preceded it. And we can do so because both Elinor and Marianne in the course of the action have had to acknowledge and bear witness to the truth about themselves and their society. In coming to terms with the reality of the world in which they live, a world embodied so substantially in Mrs. Jennings and all she stands for, they also come to terms with, learn to understand, their own natures. In the beginning, if Elinor had possessed more confidence in her feelings and less in her judgment and if Marianne had been more sensible, had acted with prudence, the affair with Willoughby would never have been allowed to develop. But for this to have occurred they would have had to be already the mature women they are to become by the end of the novel—and there would have been no story for Jane Austen to tell. And the reader would have been denied a unique chance of learning something not only about sense and sensibility but also about the human capacity both for deception and for simple honesty of feeling.

Notes

1 See Kenneth L. Moler, *Jane Austen's Art of Allusion* (Lincoln, Neb., 1968), pp. 46-58.

2 *Jane Austen and the War of Ideas* (Oxford, 1975), p. 195.

3 Ibid., p. 196.

[4] Sense Triumphant Introduced to Sensibility," in *Jane Austen:* Sense and Sensibility, Pride and Prejudice *and* Mansfield Park: *A Casebook,* ed. B. C. Southam (London, 1976), p. 139.

[5] Ibid., p. 145.

[6] Andrew Wright puts it well: "Marianne . . . does gradually acquire sense; but it is also true that Elinor becomes increasingly sensitive as the book progresses" (*Jane Austen's Novels,* [London, 1954], p. 86). More recently Joseph Wiesenfarth makes the more general point that the novel "is . . . about the reality of sense and sensibility being integral to every life that is meaningfully human, and it is about the necessity of sense and sensibility, blending harmoniously to make life meaningful" (*The Errand of Form* [New York, 1967], p. 53). A. Walton Litz argues interestingly that while this may be the intention of the novel, it is not always achieved (*Jane Austen* [London, 1965], pp. 78-79).

[7] *Some Words of Jane Austen* (Chicago, 1973), p. 96.

[8] *Sense and Sensibility,* ed. Claire Lamont (London, 1970), pp. 157-58. Subsequent references are to this edition and appear in text.

[9] See in particular Moler, *Austen's Art of Allusion,* pp. 70-71. Litz maintains that "this fine scene is ultimately negated by the reversion to literary stereotypes in the final chapter" (*Jane Austen,* p. 82), and while this may be true it does not detract from the power of the episode in itself.

[10] Sir John cannot understand why, once they are thrown into each other's company, the Misses Steele and Dashwood should not immediately become friends: "to be together was, in his opinion, to be intimate" (p. 107).

[11] Elinor, of course, cannot completely exonerate Willoughby—but the extent to which she now pities him and sympathizes with him is surprising even to her: "Willoughby, in spite of all his faults, excited a degree of commiseration for the sufferings produced by them, which made her think of him as now separated for ever from her family with a tenderness, a regret, rather in proportion, as she soon acknowledged within herself—to his wishes than his merits" (p. 292).

[12] *Emma,* ed. Stephen M. Parrish (New York, 1972), p. 283. The parallels between Emma and Elinor are worth exploring: Elinor's false assessment of Mrs. Jennings, for instance, is similar in some ways to Emma's treatment of Miss Bates; and Emma, to much greater and more dangerous degree, is like Elinor "a victim of moral-emotional blindness." (The phrase is Moler's; see *Austen's Art of Allusion,* p. 46.)

[13] "Secrecy and Sickness in *Sense and Sensibility,*" in *Jane Austen:* Sense and Sensibility, Pride and Prejudice *and* Mansfield Park: *A Casebook,* p. 137.

George E. Haggerty (essay date 1988)

SOURCE: "The Sacrifice of Privacy in *Sense and Sensibility,*" in *Tulsa Studies in Women's Literature,* Vol. 7, No. 2, Fall, 1988, pp. 221-37.

[*In the following essay, Haggerty argues that in* Sense and Sensibility *Austen is able to use the narrative to express "authentic feeling" (private desire) without hysteria and to investigate social behavior (public voice) without cool detachment and an abandonment of all emotion.*]

Sense and Sensibility remains one of Austen's "problem" texts. On the one hand, critics find it too programmatic in its analysis of the traits suggested by the title; on the other, they find the resolution of the work at best a baleful compromise.[1] Recent critics have shifted the focus of discussion from "sense" and "sensibility" in themselves to modes of perception and the "fallibility of our knowledge."[2] Claudia Johnson, for instance, suggests that "the stock terms of sensibility surface here only occasionally and somewhat vestigially. But . . . terms such as 'doubt,' 'belief,' 'conjecture,' 'certainty,' and 'probability' conspicuously dominate the novel as a whole."[3] When critics do take the title of the work seriously, they startlingly revise our sense of its implication. Nina Auerbach, for example, claims that "sense is less a medium of enlightenment than an organ of Romantic terror and confinement."[4] These controversial readings suggest not only the inherent complexity of this novel but also its ambiguous position as the final chapter in the long history of the literature of Sensibility.

"Sense" and "sensibility" establish poles of signification in the text and invite us to interpret behavior within the novel according to the tenets that these terms suggest, yet how those tenets determine judgment the novel keeps revising.[5] The more closely we watch the two heroines, Elinor and Marianne Dashwood, the more uncertain any evaluative dichotomy becomes. Austen defies the simple hierarchy that the title might suggest:

> "What a sweet woman Lady Middleton is!" said Lucy Steele.
>
> Marianne was silent; it was impossible for her to say what she did not feel, however trivial the occasion; and upon Elinor therefore the whole task of telling lies when politeness required it, always fell.[6]

Austen seems to offer the basis for easy contrast and evaluation in a passage such as this. Marianne becomes the sullen guardian of her own emotions, while Elinor accepts the implications of "polite" society and soldiers on. But from another perspective, Marianne's silence is attractive, dictated as it is by real feeling; and Elinor's polite "lies" seem a questionable basis for honest social interaction. Which response is more to be prized? Popular opinion has always felt Marianne's authentic emotionalism to be more heartwarming than Elinor's calculated coolness. To be sure, Elinor assumes responsibility in those areas in which she finds Marianne lacking; but Marianne suggests that her "cold-hearted" sister has herself areas of human response that remain undeveloped (p. 17).[7] There is something heroic about Marianne's refusal to speak in situations such as this; speech itself would be tantamount to self-betrayal.

Yet Marianne's refusal "to say what she did not feel" hints at a more serious danger than social awkwardness. Her silence at this moment is a harbinger of that longer and more threatening silence that accompanies her almost total physical collapse later in the novel. There social form is altogether rejected, and the retreat into private feeling becomes absolute. Marianne's situation becomes indistinguishable from the kind of "hysteria" that an overly excitable sensibility was assumed by contemporary psychologists to cause. Critics who celebrate Marianne's spontaneity perhaps forget that her subjection of public to private value, her reliance on emotion and imagination, can in the Age of Sensibility only lead in the direction of madness and silence. "From now on," Michel Foucault says, "one fell ill from too much feeling."[8]

But how much feeling is "too much"? This is a problem Austen explores in *Sense and Sensibility,* not just in regard to Marianne and Elinor, but also in regard to the challenges facing her as an emerging novelist. By analyzing the consequences of her characters' relations to the world and to their feelings, in other words, Austen explores for herself the possibilities of novelistic expression. Subjective emotionalism, that world of feeling already marked out for the female novelist, and objectively didactic social analysis, the possibilities of which Austen had begun to explore in her earliest writing, existed as debilitating alternatives for the aspiring female novelist.[9] I wish to argue in this essay that by examining the implications of "sense" and "sensibility," in themselves and in relation to one another, Austen was able to establish a form of narrative that could express feeling without giving way to hysteria and explore social behavior without becoming coldly analytical. In *Sense and Sensibility,* that is, Austen dramatizes her own discovery of a public voice imbued with private desire, and in doing so she expands the expressive power of fictional discourse itself.

As critics have noted, language mirrors the tension that arises between public and private experience in Jane Austen's world. "Sense" and "sensibility" are not merely different ways of reacting to experience in this novel, they are different ways of expressing that reaction as well. How the sisters use language becomes as important as what they say. Gila P. Reinstein points out that "Marianne's speeches are typically graced with rhetorical questions, apostrophe, personification, and hyperbole," while "Elinor speaks in a static prose of nouns and colorless verbs." "Marianne's verbs," she notes, "are active, and her adjectives, participles, and adverbs evoke lively pictures."[10] In the Age of Sensibility, Marianne's use of language would have been quite familiar. The same description could apply to Collins or Mackenzie or Cowper (Marianne and Austen's favorite). Claudia Johnson may be right to say that Austen does not always refer directly to sensibility, but what need is there for direct reference when a mode of response can be called up in the structure of language itself?

Writers throughout the last half of the eighteenth century were searching for a kind of authenticity in language that philosophy was rendering increasingly remote. The obsession with sensibility itself arises from an anxiety about the nature of selfhood that Locke's theories had made inevitable and that eighteenth-century philosophy deepened and intensified.[11] Such anxiety informs the literary concern with the relation of public to private experience and with the public expression of private emotion in language. What Laurence Sterne cites as the central problem for the writer of Sensibility—the ease with which language can subvert true feeling and the corollary threat that the self may have no meaning beyond its own limited consciousness—remains a problem for Austen as well. In *Sense and Sensibility,* she tries to solve the dilemma of her age in a manner both persuasive and sustaining. Marianne is the last of a long line of characters who must confront that gaping abyss between emotion and language, between authentic feeling and what Sterne calls the "pomp of words."[12] The emphasis on perception and the relation of the private to a threatening public world had been at the heart of Sensibility from the first.

When Elinor attempts to ascertain the truth of the relation between her sister and Willoughby, the paradoxical nature of the sisters' relations to language is brought into high relief. Elinor taxes Marianne about a letter she is expecting. When Marianne resists, Elinor becomes pointed:

> After a short pause, "you have no confidence in me, Marianne."
>
> "Nay, Elinor, this reproach from *you*—you who have confidence in no one!"
>
> "Me!" returned Elinor in some confusion; "indeed, Marianne, I have nothing to tell."

"Nor I," answered Marianne with energy, "our situations then are alike. We have neither of us any thing to tell; you, because you communicate, and I, because I conceal nothing." (pp. 146-47)

We know that Elinor's response to Marianne is less than honest (Lucy has insisted on secrecy regarding her engagement to Edward Ferrars) and that Marianne's accusations are justified. Paradoxically, Elinor is more suited to the public world because she has a more highly developed sense of the private. She uses secrecy as a way of protecting her deepest feelings and shielding those closest to her. She understands the nature of her emotions and therefore hides them even from herself. Language has become for Elinor a means to execute this disguise and mask her inner self with a surface of sociability. Marianne uses language merely to express what she feels.[13] Elinor considers private experience in relation to the public context, while Marianne can only understand private experience in relation to itself. Elinor thinks about her relation to the world, while Marianne primarily feels it.

Marianne, in other words, exists in a world of what Hume calls "impressions," and Elinor in a world of "ideas." "All the perceptions of the human mind," Hume says, "resolve themselves into two distinct kinds, which I shall call IMPRESSIONS and IDEAS. . . . Those perceptions, which enter with most force and violence, we may name *impressions;* and under this name I comprehend all our sensations, passions and emotions, as they make their first appearance in the soul. By *ideas* I mean the faint images of these in thinking and reasoning. . . . Every one of himself will readily perceive the difference betwixt feeling and thinking."[14] In *Sense and Sensibility,* the implied crisis for a thinking, social being is worked out in detail. "Impressions" are more vivid and immediate, according to Hume, than are "ideas," but it is upon those "faint images . . . in thinking and reasoning" that most human activity is regulated. Austen is clearly interested in the implications of this knotty contradiction, and in *Sense and Sensibility* she plays a "thinking" character against a "feeling" one as a way of unraveling it.

In another context, Hume says that "as an idea of the memory, by losing its force and vivacity, may degenerate to such a degree, as to be taken for an idea of the imagination; so on the other hand an idea of the imagination may acquire such a force and vivacity, as to pass for an idea of the memory, and counterfeit its effects on the belief and judgment."[15] It is part of Austen's subtlety that Marianne's "feelings" themselves may be predetermined by her imagination. Susan Morgan puts the case succinctly: "the conventions of sensibility, far from representing a mode of spontaneous and open response . . . are a means of predetermining truth, of dictating judgment and behavior."[16] Marianne, in other words, becomes the vic-

tim of her own delusions in the very manner that Hume describes: she is so devoted to her fantasies that she establishes them in her imagination as fact; her feelings take such precedence that she goes out of her way to create situations that will elicit them. Moreover, she does nothing to curb the pain they cause. "I must feel—I must be wretched—" she says during her first shock over Willoughby's desertion (p. 164). This is a character who has become trapped in her own self-conscious response.[17]

Marianne's emotional and physical collapse at the center of the novel is a linguistic collapse as well. Her eloquence is transformed by the pressure of self-contempt into "inarticulate sounds of complaint," "feverish wildness," and "sleepless pain and delirium," almost as if her syntactic pyrotechnics had turned on herself (pp. 271-73). We are made to feel that her collapse results from a sensibility heightened by imagination to the point that feeling has started to self-destruct.

In the eighteenth century, the word "sensibility" connoted physical as well as emotional susceptibility to pleasure and pain, as this passage from George Cheyne's *The English Malady* (1733) suggests:

> Those who stutter, stammer, have a great Difficulty with utterance, speak very low, lose their Voice without catching Cold, grow dumb, deaf, or blind, without an Accident or an acute Distemper; are quick, prompt, and passionate; are all of weak Nerves; have a great Degree of Sensibility; are quick thinkers, feel Pleasure or Pain the most readily, and are of a most lively imagination.[18]

Marianne's symptoms may not be as extreme as those described here, but the last half of the passage does call her personality to mind. Notice, too, that Cheyne's analysis relates nervous speechlessness to heightened sensibility and a lively imagination. Imagination is a faculty, as Hume's analysis has suggested, that could easily undermine the coherent structure of thought and speech, rendering the subject isolated in the silence of a world beyond speech, a world of madness.[19]

Cheyne connects amply documented "hysterical" behavior to physical disorders of a particularly suggestive kind:

> I never saw any Person labour under severe, obstinate, and strong *Nervous* Complaints, but I always found at last, the *Stomach, Guts, Liver, Spleen, Mesentery,* or some other great and necessary Organs or *Glands* of the lower Belly were obstructed, knotted, schirrous or spoil'd, and perhaps all these together.[20]

Michel Foucault, in *Madness and Civilization,* uses descriptions such as this one by Cheyne to suggest a relation between the female sexual organs and early diagnoses of hysteria.[21] In his chapter on "Hysteria and Hypochondria," Foucault centers his discussion on the notion of "irritability of fibers," thereby suggesting the relation between physiology and psychology in the eighteenth century. Foucault says that "all life was finally judged by this degree of irritation," and he shows that physical irritability easily gives way to mental instability: "once the mind becomes blind *through the very excess of sensibility*—then madness appears" (my italics).[22] It is, further, this configuration of madness with a guilty conscience, or really unconscious, that Foucault sees as the origin of modern psychiatry.

Marianne clearly borders on the kind of sexual hysteria that Foucault describes. Her imagination creates a form of desire that is impossible even for Willoughby to satisfy. She focuses her attention on Willoughby because he alone seems able to participate in her private fantasy. But that is a momentary delusion. The "violent affliction" (p. 64) she suffers when he is separated from her later becomes "excessive affliction" (p. 155) when he has proven himself false. Marianne's "irritability" is emphasized throughout the novel. For instance, Elinor wonders "that Marianne, . . . thoroughly acquainted with Mrs. Jennings' manners, and invariably disgusted by them, . . . should disregard whatever must be most wounding to her irritable feelings, in her pursuit of one object" (p. 133). Soon after, Elinor accepts Marianne's plea for silence, made "with all the eagerness of the most nervous irritability" (p. 156); and later she notes "the irritable refinement of [Marianne's] mind" and "the delicacies of a strong sensibility" (p. 175). Although we are repeatedly treated to displays of Marianne's irritability—those frequent outbursts of frustration or disgust—we are perhaps apt to miss their diagnostic significance. I would like to emphasize the degree to which the play of Marianne's private imagination has made her susceptible to the kind of self-delusions in which her character abounds. "Madness became possible," according to Foucault, "in that milieu where man's relationships with his feelings . . . were altered."[23]

The connection between "hysteria" and linguistic disturbance is implicit in Cheyne's remarks. An excess of feeling seems to disrupt the syntactic contiguity of language and to substitute private incoherence for the public coherence that language represents. At its worst, Marianne's raging fever traps her in heartbreaking isolation from those around her. Her exuberant speech, which had become almost manic in its intensity, is silenced in the misery of self-contempt. Out of this dark silence, however, she emerges to find herself in a new relation with herself and the world around her.

Whether we go so far as to apply to Marianne Foucault's sexual interpretation of hysteria probably depends on the degree to which we find it implicit in

the details of the novel. When we listen to Marianne's outburst of guilt following her illness, however, such associations are impossible to ignore:

> "Do not, my dearest Elinor, let your kindness defend what I know your judgment must censure. My illness has made me think—It has given me the leisure and calmness for serious recollection. Long before I was enough recovered to talk, I was perfectly able to reflect. . . . I saw that my own feelings had prepared my sufferings, and that my want of fortitude under them had almost led me to the grave. My illness, I well knew, had been entirely brought on by myself, by such negligence of my own health, as I had felt even at the time to be wrong. Had I died,—it would have been self-destruction. . . . I cannot express my own abhorrence of myself." (p. 303)

Marianne seems automatically to blame herself here. Guilt arises not so much from what she has done as from her nature. In Foucault's terms, her illness could be said to be "the psychological effect of a moral fault."[24] That her guilt stems from an unconscious fear of her sexuality is implicit in the terms of her rejection of her earlier self.[25]

If Marianne seems trapped in a response that at first puts her at odds with her own sexuality, we must consider, as Foucault explains in *The History of Sexuality,* that such a process was one of the "strategic unities which, beginning in the eighteenth century, formed specific mechanisms of knowledge and power centering on sex." The "nervous woman" is for him the "anchorage point" for the "hysterization of women's bodies":

> a threefold process whereby the feminine body was analyzed . . . as being thoroughly saturated with sexuality; whereby it was integrated into the sphere of medical practices, by reason of a pathology intrinsic to it; whereby, finally, it was placed in organic communication with the social body (whose regulated fecundity it was supposed to ensure), the family space (of which it had to be a substantial and functional element), and the life of children.[26]

He sees this process as a further step in the direction of psychoanalysis, a process that in his view emerges inevitably as institutionalization of the familial deployment of sexuality. Marianne's confession is in this sense a proto-case history.

Like a case history as well is Marianne's willingness to inscribe the signs of her guilt in language, not in the form of the fantastic dreamscapes of her earlier rhapsodies, but in careful and deliberate reflection on the social implications of her private desire. In terms of Elinor's rehabilitative program, that is, Marianne has begun the all-important process of self-regulation. Surely we can notice a basic change in the nature of Marianne's use of language here. This speech is the longest and most coherent that she has uttered up to this point in the novel. If she seems at first tentative, centering as she does on self-accusation, she at last becomes calmly assertive of the terms of self-judgment. "I saw that my own feelings had prepared my sufferings": Marianne's ecstatic impressions have given way to careful self-assessment. Her perceptions of her own behavior are as astute as Elinor's would be. She is able to distinguish between emotion and judgment in Elinor's response, and she applies those distinctions to herself: "My illness has made me *think*" (my italics). Marianne's physical collapse has forced her from her impressionistic response to the world and caused her to look at herself objectively. The self-abhorrence that results, we are meant to understand, is a necessary corrective to earlier indulgence. Marianne seems to have succumbed to the dictates of self-knowledge and to have accepted "ideas" as a corrective substitute for "impressions." She seems also to have settled for a linguistic compromise that sacrifices private meaning to public context in language.

What happens, then, is that Marianne becomes more and more sane as well as more suited to public position to the degree that she is willing to reject her earlier self. Indeed, Nina Auerbach sees in this novel a "pervasive philosophical awareness of the self's potential for self-betrayal."[27] But is it an act of self-betrayal for Marianne to escape the death that her sensibility had so clearly prepared her for? Do we really wish to see her sacrificed to her own spontaneity? Austen, in any case, does not. Marianne survives and Austen grudgingly celebrates that survival, not only for what it tells us about Marianne and the self, but also for what it tells us about novelistic language.

Just as Marianne tends to disrupt language with her excessive feeling, Elinor finds it natural to subvert private desire with the objectifying power of linguistic structures. We all remember the passage early in the novel when the sisters meet Edward Ferrars in the lanes near Barton Cottage:

"Have you been lately in Sussex?" said Elinor.

"I was at Norland about a month ago."

"And how does dear, dear Norland look?" cried Marianne.

"Dear, dear Norland," said Elinor, "probably looks much as it always does at this time of year. The woods and walks are thickly covered with dead leaves."

"Oh!" cried Marianne, "with what transporting sensations have I formerly seen them fall! How have I delighted, as I walked, to see them driven in showers about me by the wind! What feelings have they, the season, the air altogether inspired! Now there is no one to regard them. They are seen only as a nuisance, swept hastily off, and driven as much as possible from the sight."

"It is not everyone," said Elinor, "who has your passion for dead leaves." (pp. 75-76)

What Elinor gently ridicules as "a passion for dead leaves" is of course nothing of the kind. For Marianne, the leaves themselves are only the vehicle for a metaphor whose tenor remains finally unexpressed. Marianne is thinking about the air, to be sure, but she is also thinking about love and freedom and the possibility of defying the very limits of selfhood, which her current situation circumscribes. Metaphor for Marianne is a means of escape. But it is also a rejection of the means of effecting that escape.

Elinor seems almost brutal in her literalization of Marianne's metaphor, but her literal-mindedness represents an effort to liberate herself from the threat of Marianne's imagination. At the same time her aggressiveness on this occasion suggests a failure of her imagination, an inability to see beyond the literal. Elinor's response must also be understood in terms of Edward's presence. She is attempting to censure Marianne's enthusiasm as publicly unbecoming. She wants to compartmentalize and de-romanticize the past as well. All these activities are in the interest of creating a smooth surface and of controlling feeling so that it does not disrupt decorum.[28]

In a sense, Marianne and Elinor begin the novel trapped in linguistic patterns that veer toward the kind of "aphasic disturbances" that Jakobson describes in his now classic study, *Fundamentals of Language*.[29] Marianne has problems with contiguous relations (and relationships), inhabiting, as she does, a world of constant and ultimately debilitating metaphor. Elinor, on the other hand, if she errs, errs in the direction of an overemphasis on metonymical relations as she attempts to internalize the context and put flight to private desire. We have seen that Marianne's dependence on metaphor and imagination leads to self-consuming madness and that she begins to emerge from instability when she can order her linguistic structures so as to include a sense of a world beyond her private vision. Elinor, too, must discover that her rejection of private desire in favor of screens and surfaces and the maintenance of decorum will lead her to a desolate future.

Elinor comes early to understand that the public world will forever impinge on the indulgences of privacy. When at Barton, for instance, as Elinor thinks about Edward in the seclusion of her own drawing room, she finds herself burst in upon, not in the usual manner but as follows:

From a reverie of this kind, as she sat at her drawing-table, she was roused one morning . . . by the arrival of company. She happened to be quite alone. The closing of the little gate, at the entrance of the green court in front of the house, drew her eyes to the window, and she saw a large party walking up to the door. . . . She was sitting near the window, and as soon as Sir John perceived her, he left the rest of the party to the ceremony of knocking at the door, and stepping across the turf, obliged her to open the casement to speak to him, though the space was so short between the door and the window, as to make it hardly possible to speak at one without being heard at the other. (p. 90)

Nowhere in the novel are the demands of social intercourse so vividly dramatized, and nowhere do we have so clear an indication of what Austen considered the limits of privacy to be. Elinor can have no private thoughts but the press of the social world breaks in upon them, as it does here literally in the person of Sir John. If Elinor is to have private thoughts at all, it must be within such situations and between such intrusions. Elinor's wariness, then, seems an admirable defense in a world of intrusive and malicious society. She uses metonymical forms not just to create public relations, but also to protect herself from the potentially devastating revelation of her privacy, barely acknowledged as it is. Her dependence on public forms, however, and on truth as opposed to speculation, leads her into the trap that Lucy Steele's manipulation of those forms makes inevitable.

It takes Lucy's malicious confidence regarding Edward Ferrars to put Elinor through an ordeal as trying as that of Marianne. Only through a conscious assertion of will can Elinor keep herself from expressing the indignation she feels:

> "I gave him a lock of my hair [Lucy says] set in a ring when he was at Longstaple last, and that was some comfort to him, he said, but not equal to a picture. Perhaps you might notice the ring when you saw him?"

> "I did;" said Elinor, with a composure of voice, under which was concealed an emotion and distress beyond any thing she had ever felt before. She was mortified, shocked, confounded. (pp. 116-17)

Elinor is confounded because she has been undone even in her caution. When, a short time earlier, she saw this ring on Edward's finger, she allowed emotion to overcome reason: "That the hair was her own, she instantaneously *felt* as well satisfied as Marianne" (p. 84, my italics).

Certainly we witness here the failure of Elinor's epistemological technique.[30] She has been looking for concrete proof of Edward's love, and now she feels she has found it. Her metonymical approach to experience fails her—it does not allow her to place herself in the relationship she desires—and she abandons it in favor of an interpretation more in keeping with her own fantasy. At the moment when keenest observation is required, in other words, Elinor sees only what she wants to see. Her response is to give the ring the meaning she wants it to have: to make it a metaphor for her desire. Exposing the secret of her sexuality and confronting the implications of her mistake, as she does, puts Elinor in a position to "think and be wretched" (p. 117). Like Marianne, Elinor feels self-reproach at the danger her sexuality has occasioned, and it seems possible that she will succumb to guilty self-loathing as stunningly as Marianne.

Instead, Elinor works through her sexual disappointment intellectually and in doing so finds a way of resolving sexual desire and personal responsibility. Austen enables her to do this by devising a language that is poised between the extremes of private (metaphorical) and public (metonymical) speech. In *Sense and Sensibility,* Austen works out this resolution not just thematically but linguistically and formally as well. In exploring the implications of "sensibility" and moving from the pathetically tragic potential of that world into the "light and bright and sparkling" world of comedy, Austen is liberating herself from the threat of madness (and silence) that sensibility finally represents.

It is necessary for the novelist herself to find a language that can mediate the intensity of private vision and the complexity of public scope. We can tell that Austen is experimenting with such inner/outer language in moments like these:

> Had Edward been intentionally deceiving her? Had he feigned a regard for her which he did not feel? Was his engagement to Lucy, an engagement of the heart? No; whatever it might once have been, she could not believe it such at present. His affection was all her own. She could not be deceived in that. Her mother, sisters, Fanny, all had been conscious of his regard for her at Norland; it was not an illusion of her own vanity. He certainly loved her. What a softener of the heart was this persuasion! (pp. 119-20)

In the first place, of course, we are witnessing narrative exploration of Elinor's thoughts and feelings. The opening questions represent a challenge to earlier assumptions, assumptions that Elinor held close to her heart. Austen deftly represents this self-examination in a type of public speech that has been crafted to reflect mental processes. The rush of emotional uneasiness is mirrored in the choppiness of the prose here, and the self-assurances, timid and prolix at first, become stronger and more direct as this process of reflection continues.

The technique of Elinor's self-assurance is perhaps even more subtle. She first searches her own emotions for the truth of Edward's attachment to her; then she tests that private assurance rationally. To do so involves testing the responses of the public world, in this case, her mother, sisters, and Fanny. When she has thereby assured herself of emotional security, she can state to herself what now has value as objective fact: "He certainly loved her." After that has been articulated, she returns to the "heart" and its malleability. Rational persuasion "softens" the heart, which in its pain may have hardened, and allows human feeling to animate her response without causing her to give way to excessive emotion. Elinor finds a way to think *and* feel, without allowing one mode of response to compromise the other.

What Austen has accomplished, then, is manifold. She has developed a technique for representing mental processes in her prose while suggesting the terms whereby the tension between public and private experience is to be resolved. She introduces public, objective language into the privacy of inner emotion as a way of dispelling the ghosts that haunt inarticulate emotional response, like that of Marianne. She demonstrates how such a crisis as Marianne's can be resolved by realigning public and private value.

Marianne's illness becomes for both sisters the test of their feelings for one another and the proof that language can be a bond rather than a barrier separating them from their inmost selves. Throughout the illness, as Marianne's pulse races and she cries out in delirium, Elinor is all watchfulness and apprehension. After her interview with Willoughby, however, Elinor has something to communicate. The moment for such communication comes when Marianne has finally accepted the limitations of sensibility and expressed the self-deprecations quoted above. Now Elinor offers her communication not as a lesson to Marianne but as a way of consoling her sister and convincing her that she had been loved:

> [Elinor] managed the recital, as she hoped, with address; prepared her anxious listener with caution; related simply and honestly the chief points on which Willoughby grounded his apology; did justice to his repentance, and softened only his protestations of present regard. Marianne said not a word.—She trembled, her eyes were fixed on the ground, and her lips became whiter than even sickness had left them. A thousand inquiries sprung up from her heart, but she dared not urge one. She caught every syllable with panting eagerness; her hand, unknowingly to herself, closely pressed her sister's, and tears covered her cheeks. (p. 305)

Notice how much attention Austen pays to the manner of Elinor's presentation. We hear much more about how she addresses Marianne than about what precisely she says. The emphasis is on the act itself. Yet this simple act of communication and response quells much

of the sisterly uneasiness that the novel has dramatized. Metaphor and metonym are here combined once again to suggest that each sister has come closer to understanding the relations between public and private speech. Elinor uses tact and concern to enter Marianne's world, and she is welcomed there with a squeeze of the hand to suggest that the barriers of language have at last been broken down. Feeling is still paramount for Marianne—she presses Elinor's hand "unknowingly"— but now her feeling seems directed toward others. She edits the "inquiries sprung up from her heart" and produces instead a thoughtful request: "Tell mama," she urges Elinor (p. 305). Surely this is a Marianne who is moving beyond the incapacitating limitations of entirely private metaphor into a world in which language means communication as well. Many of the early conflicts of the novel are resolved in this scene. Marianne's recovery seems assured, and a new basis for self-affirmation seems guaranteed.

If this resolution is so affirmative, however, why has there been such dissatisfaction with the ending of the novel? Even a contemporary reader, Lady Bessborough, could write to a friend, "Have you read *Sense and Sensibility?* It is a clever novel. They were full of it at Althorpe, and tho' it ends stupidly, I was much amused by it."[31] The marriages at the close of the novel, both happy and unhappy, sit uneasily with our sense of Elinor's new self-awareness and Marianne's new self-possession. Marianne's marriage to Brandon, as peremptory as it is, comes close to parody. We might well agree with Tanner, who sees Austen's handling of Marianne as "harshly curt."[32] Gilbert and Gubar attribute this harshness to an inner conflict in Austen: *"Sense and Sensibility* is an especially painful novel to read because Austen herself seems caught between her attraction to Marianne's sincerity and spontaneity while at the same [time] identifying with the civil falsehoods and the polite silences of Elinor" (p. 177).[33]

Rather than identifying with either of these characters, however, Austen seems to be working out the claims of each for herself as a novelist. Deborah Kaplan suggests that "Austen was able to achieve authority not in assertions but in the modification, the correction of such assertions."[34] Austen also achieves authority by reformulating the configuration of thought and feeling dramatized by the sisters. She forces Elinor to come to terms with the fact of her own sexuality as a means of liberating herself from the confines of bitterness, and she establishes authority over Marianne and over such impulses toward sensibility as she sensed in herself, as a way of distancing the appalling threat of speechless emotionalism.[35] She relies on the force of a comic resolution to celebrate her discovery and to give it form.

But still for many readers the comic ending seems anything but comic. Earlier Marianne had rejected Brandon as dull and uninspiring: "his understanding has no brilliancy, his feelings no ardour, and his voice no expression" (p. 44). Now she gives him her hand out of "strong esteem and lively friendship" (p. 333). Because this is a pale reflection of her active passion for Willoughby, readers feel that Marianne has had to settle for much less than she deserved. But perhaps she was mistaken in imagining what she deserved. Once she has learned to control her passion and distrust herself, Marianne earns her position in a different kind of resolution from the one she imagined earlier. Released from the privacy of her emotions, she becomes party to the deployment of sexual power on a larger scale:

> Instead of falling a sacrifice to an irresistible passion, as once she had fondly flattered herself with expecting,—instead of remaining even for ever with her mother, and finding her only pleasures in retirement and study, as afterwards in her more calm and sober judgment she had determined on,—she found herself at nineteen, submitting to new attachments, entering on new duties, placed in a new home, a wife, the mistress of a family, and the patroness of a village. (p. 333)

Foucault has perhaps offered us the terms whereby such a realignment of public and private reality can be explained. He asserts that the hysterization of women was part of "a new distribution of pleasures, discourses, truths, and powers" on the part of the bourgeoisie: "a defense, a protection, a strengthening, and an exaltation . . . as a means of social control and political subjugation."[36] Marianne is "saved" from her hysteria in order to be swept into a social resolution at the expense, of course, of her seemingly aberrant private desire. Once her sexuality has been harnessed, she fits more readily into a position of social influence and public power. We feel the sting of what has been sacrificed to achieve this resolution, for Marianne plays her role in a power structure that excludes her as effectively as it celebrates her reconstituted self. Social relations replace the private aspirations of sensibility and establish an unfamiliar public role for the heroine. What private value is not lost is redirected toward "new attachments."

This ending represents the failure of sensibility. If the novel "ends stupidly," I think we understand this stupidity as the first harbinger of Victorian insistence on brutalizing resolutions. If the Age of Sensibility celebrated the primacy of private feeling, the resolution here works skillfully to suppress it.

What can Austen have felt she was achieving? How could so sensitive a novelist allow her work to come to so disconcerting a conclusion? The answer, it seems to me, lies in her need to find the proper novelistic voice. If Marianne is sacrificed, it is to Austen's own desire to find a language that can resolve the two extremes of linguistic behavior represented by Marianne and Elinor.

For a novelist must achieve a public voice that remains sensitive to private desire, and a great novelist must realize metonymical as well as metaphorical patterns of reference. Marianne's personal loss is therefore a gain for the "novel," and the Bennet sisters and Emma Woodhouse emerge from this new standard of novelistic discourse. If the Age of Sensibility is at an end, the Age of the Female Novelist is only just beginning. Marianne is sacrificed, in other words, in order to liberate Austen and her successors from the inarticulate emotional world that the Age of Sensibility had created for them. Words are no longer to be distrusted in the English novel; rather they will come more and more to offer the only context for self-realization in heroines throughout the century. Language becomes the arena in which thought and emotion meet, and self-expression takes the place of self-assertion. Public and private are resolved in a novelistic discourse that masters the intricacies of selfhood and achieves a version of social stature. *Sense and Sensibility* carries us, then, beyond the dichotomy of the title to a resolution, painful and peremptory as it is, that signals growth. The personal intensity of the Age of Sensibility is lost, and in its place we have a new kind of self-control, capable of preserving the heroine and earning her a place in the world. Marianne learns the meaning of public responsibility at the expense of her soul. But souls are awkward in a society that is moving toward the communal benefits of a comic vision.

Notes

[1] For a discussion of the problematical novels in the Austen canon, see Susan Morgan, *In the Meantime: Character and Perception in Jane Austen's Fiction* (Chicago and London: University of Chicago Press, 1980), pp. 1-5; also see Ruth apRoberts, "*Sense and Sensibility,* or Growing Up Dichotomous," *Nineteenth-Century Fiction,* 30 (1975), 351-65; apRoberts addresses the issue of Austen's dichotomy more imaginatively and with more useful results than most critics. For a discussion of the problematic resolution, see the chapter on *Sense and Sensibility* in Tony Tanner, *Jane Austen* (Cambridge: Harvard University Press, 1986), pp. 75-102. For even more persuasive accounts of the violence done Marianne, see Sandra M. Gilbert and Susan Gubar, *The Madwoman in the Attic: The Woman Writer and the Nineteenth-Century Literary Imagination* (New Haven and London: Yale University Press, 1979), p. 157; and Nina Auerbach, *Romantic Imprisonment: Women and Other Glorified Outcasts* (New York: Columbia University Press, 1985), pp. 11-15.

[2] Claudia Johnson, "The 'Twilight of Probability': Uncertainty and Hope in *Sense and Sensibility,*" *Philological Quarterly,* 62 (1983), 171-86; also see Morgan, *In the Meantime,* pp. 109-31.

[3] Johnson, p. 172.

[4] Auerbach, pp. 14-15.

[5] Mary Poovey suggests in *The Proper Lady and the Woman Writer: Ideology as Style in the Works of Mary Wollstonecraft, Mary Shelley, and Jane Austen* (Chicago and London: Chicago University Press, 1984) that "between these antimonies [of sense and sensibility] there is no easy choice but rather myriads of possible combinations, each understood in terms of costs and benefits, sacrifices and opportunities" (p. 44).

[6] Jane Austen, *Sense and Sensibility,* ed. James Kinsley and Claire Lamont (Oxford and New York: Oxford University Press, 1970), p. 105. All subsequent parenthetical references are to this edition.

[7] Critics have argued that Elinor is not without feeling early in the novel. See, for instance, Jean H. Hagstrum, *Sex and Sensibility: Ideal and Erotic Love from Milton to Mozart* (Chicago and London: University of Chicago Press, 1980), pp. 271-72.

[8] Michel Foucault, *Madness and Civilization: A History of Insanity in the Age of Reason,* trans. Richard Howard (1965; rpt. New York: Vintage-Random House, 1973), p. 157.

[9] Poovey says that "feeling was one significant theater of experience that could not be completely denied to women" (p. 37); she goes on to say that "although women found in the sentimental novel a subject and even a genre, these works . . . helped to drive further underground the aggressive, perhaps sexual, energies that men feared in women" (p. 38). See also Jane Spencer, *The Rise of the Woman Novelist, From Aphra Behn to Jane Austen* (Oxford: Blackwell, 1986); Spencer distinguishes "didactic" and "fantastic" strains in women's fiction in the late eighteenth century, pp. 140-213. Wollstonecraft illustrates some of the limitations of the first alternative and Radcliffe of the second.

[10] Gila P. Reinstein, "Moral Priorities in *Sense and Sensibility,*" *Renascence,* 35 (1983), 272.

[11] In *The Romantic Sublime: Studies in the Structure and Psychology of Transcendence* (Baltimore and London: Johns Hopkins University Press, 1976), Thomas Weiskel suggests that Locke's theory of the self led him to a theory of "uneasiness," in which "anxiety will always exceed its occasion because the soul can never be entirely filled by the sensations and reflections which arise from an object 'out there'—an object whose essential absence is presupposed by perception" (p. 18). Weiskel cites Tuveson as suggesting that the revisions in Locke's fourth edition anticipate the modern notion of the unconscious (p. 206, n. 35); see Ernest Tuveson, "Locke and the 'Dissolution of the Ego,'" *Modern Philology,* 52 (1955), 159-74.

[12] Laurence Sterne, *A Sentimental Journey through France and Italy,* ed. Gardner D. Stout (Berkeley and Los Angeles: University of California Press, 1967), pp. 277-78; see John A. Dussinger, "The Sensorium in the World of *A Sentimental Journey,*" *Ariel,* 13 (1982), 3-16.

[13] See Tanner, pp. 90-93; Edward Joseph Shoben, Jr., talks about the "unbridled expression of emotion" as a danger for Austen in "Impulse and Virtue in Jane Austen: *Sense and Sensibility* in Two Centuries," *Hudson Review,* 35 (1982-83), 338; Morgan suggests that Marianne "collaps[es] the distinction between feeling and expression, thus making expression spontaneous and inevitable" (p. 121). Later, Morgan calls this Marianne's "personal integrity in language" (p. 123).

[14] David Hume, *A Treatise of Human Nature,* ed. P. H. Nidditch (Oxford: Clarendon Press, 1978), pp. 1-2.

[15] Hume, p. 86.

[16] Morgan, p. 123.

[17] See John A. Dussinger, *The Discourse of the Mind in Eighteenth-Century Fiction* (The Hague: Mouton, 1974), pp. 37-39; Dussinger uses Hume's version of the "self" as an imaginary construct of continuous perceptions—"merely a habit of thinking, and the fiction of the perceiving ego"—to suggest that much of the literature of sensibility addresses the resulting uneasiness about permanence of selfhood by means of the moment to moment expression that Northrop Frye implies in his term "literature of process." See Frye, "Towards Defining an Age of Sensibility," *Fables of Identity: Studies in Poetic Mythology* (New York: Harcourt, 1963), pp. 130-31. Dussinger says further that "some of the most 'characteristic' works of fiction in this period portray the mind restless to the end and ever in doubt about the self" (p. 39).

[18] George Cheyne, *The English Malady,* ed. Eric T. Carlson, M.D. (Delmar, N.Y.: Scholar's Facsimiles and Reprints, 1976), pp. 71-72.

[19] See Tanner, pp. 109-11; see also Poovey, who demonstrates as a "paradox of propriety" the fear of sexuality implicit in the praise of a woman's "sensibility of heart" in the eighteenth century, pp. 18-19.

[20] Cheyne, p. 127.

[21] Foucault, pp. 146-50; I am indebted to Tanner's useful discussion of Foucault's analysis of madness and sensibility, pp. 82-85; see also Richard Blackmore, *Treatise of the Spleen and Vapours, or Hypochondriacal and Hysterical Affections* (London: J. Pemberton, 1725); and Robert James, "Hysteria," in *Medicinal Dictionary* (London: T. Osborne, 1743).

22 Foucault, p. 158.

23 Foucault, p. 220; see Tanner, p. 83.

24 Foucault, p. 158.

25 Poovey argues that "given the voraciousness that female desire was assumed to have, the surest safeguard against overindulgence was not to allow or admit to appetites of any kind. Thus women were encouraged to display no vanity, no passion, no assertive 'self' at all" (p. 21).

26 Michel Foucault, *The History of Sexuality: Volume I, An Introduction,* trans. Robert Hurley (New York: Vintage-Random House, 1980), pp. 103-05.

27 Auerbach, p. 15.

28 See Tanner, pp. 86-88; also see Morgan, who says that "decorum . . . is a public avowal of continued feelings and thoughts, a way of behaving which sustains the potential in experience for active and changing relations between others and ourselves" (p. 129).

29 Roman Jakobson, "Two Aspects of Language and Two Types of Aphasic Disturbances," in Roman Jakobson and Morris Halle, *Fundamentals of Language, Janua Linguarum,* Series Minor, 1 (1956; rpt. The Hague: Mouton, 1971), pp. 67-96.

30 Johnson, p. 176.

31 Quoted in Margharita Laski, *Jane Austen and Her World* (London: Thames and Hudson, 1969), p. 82.

32 Tanner, p. 100.

33 Gilbert and Gubar, p. 157.

34 Deborah Kaplan, "Achieving Authority: Jane Austen's First Published Novel," *Nineteenth-Century Fiction,* 37 (1983), 537; Poovey writes, "in *Sense and Sensibility* . . . the most fundamental conflict is between Austen's own imaginative engagement with her self-assertive characters and the moral code necessary to control their anarchic desires" (p. 183).

35 In his *Memoir of Jane Austen* (1871; rpt. Oxford: Oxford University Press, 1951), James Edward Austen-Leigh, her nephew, tells us that when "*Sense and Sensibility* came out, some persons, who knew the family slightly, surmised that the two elder Miss Dashwoods were intended by the author for her sister and herself" (p. 17).

36 Foucault, *The History of Sexuality,* p. 123.

Barbara M. Benedict (essay date 1990)

SOURCE: "Jane Austen's *Sense and Sensibility*: The Politics of Point of View," in *Philological Quarterly,* Vol. 69, No. 4, Fall, 1990, pp. 453-70.

[*In the following essay, Benedict explains how Austen negotiates between epistolary (sentimental) and objective (detached) narration in* Sense and Sensibility.]

Sense and Sensibility usually leaves modern readers cold, even irritated. They indict the book for a schematic structure which seems to segregate intelligence and warmth; for a tonal instability which seems to sneer while soliciting sympathy; and for a merciless ending which awards a crushed Marianne Dashwood "by general consent" to the flannel-waistcoated Colonel Brandon.[1] By condemning Austen's moral organization, these complaints address a general problem of interpretation: the problem of identifying the narrative attitude. This problem is epitomized by the contradiction between the sympathetic portrayal of Marianne, and the unflagging praise for her opposite, the "sensible" sister Elinor. Such a contradiction seems to weaken the authority of the narrative voice, and thus to shake the reader's faith in Austen's narrative control.

This contradiction stems from the conflict, evident in contemporary fiction, between two modes of narrative, each claiming the authority to tell human experience: the epistolary and the objective mode. While ***Sense and Sensibility*** does possess an authoritative narrative voice, Austen also admits into the novel another kind of perspective that challenges the dominance of the narrator's perspective: the epistolary point of view. These two perspectives differ in style, tone and topic: the epistolary viewpoint typically includes immediate feelings, impressions and reactions, even if multiple and contradictory, while the objective viewpoint typically delivers considered, univocal judgments after ranking the available information, excluding irrelevancies and weighing the real situation against an ideal standard.

By including both perspectives, Austen recasts the eighteenth-century opposition crystallized in the novel's title. As the novel progresses, this opposition no longer lies between behavioral models of restraint and release, between Elinor's "sense" and Marianne's "sensibility"; instead, it is shown to be an opposition between both sisters' points of view and the viewpoint of the narrative. Austen pits the sources and authority of the epistolary mode transferred to *style indirect libre* against those of objective narration. By permitting both modes expression in her novel, Austen challenges the authority of narrative control itself, predicated as this control is upon the convention of a single, coherent mode.

This contrast has political ramifications. In juxtaposing perspectives founded on literary conventions, Austen questions the very concept of a single, true vision of social relations—a concept itself indebted to the same sources as the idealized perspective of objective narration. Currently, critics are debating whether Jane Austen believes this vision by asking whether she rehearses or revises eighteenth-century conservatism. While Claudia L. Johnson finds Austen attacking the politics of personal life, Marilyn Butler sees her defending traditional political stability. While Tony Tanner reads her novels as involuntary indictments of social styles, Michael Williams locates in *Sense and Sensibility* an analysis of contemporary conceptions of taste.[2] These critical views address two relationships. One is the relationship between domestic life and "politics," i.e., the apportionment of power in the social world; the other is the relationship between Austen's fictions and their contemporary sources. Although critics have divided these relationships, in fact they are intertwined. Austen's fiction represents social relations by means of conventional, imaginative models: any flaws in the social relations she depicts reflect flaws in the literary models she uses since these models endorse specific ways of viewing relationships. By exposing the impossibility of a heroine judging with ideal impartiality, *Sense and Sensibility* shows that social politics and literary politics mirror each other in the question of the "authority" of perception.

This essay will explore the way Austen negotiates the politics of literary conventions in *Sense and Sensibility.* Originally composed as an epistolary fiction, *Sense and Sensibility* opposes the perspectives of the "sentimental," erstwhile epistolary heroines with that of the detached narrator. By granting the heroine Elinor the objective perspective conventionally accorded only to a detached narrator, Austen challenges the authority of objective narration to tell a heroine's tale. Austen, however, condemns epistolary perspectives as self-indulgent even while recognizing them as the traditional voice of female experience. It is the voice of detached narration, "objective" and hence virtuous, that translates experience into the general moral lesson didactic fiction requires. Epistolary techniques thus obstruct the narrative authority of Austen's novel by endorsing feeling when disinterest is expected. As Elinor and Marianne grow more similar, both heroines represent a source of authority and a kind of expression which opposes the values represented by the narrative voice. When Austen finally locates authority in objective narration, she eschews the point of view of "female" fiction with its value for multiplicity and feeling in favor of an ideal perspective whose organization of information into hierarchy derives from conservative literary traditions. Nevertheless, through the narrative strategy of contrasting conventions of style and topic, Austen reveals that contrast motivates moral ranking, and that this contrast is itself a matter of the conventions of literary and social perspective, conventions which favor abstract ideals and "masculine" view-

points.[3] *Sense and Sensibility,* Jane Austen's novel contrasting control and expression, in fact challenges the very power of contrast, even the power to contrast, by questioning the authority of the source of such contrast: monovocal, conventional narrative itself.

In her juvenilia, Austen explores the limits of epistolary authority. Parodying sentimental literature for selfishness and insincerity, these works indict an hypocrisy both social and literary. In the early satire "The Three Sisters," Austen conceives this hypocrisy through contrasting the moral and literary styles of two sisters: Mary Stanhope who describes her own feelings; and Georgiana who records the plot as a spectator. Writes Mary to her friend Fanny,

> I am the happiest creature in the World, for I have received an offer of marriage from Mr. Watts. . . . He is extremely disagreeable & I hate him more than any body else in the world. . . . If I refuse him he as good as told me he should offer himself to Sophia and if *she* refused him to Georgiana, & I could not bear to have either of them married before me. If I accept him I know I shall be miserable all the rest of my Life . . . He told me he should mention the affair to Mama, but I insisted upon it that he did not for very likely she would make me marry him whether I would or no; however probably he *has* before now, for he never does anything he is desired to do. I believe I shall have him.[4]

Mary's letter describes the psychology of decision, the Johnsonian vacillations between competing hopes and fears, and the impotence of the fearful will tossed between obdurate and powerful others. By eighteenth-century convention, it is typically a woman's letter: it reflects women's concerns—marriage, sexual competition, social compulsion—in a woman's style which circles ever around the subject self with its tumbling, unordered phrases and imprecise language. Whereas Austen's favorite epistolary novelists Samuel Richardson and Fanny Burney use this style to dramatize the seriousness of female interior experience, Austen mocks feminine triviality by rooting Mary's anxiety in social and material matters.[5] While proclaiming the letter authentic, this style also implies that women's thoughts and feelings are unordered. Mary's style and subject cohere as she describes the interior, female, emotional experience of a world she does not control.[6]

Mary's sister Georgiana, however, writes to her friend Anne with the detached perspective which allows the perception of contrast:

> It was in vain that Mama represented to [Mary] the impropriety she was guilty of in disliking him who was to be her Husband, for she persisted in declaring her aversion to him & hoping she might never see him again. What a Wedding will this be! Adeiu my dear Anne. (p. 67)

Emma Thompson, Kate Winslet, and Gemma Jones in a scene from the motion picture Sense and Sensibility.

Signed "Yr faithfully Sincere Georgiana Stanhope," this letter opens with an impersonal syntactical formulation, "It was," employs a Latinate vocabulary—"represented," "persisted," "aversion"—and evokes an absent ideal standard of morality through negatives—"in vain," "impropriety." This abstract and conventionally learned style accredits Georgiana as a social critic by signalling the authority of detachment: Georgiana implies that she can judge Mary's conduct against an absolute and impersonal standard. The language of contrast thus becomes the language of moral perception.[7]

This perception, however, remains an intellectual activity, without social consequences. "What a Wedding will this be!" exclaims Georgiana, but she takes no steps to prevent it. Such authority as she exercizes to judge behavior, moral authority, derives from and remains in the sphere of observation. Both Mary's mother and her sister vaunt abstract ideals which must be "represented" to the emotional subject, Mary. In conjoining the traditional social authority of the mother with the traditional moral authority of "propriety" of feeling

and behavior, this letter isolates the epistolary subject from the moral context perceived through detachment.

Sense and Sensibility explores this moral ambiguity by its "objective" narrative which describes both the internal and the external action. As scholars have remarked, the narrative style resembles "the eighteenth-century sermon or moral disquisition," partly because it "invites us to join an argument about how sense and sensibility can be combined, how they can be separated."[8] By describing the action through a narrative perspective that remains separate from, and superior to, the perspectives of either heroine, Austen dramatizes the literary authority of objectivity: the disinterested stance of the general spectator debating a public issue, a stance valorized by the eighteenth-century essay and by such narrators as Fielding uses. On the other hand, through the emotional and partisan viewpoints of the heroines, Austen describes a world of emotion modelled on epistolary fictions, and with its own kind of authority.

Elinor Dashwood, usually representing the "sense" of the novel, resembles the mediating narrator in style and function. Silent observer or attendant of others' stories, she negotiates between her sister and the repentant Willoughby; between her mother and the rude Fanny Dashwood; between Colonel Brandon and the grateful Edward. Moderating her mother's ambition for a large house by her "prudence" and "steadier judgment," she hides her own wounded feelings in order to save her family pain: she sacrifices personal relief for the general good of her society (pp. 24, 14). Although she indeed acts on her convictions, she apparently judges with detachment, supplying "inside views," as John Odmark observes, but from a distant perspective (p. 58).

Elinor's detached stance is apparent by her language. In dialogue, she uses balanced, periodical phrases which resemble those of the essayists Austen admired: Addison and Steele, and Samuel Johnson.[9] By weighing one clause against another, and by impersonal predications, this rhetorical style contrasts with Marianne's unconsidered expressions to suggest a disinterested view of characters and opinions. At the same time, however, Elinor's deliberate phrasing cumulatively results in a tautological solemnity which echoes the parodies of Austen's juvenilia. When, for example, she describes the man she loves to her sister in an early passage that must be quoted at length, she pronounces:

> "Of [Edward's] sense and his goodness . . . no one can, I think, be in doubt, who has seen him often enough to engage him in unreserved conversation. The excellence of his understanding and his principles can be concealed only by that shyness which too often keeps him silent. You know enough of him to do justice to his solid worth. But of his minuter propensities as you call them you have from peculiar circumstances been kept more ignorant than myself. He and I have been at times thrown a good deal together, while you have been wholly engrossed on the most affectionate principle by my mother. I have seen a great deal of him, have studied his sentiments, and heard his opinion on subjects of literature and taste; and, upon the whole, I venture to pronounce that his mind is well-informed, his enjoyment of books exceedingly great, his imagination lively, his observation just and correct, and his taste delicate and pure." (p. 20)

Elinor's assumption of the role of objective description highlights the function and style of the narrative, which is authorized to judge disinterestedly where a heroine is not. Her mannered parallelisms, abstract diction, and passive phrasing suggest an impartiality at comic variance with her motive in this speech: she is defending her love to her sister. With a self-consciousness reminiscent of the bookish Mary Bennet, Elinor reiterates clichés to validate her own judgment: she adopts the language of authoritative detachment.

Elinor's phrasing thus pulls in two directions. While it identifies her with the narrative and thus with the au-

thority of detachment, it also serves to characterize her, since her functional ignorance as a heroine is part of what drives the plot. Parted from narrative authority, this phrasing bespeaks excessive caution. Elinor's interjection of irrelevant modifiers and clauses—"I think," "concealed only by that shyness which keeps him silent," "At present"—separate her agency from its object, cloaking her motive in the linguistic veil of objectivity. She confesses that she has seen "a great deal of him" from "peculiar circumstances" which she then proceeds to explain as her mother's intention; she "ventures to pronounce" on his character, and belies this pomposity by what amounts to a panegyric on "minutely" dissected qualities. The objectivity of her stance thus underscores the subjectivity of her reactions, reactions so favorable to Edward that she even finds him physically handsome:

> "His abilities in every respect improve as much upon acquaintance as his manners and person. At first sight his address is certainly not striking; and his person can hardly be called handsome, till the expression of his eyes, which are uncommonly good, and the general sweetness of his countenance, is perceived. At present, I know him so well, that I think him really handsome; or, at least, almost so. What say you, Marianne?"

Elinor is attracted to Edward, yet even this most personal of responses she first expresses through passives as an objective judgment: the "expression" of his "uncommonly good" eyes and his "general sweetness," she claims, "is perceived." This aesthetic language applauds the expressive, the rare and the good-natured, concealed from the public eye. Ironically, it is this same aesthetic which characterizes the heroine opposed to "sensible" Elinor, Marianne. Whereas Marianne, however, both sees and is seen as a sentimental heroine, Elinor projects her aesthetic onto the object of her desire.[10]

By comic reversal and dramatic dialogue, this passage exposes the gender of impartiality. Just as, in the sentimental vignettes of *The Spectator,* the male speaker judges women in abstractly pictorial terms, so an infatuated Darcy admires Elizabeth's eyes in **Pride and Prejudice,** and Captain Wentworth mourns Anne's lost bloom in **Persuasion.**[11] Here, however, it is a woman who describes her lover through the sentimental aesthetic. Marianne, however, ignoring Elinor's assumption of an impartial authority, reads Elinor's description aright as a declaration of desire. When Elinor's confidence in her own impartiality breaks down, and she asks her sister's opinion, Marianne unblushingly admits that her view of Edward will follow her desires rather than a disinterested aesthetic: "'I shall very soon think him handsome, Elinor, if I do not now. When you tell me to love him as a brother, I shall no more see imperfection in his face, than I now do in his heart'" (pp. 20-21). This rhetorical shift—from Elinor to Marianne, from description to declaration, from impartial evaluation to open partiality—dramatizes the rift between the "masculine" authority of distance and the "feminine" authority of feeling. Elinor speaks now in the "female" language of hesitation and emotion, translated from an epistolary exchange into conversation itself.

In order to determine how the reader should "see" and so judge Elinor, the narrative supplies a context, or a set of terms with which to construct a contrast between Elinor's view and an objective view. This is done through describing Elinor's internal thoughts. By echoing Elinor's impersonal style, this language paradoxically reveals the self-interest in Elinor's analyses, for the narrative language is ideally disinterested whereas Elinor cannot be. After Elinor reproves Marianne's hope that Elinor will marry Edward, the narrative continues:

> Elinor had given her real opinion to her sister. She could not consider her partiality for Edward in so prosperous a state as Marianne had believed it. There was, at times, a want of spirits about him which, if it did not denote indifference, spoke a something almost as unpromising. A doubt of her regard, supposing him to feel it, need not give him more than inquietude. It would not be likely to produce that dejection of mind which frequently attended him. A more reasonable cause might be found in the dependent situation which forbad the indulgence of his affection. She knew that his mother neither behaved to him so as to make his home comfortable at present, nor to give him any assurance that he might form a home for himself, without strictly attending to her views for his aggrandizement. With such a knowledge as this, it was impossible for Elinor to feel easy on the subject. She was far from depending on that result of his preference of her, which her mother and sister still considered as certain. Nay, the longer they were together the more doubtful seemed the nature of his regard; and sometimes, for a few painful minutes, she believed it to be no more than friendship. (p. 22)

This passage imitates Elinor's speech to Marianne in moving from observations impersonally reported, through a weighing of possibilities, to a final tumbling confession of doubt, but this passage appears not in Elinor's but in the narrative voice. The contrast between impersonal narrative and emotional language centers on the ambiguous term "real." Although Elinor's internal conflict arises from the contradiction between what she sees and what she wants, the entire passage is predicated on the difference between what Elinor has said, and what she "considers," "knows," and "believes." The "real opinion" appears in the style and voice of the narrative. It is not Elinor's sincerity, nor her feelings, that are judged as "real": it is her detached observation.

This definition of "real" underscores the difference between conversation and narration, between the lan-

guages of exchange and of information. Interpreting Edward's behavior by means of comparisons—"no more than inquietude," "A more reasonable cause," "no more than friendship"—the narrative evokes an absent context, "a something" which "speaks" to the observer. When Elinor sees Edward rather than contemplating this absent standard, she experiences "painful" doubt. The narrative thus polarizes the function of contrast, prerogative of a disinterested perspective, and the experience of emotion.

The diction of the passage underscores the polarization of point of view. The mercantile language in which "prosperity" translates as "gain" rather than as "growth" illustrates the narrative predication on static contrast. This predication creates a strain between the narrative evaluation of present conditions, and Elinor's anxiety about what will happen. The impersonal "there was," and the syntactical delay of the interjected phrase "at times" mimics Elinor's careful restraint. Her authority derives from the narrative language of impersonal description, yet this conflicts with the "female" language of emotion.

The narrative reveals the limitations of Elinor's point of view through her considered opinions of other characters. Although more suspicious of Willoughby than either Mrs. Dashwood or Marianne, Elinor nevertheless does not recognize the main danger he poses.

> Elinor saw nothing to censure in him but a propensity, in which he strongly resembled and peculiarly delighted her sister, of saying too much what he thought on every occasion, without attention to persons or circumstances. In hastily forming and giving his opinion of other people, in sacrificing general politeness to the enjoyment of undivided attention where his heart was engaged, and in slighting too easily the forms of worldly propriety, he displayed a want of caution which Elinor could not approve, in spite of all that he and Marianne could say in its support. (p. 48-49).

Although she condemns Willoughby here for his "want of caution," Elinor forgives him because of it when he tells her the tale of his love of Marianne and his marriage. While Elinor rightly perceives the danger of his disregard of "persons and circumstances," his main flaw is certainly not "want of caution," but, on the contrary, a rigid adherence to a purpose his feelings oppose: marrying for money. Because of her position as a woman and a character implicated in the action, she is unable to see enough to judge with ultimate authority.

The narrative juxtaposes Elinor's evaluation of Willoughby with her similarly cautious analysis of Colonel Brandon.

> Colonel Brandon's partiality for Marianne, which had so early been discovered by her friends, now

first became perceptible to Elinor, when it had ceased be noticed by them. . . . Elinor was obliged, though unwillingly, to believe that the sentiments which Mrs. Jennings had assigned him for her own satisfaction, were now actually excited by her sister. . . . She liked him—in spite of his gravity and reserve, she beheld in him an object of interest. His manners, though serious, were mild; and his reserve appeared rather the result of some oppression of spirits than of any natural gloominess of temper. Sir John had dropt hints of past injuries and disappointments, which justified her belief of his being an unfortunate man, and she regarded him with respect and compassion. (pp. 49-50)

The careful opposition of Elinor's perception, derived from quiet distance, to those of the other characters underscores the opposition between a long and fine sight, and selfish vision. In contrast to the vulgar crowd—Mrs. Jennings—Elinor perceives "unwillingly," and with detachment, for the Colonel to her is "an object of interest," not a subject of gossip. Elinor, moreover, likes Colonel Brandon for many of the same reasons she appears to like Edward, who strikes neither Marianne nor the reader as particularly charming, unless in contrast to Willoughby. The Colonel is reserved and silent, mild-mannered and grave, like Edward; like Edward, as we learn, he conceals a past emotional attachment. Elinor perceives here from a position of disinterest, and perceives accurately, but, by virtue of her gender and her place, she can only exercise this authoritative perspective in telling the tales of others, not in judging her own story.

As a heroine like Marianne, Elinor does not possess the ultimate privilege of detachment. It is the narrative which will make this unique tale a moral example to the reader by tracing the general in the particular; when Elinor does so, or applies conventional motives to unconventional behavior, she is almost always wrong. In her attempt to explain why Marianne and Willoughby have not announced their engagement, she ignores her knowledge of her sister's character for a reasonable explanation that echoes her own beliefs and views of the general motivations of society. She attributes their silence to Willoughby's relative poverty. Since Elinor's "fortune" resembles Marianne's "competence," what she estimates as Willoughby's "independence" would appear to Marianne as poverty, as it does to Willoughby himself. Yet nothing in Marianne's character suggests that she would permit this to prevent her marriage, and indeed we learn that she never thinks of it. Elinor applies her own values to her sister's different character, and deduces the same argument to explain Marianne's situation as her own with Edward. Similarly, Elinor "sees" Edward's hair ring as her own hair, her own wedding-band, although in fact it is his engagement ring from Lucy Steele. Ironically, both men have other entanglements, other emotional claims, just as their actions would suggest. As elsewhere in the novel,

here Elinor applies pragmatic categories to sentimental tropes. The confusion between money and feeling derives from the sentimental equation of benevolence and charity, pity and alms. Like Marianne, Elinor assumes that it is the means, not the will, that is wanting: the heart is in the right place, if the purse is not. This assumption essentially qualifies her perspective and outlines the distinction between narrative authority and the point of view of a character.

Marianne sees consistently with the spontaneity of an epistolary heroine. Her judgment of people and circumstances rests on her own emotional reactions to them. The narrative demonstrates the contrast between perception quickened by emotion in Marianne, and perception retarded by detachment in Elinor in the description of their encounter with Edward. Margaret, the youngest Dashwood sister, Marianne, and Elinor are walking in the country around their cottage, and see a man in the distance riding toward their home. It is a familiar landscape scene in which distance opens possibility: Marianne, perceiving as her desires dictate, believes the man to be Willoughby while Elinor, skeptical of desire and imagination, knows only that it is not.

> [Marianne] walked eagerly on . . . and Elinor, to screen Marianne from particularity, as she felt almost certain of its not being Willoughby, quickened her pace and kept up with her. They were soon within thirty yards of the gentleman. Marianne looked again; her heart sunk within her; and abruptly turning around, she was hurrying back, when the voices of both her sisters were raised to detain her, a third, almost as well known as Willoughby's, joined them in begging her to stop, and she turned round with surprise to see and welcome Edward Ferrars. (p. 86)

The narrative begins by distinguishing Marianne's motives for her hasty action from Elinor's motives for what looks like exactly the same action, and underscores the difference by drawing a parallel literally but not metaphorically true. Whereas Elinor "keeps up with her sister" in pace, her desires lag behind her sister's. The narrative continues from Marianne's perspective: as soon as she sees that the man is not the one she desires, she sees nothing, although to her Edward's voice is "almost as well known as Willoughby's," for she perceives the two men in parallel ways, as suitors for her sister and herself. This connection points up the difference between her point of view and Elinor's. Had Elinor indeed "kept pace with her sister," she would have anticipated seeing Edward; that she only suspects the man is not Willoughby underscores the limitations of her perceptions. Although Marianne errs in permitting sensation to blind and deafen her, to govern her sight, Elinor errs in forbidding it to color her view at all. Most importantly, however, both sisters misperceive. The initial narrative distinction between them collapses. While the sisters strive to identify the particular figure on horseback, moreover, the narrative presents a conventional picture of figures meeting in a landscape, a picture accessible only to the structurally detached narrator and reader.

As the plot progresses, Elinor's role grows more active, and her observational distance gives way to an experiential perspective. After Marianne has fallen ill, and all of Elinor's fears have burst forth, Elinor rushes forward pursuing her hopes at the expense of reasoned "caution" in precisely the way she refuses to do in the above passage.

> The clock struck eight. Had it been ten, Elinor would have been convinced that at that moment she heard a carriage driving up to the house; and so strong was the persuasion that she *did,* in spite of the *almost* impossibility of [Colonel Brandon's and her mother's] being already come, that she moved into the adjoining dressing-closet and opened a window-shutter, to be satisfied of the truth. She instantly saw that her ears had not deceived her. The flaring lamps of a carriage were immediately in view. By their uncertain light, she thought she could discern it to be drawn by four horses; and this, while it told the excess of her poor mother's alarm, gave some explanation to such unexpected rapidity.

> Never in her life had Elinor found it so difficult to be calm, as at that moment. The knowledge of what her mother must be feeling as the carriage stopt at the door,—of her doubt—her dread—perhaps her despair!—and of what *she* had to tell!—with such knowledge it was impossible to be calm. All that remained to be done, was to be speedy; and therefore staying only till she could leave Mrs, Jennings's maid with her sister, she hurried down stairs.

> The bustle in the vestibule, as she passed along an inner lobby, assured her that they were already in the house. She rushed forward towards the drawing-room,—she entered it,—and saw only Willoughby. (p. 316)

Using the same techniques of violated expectation, delay, and suspense as in the passage describing the sister's encounter with Edward, the narrative here also employs the punctuation and syntax of sentimental impressionism: exclamation points, fragmented sentences, italicized words. The description also pursues sensual impressions of sight, hearing, and feeling to recount Elinor's actions. Elinor doubts time but trusts her confused senses, the pre-requisite to moving from a world of externals to a sphere governed by internal feeling. She becomes a sentimental heroine.

In the following paragraph, moreover, the narrative moves from describing Elinor's internal, sensual responses to depicting her actions in the visually vivid detail of eighteenth-century literary sentimentalism.

After Elinor has started back, a theatrical movement, and "obeyed the first impulse of her heart," we watch the movement of her hand, its symbolic power accentuated by the carefully designed contrast between Elinor's heightened expectations of emotional release with her mother, and her instant "horror" at beholding her sister's betrayer.

> Elinor, starting back with a look of horror at the sight of him, obeyed the first impulse of her heart in turning instantly to quit the room, and her hand was already on the lock, when its action was suspended by his hastily advancing, and saying, in a voice rather of command than supplication, "Miss Dashwood, for half an hour—for ten minutes—I entreat you to stay."

Elinor enacts her feelings as she "looks" at the dramatic "sight" of Marianne's betrayer. As her "passion" turns to action, Elinor has changed from witness to participant, from a disinterested judge to a sentimental heroine.

The values of detached observation, moderation and self-control that characterize Elinor derive from the literary tradition of the moral essay. These values, however, appear fully realized not in the characters, but in the narrative. By the end of the novel, the sisters speak only through tears. When Elinor learns of her mistake in thinking Edward married to Lucy, she "burst into tears of joy, which at first she thought would never cease" (p. 360). When Marianne learns of it, she reacts in almost exactly the same way: "Marianne could speak *her* happiness only by tears." (p. 363) The narrative now adopts the language of epistolary spontaneity to describe Elinor's feelings:

> But Elinor—How are *her* feelings to be described?—From the moment of learning that Lucy was married to another, that Edward was free, to the moment of his justifying the hopes which had so instantly followed, she was everything by turns but tranquil. But when the second moment had passed, when she found every doubt, every solicitude removed, compared her situation with what so lately it had been,—saw him honorably released from his former engagement, saw him instantly profiting by the release, to address herself and declare an affection as tender, as constant as she had ever supposed it to be,—she was oppressed, she was overcome by her own felicity;—and happily disposed as is the human mind to be easily familiarized with any change for the better, it required several hours to give sedateness to her spirits, or any degree of tranquillity to her heart. (p. 363)

After the opening rhetorical question on method which announces the distinction between feeling and describing, the narrative through a series of anaphoric and hasty clauses expresses Elinor's confused considerations and emotions as she witnesses and compares her situation with her fears. The narrative orders and explains this confusion by an aesthetic principle: the effect of violent contrast. The reader, with the narrator, observes the effects of the sublime on the human heart. The narrative thus frames the particular emotions Elinor experiences within a broader context that presents universal tendencies, not individuals. The narrative hence controls the sentimental particularity of the tale.

In *Sense and Sensibility,* Austen employs the stylistic patterns of literary sentimentalism within an authoritative narrative structure. Sentimental scenes appear within a discourse criticizing sentimental excess; a detached observation distinguishes a right view, yet sensation also allows a kind of truth. In *Sense and Sensibility,* Austen turns emotion into spectacle. The tensions of *Sense and Sensibility* thus do not lie between the heroines. They lie between both heroines, muffled voices of experience, and the narrative, authorized to speak by virtue of detachment. By a structure which recapitulates the literary division between "female" epistolary works narrating "authentic," internal experience, and essayistic accounts of the general truth, Austen's novel exposes the political implications of narrative authority. A language endorsing contrast, impersonality and abstract ideals opposes the language of sensation, impression, experience; consensus expressed through detachment thus rules individual experience.

Authority in Austen's world derives from detachment, the capacity (or privilege) to perceive without partiality, with what Matthew Arnold just over fifty years later would call "disinterestedness." Such a source of authority denies heroines, defined by their capacity to feel, all but the power of their feelings. This creates a paradox: how can a heroine be valued for her detachment yet also for her "feeling"? In her later novels, Austen experiments with two solutions to this paradox, both of which challenge the conventions of fiction. Her "sentimental" novels use a structure which at least partially reverses the conventional sources of narrative authority. The heroines of both *Mansfield Park* and *Persuasion,* still more marginalized than Elinor by social neglect, judge society more accurately, at least until they attempt to judge their own place in it. In these novels, furthermore, the narrative voice defends the heroine's qualifications for heroism, so that often it is the narrator who speaks with feeling and the heroines with detachment. Austen thus reveals that the creation of a heroine is itself a political act, an act in which self-interest appears dressed as ideal disinterest.

In her "satirical" novels, however, Austen creates plots dramatizing the consequences of this dilemma whereby the heroine's authority is undermined by the abstract standards of the narrative voice as it articulates social authority. Elizabeth Bennet is taught that when she judges Darcy against her ideal of a gentleman, she misjudges him: her ideals are faulty, her powers of

detached observation limited and her exercise of them an exercise of vanity. Emma learns that she sees rightly only when she sees with her heart. Indeed, these heroines go astray when they usurp the disinterested viewpoint of narrative authority, and attempt comparison in place of complacency. At the same time, by mimicking the objective perspective of narrative these heroines undermine the authority of the very structure which indicts them. Again, if they dress their self-interest as disinterest, doesn't the narrator also?

Austen's attack on the politics of literary convention reflects the conflicts, structural and political, in the works of the very authors she admired. Both Samuel Richardson and Henry Fielding attempt in their final novels to blend "female" and "male" forms of narrative authority, but both encounter difficulties similar to those that Austen explores. In his epistolary novels, Richardson presents the vacillations of female sentiment as the very process of morality, but Richardson's heroines lack social power just as the letter conventionally conjures a private audience. Austen's favorite novel, *Sir Charles Grandison,* comes closest to according a woman the power of objective judgment, for Harriet acts both as objective narrator, describing Sir Charles, and as epistolary heroine, describing her love for him. The very detachment that defines her as a heroine and qualifies her for Sir Charles, however, suggests narrative omniscience, and drives the dynamic of female vacillation out of her character to leave only structured sentiment, stagnant feelings and static letters.[12]

On the other hand, although Henry Fielding includes in his fiction inset tales as letters or stories, he subordinates these in his earlier novels entirely to an authoritative narration that presents morality as consistent feeling. *Joseph Andrews* parodies Richardson's account of moral experience in *Pamela* by dividing Pamela's virtue from her vacillations and according the former to a man and the latter to a caricatured woman. Related by an objective narrator, Lady B's hesitations—indeed female confusions—seem merely hypocrisy, as they are in *Shamela.* Moreover, although Fielding advocates "mixed" characters, Tom Jones, a sentimental hero, experiences virtually only those feelings which consistently reflect his good nature. When in his final novel Fielding attempts to combine the authority of narrative detachment with an endorsement of female interior experience, the result, *Amelia,* suffers from a structural and tonal instability similar to that of *Sense and Sensibility.* In protesting injustice through a narrative voice which is detached but not impartial, Fielding compromises his authority and control over *Amelia;* lengthy, defensive confessions by women characters further undermine the possibility of narrative objectivity by revealing that characters see their own stories in their own ways. Despite this ideological implication, however, Fielding repeats the values supported by traditional, objective narrative: the weak "hero" Booth vacillates between feelings in a fashion conventionally "female" while the titular heroine models unvarying and virtuous sentiment. Thus Fielding devalues both "female" literary forms and multiple reactions.

The methodological conflict between presenting a story from the perspective of a detached spectator, and presenting it as experienced by the character carries implications for the form of later eighteenth-century fiction. By portraying experience from the inside, novels present models of how to feel instead of proclaiming standards of how to act, a shift in emphasis with a corresponding shift in form. This shift in narrative viewpoint may contribute to what Nancy Armstrong has identified as the "feminization" of fiction: the rise of feminine authority in the novel.[13] Sentimental "autobiographies" like Laurence Sterne's *Tristram Shandy* or Henry Mackenzie's *Man of Feeling* partly represent an attempt to accord male spectators internal, quasi-epistolary expression without compromising the ideal of authoritative detachment. These fictions deliberately fragment their narratives in order to concentrate on interpreting sensation, rather than on defining moral action; however, they also mock the sentimentalism of their own heroes who lose track of their purposes in the wash of emotion. These fictions thus parody female literary conventions even while incorporating them, and hence preserve the possibility of telling the tale from an objective perspective. The supposed deletions in fact testify to the existence of a "whole" story which a detached narrator could tell.

Thus, the point of view from which judgment is delivered testifies to the authority, indeed to the author, of that judgment. Eighteenth-century fiction accords detachment moral power, the right to decide who and what is valuable. This detachment, however, is conventionally prohibited to women because it is structured by a narrative point of view founded on models of masculine writing which are informed by a neoclassical preference for generality. This viewpoint, moreover, is opposed in contemporary satire to the claims of individual feeling, portrayed in the later eighteenth century through fictions of women's experience. Austen's early challenge to this division of perspective, ***Sense and Sensibility,*** demonstrates that the language of judgment in eighteenth-century literature is the language of comparison, and that comparisons empower the judge to construct an ideal moral standard which muffles the expression and the authority of female experience. These are the politics of perspective in Austen's novel.

Notes

[1] Jane Austen, *Sense and Sensibility,* ed. R. W. Chapman (Oxford U. Press, 1923), p. 378. All citations from the novel refer to this edition. For a recent summary of critical opinions, see LeRoy W. Smith, *Jane Austen and the Drama of Woman* (London: Macmillan, 1983),

p. 69. Laura G. Mooneyham indicts the novel as a "brilliant failure" because of its rhetorical contrast of two women in *Romance, Language and Education in Jane Austen's Novels* (London: MacMillan, 1988), pp. 31-32.

[2] I am especially indebted to these studies: Claudia L. Johnson, *Jane Austen: Women, Politics and the Novel* (U. of Chicago Press, 1988), esp. pp. 49-72; Marilyn Butler, *Jane Austen and the War of Ideas* (Oxford: The Clarendon Press, 1975); Tony Tanner, *Jane Austen* (London: MacMillan, 1986); Michael Williams, *Jane Austen: Six Novels and Their Methods* (London: MacMillan, 1986), esp. pp. 31-52. Two other recent studies associate Austen's politics and her style: Margaret Kirkham's *Jane Austen: Feminism and Fiction* places Austen's work in the context of a new "female" species of writing, the novel, which exposes the "dubious moral assumptions" of familial and sexual relationships (Sussex and New Jersey: Harvester Press, and Barnes & Noble, 1983), pp. 13-14; and Mary Evans' *Jane Austen & the State* defines Austen's "feminism" as her condemnation of moral and sexual double standards, her value for women's domestic and familial role, and her portrayal of women as acting independently of men and "patriarchal interests" (London and New York: Tavistock Publications, 1987), p. 44. Recently, Julia Prewitt Brown has offered a compromise, between conventional and feminist interpretations of Austen in "Austen's Feminist Detractors," *Novel* 23, no. 3 (Spring, 1990): 300-13.

[3] The stylistic debt to epistolary fiction is noted by A. Walton Litz who argues that the language of the novel is falsified by the action in *Jane Austen: A Study of her Artistic Development* (New York: Oxford U. Press, 1965); and by Margaret Kirkham, *Jane Austen: Feminism and Fiction* (New Jersey: Barnes & Noble, 1983), pp. 86-87. For theroetical analyses of multivocal structures in fiction, see Mikhail Bakhtin, *The Dialogic Imagination,* ed. Michael Holquist (U. of Texas Press, 1981).

[4] Jane Austen, *Minor Works,* ed. R. W. Chapman (Oxford U. Press, 1954), p. 58. All citations from the juvenilia refer to this edition. For a still useful discussion of the parody in Austen's juvenilia, see Mary Lascelles, *Jane Austen and Her Art* (Oxford: The Clarendon Press, 1939). I examine this text as part of a broader argument on conflicting viewpoints in the eighteenth-century novel in my unpublished dissertation "The Tensions of Realism: Oppositions of Perception in Some Novels of Fielding and Austen" (U. of California, Berkeley, 1985).

[5] In *The Proper Lady and the Woman Writer: Mary Wollstonecraft, Mary Shelley, and Jane Austen,* Mary Poovey argues that the manipulative letters of *Lady Susan* dramatize the woman's conflict between the

desire for power and for propriety, a conflict also structuring Austen's indirection in *Sense and Sensibility* (U. of Chicago Press, 1984). *Lady Susan,* however, represents an alternative version of the juvenilia: both play with stereotypes of women's styles. For an outline the these "types" of women's writing, see Felicity Nussbaum, *The Autobiographical Subject: Gender and Ideology in Eighteenth-Century England* (Johns Hopkins U. Press, 1989), pp. 154-77.

[6] For analyses of "female" stylistics, see Ruth Perry, *Women, Letters, and the Novel* (AMS Studies in the Eighteenth Century 4. New York: AMS, 1980) and Patricia Meyer Spacks, *Imagining a Self: Autobiography and Novel in Eighteenth-Century England* (Harvard U. Press, 1976).

[7] In *Jane Austen's Novels: The Fabric of Dialogue,* Howard S. Babb lists Austen's stylistic techniques to argue that abstracts, conceptual terms and generalized statements convey authority in Austen's rhetoric (Ohio State U. Press, 1961).

[8] John Odmark, *An Understanding of Jane Austen's Novels: Character, Value and Ironic Perspective* (Oxford: Basil Blackwell, 1981), p. 58. All citations to this author will refer to this text. Michael Williams, *Jane Austen: Six Novels and Their Methods,* p. 37.

[9] Frank Bradbrook examines Austen's debt to, and ambivalence toward, Addison and Steele and Samuel Johnson in *Jane Austen and Her Predecessors* (Cambridge U. Press, 1966), pp. 3-17; J. F. Burrows defends Austen's careful stylistics and suggests that they recapitulate stereotypical gender distinctions in *Computation into Criticism: A Study of Jane Austen's Novels and an Experiment in Method* (Oxford U. Press, 1987). For a study of Austen's shifting viewpoint, see also Howard S. Babb, *Jane Austen's Novels: The Fabric of Dialogue* (Ohio State U. Press, 1962).

[10] In examining the critique of sensibility in the novel, Kenneth L. Moler argues that Austen intends us to view Elinor's "sense" skeptically in *Jane Austen's Art of Allusion* (U. of Nebraska Press, 1968), p. 44. In *The Proper Lady and the Woman Writer,* Mary Poovey suggests that Elinor experiences a conflict between feeling and control (U. of Chicago Press, 1984), pp. 185-87.

[11] John Barrell analyzes the eighteenth-century value for a detached, disinterested, comprehensive viewpoint in *English Literature in History, 1730-80: An Equal, Wide Survey* (New York: St. Martin's Press, 1983), pp. 33-40. Many of the sentimental fictions which Austen read, moreover, like Frances Moore Brooke's *The History of Lady Julia Mandeville* (1763), signal their sentimental ethic by pictorial descriptions of the heroines.

[12] Another of Austen's favorite writers, Fanny Burney, provides a variation of this solution in *Evelina* in which the heroine recounts her own social humiliation in letters, and thus to some degree experiences both feeling and transcendent judgment. Burney, however, also consigns Evelina—and her epistolary perspective—to social subordination.

[13] Nancy Armstrong, "The Rise of Feminine Authority in the Novel," *Novel: A Forum on Fiction* 15, no. 2 (Winter, 1982): 127-45.

David Kaufmann (essay date 1992)

SOURCE: "Law and Propriety, *Sense and Sensibility*: Austen on the Cusp of Modernity," in *ELH,* Vol. 59, No. 2, Summer, 1992, pp. 385-408.

[*In the following essay, Kaufmann discusses the language of law and the language of propriety as they apply to* Sense and Sensibility.]

The term "propriety," with its etymological links to property and the notion of the proper, smacks of oppression and ideological obfuscation, of outmoded ideals and outdated restraints. Accordingly, as a piece of collateral damage, *Sense and Sensibility* seems deeply, if not at times desperately, conservative. Hence perhaps the indifference and discomfort that critics have shown towards this text since Marvin Mudrick's dyspeptic dismissal of its apparently unsatisfying end.[1] A few recent commentators, most notably Julia Prewitt Brown, Susan Morgan and Claudia Johnson, have tried to redeem *Sense and Sensibility,* but they have tended to emphasize knowledge, not ethics.[2] Propriety in their discussions has constituted a sideshow, a derivative of the epistemology which comes to serve as the main attraction. In this essay I will try to recast the question. I want to ask why it is that Austen's fiction can and does make a claim on its readers. I will offer an account of propriety in Austen's first published novel in the hope of recuperating both its discursive context and its emancipatory potential.

To write about *Sense and Sensibility* entails wrangling with the problematic centrality of Elinor Dashwood. To take the novel seriously means that one should not follow Mudrick and champion Marianne at Elinor's expense. To get purchase on this text, I will begin by scrutinizing Elinor at what critics have found to be her most vulnerable moment, that fateful interview with John Willoughby.[3] Elinor, who has mistrusted Willoughby for most of the novel and loathed him since his rejection of her sister, softens towards him when, in the middle of his rake's confession, she realizes that he in fact loves Marianne.[4] She hardens her heart again when Willoughby mentions the sad story of Eliza Williams, the girl he has seduced and abandoned (316), but her cold resolve weakens anew a few pages later. That we should know how Elinor feels during this interview is significant, for the chapter is almost exclusively given over to the call-and-response of dialogue. Austen goes out of her way to chart Elinor's shifting reactions and allegiances, to show us how her emotions waver "in the course of this extraordinary conversation" (319).

Elinor is faced with a dilemma. One can see her difficulty when she says to Willoughby: "You have proved yourself, on the whole, less faulty that I had believed you. You have proved your heart less wicked, much less wicked. But I hardly know—the misery that you have inflicted—I hardly know what could have made it worse" (323). Her repetitions and the emotions signaled by her broken syntax show that she is torn between her respect for his sentiments and her distaste for the unhappiness he has caused. When Willoughby finally leaves and Elinor falls into meditation, she realizes that her regard for his emotions is based on causes that "ought not in reason to have weight" (326). And yet she pities him. She calls him "poor Willoughby" and taxes herself for the harshness of her previous thoughts about him: "[She] now blamed, now *acquitted* herself for having *judged* him so harshly before" (327; emphasis added). We should pay special attention to the use of the language of the law here. Her sense of justice comes into direct conflict with her feelings of benevolence.

That Elinor should fall prey to such a conflict is no surprise, for Austen establishes at the beginning of the novel that she has both an excellent heart and strong feelings (42). Nor should it be a surprise that Elinor is more than just a tad judgmental. In an argument about Willoughby early in the book, Mrs. Dashwood berates Elinor for being too suspicious. Mrs. Dashwood speaks in the young man's "defence," and hopes that Willoughby is "acquitted." (106-7). According to Mrs. Dashwood, then, Elinor wants to put Willoughby on trial. Her daughter's propensity "to doubt where [she] can" (105) makes "judgment"—usually meant as the power of discrimination—a quasi-legal faculty of mind. For Elinor, it signals a call before a tribunal of informal social justice. Such a view of Elinor is not unwarranted. After all, she constantly surveys and condemns those around her. Lady Middleton, Mrs. John Dashwood and Lucy Steele are all arraigned, tried and found guilty.

Elinor serves as the novel's sentinel of propriety. While this is an undoubtedly true if unsurprising statement, it does not tell us why Elinor and her mother choose to describe what are essentially private judgements in terms that come from the public realm of law. What then is the relation between propriety—the domain of manners—and the law?

John Brewer has maintained that in the eighteenth century, "Englishmen experienced government and

understood politics through their dealings with the law."[5] There is more complexity to this claim than might first appear. The eighteenth-century jurisprudential consensus—an odd site where both Whigs and Tories agreed—had it that the purpose of government was to protect property and to insure justice.[6] Here is a short florilegium. For Sir William Blackstone, the solid Establishment Whig, civil society—the conjunction of individual families who join together in order to fulfill the physical needs they cannot meet on their own—institutes government "to preserve and to keep that society in order."[7] Government's duty according to Blackstone is to make law.[8] Hume, as conservative as Blackstone in some respects, but perhaps more skeptical, concurs: "We are, therefore, to look upon all the vast apparatus of government, as having ultimately no other object or purpose but the distribution of justice."[9] And finally, that radical Whig Tom Paine maintains (with characteristic clarity) that "society is produced by our wants, and government by our wickedness; the former promotes our happiness *positively* by uniting our affections, the latter *negatively* by restraining our vices."[10] In short, then, society comes first to meet our needs and government follows quickly to protect our rights, specifically our rights to property.

Thus what I am calling the eighteenth-century jurisprudential consensus argued for a fairly strict demarcation between civil society and government, between the realm of sociability and the sphere of justice.[11] The public realm provides protection for civil society: it patrols and protects the limits of the private. But even this "private" sphere of civil society, newly freed from the trammels of government, needs regulation. Many tensions and abrasions in civil society cannot be reduced to disputes over real property. If the role of government is generally limited to the protection of goods, land and life, then what—or who—will regulate the other interactions that distinguish civil society? Hume is quite explicit on this score:

> As the mutual shocks in *society,* and the oppositions of interest and self-love have constrained mankind to establish the laws of *justice,* in order to preserve the advantages of mutual assistance and protection: in like manner, the eternal contrarieties, in *company,* of men's pride and self-conceit, have introduced the rules of Good Manners or Politeness, in order to facilitate the intercourse of minds, and an undisturbed commerce and conversation.[12]

Just as men institute justice to oversee the workings of society as a whole, so they establish good manners in the smaller spheres of friendship that Hume calls company. Note that for Hume manners are analogous to justice: they perform a similar function in a similar way for similar ends. It makes perfect sense, therefore, that Elinor Dashwood should use the language of law when she meditates on propriety: manners are the form that frontier justice takes when it enters the drawing room. We can thus qualify Brewer's point about the relation between law and politics in the eighteenth century. English men and women understood government in terms of law because justice was the primary care of government. But they also understood manners in terms of law because in the division between society and government they needed an analogy that explained how society, freed from external incursion, could regulate itself. Law became the governing metaphor for social relations: both the mandatory ones of government and the voluntary ones of society.

Manners, then, are the laws that govern the face-to-face interactions that constitute civil society. They are a necessary social lubricant that allow, as Hume says, "the intercourse of minds, and an undisturbed commerce and conversation." But if we insist that propriety was modeled on property and manners on law, we should also note that for some eighteenth-century social theorists, manners act as an origin, supplement, and corrective to the law. Burke, who, comes from the common law tradition, has a richer and more organic conception of manners than Hume, for whom law is a necessary, formal convention that has nothing to do with equity.[13] For Burke law has a definite content and so do manners, as he argues here, towards the end of his life:

> Manners are of more importance than laws. Upon them, in a great measure, the laws depend. The law touches us but here and there, and now and then. Manners are what vex or soothe, corrupt or purify, exalt or debase, barbarize or refine us, by a constant, steady, uniform insensible operation, like that of the air we breathe in. They give their whole form and color to our lives.[14]

Law depends on manners, not because civil society precedes government either historically or logically but because, for the tradition in which Burke is writing, all the law in England is really common law that, in turn, is "common custom, originating in the usages of the people and declared, interpreted and applied in the courts."[15] The law, then, articulates custom in and over time: it is nothing more or less than the formal codification of manners. But the law does not encompass all manners, for manners cast a wider net than law, and, in the end, are more inclusive.

We can get a sense of the deep importance of manners for Burke in his somewhat lurid (and often parodied) encomium to the "mixed system of opinion and sentiment" of chivalry in his *Reflections on the Revolution in France:*

> It was this, which, without confounding ranks, had produced a noble equality, and handed it down through all the gradations of social life. It was this

opinion which mitigated kings into companions, and raised private men to be fellows with kings. Without force or opposition, it subdued the fierceness of pride and power; it obliged sovereigns to submit to the soft collar of social esteem, compelled stern authority to submit to elegance, and gave a domination, vanquisher of laws, to be subdued by manners.[16]

Burke is here, of course, discussing the importance for politics of this settled system of manners. Chivalry—with its emphasis on "social esteem"—effects a number of important chiastic reversals in everyday life. The psychological effects of oppression are lessened, if not overcome, when lords can become companions of their vassals. Under chivalry, social differentiation does not disappear. Rather, the sting that comes from subordination is salved by chivalry's stress on honor. Manners supplement the constitution and make it work: they locate power less in actual domination than in mutual regard.

We can say, therefore, that Burke's notion of manners engages both conservative and radical energies: it is a prescription for social stability that masks real relations of power with the filigree-work of good behavior. By the same token, it enjoins recognition of every subject's needs. It promises not an equality of goods or of power but is a demand made on the enfranchised by the disenfranchised for an equality of respect. Furthermore, it serves as a protection for the poor and the powerless. If honor demands the regard of the poor, then the poor are rendered strong by virtue of their ability to refuse to give that regard. Thus the powerful are dependent on the poor and must serve them in their turn. While Burke's concept is conservative, it serves the interests of the disempowered, if in an apparently limited way.

We can draw several conclusions from the two passages from Burke I have just cited, conclusions that can be supported by reference to other moments in Burke's writings.[17] Manners precede law and correct its severities by restoring equity to precedence.[18] In so doing, manners attempt to mediate the apparently mutual exclusion that separates justice and benevolence in the civic jurisprudential tradition.[19] Manners are negative in that they repress, socialize, and mark mine off from thine. But they are also positive: they shape and refine the self, and render selves equal before the bar of mutual regard. They oversee aesthetic education, supervise self-creation and act to protect the powerless against the depredations of their masters.[20]

Hume and Burke come from different legal traditions and so construct the law from different premises. But we can adduce a concurrence between them and thus demarcate a field for the late eighteenth-century conception of manners: the law stands over and above civil society; it protects property and rights, and thus ensures peace in voluntary commercial associations. Manners, which resemble laws, are the rules that govern social interactions not covered by the law. They allow society to exist, free from the intervention of government. They protect the individual within "company" and from it, and in so doing they allow that company to work comfortably.

If what I have said is an accurate reconstruction of a certain complex of ideas, we can see that Elinor's reaction to John Willoughby's confession, her discomfort when she is caught between his debatable merit and his call for her sympathy, marks the residual tension within the notion of manners between the principles of justice and benevolence, between the language of rights and the demands of sympathy. Just as the law determines what is each person's right, so propriety makes sure that every person gets his due. For example: when Edward comes to Devonshire the first time, Elinor decides to temper her annoyance at his coldness. She resolves "to regulate her behaviour to him by the past rather than the present" and treats him as she thinks "he ought to be treated from the family connection" (115). This connection determines what she owes him: he deserves deference and care because he is the brother of Elinor's sister-in-law. What Edward calls Elinor's "plan of general civility" is, as Elinor points out to her sister, a way of preserving one's own opinions and feelings, while making sure that others' needs and deserts are accounted for (119). When Marianne, sickened and depressed by Willoughby's apparent dismissal, wants to leave London immediately, Elinor replies that it is impossible to quit the capital so soon: "We owe Mrs Jennings much more than civility; and civility of the commonest kind must prevent such a hasty removal as that" (202). The barest good manners insist that the Dashwood sisters take Mrs. Jennings's plans and feelings seriously. But the young women are in a position that demands more than just bare good manners: they owe her a debt. And manners, like the law, command that debts be respected.

Of course, with the fullness of time Marianne comes to recognize the values that Elinor represents. When she finally recants and agrees to practice "the civilities, the lesser duties of life, with gentleness and forebearance" (338), Marianne acknowledges that "to every common acquaintance even, [she] had been insolent and unjust; with an heart hardened against their merits" (337). Marianne, in her selfishness, has not granted others their due.

If propriety entails attention to others, a close and sometimes conflicting calculus of their needs and their deserts, it also guards with a deep jealousy the needs and deserts of the self. When, early in the novel, Elinor censures Willoughby's tendency to slight "too easily the forms of worldly propriety," she is in fact criticiz-

ing him for his "want of caution" (80). Similarly, when Elinor suggests "the propriety of some self-command" to Marianne in her attachment to Willoughby, she is not telling her younger sister to feel differently. She only wishes her feelings were "less openly shown" (84).

Circumspection is doubly necessary in *Sense and Sensibility*. It militates against the more harmful effects of gossip. As Jane Nardin has argued, propriety is needed in a social whirl that is constituted by selfish, stupid or unmannerly people.[21] Furthermore, it is important in a world where we have no immediate access to the souls of other people: we do not know what they are thinking nor what they have done. Claudia Johnson has noted that both Marianne and Elinor make mistakes about Willoughby and Edward Ferrars, not because the young women misconstrue the data they have before them, but because they do not have *sufficient* data.[22] Marianne does not know that Willoughby is a rake and Elinor does not know that Edward is secretly engaged.

The soul's opacity to the gaze of other people creates a space in which hypocrisy, that great bugbear of eighteenth-century thought, can flourish. An unprotected sincerity, such as Marianne's, leaves one vulnerable to the machinations of others. So, propriety allows for a protective secrecy. Elinor lies to Lucy Steele in order to protect her dignity, in order to circumvent Lucy's protracted assault on her feelings. Elinor is practicing a form of emotional aikido: she deflects Lucy's attacks by protecting the privacy of her affections. Just as law maintains the private realm of choice—allowing one to dispose of one's property as one wishes—so propriety allows one the privacy of sentiment.[23]

I would like to make the implications of my argument as clear as possible. For all Austen's stress on the social aspects of life, she starts from the premise that we begin as and remain individuals with feelings, needs and desires that are essentially personal. Individuality entails a danger and a challenge: we cannot know what goes on inside other people's heads and hearts. We must begin, as Elinor does, with doubt. Such radical individuality makes social interactions a minefield of conflicting interests and requires what I have called the protective secrecy of privacy. By the same token, the essentially private nature of the individual makes certain forms of candor absolutely necessary. It makes public admissions imperative. If we cannot read others' minds, we have to be able to trust their words and their actions. Hence the importance in *Sense and Sensibility* of acknowledgment.

Mrs. Dashwood makes an important mistake when she takes Willoughby's actions as a sign of his engagement. She says, "I have not wanted syllables where actions have spoken so plainly" (107). But Elinor is not so easily convinced—and rightly so, as it turns out. She says, "I confess . . . that every circumstance except one is in favor of their engagement; but that *one* is the total silence of both on the subject, and with me it almost outweighs every other" (107). Silence about attachment is one thing, but about commitment in an event of such public importance as marriage, is something else entirely. Austen depicts a society in which women's identity is determined by familial and marital connection. She presents a world whose organization and reproduction depend on connections maintained by marriage. In such a world, promises made by men to women are of deep social interest. Propriety, in this light, upholds the social order and individual dignity: it shields vulnerable emotion from public scrutiny and makes public what is of greatest note for social coherence. To put the matter plainly: those elegant decorums of Elinor's plan of general civility make sure that every individual possesses the knowledge necessary for that odd conjunction of emotional attachment and social commitment that is marriage. They also protect the individual if that knowledge is, for whatever reason, not forthcoming. Civility shows people how they should behave. It also provides a means of protecting themselves against others who do not conduct themselves as they should.

If Elinor presents a program for negotiating a world constituted by essentially obscure individuals, then we can begin to understand the contrast between the two sisters. Marianne feels that the congruence of taste that binds her to Willoughby gives her an immediate access to knowledge about him. She assumes that his heart is transparent to her. She seeks him out because they are, she feels, similar and, as any reader of the novel knows, she disdains those who are different from her. She feels she knows such people—especially Colonel Brandon—well enough to disregard them. She thus belongs to that rich tradition of eighteenth-century thought that we call sentimentalism, which sought to overcome the atomistic and rationalist reductions of social life in post-Hobbesian philosophy by positing an unmediated intersubjectivity based on feeling and sympathy. Elinor, on the other hand, doubts. But her often priggish skepticism also means that she pays attention to the differences between individuals—hence her re-evaluation of Mrs. Jennings, whose heart wins her over even though her manners are lacking. Elinor is thus a fine proof of Adorno's aperçu that tact "is the discrimination of differences."[24]

Differences is not just a norm in and for itself. It is the ground and guard of happiness. Austen is involved in an argument, mediated and disseminated by the literary marketplace, about the nature of other minds, of propriety and ultimately, of the possibilities for happiness in this sublunary world. Such an argument is overtly thematized within the novel itself. If the reader gets too involved in character analysis, he or she is likely to forget that happiness is an obsession in this book. Chapter 17 contains a lively discussion of the

relation between wealth and happiness: what constitutes female felicity; how much does a household need? Chapter 19 begins with a conversation about Edward's need for a profession. Mrs. Dashwood avers that he "would be a happier man if [he] had any profession to engage [his] time and give an interest to [his] plans and actions" (127). In the odd Horatianism of this book, male happiness, be it Edward's, Willoughby's or Sir John Middleton's, depends not on the *otium* of independence and country pursuits, but on the *negotium* of commerce (in all its designations) and professional activity. But let us not seem to claim that male happiness is without its domestic element. The last chapter of the novel provides us with a somewhat surreal spectacle of felicity: *everyone* ends up happy in their marriages, even Lucy Ferrars and John Willoughby.

Happiness is a topic of conversation in this book because its definition is up for grabs and still needs to be determined. On the risk of idealizing conversation in this novel and in Austen's other works, I want to disagree with Franco Moretti who sees in Austen not "discussion" (by which he seems to mean "rational public debate") but the desire to make oneself agreeable in company, as Hume might say.[25] *Sense and Sensibility* does not avoid revolutionary fractures any more than the confrontations between Elizabeth Bennet and Fitzwilliam Darcy avoid unpleasant social distinctions: both novels write from within overt conflict and try to make sense of the world these conflicts leave. And the discussions of happiness—of what the characters can hope for—are located in daily conversation, not, as in Voltaire or Johnson, in the abstracted forms of the *conte philosophique* or the Eastern Tale. Reasoning on happiness is not abstruse or abstract: it is the very stuff of the everyday.

If female happiness (the main subject of the novel, it seems) can be located in domesticity and can be debated in everyday life—if its boundaries and its content can be derived from common conversation and can be achieved in the prosecution of "common" activities—then happiness is resolutely secular on the one hand and fiercely apolitical on the other. Twenty years ago Gilbert Ryle noted that Austen was in essence a secular novelist.[26] For all her religious conviction, her novels do not ground their action in the will of the Allmighty. Previous novelists equate virtue and happiness, but always with a nod towards heaven, either in terms of explicit theology or providential plot-devices. *Sense and Sensibility* might contain odd coincidences, but they are never referred back to God. The norms she derives are this-worldly and depend for their determination on human experience, not divine revelation.

The location of hope in this world and in the social sphere—that is, in the realm of economic and sexual reproduction—has its own history, whose trace can be found in what I earlier called Austen's "odd Horatianism." The Horatianism of her forebears, the Augustans, is firmly aligned with that tradition of thought, excavated with such brilliance by J. G. A. Pocock, called "civic republicanism." In response to the growth of a commercial Whig order in the first decades of the eighteenth century, neo-Harringtonian political theory renewed "the ideal of the citizen, virtuous in his devotion to the public good and his engagement in relations of equality, . . . but virtuous also in his independence of any relation that might render him corrupt."[27] Corruption in this branch of thought is the result of dependence. If the citizen gets involved in exchange or patronage relations that make him vulnerable to the vagaries of others or if he hires mercenaries to fight his wars, he will inevitably fall into corruption. English Machiavellianism marks a protest against the Whig order that succeeded the Glorious Revolution. But civic republicanism, though strong, is only one voice in the debate over politics after 1688 and is marred by a serious conceptual weakness. Though it had great normative force and persuasive power in England and America, its analysis is by nature completely negative.[28] Whig modernity, with its mercenaries, standing armies, debts and placemen, could signal nothing more than the complete corruption of the state. Commerce could only reek of moral decay.

We can account for the rise of a counter-discourse to civic republicanism, then, in two ways. Whiggism needed an ideology, one that could find an adequate *normative* substitute for virtue.[29] But a discursive shift was necessary as well because civic republican ideology had a limited *descriptive* power. It could only condemn temporal change in Polybian terms, but could not discuss the new except as moral degradation. The counter-discourse that arose in the face of this deficiency, comes from the language of natural jurisprudence and that area of study that we have come to call economics.[30] This new-fangled civic jurisprudence developed a historical sociology that legitimized the radical novelty of the commercial order.[31] The legitimation of Whig modernity depended on a change of emphasis. The *telos* of the human no longer resided in political virtue (as it does in the language of the republicans) but in social manners; it moved from commitment to the public good to the pursuit of private happiness.[32]

I have shown above how jurisprudential thought divided the social from the political, the realm of society from the sphere of government. The notion of rights helped determine the proper limits of both domains. The civic jurisprudential project attempted to prove that the commercial order contained within it real utopian potential and not just moral degradation. This meant reversing the republican valorization of the public. It also meant that new attention had to be paid to civil society in all its divisions and determinations. There had to be a science of the everyday.

It is not just chance then that makes the development of civic jurisprudence in the middle decades of the eighteenth century coincide nicely with the rise of female conduct literature. The ideology of domesticity could easily be accommodated to the ideology of the new order. In fact, domesticity was necessary for the new order. The emphasis on domestic and private happiness served as the basis for the legitimacy of commerce, and the legitimation of commerce would necessarily entail the lionization of the domestic. I would thus like to add a wrinkle to Nancy Armstrong's recent discussion of the significance of domestic ideology. She argues that conduct books schematized gender differentiation in order to launch an attack on established status hierarchies, and the revolutionary bourgeoisie then organized itself around these gender divisions.[33]

There is a slight discomfort in Armstrong's account: the middle classes are constituted by a discourse that they have originated. Such a claim is less a theoretical tautology than it first may seem, but it lacks a certain force, because, as is often the case in such accounts, the bourgeoisie is its own cause. Pocock, with his usual anti-Marxist fervor, has argued on the other hand that the supposedly bourgeois ideology of possessive individualism was not, in fact, bourgeois at all, but rather the expression of the interests of the Whig magnates after the Glorious Revolution.[34] We can turn this claim to *marxisant* ends by maintaining that the hegemonizing task of defending commercial capitalism was taken over by the aristocracy. In the name of this aristocracy a discourse developed that, by exfoliating, defending and regulating the spheres of economic and sexual reproduction, could construct the gender definitions necessary for the interpellation of the middle classes. If one uses the slightly more humanistic language of "appropriation," one can see that domestic ideology—like happiness—was up for grabs: its language could be adopted by the bourgeoisie, by the gentry, or by the aristocracy.

It therefore makes perfect sense that Austen, a scion of the gentry, whose reception would make her the spokesperson for a middle class to which she most probably did not belong, should invoke manners and a secular notion of happiness that is firmly located in civil society and the domestic sphere. Hers is the logic of the civic jurisprudential tradition. Her location of happiness within civil society takes on an added historical dimension, for in the wake of the French Revolution, such a placement stands in polemical opposition to the call for political reform: hope, Austen seems to indicate, is located not in politics, but in the home.

I have therefore argued that in *Sense and Sensibility* Austen presents propriety as a contemporary norm, derived from law by analogy, as one way of protecting a secular notion of domestic happiness against the stresses of a society that is marked by selfishness, profit, and vulgarity. She thus turns manners, the *telos* presented by civic jurisprudence, against the profit-oriented behavior that civic jurisprudence was developed to defend. But Austen's position is not self-defeating: she is not attacking a money economy per se, but certain forms of action that arise in such an economy. One could argue that, like Burke, Austen understands that a certain civility is necessary if capitalism is to work.[35]

If we can thus place Austen in a certain discursive field and can see her language as the crossing point between aristocratic ideology and middle-class hegemony, we can also see her ethics as the product of a similar conjunction. Adorno's discussion of the history of tact can help us understand the sociohistorical shift that makes the contrast between Marianne and Elinor so compelling to Austen. According to Adorno, the bourgeois individual frees himself at the end of the eighteenth century from "the absolutist compulsion," that in England could be more accurately described as "aristocratic compulsion." In this brave new world, however, the social conventions tied to hierarchical divisions do not disappear: they become democratized, or rather, spread out to a more inclusive sphere of privilege. "The precondition of tact," Adorno writes, "is convention that is broken within itself yet still present."[36] This emancipated tact, no longer the acknowledgement of aristocratic privilege, tries to reconcile the claims of an assertive individuality and the demands of the social totality. It should be quite clear, then, that what Adorno means by tact, Elinor Dashwood means by civility. But this civility only has a positive normative content—the recognition of a substantive individuality—at one moment in history. It soon dissolves into either an empty formality or an intrusive intimacy.[37] Tact, that all-important moment within propriety, contains a kernel of utopian promise, a promise that is made explicit in Burke's defense of chivalry. Tact entails a vision of society in which the individual is protected and recognized within and by the whole. The utopian space created by tact is fragile and historically contingent. To us it might seem to cost too much, might seem like the product of a vicious repression. To Austen, as to Goethe, it seems like the guarantor of freedom. It not only signals the emancipation of classes but it also represents the liberation of the individual. Tact protects the mediations between the newly-derived subject and the totality that both includes and stands over it.

We can take this argument even further. The apparent repression to which Elinor submits with such tenacity can be seen as an odd form of autonomy—that is, of self-regulation. Let us take the example of her refusal to tell her family of the disappointment she has been handed by Lucy Steele: Edward Ferrars is secretly engaged to that unworthy girl. Elinor explains her prolonged silence by expounding on her duties:

> My promise to Lucy, obliged me to be secret. I owed it to her, therefore, to avoid giving any hint of the truth; and I owed it to my family and friends, not to create in them a solicitude about me, which it could not be in my power to satisfy. (263)

She has no power to satisfy their solicitude because she cannot actively intervene in or subvert the odd triangle in which she finds herself. She can only be passive because her attachment to Edward does not constitute any legitimate claim against his prior engagement. Given her powerlessness in relation to Edward and Lucy, she can only exert control over herself.

Such self-regulation seems deeply masochistic to our late twentieth-century notions of emancipation, as well it might. But it also constitutes the only autonomy readily open to the disenfranchised. One could compare Austen to Kant without doing vicious damage to either. For our purposes, however, it is worth comparing Elinor to Goethe's Werther. In an early letter, Werther expatiates on the deep restrictions which inhibit and overcome "the active, and inquiring powers of Man." In the face of a recalcitrant world, only two forms of happiness and freedom are possible: retreat into the imagination and suicide.[38] When imagination fails him and both social and emotional restraints forbid him the "active" life he seeks, Werther can only find autonomy in self-destruction.

Such an odd notion of self-regulation could be written off to the peculiarities of Werther's overheated mind (and Goethe, of course, would like us to do just this), but to do so would be to ignore the strong current of stoicism that runs through European thought in the eighteenth century. Let me offer, as another instance, this passage from Schiller:

> The highest ideal to which we aspire is to remain on good terms with the physical world as the executrix of our happiness, without thereby being obliged to fall out with the moral world that determines our dignity. Now it is well known how rarely one can succeed in serving two masters. . . . Let him be happy if he has learned to bear what he cannot alter, and to surrender with dignity what he cannot save! cases can occur in which fate surmounts all the ramparts upon which man bases his security and nothing else remains but for him to flee into the sacred freedom of the spirit—cases in which there is no other recourse in order to placate the lust for life than to will that fate . . . and by a free renunciation of all sensuous interest to kill oneself morally.[39]

Schiller is writing within a Kantian model where the subject is caught between the imperative promise of moral autonomy and the actual heteronomy imposed by the phenomenal, time-ridden world. Schiller, who published these words in 1801, lists the shipwreck of history and of revolutionary expectation as a sign of the tyranny of the physical. We might well be self-regulating subjects, he claims, but we are also subject to the vagaries of an environment we cannot control. We must therefore learn to will what we are unable to avoid. That is, we must learn to kill ourselves when necessary.

This version of *amor fati* signals a historical dilemma. On the one hand, it registers the desire for autonomy and the strength of self-determination as a norm. On the other, it admits that such autonomy is not possible, either (as Schiller would argue) because we are caught ineluctably between the noumenal and the phenomenal, or (as we might care to maintain) because the demand for autonomy has not yet found its historical outlet. Thus *amor fati* expresses both a protest against a historical situation and a sign of the subject's weakness in relation to it: it rebels against an unavoidable heteronomy that it must also accept. That Elinor, Werther and Schiller extol a self-destructive masochism is without a doubt. But this masochism is itself the last instance of power open to the powerless, be they the representatives of a revolutionary bourgeoisie or the disinherited daughters of the country gentry. Self-abnegation is the shadow of their self-assertion.

We can say then that the insistence on propriety in *Sense and Sensibility* expresses a utopian hope and a historical fear. The hope is for recognition and a kingdom of ends.[40] The fear rises from the sense that a major disjunction has taken place and that the norms that have determined behavior in the past no longer hold. It has become a commonplace that Austen's novels narrate a crisis in authority, both paternal—which is seen as inadequate—and feminine—which is dangerous and must be hidden.[41] The genealogical precision of the first pages of *Sense and Sensibility* can blind us to their thematic significance: paternal authority can no longer provide for the female Dashwoods because its norms cannot direct the selfish behavior of John Dashwood, the heir. John Dashwood is precisely one of those sophisters and economists that Burke inveighs against in his *Reflections,* a man who, once free from the manners of the past, will be guided by a purely self-seeking rationality. It is against such men that Burke invokes "the spirit of a gentleman" and the legacy of chivalry. But it is worth considering that Elinor does not use the past as her authority: she, unlike Burke, does not appeal to precedent. Her mores, her plan of general civility, have no model within the book. In fact, *Sense and Sensibility* is remarkable for the venality or impropriety of its characters, especially its older ones. Jane Nardin has pointed out that propriety is necessary in this novel because it protects the intelligent individual against a society that is blisteringly mediocre.[42] But it is also worth noting that while civility is an antidote for that society, the norms civility presents seem to arise precisely from the needs of that

society. In short, propriety is not figured here (as it is perhaps in *Mansfield Park*) as the precious because fragile inheritance of the past, but as the product of that past's inability to reproduce itself.

I want, therefore, to make a strong claim: propriety in *Sense and Sensibility* is not the atavistic outcropping of tradition but the expression of an experience of radical change. Propriety is invoked to protect the newly self-conscious subject against the anti-social interpersonal manifestations of the socioeconomic shifts that created that subject in the first place.[43] To discuss *Sense and Sensibility* in these terms (and thus to sidestep the usual questions about Austen's conservatism and her subversiveness) is to try to see her as a writer of and about modernity.

A caveat is necessary here: I do not want to engage the question of when modernity actually begins. A *structural* description and delineation of the modern is not what is at stake. Having outlined above how Austen's novel is determined by the discursive changes that occur with the advent of commercial capitalism and how the ideology of tact arises from a shift in social power that accompanies that advent, I would like now to stress the way that Austen registers the *experience* of modernity.

Following the work of Koselleck and others, I would like to suggest that beginning in the early eighteenth century, modernity (as we saw in our discussion of the derivation of the discourse of civic jurisprudence) is experienced as a qualitative break from the past.[44] Blasted out of the repetitive continuum that had marked the self-presentation of history up to that point, the modern finds itself, for better or for worse, freed from the trammels of traditional authority and example.[45] Modernity marks an openness to a future that is itself open in that it is freed from eschatalogy.[46] It signals a present moment that is conscious of itself as such but, paradoxically enough, sees itself as empty, transitory and potentially meaningless. Modernity is thus attended by both fear and utopian hope. Its orientation toward the future, the sense, born in the Enlightenment, that human institutions are historically derived and therefore susceptible to reform, and the concomitant possibility of secular progress all mean that, for the first time, utopian hope could be anchored in the sublunary world without need of divine sanction.[47] This utopianism is also made necessary by the fear that the potential meaninglessness of an apparently normless present produce. Hence the fear, the free-floating anxiety that modernity inspires requires as its antidotes hope and predictability. The shock of the new, the experience of suddenness that marks modernity, renders necessary both the collective orientation of utopia and a science of probability—that is, a sociological prognostic that can foreclose against the unpredictability of the future.[48] I have tried to show how Austen's text registers *thematically* the experience of modernity. ***Sense and Sensibility*** bodies forth the discomfort that arises from the break with authority and the past, locates a new-found horizon of hope in civil society (using the language of civic jurisprudence which is itself a theory of the modern) and gives voice to a rugged and skeptical empiricism, a tenacious lack of faith in things not actually seen.

But modernity is inscribed in the *structure* of the novel as well, in its play of affect. Moderate Whig writers of the 1790s used empiricism to redirect the utopian energies unleashed by the French Revolution toward reformist ends. The same could be argued for ***Sense and Sensibility.*** The novel uses as a pedagogical device the disappointment dealt to hope by the sheer recalcitrance of the external world. It teaches the reader to indulge in a mobile and moderate hope. It signals this teaching in Marianne's painful conversion to civility. Similarly, Elinor's plot line moves from hope to disappointment to hope fulfilled. But disappointment is not merely thematic. It recurs in visceral reactions to the text. Most critics have complained about the book's ending, about Austen's apparently cavalier treatment of Marianne. But the reader's lack of satisfaction in this marriage seems to be the whole point: the world will not allow us to have what precisely it is we want, especially when what we want—a union with Willoughby perhaps?—is marked by the dream of an all-too-easy and improbable, Rousseauistic (and therefore "Jacobin") transparency. Marianne's marriage to Brandon, this union of second loves, has not felt like much of a consolation for the inevitable disappointments that "reality" as it is constituted by Austen's novels doles out with such regularity. If we move away from the usual discussions of the epistemology of Austen's works (in which the moral worth of a character is determined by how correctly that character can understand his/her present and predict his/her future) we can see the important effect that the reader's unavoidable mistakes have. The reader, like Marianne and Elinor, is kept in the dark. And many of the hopes raised, the book is then careful to dash. We are tendered back to a limited and limiting world.

It is thus tempting to see Austen as an antiutopian, as a clear-eyed empiricist waging war against the seductions of an emancipatory imagination. Indeed, ***Sense and Sensibility*** is assiduous in its redirection of utopian energies away from revolutionary upheaval. The utopian concentration on the new, the cathexis onto a qualitative break with the past is not directed against an obdurate physical world. Rather the desire to break with a repressive past finds its outlet in the shifts within the notion of identity, within character itself. Marianne's swift and complete conversion (like Darcy's) is a *novum* that the text unleashes. The pathos of reform is located not in the image of a redeemed world but in a chastened heart. The comic marriage plot requires the

characters to change. The plot can thus appear to serve as the agent of a stiff-necked world which cannot be transformed. But the plot also argues that the world does not need to be changed, that the fault lies with our hearts, not our stars. The comic plot structure bears within it the prognostication, the predictability of happiness. To rail against the constitution of society, then, is to mistake it, to miss the opportunities it contains. The recalcitrant world, seen as external to the characters, is presented as containing within it the proper ingredients for happiness, for proper hope. Happiness does not demand revolution, but individual moral repair.

And yet, such a deeply conservative message, such a resolutely counterrevolutionary pedagogy, only tells half the story, for the apparent victory of the world over the individual as played out by the plot does not sacrifice the individual's claim against that world. While the scrutiny enacted by the use of *style indirecte libre* indicates the novel's submission of its main characters to that mediocre piece of society that it tropes as the social totality, Austen's style also deploys the full force of its ironies against the follies of that totality.

One of the most famous set pieces of ***Sense and Sensibility*** is, of course, its second chapter where Mrs. John Dashwood talks her husband out of offering financial help to "the widow and children of his father" (47). She does so by invoking the very generosity she means to strangle in its crib ("What brother on earth would do half so much for his sisters, even if *really* his sisters! And as it is—only half blood!—But you have such a generous spirit!" [44]). And John Dashwood buys it. He forgoes his original intention completely:

> This argument was irresistible. It gave to his intentions whatever of decision was wanting before; and he finally resolved, that it would be absolutely unnecessary, if not highly indecorous, to do more for the widow and children of his father, than such kind of neighbourly acts as his own wife pointed out. (47)

The irony of this passage lies in its assumption that the reader will recognize the bad faith of John Dashwood's conclusions. What could be less decorous than not helping his father's relatively impoverished family? John Dashwood, we are told earlier on, "conducted himself with propriety in the discharge of his ordinary duties" (41). The unvoiced criticism here is that he does not behave properly in the discharge of *extraordinary* duties. He would be more worthy of respect, Austen tells the reader, if he had married a more amiable woman. But the woman he has married is "a strong caricature of himself;—more narrow-minded and selfish" (41). She is an imperfect copy—a literally more humorous version—of her husband, and thus she reduces him to a poor copy of herself, or rather, of himself. The mirroring relation between the two turns John into the mere outline of a respectable man. Their respectability is vitiated by their selfishness, but they are unable to see themselves in these terms; instead they cloak their self-seeking in the garb of benevolence and decorum. The wit of John Dashwood's capitulation to his wife's version of his own worst instincts thus lies in the distance between accepted norm and actual behavior. One of the novel's great rhetorical strengths is its ability to deploy these norms tacitly as well as discuss them explicitly: it preempts the reader's disagreement by aligning the reader against characters who subscribe to but cannot live according to ideals of good manners, that is, of decorum and propriety. Following the lead Adorno has given us, we can say that Austen's irony is both the cry of an angry individuality and the negative image of that utopia whose traces we can make out in the concept and practice of propriety. This irony thus carries a radical critique which modifies the apparent conservatism of her plot.

To take Austen's vision of propriety seriously, then, would be to see her as a rather difficult writer about classical liberalism.[49] Concentrating on the promise of happiness located in civil society, she works from the premise of a radical individuality and uses a domesticated notion of rights (here troped as propriety) to mediate between the claims of the assertive subject and the social totality. The centrality of women (who are not and cannot be economic actors) in her plots underscores the implicit universality that the notion of rights entails (even in Burke's account, though Burke would limit the universe to the nation) and underlines the necessity of this global notion of rights for the orderly functioning of capitalist society. Her plots show the conflicts that seem inevitably to arise when the economic conditions which bring the language of rights to the forefront come into conflict with basic respect for these rights.

She is perhaps the first novelist of classical liberalism because she has metabolized the situation of post-revolutionary modernity and has thematized it while trying to tame its more disruptive energies. We can speculate that her canonization had to wait for several decades after her death because it was only then that the problem she sought to solve could be recognized. But by then, it seems, it was too late, for the utopian promise of tact—the interpersonal reconciliation of a fiercely-guarded autonomy with the exigencies of social existence in a market economy—was no longer a sufficient program for what had developed into a fully, self-conscious class society.[50]

The emancipatory moment of tact and propriety has therefore most probably passed, and Austen can only appear to us as a conservative. But she can still shock us with the unexpected astringencies of her tone. I would like to contend that there is still great critical

power in Austen's novel. *Sense and Sensibility* confronts us with the as-yet unsolved project of our modernity. It presents us with the demand that we reconcile our behavior with our norms, our actions with the minimal utopian hope for respect and autonomy. To read Austen nostalgically is therefore a temptation we should resist, for to do so is to misunderstand the fractures that mark the temporality of her texts. It is to mistake her irony and to see it aimed at the past, when in fact the insistent disjunctions between tenor and vehicle that scar *Sense and Sensibility* can only be healed in the future, if they are to be healed at all.[51]

Notes

[1] Here is Mudrick's summation: "Marianne, the life and center of the novel, has been betrayed; and not by Willoughby" (Marvin Mudrick, *Irony as Defence and Discovery* [Berkeley: Univ. of California Press, 1968], 72.) Mudrick's condemnation has had a long half-life. Its traces can be found in A. Walton Litz, *Jane Austen: A Study of Her Development* (New York: Oxford Univ. Press, 1965), 81-82; Sandra Gilbert and Susan Gubar, *The Madwoman in the Attic* (New Haven: Yale Univ. Press, 1979), 146-57; and Mary Poovey, *The Proper Lady and the Woman Writer* (Chicago: Univ. of Chicago Press, 1988), 172-94.

[2] Julia Prewitt Brown, *Jane Austen's Novels: Social Change and Literary Form* (Cambridge: Harvard Univ. Press, 1979), 56-60; Susan Morgan, *In the Meantime* (Chicago: Chicago Univ. Press, 1980), 109-31; Claudia Johnson, "The Twilight of Probability: Uncertainty and Hope in *Sense and Sensibility*," *Philological Quarterly* 62 (1983): 171-86, and *Jane Austen: Women, Politics and the Novel* (Chicago: Univ. of Chicago Press, 1988), 49-72.

[3] See Mudrick (note 1), 83-84; Marilyn Butler, *Jane Austen and the War of Ideas* (Oxford: Oxford Univ. Press, 1975), 191-92, D. A. Miller, *Narrative and Its Discontents* (Princeton: Princeton Univ. Press, 1981), 66-77.

[4] Jane Austen, *Sense and Sensibility,* ed. Tony Tanner (Harmondsworth: Penguin Books, 1969), 315. All further references will be included parenthetically in the text.

[5] John Brewer, "The Wilkites and the Law, 1763-74," in *An Ungovernable People,* ed. John Brewer and John Styles (New Brunswick: Rutgers Univ. Press, 1980), 133.

[6] H. T. Dickinson, *Liberty and Property* (New York: Holmes and Meier, 1977), 123-60. This Whig-Tory consensus defines itself in opposition to the Court-Country controversy, where it tends to take the Court side. Thus what I am calling a consensus here marks the survival into the eighteenth century of jurispru-

dence and not the civic republican tradition. The theory of civic republican virtue did not have to account for the foundation of government: the republic was the ground and medium of virtue. The republic was its own reward. The natural law tradition, however, had in the seventeenth century developed its own historical sociology and authropology. It sought to account for the minimum developmental conditions for the the creation of the state. The historical contingency of government presents a different problem for the civic republicans than it does for the jurists: history, which threatens the republican constitution with corruption, is the very ground of the jurisprudential derivation of the state. Jurisprudential arguments about government could provide a descriptive model for the foundation of society whereas the republicans could only find a normative one. In short, jurists could show how government comes about; republicans could only show why it should.

7 Sir William Blackstone, *Commentaries on the Laws of England* (Philadelphia, 1803), 1:2:47, 48.

8 Blackstone, 1:2:48, 53.

9 For Hume's politics, see Duncan Forbes, *Hume's Philosophical Politics* (Cambridge: Cambridge Univ. Press, 1975), 125-230. David Hume, "Of the Origin of Government," in *Essays Moral, Political and Literary,* ed. Eugene F. Miller (Indianapolis: Liberty Press, 1987), 37.

10 Tom Paine, "Common Sense," in *The Thomas Paine Reader,* ed. Isaac Kramnick and Michael Foot (Harmondsworth: Penguin, 1987), 66.

11 In David Hume's *Enquiries Concerning Human Understanding and Concerning the Principles of Morals,* ed. L. A. Selby-Bigge (Oxford: Oxford Univ. Press, 1975), 183-83, justice and benevolence seem to complement each other. Justice—the protection of property—is born of the apparently natural scarcity of goods and seems to substitute for that care for others which we call benevolence. Following the same logic, a completely benevolent race would have no need for justice even in conditions of scarcity. Justice compensates for a lack of benevolence: benevolence renders justice unnecessary. But justice and benevolence can also be seen to conflict. In Hume's description of a state of pure benevolence, property circulates according to need and there is no division of wealth. Justice, on the other hand, being a "cautious, jealous virtue," prevents this circulation by making right take precedence over need. Benevolence is centrifugal; justice, centripetal. The Whig discourse of humanist jurisprudence and the political economics that it spawned can be said to develop out of the tension between the demands of property and the claims of benevolence, out of the conflicting languages of individual right and social good.

12 Hume (note 11), 261.

13 For an elegant description of Hume's theory of justice, see Knud Haakonssen, *The Science of a Legislator* (Cambridge: Cambridge Univ. Press, 1981), 4-41.

14 Edmund Burke, "Letters on a Regicide Peace," in *The Works of the Right Honorable Edmund Burke,* 12 vols. (Boston: Little Brown, 1871), 5:310.

15 J. G. A. Pocock, "Burke and the Ancient Constitution," in *Politics, Language and Time* (Chicago: Univ. of Chicago Press, 1989), 209.

16 Burke (note 14), 3:332.

17 See, for instance, Burke, 7:320-40.

18 For the relation of equity to precedence in eighteenth-century common jurisprudence, see David Lieberman, *The Province of Legislation Determined* (New York: Cambridge Univ. Press, 1989), 75-87, 131-32, 135-36.

19 For the conflict between justice and benevolence in Hume (note 11), see paragraphs 145-63. For Adam Smith, see *The Theory of Moral Sentiments,* ed. A. L. MacFie and D. D. Raphael (Oxford: Oxford Univ. Press, 1979), 79-82. See also Haakonssen (note 13), 10-11, 85-86.

20 Thus Pocock can see the ideology of manners put forward by the civic jurisprudential tradition as an answer to the civic republican notion of virtue. Where the republicans see corruption in commerce and virtue only in an active public life, the Whig jurists locate virtue in manners and derive manners from *le doux commerce* of social and financial interaction. Where Pocock is excellent at seeing the positive goal of self-refinement that manners are given by the apologists of Whig modernity, he seems to ignore the regulatory, "negative" freedom that manners also entail. See J. G. A. Pocock, "Virtues, Rights and Manners," in *Virtue, Commerce, and History* (New York: Cambridge Univ. Press, 1985), 37-50, see especially 48-50.

21 Jane Nardin, *Those Elegant Decorums* (Albany: State Univ. of New York Press, 1973), 24-25.

22 Johnson, "Twilight of Probability" (note 2), 172-80.

23 This privacy of sentiment should not be confused with Willoughby's and Edward Ferrars's insistent secrecy about their previous attachments. Their previous commitments have a social as well as an emotional impact: their actions are, in effect, promises that change the world in which they live. They have contracted obligations and debts that do not allow them the freedom that

they seem to profess they have. To put it bluntly, the two men get secrecy wrong and invert propriety.

[24] Theodor Adorno, *Minima Moralia,* trans. E. F. N. Jephcott (London: Verso, 1974), 37.

[25] Franco Moretti, *The Way of the World* (London: Verso, 1987), 48-52.

[26] Gilbert Ryle, "Jane Austen and the Moralists," in *Critical Essays on Jane Austen,* ed. Judith O'Neill (London: George Allen and Unwin, 1970), 117.

[27] Pocock, *Virtue* (note 20), 48.

[28] See J. G. A. Pocock, *The Machiavellian Moment* (Princeton: Princeton Univ. Press, 1976), 423-552.

[29] Pocock, *Virtue* (note 20), 48-50.

[30] See Richard Tuck, "The 'modern' theory of natural law," and Istvan Hont, "The language of sociability and commerce: Samuel Pufendorf and the theoretical foundations of the 'Four-Stages Theory,'" in *The Languages of Political Theory in Early-Modern Europe,* ed. Anthony Pagden (New York: Cambridge Univ. Press, 1987), 99-122, 253-76.

[31] See Pocock, "The Mobility of Property and the Rise of Eighteenth-Century Sociology," in *Virtue* (note 20), 103-24, and "Cambridge Paradigms and Scotch Philosophers, in *Wealth and Virtue,* ed. Istvan Hont and Michael Ignatieff (Cambridge: Univ. Press, 1983), 235-52.

[32] Pocock, *Virtue,* 48; M. M. Goldsmith, "Liberty, luxury and the pursuit of happiness," in Pagden (note 30), 251.

[33] Nancy Armstrong, *Desire and Domestic Fiction* (New York: Oxford Univ. Press, 1987), 3-95.

[34] Pocock, "Authority and Property," in *Virtue,* 51-72.

[35] Pocock, "The Political Economy of Burke's Analysis of the French Revolution," in *Virtue,* 198-211; C. B. Macpherson, *Burke* (New York: Oxford Univ. Press, 1984), 39-49, 66-69.

[36] Adorno (note 24), 36. I have modified Jephcott's translation here: he has added a pun that Adorno would have liked but which the German does not authorize.

[37] Adorno, 37.

[38] "But he who perceives in all humility where this is leading, who sees how prettily the happy burgher makes a Paradise of his little garden and how even the unhappy man pursues his way willingly under his burden . . . yes, he is quiet and constructs his world

from within himself and is also happy, because he is human. And then, no matter how confined he might be, he always maintains the sweet feeling of freedom, and that he can leave this prison, when he wants to" (Johann Wolfgang von Goethe, *Werke,* 14 vols. [Munich: C. H. Beck, 1981], 6:13-14; my translation).

[39] Friedrich von Schiller, *Naive and Sentimental Poetry and On the Sublime,* trans. Julius Elias (New York: Frederick Ungar, 1966), 208. I have modified this translation.

[40] The Kantian echo might well seem a presumption here, an overburdening of Austen's text with the heaviness of German philosophy. In my defense I will juxtapose two quotations. The first is Austen's. Robert Ferrars has just married Lucy Steele and as far as the self-seeking and self-important John Dashwood is concerned, one brother is as good as the other: "Certainly, there can be no difference; for Robert will now to all intents and purposes be considered as the eldest son;—and as to any thing else, they are both very agreeable young men, I do not know that one is superior to the other" (294). Elinor holds her peace, but we may guess that the irony of John's statement rests on the reader's knowledge (a knowledge that we supposedly share with Elinor) that one brother is superior to the other, that even wealth cannot make them equal or exchangeable. Here, now, is Kant:

> "In the realm of ends everything has either a *price* [Preis] or a dignity [Würde]. Whatever has a price can be replaced by something else as its equivalent; on the other hand, whatever is above all price, and therefore admits of no equivalent, has a dignity. . . .

> Now morality is the condition under which alone a rational being can be an end in itself. . . . Thus morality and humanity, so far as it is capable of morality, alone have dignity. Skill and diligence in work have a market value; wit, lively imagination, and humor have an affective price; but fidelity in promises and benevolence . . . have intrinsic worth" (Immanuel Kant, *Groundwork of the Metaphysics of Morals,* trans. Lewis White Beck [Indianapolis: Bobbs-Merrill, 1959], 53).

Of course, John Dashwood is not a moral man: he views people as means, not ends, and cannot envision a world that consists of true dignity, that is, a world in which the worth of a person cannot be reduced to a market value. That Edward Ferrars has dignity and should command respect because he, like Elinor, is faithful in promises and benevolent from principle, is an intuition that John Dashwood is constitutionally incapable of feeling and is a conclusion that the reader, we must assume, is supposed to reach. Like Kant (and like Adorno), Austen's morality is based on the categorical distinction between dignity and price, between respect (Acht/Achtung) and the reduction of the truly human to mere returnable goods.

41 Gilbert and Gubar (note 1), 154; Poovey (note 1), 204, 208, 237-40; Deborah Kaplan, "Achieving Authority: Jane Austen's First Published Novel," *Nineteenth-Century Fiction* 37 (1983): 203-18.

42 Nardin (note 21), 24-25.

43 Tact and propriety in Austen's case serve not as a demand that social relations should change but rather as a recognition that they already have. Propriety is meant to protect the daughters of a gentry that has fallen on hard times. But to reduce Austen to her class position is to misunderstand her appeal. Though Austen might well be the spokesperson for a beleaguered country gentry, she has come to speak a language that is comprehensible to other classes whose interests are not necessarily the same as those of gentry. In other words, a class on the way down might express itself in a way that makes sense to a class on the way up. But we can go even further. Perhaps we can see in the apparent anxieties expressed in Austen's novels, a more universalizable interest which is "propped" on that of the Regency gentry. For the notion of propping, see Jean Laplanche, *Life and Death in Psychoanalysis* (Baltimore: Johns Hopkins Univ. Press, 1976), 15-18.

44 Reinhart Koselleck, *Futures Past,* trans. Keith Tribe (Cambridge: MIT Press, 1985); Jürgen Habermas, *The Philosophical Discourse of Modernity,* trans. Frederick Lawrence (Cambridge: MIT Press, 1987); Hannah Arendt, "The Concept of History," in *Between Past and Future* (New York: Penguin, 1968), 41-90; Ernst Bloch, *Natural Law and Human Dignity,* trans. Dennis J. Schmidt (Cambridge, Mass: MIT Press, 1986). In a more complicated way, my comments owe a debt to Paul de Man, "Literary History and Literary Modernity" and "Lyric and Modernity," *Blindness and Insight* (Minneapolis: Univ. of Minnesota Press, 1983), 142-65, 166-86.

45 Koselleck (note 44), "Historia Magistra Vitae," 21-38; Habermas (note 44), 7.

46 Koselleck, "Modernity and the Planes of Historicity," 3-20; "Historical Criteria of the Modern Concept of Revolution," 21-38; "Neuzeit," 231-266.

47 Koselleck, 17-18.

48 Arendt (note 44), 76-86, Koselleck, "On the Relation of Past and Future," 14-15, "Neuzeit," 262-66.

49 Mary Evans makes a similar point using a different argument in *Jane Austen and the State* (London: Tavistock, 1987), 2, 69-70.

50 Austen's belated Victorian canonization indicates the complexity of her texts. Her acceptance smacks of nostalgia. As Andrew Lang writes in 1886: "Ah, madam, what a relief it is to come back to your witty volumes, and forget the follies of today in those of Mr Collins and Mrs Bennet!" To forget the unspecified but apparently overbearing lunacies of the present for the limited humors of individual characters seems to entail dreaming anachronistically of a society whose problems can be located in personal relations with easily identifiable character-types. It marks a yearning for the universality of a certain class and gender position once the validity of that universality is seen to have been eliminated by history. It is to want to live in the parsonage when in fact one lives in the city, to tend the souls of one's cure when one is an engineer or a businessman. Austen thus represents an easier past to which it is always pleasant to return. In a similar vein, Nancy Armstrong (note 33) writes of Austen: "It was not this particular segment of society that she idealized, then, but rather the language that constituted the nuances of emotion and the ethical refinements that seemed to arise from within to modify the political meaning of signs, a new language of kinship relations capable of reproducing this privileged community on a personal scale within society at large" (160). One should perhaps read this claim (or rather this set of related claims) in juxtaposition to Raymond Williams's critique of Austen's omission of classes other than the lower aristocracy and middle gentry from her works. The ideological moment in Austen's work then is a complex one: her fascination with one class seems to give that class position a universal validity while stressing the personal aspects of social reproduction. To put it bluntly, the appeal of Austen's fiction to the Victorians might have rested on its substitution of humor and personality for the larger and more intransigent structures of class conflict. See Raymond Williams, *The Country and the City* (New York: Oxford Univ. Press, 1973), 112-19.

51 Thanks are due to the Jane Austen Society of North America and the Washington Area Romanticists' Group, which both lent a generous and critical eye to earlier versions of the work. I would also like to express my gratitude to Patricia Meyer Spacks, Deborah Kaplan, Neil Fraistat, Orrin Wang and Adrienne Donald for their insights.

Tara Ghoshal Wallace (essay date 1992)

SOURCE: "*Sense and Sensibility* and the Problem of Feminine Authority," in *Eighteenth-Century Fiction,* Vol. 4, No. 2, January, 1992, pp. 149-63.

[*In the following essay, Wallace posits that* Sense and Sensibility *is Austen's most antifeminist book because of its ambiguous position on feminine authority and power.*]

For almost two hundred years, readers of *Sense and Sensibility* have questioned Jane Austen's ambivalence towards the values of proper conduct as opposed to those of inner-directed behaviour; but this question has tended to obscure another ideological issue in the novel—the issue of feminine authority and power.[1] While readers debate whether the narrator is drawing rigid lines between sense and feeling, they may overlook the book's attitude towards female power, an attitude which is negative, cautionary, devaluing. In this essay I argue that *Sense and Sensibility* betrays Austen's anxieties about female authority; seen from this perspective the novel reveals struggles and tensions rather than ideological serenity.

The most straightforward way to begin is to assert that *Sense and Sensibility* is an account of Austen's failure to legitimate feminine authority. It is Austen's most antifeminist book, a book inhabited by monstrous women and victimized men, a book which seems to deny all possibility of sisterhood, articulated in its equivocal last words—"and among the merits and the happiness of Elinor and Marianne, let it not be ranked as the least considerable, that though sisters, and living almost within sight of each other, they could live without disagreement between themselves."[2] At the same time, feminist critics such as Patricia Meyer Spacks and Deborah Kaplan have shown that *Sense and Sensibility* criticizes patriarchal values and practices.[3] The dichotomy between fear of feminine authority and desire for it occupies Austen's novelistic imagination and informs her narrative strategies in *Sense and Sensibility.*

One antifeminist strategy that Austen consistently uses is the diversionary tactic. The sins of a man, while not ignored or excused, are overshadowed by an emphasis on the despicable behaviour of a woman. Manifested in nearly every male/female relationship in the novel, the device is pervasive. For example, although Elinor ceases to blame Charlotte Palmer for her husband's rudeness (p. 112), the dialogue that follows her re-evaluation demonstrates not the husband's ill breeding, but the wife's foolishness. What the reader *experiences,* through Elinor's conversation with Mrs Palmer, is the difficulty of responding politely to vulgarity and mindless chatter. No comparable experience of Mr Palmer is offered; instead, we are told about Elinor's mixed feelings:

> She found him, however, perfectly the gentleman in his behaviour to all visitors, and only occasionally rude to his wife and her mother; she found him very capable of being a pleasant companion, and only prevented from being so always, by too great an aptitude to fancy himself as much superior to people in general, as he must feel himself to be to Mrs. Jennings and Charlotte. (p. 304)

This evaluation not only suggests women's inadequacies, but also problematizes Elinor's judgment. We learn that her mild resistance to Mr Palmer is connected to her "remembrance of Edward's generous temper" (p. 305), and this fact personalizes and renders her evaluation less authoritative; Mr Palmer emerges more or less unscathed by the criticisms of Elinor, and Austen seems to accept his behaviour as perfectly normal.[4]

More significantly, the actions of John Dashwood and his great-uncle are allowed to become peripheral. The famous dialogue between John Dashwood and his wife obscures the patriarchal insensitivity of the old man and shades the cold selfishness of the young one. What remains prominent in the reader's mind is Fanny Dashwood's aggressive manipulation of her husband's irresolute desires. John himself describes his decision in words that give Fanny credit for it: "I believe you are perfectly right. My father certainly could mean nothing more by his request to me than what you say. I clearly understand it now, and I will strictly fulfill my engagement by such acts of assistance and kindness to them as you have described" (p. 12). He cedes agency to her, and thereby abrogates responsibility for his conduct to his sisters. Fanny wins; but so does John, for his meanness is projected onto his wife.

Another small example helps establish the pattern. When Sir John Middleton's unrestrained hospitality leads him to invite the Steele sisters to his home, "Lady Middleton was thrown into no little alarm . . . by hearing that she was very soon to receive a visit from two girls whom she had never seen in her life" (p. 118). But rather than let the reader dwell on the sensitivity and sense of a man who would so casually foist house-guests on his wife, the narrative quickly jumps to the punishment Sir John must suffer: "As it was impossible however now to prevent their coming Lady Middleton resigned herself to the idea of it, with all the philosophy of a well-bred woman, contenting herself with merely giving her husband a gentle reprimand on the subject five or six times every day" (p. 118). Male insensitivity is overshadowed by female anger, and Sir John is made to seem the victim of a nagging, unreasonable wife.

Edward Ferrars and John Willoughby are the primary beneficiaries of Austen's diversionary tactics. Edward, from the beginning, is presented as the passive victim of monstrous women—his mother, his sister, and Lucy Steele. The cold ambition of his family not only presses him towards a mercenary marriage but also prevents him from doing anything with his life. Their preference for "great men or barouches" is opposed to his desire for "domestic comfort and the quiet of a private life" (p. 16), and in such a dichotomy there is no question about the right side. Edward's participation in his aimless life and his willingness to blame his mother and sister for it, however, are muted. Although he admits to being unable to "resist the solicitations of his friends to do nothing" (p. 103), his passivity seems entirely admirable compared to their aggressive exhortations to be "smart," "genteel," "dashing and expensive" (pp. 102-3). Even his entanglement with Lucy he ascribes to his family. He falls in love with her because "instead of having anything to do, instead of having any profession chosen for me, or being allowed to chuse any myself, I returned home to be completely idle"—to a home, moreover, that "my mother did not make . . . in every respect comfortable" (p. 362). Edward's lack of energy and agency is to be explained away by the aggressive manipulations of others—of women.

Elinor's acceptance of Edward's view is a crucial moment in the tension in the novel. Elinor, like others, blames Mrs Ferrars for all that is mysterious or disappointing in Edward (just as in *Emma* the inhabitants of Highbury are eager to blame Mrs Churchill for Frank's inconsiderateness). She ascribes his coldness "to his mother's account; and it was happy for her that he had a mother whose character was so imperfectly known to her, as to be the general excuse for every thing strange on the part of her son" (p. 101). Such conviction allows her to absolve Edward and "to turn for comfort to the renewal of her confidence in Edward's affection" (p. 102), just as later she can be "consoled by the belief that Edward had done nothing to forfeit her esteem" in becoming engaged to Lucy Steele (p. 141). Actually, Elinor offers more than forgiveness; she turns away from her own sense of injury and betrayal and concentrates on Edward's misery: "if he had injured her, how much more had he injured himself; if her case were pitiable, his was hopeless. . . . She wept for him, more than for herself" (p. 140). She constructs, in effect, a hierarchy of victims and villains: Edward's "imprudence" has hurt him more than it has her, and his is a venial sin compared to the evil machinations of Mrs Ferrars and Lucy Steele.[5]

It seems to me clear that Austen does not expect the reader to accept Elinor's reading as the definitive one. Indeed, there is sufficient irony in the passages I have quoted to alert us to Elinor's evasions. But the discovery and discussion of Elinor's disingenuousness is, in fact, yet another red herring, more subtle and more successful than Elinor's own wishful excuses. If we expend sufficient energy and acuity in analysing and exposing Elinor's self-deluding justifications, we are the more likely to be diverted from remembering that Edward has in fact contracted an engagement which he is too weak to fulfil *or* to repudiate, and that he has, while thus encumbered, raised expectations in another woman. If Austen can shift the emphasis from the man's external inconsistencies to the woman's internal contradictions, she can avoid the condemnation or at least the profound doubts that his behaviour might elicit.[6]

Rather than examining Elinor's blind spot about Edward or her eventual sympathy for Willoughby, both

of which have attracted the attention of others,[7] I want to look at some connections between Edward and Willoughby less frequently discussed, and the ways in which Austen evades commentary on crucial aspects of Willoughby's confessional narrative.

Mrs Dashwood, it turns out, was partially correct in ascribing Willoughby's precipitate departure from Barton to Mrs Smith. She has indeed "exercised the privilege of riches upon a poor dependant cousin" (p. 75). But, as we learn later, this is not because of a suspected engagement with Marianne but rather because of his seduction and abandonment of Eliza Williams. While moral Mrs Smith is no mercenary Mrs Ferrars, the profound distinction is blurred in the text, left without comment.[8] Willoughby's own account of the confrontation reveals a great deal about him. He tells Elinor:

> The purity of her life, the formality of her notions, her ignorance of the world—every thing was against me. . . . She was previously disposed, I believe, to doubt the morality of my conduct in general, and was moreover discontented with the very little attention, the very little portion of my time that I had bestowed upon her, in my present visit. . . . By one measure I might have saved myself. In the height of her morality, good woman! she offered to forgive the past, if I would marry Eliza. That could not be—(p. 323)

The pejorative tone he uses to describe Mrs Smith's morality is left unchallenged by both Elinor and narrator, made irrelevant by the wonder of this man's willingness to speak openly and emotionally, to reveal "my whole heart to you" (p. 319). Such a spectacle of male candour and introspection clearly seems to deserve some reward—the reward of glossing over his actual behaviour and its effect on others. Both Elinor and Austen seem to replicate the response of Sir John Middleton, that "good-natured, honest, stupid soul" whose "heart was softened in seeing mine [Willoughby's] suffer" (p. 330). Willoughby is granted the same dispensation that Edward gets: because he is visibly miserable, the misery he causes others is less harshly judged. Marianne, on the other hand, earns no such grace; her overpowering grief is perceived as self-indulgent in part *because* she makes others aware of it.

Oddly, the text never questions why Willoughby's marrying Eliza "could not be." Presumably, Mrs Smith's forgiveness would include continued financial support, so the hindrance cannot be fear of poverty. Eliza's illegitimacy is certainly a factor, but her situation, unlike Harriet Smith's, seems not to be generally known (Brandon's story tells us that there is speculation, but no certainty about her), and Mrs Smith's support is a step towards general acceptance. In the absence of other compelling justifications, one is forced back to the notion that a fallen woman is no proper match for a gentleman. Elinor, though she condemns Willoughby's "indifference" and "cruel neglect" of Eliza (p. 322), at no time endorses Mrs Smith's position. Even Colonel Brandon, who fights a duel with Willoughby, does not suggest that Willoughby make reparation by marrying Eliza. Eliza's sin excludes her from society forever, and Austen's silence about her fate assumes that her expulsion is necessary and appropriate.

Such absolute exclusion contrasts with Austen's later treatment of fallen women. Her contempt for Lydia Bennet, for example, does not prevent her from allowing Lydia back into society—in fact, the narrative explicitly rejects Mr Collins's ungenerous view of "Christian forgiveness."[9] In *Mansfield Park* Maria Rushworth is exiled, but her adultery ranks higher in the hierarchy of sexual crimes than Eliza's unchastity. Moreover, Austen marks the contrast between Maria's "retirement and reproach, which could allow no second spring of hope or character"[10] and Crawford's "vexation": "That punishment, the public punishment of disgrace, should in a just measure attend *his* share of the offence, is, we know, not one of the barriers, which society gives to virtue. In this world, the penalty is less equal than could be wished."[11]

Willoughby, like Edward, wants to shift responsibility from himself to others—specifically, to the women who actively manipulate him. He urges Elinor to remember that Eliza is not without guilt, that he is in part victimized by "the violence of her passions" (p. 322). He blames the "unlucky circumstance" (p. 321) of exposure and the unreasonable morality of Mrs Smith for his failure to propose to Marianne. Finally, he is able to slough off responsibility for what Elinor considers his cruellest act—the "infamous letter" to Marianne (p. 325). The vulgar cruelty of the letter turns out to be his wife's. As Willoughby tells Elinor, "I had only the credit of servilely copying such sentiments as I was ashamed to put my name to. The original was all her own—her own happy thoughts and gentle diction" (p. 328). Poor Willoughby! So reduced, so unmanned by a shrewish woman that even the capacity to write his own story is taken away. Sophia Grey's "passion—her malice . . . must be appeased" (p. 321), and appeased by Willoughby's complete capitulation to her will; she will write a character for him, will be like a novelist creating a villain. Willoughby is so powerless in the face of Sophia's "ingratiating virulence" that he must cede both words and memories—he is "forced" to give up "the last relics of Marianne. Her three notes . . . the lock of hair . . . all, every memento was torn from me" (p. 329). The towering potency of Sophia extenuates Willoughby's behaviour and saves him from identification as a villain.

To some extent, Marianne joins this trio of powerful women who manipulate Willoughby. In order to rehabilitate him (even partially), the narrative must censure her. She is chastised by Elinor, by the narrator, and by some readers for creating a false relationship and a false image of Willoughby.[12] Like Emma, she has tried to be a controlling artist-figure, and we are allowed to feel that Willoughby has merely gone along with her authoritative characterization of their romance. He is led by her taste and her emphatic opinions—"If any difference appeared . . . it lasted no longer than till the force of her arguments and the brightness of her eyes could be displayed" (p. 47). Even their intimacy derives from Marianne's agency: as Willoughby tells Elinor, "To have resisted such attractions, to have withstood such tenderness!—Is there a man on earth who could have done it!—Yes, I found myself, by insensible degrees, sincerely fond of her" (p. 321). Willoughby's language here describes his sense of being a passive, even resisting, partner (who generalizes in order to distance himself—"Is there a man on earth"), and the narrative allows his language to stand without challenge. (In *Pride and Prejudice,* Darcy's similar sense of being trapped by Elizabeth's attractions is, on the contrary, explicitly criticized.)[13] There are so many women who inscribe their desires on Willoughby, who assert authority over him, that his own desire, his very self, becomes muted and blurred.

In *Sense and Sensibility* women try to bend others to their will—and often succeed. From Fanny Dashwood's manipulation of John to Lucy Steele's seduction of Robert Ferrars, we see women exerting power, sometimes directly and sometimes covertly. This novel seems to belie Spacks's contention that in eighteenth-century fiction "Women who openly express aggression, who make apparent their desire to control the behavior of others, occasionally achieve short-term success, but always fail in the long run."[14] Those who succeed in this narrative are, however, punished by the narrator. No other novel by Austen is so replete with demonic, wilful women. The destructive egoism of Fanny Dashwood, Lady Middleton, Lucy Steele, Mrs Ferrars, and Sophia Grey makes abundantly clear what sort of woman seeks authority and tries to make the world conform to her image of it. No woman in her right mind would take as a model the imperious or designing women who achieve success in *Sense and Sensibility;* if feminine power is linked to these characteristics, women and men do right to keep women unempowered, marginal, silent.

But this position presents a problem for Austen the writer: how can she, in novel after novel, keep inscribing her own desires? How can she manipulate characters and readers if to do so connects her with the monstrous women she has depicted? I do not think Austen finds a solution in *Sense and Sensibility;* rather, it seems to me that she constructs a careful vindication *and* criticism of the right-thinking authoritative woman by projecting authorial anxieties onto the figure of Elinor Dashwood.

Adrienne Rich has argued that a woman who succeeds in a patriarchal society is often appropriated by its values, so that she becomes caught up in her own specialness and thereby becomes indifferent to the lives of women who have not joined the fraternity.[15] Among such chosen women there occurs a loss of imagination, an inability to conceptualize and problematize the lives of their less fortunate sisters. In *Sense and Sensibility* this phenomenon declares itself in the narrator's silence about a number of lives: the loneliness of Mrs Smith who grants "voluntary forgiveness" (p. 367) to Willoughby, or of Mrs Ferrars to whom Lucy becomes "as necessary . . . as either Robert or Fanny" (p. 365); the disappointment of Sophia Willoughby, married to a man who values her only for her money and who abandons her shortly after marriage in order to seek Marianne's forgiveness; the helpless anger of Lucy Steele, always on the watch to improve her social position, always required to be servile and insincere in order to be accepted.[16] It may seem irrelevant or even stubbornly wrongheaded to demand interiority in relatively minor characters (this is not, after all, *Middlemarch*), but such consistent suppression of the inner lives of aggressive women argues an urgent desire to distance narrative authority from the authority claimed by aggressive female characters.

A much safer place to situate feminine authority is in the figure of Elinor, who seems to have the narrator's unqualified sympathy. The sympathy derives in part from her role as victim—as Kaplan puts it, "For Austen, authority belongs to the self-consciously powerless."[17] Moreover, Elinor's claims to authority are similar to those of her creator—a clear eye and a lively sense of the realities of life. But Austen finds ways to subvert the authority of this admirable heroine. She shows that Elinor's propriety sometimes veils sarcasm and contempt for others, and that what lurks behind her sarcasm is painful resentment at feeling marginalized. If Elinor's pain and frustration save her from being a prig, they also make her susceptible to diagnostic readings, which in turn undermine her authority.

Elinor reserves most of her sarcasm for Marianne and Willoughby, taking pleasure in deflating their romantic excesses. When, for example, Willoughby waxes sentimental about the perfections of Barton Cottage, Elinor replies "I flatter myself . . . that even under the disadvantage of better rooms and a broader staircase, you will hereafter find your own house as faultless as you now do this" (p. 73). And when Marianne is transported by a vision of Norland in autumn, Elinor drily comments: "It is not every one . . . who has your passion for dead leaves" (p. 88). Now certainly the self-indulgence and measure of hypocrisy in Willoughby and Marianne's rhapsodizing are irritating, but they hardly seem to call for such blighting ripostes. In Elinor's swift critical responses we see a version of the hasty, unvarnished irritation of "large fat sighings."[18]

The novelist's own impatience with unseemly displays of sentimentality, treated with self-conscious lightness in *Northanger Abbey,* is here projected onto Elinor.

If Marianne replicates novelistic activity in her construction of a romance hero, Elinor exhibits a different kind of authorial practice: observation and analysis. Like her creator, she is better at dissecting behaviour than at contriving an exciting plot. Moreover, like a novelist she shares her observations, sometimes in ways that defy propriety. Inserting herself into a conversation between Marianne and Edward, she takes pleasure in showing how Marianne's stated indifference to wealth masks expectations of a high income. When Edward seems to approve of Marianne's gaiety, Elinor leaps in with a corrective version: "I should hardly call her a lively girl—she is very earnest, very eager in all she does—sometimes talks a great deal and always with animation—but she is not often really merry" (p. 93). To Colonel Brandon's appreciation of Marianne's "amiable prejudices," Elinor opposes a critical view: "There are inconveniences attending such feelings as Marianne's, which all the charms of enthusiasm and ignorance of the world cannot atone for. Her systems have all the unfortunate tendency of setting propriety at naught" (p. 56). The reader, in spite of the narrator's silence here, might question the propriety of Elinor's propensity to provide hostile analysis of her sister. It may be appropriate to note the errors and deficiencies in those around us; it is a much more problematic, even dangerous proposition to make them the subject of public discourse—in conversations or in novels. The risk that Elinor takes in making public her observations and evaluations neatly replicates the danger facing the female writer: the reader may find her accurate, perceptive, even witty, but at the same time consider her crabbed, unlikeable, unfeminine.[19]

To rescue Elinor from this precarious place, the narrative turns not to an indisputable system of ethics but to the typically novelistic strategy of examining motivation and feeling. Austen knows, to use Bakhtin's phrase, that "images of official-authoritative truth . . . have never been successful in the novel."[20] She therefore moves to the discourse of psychology and invites us to locate the source of Elinor's desire for authority; and we discover that Elinor's calm superiority conceals a profound sense of frustration. Her amused contempt for the behaviour of Mrs Ferrars and Fanny, her claim that "it was not in Mrs. Ferrars's power to distress her," masks the double pain of losing Edward and being "pointedly slighted" by his family (pp. 232-33). Her anger and disappointment express themselves indirectly, in a hostile (albeit accurate) assessment of Mrs Ferrars and a grim determination to depress Lucy's sense of triumph. (Even some of Elinor's repressive sarcasm towards Marianne can be ascribed to her disappointment in Edward. Willoughby and Marianne's open devotion to each other throws into higher relief Edward's "coldness and reserve" [p. 89], and the pain of such a contrast can find consolation in censorious judgments about the propriety of public displays of affection.)

Balked expectations regarding Edward merely add to a well-established sense of frustration. The demon that drives Elinor, that leads her to embrace rigid self-control and to judge others, is the knowledge that in her own family her superiority is generally unacknowledged and her authority consistently denied. Painfully aware that Marianne will brook no interference or even inquiry from her, she resorts to indirect supervision—spying on Marianne and urging Mrs Dashwood to exert the authority denied to herself. But Marianne insists on a "privacy which eluded all her watchfulness" (p. 167) and Mrs Dashwood refuses to follow Elinor's sensible advice, so Elinor can only pass judgment: "common sense, common care, common prudence, were all sunk in Mrs. Dashwood's romantic delicacy" (p. 85). Elinor's irritability here expresses more than specific disappointment; it results from a long experience of being marginalized in her own family. Elinor may prevail in the matter of deciding upon the number of servants to take to Barton, but in more important areas, she is ignored. Mrs Dashwood, valuing Marianne's "young and ardent mind" (p. 54) more than Elinor's prudence and propensity to "doubt where you can" (p. 78), does not disguise her preference; as Elinor knows, "Whatever Marianne was desirous of, her mother would be eager to promote—she could not expect to influence the latter" (p. 155). Maternal energies in the Dashwood family are firmly centred on Marianne, to the extent that Elinor seems absent from her mother's consciousness. There is something undeniably pathetic in Elinor's early sense of exclusion from shared family grief; she tells Marianne that Edward "and I have been at times thrown a good deal together, while you have been wholly engrossed on the most affectionate principle by my mother" (p. 20). There is pathos as well as bitterness when she later witnesses Mrs Dashwood's identification with Marianne:

> Marianne continued to mend every day, and the brilliant cheerfulness of Mrs Dashwood's looks and spirits proved her to be, as she repeatedly declared herself, one of the happiest women in the world. Elinor could not hear the declaration, nor witness its proofs without sometimes wondering whether her mother ever recollected Edward. But Mrs Dashwood, trusting to the temperate account of her own disappointment which Elinor had sent her, was led away by the exuberance of her joy to think only of what would increase it. (p. 335)

This passage precisely describes Elinor's dilemma. Because she does not express her grief, she is denied the consolation, the attention that she deserves. Instead of being admired for her fortitude, instead of having others look beneath the placid surface, she is ignored. Her continuing composure in the face of such indiffer-

ence can be interpreted in the context of an absolute system of ethics, as Elinor herself wants to see it—in explaining her calmness, she uses unemotional, legalistic language: "duty," "owed," "betraying," "acquit" (pp. 262-63).[21] But it is a defence *and* a punishment. It allows Elinor to retreat from her own pain to a position of judgment on others. At times the gains are direct and obvious; confronted with Elinor's stoicism, Marianne can only "hate myself for ever," enabling Elinor to obtain "from her whatever promise she required" (p. 264). At other times Elinor wins a much more indirect and painful victory. Right after the paragraph quoted above, she finds herself alone with her mother, who promptly embarks on a recital of Marianne's happy prospects. Balked of an opportunity to discuss her own situation, and denied commendation for having had doubts about Willoughby, she can take comfort in noting her mother's foolishness. When Mrs Dashwood describes Colonel Brandon's feelings, "Elinor perceived,—not the language, not the professions of Colonel Brandon, but the natural embellishments of her mother's active fancy, which fashioned every thing delightful to her, as it chose" (p. 336). In this dialogue Mrs Dashwood seems much more foolish and self-centred than she has before; her claim that "There was always a something,—if you remember,—in Willoughby's eyes at times, which I did not like" (p. 338) is a piece of egregious self-deception worthy of Mrs Bennet. Elinor's silent criticism of her mother is her revenge for the way in which her feelings and opinions have been discounted. Dialogue and evaluation work together, one to alter a previously sympathetic character, the other to reject the belittled version.

However justified Elinor may be in her opinions, however much evidence the narrator gives us on her behalf, we cannot overlook the painful feelings that precede the judgments. To be right in one's judgments is not to be free of anguish or even of prejudice. Nor is judging a particularly enabling activity. Rather, the process of judging at all, of situating oneself in a place of authority, is open to critical scrutiny. In Elinor Dashwood, Austen seems to have inscribed a set of doubtful motives and strategies that undermine her right to authority. Elinor is subjected to a diagnostic reading: there are so many clues about her disappointments, her thwarted desire for influence, her anger at those who ignore or trivialize her pain, that the reader must interpret rather than accept her view of the world. This is not to claim that Austen does not agree with Elinor's assessments, does not identify with her values and evaluations. On the contrary, she is only too self-consciously aware that Elinor's problems mirror her own. The lack of imaginative empathy for aggressive women, the tendency to be critically observant and censorious, the desire to voice opinions and have them taken seriously are problems that confront the author as well as the heroine of *Sense and Sensibility.* The "double-voiced discourse" in this novel is not a device to distance character from author but rather to encode a female author's difficulties about her own desire for authority. Far from showing how "the writing subject cancels out the signs of his particular individuality,"[22] *Sense and Sensibility* displays the writing subject's struggles with authorship. These struggles can have no happy ending, which is perhaps why so many readers have detected a note of dysphoria at the conclusion of the novel. If female desire for a voice can be expressed only pathologically—by enslaving men or by adhering to rigid codes that perpetuate patriarchal power while they repress pain—then it is forever trapped. The best a woman writer can do is to describe her dilemma in a work that offers no solutions. In an act of courage as well as of despair, that is what Jane Austen does in *Sense and Sensibility.*

Notes

[1] Critics both sympathetic and hostile to the code of propriety agree to locate the issue at the centre of the novel. Marilyn Butler, for whom Elinor is "an active, struggling Christian in a difficult world," says of *Sense and Sensibility* that "The entire action is organized to represent Elinor and Marianne in terms of rival value systems" (*Jane Austen and the War of Ideas* [Oxford: Clarendon Press, 1975], pp. 192, 184). Marvin Mudrick sees Austen marshalling her defences against "an insurgent sympathetic committing character like Marianne" (*Jane Austen: Irony as Defense and Discovery* [Princeton: Princeton University Press, 1952], p. 91). Angela Leighton, providing a feminist revision of Mudrick, notes that "Elinor's Silences have Austen's approval; they signify heroic reticence and control, and are contained by the language of Sense. Marianne's Silences signify emotions which have escaped control, and which are therefore in opposition to Austen's art" ("Sense and Silences: Reading Jane Austen Again" in *Jane Austen: New Perspectives,* ed. Janet Todd, *Women and Literature,* n.s. 3 [New York: Holmes and Meier, 1983], 132). Those who blur or reverse the conventional identifications remain convinced of the centrality of this issue. Howard S. Babb, pointing to rhetorical evidence of overlapping, finds that "The argument remains utterly conventional, and Jane Austen's pursuit of it by tracing what might be called the double allegiance of each sister makes the novel none the less rigid" (*Jane Austen's Novels: The Fabric of Dialogue* [Columbus: Ohio State University Press, 1962], p. 56); and Jan Fergus, reversing the dichotomy, argues that "One of Austen's major interests in the novel is to define feeling and sensitive behaviour . . . This behaviour is what Elinor exhibits and Marianne violates throughout the novel. It is Marianne who must learn to behave feelingly, not Elinor" (*Jane Austen and the Didactic Novel: "Northanger Abbey," "Sense and Sensibility" and "Pride and Prejudice"* [Totowa, NJ: Barnes and Noble, 1983], pp. 40-41). Sandra M. Gilbert and Susan Gubar, in *The Madwoman in the Attic: The Woman Writer*

and the Nineteenth-Century Literary Imagination (New Haven: Yale University Press, 1979), detect a tension in the novel "because Austen herself seems caught between her attraction to Marianne's sincerity and spontaneity, while at the same time identifying with the civil falsehoods and the reserved, polite silences of Elinor, whose art is fittingly portrayed as the painting of screens" (p. 157). I believe that what Austen screens in this novel is her discomfort with her own view of the role and authority of women.

[2] *The Novels of Jane Austen,* ed. R. W. Chapman, 5 vols, 3rd edition (London: Oxford University Press, 1932), I, 380. References are to this edition.

[3] Spacks points to "the varieties of female submission" in *Sense and Sensibility* and shows how the novel exhibits the limited, constricted life of women ("The Difference It Makes," *Soundings* 64 [1981], 356-57). Kaplan, whose aim, like mine, is to examine Austen's "particular accommodation of femininity and authority," finds that Austen locates feminine authority in "a trope not of reproduction and resemblance but of revision and difference" ("Achieving Authority: Jane Austen's First Published Novel," *Nineteenth-Century Fiction* 37 [1983], 535-37). See also Mary Poovey, *The Proper Lady and the Woman Writer: Ideology as Style in the Works of Mary Wollstonecraft, Mary Shelley, and Jane Austen* (Chicago: University of Chicago Press, 1984), p. 193.

[4] Michael Williams and T. B. Tomlinson comment on Elinor's assessment of Mr Palmer. Williams sees it as both a manifestation of Elinor's growth and proof that Elinor is not always Austen's surrogate (*Jane Austen: Six Novels and Their Methods* [Houndmills, Basingstoke: Macmillan, 1986], pp. 41-42); Tomlinson connects it to the dark vision of the novel, a vision which sees negative traits "permanently embedded in human nature" (*The English Middle-Class Novel* [London: Macmillan, 1976], p. 44). While I do not disagree with these views, they omit what I believe Austen wants readers to omit: an awareness of the way in which men escape castigation in this novel.

[5] Critics have been understandably uncertain and unhelpful in their assessments of Edward Ferrars. Howard Babb is one of the more sympathetic readers when he says that Edward exhibits "only his self-distrust, not any doubts about the virtues he holds in view" (p. 64). W. A. Craik notes that Austen has to "keep him in the background" because a "man situated between two women as he is situated between Lucy and Elinor can hardly avoid looking ineffectual, if not ridiculous" (*Jane Austen: The Six Novels* [London: Methuen, 1965], p. 42), but she does not examine Austen's reasons for putting Edward in such a situation. Mudrick's language shows his distrust of Austen's strategy: "The shadow of Mrs. Ferrars falls early . . . the ogress herself does

not appear until her malevolence has been well established. When she appears at last, she is ready in all her ill-nature to devour Elinor for her presumptuous attitude toward Edward" (pp. 69-70). He does not, however, make explicit that his language criticizes a paranoid, almost hysterical attitude toward a powerful woman. Martin Price links strategy and ideology when he says, "Mrs. Ferrars' fantasies are recognized as her reality . . . since her will is almost matched by her power; and the narrative quietly accepts her vision, by a method that is akin to free indirect discourse" (*Forms of Life: Character and Moral Imagination in the Novel* [New Haven: Yale University Press, 1983], p. 71), and he too does not question the reasons for such quiet acceptance.

[6] Austen is generally successful in her attempt to deflect attention away from Edward. See, for example, Zelda Boyd's "The Language of Supposing: Modal Auxiliaries in *Sense and Sensibility*" in *Jane Austen: New Perspectives* (p. 147). One of the few readers who returns agency and focus to Edward is Jane Miller, who says "He can let himself be manipulated by his rich mother and he can tell lies. He is still acceptable to Elinor" (*Women Writing about Men* [New York: Pantheon Books, 1986], p. 63). Her insight, coded in her syntax ("he can let himself"), slips past Austen's double defence—Edward's passivity and Elinor's difficulties.

[7] See, for example, Susan Morgan on Elinor's imaginative sympathy for Willoughby (*In the Meantime: Character and Perception in Jane Austen's Fiction* [Chicago: University of Chicago Press, 1980], p. 131), and Price on Elinor's "reflux of pity" (p. 83). Among those who focus on the contradictions in the scene are Mudrick (p. 85); Kenneth Moler (*Jane Austen's Art of Allusion* [Lincoln: University of Nebraska Press, 1968], p. 72); and Poovey (pp. 186-87). Babb is a notable exception, and, significantly, is strongly anti-Willoughby.

[8] Michael Williams seems to endorse Willoughby's version of his situation when he says that in some ways Edward and Willoughby are "bluntly and consistently matched, right down to the fact that both depend for their fortunes on the whim of an elderly and irascible female relative" (p. 32). This kind of collapsing of distinction is due, I believe, to Austen's deliberate omission of narrative commentary.

[9] *The Novels of Jane Austen,* II, 364.

[10] *The Novels of Jane Austen,* III, 449.

[11] III, 468. Mary Lascelles has said that there is a "failure of power" when Austen has to deal with Eliza's story, and that this failure has to do with Austen's decision to "keep out of reach of Eliza" (*Jane Austen*

and Her Art [London: Oxford University Press, 1963, reissue of 1934 edition], p. 73). Spacks, too, notes the distance between the main plot and the Eliza narratives (p. 353). I believe that such distance has less to do with narrative skill than with Austen's uncomfortable acceptance and perpetuation of an ideology that unequally punishes male and female misconduct.

[12] See Stuart M. Tave, *Some Words of Jane Austen* (Chicago: University of Chicago Press, 1973), p. 84. Cf. Kaplan, p. 543.

[13] *The Novels of Jane Austen,* II, 190. Judith Wilt picks up Willoughby's language when she says: "The genuine love of a woman who believes herself to be genuinely loved is irresistible, and creates its counterpart. This is a kind of tentative 'embodiment' for Willougby and he values it. Tearing Marianne out of his heart to go back to his plan to marry wealth and station is exquisite pain for him" ("Jane Austen's Men: Inside/Outside 'the Mystery'" in *Men by Women,* ed. Janet Todd, *Women and Literature,* n.s. 2 [New York: Holmes and Meier, 1981], 69). Wilt replicates Willoughby's own interpretation of his experience: loving Marianne was a passive act, leaving her an active one.

[14] "Sisters" in *Fetter'd or Free? British Women Novelists 1670-1815,* ed. Mary Anne Schofield and Cecilia Macheski (Athens: Ohio University Press, 1986) p. 139.

[15] "The Antifeminist Woman" in *On Lies, Secrets, and Silence: Selected Prose 1966-1978* (New York: W. W. Norton, 1979) pp. 82-83. Echoing Rich, Gloria Steinem confesses her own pride in cracking the male code: "This is the most tragic punishment that society inflicts on any second-class group. Ultimately the brainwashing works, and we ourselves come to believe our group is inferior. Even if we achieve a little success in the world and think of ourselves as 'different,' we don't want to associate with our group. We want to identify up, not down" ("Sisterhood" in *Outrageous Acts and Everyday Rebellions* [New York: New American Library, 1986], p. 131).

[16] Babb astutely sums up the conflict in Lucy, who "is convinced in her heart that she is the equal of anyone and jealously guards her success with Edward as a token of her value. But she also recognizes that society regards her as an inferior" (p. 70). But such interiority has to be teased out of a text which wants to keep Lucy ideologically functional. As Poovey points out, "The harshness with which Austen disposes of Lucy Steele exceeds the necessities of the plot, but it is perfectly in keeping with her moral design. . . . Austen wants to convince the reader that female nature is simply inexplicable and that propriety must restrain this natural, amoral force" (p. 190).

[17] Kaplan, p. 547.

[18] *Persuasion* (*The Novels of Jane Austen,* V), p. 68.

[19] In his recent biography Park Honan accurately characterizes the dilemma facing the fledgling writer: "Nobody on record has risked more than Jane Austen when she sought a 'voice' with which to address the public. She simply had to trust that the Austens would find her agreeable and sisterly *despite* her polished jokes and knowing airs" (*Jane Austen: Her Life* [New York: St Martin's Press, 1987], p. 94). Some of her troubled hopes are unmistakably inscribed in the character of Elinor.

[20] M.M. Bakhtin, *The Dialogic Imagination: Four Essays,* trans. Caryl Emerson and Michael Holquist, ed. Michael Holquist (Austin: University of Texas Press, 1981), p. 344.

[21] Jan Fergus endorses the ideological absolute when she says that "Austen insists . . . that the consideration and self-command Elinor shows are not any the less required of her for being invariably misunderstood and unrewarded. They remain, absolutely and imperatively, an obligation" (p. 41). Such a view matches the confidence of Elinor's pronouncements, but it disallows discussion of motivation or even of psychic satisfactions gained by proper behaviour.

[22] Michel Foucault, *The Foucault Reader,* ed. Paul Ribinow (New York: Pantheon Books, 1984) pp. 102-3. Austen's problematic relationship to her text resembles that of earlier woman writers. Janet Todd in *The Sign of Angellica: Women, Writing, and Fiction, 1660-1800* (New York: Columbia University Press, 1989) points out that "In the story of women's fiction, the relation of author to authorial image and to creations will vary extremely but it will never achieve the clarity of men's relation to their ideas and creations, patented, signed and alienated from themselves" (p. 9). Austen anticipates what Margaret Homans describes as the strategy of nineteenth-century women writers: "by writing novels that represent the position of women in societies that do not accommodate their needs, these authors thematize the position of women's language in a culture that does not admit it" (*Bearing the Word: Language and Female Experience in Nineteenth-Century Women's Writing* [Chicago: University of Chicago Press, 1986], p. 20). For a discussion of Austen's sense of marginality in her family, see John Halperin, *The Life of Jane Austen* (Baltimore: Johns Hopkins University Press, 1984), especially pp. 218-19 and 237-38.

Alastair Duckworth (essay date 1994)

SOURCE: "Improving on Sensibility," in *New Casebooks: Sense and Sensibility and Pride and Prejudice,* edited by Robert Clark, St. Martin's Press, 1994, pp. 26-37.

[*In the following essay, Duckworth examines* Sense and Sensibility's *two heroines and argues that Austen did not intend for the novel's conclusion to be merely a "happy ending," but one in which the marriages are grounded in a moral society.*]

As many scholars have shown, Jane Austen works within inherited terms of aesthetic and ethical debate. Mrs Inchbald's *Art and Nature* (1796) and Maria Edgeworth's *Letters of Julia and Caroline* (1795) are only two of many novels, in the decade in which **Sense and Sensibility** had its genesis as **Elinor and Marianne,** to anticipate Jane Austen's treatment of familiar dualities of prudence and benevolence, reason and passion, discipline and freedom. While Mrs Inchbald is Godwinian in her dislike of institutions and Rousseauesque in her affirmation of the natural virtues, Maria Edgeworth is nearer the norm of the genre and Jane Austen's own position in recognising the potential excesses of sensibility and the need for the temporising effect of reason. Another novel, Mme d'Arblay's *Camilla* (1796), suggests in its description of the heroine a common view of the 'wayward' faculty:

> [Her] every propensity was pure, and, when reflection came to her aid, her conduct was as exemplary as her wishes. But the ardour of her imagination, acted upon by every passing idea, shook her Judgment from its yet unsteady seat, and left her at the mercy of wayward Sensibility—that delicate, but irregular power, which now impels to all that is most disinterested for others, now forgets all mankind, to watch the pulsations of its own fancies.[1]

Jane Austen is listed among the subscribers to the first edition of *Camilla,* and she would, on the whole, subscribe to these reflections.

Her achievement in **Sense and Sensibility** is not, however, to be assessed merely in terms of her ability to reveal the dangers of excessive sensibility, or, for that matter, to modify a strictly rational outlook. Given her awareness of the widespread corruption of traditional moral assumptions, more than a mere accommodation of her inherited—almost hackneyed—terms was needed. The resolution of the novel was intended, I believe, not merely to discover the private happiness of the central characters, but to reconstitute around these unions the grounds of a moral society. It cannot be said that this intention is convincingly achieved—Marianne's marriage to the rheumatic Colonel Brandon is a gross over-compensation for her misguided sensibility—but it is wrong to imply, as Marvin Mudrick does, that the novel's failure reveals bad faith on Jane Austen's part, that Marianne's vitality and enthusiasm are betrayed not by Willoughby, but by an author who has here substituted for a personal commitment to feeling a dull conformity to social conventions.[2]

Marianne is one of the most interesting characters in Jane Austen's fiction. More than Emma even, she anticipates the tragically Quixotic heroines of the nineteenth-century novel, whose visions of existence can find no fulfilment within the limitations of their societies. But while Jane Austen permits Marianne's quixotism to act as an implicit criticism of what is limited and pedestrian in her society, she also, quite convincingly, reveals the deficiencies of her idealism.

Nothing is clearer initially than that we are to view Marianne with a good deal of sympathy: she has 'a life, a spirit, an eagerness which could hardly be seen without delight' (p. 46). At first it seems she is to exhibit 'heroic' qualities, conspicuous by their absence in the young Catherine Morland. Like her mother, she 'can feel no sentiment of approbation inferior to love' (p. 16); she is passionately fond of music and drawing; she objects to Elinor's friend, Edward Ferrars, because 'he has no real taste' (p. 17); and when they leave Norland, she sheds tears for a 'place so much beloved' (p. 27). But although her enthusiasms are occasionally those of the romantic heroines Jane Austen had delighted in burlesquing in her juvenilia, the parodic satire here is not harsh. What vindicates Marianne in the early scenes is the sincerity behind her enthusiasms, the personal quality present even when her sensibility is mediated through her reading. That she is not merely fashionable is shown in her dislike of Gilpinesque 'jargon', indeed of 'jargon of every kind' (p. 97). During her conversation with Edward about landscape scenery she observes: 'sometimes I have kept my feelings to myself, because I could find no language to describe them in but what was worn and hackneyed out of all sense and meaning' (p. 97). And when Sir John Middleton suggests that she 'will be setting [her] cap' at Willoughby, her caustic reply, though somewhat outspoken from a seventeen-year-old, is no less than his use of cliché deserves (p. 45).

Strongly individualistic, Marianne's attitudes are often without egoism, and her disregard of 'every common-place notion of decorum' (p. 48) is on occasions magnificent. When Mrs Ferrars, in the drawing room of her home in Harley Street, ignores the painted screens of Elinor to praise the absent art of the absent Miss Morton, Marianne's reaction is superb:

> 'This is admiration of a very particular kind—what is Miss Morton to us?—who knows, or who cares, for her?—it is Elinor of whom *we* think and speak.'

> And so saying, she took the screens out of her sister-in-law's hands, to admire them herself as they ought to be admired.

> Mrs Ferrars looked exceedingly angry, and drawing herself up more stiffly than ever, pronounced in

retort this bitter phillippic: 'Miss Morton is Lord Morton's daughter.' (pp. 235-6)

Given the mercenary and mediocre world in which she lives, Marianne's responses are often admirable, and one can understand why Mudrick sees in her a 'passionate, discriminating, instantaneous sympathy for worthy people and beautiful things', a 'basic opposition to lying and the forms of lying'.[3] But if one sees Marianne not only as an aspect of her author (which she is, I think) but also as a representative of sensibility, then her outlook is not so unequivocally to be affirmed nor her subsequent chastening wholly deplored. Rather than unconsciously destroying what is authentic in her nature, I would argue that Jane Austen is consciously rejecting a tendency, in herself as in her time, which she sees to be mistaken and, when taken to an extreme, immoral.

Marianne is the legatee of a philosophy of sentiment, which, wherever its roots are exactly to be located, was generally considered to have begun in the *Characteristics of Men, Manners, Opinions, Times* (1711) of the third Earl of Shaftesbury.[4] Happiness for the sentimental philosopher, in opposition to the Calvinist view of man's innate depravity and necessarily troubled life in this world, is possible for the individual who recognises the promptings of virtue and exercises his innate benevolence. Morality is discoverable in the 'heart' rather than the 'head', in feelings rather than in conformity with received precepts. Shaftesbury's thought did not deny a rational access to truth, but his emphasis on an innate moral sense tended in later writers to become a full-fledged sentimentalism, and when his views were joined with the sensationalist epistemology of the empiricists, who were reducing the function of the mind to that of passive receptor of external impressions, ethical rationalism was frequently discredited. In Hume's moral philosophy, for example, morality is 'more properly felt than judged of'.[5] The tendency toward ethical sentimentalism did not go unchallenged; Bishop Butler, for example, opposed it, arguing that any theory of ethics must include judgement as a primary component;[6] but when the rapprochement of Shaftesburian rationalism and Humean empiricism was aided by Adam Smith's theory of sympathy and Rousseau's immense influence as a philosopher of 'natural' goodness, not only was a rational access to moral truth frequently denied, but the validity of all external structures was called into question.

Jane Austen sets herself against these tendencies in **Sense and Sensibility,** insisting on the necessary aid of judgement in the process of moral decision, and requiring, as she will elsewhere in her fiction, that the individual respect and support his cultural heritage. The major limitations of Marianne's sensibility, adequately dramatised as we will see, are that it places excessive faith in the self's inner ability to reach moral decisions intuitively and rejects entirely the need for living within conventional limits.

The dangerous tendencies of Marianne's individualism only become apparent in her relationship with Willoughby, who is, like Anna Karenina's Vronsky, to a large degree an invention of the imaginative mind. This is not to deny that he is handsome and possessed of 'ardour', 'talents', and 'spirit', which put Ferrars and Brandon in the shade, merely to note that from the moment he becomes her 'preserver' (p. 46), Willoughby is defined, and is willing to be defined, in terms of 'the hero of a favourite story' (p. 43). Hearing of his indefatigable dancing powers, Marianne cries: 'That is what I like; that is what a young man ought to be. Whatever be his pursuits, his eagerness in them should know no moderation, and leave him no sense of fatigue' (p. 45)—and his expressed passion for dancing on their first meeting is sufficient to earn him from Marianne 'such a look of approbation' (p. 46). Thereafter, the 'general conformity of judgement' that is discovered between them is not a little due to her enthusiasm and his compliance. It is she who brings forward and rapturously describes her favourite authors, while Willoughby 'acquiesced in all her decisions, caught all her enthusiasm' (p. 47).

In company with Willoughby, Marianne is drawn into increasingly serious acts of impropriety. She accepts from Willoughby the gift of a horse, forgetting that the expense of keeping it will be a burden to the family's reduced income. Faced with the additional charge that it may be improper to accept a gift of this kind from a man so lately known to her, Marianne answers with spirit that 'it is not time or opportunity that is to determine intimacy;—it is disposition alone' (p. 59). Though Marianne is persuaded by Elinor to give up the horse, Willoughby is heard to promise that 'when you leave Barton to form your own establishment in a more lasting home, Queen Mab shall receive you' (p. 59), and this hint, together with his use of Marianne's Christian name, is sufficient to convince Elinor of their being engaged.

Such instances of their disregard of decorum culminate in their unchaperoned visit to Allenham, the home of Mrs Smith, the elderly relative and benefactress of Willoughby. This trip is not only indecorous, it more seriously shows an entire lack of concern for the feelings of others. From the point of view of the present owner, the unannounced visit of her heir and a young female companion can only indicate barely concealed impatience for her death. In her Shaftesburian defence of her conduct on this occasion the weakness of Marianne's position is evident: 'If there had been any real impropriety in what I did, I should have been sensible of it at the time, for we always know when we are acting wrong, and with such a conviction I could have had no pleasure' (p. 68).

In keeping with the tenets of the tradition she represents, propriety and morality in Marianne's definition are innate qualities of the self and not conformity to any set of social rules. She has responded to her experience of seemingly universal selfishness by retiring into a subjective world into which she will allow only a few privileged and manifestly worthy people. When Willoughby comes dramatically into view, Marianne looks to him for the limits of her happiness, and, like Hester Prynne in *The Scarlet Letter,* argues that what she and her lover do together has 'a consecration of its own'. Like Hawthorne, however, Jane Austen refuses to sanction the spiritual autonomy of a relationship.

In rejecting the forms of this world in her passion for Willoughby, Marianne has substituted emotional laws for social laws: 'I felt myself . . . to be as solemnly engaged to him, as if the strictest legal covenant had bound us to each other' (p. 188). Willoughby, however is unwilling to obey the unwritten laws of Marianne's private world, and instead prudently adheres to the propriety of society for his own selfish ends. Thus it is that in the climactic scene of their meeting in London, the sincerity of her sensibility is noticeable in her manner of speech and salutation, while the falsity of his sensibility (and its prudent content) is seen in the reserved manner of his response. Marianne, on sighting him across the room,

> started up, and pronouncing his name in a tone of affection, held out her hand to him. He approached, and addressing himself rather to Elinor than Marianne, as if wishing to avoid her eye, and determined not to observe her attitude, inquired in a hurried manner after Mrs Dashwood, and asked how long they had been in town. Elinor was robbed of all presence of mind by such an address, and was unable to say a word. But the feelings of her sister were instantly expressed. Her face was crimsoned over, and she exclaimed in a voice of the greatest emotion, 'Good God! Willoughby, what is the meaning of this? Have you not received my letters? Will you not shake hands with me? (p. 176)

Whereas at Barton the ancillary features of sensibility—extravagant language, the shaking of hands—had been found in both Willoughby and Marianne, in the London assembly Willoughby is aloof, 'her touch seemed painful to him, and he held her hand only for a moment' (p. 177).

Her relationship to Willoughby has been for Marianne the constitution of a society of two, and when this is lost through the defection of one of its members, Marianne has no rule for living, no motive for action, no 'ground' on which to stand. Misery like hers, she admits, has no pride, and in keeping with the anti-stoical strain of the sentimental philosophy in which tears are considered the evidence of feeling, Marianne's subsequent behaviour is an active soliciting of grief. Her illness at Cleveland is spiritual, and the death to which it might easily have led would have been suicide. We should not discount the solemnity of Marianne's retrospections on her recovery. Recognising that, 'Had I died—it would have been self-destruction' (p. 345), she wonders that she has been allowed to live, 'to have time for atonement to my God' (p. 346).

In Marianne's subjective attitudes Jane Austen has revealed how the self, unaided by the forms of culture and the administration of self-discipline, finds itself alienated from society and friends. By considering her internal inclinations sufficient arbiters of moral action, Marianne has denied external sources of obligation in family, society, and religion. The inevitably negative effects of her extreme, individualistic response are sufficiently clear, but even if they were not so, Elinor's contrasting behaviour in regard to personal grief, no less than in regard to the maintenance of a decorous politeness even in the company of fools, would indicate her author's requirement for a positive and social response. When Elinor discovers that Edward is engaged to Lucy Steele, 'she wept for him, more than for herself' (p. 140), yet when she joins Mrs Jennings and Marianne at dinner, 'no one would have supposed . . . that Elinor was mourning in secret over obstacles which must divide her for ever from the object of her love' (p. 141).

Elinor's characterisation in *Sense and Sensibility* is more successful than has generally been recognised in critical discussion. She starts off with the disadvantage of being the single normative representative of 'sense' in the novel. Other characters—the John Dashwoods, Lady Middleton, Mrs Ferrars, Lucy Steele—exhibit 'sense', as well as 'prudence' and 'reserve', only in debased and 'economic' meanings. Added to this, the two possible male representatives of the term fail entirely to provide an effective counterbalance to the selfishness and expedient behaviour everywhere evident. (In later novels, Darcy and Knightley will successfully provide such counterbalance.) Elinor's task of upholding the true moral conception of the word is, therefore, large—too large for her to achieve unaided. Yet Elinor is not quite the bloodless figure of sense she has been considered. It is clear, for example, that Marianne's vital and central position in the novel is in part accounted for by the fact that she is the object of Elinor's observation. If the first volume describes the rise of Marianne's hopes and their temporary disappointment on Willoughby's departure from Devonshire, the second volume her renewed hopes in London and their cruel destruction, and the third volume her near fatal illness and gradual recovery, they describe these events often through Elinor's consciousness. Consequently, while it is Marianne's acts that are described, they are frequently filtered through Elinor's subjective experience of them. Edmund Wilson was perhaps the first to understand the importance of this when he

commented upon the scene in which Marianne meets Willoughby in London (the scene which for George Moore revealed the 'burning human heart in English prose fiction for the first and alas the last time'). 'Isn't it rather', Wilson asks, 'the emotion of Elinor as she witnesses her sister's disaster than Marianne's emotion over Willoughby of which the poignancy is communicated to the reader?'[7]

In this partial internalisation of the debate in Elinor's consciousness—as Marianne's actions and Elinor's perception of these actions merge—Jane Austen's technical advance over *Northanger Abbey,* and her movement in the direction of *Pride and Prejudice,* are evident. Elinor may seem to others to be reserved, rational, and cold, but the reader is given access to her continued inner struggle, not only with respect to her own love affair, but vicariously, as she watches Marianne impetuously fall in love, and, her love slighted, no less passionately give way to melancholy. Elinor, much more than Catherine Morland, though less than Emma, has become a centre of consciousness. She is the only character (apart from Mrs Jennings on one occasion ([III, iii] which must be judged a technical lapse) whose mind the reader is allowed to enter. Opaque to the other characters, Elinor is transparent to the reader. By allowing us frequent access to Elinor's observing mind, the narrator reveals that 'sense' need not be cold, nor introspection selfish.

Elinor's sense is neither a Mandevillian self-interest nor an emotionless calculation. In its affirmation of social principles it resembles, rather, the 'early received and uniformly continued sense of mankind',[8] which Burke considered had not only built up the 'august fabric of states' but had continued to preserve it from ruin. Like her lover Edward, Elinor accepts the validity of social institutions and acts within received principles of ethical and social conduct. Against the private instinct of her sister, as against the selfish motivations of those around her, Elinor opposes a stoical fidelity to traditional and basically Christian values. Her withdrawal into a personal reserve is a committed withdrawal.

The theme of profession, so central to *Mansfield Park,* and found in all the mature novels, is relevant here. In the moment of social discontinuity, the responsible individual can only look conscientiously to his duty and actively profess his role. Unlike Willoughby, who is 'of no profession at all' (p. 61), or Mr Palmer, who 'idled away the mornings at billiards, which ought to have been devoted to business' (p. 305), or John Dashwood, who is always 'thinking about writing a letter to his steward in the country' (p. 259), but never does, the responsible characters of the novel, Ferrars and Brandon, are characterised by their commitment to their roles. Edward, indeed, agrees with Mrs Dashwood when she suggests that he would 'be a happier man if [he] had any profession' to engage his time (p. 102). He admits, 'It has been, and is, and probably will always be a heavy misfortune to me, that I have no necessary business to engage me, no profession to give me employment' (p. 102). And, later, looking back on the foolish infatuation which caused him to engage himself to Lucy, he recognises that his error sprang from his ignorance of the world, his 'want of employment', and his lack of an 'active profession' (p. 362). Yet, having made the betrothal, Edward has proved himself willing to take responsibility for his actions, as Willoughby for all his superior appearance and talents has not.

The need for 'employment', 'duty', 'responsibility', is sounded again and again in Jane Austen's novels, as her heroines all learn that the act of living itself is a profession. After Edward has left the Barton cottage, his melancholy over his commitment to Lucy having communicated itself to Elinor, her reaction may be taken as the positive response that is to be affirmed: she '*busily* employed herself the whole day' and addressed herself to the '*business* of self-command' (p. 104; my italics). In comparison with this self-discipline, Marianne's 'indulgence of feeling' and 'nourishment of grief' (p. 83) are hardly admirable.

Only when Marianne's recovery is assured by the attentions of Elinor and the much maligned Mrs Jennings may Elinor's self-discipline be relaxed. At the end of the novel we are given explicit indications of Elinor's sensibility. First she feels for Marianne, who, 'restored to life, health, friends . . . was an idea to fill her heart with sensations of exquisite comfort, and expand it in fervent gratitude' (p. 315). Then she responds sympathetically to Willoughby's tempestuous arrival and self-pitying tale, and for a time, 'Willoughby, "poor Willoughby", as she now allowed herself to call him, was constantly in her thoughts' (p. 334). Finally with Edward's arrival the question becomes, 'How are [Elinor's] feelings to be described?' (p. 363), and on news of Edward's freedom from the duty of his engagement to Lucy, we are given the answer:

> Elinor could sit it no longer. She almost ran out of the room, and as soon as the door was closed, burst into tears of joy, which at first she thought would never cease. Edward, who had till then looked any where, rather than at her, saw her hurry away, and perhaps saw—or even heard, her emotion. . . . (p. 360)

Marianne's danger over, her morality now properly directed, Elinor may release the emotional tension thus far contained, and herself give way to a temporary display of feeling. By choosing sense as her point of view over sensibility, Jane Austen has made a statement about the priority of discipline to freedom, and of social principles to individual propensities; but, that

statement made, she has also recognised in Elinor's emotion the necessary presence of feeling in the ethical constitution of the individual, if rationality is not to become cold and inhuman.

The novel ends with a union of terms similar to that which will be more successfully achieved in *Pride and Prejudice.* Marianne, like Elizabeth Bennet, comes to the recognition of the need for self-discipline. She promises that '[her] feelings shall be governed and [her] temper improved' (p. 347), and instead of further indulging her grief, she exercises a 'reasonable exertion' (p. 342). Coming to a gradual awareness of Willoughby's false sensibility, his prudent core of self, she compares her conduct to 'what it ought to have been' (p. 345). Her language is characterised now by its ethical vocabulary, and while her sister may show that the individual emotion is a component part of the social response, Marianne determines that, though Willoughby can never be forgotten, his remembrance 'shall be regulated, it shall be checked by religion, by reason, by constant employment' (p. 347). Although her marriage to Colonel Brandon fails to convince, it at least demonstrates the imprudence of her previous arguments that wealth had nothing to do with happiness, for with Brandon's £2,000 a year Marianne gains for herself the 'competence' which Elinor earlier had laughingly considered her own idea of 'wealth' (p. 91).

There is no doubt that the decision to portray two heroines, and the selection of the 'sensible' sister as point of view, led Jane Austen into aesthetic difficulties from which she could not entirely escape. Given the vivacity of Marianne, Elinor's explicitly normative function can only seem didactic on occasions, though this is less often so than is sometimes charged. By looking through the eyes of one of the heroines, Jane Austen has escaped the narrative problem of *Northanger Abbey* without discovering the solutions of *Pride and Prejudice* and *Emma.* She has to some degree dramatised her standards in the psychology of Elinor (as she failed to do in either Henry Tilney or Catherine [in *Northanger Abbey*]) and has thus escaped the problems that arise when judgements remain at the level of the presiding and anonymous narrative consciousness, but she has still left herself with a task of persuasion, of making art and morality coincident. The reader must be made to accept the priority of one sister's moral vision, and the task is complicated by the author's refusal in any way to limit the attractive individualism of the other sister. In *Pride and Prejudice* and *Emma* this problem is successfully avoided by making the individualistic heroines also the central intelligences of their novels, and by allowing these heroines to come to a gradual internal awareness of the insufficiency of their outlooks. Whereas in *Sense and Sensibility* there is a bifurcation of action and reflection, in the later novels the two modes are one in the actions and retrospective reflections of the heroine. In **Sense and Sensibility,** Marianne's moral growth can only be seen externally in her words and actions, frequently as they are observed through Elinor's consciousness of them. Elinor herself does not so much evince a moral growth as a constant internal moral struggle. In **Pride and Prejudice** and **Emma** (though in ways to be distinguished), the movement from an individualistic to a social morality is followed within the psyche of a single heroine.

Notes

[Duckworth sees Marianne as the representative of sensibility, a movement in thought, manners and opinion in the late eighteenth century which seemed superior to the mercenary values of many of Austen's contemporaries, yet also dangerously immoral because prioritising individual subjective feelings over objective social conventions. Duckworth notices that rather than Elinor being a rather dull and repressive foil to Marianne's transgressive liveliness, she stands for a very complex and discriminating kind of sense when she is compared with characters whose minds are narrowly concerned with their own economic betterment. Her tendency to self-repression is born of a responsible Christian appreciation of her place in society and of the needs of others. Duckworth's account appears to be a very perceptive reading *along the grain* of Austen's world view and illuminates the sophisticated discriminations to which the contemporary reader of Austen might have been attuned.

References to Jane Austen's work are to *The Works of Jane Austen,* ed. R. W. Chapman, 3rd edn, 5 vols (London, 1933), and vol. 6, *Minor Works,* ed. R. W. Chapman (London, 1954). References to Austen's letters are to *Jane Austen's Letters to her Sister Cassandra and Others,* ed. R. W. Chapman, 2 vols (Oxford, 1932), cited as *Letters.* Ed.]

[1] *Camilla* (London, 1796), IV, 399. For studies treating the literary background to *Sense and Sensibility,* see the relevant portions of Henrietta Ten Harmsel, *Jane Austen: A Study in Fictional Conventions* (The Hague, 1934); A. Walton Litz, *Jane Austen: A Study of her Artistic Development* (London, 1965); Kenneth Moler, *Jane Austen's Art of Allusion* (Lincoln, 1968); also Alan D. McKillop, 'The Context of *Sense and Sensibility*', *The Rice Institute Pamphlet,* 44 (April 1957), 65-78. J. M. S. Tompkins, '"Elinor and Marianne": A Note on Jane Austen', *The Review of English Studies,* 16 (1940), 33-43, suggests Jane West's *A Gossip's Story* (London, 1796) as a single model of *Sense and Sensibility,* but Kenneth Moler, while not denying Jane West's influence, is one of several critics to see affinities with a number of other sentimental novels.

[2] For an excellent brief rebuttal to Mudrick's view contained in *Jane Austen: Irony as Defense and Dis-* covery (Princeton, 1952), see A. Walton Litz, *Artistic Development,* pp. 81-3. Litz argues that 'the alternative to Willoughby is Colonel Brandon not because this was Jane Austen's heritage from life, but because it was her heritage from the broad antitheses of moralistic fiction', and that Jane Austen in *Sense and Sensibility* was 'the victim of conventions, but these were primarily artistic, not social'.

[3] Mudrick, *Irony as Defense,* pp. 75, 74.

[4] Ronald Crane, 'Suggestions Toward a Genealogy of the "Man of Feeling"', *Journal of English Literary History,* 1 (1934), 205-30, argues for an earlier expression of the sentimental outlook in the latitudinarian preachers of the late seventeenth and early eighteenth centuries. Other critical studies which consider the philosophy of sentiment and its development in the eighteenth century are: A. S. P. Woodhouse, 'Romanticism and the History of Ideas', *English Studies Today* (Oxford, 1951), pp. 120-41, and Walter Jackson Bate, 'The Premise of Feeling', in *From Classic to Romantic: Premises of Taste in Eighteenth Century England* (1946; rpt New York, 1961), pp. 129-60. Perhaps the best treatment of the idea in Jane Austen's novel is found in Ian Watt's Introduction to *Sense and Sensibility* (New York, 1961), reprinted in *Jane Austen: A Collection of Critical Essays,* ed. Ian Watt (Englewood Cliff, N J, 1963).

[5] *Treatise on Human Nature,* ed. T. H. Green and T. H. Grose (London, 1874), p. 235.

[6] *The Works of Joseph Butler,* ed. W. E. Gladstone (Oxford, 1896), vol. 2, pp. 14-15.

[7] 'A Long Talk About Jane Austen', *Classics and Commercials: A Literary Chronicle of the Forties* (New York, 1950), p. 203.

[8] Edmund Burke, *Reflections on the Revolution in France,* ed. William B. Todd (New York, 1959), p. 111.

Moreland Perkins (essay date 1998)

SOURCE: "Elinor Dashwood: The Heroine as Intellectual," in *Reshaping the Sexes in* Sense and Sensibility, University Press of Virginia, 1998, pp. 11-36.

[*In the following essay, Perkins advances the theory that* Sense and Sensibility *is Elinor Dashwood's story, not Marianne's, and argues that her special interest lies in her position as a female intellectual.*]

Because many first-time readers of **Sense and Sensibility** find Marianne the more appealing of the two elder Dashwood sisters, they may think of her as the primary heroine. For those readers, Marianne's early disappointment, long suffering, and ultimate fade-out can figure as a major disincentive for rereading the novel. However, once we start to understand how much there is in Austin's rendering of Elinor Dashwood that is not only appealing but politically significant, the realization that the novel is written as her story may awaken in us a desire to return to it and read her closely. No one has more cogently made the case for the novel's being Elinor's story than Stuart Tave:

> **Sense and Sensibility** is the story of Elinor Dashwood.... The whole of Marianne's story is included within Elinor's: Marianne's begins later and it ends earlier. . . . The whole of the story comes to us through Elinor.... There may be things that Elinor doesn't know [about Marianne] . . . but if Elinor doesn't know . . . we don't know. . . . Marianne's story could not be resolved except for what Elinor does, advising her, protecting her, providing her an example . . . ; even the two men in Marianne's life are understood by the reader, and by Marianne, as they speak to and are interpreted by Elinor. There is no part of Marianne's story that is not a part of Elinor's, but there are large and important parts of Elinor's story that are not part of Marianne's.[1]

Professor Tave's perception of Elinor's centrality perfectly coheres with my own experience of the novel. However, neither he nor any other critic I have read finds quite the elements of her characterization that I believe account for her special interest. These features can all, I think, be tied to Austen's intention to reshape gender in this early novel. And the most fecund characteristic is the following. In depicting Elinor Dashwood, Jane Austen achieved something uncommon in our major ficiton: the rendering of an intellectual. Even more unheard of, a female intellectual. In her first morally ambitious drafting of a heroine, Jane Austen accorded herself the political freedom, not to be indulged again, of creating one who is nearly as gender dissonant, because nearly as accomplished an intellectual, as Austen herself would have been when precociously composing the first version of this novel, probably in 1795 at about Elinor's age of nineteen.[2]

To judge from the absence of acknowledgment by critics, even today an intellectual is not easy to recognize if she is female, and both her experience and her immediate subject matter are chiefly found in domestic, personal, and small-scale social life, especially if it is known that she was born and raised in the eighteenth century. This block has somewhat blurred critical perception of both Elinor and Jane Austen. Critics' resistance is not explained by the fact that our current understanding of the phrase "an intellectual" has come so much later than those times. Austen's peers never spoke of the ruling class's ideology either, but that doesn't mean they didn't have one. Part of the point of Julia Prewitt Brown's remark, that "Jane Austen was

not an intellectual in the sense in which George Eliot was" (try to picture Austen translating Spinoza, as Eliot did), is that Austen *was* of course an intellectual.[3]

My thesis about Elinor Dashwood is that Austen endowed her with enough of the habits and powers of thought belonging to Austen herself to qualify Elinor also as an intellectual, to wit: unrelenting, dispassionate, analytical inquiry into the causes, contents, contexts, and outcomes of individual persons' conduct and experience, all conceived as ineluctably social; and the habit of taking pleasure in the pure play of ideas over her subject matter. If we acknowledge, as we do, that today a rigorously thoughtful but non-publishing psychoanalyst or art critic or urban anthropologist may be an intellectual, then we must allow the same stature to a talented analyst of human conduct, character, and convention who is equally dedicated to concretely applied reason—although we imagine her functioning this way long before the phrase "an intellectual" was put to its current use.

The (apparently unwitting) disciple of Austen whose moral sensibility was possibly closest to hers, Henry James, never, I think, created as protagonist that rare creature in major English fiction, a convincing intellectual; but James's own disciple Ford Madox Ford gave us, in Christopher Tietjens, an intellectual who makes in several respects an interesting contrast with Elinor Dashwood. Tietjens, younger son of an ancient Yorkshire landed family, is a brilliant mathematician working with precocious distinction in "the Imperial Department of Statistics." He is also endowed with an encyclopedic curiosity and memory. By quick brush strokes the first novel of Ford's four-volume work, *Parade's End,* succeeds, with Tietjens, in painting a charismatic portrait of an intellectual. Because Tietjens' intellectuality operates in his romantic life not discernibly at all or else in ways that are largely either irrelevant to important concerns or just plain eccentric, Ford is left free to make Tietjens sometimes impulsive or moody or irrational in personal action without ceasing to seem an intellectual.

Tietjens' versatility of temperament means that Ford's fabrication of this intellectual was in two respects less demanding than Austen's creation of *her* fictional intellectual. First, because Tietjens' intellectuality only occasionally manifests itself in his romantic life, he can be rendered as a man of dramatically opposing aspects, hence fascinating in his variety and unpredictability. Second, Tietjens' eccentricity and suppressed yet evident emotionality can quickly endear him to many readers. On the other hand, because Elinor is not, could not then be, a professional person and is the heroine of one troubled love story and the anxious monitor of another, the domain of application for her intellect is almost entirely the actions, circumstances, and feelings that figure in affairs of the heart. Because of this limitation, Elinor's intellect must be steadily—hence for some readers dauntingly—on display; and for the same reasons, her orientation to her own emotions will be more rational than many readers can find attractive. Permeating all this is Elinor's gender dissonance: many readers then and now will experience intellectual display in a *man's* informal conversation, and rational self-control in *his* conduct, as more natural and attractive than they find either in a woman. For immediate reader appeal, Ford's fictional intellectual has a head start over Austen's.

Austen spent the first twenty-five years of her life in the rectory of her Oxford-educated father, who was both a scholarly minister and a teacher. Two of her older brothers, also Oxford graduates, became ministers, and the eldest, ten years her senior, had strong literary interests and showed some poetic skill as a young man. Had she wished to, she could have created a scholar-clergyman whom we today would call (though she wouldn't) a professional intellectual. (To be sure, she would need to expend some ingenuity to conform to her self-injunction never to write of men talking only with men.)

In her next novel she will make a gesture toward a male intellectual, secular Mr. Bennet. But at the start, if she wanted an intellectual, she wanted a fictional translation of her own disproof of patriarchy's gender paradigm: it would be a woman. This could gratify her.

Elinor's being an intellectual but not a professional one has the effect that she will be "at work" full-time: there will be no holidays from intellectual work while away from office, lab, or study. No matter how strongly Elinor's own interest is affected or her desire engaged or her emotions aroused, in almost every emotionally potent situation her chief expense of energy will go first toward understanding and next to bringing her action and her feeling into accord with reason. No more for Elinor than for Jane Austen is the habit of dispassionate analysis a matter of choice: it composes the very texture of Elinor's temperament.

As narrator of her fictions, Jane Austen had an intimate relationship to her heroines. This intimacy has several interesting aspects. Just now I attend to only one of them: the harmony she creates between the habits of thought—especially the analytical wit and irony—of herself as narrator and Elinor. This is a two-way street: the narrator's thought patterns are as much colored by her heroine's as the latter's are borrowed from the author's.

For example, the narrator of *Sense and Sensibility* is more inclined to an abstruse, mock-metaphysical wit than is the narrator of *Pride and Prejudice.* The same contrast holds between Elinor Dashwood and Elizabeth Bennet. Although bright, Elizabeth is not an intellectual. She falls short of Elinor in this way despite the fact that she is witty in a way Elinor is not; for Elinor's wit is scarcely social and never sociable, whereas Elizabeth's is always part of her gaiety and sometimes part of her sexuality. The mock-metaphysical wit of Elinor and her narrator reinforce each other in helping render Elinor's portrait as an intellectual; the narrator's higher flights raise the altitude of her heroine's by a kind of attraction or osmosis.

Consider the private meditation below in which Austen shares with Elinor the narrator's disposition to a witty abstruseness in condemning Edward's disagreeable mother: they (she) imagine(s), as (a) mock-philosopher(s), a uselessly *hypothetical* because utterly imaginary *duty* of Elinor's to *rejoice!* Elinor has at last met Mrs. Ferrars, but only after her love for Edward has been thwarted by her learning of his secret engagement to Lucy Steele:

> Elinor's curiosity to see Mrs Ferrars was satisfied.—she had found in her every thing that could tend to make a farther connection between the families, undesirable.—She had seen enough of her pride, her meanness, and her determined prejudice against herself, to comprehend all the difficulties that must have perplexed the engagement, and retarded the marriage, of Edward and herself, had he been otherwise free;—and she had seen almost enough to be thankful for her *own* sake, that one greater obstacle preserved her from suffering under any other of Mrs Ferrars's creation, preserved her from all dependence upon her caprice, or any solicitude for her good opinion. Or at least, if she did not bring herself quite to rejoice in Edward's being fettered to Lucy, she determined, that had Lucy been more amiable, she *ought* to have rejoiced. (ch. 41:293)

With the climactic "she determined," the narrator makes conclusive the transfer to Elinor of the most abstruse element in this reflection. Jane Austen does not assign to Elizabeth Bennet such an intricate mental construction by displaying, for example, Elizabeth's dismay over an encounter with Lady Catherine de Bourgh. What pleases us in Elizabeth is a very different sort of wit. Lady Catherine pays her meddling visit to Elizabeth and asks her whether she knows that a report is being spread with the news she will marry Lady Catherine's nephew, Mr. Darcy:

> "I never heard that it was."

> "And can you likewise declare, that there is no *foundation* for it?"

> "I do not pretend to possess equal frankness with your ladyship. *You* may ask questions which *I* shall not choose to answer."

> " . . . Has he, has my nephew, made you an offer of marriage?"

"Your ladyship has declared it to be impossible."

" . . . You may have drawn him in."

"If I had, I shall be the last person to confess it."

" . . . Your alliance will be a disgrace; your name will never even be mentioned by any of us."

"These are heavy misfortunes. . . . But the wife of Mr. Darcy must have such extraordinary sources of happiness necessarily attached to her situation, that she could, upon the whole, have no cause to repine." (*PP,* ch. 56: 363-65)

Elizabeth does here display an exceptionally nimble wit. In its context, "I do not pretend to possess equal frankness with your ladyship" is an almost-polite parry that turns her opponent's blow against herself. And "Your ladyship has declared it to be impossible"— also fired off fast—is enough, one would think, to make Lady Catherine feel she is defeating herself. Amazingly, "If I have, I shall be the last person to confess it" maintains the wickedly creative trick of making Lady de Bourgh's words come back at her like boomerangs. Elizabeth Bennet's intellect here functions like that of a nimble defense attorney. Elinor Dashwood's works more like a philosopher's.

In a moment we'll contemplate Elinor being openly aggressive, though at second-hand, toward Mrs. Ferrars, but first let us enjoy an example of the author-narrator's aggression toward the same woman, so that we may notice the kinship between the narrator's attack and Elinor's. One way that Edward Ferrars's mother is depicted as something of a monster is through Austen's ironically mock-metaphysical account of Mrs. Ferrars's habit of disowning a son from time to time. In the last chapter of the book, Austen goes after this favorite target in a way that, when we reread the book, affects our experience of an earlier attack on the same woman by Elinor. (Remember, Edward is the eldest son.) Thus the narrator on Mrs. Ferrars:

Her family had of late been exceedingly fluctuating. For many years of her life she had had two sons; but the crime and annihilation of Edward a few weeks ago, had robbed her of one; the similar annihilation of Robert had left her for a fortnight without any; and now, by the resuscitation of Edward, she had one again.

In spite of his being allowed once more to live, however, he did not feel the continuance of his existence secure, till he had revealed his present engagement; for the publication of that circumstance, he feared, might give a sudden turn to his constitution, and carry him off as rapidly as before. With apprehensive caution therefore it was revealed, and he was listened to with unexpected calmness. . . .

What she would engage to do towards augmenting their income, was next to be considered; and here it plainly appeared, that though Edward was now her only son, he was by no means her eldest; for while Robert was inevitably endowed with a thousand pounds a-year, not the smallest objection was made against Edward's taking orders for the sake of two hundred and fifty at the utmost. (ch. 50:362-63)

Now look at Elinor's way of openly deriding Mrs. Ferrars to her brother, John Dashwood, the older woman's son-in-law. John has just queried his sister about Colonel Brandon's motive in bestowing a rector's living upon Edward Ferrars. Edward had been disowned by his mother for refusing to break his engagement to Lucy Steele. Now John assumes the living from Brandon will enable Edward and Lucy to marry. Rereading this exchange from chapter 41, one remembers the just quoted, more brilliant development in chapter 50 of the same theme by the narrator, and Elinor as intellectual benefits by a kind of fusion of the narrator's developed metaphor with Elinor's embryonic one. John is speaking of Brandon's gift of a living to Edward:

"Mrs Ferrars," added he, lowering his voice to the tone becoming so important a subject, "knows nothing about it at present, and I believe it will be best to keep it entirely concealed from her as long as may be.—When the marriage takes place, I fear she must hear of it all."

"But why should such precaution be used?—Though it is not to be supposed that Mrs Ferrars can have the smallest satisfaction in knowing that her son has money enough to live upon,—for *that* must be quite out of the question; yet why, after her late behaviour, is she supposed to feel at all?—she has done with her son, she has cast him off for ever, and has made all those over whom she had any influence, cast him off likewise. Surely, after doing so, she cannot be imagined liable to any impression of sorrow or of joy on his account—she cannot be interested in any thing that befalls him.—She would not be so weak as to throw away the comfort of a child, and yet retain the anxiety of a parent!" (ch. 41:293)

One has to do no more than compare this attack with any to be found in another Austen heroine to realize that nowhere else will so much intellectual energy be given over to the meticulous development of an ironic metaphor in order merely to register contempt. Only an intellectual would spontaneously express her abhorrence of such conduct by presenting it as a mock-logical scandal created by the mock-paradox of Mrs. Ferrars's expected maternal distress from the news of good fortune befalling a son who is no longer a son. It is as if Elinor can enjoy her personal aggression only if she can embed it within—and offer to her proxy target, John Dashwood—the purer pleasure of the play of ideas.

When Elizabeth Bennet tells her sister Jane the story from Wickham that alleges dastardly behavior on the part of Bingley's best friend, Darcy, Jane—who habitually thinks the best of everyone—seeks a way to believe neither man dishonorable:

> "They have both," she said, "been deceived, I dare say, in some way or other, of which we can form no idea. Interested people have perhaps misrepresented each to the other. . . . "

> "Very true, indeed; and now, my dear Jane, what have you got to say in behalf of the interested people who have probably been concerned in the business? Do clear *them* too, or we shall be obliged to think ill of somebody." (*PP,* ch. 17:128)

Here as always Elizabeth's repartee adds a small piece to the picture of a very bright person. But neither here nor elsewhere does it suggest that Elizabeth takes the kind of pleasure Elinor does in the play of ideas for its own sake. And yet it is not that Elinor ever ascends into the realm of pure theory. On the contrary, she indulges in her intellectual pleasures only when the play of ideas is embedded within pursuit of a practical end she deems worthy, or anyhow necessary.

Examples of Elinor's (and her narrator's) mock-metaphysical wit add color, scope, and a larger coherence to the central element in Austen's portrait of Elinor as intellectual, that is, to Elinor's analyses of character, conduct, and human causality. Surely exemplary here and proving the value, for appreciating Elinor, of having read to the end of the novel in reading its beginning, are Elinor's explanations of Willoughby, late in the story, after his visit with her when Marianne is ill. I pick three passages, in order of ascending level of abstraction. First, Elinor to Marianne on how a marriage to Willoughby would have faltered:

> "Your marriage must have involved you in many certain troubles and disappointments, in which you would have been poorly supported by an affection, on his side, much less certain. Had you married, you must have been always poor. His expensiveness is acknowledged even by himself, and his whole conduct declares that self-denial is a word hardly understood by him. His demands and your inexperience together on a small, very small income, must have brought on distresses which would not be the *less* grievous to you, from having been entirely unknown and unthought of before. *Your* sense of honour and honesty would have led you, I know, when aware of your situation, to attempt all the economy that would appear to you possible; and perhaps, as long as your frugality retrenched only on your own comfort, you might have been suffered to practise it, but beyond that—and how little could the utmost of your single management do to stop the ruin which had begun before your marriage?—Beyond *that,* had you endeavoured, however reasonably,

to abridge *his* enjoyments, is it not to be feared, that instead of prevailing on feelings so selfish to consent to it, you would have lessened your own influence on his heart, and made him regret the connection which had involved him in such difficulties?" (ch. 47:341-42)

This is dense causal reasoning that packs into a very short passage a multitude of factors figuring in several different causal chains that convincingly converge on a single result, the alienation of Willoughby's affections from Marianne. I have made no survey to warrant saying that the single sentence beginning "*Your* sense of honour," which makes up the entire second half of this passage, is the longest assigned to an Austen heroine, but I suspect it is the most complex bit of causal reasoning to be found in a single sentence so assigned. Compare the whole passage with a rejoinder in *Emma* by Emma Woodhouse to Mr. Knightley, who has been arguing that Harriet Smith can do no better than to marry Robert Martin, farmer, because of the limits set by Harriet's origins, upbringing, present circumstances, and abilities:

> "You are a very warm friend to Mr Martin; but, as I said before, are unjust to Harriet. Harriet's claims to marry well are not so contemptible as you represent them. She is not a clever girl, but she has better sense than you are aware of, and does not deserve to have her understanding spoken of so slightingly. Waving that point, however, and supposing her to be, as you describe her, only pretty and good-natured, let me tell you, that in the degree she possesses them, they are not trivial recommendations to the world in general, for she is, in fact, a beautiful girl, and must be thought so by ninety-nine people out of an hundred; and till it appears that men are much more philosophic on the subject of beauty than they are generally supposed, till they do fall in love with well-informed minds instead of handsome faces, a girl, with such loveliness as Harriet, has a certainty of being admired and sought after, of having the power of choosing from among many, consequently a claim to be nice. Her good-nature, too, is not so very slight a claim, comprehending as it does, real, thorough sweetness of temper and manner, a very humble opinion of herself, and a great readiness to be pleased with other people. I am very much mistaken if your sex in general would not think such beauty, and such temper, the highest claims a woman could possess." (*E,* ch. 8:89-90)

If in comparison with Elinor's temperament of an intellectual Elizabeth Bennet appears no more than bright, it may be fair to say Emma, with respect to analytical and argumentative bent, seems merely clever.

Like a true intellectual, Elinor can go over much the same ground a second time and give an explanation that coheres with the first yet is fresh:

"At present," continued Elinor, "he regrets what he has done. And why does he regret it?—Because he finds it has not answered towards himself. It has not made him happy. His circumstances are now unembarrassed—he suffers from no evil of that kind; and he thinks only that he has married a woman of a less amiable temper than yourself. But does it thence follow that had he married you, he would have been happy?—The inconveniences would have been different. He would then have suffered under the pecuniary distresses which, because they are removed he now reckons as nothing. He would have.had a wife of whose temper he could make no complaint, but he would have been always necessitous—always poor; and probably would soon have learnt to rank the innumerable comforts of a clear estate and good income as of far more importance, even to domestic happiness, than the mere temper of a wife." (ch. 47:342)

By now a student of the eighteenth century may be perceiving—or recalling—that Elinor Dashwood's modes of thought resemble, possibly more than those of any other of her author's creations do, those of Samuel Johnson, one of the intellectuals of that century most admired by Jane Austen. Not only the lucidity, the balanced symmetry in explanatory structure, but also the fluid movement of the argument, the centrality of familiar abstractions, and the extended reach of a single sentence's thought remind us of Elinor's affinity to the great Johnson. Moreover, a similarity of moral sensibility emerges when we consider, on the one hand, the dispassionate objectivity with which, near the end of the novel, Elinor appraises Willoughby's character, given her sympathy for him after their dramatic late interview, and on the other, that sympathy itself, given the horrors in her family life for which she justly blames Willoughby. All this shows most vividly in the analysis Elinor meditates within herself when Willoughby has concluded his explanation of his behavior toward Marianne with, "Now you know all."

> Elinor made no answer. Her thoughts were silently fixed on the irreparable injury which too early an independence and its consequent habits of idleness, dissipation, and luxury, had made in the mind, the character, the happiness, of a man who, to every advantage of person and talents, united a disposition naturally open and honest, and a feeling, affectionate temper. The world had made him extravagant and vain—Extravagance and vanity had made him cold-hearted and selfish. Vanity, while seeking its own guilty triumph at the expense of another, had involved him in a real attachment, which extravagance, or at least its offspring, necessity, had required to be sacrificed. Each faulty propensity in leading him to evil, had led him likewise to punishment. The attachment, from which against honour, against feeling, against every better interest he had outwardly torn himself, now, when no longer allowable, governed every thought; and the connection, for the sake of which he had, with little

scruple, left her sister to misery, was likely to prove a source of unhappiness to himself of a far more incurable nature. (ch. 44:324)

In somewhat the way Elinor needed to filter her hostility toward Mrs. Ferrars through the metaphor of a mock-paradox, here her charity for Willoughby reaches him from almost the height of a Platonic Realm of Universals to which the misfortune of his depravity is ascribed: independence generated in him idleness, dissipation, and luxury; the world introduced into his disposition extravagance and vanity, which in turn brought on coldheartedness and selfishness; for vanity (personified) sought its triumph, accidentally leading him—because of his openness and affectionate temper—into an attachment which . . . and so on and so on. Both Willoughby and his environment have been analyzed into causally determining "propensities." Under the explanatory projects of the theorizing intellect, all individuals tend to become, for the moment, intersections of causally effective abstractions. In this abstractionism Elinor surpasses Samuel Johnson.

Reading the following representative passage of similar analysis by Johnson, one perceives the affinity but also notes that Johnson makes less frequent use of abstractions as the subjects of verbs than Elinor did. The passage is taken from the last six or seven paragraphs of Johnson's life of Richard Savage, in his *Lives of the English Poets:*

> It cannot be said that he made use of his abilities for the direction of his own conduct: an irregular and dissipated manner of life had made him the slave of every passion that happened to be excited by the presence of its object, and that slavery to his passions reciprocally produced a life irregular and dissipated. He was not master of his own motions, nor could promise anything for the next day. . . .

> His friendship was . . . of little value; for . . . it was always dangerous to trust him, because he considered himself as discharged by the first quarrel from all ties of honour or gratitude . . . he could not bear to conceive himself in a state of dependence, his pride being equally powerful with his other passions, and appearing in the form of insolence at one time, and of vanity at another.

Quite possibly Elinor's revaluation of Willoughby on the occasion of his late visit to her reminds a reader of Elizabeth Bennet's revaluation of Wickham, in **Pride and Prejudice,** when she read the explanatory letter Darcy wrote her after she refused him in marriage. Of course there are similarities. But to return to Elizabeth's mind at work on a project that is somewhat similar to the one we just examined is to become convinced that Austen had no intention of making Elizabeth an intellectual, and to be made more sure of one's impression of Elinor as just that. Elizabeth is passionate, variable, swiftly moving in both thought and feeling, the two always interlocked. Sustained independent analysis is not her way. From Elinor's analysis of a complex personality and its rich societal context we feel we receive illumination; by contrast, Elizabeth merely absorbs an explicitly told story we already know, and connects it with her experience.

> She read, with an eagerness which hardly left her power of comprehension, and from impatience of knowing what the next sentence might bring, was incapable of attending to the sense of the one before her eyes. His belief of her sister's insensibility, she instantly resolved to be false, and his account of the real, the worst objections to the match, made her too angry to have any wish of doing him justice. He expressed no regret for what he had done which satisfied her; his style was not penitent, but haughty. It was all pride and insolence.
>
> But when this subject was succeeded by his account of Mr Wickham, when she read with somewhat clearer attention, a relation of events, which, if true, must overthrow every cherished opinion of his worth, and which bore so alarming an affinity to his own history of himself, her feelings were yet more acutely painful and more difficult of definition. Astonishment, apprehension, and even horror, oppressed her. She wished to discredit it entirely, repeatedly exclaiming, "This must be false! This cannot be! This must be the grossest falsehood!"— and when she had gone through the whole letter, though scarcely knowing any thing of the last page or two, put it hastily away, protesting that she would not regard it, that she would never look in it again.
>
> In this perturbed state of mind, with thoughts that could rest on nothing, she walked on; but it would not do; in half a minute the letter was unfolded again, and collecting herself as well as she could, she again began the mortifying perusal of all that related to Wickham, and commanded herself so far as to examine the meaning of every sentence. . . . She put down the letter, weighed every circumstance with what she meant to be impartiality—deliberated on the probability of each statement—but with little success. On both sides it was only assertion. Again she read on. But every line proved more clearly that the affair, which she had believed it impossible that any contrivance could so represent, as to render Mr Darcy's conduct it less than infamous, was capable of a turn which must make him entirely blameless throughout the whole. (***PP,*** ch. 36:233-34)

Against my use of this contrast between Elinor and Elizabeth it might be objected that Willoughby is merely the lover of Elinor's sister whereas Darcy and Wickham belong to Elizabeth's own amorous adventures; so Elinor *should* be more dispassionate than Elizabeth. But this is the closest Elizabeth comes to the kind of analysis Austen assigns to Elinor. If for

Elizabeth personal engagement alone will generate even this much mental work, this too contributes to the difference in nature that Austen has rendered in her two portraits.

However, we do have presented to us Elinor's mind in play when her own romantic life is smashed by Lucy Steele's revelation of her engagement to Edward Ferrars. It is, I think, only if we conceive Elinor as uniquely invested by Austen with the private vocation of the lay intellectual that her response in this crisis can seem credible, natural, true. Here it is:

> However small Elinor's general dependance on Lucy's veracity might be, it was impossible for her on serious reflection to suspect it in the present case, where no temptation could be answerable to the folly of inventing a falsehood of such a description. What Lucy had asserted to be true, therefore, Elinor could not, dared not longer doubt; supported as it was too on every side by such probabilities and proofs, and contradicted by nothing but her own wishes. Their opportunity of acquaintance in the house of Mr Pratt was a foundation for the rest, at once indisputable and alarming; and Edward's visit near Plymouth, his melancholy state of mind, his dissatisfaction at his own prospects, his uncertain behaviour towards herself, the intimate knowledge of the Miss Steeles as to Norland and their family connections, which had often surprised her, the picture, the letter, the ring, formed altogether such a body of evidence, as overcame every fear of condemning him unfairly, and established as a fact, which no partiality could set aside, his ill-treatment of herself.—Her resentment of such behaviour, her indignation at having been its dupe, for a short time made her feel only for herself; but other ideas, other considerations soon arose. Had Edward been intentionally deceiving her? Had he feigned a regard for her which he did not feel? Was his engagement to Lucy, an engagement of the heart? No; whatever it might once have been, she could not believe it such at present. His affection was all her own. She could not be deceived in that. Her mother, sisters, Fanny, all had been conscious of his regard for her at Norland; it was not an illusion of her own vanity. He certainly loved her. What a softener of the heart was this persuasion! How much could it not tempt her to forgive! He had been blameable, highly blameable, in remaining at Norland after he first felt her influence over him to be more than it ought to be. In that, he could not be defended; but if he had injured her, how much more had he injured himself; if her case were pitiable, his was hopeless. His imprudence had made her miserable for a while; but it seemed to have deprived himself of all chance of ever being otherwise. She might in time regain tranquillity, but *he,* what had he to look forward to? Could he ever be tolerably happy with Lucy Steele; could he, were his affection for herself out of the question, with his integrity, his delicacy, and well-informed mind, be satisfied with a wife like her—illiterate, artful, and selfish?

The youthful infatuation of nineteen would naturally blind him to every thing but her beauty and good nature; but the four succeeding years—years, which if rationally spent, give such improvement to the understanding, must have opened his eyes to her defects of education, while the same period of time, spent on her side in inferior society and more frivolous pursuits, had perhaps robbed her of that simplicity, which might once have given an interesting character to her beauty.

If in the supposition of his seeking to marry herself, his difficulties from his mother had seemed great, how much greater were they now likely to be, when the object of his engagement was undoubtedly inferior in connections, and probably inferior in fortune to herself. These difficulties, indeed, with an heart so alienated from Lucy, might not press very hard upon his patience; but melancholy was the state of the person, by whom the expectation of family opposition and unkindness, could be felt as a relief!

As these considerations occurred to her in painful succession, she wept for him, more than for herself. Supported by the conviction of having done nothing to merit her present unhappiness, and consoled by the belief that Edward had done nothing to forfeit her esteem, she thought she could even now, under the first smart of the heavy blow, command herself enough to guard every suspicion of the truth from her mother and sisters. . . .

The necessity of concealing from her mother and Marianne, what had been entrusted in confidence to herself, though it obliged her to unceasing exertion, was no aggravation of Elinor's distress. . . .

From their counsel, or their conversation she knew she could receive to assistance, their tenderness and sorrow must add to her distress, while her self-command would neither receive encouragement from their example nor from their praise. She was stronger alone, and her own good sense so well supported her, that her firmness was as unshaken, her appearance of cheerfulness as invariable, as with regrets so poignant and so fresh, it was possible for them to be. (ch. 23:157-59)

If we have read the whole novel—especially through to the end of chapter 48, when Elinor learns Edward is unmarried, unengaged, and free to marry her—we now read this passage believing Elinor does love Edward because we have "seen" that she does. However, we also believe that for months before this revelation she had, from prudence based on Edward's inconsistent behavior toward her, suppressed the feeling of love. Her mental control had showed itself clearly in an early exchange with Marianne, who complained because Elinor refused to acknowledge her feelings of love for

Edward, referring to them instead as (mere) "esteem" and "liking." Provoked by this evasion, Marianne says, "Use those words again and I will leave the room this moment." Elinor replies, "Till his sentiments are fully known, you cannot wonder at my wishing to avoid any encouragement of my own partiality by believing or calling it more than it is" (ch. 4:55). Surely this was reasonable—and even more provident than she knew. But now, with Lucy's news of her engagement to Edward, something is needed other than prudence, which has little application to this sudden "extinction of all her dearest hopes" (ch. 23:158). Intellectually and morally—here these two are one—her response is imaginative and creative. It is guided in part by a conservative principle of moral appraisal, that is, a principle that says: in any trying situation, conserve the highest goods that *can* be conserved consistent with the truth. She finds that Edward loves her, a conclusion needing a clear head and some courage in these unfavoring circumstances. She finds that Edward's injury to her is redeemed by its source in love of her. She concludes Edward "had done nothing to forfeit her esteem." And that she herself has "done nothing to merit her present unhappiness": the only part of the world she *can* control she has managed responsibly. Also she helps herself conserve, in her appraisal, not only justice but her own feeling for Edward by finding that his conduct of his affairs of the heart has far more seriously injured himself than her. This judgment is just, but it causes her to weep for him more than for herself—thus it helps conserve her feeling of love for him. Along the way she explains Edward's early infatuation with Lucy and subsequent disaffection in a manner both insightful and conservative of Edward's character and his mature taste and judgment. It is a tribute to Austen's own imagination that she invented for Elinor, in a situation so poignant with loss, an analysis that is so creatively useful to Elinor's emotional equilibrium yet does not depart from the truth. For a woman to be moved to forgive an offense because the offender has softened her heart by loving her is to abandon neither the truth nor high moral ground, although in itself it appeals to neither of these: it is simply an impeccable movement of the heart. The head has not surrendered to the heart, nothing is more evident; but neither has it suppressed the heart, which in Elinor is not something readers may feel they can always count on.

The integration in Elinor of analytical intellect, affective imagination, a disciplined will governed by a sensitive conscience, and a habit of conserving the good is in these circumstances so exceptional that we may now for the first time recognize Austen's intention to achieve in Elinor this difficult outcome: a credible idealization. . . . Perhaps in order quickly to improve the balance in Elinor's portrait by bringing into our view baser elements of her temperament, in the very next chapter of the novel Austen lowers Elinor into her nasty battle with Lucy Steele.

The next occasion of Elinor's analyzing the unhappy triangle comes four months later, when she has to tell Marianne of its existence because Edward's engagement to Lucy is about to become public knowledge. At this point the reader may feel Elinor does fall into distortion of the truth:

> "Now, I can think and speak of it with little emotion. I would not have you suffer on my account; for I assure you I no longer suffer materially myself. I have many things to support me. I am not conscious of having provoked the disappointment by any imprudence of my own, and I have borne it as much as possible without spreading it further. I acquit Edward of all essential misconduct. I wish him very happy; and I am so sure of his always doing his duty, that though now he may harbour some regret, in the end he must become so. Lucy does not want sense, and that is the foundation on which every thing good may be built.—And after all, Marianne, after all that is bewitching in the idea of a single and constant attachment, and all that can be said of one's happiness depending entirely on any particular person, it is not meant—it is not fit— it is not possible that it should be so.—Edward will marry Lucy; he will marry a woman superior in person and understanding to half her sex; and time and habit will teach him to forget that he ever thought another superior to *her*." (ch. 37:264)

Does Elinor by now believe Edward and Lucy will somehow marry? Possibly, for when, a short time later, Edward leaves her after she has extended to him Colonel Brandon's offer of a living, we have this: "'When I see him again,' said Elinor to herself, as the door shut him out, 'I shall see him the husband of Lucy'" (ch. 40:289). On the other hand, not quite; for when she is (mis)informed that Edward and Lucy have married, near the end of the book, we read this:

> Elinor now found the difference between the expectation of an unpleasant event, however certain the mind may be told to consider it, and certainty itself. She now found, that in spite of herself, she had always admitted a hope, while Edward remained single, that something would occur to prevent his marrying Lucy; that some resolution of his own, some mediation of friends, or some more eligible opportunity of establishment for the lady, would arise to assist the happiness of all. But he was now married, and she condemned her heart for the lurking flattery, which so much heightened the pain of the intelligence. (ch. 48:347)

To complete this picture of Elinor's frail normality under the utter certainty of her loss, the passage continues, a little further on:

She saw them in an instant in their parsonage-house; saw in Lucy, the active, contriving manager, uniting at once a desire of smart appearance, with the utmost frugality, and ashamed to be suspected of half her economical practices;—pursuing her own interest in every thought, courting the favour of Colonel Brandon, of Mrs. Jennings, and of every wealthy friend. In Edward—she knew not what she saw, nor what she wished to see;—happy or unhappy,—nothing pleased her; she turned away her head from every sketch of him. (ch. 48:347)

> We may believe, then, that when Elinor expounded the Edward-Lucy-Elinor situation for her sister, her spirits were still being severely tried by it.

I think we must admit the intellectual in Elinor somewhat flounders here. We remember that at the end of her constrained battle with Lucy, an ending "to which both of them submitted without any reluctance," Elinor had "sat down to the card table with the melancholy persuasion that Edward . . . had not even the chance of being tolerably happy in marriage, which sincere affection on [Lucy's] side would have given" (ch. 24:168). Elinor is nonetheless entitled upon cooler reflection to revise an opinion formed immediately after an unpleasant verbal duel, without being read as dishonest with Marianne. The two grounds on which she founds her belief in Edward's prospective happiness with Lucy may manifest more the rationalist in Elinor than the rationalizer. First is the view, of ancient and respectable lineage, that a man who always does his duty must in the long run be happy. Second, and perhaps more surprising in Elinor, is the view that "sense . . . is the foundation upon which every thing good may be built." (She puts sense before character?) Nevertheless, if we allow "sense" to mean here being thoroughly sensible in the ordinary affairs of life, this is, though somewhat pagan, surely a respectable view. Did she believe Lucy had this sort of intelligence? Yes. That is how one reads Elinor's early observation that "Lucy was naturally clever; her remarks were often just and amusing . . . but her powers had received no aid from education. . . . Elinor saw, and pitied her for, the neglect of abilities which education might have rendered respectable" (ch. 22:149). However, Elinor is now simply discounting, without justification offered, what she is also reported as seeing in Lucy: her "thorough want of delicacy, of rectitude, and integrity of mind," not to mention her being "illiterate, artful, and selfish," while Edward is so much the opposite (ch. 22:149, 23:158). Of course the fact that Elinor picks out only sense in Lucy as the basis for being hopeful shows that she has not forgotten Lucy's failings. But in reassuring Marianne she discounts these failings, without offering an explanation for doing so.

As to the antiromantic arrow she lets loose at Marianne in favor of the possible ending of one love and growth of another, there is no doubt Elinor does believe in this, for it came up in an earlier discussion with Colonel Brandon, who remarked:

"Your sister, I understand, does not approve of second attachments."

"No," replied Elinor, "her opinions are all romantic."

"Or rather, as I believe, she considers them impossible to exist."

"I believe she does. But how she contrives it without reflecting on the character of her own father, who had himself two wives, I know not." (ch. 12:86)

This is eminently reasonable. Its application to Edward and his two loves, however, is less so. In short, Elinor as intellectual is human enough: I cannot make out her hopeful prognosis for Edward as a calculated effort merely to mislead Marianne; rather, in her own interest Elinor seems to succumb to some contortion of her thought—at least for the moment.

Having read Elinor's explanation with Marianne that way, I have to admit that an alternative interpretation is not implausible: this reading takes Elinor's contortional moves to be more strongly motivated by her desire to keep Marianne's emotional temperature down than I find them to be, so that Elinor is not deceiving herself, only Marianne. My own belief is that Austen would have given us some explicit sign if she had meant Elinor to be here disingenuous with Marianne; but I find none.

I end my focus on Elinor Dashwood as an intellectual with a rather striking instance of what Alison Sulloway calls Austen's "techniques of simultaneous revelation and concealment" of her feminist sorties.[4] The "concealment" on this occasion consists in a largely indirect manifestation of Elinor's life as an intellectual; the "revelation" occurs through her mother's mimicking the logician's skeptical questioning she anticipates from conversation with Elinor when matters of moment are in hand. In this camouflaged maneuver, the gender reform embodied in Elinor is nonetheless revealed by the paradigmatically patriarchal role the mother assigns to her daughter: Elinor is enacted by her mother as an analytical intellect dashing with cold logic the romantic hope dear to a more "feminine" heart.

Indeed by returning all the way to the first chapter, we find Elinor there portrayed in a role clearly far more "standard" for the husband of a mother of marriageable daughters than for either a daughter or even the mother herself. There Elinor is said to have the "strength of understanding, and coolness of judgment . . . to be the counselor of her mother and . . . frequently to counteract . . . that eagerness of mind in Mrs. Dashwood which must generally have led to imprudence" (ch. 1:42).

Much later, in chapter 15, Elinor and her mother try to understand the shocking manner of Willoughby's departure from their neighborhood. The "simultaneous revelation and concealment" of Austen's gender reform works here in this way: the style of skeptical logician shows itself not directly in Elinor's conversation but in emotionally romantic Mrs. Dashwood, who is presented as shaping at least the rhetorical form of her reasoning discourse with Elinor into a structure not natural to her but learned by her from long experience of Elinor's critical, even skeptical habits of thought. Mrs. Dashwood begins a reassuring explanation of Willoughby's behavior with unnatural awareness of her own fallibility: "You, Elinor, who love to doubt where you can—it will not satisfy you, I know." She ends her hopeful interpretation of Willoughby's conduct with an equally uncharacteristic acknowledgment of alternative explanations:

"You will tell me, I know, that this may, or may *not* have happened; but I will listen to no cavil, unless you can point out any other method of understanding the affair as satisfactory as this. And now, Elinor, what have you to say?"

"Nothing, for you have anticipated my answer."

"Then you would have told me that it might or might not have happened. Oh! Elinor, how incomprehensible are your feelings! You had rather take evil upon credit than good. You had rather look out for misery for Marianne and guilt for poor Willoughby, than an apology for the latter. . . . Are no probabilities to be accepted, merely because they are not certainties? Is nothing due to the man whom we have all so much reason to love, and no reason in the world to think ill of?" (ch. 15:105-6)

Of course clearheaded Elinor's problem with this last remark is that they now have one reason to think ill of Willoughby, his sudden, strange departure. Of the role of another piece of disconfirming evidence, Elinor has this to say: "I confess . . . that every circumstance except *one* is in favour of their engagement; but that *one* is the total silence of both on the subject, and with me it almost outweighs every other" (ch. 15:107). Mrs. Dashwood exemplifies a common confusion of skepticism with both cynicism and pessimism when she upbraids Elinor with "You had rather take evil upon credit than good." The outlook of the cynic is itself a failing considered so stereotypically masculine that it is more or less tolerated in men but abhorred in women. In fact, Elinor has no inclination toward either cynicism or pessimism; her principled skepticism is nonetheless both a common mark of the intellectual, hence of the male in her era, and an excluded ingredient of the socially constructed concept of genteel feminine gender.

Austen has been careful, however, to make Elinor's skepticism subject to lapses where love enters. When Edward sprang on them his own milder version of an unexpected and incomprehensibly early departure from them,

> Elinor placed all that was astonishing in this way of acting to his mother's account; and it was happy for her that he had a mother whose character was so imperfectly known to her, as to be the general excuse for everything strange on the part of her son. . . . She was very well disposed . . . to regard his actions with all the . . . generous qualifications, which had been rather more painfully extorted from her, for Willoughby's service, by her mother. (ch. 19:126)

This is all very well, but the cases of Edward and Willoughby are so different that Austen's conflating them must be taken as only half serious. Perhaps, too, on behalf of Elinor's larger generosity, we should not let pass unnoticed how tender her earliest response to Willoughby had been. When Elinor's mother rhetorically asked about Willoughby, "Can he be deceitful?" Elinor replied: "I hope not, I believe not. . . . I love Willoughby, sincerely love him; and suspicion of his integrity cannot be more painful to yourself than to me" (ch. 15:108). The novel as a whole confirms as truthful this spontaneous expression of her early—and renewable—affection for Willoughby. We shall find occasion, two chapters further on, to take a closer look at Elinor's emotional life. She *is* an intellectual. She is *not* a cold one.

Notes

[1] Stuart Tave, *Some Words of Jane Austen* (Chicago: Univ. of Chicago Press, 1973), 96-97.

[2] Since Austen was born in December 1775, she would not have been twenty until the last month of 1795. She rewrote the novel in 1797 and revised it again in her mid-thirties before submitting it to the public in 1811.

[3] Julia Prewitt Brown, *Jane Austen's Novels: Social Change and Literary Form,* (Cambridge: Harvard Univ. Press, 1979), 45. My epigraph for the present book can be found on p. 155.

[4] [Alison G.] Sulloway, *Jane Austen and the Province of Womanhood* [(Philadelphia: Univ. of Pennsylvania Press, 1989),] 167.

FURTHER READING

Criticism

Easton, Celia A. "*Sense and Sensibility* and Joke of Substitution." *The Journal of Narrative Technique* 23, No. 2 (Spring 1993): 114-26.

Discusses how Austen's use of the ironic "stand-in effect" keeps the reader and the novel's characters in suspenseful delusion.

Harding, D. W. "The Supposed Letter Form of *Sense and Sensibility.*" *Notes and Queries* n.s. 40, No. 4 (December 1993): 464-66.

Disputes the notion that *Sense and Sensibility* was originally in letter form and proposes that *Pride and Prejudice* was the far likelier candidate.

Kaplan, Deborah. "Achieving Authority: Jane Austen's First Published Novel." *Nineteenth-Century Literature* 37, No. 4 (March 1983): 531-51.

Examines *Sense and Sensibility* to discover Austen's accommodation of femininity and authority.

Lock, F. P. "The Geology of *Sense and Sensibility.*" In *The Yearbook of English Studies.* Theatrical Literature Special Number, Vol. 9. Edited by G. K. Hunter and C. J. Rawson, pp. 246-55. Modern Humanities Research Association, 1979.

Discusses various critics' interpretations of the origins and shaping of *Sense and Sensibility.*

Meyersohn, Marylea. "Jane Austen's Garrulous Speakers: Social Criticism in *Sense and Sensibility, Emma,* and *Persuasion.*" In *Reading and Writing Women's Lives: A Study of the Novel of Manners,* edited by Bege K. Bowers and Barbara Brothers, pp. 35-48. Ann Arbor: UMI Research Press, 1990.

Demonstrates how the dialogues of Austen's characters in her "novels of manners" offer insights into her beliefs about the social function of rational discourse.

Moler, Kenneth L. "*Sense and Sensibility* and the 'Sensible Sister.'" In *Jane Austen's Art of Illusion,* by Kenneth L. Moler, pp. 43-74. Lincoln: University of Nebraska Press, 1968.

Refutes the common perception by readers that Austen favors Elinor over Marianne.

Monaghan, David, ed. *Jane Austen in a Social Context.* London: Macmillan, 1981, 199 p.

Collection of eleven essays on various aspects of Austen's novels.

Nollen, Elizabeth. "Ann Radcliffe's *A Sicilian Romance*: A New Source for Jane Austen's *Sense and Sensibility.*" *English Language Notes* 22, No. 2 (December 1984): 30-37.

Briefly discusses the similarities between the two novels, focusing on each pair of sisters.

Schaffer, Julie A. "The Ideological Intervention of Ambiguities in the Marriage Plot: Who Fails Marianne in Austen's *Sense and Sensibility?,*" pp. 128-51. In *A Dialogue of Voices: Feminist Literary Theory and Bakhtin,* edited by Karen Hohne and Helen Wussow, Minneapolis: University of Minnesota Press, 1994.

Argues that uniting the interests of feminist criticism with a Bakhtinian view of novels as dialogic discourse makes possible the likeability of Marianne and her view of life and makes it meaningful to the novel's overall project.

Shoben, Edward Joseph, Jr. "Impulse and Virtue in Jane Austen: *Sense and Sensibility* in Two Centuries." *The Hudson Review* 35, No. 4 (Winter 1982-83): 521-39.

Uses the two primary characters to illustrate the "complexity and depth of Jane Austen's psychological insights."

Smith, Phoebe A. "*Sense and Sensibility* and 'The Lady's Law': The Failure of Benevolent Paternalism." *The CEA Critic* 55, No. 3 (Spring/Summer 1993): 3-25.

Shows how the legal situation of women in the late eighteenth and early nineteenth centuries affects the narrative movement and participates in the construction of character in the novel.

Spacks, Patricia Meyer. "The Difference It Makes." *Soundings* 64, No. 4 (Winter 1981): 343-60.

Overview of how feminist criticism offers new "ways of seeing" and valuing female experience, using Austen's novels as examples.

Additional coverage of Austen's life and career is contained in the following source published by The Gale Group: *World Literature Criticism, 1500 to the Present.*

Oliver Wendell Holmes

1809-1894

American essayist, poet, novelist, and biographer.

For additional information on Holmes's life and works, see *NCLC*, Volume 14.

INTRODUCTION

Oliver Wendell Holmes is considered one of the most versatile American authors of the nineteenth-century. Although he wrote in a wide variety of genres, he is best known for his popular collection of essays, *The Breakfast-Table Series*. Critics believe that these fictional conversations provided Holmes with the ideal medium for expressing his views on humankind and its institutions and for acting, as he put it, as "his own Boswell." Holmes's novels, too, have attracted the interest of scholars. In these, most notably in *Elsie Venner*, Holmes incorporated his pioneering theories of psychology and clarified his arguments against Calvinism and the concept of original sin. In addition to his literary works, Holmes was respected for his controversial scientific essays and for his brilliant skill as a conversationalist. Holmes's reputation has diminished considerably in recent years. Perhaps the most famous and important figure in Boston intellectual circles during the second half of the nineteenth-century, he is remembered now chiefly for the sparkling wit of *The Autocrat* and for the spirit of free inquiry demonstrated by the wide range of his interests.

Biographical Information

Holmes was born in Cambridge, Massachusetts, in 1809 to Sarah Wendell Holmes and the Reverend Abiel Holmes. A Calvinist minister, the Reverend Holmes was forced out of his parish in 1829 as a result of a conflict between the conservative and liberal factions within his congregation. For the young Oliver Holmes, this event, as well as his early religious training, engendered a lifelong antagonism toward the Puritan strictures of Calvinism—an antagonism that critics trace throughout his literary and scientific writings. Holmes attended Phillips Academy at Andover from 1824 to 1825 and then entered Harvard University. Losing interest in his law studies, he transferred to medicine. After taking advanced courses in Paris in 1833, he returned to Harvard and completed the requirements for his medical degree in 1836. Holmes practiced as a personal physician until 1839 when he was appointed to a professorship at

Dartmouth College. The following year, he married Amelia Lee Jackson with whom he had three children. Holmes achieved distinction during the 1840s and 1850s as a teacher and scientific writer, and he later won great respect as Dean of the Harvard Medical School. He was also active on the lecture circuit, speaking on a wide variety of medical topics. In his 1842 essay, *Homeopathy and Its Kindred Delusions*, Holmes demonstrated the futility and danger of some existing medical treatments. For example, in *The Contagiousness of Puerperal Fever* (1843), he suggested that physicians themselves could be the carriers of disease. Despite the uproar of criticism that his essays elicited, he held his ground. Holmes retired from Harvard in 1882 and remained active as a writer and public speaker. Having outlived most of his family and friends, he died at the age of eighty-five.

Major Works

While his medical career was flourishing, Holmes was also gaining respect as a poet. He first caught the attention of the public in 1830 with the publication in a Boston newspaper of "Old Ironsides," a poem protesting the government's plans to dismantle the frigate *U.S.S. Constitution*. The poem touched a patriotic nerve, and the ensuing public outcry saved the ship from destruction. Buoyed by his early popular success, Holmes published *Poems* in 1836; expanded and revised editions of the collection followed in 1846, 1848, and 1849. Holmes wrote much serious poetry but his output also included a large number of occasional verses composed in either heroic and octosyllabic couplets or in the meter of the folk ballad. Most of Holmes's poems express his views about the human condition and his hopes for its improvement. In "The Chambered Nautilus," for example, Holmes speculated on the growth of the soul and in "The Last Leaf," he depicted the problems of old age. Holmes is generally considered neither an innovator nor an influence on the development of American poetry, and many commentators point out that his style derives from the neo-classicism of the Augustan age of eighteenth-century England. Nevertheless, critics consistently note that he successfully used poetry as a forum for expressing his philosophy, particularly in such pieces as "The Deacon's Masterpiece; or The Wonderful 'One-Hoss Shay,'" his strongest poetic statement against Calvinism. Holmes's approach to writing also demonstrates his scientific bent: he claimed that his meter was modeled on the pulse and respiration rate of a speaker reading poetry aloud. Scholars affirm that his many later collections, including *Songs in Many Keys*, *Soundings from the Atlantic*, *Songs of Many Seasons*, and *The Last Leaf*, attest to the endurance of Holmes's poetic gift.

Already an established poet, Holmes began writing prose pieces in 1858 for the *Atlantic Monthly* at the invitation of its editor, James Russell Lowell. Holmes's first contributions, which were later collected as *The Autocrat*, present the breakfast-table conversations of a fictional group of boarding house residents, narrated by a member nicknamed "the autocrat." Complete with well-developed characters and plot this work is difficult to place within a genre but is most often classified as a collection of essays. *The Autocrat* achieved enormous popular and critical success and helped to establish the *Atlantic Monthly*'s reputation. While some pieces were humorous, others contained Holmes's ideas for changing society and still others satirized various aspects of Calvinism. Holmes especially delighted in debunking "any logical system . . . supposed by its authors to be perfect, uncorrectable, and therefore, everlasting." *The Autocrat* was followed by *The Professor at the Breakfast-Table* (1860), *The Poet at the Breakfast-Table* (1872), and *Over the Teacups* (1891). These four collections comprise what is usually referred to as the Breakfast-Table series.

Just as he had used the Breakfast-Table books to present his views on society, Holmes utilized his so-called "medicated novels" to explore the causes and treatment of aberrant behavior. *Elsie Venner*, *The Guardian Angel*, and *A Mortal Antipathy* strongly attest to Holmes's scientific interest. Critics are divided on how to categorize these works: some consider them novels concerned with psychology, some regard them as scientific treatises presented in a fictional framework, and others claim that Holmes's novels are not about science, but about morality. In the first, *Elsie Venner*, which originally appeared serially in the *Atlantic Monthly* as *The Professor's Story*, Holmes created a protagonist who is believed to be part human and part serpent as a result of a prenatal snakebite. In this novel, Holmes presents discourses on topics such as prejudice, the Calvinist concept of original sin, and human psychology and sexuality. Most critics contend that *Elsie Venner* lacks artistic merit although the same critics argue that Holmes's perceptive character studies anticipate the psychological theories of Sigmund Freud and Carl Jung. In *The Guardian Angel*, Holmes discussed the influences of heredity and environment on mental and physical health. The novel also warns against a Puritan upbringing for children. *A Moral Antipathy*, which ran serially in the *Atlantic Monthly* as *The New Portfolio*, deals with the causes and cures of childhood trauma. Commentators stress that the issues in these "medicated novels" derive from their author's background as a scientist. Indeed, in each, the characters seek out doctors and professors for help—suggesting that Holmes looked to science, not theology, to provide the answers for humanity's complex problems.

Critical Reception

Criticism of Holmes's literary efforts is as varied as his fields of expertise, and a consensus of opinion is difficult to find. Scholars have debated whether he is predominantly a literary figure or predominantly a scientist, focusing on the frequent incorporation of medical themes and terminology into his works. Critics S. I. Hayakawa and Howard Mumford Jones argued that those who view Holmes primarily as an artist overlook his most important quality: his scientific interest. They also point out that his essays on medical topics exhibit his best prose, free of Victorian constraints. Other commentators, both in the nineteenth and twentieth centuries, have chosen not to acknowledge Holmes's scientific career as a primary element of his work, having emphasized, instead, his role as an author.

In assessments of Holmes as a writer, emphasis has shifted over time from his poetry to his fictional essays and then to his novels. While early critics of his poetry stressed his humor, wit, and patriotism, some stated that his poetry was shallow and dilettantish, and Holmes himself noted in a preface to an 1862 collection that his poetic promise remained unfulfilled. After he published *The Autocrat*, critics transferred their attention to his prose. Some reviewers praised his versatility and wit, while others denounced the provincialism, elitism, and political conservatism of his sketches. In addition, Holmes's privileged financial and social position led to charges of insularity: many critics faulted his failure to support the abolitionist and women's rights movements. Conversely, his sympathizers point out that despite his limited contact with persons and ideas outside of New England, Holmes was expansive in his interests and expertise, and the didactic tone of much of his writing can be read as his concern for the welfare of others. However, it is Holmes's novels that have proven most interesting to twentieth-century critics. Controversial when published because of their intimate look at human physiology and psychology, they remain so today. While *The Autocrat* is still considered his best work, all of Holmes's novels have attracted attention from modern critics who praise them as important early psychological studies.

Although still valued for his contributions to literature, science, theology, and psychology, Holmes is no longer as popular with readers as he once was. Despite this diminution of his reputation, which many critics attribute to the decline of New England's influence on American culture, Holmes and his writings still attract considerable commentary. Today, *The Autocrat*, likened by Virginia Woolf to the taste of "champagne after breakfast cups of weak tea," continues to occupy an important place in American literature.

---

*PRINCIPAL WORKS

Poems (poetry) 1836; also published in revised form as *Poems*, 1846, 1848, 1849
Homeopathy and Its Kindred Delusions (essay) 1842
The Contagiousness of Puerperal Fever (essay) 1843
Urania: A Rhymed Lesson (poetry) 1846
Astraea: The Balance of Illusions (poetry) 1850
The Autocrat of the Breakfast-Table (essays) 1858
The Professor at the Breakfast-Table (essays) 1860
Currents and Counter-Currents in Medical Science (essays) 1861
Elsie Venner: A Romance of Destiny (novel) 1861
Songs in Many Keys (poetry) 1862
Soundings from the Atlantic (poetry) 1864
The Guardian Angel (novel) 1867
Mechanism in Thought and Morals (essay) 1871
The Poet at the Breakfast-Table (essays) 1872
"Crime and Automatism" (essay) 1875; published in periodical *Atlantic Monthly*

Songs of Many Seasons (poetry) 1875
John Lothrop Motley (memoir) 1879
The School-Boy (poetry) 1879
The Iron Gate, and Other Poems (poetry) 1880
Medical Essays, 1842-1882 (essays) 1883
Pages from an Old Volume of Life (essays) 1883
A Moral Antipathy: First Opening of the New Portfolio (novel) 1885
Ralph Waldo Emerson (biography) 1885
The Last Leaf (poetry) 1886
One Hundred Days in Europe (diary) 1887
Before the Curfew, and Other Poems (poetry) 1888
Memoir of Henry Jacob Bigelow (memoir) 1891
Over the Teacups (essays) 1891
The Writings of Oliver Wendell Holmes. 13 vols. (novels, essays, poetry, diary, biography, and memoir) 1891-92
The Poetical Works of Oliver Wendell Holmes (poetry) 1975

*Many of Holmes's works were first published in the *Atlantic Monthly*.

CRITICISM

Miriam Rossiter Small (essay date 1962)

SOURCE: "The Breakfast-Table Series," in *Oliver Wendell Holmes,* Twayne Publishers, Inc., 1962, pp. 88-115.

[*In the following essay, Small analyzes the various pieces that make up the Breakfast-Table series. In each, Holmes created a different main character in order to emphasize and illustrate various issues in society that concerned him.*]

In December, 1884, when Holmes was opening the "New Portfolio" with his third and last novel *A Mortal Antipathy,* he devoted the first number to an introduction in which he talked over with "the whole family of readers belonging to my list of intimates" (VII [1]-32) his career as a man of letters up to that time. His first Portfolio began with the poems for occasions and for the "showy annuals," but its contents had "boyhood written on every page." The "best scraps" he justly selected from the first Portfolio were "Old Ironsides . . . a single passionate outcry when the old war-ship I had read about . . . was threatened with demolition"; and "The Last Leaf" suggested by old Major Melville in his cocked hat and breeches. The second Portfolio was opened in the autumn of 1857, when the *Atlantic Monthly* "which I had the honor of naming was started by the enterprising firm of Phillips & Sampson, under the editorship of Mr. James Russell Lowell."

After the success of the magazine was assured, Holmes and Lowell each generously cited the part the other had played in that achievement. It cannot now be accurately measured how much urging Holmes needed to set down in print the kind of talk which had made him sought after as companion and speaker at gatherings formal and informal. Whether coincidental or causative, Lowell as editor and Holmes as the writer of an easy, concrete prose neatly alternating with poems that gave emphasis or variety, helped to make successful the first literary magazine in this country to have an enduring life. The *Atlantic* could take advantage of many talents: the melody of Longfellow; the lyric intensity of Whittier; the fascinating thought and expression of Emerson; the haunting power of Hawthorne, "the great Romancer"; and the vivid exposition of the scientist Agassiz and the diplomat Motley. Besides all these, to balance the more radical reformers like Underwood and Lowell who had cut their editorial teeth on abolitionist papers, Holmes's record indicated he could be counted upon for brief and witty comment; if he did ridicule, surprise and recognition removed the sting.

I The Autocrat

When Holmes wrote the opening number of *The Autocrat of the Breakfast-Table,* as Autocrat he took up the advantages of Societies of Mutual Admiration, with "the young man named John" and the divinity student dissenting. He cited as an example the *Société de l'Observation Médicale* to which he had belonged in Paris, and an American club of which he was not a member but which thrived on the well-deserved admiration exchanged among the generous company of "artists, authors, philanthropists, men of science." That he was not a member of the Saturday Club until October 31, before the first number of the *Atlantic* appeared in November, 1857, was probably because, with other studies and duties, he was "outside of the charmed circle drawn around the scholars and poets of Cambridge and Concord" (VII, 10). The club met the last Saturday of each month at the Parker House in Boston.

At his class dinners Holmes had come to take it for granted that he would play an important part, by warm loyalty, by quick repartee, and by reading at least one poem. Although many of "The Boys" were wealthier or of higher social background than he, his place was secure. But the Saturday Club was a place of exchange rather than performance; and although both Lowell and Holmes inclined to take over as if on the lecture platform, such self-indulgence came later rather than at the beginning of his membership, when Holmes was gratified to be accepted in the group headed by Longfellow and Agassiz and including Emerson and Hawthorne, the lawyers Rockwood Hoar and Richard Henry Dana, and the society leaders Sam Ward and Tom Appleton. The anecdote which tells of the meeting of the club after the *Atlantic* had just come out when each member sat down quietly to read his own contribution is probably not a gross exaggeration. That both Lowell and Holmes were quick of wit and word and enjoyed a verbal fencing-match gives substance to the story that when the Saturday Club entertained the Reverend Calvin Stowe and his wife Harriet Beecher, at one end of the table Lowell was busy proving to the daughter of the crusading Beechers and the author of *Uncle Tom's Cabin* that Fielding's lusty *Tom Jones* was the greatest novel ever written while at the other end Holmes was explaining to the Reverend Calvin Stowe that people learned their swearing from ministers in the pulpit.

The Saturday Club and the *Atlantic Monthly* were two important outlets for Holmes which also enriched his life. The people concerned with the new magazine were frankly amazed at the immediate popularity of *The Autocrat of the Breakfast-Table.* The title and pattern depended on the dramatic scene Holmes had first created twenty-five years earlier; the Autocrat was now more experienced and assured and the other figures more sharply etched, often more recognizable as types, like "the economically organized female in the black bombazine." Holmes remarked it was "dipped from the running stream of my thoughts." An important key to its success was that it answered so well the second reason Holmes gave as justification for an author: the first was if he had a story to tell that everyone wanted to hear; the second, "if he can put in fitting words any common experiences not already well told, so that readers will say, 'Why, yes! I have had that sensation, thought, emotion, a hundred times, but I never heard it spoken of before, and I never saw any mention of it in print'" (I, 12).

The pleasure readers still derive from the books of the Breakfast-Table series is that of recognition, with a subsequent quickening of interest to find out what the author has made of the human interplay he has developed. The richness Holmes offered in his treatment was only rarely of philosophical depth or lyrical intensity, but frequent analogies with concrete vividness threw light on some aspect of a situation we all recognize. Thus Truth was contrasted with "an old lying falsehood" in the shape of a flat stone that kills normal growth and breeds "hideous crawling creatures" which come to light when the stone is turned over by one who "puts the staff of truth to the old lying incubus"; children are early given a choice between the cubes of truth which won't roll, have "a great talent for standing still, and always keep right side up" and the spheres of lies "which are the most convenient things in the world" because they roll so easily, but "are apt to roll into the wrong corner, and to get out of his way when he most wants them" (I, 111-16). Sprinkled among these concrete images which suggest more than they say are brief quotable statements: "Good feeling helps society to make liars of most of us—not absolute liars, but such careless handlers of truth that its sharp corners get terribly rounded"; or, at the opening of the next number, "Sin has many tools, but a lie is the handle which fits them all."

Familiar diction gives an extra tang to comments like "All lecturers, all professors, all schoolmasters, have ruts and grooves into which their conversation is perpetually sliding" (I, 65): "habit is a labor-saving invention which enables a man to get along with less fuel" (I, 155); "They [cant or slang terms instead of precise words] are the blank checks of intellectual bankruptcy;—you may fill them up with what idea you like; it makes no difference, for there are no funds in the treasury upon which they are drawn" (I, 256). Figures contributed to the sharp effects, and were quick and suggested in a word or two or followed through with growing relevance, as in his picture of human feelings:

> Every person's feelings have a front-door and a side-door by which they must be entered. The front-door is on the street. . . . This front-door leads into a passage which opens into an anteroom, and this into the interior apartments. The side-door opens at once into the sacred chambers. . . .
>
> Be very careful to whom you trust one of these keys of the side-door. The fact of possessing one renders those even who are dear to you very terrible at times. You can keep the world from your front-door, or receive visitors only when you are ready for them; but those of your own flesh and blood, or of certain grades of intimacy, can come in at the side-door, if they will, at any hour or in any mood. . . .
>
> No stranger can get a great many notes of torture out of a human soul; it takes one that knows it well,—parent, child, brother, sister, intimate. Be very careful to whom you give a side-door key; too many have them already (I, 128-30).

Dramatic interplay gives variety, and makes extreme statements acceptable or ridiculous. The landlady is primarily concerned with keeping her boarders; her son Benjamin Franklin proves convenient for errands, for interruptions, for instruction in French and Latin. The Poor Relation provides an acid touch, but the most effective dissenter is the young fellow named John, who has both feet on the ground as well as active voice and hands. When the Autocrat has outlined psychologically the six personalities taking part in a dialogue between John and Thomas—"I. The real John; known only to his Maker. / 2. John's ideal John; never the real one, and often very unlike him. / 3. Thomas's ideal John; never the real John, nor John's John, but often very unlike either" and three similar

Thomases (I, 53)—the literal John took the remaining peaches in the basket before it reached the Autocrat, since "there was just one apiece for him." The divinity student and the old gentleman opposite speak up less frequently; the former is the voice of dogma, the latter is wise in years and experience. The school-mistress is a contrast to the landlady's daughter in appearance, taste, and manner, and she provides the romantic finale as she and the Autocrat take "the long path together." The Autocrat hints that the romance comes at the request of his readers: they, especially the women, were as advisory as to what should happen in the next number as Richardson's had been about what should happen to Pamela and Clarissa Harlowe. It was Holmes's fault; he admitted, "I purr very loud over a good honest letter that says pretty things to me" (I, 289).

Holmes often uses his intimacy with his readers to give them advice: although he is not so didactic as the modern *How To Read A Book* (he would surely have preferred *How To Read Two Books*), he asks that his readers be creative; that they realize the "saturation-point of each mind differs" (I, 133); that the reader's imagination is needed to transfigure "a string of trivialities" (I, 199). Holmes states a preference for life over books that recalls Emerson's *American Scholar* which he had heard at Harvard in 1837. After distinguishing between the use and abuse of books, Emerson asserted: "Books are for the scholar's idle times. When he can read God directly, the hour is too precious to be wasted in other men's transcripts of their readings." Holmes accents the mind: "there are times in which every active mind feels itself above any and all human books"; or he asserts: "I always believed in life rather than in books" (I, 132, 134). Like Dr. Johnson too in finding books no substitute for life, Holmes announced the game he was playing with the eighteenth-century *magister* by his subtitle here: "Every Man His Own Boswell." The most detailed account of the game of identity Holmes gave on December 13, 1884, when "I have just lost my dear and honored contemporary of the last century." Since Johnson was baptized on the day he was born and Holmes not for three weeks, the date, September 18, was the same in 1709 and 1809. "Year by year, and almost month by month, my life has kept pace in this century with his life in the last century. . . . It was for me a kind of unison between two instruments, both playing that old familiar air, 'Life,'—one a bassoon, if you will, and the other an oaten pipe" (VII, 20-21).

The Autocrat has to share the stage with two facets of Holmes's career already established—the Poet and the Professor: " . . . I think myself fortunate in having the Poet and the Professor for my intimates. We are so much together, that we no doubt think and talk a good deal alike; yet our points of view are in many respects individual and peculiar" (I, 178-79). The Poet offers only one poem, the occasional **"A Good Time Go-ing"** (I, 223-24; 155-56), which Holmes had written for a farewell dinner for Charles Mackay on May 18, 1858. The preface to the poem in the *Autocrat* explains how eager the Poet is to leave town before the anniversaries begin and he will have to "get up and make speeches, or songs, or toasts." Like the poem, the protest here is perfunctory and lifeless compared to the fireworks of the Autocrat's talk or the vivacity Holmes could muster on this subject in a letter to T. W. Higginson on September 30, 1872, after he had been succumbing to such demands for another ten years.

> Your kind words are pleasant and your request is far from unreasonable, yet I must excuse myself from the very slight task—as it seems at least—to which you invite me.
>
> I am thoroughly tired of my own voice at all sorts of occasional gatherings. I have handled the epithets of eulogy until the mere touch of a warm adjective blisters my palm. I have tried not to do myself discredit by unseemly flattery, but I do really feel as if by force of repetition my welcomes were growing if not unwelcome, at least outworn, and should in common propriety give place to something a little fresher. I have greeted representatives from all parts of the civilized and half-civilized world and am expecting to be called on whenever the King of Dahomey or a minister from Ujiji makes his appearance.
>
> The most desperate attempts were made by men with argument and women with entreaty to get me to play Orpheus to the stones of the Pittsfield monument, but I resisted both successfully. These invitations keep coming to me all the time, and I mean to decline them all unless for some very special reason that happens to strike me full in the centre of volition. Here are Froude, and Edmund Yates, and George MacDonald, and nobody knows how many more—Tyndall and by and by perhaps Huxley and one must draw the line somewhere—suppose we say "Rhyming done here only for crowned heads or their representatives?" I have done England, France, Russia (twice), China, Japan, Germany (in the person of Ehrenberg) and so belabored my own countrymen of every degree with occasional verses that I must have coupled "name" and "fame" together scores of times and made "story" and "glory" as intimate as if they had been born twins.
>
> I know you are on your knees by this time asking the Lord to forgive you for making a suggestion that I should try this last experiment on the patience of mankind. I cannot say whether He will forgive you or not but you have my full pardon inasmuch as you have joined a very complimentary request with a word of praise which coming from so good a judge of what will bear praising makes me willing to do almost anything except what you ask me to.[1]

This delightful play of concrete detail, exaggeration, colorful diction combined with the winning personal tone of the verbal *tour de force* at the end reveals Holmes still writing, on occasion in 1872, as he had written for *The Autocrat* in 1857-58. It is as Holmes the talker that the Autocrat shines: "Sometimes it becomes almost a physical necessity to talk out what is in the mind, before putting anything else into it" (I, 134) helps explain the social trait he was famous for. "Real talkers" are defined as "people with fresh ideas, of course, and plenty of good warm words to dress them in" (I, 143). But the Autocrat warns against wit; an author is not pleased to be told he is droll because he knows, like the clown, that the women are not in love with him but with "the fellow in the black coat and plumed hat" and that his place is "at the tail of the procession." A figure of white light in contrast to colored lights, which is one of the "grooves" into which Holmes's "conversation is perpetually sliding," illuminates his estimate of wit. A single ray of color—red, yellow, blue—illustrates that wit. "consists in a partial and incomplete view of whatever it touches. . . . We get beautiful effects from wit,—all the prismatic colors,—but never the object as it is in fair daylight. . . . Poetry uses the rainbow tints for special effects, but always keeps its essential object in the purest white light of truth" (I, 50). Within a paragraph contrasting lights have led him from *wit* to *poetry*. To illustrate how easily he could slide into this "groove" and how genuinely he could fuse the truth of poetry with the truth of religion, another use of this figure in a letter to a lady who was trying to interest him in her newly adopted religion, Roman Catholicism, may be cited:

> I think myself that this planet is lighted by a stained window. One sees through a blue pane, another through a red or yellow one—but outside the light is white, and those see it most truly who are next an *open* window.
>
> But I do not quarrel with this saint because he (or she more likely) is in a patch of blue light or with that other because she is in a yellow one. The accidents of your church please my taste and stimulate my imagination. I love the pictures, the incense, the tingling of the boyish choristers' voices. There is the difference between your service and the puritan preachment that there is between the maple in October, dressed in its flaming robes, and the same tree in January naked in the blast. But the course of nature is that the painted leaves must fall, and the bare tree bud with new foliage.[2]

The Autocrat is rich in biographical intimacies of Holmes. His moving to Charles Street in 1858 had meant that the Charles River was his backyard, and he could indulge in boating, the outdoor activity he enjoyed next after riding and driving fast horses, which had become expensive and inconvenient with the

Pittsfield vacations gone. The Autocrat gives a full account of the three boats Holmes owned and used on the river, especially the race-boat and the pride he took in his speed and skill rowing on the river and in the bay. Travel in Italy and the voice of a child in Paris are part of the Autocrat's memories, and he uses Holmes's Class Poem for 1854, **"The Old Man Dreams."** He begins a series of three figures with the class and its log of competition, the opening epigrammatic: "I find the great thing in this world is not so much where we stand, as in what direction we are moving" (I, 93). The Derby is used as the image for commencement, and the log is checked through the decades against individual achievements. The third figure is of the sea-shell, the Pearly Nautilus, and the passage closes with Holmes's poetic masterpiece **"The Chambered Nautilus"** (I, 97; 149-50).

The success of this poem, growing out of a close following of one idea through many pages and using as concrete image an object he had long known and studied, argues for the truth of his statement: "Certain things are good for nothing until they have been kept for a long while; and some are good for nothing until they have been kept and used. . . . Of those which must be kept and used I will name three,— meerschaum pipes, violins, and poems" (I, 101). In the poem, "The ship of pearl" is described in the first stanza and wrecked in the second with such suggestive diction as "shadowed main," "webs of living gauze," and "irised ceiling"; the stanza has a special lyric beauty, with the change to the short lines Holmes had early displayed a mastery of. The brevity, the melody, and the artful consistency of image have won it continuing praise, although the proportion of two stanzas for the exposition of the idea as against three for the concrete image is almost too much for the twentieth-century aversion to any *So live's*. But the vocabulary keeps the coils of the shell with the lesson to the end: "Leaving thine outgrown shell by life's unresting sea!"

This poem was one of the two that Osler suggested when he expressed the wish that Holmes would evaluate his own contributions to medicine and to poetry. Osler was writing of doctors who were also men of letters; and, after mentioning Goldsmith and Keats, he continued:

> The most conspicuous modern example of success in both fields is offered by the Autocrat of the Breakfast Table, who for many years occupied the Chair of Anatomy at Harvard, and who as a young man made permanent contributions to practical medicine. In his last book, "Our Hundred Days in Europe," he mentions having sat next to Mr. Lawson Tait at dinner and he suggests the question, "Which would give most satisfaction to a thoroughly humane and unselfish being of cultivated intelligence and lively sense—to have written the plays which Shakespeare

has left for an inheritance to mankind, or to have snatched from the jaws of death scores of suffering women and restored them to a sound and comfortable existence?" I know of no man who could so well make answer to this question as the Autocrat himself. Would he rather go down to posterity as the man who, in this country at least, first roused the profession to a sense of the perils of puerperal fever as an infectious disease—and who thereby has probably saved more lives than Lawson Tait—and whose essay on the subject—*pace* shades of Meigs and Hodge— is a classic in American literature, or would he choose to be remembered as the author of "The Pearly Nautilus" and "The Last Leaf"?

The printed query came to Holmes's attention, and in his reply to Osler he chose to consider only **"The Chambered Nautilus"** as the poem.

> I have rarely been more pleased than by your allusions to an old paper of mine. There was a time certainly in which I would have said that the best page of my record was that in which I had fought my battle for the poor poisoned women. I am reminded of that essay from time to time, but it was published in a periodical which died after one year's life, and therefore escaped the wider notice it would have found if printed in the *American Journal of Medical Sciences*. A lecturer at one of the great London hospitals referred to it the other day and coupled it with some fine phrases about myself which made me blush, either with modesty or vanity, I forget which.

> I think I will not answer the question you put me. I think oftenest of **"The Chambered Nautilus,"** which is a favorite poem of mine, though I wrote it myself. The essay only comes up at long intervals, the poem repeats itself in my memory. And is very often spoken of by correspondents in terms of more than ordinary praise. I had a savage pleasure, I confess, in handling those two Professors—learned men both of them, skillful experts, but babies, as it seemed to me, in their capacity of reasoning and arguing. But in writing the poem I was filled with a better feeling, the highest state of mental exaltation and the most crystalline clairvoyance, as it seemed to me, that had ever been granted to me—I mean that lucid vision of one's thought and all forms of expression which will be at once precise and musical, which is the poet's special gift, however large or small in amount or value. There is more selfish pleasure to be had out of the poem—perhaps a nobler satisfaction from the life-saving labor.[3]

Once again Holmes reveals that he held firm ideas about a poet's experience and expression.

Of the poems the Autocrat gave as his own, the most sentimental and the one which drew the most popular response, especially from women, was **"The Voiceless"** (I, 306-7; 99). It appeared in the parenthesis **"The**

Long Path" which the Autocrat was taking with the schoolmistress, and it was addressed to "hearts that break and give no sign." The last four lines of the stanza were the ones most often requested by autograph collectors or for sale at the many charitable fairs during and after the Civil War. To such charities Holmes sometimes sent as many as a hundred signed autograph copies of specified lines.

> A few can touch the magic string,
> And noisy Fame is proud to win them;—
> Alas for those who never sing,
> And die with all their music in them!

The humorous play the Autocrat often indulged in is illustrated by two of the poems he recited for the group at the Breakfast-Table. One was later given the title **"Ode for a Social Meeting / With slight alterations by a teetotaler"** (I, 48; 162), and it shows Holmes completely recovered from any restraint Lowell's objections might have suggested: in the line " . . . summer's last roses lie hid in the wines," *last roses* is crossed out and *rank poisons* written in, and the last line is altered from "Long live the gay servant that laughs for us all" to "Down, down with the tyrant that masters us all." The poem **"Contentment"** with the epigraph "Man wants but little here below" (I, 268-70; 157-58) reveals a more subtly developed irony than this exercise, and it shows the Autocrat—and Holmes— laughing at the importance both give to ancestors, a library and family portraits, and tasteful elegance. "Simple tastes" are defined as content with "Titians and Raphaels three or four," *one* Stradivarius but *two* Meerschaums, "A ruby and a pearl or so":

> Wealth's wasteful tricks I will not learn,
> Nor ape the glittering upstart fool;—
>
>   . . . . .
>
> Thus humble let me live and die,
> Nor long for Midas' golden touch,
> If Heaven more generous gifts deny,
> I shall not miss them *much,—*
>
>   . . . . .

In *The Autocrat* Holmes saved some of his reminiscences and characteristic verses for the Professor; like Holmes, he had resided at Central Court, at Dartmouth, and along the Housatonic. Literary allusions were divided between the Professor and the Autocrat: the latter spoke tenderly of Cowper's poem about his mother's picture and composed a Houyhnhnm Gazette in which his horses won Swift's Gulliver by offering lilac leaves and hyacinths till his "eyes filled as if with raindrops"; the Professor turned Cicero's "De Senectute" into journalistic English remarks on old age, revising some Latin phrases to match the

familiar English. He shared Holmes's preference for "old-fashioned heroics," although the most professional poem Holmes ever wrote, **"The Living Temple"** (I, 175-76; 101-2), called by the Professor **"The Anatomist's Hymn,"** was in octosyllabic couplets arranged in eight-line stanzas. It shares the wonder at the human body of Fletcher's "Purple Island," but it begins and ends with a tribute to the Divine Maker of "these mystic temples." The Professor also contributed the Class Poem for 1858, **"Mare Rubrum,"** and the farewell to Motley of 1857.

But the professor's real triumph, again in the octosyllabic couplet, was **"The Deacon's Masterpiece; or the Wonderful 'One-Hoss Shay'"** (I, 252-56; 158-60), the success of which puffed him up ridiculously— until he found he could not repeat his success. Anyone familiar with New England dialect is delighted with the "Settler's ellum" that rhymes perfectly with "Couldn't sell 'em." The picturesque narrative is so entertaining that to lay on it a burden of allegory seems intrusive. But the dates of 1755 and 1855 are as carefully given as the proper wood for spokes and thills, crossbars and panels; and, reluctant as the reader may be to accept the tale as an account of the downfall of Calvinism, the stress on *logic*—the subtitle is a "A Logical Story" and the last line is "Logic is logic. That's all I say"—surely points in that direction, especially as the principle of Calvinism developed by Jonathan Edwards and rejected by Holmes was its irrefutable logic. This allegorical reading of the poem is the strongest argument that may be offered against Holmes's being "crippled" by his early orthodox exposure, as he had remarked a child brought up under the shadow of the doctrine of original sin must be. The wound was surely there; but, as Holmes often urged in his medical addresses, nothing is more healing than fresh air and sunshine, here the sunshine of wholesome laughter.

When *The Autocrat of the Breakfast-Table* appeared as a book late in 1859, it was warmly welcomed, as had been the numbers appearing in the *Atlantic Monthly*. It has been the most popular of Holmes's books, and generally regarded as best preserving the talk which his contemporaries maintained was more scintillating and delightful than any of his printed works. Henry James, Sr., told him once: "Holmes, you are intellectually the most alive man I know." As the first of its kind, it had the advantages of originality of form, variety of subject matter, imaginative play with history and literature, and a warm familiar style which won loyal friends then and has continued to win them.[4]

II The Professor

The Professor at the Breakfast-Table suffered from being second on the scene, from being only the *alter ego* of the more lively Autocrat, and from too many serious openings like "I have a long theological talk to relate." As the Autocrat took his leave, hoping "you will love me none the less for anything I have told you," he announced that the Professor was to be his successor. That was in the *Atlantic* for October, 1858, but the Autocrat continued to appear in titles of articles for the November and December numbers in order to get the twelve numbers on a calendar-year basis, a program which the other two in the series and the novels followed. The titles in the November and December issues explained they were filling in: **"A Visit to the Autocrat's Landlady"** and **"The Autocrat gives a Breakfast to the Public."** When the Professor took over in January, 1859, a change was immediately apparent, particularly during the early numbers. The Professor tried to take up his subject, "the great end of being is . . . ," but was interrupted. A new boarder, a vulgar man with dyed hair and a diamond pin dubbed the "Kohinoor," was paying attention to the landlady's daughter; but these, the young man named John, and the divinity student—all are perfunctory and lifeless until the drama of the cripple Little Boston and the warm-hearted Iris develops.

Statements are still made memorable by brief figurative phrasing, as when the Professor replies to the divinity student's warning to stay off important subjects like religion: "Truth is tough. It will not break like a bubble at a touch; nay, you may kick it about all day, like a football, and it will be round and full at evening" (II, 109). Or when he notes wisely of the true artist: "A moment's insight is sometimes worth a life's experience" (II, 239). The Professor is careful to explain he does not call phrenology a pseudo-science; but he points out how it imposes on human gullibility, uses the name of Bumpus & Crane for his practitioners, and by the way they go through a group concludes "They go only by the bumps"— and is interrupted by the boarders' laughter. His incidental comment sometimes gives the same pleasure and surprise of recognition as the Autocrat's did so often, as when he notes we are all surprised by our own pictures; we think we know how we look, but "no genuine expression can be studied by the subject of it in the looking-glass" (II, 190). He also takes a shot at the portrayals of children in contemporary publications; "these tearful records of premature decay" is an apt summary of the popular engravings of ill or dying children in gift-books or the moral tales in a period when Poe gave us Annabel Lee and Harriet Beecher Stowe, little Eva.

Such apt and amusing comment is less frequent in *The Professor* than in *The Autocrat;* also less frequent are vivid scenes from Holmes's experience. An exception is the poem **"The Opening of the Piano"** (II, 73-74; 166-67), when Holmes takes us back to the family in the gambrel-roofed house as the "London-made piano" was opened to the eager

cries of pushing children quieted by the grave father, and the mother's "'Now, Mary, play.'"

The emphasis in this book is more serious and more theological, although in his first indictment the Professor links medicine with religion: homeopathy in medicine and spiritualism in religion are "out of the mouths of fools and cheats" and "the folly of the world . . . confounds the wisdom" (II, 13). The strong language called forth attacks in many church papers and caused some ministers to warn their congregations away from heresy. Many subscriptions to the *Atlantic* were canceled, but not enough to worry the publishers. Holmes did make a scrap-book[5] out of the clippings sent to him or to the editor of attacks in newspapers or magazines; he did not, therefore, so entirely ignore them as he pretended in the prefaces he wrote later and in his refusal to answer.

The Professor uses strong language again when he adds law to medicine and religion: "The three learned professions have but recently emerged from a state of *quasi* barbarism." After citing examples of superstition and cruelty, with all too recent dates, he concludes that primal instincts are violated "when the ideas of the healing art, of the administration of justice, of Christian love, could not exclude systematic poisoning, judicial dueling, and murder for opinion's sake" (II, 105-6). In this book Holmes combines *logic* and Jonathan Edwards in a way which argues that the *logic* in **"The Deacon's Masterpiece"** did point to an allegory of orthodox Calvinism; after reference to the Northampton church's dismissing Edwards, he closes the paragraph: "A man's logical and analytical adjustments are of little consequence, compared to his primary relations with Nature and truth; and people have sense enough to find it out in the long run; they know what 'logic' is worth" (II, 114)—a phrasing only slightly different from "Logic is logic. That's all I say."

The Professor does not use merely the weapon of straight attack, however. Like Swift, Holmes made up names: *Bumpus & Crane* ridiculed phrenology; the *Muggletonians* are called to mind by the divinity student's stubborn dogma. But the figures still do the most to clarify and interest, as with the classification of Broad Church and Narrow. The latter is a garden fenced in; without a forcing system only plants of one zone—arctic, tropical, or temperate—will grow there together. More vivid is the contrast of Broad and Narrow in the figure of boats: the Broad working the pumps on board to save all; the Narrow "in the long boat, in the jolly boat, in the captain's gig, lying off the poor old vessel, thanking God that *they* are safe" (II, 296-98).

The theological issues become poignant and dramatic when they concern the cripple and Iris. The latter is a sensitive, beautiful orphan who has been given study and training in the city by her patroness, "the Model of all Virtues." Her week at the boarding house did not add to the enjoyment of any—"that excellent lady whose only fault was, that Nature had written out her list of virtues on ruled paper, and forgotten to rub out the lines" (II, 316). Holmes reminds us we must find "a weak spot or two in a character before we can love it much." The cripple's changing status in the group is indicated by his names: at first he is the Sculpin; as pity and respect for him grow but, as he harps on Boston as the Hub of the Universe and the view from the State House as unequaled for what is worth seeing, he becomes Little Boston; by the closing pages he is the Little Gentleman. He talks much about making our religion match our politics: "a man's soul has a vote in the spiritual community; and it doesn't do, Sir, or it won't do long, to call him 'schismatic' or 'heretic' and those other wicked names that old murderous Inquisitors have left us to help along 'peace and good-will to men'" (II, 207). After he has said we are battling for a new faith in the United States and the divinity student remarks it is late in the world's history to be looking for a new faith, his reply is consciously American: "I didn't say a new faith . . . old or new, it can't help being different here in this American mind of ours from anything that ever was before; the *people* are new, Sir, and that makes the difference" (II, 218). The Professor also expresses faith in our national growth toward more freedom from Old World traditions and superstitions, and waxes eloquent with the vision:

> Never, since man came into this atmosphere of oxygen and azote, was there anything like the condition of the young American of the nineteenth century. . . . heir of all old civilizations, founder of that new one which, if all the prophecies of the human heart are not lies, is to be the noblest, as it is the last; isolated in space from the races that are governed by dynasties whose divine right grows out of human wrong, yet knit into the most absolute solidarity with mankind of all times and places by the one great thought he inherits as his national birthright; free to form and express his opinions on almost every subject, and assured that he will soon acquire the last franchise which men withhold from man,—that of stating the laws of his spiritual being and the beliefs he accepts without hindrance except from clearer views of truth,—he seems to want nothing for a large, wholesome, noble, beneficient life. In fact, the chief danger is that he will think the whole planet is made for him, and forget that there are some possibilities left in the *débris* of the old-world civilization which deserve a certain respectful consideration at his hands (II, 284).

Walt Whitman was not the only American who had a vision and a faith during those politically troubled years before the firing on Fort Sumter. But Holmes's enthusiasm is rationally tied down by the play with scientific terms for *atmosphere* at the beginning and by the wry warning at the end.

The romance between the young Marylander and Iris, as they sit nearer each other at table and walk together, is less tense and moving than the growing tenderness between the Little Gentleman and Iris. The high point, emotionally and theologically, is when the Little Gentleman is ill, probably fatally, and the Professor attends him while the divinity student prays for him. When he asks the Little Gentleman conventional questions about repenting of his human sins, the latter passionately denies having in any way shared the life of men in this world. His left arm alone has escaped the curse of crippling; its beauty of form and movement is often mentioned. It contrasts sharply with the misshapen body, where even the heart is misplaced: it is on the right side instead of the left. All he has ever known in his encounters with other mortals has been curiosity, repulsion, sometimes pity. As he ends his passionate avowal of how completely he has been isolated from all ordinary human experience, of his loneliness without love of man or caress of woman, Iris leans to kiss him, and is repaid by his grateful tears. Even the divinity student realizes "he could trust this crippled child of sorrow to the Infinite Parent" (II, 302), and he asks to pray with rather than for him.

The end comes quickly, with the Little Gentleman crushing Iris' hand in a last desperate struggle to make up for a lifetime of isolation from his kind. The mystery which has gathered about his rooms because of the strange sounds of heavy movements at night and of a human voice in pain is solved a trifle arbitrarily. During sleepless nights he relieved his suffering by sharing it with the loving Saviour on the Cross, whose statue he could not reach without pulling out a heavy cabinet; the voice in pain is the *vox humana* stop on the fine organ which he has willed to the Professor. Holmes's lively interest in musical instruments, especially in any new invention, is reflected here. The note of scientific curiosity is odd in the midst of slightly Gothic shadows and suspense. But this mixture of shadowy mystery with active contemporary curiosity counts less as an artistic flaw because all is relaxed and anticlimactic after the death of the cripple. One detail is stressed and carries symbolic tension: Little Boston had wanted a six-foot coffin and a grave to match so that, after death, he could take his place in the world of men without the blunted deformity he had carried while living. His wish is fulfilled and Iris' annual return from Maryland to visit that grave, later with children, leaves all happily taken care of at the end.

It is appropriate to the prevailingly serious tone of the arguments and the dramatic intensity of Little Boston's proud struggle that the two best-known poems from this book are hymns. Iris' tender **"Hymn of Trust"** (II, 282; 163), "O Love Divine, that stooped to share / Our sharpest pang, our bitterest tear," has brought surcease from pain to others besides Little Boston, with its closing "Content to suffer while we know, / Living or dying, Thou art near." At the end the Professor asks all his readers—the friends and the vexed alike—to join in singing his hymn to "the warmth that alone can make us all brothers." It is called **"A Sun-Day Hymn"** (II, 319; 163-64), and begins "Lord of all being! throned afar"; the lines most characteristically Holmes's are "Lord of all life, below, above, / Whose light is truth, whose warmth is love." Less devotional than the other, it has become one of the great hymns of the Protestant church.[6]

The subtitle of *The Professor* was changed for book publication in 1860. In the magazine under the title had been, in italics, "What he said, what he heard, and what he saw." In his farewell remarks the Professor made reference to this: "The Professor has talked less than his predecessor, but he has heard and seen more," a fair estimate of the way interest shifted from the talk of the Professor to the tender relations between the cripple and Iris. It was artistically fitting that the subtitle in the book be changed to "With the Story of Iris."[7]

III Medical Lecturer

Chronologically and thematically a medical lecture, "Currents and Counter-Currents in Medical Science," deserves mention. On May 20, 1860, Holmes addressed the Annual Meeting of the Massachusetts Medical Society, and he argued as eloquently against entrenched ignorance in medical practice as the Professor and Little Boston had argued against the narrow fencing-in by creeds in religion. He first exposed the delusion doctors suffered when they supposed they were treating their patients according to the techniques of experience. All too often the treatment was based merely on some prevalent fashionable belief which was accepted without testing because it had prevailed for so long. He warned the physician who prided himself on being a practical man and on leaving mere theorists to watch the currents of progress that he needed to look out and up and find out where he was going. Colorful examples are introduced of an arctic expedition on which no traveler would have known he was traveling backward if he had not lifted his eyes from the track; of the workman who covered the niche in the wall without noticing the human figure within; of the Jewish artisan who nailed together two pieces of timber for Pontius Pilate. Then these examples are pointed home in one sentence: " . . . with subtler tool than trowels and axes, the statesman who works in policy without principle, the theologian who works in forms without a soul, the physician who, calling himself a practical man, refuses to recognize the larger laws which govern his changing practice,

may all find that they have been building truth into the wall, and hanging humanity upon the cross" (IX, 176-77).

The fact that there was a closer relation between the medical sciences and the prevailing social and political thought of a period than most people realized, was made persuasive—as had been his previous handling of **"Homeopathy and Its Kindred Delusions,"**—by his beginning with examples far enough in the past to be seen objectively. Andreas Vesalius was linked with Luther in his defiance of a church authority that forbade investigation and protected corruption; Marie François Xavier Bichat's practice caused as great an upheaval in surgical circles as Napoleon's in military and political ones; Dr. Benjamin Rush, who emancipated American medicine from slavish following of European practices, was a contemporary of men who founded a new nation.

Holmes prepared his audience psychologically for what he wanted it to give undivided attention to. "The more positive knowledge we gain, the more we incline to question all that has been received without absolute proof" (IX, 181). Homeopathy and Spiritualism were paired, as they were in *The Professor,* as caves of folly to which the frightened retreated when their old beliefs were threatened. But the real target here was overmedication, the resort to drugs and specifics with no attempt to find out the causes in order to prevent the diseases. Hippocrates' distinction between Nature and Art—what the body will do on its own and what should be done by the attending doctor—was traced through the centuries as it had been passionately defended or as passionately denounced. Dr. Rush was cited again and his denunciation quoted; his connection with the American Revolution was used with different effect from the first citation: the huge doses he prescribed were as "heroic" as the times in which he lived. Holmes was too serious here to indulge in the colloquial or the amusing, but the witty turning of the coin to see both sides marked poise of intellect rather than unleashed invective. He recommended the life and writings of Rush to the student who wished "to understand the tendencies of the American medical mind, its sanguine enterprise, its self-confidence, its audacious handling of Nature, its impatience with her old-fashioned ways of taking time to get a sick man well" (IX, 192).

Although the science of semantics would not be born till the next century, Holmes was practicing it when he pointed out the need to find workable definitions for words that had become emotionally confused such as *Nature, Art, Disease, Food, Medicine, Physic;* he went on to offer such definitions (IX, 196-97). One attack sounds like a page out of today's newspaper: "Add to this the great number of Medical Journals . . . many of them excellently well conducted, but which must find something to fill their columns, and so print all the new plans of treatment and new remedies they can get hold of . . ." (IX, 193-94). A modern reader misses only the stress on the income from advertising which paves the way for quack remedies in large type. After several examples of widespread misuse of such drugs as opiates, Holmes recommended the following for consideration: "The *presumption* always is that every noxious agent, including medicines proper, which hurts a well man, hurts a sick one" (IX, 201). He cited his experience as physician at the Boston Dispensary as his chance to learn that "medication without insuring hygienic conditions is like amputation without ligatures" (IX, 203).

In his closing words Holmes exhorted his "friends and brothers in Art . . . to save all our old treasures of knowledge and mine deeply for new, . . . to stand together for truth." Self-governing Americans were reminded that our history, unlike the Old World's, was not a history of "mounted majorities, clad in iron," but of a land where "the majority is only the flower of the passing noon, and the minority is the bud which may open in the next morning's sun." The attack here on traditional authority not tested by close and constant observation is the characteristic attack of Holmes the scientific thinker: he used as an example of failure to study actual cases the opposition to **"The Contagiousness of Puerperal Fever."** But his respect for the great medical works of the past was, as the word *treasures* indicates, more than intellectual respect; it was combined with a lover's delight in old books and a collector's joy in knowing their fine points.

> Shall I ever forget that rainy day in Lyons, that dingy bookshop, where I found the Aëtius, long missing from my Artis Medicae Principes, and where I bought for a small pecuniary consideration, though it was marked *rare,* and was really *très rare,* the Aphorisms of Hippocrates, edited by and with a preface from the hand of Francis Rabelais? And the vellum-bound Tulpius, which I came upon in Venice, afterwards my only reading when imprisoned in quarantine at Marseilles, so that the two hundred and twenty-eight cases he has recorded are, many of them, to this day still fresh in my memory. And the Schenckius,—the folio filled with *casus rariores,* which had strayed in among the rubbish of the bookstall on the boulevard,—and the noble old Vesalius with its grand frontispiece not unworthy of Titian, and the fine old Ambroise Paré, long waited for even in Paris and long ago, and the colossal Spigelius with his eviscerated beauties, and Dutch Bidloo with its miracles of fine engraving and bad dissection, and Italian Mascagni, the despair of all would-be imitators, and pre-Adamite John de Ketam, and antediluvian Berengarius Carpensis,— but why multiply names, every one of which brings back the accession of a book which was an event almost like the birth of an infant? (IX, 410-11)

I quote these remarks here, which are from his Dedicatory Address at the Opening of the Boston Medical Library on December 3, 1878, because they convey so vividly the loving attention he lavished on medical works of the past, estimating justly their excellences and their mistakes. The purchases he was recounting in intimate detail were made during his study years in Europe, more than forty years before. Hence the warning sounded to students in the medical sciences in 1860 arose from a deep-seated concern for human welfare, not from impatience with the past or personal desire for novelty or notoriety. Although "Currents and Counter-Currents in Medical Science" was printed by the society in June, opposition to Dr. Holmes's stand arose: at an adjourned meeting on May 31, Dr. Childs of Pittsfield introduced a motion that "the Society disclaim all responsibility for the sentiments," and it was passed by a vote of nine to seven. The implied censure was recalled at a regular meeting on October 3, 1860, by a vote of twenty-seven to seventeen. Dr. Holmes was not disturbed by this opposition as he had been when authorities attacked his diagnosis of puerperal fever; nor did he need to be, for the doctors he respected shared his convictions and applauded his vigor and leadership. This serious professional address by Holmes at a time when he was capturing a large lay audience with his essays in the *Atlantic* illustrates the facility with which he moved from one area to the other. Examples and analogies are no more picturesque and only slightly more frequent for the lay reader. If anything, the concentration and close thought of the medical address lend it as much interest and even greater force.

IV The Poet

Holmes's next two long writings for the *Atlantic* were novels, **Elsie Venner** and **The Guardian Angel.** The Autocrat had stated that every man has at least one novel in him; the direction **The Professor** had taken *With the Story of Iris* had given him a taste of the excitement which might await him, and his alert mind was always eager to branch out into new fields of human study. I shall consider the novels together in the next chapter, since they, like the three books of the Breakfast-Table series, share features which emerge more clearly when examined comparatively.

The Poet at the Breakfast-Table did not begin in the *Atlantic* until January, 1872, and it was published as a book at the end of that year. Besides the two novels in the 1860's **Soundings From the Atlantic** appeared in 1864—a collection of essays reprinted from the magazine. Three of the articles have been mentioned previously in connection with the Civil War: **"Bread and the Newspaper," "My Hunt After 'The Captain,' "** and **"The Inevitable Trial."** The last-named oration of July 4, 1863, had not appeared in the *Atlantic* because it had been immediately printed separately and widely distributed. Other essays dealt with new inventions which had caught Holmes's interest, usually through their similarity to natural processes of the human anatomy or of the natural world. Thus the titles of two of the three essays dealing with photography used "sun": **"Doings of the Sun Beam"** and **"Sun-Painting and Sun-Sculpture"**; the other was about the stereoscope, the use and study of which Holmes found so absorbing that by 1868 he had investigated "The History of the American Stereoscope." The subtitles of two essays explained the analogies he developed: "The Great Instrument: The organ in the Boston Music Hall, with a brief description of the anatomy of the human ear" and "The Human Wheel: The Physiology of Walking."

Occasional poems were still called for, and from farther away or for more distant celebrations. Besides appearing with Liszt, the piano virtuoso, and Ole Bull, the violinist, at Boston's overblown Peace Jubilee in June, 1869, he wrote poems for two anniversaries in Germany: President Barnard of Columbia University asked him to contribute to the Fiftieth Anniversary of Ehrenberg as Doctor of Medicine in November, 1868, and in 1869 Holmes and Agassiz helped make Boston aware of the centennial of the birth of Friedrich Humboldt. The subtitle of Holmes's poem **"Humboldt's Birthday"** (213-14) showed him still drawing a parallel between medicine and politics, "Bonaparte, August 11, 1769.—Humboldt, September 14, 1769." In 1869, Holmes was one of the members of the Massachusetts Historical Society who gave the Lowell Institute Lectures. His lecture, "The Medical Profession in Massachusetts," took him again to Colonial records, but he developed the relation between local practices and the general state of medical science instead of proceeding as he had with intermittent fever to a narrow but substantially supported conclusion—a contrast between broad and narrow that he had illustrated in religion in *The Professor* and that he would investigate in science in *The Poet.*

The inauguration of a new president at Harvard in 1869, Charles William Eliot, had brought the new emphasis on specialization into Holmes's professional life; he was made Professor of Anatomy, and Physiology was set off in a field of its own. President Eliot, who was affecting all people connected with Harvard, was "proposing in the calmest way to turn everything topsy-turvy," according to Holmes. Although Holmes was suspicious of the new emphasis on more lectures in the medical school instead of so much clinical work as he advocated, his position was more moderate than belligerent, and he wanted to reconcile the opposing sides. This position is echoed in the ambivalent arguments delivered in *The Poet.* Another personal effect *The Poet* echoed was the sale of the Holmes house in Cambridge to Harvard to make way for Eliot's program of change and of building which was soon to change or convert many familiar landmarks.

The necessity of cleaning out the old gambrel-roofed house took John and Wendell and Ann Upham back to the old days. The memories that found their way into Holmes's writing were published in the *Atlantic Monthly* in January of 1871 and 1872. The first was the poem **"Dorothy Q."** (186-87), delightful in its combination of pride, humor, and tenderness caught in quick rhyming couplets, about the portrait whose "rent the light shines through." He had learned as a child that the rent was made by a British "Redcoat's rapier thrust." He included early in the new book in the Breakfast-Table series his essay on **"The Gambrel-Roofed House and its Outlook"** (III, 10-31), and in it he not only indulged his own pleasure in going over experiences of his early years but also sketched a vivid and valuable picture of the old village Cambridge had been.

The immediate opening of *The Poet* identified some of the people now at the Breakfast-Table, which had been out of sight for twelve years: the gently satirized **"Member of the Haouse"** with his dialect and huckleberry-conscious constituents; the six-year-old Boy, whom the Poet refused to call *Bub,* because he knew that was the diminutive of *Beelzebub;* the Old Master, who had prejudices strong enough to rub against; and the Landlady, who was always interrupting. The Poet used her interruptions to introduce a comic literary interlude, like the Professor's Houhynhym Gazette, in which Shakespeare was imagined being likewise interrupted by Anne's query about his preference for pudding or flapjacks today when he was in the midst of composing Hamlet's "To be or not to be" speech. The looser organization of this book is one reason its effect is more diffused. The essay on early Cambridge comes before the introduction of the opponents of the Old Master; they are the scientists called the Scarabee and the Young Astronomer, and their absorption in special studies means narrow living and narrow loving. The Lady and Scheherezade appear later and are less sharply contrasted than the other feminine pairs. Holmes is determinedly seeing good in the young who are breaking up the old patterns. The Young Girl's being called Scheherezade has the old refreshing play: she too keeps herself alive by telling stories—only hers are sold to newspapers and magazines, a far cry from any Arabian nights. She differs from the Lady only in background and in enjoying the scientific discussions the latter finds tiresome and distressing. The link with the earlier books is managed through the Landlady and her family. Her daughter is now married to an undertaker, a cheerful soul when not on professional duty, and the Landlady goes to live with her when she gives up her boarding-house at the end. Benjamin Franklin has become a medical doctor, and Holmes ridicules him for his enthusiasm about all the new gadgets in his profession and for insisting on getting every detail of his patient's history before he will venture a diagnosis—Dr. Holmes laughing at the medical innovations he had proudly brought back from Paris, as he had earlier invited laughter at himself in "The Stethoscope Ballad." Minor figures like the Register of Deeds, the Capitalist, and Mrs. Midas Goldenrod (who takes up with the Lady again as soon as the Register of Deeds has restored her wealth by finding an old paper) remain names for dominant traits rather than human beings.

An inner circle is composed of the Old Master, the Poet, the Young Astronomer, the Scarabee, and occasionally Scheherezade. The Young Astronomer's poem **"Wind-Clouds and Star-Drifts"** closes seven chapters and is written in blank verse; both the form and the subject matter are attempts by Holmes to present sympathetically a reconciliation of his "narrow" and "broad." The compromise is only dimly etched in; the real life is in the Old Master and the Scarabee. The Young Astronomer may be a failure because of Holmes's lack of conviction or because he was trying to understand and interpret a young man near and dear to him, his son Oliver Wendell Holmes who was pursuing an independent course of life with marked success, was devoted to his law profession and was writing brilliant studies based on close and concentrated analysis, and who was rescued from lonely eccentricity by his brilliant wife and their richly shared social relations. The Poet gives an accurate estimate of the book when he is reflecting on the doubt the Lady expressed as to "whether she would find better company in any circle she was like to move in than she left behind her at our boarding-house. I give the Old Master the credit of this compliment. If one does not agree with half of what he says, at any rate he always has something to say, and entertains and lets out opinions and whims and notions of one kind and another that one can quarrel with if he is out of humor, or carry away to think about if he happens to be in the receptive mood" (III, 297).

The Old Master has an occasional epigrammatic sentence: "Sin, like disease, is a vital process" (III, 306). An elaborate figure he develops to illustrate "broad" and "narrow" is emotionally slanted: the eagle's flight leaves no track while the patient mollusc's boring into a marble column outlasts the temple. He sees it as a just picture of his ranging far and wide to investigate the "Order of Things" in contrast to the Scarabee's confining himself to beetles and thereby leaving a single point "finally settled for the instruction and, it may be, the admiration of all coming time" (III, 251-52). The Old Master summarizes Holmes's treatment of new inventions in *Soundings:* "There are many modern contrivances that are of as early date as the first man, if not thousands of centuries older" (III, 322-23). Telescope and microscope are related to the human eye, instruments to the larynx, and the new heating apparatuses of furnace and radiators to the human frame. Like

the Professor, he is interrupted in his statement *"The one central fact in the Order of Things which solves all questions is,"* and when the Young Astronomer and the Poet want him to give his conclusion, he replies it is all there in his books and advises them to reach individual conclusions with a characteristically colloquial figure of speech: "It's quite as well to crack your own filberts as to borrow the use of other people's teeth" (III, 339; 344).

The vivid colloquial language and memorable figure are less frequent in *The Poet* than in earlier works; nevertheless the Poet's classification of men into one-story, two-story, and three-story intellects has been echoed so often, with or without attribution, that it may justly be named one of his famous figures. Its clarity and brevity are part of its power: "All fact-collectors who have no aim beyond the facts, are one-story men. Two-story men compare, reason, generalize, using the labors of the fact-collectors as well as their own. Three-story men idealize, imagine, predict; their best illumination comes from above, through the skylight" (III, 43). Some librarians are noted as examples of the one-story mind which stops at the fact; lawyers, as examples of the two-story; poets, of the three-story, "full of light, if sometimes rather bare of furniture, in the attics." The colloquial humor placed at the end to relieve the sharp classifications, would seem desirable for a man who made lawyers second-story intellects when his mother's father was a distinguished judge, his wife's father was equally renowned as a judge in his day, and his eldest son was already exhibiting, besides an intense devotion to his work, a range of imaginative thought and phrase and a poise of intellect which could employ the comic to advantage. For three decades of the twentieth century these characteristics would make the name Oliver Wendell Holmes mean to the public the brilliant judge and legal writer.

Though the Old Master sets the tone of the book and we are at home with him in his library, or reading from his published book or his new notes, no such emotional quickening takes place as Little Boston and Iris gave to *The Professor.* The Scarabee lives his part, and does finally manage one smile, but his correspondence is only with professional colleagues who are suspected as competitors eager to publish their papers ahead of his, and only his spider loves him. He and the Young Astronomer often refer to Darwin, and to the great logical advantages to be found in his theory of species as contrasted to the universe conceived in the Old Testament. Our national love of display is ridiculed, but gently, as when the Poet admits to the inordinate pride he takes in wearing a tiny particolored ribbon in his buttonhole. The most amusing puncturing of the inflated diction that Holmes, like Mencken later, finds characteristic of our national vainglory, is the Scarabee's *Muscarium,* which he explains is "my home for house-flies" (III, 244). A reference is made to the crusade for women's rights, but it is only gently satiric. There may be humorous diction or an incongruous comparison, but the tone is never one of attack or satire.

Besides the seven parts of the long poem the Young Astronomer is working on, the Poet closes his return to the gambrel-roofed house with the tender and comforting **"Homesick in Heaven."** The Angel is gentle as he helps the mourners seeking earthly forms in Heaven to comprehend that these forms belong only to the earth left behind. Only two poems offer comic relief. In **"Aunt Tabitha"** (III, 87-88; 171), Scheherezade makes Aunt Tabitha's manners amusing "When *she* was a girl (forty summers ago) . . . How wicked we are, and how good they were then." The book closes with an "Epilogue to the Breakfast-Table Series: Autocrat—Professor—Poet. At a Book store. *Anno Domini* 1972" (III, 349-51; 183-84). A passerby stops to look through "Your choice among these books, 1 Dime," and finds "A Boswell, writing out himself. . . . One actor in a dozen parts . . . Thy years on every page confessed . . . Thy hopeful nature, light and free, / I start to find myself in thee." His start of recognition makes him take all three, but he puts them in a class we also recognize: "Read you,—perhaps,—some other time."

At least for **The Autocrat** this prediction was wrong. In **The Poet** Holmes has talked frankly with his readers about the likelihood that the series will now have a diminished audience: he follows this by deciding he will take advantage of it and be more intimate with his one reader.[8] The first time this one reader is addressed as "Beloved," the effect is disconcerting, but gradually the reader begins to enjoy it. The tone is frequently less intimate than in **The Autocrat**—necessarily so when serious speakers and subjects are present—but it is as easy and more tender. The form is less developed, for fewer characters are brought to life and divisions are acknowledged and named; the range is narrowed and the sparkle dimmed. The Old Master and the Scarabee are alive and appealing each in his way, but the solution by way of the Young Astronomer is dim and contrived. He is saved from the lonely fate of the Scarabee by marrying the alert and independent Scheherezade, but his problem, variously presented in **"Wind-Clouds and Star-Drift,"**[9] remains the dilemma of the scientific humanist: to dedicate himself utterly to his work and, like the Scarabee, become important only to and for his beetles; or to respond freely to all living situations and creatures and to be welcome, like the Old Master, in any group because he wears his learning lightly, is tolerant, humorous, and wise. Little wonder that Holmes, by 1872 a confirmed occasional

poet, skillful lecturer, and popular essayist, gave the Old Master all the advantages—except the lasting renown of a single achievement.

Notes

[1] Although this a.l.s. was marked "Private" at the top of the first leaf, it was printed in fascimile in Higginson and Boynton, *A Reader's History of American Literature* (Boston [1903]), facing p. 158. The reading here is from the autograph owned by the late discriminating collector-scholar Carroll A. Wilson, and called by him the finest Holmes letter he owned.

[2] a.l.s. Holmes to Miss Charlotte Dana, April 18, 1863, in the Massachusetts Historical Society, Dana Papers; used here with the permission of Director Stephen T. Riley.

[3] Osler's first reference to this question was in the "Notes and Commentaries" he had been writing for the *Montreal Medical Journal* (January, 1889). Holmes's reply was written on Jan. 21, 1889, and was twice printed by Osler. The original letter is now in the collection of Osleriana in the McGill Medical Library in Montreal. For a full account of Osler's regard for Holmes, see Harvey Cushing, *Life of Sir William Osler* (Oxford, 1926), I, 301-2.

[4] Four editions of *The Autocrat* appeared in this country before the new and revised edition in 1883; five issues of it came before Holmes's death in 1894, five after. Modern reprints have appeared in Oxford's World's Classics in 1904 (reprinted 1906, 1909, 1923, then allowed to lapse); in Macmillan's Modern Readers' series in 1927; and in the New American Library of World Literature's Signet Classics in 1961.

Both the first and the revised editions appeared promptly in Edinburgh: the first, 1859; the revised, 1883. Although there were only two English editions—one in 1859, and an illustrated edition in 1865—*The Autocrat* won an enthusiastic audience there, as a result of which Holmes's distaste for that country began to give way to an eager desire to visit it again, especially after his friends Lowell and Motley were writing him of English experiences he could wish to share. A German translation came out in Stuttgart in 1876, *Der Tisch-Despot;* in Leipzig, a Tauchnitz edition in 1883. In 1922, it was published in Japan as one of the Kenkyusha English Classics.

Besides these single printings, it was Volume I in the collected editions of 1891, 1892, and 1893.

[5] This scrapbook is now in the Oliver Wendell Holmes Library of Phillips-Andover Academy.

[6] I omit *American* here intentionally. In 1933, when I attended at the Crystal Palace in London a service of song presided over by the Archbishop of Canterbury and performed by the different cathedral choirs of England in their robes of varying colors and with their choir-masters and organists, this hymn by Holmes was chosen to close the program.

[7] That *The Professor* by no means matched *The Autocrat* in popularity is shown by a brief review of the printings. Under the title *The Story of Iris,* the parts concerning her were published separately in 1877; a reprint of this, with a section of *Favorite Poems* by Holmes and another section of five sermons by Dr. John Brown was issued in the Modern Classics, No. 30, in 1882. A revised edition, to match that of *The Autocrat,* appeared in 1883. A Birthday edition in two volumes was put out in 1891, the same year it became Vol. II of the Riverside edition of the *Writings,* and of the subsequent editions of 1892 and 1893. Only two editions have appeared since Holmes's death in 1894; one in Boston and London, 1902, which ran to four issues; the last, Boston, 1916. An English edition came out the same year as the first book publication here (1860), making only two; the revised edition, in two volumes, came out in Edinburgh in 1883.

[8] When *The Poet* came out as a book in 1872, the subtitle emphasized the supposed single reader: "His [changed in 1883 to *He*] talks with his Fellow-Boarders and the Reader." The London edition, in 1872, omitted the subtitle, but noted the author was the author of *The Autocrat.* Editions followed the pattern of *The Professor:* a revised edition, 1883; a two-volume Edinburgh edition, 1884; the Birthday, 1890; the three in the collected *Writings* of 1891, 1892, and 1893; an edition in Boston and London, 1902; in Boston, 1916. Sales were also about the same; the marked difference was between them and *The Autocrat,* which has sold about twice as many copies as any other of Holmes's works.

[9] That Holmes worked hard over "Wind-Clouds and Star-Drifts" (pp. 171-84) as central to the problem he was treating in *The Poet,* is proven by the changes he made when it was published in editions of his poems. He shortened the sections, making twelve instead of seven, and gave each a title. From "Ambition," the progress of the young scientist was marked by "Regrets," "Sympathies," the comfort of "Master and Scholar" to the isolation of "Alone"; he proceeded to brave "Questioning" and "Worship" (a significant juxtaposition); achieved "Manhood" with its "Rights" and "Truths"; but was tempted by "Idols" until finally rescued by "Love." Middle sections were rearranged and sharpened by rewriting some lines and omitting many. Indicative not only of how real to Holmes was the problem of the young

scientist but also of how natural to his poetic expression were rhyme and stanza, especially the rhyming couplet for long poems, are the effort, revision, and ultimate failure of this venture into blank verse. I note these changes because they reveal Holmes's special poetic taste and gift; also because it is one of the few instances where textual changes are not carefully recorded in *Bibliog.*

John Martin (essay date 1986)

SOURCE: "This is the ship of pearl . . ." in *Books at Iowa,* No. 45, November, 1986, pp. 17-25.

[*In the following essay, Martin compares Holmes's life and writing with that of his contemporaries and fellow New Englanders, Henry David Thoreau and Ralph Waldo Emerson.*]

The nineteenth century saw a starveling infant nation grow into a muscular, prosperous giant whose strong arms spanned the land from the Atlantic to the Pacific. Aggressive, assertive, brawling; ridden by political scandal and social strife; hungering for land and getting it by purchase, treaty, war (Mexico), or disenfranchisement of the aboriginals (that is, decimation of the American Indians), the United States seemed more concerned with power and material gain than with "human rights" and spiritual development. Yet there was a brighter side to this country in that noisy century. Movements for social reform were many (the abolitionists, the attempts at communism at New England's Brook Farm and Fruitland). The festering wound of slavery was closed at great cost, though the pain lingered on. Science and education flourished, to create a better life for the teeming new millions. A new breed of intellectuals dared to break the bonds of Europe, which had for too long restrained independent thought. Most surprisingly, amidst all the ongoing turmoil and possibly because of it, there grew a body of literature uniquely American, expressing basic philosophies with new voices and a spirituality which must have puzzled certain foreign contemporaries.

The list is long and familiar: Hawthorne, Poe, Lowell, Bryant, Longfellow, Prescott, Parkman, Clemens, Harte, Greeley, Cooper, Whitman, Thoreau, Emerson, Holmes, and still others. Each sang his own song and each was his own man in his own special way; each left his personal stamp on world literature and on the American conscience. To read them is to savor some of the world's most satisfying classics.

The last three named, Henry David Thoreau (1817-62), Ralph Waldo Emerson (1803-82), and Oliver Wendell Holmes (1809-94), hold a special attraction for this writer, with an admitted choice of Holmes for first place. These three quintessential New Englanders had much in common and yet were so different in many ways. But in this they were alike: undeterred by the barbs of critics, they trod their own particular paths and produced their written works under the command of their own unswerving convictions.

· · · · ·

Of these three, Holmes was more in the world, more with his fellow men, tolerant yet critical of fools, cool and smooth in that speech rich with just the right metaphor, ever ready with the right anecdote to drive home a point. His head may have been too large for his body, his sloping shoulders too narrow, his waistline a bit too full, but before his audience, be it in a public lecture, with his cronies at the Saturday Club, or before his class at Harvard Medical School, he enlivened his listeners with his fresh spirit, sparkling wit, and astounding fund of information. He was a happy man, enjoyed a long life, and surely must never have allowed himself an idle moment. No worried introvert, he. Thoreau said, "The mass of men lead lives of quiet desperation. What is called resignation is confirmed desperation" *(Walden: Economy)*. He wasn't thinking of Oliver Wendell Holmes when he wrote that. Holmes was neither desperate nor resigned. He enjoyed his old age when he was widowed and had as his joyful companion his daughter Amelia. His son was for many years one of the most honored jurists ever to serve on the United States Supreme Court.

Most likely the informed scholar of American Poetry would not place Holmes's work in the front rank. Yet it is all eminently readable and above all else it is *understandable.* His poetry was not made up of fragments of thought obscure to all but himself. They are poems of defined structure, with the clarity that comes with the use of simple words. They could tell a story with appealing whimsy and a gentle smile (*The Last Leaf,* 1831). They could poke the ribs of his own medical profession (*The Stethoscope Song,* 1848). They could rattle the pomposity of his own Calvinistic background and the Unitarian Church, with the collapse of the cart, the parson, and "logic" in front of the meetin' house (*The Deacon's Masterpiece, or The Wonderful 'One-Hoss Shay,'* 1858). What finer prayer than his *A Sun-day Hymn* (1859)? Bryant's *Thanatopsis* (1811) is one of America's hallowed poems, and rightly so. But even more lyrical, even richer in hopeful outlook and without the somber overtones of *Thanatopsis,* Holmes's *The Chambered Nautilus* (1858) routs depression and makes the spirit soar. "Build thee more stately mansions, O my soul. . . . " How could that last stanza be improved? No wonder the *Atlantic Monthly,* to which Holmes was a major contributor, was a continuing publishing success. To me it is a great poem and his finest.

Besides the well-known *Breakfast Table Series,* which were poems and essays written as early as 1833,

Holmes's prose works include that delightful account of a vacation in Europe with Amelia in the spring and summer of 1886. He visited old haunts from his student days in medical training at the University of Paris, but most of the trip was spent touring the cities, countryside, cathedrals, and historic sites of England. In this, *Our Hundred Days in Europe* (1887), the reader will make an armchair visit to places hallowed in British history, meet the cream of literary and social life, make the acquaintance of a direct descendant of that old curiosity, Sir Kenelm Digby, visit the shop of Bernard Quaritch, meet the founder-owner of that still-flourishing establishment, and wonder with Holmes at the collection of rare books and manuscripts there. (He remarked that the prices asked were high. Alas! they still are.) The reader is granted a brief visit with Tennyson and Palgrave and others equally famous and well-known to us.

A vein of kindly satire runs through all of Holmes's essays. These varied works, covering a wide range of subjects, are written with a steady flow of elegant prose backed by a massive knowledge of world history and literature from the time of the early classics, and especially with a knowledge of human nature with all its beauty as well as its meanness and warts. The essays and poetry have kept Holmes before us, for they are common readings in high school and college literature courses. His three novels, *A Mortal Antipathy, The Guardian Angel,* and *Elsie Venner* are less well-known. All are now dated, "unmodern." However, *Elsie Venner* (1861), if not the perfect novel as judged by structure, is nevertheless a powerful work, a masterful depiction of abnormal psychology, and proof of his ability as a physician to probe the psyche. It is a hint as to why Holmes was both a successful practitioner of medicine and a clear-eyed critic of the world about him.

With his education at Phillips Academy at Andover and his degree from Harvard in 1829, and with his father a learned historian and Congregational minister, the young Wendell of that era might have been expected to go into the ministry, devote himself to literature, or even study law, but instead he chose science. Though he continued to write poetry and essays throughout his life, Holmes was, by career, a physician. He had some of his first medical training in Boston, but the more formal part of it was in Paris, where his mentor was the famous general practitioner and pulmonary specialist, P. C. A. Louis at the Pitié Hospital. The first half of the nineteenth century were heady days in French medicine. That was the time of Magendie, of bloody Broussais and Bouillaud, of irreverent Ricord, of Malgaigne, Andral, Dupuytren, Duchenne, Brown-Séquard, Leuret, and Velpeau. Thus the young medical student was exposed to the best of contemporary French medical practice. He returned home with an appreciation for all of it except the unbridled bloodletting of certain of his teachers. For a man so honest, so direct and simple in his care of the sick, and for a man of his sensitive nature, such practices as that and overdosing the patient with useless and dangerous drugs was totally repugnant. His indignation is strongly stated in *Medical Essays,* published in 1861 and in many later editions.

In his lectures before various medical societies in and around Boston, in essays written especially for publication, and in his classroom lectures to medical students, the only strident notes one finds in the words of this kind man were directed toward all that is dishonest and incompetent in medical practice. In the essay *Homeopathy and Its Kindred Delusions* (1842), such patent fakes as Perkin's Metallic Tractors and Digby's "powders of sympathy," along with other quackery, were effectively reduced to their proper level. Hahnemann and homeopathy receive rough handling in this essay. To fully understand Holmes as a physician, one must have read these essays. His admonitions to medical students are as valid today as they were then, and could reasonably be required reading in the modern medical curriculum. He urged the teaching of medicine at the bedside, apprentice with master, directly observing the sick person. Much in books and lectures, he felt, was useless and a waste of time. These pungent essays, packed with wit and keen, sane observations, rich in historical lore, are impassioned with Holmes's great wish to clear out all the old fallacies and pretensions and to make simpler and more humane the medical career which he so highly esteemed. At times he was prophetic and accurately so, as one sees in his appreciation of Florence Nightingale, and in his belief that a day would come when nursing would be an honored profession, based on a structured plan for training.

Holmes accurately described the cause, nature, and prevention of puerperal fever before Ignaz Semmelweis took up the fight and published his famous book in 1861. Like Semmelweis, Holmes suffered bitter criticism and vicious attacks from such contemporaries as the famous and influential Charles D. Meigs of Jefferson Medical College in Philadelphia. But Holmes, knowing he was right and having a tougher skin than Semmelweis, let all this roll off his back and continued a successful fight, not suffering the fate of that tragic Viennese. American medicine was fortunate to have Oliver Wendell Holmes on stage at a time of ferment and change in medical knowledge and teaching, to have him set the facts straight in candid, unmistakable language, and boldly to associate errors with names, dates, and places.

Sometimes I have thought how much more pleasant some of my medical classes would have been if Oliver Wendell Holmes had been my teacher. A successful practitioner early in his career, he was thereafter for the rest of his life professor of anatomy at Harvard Medical School, where he was a much-beloved teacher.

He did not slavishly follow the prescribed plan of lectures. Many "facts" that students must memorize he considered a wasteful approach to the actual care of the patient. He accused the curriculum of redundancy, too often concerned with science for science's sake. His lectures could ramble far and wide, only loosely related to the cadaver or skeleton under discussion, for his mind bubbled with historical allusions and colorful metaphors, making his lectures much more than a recitation of the facts of anatomy.

Long ago I heard a story told of Dr. Holmes that I like to believe is true and not apocryphal. One day this uniquely humane genius stood before his class, a skull in hand, intending to describe that most complicated of bones, the bone which has been the downfall of many a freshman medical student on examination day—the dreaded sphenoid bone. The greater and lesser wings, the various processes, canals, foramina and tuberosities, the fissures, margins, plates and recesses—Holmes did his best to put it together into a sensible, coherent demonstration. He became more and more entangled and hopelessly lost, and he for one time lacked words to say what he wished. So he abruptly stopped speaking, looked at the class, smiled, put the skull on the table before him, and quietly said, "Gentlemen, to hell with the sphenoid bone."

Anne Dalke (essay date 1988)

SOURCE: "Economics, or the Bosom Serpent: Oliver Wendell Holmes's *Elsie Venner: A Romance of Destiny*" in *American Transcendental Quarterly,* N. S., Vol. 2, No. 1, March, 1988, pp. 57-68.

[*In the following essay, Dalke examines Holmes's intent in* Elsie Venner: A Romance of Destiny, *in which he argues that human beings cannot be held accountable for misdeeds because of their heredity.*]

Oliver Wendell Holmes's first novel, *Elsie Venner,* has three prefaces, each allowing the reader less license than its predecessor. In the first, Holmes describes the book as a "romance," and leaves the reader to "judge for himself" what "actually happened," what is "possible" and what "more or less probable" (vii). In the second preface Holmes much more pointedly explains that the aim of his story is "to test the doctrine of 'original sin' and human responsibility." The thesis of the story is here presented in the form of a question: "Was Elsie Venner, poisoned by the venom of a crotalus before she was born, morally responsible . . . ?" (ix-x). In the third preface Holmes says even more expressly that his novel is a tract, in which he "tried to make out a case for my poor Elsie, whom the most hardened theologian would find it hard to blame for her inherited ophidian tastes and tendencies." The "only use of the story," Holmes this time asserts, "is to bring the dogmas of inherited guilt and its consequences into a clearer point of view" (xii).

Critics have long observed that, by strongly emphasizing heredity and environment, Holmes "seemed to be teaching materialistic determinism no less binding than the Calvinistic predestination which he ridiculed" (*LHUS*, 1:598). In the novel the young schoolmaster Bernard Langdon argues, for example, that "Each of us is only the footing-up of a long sum in addition and subtraction" (74). Bernard's general equation is applied to a specific example, when Dudley Venner reflects on his daughter's strange behavior and detects "the impressive movement of hereditary impulse in looks and acts. To be a parent is almost to be a fatalist" (271). Holmes's theory, expressed by these characters, was that "our ancestors' lives shape ours; we cannot be held accountable. This was the doctrine of original sin turned inside out" (Parker 52).

The snake bite which Catalina Venner suffers, and which poisons Elsie before birth, thus functions both as a discounted symbol for original sin, and as a representative of inherited genetic tendencies. It also carries a range of association not described in Holmes's introduction. As Stanton Garner has suggested, the snake clearly has sexual implications (293). Mrs. Venner is vulnerable to attack because she is immobilized at home, and she is immobile because she is pregnant. The original sin, in Holmes's retelling of the story of Genesis, is a sexual transgression, and the knowledge attained is purely carnal. Catalina and Dudley Venner share that knowledge, "that one early summer when they walked arm in arm through the wilderness of roses that ran riot in the garden" (243). Their sympathetic union results in Elsie's isolation of being; the punishment for their Edenic experience is a child who is the embodiment of sexuality (Garner 293), but unable to love.

Gail Parker has discussed in detail the degree to which Holmes portrayed his anxiety and guilt about sexual impulses in his fiction, and the means he used to "make the evil phallic principle clear" (56). She has also suggested that "Holmes could never really sort out the components of the male role in his mind," that "concentrated sexual energy" and "concentrated mental energy," "phallicism" and "professionalism" become confused in his work (57). In *Elsie Venner,* the concentrated pursuit of economic success in particular becomes a substitute for sexual activity.

For characters other than Elsie, the forbidden activity of sex is transmuted not into isolation, but into financial engagement. With curious obliquity, sexuality is displayed as monetary desire throughout *Elsie Venner.* What Holmes presents as a disquisition on original/sexual sin is also the story of a "new" society in which money-getting replaces all other concerns, particularly the affectional.

Holmes's insistence that people should not be held morally responsible for misbehavior conditioned before birth is clearly central to *Elsie Venner;* asserted with increasing strength in each of his three introductions, it is also argued consistently by his spokesman in the novel proper, Dr. Kittredge. But Holmes does hold his characters accountable for one form of willed activity, in which all of them but Elsie engage: that of economic practice.

The money-grubbing world of this novel is a world which Holmes condemns, sometimes obliquely or ironically, sometimes roundly. All "commercial transactions in regard to the most sacred interests of life are hateful even to those who profit by them," he explains.

> The clergyman, the physician, the teacher, must be paid; but each of them, if his duty be performed in the true spirit, can hardly help a shiver of disgust when money is counted out to him for administering the consolations of religion, for saving some precious life, for sowing the seeds of Christian civilization in young ingenuous souls. (171-172)

This catalogue omits the "sacred interest" of love, as expressed in courtship, but that interest clearly and repeatedly becomes an economic transaction in the course of the novel.

Holmes thus puts *Elsie Venner* to a use not mentioned in the multiple qualifications and restatements which preface the book, a use less time-worn than his explicit argument with Calvinism (which, by 1860, was a "negligible opponent" anyway; cf. Garner 283, Martin 115). By substituting economics for sex as a central motivation throughout the novel, Holmes explores the degree to which financial necessity and desire influence behavior. The economic motive impels all but the title character, who proves unfit to live in a "new" world where even Brahmins accomodate themselves to monetary considerations.

When the novel begins, Elsie Venner is attending classes at the Apollinean Institute, a school where the "business of instruction" is "incidental"; "its real business was making money by taking young girls in as boarders." The principal of the school has a single-minded intention: to make "just as much money in just as few years as could be safely done" (48). Silas Peckham tries very hard to get "the most work for the least money out of his assistants" and so "pocket[s]" the "profits" of their hard work (129). His establishment, "got up on commercial principles" (68), is a "rude market" in which at least one of his teachers, Helen Darley, has "bartered away the life of her youth" (124).

Silas Peckham and his employees are only the first of the residents of Rockland, Maine, who are introduced in monetary terms. The principal's "commercial spirit" is an accurate reflection of the whole town's (131). Even the most minor, and the most positive, characters are described in economic terms. Dr. Kittredge's hired man Abel Stebbins, for instance, "sold his time to the Doctor, and, having sold it . . . took care to fulfil his half of the bargain" (135).

If economics are an explicit concern in the town of Rockland, sex is a subliminal obsession for its residents. When Bernard Langdon arrives at the Apollinean Female Institute to begin his duties as schoolmaster, for example, he moves

> about among these young girls day after day, his eyes meeting theirs, his breath mingling with theirs, his voice growing familiar to them . . . with its male depth and breadth of sound among the chorus of trebles, as if it were a river in which a hundred of these little piping streamlets might lose themselves. (174)

Such an attraction is unconscious, not quite understood: "Dear souls! they only half knew what they were doing" (175).

Holmes reinforces the obsession which underpins his novel by multiple allusions to the Biblical fall, in which he makes the sexual element paramount. Bernard Langdon, for example, experiences schoolteaching as a modern-day Adam responding to the overwhelming sexual attractions of Eve. The knowledge his pupil desires is clearly sensual as well:

> What was there to distract him or disturb him? He did not know,—but there was something. This sumptuous creature, this Eve just within the gate of an untried Paradise, untutored in the ways of the world, but on tiptoe to reach the fruit of the tree of knowledge,—alive to the moist vitality of that warm atmosphere palpitating with voices and music. . . . —this almost overwomanized woman might well have bewitched him. (105)

Schoolgirls entice Bernard Langdon to sexual consciousness; Elsie has done the same for her cousin Dick: "when those who parted as children meet as man and woman, there is always a renewal of that early experience which followed the taste of the forbidden fruit—a natural blush of consciousness, not without its charm" (157). Elsie herself describes Eve as "a good woman," and asserts that "she'd have done just so, if she'd been there" (256).

Significantly and repeatedly in this novel, such forces, which are implicitly sexual, are made literally economic. Sentimental relations become business operations, described in the language of finance, and with decided economic consequences. Economics replace affection, as financial interest becomes not only a means of expression but an open substitution for love. Sexual

attraction is displaced by financial dealing, sentimental relations supplemented with economic ones. Sexual fantasies are presented as economic fears (cf. Baym 20, 28, 45; Dalke 295-296; Michaels 279).

The Widow Rowens, for example, is in search of a gentleman "with an ample fortune" (289); her hunt duplicates that of numerous "fair . . . dowerless ladies," who are "smiling and singing and fading" away (182). Those faded gentlewomen form a marked contrast to the flourishing Colonel Sprowle, who succeeds "in trade, and also by matrimony" (82) in achieving what they pursue so fruitlessly. The Colonel and his wife plan a great party as a quite literal means of offering their daughter for marriage in turn: "'There's one piece of goods,' said the Colonel to his wife, 'that we ha'n't disposed of, nor got a customer for yet. . . . Let's have a party, and give her a chance to show herself'" (83).

The Colonel describes his daughter as if she were an item of merchandise for sale. The young clerks who walk by the Institute, hoping to catch a word or a glance from the young ladies there, describe themselves in the same way: they use

> that style of address . . . acquired in the retail business, as if the salesman were recommending himself to a customer,—"First-rate family article, Ma'am; warranted to wear a lifetime; just one yard and three quarters in this pattern, Ma'am; sha'n't I have the pleasure?" (174)

The replacement of affectional by financial language is perhaps most succinctly accomplished by Silas Peckham, who taunts Helen Darley on her return from the Dudley mansion-house:

> "Hope the Squire treated you hahnsomely,—liberal pecooniary compensation,—hey? A'n't much of a loser, I guess, by acceptin' his propositions?" Helen blushed at this last question, as if Silas had meant something by it beyond asking what money she had received; but his own double-meaning expression and her blush were too nice points for him to have taken cognizance of. (471)

The distinction between the languages of love and of economics is too fine not only for Silas Peckham, but for most of the characters in this novel, who have substituted financial interest for affection. Their confusion is made explicit when Holmes describes love as a treasure which costs a great deal. It involves an expenditure which most people are unable to pay:

> No man or woman can appropriate beauty without paying for it,—in endowments, in fortune, in position, in self-surrender, or other valuable stock; and there are a great many who are too

poor, too ordinary, too humble, too busy, too proud, to pay any of these prices for it. (126)

The wealthiest family in Rockland remain, of course, as oblivious to financial concerns as they are to financial need. But it is precisely the inattention of Elsie Venner and her father to such matters which makes them vulnerable to the economic schemes of their closest relative. Dudley Venner does not imagine that his nephew Dick might "wish to become his son-in-law for the sake of his property" (271).

Dick carefully catalogues the attractions of his uncle's home—"The old house . . . fat with the deposits of rich generations which had gone before" (197)—and, with the air of an accountant, weighs them against the drawbacks "of establishing himself as the heir of the Dudley mansion house and fortune":

> There was much to be said on both sides. It was a balance to be struck after the two columns were added up. He struck the balance, and came to the conclusion that he would fall in love with Elsie Venner. . . . business is business. . . . (198-199)

> It was plain enough to him that the road to fortune was before him and that the first thing was to marry Elsie. . . . In short, he must have the property, and Elsie Venner, as she was to go with it. . . . (262-263)

For Dick, as for the smaller-minded schemer Silas Peckham, monetary gain is the single aim. All other actions are judged by that standard. Dick reflects, for instance, that he himself "was not principled against virtue, provided virtue were a better *investment* than its opposite" (264, my emphasis). Even moral issues are expressed in economic terms.

A confirmed fortune hunter, Dick assumes that all others share his motives. He attributes Elsie's attraction to Bernard Langdon to the scheming of the latter: "Estates like the Dudley property were not to had every day, and no doubt the Yankee usher was willing to take some pains to make sure of Elsie" (310). When Dick attempts to kill the schoolmaster, and so dispose of what he views as an economic rival, he is driven from town. But his departure fails to cleanse Rockland of the fortune-hunting impulse. It is embraced, and successfully realized, by his supposed opponent.

The keynote of Bernard Langdon's concern is sounded in the first chapter of the novel, "The Brahmin Caste of New England." There Holmes explains the lack of an American aristocracy, by tracing the usual cycle of large fortunes: "subdivided and distributed," they "diminish rapidly": "the millionocracy . . . is not at all an affair of persons and families, but a perpetual fact of money with a variable human el-

ement" (2). Money is long-standing, even permanent; its owners, however, change constantly.

Against this unsettled order Holmes juxtaposes the constancy of the Brahmins, a "harmless. inoffensive, untitled aristocracy" distinguished by its aptitude for learning (4). This "race of the hereditary scholar has exchanged a certain portion of its animal vigor for its new instincts"; it possesses only a "compromised and lowered vitality" (5).

It becomes very clear in the second chapter, when Holmes turns to the consideration of a particular young Brahmin, that the lack of vitality attributed to this class is less physiological than economic. To be sure, Bernard Langdon's face is a "little too place" (7), his jaw slightly narrowed, his whiskers thin; altogether he is a "delicate" and "reflective" "form of physical life" (8). But when Bernard speaks for the first time, the lack he displays is not one of physical vitality, but rather an habitual financial failing:

> "There's trouble at home, and they cannot keep me here as they have done. So I must look out for myself for a while. It's what I've done before, and am ready to do again". . . . our young man had been obliged, from an early period, to do something to support himself, and found himself stopped short in his studies by the inability of the good people at home to furnish him the present means of support as a student. (16)

The first act of Holmes's story, the decision of an impoverished young man to teach in a provincial town, is thus motivated by a need for cash. Like most other significant acts in ***Elsie Venner,*** Bernard's behavior has an economic cause. The young man goes into service for the money it will bring; he gives up his first position, in Pigwacket Centre, for "a proposition so much more agreeable and advantageous"—that is, with higher wages—in Rockland (40).

He there encounters a young lady assistant, who finds herself in precisely the same position as he:

> She was dependent, frail, sensitive, conscientious. She was in the power of a hard, grasping, thin-blooded, tough-fibred, trading educator, who . . . meant to have his money's worth out of her brains, and as much more than his money's worth as he could get. (69)

Bernard Langdon discovers in Helen Darley a kindred spirit. Their companionship is one of displaced class:

> When two persons of this exceptional breeding meet. . . . they seek each other's company at once by the natural law of elective affinity. It is wonderful how men and women know their peers. If two stranger queens, sole survivors of two shipwrecked

vessels, were cast, half-naked, on a rock together, each would at once address the other as "Our Royal Sister." (74-75)

Like two dethroned monarchs, Bernard and Helen meet in the desolation that is *Rock*land (my emphasis), and revel in one another's gentle breeding. Bernard discovers, to his great pleasure, that Helen is a "lady"; "that word meant a good deal to the descendent of the courtly Wentworths and the scholarly Langdons" (75).

Much as Bernard comes to care for Helen Darley, he never considers her as a possible mate. She may be noble, but she is also poor. When the schoolmaster discovers that same nobility at the Widow Rowens' tea-party, attached to a fortune that is intact, the displacement of one companion by another is palpable. Bernard acknowledges that Helen "never looked more charmingly . . . but, to be sure, he had just been looking at the young girl next him, so that his eyes were brimful of beauty" (305). If Holmes presented Helen as a dethroned queen, Bernard imagines Letty Forrester as a princess, a potential ruler:

This thorough-bred schoolgirl quite enchanted Mr. Bernard. He could not understand where she got her style, her way of dress, her enunciation, her easy manners . . . this young girl [was] fit to be a Crown Prince's partner where there were a thousand to choose from. (304-305)

The use of the queenly metaphor points accurately to the relative finances of the two women, as well as to their relationships with Bernard. Helen has no estate but her breeding, while Letty is soon to add to her good breeding immense wealth. As decidedly as Dick Venner pursued his wealthy cousin, Bernard sets out to capture the heiress.

Fortune-hunting is not foreign to Bernard's family. His grandfather had engaged in that pursuit with some success:

It is a charming thing for the scholar, when his fortune carries him in this way. . . . His narrow study expands into a stately library, his books are counted by thousands . . . and his favorites are dressed in gilded calf. . . . The Reverend Jedediah Langdon, grandfather of our young gentleman, had made an advantageous alliance of this kind. (10-11)

If this minister did not worship the golden calf, he most assuredly surrounded himself with its images.

The activity which Holmes implicitly rebukes in the grandfather is pursued even more successfully by the grandson. In the mercenary world of this novel, as Bernard's professor makes clear from the first, it is imperative to sublimate the sexual urges to achieve monetary success. When the professor writes Bernard's recommendation, he hesitates to recommend him as a teacher for either sex, in fear that sexual dalliance, or "misalliance" (17), will hamper his career:

He should . . . work his way up to a better kind of practice,—better, that is, in the vulgar, worldly sense. . . . there would soon be an opening into the Doctor's Paradise. . . . I would not have him marry until he knew his level,—that is, again, looking at the matter in a purely worldly point of view, and not taking the sentiments at all into consideration. (19-20)

Bernard follows the professor's advice not to "undervalue" himself (482): he "took a genteel office, furnished it neatly, dressed with a certain elegance, soon made a circle of acquaintances, and began to work his way into the right kind of business" (484). This list of material successes is crowned by the announcement of Bernard's engagement to a woman who is ironically presented as the product, not of her parents, but of a financial concern: " 'that is neither more nor less than Miss Letitia Forrester, daughter of—of—why, the great banking firm, you know, Bilyums Brothers and Forrester' " (485). Bernard ends the novel having surpassed not only his grandfather's achievement, but those of the "millionocracy" of Chapter One: he contemplates, in the novel's final pages, the potential billions of his wife's estate.

The real "romance of destiny" of the novel's subtitle thus belongs, quite clearly, to Bernard. It is he, and not Elsie, who realizes the destiny offered tantalizingly throughout the novel which bears her name, a destiny from which she is pointedly excluded: the possibility of improving oneself by marriage to money.

Bernard's romantic fate is not far different from that of Helen Darley, whose forthcoming marriage is also imagined in monetary terms. Dudley Venner's proposal surprises Helen because of the enormous economic difference between them:

a man like this . . . [who] lived in another sphere than hers, working as she was for her bread [,] a poor operative in the factory of a hard master and jealous overseer, the salaried drudge of Mr. Silas Peckham. . . . [was] a man so far removed from her in outward circumstance. (468).

Dudley Venner hopes to enjoy with his second wife the same unity of spirit he knew with his first. But that unity has a decidedly materialistic beginning. He makes his marriage plans public at the moment when Helen is deprived of her salary. Once more, the metaphor of queenship is invoked, this time to describe Helen's belated coming into wealth. Bernard begs Mr. Venner, "as one of the Trustees of this Institution, to look at the manner in which its Principal has attempted to swindle this faithful teacher". . . . Dudley Venner took the account and read it through. . . . Then he turned to Silas Peckham.

"You may make arrangements for a new assistant in the branches this lady has taught. Miss Helen Darley is to be my wife". . . . Mr. Bernard . . . turned to Dudley Venner, and said,—

"She is a queen, but has never found it out. The world has nothing nobler than this dear woman, whom you have discovered in the disguise of a teacher." (479)

Helen Darley's marriage involves, as clearly as does Bernard Langdon's, a displacement. Helen can only marry Dudley Venner after his daughter has died, and after she herself has undertaken "the sisterly task" of nursing Elsie in her last illness (431). As Michael Paul Rogin observes,

Elsie Venner addressed anxieties over female sexual power and family breakdown. Holmes titillated those anxieties, [but then] defused them. . . . Elsie's death . . . frees the other characters. . . . After she dies, [her father] marries the school teacher. . . . [a] restoration of family happiness. . . . (185-186)

Indeed, the structural principle of **Elsie Venner** seems to be one of displacement. There is a continual shift in focus and emphasis throughout the novel. Its original narrator, the professor, is replaced by Dr. Kittredge as advisor to young Langdon. Dick's fortune-hunting activities are taken over by Bernard. Bernard's interest shifts from Helen to Letty, as Dudley's shifts from Elsie to Helen. Yet another significant displacement involves the two types of women Holmes portrays in this novel. The original means of distinguishing between them is purely aesthetic. The schoolgirls, for example, are contrasted by hue (50-51). Helen and Elsie are likewise first brought together in a chapter entitled "Sunbeam and Shadow." The Widow Rowens attempts—mistakenly—to plan her tea-party on the same principle of contrast, with Helen Darley as a faded foil to her own brilliant coloring:

"—why, yes, just the thing,—light brown hair, blue eyes,—won't my pattern show off well against her? . . . nobody knows what a 'thunder-and-lightening woman' . . . is, till she gets alongside one of those old-maidish girls, with hair the color of brown sugar, and eyes like the blue of a teacup." (292)

The varied complexions of these women represent, surely, their relative sexual natures. Holmes hints as much when he describes the "probable want of force" of Helen Darley (128), or when he compares her "femineity" with the "muliebrity," the "color and flavor" of the "tropical" young girls she teaches (126). But the sexual rivalry of such women is essentially an economic one, as the outcome of the tea-party makes clear. When Helen captivates Dudley's attention, and Letty Bernard's, the loss of the dark women is primarily monetary.

In an extended discussion, Leslie Fiedler argues that "the Dark Lady" represents "the hunger of the Protestant, Anglo-Saxon male . . . for the rich sexuality, the dangerous warmth he rejected as unworthy of his wife"—who is, of course, always a Fair Maiden. Fiedler suggests that Holmes deliberately exploits such a contrast in *Elsie Venner,*

where he sets up with some care the customary opposition of a "dependent, frail, sensitive" blue-eyed lady . . . and the darkeyed "ophidian" girl, Elsie, but he does not permit them to enter into the archetypal contest for the soul of the hero. (300-301)

That contest has been forestalled by another: Bernard is not an object of rivalry between Helen and Elsie because he himself is engaged in a different pursuit, that of getting cash from a well-to-do student. It is significant that the girl he marries, like Dudley Venner's second wife, is younger than her husband: he retains thereby a measure of superiority in a marriage to which she brings all the financial resources.

Fiedler maintains that the "class-war meanings" of the English sentimental novel are lost in America, whose culture could provide no artistocratic seducers to prey on poor young maidens (89). But those meanings have been transmuted: in the land without aristocracy which Holmes portrays in his first chapter, everyone is scrambling for cash. Bernard is in no position to play Lovelace or Don Juan, but he engages quite successfully in the pursuit of a wealthy wife.

The same novel which charts Bernard Langdon's accumulation of wealth, by hard work, good breeding and marriage, and the duplication of that accomplishment by Helen Darley, demonstrates as well Elsie Venner's exclusion from such activity. Elsie's stigmata prevent her from expressing or receiving affection. More remarkably, they represent her exclusion from the act of buying and selling which defines marriage for the other characters of this novel. In the climactic scene of this book, Elsie doesn't ask Bernard for money, nor—as she could easily do—offer it to him, but begs him instead for love. Bernard is patently unable to offer her the affection she so desperately needs: " 'Give me your hand, dear Elsie, and trust me that I will be as true a friend to you as if we were children of the same mother' " (423).

Bernard offers Elsie a form of love not demonstrated anywhere in the world of this novel, where siblings do not exist. He offers a similar brotherly substitution to Helen Darley, who, in pursuit of her own fortune, accepts the appelation. But Elsie cannot accept, much less understand, the terms on which marriage is concluded by her peers. Her infection has disabled her for life in plutocratic society. She is a woman entirely out of date in Holmes's fiction: she seeks affection in a world in which destiny is, immutably, economic.

The exclusion of Elsie Venner thus becomes not only a judgment on out-moded theology, not only an exploration of genetic determinism, but also a commentary on the destructive economic practices of a "new" social order. What began as a treatise on original sin becomes criticism of a society in which wealth is the central obsession (cf. Garner 292, Martin 119).

Destiny in this book seems to be shaped as much by financial motive as by heredity. The "new" society is congenial only to certain genetic traits, those which involve an obsession with moneygetting. Holmes's targets are both old dogma and new belief: he passes judgment on forms of determinism that are theological and physiological, but he also criticizes financial motives. He supplements the predestination of the Calvinists and the blood line of the family with an equally powerful but much more worldly form of influence, that of money. The snake which bites Catalina Venner represents original sin, of a sexual nature, as well as inherited genetic tendencies; but it also represents a fall into the world of economics. The bite of the serpent, and the disruption which results, usher in an era in which, distressingly, all relationships are based on cash.

Works Cited

Baym, Nina. *Women's Fiction: A Guide to Novels by and about Women in America, 1820-70.* Ithaca, New York: Cornell University Press, 1978.

Dalke, Anne. "'The Shameless Woman is the Worst of Men': Sexual Aggression in Nineteenth-Century Sensational Novels." *Studies in the Novel* 18 (Fall 1986): 291-303.

Fiedler, Leslie. *Love and Death in the American Novel.* Rev. ed. New York: Stein and Day, 1966.

Gallagher, Kathleen. "The Art of Snake Handling: *Lamia, Elsie Venner,* and 'Rappaccini's Daughter.'" *Studies in American Fiction* 3 (Spring 1975): 51-64.

Garner, Stanton. "*Elsie Venner:* Holmes's Deadly 'Book of Life.'" *Huntington Library Quarterly* 37 (May 1974): 283-298.

Holmes, Oliver Wendell. *Elsie Venner: A Romance of Destiny.* 1861; rpt. Standard Library Edition, 15 vols. Vol. 5. New York: Arno, 1976.

Martin, John Stephen. "The Novels of Oliver Wendell Holmes: A Re-interpretation." *Literature and Ideas in America.* Ed. Robert Falk. Columbus: Ohio University Press, 1975. 111-127.

Michaels, Walter Benn. "Dreiser's *Financier:* The Man of Business as a Man of Letters." *American Realism: New Essays.* Ed. Eric Sundquist. Baltimore: Johns Hopkins University Press, 1982. 278-294.

Parker, Gail Thain. "Sex, Sentiment, and Oliver Wendell Holmes." *Women's Studies* 1 (1972): 47-63.

Rogin, Michael Paul. *Subversive Geneology: The Politics and Art of Herman Melville.* New York: Knopf, 1983.

Spiller, Robert E. et al., eds. "The New England Triumvirate: Longfellow, Holmes, Lowell." *Literary History of the United States: History.* 4th ed. rev. New York: Macmillan, 1974. 587-606.

Len Gougeon (essay date 1994)

SOURCE: "Holmes's Emerson and the Conservative Critique of Realism," in *South Atlantic Review,* Vol. 59, No. 1, January, 1994, pp. 107-25.

[*In the following essay, Gougeon examines Holmes's attempt in his biography,* Ralph Waldo Emerson, *to make Emerson into an icon of cultural conservatism.*]

The controversy generated by the emergence of American realism and naturalism in the post-Civil War period affected not only the criticism directed toward contemporary representatives of the movement but also critical interpretations of the works of previously established and highly regarded authors. Not surprisingly, in some cases deliberate efforts were made by opposing camps to appropriate the authority of past idols in order to reinforce arguments for or against the new realism and naturalism. Nowhere is evidence of this historic literary controversy more apparent than in the critical discussions of Ralph Waldo Emerson that appeared at this time. The following narrative documents the redoubtable efforts of Oliver Wendell Holmes to create, in his 1884 biography of Emerson, and later in the pages of the *Atlantic Monthly,* an icon of cultural conservatism. Holmes's efforts would, in turn, find a counterpoint in a critical response from one of America's foremost literary figures of the time, William Dean Howells. For Howells, Emerson was a harbinger of literary revolution.

Oliver Wendell Holmes was one of the nineteenth century's most prominent custodians of the "genteel tradition" in American culture. These individuals are described by Daniel Aaron as "men and women of culture and taste who did their best to mitigate the crudities of the Gilded Age" and who "glanced back nostalgically to the myth of unspoiled homogeneous America, and shrank from the squalor, violence, and vulgarity of their own times." Offering more than a brief stay against confusion, these stalwart souls "plumped for unchanging moral values and traditional culture. They closed ranks against naturalism, literary experimentation, and social heterodoxy, against any movement that might endanger . . . the 'spiritual rootage of art' " (734, 735). All of these values would emerge conspicuously in Holmes's popular biography *Ralph Waldo Emerson,* published by Houghton, Mifflin and Company in their prestigious American Men of Letters series in 1884. This biography has always been an influential work, and it remains very firmly established in the canon of Emerson scholarship to this day.[1]

Holmes's conservative and genteel values are expressed throughout the biography in a variety of subtle and sometimes surprising ways, not the least of which are the unflattering allusions he makes to two of Emerson's best-known literary contemporaries and friends, Henry David Thoreau and Walt Whitman. While these references are relatively brief, it is clear from Holmes's working notes in his papers at the Library of Congress that the Brahmin saw them both as representatives of the Zola school of literary realism, that is, as writers who rejected the traditional rules of both literary and social decorum. In his view these individuals sought to nullify civilization and in the process reduce literary subject matter to a disgusting "slop-pail" level. The notes also suggest that Holmes was clearly disturbed by Emerson's consistent admiration for, and support of, both Thoreau and Whitman. While readers familiar with Emerson's essay "The Poet" would have no trouble in understanding his admiration for Whitman, and those familiar with "Self-Reliance" could not be puzzled by his high regard for Thoreau, for Holmes these relationships presented a problem, and possibly an opportunity. By criticizing both Thoreau and Whitman for what he considered to be their degenerate eccentricities, Holmes could deflect such criticisms from Emerson and thus preserve, for the most part, a decidedly conservative view of the man.

In the large bound volume of handwritten notes used in preparing the biography, Holmes initially associates Thoreau's experiment at Walden Pond with the failed transcendentalist community at Brook Farm.[2] For Holmes, both of these enterprises were the products of a pernicious tendency toward whimsy. Of course it was Emerson himself who had once claimed in "Self Reliance," "I would write on the lintels of the door-post, *Whim.* I hope it is somewhat better than whim at last, but we cannot spend the day in explanation" (*Collected Works* 2: 30). And it was also Emerson who consistently encouraged others to challenge the placid assumptions of the world about and

to follow their instincts regardless of society's judgments. For Holmes such inclinations could lead to unwholesome consequences that he felt, or chose to assert, Emerson would never have approved. In his view Thoreau and Whitman provided two good examples of such excess. Holmes's notation reads as follows:

> Brook Farm
>
> Its failure. Conduct of Life 112.[3]
>
> Thoreau who worked out one whim as Brook Farm worked out another.

He goes on to note:

> Thoreau a great boy—we all like to build huts when we are boys and make ourselves uncomfortable in every ingenious way possible. (1)

While this Thoreauvian whimsy may appear innocuous enough to most, for Holmes such puerile lawlessness inevitably leads one away from conventional civilization and its standards and discipline. Inevitably, it is a course fraught with danger. Hence, he notes further:

> Thoreau, Walt Whitman. One dispensed with the architect and the cook, the other with the tailor, at last in Zola we reached the scavenger and the slop-pail. Antisthenes the first cynic with the holes in his coat. (2)

These observations then lead Holmes into something of a conundrum. What did Emerson, whom Holmes depicts as the epitome of conservative, civilized, and "genteel" values, see in these individuals during his lifelong relationships with them? How could he admire such men? When considering the topic of the "Influence of others on E.," Holmes asks in his notebook: "What was the meaning for his fancy for Walt Whitman? Of his liking for Thoreau and for *others.*"

A typescript of these handwritten notes provides some additional materials, as well as some further insights into Holmes's view of Whitman and Thoreau.[4] This typescript includes the following statement under the heading "Influence of E. on others."

> Influence on Thoreau, Whitman, Alcott, Channing and others.
>
> Relation between Thoreau and Whitman; what they had in common.

Under the heading "Influence of others on E." in the typescript, Holmes again asks, "What is the meaning of his fancy for Walt Whitman? Of his liking for Thoreau and *others?*" and he then records the following "Comments."

> Thoreau, Walt Whitman, Zola. Scavenger and slop pail.
>
> E's mind acted on a second series of minds and his force was by them converted into definite action. Th. Parker was the best example of this. But look at Brownson, Father Hecker, W. Channing, Mrs. Ripley. The ridiculous in Transcendentalism, see Cranch's caricatures. Also Conway page 233.[5]

These comments suggest the strategy that Holmes eventually devised for the troublesome conundrum of Emerson's personal relationships. He simply asserted that Emerson's influence on others was a philosophical rather than a practical one. These "others," Holmes insists, would put into practice what Emerson preached, but not necessarily in ways he would have approved. By offering this condemnation of the other two, Holmes could implicitly defend Emerson against similar charges by insisting that he would not have approved such conduct and never intended to encourage such "excess." Thus we have the "ridiculousness" of transcendentalism, especially as represented in the example of Brook Farm; the pernicious "whimsy" of Thoreau's experiment at Walden Pond; and the "slop-pail" poetry of Walt Whitman. Holmes goes on to note:

> E's assertion of the individual to be found in Thoreau's cabin, in Brook farm, Walt Whitman, T. Parker, etc.
>
> See E's lect. on the Times what he says about reforms, abolition, etc.
>
> Walt Whitman threw the sponge and thought he should make a picture.

All of these views are finally developed in the biography but in a somewhat adumbrated way. For example, Holmes's first reference to Thoreau in the work itself does not mention him by name but his identity is obvious enough. In discussing Concord's reputation for producing unique characters, Holmes refers, among others, to "that unique individual, half college-graduate and half Algonquin, the Robinson Crusoe of Walden Pond, who carried out a school-boy whim to its full proportions, and told the story of Nature in undress as only one who had hidden in her bedroom could have told it" (72).[6] The associations Holmes makes here are clear and certainly less than flattering to say the least. Not only is Thoreau's sojourn at Walden Pond seen as little more than a schoolboy's whim, as suggested in Holmes's notes, but Thoreau's exposure to raw nature seems almost prurient—which is undoubtedly, in his mind at least, one of the untoward consequences of nullifying civilization.

Additionally, for Holmes, Thoreau's primitive sojourn at Walden was lacking in "common sense," and in the biography he is at pains to distance Emerson from it. Even though Emerson was known to have experimented with a variety of social schemes in his own household and was open to a variety of strategies for bringing about the general reform of society, Holmes assures his readers that "[i]t would never have occurred to him [Emerson] to leave all the conveniences and comforts of life to go and dwell in a shanty, so as to prove to himself that he could live like a savage, or like his friends 'Teague and his jade,' as he called the man and brother and sister, more commonly known nowadays as Pat, or Patrick, and his old woman" (143). As Holmes would have it, Thoreau's move to Walden Pond would have been seen by Emerson as tantamount to an atavistic reversion to a life-style characteristic of the poor and primitive Irish, a life-style from which civilized New Englanders had long ago evolved.

As suggested by his notes, Holmes saw the failure of Brook Farm as the result of the same kind of whimsy and impracticality represented in Thoreau's experiment. At one point, when discussing Emerson's 1844 lecture "New England Reformers," he points out that "[t]he Brook Farm experiment was an index of the state of mind among one section of the Reformers of whom he [Emerson] was writing." The purpose of this group, according to Holmes, was "[t]o remodel society and the world into a 'happy family' . . ." (189). Thus, "Some attacked one part of the old system, some another; . . . one was for a phalanstery, where all should live in common, and another was meditating the plan and place of the wigwam where he was to dwell apart in the proud independence of the woodchuck and the musquash." In Holmes's view Emerson could never have approved of such an addled enterprise. He goes on to note that while "Emerson had the largest and kindliest sympathy with their ideals and aims, . . . he was too cleareyed not to see through the whims and extravagances of the unpractical experiments" (189). To reinforce even further this dissociation of Emerson from the extravagant "whimsy" of such reformers, Holmes assures his readers that "Emerson has had the name of being a leader in many movements in which he had very limited confidence" and that, while "the idealizing impulse derived from him lent its force" to such groups, "he was in no sense responsible" for their organization. According to Holmes, Emerson's "sympathies were not allowed to mislead him; he knew human nature too well to believe in a Noah's ark full of idealists" (191).

If Thoreau did have a redeeming characteristic for Holmes, it was his clarity of vision in perceiving the natural world. "Thoreau," says Holmes, lent Emerson "a new set of organs of sense of wonderful delicacy." While Emerson "looked at nature as a poet, and his natural history, if left to himself, would have been as vague as that of Polonius, . . . Thoreau had a pair of eyes which, like those of the Indian deity, could see the smallest emmet on the blackest stone in the darkest night,—or come nearer to seeing it than those of most mortals." According to Holmes, "Emerson's long intimacy with [Thoreau] taught him to give an outline to many natural objects which would have been poetic nebulae to him but for this companionship" (389).

Here again, however, this closeness to nature was fraught with danger, as Holmes would point out when speaking of Whitman. Interestingly enough, the unusual association of Thoreau and Whitman and Zola is only suggested in the biography and never overtly made as it is in the notes. As Holmes's notes make clear, however, he saw all three as being in the same literary boat. Additionally, Holmes's concern with distancing Emerson from Whitman at this time was undoubtedly amplified because just two years earlier *Leaves of Grass* had been "banned in Boston." On 1 March 1882 the District Attorney of Boston notified Whitman's publisher, Osgood and Company, that he had officially classified *Leaves of Grass* as obscene literature and demanded substantive deletions of offensive materials from the work. After a brief and unsuccessful negotiation with Whitman, who refused to make the changes, Osgood ceased publication of the book. The case caused a great deal of notoriety at the time (Allen 498-99).

When speaking of the natural quality of Emerson's poetic diction, a characteristic that he attributes in part to Thoreau's influence in the statement above, Holmes asserts that Emerson "called upon the poet to 'Tell men what they knew before;/Paint the prospect from their door,' "[7] and he insists that "his practice was like his counsel." Emerson, he says, "saw our plain New England life with as honest New England eyes as ever looked at a huckleberry-bush or into a milking-pail." However, according to Holmes, "this noble quality of his had its dangerous side. In one of his exalted moods he would have us 'Give to barrows, trays and pans/ Grace and glimmer of romance' " (324-25).[8] The "danger" here, of course, is that by directing the poet's attention to the mundane and potentially tawdry elements of the real world about, the elegant, the civilized, and, for Holmes, the truly poetic quality of life is lost. Consequently, to compensate for this dangerous tendency, Holmes offers an ingenious corrective taken from Emerson's own writings. From Emerson's lecture "Poetry and Imagination," he quotes the following: "What we once admired as poetry has long since come to be a sound of tin pans; and many of our later books we have outgrown. Perhaps Homer and Milton will be tin pans yet" (Emerson *Complete Works* 8: 68; qtd. in Holmes, **Ralph Waldo Emerson** 325). While Emerson's point here is obviously that the poetry of the past does not always wear well, that it eventually becomes like the sound of "tin pans" and must be foregone in favor of the new, Holmes offers

the following interpretation that makes the tin pans, not poetry, the object of Emerson's comment: "The 'grace and glimmer of romance' which were to invest the tin pan are," he says, "forgotten," and Emerson "uses it as a belittling object for comparison." Following this rather extraordinary feat of verbal legerdemain, Holmes assures his readers that Emerson himself "was not often betrayed into the mistake of confounding the prosaic with the poetical, but his followers, so far as the 'realists' have taken their hint from him, have done it most thoroughly" (325).

In this discussion of Emerson's poetics, Holmes goes on to make specific reference to Whitman. In Holmes's view the poetic principles articulated by Emerson must be interpreted with common sense and reasonable restraint lest they mislead one. Unfortunately, in Holmes's opinion, it is the latter that has frequently happened. Just as Emerson's philosophy of individualism had been perverted into an uncivilized and whimsical impracticality at Walden Pond and Brook Farm, so too the literary "realists" are now perverting his poetic principles into a disgusting preference for the lowly and offensive. For Holmes this addled "realistic" tendency of some who claim to be Emerson's cohorts is indicative of the assault on established literary values generally. One of the chief American offenders in this regard, as Holmes would have it, is Walt Whitman. "Mr. Whitman," says Holmes, "enumerates all the objects he happens to be looking at as if they were equally suggestive to the poetical mind, furnishing his reader a large assortment on which he may exercise the fullest freedom of selection." This, he says, "is only giving him the same liberty that Lord Timothy Dexter allowed his readers in the matter of punctuation, by leaving all stops out of his sentences, and printing at the end of his book a page of commas, semicolons, colons, periods, notes of interrogation and exclamation, with which the reader is expected to 'pepper' the pages as he might see fit" (325-26).[9]

The criticism here is tame enough but for Holmes, as his notes make clear, this tendency leaves both Thoreau and Whitman dangerously close to the corruption of European realism and naturalism, the influence of which was manifesting itself just then in the rise of a new generation of American writers that included Mark Twain, Henry James, William Dean Howells, and several others. Shoring up the crumbling literary citadel of Boston in the face of this onslaught was a constant concern to Holmes, and he never missed an opportunity to fire a shot. Consequently, making what must have seemed something of a surprising leap to his readers, Holmes goes on directly to state: "French realism does not stop at the tin pan, but must deal with the slop-pail and the wash-tub as if it were literally true that 'In the mud and scum of things/There alway, alway something sings.'"[10] Holmes further states; "Happy were it for the world if M. Zola and his tribe would stop even there; but when they cross the borders of science into its infected districts, leaving behind them the reserve and delicacy which the genuine scientific observer never forgets to carry with him, they disgust even those to whom the worst scenes they describe are too wretchedly familiar" (326). Holmes always felt a strong antipathy toward Zola and the corrupting realistic/naturalistic movement in literature that he represented. Eleanor Tilton notes that Holmes told a correspondent in September of 1885 that "the naturalism of 'unwashed Zola' offered him nothing"; she notes further that, in his notebook for his appropriately titled novel, *A Mortal Antipathy* (1885), he expressed the opinion that it was "time for the decently immoral to interfere with the nauseating realism of Zola and the rest" (352, 353). "The rest" in this case would include Flaubert, whose *Madame Bovary* (1857) Holmes found particularly offensive.

Following the publication of his biography, Holmes would frequently invoke his conservative image of Emerson while continuing the struggle against literary innovation. For the most part, he relied upon his easy access to the pages of the *Atlantic Monthly* to provide an outlet for his views. However, with changing times and the accelerating acceptance of realism and naturalism in the late 1880s and early 1890s, his position would become increasingly difficult to maintain. Additionally, there were other powerful figures on the literary scene who would frequently turn to Emerson's writings in defending the dreaded infidels. Not the least of these champions of realism was William Dean Howells.

It is somewhat ironic that very early in his literary career Howells was declared the heir apparent to the New England literary tradition by Oliver Wendell Holmes.[11] During his years as editor of the *Atlantic Monthly,* 1871-81, Holmes was something of a mentor, and a nemesis, to him. Howells, in return, was dutiful. As Kenneth Lynn points out, during the time of his editorship, when Holmes "submitted his literary work to the *Atlantic, . . .* Howells never failed to accept it. [And] after Howells began to write novels in the early 1870s, Holmes not only read them, but also monitored them for social errors" (96). Eventually, however, Howells came to feel an increasing tension between his growing commitment to the principles and practices of literary realism and the traditional dedication of the *Atlantic* to an increasingly effete romantic idealism, represented most immediately to Howells by the aging Holmes as well as Longfellow, Lowell, and others. By 1882 Howells was, as he told a correspondent at the time, "reading everything of Zola's that [he could] get [his] hands on" and feeling increasingly cramped by his Boston environment (qtd. in Lynn 258). (Holmes literally lived two doors down from him on Beacon Street.) After moving to New York in 1889, a cultural world away from Boston, Howells would continue to

show a public deference toward the aged Holmes, but in his monthly "Editor's Study" column, he would openly promote the cause of realism and the works of continental and British authors in words that must have made Holmes's ears burn. Indeed, Lynn indicates "that Howells was possessed by a new boldness of purpose and imaginative freedom [that were] made explicit at the very outset of his career at *Harper's.* . . . The proprietor of 'The Editor's Study' made it clear that he would review mostly novels, because in his bluntly stated opinion they constituted 'the only living movement in imaginative literature.' Various 'professors' were given to denunciations of this new literature, which they justified by pointing to 'certain objectionable French novels,' yet Howells not only went on to defend the masters of the modern novel, but he did so with a flamboyant scorn for the detractors that reminded some observers of Mark Twain's remarkable zest for verbal battle" (285).[12]

Holmes was undoubtedly hurt by his protégé's transition from apostle to apostate but he never said so publicly. However, from the pages of his own *Atlantic Monthly* column, "Over the Teacups," Holmes continued the good fight against the emerging realism and naturalism and often seemed to engage his former protégé in a point-counterpoint argument on the question of literary tastes and values. Eventually in 1891 both writers published selections from their columns. Howells's appeared as the well-known *Criticism and Fiction,* while Holmes retained **Over the Teacups** for his title. Holmes was no doubt encouraged in his efforts to defend gentility in literature by Thomas Bailey Aldrich, who had assumed editorship of the *Atlantic* in 1881 after Howells's departure. As Willard Thorp has pointed out, Aldrich "and his friends R. H. Stoddard and E. C. Stedman . . . were bent on upholding the Ideal in literature. They despised naturalism (an abominable Gaulish invention of Zola and Flaubert) and fought to keep American letters free from its taint." In their eyes, literature should always "be the preserver of the True and the Beautiful" (4).

In his columns Holmes not only frequently invoked Emerson's name and reputation in making his arguments against literary innovation, but he also continued his simultaneous attacks on Whitman, who was himself an increasingly important figure on the American literary scene. For his part, Howells frequently invoked Emerson in his defense of realism and naturalism and, additionally, often praised Walt Whitman for his literary innovation and boldness. The following exchange is representative.

In his "Editor's Study" column in the February 1888 issue of *Harper's,* Howells published a brief review of James Elliot Cabot's recent biography, *A Memoir of Ralph Waldo Emerson.* The *Memoir* itself, while in no way radically revisionist, did serve as something of a corrective to the image of Emerson projected by Holmes. Among other things, it brought forward more clearly Emerson's role as social reformer and literary nonconformist. In his review Howells respectfully asserts that "in humanity, as in his theories of what literature should be to us, Emerson is still the foremost of all our seers, and will be so a hundred years hence." It is, however, primarily Emerson's revolutionary spirit that appeals to Howells, who was promoting literary revolution himself. He goes on to say of Emerson, "every new thing, every new thought, challenged him: abolition, Brook Farm, Walt Whitman: he was just to each and, with Emerson as with all high souls, to be just was to be generous" (478), a position diametrically opposite to that taken by Holmes in his biographical study.

Howells is particularly interested in the Emerson/ Whitman relationship and the one flaw that he finds in Cabot's study is that "he has not touched at all one of the most interesting facts, from a literary point of view, in Emerson's history," namely, Emerson's "perception of the great and fruitful elements in Walt Whitman's work" (478). While allowing for certain occasional reservations on the moral side, Howells asserts that "there is no doubt that Emerson felt a keen sympathy with the aesthetic revolt so courageously embodied" in Whitman's *Leaves of Grass.* Comparing Whitman and Emerson as poets, Howells contends that the former is clearly the greater of the two, but he does point out that Emerson's verse was also often unconventional and innovative, and "in a certain beautiful lawlessness expresses . . . his impatience with smoothness and regularity, his joy in a fractured surface, a broken edge, his exultation in a pace or two outside the traces." Ultimately, according to Howells, both Whitman and Emerson "could foresee the advantages of bringing poetry nearer to the language and the carriage of life" (479), which, of course, was the agenda of the realistic movement.

Not surprisingly, then, as if to confirm Holmes's very fears in this regard, Howells suggests just such an association in terms of the realistic movement. He says of Emerson and Whitman, "[W]e have been thinking of them in connection with a passage of recent criticism in the *World* newspaper reviewing one of the late translations of Tolstoi. The writer has discovered that 'the Russian absolutely ignores all rules, all efforts at an artistic roundness and finish. He finds life without artistic roundness, and he draws it as he sees it.' " While Howells allows that Whitman has more of a "literary consciousness" than Tolstoi, on the basis of Whitman's conscious rebellion against such a literary consciousness, the result is very much the same in each case, a new and realistic depiction of life without the intervention of literary convention. A few lines later in the article, Howells suggests that Zola is also reasonably successful in this regard since only "half the time

[does he] give you the sense of book-making" (479). In his *Harper's* column of February 1889, Howells returns to the subject of literary realism again in a review of Whitman's recently published *November Boughs.* In the review he again reflects upon Whitman's revolutionary greatness as a poet and contends that Whitman "produced a new kind in literature, which we may or may not allow to be poetry, but which we cannot deny is something eloquent, suggestive, moving, with a lawless, formless beauty of its own." Because of this, Whitman "dealt literary conventionality one of those blows which eventually show as internal injuries, whatever the immediate effect seems to be." The end result is that "he made it possible for poetry hereafter to be more direct and natural than hitherto." This "naturalness" Howells also finds characteristic of Whitman's prose, and once again he connects him with the Russian realists. The prose passages in Whitman's volume, says Howells, "are alive with a simple pathos and instinct with a love of truth which recall the best new Russian work" (488). Later in the same article, Howells again dutifully refers to Emerson as America's most outstanding writer by the consensus of critics (489). However, Howells's concept of greatness undoubtedly derives from criteria much different from those which might be employed by the likes of Holmes.

Later, in his November 1889 "Editor's Study" column, Howells would make what is probably his most direct and sustained argument for the new realism and naturalism. Not surprisingly, he once again invokes Emerson in justifying his literary values. The lengthy article begins by addressing the question of degeneracy in literary art, a degeneracy wherein "the ugly can come to be preferred to the beautiful" (962). This, of course, was the very danger that Holmes and other genteel critics warned about, the descent to the "slop-pail." In answering charges that realism and naturalism lead inevitably to such decline, Howells turns to the Spanish novelist Armando Placio Valdes, long a favorite of his, and the essay on fiction "with which he prefaces his last novel," *The Sister of San Sulpizio,* which had not yet been translated from the Spanish. "Señor Valdes," says Howells, "is a realist but a realist according to his own conception of realism, and he has some words of just censure for the French naturalists, whom he finds unnecessarily . . . nasty." The censure, however, is not universal, and Valdes himself holds that "naturalistic art . . . is not immoral in itself.' " In fact, when referring to the " 'prototype of this literature, . . . *Madame Bovary* of Flaubert,' " Valdes states, " 'I am an admirer of this novelist, and especially of this novel.'' ' The naturalistic form, then, is immoral only when pushed to unnecessary extremes by unscrupulous practitioners. For his part, Howells adds that "French naturalism is better at its worst than French unnaturalism at its best" (963).

The ideal, according to both Valdes and Howells, and in direct opposition to Holmes, is to depict things as they are and to exclude nothing a priori from artistic view. Paraphrasing Valdes, Howells writes that "beauty . . . exists in the human spirit, and is the beautiful effect which it receives from the true meaning of things; it does not matter what the things are, and it is the function of the artist who feels this effect to impart it to others." He goes on, extrapolating from Valdes: "[W]e might add that there is no joy in art except this perception of the meaning of things and its communication; when you have felt it, and told it in a poem, a symphony, a novel, a statue, a picture, an edifice, you have fulfilled the purpose for which you were born as an artist" (963). All of this, of course, sounds very Emersonian (or Thoreauvian, or Whitmanesque for that matter), as Howells is undoubtedly well aware. However, it is not the romanticism of these classic authors that he admires, but their realism, their dedication to the notion that literature should address immediate life in all its forms without concern for effete (or genteel) concepts of literary propriety regarding subject matter and style. The past is past for Howells, and "those who continue to celebrate the heroic adventures of Puss in Boots and the hairbreadth escapes of Tom Thumb, under various aliases, only cast disrespect upon the immortals, who have passed beyond these noises" (964).

At the conclusion of his lengthy article—which touches upon the writings of Jane Austen, Tolstoi, Dostoyevsky, George Sand, and Charles Dickens, among others—Howells, quoting from Emerson, contends that, like Emerson, Valdes "believes that 'the foolish man wonders at the unusual, but the wise man at the usual'; that 'the perception of the worth of the vulgar is fruitful in discoveries.' Like Emerson, he 'asks not for the great, the remote, the romantic'; he 'embraces the common,' he 'sits at the feet of the familiar and the low.' " Using Valdes's words, he states: " '[T]hings that appear ugliest in reality to the spectator who is not an artist are transformed into beauty and poetry when the spirit of the artist possesses itself of them' " (966), a thought that clearly echoes Emerson's view of the artist as expressed in "The Poet," where he says, "For it is dislocation and detachment from the life of God, that makes things ugly, the poet, who re-attaches things to nature and the Whole—re-attaching even artificial things, and violations of nature, to nature, by a deeper insight,—disposes very easily of the most disagreeable facts" (*Collected Works* 3:11). In this context the sentiment leads directly to the notion that all matters, regardless of their ugliness, are potentially fit subjects for a truthful literature and, hence, to Howells's famous dictum: "Realism is nothing more and nothing less than the truthful treatment of material."[13]

Holmes may very well have taken notice of his former protégé's exposition of literary theory conjoining Emerson, Whitman, and the new realists and naturalists; very shortly he attacked Flaubert specifically, along with Whitman and Zola, in articles in the *Atlantic*

Monthly, both repeating and expanding upon the charges first made in his biography of Emerson. In his "Over the Teacups" column in the April 1890 issue, Holmes admits that *Madame Bovary* is "famous for its realism" and "is recognized as one of the earliest and most brilliant examples of that modern style of novel which, beginning where Balzac left off, attempted to do for literature what the photograph has done for art." However, he goes on to note that "for those who take the trouble to drink out of the cup below the rim of honey, there is a scene where realism is carried to its extreme,—surpassed in horror by no writer, unless it be the one whose name must be looked for at the bottom of the alphabet [Zola], as if its natural place were as low down in the dregs of realism as it could find itself." The scene Holmes found so repulsive was "the death bed where Madame Bovary expires in convulsions" (555). For Holmes, the offensiveness of this scene suggests the fundamental flaw of contemporary realistic and naturalistic writing. As he goes on to note, "the first great mistake made by the ultra-realists like Flaubert and Zola is . . . their ignoring the line of distinction between imaginative art and science. We can find realism enough in books of anatomy, surgery, and medicine. In studying the human figure, we want to see it clothed in its natural integuments." For the genteel Boston physician, "this is the gravest accusation to bring against realism, old or recent. . . . Leave the description of the drains and cesspools to the physician, the details of the laundry to the washerwoman." Obviously, for Holmes, not all subjects are elevating, or proper, or fit for literary treatment. Ultimately he suggests, "[I]f we are to have realism in its tedious descriptions of unimportant particulars, let it be of particulars which do not excite disgust" (556).

Later in the year, in the September issue of the *Atlantic,* Holmes would make essentially the same charge of literary crudity against Whitman, while offering Emerson as a sterling example of literary decorum, thus carrying on the dichotomy first suggested in the biography six years earlier. In the article Holmes points to Emerson as a literary innovator and, speaking of his own study, notes that "one of Mr. Emerson's biographers has claimed that his Phi Beta Kappa Oration was our Declaration of Literary Independence." However, as Holmes would now have it, independence has its limits, and he is quick to remind his audience that "Mr. Emerson did not cut himself loose from all the traditions of Old World scholarship. He spelt his words correctly, he constructed his sentences grammatically. He adhered to the slavish rules of propriety, and observed the reticences which a traditional delicacy has considered inviolable in decent society." To make his point absolutely clear, Holmes goes on to note that when Emerson "wrote poetry he commonly selected subjects which seemed adapted to poetical treatment,—apparently thinking that all things were not equally calculated to inspire the true poet's genius." While recognizing that Emerson did, in fact, make an effort throughout his career to expand the traditional horizons of the artist, Holmes insists that, nevertheless, Emerson "chiefly restricted himself to subjects such as a fastidious conventionalism would approve as having a certain fitness for poetical treatment" (388).

Whitman, however, is another story. In what appears to be a direct response to Howells's recent linkage of the two, Holmes is once again at pains to point out that there is a world of difference between them. For Holmes, Whitman's sins remain legion and, perhaps most distressingly, they place him, as Howells had so recently demonstrated, squarely in the vanguard of the disgusting "ultra-realists" who had been now for some time battering the foundations of polite civilization. Whitman, says Holmes, "takes into his hospitable vocabulary words which no English dictionary recognizes as belonging to the language,—words which will be looked for in vain outside of his own pages." This stylisticl sinfulness, however, is only a symptom of a more serious literary corruption, namely, that Whitman, like Zola, Flaubert, and the other "ultra-realists," "accepts as poetical subjects all things alike, common and unclean, without discrimination, miscellaneous as the contents of the great sheet which Peter saw let down from heaven" (388).

Holmes, of course, was not alone among the New England Brahmins in associating Whitman with such slop-pail realism. As Gay Wilson Allen points out, "the more genteel poets, like Longfellow, Holmes, and Lowell, were never to find anything to admire in *Leaves of Grass*" (174). Indeed, the Brahmins seemed agreed on the unacceptable crudity and "realism" reflected in the style and diction as well as the subject matter of most of Whitman's work, and they were undoubtedly chagrined by Howells's defense of such muck. In a poem prepared in February of 1889, the same month as Howells's *Harper's* article praising Whitman's *November Boughs,* Holmes satirizes Whitman's work for its randomness and barbarity:

> Or is it he whose random venture throws
> His lawless whimseys into moonstruck prose,
> Where they who worship the barbarian's creed
> Will find a rhythmic cadence as they read.
> (qtd. in Tilton 375)

The occasion for the piece was, appropriately, a birthday gathering for James Russell Lowell.

Oliver Wendell Holmes died in 1894 and Howells, in 1920. Slowly, and inevitably, the "genteel tradition," which the former had so gallantly championed throughout his lifetime, gave way to the inexorable forces of cultural change. The battle, of course, was lost even before Holmes drew his last breath, as American writers such as Mark Twain, Henry James, and Howells himself, as well as many others, achieved prominence and recognition as "realists." By the turn of the century, American naturalism would achieve maturity in the powerful Zolaesque writings of Frank Norris, Stephen Crane, Theodore Dreiser, and others. Holmes might have taken some comfort from the fact that the reputation of Ralph Waldo Emerson would endure throughout the long process of evolutionary change, although he undoubtedly would not have recognized today's Emerson as the subject of his own conservative writings.

Notes

[1] Holmes's Emerson biography has been reprinted many times since its original publication; opinions of the work, however, have not been uniformly positive. Eleanor Tilton, in her definitive biography of Holmes, states that the work is "useless for the modern student of Emerson" (344). Many Emerson scholars, however, hold a generally favorable view. Frederick Carpenter, in his influential *Emerson Handbook,* refers to the work as "a readable biography containing much original material, and emphasizing Emerson's social relations. Good as biography . . . but often poor as criticism" (47). Joel Porte, in his introduction to the Chelsea House edition of the work, states that "Holmes and Emerson had much in common" and that the biography is "peppered with shrewd observations and sound judgments" (xvii, xxv). John McAleer in his biography, *Ralph Waldo Emerson: Days of Encounter,* affirms Holmes's conservative presentation of Emerson's social views and insists that "Holmes assessed Emerson's role correctly" in such matters (518).

[2] Oliver Wendell Holmes, Sr., Papers, Library of Congress, Washington, DC, vol. 6.

[3] The passage in *Conduct of Life* to which Holmes refers here emphasizes the uniqueness of the individual worker, something that would presumably have worked against the communal approach of Brook Farm. *(Complete Works* 6: 112).

[4] The ts. is located in the Oliver Wendell Holmes, Sr., Papers at the Houghton Library, Harvard University ("Memoranda Books on Emerson," bMS AM 1234.8); quoted with permission. Holmes apparently preferred to work with printed material whenever possible. Since these typed notes largely replicate the handwritten notes at the Library of Congress and then go beyond them a bit, it seems likely that Holmes typed them, or had them typed, sometime after penning the handwritten notes. Because of the similarity between the handwritten notes and the typed notes, and because the latter are included and cataloged at the Houghton with the "Memoranda Books

on Emerson," a title that designates the materials generated by Holmes in writing the biography, there can be little doubt as to their authority.

[5] Christopher Pearse Cranch was a writer, editor, painter, and sometime contributor to *The Dial*. He is probably best remembered today for his "New Philosophy Scrapbook," which contains humorous caricatures based on statements from Emerson's writings, the most famous of which is the long-legged, barefoot, dinner-coat-clad, transparent eyeball (Myerson 133-39). Moncure Conway, in his biographical study *Emerson at Home and Abroad*, offers a humorous and unsympathetic view of transcendentalists generally, a view that Holmes obviously shared.

[6] Edward Wagenknecht refers to this statement as indicative of the "ungenerous" attitude of some New England Brahmins toward Thoreau's work (1).

[7] Holmes quotes here from Emerson's poem "Life" (*Complete Works* 9: 354).

[8] Holmes quotes here from Emerson's poem "Art" (*Complete Works* 9: 277).

[9] Timothy Dexter (1747-1806) was a minor literary figure known for his highly experimental techniques. The work to which Holmes refers here is the second edition of *A Pickle for the Knowing Ones* (1802).

[10] From Emerson's poem "Music" (*Complete Works* 9: 365). Apparently this couplet was the cause of long-term consternation for Holmes. In an annotation to the piece, Edward Emerson states: "The present editor obtained Mr. Cabot's permission to include this among the minor poems in the Appendix to the posthumous edition of the Works in 1883, even though Dr. Holmes made some protest against allowing the 'mud and scum of things' to have a voice. At the celebration of the recent centenary of Mr. Emerson's birth, it was pleasant to see that the poem had become a favorite, even with children, and was often quoted" (*Complete Works* 9: 512).

[11] At a Parker House dinner that the young Howells attended in 1860 with James T. Fields, then the publisher of the *Atlantic,* and Oliver Wendell Holmes, Holmes reportedly remarked to Fields regarding their young guest of honor, "Well, James, this is something like the apostolic succession; this is the laying on of hands" (Lynn 96).

Howell's attitude toward Holmes became more critical with the passage of time. In his *Literary Friends and Acquaintances* he says of him, "He was not a prophet like Emerson, nor even a voice crying in the wilderness like Whittier or Lowell. His note was heard rather amid the sweet security of streets, but it was always for a finer and gentler civility. He imagined no new rule of life, and no philosophy or theory of life will be known by his name. He was not constructive. . . . First to last he was a censor, but a winning and most delightful censor" (71).

[12] It is interesting to note here, given Howells's derogatory use of the term "professors," that one of Holmes's best-known works is *The Professor at the Breakfast-Table* (1860).

[13] It should be noted that Howells revised this section of his essay substantially when he published it in *Criticism and Fiction,* separating the comments by Emerson and Valdes into different chapters (see *Criticism and Fiction and Other Writings* 37-38, 40).

Works Cited

Aaron, Daniel. "Literary Scenes and Literary Movements." *Columbia Literary History of the United States.* Gen. ed. Emory Elliott. New York: Columbia UP, 1988. 733-57.

Allen, Gay Wilson, *Solitary Singer: A Critical Biography of Walt Whitman.* New York: Macmillan, 1955.

Cabot, James Elliot. *A Memoir of Ralph Waldo Emerson.* Boston: Houghton, 1887.

Carpenter, Frederick, *Emerson Handbook.* New York: Hendricks, 1953.

Conway, Moncure Daniel. *Emerson at Home and Abroad.* Boston: Houghton, 1882.

Emerson, Ralph Waldo. *The Complete Works of Ralph Waldo Emerson.* 12 vols. Ed. Edward Waldo Emerson. Boston: Houghton, 1903-04.

———. *The Collected Works of Ralph Waldo Emerson.* 4 vols. to date. Eds. Robert Spiller et al. Cambridge, MA: Harvard, 1979-.

Holmes, Oliver Wendell, Sr. *Ralph Waldo Emerson.* Boston: Houghton, 1884.

———. *Over the Teacups.* Boston: Houghton, 1891.

———. "Over the Teacups." *The Atlantic Monthly* April 1890: 549-60.

———. "Over the Teacups." *The Atlantic Monthly* September 1890: 387-400.

———. Oliver Wendell Holmes, Sr., Papers. Vol. 6. Library of Congress, Washington, DC.

———. "Memoranda Book on Emerson," bMS AM 1234.8. Oliver Wendell Holmes, Sr., Papers. Houghton Library, Harvard University. Quoted with permission.

Howells, William Dean. *Literary Friends and Acquaintances.* New York: Harper, 1901.

———. "Editor's Study" *Harper's* February 1888: 476-82.

———. "Editor's Study" *Harper's* February 1889: 488-92.

———. "Editor's Study" *Harper's* November 1889: 962-67.

———. *Criticism and Fiction and Other Writings.* Ed. Clara Kirk and Rudolf Kirk. New York: New York UP, 1959.

Lynn, Kenneth S. *William Dean Howells: An American Life.* New York: Harcourt, 1970.

McAleer, John. *Ralph Waldo Emerson: Days of Encounter.* Boston: Little, 1984.

Myerson, Joel. *The New England Transcendentalists and the Dial.* Rutherford, NJ: Fairleigh Dickinson UP, 1980.

Porte, Joel. Introduction. *Ralph Waldo Emerson.* By Oliver Wendell Holmes, Sr. New York: Chelsea, 1980.

Thorp, Willard. *American Writing in the Twentieth Century.* Cambridge, MA: Harvard UP, 1960.

Tilton, Eleanor. *Amiable Autocrat: A Biography of Dr. Oliver Wendell Holmes.* New York: Schumann, 1947.

Wagenknecht, Edward. *Henry Thoreau: What Manner of Man?* Amherst: U of Massachusetts P, 1981.

David D. Yuan (essay date 1997)

SOURCE: "Disfigurement and Reconstruction in Oliver Wendell Holmes's 'The Human Wheel, Its Spokes and Felloes,'" in *The Body and Physical Difference: Discourses of Disability,* The University of Michigan Press, 1997, pp. 71-88.

[In the following essay, Yuan analyzes Holmes's main work on disability and prosthetics and considers his philosophy that disabled citizens be rehabilitated and assimilated back into society.]

Susan Reynolds Whyte, summarizing Henri-Jacques Stiker's monumental history of the discourse on bodily abnormality in the West, *Corps infirmes et sociétés,* writes that after World War I "a broad paradigm shift" occurred in Europe and the United States: now "damaged people" were to be "rehabilitated," that is, they were to be "returned to a real or postulated preexisting norm of reference, and reassimilated into society"; "[w]hereas earlier epochs situated the infirm as exceptional in some way, the modern intention (or pretension) is that they are ordinary and should be integrated into ordinary life and work."[1] From this perspective, the quintessentially modern concept of rehabilitation began as a strategy for winning "professional control over the damaged bodies" of World War I veterans and preventing old war wounds from hindering the post-world war economy.[2] For Stiker, this move was critical, as it marked the "beginning of the denial of difference" that is "characteristic of our time."[3] But this "broad paradigm shift" in the treatment of the disabled, as singular as it may have seemed in the wake of the almost unimaginable carnage of World War I, was not entirely unprecedented: many of the tenets of the new ideology (rehabilitation, reassimilation, the social "invisibility" of the disabled) had in fact been anticipated during the aftermath of the American Civil War.

Regarding military technology and strategy, the importance of the American Civil War as a precedent for World War I has been widely acknowledged: the Civil War, after all, introduced ironclad warships, repeating rifles, telegraphy, and the importance of controlling the railways to Western war making. Because weapons technology outstripped medical technology between 1861 and 1865, the Civil War was one of the most injurious wars in history: over 600,000 Americans died as a direct consequence of the Civil War, more than died in both world wars, the Korean War, and the Vietnam War combined.[4] In addition, the Civil War produced more amputees than any other war Americans have fought in; three out of every four operations performed on Union soldiers were amputations, and altogether 130,000 men were "scarred or disfigured for life" during the war.[5]

Thus it is not surprising that the Civil War and Reconstruction not only redefined war but also helped to redefine disability for the modern state.[6] Looking past the war that was still convulsing the country, Oliver Wendell Holmes Sr.—physician, poet, inventor, and futurist—was one of the first to propose that, in effect, rehabilitation and reassimilation should become critical components of a new paradigm for the treatment of the disabled (albeit Holmes, already in his fifties by the start of the war, sometimes shrank from his own vision of the future). But equally important to the modern history of physical difference, Holmes adumbrated what might be called a nationalist body aesthetics whose implications went well beyond the practical task of rehabilitating disabled workers. For Holmes, it was important not only that the disabled citizen be rehabilitated into the workforce but also that his or her body—like the bodies of all citizens—properly emblematized the body politic. For Holmes, the disabled body was not a correct emblem for the Reconstructed United States.

Holmes published his seminal article on disability and prosthetics, **"The Human Wheel, Its Spokes and Felloes,"** in the *Atlantic Monthly* in May 1863. By then any illusion that the Civil War would be brief and casualties few had long been shattered. Holmes writes at the start that the raison d'être for his article is the sudden, alarming ubiquitousness of the amputee.

> The starting point of this paper was a desire to call attention to certain remarkable AMERICAN INVENTIONS, especially to one class of mechanical contrivances, which, at the present time, assumes a vast importance and interests great multitudes. The limbs of our friends and countrymen are a part of the melancholy harvest which war is sweeping down with Dahlgren's mowing-machine[7] and the patent reapers of Springfield and Hartford. The admirable contrivances of an American inventor, prized as they were in ordinary times, have risen into the character of great national blessings since the necessity for them has become so widely felt. While the weapons that have gone from Mr. Colt's armories have been carrying death to friend and foe, the beneficent and ingenious inventions of MR. PALMER have been repairing the losses inflicted by the implements of war.[8]

The American inventor B. Frank Palmer (whom Holmes surmises was aptly named for the inventive Benjamin Franklin), an amputee from childhood, designed his own prosthetic leg, allegedly because he was disgusted with the simple "peg leg" that he had worn since childhood. The "Palmer leg" was designed to replace an entire limb—including the complex knee joint. Unlike the peg leg, the Palmer leg was carefully shaped to resemble a natural limb from thigh to foot. Most important, the artificial knee was articulated, thanks to an intricate system of springs and pulleys hidden inside the prosthesis, allowing the amputee to walk much more naturally.

While the Palmer leg is Holmes's ostensible subject, **"The Human Wheel"** also includes a brief lecture on human locomotion, another on the mass production of boots and shoes, and, to conclude, a chauvinist harangue on American ingenuity. The essay's title refers to the then recent discovery of the true nature of human locomotion, a discovery that could not be made, according to Holmes, until the advent of instantaneous photography made it possible to freeze each moment of the marvelously integrated process that is the act of walking. Instantaneous photography revealed that "Man is a *wheel,* with two spokes, his legs, and two fragments of a tire, his feet. He *rolls* successively on each of these fragments from the heel to the toe"; "Walking, then, is a perpetual self-recovery. It is a complex, violent, and perilous operation, which we divest of its extreme danger only by continual practice from a very early period of life . . . We discover how dangerous it is, when we slip or trip . . . or overlook the last step of a flight of stairs, and discover with what headlong

violence we have been hurling ourselves forward" (571). Like much of Holmes's writing, **"The Human Wheel"** has allegorical overtones. By 1863, the Civil War, already far from the brief affair that the young recruits had expected, could be allegorized as a national Fall, a Fall that revealed with what headlong violence the young nation had been hurling itself into the future.

The photograph (like the microscope) has the power to reveal the invisible; we would not know that "Man is a wheel" without photography. But the goal of the Palmer leg is a kind of invisibility: its goal is to fool the observer into thinking that the amputee is not an amputee. The highest compliment that Holmes can pay the Palmer leg is that "No victim of the thimblerigger's trickery was ever more completely taken in than we were by the contrivance of the ingenious Surgeon-Artist" (577). Holmes, who begins his essay by making visible the hitherto invisible act of human locomotion, concludes by championing the Palmer leg, a device intended not so much to improve the amputee's mobility as to improve his appearance by rendering his injury invisible: "counterfeiting its aspect so far as possible" (575). Holmes insists that for "polite society" the sight of the "odious 'peg' " is simply intolerable: "misfortunes of a certain obtrusiveness may be pitied, but are never tolerated under the chandeliers" (574). In other words, polite society does not wish to see certain realities, and Holmes recognizes that American ingenuity exists not only to reveal truth but also to hide it.

Holmes, summing up, writes that the United States finds itself in an "age when appearances are realities"; thus the technology of disguise becomes crucial. The fact that the Palmer artificial leg does not quite achieve a perfect illusion of normalcy (see 576) is beside the point. **"The Human Wheel"** implies that eventually the amputee will be able to "pass" for a whole-limbed person with the aid of an ever-improving American technology: "As we wean ourselves from the Old World, and become more and more nationalized in our great struggle for existence as a free people, we shall carry this aptness for the production of beautiful forms more and more into common life" (578).

"The Human Wheel" recalls the dilemma of photographers who sought to capture the sights of the Civil War. Even as the advent of photography helps to reveal the true nature of war and deconstructs the glamorous image that had long protected society from war's horrors, it provokes the question, To what extent is it desirable to know the truth about war? For Holmes it seems enough for the revelatory photograph (the photograph that reveals the mundane violence of locomotion) to return the secrets of human anatomy and physiology to the realm of the invisible: if the Civil War is reaping a "melancholy harvest" of limbs, then American ingenuity is just as rapidly replacing them with its prostheses. And if the war's devastations can be reversed in this way, then the extent to which the war appears to inflict permanent damage is mitigated. As Timothy Sweet has argued, the very notion of "harvest" that is promulgated by Holmes and others suggests the hopefulness of renewal and rebirth, a rebirth to follow the holocaust of the war.[9]

Holmes's other analogy for the war is the bloody but lifesaving surgical operation: "We are in trouble just now, on account of a neglected hereditary *melanosis*"; we must "eliminate the *materies morbi*" if the body politic is to be cured (580). Like the pastoral analogy, the medical analogy was very popular with intellectuals who sought to explain the Civil War's necessity.

Anticipating a Union victory and the postbellum society that will follow, Holmes finds that not only is the Civil War a kind of surgery but that the prosthesis will assist in a kind of social reconstruction even as it completes the body's reconstruction. Undisguised limblessness is simply not to be tolerated in the postbellum society. But it requires a new technology to create an artificial limb that will convincingly disguise the intolerable fact of the incomplete body. Holmes understands well the broader implications of the problem: "Reconstruction," in all senses of the term, will require new technologies of disguise. Reconstruction will require a national ideology that privileges the new, while disguising or even displacing the past. Holmes even theorizes why Europeans tolerate the sight of the peg leg while Americans do not: it is the fineness of the "national eye for the harmonies of form and color," the superiority of the American's visual aesthetic (578). In short, appearances matter more in America than they do in the Old World

In an earlier article, **"The Doings of the Sunbeam,"** Holmes reveals the mysterious process of production at a commercial photograph factory.[10] In "The Human Wheel," Holmes seeks to convey Palmer's extraordinary achievement by dissecting what Holmes calls an *Autoperipatetikos*, a "walking" automaton, which Holmes gleefully exposes as an impostor. One *Autoperipatetikos* in particular has become famous because she "toddle[s]" behind a shop window, attracting great crowds of spectators.

> An autopsy of one of her family which fell into our hands reveals the secret springs of her action. Wishing to spare her as a member of the defenseless sex, it pains us to say, that, ingenious as her counterfeit walking is, she is an imposter. Worse than this . . . duty compels us to reveal a fact concerning her which will shock the feelings of those who have watched the stately rigidity of decorum with which she moves . . . *She is a quadruped!* Inside of her great golden boots, which represent one pair of feet, is another smaller pair, which move freely through these hollow casings . . . Her movement, then, is

not walking . . . it is more like that of a person walking with two crutches besides his two legs. (572)

Holmes's ostensible point here is to highlight the ingenuity of the Palmer prosthesis by revealing the authomaton's failings, but the very act of comparing the automaton and the amputee-with-prosthesis suggests the conflation of humans and machines, an idea that Holmes explicitly evokes later in the essay: "gradually the wooden limb seems to become, as it were, penetrated by the nerves, and the intelligence to run downwards until it reaches the last joint of the member" (576-77). Moreover, the conflation of machine and person is further suggested by the way in which Holmes goes on to "dissect" B. Frank Palmer in much the same way as he dissects and explains the prosthesis and the *Autoperipatetikos*: analyzing Palmer's exterior and interior, extracting his motivation and character. Holmes explains Palmer's motivation, imagining the emotional burden of Palmer's "unsightly appendage" (his peg leg) during "adolescence" and how this misery proved to be the source of his inventiveness (574). Then Holmes explicates and evaluates both the mechanics of Palmer's novel prosthesis as such (the "ingenious arrangement of springs and cords in the *inside* of the limb") and the mechanics of inventor and invention (amputee and prosthesis) in combination: "He puts his vegetable leg through many of the movements which would seem to demand the contractile animal fibre. He goes up and down stairs with very tolerable ease and dispatch. Only when he comes to *stand* upon the human limb, we begin to find that it is not in all respects equal to the divine one" (576). If this man-machine hybrid does not perfectly imitate the divine creation, it is a better illusion than the "walking" automaton, which transfixed the crowds gathering around the shop window.

What **"The Human Wheel"** offers, as Holmes is well aware, is a vision of American society in the near future for which the boundary between bodies and machines has become ambiguous. In other words, Holmes anticipates the "machine culture" (or "prosthetic culture") that was to become dominant in the latter nineteenth century, a culture whose paradigmatic issue is "the problem of the body."[11] Holmes's use of the feminized *Autoperipatetikos* anticipates what Mark Seltzer identifies as the naturalist novel's exploration of "the mechanism of the feminine."[12] Furthermore, Holmes's interior and exterior dissection of Palmer (the psychoanalytic pursuit of "what makes Palmer tick" alongside the analysis of how he physically moves) coupled with his dissection of the female automaton anticipates the postbellum assumption *"that bodies and persons are things that can be made."*[13]

As noted, production fascinates Holmes. Holmes, who was delighted with the primitive assembly line used by the E. T. Anthony firm to produce thousands of photographs in a day, visits the Palmer factory where "legs are organized," expecting to see another example of machine-driven efficiency (577). But at the Palmer factory, Holmes is surprised to discover that the shaping of the wooden limbs "is all done by hand".

> We had expected to see great lathes, worked by steam-power, taking in a rough stick and turning out a finished limb. But it is shaped very much as a sculptor finishes his marble, with an eye to artistic effect,—not so much in the view of the stranger, who does not look upon its naked loveliness, as in that of the wearer, who is seduced by its harmonious outlines into its purchase, and solaced with the consciousness that he carries so much beauty and symmetry about with him. (577)

Holmes's expectation of steam-powered lathes evokes not only the changing face of Northern industry (like the textile factory) but also the role of steam power in the Civil War, with armored steamships skirmishing in the bays and rivers and steam locomotives hauling supplies by rail to the front lines. Melville wrote derisively of the Monitor's battle with the Merrimac: "all went on by crank / Pivot, and screw." Melville recognized that the Civil War had ushered in a new kind of combat, as well as a new kind of soldier: "War yet shall be, but warriors / Are now but operatives."[14] Holmes himself has made the connection between a vital new mechanized industry and both the removal and the replacement of limbs, but here at the Palmer factory he is initially both surprised and gratified to discover that production is less an anticipation of the assembly line than a throwback to a vanishing era of handcrafted artisanship. Nevertheless, as we have already glimpsed, there is a disturbing subtext to **"The Human Wheel"**: workers and soldiers seem to be not so much "operatives" as mechanical parts that are being operated. And because they are cogs in the war machine (human wheels), the implication is that they may be summarily repaired or replaced as needed. The Civil War, then, conflated the prosthesis and the soldier, as the industrial revolution conflated the prosthesis and the worker.

Henry Ford, writing sixty years after Holmes, dramatically expands the conflation of worker and prosthesis. Ford, writing about the Model T assembly line in his autobiographical *My Life and Work* (1923), notes that only 12 percent of the 7,882 work operations along the line required "strong, able-bodied, and practically physically perfect men." The vast majority of operations could be performed by workers who were less than "able bodied": "we found that 670 could be filled by legless men, 2,637 by one-legged men, two by armless men, 715 by one-armed men and ten by blind men."[15] Ford, like Holmes, is pondering the problem of reconstruction in the wake of a war of unprecedented mechanization and carnage.[16]

Ford's analysis suggests a future where the conflation of worker and prosthesis is virtually complete. The "worker" as such is no longer relevant; industry has become so specialized that it is now appropriate to speak of the laboring body part or function rather than the laborer.[17] What is striking about Ford's comment is the contrast it presents when compared to Holmes's argument in the **"Human Wheel."** For Ford, the literal prosthesis has become irrelevant. Instead of a worker needing a prosthesis to appear or perform as if whole bodied, he or she can dispense with this pretense altogether. Thus when industry begins to think of labor "prosthetically," the amputee laborer is liberated from the prosthesis; the 'incomplete' worker is redeemed. Appearances, so important to Holmes, seem to have lost their relevance for Ford, who is concerned with the part of each worker performing its discrete task rather than with the appearance of "wholeness."[18]

But while Ford, perhaps, felt that he was already living in a prosthetic culture, Holmes, in 1863, is somewhat nervously anticipating its arrival. Holmes unabashedly celebrates the triumphs of mechanized industry elsewhere (as in **"The Doings of the Sunbeam"**), but in **"The Human Wheel"** he seems to hesitate before its inexorable advance. At the Palmer factory, Holmes is deeply impressed by the fact that the Palmer leg is not purely an anonymous, machine-molded tool (like the weapons that had proved so proficient at removing limbs), calling it a "true artist's limb" (579). The Palmer leg is a commodity imbued with a soul. But Holmes's ambivalence toward the nascent machine-prosthetic culture is evident in the language he uses to describe the final phase of the Palmer leg's construction: "The hollowing-out of the interior is done by wicked-looking blades and scoops at the end of long stems, suggesting the thought of dentists' instruments as they might have been in the days of the giants" (577). Thus while the *exterior* shaping of the Palmer leg is done by hand, as "a sculptor finishes his marble," the *interior* of the prosthesis is prepared by the very sort of intimidating machines that Holmes had expected to see in the first place (there is a resemblance between Holmes's description of the factory machines and his earlier description of the peg leg [which is quoted later in this article]: the latter is "fearful-looking," the former "wicked-looking"). Thus the Palmer leg is not simply useful sculpture, it is a peculiar combination of art and machine-produced artifact: the artist handing off the half-completed limb to the "wicked-looking" machinery to finish.

Holmes's mixed reaction to the Palmer factory is a sort of prototype for the ambivalence and confusion that would become a characteristic response as Americans confronted or evaded the implications of the body-machine complex. Like the responses of his later counterparts, Holmes's response to scenes of the "miscegenation of nature and culture," as Seltzer puts it, is itself mixed (21). Holmes is both eager and reluctant to gaze on the new society that machines are ushering into being, and he projects onto the hero of **"The Human Wheel"** this ambivalence in his very reading of the hero's name (B. Frank Palmer). Holmes initially draws out only the name's evocation of Benjamin Franklin, as noted. But later, Homes alludes to another Palmer "namesake": "We owe the well-shaped, intelligent, docile limb, the half-reasoning willow of Mr. Palmer, to the same sense of beauty and fitness which moulded the soft outlines of the Indian girl and the White Captive in the studio of his namesake in Albany" (578). The Albany namesake is Erastus Dow Palmer (1817-1904), the noted New York sculptor whose two most famous pieces are the *Indian Girl* (1856) and the *White Captive* (1858). Thus "B. Frank Palmer" signifies, for Holmes, the combined sensibilities of the artist and the scientist. The inventor is as much a hybrid as his invention.[19]

In another telling move, Holmes deliberately feminizes the prosthesis: the amputee is "seduced" into buying the beautiful limb, and he relishes its "naked loveliness" even though the public (which he intends to dupe with this counterfeit) will never see it, any more than they would see the naked loveliness of a genuine limb in a polite social context. A romantic description like this one softens the impression, given elsewhere in the essay, that the body itself has been reduced by medicine and technology to its mechanical essentials and that beauty and grace are no longer the body's most important attributes. Holmes's description represents an intriguing regendering of the Palmer leg from the obviously phallic (the Palmer leg "would almost persuade a man with two good legs to provide himself with a third") to the "feminine" as Holmes would define it (the leg is "well-shaped," "docile," and both "intelligent" and "half-reasoning" [577-78]). I will explore the political utility of this regendering of the prosthesis later on, but for now I only want to point out the range of examples of hybridity in Holmes's text: the "female" automaton, a counterfeit woman, is revealed to be a "quadruped"; "B. Frank Palmer" refers to two divergent antecedents; and the Palmer leg is a complex hybrid, emblematic of the complex nation that produced it. The Palmer leg is organic and inorganic, rational and romantic, masculine and feminine, intelligent and half-reasoning. Moreover, the Palmer leg becomes even more complex when it is conjoined with the amputee.

Holmes takes great pains to establish a stark contrast between the peg leg and the Palmer leg. The image of the former is grotesque, the amputee stumping about on the crude peg; the image of the latter is all symmetry and grace. Interestingly the wound itself, the stump that marks the place where the natural limb should be, is not discussed (even though Holmes as a physician would be eminently equipped to discuss amputation and its aftereffects). It is not the absence of the limb that is grotesque or hideous; it is the peg leg's crudity, the rude transparency of its counterfeit, that offends. Or rather it is the *lack* of disguise that offends: the fact that the peg leg is actually no counterfeit limb at all but is simply a pragmatic response to the amputee's desire to move about. The Palmer leg's "naked loveliness" is enjoyed only by the amputee himself (in Holmes's imagining of it), but the nakedness of the peg leg is seen by all and disgusts all.

According to Holmes, B. Frank Palmer's leg was amputated when he was ten years old; Holmes does not give us the details of the accident, telling us only that the limb was "crushed." Holmes's truncated biography moves directly from the accident to Palmer's adolescence, because it is with the dawning of sexual possibility that the weight of Palmer's aesthetic disability begins to be felt.

> We can imagine what he suffered as he grew into adolescence under the cross of this unsightly appendage. He was of comely aspect, tall, well-shaped, with well-marked, regular features. But just at the period when personal graces are most valued, when a good presence is a blank check on the Bank of Fortune, with Nature's signature at the bottom, he found himself made hideous by this fearful-looking counterfeit of a limb. (574)

The peg leg is "hideous," "unsightly," and, perhaps most significantly of all, "fearful-looking." The horror of Palmer's condition is enhanced by the fact that he was otherwise a handsome, well-proportioned young man. Incongruity is a hallmark of the grotesque, and the incongruity of an otherwise thoroughly presentable young man stumping around on the rude peg makes this scenario not only pathetic but hideous. Indeed, the effect is so terrible that young Palmer could not tolerate it, and he abandons the peg leg for the "tender mercies of the crutch," as Holmes cryptically puts it. But the crutch is "at best an instrument of torture," pressing upon a "great bundle of nerves" in the armpit, distorting the figure, perhaps even "distempering the mind itself" (575). It seems remarkable that young Palmer would ever have thought the crutch a "tender merc[y]" for even a moment, but such is society's horror of "the odious 'peg'" that Palmer was driven to the attempt. Finally, the ingenous Palmer invents his superior prosthesis and resolves his aesthetic dilemma. Since it is allegedly the public appearance that counts in **"The Human Wheel,"** it does not seem to matter that Palmer must still remove the artificial leg at night and expose his stump to plain view. Holmes is too discreet to imagine a Mrs. Palmer or how she might react to the real state of his bodily affairs.

Holmes's **"The Human Wheel,"** like Thomas Jefferson's *Notes on the State of Virginia,* extrapolates from the individual to the national and addresses the place of the United States in the world scene. **"The Human Wheel"** is as much a reaction to the national crisis as it is to the specific plight of the amputee. Holmes, who is fond of offering readers the obvious analogy, fails to consider the Civil War as an amputation of the body politic: the nation losing its Southern half. But he does refer to the war as "a neglected hereditary *melanosis,*" which requires the elimination of "the *materies morbi*" (580). But what are the *materies morbi* for Holmes? The Confederate government? The institution of slavery? The blacks themselves? A "hereditary *melanosis*" suggests the origin of the national illness in the black slaves, but are they the cause or only the symptom of the disease?[20] Eliminating the *materies morbi,* in the medical sense, refers to the surgical removal of dead tissue; Holmes probably had the removal of a gangrenous limb in mind. Thus figurative amputation, like literal amputation, is for Holmes a beneficent, life-saving procedure: the *materies morbi* are eliminated, and the patient survives. But an unsightly appearance in polite society is intolerable, and the scorn that a critical Europe might have for the struggling United States concerns Holmes. To European critics, Holmes offers a raw rebuttal: "We profess to make men and women out of human beings better than any of the joint-stock companies called dynasties have done or can do it" (580). Holmes will not allow Europe to believe that the United States itself is grotesque; the United States must not be viewed as a cripple among the nations nor a crude yokel whom genteel Europe finds intolerable.

Holmes blatantly uses the invention of the Palmer leg to refute the unexamined notion that Europe always surpasses the United States in the achievement of symmetry, harmony, and beauty. Holmes does not argue that American civilization is catching up with Europe, he argues that it is already surpassing Europe. Holmes proudly proclaims: "American taste was offended, outraged, by the odious 'peg' which the Old-World soldier or beggar was proud to show" (578).

Holmes's pride in the Palmer leg can be read as a remarkable evasion of the Civil War, which, after all, was the severest test that "American civilization" had ever faced. Holmes, in the middle of the most destructive war in history, finds in the very fact of unprecedented carnage the proof of American superiority. First, Holmes finds that the war is proving America's technical prowess: American ingenuity has produced both the best weapons for killing and wounding and the best prostheses. Second, it is not in spite of the war that "American civilization" aspires to a higher aesthetic plane, but, Holmes implies, partly *because* of the war: "As we wean ourselves from the Old World, and become more and more nationalized in our great struggle for existence as a free people, we shall carry this aptness for the production of beautiful forms more

and more into common life" (578). The Civil War, then, is a continuation of the American Revolution; it is another milestone in the nation's growing up and away from the Old World. As most contemporary historians would be quick to agree, the Civil War was, as Holmes suggests, the introduction to a vast expansion of American nationalism. It is true that Holmes qualifies his cultural chauvinism a bit. He admits that "the national car for music is not so acute [as Europe's]," but he insists that "the national eye for the harmonies of form and color is better than we often find in older communities" (578). The image of the peg-legged "beggar" (which is presumably more ubiquitous in the dynastic Old World than in democratic America) subtly invokes Poe's Europe of gothic horrors and grotesques: catacombs, plagues, madhouses, slums replete with the crippled and deformed.

But what is it that allows the European soldier to proudly display his peg, while the American soldier is ashamed to show his? Unlike the beggar's condition, whose meaning may be ambiguous, the veteran's wound is presumably a badge of courage and honor. Holmes implies that the American "eye" is not only more aesthetically refined and demanding but more democratic: American has less tolerance for the sight of the disfigured dregs of society. In the United States, the misshapen cannot be so cavalierly discarded and relegated to the interstices of polite society. American society has an obligation to recuperate the disfigured and offer them the opportunity to make themselves presentable. Importantly, Holmes refutes the idea that the democratic society drags the elite down to the level of the lowest denominator. Rather, it is the task of American technology and culture to raise the coarse and vulgar to the plane of symmetry and refinement—this is precisely what is involved in the process of weaning "ourselves from the Old World."

As an introduction to his analysis of the Palmer leg, Holmes presents Plumer's last: the shoe mold designed by the pioneering American podiatrist Dr. J. C. Plumer. Plumer last produced shoes and boots that conformed well to the actual shape of the human foot, in contrast to the typical nineteenth-century shoe, which forced the foot to do most of the conforming. The standard-issue boots supplied to the soldiers in the Union army were notoriously punishing, and it often took weeks of use before they could be worn without pain. (The Confederate soldiers were often not issued boots at all.) Along the way, the recruits were made uncomfortable, and some were even disabled by the boots—thwarting the men's morale and their readiness to fight. Dr. Plumer, the foot's great liberator, came to the rescue with his innovative last. Holmes applauds him as "the Garrison of these oppressed members of the body corporeal" and declares: "The foot's fingers are the slaves in the republic of the body. Their black leathern integument is only the mask of their servile condition. They bear the burdens, while the hands, their white masters, handle the money and wear the rings" (572). "[B]lack integument" here obviously invokes the slave's black skin, and black skin—to pursue Holmes's analogy—is a mask that helps to disguise the slave's essential humanity, thus justifying the misconception that the African American is a separate species and is biologically suited for subjugation. (Holmes's discourse on toes as slaves and shoes as black skin is echoed later in the essay's closing description of the war as a "hereditary *melanosis*.")

Beneath the innocuous sheen of patent leather, the feet are performing the hardest labor in the republic of the body. Holmes's discourse on feet is comparable to his discourse on photography: in both discourses the overarching theme is the dis-covering of a hitherto invisible labor process. The wider implication of **"The Human Wheel"** is that medicine and physiology themselves may be understood in the same terms: they are the sciences dedicated to revealing how the body, which is a kind of organic labor process, or organic industry, is ordered and run. The feet suffer, in part, because we do not penetrate their "narrow prisons" to see how they labor. The feet, like the slaves, are de-formed by the severity of their labor and their harsh environment: "they grow into ignoble shapes, they become callous by long abuse, and all their natural gifts are crushed and trodden out of them" (572). The horror of slavery, then, is not simply that the slave suffers but that he literally becomes something grotesque and ignoble. It is not the "black integument"—the slave's physiognomy—that is grotesque, nor is the African American intrinsically benighted; it is the institution of slavery that deforms the slave.

Holmes's discussion of the body corporeal constantly evokes the body politic and vice versa; it seems he cannot investigate the one without investigating the other. As Holmes recounts it, Dr. Plumer began his research by "contemplating the natural foot as it appears in infancy, unspoiled as yet by social corruptions, in adults fortunate enough to have escaped these destructive influences, in the grim skeleton aspect divested of its outward designs" (572). Reading analogically again, it is not only the idea that the slave has been warped and corrupted that is conveyed here but also the idea that the master has been corrupted, which is a familiar, even predominant argument of the abolitionists. Holmes also returns to the contrast between appearance and the deep structures underlying appearance. The "grim skeleton" is "divested of its outward designs," and like the skull grinning in at the banquet that William James posits, the "skeleton" insists that we examine the true nature of our existence and our experience. Holmes directs the reader to dis-cover labor and production. Similarly, he asks the reader to look beneath the surface of the corporeal body and the body politic to view the complex stresses on bone and tendon, the delicate chemical negotiations occurring in the blood, and the despair attending a slave economy content to conduct business as usual.

Ultimately in **"The Human Wheel,"** Holmes capitulates to the demands of appearance and the sanctity of socially approved disguise. But it is important to recognize the polarity in Holmes's thought: the tension between the tyranny of appearance and the need to deconstruct appearance (i.e., to estrange aspects of our experience in order to truly see and understand it). Thus toes are liberated by Plumer's last, but Palmer's wooden leg, schooled by the amputee himself, submits to the amputee's command, and the amputee himself—in wearing the Palmer leg—submits to the command of "American civilization" and conforms to the new code of public appearance.

> America has made implements . . . which out-mow and out-reap the world. She has contrived man-slaying engines which kill people faster than any others . . . She has bestowed upon you and the world an anodyne which enables you to cut arms and legs off without hurting the patient; and when his leg is cut off, she has given you a true artist's limb for your cripple to walk upon, instead of the peg on which he has stumped from the days of Guy de Chauliac. (579)

Holmes correctly anticipates a postbellum America that will lead rather than follow the other nations. Holmes's description recalls "Harvest of Death," Timothy O'Sullivan's famous photograph of corpses lying on the fields of Gettysburg. But this Civil War pastoralism (which Timothy Sweet correctly explains as an effort to make the carnage "natural" and thus more acceptable) is undercut by mechanoindustrial undertones ("implements" for mowing and reaping; "man-slaying engines"). Such language conveys the opposite idea of "unnatural" processes of production and destruction: farming as agribusiness; war and medicine as industry; the foreshadowing of the assembly line. Holmes seems reluctant to push the parallel he draws between harvesting/replanting and war/medicine (war removes limbs, medicine replaces them) to its conclusion. But what makes Holmes hesitate? Is it a reluctance to "naturalize" war, or is it a reluctance to recuperate a fallen America via the familiar naturalizing imagery?

. . . The human wheel emblem's evoking of the anthropometric studies of Leonardo da Vinci is probably intentional, and it serves to underscore one of Holmes's objectives: to provide a more accurate measure and definition of humanity—especially of humanity acting, of humanity moving, as opposed to humanity simply being.[21] As instantaneous photography allows us to understand human locomotion, so the arts of historical and cultural analysis allow us to trace the trajectory of the human species through time.

The human wheel as an emblem for the essay is appropriately paradoxical. The figure of the wheel suggests both returning and forward progress—and both ideas are powerfully attractive to Holmes, who is writing, despite his air of assurance, at a time of uncertainty and anxious confusion. Nevertheless, the surface of Holmes's text optimistically declares his dedication to forward progress. Holmes boasts that the "American Wheel is moving through the miseries of the Civil War to a better place in history, a place which will be envied by the great nations of the world." The amputee, the cripple, the grizzled veteran "stumping" around on his peg do not present the image appropriate to a young nation boldly on the rise. The "peg" is neatly opposed to the wheel in Holmes's essay: if America is the efficient, smoothly rolling wheel, then Europe is the splintery, inefficient, old peg.

The wheel does seem an apt metaphor for the United States—the Civil War was itself a demonstration on a vast scale of the wheel's power. First, the Civil War was "the first American conflict in which railroads played a major role."[22] The North's rail superiority was a key factor in securing its victory. Second, other innovative wheeled or wheel-like machines, from the field ambulance to the wheeled gun battery that was mounted on its own steel rails, were prominent during this war. And even as the war raged on, the transcontinental railway project was already underway; by 1869 the recently re-United States was spanned by rails from the Pacific to the Atlantic, greatly facilitating Easterners' migration to Western lands. (As the United States entered the twentieth century, the automobile allowed the wheel as national paradigm to continue to dominate the American landscape and imagination, replacing the railroad train as the quintessential wheeled machine.)

But while Holmes seems to believe that the future he envisions will come to pass, **"The Human Wheel"**'s subtext, as we have already seen, belies this rather bellicose optimism. Beneath Holmes's eager modernism is a deep desire to redeem the past and avoid the full consequences of the modernity Holmes sees hurtling toward him; Holmes hesitates before the prosthetic culture that he has insightfully anticipated. Even as Holmes professes the recuperation of amputees into society via the invisible prosthesis (the Palmer leg), he is compelled to confront the prostheticization of society, that is, the "dismemberment of the natural body" that Seltzer recognizes in Henry Ford's industrial "fantasy."[23]

We need to return to the most basic question about **"The Human Wheel"**: why should Holmes demand that the prosthesis be invisible? The essay offers several explicit answers: America's highly developed aesthetic sense, the desire to demonstrate technical prowess, the stigma that the amputee must bear. But it is Holmes's stark maxim that "[a]ppearances are realities" that needs to be reexamined. The subtext of

the maxim is that the visible prosthesis serves to remind us of the way in which prosthetic culture is enveloping all of society, not only the disabled and disfigured. Despite Holmes's huffing and puffing about the peg leg and the Old World, the visible prosthesis is as much an emblem of encroaching modernity as it is an emblem of the old order (like the human wheel, which stands for returning as well as for progress). If prostheses are invisible, then they do not exist; if we can convince ourselves that we are not living in a prosthetic culture, then we will not confront the political implications of the new order. Things will seem to be the way they have always been.[24] Holmes writes glowingly of liberation and freedom, but through his essay the reader may glimpse a rather different future American society: a society where no workers will be slaves but where workers will be not unlike the "well-shaped, intelligent, docile limb, the half-reasoning willow of Mr. Palmer" (578). The political expediency of Holmes's regendering of the phallic prosthesis is now clear: Holmes identifies as feminine the qualities of docility, gracefulness, and half-reasoning intelligence. And these are the qualities that should characterize the worker, who, like the willow limb, is "stupid until practice has taught . . . just what is expected" of him: this is what Holmes means by half-reasoning intelligence. If it is understood that the Civil War has conflated the soldier and the prosthesis, then it becomes apparent that the disciplinary strategies that served to order the soldier might also serve to order the postbellum worker. Like the well-disciplined soldier, the worker should be intelligent enough to perform assigned tasks but not intelligent enough to question them; the worker should be "free" yet subordinate.

Notes

[1] Benedicte Ingstad and Susan Reynolds Whyte, eds., *Disability and Culture* (Berkeley, CA: University of California Press, 1995), 270. Whyte, an anthropologist, suggests in her well-named essay "Disability between Discourse and Experience" that it is necessary to include both a historicizing discourse analysis and a thoughtful "appreciation of narratives and case studies" if one is to have a truly comprehensive disability studies (280). I concur with Whyte's integrationist view, and I would argue further that disability studies is not exclusively an inquiry into the construction of disability as it affects the disabled, but an inquiry into how the construction of disability affects and reflects an entire culture. To interrogate a culture's idea of disability is to interrogate that culture.

[2] Ibid., 9.

[3] Ibid., 270.

[4] John Keegan, *A History of Warfare* (1993; reprint, New York: Vintage-Random House, 1994), 356. Over

400,000 Civil War deaths were the result of infection and disease contracted after battle, often after surgery (antiseptic measures did not become standard medical procedure in the United States until after the Civil War).

[5] Stewart Brooks, *Civil War Medicine* (Springfield, IL: Charles C. Thomas, 1966), 74, 97.

[6] Hillel Schwartz has discussed the importance of the American Civil War in the history of prosthetics and has argued for a distinctive period of prosthetic innovation beginning in 1865 (Reconstruction) and culminating in 1920 (the post-World War I period). Schwartz writes that after the Civil War, "the United States became a leading innovator in the production and fitting of artificial limbs. These would subsequently be adapted and improved by the English, French and Germans during World War I" ("Torque: The New Kinaesthetic of the Twentieth Century," in *Incorporations,* ed. Jonathan Crary and Sanford Kwinter [New York: Zone Books, 1992], 102).

[7] "Dahlgren's mowing-machine" refers to a devastating naval gun deployed by the Union Navy. Abraham Lincoln delighted "in the big splash eleven-inch shells made when fired into the Potomac by the great bottle-shaped Dahlgren guns" (Geoffrey Ward, *The Civil War: An Illustrated History* [New York: Alfred Knopf, 1990], 130).

[8] Oliver Wendell Holmes Sr., "'The Human Wheel, Its Spokes and Felloes,'" *Atlantic Monthly,* May 1863, 567-80. Hereafter referred to as "The Human Wheel"; subsequent quotations from this work will be noted parenthetically in the text. All emphases in quotations from "The Human Wheel," unless otherwise indicated, are Holmes's.

[9] Timothy Sweet, *Traces of War: Poetry, Photography, and the Crisis of the Union* (Baltimore, MD: Johns Hopkins University Press, 1990), 114.

[10] Oliver Wendell Holmes Sr., "The Doings of the Sunbeam," *Atlantic Monthly,* July 1863, 1-15.

[11] Mark Seltzer, *Bodies and Machines* (New York: Routledge, 1992), 3.

[12] Ibid., 65.

[13] Ibid., 152 (Seltzer's emphasis).

[14] Herman Melville, "A Utilitarian View of the Monitor's Fight," in *Battle-Pieces and Aspects of the War* (1866; reprint, Amherst, MA: University of Massachusetts Press, 1972), 62.

[15] Henry Ford, *My Life and Work* (Garden City, NJ: Doubleday, Page, 1923), 108-9.

[16] The Ford Motor Company began building cars on the moving assembly line in 1913-14, at the same time as Europe was utilizing similar technological strategies to mobilize its armies (World War I is remembered as the first fully motorized war: the war that introduced the armed tank, submarine, and airplane). Holmes, writing in 1863, the year Henry Ford is born, anticipates the machine-driven (prosthetic) culture that would become so deeply associated with Ford in the twentieth century (the automobile, after all, is modern society's ultimate prosthesis).

[17] Bill Brown has helpfully summarized the move by which labor is prostheticized: "Human labor is analytically and materially reduced to the operation of the body part, and the individual human functions only as a part, the 'conscious limb,' within the machine system" ("Science Fiction, the World's Fair, and the Prosthetics of Empire, 1910-1915," in *Cultures of United States Imperialism,* ed. Amy Kaplan and Donald E. Pease [Durham, NC: Duke University Press, 1993], 136).

[18] Ford, as one might expect, is more concerned than is Holmes with the disabled veteran's capacity to hold a factory job. Inside the factory's secure walls (and Ford always valued security), remote from the ballroom that is uppermost in Holmes's mind, the amputee's appearance would not matter as it would "under the chandeliers." The bold new ideology of the body that Holmes argues is peculiarly American is somewhat belied by Holmes's Old World attitude toward the disabled and work. When Holmes notes that Palmer's artificial arm (invented after Palmer's success with his artificial leg) "cannot serve a pianist or violinist" but "is yet equal to holding the reins in driving, receiving fees for professional services, and similar easy labors," he affirms the old notion that the disabled are incapable of performing complex or strenuous tasks (578).

[19] I have found no evidence that B. Frank Palmer was actually named for Erastus Dow Palmer. I believe Holmes is simply using the coincidence of the two having the same name to amplify his point that the inventor has both technological ingenuity and a "sense of beauty and fitness." The patent that Palmer received in 1846 for his artificial leg (Patent No. 4,834) was granted to "Benjamin F. Palmer," suggesting that "B. Frank Palmer" was a variant he adopted later (Joseph Nathan Kane, *Famous First Facts* [New York: H. W. Wilson, 1981], 321).

[20] While the *Oxford English Dictionary,* second edition, asserts that the primary meaning for *melanosis* in the mid-nineteenth century was "a morbid deposit or abnormal development of a black pigment in some tissue" (or hyperpigmentation), it seems more likely that Holmes had the more sinister secondary meaning of the word in mind here: a "black cancer" ([Oxford: Oxford-Clarendon University Press, 1989], volume IX,

576). "Black cancer" probably referred to what today is called melanoma: the highly malignant, dark-colored skin tumor that is often deadly if untreated.

[21] And note that like Leonardo da Vinci, B. Frank Palmer and Holmes himself combine the roles of artist and scientist.

[22] Eric Foner and John A. Garraty, eds., *The Reader's Companion to American History* (Boston, MA: Houghton and Mifflin Co., 1991), 907.

[23] Seltzer, 157. The Palmer prosthesis, although admittedly imperfect, clearly represents Holmes's ideal (an ideal that I am calling the "invisible prosthesis").

[24] This is the human wheel as conservative emblem (the human wheel returning). From this perspective, the object of Palmer's innovative invention is conservative: to return the body to its stainless antebellum state (Holmes, as indicated, already reads antebellum America as corresponding to a prelapsarian age in the national mythos). Thus missing limbs and other traces of conflict will be erased. Bill Brown, writing about nineteenth-century science fiction, describes the postbellum idealized male body as "a body on which history is not written but erased, a body without memory, a national body with no nation" (Brown, "Science Fiction," 155).

FURTHER READING

Brenner, Rica, "Oliver Wendell Holmes." In her *Twelve American Poets before 1900,* pp. 169-98. New York: Harcourt, Brace and Co., 1933.

Assesses Holmes's literary career and claims that his works help to illuminate his life.

Fields, Annie. "Oliver Wendell Holmes: Personal Recollections and Unpublished Letters." In her *Authors and Friends,* pp. 107-55. 1897. Reprint. Grosse Pointe, Mich.: Scholarly Press, 1969.

A friend's memories of Holmes.

Grattan, C. Hartley. "Oliver Wendell Holmes." *The American Mercury* IV, No. 13 (January 1925): 37-41.

Proposes reducing Holmes's literary fame to a "footnote," contending that most of his poetry is 'dusty' and his prose work barren.

Hoyt, Edwin P. *The Improper Bostonian: Dr. Oliver Wendell Holmes.* New York: William Morrow and Co., 1979, 319 p.

A detailed, anecdotal, and fully illustrated biography of Holmes.

Kreymborg, Alfred. "Dr. Holmes and the New England Decline." In his *Our Singing Strength: An Outline of American Poetry (1620-1930),* pp. 134-50. New York: Coward-McCann, 1929.

Claims that Holmes's "wittiest warfare" was directed against Calvinism and adds that the author was an intellectual whose poetical style was reminiscent of the eighteenth century.

Morse, John T., Jr. *Life and Letters of Oliver Wendell Holmes.* Boston and New York: Houghton, Mifflin and Company, 1896, 293 p.

A detailed and illustrated biography of Holmes. Morse discusses Holmes's careers in medicine and literature and includes excerpts from the author's notes and correspondence.

Conrad Ferdinand Meyer

1825-1898

Swiss novelist and poet.

INTRODUCTION

As the author of some of the most intricate psychological narratives of nineteenth-century European literature, Meyer exemplifies the artistic movement known as poetic realism, which sought to objectify the inner life of characters through the use of stylized gestures, settings, and images. Meyer is perhaps best known for his sophisticated use of narrative frames in his prose, as well as for his perceptive attention to detail. Although his major novellas are set in the past, his work reflects the transitional character of his time; his relatively conventional political and religious outlook contrasts with the innovative complexity of his narratives and his modernist representation of the ambiguity of human thought and feeling.

Biographical Information

Born in Zurich, Switzerland, on October 11, 1825, to a bourgeois family, Meyer grew up in an intellectual environment. His father held a position as a history teacher at a gymnasium, or high school, and had close ties to the incipient University of Zurich. After his father's death in 1840, Meyer's mother, a pious and intelligent woman, strongly influenced both Meyer and his younger sister, Betsy, who would later become Meyer's secretary and close companion. As a young man, Meyer oscillated between listlessness and hyperactivity, and he pursued an interest in German history and literature. Between 1837 and 1843, Meyer attended the Zurich Gymnasium, but he found it difficult to concentrate on his studies. In 1843, he was sent to Lausanne for a year, where he was introduced to French literature, began composing Romantic poetry, and decided to pursue a writing career. He recognized the mediocrity of his early poetic efforts, however, and plagued by depression, isolated himself from all social contact beyond his immediate family and a few close friends.

During this period he read voraciously—primarily historical works and German Romantic novels—and became increasingly discouraged about his own artistic prospects. He began to suffer from neurotic symptoms and hinted to his family that he planned to commit suicide. His mother, concerned by his mental deterioration, took him to the Préfargier mental hospital in 1852, where he was diagnosed with an "irritation of

the nerves." In 1853 Meyer moved back to Lausanne to study French and there resumed the relationships he had abandoned in 1844, including his friendship with the translator and historian Louis Vulliemin, who supported his literary ambitions and intensified Meyer's interest in history. Because of Vulliemin's influence, Meyer secured a position teaching history and soon began translating Augustin Thierry's *Récits des temps Mérovingiens* (1840), which earned critical praise and provided him with an introduction into the Romantic literary scene. Unimpressed by these accomplishments, Meyer's mother convinced him to return to Zurich at the end of 1853. Meyer again found himself alienated amid bourgeois social life; he continued to translate French historical works and to write poetry, and he produced his first novella, *Clara* (first published in 1938). In 1856 his mother's mental health had degenerated to the point that she was institutionalized at Préfargier, where she committed suicide. At the same time, Meyer and his sister, Betsy, inherited from a longtime friend a large estate, which brought them financial independence.

After spending time in Paris, the Swiss Alps, and Italy, Meyer returned to his translating work and to writing poems, 20 of which eventually were published anonymously as *Zwanzig Balladen von einem Schweizer* (1864). Still others were published in periodicals beginning in 1865. During this period, Betsy became the principal supporter of his literary work, and for most of his career his works were dictated to her. In 1869 Meyer published at his own expense a collection of poems, *Romanzen und Bilder,* and in 1871 had his first major literary success with the publication of *Huttens letzte Tage* [*Hutten's Last Days*], a verse portrayal of the Reformation hero Ulrich von Hutten. During the next 20 years Meyer published a total of 11 novellas and 5 editions of his collected poems. He enjoyed both popular and critical adulation. In recognition of his accomplishments, he was awarded an honorary doctorate by the University of Zurich in 1880.

In 1875 Meyer had married Luise Ziegler, the daughter of a wealthy Zurich family. His marriage inaugurated a tense relationship between Betsy and Luise that would increasingly disrupt Meyer's ability to write, and may have contributed to a mental and physical breakdown that culminated in a year-long hospitalization in 1892-93. For the remaining six years of his life, Meyer wrote very little, while his sister continued to supervise new editions of his work. He died of a heart attack in November 1898.

Major Works

Meyer's work tends to focus on heroic figures of European history—including Thomas à Becket, the Swiss leader Jürg Jenatsch, the Spanish general Fernando Avalos, and the Swedish king Gustav Adolf. Many of these historical figures had not only political, and specifically nationalist, significance, but played a part in religious conflicts as well. Although Meyer researched these figures and their time, he also frequently modified historical details to introduce ambiguities of motivation, complexity of character, and dramatic tension in his writings. The historical novellas are notable for Meyer's sophisticated employment of frame narratives, particularly in *Der Heilige* [*The Saint*] (1880), *Das Leiden eines Knaben* [*A Boy Suffers*] (1883), and *Die Hochzeit des Mönchs* [*The Monk's Wedding*] (1883). The frames do not function merely as transparent vehicles for the internal story. Rather, the interaction between frame and narrative calls attention to the ambiguous nature of artistic construction: the narrators often claim to be confused by the very story they are recounting. Similarly, Meyer's work manifests a fundamental indeterminateness with regard to the central characters' intentions, thus allowing contradictory but equally plausible interpretations of the narratives. Meyer's subtle characterizations correspond to what George F. Folkers

has called an "ambivalent objectivity"—his insistence on describing events, actions and gestures in the fullness of their opacity. The resulting pessimistic tone of his novellas has been read by recent scholars as an implicit critique of the bourgeois mores and self-satisfaction of Meyer's Europe.

In addition to prose works, Meyer wrote two verse narratives early in his career, *Huttens letzte Tage* and *Engelberg* (1872), and in his lifetime published five editions of his collected poems. The poems particularly show the arduous revisions of his work that Meyer undertook as a regular part of the writing process. The poems, like the novellas, employ naturalist motifs in both traditional and original symbolism, and often contain Meyer's deeply personal reflections on his own intimate relationships, his interest in the tension between piety and sensuality, and the anticipation of his own death.

Critical Reception

Although Meyer's earliest writings met with critical indifference, *Huttens letzte Tage* was proclaimed a literary success at its publication and has remained one of Meyer's most popular works. The stylistic precision, psychological insight, and complex structure of this and other novellas are consistently praised by both Meyer's contemporaries and more recent critics. Many consider his masterwork to be *Der Heilige;* as Tiiu V. Laane has written, "His tendency toward the pictorial and dramatic; his striving for symbolization, concentration, and the grand gesture; and his demand for strict objectivity reach their epitome in this novella." Meyer's own favorite work, *Die Richterin* [*The Judge*] (1885), became the subject of one of Sigmund Freud's essays. He considered the dramatic narrative dealing with incest, murder, and justice a confirmation, in nascent form, of his own psychoanalytic concepts. Although Meyer himself thought his poetry secondary to his novellas, he is viewed by critics as a precursor of the German symbolist movement for his use of imagery.

Critics of Meyer's work point to the contrived plots, the occasionally cumbersome and over-explicit use of symbolism, and to his refusal to affirm any single interpretation of events—an insistence that leaves some readers feeling the narrative has been left unresolved. Yet this last characteristic is also applauded by more recent critics as a further manifestation of Meyer's abiding interest in the enigmatic aspects of reality and the contradictory nature of inner life. Meyer's work is generally considered reflective of both the strengths and weaknesses of the transition from Romantic to modern literature: his cosmopolitanism, attention to psychological detail, and objective style contrast with his instinctive patriotism, anti-Catholicism, and apolitical stance.

PRINCIPAL WORKS

Zwanzig Balladen von einem Schwezer (poetry) 1864
Romanzen und Bilder (poetry) 1869
Huttens letzte Tage [*Hutten's Last Days*] (poetry) 1871
Engelberg (poetry) 1872
Das Amulett [*The Amulet*] (novella) 1873
Der Schuss von der Kanzel [*The Shot from the Pulpit*] (novella) 1878
Der Heilige [*The Saint*] (novella) 1880
Gedichte [*Poems*] (poetry) 1882
Gustav Adolfs Page [*Gustav Adolf's Page*] (novella) 1882
Die Hochzeit des Mönchs [*The Monk's Wedding*] (novella) 1883
Jürg Jenatsch: Eine Bündnergeschichte [*Jürg Jenatsch: A Story of Bünden*] (novella) 1883
Das Leiden eines Knaben [*A Boy Suffers*] (novella) 1883
Die Richterin [*The Judge*] (novella) 1885
Die Versuchung des Pescara [*The Tempting of Pescara*] (novella) 1887
Angela Borgia (novella) 1891
Clara (novella) 1938

CRITICISM

Georg Lukács (essay date 1936-37)

SOURCE: "Conrad Ferdinand Meyer and the New Type of Historical Novel," in *The Historical Novel,* translated by Hannah and Stanley Mitchell, Merlin Press, 1962, pp. 221-30.

[*In the following essay, first published in Russian in 1936-37, Lukács reads Meyer's historical portrayals as critical reflections on the "innermost conflicts" of modern bourgeois sensibility.*]

The real representative of the historical novel in this period is Conrad Ferdinand Meyer, who along with Gottfried Keller—likewise a native of Switzerland—is one of the most important realistic narrative writers of the period following 1848. Both, however differently, have stronger ties with the classical traditions of narrative art than most of their German contemporaries and hence surpass them far in respect of a realism which comes to grips with essentials. But Meyer already shows marked features in both his outlook and art of the decline of realism. Yet this did not prevent his exercising a powerful influence far beyond the German speaking world. On the contrary, precisely because he appeared to combine a classical containment of form with a modern hypertrophy of sensibility

and subjectivism, an objectivity of historical tone with a wholesale modernization of characters' emotions, and did so with artistry—he became the true classic of the modern historical novel.

In Meyer the conflicting tendencies of the new phase of development cohere in a new form. Yet his essential problems are strikingly similar in many respects to those of Flaubert. This is particularly interesting because the concrete historical situation of the two writers and hence their concrete attitudes to historical problems are so very different. Flaubert's decisive historical experience is the Revolution of 1848 (in *L'Education Sentimentale* one can clearly see its effect on him). Conrad Ferdinand Meyer's great historical experience, on the other hand, is the dawning of German unity, its struggle and realization. The fact that Meyer is the living contemporary of this conclusion to the bourgeois-democratic struggles for German unity, and particularly the contemporary of their capitulation to the "Bonapartist monarchy" of the Hohenzollerns under Bismarck's leadership, this makes his historical subject-matter less arbitrary than Flaubert's. Admittedly the decorative contrast between a "grandiose" past and a trivial present plays an important part in his work, too, and determines his predilection for the Renaissance. But even so, considerable importance is attached to struggles for national unification and national unity (***Jürg Jenatsch, The Temptation of Pescara,*** etc.)

However, the treatment of these themes suffers disastrously from the central position of Bismark in this period, which affected even Meyer. Meyer speaks quite openly on the subject, particularly in reference to Jürg Jenatsch. He complains in a letter that his hero's resemblance to Bismarck is "not palpable enough"; in another place: "and how petty, despite murder and killing, is the confederate (Jenatsch—G.L.) compared with the prince". This Bismarck adulation is very closely connected with the fact that Meyer, like the German liberal middle class in general, after the 1848 Revolution no longer regards the establishment of national unity and the defence of national independence as the cause of the people to be carried out by the people themselves under the leadership of "world-historical individuals", but as a historical destiny whose executive organ is some enigmatic, lonely "hero" or "genius". Pescara especially is portrayed in this way—a lonely figure who decides in lonely ruminations whether Italy is to be freed from foreign domination and of course decides negatively: "Does Italy deserve freedom at this hour and is she of sufficient worth, as constituted, to receive and preserve it? I think not," says Pescara. But this statement is simply an expression of his secluded personality, it does not relate in the novel itself to any popular movement which has such an aim; he says this only among the higher circle of diplomats and generals etc.

Naturally, one cannot make a simple comparison between the Swiss patrician and the vulgar-liberal supporters of Bismarck in Germany. Meyer's superiority to them, however, is chiefly one of taste, moral feeling and psychological sensitivity, not of political vision or of deeper solidarity with the people. Thus Meyer's remoulding of the problems of his age, once he has projected them into history, is purely a matter of aesthetic feeling and taste; he turns the fatalistic geniuses, the supposed makers of history into decorative and superb decadents. His aesthetic and moral superiority to his German contemporaries simply means that he introduces moral problems and scruples into the Bismarck conception of history as a question of naked power. (We recall the similar position of Jacob Burckhardt.)

The abstract ideology of power and the mystical and fatalistic mission of "great men" remains unchanged and uncriticized in Meyer. He says in his novel on Pescara: "He believes in power alone and in the single duty of great men to attain to their full stature through the means and tasks of the age." As a result the tasks themselves shrink more and more into power intrigues within the upper stratum and the real historical problems, whose executive organs these men were in reality, fade increasingly from sight. It is very characteristic of Meyer's development that in *Jürg Jenatsch* there was still some rudimentary connection with real popular aims even though it was expressed, à la Bismarck, solely through the "genius" of the hero. In *Pescara* such connections have disappeared and the other historical novels are even further away from the historical life of the people; in them the dualism between questions of power and subjective moral rumination becomes even more the exclusive preoccupation.

This conception of heroes is linked in Meyer with a fatalistic view of the unknowability of the paths of history, with a mystique of "great men" as the executors of the fatalistic will of an unknowable divinity. In his youthful and lyrical-historical work on the fortunes of Ulrich von Hutten he states this view quite clearly:

> "Wir ziehn! Die Trommel schlägt! Die Fahne weht!
> Nicht weiss ich, welchen Weg die Heerfahrt geht.
>
> Genug, dass ihn der Herr des Krieges weiss—
> *Sein* Plan und Losung! *Unser* Kampf und Schweiss."

> ("We're off! The drum strikes up! The flag is flying!
> I do not know the way the expedition goes.
>
> Enough that the Lord of war knows it—
> *His* plan and battle-cry! *Our* struggle and sweat.")

The unknowability of the ways and ends of the historical process is exactly countered by the unknowability of the individuals acting in history. They are not temporarily isolated, as a result of definite objective or subjective circumstances, but fundamentally lonely.

This loneliness is connected in Meyer, as in almost all the important writers of this period, very deeply with his general outlook, with his belief that man and his destiny are fundamentally unknowable. The inevitable result of the loss of interaction between man and society, of blindness to the fact that if man is formed by society, then this is also a process of his own inner life, is to make the words and deeds of men appear to the writer as impenetrable masks, behind which the most varied motives may be at work. Meyer has stated this feeling clearly several times, most plastically in the *Novelle*, **The Monk's Wedding.** Dante tells a story in which the Hohenstaufen Emperor, Frederick II, and his Chancellor, Petrus de Vines, appear episodically. To the question of the listening tyrant of Verona, Cangrande, as to whether he, Dante, really believes that Frederick was the author of the piece *Of the Three Impostors,* Dante replies "non liquet" (it is not clear); and to the question as to whether he believes in the Chancellor's treachery he replies in a similar fashion. Cangrande then reproaches him for having shown Frederick guilty and Petrus asserting his innocence in the *Divine Comedy:* "You do not believe in the guilt and you condemn. You believe in the guilt and you exonerate." The real Dante certainly had no such doubts. It is only Meyer who makes of him an agnostic in his attitude to people. In this way the decorative robes of the Renaissance conceal the most modern agnosticism and nihilism.

There is apparent self-criticism on Meyer's part in Cangrande's reproaches to Dante. Yet at best it is but one side of his conception. For Meyer feels that Dante has every right to portray history and people, whom he admits he cannot really penetrate, in an autocratic manner, according to his own lights; the more so, as this loneliness and unknowability is in Meyer's eyes a *merit:* the greater a person's stature, the greater his loneliness and unknowability.

This sentiment becomes more and more pronounced in the course of Meyer's development and, as a result, his heroes, too, acquire more and more of this enigmatic loneliness, they become more and more eccentric in their attitudes to the events of history in which they are the heroes. Already in **The Saint** Meyer turns the struggle of crown and church in medieval England into a psychological problem of Thomas Beckett. The tendency is still more pronounced in **Pescara.** What appears to be a highly dramatic action, the question namely of whether General Pescara will renounce the Spaniards and fight for the unification of Italy is no more than the illusion of a conflict. Pescara wanders through the novel, an enigmatic sphinx whose farsighted plans nobody understands. And why? Because Pescara has no such plans. He is dangerously ill and knows that he soon must die, that he can never again take part in any great enterprise. He says himself: "For no choice ever appeared before me, I stood outside of things . . . The knot of my existence is inextricable, it (that is death, G.L.) will cut it apart."

Here we see in a different form a similar problem to the one we observed in Flaubert: the combination of a desire for great deeds with a personal and social inability to accomplish them in reality is projected into the past, in the hope that this social impotence may lose its modern pettiness in the ostentatious attire of the Renaissance. However, this projection into an illusory monumentality—a monumentality merely of picturesque gestures, hiding the decadent, tormented broodings of the modern bourgeois—produces in the general tone of the writing notes as false and feelings and experiences as distorted as in Flaubert.

Here also is the real source of Meyer's modernization of history. Meyer, like Flaubert, always gives an accurate picture of the externals of historical life, except that he is more concentrated, decorative and less prone to naturalistic detail. Brandes's criticism of Scott's naïve handling of contemporary plastic arts in his historical novels could never be levelled against Meyer. Yet the *innermost conflicts* of his heroes do not grow out of the real historical conditions of the given period, out of the popular life of the period. Instead they are specifically modern conflicts of passion and conscience in an individual artificially isolated by capitalist life, just as Flaubert's conflicts were conflicts of desire and fulfilment in present-day bourgeois society. For this reason the psychology of Meyer's heroes—despite the fine gradations and picturesque portrayals of historical attire—is throughout the same or almost so; it is immaterial which country or which age is chosen as the arena of the historical plot.

Meyer was quite aware of this "problematic" in his art. In a letter he writes of his aims and attitude in regard to the form of the historical novel: "I use the form of the historical *Novelle* simply and solely to express my experiences and my personal feelings, I prefer it to the 'period novel', because it gives me a better mask and puts the reader at a greater distance. Thus within a very objective and highly artistic form I am essentially very individual and subjective." This subjectivity appears chiefly in the fact that the heroes are spectators rather than executors of their own deeds, that their real interest is the moral-metaphysical scruples and broodings which have as their object the "questions of power" in the foreground of the story.

Because of this attitude Meyer follows on from Vigny rather than from Scott in the historical novel. But he makes history even less historical. Vigny and similar Romantic historical novelists see the historical process incorrectly, standing on its head. But they nevertheless see some kind of historical process, even if it is of their own false construction. And their "great men" act within this historical process. In Meyer, apart from certain attempts and survivals, the historical process itself has disappeared, and with it man disappears as the real actor in world history. It is very interesting to see that in Meyer's original plan for *Pescara* the fatal illness was absent. He says in a conversation: "I could have done it differently, and that would have had its attractions, too: Pescara's wound was not mortal; he is tempted, fights the temptation, overcomes and repudiates it. And then afterwards seeing the gratitude of the House of Habsburg, he regrets having done so. He can also then fall in the battle outside Milan." One observes how, even in this plan, the psychological-moral element prevails over the historical-political motifs. And it is no accident that Meyer in subsequent work on the material takes it further in this direction, giving his hero an irrational, biological "depth". In so doing Meyer produces on the one hand the fatalistic-melancholic groundnote of the novel, on the other the enigmatic loneliness of his hero. He himself says on one occasion: "One does not know what Pescara would have done without his wound."

Thus by having only protagonists of history at the centre of his novels and almost totally neglecting the people and their lives, the real broad forces of history, Meyer has reached a much more advanced stage of the liquidation of history than the earlier Romantics. History has become something purely irrational for him. The great men are eccentric and lonely figures caught up within meaningless events which never touch them at the centre. History is a complex of decorative *tableaux,* great pathetic moments, in which this loneliness and eccentricity gives vent to itself with a lyrical psychological force that is often very moving. Meyer is an important writer because he does not conceal his "problematic" with art; the modern bourgeois incapacity of his heroes breaks through the historical costume again and again. But this very artistic honesty and uprightness is what shatters the fine structure of his works. Again and again his history is unmasked as mere costumery.

Yet from a formal point of view the structure of Meyer's works is of a very high quality, outwardly well-nigh perfect. His exploitation of the decorative possibilities does not, as in Flaubert, lead to excessive description. Meyer, on the contrary, is unusually economical in his descriptions. He concentrates his action round the pathos and drama of a few scenes and his description of surrounding objects is always subject to the psychological problems of the characters. His model is the strict compactness of the old *Novelle*. But this compactness serves for him a double purpose: at once to mask decoratively and unmask lyrically the subjective projection of present-day feelings into history. His plots are constructed with the deliberate aim of stressing the enigma of his heroes. The form of a story within a story serves to make events, conceived as incomprehensible and irrational in themselves, actually appear so, and in particular to underline the impenetrable enigma of the main characters.

Meyer already belongs quite consciously with those modern writers for whom the charm of storytelling lies no longer in the elucidation of an apparently incomprehensible event, in the elucidation of deeper connections of life which comprehend the apparently incomprehensible, but in the mystery itself, in portraying the irrational "unfathomable depth" of human existence. Meyer, for example, lets a simple archer, who naturally understands nothing of the deeper connections, recount the fortunes of Thomas Beckett. He tells of events which were "astounding and inconceivable" not only for distant observers but also for the participants.

Meyer hopes by this strict composition to avoid the modern writer's submergence in psychological analysis. But his way out is illusory, for the psychologism of the moderns had nothing to do with analysis as a form of expression, it springs from the writer's orientation on the inner spiritual life of his characters, which he believes to be independent of the total coherence of life and to move according to its own laws. Meyer's decorative concentration is thus no less psychologistic than the writings of those of his contemporaries who were open adherents of psychological analysis. Simply that with him the discrepancy between the decorative outward spectacle of history and the modern psychology of the characters is sharper.

This discrepancy is further underlined by the fact that Meyer, like Flaubert, inclines to see the greatness of vanished ages in the brutal excesses of the people of the past. Gottfried Keller, his great democratic contemporary, who had a high regard for Meyer's honest artistic aims, continually jibes in his letters at this passionate weakness of the humanly very sensitive writer for cruelty and brutality in his stories.

All these features, as with Flaubert, express opposition to the triviality of bourgeois life. But because of the different social historical circumstances they do so in quite a different way. Flaubert's rejection of modern bourgeois life has very romantic sources and modes of expression, yet it is full of a passionate radicalism. Meyer has much more the weary melancholy of the liberal bourgeois, who watches with repudiation and bewilderment the evolution of his own class amid the vehement advances of capitalism while at the same time timidly admiring the power that is manifested therein.

Meyer's portrayal of historical protagonists is interesting and important because it shows so vividly how the once democratic aims of the bourgeois class are transformed, even in the case of honest and highly gifted writers, into a compromising liberalism. Meyer cherishes a great admiration for the men and theories of the Renaissance. But the fiery wine of this admiration is always mixed with a goodly measure of liberal water. We have already seen the overdone moral-psychological reflections which are mixed up with the question of "power in itself". This mixture appears again and again in Meyer's novels as a longing for the "beyond Good and Evil" world of the Renaissance mingled with liberal reservations and extenuations. Thus in the Pescara novel, for example: "Caesar Borgia, he tried with pure Evil. But . . . Evil must be used only in small portions and with caution, otherwise it kills." Or as Pescara himself says—in a very Bismarckian way—of Macchiavelli: "There are political principles which are meaningful to intelligent minds and prudent hands, but which become corrupt and wicked as soon as a rude mouth utters or a criminal pen inscribes them." So we see that Meyer's enthusiasm for the Renaissance is not based upon the recognition and acknowledgment of a great and unsurpassed period of progress, as it was with Goethe or Stendhal, Heine or Engels. His contemporary, Burckhardt, played a decisive part in popularizing the Renaissance. Yet despite important individual discoveries, he is already waging an ideological rearguard action: correct insights are frequently obscured by infusions of liberal "problematic". In Meyer this tendency is more marked as is his formalist-decorative conception of the Renaissance.

This "problematic" leads on to the liberal hero-cult of Bismarck. For while the principle of "beyond Good and Evil" is permissible to the "man of destiny", woe betide should it become the property of the people. Behind Meyer's conception of history lies his admiration for Bismarckian *Realpolitik,* for the superior skulduggery of the uppermost spheres of society, for a form of politics which in the eyes of the liberal ideologists has become an "art", an "end-in-itself".

Thus the virtual disappearance of popular life in these novels, the fact that it is only an artificially isolated upper stratum which acts in the foreground, is only apparently an artistic problem. In Vigny this expressed a reactionary-Romantic opposition to the progressive, popular character of Scott's conception of history. In Meyer, who personally was not nearly so openly reactionary as Vigny, it shows the triumph of the National Liberalism into which the liberalism of the German speaking world had turned. The Swiss, Meyer, is sufficiently independent socially and sufficiently honest, personally and artistically, not to succumb entirely to the apologist excesses of the German national-liberal bourgeoisie. He creates works of art superior in every respect to contemporary productions in Germany, yet for precisely this reason the effect of national liberalism and its estrangement from the people on the historical novel is in his case all the more important and fatal.

In most of Meyer's works this estrangement is expressed directly: the historical events take place exclusively "above"; the inscrutable course of history manifests itself in the power-political deeds and moral scruples of individuals who are completely isolated and uncomprehended even within the upper stratum. If the people are shown at all, then it is simply as an amorphous, spontaneous, blind and savage mass, usually as wax in the hands of the lonely hero (Jürg Jenatsch). Popular figures which are given any independence and individuality express in the main only blind devotion to (archer in **The Saint**) or blind enthusiasm for (Leubelfing in **Gustav Adolf's Page**) the great historical hero.

But when Meyer, very exceptionally, gives us a popular story, even in the form of an episode, the contrast between his characterization and that of the classical period of the historical novel comes out with particular clarity. In the *Novelle,* **Plautus in the Convent** (**Plautus im Nonnenkloster**), the story is told of a brave and determined peasant girl, Gertrude, rigorously bound by the Catholic Faith of her time. She has taken a vow to become a nun which she wishes to fulfil despite the resistance of her whole being, despite her love for a youth whom she would like to marry. When the novices are received into the convent "miracles" are made to occur: the novice is expected to carry a heavy cross (with a crown of thorns on her head). Only if she does not collapse under its weight will she be accepted as a nun. According to superstition the holy Virgin assists; in actual fact the novice is given quite a light cross, outwardly similar to the heavy one. Poggio, the narrator of this story, succeeds through various circumstances of the main plot to reveal this deception to the girl. Gertrude now chooses the really heavy cross in order to test in fact whether the holy Virgin really wants her to become a nun. After heroic efforts she collapses, and now she is able to become the happy wife of her loved one.

But how does Poggio—and with him surely C. F. Meyer—react to this? Poggio relates:

> "This she did and calmly descended from step to step radiant with joy, once more the simple peasant girl, who, now that her modest human wish had been granted and she could return to everyday life, would no doubt quickly and happily forget the moving spectacle which she had afforded the crowd in her despair. For a brief while the peasant girl had stood before me, and I with my excited senses had seen her as the embodiment of a higher being, a demonic creature, truth jubilantly destroying illusion. But what is truth asked Pilate?"

We have quoted this passage in full, because if one compares the story of Gertrude with that of Goethe's

Dorothea or Scott's Jeannie Deans the contrast between the two periods is vividly apparent. At the same time the comparison reveals the social and human foundations of this new type of historical novel. We have to limit ourselves here to the most essential features of the contrast. First of all, the bravery of Meyer's peasant girl has something eccentric and decorative about it. We do not see its significant human qualities; instead we have one short, unique act which shows physical strain on the one hand and pictorial effect (cross and crown of thorns) on the other. Secondly, Meyer views the moment of heroism in isolation from life, indeed as a complete antithesis to life. The return to everyday life is not, as in Goethe and Scott, a broad epic destiny, it does not suggest the slumbering presence of similar forces in countless ordinary people which, for personal or historical reasons, have simply never been released or tested. For Meyer it is determined by the antithesis between the "demonic" and the "everyday", so that the return to everyday life in fact nullifies the "heroic moment", whereas in Goethe and Scott the heroism is "sublated" (aufgehoben) in the dialectical, two-fold sense.

Meyer proves himself to be an important artist amid the onset of decline by portraying a completely normal heroine and not, as Huysmans, Wilde or d'Annunzio would have done, a really "demonic" and hysterical creature. But he is already sufficiently contaminated by decadence to treat his own rightness of view with a certain sceptical melancholy.

This type of sensibility reveals the spirit of the new times. Meyer's heroes stand spiritually and morally on tiptoe in order to appear to others and particularly to themselves greater than they are, in order to convince others and themselves that the height which they have attained or at least dreamed of attaining at individual moments of their lives is theirs at all times. The decorative historical costume serves to conceal this tiptoe posture.

It is clear that this inner weakness, coupled with the morbid longing for greatness, is due to the divorce from popular life. The everyday life of the people appears as dull, degrading prose, nothing more. No longer is an organic connection seen between this life and an historical upsurge. The hero, as Burckhardt says, is "what we are not".

The German bourgeoisie became national-liberal; it betrayed the bourgeois-democratic Revolution of 1848 and later, with ever fewer reservations, chose the Bismarck way to German unity. In German literature of the time this path of development takes the form ideologically of pure apologia and artistically of the wholesale decline of classical traditions and the most superficial assimilation of a second-class West European realism.

Whatever Meyer's superiority aesthetically and ethically to these German bourgeois, who from 1848 to 1870 turned from democrats into national-liberals, and however complex the connections between the development of his art and this social-historical development, he nevertheless mirrors this process in the most intimate, spiritual and artistic problems of his life's work. His Renaissance figures reflect liberal timidity and faint-heartedness. His "lonely" heroes bear typical traits of the decline of German democracy.

Heinrich Henel (essay date 1954)

SOURCE: "Bread and Wine," in *The Poetry of Conrad Ferdinand Meyer,* University of Wisconsin Press, 1954, pp. 194-234.

[*In the following excerpt, Henel discusses the evolution of one of the central themes in Meyer's poetry of the seasons—the "conflict between pagan and Christian imagery."*]

Conrad Ferdinand Meyer's poems on summer and fall provide an example of proliferation which is almost overwhelming in its complexity and complication. However, there would be little point in following their evolution if such a study provided merely additional proof of what has been amply demonstrated already. Interest is aroused, not so much by the fact that twelve poems in *Gedichte* and four in *Huttens letzte Tage* are based on a small number of related motifs and can be traced back to common origins, but rather by the great difference between the earlier and the later poems, and especially by the violent contrasts among the later poems themselves. The *amor fati* expressed in "Säerspruch" is so totally different from the *amor fati* expressed in "Schnitterlied," the pious acceptance of death in "Hussens Kerker" clashes so sharply with the pagan desire for destruction in "Die Veltlinertraube," that no view of Meyer's poetry, and perhaps of Meyer the man, can be adequate which does not attempt to explain this remarkable group of poems. To an even higher degree than is usual with Meyer, these poems are conceptual in origin and metaphoric in character, yet their thought is confused and their images are of changing significance. The idea of the return or the homecoming, which we met in several of his wanderer and mountain poems, underlies all of Meyer's poetry on summer and fall, but here it is elusive and baffling. The return may be a return home ("Heimkehr"), or cyclical return ("Wiederkehr"), or a return to God ("Einkehr"), and sometimes it is two or all three of these things at once. The poet seems to be struggling with conflicting emotions and urges, or perhaps he is reaching for something which he can never attain. The impression is confirmed by the devious routes he takes in elaborating these poems and by the inferior poetic worth of some of the final products.

None of them has the scenic interest of Meyer's great Alpine poems. We see fields, harvesters, sowers, vintagers, grapes, and falling leaves, but these figures and objects are not placed in settings which give the impression of reality. They remain metaphors, ideas in disguise. It is fair to conclude that the sight of fields and of farmers, of vineyards and of vintagers, never gripped Meyer and never gave him the happiness he felt in beholding the mountains. For this an another, and perhaps the most revealing, quality of the poems on the seasons: they are joyless. The early poems and some later ones are elegiac in mood, while five of the later poems change over to a desperate exuberance.

In the Alpine poems, the poet is received into a world of vastness, solitude, and silence. The return means a turning to the true self and to lonely contemplation— to a state which is sometimes merely resigned but often filled with gladness. There is only one seasonal poem, **"Ewig jung ist nur die Sonne,"** in which the poet returns to a lonely place, and this poem is an elegy. The other poems speak of activity, the activity of nature or of people, and the poet, while not actually taking part in the work, is somehow involved in it. He praises the sacredness of labor in **"Auf Goldgrund"** and **"Der Uli"**; in **"Der Erntewagen,"** he is at pains (somewhat embarrassingly) to assure us that he, too, is not idle; and in **"An die Natur im Spätsommer"** and **"Spätjahr"** he compares himself with the seed grain lying dormant in the ground but secretly getting ready to produce growth. **"Schnitterlied"** glorifies man's defiance of nature and the work he does in the teeth of mortal danger. **"Der Triumphbogen"** pictures Clio as a reaper who cuts down the crop seeded by the past, intimating thereby that what has come to maturity must perish. Most remarkable of all, **"Der Musensaal"** transforms the muses into harvesters who stride about in agitated groups and render judgment on men and nations. And the poet not only watches these diverse activities, but sympathizes with them all and nods his approval.

The contrast between the poems about lake, forest, and mountains and those about the seasons is very striking. While the former speak of solitude, withdrawal, and contemplation, the latter speak of action and of participation. They are the records of Meyer's struggle to break out of his lonely state and to win himself a place in society—or if not that, then in the divine order of things. They voice his desire to merge the self in a larger whole, and his need for reassurance that his life is not useless and wasted. They defend the position of the poet who, though he must necessarily be different from other men, renders them service as prophet and judge. What holds the poems on the seasons together and constitutes them as a group is, beyond their genetic relationship, the fact that they deal with the individual's relation to the community and with his share in the common destiny of man.

However, it is only when one speaks in such general terms that the unity of Meyer's poems on the seasons can be seen, for, as has been said before, their differences and even inconsistencies are very great. The early versions of his poetry offer abundant evidence of uncertainty as to how he should convey his message, but the message itself is mostly clear from the start. Usually he knows what he wants to say and lacks only the means of saying it effectively. It is different with the poems about the seasons, where several ideas rival each other even in the earliest versions. The return in **"Die Heimkehr"** is both a return to God and a return to a congenial human community. In **"Der Erntewagen"** and **"Morgenlied,"** the poet puts his trust in the future fruits of faithful and persistent labor, but in the latter poem he also paraphrases the Lord's prayer and asks that bread may be given him today. **"An die Natur im Spätsommer"** and **"Spätjahr"** retain the gentle and elegiac note of the earlier poems but replace the worship of God by worship of nature. Now it is the cyclical return of the seasons which inspires the poet with confidence and hope, but he identifies himself also, and more specifically, with the seed grain which is sheltered in the earth and bides its time. He seeks peace and security, and he craves assurance of future productivity. Still later, **"Säerspruch"** teaches complete submission to the will of God and acceptance with equal readiness of either life or death; and it praises even the seed which perishes and never bears fruit. Written at about the same time, **"Das fallende Laub"** and **"Hussens Kerker"** bless the man who is called home by God when his work is done, but **"Die Veltlinertraube"** and **"Erntegewitter"** give a very different meaning to the words, "Ripeness is all"—words which formed the motto of the first two editions of **"Huttens letzte Tage."** In these poems the poet asks for extinction at the moment when life is fullest, and in them, as in **"Mein Jahr,"** he seeks fulfillment, not in patient labor conforming to a universal order or higher will, but in a supreme moment of glowing passion and reckless surrender.[1]

It is not possible, then, to say that the religious spirit of Meyer's early poems on the seasons gave way, later on, to secularism or paganism; nor that his search for a congenial society was replaced by his desire to merge with nature; nor that his patience became exhausted and made him wish for a sudden and violent end. Inconsistencies and ambiguities exist not only between poems written at different times but also between contemporary poems and even within a single poem, so that they cannot be resolved by drawing a line of development. Rather, we must conclude that Meyer's concern with society and with his own position in it was uncertain and mutable, that it expressed only a secondary need, and that it was constantly interfered with and modified by more vital concerns. He needed solitude more than company, calm more than applause. Of course it was natural that a man of his

powers should, sometimes at least, have felt bitterly his separation from the world and the apparent sterility of his existence; that there were times when he might have cried with Faust in his despair:

> Der Gott, der mir im Busen wohnt,
> Kann tief mein Innerstes erregen;
> Der über allen meinen Kräften thront,
> Er kann nach außen nichts bewegen.

But it was not easy to see what he could do to remedy this situation and yet remain true to himself. In the poems on the seasons Meyer tried to persuade himself that the active and the contemplative life could be complementary, but the poems themselves prove the futility of this hope. He has no sooner established his place in some larger order than he tries to escape or transcend it. He admires the workers in the fields in **"Der Erntewagen,"** but returns to his study to emulate them. He praises their labor in **"Auf Goldgrund,"** but likens them to the saints whose pictures he saw in a museum. He is received back into a community in **"Die Heimkehr,"** but the father who welcomes him home is really the Father in heaven. In **"Spätjahr"** he trusts that he will grow like the seed, but finds in **"Säerspruch"** that death is as welcome as life. Always there is an escape clause in the compacts he makes with the world, and the more he is committed the more violent becomes his desire to free himself. It is thus, I believe, that we must understand the note of desperateness in his poems glorifying the supreme moment—the only note not present from the beginning in his poetry on the seasons.

When he was young, Meyer could persuade himself that his time for action lay in the future, that winter comes before summer, and that the seed must rest undisturbed in the ground if it is to bear fruit later on. This allowed him to continue his secluded life and yet to feel that his existence was not abnormal or damnable but on the contrary conformed to universal order. But as he grew older, activity and production could no longer be postponed, and indeed he could have displayed the products of his labor with pride. Now, however, he had to admit openly what he had secretly known and suggested all along: the real attraction of the concept of the seed lay not in its promise of a future harvest but in its closeness to death. In similar fashion, Meyer's symbols for fertility and achievement, the grape and the harvest, were at the same time symbols of death. For him, the consummation of life was not achievement as such but the honorable release which it afforded. He resisted a lifelong temptation to take his life only because he had a task to perform, because of his poet's vocation. Had he ever felt that his work was done, he would have spoken his "Nunc dimittis." In his poetry, he anticipated the hour of release, asking for it in pious accents in **"Das fallende Laub"** and **"Hussens Kerker,"** and desiring it impatiently in

"Schnitterlied" and **"Die Veltlinertraube."** No matter how flattered Meyer may have been by his reacceptance into the Zürich patriciate and his gathering fame as an author, his deeper self, his poetic self, remained bound to the lonely life and made him feel that success was like treason and should be atoned for through death.

Ultimately, the active life held out only one satisfaction to Meyer, but this he was not able to attain. He shrank from the thought of suicide, but if he could have died for his country, died on the field of battle, he would have blessed his fate, for then he would have given his life and not flung it away. Perhaps such speculations are not permissible, although there is much to confirm them. The eagerness with which Meyer listened to Conrad Nüscheler's reports about the battles he fought in Italy;[2] the enthusiasm with which, despite moral qualms, he followed Prussia's wars under Bismarck; poems like **"Der Ritt in den Tod"** and **"Das Weib des Admirals"**—all these show an interest in war and in fighting which can be explained, in a man as peaceable as Meyer, only as expressing his desire for a sacrificial death. It is deeply significant that among his early poems there is one on Winkelried,[3] the Swiss hero who deliberately sacrificed his life at the battle of Sempach to gain victory and freedom for his country. This poem was written at about the same time as **"Die Heimkehr"** and parallels it in a remarkable way. Embellishing the legend, Meyer says that Winkelried has just returned to his native land when he obeys the call to arms and is presently killed. Thus, just as the prodigal son in **"Die Heimkehr"** returns to his family but also to the Father in heaven, so Winkelried returns to his country but also to God. Even in this early poem, the desire to live in a community is surpassed by the desire to die for it.

There is one poem, **"Am Wassersturz,"**[4] in which Meyer sheds all disguises and simply speaks of himself, but it was precisely for this reason that he withheld it from print. Yet even this poem, consciously or unconsciously, harks back to Winkelried's deed. Winkelried grasped the spears of the enemies and pressed them into his breast, thus opening a path for his comrades. Meyer, longing for death, would receive the full force of an Alpine torrent on his unprotected breast:

> Seh' ich dieser Wasser wilde Kraft
> Donnernd stürzen, daß die Felsen zittern,
> Wird es mir, als müßte Leidenschaft
> Einmal noch mich auf den Grund erschüttern.
>
> Und ich möchte, der Gefahr bewußt,
> Ihr die Arme breiten ohne Bangen
> Und den vollen Sturz mit Todeslust
> Auf der unbewehrten Brust empfangen.

This is so powerful an outburst that none can doubt its genuineness. It is a desperate plea to be granted the life of passion and a violent end. However, fulfillment of this desire was denied to Meyer—and it was denied not so much because of external circumstances as because there were other sides in his nature which prevented satisfaction of his more violent urges. He knew this, and he admitted, in the sad and reluctant end of the poem **"Reisephantasie,"**[5] that the passionate life was not for him:

> Daß ich einem ganzen vollen Glücke
> Stillen Kuß auf stumme Lippen drücke
> Einmal nur in einem Menschenleben—
> Aber nimmer wird es sich begeben.

In actual life, Meyer was never overwhelmed by desperate love, and he never knew the desperate danger and exultation of battle. He was not allowed to give his life for his country, but he was allowed to give it his poetry. At times, this must have seemed to him like bitter renunciation. To adapt the words of **"Firnelicht,"** instead of "ein großes wildes Leuchten," he gave merely "ein kleines stilles Leuchten."

But of course there is a measure of false modesty in **"Firnelicht;"** it hardly does justice to Meyer's greatness as a poet. Greatness his poetry gained much less from his hankering after the active life and his imaginative experience of death in action than from his solitary life and its nearness to death and to God. Solitude gave him "Leidlosigkeit" at the least, and sometimes true gladness. All he could ever imagine himself gaining from the active life was "Freudlosigkeit," the dreariness of dogged persistence or a violent rapture followed by sudden extinction. Few of his poems on the supreme moment are as flawless as **"Der Ritt in den Tod"** and **"Am Wassersturz"**; most of them are marred by excessive violence or adolescent boastfulness. To be sure, many of his poems springing from his solitary musing are weak or sentimental, and some are even mawkish; but many remain which appeal through their somber grandeur, and in some the poet's spiritual elation is radiant and pure. He was earnest enough in desiring a sacrificial death, but, stout Protestant that he was, Meyer had to work out his salvation alone.

It is almost impossible to describe in discursive language the conflicting emotions and wishes expressed in Meyer's poems on the seasons—there are far too many "buts" in the preceding pages. We have made various suggestions to account for what is ultimately unaccountable, and it would be easy to see contradictions where alternative explanations are intended. We have said that the poems express Meyer's desire for communion and approval, and had to admit that his longing for withdrawal also enters into them. We have seen in them an attempt to vindicate the poet's position in society, but also a craving to give to society something more than mere poetry. We have suggested that he sought death as release from an unwanted life, or as atonement for respectability and prosperity, or as a sacrifice—and we have denied all these possibilities by saying that it was not really death that he wanted but "Leidlosigkeit," a resting place this side of the grave. Who can know these things? There is some evidence for all our suggestions, but the sphere of thought and feeling in which the poet moved will always remain shrouded in mystery. We have only the poems to go by, and only individual poems can be clearly defined. To this task we must now address ourselves.

The parent poem of the whole group of poems on summer and fall is **"Die Heimkehr."**[6] Just as the scene of **"Das Glöcklein,"** which introduces Meyer's Alpine poetry, is not laid in the mountains, so the subject of **"Die Heimkehr"** is not the seasons. But just as the mountains have a symbolic function in the one poem, so symbols related to the seasons are used in the other. That is to say, both groups of poems originated from concepts, and the central concept of the seasonal poetry is, as the title of the parent poem suggests, the return. On the other hand, the subject of this poem is the story of the prodigal son. What interested Meyer in the Biblical parable, and what he made of it, can be shown best by first quoting Mr. Bodmer's criticism of **"Die Heimkehr":**[7]

> The very elaborate narrative poem treats the story of the prodigal son, but strangely enough its first part only, the confession of the returned son, whose experiences abroad form the main content. However, the center of the parable, the conflict which makes the real poetic material, surely lies in the contrast between the obedient and the disobedient son, and in the father's joy over the one sinner that repenteth. . . . The poet needs almost four times as many words to say the same as Scripture.

Mr. Bodmer is right in complaining that the poem is prolix. However, when he charges that Meyer missed the point of the parable he merely shows that he himself missed the point of the poem; for Meyer's concern was not to decide whether righteousness or repentance is the higher virtue, but to find a way of merging his highly individualistic existence in a larger whole. The introductory two stanzas of **"Die Heimkehr"** describe the harmonious working of a patriarchal peasant economy, and the prodigal son's account of his experiences abroad is climaxed by his vision of life in his father's house, "where each has his assigned duty, and all are bound together in one community." It is this vision of "a lovely circle, clear order, and a steady course" which has decided him to come home. He returns to a community which moves with the rhythm of nature, finding satisfaction in tilling the soil and joy in gathering its gifts; but he returns also to his father who, in Meyer's poem no less clearly than in the Bible, is an image of the Father in heaven. At the end of the poem, night has fallen on the land, and the returned traveler, walking hand in hand with his father, steps through the gate into the light.

"Die Heimkehr" voices the poet's aversion to a forced pursuit of happiness, his revulsion from noisy feasting and sharp regret. The life free from exuberance and free from sorrow, the "Leidlosigkeit" which he sought, is in this world most nearly gained in an existence close to nature, but ultimately it is gained only in death. This is the meaning of the poem, but, as with all Meyer's inferior works, it is not wholly apparent from the story alone. It resides, rather, in the motifs, and these are superimposed on the story as diacritical marks are placed over a scanned line of verse. There are too many such motifs; none of them is central; none has inspired the poem as a whole. Hence its diffuseness as well as the elusiveness of its import.

The motifs of the sower (the only one hitherto observed in this poem)[8] and of the harvest (stanzas 15, 16) are the most prominent, for they occur in the vision of the son who has failed to sow and therefore cannot reap. All the other motifs are so imperfectly realized that they would hardly be noticed if they did not appear more prominently in poems later derived from **"Die Heimkehr."** Thus the motif of the roundelay, which is so firmly linked with much of Meyer's later poetry of the seasons, is here but faintly suggested in the contrast between a round dance in a foreign city and the friendly circle at home (stanzas 9, 16). The motif of the ruin, familiar from Meyer's poems about ancient castles as well as from **"Der Mönch von Bonifazio,"** is forced rather harshly into the son's account of his life in the fields (stanza 12). The phrase, "morning climbs through the window," (stanza 9) reminds one of a most curious motif of Meyer's. It contributes practically nothing here, but its symbolism may be gathered from such diverse poems as **"Tag, schein' herein,"** **"Das Gemälde,"** **"Das tote Kind,"** and **"Hussens Kerker."**[9] The archway in the rock (stanzas 22, 24), finally . . . symbolizes the son's sense of salvation as he approaches his home.

Just as the motifs fail to enlighten the reader, so the scenes fail to please him. Again one must turn to later poems to understand the poet's intentions. Stanzas 3 and 24 anticipate but vaguely the setting of **"Am Himmelstor";** stanza 9 gives little promise of its later perfection in **"Das Ende des Festes;"** and stanza 22, while it has most of the materials of **"Ewig jung ist nur die Sonne,"** has none of its assurance. Small wonder, then, that instead of attempting to revise **"Die Heimkehr"** Meyer scrapped the poem entirely and made a completely fresh attempt to realize his concept of the return. He had wedged the ideas of the cycle of the seasons and of a life close to nature into the Biblical parable; now he dropped the constraining framework and made nature itself the image of his thought.

In the years between 1860 and 1865 Meyer wrote several poems in which, as it were, he tried out his new plan by speaking of a return now to the mountains, now to field, forest, or river. That is, he chose places dear and familiar to him since boyhood as symbols of peacefulness and fulfillment. The poems describing the return to the mountains have been discussed already. They began with **"Das Glöcklein"** (1861) and developed through **"Auf der Wanderung"** (1865) to **"Das weiße Spitzchen."** The return to the forest appears for the first time in a poem of the year 1862 which begins with these lines:

> Ich wandle wieder durch die Waldesspitze
> Wo sich ein Fluß mit einem Strom vereint.

The unusual locale is obviously chosen only because the poet wishes to identify his existence both with the woods and the water. We have seen earlier that the forest scene and its symbolism ultimately gave rise to **"Jetzt rede du"**; and we shall see that the other element in the poem, the return to the water, was revived in **"Ewig jung ist nur die Sonne."** The return to the fields, finally, occurs for the first time in the second version of **"Der Erntewagen"** (1864), and while it was eliminated in the later versions of this poem, it persists in poems which might be called its lateral descendants.

These early poems are usually overloaded with scenic elements, and their symbolism is correspondingly vague. Moreover, most of them tell of a return to lonely places and thereby suggest that salvation is found in solitude. But that was not the meaning of **"Die Heimkehr,"** where naturalness and happiness were found in the life of a community. The return to nature in this latter sense, not to its solitude but to its cyclical order and enfolding protection, is symbolized in Meyer's poetry by the seasons and especially by the fields and the harvest. For it is in late summer and fall that nature yields its fruits and that the interdependence of all things becomes apparent. As life in the fields dies down, man receives his bread. But he, too, must make a return for his blessings, and he must ultimately return to God—the *double entendre* is in keeping with the ambiguity of Meyer's concept.

A short poem written about 1861 describes a traveler's return home but at the same time the fall of the year. The traveler is greeted by a familiar mountain, and he arrives at the time of the ripening grapes. The implication is, of course, that the traveler himself has matured and now knows the road to the good life, and that peace and security lie at his journey's end:

> In raschem Schritt! Es wandert sich so leicht
> Der Heimat zu, wenn früh die Sonne neigt.
> Schon naht der Herbst, wie naht er reif und
>   mild,
> Der tiefe Himmel ohne Wolke schwebt,

> Und über goldnem Rebenlaub erhebt
> Der Schneeberg sein bekanntes Bild.

What is hinted here is elaborated in a longer poem, different versions of which were published in 1865 and 1869.[10] . . .

AN DIE NATUR IM SPÄTSOMMER

> Ihr Wolken und ihr Winde,
> Die sich gemerkt der Knabe,
> Ihr heimatlichen Gründe,
> Die ich verlassen habe!
> Auf langentbehrten Wegen
> Laßt wiederum mich gehn,
> Vergönnt mir euern Segen,
> Laßt eure Sprache mich verstehn.

> Verweht ist längst der Schleier,
> Der blaue, mit dem Lenze,
> Es naht die Erntefeier,
> Des Sommers goldne Grenze.
> Schon rötet sich die Traube
> Im grünen Rebenblatt,
> Bald deckt mit gelbem Laube
> Die Erde ihre Ruhestatt.

> Ein jedes Werk des Jahres
> Hat seine eigne Weihe
> Und ist ein Wunderbares
> In wunderbarer Reihe;
> Das letzte kommt von allen
> Des Sämanns stiller Gang
> Und seiner Körner Fallen
> Der Furche dunkle Flucht entlang.

> Wenn deine sanften Freuden
> Nicht selber ich mir trübe,
> Natur, wer will mich scheiden
> Von deiner Mutterliebe,
> So lang du, Totgeglaubte,
> Dich wonnevoll erneust,
> Bis du mir einst zu Haupte
> Die dunkelbraunen Schollen streust!

SPÄTJAHR

> Verweht ist längst der Schleier
> Der Ahnung mit dem Lenze,
> Vorbei die Erntefeier,
> Des Sommers goldne Grenze,
> Entnommen ist die Traube
> Dem rothen Rebenblatt,
> Der Wald bestreut mit Laube
> Der Erde Ruhestatt.

> Ein jedes Werk des Jahres
> Hat seine eigne Weihe
> Und ist ein wunderbares

In wunderbarer Reihe;
Das liebste doch von allen
Ist mir des Sämanns Gang
Und seiner Körner Fallen
Der Furche Flucht entlang.

Nun träumen ohne Leiden
Des Lebens neue Triebe—
Natur, wer kann mich scheiden
Von deiner Mutterliebe,
So lang du, Todtgeglaubte,
Dich wonnevoll erneust,
Bis du mir auch zu Haupte
Die braunen Schollen streust!

Compared with **"Die Heimkehr,"** this poem is much simpler and much more readily intelligible. Simplification has worked in three ways: the poet speaks of himself, not of the prodigal son; the harmonious existence which he seeks is represented by nature itself, not by a rural community close to nature; and the theme of the poem is now taken from the same sphere as its governing motifs. The result is an enormous gain in directness, in ease, and in genuineness. The 144 lines of **"Die Heimkehr"** have shrunk, first to thirty-two, and then to twenty-four lines. The middle stanzas of **"An die Natur im Spätsommer"** give a simple picture of nature in summer, fall, and winter. The motifs of the harvest, the falling leaves, and the sower are the only ones that are retained from **"Die Heimkehr,"** and they fit in so naturally with the subject of the poem that they yield their symbolism without constraint. They have become true symbols, for even without the interpretative last stanza their force would be felt: the cyclical life in nature inspires both contentment and hope. In **"Die Heimkehr,"** on the other hand, where the poet struggled with a disparity between his motifs and his theme, the same three motifs could be used only as metaphors. Thus, for example, the prodigal son sums up his wasted youth in this simile:

Wie welke Blätter, aufgerafft
Vom Sturm, so flog der Leidenschaft
Verlorne Zeit von hinnen.

The simile is forced, and it obscures the meaning of Meyer's motif. Falling leaves are a premonition of death—that is their significance in **"Spätjahr"** and again in **"Das fallende Laub,"** a poem in the **"Hutten"** cycle which descended from **"Spätjahr."**

Above all, **"An die Natur im Spätsommer"** really says what it is meant to say. Meyer was no prodigal son. His youth was wasted not because of an excess of pleasures, but because it was utterly lacking in joy, as he says in **"Ein bißchen Freude."** He needed release from loneliness, not from gay companions. What he sought was reassurance, not forgiveness. In seizing upon the parable in Luke, Meyer had chosen the wrong subject, and it had distorted his meaning.

However, it is not enough to say that **"An die Natur im Spätsommer"** expresses well what was badly expressed in **"Die Heimkehr."** There is also a change of meaning, or at least a significant change of emphasis. Meyer's prodigal son returned home not only to find security but also to take his place in the community and to do his share:

Da wird die Arbeit ausgetheilt
Und Jeder auf den Posten eilt,
Das Seine zu vollenden; . . .

Und Jeder hat sein eigen Amt,
Und wieder sind sie allesammt
In einen Bund geschlossen.

The echo of these lines in the later poem is gentler, but it is also much less determined:

Ein jedes Werk des Jahres
Hat seine eigne Weihe
Und ist ein Wunderbares
In wunderbarer Reihe.

The cycle of the seasons has taken the place of the family circle, and of all the many activities of the farmer the sower's work is singled out as dearest to the poet. The time for productivity is seen to lie in the future, and the present task is merely to trust and be patient. Clearly, Meyer is here alluding to his own most pressing problem, the slowness of his development. In comparing his state with the secret readying which precedes growth in nature, he reassures himself that he is a poet in spite of his many failures, and that his apparently barren life is nevertheless meaningful and promising. "They also serve who only stand and wait." And even if this hope should fail, if the seed should die and never bear fruit, the poet will be received back into the wider life of nature as the prodigal son was received by his father. **"Die Heimkehr"** promised a mansion in the Father's house to him who, however late, contributed his share to the welfare of the community; the present poem makes a similar promise even to the man who has spent his life in lonely contemplation. Meyer's individualism has reasserted itself.

The first metamorphosis of Meyer's poem on the return, then, has consisted mainly in a change of theme. We have observed before how secondary and therefore interchangeable the themes of his poetry were. To find the adequate objective form for a poetic concept was indeed of supreme importance for his success, but any given theme was important to him only in proportion to its adequacy to the idea. The further development of **"An die Natur im Spätsommer"** also conforms to Meyer's general habits of production and could almost be predicted: the narration will be frozen into situations or pictures; the confession will be absorbed by the symbols; and the symbols will attract additional aspects of reality, the settings in which they appear will be rounded out, so that the one original poem will at last fall apart and produce several new ones. The process of proliferation is then complete.

The most obvious difference between **"An die Natur im Spätsommer"** and **"Spätjahr"** is the omission of the original first stanza. Actually, however, the stanza was not omitted so much as split off. It lived on independently in the poet's mind so that, much later and greatly strengthened, it could re-emerge as the poem **"Ewig jung ist nur die Sonne."** Through the ommission of this stanza, **"Spätjahr"** is freed of all the narrative elements and of part of the direct confession contained in the earlier version. With the exception of the last stanza, it is a descriptive poem of symbolic significance. The idea of the return, which was made explicit in the omitted stanza, is conveyed only by the symbol of the seed which returns to the maternal soil. And since it is now all-important that the symbolism should be understood, the scene of the poem is adjusted to it: as the title says, the time is no longer late summer but late fall; the harvest is over, not approaching; the grapes are gathered, not ripening. In the last stanza, finally, a weak, moralizing passage is replaced by an express interpretation of the symbol of the seed. It lies dreaming, without pain, waiting for fresh life.

It is not difficult to imagine what Meyer would have done had he revised **"Spätjahr"** for inclusion in the **Gedichte**. The last stanza would have to go. Without one word of explanation, the image of the dormant seed would have to convey the idea of "Leidlosigkeit" and all it meant for the poet. However, he either did not attempt or did not achieve such a revision, for the poem contained a fatal flaw. He had set out to write a poem on the cycle of the seasons and on the harmonious life of nature. **"An die Natur im Spätsommer"** characterizes briefly each of the four seasons in its second stanza and sums up their rhythmic sequence in the third. In **"Spätjahr,"** however, the symbolism depends on the one season, late fall. Its second stanza no longer accords with the first half of the third. There was only one way out of this difficulty: the conflicting elements of the poem had to be released so that each could develop in its own way. Thus, the symbols of the seasons, harvest, grape, falling leaves, and seed (significantly, there is none for spring), each acquired a body of its own and grew into a separate poem. At the same time, however, Meyer gave up neither the idea of a poem on the cycle of the seasons nor that of a poem on late autumn. He realized them both, although with entirely new means.

At this point, then, there is not only bifurcation but separation in several directions. The process is so complex that Mr. Kraeger,[11] who studied the later transformation of the poems in **"Romanzen und Bilder,"** thought that *Spätjahr* had vanished entirely and left no trace in the **Gedichte**. Actually, it is one of Meyer's most prolific poems. **"Der Uli," "Das fallende Laub," "Reife,"** and **"Die Traube"** in **"Huttens letzte Tage"** are related to it no less clearly than a block of eleven poems in the section "Hour" of the **"Gedichte,"** from **"Vor der Ernte"** to **"Novembersonne."** The latter are interrupted by only four poems of different origin, **"Requiem," "Abendwolke," "Mein Stern,"** and **"Weinsegen,"** and two of these were added only in the fourth edition (1891).[12] Thus almost all the poems on summer and fall in the **Gedichte** are related to **"An die Natur im Spätsommer,"** and they betray their common origin by being so closely grouped together.

They are all related to the one early poem, but of course they are not derived from it alone. They are woven from many strands and are indebted to, or overlap with, many poems in addition to **"Spätjahr";** only it is impossible to unravel all the threads, and even those which can be picked out must be followed one at a time. We shall proceed in this order: first we shall see what Meyer made of his poem on autumn; next how he realized the idea of the return; then what poems arose from his four symbols of falling leaves, seed, grape, and harvest; and finally what became of his concept of the cycle of the seasons.

"Nach der Lese," later called **"Novembersonne,"**[13] is the most direct descendant of **"Spätjahr."** The titles indicate that this is the final form of the poem on late fall. A comparison of the lines in **"Spätjahr,"**

> Entnommen ist die Traube
> Dem rothen Rebenblatt,
> Der Wald bestreut mit Laube
> Der Erde Ruhestatt

with the new opening,

> In den ächzenden Gewinden
> Hat die Kelter sich gedreht,
> Unter meinen alten Linden
> Liegt das Laub hoch aufgeweht

confirms the link between **"Spätjahr"** and **"Novembersonne,"** while it shows at the same time an astonishing gain in vividness and felicity. The review of the seasons is retained in **"Novembersonne,"** but they are now related to the sun through a series of metonyms. In spring the sun is a worker in the fields, later a harvester, then a vintager, and at last, when its work is done for the year, it becomes a gentleman of leisure. The sun's labors through the year are climaxed by its leisure, and all its useful gifts are surpassed by the gifts of wine and poetry. The sun is both Bacchus and Apollo, god of the grape and leader of the muses. The last stanza, in which this final metamorphosis is revealed, also resumes the idea of the return. The winter session of German and Swiss universities opens on the first of November. So the poem ends with a picture of students returning to their alma mater and enjoying the sunny days of an Indian summer. They, devotees of the muses, are glad enough to toast Apollo with the gift of Bacchus. Vivacious though it is, this finale is contrived rather too ingeniously.

Meyer's definitive poem on the concept of the return is **"Ewig jung ist nur die Sonne"** (1887), and in this poem, too, the sun is the central symbol. Three elements may be distinguished: the scene, the motif of the cowbells, and the refrain about the eternally youthful sun. For the scene, Meyer refurbished the situation of a traveler coming home to his native valley. Characteristically enough, he drew not only on the first stanza of **"An die Natur im Spätsommer"** but went even farther back and reintroduced some elements from stanza 22 of **"Die Heimkehr"** and from the poem **"Ich wandle wieder durch die Waldesspitze."** However, whereas in the early poems the wanderer recognizes familiar landmarks and therefore feels happy and reassured, he finds the scene deserted and sadly changed in **"Ewig jung ist nur die Sonne."** The poem is an elegy, an old man's lament about the brief span of human existence, and its setting has been adapted to this mood. The motif of the cowbells is borrowed from Meyer's Alpine poetry. It reinforces the elegiac note, for, as we saw in the preceding chapter, it is a reminder of death. The refrain, finally, rounds out the poem by contrasting man's mortality with the eternal youthfulness and splendor of the sun.

This refrain has its own, and a rather surprising, history. It occurs first in a poem of totally different import. Among Meyer's earlier love lyrics there is a short piece, **"Kurze Freude"** (1871), in which the brief appearance of the evening star is symbolic of love aroused but soon thwarted. A revised version, **"Wintertag,"** found in a letter Meyer wrote in November, 1883, substitutes the winter sun for the star to express the same symbolism. With slight changes, this version was printed in Wolff's *Poetischer Hausschatz:*[14]

> Über schneebedeckter Erde
> blaut der Himmel, haucht der Föhn—
> ewig jung ist nur die Sonne!
> sie allein ist ewig schön!
>
> Heute steigt sie spät am Himmel,
> und am Himmel sinkt sie bald
> wie das Glück und wie die Liebe
> hinter dem entlaubten Wald.

Here, then, we have literally the same refrain as in **"Ewig jung,"** but in a poem which in all other respects is entirely different. Once again we face the strangeness of Meyer's methods and the unpredictability of his success; for who would expect that an elegy could be made out of a scene taken from a Biblical poem written more than three decades earlier, a motif borrowed from an Alpine poem equally old, and a refrain transferred from an insignificant love poem? Yet the result is a fine poem. Its symbolic use of sun and cowbells is delicate, and its emotional balance is perfect, for it avoids both the robustness of **"Novembersonne"** and the mawkishness of **"Das Glöcklein."**

While there is no doubt that **"Novembersonne"** and **"Ewig jung"** derive from **"An die Natur im Spätsommer"** and the other early poems which we have mentioned, they show remarkable changes of mood. Late fall was associated with sadness, but **"Novembersonne"** is cheerful and almost gay. On the other hand, the returning traveler found security and harmony, but in **"Ewig jung"** he is lonely and sad. If it is true, as we have repeatedly suggested, that the emotional values of Meyer's poetry are bound to its motifs, the changes in mood must be due to the introduction of the new motif, the sun. In most of Meyer's poems where the sun occurs he speaks of the setting sun, and this is a death symbol, as Mr. Brecht has pointed out. However, in at least one poem, **"Die Pythagoräer,"** he speaks of the rising sun and celebrates it as a power which incites men to activity and struggle. This poem is explained by a remarkable passage in a letter which Betsy Meyer wrote to Lina Frey: "Conrad's early 'sun worship,' which was not really a faith but in all seriousness the philosophy of his youth, his original *paganism,* remained—even after . . . he had changed completely—the natural *basis* of his poetry." Whatever one may think of the statement—and it is certainly difficult to take it quite literally—it confirms one's feeling that **"Die Pythagoräer"** is an expression of paganism. To be sure, the end of the poem (it is a prayer to the sun) asks for the gift of kindness, but this gift is to be bestowed only when the day fades in the gentle gold of the twilight. These lines bring to mind the poem **"Zwiegespräch,"** where the sun represents the masculine, active, heroic principle, and the evening glow represents femininity, passiveness, and gentleness. Now if we also adduce **"Unter den Sternen,"** which identifies the sun with struggle and ruthlessness, and the stars with holiness and justice, we are ready to interpret the two poems under discussion.[15] **"Novembersonne"** describes the attitude of youth, and **"Ewig jung"** that of old age. Youth is not troubled by the thought of impending winter, it trusts in its own future as it trusts in the cyclical return of the sun, and it enjoys the sun's gifts in a carefree spirit. It thinks of human life as not different from life in nature—to be enjoyed while it lasts. The paganism of the poem is underlined by its references to the sun as Bacchus and Apollo. In **"Ewig jung,"** on the other hand, an old man discovers, sadly enough, that man's return to nature is not like the daily and annual return of the sun. He returns to die, not to be born again. The pagan symbol—we remember that the sun replaced the star in the evolution of the poem—holds no comfort for him who has run his course on earth. To be sure, the title of Meyer's central poem on the sun, **"Die Pythagoräer,"** might suggest the idea of transmigration, but there is not a trace of such a hope in **"Ewig jung."** Here at last Meyer distinguishes "Wiederkehr," the cyclical return, from the other meanings of his concept and finds that if this is its true meaning for man, he must end in sadness. It would be a mistake, however, to take **"Novembersonne"** and **"Ewig jung"** as confessions of faith. The former poem does not prove Meyer's paganism, nor does the latter disprove it. Although it was written much earlier, Meyer placed **"Novembersonne"** after **"Ewig jung"** in the *Gedichte* and thereby conceded at least a relative justification to worldliness. He who felt old in his youth and young in his later years was not ready to commit himself finally even when he had passed his sixtieth year.

Of the four symbols which characterize the seasons in **"An die Natur im Spätsommer,"** the motif of the falling leaves has the simplest history. It dominates only one later poem, **"Das fallende Laub."** In **"An die Natur im Spätsommer"** and **"Spätjahr,"** the dry, brown leaves cover the wintry earth, as the brown earth itself will some time cover the poet's grave. This symbolism is elaborated in **"Das fallende Laub."** When the sick and weary Hutten sits pondering over the labors and struggles of his past, a falling leaf touches his shoulder, and he regards this as a message from his Master telling him that his work is done and that he may now go to rest:

> Mich schauderte, da ich das Blatt gespürt,
> Als hätte mich des Meisters Hand berührt
> Und mich gemahnt: Genug! Die Sonn' ist
>   fern,
> Geh ein, du Knecht, zur Ruhe deines Herrn!

The symbol of the seed produced two poems: **"Der Uli"** was added to the **"Hutten"** cycle in 1881, and **"Säerspruch"** was published in the *Gedichte* in the following year.[16] Both poems are again religious, and both betray unmistakably their derivation from **"Die Heimkehr"** and the season poems of 1865 and 1869. Specifically, it seems that Meyer first took the middle strophe of **"Spätjahr"** as a starting point for **"Der Uli"** and then, not satisfied that he had exhausted the meaning of his motif, went back still further and fashioned a passage from **"Die Heimkehr"** into the opening of **"Säerspruch"**; witness these verbal echoes:

> Ein jedes Werk des Jahres
> Hat seine eigne Weihe
> Und ist ein wunderbares
> In wunderbarer Reihe;
> Das liebste doch von allen
> Ist mir des Sämanns Gang
> Und seiner Körner Fallen
> Der Furche Flucht entlang.

(Spätjahr)

> Schön ist ein jedes Werk das Jahr entlang,
> Am liebsten doch ist mir des Säers Gang.

(Der Uli)

> Die Schritte zählt der Ackersmann
> Und schleudert in die Schollen dann
> Das Korn aus vollen Händen.

(Die Heimkehr)

> Bemeßt den Schritt! Bemeßt den Schwung!

(Säerspruch)

"Der Uli" is a comfortable poem with an anecdotal flavor. The Swiss reformer Ulrich Zwingli, so it tells, grew up in so high and barren an Alpine valley that he was ten years old before he saw sowers scatter the seed. Their motions seemed to him like the gestures of priests celebrating mass, and the solemnity of the scene brought tears to his eyes. The scattering of the "wondrous grains," of "God's bread," inspired him with awe and reverence. **"Säerspruch,"** on the other hand, is a most energetically concentrated poem. Its eight short lines and its still shorter sentences are monumental as if graven into rock, and its thought is equally severe. Based on the parable of the sower in Matthew, the poem teaches complete submission to the will of God. It praises the seed that falls on stony places, for in death it finds sweet repose; and it praises also the seed that springs up, for sweet is its life in the light.

"Säerspruch" is one of Meyer's noblest achievements. It is one of those poems which accomplish triumphantly what his early verse so vainly essayed: it compares with the best in earlier German verse, and it pioneers a poetic mode which remained exemplary for the later symbolists. It recalls the sower passage in Hölderlin's "Patmos," and it foreshadows poems like Ricarda Huch's "Tod Sämann" (which is a rather obvious combination of Meyer's **"Schnitterlied** and **"Säerspruch"**) and even masterpieces like Rilke's **"Herbst"** ("Die Blätter fallen") and **"Herbsttag."** True, Meyer's language does not match the suppleness of Hölderlin's or Rilke's, and his poem on the falling leaves has no imaginative phrase such as Rilke's "Sie fallen mit verneinender Gebärde." But the austerity and almost haughty grandeur of **"Säerspruch"** equal the same qualities in **"Herbsttag,"** and its end stands comparison with the end of Rilke's *Herbst*.

The motif of the grape, which had only incidental significance in **"An die Natur im Spätsommer,"** gave rise later to four poems. Its meaning was explained by Meyer himself in his account of the origin of **"Huttens letzte Tage:"** [17]

Among my poetic sketches there was a draft depicting the sick knight as he gazes into the fading sunset glow, while a Holbeinesque Death cuts a golden cluster from the grapevine on the arched window. The grape's meaning was, "Ripeness is all." That is the seed from which my **"Hutten"** arose. I did not include the poem in any of my collections, dimly feeling that it failed to present the whole Hutten. So it lay for years.

The collections from which the poem was excluded can only be those of 1860 or 1864, so that Meyer's **"Hutten"** poetry and his motif of the grape had their inception in 1864 at the very latest. More important than the date, however, is the poet's statement that the whole **"Hutten"** cycle developed out of a single poem and indeed out of a single motif; only in **"Liederseelen"** has Meyer said with equal precision that with him motifs were the starting point of the poetic process. The passage is remarkable also for offering an explicit interpretation of a poetic motif, for Meyer did not often give such explanations. His interpretation is, of course, a quotation from *King Lear,* V, ii:

> Men must endure
> Their going hence, even as their coming
>   hither.
> Ripeness is all.

When, in 1870, Meyer began to work in earnest on his **"Hutten,"** the motif of the grape again dominated the first new drafts he made,[18] and in the completed work published the following year it informed the poems **"Reife"** and **"Die Traube."** **"Die Traube"** is not substantially different from that earliest poem described in Meyer's essay. The dying knight imagines a picture of himself done by Holbein. Death is to stand beside him, but instead of the "horrid scythe" he shall hold a vintager's knife and cut a cluster of grapes. It will be understood, Hutten thinks, that he is the grape, cut down today but inspiring all Germany with his fiery spirit tomorrow. The poem is not very pleasing. Its genre quality dates it and makes it as unpalatable to us as is the sort of nineteenth-century painting on which it may have been patterned.[19] The connection between symbol and story is not clear, and although Hutten says it is obvious, this is merely an excuse for offering an explanation. The note of boastfulness is yet another flaw.

"Reife," on the other hand, is not foreshadowed in the early **"Hutten"** drafts but is derived from the first stanza of **"Spätjahr."** To be sure, there is not much specific similarity beyond the time of the year (after the harvest in **"Spätjahr"*;* the equinox in **"Reife"**) and the mention of haze, but **"Reife"** is primarily a nature poem, and it is preceded in the cycle by **"Das fallende Laub,"** which also goes back to **"Spätjahr."** The poem gives a delicate picture of an early morning scene in autumn, a picture in which grapes are both the most vivid sense

impression and a monitory symbol. The scene itself suggests that Hutten, too, has reached the fall of his life and must now endure his going hence. And just as **"Säerspruch"** and **"Das fallende Laub"** reminded us of Rilke, so the lines,

> Und schwerer hangt die Traube schon am
>   Schaft,
> Sie schwillt und läutert ihren Purpursaft,
> Sie fördert ihre Reife früh und spat—
> Was meinst du, Hutten? Auch die deine naht,

would again seem to prefigure Rilke:

> Befiehl den letzten Früchten voll zu sein;
> gib ihnen noch zwei südlichere Tage,
> dränge sie zur Vollendung hin und jage
> die letzte Süße in den schweren Wein.

However, the development does not end here, for Meyer achieved a blend of **"Reife"** and **"Die Traube"** which far surpasses either poem. **"Hussens Kerker,"**[20] one of his most mellow poems, and one of the few historical poems of his which are flawless, may very properly be called the definitive Hutten poem. Both Hus and Hutten were steadfast Protestants, martyrs of their faith. Both are shown in the evening of their lives, nearing the end after manly struggles and sturdy deeds. Hence scenes and imagery of the **"Hutten"** poems could be used in **"Hussens Kerker."** Hus, awaiting death in his prison cell, gazes through the bars at Lake Constance and the Alpine peaks beyond, while a cluster of grapes with its red foliage hangs heavily in the window. Here, then, the indoor scene of **"Die Traube"** is combined with the view of calm waters in **"Reife."** There is no skeleton Death; the symbol of the grape is allowed to speak for itself:

> Es ist die Zeit zu feiern!
> Es kommt die große Ruh!

Manliness and gentleness, resignation and hope are exquisitely balanced. The whole poem is as drenched with the coolness of the lake, and the sail which the prisoner perceives in the distance is one of Meyer's strongest symbols of reassurance and hope. Hus knows that his fate now rests in the hands of God, and he sees the Son of Man coming down in a cloud to receive him.[21] He praises his prison, and in its bars he recognizes the cross. And just as the end of **"Das fallende Laub"** is reminiscent of Simeon's "Nunc dimittis" in Luke, 2:29, so the end of "Hussens Kerker" calls to mind Christ's words in Matt. 10:29-31.

"Hussens Kerker" is so very great a poem because it fuses Meyer's feeling for nature, for history, and for the divine; because its straightforward and apparently simple language carries so many overtones; and because earliest impulses, the religious emotions of poems like **"Die Heimkehr,"** are revived and realized in it. It is Meyer's loveliest and profoundest poem on the homecoming.

The other branch in the development of the motif of the grape led from **"Spätjahr** to **"Im Veltlin"** (1879), **"Wunsch"** (1882), and **"Die Veltlinertraube"** (1882).[22] The three titles represent successive versions of one and the same poem, but in the course of revision this poem lost in spontaneity what it may have gained in firmness. **"Im Veltlin"** describes vineyards in late fall, just before the gathering of the grapes. The country seems as if soaked with heat, a sultry silence is spread heavily over it. The meaning of the poem lies in the contrast between this silence and the fiery juices held captive within grapes swelled almost to bursting. On the morrow, their passion will break out in the joyous cries of the gatherers. Ah, says the poet, to be a grape in such a warm, purple cluster! In **"Wunsch,"** the symmetry of the poem is enhanced by the omission of the third (middle) stanza, and the contrast between present calm and coming excitement is brought out more sharply by a number of minor changes. In the final version, **"Die Veltlinertraube,"** the symbolic reference to the poet himself has become paramount. Now the descriptive first stanza is dropped, and the omitted third stanza, which is the most violent, is re-introduced. The poet identifies himself directly with the grape, his unruly blood teems with the vigor of the soil, he is drunken with the light of the sun and burning from its heat. He imagines himself hanging over a red mouth, like a darkly purple, shiny, lush grape, ready to be eaten.

"Die Veltlinertraube" brings out aspects of the motif of the grape which are suggested in **"Die Traube"** but are neglected in **"Reife"** and **"Hussens Kerker."** The two latter poems illustrate Meyer's motto from Shakespeare, "Ripeness is all." That is, they speak of the individual and his readiness for death. Although in history Hus gave his life for his faith and through his martyrdom inspired and even inflamed his people, Meyer's poem on Hus is concerned only with personal salvation. In **"Die Traube"** and **"Die Veltlinertraube,"** on the other hand, the grape not only symbolizes a life well lived and death courageously faced, but suggests that man must live and die like the things in nature and that, like them, he must be sacrificed for the good of others. These poems reveal a startling combination of Christian and pagan impulses. It is sheer naturalism to say that man, like fruit, will spoil quickly once he has reached maturity, and it was the paganism of the ancients (and of Nietzsche) which taught that "whom the gods love die young." On the other hand, the thought that life must be sacrificed to sustain life is not necessarily naturalistic or pagan but underlies also the sacrament of Holy Communion. In **"Die Traube,"** the fiery juices of the grape symbolize Hutten's fiery spirit which will spread throughout Germany when he is dead.

And even in **"Die Veltlinertraube"** there is a faint suggestion of the eucharist, of the wine which symbolizes Christ's blood spilt for the salvation of mankind.

Primarily, however, **"Die Veltlinertraube"** is an erotic poem. It is aglow with an undefined passion, a blind yearning for an abundant life and an early death. Its ecstatic language and its spirit of self-surrender have been much admired, but I cannot join in the applause.[23] Even without knowing Meyer and his life one would feel that **"Die Veltlinertraube"** is as forced and overheated a poem as **"Hussens Kerker"** is cool and controlled. That this shy and modest man should have felt the mighty powers of his soul, and that he should have wished, at times, to give them violent release, is understandable enough. He was great, however, precisely because he restrained himself, because he saved his strength and did not spend it foolishly in one glorious blaze of self-destruction. The essence of the symbol is that the grape's fiery strength is within, hidden and contained. Grapes must indeed be crushed to yield their goodness, but surely the pleasure is not theirs but the eater's. As an expression of *amor fati,* **"Die Veltlinertraube"** is as inept and ludicrous as **"Hussens Kerker"** is fitting and noble.

The motif of the harvest parallels the motif of the grape in its development. It, too, is a symbol of resignation which, in some later poems, becomes a symbol of exultant surrender. Its earliest occurrence is found in the poem **"Der Erntewagen"** (1860), which is included in the same collection, **"Bilder und Balladen,"** as **"Die Heimkehr."** The version of 1860 has never been printed, but two later versions were published by the poet in 1865 and 1869, and a complete recasting of the poem, entitled **"Auf Goldgrund,"** appeared in three successive versions in 1879, 1882, and 1883.[24]

In its earliest form, **"Der Erntewagen"** merely gives a picture of harvesters who pile sheaves on a wagon, their dark figures silhouetted against the pale evening sky. A moral is faintly suggested in the closing lines:

> Bleichen auch des Lebens Farben,
> Dauert noch der rege Fleiß.

The next version is augmented by two introductory stanzas. The poet, walking near his home, is startled by the unusual clarity of the air and by the rich colors and sharp contours of the country. He is reminded of Italy and of the restless travels of his youth, and he is almost overcome by his former wanderlust; but when he sees the harvesters, their untiring industry is an example to him, and his restlessness is gone. He remembers that for him, too, the time has come to labor long and late and to bring in the crop:

> Der Arbeit stille Stunden
> Sind wie die Ernte reich.

The version of 1869 reduces the poem again from four stanzas to two. The narrative introduction is omitted, the poet's conflicting emotions are no longer mentioned; only the picture of a tall wagon and of busy harvesters etched against a golden sky remains. Both confession and moral have been absorbed into the image: evening, usually given to rest, hallows the labor of tired arms with a background of gold. Now, however, the poet was afraid lest the meaning of the scene should be missed. Therefore in **"Auf Goldgrund"** he changed the title and added an express juxtaposition of ancient pictures of saints on a background of gold and of the living tableau of the harvesters. The last two versions give ultimate precision and compactness to both the language and the symbolism of the poem.

"Auf Goldgrund," restrained and refined though it is, is not a little precious. This visit to a museum followed by a walk through fields results in nothing more profound than the observation that faithful labor also has its solemn dignity. The poet has overexternalized his emotion; experience has been translated into a picture, but below its gleaming surface no more than a stale moral can be found. The disturbed, uneasy poet of **"Der Erntewagen"** has become an idle museum-goer whose calm is all too complacent. What Meyer really intended by **"Der Erntewagen"** and **"Auf Goldgrund"** is indicated by the fact that he introduced the motif of the returning wanderer into the second version. The poems on the harvest, just like those more directly derived from **"Die Heimkehr,"** deal with the return to nature and to a harmonious life. There is one difference, however. Whereas in **"Die Heimkehr"** and **"An die Natur im Spätsommer"** the traveler returns disillusioned and weary, he has been home for some years in **"Der Erntewagen"** and, seized with unrest, wants to set out again. That is, his return has been accomplished physically but not psychologically. We said earlier that the prodigal son of **"Die Heimkehr"** returns to his father not only to find security but also to find usefulness. For Meyer himself, usefulness meant poetic productivity, and this, given his peculiar talents and lack of talents, meant keeping late hours and working until late in life so as to garner the crop. In this sense, his poems on the harvest are a complement and a continuation of his poems on the return.

However, there is also more tangible evidence that these two streams in Meyer's production belong together. *Clara*, a short story which he wrote very early (between 1850 and 1860), contains the earliest mention of the prodigal son side by side with the picture of men toiling late and silhouetted against the sunset glow. The context shows that Meyer's purpose in drawing the scene was didactic. The hero of the story has returned like the prodigal son, but, unlike the Biblical father, the heroine is not willing to accept his repentance. She insists that he rehabilitate himself through labor more faithful and prolonged than is ordinarily demanded of men.[25]

Meyer's insistence on the dignity of labor might seem strange in a man who was financially independent and never worked to support himself and his family. It was due to a combination of practical concerns and religious emotions—symbolized by the loaded wagon and the golden evening sky. He gained fresh confidence when he persuaded himself that the laborious processes by which he produced his works were not unworthy of a poet (who, according to German tradition especially, was supposed to write spontaneously, guided by genius and by flashes of inspiration); and he felt that he would have earned release only when his task was performed. These thoughts appear clearly in his **"Morgenlied,"**[26] a devotional song written in the same year 1865 in which **"Der Erntewagen"** was first published. Here the poet asks for patience and strength, and he hopes that the "distant evening" may suffuse his harvest with a golden light. Prophetically he says that he will not bring home the sheaves until his last hours, in the last glow of evening, staggering under their weight. Six years later he changed the song into a prayer, still asking for nothing better than peace and toil:

> Gieb mir heute Müh' in Frieden,
> Gieb, daß dieser helle Tag
> Unter Garben, gleich dem müden
> Schnitter, abends schwanken mag.

There is, however, a sense of urgency in this poem which is not found in the earlier poems on the harvest. The emphasis is no longer on the sanctity of labor but on the laborer's need for his reward. The poet asks to be spared futile regret of the past, and he is no longer content with mere hope for the future. He wants courage to face this day's labor, and he wants this day to bring its reward:

> Unerschöpfter Quell des Lebens
> Gieb mir heut mein täglich Brot.

"Morgenlied" is a simple confession. It expresses Meyer's thoughts and aspirations much more clearly than **"Der Erntewagen"** and **"Auf Goldgrund,"** but, moving as it is, he could not be satisfied with it as a poet, and he never published it. He imitated the romantic manner not only in his youth but fell back on it often when his symbols and his message would not harmonize; but such poems formed only a transitional stage and were soon suppressed by renewed efforts to convey the message symbolically. It was in this way that **"Morgenlied"** followed **"Der Erntewagen"** and was in its turn supplanted by a poem of which we have four manuscript versions, variously entitled **"Sommernacht,"** **"Nacht in der Ernte,"** and **"Erntenacht."**[27] The poem is difficult to date, but I believe that all four versions were written in 1871, and actually at harvest time. It represents an entirely fresh beginning, and like many of Meyer's first drafts it contains too many and conflicting elements—a result of his attempt to render a complex emotion. Three elements may be distinguished: the fields, the harvesters, and the night sky. The description of the sheaves—the poet calls them "the staff of our lives"—and of the fading glow on the horizon resembles the description in **"Der Erntewagen"** and evokes a similar mood. Now, however, the harvesters are no longer at work but are gathering and preparing to go home. They are told that they have earned their rest, and as they walk over the fields they sing a song. It must be a hymn, one feels, for their song is answered by the music of the spheres. The stars have risen, and their music sounds like a sickle cutting in the distance—assurance that the heavenly powers which ripened the grain will also help with the harvest, that they will take over from the exhausted harvesters and finish their work.

The stars are the new image in this poem, not found in **"Der Erntewagen,"** and its introduction has changed the meaning completely. It is difficult not to connect this change with the change which had taken place in Meyer's position as a poet. Late in 1869 he had published **"Romanzen und Bilder,"** and in June, 1871 he had completed **"Huttens letzte Tage"** and sent off the manuscript. At last he could feel that his work was done, or at least that one day's work was done, and immediately his hope that he might now have earned rest and release asserted itself. He himself is the weary harvester who raises his voice in a song of praise and who looks up yearningly to the eternal stars.

The seven stanzas of **"Erntenacht"** (we shall call the poem by this name) are quite loosely connected, and they are shuffled around, omitted, and readmitted in the four successive versions. Nevertheless the intended or potential structure of the poem can be discerned. The music of the spheres echoes the song of the harvesters, but it also resembles the sound of a sickle. The stars as the central symbol hold the other two elements of the poem together, they relate to both harvest and harvesters: the eternal mediates between man and nature. However, the imagery by which this idea is expressed is so far-fetched and capricious that Meyer felt it necessary to supplement the symbol of the stars by the symbol of the crescent moon. Just as the sound of the sickle is equated with the music of the spheres, so its shape is compared with the moon. The latter image, though conventional, is plausible enough, but unfortunately it does not convey the meaning of the poem. Meyer must have found it impossible to remedy the faults of his poem satisfactorily, for in the further elaboration of the motif of the harvest he sacrificed (as he did only too often) the complexity and profundity of his thought, broke his poem apart, and developed only those of its elements which were sound in technique. In this fashion, **"Erntenacht"** gave rise to **"Vor der Ernte," "Ernteabend,"** and **"Erntelied,"** while it supplied also some material for **"Auf Goldgrund"** and **"Der Gesang der Klio."**

"Vor der Ernte"[28] paints a picture of grain fields the night before they are cut, but what this picture is intended to mean must baffle even the shrewdest reader. The poem picks up the equation of the crescent moon with the sickle, and it says that the moon travels "melodiously" high above the land. There is a suggestion of impending doom in the violence with which the Föhn—the Swiss chinook—sweeps through the grain, but on the other hand the night is clear and the moon is lovely. The poem cannot be read simply as a nature poem, for the identification of sickle and moon and the contrast between the clear sky and the violent gusts of wind point to some ulterior purpose or hidden meaning. Only those who know **"Erntenacht"** and therefore understand the function of the phrase "voller Melodie" can perceive that this apparently harmless poem touches upon one of the great and fearful mysteries of existence, namely that life must be sacrificed to sustain life, and that the heavens look calmly upon this spectacle which is in harmony with the eternal order of things. Let him who thinks that we are reading ideas into the poem never intended by its author compare it with Martin Greif's "Vor der Ernte." He will find a pure nature poem, very similar to Meyer's in its subject and yet totally different in tone. Greif's lines are much more melodious and more perfect than Meyer's, but they still have some Goethean echoes, whereas Meyer's poem does not hark back to earlier poetry, just as his **"Schnitterlied"** challenges comparison with such later symbolic poems as Dehmel's *Erntelied* or Stadler's *Sommer*.

In the early manuscript collection **"Bilder und Balladen"** (1860) there is, side by side with the earliest version of **"Der Erntewagen,"** a short poem called **"Stimmung."**[29] It describes sheaves lying in the fields, the cheerful activity of the harvesters, and the gay tints of valley and mountain. Then a cloud comes up and casts the ashen color of rotting wood over the scene which a moment before seemed so cheerful. It is obvious that **"Stimmung"** is a forerunner of *Vor der Ernte,* but it leaves the reader even more puzzled. Few who do not know Meyer's other poems on the harvest will guess that the dark cloud stands for the sudden realization that all things in nature feed on each other.

"Ernteabend," a poem written between 1882 and 1887,[30] separates out the second element in **"Erntenacht,"** namely the correspondence between the song of the harvesters and the heavenly music. It speaks of the sound of harps and lyres streaming down from the "pure spaces" above, and of angels who bring in the crop. The latter image reveals, suddenly and surprisingly, where Meyer got the concept of the harvest in heaven and what it meant for him. It goes back to the Biblical verse, "The harvest is the end of the world; and the reapers are the angels" (Matt. 13:39). **"Ernteabend"** expresses its meaning more clearly than **"Erntenacht,"** especially in describing the song of the harvesters as a song of praise ("Lobgesang"), but as a poem it is ruined by its sentimentality. Meyer did not publish it, but its thought was too important for him to lose it altogether. So he worked it, rather neatly, into the novel, **"Die Versuchung des Pescara"** (1887). There, in the fourth chapter, Pescara remembers a song about singing and harvesting in the fields and in heaven, and he even remembers a rhyme, "Schnitter und Zither," which occurs in **"Ernteabend."** There is no doubt that the half-forgotten song in **"Pescara"** is identical with the rejected poem.

The motif of the harvest runs through the whole of **"Pescara."** A picture of harvesters resting at noon in the Lombard plains is described on the first page; a picture of Pescara himself on a background of gold is mentioned in Chapter IV; he speaks of death as the grim reaper in Chapter V; and he is himself shown in that role as he leads an attack in the last chapter. At the end, where Pescara's death is described, two pictures are flashed on the screen in quick succession: the first is a Pietà, showing the dead general's head resting on the knees of his friend, and the second shows him again as a reaper: "The mighty energy of his features was relaxed, and his hair had fallen over his brow. Thus he looked like a young, lean reaper who, exhausted from the harvest, lay asleep on his sheaf." Meyer's narrative technique often resembles that of the motion picture. Instead of letting narration flow evenly, he pieces his story together by adding picture to picture, and many of these pictures are really lyrical motifs transferred from his poetry. Thus, in the present instance, the sequence of references to the harvest in **"Pescara"** can be identified with the poems **"Der Triumphbogen," "Auf Goldgrund," "Schnitterlied," "Vor der Ernte"** (if the sickle may stand for the more common attribute of death, the scythe), and **"Ernteabend."** The last of these poems begins with a picture of the poet himself who, tired from the day's work, has gone out to the fields and rests on a sheaf.

"Erntelied," the third poem derived from **"Erntenacht,"** exists in seven versions, of which the last three are entitled **"Schnitterlied."**[31] The poem was written in 1875 and first published in 1877. It drops the metaphoric correspondence between heaven and earth and concentrates on the harvesters and the grain. It is based on the thought that the harvest not only provides sustenance for life but also ends the life which falls before sickle and scythe. Now, however, the harvesters themselves are aware of this, and they are also aware of how short and endangered their own lives are. The thought inspires them with an exultant defiance. They finish their work as a storm breaks, they sing of love and of death, they drink to the flaring sheets of lightning. Success, so the poem says, is gained by defiance, by persistence in the teeth of danger; and courage will also gain the highest prize, the love of woman. Having saved the grain, their work accomplished, the harvesters are

equally ready for love and for death, indeed they yearn for both in their desire to achieve an ultimate intensity of triumph. The poem ends with an adaptation of the familiar saying, "There is many a slip 'twixt the cup and the lip," a saying which is widespread in European literature and has been traced back as far as Aristotle.[32] But whereas the proverb is a caution, a sceptical warning that success may be thwarted in the last moment, Meyer has changed it into an expression of defiance. To stress the erotic nature of the poem, the lines of the first version,

> Vom schäumenden Becher zum durstigen Munde
>
>   Ist Raum für den Tod

were finally changed to

> Von Munde zu Munde
> Ist Raum für den Tod.

Walther Brecht noted the close similarity between **"Erntegewitter"** and **"Schnitterlied"** and concluded that the latter poem developed from the former.[33] The evidence of the manuscripts leaves no doubt that the opposite was the case and that **"Erntegewitter"** was not written until shortly before publication of the *Gedichte* in 1882. **"Erntegewitter"** is a close-up of **"Erntelied"**; specifically, it is an elaboration of the lines (here quoted from the first version):

> Hoch thronet ihr Schönen, umschimmert von Blitzen,
> Mit flatternden Haaren auf güldenen Sitzen.

The storm which threatened in **"Erntelied"** has broken in **"Erntegewitter,"** and the threat of sudden death is realized. A "wicked maiden" with naked arms and hair undone rides high on a grain wagon, stays and drinks to the flaming light when others seek shelter, tosses away the empty cup, and glides herself into the darkness. If this unlovable poem means anything at all, it must mean that she is struck down.

All Meyer's poems on the harvest make prominent use of color and light. Their dominant sense impression is the golden yellow of the ripened crops in the fields. In **"Auf Goldgrund,"** the golden color is perceived also in the evening sky, and this is in turn compared with the background of gold in ancient pictures of saints: the harvest is sacred, and sacred, too, is the toil by which it is secured. In **"Schnitterlied"** and **"Erntegewitter,"** on the other hand, the harvesters' work is not transfigured by a golden horizon but is illumined instead by the fitful flashes of lightning. The motif of lightning, here as in **"Wetterleuchten"** and **"Mein Jahr,"** is the symbol of the passionate life and of the supreme moment. It is again hard not to connect the totally changed tone of **"Schnitterlied"** and **"Erntegewitter"** with the changes in Meyer's life. The first version of **"Schnitterlied"** was written in April, 1875, three months before Meyer's engagement. The poems about their engagement which he wrote for his fiancée in the summer of 1875 are governed by the motif of the star, but the poem which he included in *Gedichte*, **"Liebesjahr,"** is governed by the motifs of the harvest and of lightning.[34] We have noted a similar change of imagery in the transition from **"Erntenacht"** to **"Erntelied."** May one conclude that happiness and marriage had very different meanings for Meyer the man and Meyer the poet? Some corroborating evidence could be adduced from his biography, but even the poems alone, I think, show that it took an enormous effort to break away from the lonely life and that he had to work himself into a state of high excitement to overcome his sense of betrayal. He could forgive himself only because he yearned for death as ardently as for love and sought happiness as one plunges into a desperate venture.

Apart from incidental occurrences,[35] the motif of the harvest plays a part in two more poems, **"Der Musensaal"** and **"Der Triumphbogen."** In **"Der Musensaal"** the poet, using the fiction of a dream, gives a highly fanciful and none too pleasing interpretation of the statues of the muses in the Vatican. He sees them, not gravely grouped around their leader, Apollo, but moving about in violent agitation:

> In wilder Gruppe schritten eilig sie,
> Wie Schnitterinnen, die auf blachem Feld
> Ein flammendes Gewitter überrascht.

Surely this is a remarkable simile to use of a group of rather solemn statues. Descriptive value it has none, and indeed the introduction of the poem disclaims any intention to describe. As has been shown, the harvest symbolized for Meyer not only fulfillment but also extinction: what has come to perfection perishes. It is in this sense that the simile of the reapers applies to the muses. They do not merely represent the arts, but weigh and actually decide the present fate of men and of nations: what justice in destruction, what hope of peace, what value in the heroic and in the idyllic life? In the first edition of *Gedichte* there were clear references to the fall of France and Germany's victory in 1871 (deleted in the second and subsequent editions),[36] and the event was shown in its dual aspect of end and beginning, as a necessary stage in European history, whether desirable or not. Thus, in effect, the muses have become Fates in Meyer's hands; they are reapers at work as the storms of destiny flame over the peoples of the earth. It is a metamorphosis characteristic of him who was so fond of transforming life into art, and art back into life.

When all is said and done, though, the application of the motifs of lightning and the harvest to the muses remains forced, and indeed it is an extension of an earlier, simpler, and more plausible concept. In the older versions of the poem, the motifs apply not to the muses in general but only to Clio. There history is represented as tired of the perusal of parchments and is changed from a recorder of the past into a herald of the future. She becomes "the mistress of the present, binding the ripened sheaf" and "the reaper, hastening as lightning and thunder roar." The idea that the seeds sown in the past bear fruit in the present, that history is the determinant of the day, is represented naturally and with ease by the motif of the harvest, but when the motif was extended to symbolize the activity of all the muses it was strained and hence became obscure. The extension succeeds most nearly in the case of the Tragic and the Comic Muse. Melpomene leads the muses in **"Der Musensaal,"** carrying the sword and avenging the father's guilt upon the sons. Thus she stands for the tragic cycle of guilt and punishment, of violence and violent revenge which has held the peoples of the earth in its grip throughout recorded history. The role of Thalia is even more striking. In his early poem, **"Das Lustspiel"** (1860),[37] Meyer described Comedy as cruel but true, harsh but healthy. The idea is developed further in Thalia's words in **"Der Musensaal":**

> Ich morde lachend, was nicht sterben kann,
> In trunkner Lust, wie die Bacchante jach
> Ein Zicklein oder Reh in Stücke reißt.

The Comic Muse, then, is the destroyer of what cannot find a natural death and would otherwise drag out an intolerable existence. **"Das Lustspiel"** speaks only of the human individual, but in **"Der Musensaal"** the cleansing function of Comedy applies to whole nations. Meyer may have known, perhaps through Burckhardt, the Greek idea of the athanasia of cities,[38] and he uses it here as well as at the end of **"Die wunderbare Rede,"** where he gives a gloomy turn to the ancient boast that Rome is eternal:

> Ach wie lange noch, wie lange noch?
> Stürbest, Göttin Roma, stürbst du doch!
> Aber du bist voll Unsterblichkeit!

Although **"Der Musensaal"** introduces the muses as "The Nine," only eight of them are described. Curiously enought it is Clio who is absent. The reason for the omission must be sought in the fact that she has been given a poem of her own, **"Der Triumphbogen,"** . . . is an offshoot of **"Der Musensaal."** The scene and the main figure of **"Der Triumph-bogen"** bear a striking resemblance to those of **"Erntegewitter,"** and imagery and ethos of the two poems are also much alike. Thus, while **"Der Musensaal"** and **"Der Triumphbogen"** are not directly derived from **"Der Erntewagen,"** they are interrelated with its descendants, **"Erntelied"** and **"Erntegewitter."** What is said of man in the one group of poems is said of mankind in the other.

Any attempt to define a group within the total body of Meyer's poetry is more or less arbitrary, for all his poems are interlinked. Thus one might go on to show how **"Friede auf Erden"** is related to the thought of **"Der Musensaal,"** and **"Die gefesselten Musen"** to its theme; how **"Einem Tagelöhner"** (1883) and **"Wander-füße"** (1891) were inserted in the *Gedichte* among the poems on the seasons because they, too, refer to seasonal change and to the concept of the cycle; or how the idea of the return is expressed also in such diverse poems as **"Der Gesang des Meeres," "Die erste Nacht,"** and **"Engelberg";**[39] and so on. The student and expositor of Meyer must draw a line somewhere, must come to a stop sometime, but in doing so he obeys convenience rather than the logic of his subject.

Before summarizing we must, however, redeem our promise to show what became of Meyer's concept of the cycle of the seasons. It plays some part in several poems discussed in this chapter but is not fully worked out in them because it is jostled by other ideas and motifs. However, it is finally realized in **"Mein Jahr,"** a poem so late that it could be included only in the fourth edition of *Gedichte* (1891).[40] This realization is again achieved with entirely new means. We saw earlier that **"Mein Jahr"** is related to the love poems of the white blossoms cycle and to the motif of the roundelay. It agrees with them, rather than with **"An die Natur im Spätsommer,"** in its description of the four seasons, for harvest, grape, leaves, and seed are not mentioned. More important still, the emotional accent is again completely shifted. To the poet of **"Spätjahr,"** early winter is the dearest season and the sower's walk over the fields is the most sacred event. In **"Mein Jahr,"** on the other hand, early summer is the peak of the year, and the first flash of lightning sanctifies it. Both poems have religious undertones, but while the young poet trusts in slow growth and secret guidance, the older poet trusts in violent rejuvenation and the palpable sign. Or rather, he pretends to have such trust, for it is difficult to take **"Mein Jahr"** at face value. It is one of the poems which attempts to fulfill the program laid down in **"Fülle"** and shares with it that boastfulness and strident virility of which Gottfried Keller complained.

However, it is not necessary to appeal to Keller's judgment. Meyer himself wrote the most pertinent criticism of **"Mein Jahr,"** in a passage of his novel *Gustav Adolfs Page.*[41] In this passage, King Gustavus Adolphus and his page discuss the meaning of the motto, "Courte et bonne." The page, who likes the motto, offers this interpretation: "I wish all the rays of my life were gathered into one sheaf of flame and crowded into the space of one hour, so that not a dull twilight but a refulgent light of happiness would appear and then vanish like a flash of lightning." Then Meyer goes on: "The king did not seem to be pleased by this kind of talk, nor by this 'flash of lightning.' " And he has the king say: "This questionable motto was thought up by a worldling, an epicurean, as Doctor

Luther used to call such people. Our life is God's gift. We must not desire it to be either long or short, but take it as He ordains." Here, then, is a clear admission by the poet himself that the flash of lightning is an adolescent's rather than a mature man's symbol for the good and worthy life. The symbol represents a pagan view and offends the Christian. Meyer can have adopted it only in moments of acute impatience with his renunciative life and only by doing violence to his truer self.

Conrad Ferdinand Meyer was a poet, not a philosopher. It was not his task to fashion a consistent system of thought, but rather to give convincing expression to his feelings.[42] Nor can it be the critic's task to reduce the complexities of poetic genius to the dogmatic clarity of a platitude. His explanation may carry the poet's work a little further, but it must not attempt too much. By divining the poet's intent the critic can throw some light on the obscurities in poetic products, and by comparing these with each other he can explain some of their inconsistencies; but he must not forget that what matters in poetry is the problems and not their solutions.

The most disturbing problem in Meyer's poetry on the seasons is that which we have described as a conflict between pagan and Christian imagery. **"Die Heimkehr,"** the parent poem of the whole cycle, paraphrases the parable of the prodigal son, and **"Das fallende Laub," "Säerspruch," "Hussens Kerker,"** and **"Ernteabend"** allude to the verses of the Bible which we have quoted. In similar fashion, **"Der Erntewagen"** is based on Matt. 9:37-38, and **"Morgenlied"** on the Lord's prayer. On the other hand, the sun in **"Novembersonne"** and **"Ewig jung"** and even more clearly the lightning in **"Schnitterlied," "Erntegewitter,"** and **"Mein Jahr"** are pagan symbols, and in **"Ewig jung"** and **"Schnitterlied"** (so we have seen) these symbols superseded the Christian symbol of the star. The most difficult poems are **"Schnitterlied"** and **"Die Veltlinertraube,"** for in them bread and wine are honored both because they provide sustenance and pleasure and because they are the elements of the Christian sacrament. These poems speak of life boldly enjoyed and of death wantonly sought, and yet they also commemorate, like the sacrament, Christ's vicarious suffering and sacrificial death.

In attempting to explain the conflict we should admit, first of all, that by choosing the word "pagan" to describe the quality of certain symbols and poems we have stated the case rather drastically. We have chosen the word because Meyer himself used it, but we must now add that he used "Christian" and "pagan" not only as opposite but also as complementary terms. Thus, in the poem **"Die Zeichen"** (written in 1871),[43] Meyer tells how climbing in the mountains one day he saw an eagle soaring into the sky and, a little later, a young tree growing from a tree trunk split by lightning. He calls the one a pagan symbol and the other a Christian symbol, and he decides that both are omens of his future: they promise him life. In a similar way, Meyer places side by side in **"Huttens letzte Tage"** the poems **"Ein christliches Sprüchlein"** and **"Ein heidnisches Sprüchlein"** (these poems were added to the third edition, 1881), quoting what St. Paul and what Socrates said about death and eternity. What Meyer is trying to show is that the ideas of the Greek philosopher and those of the apostle were not too far apart, and that Hutten, a Renaissance man nourished by pagan as well as Christian philosophy, could draw solace from them both. Again in **"Gloriola"** (also added to the **"Hutten"** cycle in 1881) Meyer quotes the Latin inscription on a sundial, "Ultima latet," and says that it expresses the spirit of antiquity, but the Christian spirit as well. The poems on the harvest supply yet another example. It will be remembered that the reapers in **"Erntenacht"** sing a song, but that we are not told what kind of song it is. In **"Ernteabend,"** their song is a song of praise, a hymn, but in **"Schnitterlied"** it is a song about dancing and drinking. Both these poems are derived from **"Erntenacht,"** so that in this case the manifestations of Christian and of pagan sentiments are not only complementary but go back to a common origin. I might add that I have interpreted **"Mein Jahr"** as a Christian poem [elsewhere] and as a pagan poem in the present chapter, that I do not consider these interpretations to be mutually exclusive, and that I am willing to defend them both.

What these examples teach is that Meyer's religious feeling was neither pagan nor Christian in the traditional sense, but that sometimes he was able to convey his meaning only by representing himself as being both Christian and pagan. The key to his meaning is to be found, I believe, in the philosophy of the German romanticists. Adolf Frey has told us that Meyer was intimately familiar with the works of Novalis and other German romanticists, and we ourselves have found that Meyer's concepts of the "sweet terror" and of the mountains as a border land between heaven and earth were borrowed from romantic literature.[44] The romanticists attempted to redefine the Christian religion in such a way as to satisfy both the greater spirituality of modern man and his conviction that the material world is real and autonomous. Hence their religion of immanence, that is their doctrine that the infinite is revealed in the finite and that it is the task of man to spiritualize ("etherealize," said Novalis) matter through transforming it into thought.[45] The great danger of this philosophy is that it is easily confused with the naïve spiritualism of primitive peoples or of the ancient Greeks, who thought of material objects as being inhabited by spirits or actually identical with them. The difference can be stated readily enough in philosophic terms—it is the difference between monotheism and polytheism, between thinking of objects as partaking in the divine or as being divine—but it is easily obscured in emotional experience. That is, it is difficult not to lapse from the romantic position either into the medieval (or fundamentalist) Christian view that the material world is finite and deserted by the divine, or into the pagan view that it is itself infinite and divine.

Conrad Ferdinand Meyer struggled with this difficulty, and this accounts for the ambiguities and inconsistencies in his poetry. In a rather remarkable early poem he describes a sunrise in the Alps and notes the sharp contrast between the light on the peaks and the darkness in the valleys. Then, abruptly, he adds this stanza:[46]

> Das Himmelskind, das Erdenkind,
> Das muß sich nicht vermengen,
> Was so verschied'ne Wesen sind,
> Das kann sich nur bedrängen.

Here Meyer falls back on the fundamentalist Christian view, but we know that at almost the same time (in the poem **"Das Glöcklein"**)[47] he made the mountains a symbol of his religion of immanence, and that he developed this symbol with ever increasing firmness and precision. He was able to do this because dead nature, and especially the grandiose Alpine scene, viewed by a person who is alone and in a contemplative frame of mind does seem to reveal the eternal or at least inspires thoughts of eternity. It is a different matter, however, when nature is seen as the scene of struggle and destruction, where all creatures feed on others and where man takes his place not as a detached spectator but as a participant in strife, both terrible and terrified. Meyer's poems on the seasons, particularly those on the harvest, attempt to maintain his religion of immanence in the face of this second aspect of the physical world, but they do not always maintain the balance of his Alpine poetry. To say that the divine order is revealed in the material world and in all its aspects is to approve the working of blind accident—**"Säerspruch"** does just this; it is to assert the right of the stronger to feed on the weaker—**"Schnitterlied"** makes the assertion; it is to sanction the destruction of whole nations—as **"Der Musensaal"** and **"Der Triumphbogen"** do. But the more Meyer tried to defend his faith the more he was driven to glorify, not nature as a revelation of the divine, but physical life as such with all its joys, passions, cruelties, and horrors. And the more he did this the more he was revolted and longed for escape and for death. To be sure, he tried to keep his distinctions intact. **"Schnitterlied,"** I take it, is to show the permissible limit to which man may go in his enjoyment of life—pleasure is permissible when it is earned by hard work and especially when it is mingled with a sense of awe ("Wir sind die Verschonten," says an earlier version). **"Erntegewitter"** on the other hand, is a warning example of recklessness and impiousness. The poem was developed from **"Schnitterlied"** and placed beside it in *Gedichte* to guard against misunderstanding. Yet the very fact that such a warning was necessary shows how dangerously close Meyer had come to pure secularism in **"Schnitterlied"** and the other poems which we have mentioned.

The arrangement of the four poems on the harvest in *Gedichte* is significant. They begin with **"Vor der Ernte,"** where the harvest as the giver of life and the sickle as the symbol of death are introduced but not explained. Then follows **"Erntegewitter,"** which says that the wages of sin is death. Next **"Schnitterlied,"** in which the reapers (unlike the maiden in **"Erntegewitter"**) understand that the lightning is not only a symbol of the supreme moment but also of God's might. And finally **"Auf Goldgrund,"** where self-denying labor and reverence are honored. If **"Auf Goldgrund"** were a better poem, and if **"Schnitterlied"** did not stray from the exact center which it is intended to hold, it would be easier to see that the sequence of poems is meant to expound the religion of immanence. But of course, as we have said, it is difficult to uphold such a faith—not only in poetry but in actual living as well.

Meyer's habit of splitting complexity into antitheses was primarily a method of making poetry. In his greatest poems he presented complex states of mind as such, but when his powers failed him, he was content with saying in two or several poems what he could not say in one. Beyond this, however, his antitheses sprang from his attempt to explain and to defend his monism. I do not agree with Mr. Brecht that Meyer was a dualist or that his was "an antithetical nature." Nor do I agree with Mr. Baumgarten that Meyer's monism was a passing phase.[48] He approved life as a revelation of divine will, but he did not always find it easy to justify it. That he loved life the better the farther he was removed from its more violent manifestations, that he saw its justice more clearly while he kept aloof, does not deny the essential unity of his vision. Unlike the poets and artists of the baroque with whom he is so often compared, Meyer was not saddened by the ruins of ancient Rome; they gave him joy. They reminded him not of the transitoriness and vanity of life but of its permanence. And that the thought of death as the true goal of life was constantly before him is merely additional, indeed conclusive evidence of his realization of the unity and continuity of existence. For Meyer, death was the comrade even of the lover.

It is not a little moving to see how early Meyer found this faith and how firmly he adhered to it. In a poem written when he was not much over twenty[49] he used a legend about Walther von der Vogelweide, the minnesinger, to express his conviction that fresh life rises from death and that, should his hope for an early death be fulfilled, others would sing the songs which he might have composed. According to the legend, Walther had asked that the birds should be fed on his grave,

> Daß aus einer toten Brust
> Steige junge Lebenslust,

> Daß ein neues Lied beginn'
> Da wo ich begraben bin.

In his middle years, Meyer wrote a New Year's poem, **"Am Sylvester,"**[50] in which he stated his thought in general terms and then gave it a multiple interpretation. The lines,

> Tief Gesetz in allem Sein,
> Nur durch Tod zum neuen Leben,

affirm in the first place the Christian's faith that there is a life after death. But they mean also—and this Meyer explains through the symbol of the seed—that life on this earth continues because of the sacrifice, willing or enforced, of other life. And they mean, finally, that individual men (and poets) can gain true life only by a continuous process of death and resurrection, of rejuvenation through casting off the outworn and the moribund. That is, Meyer understood both Goethe's "Selige Sehnsucht" and the Biblical admonition, "He that findeth his life shall lose it; and he that loseth his life shall find it." And thus, because he was both pagan and Christian, mortal man and immortal poet, fond of death but also fond of life, Conrad Ferdinand Meyer could direct that on his grave there should be an obelisk and not a cross, but that it should bear the inscription,

> Ich lebe, und ihr sollt auch leben.

Notes

[1] See Betty L. Fletcher, "The Supreme Moment as a Motiv in C. F. Meyer's Poems," *Monatshefte* (University of Wisconsin), XLII (1950), 27-32.

[2] See [Adolf] Frey, [*Conrad Ferdinand Meyer, Sein Leben und seine Werke,* 3rd ed., Stuttgart and Berlin, 1919] p. 53.

[3] See above, Ch. VII, n. 3.

[4] "Am Wassersturz" is found in CFM 171e, calendar page of Aug. 3, 1871, and is printed by Frey, p. 230, and [Conrad Ferdinand Meyer, *Leuchtende Saat, Eine neue Sammlung von Gedichter und Sprüchen,* (ed. Friedrich Kempter, Engelberg: Württ, 1951),], p. 38. Kempter corrects one error in Frey.

[5] "Reisephantasie" appeared in [C.F. Meyer, *Gedichte (G²)*] (1883). There are no MSS. Dahme's assertion ([Lena F. Dahme, *Women in the Life and Art of Conrad Ferdinand Meyer,* Columbia University Germanic Studies, New Series, IV, New York, 1936] pp. 146f.) that the poem refers to a trip taken in 1853 and to Meyer's alleged infatuation with Alexandrine Marquis is unfounded. As is so often the case with Meyer, the poem seems to have been inspired by literary sources,

especially romantic literature. Its similarity with Heine's "Der Herbstwind rüttelt die Bäume" is striking, and it is even closer to Browning's "Love among the Ruins" and to Schiller's "Resignation". The story of Browning's lover who knows "That a girl with eager eyes and yellow hair / Waits me there / In the turret . . ." is, in its turn, connected with a long tradition in literature and the arts. The tradition derives from the baroque paintings of Guercino and Nicolas Poussin which show shepherds gazing at the inscription, "Et in Arcadia ego," on ancient ruins. This is a very large subject. We must be content in this place to say that Meyer's motif of "Verwischte Inschrift" is in all probability connected with this tradition, and that he changed the subject of "love among the ruins" in characteristic fashion—his lady love is a ghost, a figment of the imagination. See Herbert von Einem's notes to Goethe's *Italienische Reise* (Hamburger Ausgabe, XI, 575ff.) and C. B. Tinker, *The Good Estate of Poetry* (Boston, 1929), pp. 153ff.

[6] There are three MSS of "Die Heimkehr": (1) CFM 177.34, autograph, dated Oct. 28, 1860; (2) [Martin Bodmer (ed.), *Frühe Balladen von Conrad Ferdinand Meyer,* Leipzig, 1922 (*FB*)], pp. 45f., dated June 22, 1860; and (3) [C. F. Meyer, *Bilder und Balladen von Ulrich Meister* (*BB*)], No. 85. The three versions differ only slightly, but they seem to have arisen in the order indicated rather than the order suggested by the dates of the MSS. See [Theodor] Bohnenblust, [*Anfänge des Künstlertums bei C. F. Meyer. Studie auf Grund ungedruckter Gedichte,* Leipzig, 1922] pp. 42f.

[7] *FB*, p. 55.

[8] *FB*, p. 56.

[9] See p. 141, above.

[10] "An die Natur im Spätsommer" appeared in Cotta's *Morgenblatt* (1865) and is reprinted by [Heinrich Moser, *Wandlungen der Gedichte Conrad Ferdinand Meyers,* Leipzig, 1900], p. 6. "Spätjahr" appeared in [C. F. Meyer, *Romanzen und Bilder* (*RB*)] and is reprinted by Kempter, p. 22. There are also two MS versions of "Spätjahr". CFM 174.8 is identical with *RB* except that it lacks the title and has one variant. A version of "Der Erntewagen," also close to the text in *RB,* is found in the same MS. On the other hand, CFM 77.3r, entitled "Frühwinter," has only the second and third stanzas, and these read like an improved version written later than *RB.* However, MS. CFM 77.3r also contains early versions of "Der römische Brunnen" and "Stapfen," and these agree closely with the versions of these poems published in 1865 (see above, Ch. IV, n. 23). Moreover, "Der erste Schnee," of which we have a MS dated Nov. 25, 1865 (see above, Ch. I, n. 55), would seem to be derived from "Frühwinter," so that the latter poem should likewise date from the year 1865. I can explain the conflict between internal and external

evidence only by assuming that when Meyer wrote "Spätjahr" in 1869 he forgot that he had made a superior version, "Frühwinter," four years earlier. Instead of using it, he based his revision on "An die Natur im Spätsommer," which may have been more readily accessible because it had appeared in print.

[11] [Heinrich Kraeger, *Conrad Ferdinand Meyer. Quellen und Wandlungen seiner Gedichte,* Pelaestra, XVI, Berlin, 1901], p. xxx.

[12] See [Walther Brecht, *Conrad Ferdinand Meyer und das Kunstwerk seiner Gedichtsammlung,* Vienne and Leipzig, 1908], p. 211. In G^1, the group of poems on summer and fall comprised only nine poems, seven derived from "Spätjahr" and two others: "Requiem was attached to "Auf Goldgrund" (both being poems about evening), and "Weinsegen" to Die Veltlinertraube" (both being poems about the grape). In G^2 through G^4, six poems were added. Of these, "Mein Jahr" and "Ewig jung" are derived from "Spätjahr;" "Wanderfüße" and "Einem Tagelöhner" are related to it; and "Abendwolke" and "Mein Stern" are unrelated. Since "Wanderfüße" and "Einem Tagelöhner" are less closely related to "Spätjahr" than the other nine poems, I have touched on them only briefly in the text (see below, p. 228) and have not included them in the chart at the end of the chapter. At the beginning of this chapter, where I speak of twelve poems on summer and fall, I have in mind the nine in the section "Hour," plus "Der Triumphbogen," "Der Musensaal," and "Hussens Kerker". These are the final products of Meyer's poetry on the seasons, and they appear in the bottom line of the chart.

[13] There are four versions of "Novembersonne": the MSS. CFM 45.1 and 45.2, the text printed in Deutsche Dichterhalle, IX (1879), 58, and the text in *G.* The MSS are in Betsy's hand. There is no indication of their date except the note, "4 Feb. (definitiv)," in CFM 45.2. This may mean that they were written early in 1879. The title is "Novembersonne" except in the magazine version, where it is "Nach der Lese". This version is reprinted by Moser (p. 21), who, however, dates it 1880 instead of 1879.

[14] For "Kurze Freude" see above, Ch. V, n. 44. "Wintertag" is found in *Briefe,* I, 168, and in Wolff's *Poetischer Hausschatz,* 30th edition, 1907. The version in the letter differs somewhat from the version in the anthology. In the letter, Meyer says that he jotted down the poem for a young visitor from Leipzig. When and how the poem got into the anthology I do not know.

[15] "Die Pythagoräer" is printed in *Corona,* p. 394. The poem is preserved in CFM 177.7, which was written ca. 1885 and has also the beginning of a second version. For the sun as a death symbol see Brecht, pp. 50-53, 84, and [Martin Bodmer, *Conrad Ferdinand Meyer. Her Kommer und Umwelt.* Ver off entlichung

der Vereinigung Oltner Bücherfreunde, XXIII, Olten, 1944], *Corona,* p. 390. Betsy Meyer's letter is printed in *Corona,* p. 455; Bodmer (*ibid.*) would seem to underrate its importance.

I know five MSS of "Zwiegespräch". The first two versions, both entitled "Tagesneige", are found in CFM 171e, calendar pages of Aug. 14-15 and Aug. 16-17, 1871. Frey, p. 231, printed the second version. The third version, entitled "Abendrot," is found in CFM 176.18, No. 12 and in CFM 87.1, a copy by Adolf Frey. This is a love poem, presumably written for Luise Ziegler in or after 1875. The fourth version is found in CFM 87.2, an autograph written ca. 1881 in preparation of *G. Unter den Sternen* appeared in *G²* (1883). There are no MSS.

[16] There is only one MS of "Säerspruch," CFM 43*r,* which was written by Meyer himself when he prepared the *Gedichte.* The text is identical with *G.*

[17] C. F. Meyer, "Mein Erstling *Huttens letzte Tage,*" *Deutsche Dichtung,* IX (1891), 172-74; reprinted in *Briefe,* II, 520.

[18] Printed in Frey, pp. 221-24; excerpts in [Robert Faesi, *Conrad Ferdinand Meyer,* 2nd ed., Frauenfeld, 1948], pp. 98f.

[19] See Frey, pp. 220, 408.

[20] *Schloß Gottlieben* (*BB,* No. 88) is the earliest form of *Hussens Kerker.* There are three further MSS: CFM 156.1, an autograph dated Feb. 21, 1865; CFM 156.2, written by Betsy, with numerous corrections by Meyer which point to ca. 1865; and CFM 156.3, an autograph written shortly before the poem appeared in *G¹.*

[21] Titian's *Assunta,* which Meyer saw in Venice, made a lasting impression on him and colored all assumption scenes in his works to a greater or lesser extent. See the poem "Venedig"; *Engelberg,* Canto I, pp. 10-13; *Page,* Ch. IV, p. 268; and *Pescara,* Ch. III, p. 118. Cf. [Betsy Meyer, *Conrad Ferdinand Meyer in der Erinnerung seiner Schwester,* 2nd ed., Berlin, 1903], p. 169; Frey, p. 242; [Erwin Kalischer, *Conrad Ferdinand Meyer in seinem Verhältnis zur* italienischen Renaissance, Palaestra, LXIV, Berlin, 1907], pp. 13f. and 17; [Emil Sulger-Gebing, "C. F. Meyers Werke in ihren Beziehungen zur bildenden Kunst," *Euphorion* XXIII (1921)], (1921), pp. 448f.; and [Walther Linden, *Conrad Ferdinand Meyer. Entwicklung und Gestalt,* München, 1922], p. 105.

[22] "Im Veltlin" appeared in 1879 (not 1880, as stated by Moser and Linden) in *Deutsche Dichterhalle,* IX, 41, and "Wunsch" in *Zürcher Dichterkränzchen,* 1882. Both versions are reprinted in Moser, pp. 45f. and in *Wandlungen,* p. 68. Meyer added a stanza to a copy of *Wunsch* which he sent to Louise von François (printed by [Anton Bettelheim (ed.), *Louise von François und Conrad Ferdinand Meyer. Ein Briefwechsel,* 2nd ed., Berlin, 1920], p. 287), and he added two stanzas to a copy found among his papers (CFM 41).

[23] Louise von François (ed. Bettelheim, p. 45) named "Wunsch" among the poems by Meyer which she liked best. Six of the twenty-four anthologies which I have consulted include "Die Veltlinertraube"; only three include "Hussens Kerker".

[24] There are five versions of "Der Erntewagen": *BB,* No. 47 (1860); CFM 37 (dated July, 1864); "Morgenblatt," 1865; CFM 174.8*v* (an autograph written ca. 1869; see note 10, above); and *RB.* There are no MSS of "Auf Goldgrund". The three versions mentioned in the text appeared in *Sänger aus Helvetiens Gauen* (1879), *G¹,* and *G².* For reprints see Moser, pp. 7f. and *Wandlungen,* pp. 71f.

[25] "Clara" was published by Constanze Speyer in *Corona,* VIII (1938), 395-411. The passage in question is found on page 400. Speyer thinks the story was written between 1849 and 1851; Frey (pp. 72-75) dates it ca. 1855. However, Kalischer (p. 24, n. 2) points out the similarity between "Auf Goldgrund" and a painting by Leopold Robert which Meyer saw in Paris in 1857 (see Frey, p. 97), and since this similarity would also exist between the painting and the passage in "Clara," the story may have been written after 1857. That the scene in *Clara* adumbrates "Auf Goldgrund" was observed by Frey in a letter to Betsy of Jan. 31, 1893 (*Corona,* VIII, 429) and by [Constanze Speyer (ed.), *Conrad Ferdinand Meyers Gedichte en Seine Breut Luise Ziegler,* Zürich and New York, 1940] (*ibid.,* p. 415).

[26] See above, Ch. I, n. 54.

[27] MSS. CFM 36.1-4 are all in Betsy's hand. The catalogue numbers indicate their chronological order. In CFM 36.1, which bears the note, "13 Juli. Erster Entwurf," the title "Nacht in der Ernte" is crossed out and replaced by "Sommernacht". The other three versions are entitled "Erntenacht". As for the date of the poem, these clues seem significant to me: (1) The publication of "Der Erntewagen" in *RB* (1869) concludes the first phase of Meyer's attempt to realize his motif of the harvest. "Erntenacht" marks a fresh beginning and must have been written after 1869. (2) On the other hand, the style of "Erntenacht" is not yet markedly different from the style of the poems in *RB.* There is, for example, a striking similarity in the melody and rhyming technique of this stanza in "Auf dem" See 3,

> Zeit ist's, daß der Sanfte weiche,
> Schon in seiner vollen Pracht

Hebt sich der verhängnisreiche
Jupiter in blauer Nacht,

with stanza 5 of "Sommernacht":

An der Ernte, die er hegte,
Die er reifte bis zum Schnitt,
Hülfe gern der leisbewegte
Kräftereiche Himmel mit.

(3) CFM 36.4 has on its verso a version of "Das Nachtboot" which must have been written in, or shortly after, 1871 (see above, Ch. VI, n. 42). (4) The close similarity of "Erntenacht" with the "Morgenlied" in CFM 171e also points to the summer of 1871.

[28] The first version of "Vor der Ernte" is found in CFM 43v, the second and third in CFM 36.7v, the fourth in G^1, and the final one in the later versions of *G*. The first version is called "Mondensiche" l; the second, "Die Sichel"; the later ones, *Vor der Ernte*. Both the MSS are in Meyer's hand of 1881-82.

[29] "Stimmung" is printed by Bohnenblust, p. 53. It is No. 46 in *BB;* "Der Erntewagen" is No. 47.

[30] "Ernteabend," found in CFM 177.17, is written in Fritz Meyer's hand and must therefore be later than 1881. It must be earlier than 1887, when *Pescara* was published. Printed by [August Langmesser, *Conrad Ferdinand Meyer. Sein Leben, seine Werke und sein Nachlaß,* 3rd ed., Berlin, 1905], p. 522, and Kempter, p. 9.

[31] "Erntelied" is found in CFM 36.5r; CFM. 36.6; *Das Schweizerhaus,* VI (1877), 129 (reprinted by Moser, p. 81, and Brecht, p. 48); and CFM 43r. The first two versions were written by Betsy on note paper with the monogram "CFM" which Meyer used in and about 1875. In addition, CFM 36.6 is dated, "April '75." Three additional versions, with the title changed to "Schnitterlied," are found in CFM 36.7, G^1, and the later versions of *G*. CFM 43 and 36.7 are autographs of 1881-82.

[32] In Germany, the saying is usually quoted in the form given it by Friedrich Kind (1768-1843): "Zwischen Lipp' und Kelchesrand / Schwebt der finstern Mächte Hand." The line, "Von Becher zu Munde," is still found in G^1 and was changed to "Von Munde zu Munde" only in the later editions of *G*.

[33] Brecht, pp. 45-49. "Erntegewitter" is found in CFM 43v and CFM 35, both autographs of ca. 1881-82. The first MS is obviously a first draft. It has numerous corrections. The reapers are compared with witches, and the main figure is called "eine frevle Höllenkönigin." The second MS is identical with *G*, except that lines 9-10 of *G* are omitted—perhaps inadvertently, since they are found in CFM 43.

[34] See Speyer, pp. 41, 49, and above, pp. 82-84. Cf. the poem "Ihr Heim".

[35] See, for example, "Cäsar Borjas Ohnmacht" and "Pergoleses Ständchen".

[36] See Kraeger, p. 220; [Max Nußberger, *Conrad Ferdinand Mayer. Leben und Werke,* Freuenfeld, 1919], p. 254. The references to the Franco-German War are, of course, not found in the five versions of "Der Musensaal" written between 1864 and 1869 (see above, Ch. VI, n. 22), but appear for the first time in G^1. It is possible that they were transferred from a poem, "Germanias Sieg," which Meyer wrote in 1870 but never published. This poem is preserved in three MSS: (1) CFM 177.72, an autograph which has also versions of "Das Bild des Vaters" (other MSS are *BB*, No. 29, CFM 177.18, 177.75, 177.76, and 177.77) and of "Der deutsche Schmied" (other MSS are CFM 177.7v and 177.78v; cf. Betsy, p. 157; Frey, pp. 226, 408; [Conrad Ferdinand Meyer, *Huttens letzte Tage,* ed. Robert Bruce Roulston, Baltimore, 1933], p. 104); (2) CFM 177.74, Betsy's copy of version 1; and (3) CFM 177.73, an autograph dated Dec. 10, 1870, which improves on the other two versions in a few places. Stanza 4 of "Germanias Sieg" corresponds to lines 37-38 of "Der Musensaal" in G^1, and stanza 9 to lines 41-44. The former passages say that Germany in 1870 was the instrument of historic justice, while the latter prophesy a future of universal peace. For the ideological connection of "Der Musensaal" with the poems "Alle," "Friede auf Erden," and "Die Menschheit" (*Hutten,* No. LX) see Kraeger, p. 217, and Brecht, pp. 116f.

[37] *Das Lustspiel* is found in *BB*, No. 14 and in CFM 177.37v. It is printed by Frey, p. 158, and Kempter, p. 78.

[38] Brecht, p. 111, n. 3.

[39] In *Engelberg,* the return is the central idea as well as a motif used in specific situations. See especially the end. Kurd's return home in Canto XI, p. 84, is reminiscent of stanza 22 of "Die Heimkehr". "Die erste Nacht" is the second poem in *Huttens letzte Tage.*

[40] The MS versions CFM 39.1 and 39.2 are in Fritz Meyer's hand, dated July 12, 1889, and entitled "Jahresrechnung". CFM 39.3 is an undated autograph called "Mein Jahr". Its text is practically identical with *G*. The three MSS were written in the order in which they are catalogued.

[41] *Page,* Ch. II, p. 234.

[42] See the lines from "Homo sum" which Meyer used as a motto for *Huttens letzte Tage.*

[43] "Die Zeichen" is found in CFM 171e, calendar page of Aug. 1, 1871.

[44] See Frey, p. 52, and pp. 90f. and 177f., above.

[45] "Man halte das Unendliche nicht etwan für eine philosophische Fiktion, man suche es nicht jenseits der Welt: es umgibt uns überall, wir können ihm niemals entgehen; wir leben, weben und sind im Unendlichen."—A. W. Schlegel, *Vorlesungen über schöne Literatur und Kunst,* ed. J. Minor (Heilbronn, 1884), I, 90. "Dies mystische Erscheinen unseres tiefsten Gemütes im Bilde, dies Hervortreten der Weltgeister, diese Menschwerdung des Göttlichen, mit einem Worte: dies Ahnen des Unendlichen in den Anschauungen ist das Romantische."—Ludwig Uhland, *Über das Romantische, Werke,* ed. H. Brömse (Leipzig, n.d.), III, 15. "Einst soll keine Natur mehr sein. In eine Geisterwelt soll sie allmählich übergehen."—Novalis. See also the fourth of Novalis' *Hymnen an die Nacht.*

[46] The poem begins, "Ihr hohen Warten in der Nacht." See above, Ch. VII, n. 15.

[47] See pp. 177f., above.

[48] Brecht, pp. 7, 11, and 13, n. 2; [Franz Ferdinand Baumgarten. *Das Werk Conrad Ferdinand Meyers,* ed. Hans Schumacher, Zürich, 1947], p. 75.

[49] "Walter von der Vogelweid" is preserved in CFM 178.6, an autograph which according to Betsy Meyer's note to Frey (CFM 178.4) was written ca. 1847-50.

[50] "Am Sylvester" is found in CFM 177.94, which is dated Monday, Mar. 14. The date would fit the years 1859, 1864, 1870, 1881, 1887, etc. The poem was probably written in 1864, perhaps in 1870.

Frederick J. Beharriell (essay date 1955)

SOURCE: "C. F. Meyer and the Origins of Psychoanalysis," in *Monatshefte für Deutschen Unterricht, Deutsche Sprache und Literatur,* Vol. XLVII, No. 3, March, 1955, pp. 140-48.

[In the essay that follows, Beharriell examines Freud's interest in Meyer's writing as it anticipates major elements of psychoanalytic theory, such as wish-fulfillment, the fantasy Freud names 'the family romance,' and the psychological significance of art.]

In "Freud and Literature," an eminently sane and balanced essay, Lionel Trilling commented on the lack of evidence concerning the literary influences on the founder of psychoanalysis.[1] That there were such influences has of course always appeared certain. The importance of *Hamlet* and *Oedipus* in Freud's early thinking is well known. The similarity between his theory of dream meaning and the process of literary symbolism was apparent from the first. Innumerable allusions to literature in his writings reveal a wide acquaintance with literature and a striking respect for the insight of the writer. And if, as Trilling says, Freud "ultimately did more for our understanding of art than any other writer since Aristotle,". . . it is no secret that Freud approached the other arts through literature. On the other hand, specific information was lacking. Not much light on the subject could be found in Freud's various autobiographical sketches. It must be remembered that all his life he had to suffer allegations that he was a theorist only, a philosopher whose claims had no firm basis in verifiable fact; his claim to be a scientist was ever nearest his heart. Thus it is not surprising that he did not emphasize the debt he owed to literature. His "discoveries," he repeatedly asserts, were forced upon him by his clinical experience.

Another circumstance contributed to the obscurity surrounding his early work. Like not a few of his contemporaries—one thinks of Henry James and Stefan George—Freud felt a curious animosity toward unknown future biographers. Ernest Jones, the official biographer, says that on more than one occasion Freud carefully destroyed, as far as he had the power, all his correspondence, notes, diaries, and manuscripts. And like James he gloated at the thought of the future biographers' discomfiture.[2]

These facts lent interest to the appearance in 1950 of *Aus den Anfängen der Psychoanalyse,* a collection of previously unknown letters and documents penned by Freud in the years 1887 to 1902.[3] Most of the material dates from precisely the years 1895 to 1900 when his most important ideas were born. Freud's work on the *Traumdeutung,* the famous self-analysis that went hand in hand with it, and the birth of the Oedipus concept all date from this period. These new documents, preserved in spite of Freud's efforts to destroy them, reveal among other things the hitherto unsuspected part played by the works of Conrad Ferdinand Meyer in the origins of psychoanalysis. An intensive systematic study of Meyer's works is now seen to have been Freud's basic reading, outside of technical material, throughout the most crucial period. It is also not without interest that psychoanalytical criticism by Freud of one of Meyer's stories must now be regarded as the earliest application of psychoanalytic methods to a work of literature, anticipating by almost ten years the essay, "Der Wahn und die Träume in W. Jensens 'Gradiva.' "

Freud's attention was drawn to Meyer by Wilhelm Fliess, the Berlin physician to whom the letters of *Aus den Anfängen der Psychoanalyse* are addressed. Fliess, although a nose and throat specialist, had developed a consuming interest in certain aspects of neurosis, and here, of course, his research coincided with Freud's. From 1887 to 1902 Freud enjoyed with Fliess a friendship so close that his biographer has called it "the only really extraordinary experience in Freud's life" (Jones,

287). During these years the two men maintained a regular correspondence, reporting their findings and theories to one another and exchanging criticism and encouragement. Fliess was Freud's only confidant.

Freud's first recorded reference to Meyer dates from March 15, 1898, when Freud was at work on the manuscript of the *Traumdeutung*. His letters to Fliess of that date begins abruptly, "Teurer Wilhelm! Habe ich Conrad Ferdinand je unterschätzt, so bin ich seit dem Himmelstor durch Dich längst bekehrt." The reference is of course to Meyer's poem, **"Am Himmelstor."** As Freud destroyed all the letters Fliess wrote to him, we can only surmise what may have preceded this enthusiastic comment. It seems clear that Fliess had recommended the poem to Freud, and that the latter had found in it some decisive merit. The poem itself offers some assistance. Its purely poetic qualities are not such as to explain Freud's interest. On the other hand it does purport to describe a dream. Freud was struggling every evening with the manuscript of his dream theory, and the letters show how completely this work monopolized his time. His part of the correspondence, moreover, deals predominantly with his progress on the *Traumdeutung*. Everything suggests that Fliess had recommended Meyer's works, and particularly this dream poem, as illustration or corroboration of Freud's dream theory.

"Am Himmelstor" is of course the short poem in which the poet dreams he finds his beloved weeping outside the gate of heaven, incessantly washing her feet; he does not understand why, and the poem ends with her cryptic explanation, "Weil ich im Staub mit dir, / So tief im Staub gegangen." In view of the sharply conflicting interpretations that have been given to the poem,[4] it is regrettable that we do not have Freud's opinion on its meaning. Nor would it be wise to indulge in speculation, for his dream theory itself was undergoing daily revision as he simultaneously developed and recorded it. The letter preceding this one, for example, communicates a basic idea, just evolved, which was very soon to be discarded. Thus it is not possible to determine precisely what the theory was on this date. All that can be said with certainty is that Freud saw in Meyer's dream-poem a gratifying confirmation, firstly, of the basic idea of wish-fulfilment, and secondly, of that process of symbolic distortion in which Freud also believed from the very outset.

The precise point Freud had reached in his speculations on the Oedipus theme is revealed in an interesting passage in this same letter (March 15, 1898). Freud says he is transmitting a portion of the *Traumdeutung* manuscript for Fliess to read. Two of the dreams there described, he writes, will be explained later: "Bemerkungen über König Ödipus, das Talismanmärchen, vielleicht den Hamlet werden ihre Stelle finden. Vorher muß ich über die Ödipussage nachlesen, weiß noch nicht, wo." It is

a time of seminal thinking for Freud, and his steady reading of Meyer proceeds, it will be seen, through the time of the working out of the Oedipus idea. Moreover, Freud can have found time for little else in the way of imaginative literature at this period. His typical work day in early 1898 began with nine to twelve hours of work with patients, finishing around nine in the evening. "Then," reports Ernest Jones, "came writing *The Interpretation of Dreams,* correspondence, and the self-analysis" (Jones, 338; cf. *Anfänge,* 264). That Freud read Meyer under such pressure of work suggests he was seeking more than entertainment. There was little time for reading for pleasure.

Freud wrote about Meyer again only three weeks later, on June 9, 1898. He had meanwhile had a brief vacation in Istrea, but is back at work and once again lamenting his difficulties with the dream manuscript. He reports he is still finding great enjoyment in Meyer, and has now finished *Gustav Adolfs Page.* Fliess had recommended this story too, drawing Freud's attention particularly to an example of the phenomenon or theory which Freud had labeled "deferred action" (*Nachträglichkeit*). In the story, it will be recalled, the colonel upbraids the heroine for her irrational adoration of the king, with the words, "Nun sag' ich: man soll die Kinder nicht küssen! So'n Kuß schläft und lodert wieder auf, wann die Lippen wachsen und schwellen. Und wahr ist's und bleibt's, der König hat dich mir einmal von den Armen genommen, Patchen, und hat dich geherzt und abgeküßt, daß es nur so klatschte. Denn du warest ein keckes und hübsches Kind."[4] The "deferred action" that Freud and Fliess both saw in this remark is of course the idea of the previously unrecognized psychological importance of childhood experiences. This was still a very new idea with Freud, one he had just "discovered" in his self-analysis and was still working out in the *Traumdeutung* manuscript. The letter of March 10, for example, contains lengthy speculations on the supreme importance of the years from one to three, "the source of the unconscious." Freud is thus using Meyer's story as he might use a patient, as "raw material" for the working out of still-developing theories.

A second example of *"Nachträglichkeit"* in *Gustav Adolfs Page* was discovered by Freud himself in the anecdote concerning Gustav Adolf's daughter Christina. Meyer relates that a scheming Jesuit fanatic, posing as a Lutheran in order to obtain a post as the child's tutor, had taken advantage of his position to influence her religious attitude. When the child's governess discovered her secretly praying with a rosary, the fraudulent tutor was banished. This incident occurred in 1632, when Christina was six, and Freud interpreted it as a foreshadowing by Meyer of her later abdication and conversion to Catholicism at the age of twenty-nine.

It may be pertinent to observe that of these two examples of *Nachträglichkeit,* the first is a rather striking confirmation of what was in 1898 a new theory, while the second is much less impressive. The first, the reference to the king's kissing the infant, is in fact a gratuitous intrusion on the narrative, an intrusion in which we must see with Freud a kind of "psychologizing" by Meyer. If it means anything, it must mean what Freud claims. The incident of the fraudulent tutor, on the other hand, can be amply explained as an example of Meyer's fondness for repeated variations on a theme, in this case the central theme of disguise and deception. This previous victimization of the king renders the "page's" deception of him more dangerous. And of course it is most significant that the story makes no reference to Christina's later actions. If Meyer really intended *Nachträglichkeit,* the historical consequences of the act would surely have been incorporated in the story. With regard to this same incident, further, it is not ascertainable whether Freud meant that Meyer consciously proposed this explanation of Christina's later conversion, or that Meyer unconsciously selected this anecdote because of Christina's later acts, or simply that Freud himself took the incident as a plausible explanation of the conversion. It is interesting to observe in this earliest Freudian criticism a lack of clear distinction between analysis of the artist and analysis of his art. This lack, inevitable in the Freudian system, has of course continued to this day to alienate non-Freudian critics.

Freud's remarks on *Gustav Adolfs Page* close with a much less controversial criticism: "Sonst aber stehe ich ratlos vor der Willkürlichkeit der Annahme, auf der die Verknotung beruht. Die Ähnlichkeit des Pagen mit dem Lauenburger in Hand und Stimme, an sich so unwahrscheinlich und gar nicht weiter begründet." Most critics will agree that this complaint is a just one.

In the letter in which he discussed *Gustav Adolfs Page* Freud had included a promise that he would soon forward a short essay on Meyer's *Die Richterin.* This essay is now recognized as Freud's first formal application of analysis to a work of literature (see *Anfänge,* 273, note 1). Indeed it seems to be the first such application to any work of art, and shares with the dream theory the distinction of inaugurating that ever-widening application of Freudian analysis which was eventually to bring under scrutiny so many aspects of behavior and culture. The essay was apparently written between June 9 and June 20, 1898, and was sent to Fliess on the latter date when Freud returned to Vienna from a visit in Aussee.

Again Freud uses Meyer's work to test the theories which are taking form in his mind. *Die Richterin* is the story in which Meyer incorporated a somewhat imperfect union of two main themes: the (female) judge who herself stands in need of judgment; and the forbidden love of a brother and sister. Needless to say it was the latter theme which seemed to Freud to hold the

essence of the story. His essay begins on a typically confident note: "Kein Zweifel, daß es sich um die poetische Abwehr der Erinnerung an ein Verhältnis mit der Schwester handelt. Merkwürdig nur, daß diese *genau* so geschieht wie in der Neurose. Alle Neurotiker bilden den sogenannten Familienroman . . . , der einerseits dem Größenbedürfnis dient, andererseits der Abwehr des Inzestes. Wenn die Schwester nicht das Kind der Mutter ist, so ist man ja des Vorwurfes ledig." It is relevant here that at this time Freud probably was acquainted with the most superficial facts of Meyer's life—Meyer was by then a public figure—but no more. His speculations are based on the stories. Some six months later (December 5, 1898), he laments his ignorance of Meyer's *"Lebensgeschichte"* particularly the order in which the works were written, "was ich zur Deutung nicht entbehren könnte."[5] And in January, 1900, he procures and reads a copy of Adolf Frey's biography of Meyer as soon as it is published.

The *"Familienroman"* or family romance with which Freud identifies *Die Richterin* is the name he gave to a recurring pattern of phantasy reported by neurotic patients. Although Freud later came to regard it as a function of the normal personality, he at first believed it to be a regular symptom of paranoia. His neurotic patients, he said, frequently claimed that as children they had come to believe themselves stepchildren or adopted children. Freud later asserted that many normal adults can recall the same childhood phantasy. A second phase of this phantasy is a feature common to neurosis and to every higher gift, such as the poetic temperament. In this stage the child's phantasy busied itself with the task of doing away with the "despised" parents and replacing them with phantasy parents who are usually higher in the social scale. (Certain well-known writers come instantly to mind.) In a third and final stage, having learned, as Freud puts it, that *pater semper incertus est* while the mother *certissima est,* the child was content to imagine an unknown aristocratic father. At this stage also, the original motive of revenge on insufficiently doting parents is strengthened by a developing Oedipus desire to imagine the mother as untrue to the father.[6]

Freud did not publish his concept of the family romance until 1909 (see *Anfänge,* 219, note 2). All the main features of the theory, however, are stated in his analysis of *Die Richterin.* On the available evidence it appears that it was on this story that Freud based his first seriously worked-out identification of the poetic temperament with the neurotic, an identification which has had the most sweeping consequences although Freud himself at last virtually abandoned it. It is true that a year before the *Richterin* essay he had jotted down, "Der Mechanismus der Dichtung ist derselbe wie der hysterischen Phantasien. . . . So behält Shakespeares Zusammensetzung von Dichtung und Wahn recht (fine frenzy)." (*Anfänge,* 222). When he wrote this, however, his attention was fully engaged by the still unsolved problem of the hysterical phantasies, and not at all by the mechanism of creative writing. The Oedipus idea had not then occurred to him. The quoted remark about Shakespeare seems no more than a fleeting *aperçu.* Then in a letter of October 15, 1897, come the first tentative speculations on the Oedipus complex, suggesting: "Jeder der Hörer war einmal im Keime und in der Phantasie ein solcher Ödipus," and that Hamlet was a "typical hysteric." The crucial labeling of the creative process itself as identical with a neurotic defense mechanism, however, together with a formal working out of the thesis, does not appear until the analysis of *Die Richterin.* Thus while it is most unlikely that any one author provided the whole pattern for Freud's original concept of the artist, the available evidence does suggest that that concept drew from Meyer, Sophocles, and Shakespeare, in that order of importance.

In *Die Richterin* Freud was impressed by the double occurrence of the motif of the faithless mother, once in the figure of the heroine, and again in that of her servant Faustine. This weakness in composition, he said, was reminiscent of his patients, who always insisted on telling him the same story twice. In both the family romance and the story, further, there is discernible a desire for revenge against the sternly punishing mother: this bitterness against her makes her a stepmother in the story. The aloof father, towering majestically above the child, is symbolized in the story by Charlemagne. The dispatching of Wulfrin's father by means of poison satisfies the family romance dream of encompassing the death of the father. Freud's attention to "significant detail" in this essay foreshadows the future nature of most psychoanalytic criticism: the incident of the taking away of the hero's horn, its recovery, the sister's anorexia, the hurling of the sister on the rocks, the schoolmaster motif, all are, according to Freud, characteristic of the phantasies of neurotics: "Also in jedem einzelnen Zug identisch mit einem der Rache- und Entlastungsromane, den meine Hysteriker gegen ihre Mutter dichten, wenn sie Knaben sind."[7]

The study of Meyer continued. Less than three weeks after the historic essay on *Die Richterin,* on July 7, 1898, a letter from Freud contains a paragraph of analysis on *Die Hochzeit des Mönchs.* Here for the first time Freud uses the concept of latent and manifest themes. This concept has of course had a decisive impact on twentieth-century criticism; in Lionel Trilling's view it has been Freud's most valuable contribution to understanding of the literary work (op. cit., page 48). In *Die Hochzeit des Mönchs,* Freud thought, the latent or secret theme, rooted in Meyer's childhood, is unsatisfied revenge and inevitable punishment; Dante's presence suggests that this revenge and punishment are to be eternal. The manifest or apparent theme, on the other hand, is the loss of

equilibrium (*Haltlosigkeit*) that follows when a man abandons his firm support in life, and this theme has in common with the latent theme, and with *Die Richterin,* that "blow follows on blow." Thus, just as *Die Richterin* was found to conceal the reaction to infantile misdeeds that were discovered by the avenging mother, *Die Hochzeit des Mönchs* is a reaction to infantile misdeeds (Freud might later have written "thoughts" for "deeds") which were not detected. "Der Mönch ist der Bruder, 'Frate,'" Freud concluded. "Als ob es vor seiner eigenen Ehe phantasiert wäre, und besagen wollte, so ein Frater wie ich soll nicht heiraten, sonst rächt sich die Kinderliebe an der späteren Ehefrau."

On November 28, 1898, Meyer died. Freud "marked the occasion" by purchasing the volumes he still lacked—*Hutten, Pescara, Der Heilige*—and wrote to Fliess, "Ich glaube, jetzt tue ich es Dir an Begeisterung für ihn gleich. Vom Pescara konnte ich mich kaum losreißen" (*Anfänge,* 288). He finally obtained a biography of Meyer when Adolf Frey's book became available late in 1899. His comment on Frey was, "Er weiß das Interne nicht oder darf es aus Diskretion nicht sagen. Es ist auch gerade nicht viel zwischen den Zeilen zu lesen" (*Anfänge,* 330).

Freud retained his interest in Meyer's works and his easy familiarity with them for the rest of his life. "Ich bin kein ausgeklügelt Buch, / Ich bin ein Mensch mit seinem Widerspruch," the lines from *Hutten* so suggestive of Freud's own view, are quoted at the end of a case history written in 1899 (*Anfänge,* 297), and cited again ten years later in another work (*GW* VII, 347). In his book, *Freud, Master and Friend* (Cambridge, Mass., 1944), page 52, Hanns Sachs recalls that Freud's lectures at the Psychiatric Clinic were marked by quotations and other hints of his partiality to Meyer, and that at the first personal interview between Freud and himself, the two "joined in praise of Conrad Ferdinand Meyer."

There is one last testimonial to the unique importance of Meyer for Freud's early thinking. After Freud had become famous he was asked on one occasion to recommend a list of ten good books, the request apparently not defining the word "good" more closely. On the list which he returned Freud included Meyer's *Huttens letzte Tage,* and the comment he appended is of peculiar relevance here. Emphasizing that his list does not represent the ten "greatest" works, nor the "most significant," nor even his favorites, Freud interprets "good" as meaning "Bücher, mit denen man etwa so steht wie mit 'guten' Freunden, denen man ein Stück seiner Lebenskenntnis und Weltanschauung verdankt, die man selbst genossen hat und anderen gerne anpreist, ohne daß aber in dieser Beziehung das Moment der scheuen Ehrfurcht, die Empfindung der eigenen Kleinheit vor deren Größe, besonders hervorträte." He stresses the importance of the relationship between the author and his works, and concludes significantly, "bei C. F. Meyers **Hutten** muß ich die 'Güte' weit über die Schönheit, die 'Erbauung' über den ästhetischen Genuß stellen."[8] An admission, it would appear in view of all the evidence, that from Meyer as from few other authors he had deduced basic ideas about the connection between the artistic personality and its imaginative creations.

There was more than one reason for Freud's interest in Meyer. In view of Meyer's emotional instability, it is relevant that Freud himself suffered for ten years from "a very considerable psychoneurosis," and that for those ten years, which included the years of original work discussed in this paper, he experienced "only occasional intervals when life seemed much worth living" (Jones, 304-305). Meyer was preoccupied with the idea of death;[9] Freud suffered attacks of *Todesangst,* and once, as he was regaining consciousness after a fainting spell, his first words were, "How sweet it must be to die!"—one of many indications, his biographer observes, that "the idea of dying had some esoteric meaning for him" (Jones, 317). And recalling that curious and decisive period of Meyer's youth which Meyer called his *"dumpfe Zeit,"* it is significant to find the following concerning Freud: "In the depressed moods he could neither write nor concentrate his thoughts. . . . He would spend leisure hours of extreme boredom, turning from one thing to another . . . (in) a state of restless paralysis. Sometimes there were spells where consciousness would be greatly narrowed: *states, difficult to describe, with a veil that produced almost a twilight condition of the mind*" (Jones, 306; italics mine). It was precisely during the period of these "spells" that Freud discovered and studied Meyer.

Last and most important is the striking correspondence between the new symbolism of Meyer's creative process and the very similar symbolism on which Freud was building his theory of dreams. Indeed Meyer's peculiar creative process affords a striking example of the precise theory of poetry toward which Freud was moving. In essence Freud's theory was that the present experience which occasions the poem awakens in the poet a forgotten earlier (frequently childhood) experience; the poem, then, will contain elements of the old experience as well as of the fresh stimulus. Of the two, the childhood experience, dating from the formative period, is of course the fundamental and determining one (*GW* VII, 221). This is very similar to the dichotomy which Professor Henel has demonstrated in Meyer between past and present, motif and theme, subconscious and conscious content.[10]

For some or all of these reasons Meyer was intensively read and studied by Freud during the most critical period of the birth of psychoanalysis. Meyer's work was an important source, or at the least a first "proving ground"

for the key concepts of *Nachträglichkeit,* the family romance, the Oedipus complex, art as neurosis, and the roots of art in childhood experience. The essay on *Die Richterin* is Freud's first formal application of analysis to a literary work, and thus the first step toward the application of analytical ideas far beyond the consultation room. Freud may have been thinking of Meyer when in 1928, as he frequently did, he paid envious tribute to the insight of poets, to whom it is granted, "aus dem Wirbel der eigenen Gefühle die tiefsten Einsichten doch eigentlich mühelos heraufzuholen, zu denen wir Anderen uns durch qualvolle Unsicherheiten und rastloses Tasten den Weg zu bahnen haben."[11]

Notes

[1] Lionel Trilling, *The Liberal Imagination* (New York, 1953), p. 44.

[2] Ernest Jones, *The Life and Work of Sigmund Freud,* Vol. I (New York, 1953), pp. xii-xiii, hereafter referred to as "Jones."

[3] Sigmund Freud, *Aus den Anfängen der Psychoanalyse* (London, 1950); hereafter referred to as *"Anfänge";* letters identified in the text by date are in this volume.

[4] See Heinrich Henel, *The Poetry of Conrad Ferdinand Meyer* (Madison, 1954), p. 145.

[5] If Freud contemplated any "Deutung" beyond his essays for Fliess he apparently abandoned it; he probably was thinking of his own understanding of the works as a whole.

[6] Paraphrased from Freud, *Gesammelt Werke,* 18 vols. (London, 1940-52), Vol. VII, 227-231; hereafter cited as *"GW."*

[7] The same interpretation of *Die Richterin* reappears in a much more elaborate form in Otto Rank, *Das Inzest-Motiv in Dichtung und Sage* (Leipzig and Vienna, 1926), pp. 499ff.

[8] Hugo von Hofmannsthal, "Vom Lesen und von guten Büchern," *Jahrbuch deutscher Bibliophilen und Literaturfreunde,* 1931, pp. 108-127.

[9] See Henel, *The Poetry of C. F. M.,* Chapters IV and V.

[10] Ibid., particularly Chapter I.

[11] Quoted from *Anfänge,* p. 20.

Edward M. V. Plater (essay date 1972)

SOURCE: "The Banquet of Life: Conrad Ferdinand Meyer's *Die Versuchung des Pescara,*" in *Seminar: A Journal of Germanic Studies,* Vol. VIII, No. 2, June, 1972, pp. 88-98.

[*In the essay that follows, Plater argues that the allegorical complexity of Meyer's narratives allows him to represent the ambivalence and self-contradiction of human thought and emotion.*]

This investigation concerns itself with the significance of the frescoes that Meyer describes at the beginning of his novella **Die Versuchung des Pescara:**

> Links von der Tür hielt Bacchus ein Gelag mit seinem mythologischen Gesinde, und rechts war als Gegenstück die Speisung in der Wüste behandelt von einer flotten, aber gedankenlosen, den heiligen Gegenstand bis an die Grenzen der Ausgelassenheit verweltlichenden Hand. Oben auf der Höhe, klein und kaum sichtbar, saß der göttliche Wirt, während sich im Vordergrunde eine lustige Gesellschaft ausbreitete, die an Tracht und Miene nicht übel einer Mittag haltenden lombardischen Schnitterbande glich und zum Lachen alle Gebärden eines gesunden Appetites versinnlichte.[1]

The functions and significance of the fresco with the biblical theme in particular have never been fully recognized and appreciated. Scholars have pointed out, it is true, how both frescoes reflect the historical period in which the novella is set, the late Italian Renaissance. Marianne Burkhard, for example, states that the superficial and intentionally frivolous parallels between the Bacchanalian revel and the feeding of the multitude in the wilderness reflect the moral and ethical bankruptcy of the Italians, for whom the divine is no longer a mysterious power operative in man's soul, but has been reduced "zu jederzeit verfügbaren Requisiten des Kunstverstandes." These Italians, she continues, cannot appreciate moral values with all their heart and soul but only in a detached way, as an aesthetic experience.[2]

A somewhat different emphasis is given the frescoes by Louis Wiesmann, who points out how their significance shifts in the course of the narrative. He maintains that the dominant spirit of worldly merriment in both frescoes is echoed in the first half of the novella, where the author focuses on the here-and-now and on the villainous undertaking in which the pagan conspirators are engaged. The divine element, on the other hand, which is so minute and distant in the fresco with the biblical theme, gradually moves closer in the second half of the novella as Pescara's end approaches.[3] William D. Williams also points out that the two frescoes reflect the mixture of the worldly and the divine in the story. He makes the additional observation that the fresco with the multitude resembling a band of reapers introduces a grim reminder of death into the midst of gaiety and worldly pursuits.[4] Finally, Henry H.H. Remak dismisses the frescoes as mere allegories, whose meanings are shallow and obvious.[5] I agree with the observations of all but the last-mentioned critic but believe that the frescoes do much more than reflect in a general way the moral and intellectual atmosphere of the

historical period and introduce a vague hint of death. I hope to show that the fresco of the feeding of the multitude in the wilderness, with which the following discussion will be chiefly concerned, is far more complex in its functions and significance than has been noted before, that it is in fact a central anticipatory device, an intricate allegory, and a variation of one of Meyer's complex symbolic motifs. Let us approach the fresco first as an anticipatory device.

One type of anticipation consists of referring to something outside the story—some momentous historical juncture, for example, or a legendary hero, a fictional event, and so on. Such a reference may, for a variety of reasons, strike the reader's curiosity and arouse in him the suspicion that the author had a hidden motive for introducing it into the text, that it may, in fact, point ahead to something which occurs later in the narrative. The effectiveness of such anticipation depends, of course, on the reader's knowledge of the extraneous person or event but also on how greatly it strikes and holds his attention. If in the present case the reader is acquainted with the biblical story of the feeding of the multitude, its relevance to Meyer's story, though not immediately evident, will become increasingly clear to him as he proceeds in his reading. A comparison of the fresco of the feeding of the multitude with another comprehensive prefiguration, the stucco relief of the sacrifice of Isaac by Abraham at the beginning of **Gustav Adolfs Page,** will illustrate this point: "Kaum aber hatte er [Leubelfing's father] die wenigen Zeilen des in königlicher Kürze verfaßten Schreibens überflogen, wurde er bleich wie über ihm die Stukkatur der Decke, welche in hervorquellenden Massen und aufdringlicher Gruppe die Opferung Isaaks durch den eigenen Vater Abraham darstellte" (XI, 167).

The contexts of the two works of art are similar. In both novellas the characters are presented going over lists of financial figures; and in both cases the reader's attention is drawn to the art works when the characters look up, in desperation, as though to escape from the pressing crises which threaten to destroy them. In **Gustav Adolfs Page** the reader is immediately alerted to the possibility of the presence of foreshadowing, for the potential parallel between the sacrifice of Isaac by his own father and Leubelfing's vainglorious and impulsive declaration that his fainthearted son longed to serve as the King's page is at once obvious. Partial confirmation of the stucco relief as an anticipatory device at the end of the first chapter, when Gustel agrees at the last moment to respond to the King's request in her cousin's place—just as the sacrifice of Isaac was halted at the last moment and a ram offered in his place—encourages speculation that the parallel to the biblical story will continue. The slaying of the substituted animal in the Bible prepares the reader to expect the death of Gustel. Thus the ceiling decoration of the sacrifice of Isaac impends ominously over the entire novella.

In *Die Versuchung des Pescara,* on the other hand, the possible relevance of the fresco to the story is not immediately apparent but only gradually suggests itself as the story progresses and the parallels between Pescara and Christ increase. The earliest hints that Pescara is to be associated with the figure of Christ in the fresco are at best tenuous. Perhaps the least obscure ones are the title of the novella, which might suggest to the reader the temptation of Christ in the wilderness, and the reference in the first chapter to Pescara's spear wound, which might bring to mind that on the cross Christ's side was pierced by a soldier's spear (John 19:34). Actually the association of Pescara with Christ does not become insistent until the vision which Pescara's wife Victoria experiences toward the end of the second chapter. Moreover, the fresco of the feeding of the multitude is overshadowed and obscured shortly after it is described by the introduction of a work of art whose potential relevance to the plot is far more obvious, the painting of Pescara and Victoria at a game of chess.

Nevertheless, the biblical story of the feeding of the multitude does have much in common with the story of Pescara, and Meyer's reference to it at the start of his narrative is therefore anticipatory, even though this aspect of the fresco may not be detected immediately by the reader. There is first of all a foreshadowing parallel between the crowds that follow Christ about (Mark 6:33-4) and the people all over Italy who are keenly interested in whether Pescara will defect from the Emperor and assume command of the forces of the Holy League. The compassion which Christ shows toward the multitude, both by healing and by providing food for them, is echoed by the compassion which Pescara demonstrates toward Italy.[6] Pescara's silence in regard to his "identity," that is, in regard to whether his features are "die eines Italieners oder die eines Spaniers" (XIII, 165), parallels Christ's admonition to his disciples after the miraculous feeding of the multitude that they not betray his identity (Luke 9:18-21). Still another similarity between the biblical accounts of the event depicted by the fresco and the story of Pescara consists in the rejection by both Christ and Pescara of worldly enticements. Just as Christ flees from the multitude when he sees that they wish to make him a king (John 6:14-15), so Pescara rejects the Holy League's attempt to entice him with the "Fabel- und Traumkrone von Italien" (XIII, 170). Finally, that Christ begins to foretell his passion after the feeding of the multitude (Luke 9:22, 44-5) is echoed in Meyer's story by Pescara's hints, usually uncomprehended or unregarded by the other characters, of his approaching death.

In spite of all these parallels, however, it cannot be overlooked that the most important and obvious element of the biblical story, the miracle that Christ works, finds no echo in *Die Versuchung des Pescara.* The liberation of the Italian states, the "miracle" that the Italians hope for from Pescara, does not take place. Thus the reader who detects the anticipatory nature of the reference to the feeding of the multitude and looks for the parallel to be completed will be disappointed. If, however, the reader also takes into consideration the fresco itself, and not only the biblical accounts of the event it depicts, he will not be misled. A careful examination of the fresco reveals it to be a meticulously devised allegory in which the basic situation, the general plot, and the outcome of the novella are all prefigured.

The term "allegory" may be defined as a "form of extended metaphor in which objects and persons in a narrative . . . are equated with meanings that lie outside the narrative itself."[7] The key to the interpretation of the fresco as an allegory lies in the detail on which the Duke's eyes come to rest when he looks up from the distressing list of expenses incurred in the fortifying of Milan:

> Der Blick des Herzogs und der demselben aufmerksam folgende seines Kanzlers fielen auf ein schäkerndes Mädchen, das, einen großen Korb am Arme, wohl um die überbleibenden Brocken zu sammeln, sich von dem neben ihr gelagerten Jüngling umfangen und einen gerösteten Fisch zwischen das blendend blanke Gebiß schieben ließ. 'Die da wenigstens verhungert noch nicht,' scherzte der Kanzler mit mutwilligen Augen" (XIII, 151).

The roasted fish which the young man playfully stuffs into the girl's mouth establishes at least a tentative link with the title character of the story, for the Spanish word for "to fish," *pescar,* suggests his name. Once this association is established, we may proceed to the question of the meaning to be attached to the young couple in the detail. A partial answer to this question is provided by the description of the group representing the multitude as resembling a band of Lombardic reapers taking a noonday rest. The traditional association of the reaper with both ripeness and death might come to mind. One need not adduce evidence from outside the text, however, in order to establish this association. Pescara's reference to his "Todesengel" as the "Schnitter" (XIII, 252) and the circumstance that he is overtaken by death in the prime of life make both aspects of the motif sufficiently clear.[8] It would seem, then, that the couple in the foreground of the fresco— both reapers—is to be associated somehow with ripeness or death or a combination of the two. Another factor to be considered is the relationship in which the couple is depicted. The comportment of the young man, his amorous advances toward the girl, is echoed in the story by Italy's posture with respect to Pescara, by the efforts of the Holy League to woo him away from the Emperor. Meyer encourages this interpretation when he has Pescara refer to the Italians as being in a sense dead, thus giving explicit support for the identification of the Italians with the reaper: "Ich spiele mit Italien, sagst du? Im Gegenteil, deine Landsleute, Numa, spielen mit mir: sie heucheln Leben und sind tot in ihren Übertretungen und Sünden" (XIII, 224).

If the male reaper represents Italy, or more specifically the Holy League, then perhaps the other reaper in the detail, the young, flirtatious girl, represents Pescara's wife, Victoria Colonna, who is courted by the Holy League in the person of its head, Pope Clemens, one of its principal advocates, Girolamo Morone, and its chief propagandist, Aretino, all of whom hope to persuade her to attempt to win over her husband to their cause. Two factors, however, discourage this line of reasoning: neither the coquetry of the girl in the fresco nor the meaning of death attached to her by virtue of her resemblance to a reaper apply to Victoria. But whom else in the story could this female allegorical figure represent? The answer, in the words of Morone, appears to be: "Pescara, ihn selber!" (XIII, 168). Again Meyer has his title character furnish evidence that this is his intent: " ' . . . Und ich habe das Leben geheuchelt, so gut, daß mir Italien den Brautring bot!' Er lächelte" (XIII, 246). The situation in which the girl in the fresco finds herself, as the object of the young man's bold advances, is the main basis for a first, tentative identification of her with Pescara; the fact that it is a girl actually strengthens rather than weakens the analogy, for it expresses the passive, "female" role that Pescara plays in the temptation.

The coquetry of the figure in the fresco is also echoed by Pescara. It is true, the General does not flirt in the sense of entertaining even for a moment illusions about the course of action open to him.[9] Nor is it his purpose to play games with his tempters, deliberately to lead Morone on as a ruthless joke, only to disappoint him in the end. Yet Pescara does appear to some to engage in political coquetry. Both Victoria and his physician Numa Dati accuse him of playing a cruel game with the Italians, and Morone cannot help but consider this too,[10] along with the possibility that Pescara might after all be flirting with the idea of defecting from the Emperor and offering his services to the Holy League. On the other hand, his request that Del Guasto and Bourbon conceal themselves behind a curtain in order to listen in secret to his interview with Morone, his willingness to let Morone make his proposal, his deferment of a final answer to it, and his detention of the Chancellor under house arrest are all politically wise decisions intended to protect himself and to gain as much information and advantage from the enemy as possible. In making these moves Pescara merely carries out his duty to his Emperor and to himself. His coquetry has serious and respectable purposes, for though he gives the appearance of being interested in the generalship of the Holy League, his motives for doing so are not arbitrary or frivolous.

Besides this somewhat deceptive appearance of political coquetry the secret of Pescara's real position is also prefigured by the fresco. The roasted fish in the girl's mouth, which, as now seems probable, is intended to help establish a connection between this figure and Pescara, also links Pescara with the figure of Christ in the fresco, for the likeness of a fish as used by the early Christians is a symbol of Christ, the Greek word for "fish" forming a monogram of the words "Jesus Christ, Son of God, Saviour." This link is reinforced by the parallels discussed earlier between the story of Pescara and the biblical accounts of the feeding of the multitude, and there are many other parallels between Pescara and Christ throughout the novella which strengthen the link still further.[11]

In the fresco the figure of Christ appears sitting on a hilltop, small and hardly visible, above the merry group in the foreground. Here too is Pescara. The minute size and remoteness of the figure of Christ reflect the apostasy of the Italian Renaissance, this period of man's proud assertion of his own importance and the spiritual defection of the church. In its application to Pescara, however, this remote, almost imperceptible figure suggests the General's already accomplished spiritual departure from the arena of life. That is to say, although Pescara is still physically present down below in the midst of the multitude, his awareness of the approaching Reaper Death has already removed him in spirit from the world of ambition and intrigue, made him immune to the temptations of power and revenge. He is "aus der Mitte gehoben, ein Erlöster" (XIII, 253).

The preceding interpretation has been concerned with establishing the two sides of the equation referred to in the definition of allegory given earlier. It now remains to investigate whether the fresco also functions symbolically. To do this it must be important in itself, for, in contrast to an allegory, a symbol "has permanent objective value, independent of the meanings which it may suggest."[12] In other words, the fresco must seem appropriate in its context, must be so natural a part of the fictional world in which it is placed that the reader accepts it for its objective, concrete reality alone. This condition is met from the standpoint of both the subject matter of the fresco—biblical—and the manner in which it is executed—"von einer flotten, aber gedankenlosen, den heiligen Gegenstand bis an die Grenzen der Ausgelassenheit verweltlichenden Hand" (XIII, 151). Many frescoes with biblical themes were produced by the artists of the period in which the story takes place, and the profane treatment of such themes reflects the historically documented corruption of the church and the widespread non-belief and worldliness of the Renaissance. The other basic requirement of a symbol is that the objective, concrete reality evoked by it suggest another level of meaning.[13] This meaning must be embodied in the symbol or symbolic configuration itself. Thus, the symbolic meaning of the fresco is not to be sought outside of it, as its allegorical meaning is, but rather must be suggested by it.

Restricting one's attention exclusively to the fresco itself, one finds that the concrete reality evoked by its description does indeed suggest another level of meaning. To begin with, the subject matter of the fresco suggests life in the most basic sense of the word: the miracle Christ performs provides the multitude with the nourishment necessary to sustain physical life. The manner in which the subject matter is depicted also suggests life, but life in a figurative sense. The artist, by reducing Christ to a small, scarcely visible figure in the background while placing a merry company of Lombardic picnickers with healthy appetites in the foreground, emphasizes the enjoyment of worldly pleasures, of the here-and-now, and a general disregard for spiritual values. The feeding of the multitude, then, suggesting life in this dual sense, is an objectification of the concept of life as a banquet, which, as Heinrich Henel has demonstrated, is one of Meyer's symbolic motifs.[14]

The attitude toward life conveyed by the fresco is, however, by no means entirely pleasure-seeking and carefree. The threat of death is suggested by the setting in which the feeding of the multitude occurs, the wilderness, with its extremely limited capacity to support life. Death is also brought to mind by the comparison of the merry group in the foreground with a band of reapers, for the reaper cuts down the ripened grain, thus terminating life in its prime.

The symbolism of the fresco increases in complexity with the addition of the meaning suggested by the girl in the foreground, the one member of the multitude whom Meyer singles out for special attention. The circumstance that she carries a large basket on her arm for gathering up what remains of the meal suggests concern at the approach of the end of life's banquet and hope of delaying its arrival. At the same time the girl's response to the advances of the young man is restrained. She does not surrender to temptation but appears merely to flirt with it. Thus while desiring to hold on to life she seems reluctant or perhaps even unable to give herself completely to it.

This symbolic interpretation of the fresco accords with Heinrich Henel's discussion of the banquet motif in Meyer's poetry. Henel points out that the emotional value of the motif ranges from an exuberant desire for a full, rich life in the poem **"Fülle"** to an awareness of the transitoriness of such a life, and indeed of life in general, in **"Das Ende des Festes."**[15] But whereas each of these poems reveals only one pole of the emotional range of the motif, the fresco presents the reader with both simultaneously and thus preserves the motif's basic duality. This duality, this suggestion of conflicting feelings, which stems as much from the worldly spirit in which the religious subject is depicted as from the

contrasting individual details that comprise the subject, prevents one from dismissing the fresco as a mere allegory, a mere equating of concrete imagery with specific abstract meaning. One cannot determine precisely in what proportion the conflicting ingredients are present in the over-all feeling toward life expressed by the fresco. This ultimate indefiniteness, this suggestive quality, is what makes the fresco symbolic.

The relevance of the fresco's symbolism to the story of Pescara is suggested by the following words, recalling the banquet motif, which the General once spoke to Victoria: "Menschen und Dinge mit unsichtbaren Händen zu lenken, sei *das Feinste des Lebens,* und wer das einmal kenne, möge von nichts anderem mehr *kosten*" (XIII, 186, italics mine). But just as death is an ever present threat in the view of life conveyed by the fresco, so it has been close to Pescara on every battlefield and is now, as the result of his fatal wound, an imminent certainty to which he has become reconciled. Yet there are still moments when the will to live flares up again within him—as, for example, when he takes final leave of Victoria—and he would like to be able to postpone death, like the girl in the fresco who gathers up the remnants from the banquet of life. Thus a mixture of the same conflicting feelings suggested by the fresco is also present in Pescara. The feeding of the multitude, then, besides foreshadowing and expressing allegorically the content of the novella, gives symbolic expression to the hero's ambivalent feelings toward life.

Let us now return briefly to the other fresco mentioned at the beginning of this discussion, the depiction of the Bacchanalian revel. The author, it will be remembered, does not describe any details of the fresco. He merely states: "Links von der Tür hielt Bacchus ein Gelag mit seinem mythologischen Gesinde . . ." (XIII, 151). In the light of the preceding discussion it now seems apparent that this fresco too is a variation of the motif of the banquet of life. Unlike the fresco of the feeding of the multitude, however, it is neither an allegory, whose elements correspond exactly to elements of the story, nor a symbol, whose meaning is embodied in and suggested by itself. It is merely a mythological allusion. As such it has little functional value beyond that discussed earlier, namely that it reflects the moral and intellectual atmosphere of the historical period. Like its companion piece it does contain, it is true, a suggestion of death, but this is so obscure and indirect that its foreshadowing force is insignificant. It would be effective only if the reader were familiar with other occurrences of Meyer's Bacchus symbolism, which, as Louis Wiesmann has demonstrated, carries an unmistakable connotation of death,[16] or if the reader were acquainted with the mythological stories of Bacchus. The savage brutality connected with the worship of Bacchus, however, hardly accords with the lyrical, elegiac manner in which Pescara's death is presented.

It is clear, then, that the fresco of the feeding of the multitude in the wilderness is far more significant to the whole work than its companion piece, the Bacchanalian revel. It is a comprehensive prefiguration, a complex allegory, a central symbolic configuration, and a natural part of the setting, reflecting the intellectual and moral atmosphere of the historical period. Of these functions only the last one can be claimed for the fresco of the Bacchanalian revel. Yet as a variation of the motif of the banquet of life this fresco does act in concert with that of the feeding of the multitude to provide the starting point and secret basis of the story of life and death that follows.

Only now that the hidden significance of the frescoes has been revealed can one appreciate fully their appearance in the opening scene of the novella. Suddenly one realizes what an ironic touch Meyer has introduced here. For what could be more ironic than the Duke's finding refuge from his apprehensive questioning of the wisdom of Morone's political strategy in the contemplation of a painting which, unknown to him, has concealed in it the very answers he seeks. And how ironic Morone's feeble joke about the girl in the fresco now appears, when one considers the identity of this allegorical figure and the symbolic meaning of the banquet. Of course, neither the Duke nor the chancellor can see the fresco's hidden meaning, just as neither can see into the future. But their blindness goes beyond the normal inability of man to know what the future has in store, and herein lies the deeper significance of their failure to comprehend the fresco's message. Both are prevented by their own weaknesses from assuming a more cautious attitude—Sforza by his youth and inexperience and by his dependence on the cunning Chancellor, and Morone by his emotionally charged patriotism, his excitability, and his taste for intrigue. They are so blinded by these shortcomings, the implication is, that even when brought face-to-face with the answer to the question uppermost in their minds they fail to grasp it, a fact revealed in the further course of the story.

Basically what applies here to the Duke and his chancellor also applies by extension to us, the readers of the novella. We too must be cautious and discerning, must approach the novella with an open mind prepared to discover just such things as this investigation has brought to light. In fact, we must approach all of Meyer's novellas in this way, for the hidden subtleties and complexities exhibited by the fresco of the feeding of the multitude are characteristic of Meyer's narrative art in general. It is the nature of his creative process to use already existing materials, such as history and biblical stories, and to infuse these materials with the content of his own poetic world. This process gives rise to the allegorical and symbolic configurations which form such an integral part of his novellas. Not all such configurations, it is true, are as versatile in

their functions, as skilfully assimilated to the stories in which they occur, nor as central to the meaning of these stories as the fresco of the feeding of the multitude; one sometimes encounters obvious and irritating allegories too. When, however, Meyer succeeds in his creative process, as he does here, the reader is treated to a satisfying aesthetic experience. He becomes conscious of not only the author's meticulous craftsmanship but also his inner world of deep and ambivalent feelings, which constitute the real life of Meyer's novellas.

Notes

[1] *Conrad Ferdinand Meyer: Sämtliche Werke. Historisch-kritische Ausgabe,* ed. Hans Zeller and Alfred Zäch (Bern, 1958-), XIII, 151. Subsequent references to this edition will appear in the text and provide volume and page numbers.

[2] *C.F. Meyer und die antike Mythologie* (Zürich, 1966), pp. 36-7.

[3] Louis Wiesmann, *Conrad Ferdinand Meyer: Der Dichter des Todes und der Maske* (Bern, 1958), p. 134.

[4] *The Stories of C.F. Meyer* (Oxford Univ. Press, 1962), pp. 152-3.

[5] "Vinegar and Water: Allegory and Symbolism in the German *Novelle* between Keller and Bergengruen," in *Literary Symbolism: A Symposium,* ed. Helmut Rehder (Univ. of Texas Press, 1965), pp. 41-2.

[6] Pescara shows compassion toward Italy when he appoints Bourbon his successor (XIII, 231), when he contrasts Italy's humaneness to the horror of Spain's world domination (XIII, 253), when he refuses to permit a reign of terror to be instituted in Milan (XIII, 226), and when he requests that the Emperor protect Sforza, pardon Morone, and give his command to Bourbon (XIII, 274).

[7] William Flint Thrall and Addison Hibbard, *A Handbook to Literature,* rev. and enl. C. Hugh Holman (New York, 1960).

[8] Still other occurrences of the motif in the novella are given by Heinrich Henel in his book *The Poetry of Conrad Ferdinand Meyer* (Univ. of Wisconsin Press, 1954), where he treats the symbol of the harvest. See esp. pp. 223-4.

[9] His unwavering loyalty to the Emperor and the reason for it are indicated in his words to Victoria: " . . . [ich] habe nicht geschwankt, nicht einen Augenblick, mit dem leisesten Gedanken nicht. Denn keine Wahl ist an mich herangetreten, ich gehörte nicht mir, ich stand außerhalb der Dinge" (XIII, 242).

[10] According to Giucciardin, Morone did, in fact, once describe Pescara as "falsch, grausam und geizig" (XIII, 165).

[11] The spear wound common to both and Victoria's vision toward the end of the second chapter have already been mentioned. Other bases for comparison include the altar painting at Heiligenwunden, Pescara's speaking to Bourbon of his approaching death in the manner of a missionary to his disciple (XIII, 231), and the final scene of the novella, where Pescara's body lies on a gold brocade, his head resting in his faithful friend's lap, a pose similar to the Pietà, as Heinrich Henel points out (p. 223).

[12] Thrall and Hibbard, p. 478.

[13] Ibid.

[14] Henel, pp. 127-34, where Mr Henel discusses the banquet motif in Meyer's poetry. Meyer expressly relates the banquet motif to his own life in a letter dated 22 October 1888, written after he had recovered from a severe and protracted illness: " . . . ich fühle mich doch . . . lebensstärker als seit lange . . . Mir sollte es recht sein, noch einen Gang *du banquet de la vie* mitzumachen . . ." (Letter to François Wille, in *Briefe Conrad Ferdinand Meyers,* ed. Adolf Frey [Leipzig, 1908], I, 197-8.)

[15] Henel, pp. 128, 132.

[16] Wiesmann, pp. 162-7.

Manfred R. Jacobson (essay date 1974)

SOURCE: "The Narrator's Allusions to Art and Ambiguity: A Note on C. F. Meyer's *Der Heilige,*" in *Seminar: A Journal of Germanic Studies,* Vol. X, No. 4, November, 1974, pp. 265-73.

[*In the following essay, Jacobson contends that the narrator's attempt to understand Thomas à Becket in* Die Heilige *exposes a distinction, crucial for Meyer, between inherent and artificial ambiguity in art.*]

The general significance of Meyer's frequent symbolic use of art and artefacts has already been ably treated by Karl S. Guthke. In his essay, 'Kunstsymbolik im Werke Meyers,' he argues convincingly that these works of art and artefacts not only serve a proleptic purpose, but also function as prototypes which illuminate human character and human situations—that, in other words, life tends to imitate art in Meyer's work.[1] This note is not intended either to challenge or to substantiate further this well documented thesis. It is simply an attempt to determine the specific function of two extremely prominent passages on art

in *Der Heilige* that were not mentioned by Guthke and have received scant attention elsewhere.

Hans, the dramatized narrator of *Der Heilige,* makes two references to works of art whose ultimate intent derives from a remarkable parallelism between them which has been overlooked completely in the critical literature. To facilitate comparison and provide a point of reference for the ensuing discussion, the two passages are given here:

> So vergnügte er sein Auge—wenngleich der große falsche Prophet den Seinigen diese bildlichen Ergötzungen untersagt hat—oft an den weißen und ruhigen Gliedmaßen der keuschen Marmorweiber, die er in seinen Palästen aufgestellt hatte. Ihr habet wohl noch keine gesehen. Sie werden aus dem Schutte zerstörter Griechentempel hervorgezogen, und der Herr von Byzanz hatte dem Kanzler für eine politische Gefälligkeit deren einige zugeschickt. Es sind tote Steine ohne Blick und Kraft der Augen, aber betrachtet man sie länger, so fangen sie an zu leben, und nicht selten bin auch ich vor diesen kalten Geschöpfen stehen geblieben, um zu ergründen, ob sie heitern oder traurigen Gemütes sind. (XIII, 41)[2]

> Habt Ihr das aus Byzanz gekommene Bild gesehen, das die Mönche in Allerheiligen als ihren besten Schatz hüten? Es ist ein toter Salvator mit eingesunkenen Augen und geschlossenen Lidern; aber betrachtet man ihn länger, so ändert er durch eine List der Zeichnung und Verteilung der Schatten die Miene und sieht Euch mit offenen Schmerzensaugen traurig an. Eine unehrliche Kunst, Herr! Denn der Maler soll nicht zweideutig, sondern klar seine Striche ziehen. (XIII, 72)

Any attempt at an exegesis of these two digressions should begin with some remarks about Hans who is the source for both of them and whose qualities and attitudes may thus be assumed to play an important role in how the reader is to evaluate them. The consideration of Hans himself is especially urgent in connection with these two passages, for in them he speaks about art and Thomas à Becket, subjects on which his competence and objectivity may indeed be challenged. The published assessments of Hans are many and varied. Meyer's own explicit comments on Hans, although they should not necessarily be accepted as authoritative, are sufficiently helpful to be summarized here. In a letter to Lingg he describes Hans as a person 'der den gesunden Menschenverstand personificiert,' and 'als naiven Augenzeugen eines einzigartigen Characters.'[3] In response to inquiries from Betty Paoli Meyer discusses Hans and his function, stressing his mediaeval limitations: 'Energische Angabe des Kostüms durch ein lebendiges Stück Mittelalter, ich meine den Armbruster mit seinem Vorleben und seinen Raisonnements.'[4] In a subsequent letter to Paoli he writes that, ' . . . der in seinem Zeitalter befangene

Hans nur das Äußerliche der Geschichte, allerdings mit scharfen Sinnen, auffaßt, das Urtheil des Lesers aber über Beckets Wesen durchaus frei läßt.'[5] The image of Hans that emerges from these comments does not serve to inspire confidence in him as a reliable judge of so complex, unusual, and modern a character as the Becket of *Der Heilige.* Meyer, of course, concedes Hans's inability to penetrate Becket's surface, but he does suggest that what Hans reports is at least accurate and objective.[6]

Although in the past most critics have been satisfied with and have echoed Meyer's view, more recent criticism has attempted to revise the generally accepted image of Hans. George Fulton Folkers argues for an extremely positive evaluation of Hans as 'circumspect,' 'devout,' 'pious,' 'loyal,' 'trustworthy,' and, unlike Becket and Henry, embodying 'the fusion of two otherwise exclusive entities, body and spirit,'[7] while Michael Shaw, at the other extreme, characterizes him as essentially base, hypocritical, untrustworthy, and extremely hostile to Becket.[8] A more moderate account of Hans is given by William D. Williams, but he too suspects that his fierce loyalty to Henry makes him unfit to discuss or judge Becket objectively.[9] Good arguments can and have been made for most of the divergent views of Hans set forth in the critical literature and this is a consequence of the drastic ambiguity of the novella. I mention all this only as a reminder that there is no incontrovertible authority or critical concensus to which one might turn for a truly reliable opinion of Hans's character. This makes any attempt to interpret the two passages under consideration here an especially hazardous and subjective undertaking, since it involves speculations on the tone and import of two statements by a speaker whose true character has proved most elusive.

Before attempting to discern the intent of the two digressions when seen in conjunction, it will be necessary to explore their possible individual functions. The occasion for the first digression is the introduction of Queen Ellenor, Henry's promiscuous and vindictive wife. Hans describes Becket's behaviour towards the queen as unfailingly proper, but reveals that he suspects that Becket was actually revolted by her, since what he admired in women were delicacy and decency: 'Der Kanzler begegnete ihr, wo er ihr nicht ausweichen konnte, mit tiefer Ehrerbietung, während ich glaube, daß sie ihm zuwider war; denn er liebte an Frauen das Zarte und Anständige' (XIII, 41). The remarks about Becket and the Greek statues follow this statement, ostensibly to illustrate and confirm Hans's appraisal of the qualities Becket valued in women. While Hans seems only to point to a praiseworthy element in Becket's character, his use of the statues to confirm this is very suggestive and problematical. Had he simply cited an example of Becket's admiration of a real woman who possessed the virtues of decency

and delicacy in a high degree, he would have made his point and eliminated the suspicion that he may mean something different from what he says. Instead, in bypassing the human realm and in choosing to substantiate his claim with an example of Becket's admiration for works of art which embody the virtues in question in idealized form, he opens the way for a variety of interpretations. Hans may simply adduce the statues in support of his claim because no example from real life comes to mind; his use of the statues is then free of any ulterior motive or special intent. Perhaps, however, he wishes to stress Becket's extreme fastidiousness by introducing the statues. Or he may have chosen the statues to illustrate his assertion in order to subvert its apparent praise of Becket by suggesting that he lacks the capacity to respond to real people and can only find satisfaction in art. Whatever Hans's intention may be, his special use of the statues leaves the reader with the impression, which is of course borne out elsewhere in the text, that Becket shies away from contact with real life, that he is an aesthete *par excellence.* Therefore Hans praises Becket in such a way that we are led to wonder about his motives and intentions, and while we cannot determine with certainty what he wished to suggest, a great deal more comes to the reader's mind than he could have intended.

Interestingly, the digression contains a parenthetical remark that essentially parallels the peculiar complexity and suggestiveness of the passage as a whole. Hans comments on Becket's delight in viewing the statues with the remark: ' . . . wenngleich der große falsche Prophet den seinigen diese bildlichen Ergötzungen untersagt hat . . . ' The great false prophet is of course a reference to Mohammed and the implication here is that Becket is a believing Mohammedan.[10] It is not clear whether Hans brings this up simply because he cannot resist the opportunity to take a thrust at Becket, or whether he takes Becket's Mohammedanism for granted and alludes to it here to emphasize his admiration for the statues by pointing out that he is willing to violate a tenet of his religion for the sake of the pleasure he derives from them. Whatever Hans's intention is here, he makes use of the statues to label Becket a heathen. Becket, he asserts, is a Mohammedan and thus a heathen and this view of him seems to be reinforced by his liking for the statues which are heathen art.[11] Surprisingly, however, Hans inadvertently undermines his own apparent intentions by asserting that Becket has to violate a tenet of his heathen faith in order to gaze upon heathen art. Thus the term heathen is allowed to emerge as complex enough to contain mutually exclusive attitudes. It could certainly not have been Hans's intention to point up the complexities and render essentially meaningless a term which he so often uses as a facile pejorative. Once again, and within the same passage, Hans must serve a double purpose: he must act in character and at the same time suggest a different, more sophisticated, and opposite view—

possibly Meyer's own. Even after all these considerations there remains a residue of detail in the digression that resists explanation unless it is viewed in conjunction with Hans's second digression.

A most important event transpires between these two passages: the seduction and death of Becket's daughter Gnade. Gnade's death produces a marked change in Becket's behaviour[12] and Hans even claims to observe a physical change in him, which he illustrates in the digression on the painting of Christ. The mark of death, which he observed on Becket's face when he surprised him leaning over Gnade's coffin, has now become a permanent feature. After describing the painting, he concludes: 'Mit dem Kanzler aber ging es mir umgekehrt. Wenn ich sein Antlitz länger betrachtete und er schwieg, so war es, als schlössen sich seine Lider und es sitze ein Gestorbener mit dem Könige am Tische' (XIII, 72). Since the gist of this conclusion is that Hans believes that Becket is already essentially dead to the world,[13] one wonders whether the relatively lengthy description of the painting was really necessary to prepare for it. Indeed the initial sentence of the conclusion—'Mit dem Kanzler aber ging es mir *umgekehrt*' (italics mine)—gives one the impression that the connection between the description of the painting and the conclusion is somewhat forced; that the author created a reason or excuse to introduce the painting. Thus the suspicion arises that here, just as in the first digression, the narrator's and the author's intentions, which are in no way congruent, may be in conflict.

One of the more difficult and confusing aspects of the reference to the painting is that Hans here juxtaposes Christ, or more specifically, a certain representation of Christ, and Becket. Two factors differentiate this passage from the usual literary suggestions that a certain character is a Christ figure: the use of the term 'umgekehrt' to establish the relationship between Becket and the painting and Hans's negative evaluation of this particular representation of Christ. Because of these factors it seems clear that Hans wishes to suggest something other than that Becket is Christlike. Christ comes to life while Becket seems to die; a positive development in the first instance and a negative one in the second. An invidious comparison in favour of Christ, one might be tempted to conclude, but this cannot be Hans's intention here since it is specifically the painting of Christ to which he objects. Since Hans believes that the painting depicts a kind of false Christ we are perhaps intended to conclude that Becket is a kind of false saint. While we can be quite sure that Hans does not introduce the painting to suggest a similarity between Becket and Christ, from this point on Becket is in fact more and more identified with Christ or identifies with him.[14] Perhaps the digression on the painting is intended as a warning that Becket is really hypocritical. This in fact seems to be Hans's

basic attitude towards him, but the question is really whether the reader should share this attitude.

Specifically, however, Hans objects to the painting's ambiguity and it is this quality too which seems to disturb him in Becket. Thus Hans may simply, perhaps subconsciously, wish to vent his annoyance at being unable to fathom Becket by castigating the painting. Another possibility is that Hans, naive, commonsensical, and intellectually circumscribed, is unable to accept ambiguity in either art or life. Hans's seemingly categorical rejection of ambiguity is particularly perplexing in the light of Meyer's own accurate characterization of the novella in which it occurs as 'absichtlich mehrdeutig.'[15] Even this aspect of the passage has drawn very little critical attention. Faesi dismisses it as gratuitous irony,[16] while Williams is the only critic who has offered an exegesis for it: 'Here Meyer is going out of his way to forestall objections. This altar-picture exactly parallels Meyer's own technique in this story, and that Hans calls it *unehrlich* draws our attention deliberately to it. There is no need to argue whether a distinction is being drawn between what is proper to painting and what to narrative—the artistic purpose of the episode lies simply in calling attention to the technique of the narrative.'[17]

Within limits Williams's assessment of this passage and its function is accurate. Hans's comments do indeed call attention to the general question of ambiguity in art and therefore also to the ambiguity of the novella. Also it must be assumed that Meyer wishes to forestall objections to his use of ambiguity in this work rather than to encourage them with this passage. But Williams fails to point out just how the passage achieves this purpose. Nor does he prove that there is no distinction between the technique of the painting and that of the novella. Both works do indeed make use of ambiguity, but are they, as Williams asserts, exact parallels of each other? Is it not possible that Hans's generalization about the value of ambiguity in art is to be rejected, but that his specific judgment of the painting is completely accurate? This question can best be answered with reference to the earlier digression, for the two digressions are intended to function together to convey something beyond and more significant than what we have seen to be their individual suggestiveness.

The two passages exhibit a sufficient number of similarities to warrant the suspicion that they are intended to elicit a comparison from the reader. The use of the same phrase in both passages—'betrachtet man . . . länger'—not only establishes a link between them, but invites the reader to consider them with special care. Indeed, only when seen in conjunction does Hans's criticism of the altar-picture and ambiguity come to make sense as a defence of Meyer's own technique in *Der Heilige.*

Both the painting and the statues are mentioned in digressions and brought into conjunction with Becket.

Both of these works originated in Byzantium and in both descriptions our attention is focused on the eyes. Although the painting and the statues are executed in different media, belong to two completely different historical periods, and depict totally different subjects, they share one most salient feature: ambiguity. The source of the ambiguity in the painting and the statues resides in the eyes. Christ's eyes are closed and those of the statues lifeless. Thus both Christ and the women give the initial impression of being dead. As one continues to gaze at them, however, both the painting and the statues seem to come to life. Yet, according to Hans, there is a crucial difference in how this is achieved and in the effect it has on the viewer. While the eyes of the dead Christ seem to open up and look at the viewer with an expression of pain and sadness, those of the statues are and remain lifeless. The coming alive of Christ is an optical illusion and, as such, is produced by a trick, 'eine List der Zeichnung und Verteilung der Schatten.' The ambiguity of the work resides completely in the technique. There seems to be no inner necessity for it and it reflects no insoluble mystery. Hans describes the ambiguity of this work as dishonest. The Greek statues are an entirely different matter. No trick has been employed by the sculptor. They are not both dead and alive. Their aliveness is inherent and needs only to be discovered by the viewer. Even after he has made this discovery, however, an insoluble mystery remains. In Hans's words: ' . . . ob sie traurigen oder heitern Gemütes sind.'

Although the ambiguity in both the painting and the statues is stressed, a clear distinction is drawn between them concerning both the nature and the value of this feature. The ambiguity of the painting is arbitrarily imposed from without by means of a trick and is not an organic part of the work. It is therefore explicitly rejected. The ambiguity of the statues, on the other hand, is inherent and artistically true. It is the ambiguity of life itself. The pleasure that a man of Becket's sensibilities and tastes derives from them and Hans's repeated efforts to fathom them testify to their genuineness, charm, and mystery. The two passages suggest that there are at least two reasons for ambiguity in art and, if we rely on Hans's judgment, one good and one bad. Meyer, then, being fully conscious of the ambiguity of **Der Heilige** and anticipating the objections that indeed were forthcoming to this feature of his work, may have introduced these two digressions on art to indicate that he was not purposely attempting to confuse the reader, but rather to show that Becket's nature was itself ambiguous, while the portrayal is artistically true. Only if one accepts the connection between the two digressions as intended and their function to be that described above, can one speak of an effort to forestall objections that might be truly effective.

I hope to have brought out at least some of the possible functions of the two digressions on art when viewed independently and to have shown that, whatever Hans may have wished to suggest by them, they cause the reader to consider possibilities that Hans would certainly not have intended and which, perhaps, represent the author's views to which the reader should give priority. Since the entire story is told from the narrow and biased perspective of the dramatized narrator, the author may or must occasionally intrude in some subtle way and offer correctives for his narrator's assertions. In the two digressions under discussion I believe that we feel the author's presence more than anywhere else in the text. The two passages on works of art do very little actually to support the contentions for which they are ostensibly adduced. Rather, they tend to suggest possibilities about both Hans and Becket that we could not expect the narrator to be able or willing to reveal. Even after attempting to exhaust the possible intentions or suggestions of the individual passages, a residue remains which can only be accounted for if they are seen in conjunction and interpreted as the author's defence of his use of ambiguity.

Notes

[1] Karl S. Guthke, 'Kunstsymbolik im Werke Meyers,' *Wirkendes Wort,* 8 (1958), 336-47.

[2] Conrad Ferdinand Meyer, *Der Heilige* in *Sämtliche Werke,* 14 vols., ed. Hans Zeller and Alfred Zäch (Bern, 1962), vol. XIII. Subsequent references to the text will be indicated by volume and page numbers in parentheses.

[3] *Briefe Conrad Ferdinand Meyers,* ed. Adolf Frey, 2 vols. (Leipzig, 1908), II, 305-6.

[4] Letter of 19 April 1880, quoted by Alfred Zäch in C.F. Meyer, *Sämtliche Werke,* XIII, 296.

[5] Letter of 17 January 1881, quoted by Alfred Zäch in C.F. Meyer, *Sämtliche Werke,* XIII, 297. XIII, 296.

[6] For a full discussion of Hans as an unreliable narrator see Manfred R. Jacobson, 'The Narrator in C.F. Meyer's Prose Work,' PH D dissertation, University of Chicago, 1972, pp. 44-95.

[7] George Fulton Folkers, 'The Narrative Techniques of C.F. Meyer in *Der Heilige'* PH D dissertation, Princeton University, 1967, pp. 98-112.

[8] Michael Shaw, 'C.F. Meyer's Resolute Heroes,' *Deutsche Vierteljahrsschrift,* 40 (1966), 360-90.

[9] William D. Williams, *The Stories of C.F. Meyer* (Oxford, 1962), p. 53.

[10] The novella abounds in suggestions that Becket is in secret a Mohammedan, but usually in the sense that he

has certain affinities or sympathies for the Arabs. In this passage, however, the implication is that Becket subscribes to Mohammed's teaching.

[11] The correlation Mohammedan = heathen and statues = heathen is only implicit in the final version of this passage and must be deduced by the careful reader. Earlier versions (cf. *Sämtliche Werke*, XIII, 331) made this point explicit. For 'den Seinigen' of the final edition, 'den Heiden' had been written, and 'Griechentempel' replaces the earlier 'Heidentempel.'

[12] Cf. XIII, 78: 'Waren aber die Worte des Kanzlers nicht allesamt christlich, so wurden es seine Werke je mehr und mehr.' It should also be noted that Hans here remarks on Becket's addressing the crucifix which he had regarded with aversion earlier, although Hans emphasizes that he addresses Christ as a kind of equal. Thus Becket's attitude toward the crucifix and, by implication, Christ is still ambiguous and this change of attitude does not vouch for a genuine conversion. What has drawn Becket closer to Christ is, apparently, the suffering that they have shared in common. It is suffering that Becket had tried to hold at bay until Gnade's demise proved his efforts futile. He is now ready to deal with this aspect of human existence more realistically.

[13] There is both parallelism and progression in the two digressions under consideration. In the first one the implication is that Becket is removed from life, and in the second that he is already essentially dead to the world. This is just one of many factors that links the two passages.

[14] To cite just a few examples: XIII, 76-7, 84-5, 120, 124, 129ff.

[15] *Louise von François und Conrad Ferdinand Meyer: Ein Briefwechsel,* ed. Anton Bettelheim (Berlin, 1920), p. 2.

[16] Robert Faesi, *C.F. Meyer* (Leipzig, 1925), pp. 87-8.

[17] Williams, p. 65, n. 1.

Martin Swales (essay date 1977)

SOURCE: "Fagon's Defeat: Some Remarks on C. F. Meyer's *Das Leiden eines Knaben,*" in *The Germanic Review,* Vol. LII, No. 1, January, 1977, pp. 29-43.

[*In the following essay, Swales claims that Meyer's* Das Leiden eines Knaben *dramatizes the problem of artistic construction, which, through its very engagement with experience, introduces a certain mediation and detachment from the world represented in the work of art.*]

Das Leiden eines Knaben is, like many of C. F. Meyer's stories, a "Rahmenerzählung," and Meyer spends much

time and space on the framework situation. King Louis XIV of France goes, as is his wont, to the rooms of Madame de Maintenon in the early evening. He complains to her of the impolite treatment which Fagon, his personal physician, has accorded to Père Tellier, the King's newly appointed father confessor. Fagon appears, and renews the attack on Tellier in terms of extraordinary virulence:

> Es war [. . .] etwas ganz Abscheuliches und Teuflisches, was ich gerächt habe, leider nur mit Worten: eine Missetat, ein Verbrechen, welche der unerwartete Anblick dieses tückischen Wolfes mir wieder so gegenwärtig vor das Auge stellte, dass die karge Neige meines Blutes zu kochen begann. Denn, Sire, dieser Bösewicht hat einen edeln Knaben gemordet! (105)[1]

The King, not surprisingly in view of the fact that the object of this onslaught has just received a royal appointment, resists Fagon's accusations: "Ich bitte dich, Fagon [. . .] welch ein Märchen!" (105) However, the King is intrigued and asks who the boy in question was. But on being told that it was one Julian Boufflers, he is disappointed: he has already heard the outline of the story from the boy's father. He knows that Julian was totally ungifted intellectually, that he ruined his health in desperate attempts to make himself learn his schoolwork, and the King therefore concludes that, as Père Tellier was in charge of the college where the boy was a pupil, the Jesuit is, in Fagon's eyes, responsible for Julian's sorry end. And we read: "Ludwig zuckte die Achseln. Nichts weiter. Er hatte etwas Interessanteres erwartet." (105) But the matter is not left there: the King recalls his one and only meeting with Julian, a meeting which Madame de Maintenon, who was very close to the boy's mother, also witnessed. And she reminds the King of the nickname—"le bel idiot"—which Saint-Simon bestowed upon the boy. Fagon asserts that even Saint-Simon would have pitied the boy if he had known the full facts, and above all, if he could have witnessed how Julian died: "wäre er, wie ich, bei dem Ende des Kindes zugegen gewesen, wie es in der Illusion des Fiebers, den Namen seines Königs auf den Lippen, in das feindliche Feuer zu stürzen glaubte." (107) At this—and perhaps particularly because of the gratifying reference to himself—the King's interest is roused, and he invites Fagon to tell him the story.

All this may seem at first sight an over-leisurely—and largely unnecessary—prelude to the events of Julian Boufflers' life which constitute the substance of the story Meyer has to tell. But, on closer examination, one finds that the frame situation plays a role of particular significance in the overall import of Meyer's tale. We are rarely, if ever, allowed to forget that the story of Julian Boufflers is told within a specific context—and with a particular aim in view. Indeed, the frame is the setting for a full-blooded battle of wills, and the story is a vital ingredient in that battle. Hence, the lead-in which I have summarized above is a necessary part in the all-important process of defining the frame situation, of defining Fagon's position as narrator.

One notes in these opening pages the King's irritation with Fagon's behaviour, his insistence that Fagon has overstepped the bounds of decency by hissing insults at Père Tellier: "Er erlaubt sich zuviel." (103) Strangely enough, when Fagon appears, he makes no attempt to be less provocative. In fact, he adopts the opposite approach and seems to be attempting to capture the attention of the King by the very fury and outrageousness of his onslaught on Père Tellier. And Fagon's promise of narrative fireworks is effective: for, while Louis XIV immediately repudiates the accusations against Tellier, he is obviously intrigued in spite of himself—hence his disappointment when he discovers that the story Fagon has to tell is one he already knows. Fagon has, then, managed to capture the King's attention and has, in effect, persuaded him that at the very least the details of Julian's story will make a gripping tale. But the crucial issue is, of course, still left open. Fagon is telling the story not simply to lament the sad fate of a helpless, innocent boy, but in order to justify his dislike of Père Tellier and thereby to enlighten the King as to the kind of man he has raised to the influential position of royal confessor. For this reason, the suspense and tension generated by **Das Leiden eines Knaben** derives less from the plot sequence of the "Binnenerzählung" than from the possible effect which the telling of that story can have on the "Rahmensituation." Fagon has promised the King high drama, a story full of "Missetat" and "Verbrechen," with a cast that includes a "tückischer Wolf" and an "edler Knabe." Louis has already described Fagon's outline of events as a "Märchen"—but he is prepared to listen to this "Märchen" for its colorful events, for its sharply delineated characters, for its simple narrative appeal. Fagon, of course, is after more: he wants to persuade the King that the enormity he is about to recount is not a "Märchen": that it happened in the real world of the Sun King's Paris, that it is relevant to the present constellations of power and influence about the person of the monarch. The frame situation is, then, fraught with considerable political tension: for this reason, the *act* of narrating is as important as what is narrated.

As if aware of the risks involved, Fagon begins by capitalizing on the King's evident eagerness to hear the story of Julian Boufflers and covers himself against possible offence which the story might give. He asks for three "freedoms," for three "lives" as narrator. And the King grants them. This exchange between Fagon and his master has several important implications for the former's position as narrator. The King knows—and Fagon knows—that there are certain limits of decency and decorum which must be observed. In a sense, Fagon's very undertaking is an offence against these limits—because it involves virulent criticism of a decision which the King has taken. However, the device of story-telling does give Fagon certain advantages: it can, as it were, allow him to have his cake and eat it—to both offend the King and please him, to tell a story whose import is offensive, but whose sheer narrative energy makes it a thoroughly engrossing tale. Fagon is, in many respects, in the situation of the fool or court jester: because of the aesthetic pleasure he can give, he is allowed a certain amount of licence. And he can exploit this licence in order to formulate cogent criticisms of his master. But at all times the pill has to be coated with sugar. And there is, of course, always the danger that the monarch will take the sugar without swallowing the pill. It is this tension between narrative (artistic) success and polemical import that gives especial fascination to Fagon's performance within the frame situation.

Having obtained his three "freedoms," Fagon begins his tale. He opens at a leisurely pace with a disarmingly chatty introduction. He recalls to Louis XIV the time when Molière was at the height of his powers. He refers to *Le Malade Imaginaire,* and reminds the King of a passage in the play where a father praises the limitations of his utterly stupid son in such a way that the whole speech becomes an implicit ironization of the character speaking. Here Fagon breaks off and says: "Doch die Majestät kennt die Stelle," to which Louis replies: "Mache mir das Vergnügen, Fagon, und rezitiere sie mir." (109) And this Fagon proceeds to do at some length. The point of this introduction is only reached when Fagon explains how, on the occasion of a specific performance, he noticed a woman in the audience whose laughter gradually turned to tears. Her reactions told him that she had a stupid son, and that her anxieties were being cruelly parodied on stage. The woman was none other than Julian's mother. Only now does Fagon's narration proper get under way as he goes on to describe how Madame Boufflers, shortly before her death, asked him to keep a careful eye on Julian.

The opening to Fagon's narration would seem, at first sight, to be over-long and superfluous. But on closer examination, one finds that it has a quite specific purpose, one which can only be appreciated in the context of Fagon's undertaking as narrator. He clearly uses this introduction to capture the King's attention in the most agreeable way possible. The opening is a calculated piece of salesmanship. The mention of Molière is pleasing to Louis: it recalls happy memories of a much more secure and brilliant period of his reign. Furthermore, it reminds him of something that used to give him intense pleasure. We read that his "Lachmuskeln [. . .] unwillkürlich zuckten in der Erinnerung des guten Gesellen, den er einst gern um sich gelitten und an dessen Masken er sich ergötzt hatte." (109) Furthermore, one should note how carefully Fagon controls the response of the King: his remark "Doch die Majestät kennt die Stelle" implants in the King the wish to hear the passage and also subtly suggests that Fagon knows the passage (but that there is no point in reciting it because it is too familiar to his hearers). Fagon is, of course, invited to perform, and we read: "'Es ist nicht darum,' spielte Fagon den Doktor Diaforius, dessen Rolle er seltsamerweise auswendig wusste, 'weil ich der Vater bin . . . '" (109) One notices the authorial comment "seltsamerweise," a comment in which Meyer draws specific attention to Fagon's remarkable feat of memory. The implications of this are obvious. Fagon is able to recite by heart a lengthy passage from the Molière play for the simple reason that he has learnt it for the occasion, that he has carefully prepared the story he is going to tell the King, and has deliberately made the opening engaging, unpolemical, light-hearted. Thereby Fagon establishes his capabilities as entertainer, his skill as performing artist. And it should be noted that the opening register of theatricality is sustained throughout. Over and over again Fagon does not simply report the gist of a conversation he has had with somebody, but he renders it in direct speech, thus extracting the greatest possible dramatic immediacy from it. It is a technique which reaches its climax at the end of the story in the interview with Père Tellier and in Julian's death. Moreover, it is clear from one revealing comment Fagon makes that he knows full well the potentially critical and polemical power of art, a power on which he is trying to capitalize. He says that he made a point of seeing *Le Malade Imaginaire*—"ich durfte nicht wegbleiben da, wo mein Stand verspottet und vielleicht, wer wusste, ich selbst und meine Krücke [. . .] abbildlich zu sehen waren." (108) Here he suggests to the King something that the latter presumably recalls very precisely: the experience of confronting a work of art which had an unmistakably direct—and critical—relationship to the actual situation of its audience, even to specific persons or classes. It is for this kind of relevance that Fagon himself strives in telling the story of Julian Boufflers.

Hence, Fagon's set piece from Molière has a quite specific purpose. Indeed, when he goes on to report his interview with Madame Boufflers, he also recites her speech (in which she commends Julian to his care) at great length. One notes how he controls the rhythm of the scene changes. He introduces the description of his interview in the following words: "Wenige Tage vor inhrem letzten beschied sie mich zu sich . . ." (111) He then plays the role of Madame Boufflers, ending with her last words:

> "Also, du versprichst es mir, bei dem Knaben meine Stelle zu vertreten . . . Du hältst Wort und darüber hinaus . . ."

> Ich gelobte es der Marschallin, und sie starb nicht schwer.

> Vor dem Bette, darauf sie lag, beobachtete ich den mir anvertrauten Knaben. Er war aufgelöst in Tränen [. . .] (112)

And yet, on Fagon's own admission, there was a gap of several days between these words spoken by Madame Boufflers and her actual death. What Fagon has done in his narration is to telescope the two scenes into one: to make the mother's plea, which is "acted out," even more poignant by the suggestion that these are her last words, a testament made on her death bed.

Fagon then describes the decision to entrust the boy to a Jesuit College and his own careful precautions to make sure that Julian is treated well by the fathers. (Only later do we discover the precise nature of these "precautions"—and it will cost Fagon one of his "freedoms"). We then hear of Marshall Boufflers' successful unmasking of an attempted financial swindle by certain Jesuits, and how this action of his father's makes Julian the object of consistent and vengeful persecution at school. And at this point in the story Fagon begins to introduce a polemical note. Having praised the Jesuits for their pedagogic skill (a skill which led him to recommend that Julian be entrusted to their care), he now paints them in the blackest possible colors, referring to their "verbissener Hass," "verschluckte Groll," "getäuschte Habgier," "entlarvte Schurkerei," to the "feine Giftluft schleichender Rache" (118) which destroys Julian. Here the King raises objections, and accuses Fagon of wilful distortion: "Du sieht Gespenster, Fagon. Du bist hier Partei und hast vielleicht, wer weiss, gegen den verdienten Orden neben deinem ererbten Vorteil noch irgendeine persönliche Feindschaft." (119) For the first time, open and violent conflict flares in the "Rahmensituation."

For all Fagon's narrative success so far—the King has raised no objection and has clearly listened intently—we now come to the crucial issue. And, quite clearly, the King repudiates all the tendentious aspects of his physician's story as fantasies, as "Gespenster." "Märchen" was the word Louis had used initially to Fagon. However much he has enjoyed the story up to this point, the King has neither been convinced by Fagon's onslaught on the Jesuits, nor has he been lulled by the sheer drama of Fagon's narration into a suspension of disbelief. Fagon is furious, and in almost incoherent anger, he turns on the King "und seine Worte stürzten durcheinander, wie Krieger zu den Waffen." (119) Here Meyer reminds us of the desperate seriousness that underlies Fagon's act of story-telling—and of the sheer precariousness of his position: as personal physician he enjoys a certain freedom in that he can allow himself a degree of direct criticism of his master that is quite exceptional: "Frau von Maintenon wusste, dass der heftige Alte, wenn er gereizt wurde, gänzlich ausser sich geriet und unglaubliche Worte wagte, selbst dem Könige gegenüber, welcher freilich dem langjährigen und tiefen Kenner seiner Leiblichkeit nachsah, was er keinem andern so leicht vergeben hätte." (119) It is, of course, this general situation of Fagon's which informs his present position as narrator. He is allowed certain "freedoms," but there is a limit to how many. Furthermore, there is the danger that Fagon is allowed these freedoms because the King does not quite take him seriously: because anything offensive which Fagon says can be excused as an example of his irascibility. Fagon now turns on the King and accuses him of simply refusing to believe unwelcome truths. Fagon's attack here is savage, and encompasses both scathing sarcasm ("Sage mir, König, du Kenner der Wirklichkeit") and the reference to a highly loaded political issue: "Kannst du auch nicht glauben, dass in deinem Reiche bei der Bekehrung der Protestanten Gewalt angewendet wird?" (120) In reply, the King warns Fagon that he has now used up the first of his three "freedoms," but he answers the charge. And Louis' answer is, in effect, an answer not simply to Fagon's question but also to his whole behaviour. The King quite simply asserts his power as absolute monarch: "Es wird, verschwindend wenige Fälle ausgenommen, bei diesen Bekehrungen keine Gewalt angewendet, weil ich es ein für allemal ausdrücklich untersagt habe und weil meinen Befehlen nachgelebt wird." (120)

At this point Fagon has to lose. Once the argument between them comes into the open, then Fagon has no weapons left. The King, as despot, can simply terminate any conversation at will, and can enforce silence on the other. And if the battle becomes a simple—and overt—power struggle, there can be no doubt as to the outcome. Fagon makes one last attempt to prove his point. He recounts how pressure was put on his father to convert to catholicism. He was a chemist who found that the community simply refused to buy from a Calvinist. So, the father abjured his Calvinism, but only to find that his conscience gave him no peace. In despair he hanged himself. Obviously, Fagon's little inset story here has the force of personal experience and conviction. In this sense, it is unanswerable. The King replies by reproaching Fagon with tactlessness and crudity. As he puts its, "unselige Dinge verlangen einen Schleier." (121) At this level too Fagon is beaten. With as much grace as he can muster, he accepts the reproach and "buys" forgiveness by surrendering his second "freedom." Hence, Fagon is driven back to the one weapon he has—his story. His only chance of confronting the King with certain unpalatable truths is by veiling the "unselige Dinge"—veiling them in his performance as narrator. The image of the veil raises what is the central issue in the "Rahmensituation," namely the relationship between the "Schleier" and the "unselige Dinge." One is tempted to reflect that much depends on the thickness of the veil: if it is too thin, then the King will simply know how fiercely he is being button-holed; if it is too thick, then there is the danger that the "unselige Dinge" disappear from sight altogether.

Understandably, when Fagon resumes his narration, he does so with the kind of leisurely lead-in with which he began his story: "'Sire,' fragte Fagon fast leichtsinnig, 'habt Ihr Euern Untertan, den Tiermaler Mouton gekannt?'" (121) We have a lengthy digression on the character and talents of Mouton, liberally laced with flattery:

Hat Mouton die Sonne unserer Zeit gekannt? Wusste er von deinem Dasein, Majestät? Unglaublich zu sagen: den Namen, welcher die Welt und die Geschichte füllt—vielleicht hat er nicht einmal deinen Namen gewusst, wenn ihm auch, selten genug, deine Goldstücke durch die Hände laufen mochten. (122)

This long and harmless prelude leads to another of Fagon's theatrical performances as he reports in direct speech a dialogue between Mouton and Julian. He then goes on to refer to the growing love between Julian and Mirabelle, and to his affection for the boy. On the whole, the material is, from the King's point of view, uncontentious. But Fagon wrings as much special pleading as he can out of his direct quotation of the words the boy speaks. And at one point he quotes his own advice to Julian, advice which, as reported in the present context, represents an attempt to involve the King in a kind of vicarious assent to Julian:

Du gehst ins Feld und kämpfst in unsern Reihen für den König [. . .] Dann wirst du ein einfacher Diener deines Königs [. . .] Du hast Ehre und Treue, und deren bedarf die Majestät [. . .] Die Majestät, wenn sie sich im Rate müde gearbeitet hat, liebt es, ein zwangloses Wort an einen Schweigsamen und unbedingt Gehorsamen zu richten. (139)

This is a very potent emotional appeal, an attempt to achieve empathy between the King and Julian which can then be channelled into disgust at the cruelty of Julian's tormentor. But Fagon is aware of the danger of overplaying his hand, of trying too hard for emotional assent. And he then goes on to describe—and to ironize—his own personal revelations to Julian: "Fagon trug, was ihn vielleicht in seiner Jugend schwer bedrängt hatte, mit einem so komischen Pathos vor, dass den König belustigte und der Marquise schmeichelte." (140)

Fagon then comes to the climactic scene of his story: the beating of Julian and the interview with Père Tellier. At this stage, he has to admit something that he has already hinted at: that, in order to protect Julian, he had circulated the rumor that the boy was perhaps the illegitimate son of the King. Louis is deeply offended, and makes it clear to Fagon that the latter has now used up his third and last "freedom":

"Spieltest du so leichtsinnig mit meinem Namen und dem Rufe eines von dir angebeteten Weibes, hättest du mir wenigstens diesen Frevel verschweigen sollen, selbst wenn deine Geschichte dadurch unverständlicher geworden wäre. Und sage mir Fagon: Hast du da nicht nach dem verrufenen Satze gehandelt, dass der Zweck die Mittel heilige? Bist du in den Orden getreten?"

"Wir alle sind es ein bisschen, Majestät," lächelte Fagon [. . .] (146f.)

This is a revealing exchange. Fagon has given offence not only by what he did—but also by the act of recounting it to the King. But Fagon is caught either way: either he conceals his behaviour and renders the story less comprehensible, or he reveals it and the story gives offense. His only comment is the wry recognition that, in so many spheres of human activity, man finds himself having to compromise over the means for the sake of the end, a comment which also contains a political dig at the increasing influence of the Jesuits at court.

Whether Fagon's undertaking will be successful is, at this stage of the story, still undecided. But the decision follows almost immediately. In his account of the argument with Tellier, Fagon makes no attempt to play down the tendentiousness of his narrative, and at one point he breaks out of the dramatic mode and addresses the King directly: "Ich glaubte zu sehen, Sire, wie Hochmut und Ehrgeiz sich in den düstern Zügen Eures Beichtvaters bekämpften, aber ich konnte den Sieger nicht erraten." (151) Fagon describes how Tellier contrives to slip away, having broken his word with Argenson. This section is the climax of Fagon's onslaught on the figure of the King's new confessor and the decisive point in the battle enacted in the "Rahmen" has now arrived:

> Fagon betrachtete den König unter seinen buschigen greisen Brauen hervor, welchen Eindruck auf diesen die ihm entgegengehaltene Larve seines Beichtigers gemacht hätte. Nicht dass er sich schmeichelte, Ludwig werde seine Wahl widerrufen. Warnen aber hatte er den König wollen vor diesem Feinde der Menschheit, der mit seinen Dämonenflügeln das Ende einer glänzenden Regierung verschatten sollte.

> Allein Fagon las in den Augen des Allerchristlichsten nichts als ein natürliches Mitleid mit dem Lose des Sohnes einer Frau, die dem Gebieter flüchtig gefallen hatte, und das Behagen an einer Erzählung, deren Wege wie die eines Gartens in einen und denselben Mittelpunkt zusammenliefen: der König, immer wieder der König!

> "Weiter, Fagon," bat die Majestät, und dieser gehorchte, gereizt und in verschärfter Laune. (152f.)

The outcome of the struggle is clear: Fagon has, quite simply, lost. Louis, we are told, is impressed by the story, he is moved by what he has heard. But his response does not go beyond pity for Julian: the social and political implications of the story do not strike home. Furthermore, the King's pleasure in the tale is not without its selfish features: it is even implied that such pity as he feels for Julian is to a certain extent dependent on the fact that he found the boy's mother particularly attractive. In E.T.A. Hoffmann's story *Das Fräulein von Scudéry,* Louis XIV is so moved by the resemblance between a young girl and a previous mistress of his that he exercises his prerogative of royal pardon. In Hoffmann's story there is a resolution, a "happy ending," although the process by which this is brought about means that the conclusion is particularly precarious and tentative. But in Meyer's story, not even a tentative "happy ending" is possible. Moreover, it is made clear that one of the chief sources of the King's involvement in the story is the fact that it by implication appeals to his vanity, that he finds himself to be the unspoken center of all the events which are reported. The King has, then, been moved by the pathos of Fagon's narration, by its nostalgic appeal, by its flattery—but there is no more to it than this. He has, as it were, swallowed the sugar coating, but rejected the unpalatable center. And he forces Fagon into the uncontentious role of royal entertainer. He orders him to continue with the story, and Fagon has no option but to obey. A few minutes later, Dubois, a servant, comes in to announce that dinner is served: the King chides him—"Du störst, Dubois"—and the latter leaves "mit einem leisen Ausdrucke des Erstaunens in den geschulten Mienen, denn der König war die Pünktlichkeit selber." (153) In this little incident we sense that something remarkable has happened: King Louis XIV is so caught up in the story of Julian Boufflers that he breaks with his deeply ingrained habit of dining punctually. As story-teller, Fagon could hardly ask for a higher tribute to his narrative powers: but it is an achievement that succeeds brilliantly on all levels but the one which matters most.[2] It is significant that, at this crucial point in the story, Meyer should add a particularly telling authorial comment: he says that Fagon knew that nothing would induce the King to revoke his nomination of Tellier, but that he, Fagon, simply wanted to warn his master "vor diesem Feinde der Menschheit, der mit seinen Dämonenflügeln das Ende einer glänzenden Regierung verschatten sollte." (153) What Meyer adds here is the uniquely authorial perspective of historical hindsight: the modal verb "sollte" gives authoritative assent to the rightness of Fagon's understanding of the political situation, and underlines the desperate seriousness of what he attempts in his narration. Until this point in the story, we the readers cannot be sure how right Fagon is: we are made consistently aware of his dislike of the Jesuits, of his especial hatred for Père Tellier, but we have no means of knowing how far this is personal prejudice, and how far it is genuine insight into an objective danger in the real social world. But when it finally comes, Meyer's all-important endorsement of Fagon's aim coincides with the clear statement of Fagon's failure to achieve that aim. And this gives bitterness and poignancy to the end of the story.

Fagon now concludes his narration swiftly. He recounts the gradual deterioration of the boy's condition, his delirium and death. The polemic is as strong as ever, but it is, as we now know, a polemic to no avail. Even the reference to Julian's agony at the hands of Père Tellier as "das Golgotha bei den Jesuiten" (156) is presumably reduced, in the King's mind, to a vivid figure of speech which adds color and urgency to the narrative but which is bereft of any capacity to shock. The story closes as follows:

> Fagon hatte geendet und erhob sich. Die Marquise war gerührt.

> "Armes Kind!" seufzte der König und erhob sich gleichfalls.

> "Warum arm," fragte Fagon heiter, "da er hingegangen ist als ein Held?" (157)

The King sighs and expresses his pity for Julian—and in so doing, expresses once again his refusal to draw any conclusion from the events he has heard. There is no blame to be apportioned, no action to be taken, no lesson to be learnt. Fagon has been kept firmly in the role of entertainer. And he has no option at the end of the story but to accept that role. His last words, we are told, are "heiter" in tone. He can only conclude on a register of harmlessness, a register that removes all sting from his narration. The tone may be "heiter," but the import of his last words is anything but conciliatory. He asserts that Julian died like a hero, that his was, in effect, a martyr's death. And Julian is martyred by political intrigue, by the corrupt manipulations of the world of the Sun King's court.

While in specific terms Fagon's narration is a denunciation of the Jesuits, in a more general sense it offers a devastating picture of life at court. The court has no place for a Julian or for those like him. Of Mirabelle we are told: "die Luft, die sie aushaucht ist reiner als die, welche sie einatmet," (133) and her innocence is the measure of her unacceptability to the world in which she finds herself. Fagon's passionate involvement with Julian leads him to a total devaluation of all that Louis XIV's court stands for. When he goes to Versailles on the day of Julian's death, Fagon finds the following figures together:

> In Versailles [. . .] fand ich den Marschall tafelnd mit einigen seiner Standesgenossen. Da war Villars, jeder Zoll ein Prahler, ein Heros, wie man behauptet und ich nicht widerspreche, und der unverschämteste Bettler, wie du ihn kennst, Majestät; da war Villeroy, der Schlachtenverlierer, der nichtigste der Sterblichen, der von den Abfällen deiner Gnade lebt, mit seinem unzerstörlichen Dünkel und seinen grossartigen Manieren; Grammont mit dem vornehmen Kopfe, der mich gestern in deinem Saale, Majestät, und an deinen Spieltischen mit gezeichneten Karten betrogen hat, und Lauzun, der unter seiner sanften Miene gründlich Verbitterte und Boshafte. Vergib, ich sah deine Höflinge verzerrt im grellen Lichte meiner Herzensangst. (153f.)

Fagon apologizes for this description, and attributes it to his fear for Julian's health. But the disclaimer is clearly only a tactful manoeuvre, because there is a sense in which the "Verzerrung" is not wilful distortion, but is profoundly revelatory. It is this disillusioned—and disillusioning—perspective that obtains throughout Fagon's passionate narration, that accounts for its overt theatricality and special pleading. It is also, we remember, the perspective of Molière's art as Fagon describes it, an art that works with "grellen Lampen und den verzerrten Gesichtern der auf die Bühne gebrachten Gegenwart." (108) For Fagon—and for any who are prepared to share his "Herzensangst" at the fate of Julian—society is a jungle made up of, at best, indifference, and, at worst, unadulterated malice. What Fagon's story offers the King is not simply "die ihm entgegengehaltene Larve seines Beichtigers," (152f.) but the distorted yet revealing mask of the world over which he presides. The harsh illumination of the "grellen Lampen" of Molière's art becomes the savage narrative viewpoint of Fagon. But the only response this elicits from the King is pity for the individual who is destroyed by the social machinery. There is no critical awareness of this machinery as such, nor, of course, of the position of its lynch-pin, "der König, immer wieder der König." (153)

At one point in **Das Leiden eines Knaben,** Fagon comes across a sketch done by Mouton the painter, and he describes it as follows:

> Ich studierte das Blatt, welches die wunderliche Parodie einer ovidschen Szene enthielt: jener, wo Pentheus rennt, von den Mänaden gejagt, und Bacchus, der grausame Gott, um den Flüchtenden zu verderben, ein senkrechtes Gebirge vor ihm in die Höhe wachsen lässt. Wahrscheinlich hatte Mouton den Knaben, der zuweilen seinen Aufgaben in der Malkammer oblag, die Verse Ovids mühselig genug übersetzen hören und daraus seinen Stoff geschöpft. Ein Jüngling, unverkennbar Julian in allen seinen Körperformen [. . .] ein schlanker Renner, floh, den Kopf mit einem Ausdrucke tödlicher Angst nach ein paar ihm nachjagenden Gespenstern umgewendet. Keine Bacchantinnen [. . .]—eines dieser Scheusale trug einen langen Jesuitenhut auf dem geschorenen Schädel und einen Folianten in der Hand [. . .] (135)

The painting can, in my view, be seen as a kind of cipher for Conrad Ferdinand Meyer's art. All Meyer's "Novellen" have an historical setting. And this fact has given rise to certain commonplaces about his work. Most obviously, there is the frequently made generalization that Meyer himself was a desperately nervous and insecure person who sought refuge in the past and turned, for this reason, to the historical "Novelle." The danger of this argument is that it implies a certain facile escapism on Meyer's part, and often leads to a misreading of his work. One cannot, for example, help feeling that if Meyer had wanted a refuge from present turmoil and distress, he could have chosen his sanctuaries rather better than he did. His stories are almost without exception concerned with bloodshed, violence, intrigue, betrayal. Furthermore, while there may be a certain truth in the arguments of both Leo Löwenthal and Jost Hermand that Meyer's work is the perfect expression of "gründerzeitlich" monumentalism,[3] yet it seems to me that in his finest work he is concerned not with celebrating unequivocally the great historical figure, the sharply profiled man of destiny, but rather with unmasking history, with showing the great historical age as a largely squalid and malignant confusion. Meyer himself commented on his relationship as creative writer to the past in the following terms:

> Je me sers de la nouvelle historique purement et simplement pour y loger mes expériences et mes sentiments personnels, la préférant au "Zeitroman" parce qu'elle masque mieux et qu'elle distance davantage le lecteur. Ainsi, sous une forme très objective et éminément artistique, je suis au dedans tout individuel et subjectif. Dans tous les personnages du *Pescare,* même dans ce vilain Moroni, il y a du C.F.M.[4]

Here Meyer himself talks of the historical "Novelle" as something that conceals his own persona, that distances the reader. But he goes on to lay particular stress on the *artistic* gain of this distance: he says that his work is intensely personal, but that the historical "Novelle" allows him a re-working of these experiences that is "éminément artistique." The distance Meyer gains by his use of history, then, is aesthetic distance: it is not the distance of escapist evasion. And, similarly, the distance which Mouton gains by basing his picture of Julian on a scene from Ovid is the distance of controlled artistic illumination and statement.

Meyer often makes particularly elaborate use of the frame technique. This, too, it has often been suggested, is symptomatic of his attempt to escape his problematic self, to keep even the act of narrating separate from his own persona. But this argument does not account for the use of the fully developed "Rahmensituation." Why should he bother to create not only a fictitious narrator but also a fictitious audience? The answer, in my view, lies in the fact that the nature of art itself is a central thematic preoccupation within his greatest "Rahmenerzählungen." Over and over again he shows himself to be acutely aware of the nature of his own artistic creations. In a letter he speaks of "mein starkes Stilisieren,"[5] and the influence of the plastic arts on his technique—his fondness for the denotative tableau—has often been commented upon. Elsewhere he writes: "am liebsten vertiefe ich mich in vergangene Zeiten, [. . .] die mir erlauben, das Ewig-Menschliche künstlerischer zu behandeln, als die brutale Aktualität zeitgenössischer Stoffe mir nicht gestatten würde."[6] Art,

then, implies interperative control, implies a degree of distance from the material to be treated. In history Meyer finds the artistically manageable correlative for his own problems and anxieties. And the presence of a developed "Rahmensituation" makes the nature of artistic achievement a manifest thematic presence in the work as a whole.

In one of his finest stories, *Die Hochzeit des Mönchs,* Meyer uses the "Rahmen" in order to ask what impact the narrative interpretation of a specific world can have on an audience that inhabits that world. Both Fagon's and Dante's narrations have a formal and interpretative control that derives from the careful artistic shaping of material. (The same is true of the stylization of Mouton's painting). And in both stories, the "Rahmensituation" shows what the audience makes of this kind of art. Both Fagon's and Dante's stories are, by implication, savage indictments of the society to which they are told: their artistic sharpness is the measure of their interpretative energy. But in both cases, the society does not heed the image of itself which the narrators give. It ignores the voice of Dante, the "Wanderer durch die Hölle"[7] (and the Hell referred to is not only the *Inferno* but also the world which Dante recreates before the eyes of Cangrande and his courtiers); it ignores the voice of Fagon, the physician who diagnoses the sickness of Louis XIV's court. It is not that the social world refuses to listen to what Fagon and Dante recount: the audience follows with rapt attention, but with an attention that degrades both narrators to entertainers. At the end of *Die Hochzeit des Mönchs* Dante takes his leave of Cangrande's court with words which, in essence, could have come from Fagon: "Ich habe meinen Platz am Feuer bezahlt."[8] The court audience enjoys the entertainment afforded by a narrative *tour de force:* but there is no more to it than this. Both rulers—Cangrande and Louis XIV—are flattered by what they hear. But the implications are lost on them. In these two stories Meyer uses the "Rahmen" to express devastating doubts about the value of art, about its ability to have any decisive effect on the real world at which it is directed. Art can order and control experience, art can, thereby, interpret the world of man: but, in a strange way, art can neither answer nor help towards the solution of the problems which it so precisely uncovers. The clarity it attains remains a function of its specifically fictional existence. As Meyer himself put it:

> Wo die Kunst die Leidenschaft reinigt, d.h. der Mensch sich selbst beruhigt und begnügt, entsteht die Vorstellung einer trügerischen Einheit, während wir (und so photographiert uns auch die realistische Kunst) doch so gründlich zwiespältig und nur durch ein anderes als wir, durch Gott, zu heilen sind.[9]

Meyer's historical fiction allowed him to impose artistic control and interpretive insight on the threatening flux of his experience. But he was bitterly aware that he had not thereby brought a solution any nearer. He knew that art could reveal profound truths, but that there was no guaranteed mediation between the artistic vision and the real world on which it commented so powerfully. And in *Das Leiden eines Knaben* and *Die Hochzeit des Mönchs* he faces the possibility that an audience can listen carefully to a story and can, quite simply, evade the issue with which it is being so cogently confronted.

The implications of this argument are, in my view, important for an understanding of Meyer's place within certain literary-historical developments. It is interesting to note that many commentators have suggested that the "Novelle" is born in the Renaissance, at a time when individualism becomes a governing principle in human affairs. It is particularly noteworthy that C. F. Meyer, who is in many ways the writer who pens the epitaph to the great line of nineteenth-century "Novellen," should turn his attention so frequently to the Renaissance, should go back to the starting point of the genre in order, as it were, to proclaim its demise. Obviously, any such argument, while suggestive in itself, savours of a suspect schematism. But clearly Meyer was a writer who stood in a thoroughly critical relationship to the narrative tradition within which he worked. And this relationship becomes strikingly apparent in his handling of the "Rahmen." The situation of the threatened narrator is one of the oldest ingredients of the "Rahmensituation." In the *Arabian Nights* that threat is execution, in Boccaccio the threat is the plague and the moral and social chaos it entails, in Goethe's *Unterhaltungen deutscher Ausgewanderten* it is the social and political turmoil of the French Revolution. And in all these cases, the act of narration is an attempt to answer a danger, to overcome a threat by the—in both the aesthetic and the social sense—*formal* art of storytelling. C. F. Meyer clearly draws on this tradition in *Das Leiden eines Knaben,* but only to reach a conclusion of disturbing implications for his situation as artist. Fagon's story does not work: it is powerless before the corruption, nastiness, and bigotry of the social world, it is unable to modify the consciousness of its hearers.

At the deepest level, a story such as *Das Leiden eines Knaben* questions the value of the achieved work of art. Formal control is the source of the narrative energy in Fagon's story, and yet it seems to achieve so little: form is not allowed to acquire the status of an unequivocal value. Here Meyer is both part of the late nineteenth century and a precursor of the moderns. In a suggestive essay entitled "Bürgerlichkeit und l'art pour l'art" Georg Lukács argues[10] that many of the great writers of the second half of the nineteenth century in Germany were obsessed by the notion of art as a carefully wrought construct which demanded from its maker the sheer hard work and regular working hours of any other craftsman. Lukács argues that for Mörike, Keller, and Storm, art involved solid workmanship rather than inspiration, that for them the carefully achieved form was proof of the solidity—in both moral and aesthetic terms—of the artist's endeavour. Meyer, too, was part of this ambience, but at the same time he saw its problematic aspects. And for this reason his art looks forward to that work which offers the most radical exploration—and critique—of this ethos: Thomas Mann's *Der Tod in Venedig.*

Notes

[1] References throughout are to C. F. Meyer, *Sämtliche Werke* (ed. Zeller and Zäch), XII, Bern, 1961.

[2] I have derived much pleasure and profit from W. D. Williams' *The Stories of C. F. Meyer,* Oxford, 1962. He, too, devotes a great deal of discussion to the "Rahmen," and insists that Fagon's undertaking is, in the last analysis, a failure (p. 84). In my view, however, he fails to see the implications of this defeat—both for the specific story and for Meyer's art as a whole. I have hoped both to underpin and to go beyond Williams' analysis in this present paper.

[3] See Leo Löwenthal, *Erzählkunst und Gesellschaft,* Neuwied/Berlin, 1971, pp. 176ff., and R. Hamann and J. Hermand, *Gründerzeit,* Munich, 1971.

[4] Letter dated January 14, 1888 in *Briefe* (ed. Frey), I, Leipzig, 1908, pp. 138f.

[5] *Briefe,* I, p. 411.

[6] *Louise von François und C. F. Meyer: Ein Briefwechsel* (ed. Bettelheim), Berlin, 1920, p. 12.

[7] Meyer, *Sämtliche Werke,* XII, p. 57.

[8] Ibid., p. 98.

[9] *Briefe,* I, p. 60.

[10] The study is to be found in the early collection of essays *Die Seele und die Formen,* which has appeared both in the "Sammlung Luchterhand" (Neuwied/Berlin, 1971) and in Volume I (Frühschriften, I) of the complete edition of the *Werke* (Neuwied/Berlin, 1963ff.).

Dennis McCort (essay date 1978)

SOURCE: "Historical Consciousness versus Action in C. F. Meyer's *Das Amulett,*" in *Symposium,* Vol. XXXII, No. 2, Summer, 1978, pp. 114-32.

[*In the essay that follows, McCort traces the conflict in Meyer's* Das Amulett *between nostalgia for an existentially comforting world order and a persistent skepticism regarding the possibility of transcending limited and subjective comprehension.*]

It has been long in coming, but due recognition is finally being accorded Conrad Ferdinand Meyer's earliest novella, **Das Amulett.** As sometimes happens with works whose artistry is subtle, critical evaluation has come full circle. Deemed a triumph on publication for its integrity of plot structure,[1] in the critical canon of our own century the novella fell to the status of an apprenticeship-exercise, faulted variously, even contradictorily, for awkward organization, strained symbolism, hedging on questions of destiny versus free will, and outright fatalism.[2] Sporadic attempts to "rehabilitate" the work,[3] from the mid-thirties through the late fifties, finally issued in a groundswell of positive revaluation in the late sixties and early seventies, a full century after its appearance.[4]

The irony of the critical picture as it now stands is that contemporary critics who have taken a close look at the text of **Das Amulett** and found it meritorious are in no more agreement as to the source of that merit than were the earlier critics with regard to its defects. The confusion seems to revolve around a basic uncertainty over the light in which Meyer intends us to regard his Calvinist hero, Hans von Schadau. D. A. Jackson stresses "the distinction to be made between Schadau's [bigoted] mental consciousness and Meyer's own,"[5] and argues that "Forty years after the massacre [of St. Bartholomew's Day], Schadau is as blind as he was at the time. His creator Meyer has no love for him."[6] Gunter Hertling, on the other hand, tries to persuade us that Schadau does indeed outgrow his religious fanaticism and that Meyer is really portraying "die Wandlung eines orthodoxen Protestanten zum toleranten Menschen, dem die Gnade Gottes teilhaftig wird,"[7] replete with autobiographical resonances. Consistent with this more charitable view of Schadau's character is Paul Schimmelpfennig's interpretation, according to which Schadau's spontaneous acts of generosity toward those proscribed by his faith—his uncommitted uncle, the old Catholic Boccard and the areligious Bohemian fencing-master—gradually undermine his narrow Calvinist precepts, ultimately enabling him, during the civil crisis, to "appeal to Boccard to help save Gasparde 'im Namen der Muttergottes von Einsiedeln,'" this last "a clear manifestation of heightened spiritual flexibility" (p. 190). Finally, George W. Reinhardt takes a completely different tack viewing Schadau and the novella as a whole, along with the lyric, "Die Karyatide," as Meyer's vehicles for an indictment of "French bloodlust as manifested by the Massacre of St. Bartholomew as well as by the excesses of the French Revolution and the Commune of 1871." Between the lines Reinhardt would have us detect Meyer's need to rationalize his own enthusiasm for the *Realpolitik* of the new *Reich*. Showing the French Catholics as demoniacally possessed fanatics "enables the moral absolutist in Meyer to accept the Franco-Prussian War as a Manichean struggle between the armies of light and darkness" (p. 283).

Reinhardt's political extrapolations show the interpretative extremes to which the puzzling character of Schadau can give rise. The question remains: How are we to take Meyer's hero? As reminiscing first-person narrator, is he essentially the same hardheaded partisan he was forty years ago; or have the atrocities he has lived through, committed by both sides in the name of religion, made him more aware of the mindless, mechanical nature of fanaticism? Any interpretation of **Das Amulett** hinges on the question of whether Schadau has learned from the experiences he relates to us. At the risk of compounding the confusion of critical voices, but also with the hope of resolving it, I offer an interpretation of the novella centered on a scene almost all the various readings acknowledge as revelatory of Meyer's intent but which I believe has eluded correct interpretation up to now: Schadau's vision during his night of imprisonment in the Louvre. Close examination of this scene and its function within the novella's inner form will show that the meaning of **Das Amulett** *as literature* has little to do with pronouncements against religious bigotry—or any other moral issue—and everything to do with the portrayal of the characters' varied levels of historical consciousness in relation to their respective roles in contemporary events. This interpretation opens upon a discussion of some of the intellectual issues surrounding Meyer's artistic conception and calls for a general comment on the quality of realism in the novella which such a reading discloses.

The scene in question is brief: Boccard, whose loyalty to Schadau as a fellow Swiss overshadows religious differences, has locked Schadau in his room in the Louvre to protect him from the impending massacre of the Huguenots. Schadau is unaware of his countryman's friendly motives and suspects him of betrayal. The shock of imagined betrayal jolts Schadau into a crisis of doubt and panic. Perhaps the king has gone mad and turned against the Huguenots. Could his warm affection for Admiral Coligny have turned to bitter hatred within a few hours? Worried over these matters and over his unexplained lateness at home, where his new bride, Gasparde, awaits him, Schadau sees his darkest fears confirmed as he peers out through the bars of an elevated window at three sinister figures on a balcony just above him: King Charles, his brother, Duke of Anjou, and Catherine de Medici, the queen mother. The first shot rings out and Schadau witnesses Catherine's "benediction" of the massacre: "'Endlich!' flüsterte die Königin erleichtert und die drei Nachtgestalten verschwanden von der Zinne."[8] Schadau's panic mounts to fever pitch as he realizes his utter helplessness in a situation involving grave danger to his wife: "Das Haar stand mir zu Berge, das Blut gerann mir in den Adern" (XI, 62). Reduced to the desperate situation of a trapped animal, whose instincts of rage and fear merge in the single all-consuming urge to escape, Schadau flails away in vain at the heavy oaken door and the barred window.

To understand the true significance of the vision that Schadau is to have later during this agonized night of incarceration, we must take careful note of the distraught quality of his emotional state at this point, especially its physiological manifestations: "Das Haar stand mir zu Berge, das Blut gerann mir in den Adern. . . . Ein Fieberfrost ergriff mich und meine Zähne schlugen auf einander. Dem Wahnsinne nahe warf ich mich auf Boccards Lager und wälzte mich in tödlicher Bangigkeit" (XI, 62). Hair raised, blood coursing, chills, chattering teeth, convulsions, a sense of impending madness—these are symptoms of a body operating on an emergency level and poised for survival action but to which every path of action has been blocked. Meyer does not present such physiological details simply as strokes of sensationalism to intensify the melodrama; rather, they form an essential prelude to a mode of escape Schadau would never have thought to attempt deliberately—escape from his own body into a sphere of metaphysical truth.

Curiously, Schadau, who is recording these events some forty years after their occurrence "so mein Gemüt zu erleichtern" (XI, 8), tells us nothing of the few hours between his convulsive "tödlicher Bangigkeit" and this exosomatic deliverance. Perhaps the unnarrated interval, during which his consciousness could only have congealed into a numbed despair, is too painful to recall. It may also indicate a transitional nimbus between normal conscious awareness and the limpid breadth of vision to come. In any case, toward dawn it yields to an event that defies all known natural law. Inexplicably, Schadau finds himself back up at the barred window. Peering through, he witnesses a dialog on the folly of religious fanaticism between the goddess of the Seine and a caryatid supporting the balcony just outside his room. There are several indications in the text that Schadau's experience of these extraordinary beings is not meant to be taken as merely a dream of gratuitous "vision" of the *deus-ex-machina* sort, but as an actual out-of-the-body experience (OOBE) leading to metaphysical insight.[9] This phenomenon, akin to satori, mystical release, and similar ecstatic states of consciousness, only gradually is coming to be understood by psychologists; but OOBE's have been spontaneously happening to people both in life and in literature from time immemorial. Robert Crookall's landmark *Study and Practice of Astral Projection* contains hundreds of "accounts of people who claimed temporarily to leave the body, to be conscious apart from it, and to 'return' and recount their experiences."[10] Similarly, Charles Tart, in *States of Consciousness,* discusses "people [who] report existing at space/time locations different from that of their physical bodies, or being outside of space/time altogether" (p. 285). Meyer provides sufficient clues to indicate that Schadau's perception of the caryatid and the river-goddess occurs in just such a state of consciousness apart from his physical body. That Schadau's experience is not simply a dream or a "vision" but a bodiless waking state of expanded consciousness has important implications for Meyer's central purpose: showing the dichotomy within his major characters between historical awareness and decisive action.

One of the typical features of OOBE's is that they are only partially remembered, or remembered as dreams (Crookall, pp. 1, 28, 177). In recalling his experience, Schadau is hesitant to label it a dream, even though his reason has no other convenient category for it. He is intuitively aware of its uncanny nature, since he admits he had drifted "in einen Zustand zwischen Wachen und Schlummern, der sich nicht beschreiben läßt" (XI, 62). This hypnagogic or twilight area of consciousness, when one is no longer awake but not yet asleep, is most conducive to the occurrence of an OOBE, especially when one is self-preoccupied and observing oneself "in the process of falling asleep" (Crookall, p. 19). Schadau is not merely self-preoccupied but obsessed with the desperate impotence of his incarceration. Unconsciously he is seeking the only way out of his prison left to him. The complete frustration of a life-and-death need to get to another location can nudge the psychic body loose from its moorings in the physical body. Without explaining how he got there, since he himself does not know, he says simply: "Ich meinte mich noch an die Eisenstäbe zu klammern und hinaus zu blicken auf die rastlos flutende Seine" (XI, 62). This is no dream, any more than his first glimpse through the barred window at the Machiavellian triumvirate, earlier on. Dreams, even "Fieberträume,"[11] occur during sleep. To assume Schadau capable of attaining sleep in his present predicament is to fly in the face of the most elementary logic of emotions. Moreover, as in reality, dreams in Meyer's fiction—witness Pfannenstiel's erotic dream in *Der Schuß von der Kanzel* or Leubelfing's guilt-ridden nightmares in *Gustav Adolfs Page*—are intimate expressions of a character's deep-rooted wishes and fears. By contrast, Schadau's vision is oddly impersonal; it strikes us as less psychological manifestation than metaphysical revelation. And he is not directly involved in it at all, but simply witness to a dialog between two larger-than-life entities that take no notice of him. One is led to conclude that Schadau's consciousness has left his body. While his physical body remains on Boccard's bed in cataleptic stupor, the psychic body in which his consciousness is now draped drifts up to the barred window just beneath the ceiling. Ironically, the cell from which Schadau is liberated is not the object of his violent protestations but the mortal coil that entwines all men, obscuring the clarity of vision Schadau now attains.

In this radically altered state of consciousness, Schadau is present at a most enlightening scene between the goddess of the Seine who has just risen from its waves, "ein halbnacktes, vom Mondlichte beglänztes Weib," and "eine Steinfrau, die dicht neben mir die Zinne trug, auf welcher die drei fürstlichen Verschwörer gestanden" (XI, 62-63). Complaining of the procession of blood-drenched corpses staining her waters, the river-goddess expresses her annoyance in decidedly un-godlike language, "Pfui, pfui!" and asks her "Schwester" the reason for all the killing: "Machen vielleicht die Bettler, die ich abends ihre Lumpen in meinem Wasser waschen sehe, den Reichen den Garaus?" (XI, 63). The caryatid whispers in response, "Nein . . . sie morden sich, weil sie nicht einig sind über den richtigen Weg zur Seligkeit." At this point Schadau notes, "ihr kaltes Antlitz verzog sich zum Hohn, als belache sie eine ungeheure Dummheit . . ." (XI, 63).

Within the context of Schadau's OOBE it is impossible to know with certainty whether the river-goddess and the caryatid exist subjectively or objectively. Meyer does not elaborate on their mode of existence. They may be archetypes from Schadau's unconscious, projected outward onto the embattled cityscape, since the inner barriers between the conscious and unconscious mind are lifted with release from the body during an OOBE. On the other hand, they may be veridical hallucinations, i.e., objectively valid astral beings that exist in a dimension outside the normal space-time continuum and can only be perceived from within that dimension.[12] It is also well to bear in mind that the subject-object distinction is regarded by mystics as an illusion of conventional consciousness so that the whole question of ontology may be inappropriate. In any case, their function within the narrative remains the same and it is a more complex function than has been assumed generally. Critics have focussed exclusively on the caryatid's ironic remark, accompanied by mocking grimace, about the stupidity of religious fanaticism, identifying this as Schadau's profound insight and/or Meyer's own point of view.[13] They have failed to see that Schadau's perception is here clairvoyant and must be regarded in its entirety as a *Gestalt*. Reducing it to a propositional statement about religious fanaticism robs it of its vibrant symbolic resonances, both concretely visual and abstract intellectual. This means missing the function of the entire scene within the novella as a whole. It is essential to note that, whatever their ontological status, the river-goddess and the caryatid manifest themselves to Schadau as intimately related entities. "Flußgöttin" addresses "Steinfrau" as "Schwester." If we take this sibling form of address, in whatever sense the river-goddess may intend it, as a clue to a dialectical relationship between the two, then Schadau's profound insight takes on a decidedly different cast from the usual interpretation of his moral transcendence of religious bias. In fact, we move out of the moral sphere altogether and into the metaphysical or cosmological. The river-goddess is the spirit of changing social forms, of transitions from old to new orders. Her bloody stream is the violent flux of historical cataclysm. She is the upstart, the trouble-maker, and speaks appropriately in the street idiom of the revolutionary.[14] Her movement is as inevitable as the flowing of the Seine itself. The caryatid is the solid bulwark of cultural tradition. She is not, as Hertling claims, the "Trägerin des Louvredaches,"[15] but the bearer of the balcony "auf welcher die drei fürstlichen Verschwörer gestanden" (XI, 63), hence the "bedrock" ("*Stein*frau") of the established order. Though opposites, these historical forces are nevertheless "Geschwister," each eternally evolving out of the other in dialectical interdependence. Seen together, they embody allegorically not merely the struggle of the Huguenots, bound by particulars of time and place, to broaden the scope of the rigid Catholic establishment, but the very cosmology of historical movement itself. Meyer portrays a similar symbiotic relationship between change and tradition or movement and stasis in the famous lyric, "Der römische Brunnen."

It is not only in their visual aspect that the river-goddess and the caryatid symbolize history as dialectical movement. The very form of their verbal exchange, the question and answer, is also dialectical on the level of logic or thought process. Meyer was certainly no Hegelian; his historian-mentors were, among others, Ranke, an outspoken opponent of Hegel, Burckhardt and Michelet. Still, the dialectical principle, whether in the triadic form given it by Hegel or otherwise, was part and parcel of nineteenth-century intellectual life, and the notion of the extension of this principle from the realm of thought and language into nature and history was in Meyer's time an internationally popular one. It had its ancient origins in such thinkers as Heraclitus and Proclus and its nineteenth-century exponents, even apart from Hegel and the german romantics, in Coleridge, Emerson and the French philosopher, Victor Cousin.[16] Meyer, a voracious reader in French history and philosophy, may well have read Cousin's Hegelian *Introduction à l'histoire de la philosophie,* although there is no evidence that he did. In any case, he makes creative use of the dialectical idea by having the verbal exchange between "Flußgöttin" and "Steinfrau" imply through its dialectical form an extension into the metaphysical process of history, which the two figures visually symbolize.

If, then, we view this scene as Schadau's attainment of metaphysical rather than moral insight, if his epiphany is the realization, not that fanaticism is evil, but that history will take its inevitable course, using human conflict as its vehicle of self-realization, then the caryatid's sarcastic response to her "sister"'s question is a comment on the inability of most mortals in their shrouded consciousness to perceive the true pattern of history rather than a preachment against the moral deficiencies of human character: "'sie morden sich, weil sie nicht einig sind über den richtigen Weg zur Seligkeit.'—Und ihr kaltes Antlitz verzog sich zum Hohn, als belache sie eine ungeheure Dummheit . . ." (XI, 63). It is human ignorance that the caryatid mocks, not evil behavior. It is man's remoteness from the cosmic perspective, not his malevolence, that makes him an object of "the laughter of the gods." The distinction between the metaphysical and the moral is crucial, because on it rests the entire matter of Meyer's thematic and formal intent in *Das Amulett.*

Schadau's insight into the cosmic pattern of history, accessible only in a bodiless state of clairvoyance, is the most dramatic sequence in a novella whose inner compositional principle is the problem of discontinuous levels of historical consciousness. It is Meyer's artistic preoccupation with this problem of human consciousness, cast in its contemporary historistic mold, and not his moral interest in indicting human bigotry, that provides the key to *Das Amulett.*

The rich vein of irony inherent in Meyer's theme becomes apparent the instant Boccard enters the room, for it is at this point that Schadau loses the cosmic vision attained during his OOBE. Boccard's sudden entrance dispels the vision and forces Schadau's consciousness back into his body: "In diesem Augenblicke knarrte die Türe, ich fuhr auf aus meinem Halbschlummer und erblickte Boccard" (XI, 63). Immediately it is evident that Schadau has lost the significance of this rare experience, since he implores Boccard for information regarding the violent events whose underlying meaning he has just penetrated more deeply than anyone else: "'Um Gotteswillen, Boccard', rief ich und stürzte ihm entgegen, 'was ist heute nacht vorgegangen? . . . Sprich! . . . Ist das Blutbad beendigt?'" (XI, 63). Re-entry into the body has resulted in contraction of Schadau's consciousness from the dispassionate, Olympian perception of universals to impassioned, self-interested concern for specific details, above all, concern for his wife: "Jetzt zuckte mir der Gedanke an Gasparde wie ein glühender Blitz durchs Gehirn und alles andere verschwand im Dunkel" (XI, 63). The irony of this last clause is that the first-person narrator is telling us more than he knows. Unlike the reader, he himself has no inkling of what "alles andere" involves. Looking back on this episode from a temporal remove of forty years, as Jackson says, Schadau "is as blind as he was at the time." Jackson errs, however, in concluding from this that "His creator Meyer has no love for him," i.e., that Meyer's chief concern is to portray a hero whose lifelong moral intransigence he can condemn. Schadau's "blindness," even forty years after the massacre at the time of narration, is less moral than metaphysical. The function of the initial frame

chapter, in which he displays a singular lack of sympathy for the wretched condition of the old Catholic Boccard, is to show that his Calvinist partisanship is as much a shroud over his perception of historical movement in old age as in his youth. Having occurred on a bodiless plane of existence discontinuous with embodied consciousness, (his momentary God's-eye view of history) has had no broadening effect on his historical myopia.

In the frame chapter, we also see how Schadau's retention of his narrow Calvinist outlook into old age has assuaged his guilt over the death of his Catholic friend, Boccard, who had helped him and Gasparde escape the massacre. Observing the old man's frugality, he remarks with a sneer, "Rafft und sammelt er doch in seinen alten Tagen, uneingedenk daß sein Stamm mit ihm verdorren und er seine Habe lachenden Erben lassen wird" (XI, 7). Only a rigid Calvinist convinced of the hand of providence in Boccard's death could regard the old man's pathetic situation with such disdain. On the ride home after concluding his business with old Boccard, Schadau is overwhelmed by a flood of memories: "die Bilder der Vergangenheit [stiegen] vor mir auf mit einer so drängenden Gewalt, in einer solchen Frische, in so scharfen und einschneidenden Zügen, daß sie mich peinigten" (XI, 8). But it is not the need to confess and expiate on guilt that induces Schadau to record past events "so mein Gemüt zu erleichtern" (XI, 8), since his religion has provided him with a convenient rationalization for any guilt. Schadau's need for relief is really a need for bodily release, a need to recover and assimilate the lost vision of his OOBE, which has left an indelible imprint on his unconscious. The tragic irony of his "narrative search" is that it yields no result beyond recollection of a "dream" that took place upon his lapse "in einen Zustand zwischen Wachen und Schlummern, der sich nicht beschreiben läßt" (XI, 62). His admission that his descriptive powers fail to do justice to this condition indicates his vague inkling that there is more to the phenomenon he is about to relate than his memory is able to get at. The visual and auditory components of the OOBE are recalled and related. But the immediacy of metaphysical truth and the entire paranormal significance of the event are irrevocably lost to a reminiscing narrative consciousness that remains shrouded by the body.[17]

The split between mind and body, consciousness and action, grasping the pattern of history and participating in that pattern—this is the thematic and formal principle of *Das Amulett.* It appears in stark dichotomous outline when we place Schadau's OOBE, his sole moment of enlightenment, next to any number of incidents occurring before and after it that portray his historical vision as severely myopic: his duel with Guiche and its profound political repercussions to which he is blind; his confident dismissal of his landlord's fear of bloody reprisals against the Huguenots in Paris: "'Habt keine Angst', beruhigte ich, 'diese Zeiten sind vorüber und das Friedensedikt gewährleistet uns allen freie Religionsübung'" (XI, 50); his Calvinist scruples, resurfacing only moments after his vision, about appealing to Boccard for help "Im Namen der Muttergottes von Einsiedeln!" (XI, 64), an appeal he can bring himself to make only after all others have failed; or his bigoted coldness toward old Boccard's misery forty years later.

Implicitly *Das Amulett* poses the questions: Is there some goal-directed pattern informing the chaotic events of history and, if so, under what conditions can men perceive this pattern? Meyer depicts an optimistic answer to the first question but a pessimistic one to the second. The dialectical relationship between the river-goddess and the caryatid reveals history's telic pattern of movement, but Schadau's capacity to perceive this truth only in a condition in which he is impotent to act on it, i.e., out of his body, dramatizes the tragic darkness of conventional human consciousness. After Hegel and Darwin, the problem of discerning general laws governing historical change was one no serious writer of historical fiction could avoid. Tolstoy, for whom Meyer often professed admiration,[18] wrestled with it in *War and Peace* (1869), which appeared at the time Meyer was resuming work on *Das Amulett.* In his paragon of historical novels Tolstoy poses the problem of human historical consciousness in terms that could serve as the perfect thematic abstract for Meyer's novella. Grimly the "omniscient" narrator declares: "nowhere is the commandment not to taste of the fruit of the tree of knowledge so clearly written as in the course of history. Only unconscious activity bears fruit, and the individual who plays a part in historical events never understands their significance. If he attempts to understand them, he is struck with sterility."[19] This is precisely what happens to Schadau during his night in the Louvre. Up to now he has been a blind participant in the pattern of historical events. In killing Guiche, he unwittingly triggered the outbreak of violence against the Huguenots. There he was an *actor* on the stage of history. But as disembodied witness to the cosmic dialog, he is a *seer,* and in seeing, he is "struck with sterility," for his insight is conditional upon the loss of the only instrument through which historical actions can be realized—the body.

The tragic split between grasping and making history is epitomized in Schadau. But, to one degree or another, it is a shaping principle of the other characters as well. The wise scholar, Chatillon, whose sense of history has matured far beyond the partisan squabbling of Schadau and Boccard, is to that extent impotent to act. Historical actions in *Das Amulett* are impelled by narrow factionalism, by more or less unquestioning commitment to either religious cause. Chatillon is isolated by his capacity to achieve an overview of the conflict, to see it in its historical inevitability as a *Gestalt*. His broadened consciousness depletes his motivation to act on behalf of his Huguenot comrades. Despite a firm intellectual commitment to their cause, "doch bewahrt er," as Brückner says, "seiner Natur gemäss den Abstand von den Dingen" (p. 46). His niece, Gasparde, recognizes and accepts his deep-rooted pacifism out of love, though she has no inkling of its source. It is Schadau, and not her uncle, to whom she turns for help against the insulting Guiche: "Ich mag dem lieben Ohm bei seiner erregbaren und etwas ängstlichen Natur nichts davon sagen. Es würde ihn beunruhigen, ohne daß er mich beschützen könnte" (XI, 36).

Chatillon's tragic death at the hands of the rioting Catholics is also, at least partially, a result of what Tolstoy means by the sterility of understanding. No one could have sensed the explosive situation in Paris more acutely than Chatillon. Yet he takes no steps to protect Gasparde and himself from danger. His ostensible reason for staying in the city is that he wants to renew a commitment to his fellow Huguenots that he has failed in the past to uphold by deeds. Even here, however, his words betray rather doom-ridden resignation than commitment to decisive action: "ich stand nicht zu meinen Glaubensgenossen, wie ich sollte; in dieser letzten Stunde aber will ich sie nicht verlassen" (XI, 56). The perspicacious Montaigne senses something of this when he chides the old man good-naturedly: "Alter Junge, du betrügst dich selbst, wenn du glaubst, daß du aus Heldenmut so handelst. Du tust es aus Bequemlichkeit. Du bist zu träge geworden, dein behagliches Nest zu verlassen selbst auf die Gefahr hin, daß der Sturm es morgen wegfegt" (XI, 57). But Chatillon is far from deceiving himself. To the contrary, the tragic irony implicit in his ominous words "in dieser letzten Stunde" is that his heightened awareness transcends even itself: he realizes that his own awareness has rendered him impotent to act, even in order to survive.

Other characters in the novella may also be seen as variations on the inverse proportion between historical consciousness and action. Montaigne and Schadau's uncle both resemble Chatillon in their libertarian social attitudes formed from a broad overview of historical currents. Also like Chatillon, their heightened consciousness keeps them aloof from the scene of action. Montaigne, a freethinker, has left Paris by the time violence erupts, and Schadau's uncle spends his years in scholarly seclusion on the lake of Biel in Switzerland, well out of range of the religious cold war being waged in the cantons. Gasparde and Boccard bring up the opposite end of the consciousness-action spectrum. Though she has little interest in doctrinal matters, Gasparde is a devout Huguenot and shares responsibility with Schadau for the fateful action taken against the hated Catholic Guiche. In using Schadau as her instrument to avenge an insult magnified out of all proportion by her own religious prejudice, she becomes in turn an instrument of the process by which history manifests itself. Boccard is a superficial hotblood little given to conscious reflection. His actions are impulsive, motivated as they are by two unexamined and at times even conflicting biases—religion and nationalism. His resentment of Schadau's Calvinism is mitigated only by his loyalty to Schadau as a fellow Swiss. Aiding Schadau during the massacre he does not reach out to a human being in need but makes a concession to a Swiss compatriot who, in desperation, finally patronizes his superstitious devotion to the Virgin of Einsiedeln. It is "isms" that automatically determine Boccard's attitudes and behavior. His is a darkened consciousness that reduces him to the status of a pawn in the conflict of historical forces. For this reason, he is Chatillon's antipode.

One other character, or rather fictional presence, is vital to the theme of levels of consciousness and to the form of the novella. Between title and first chapter Meyer inserts himself as translator of Schadau's memoirs with the announcement: "Alte vergilbte Blätter liegen vor mir mit Aufzeichnungen aus dem Anfange des siebzehnten Jahrhunderts. Ich übersetze sie in die Sprache unserer Zeit" (XI, n. pag.). Commentators have noted the function of this device as a means of enhancing the verisimilitude and quasi-historical authenticity of Schadau's chronicle.[20] Beyond this, however, the fictional translator serves as a transcendent consciousness, a disinterested point of view located in both a literal and a figurative sense over and above the work, encompassing the limited visions of the characters and, together with them, forms a hierarchy of historical consciousness. This perspectivistic hierarchy constitutes the novella's inner form. One might visualize it metaphorically as a set of Chinese boxes of awareness ranging from the all-enclosing historical vision of the author-translator-(hence) reader through a median area of enlightenment provided by Chatillon, Montaigne and Schadau's uncle down to the smallest, innermost boxes of myopic partisanship evidenced by Boccard and Gasparde. Schadau, as the central character who experiences a radical, though temporary, transformation of consciousness through his OOBE, moves from the innermost to the outermost box and back to the innermost. His momentary elevation to the God's-eye-view of the translator imbues the inner form of the novella with tragic dynamism, for his inevitable return to the body is a return to his role as blind instrument of the self-actualizing process of history.

Meyer's portrayal of historical consciousness over against action as a tragic polarity reflects the strong ambivalence he must have felt toward the prescriptive ideals of his "historian-father," Leopold von Ranke. Meyer read nearly everything Ranke wrote, and we know from his letter of May 4, 1868, to his good friend, the Swiss historian Georg von Wyß, that he

had consulted Ranke's *Französische Geschichte, vornehmlich im sechzehnten und siebzehnten Jahrhundert* (1852-54) as a source for his depiction of the St. Bartholomew's Day Massacre in *Das Amulett*.[21] However, it is less Ranke's historical studies than his historiographical principles that are relevant here. In *Über die Epochen der neueren Geschichte* (1854) Ranke poses a formidable challenge to the historian: "Die Gottheit—wenn ich diese Bemerkung wagen darf—denke ich mir so, daß sie, da ja keine Zeit vor ihr liegt, die ganze historische Menschheit in ihrer Gesamtheit überschaut und überall gleich wert findet. . . . vor Gott erscheinen alle Generationen der Menschen gleichberechtigt, und so muß auch der Historiker die Sache ansehen."[22] Later, in a letter to King Max II of Bavaria (Nov. 26, 1859), Ranke speaks of the ideal that "darin liegen [würde], daß das Subject [i.e., the observer of history] sich rein zum Organ des Objects . . . machen könnte."[23] Intellectually, Meyer subscribed to this ideal state of historical consciousness in which all bias falls away as the historian becomes the pristine mirror ("Organ") in which events are reflected. As Karl Fehr points out, it is precisely such an Olympian posture of "historisch-pragmatische[r] Objektivität" that Meyer adopted from Ranke and claimed for himself as author of *Das Amulett*.[24] But Meyer's underlying ambivalence toward this ideal, particularly his doubting man's capacity to perceive the pattern of contemporary history in which he is himself swept up and then with wisdom to act on that perception, is seen in the tension between intellectual assent and artistic intent in *Das Amulett*. While Meyer, as historical novelist temporally removed from his subject, can answer the Rankian challenge, his protagonist Schadau can only do so by relinquishing his sole instrument of historical action, his body. In an ironic sense, it is only as a bodiless consciousness that either author or protagonist can penetrate the metaphysical meaning of the conflict between Catholics and Huguenots. Obviously Meyer, for whom these events are past, can have no physical impact on them; his relationship to them is limited to the rarefied sphere of authorial consciousness. By the same token, Schadau, though a contemporary to the conflict, is no less impotent to act during his moment of illumination. And his actions after that moment has passed show no trace of that illumination. Both author and character are caught up in the mind-body split.

Even Meyer's intellectual assent to Ranke was not unwavering. Although able in his better moments to affirm a divine consciousness that both viewed and permeated history in its totality, he as often questioned his own capacity, and by extension man's, to rise above the constraints of ego and identify with its cosmic vision. Thus in a letter to his cousin, Friedrich von Wyß (July 27, 1866), recalling the beauty of an Alpine landscape: "so sage ich mir, daß derselbe Meister; der dies geordnet hat, auf dem ganz anderen Gebiete der Geschichte gewiß auch seine, wenn auch für mich verborgenen Linien gezogen hat, die das Ganze leiten und zusammenhalten."[25] This concept of immanent justice, a suprarational sense of the inherent rightness of events which Heinrich Henel has aptly called "a manifestation of mystic thinking in the realm of ethics,"[26] is the informing principle of Meyer's philosophy of history. It is just such immanent justice, the inexorable working-out of the mysterious "verborgenen Linien" of historical evolution, that Schadau glimpses in the dialog between river-goddess and caryatid. The pity is that it is only for a flickering instant of transfigured consciousness that Schadau can, as Henel says of Meyer the lyricist, "surrender to powers (both without and within him) that are mightier than his reason and larger than his conscious self" (p. 68). It was Meyer's ambivalence toward Ranke that generated the esthetic impulse to **Das Amulett**, his attraction to Ranke's ideal of godlike historical consciousness and his simultaneous skepticism of man's ability to grasp those historical currents, and in grasping to shape them, "larger than his conscious self," in which he is bodily embedded. The simple, unalterable fact of the physical grounding of consciousness in the present would prevent man forever, whether as historian, novelist or otherwise, from fashioning for that present something Stendhal, with reference to the novel, called a "mirror of life," reflecting, as it "journeys down the highway," the "blue of the skies and the mire in the road below."[27]

In a larger sense, the ephemeral quality of Schadau's insight reflects Meyer's nostalgia, the nostalgia of a self-designated "Kind[es] des neunzehnten Jahrhunderts"[28] who felt himself an exile in his own time for a bygone era before the all-embracing mystico-metaphysical world views began to be eclipsed by the piecemeal truths of an objective science. Although it is impossible to cite direct sources from this longed-for past for Meyer's portrayal of the out-of-the-body experience, or even to know whether he had any specific antecedent in mind, it is a fairly simple matter to identify various conceptions of the phenomenon from the recent and remote past which he doubtless encountered in his lifelong study of history and literature. One could point to the Platonic view of the body as the temporary prison of the incorporeal, conscious component of man; or the out-of-the-body experiences reported by the Swedish theosopher, Emanuel Swedenborg; or the allegory of Homunculus, the incandescent entelechy in quest of a body in *Faust II*. Meyer was well acquainted with these and other philosophical, mystical and artistic permutations of the mind-body mystery.[29] In his historical sketch of eighteenth-century Swiss town life written for the *Zürcher Taschenbuch* in 1881, "Kleinstadt und Dorf um die Mitte des vorigen Jahrhunderts," he relates an anecdote about an out-of-the-body experience involving the wife of a close friend of the young Lavater that had provided the inspiration for Lavater's first literary success, *Die Aussichten in die Ewigkeit* (1768-78).[30]

Even in his own experience Meyer the "realist" seems to have had at least a nodding acquaintance with mystical states of consciousness. During his recuperation from a nervous disorder in the pietistic asylum at Préfargier in 1852, he had employed some mystical technique or other as a means of establishing distance between himself and his illness. This momentary rising to a less ego-bound perspective on one's own oppressive situation—one way of describing what happens to Schadau—is mentioned in a letter to A. Meißner of November 24, 1877: "In meinen ganz schlimmen Zeiten [at Préfargier] habe ich mich oft mit etwas bescheidenem Mysticismus gefristet und ihn—in kleinen Dosen—probat gefunden d.h. über die Unterwerfung unter das Notwendige . . . hinaus suchte ich im Schicksal, wie es falle, etwas zu lieben."[31] Meyer does not say whether these "mild doses" of mysticism were self-administered during the hypnagogic moment between waking and sleeping, as is the case with Schadau, but we do know from Henel's searching study of Meyer's lyrics that this transitional phase of consciousness, this threshold to an awareness far superior to either waking or dreaming, had a special significance for the poet: "The dream states which Meyer describes [in the lyrics] are complicated by the fact . . . that both the subconscious and the conscious mind are active in them. They resemble the moment just before waking up, when reality intrudes upon the sleeper's visions, when he tries to 'get a grip on himself,' and when he is painfully aware of two worlds" (p. 30). Schadau, of course, is not on the verge of waking up but, conversely, sinking into a kind of numbed hysteria, "in einen Zustand zwischen Wachen und Schlummern, der sich nicht beschreiben rlaßt' " (XI, 62). Functionally, however, the two conditions are the same, each a potential point of entry to a sphere of awareness lying above and beyond the normal waking-sleeping zone. All that is needed to reach this sphere is an impetus, which for Schadau assumes the form of a profound frustration of his need to escape, that pushes him out of the waking-sleeping zone into a bodiless state of metaphysical illumination.

Perhaps the most intriguing speculation on possible prototypes for Schadau's OOBE is occasioned by the fact of Meyer's strong attraction to St. Paul. Although Meyer never overcame his ambivalence toward the dogmatic aspect of Christianity, his admiration for the aggressive confidence with which Paul pursued his mission was unwavering. Through the spring and summer of 1860 in Lausanne, Meyer steeped himself in Paul's letters and in the *Acts of the Apostles,* intending to write a biographical sketch of the apostle.[32] The sketch was never realized, but the effects of Meyer's intense preoccupation with this charismatic personality were deep and durable. The influence of Pauline thought on **Das Amulett,** completed over a decade later, has been observed by Schimmelpfennig. It is an influence that extends even to the language that Meyer has issue from Schadau's mouth.[33] Whether Meyer resumed his study of Paul's letters during the writing of the novella or knew them well enough to paraphrase them in the novella from memory, we do not know. In either case, it is not unreasonable to suppose Meyer was also familiar with Paul's concept of the psychic or spiritual body: "there are bodies that belong to earth and bodies that belong to heaven. . . . If there is such a thing as a natural body, there must be a spiritual body too" (I Cor. 15: 40, 44). And in following the exciting account of Paul's conversion in *Acts* 9, Meyer may well have had a lingering impression of an episode strongly resembling an OOBE related in the previous chapter in which we are told that Philip, after baptizing a eunuch, "was carried off by the spirit of the Lord, and the eunuch did not see him any longer; he went on his way rejoicing. As for Philip, he was next heard of at Azotus" (Acts 8: 39-40).

In its historical setting and its implicit reference to various traditional configurations of the out-of-the-body experience, **Das Amulett** certainly reveals Meyer's strong intellectual and emotional ties to the past. Paradoxically, however, it is this very retrospective attitude that makes the novella a distinctly contemporary work of fiction. Through Schadau's out-of-the-body experience, Meyer looks back wistfully to a time when it was still possible to conceive of the world and history as making metaphysical sense. But the futility of Schadau's moment of total historical consciousness, the immediate loss of something gratuitously attained, echoes a most contemporary nineteenth-century dwindling of faith in man's capacity to perceive himself as part of what Fritz Martini calls "einen gemeinsamen Bedingungs- and Ordnungszusammenhang des Lebens."[34] The fading of a transpersonal vision of life, of a world whose ordering principle emanates from a center beyond the narrow constructs of individual consciousness, lies at the core of German realism. Meyer's portraits of characters who stand at either end of the consciousness-action spectrum, characters who act without awareness or are aware but impotent to act, reflect his own and his era's increasing perception of human behavior as little more than a stimulus-response mechanism, and of historical awareness as having no impact on historical reality. In Schadau's out-of-the-body experience it is as if Meyer is lifting his hero up above the stifling miasma of his belief-system by the scruff of the neck and demanding he see, at least for once in his life, a transpersonal pattern of wisdom informing his own narrowly partisan actions. Through Schadau, Meyer objectifies and symbolically dramatizes his own crisis of metaphysical doubt. But the atmosphere in which the river-goddess and caryatid reside is too heady for Schadau, and the author must soon allow him to be pulled down by the weight of an ego-bound consciousness rooted in the body.

The transitory character of Schadau's historical vision shows it to be an example of what Richard Brinkmann calls the "hypostasierte Ganzheiten" or reconstructed cosmologies from an earlier, more idealistic era that are built into many works of German realistic fiction. Thus do realistic authors take pains to elaborate the limited, perspectivistic nature of their characters' consciousnesses and proceed then to sew these tight pockets of awareness onto the comforting mantles of metaphysically ordered worlds, worlds that are, however, more products of nostalgic longing than confident conviction, worlds, as Brinkmann says, "die nicht aus der erfahrenen Tatsächlichkeit abgelesen sein wollen, sondern nach denen das in der Erfahrung isolierte Einzelne normativ angerordnet wird."[35] Schadau's out-of-the-body experience symbolizes the spiritual need of an author who has "Gottvertrauen, so viel ein Kind des neunzehnten Jahrhunderts haben kann,"[36] to get beyond a historistic world view that is merely hypostasized to one that is manifestly real. It is probably fortunate for us that Meyer never fully exorcized his own demons of doubt. If he had, the corpus of realistic fiction might well have been the poorer for it.

Notes

[1] For a sampling of the first reviews, see the "Anhang" to Adolf Frey's biography, *Conrad Ferdinand Meyer: Sein Leben und seine Werke,* 2nd ed. (Stuttgart: Cotta, 1909), pp. 387-90.

[2] G[unter] H. Hertling, "Religiosität ohne Vorurteil: Zum Wendepunkt in C. F. Meyer's 'Das Amulett,' " *ZfDP,* 90 (1971), 526-45, and Paul Schimmelpfenning, "C. F. Meyer's Religion of the Heart: A Reevaluation of *Das Amulett,*" *GR,* 47 (1972), 181-202, present excellent summaries of the novella's long critical nadir that has extended to our own decade with Karl Fehr's assertion of "Anfangs-Schwächen" in his book, *Conrad Ferdinand Meyer* (Stuttgart: Metzler, 1971), p. 48.

[3] These include John C. Blankenagel, "Conrad Ferdinand Meyer: *Das Amulett,*" *JEGP,* 33 (1934), 270-79; Helene von Lerber, *Conrad Ferdinand Meyer: Der Mensch in der Spannung* (Basel: Reinhardt, 1949), pp. 314-17; James M. Clark, "Introduction" to *Das Amulett,* ed. James M. Clark (London: T. Nelson, 1955), i-xxii; Louis Wiesmann, *Conrad Ferdinand Meyer: Der Dichter des Todes und der Maske,* Baseler Studien zur deutschen Sprache und Literatur, 19, ed. Friedrich Ranke and Walter Muschg (Bern: Francke, 1958), pp. 42, 185; Ipke Nommensen, *Erläuterungen zu Conrad Ferdinand Meyers "Das Amulett,"* 7th revised ed., Erläuterungen zu den Klassikern, 273 (Hollfeld/Obfr.: C. Bange, 1958); and Keith Leopold, "Meyer and Mérimée: A Study of Conrad Ferdinand Meyer's *Das Amulett* and its Relationship to Prosper Mérimée's *Chronique du règne de Charles IX,*" *University of Queensland Papers,* I (1960), 1-13.

[4] The novella's present prestige is largely the result of efforts by D. A. Jackson, "Recent Meyer Criticism:

New Avenues or Cul-de-sac?" *Revue des Langues Vivantes,* 34 (1968), 620-36, and "Schadau, the Satirized Narrator, in C. F. Meyer's *Das Amulett,*" *Trivium,* 7 (1972), 61-69; Hans-Dieter Brückner, *Heldengestaltung im Prosawerk Conrad Ferdinand Meyers,* Europäische Hochschulschriften: Deutsche Literatur und Germanistik, Series 1, 38 (Bern: Herbert Lang, 1970), pp. 22-23, 44-47; Hertling, "Religiosität," and *Conrad Ferdinand Meyers Epik: Traumbeseelung, Traumbesinnung und Traumbesitz* (Bern: Francke, 1973), pp. 73-82, which states the interpretation given in the earlier article, Schimmelpfennig, "C. F. Meyer's Religion of the Heart," and George W. Reinhardt, "The Political Views of the Young Conrad Ferdinand Meyer with a Note on *Das Amulett,*" *GQ,* 45 (1972), 270-94.

⁵ Jackson, "Recent Meyer Criticism," p. 633.

⁶ Jackson, "Schadau, the Satirized Narrator," p. 68.

⁷ Hertling, "Religiosität," p. 529; similarly in his book, *Conrad Ferdinand Meyers Epik,* pp. 81-82.

⁸ Conrad Ferdinand Meyer, *Sämtliche Werke. Historisch-kritische Ausgabe,* ed. Hans Zeller and Alfred Zäch (Bern: Benteli, 1959), XI, 62. Subsequent parenthetical volume and page references are to this edition.

⁹ Jackson, "Schadau, the Satirized Narrator," p. 69, places no importance on this scene and does not bother to identify the nature of Schadau's experience. He is content with the generalized statement that "he [Schadau] glimpses the folly of man murdering man because of disagreements about the right way to salvation." Hertling, "Religiosität," p. 535, characterizes Schadau's experience variously as "Traumbild," "Fiebertraum" and "Vision," which, nevertheless, somehow remains an "in sich selbst realistisches Erlebnis" that is "wirklichkeitsnah. . . . Nymphe und Steinfrau sind für ihn keine Märchengestalten, denn er erlebt sie empirisch: er sieht und hört sie." With less confusion but ultimately no more enlightenment, Schimmelpfennig refers to the experience as a "dream" (p. 190) and as "a religious epiphany" (p. 194). Like Jackson, Reinhardt makes no attempt to identify the nature or quality of Schadau's experience, simply remarking that "The goddess of the Seine rises from the blood-stained river to converse with her 'sister,' one of the caryatids of the Louvre" (p. 283).

¹⁰ Robert Crookall, *The Study and Practice of Astral Projection* (1960; rpt. Secaucus, New Jersey: Citadel, 1976), p. 1. My references to typical characteristics of the OOBE rely mainly on Crookall's study. Readers interested in the results of laboratory experimentation with this phenomenon are referred to Charles T. Tart's chapter, "Out-of-the-Body Experiences," in *Psychic Exploration,* ed. E. Mitchell and J. White (New York: Putnam, 1974),

pp. 349-74, and to Tart's book, *States of Consciousness* (New York: E. P. Dutton, 1975), p. 285.

¹¹ See reference to Hertling in note 9.

¹² Cf., e.g., Crookall, p. 185.

¹³ Jackson, "Schadau, the Satirized Narrator," p. 68; Hertling, "Religiosität," pp. 535-36; Schimmelpfennig, p. 190; and Reinhardt, p. 283.

¹⁴ The river-goddess' slang is a vital aspect of her symbolic function as historical gadfly. This becomes clear when one considers that Meyer almost never allows his mortal characters, much less a goddess, to speak in less than declamatory heroic style. As Arthur Burkhard has observed, "[Meyer] . . . avoids colloquial words, common foreign terms, and the dialect expressions of provincial speech." See *Conrad Ferdinand Meyer: The Style and the Man* (Cambridge, Mass.: Harvard University Press, 1932), p. 29.

¹⁵ Hertling, "Religiosität," pp. 535-36, in support of his argument that she speaks "von oben," i.e., from a transcendent perspective.

¹⁶ Gustaaf van Cromphout, "Emerson and the Dialectics of History," *PMLA,* 91 (1976), 54, 64, provides a good summary discussion of the issue.

¹⁷ Hertling's contention, in "Religiosität," p. 529, that Schadau's vision transforms him from doctrinaire Calvinist into liberal Christian is contradictory, inasmuch as this "conversion experience" supposedly takes place without Schadau's awareness: "Vielmehr möchten wir zeigen, . . . daß der Dichter gerade die innere, wenn auch seinem Helden Schadau selber nicht bewußte Gesinnungswandlung gestaltet: Es ist die Wandlung eines orthodoxen Protestanten zum toleranten Menschen, dem die Gnade Gottes teilhaftig wird." It is hard to conceive of a conversion experience that leaves the conscious mind unaffected. Schadau's moment of enlightenment, his "Gesinnungswandlung," is tragically fleeting, limited as it is to the brief duration of his OOBE, and, in subsequently becoming partially lost to memory, leads to no substantial change of character.

¹⁸ See Harry Maync, *Conrad Ferdinand Meyer und sein Werk* (Frauenfeld: von Huber, 1925), p. 223.

¹⁹ Quoted and translated by Isaiah Berlin, *The Hedgehog and the Fox: An Essay on Tolstoy's View of History* (New York: Touchstone, 1953), p. 18.

²⁰ See Jackson, "Schadau, the Satirized Narrator," pp. 62-63; Schimmelpfennig, p. 195; and Leopold, p. 8.

²¹ See Conrad Ferdinand Meyer, *Briefe Conrad Ferdinand Meyers nebst seinen Rezensionen und*

Aufsätzen, ed. Adolf Frey (Leipzig: H. Haessel, 1908), I, 32; also Meyer, *Sämtliche Werke,* XI, 227.

[22] Leopold von Ranke, *Über die Epochen der neueren Geschichte. Vorträge dem Könige Maximilian II. von Bayern im Herbst 1854 zu Berchtesgaden gehalten,* in *German Literature since Goethe,* ed. Ernst Feise and Harry Steinhauer (Boston: Houghton Mifflin, 1958), I, 163.

[23] Quoted by Richard Brinkmann, "Zum Begriff des Realismus für die erzählende Dichtung des neunzehnten Jahrhunderts," in *Begriffsbestimmung des literarischen Realismus,* Wege der Forschung, 212, ed. Richard Brinkmann (Darmstadt: Wissenschaftliche Buchgesellschaft, 1969), p. 226.

[24] Fehr, p. 49; see also Schimmelpfennig, p. 196, for a discussion of Meyer's claims to authorial impartiality in letters to Hermann Haessel (May 26, 1873) and Franz Brümmer (March 11, 1874).

[25] Meyer, *Briefe,* I, 65.

[26] In *The Poetry of Conrad Ferdinand Meyer* (Madison, Wisconsin: University of Wisconsin Press, 1954), p. 68.

[27] Quoted by Margaret R. B. Shaw, "Introduction" to *Scarlet and Black,* by Stendhal (Baltimore: Penguin, 1969), p. 11.

[28] In a letter, Meyer says of himself: "Ich habe . . . Gottvertrauen, so viel ein Kind des neunzehnten Jahrhunderts haben kann." Quoted by Wiesmann, p. 43.

[29] Meyer's acquaintance with Platonic thought is documented in Frey's biography, p. 97. Although there is no reference to Swedenborg in either the letters or Frey's biography, it is inconceivable that Meyer had no knowledge of this most influential of Swedish thinkers, particularly when one considers Meyer's studies of Swedish affairs preparatory to writing *Gustav Adolfs Page* (see Meyer, *Sämtliche Werke,* XI, 279-86) and the prominence of Swedenborgian societies in Switzerland well into our own country. As for *Faust,* a perusal of the *Briefe,* e.g. II, 206-07, shows that Meyer knew the drama well enough to cite textual differences between the prose *Urfaust* of 1775 and the final version in verse.

[30] See "Vermischte Aufsätze," in *Briefe,* II, 473-74.

[31] Meyer, *Briefe,* II, 272. For an account of Meyer's dabbling in mysticism at Préfargier, see also Lena F. Dahme, *Women in the Life and Art of Conrad Ferdinand Meyer* (1936; rpt. New York: AMS press, 1966), pp. 41-42.

[32] Frey, *Conrad Ferdinand Meyer: Sein Leben und seine Werke,* pp. 144-45, and Fehr, p. 35.

[33] Schimmelpfennig, pp. 193-94, points out Meyer's paraphrase of a verse from Paul's letter to the Romans: When Schadau, in reflecting on his mixed feelings about Boccard's death, says, "meine Gedanken verklagten und entschuldigten sich unter einander," he is paraphrasing Paul, who says of the heathens with their innate sense of conscience "daß sie beweisen, des Gesetzes Werk sei beschrieben in ihren *Herzen,* sintemal ihr Gewissen sie bezeugt, dazu auch die *Gedanken, die sich unter einander verklagen oder entschuldigen. . ."* (Rom. 2: 14-15; italics Schimmelpfennig's).

[34] Fritz Martini, "Wilhelm Raabes 'Prinzessin Fisch': Wirklichkeit und Dichtung im erzählenden Realismus des 19. Jahrhunderts," in *Begriffsbestimmung des literarischen Realismus,* p. 304.

[35] Brinkmann, p. 227. For a fuller discussion of Brinkmann's position, see his book, *Wirklichkeit und Illusion: Studien über Gehalt und Grenzen des Begriffs Realismus für die erzählende Dichtung des neunzehnten Jahrhunderts* (Tübingen: Niemeyer, 1957), especially the last chapter.

[36] See note 29.

Edward M. V. Plater (essay date 1978)

SOURCE: "'Der schöne Leib' in the Prose of Conrad Ferdinand Meyer," in *Seminar: A Journal of Germanic Studies,* Vol. XIV, No. 4, November, 1978, pp. 255-67.

[*In the following essay, Plater examines the significance of the complex objectification of inner life in Meyer's novellas.*]

The underlying principle of Conrad Ferdinand Meyer's narrative art was expressed by his sister Betsy as follows:

> 'Mein Bruder sehnte sich von jeher, so zu dichten, daß durch sein Wort nicht Gedanken ausgedrückt, sondern handelnde Gestalten geschaffen würden. "Jeder Gedanke muß seinen schönen Leib haben," meinte er . . . "In der Poesie muß jeder Gedanke sich als sichtbare Gestalt bewegen. Es darf kein Raisonnement, nichts gedankenhaft Beschreibendes als unaufgelöster Rest übrig bleiben. Es muß alles Bewegung sein und Schönheit!" sagte er mir oft.'[1]

Meyer's stories abound with examples of the principle stated here. Unspoken thoughts and feelings are revealed through significant gestures and poses, and hidden levels of meaning are expressed through significant works of art and craftsmanship, features of the landscape, and atmospheric phenomena. Thus Meyer's narratives often operate on two levels—a literal and a non-literal, the latter level arising from the process of externalizing or objectifying the inner world of thought and feeling, of giving it its 'schönen Leib.'[2]

Much of this objectification involves the description of gestures and facial expressions which result from and are a natural externalization of a character's inner reaction to a given situation, or the description of physical features which express one's character and/or intelligence. Such objectification reflects the eyewitness's point of view, which is characteristic of all of Meyer's novellas, even of *Die Hochzeit des Mönchs,* in which Dante, the fictitious narrator, states at the outset that he is going to invent his story, taking a tombstone inscription as his point of departure.[3] It is not this type of objectification, however, with which the following pages will be concerned. It is, rather, a more complex type which suggests hidden significance beyond its immediate context. In it character and setting interact in such a way as to reveal something of the inner life of the character or to uncover some privileged information or some secret communication from the narrator.

In the following pages I shall examine this type of objectification in scenes from three of Meyer's novellas. The scenes were selected with two general purposes in mind: first, to explore the range of such objectification; secondly, to increase the reader's understanding and appreciation of the works in which the scenes occur. There are, to be sure, other examples which would have served these purposes equally well. Ultimately my choice was based on the question of which scenes that had not been analysed before would serve these purposes and at the same time demonstrate the varied success in Meyer's use of this more complex objectification.

Heinrich Henel considers as the most important criterion for judging Meyer's achievement in his poetry the question of whether he succeeds in fusing completely theme and motif, that is, whether the subjective content of his poems finds perfect expression in the figures and forms of objective reality that he uses to embody it.[4] This criterion is applicable not only to Meyer's poetry, but wherever he uses objective reality to suggest the incorporeal world of thought and feeling. If complete fusion is achieved, then such qualities as subtlety, genuineness, and immediacy will result. There will be no impression of clumsiness or artificiality. The scenes will be convincing on their literal level and will suggest without the necessity of explanation or outside point of reference their unarticulated, subjective meaning. The perfect fusion of inner and outer worlds, then, is what I shall have in mind in evaluating the artistic success of the scenes I have chosen.

I shall begin with a relatively simple example of objectification and proceed to ones of increasing complexity. In the scene from *Der Heilige* in which King Henry receives the news that Thomas Becket has secretly entered England with a papal bull directed against the Bishop of York, the following incident occurs: 'Herr Heinrich, von dem Aufruhr oder der Demut des Primas gleicherweise empört, sprang in sinnlosem Zorne vom Sitz empor und stieß seinen Becher so hart von sich, daß er weit über die Tafel rollte, den Wein in roten Strömen auf das Linnen vergießend, wie Blut in den Schnee.'[5] The image of the red wine spilled on the white tablecloth is a concrete representation foreshadowing Becket's death. It is not an objectification of what is going through the King's mind, or only accidentally so; it is, rather, an objectification of the author's knowledge of the outcome of the conflict between King and Archbishop. It depends for its primary meaning, then, on something outside the scene.

The meaning of the image would be obvious even without the simile likening the wine to blood and without all the reminders throughout the narrative of Becket's violent death at the hands of the King's henchmen, for the association of spilled wine with bloodshed has a long tradition in literature and art and therefore comes readily to mind. In this case, however, lack of subtlety is not an artistic fault. First, it is not as if the author had made a clumsy attempt to communicate surreptitiously some secret information; for, as just indicated, the fact of Becket's death is clear from the outset. Secondly, the author has chosen in Hans the Crossbowman a naive centre of consciousness through which to communicate his story; and the conventional image and superfluous simile are consistent with this purpose. If, however, if had not been Meyer's wish to communicate his story through a naive centre of consciousness, one would have to consider the objectification from an aesthetic point of view as a failure; for it would be as if the author were challenging the reader to uncover the obvious, and the reader would be justifiably annoyed by the inept attempt at veiled communication.

My next example of objectification, also from *Der Heilige,* is more complex. It is the scene in which King Henry and the narrator Hans come by accident upon the ornate little Moorish castle in the forest where they have been hunting. Hans relates:

> Bald sah ich die Glut der sinkenden Sonne purpurn vor mir auf den Stämmen blinken. Ich wandte mich um nach dem Könige, er aber drang ungeduldig an mir vorüber der rötlichen Helle entgegen, so heftig, daß ich Mühe hatte, ihm auf den Fersen zu bleiben.

> Da sah ich ihn plötzlich verwundert den Schritt hemmen. Am Waldsaume stand er unter den tröpfelnden Zweigen und lugte, die Augen mit der erhobenen Rechten beschattend, unverwandt in die untergehende Sonne hinaus.

(XIII, 45)

Hans, by describing the King's reaction to the scene they have chanced upon from the point of view of an eyewitness, gives an objective representation of Henry's inner state. His movements and gestures reveal in themselves, aside from an impatient, peremptory manner, only a perfectly natural reaction to the unexpected and marvellous vision he beholds and an instinctive desire to spare his eyes from the blinding rays of the setting sun. In other words, his movements and gestures in themselves suggest nothing beyond what is self-evident.

The setting sun, however, does have a hidden meaning beyond its literal one. Walter Morris states that the setting sun is often associated with tragedy and death in Meyer's work and cites examples from *Die Richterin* and *Die Versuchung des Pescara* to support his assertion. In the above passage he sees a foreshadowing of Gnade's death.[6] It seems more appropriate, however, to associate the foreshadowing with King Henry. In the first place, the colour of the sun reflected by the wet tree trunks, purple, traditionally signifies royalty. Secondly, only eleven pages earlier Rollo states in reference to the Norman kings: 'Die hohen Herren haben allesamt ein böses Sterben. Dieser Bolz—Gott und der Teufel wissen, wer ihn abschoß—hat Herrn Wilhelm dem Rothaarigen mitten im lustigen Jagen den Lebensfaden zerschnitten. Aber was tut's? Glänzende Sonnen gehen blutig unter' (XIII, 34). This passage establishes the association of the setting sun with the Norman kings and with death. It is, moreover, literally 'mitten im lustigen Jagen' that the reckless adventure begins which leads to Henry's destruction.

The image of the sun is also applied specifically to the person of King Henry. Hans states that Thomas Becket was the only Saxon, 'der im Sonnenlichte der königlichen Gnade wandelte' (XIII, 28). And speaking of the Chancellor he says: 'dieser sonnte sich, wie eine schlanke weiße Schlange, in den Strahlen der fürstlichen Gunst' (XIII, 36).

The explicit association of the sun with King Henry and of the setting sun with death gives this scene foreshadowing force. This is not to say that Meyer's primary purpose here was to foreshadow. Such a contention ignores the fact that the reader already knows from the narrator's transition to this segment of the story that the episode he is about to relate led ultimately to King Henry's death: 'Jetzt komme ich zu reden auf ein Geheimnis der Ungerechtigkeit, das zwar in keiner Chronik wird verzeichnet stehen, aber doch die Grabschaufel ist, Herrn Thomas und Herrn Heinrich, einem nach dem andern, seine Grube gemacht hat' (XIII, 43). Meyer's main purpose was, rather, to render the idea stated here, which is by definition abstract, in concrete form, to give it its 'schönen Leib'. When the King's reaction to the scene is viewed in this light, it takes on meaning which it does not by itself suggest. His starting in wonder at the graceful, shimmering

castle, as if a spell had rooted him to the spot, now suggests his complete enchantment with the irresistible beauty and charm of Gnade and his powerlessness to resist his virile impulses when confronted with this lovely creature, even though he realizes from the first evening that she is Thomas Becket's daughter. His position and posture with respect to the sun are also significant. In order to see the castle the King must look directly into the sun. Figuratively this means that Meyer brings the King face to face with his fate. The King, however, shields his eyes from the sun's rays— a perfectly natural gesture, it is true, but in the context of this scene it suggests his refusal to see the consequences of the treachery he commits, his wilful disregard of the enormity of his violation of Becket's sanctuary. This, the King's reaction to the scene tells us, is how his downfall, indicated by the setting sun, comes about.

Two points are important here. First, although the King's reaction to the scene does give us some privileged information about him, this information depends on the rather artificial identification of the King with the sun. Secondly, the information we obtain on this non-literal level concerns the further course of the action rather than the inner life of the character or some universal truth. For these reasons the scene is primarily allegorical: its meaning derives in large part from outside the scene and relates to events that lie beyond it.[7]

The next scene I have selected for analysis is from *Die Hochzeit des Mönchs*. It is the scene with which the action resumes a week after the tragedy on the Brenta that claimed the life of Astorre's brother and resulted in the monk's betrothal to Diana.

> An einem leuchtenden Morgen, sieben Tage nach der Totenfeier, saß im schwarzen Schatten einer Zeder, den Rücken an den Stamm gelehnt und die Schnäbel seiner Schuhe in das brennende Sonnenlicht streckend, der Mönch Astorre; denn diesen Namen behielt er unter den Paduanern, obwohl er weltlich geworden war, während seines kurzen Wandels auf der Erde. Er saß oder lag einem Brunnen gegenüber, der aus dem Mund einer gleichgültigen Maske eine kühle Flut sprudelte, unfern einer Steinbank, welcher er das weiche Polster des schwellenden Rasens vorgezogen hatte (XII, 32).

Astorre's preference for the soft cushion of luxuriant grass over the stone bench suggests his basically sensuous nature. This quality was revealed earlier, when Ezzelin asked Astorre how much it had cost him to accept his monastic vows. He replied: ' "Armut und Gehorsam nichts." . . . "Und das dritte?" holte Ezzelin nach . . . "Es ist mir nicht leicht geworden, doch ich vermochte es wie andere Mönche, wenn sie gut beraten sind, und das war ich" ' (XII, 24-5). It is also significant that, though sitting in the shade of the tree, he stretches his legs so that the tips of his shoes extend into the burning sunlight. The dark, cool shade of the tree and the bright, burning sun suggest the contrast between the sheltered, subdued life in the monastery and the energetic, pulsating life of action outside its walls, where there is no vow of chastity to restrain one's passionate nature. Hence, by describing Astorre reclining on the soft grass in the shade of the tree with the tips of his shoes in the sunlight, Meyer creates an objective representation of a natural appetite that is beginning to assert itself in him now he has shed his monk's habit.

This idea is supported by a passage that occurs somewhat later in the novella. When Astorre leaves the grounds of his palace for the first time since his father's death, in order to purchase a ring for Diana, he dons a summer mantle which has a hood attached to it. 'Auf der Straße zog sich Astorre dieselbe tief ins Gesicht, weniger gegen die brennenden Strahlen der Sonne als aus langer Gewöhnung . . . ' (XII, 51). It is not, so we are told, out of natural inclination that Astorre pulls the hood down over his forehead and shades himself from the sun, that he protects himself from the fiery passions of his true nature, but out of habit, developed over a period of fifteen years in the monastery, imposed by his vow of chastity. A single spark could cause this sensual nature to ignite and burst forth in its full vitality, and this spark is provided by Antiope. 'Ein schöpferisches Feuer war aus der Hand Antiopes in die seinige gefahren und begann zuerst zart und sanft, dann immer heißer und schärfer in seinen Adern zu brennen' (XII, 66), Dante says, after Astorre has returned from escorting Antiope home.

The psychological content of the picture of Astorre reclining under the cedar tree is substantiated later in the scene, after the author introduces Ascanio and Germano. Ascanio calls the gardener's daughter over. 'Er legte die Linke um die schlanke Seite des Mädchens und holte sich mit der Rechten aus dem Korb eine Traube. Zugleich suchte sein Mund die schwellended Lippen. "Mich durstet", sagte er' (XII, 38). He playfully makes an association between the voluptuous lips of the girl and the juicy grapes. Terrified by Astorre's visible displeasure, the girl then runs off, spilling some of the fruit from her basket. Ascanio picks up two bunches of grapes, one of which he offers to Germano. Significantly, this innocent man in armour, whose brusque manner repels the opposite sex, rejects the fruit. 'Die andere reichte der Mutwillige dem Mönche, der sie eine Weile ebenfalls unberührt ließ, dann aber gedankenlos eine saftige Beere und bald noch eine zweite und die dritte kostete' (XII, 39). Again Astorre unconsciously reveals the presence of a sensual appetite stirring within him.

If Astorre's tasting of the grapes is an objectification of his awakening physical passion, then the consumption of these grapes would seem to suggest the satisfaction of this appetite. On the other hand, to consume the ripe grapes is to destroy them. Hence, the possibility arises that Meyer intended to suggest by means of the monk's distracted response to the grapes the unexpected intrusion of death in the prime of life.[8] Both interpretations seem possible at this point in the story in view of Dante's announcement at the outset that he would develop his story from a tombstone inscription which he had come across years before in Padua and which read: 'Hic jacet monachus Astorre cum uxore Antiope. Sepeliebat Azzolinus' (XII, 11). Cangrande translates: 'Hier schlummert der Mönch Astorre neben seiner Gattin Antiope. Beide begrub Ezzelin' (XII, 11). Astorre's absent-minded tasting of the fruit, then, seems intended as a veiled hint of the eruption of his passionate nature and its extinction in death.

It should be noted here that the scene, which began symbolically, has now veered in the direction of allegory by suggesting something external to itself. As long as the simple act of tasting the grapes suggests something about Astorre's emotional make-up, it is a symbolic act, but as soon as its meaning depends on something that lies outside the scene—in this case Astorre's death at the hands of Germano at the end of the novella—it becomes allegorical.[9]

The fountain opposite Astorre is also allegorical in nature. Its cool water bubbles out of the mouth of a mask bearing an expression of indifference. The water issuing from the fountain is, to be sure, a universal symbol, embodying in itself the suggestion of the interminable flow of life; and the mask with its unconcerned countenance symbolizes the absolute impartiality of the laws which govern life, the laws of creation. But these symbols also apply to the specific events which Dante relates and thus they function allegorically. The interminable flow of life suggested by the bubbling fountain becomes the metaphorical river of which Dante speaks when he describes the monk's reaction to his friends' discussion of the consequences if the Emperor should die: 'der Mönch erstaunte über die Macht der Sterne, den weiten Ehrgeiz der Herrscher und den alles mitreißenden Strom der Welt' (XII, 40). The mask of indifference, in its specific application to the events of the story, becomes associated with Ezzelin. When Ezzelin suddenly appears behind Ascanio, Dante describes his face as 'ruhig wie die Maske des Brunnens' (XII, 40). Significantly, Ezzelin sits down upon the hard, cold, unyielding stone bench which Astorre had eschewed; he is, after all, in affairs of state a cold, calculating, dispassionate man, as, for example, his handling of the suspected treason of Petrus de Vinea reveals (XII, 42). He is also a fatalist and at the same time seems to be an unwilling instrument of the impersonal fate in which he believes. His sudden appearance in the doorway at the end of the story just at the moment when Germano, facing the entrance to the room, is holding off Astorre's arrow with his sword, results in the very catastrophe he had sought to avert. Thus the mask of the fountain, through its association with Ezzelin, suggests the absolute impartiality of the laws which govern life in the world outside the monastery; and Astorre, whose passion and compassion bring him into conflict with this uncompromising world, is swept by the 'alles mitreißenden Strom der Welt' to his destruction.

In both this scene and the scene in the English forest in *Der Heilige* an individual is brought, figuratively speaking, face to face with his fate. But, whereas King Henry is explicitly linked with the sunset and thus with what it represents, Astorre's connection with the fountain and its significance is left open. We are inclined, to be sure, to make the connection because of Astorre's position with respect to the fountain—he is described as reclining opposite it—and because of our knowledge of the outcome, of which Dante reminds us— 'während seines kurzen Wandels auf der Erde' (XII, 32)—in the very midst of placing Astorre in the scene. Furthermore, what the fountain with its bubbling water and its mask of indifference suggests is less specific than the rather precise indication of downfall and destruction associated with the setting sun. This greater dependence on suggestiveness together with the more complex configuration of the scene and its symbolism make it a greater artistic achievement than the scene from *Der Heilige.*

The last scene I have chosen to examine is from *Die Richterin.* It is the scene in Chapter III in which Palma and Wulfrin rest on the shore of a mountain lake (XII, 204-6). The lake is a favourite spot of Palma's. She refers to it in fact as *her* lake (XII, 202) and is eager to show it to her brother. Around the shore of the lake are strewn huge boulders, and opposite the prominence on which the alleged siblings sit there rises a majestic, snow-capped mountain that reaches to the clouds. The soaring mountain peaks covered with eternal snow and often shrouded in mist suggest in their ethereal appearance the spiritual nature of man. They provide an apt image, as Henel has pointed out, to symbolize the 'border land between heaven and earth,' where the soul finds tranquility 'beyond the reach of the passions,' 'its state before incarnation.'[10] By contrast the huge boulders in their heavy, earthbound solidity suggest the physical nature of man and all that that implies. The snow-capped mountain peak and the huge boulders thus furnish a significant and, as we shall see, appropriate setting for what transpires here.

Palma tells Wulfrin of often having experienced a sense of disengagement from herself while swimming and splashing about in the water of the lake. This experience can be attributed in part to the relative weightlessness one feels in the denser medium of water, as if one did indeed shed to some degree one's corporeality.

But the author means 'disengagement' in another sense too. Palma is at the age of adolescence. Her whole being is roused by her awakening womanhood. She is driven unconsciously by an overwhelming need to express her love. The chilling water of the shaded mountain lake calms her agitated heart, the womanly love stirring within her young body. She experiences a release from this emotional and physiological turmoil, so that it is as if her soul freed itself from the needs and desires of her physical being and bathed thus disencumbered in the cool, calming water. Palma's mountain lake with its pure, cool water becomes, like the mountain peak with its perpetual snow, a symbol suggesting the state of her soul before incarnation and thus its eternal home; and her play in the water is a symbolic act of cleansing, of restoring the soul.

Just as Palma finishes relating her experience of disengagement from herself, the clouds break up and the snow-capped mountain peak comes into view. The mountain appears outlined in a brilliant radiance against the clear, blue sky; and its lines are described as suggesting both seriousness and charm, strength and loveliness, as if they had been formed before creation separated into man and woman, youth and old age. This description suggesting a state of pure spirit is in keeping with Meyer's use of snow-capped mountain peaks as a symbol for the home of the pre-incarnated soul. At the same time the combination of masculine and feminine qualities in the radiant lines of the mountain, suggesting the union of man and woman, seems intended as an objectification of the desire that Palma innocently cherishes. Her reaction to the appearance of the mountain peak shows, to be sure, her ignorance of this desire—she says only: 'Jetzt prangt und jubelt der Schneeberg' (XII, 205). It is only the author's purpose I am speaking of here, which he seems to betray through the intimation of sexual union in his description of the mountain.

Palma goes on to speak of how the snow-capped mountain towering above them takes on a bluish 'Gewand' in the moonlight and speaks secretively and ardently. Recently, she says, this bluish gleam of the mountain brought tears to her eyes and wrung her heart. This bewildering experience is doubtlessly attributable to Palma's awakening womanhood, to the strong natural drives stirring within her which she does not understand and which therefore cause her anguish. All the details of her account point to such an interpretation: the moonlight, with which a romantic spell is traditionally associated; the ardent manner in which the mountain 'spoke'; the tears; and the heart, the seat of emotions, as the organ affected by the experience she describes.

No sooner does Palma finish relating this experience than a cloud formation floating above the snow-white peaks attracts her attention. The author describes it as a heavenly banquet. An arm is seen raising a cup and friends or lovers—Meyer is purposefully ambiguous here—incline towards each other. As the cloud formation threatens to dissolve, Palma cries out: 'Bleibet! oder gehet nur! . . . wir sind Selige wie ihr! Nicht wahr, Bruder?' (XII, 205). The author then relates how Palma looks into the depths of her presumed brother's eyes and embraces him in love and innocence. Here, as indeed throughout this scene, the author has Palma react to the natural setting in such a way as to suggest the feelings stirring within her, which she in her helpless innocence could not realistically articulate.

Although Palma enjoys here at the edge of her mountain lake a taste of the bliss which her whole being longs for, her unclouded happiness is of brief duration. After resting for a while in Wulfrin's arms, she draws his attention to their reflection in the water. 'Da rief eine kindliche Stimme: "Sieh doch, Wulfrin, wie sie sich in der Tiefe unarmen!" ' (XII, 205). While Palma points to their reflection in childlike innocence, Wulfrin shudders in horror at the same image and immediately leaps to his feet and runs off, thus bringing to an abrupt end the moment of hushed bliss. The reflected image is, of course, a mere illusion and not the real thing. Hence it does not reveal the inner reality of the two characters. It merely reflects in a strictly objective way their outward appearance. Their inner reality, their truest feelings, are revealed, rather, in the way in which each reacts to the reflection. Wulfrin, who had earlier expressed his resentment of Palma's excessive attentions to him (XII, 201), shudders in horror because he is beginning to realize that he desires the young girl whom he assumes to be his sister.

Both this incident and the cloud formation described above are echoed later when the two join Gnadenreich at Pratum. The 'himmlisches Fest' (XII, 205) discernible in the clouds is repeated as the three sit down to a repast for the betrothed in the open air atop the tower of the bishop's castle. The arm raising a cup, visible in the cloud formation, is repeated by Wulfrin's congratulatory gesture with the pitcher of wine; and the image of the friends or lovers inclining towards each other is repeated not by Palma and Gnadenreich, as one might expect, since it is their betrothal that is being solemnized, but by Palma and Wulfrin, who leans over and awakens his presumed sister with a kiss on the back of her neck.

Palma then asks Gnadenreich to bring the book which he had shown to her mother on their last visit and which she insists contains a picture of her brother. The picture is actually an illustration of the story of Byblis's passionate love for her brother Caunus. Ovid relates in his *Metamorphoses* that Byblis followed her brother through many lands, hoping in vain that he would return her love. Finally she gave in to despair and wept inconsolably. From her tears there arose an eternally flowing spring.[11] As Wulfrin looks at the girl in the picture, he sees increasingly a resemblance to Palma. When Gnadenreich reveals to Wulfrin what the story of Byblis is about, Wulfrin turns pale, tears the picture to shreds, throws these into the whirlwind overhead, and even draws his sword on Palma, whom he orders to return home at once and threatens to throw into the stream if she should meet him on the way.

The illustration to the story of Byblis and Caunus is like the reflection of Palma and Wulfrin in the water of the mountain lake; and, as in that scene by the lake, it is Palma who innocently draws her presumed brother's attention to the picture that seems to depict them. And again one can say that the different way in which the two react to their reflected image mirrors the truest feelings of their souls. In both cases, then, Meyer uses reflections to provoke reactions; and it is the reactions which reflect the inner world of the characters, while the reflections, like the cloud formation, in the description of which the author himself felt compelled to equivocate, symbolize the ambiguity of outward appearances.

The scene by the shore of the mountain lake is truly a remarkable piece of writing. It is like a brilliant performance by a great artist, in which one small triumph after another in rapid succession finally brings the astonished audience to its feet. The scene pulsates with suggestiveness, as physical reality takes on symbolic force and the characters react to the setting in such a way that they reveal unwittingly the depths of their souls. What makes the achievement even more exciting is that, though the symbolism is present in such extraordinary density, it arises so naturally from the setting and the characters' reaction to the setting that it is completely unobtrusive. One can in fact read the scene as a straightforward, realistic account without even becoming aware of its symbolic content.

As the foregoing analyses indicate, objectification in Meyer's prose may range from simple, obvious allusions of an allegorical nature to complex, symbolic configurations of subtle suggestiveness. They further indicate that naturalness is the most important criterion for judging the aesthetic quality of the objectification, at least in works like Meyer's that strive to create the illusion of reality. Whenever Meyer succeeds in making things in the outer world suggest in themselves aspects of the inner world and in making characters reveal their desires, moods, attitudes, etc by their reaction to these things, the result is an aesthetically satisfying, secret communing with the reader. When, however, the reader must rely on sources outside the scene for the meaning of the objectification, then the artificial nature of the secret communing is more likely to call attention to itself. The reason for this is that the mental leaps required to make the connection between image and outside point of reference break the illusion of reality, and one becomes aware of the conscious artistry of the author. This is not to say that objectification of an allegorical nature should be avoided at all costs. It merely means that the author must exercise great care to avoid allegorical allusions that are so obvious as to offend the reader's intelligence and forcefully draw attention to the contrived nature of the fictional world.

Generally speaking, the more obvious the connection with the outside point of reference, whether this exists in the same work or in literary tradition, the less satisfying the objectification. Thus the image of the red wine spilling across the white tablecloth is artistically less satisfying than the image of King Henry staring in wonder at the Moorish castle. Other factors do enter into aesthetic judgments; and one of these, as we have seen, is the characterization of the fictitious narrator. Because Hans the Crossbowman is a relatively simple, unsophisticated man, one is inclined to forgive such obvious allegorical references as the spilled wine, which one would regard less charitably under other circumstances.

As we have also seen, however, allegory can stand on its own merits in the fictional world of Meyer's prose. The subtle touch of the King's shading his eyes from the rays of the allegorical sunset in *Der Heilige* or the allegorical content of the scene from *Die Hochzeit des Mönchs* are two cases in point. Indeed, the discovery of non-literal meaning arising from a character's reaction to or placement within a setting and depending on outside points of reference is one of the major pleasures afforded by the reading of Meyer's prose. Such allegorical configurations, when skilfully introduced into the narrative, can provide almost as much excitement for the reader as the subtle symbolic passages. These, however, are beyond question the supreme achievement of Meyer's narrative art, for in them outer and inner world are so perfectly matched that thought and feeling suggest themselves without the aid of an outside point of reference. Abstract meaning finds complete embodiment in concrete imagery and has in the fullest sense of the phrase its 'schönen Leib.'

Notes

[1] Betsy Meyer, *Conrad Ferdinand Meyer in der Erinnerung seiner Schwester* (Berlin, 1903), pp. 161, 163.

[2] Objectification is, to be sure, not a new discovery. Many critics have referred to this aspect of Meyer's narrative art, among them Franz Ferdinand Baumgarten in *Das Werk Conrad Ferdinand Meyers/Renaissance-Empfinden und Stilkunst,* 2nd ed. (Munich, 1920), especially the fourth chapter, 'Die Novellenform.' More recently Heinrich Henel, in *The Poetry of Conrad Ferdinand Meyer* (Madison, 1954), has focused on this principle of Meyer's creative process, which he finds not only in his poetry but in his fiction as well. See, for example, Henel's discussion of the opening of *Die Hochzeit des Mönchs,* pp. 45-6.

[3] Baumgarten points out that Meyer's stories are narrated from the vantage point of an eyewitness to the events and that the thoughts and feelings of the characters are communicated by describing their gestures and facial expressions (pp. 128, 148-9). In this connection Meyer himself stated: 'Die Personen schildere ich möglichst nur so wie sie den Mithandelnden erscheinen' (quoted in Harry Maync *Conrad Ferdinand Meyer und sein Werk* [Frauenfeld, 1925], p. 342).

[4] Henel, p. 46.

[5] *Conrad Ferdinand Meyer: Sämtliche Werke. Historisch-kritische Ausgabe,* ed. Hans Zeller and Alfred Zäch (Bern, 1958-), XIII, 125. Subsequent references to this source are cited in the text by volume and page number.

[6] 'Poetic Images and Motifs in Conrad Ferdinand Meyer's Prose Works' (diss. University of Texas, 1959), p. 48. Walther Brecht first pointed out the association between the sunset and death in Meyer's works in *Conrad Ferdinand Meyer und das Kunstwerk seiner Gedichtsammlung* (Wien, 1918), pp. 50-2.

[7] These two characteristics, the outside referent and the element of action, are basic to allegory. See, for example, the discussion of allegory in C. Hugh Holman, *A Handbook to Literature,* 3rd ed., based on the original by William Flint Thrall and Addison Hibbard (Indianapolis, 1972).

[8] Henel points out, p. 214, that the grape is one of Meyer's poetic motifs, a symbol both of ripeness and death, and that its meaning comes from *King Lear,* v.ii: 'Men must endure / Their going hence, even as their coming hither. / Ripeness is all.'

[9] This distinction conforms to the usual definitions of symbol and allegory. See, for example, the discussion of symbol and its differentiation from allegory in Holman, p. 519.

[10] Henel, pp. 178, 174, 178.

[11] Marianne Burkhard refers to this story in her book *C.F. Meyer und die antike Mythologie* (Zürich, 1966), p. 33, as do the editors of the critical edition of C.F. Meyer (*Werke,* XII, 380). Neither reference, however, attempts to connect the story with Meyer's use of reflections.

Marianne Burkhard (essay date 1978)

SOURCE: "Flaming Signals on Dark Waters: Meyer's Poetry" in *Conrad Ferdinand Meyer,* Twayne Publishers, 1978, pp. 95-122.

[*In the essay that follows, Burkhard discusses Meyer's careful experimentation with poetic structure, particularly in his aesthetic treatment of death.*]

For all his extensive work in prose since 1872, Meyer was far from neglecting his poetry which, for long, had been his prime endeavor. And it is in poetry that, after an arduous working process, he was to reach his most innovative accomplishments. Letters and manuscripts of the 1870s reveal continuous work on poems which were published individually or in small groups in several poetry journals. For years, Meyer and Haessel could not agree on the terms for a poetry collection which Meyer had proposed as early as 1873 (*W,* II, 8-10). Thus, the preparation of such a collection—simply entitled *Gedichte (Poems)*—in 1881-1882 meant for him the realization of a cherished plan.

With utmost care Meyer reviewed all his poems written before 1881, many of which had already been revised several times. Among those chosen for the collection there is scarcely one that was not altered, at least in some minor way, and almost half of them were recast into a *Neufassung* differing from the preceding version in meter, length, and at times even in crucial imagery.[1] The *Gedichte* of 1882 thus represent a sort of poetic *summa,* the result of Meyer's unique effort of patient revising and experimenting. Spanning two decades, this effort proceeds from mediocre beginnings to original poems, from wordy, long-winded narrative poems to concise, dramatic ballads, from conventional lyrics to delicately wrought images and to symbolist poems unfolding new poetic possibilities and, in some cases, highest perfection. Thanks to Betsy, this whole process can be closely traced in the hundreds of manuscripts which, over the long years of her collaboration, she had set aside one by one as soon as they had become obsolete. Thus she saved this material from certain destruction by Meyer himself, who was not at all interested in work which he had already surpassed.[2] The entire manuscript material is being published by Hans Zeller in the critical Meyer edition: Volumes 2-5 will contain the material relating to the *Gedichte,* Volumes 6 and 7 the collections *Zwanzig Balladen von einem Schweizer* (*Twenty Ballads by a Swiss,* 1864) and *Romanzen und Bilder* (*Ballads and Images,* 1869) as well as the material relating to all other poems. Thus, Zeller's edition will offer an unusual opportunity for observing a poet at work.

I *Toward a New Lyricism*

To be sure, Meyer is not the only poet who diligently reworked his poems. Yet his travail is singular in the persistence he applied to a relatively small body of poems which, at that, contains an even smaller number of concepts and motifs. In the course of rewriting, Meyer often achieves astonishing results by refining images, by slowly unveiling the full depths of symbols, by isolating, developing, and interchanging motifs. One motif often becomes the focus for several related yet still diverse poems, for example, Charon's boat for the so-called lake poems, namely, **"Die toten Freunde"** (**"Dead Friends"**), **"Schwüle"** (**"Sultry Day"**), **"Eingelegte Ruder"** (**"Oars at Rest"**), **"Im Spätboot"** (**"Nocturnal Boat"**); or the figure of the dead beloved for a group of love poems, **"Weihgeschenk"** (**"Votive Offering"**), **"Der Blutstropfen"** (**"A Drop of Blood"**), **"Wetterleuchten"** (**"Heat Lightning"**), **"Lethe,"** **"Stapfen"** (**"Footsteps"**). Repeatedly, two or three different pieces derive from the same early poem, for example, the early versions of **"Der tote Achill"** (**"Dead Achilles"**) are also the basis for **"Der Gesang des Meeres"** (**"Song of the Sea"**) and **"Möwenflug"** (**"Sea Gulls in Flight"**), and the poem **"Der Triumphbogen"** (**"Triumphal Arch"**) uses an isolated motif from **"Der Musensaal"** (**"Hall of the Muses"**). In his fundamental study *The Poetry of Conrad Ferdinand Meyer,* Heinrich Henel characterizes this development as "proliferation" which, in an intriguing way, combines "organic growth and conscious manipulation."[3] Several charts exhibit the complexity of a creative process the strength of which lies less in imagining new motifs and symbols than in elaborating and interlinking the ones that his imagination had produced quite early—in the 1860s when he concentrated on poetry—but in embryonic form. Like Schiller, Meyer builds his poetic world with "a small family of concepts." Therefore, it is no surprise to find topics from ballads in the novellas, for example, **"Der Mars von Florenz"** (**"Mars of Florence"**) in *Die Hochzeit des Mönchs,* **"Mit zwei Worten"** (**"With Two Words"**) in *Der Heilige,* **"Cäsar Borgias Ohnmacht"** (**"Cesar Borgia Powerless"**) in *Angela Borgia,* and to recognize many lyric motifs in the novellas.

Meyer's persistence in reworking his poems shows, more than anything else, how much importance he attached to his poetry. His comments, however, are quite contradictory. Only seldom does he speak positively about his poetic endeavors, so when he describes his lyric poems as "most delicate" (*W,* II, 28) and ventures the opinion that "on the whole, the collection holds—if I am not mistaken—its own" (*W,* II, 29). Much more often he takes a disparaging view, calling his poetry "sentimental," "not true enough," "rarely more than a play or, at the most, an expression of an inferior part of my nature" (*W,* II, 28-29). This ambivalence is rooted in his own uncertainty with regard to his poetry which he knew to be out of tune with the conventional lyric production of the time, and which, moreover, affords some rare—though still veiled—glimpses into his most personal experiences. Among the contemporary readers only a few—for instance, Gottfried Keller and Carl Spitteler—recognized the unusual beauty of Meyer's lyrics; most critics of the time preferred his historical ballads because they felt the lack of direct expression of emotions in the lyric poems. This opinion is summed up in Theodor Storm's words: " . . . for real lyric poetry he lacks the true 'tirili' of the soul. . . . [he lacks] the immediate, captivating expression of feeling, maybe even the immediate feeling itself" (*W,* II, 34). In the twentieth century, this assessment has been reversed, and the lyric poems are being appreciated as an important link in the emergence of symbolist poetry in German literature. Yet a comprehensive evaluation of both ballads and lyrics and their respective styles, their differences and similarities, is still lacking.

A look at German lyric poetry after 1860 makes us realize that the style created by Goethe and the romantics was still the prevalent model: the words "lyric" and "poetic" were tantamount to immediacy of feeling and expression, and a supple, melodious language. Reluctant, even unable, to bare his soul and with little talent for melodious verses Meyer was—as Storm rightly observes—ill suited for this kind of confessional poetry, or *Erlebnisdichtung.* Yet other models, though available in Goethe's nonconfessional objective poetry, or in Mörike's delicate epigrams, were overlooked and not recognized as such. In the many revisions of his poems Meyer, therefore, had to grope his way toward a style more akin to his own temperament. It was a slow, empirical process, and the results are varied in nature and, at times, uneven in quality but basically similar in their thrust toward a poetry in which immediacy is replaced by contemplation and objective description. The most striking achievement in this development are some consummate examples of symbolist poetry, a style which, rooted in German romanticism, first came into prominence in France in the work of Charles Baudelaire (1821-1869) and Stéphane Mallarmé (1842-1898) before it appeared in Germany in Stefan George's poetry in the 1890s and in Rainer Maria Rilke's *Neue Gedichte* in 1907-1908. In symbolism, the poet conveys his emotions indirectly in images which reveal subjective meaning mainly in their objective shape. The symbolist poet also stresses conscious composition over inspiration. In short, symbolism is antithetical to *Erlebnisdichtung* and, thus, an appropriate style for Meyer. Despite his interests in French literature, he had, however, no cognizance of Baudelaire or later symbolists;[4] in virtual isolation and without specific theoretical aims, he broke new ground in German poetry. From this stylistic point of view, Meyer's numerous revisions are most valuable documents because they allow us to trace the transition from romantic to symbolist poetry in the very particulars of creative work. Analyzing the entire development of individual poems is a rewarding task but too extensive for the limited space of this book, so that we have to refer the reader to the studies of Heinrich Henel, Emil Staiger, and other scholars.[5]

The decided focus on the outer world gives rise to two types of poems characteristic of Meyer's more modern poetry. Using the principle of analogy he likens the description of an external phenomenon to a trait of internal life. On the basis of detached contemplation he provides a visual image with an invisible, sometimes emotional correspondence giving the poem a transparency unwonted at the time. One of the best examples for this type, which Henel calls *Gleichungsgedicht* ("poem of equation"),[6] is the short poem **"Eppich" ("Ivy")** whose structure perfectly mirrors the correlation of the two worlds in the two equal stanzas as well as in the rhetorical form of a dialogue between the poet and the ivy. While some of these poems, such as **"Der verwundete Baum" ("The Injured Tree")**, are somewhat contrived, felicitous poems like **"Möwenflug" ("Sea Gulls in Flight")** and **"Das Ende des Festes" ("The Banquet's End")** show that the lucid correspondence between the two parts need not destroy the delicate veil of a poetic vision.

In another group of poems Meyer goes a step further: eliminating the explicit comparison he concentrates on describing an object, a visible image in such a way that the mere dispassionate description reveals the deeper symbolic meaning of the object. This so-called *Dinggedicht* ("object poem") finds a perfect example in **"Der römische Brunnen" ("The Roman Fountain")**, probably Meyer's best known poem:

> Aufsteigt der Strahl und fallend giesst
> Er voll der Marmorschale Rund,
> Die, sich verschleiernd, überfliesst
> In einer zweiten Schale Grund;
> Die zweite gibt, sie wird zu reich,
> Der dritten wallend ihre Flut,
> Und jede nimmt und gibt zugleich
>   Und strömt und ruht.

> Up rises the jet and falling
> Fills the marble bowl to its round rim,
> Which, veiling itself, flows over
> Into the depths of a second bowl;
> The second, becoming too rich, gives,
> Swelling up, its flood to the third,
> And each takes and gives at the same time
>   And flows and rests.

In this depiction, devoid of any comment or even an emotional tone, the reader recognizes the fountain as a symbol of life with its continuous flux and eternal permanence, as a living symbol of beauty with its balance between movement and rest, and a symbol of art that unites the all too often disparate elements of giving and taking. The image of the fountain with the water in endless cycle is delightful in its simplicity, which is, however, the result of much conscious work, as is evident from the poem's development through seven stages and twelve manuscripts (*W,* III, 242-49). Over the years this small work has generated numerous interpretations, among which is the recent one by

Thomas E. Hart.[7] Analyzing the poem's language with the tools of precise linguistic description, Hart convincingly shows how sound patterns, metric and linguistic structures reflect the contrasts and parallels in imagery and meaning, how—in Hart's words—the poet "enlisted calculation to support inspiration." **"Der römische Brunnen"** is a poetic triumph representing, as it does, harmonious beauty in an immediately engaging, understandable image which, though elaborately wrought, preserves the simplicity of beauty that needs no explanation.

The poem **"Zwei Segel"** (**"Two Sails"**) discloses another facet of the *Dinggedicht*. Meyer's subtle use of personalized words such as *empfinden, begehren, Gesell* impart an inner dimension to the otherwise wholly visual scene; thus the two boats following each other in unison come to symbolize love. The dominance of the external image makes it possible for Meyer to express inner, in some cases even personal feelings in a veiled, nonconfessional form. Thus the symbol in **"Das Seelchen"** (**"Little Soul"**) contains an indication about his innermost self: using the classical symbol for the soul, the butterfly, he imagines it in a personal way when concluding with the lines: "Wie sind die Schwingen ihm gefärbt? / Sie leuchten blank, betupft mit Blut" ("How are his wings dyed? / They gleam brightly, flecked with blood"). The mottling of blood indicates the wounding of the unprotected, delicate soul. Other details hint at suffering as well: in contrast to the earth, the sky appears as "blissful blue," and the butterfly, ready to fly off, conveys the poet's—man's—yearning to leave a painful life.

Brevity and concentration on a single motif are characteristic of Meyer's symbolist poetry; they are the outward signs of an intrinsically different way of writing. In romantic poetry, symbols emerge from an experience in which the poet identifies his inner state with the external world, and such identification generates a number of symbols related to the experience and employed in one poem. In symbolist poetry, however, an external image, or a series of images is described in such ways that the depiction alone reveals the symbolic meaning that this object assumes for the poet with regard to life or to a personal experience.[8] The poet's basic attitude has changed from identification to contemplation. Like Hutten on the Ufenau, Meyer contemplates the world around him and his own experiences, and then carefully chooses individual external phenomena that lend themselves to being matched with and to express this or that internal feeling. In the poem **"Liederseelen"** (**"Souls of Songs"**), which is reminiscent of the early Hutten poem **"Der Zecher,"**[9] Meyer outlines this procedure of seeing isolated motifs and of developing each one individually into a poem. And it is significant that the concluding lines give equal importance both to the inspiration and the poet's

conscious selection: " 'Und die du wählst, und der's beschied / Die Gunst der Stunde, die wird ein Lied' " ("And the one you choose and the one destined / By a favorable hour becomes a song"). Thus **"Liederseelen"** constitutes—so to speak—Meyer's symbolist poetics *en miniature*. While the romantic group of symbols may encompass a wide world of feeling, these isolated motifs are more limited; even in their most elaborate form they express only the one aspect of the poet's world, of human emotions. Therefore, no one motif can express all of Meyer's world, and while some of them do have special weight, they still must be seen in the larger context of associated motifs. On the following pages, the main motifs will be discussed, starting with the ones relating to death and moving on to the motifs of the mountains, the harvest and Dionysian life, and continuing from there to the ballads.

II *Dark Waters: The Lake Poems*

Original in content and accomplished in form, Meyer's lake poems **"Eingelegte Ruder," "Schwüle," "Im Spätboot,"** and **"Nachtgeräusche"** are among his finest lyric creations. With some variations they focus on the motif of a lonely boat on the lake at dusk or at night and on the dark and silent waters. Meyer's personal feeling of being close to death, his classical knowledge, and the familiar landscape coalesce in a quietly impressive image of weariness, ennui, and death. **"Eingelegte Ruder"** (**"Oars at Rest"**) opens with an image which, in its lack of scenery and its dull calm, conveys the impression of total emptiness:

> Meine eingelegten Ruder triefen,
> Tropfen fallen langsam in die Tiefen.
>
> Nichts das mich verdross! Nichts das mich freute!
> Niederrinnt ein schmerzenloses Heute!
>
> Unter mir—ach, aus dem Licht verschwunden—
> Träumen schon die schönern meiner Stunden.
>
> Aus der blauen Tiefe ruft das Gestern:
> Sind im Licht noch manche meiner Schwestern?

> My locked oars drip,
> Drops fall slowly to the depths.
>
> Nothing pains me! Nothing gives me joy!
> Down drips a painless today!
>
> Beneath me—oh gone from the light—
> My more beautiful hours are already dreaming.
>
> From the blue depths yesterday calls:
> Are many of my sisters still in the light?

This external emptiness of the first stanza corresponds to an internal one described in the following three stanzas. Nothing moves the poet, the present has no emotional content, no hold on him—like the drops of water from the oars it drips down without touching him. Whatever was worthwhile has long sunk to the depths of the lake. Nothing but the passing of time remains visible in the slowly falling drops, and this last trace of motion renders the calm even heavier. This leaden stillness is palpable in the form as well: the long trochaic line with its many long vowels is heavy and slow, and the simple rhyme couplets create a monotonous, falling cadence comparable to the falling drops. The weariness of life Meyer must have felt himself transcends the purely personal, because it is rooted in a deep disillusion with life that was newly growing in the nineteenth century and that Georg Büchner describes as *Langeweile* ("boredom") and Charles Baudelaire as ennui.

In **"Schwüle" ("Sultry Day")** the feeling of emptiness is given a more alarming dimension. In the face of a wan, hollow world, the call from the depths assumes a dreadful, yet alluring insistency which makes the need for even the faintest hope—the stars—desperately felt.

> Trüb verglomm der schwüle Sommertag,
> Dumpf und traurig tönt mein Ruderschlag—
> Sterne, Sterne—Abend ist es ja—
> Sterne, warum seid ihr noch nicht da?
>
> Bleich das Leben! Bleich der Felsenhang!
> Schilf, was flüsterst du so frech und bang?
> Fern der Himmel und die Tiefe nah—
> Sterne, warum seid ihr noch nicht da?
>
> Eine liebe, liebe Stimme ruft
> Mich beständig aus der Wassergruft—
> Weg, Gespenst, das oft ich winken sah!
> Sterne, Sterne, seid ihr nicht mehr da?
>
> Endlich, endlich durch das Dunkel bricht—
> Es war Zeit!—ein schwaches Flimmerlicht—
> Denn ich wusste nicht wie mir geschah.
> Sterne, Sterne, bleibt mir immer nah!

> Gloomily the sultry summer day vanished,
> Dull and sad the sound of my oars strikes—
> Stars, stars—it is evening—
> Stars, why are you not yet out?
>
> Pale is life! Pale the rocky cliff!
> Sedge; what is your brazen, frightened
>   whisper?
> Far the sky and the depths near—
> Stars, why are you not yet out?
>
> A dear, dear voice ceaselessly
> Calls me from the watery grave—

> Away, ghost, whom often I saw beckon!
> Stars, stars, are you no longer there?
>
> Finally, finally through the darkness breaks—
> High time!—faint glimmering light—
> For I did not know what was happening to
>   me.
> Stars, stars, remain ever close to me!

For several reasons, the third stanza is of special significance. It contains a rarely occurring personal element by alluding to Meyer's mother, who drowned herself, and to his own occasional desire to end his life. The manuscripts reveal that this biographical reference was only added when Meyer revised the 1869 version in 1881-1882. Such a remark about the dark period of his life which he consistently passes over in silence is only possible when form and imagery for a poem are already established.[10] Nevertheless, this last touch proves to be the symbolic core of the poem. Only when the water is identified as the realm of death, the anxiety—caused by the empty sky, the livid landscape, the eerily rustling reeds, the close depths—is understandable in its full threat. Only now the repeated cry for the stars acquires its full significance as a dramatic emphasis of man's forlornness, his exposure to dark, destructive forces. The simple forms of rhyme and stanza as well as the many word repetitions, function as a sort of formal dam set up against the forces of the depths that threaten to dissolve—as is evident in the chopped sentences—all order and meaning of life.

The full symbolism of the boat at night emerges in the poem **"Im Spätboot" ("Nocturnal Boat")**:

> Aus der Schiffsbank mach ich meinen Pfühl,
> Endlich wird die heiße Stirne kühl!
> O wie süss erkaltet mir das Herz!
> O wie weich verstummen Lust und Schmerz!
> Ueber mir des Rohres schwarzer Rauch
> Wiegt und biegt sich in des Windes Hauch.
> Hüben hier und wieder drüben dort
> Hält das Boot an manchem kleinen Port:
> Bei der Schiffslaterne kargem Schein
> Steigt ein Schatten aus und niemand ein.
> Nur der Steurer noch, der wacht und steht!
> Nur der Wind, der mir im Haare weht!
> Schmerz und Lust erleiden sanften Tod:
> Einen Schlummrer trägt das dunkle Boot.

> On the ship's bench I rest my head,
> Finally my hot forehead cools!
> Oh how sweetly my heart grows cold!
> Oh how softly desire and pain grow silent!
> Above me, the black smoke from the stack
> Waves and bows to the wind's breath.
> Over here and then again over there
> The boat stops at several small ports:
> In the dim light of the ship's lantern

A shadow climbs aboard, no one debarks.
Only the helmsman, he still watches and
   stands!
Only the wind which blows in my hair!
Pain and desire suffer gentle death:
The dark boat carries a slumberer.

As in **"Die toten Freunde,"** Meyer is here bold enough to use the modern steam boat—at the time considered unlyrical—for the poem's setting. In his sparing description, the boat with her steadfast helmsman and the lone passenger turns into the symbol of Charon's boat crossing from the shore of life to the land of the dead. Death is shown as a barely perceptible passage: emotions are dying down "sweetly" and "softly," resulting in an inner stillness that is welcome as a long-awaited relief. Reality is fading away, too: passengers leaving the boat and returning to reality appear as mere shadows; death personified in the ever watchful helmsman is the only reality left. For even the poet's "I," present in the last traces of feelings at the beginning, even his consciousness is being effaced when, in the last line, he is referred to in the third person. With an everyday image and an almost prosaic language Meyer evokes a suggestive vision of death as a gentle passage into ultimate sleep and lasting peace.

A variation of this passage is found in **"Nachtgeräusche"** (**"Night Sounds"**):

Melde mir die Nachtgeräusche, Muse,
Die ans Ohr des Schlummerlosen fluten!
Erst das traute Wachtgebell der Hunde,
Dann der abgezählte Schlag der Stunde,
Dann ein Fischer-Zwiegespräch am Ufer,
Dann? Nichts weiter als der ungewisse
Geisterlaut der ungebrochnen Stille,
Wie das Atmen eines jungen Busens,
Wie das Murmeln eines tiefen Brunnens,
Wie das Schlagen eines dumpfen Ruders,
Dann der ungehörte Tritt des Schlummers.

Announce the night sounds to me, Muse,
Which lap at the ear of him who cannot
   sleep!
First the familiar watchful bark of dogs,
Then the strokes of the hour measured,
Then two fishermen talking on the shore,
Then? Nothing more than the uncertain
Phantom sound of unbroken stillness,
Like a young bosom's breathing,
Like a deep well's murmuring,
Like a muffled oar's beat,
Then the unheard footfall of slumber.

Modest looking, this little poem is, on closer examination, a stunning poetic accomplishment. Focusing on familiar sounds audible at night and using the simplest form of enumeration, Meyer succeeds in creating a magic atmosphere of deepening silence. The sounds of dogs, clock, and fishermen are the last traces of wonted daily life. The third suspended "Dann" marks the point where silence becomes prevalent in the outside world. Yet Meyer penetrates this silence by noting another series of sounds echoing an internal realm of unfathomable depths. The "stroke of a muffled oar" at the end suggests the beat of a pulse, a sound of life that is even more internal than that of breathing mentioned before. Together with the stroke of the clock, this beat points to the outer and inner world, to outer and inner time. And finally, the idea of the "muffled oar" is reminiscent of Charon's boat; thus the approaching sleep can also be understood as death.

Here, to an even greater extent than in **"Spätboot,"** Meyer expands the realm of the expressible to the very limits of consciousness. He does this with seemingly simple means. The motif of the external sounds is quite plain, only the invocation of the muse is openly poetic. The language is simple, too: with the exception of one enjambment (lines 6-7) each syntactical unit fills a line. As in **"Eingelegte Ruder"** and **"Spätboot,"** Meyer uses the trochaic pentameter, which here, however, is rhymeless except for one rhyme (lines 4-5). In conjunction with the prevailing *u* assonances, this rhyme provides a certain melodious quality. Only once the *u* sounds are interrupted by an *i* assonance (lines 6-7) at the point where the silence itself becomes audible. Moreover, the suspended "Dann?" and the following enjambment create the impression that the silence is expanding until, in the last line, it pervades everything.

III *Death and Distance: The Love Poems*

These lake poems clearly demonstrate how far Meyer had departed from romantic poetry. Night, for the romantics, was a realm filled with intense yearning and promise, suggestive of a wide, enticing world; for Meyer, night has become almost void, a realm open only toward the depths, promising only peace in sleep or death. And while romantic poets follow rushing streams while fascinated by the mysteries of ever changing life, Meyer focuses on the stagnating waters of a lake while attracted by death. The significance which death has for Meyer separates him from the romantics in yet another way: in a group of beautiful love poems he sees the beloved as a young girl who died years ago unfulfilled. Love, since Goethe the epitome of immediate lyric expression, is presented not only in retrospect but also transfixed by death. Earlier scholars, especially Lena F. Dahme, established biographical connections between this "junggebliebne Tote" ("eternally youthful dead") in the poems and two young women who briefly played a role in Meyer's emotional life: Constance von Rodt (1839-1858) whom he knew in 1853, and Clelia Weydmann (1837-1866) whom he admired in 1860. But neither the scant biographical material nor the genesis of the poems support such a directly biographical interpretation;[11] instead these poems epitomize the nonconfessional nature of Meyer's poetry. His unfulfilled dreams about love are depersonalized and condensed in the basic figures of the dead beloved who is characterized—if at all—as a shy, untamed stranger in this world. Henel explains that unrequited love made Meyer keenly aware of his lacking access to life and that, consequently, he felt the need to picture this failure in the form of adverse fate, of death depriving him of his beloved before their love could mature.[12]

Death is important in another sense as well. By arresting the flow of life, by eliminating any further changes, it enables Meyer to contemplate his painful feelings from a distance growing with time. This contemplation turns into objectification, into art which—like death—isolates an experience from the transience of life and gives it lasting form. This view of art is crucial for Meyer and is illustrated in the poem **"Michelangelo und seine Statuen"** (**"Michelangelo and His Statues"**) in which the sculptor addresses some of his works:

> Du öffnest, Sklave, deinen Mund,
> Doch stöhnst du nicht. Die Lippe schweigt.
> Nicht drückt, Gedankenvoller, dich
> Die Bürde der behelmten Stirn.
> Du packst mit nervger Hand den Bart,
> Doch springst du, Moses, nicht empor.
> Maria mit dem toten Sohn,
> Du weinst, doch rinnt die Träne nicht.
> Ihr stellt des Leids Gebärde dar,
> Ihr meine Kinder, ohne Leid!
> So sieht der freigewordne Geist
> Des Lebens überwundne Qual.
> Was martert die lebendge Brust,
> Beseligt und ergötzt im Stein.
> Den Augenblick verewigt ihr,
> Und sterbt ihr, sterbt ihr ohne Tod.
> Im Schilfe wartet Charnon mein,
> Der pfeifend sich die Zeit vertreibt.

> You, slave, open your mouth,
> Yet you do not moan. Your lips are silent.
> You, full of thought, you are not weighted
> By the burden of a helmeted brow.
> With sinewy hand, you grasp your beard,
> Yet you, Moses, do not jump up.
> Mary with your dead son,
> You cry, yet your tears do now flow.
> You manifest the gesture of sorrow,
> You, my children, without sorrow.
> This is how the liberated spirit
> Sees life's sorrow overcome.
> What tortures the living breast
> Elevates and delights in marble.
> You render the moment eternal,
> And if you die, you die without death.

> In the sedge Charon waits for me
> Who whistling whiles away the time.

The expression of emotions, however painful or violent they may be, acquires an artistic beauty that comes from detachment. In the act of creating the gesture of pain its acutest sting is already overcome. Released from the actual throes of suffering the artist is able to embody its vivid memory in a permanent form of consoling, even delightful beauty. The reference to Charon, however, indicates that such artists are always close to death, even in their active life.

Viewing his experiences of frustrated love through death and distance, Meyer produced a group of unusual love poems. Closest to the forceful expressiveness he admired so much in Michelangelo is **"Wetterleuchten"** (**"Heat Lightning"**). Here the pale face of the dead girl appears amid spring blossoms, and sudden flashes of heat lightning cast on her a glow reminiscent of her blushing "way back / When the first word of love startled you." In its short intensity this image symbolizes both the force of love and its early evanescence. A painting by Charles Gleyre (1806-1874) inspired Meyer, in **"Lethe,"** to picture the dead beloved in Charon's boat gliding away from life. When the poet immerses himself in the water that has a "strange chill," when he tries to break into the boat, Meyer actually creates an image of himself and of his need to draw his poetry from the depths of death. As Henel shows in his interpretation, the beloved is also a symbol of Meyer's art, as is the boat gliding away noiselessly and without oars. This fine symbolism is, however, abandoned at the end where, for the sake of a dramatic conclusion, the beloved vanishes, leaving the poet empty-handed. Meyer did not bring this poem to full maturity, and it is thus very instructive in that it indicates how difficult it must have been for him fully to develop his unusual symbols without slipping back—as is the case here—into conventional imagery. Such imperfect poems set the accomplishment of others into full relief.

Felicitous unity of symbols and form is reached in **"Stapfen"** (**"Footsteps"**). Skillfully, Meyer develops another modest image into a suggestive symbol: returning alone from a walk with his beloved on a rainy day, the poet contemplates her footsteps which, imprinted in the wet soil of the woods, slowly disappear. The concluding lines read: "Fast unter meinem Blick verwischten sich / Die Spuren deines letzten Gangs mit mir" ("Almost under my glance vanished / The traces of your last walk with me"). The adjective "last" provides the key to the poem's subtle symbolism. The girl's vanishing footsteps presage her early death, the untimely end of a shy love. This adjective illuminates the significance of the girl's attributes: she is a guest at his neighbor's house, she is wearing a traveler's cloak and talking about another, longer voyage. Simple external circumstances thus become transparent for the transience of life. Her inner nature is characterized by such corresponding traits as "wandering, wayfaring, / Delicate, pure, dark as woods, but oh how sweet!" Again, an adjective opens up deeper dimensions: coining the compound "walddunkel," the poet endows the girl with an element of deep, yet charming reserve. As shown in the poems about the forest, for example, **"Abendrot im Walde"** (**"Sunset in the Forest"**), **"Jetzt rede du"** (**"Now You Shall Speak"**), and **"Sonntags"** (**"On a Sunday"**), the woods are for Meyer a realm of comforting refuge from the noise and the pains of the world. Congenial with the forest, the girl's nature is recondite, alien in the everyday world, and therefore all the more appealing. The description of her inner nature conjures up her delicate body before the poet's eyes; but it is "a dream figure" passing by. At the moment of intense recollection her strangeness too becomes palpable as the silent passing of someone whose footsteps, her contact with and imprint on the earth, are fading away.

The form of the poem is as light and unobtrusive as the symbol of the footsteps. Both language and vocabulary are evocative but never poetizing, and the rhymeless iambic pentameter lines prove to be marvellously pliable and quite soft despite their stressed endings. In addition, enjambments and an intricate syntax blur the metrical form, and this blurring perfectly corresponds to the main symbol, to the impressionistic light touch characterizing the entire poem. Here as well as in **"Der Blustropfen"** (**"A Drop of Blood"**) Meyer infuses the iambic pentameter, the blank verse of the classical German drama, with a new lyric quality. In the most sensitive review published in Meyer's lifetime, Carl Spitteler wrote in 1891 about the poet's use of this verse: "The art to create a sublime mood—without any melody, solely with the images in words—in an unassuming meter . . . has here reached absolute perfection. . . . And this art is new. Classical poets do not show us anything similar. Poems such as 'Stapfen' . . . are in content and form of exemplary perfection and open new realms to lyric poetry for all times" (*W,* II, 39).

The beginning and end of **"Stapfen"** mark the poem's content as a remembrance. In **"Der Blutstropfen,"** the temporal distance involved in remembering becomes visible in the symbol of the blood drop which, over the years, has faded but not disappeared. Tribute to the dead is the theme of **"Weihgeschenk"** (**"Votive Offering"**)—a poem of a melodious charm rare in Meyer's entire lyric oeuvre—and of **"Einer Toten"** (**"To a Dead Woman"**) where the poet's remembering is contrasted with the world's forgetfulness. For Meyer, remembrance is the main source of inspiration, both in the small scale of personal memories and on the larger scale of history. In **"Chor der Toten"** (**"Chorus of the Dead"**) he expresses the significance of remembering:

Wir Toten, wir Toten sind grössere Heere
Als ihr auf der Erde, als ihr auf dem Meere!
Wir pflügten das Feld mit geduldigen Taten,
Ihr schwinget die Sicheln und schneidet die
　　Saaten,
Und was wir vollendet und was wir begonnen,
Das füllt noch dort oben die rauschenden
　　Bronnen,
Und all unser Lieben und Hassen und Hadern,
Das klopft noch dort oben in sterblichen
　　Adern,
Und was wir an gültigen Sätzen gefunden,
Dran bleibt aller irdische Wandel gebunden,
Und unsere Töne, Gebilde, Gedichte
Erkämpfen den Lorbeer im strahlenden Lichte,
Wir suchen noch immer die menschlichen
　　Ziele—
Drum ehret und opfert! Denn unser sind viele!

We, the dead, the dead form greater armies
Than you on the earth, than you on the sea!
We plowed the fields with patient deeds,
You wield the sickles and cut the seed,
And what we completed and what we began
Is still filling the rushing fountains above,
And all our loving and hating and quarreling
Still beats up above in mortal veins,
And all earthly change remains bound
To whatever valid maxims we have found,
And our music, sculpture and poems
Vie for the laurel in the glowing light,
We still seek human goals,
Therefore, honor and sacrifice! For we are
　　many!

In the unusual form of four-stress dactylic lines rhyming in couplets Meyer forges a powerful rhythm and a solemn tone, resounding, as it were, with a multitude of voices. References to the dead "down here" and to the living "up there" regularly alternate, each reference filling one line, but every contrasted pair is tied into a single syntactical unit. Thus, the structure reinforces the idea that the dead with their deeds, thoughts, and emotions are inseparably bound up with whatever the living do, that the past inevitably conditions the present. **"Chor der Toten"** marks the point where Meyer's personal experience of death as an essential element in his life fuses with his interest in history. In other words, his way of seeing persons and feelings through a distance interposed by death, his emphasis on remembrance are the lyric equivalent of his proclivity for historical topics in his ballads and larger narrative works.

IV *Dionysian Life*

Yet there are other facets to Meyer's poetic world. The realm of the high mountains, evoked in many poems, is not only removed from the world as are the woods, it is also free of pain, of limitations; it is unimpeded by remembrance. The mountain landscape in the beautiful poems **"Himmelsnähe"** (**"Close to the Sky"**) and **"Noch einmal"** (**"Once Again"**) is striking in its combination of snow and ice, flowers, and rushing waters, all uniting to form an image of eternally living, timeless nature. In **"Himmelsnähe,"** air and wind, the silence itself are felt as the spirit of life itself—breath, prayer, and divine presence at once. **"Noch einmal"** adds a quietly gliding eagle as a symbol of inner freedom experienced in such surroundings, of deliverance from earthly heaviness. Clearly, the mountain landscape is the symbolic place for the poem **"Das Seelchen"** mentioned earlier. Here the soul is free enough to be contemplated. It has acquired the lightness of a butterfly and a transparency which is not destroyed but enhanced by the red mottling symbolizing past earthly pain. In the sense of the Michelangelo poem this is another example of the poet's freedom to transform past suffering into a symbol of quietly radiant beauty.

Between the realm of dark waters and that of bright mountains there is the realm of the harvest characterized by vivid, even glaring colors, intense emotions, and dramatic contrasts. In compact form, **"Schnitterlied"** (**"Harvest Song"**) illustrates the nature of this world. The scene with its vigorous work and the fervid emotions of the harvest celebration represents abounding life. But at this high-point of life death, too, is near:

> Von Garbe zu Garbe
> Ist Raum für den Tod—
> Wie schwellen die Lippen des Lebens so rot!

> From sheaf to sheaf
> There is room for death—
> How the lips of life swell red!

The juxtaposition of life and death is also suggested by the thunder and lightning in the background. In **"Erntegewitter"** (**"Harvest Storm"**) all these elements appear in an even more dramatic form. The blazing light of the lightning flashes and the girl's gesture of ebullient life—emptying a full glass in one gulp—are but momentary pictures immediately absorbed in darkness. The abrupt changes from light to darkness are designed to intensify exuberant life unmindful of anything else. The poem is a prime example of Meyer's monumental style which carries gestures, emotions, and contrasts to the extreme. The result here is highly theatrical, wrought with art—there are three flashes of lightning, two scenes with girls, the second one being an intensification of the first—but with such obvious intent that the exuberance is not really convincing.

An interesting companion piece is the poem **"Auf Goldgrund"** (**"On Golden Ground"**). Aiming at an image of quiet richness, Meyer here compares a harvest scene, bathed in the light of the setting sun, to medieval paintings in which "the saints, the praying / Shine on golden grounds." By thus borrowing heightened significance—"divine grandeur" (*heilige Würde*)—for life from art it becomes evident how important forms already condensed and stylized are from Meyer's art. In the light of art he more readily recognizes life's higher meanings. It is no accident that the external world started to fascinate him in Rome, where he was surrounded by great art and where the emotional expressiveness of a Southern people endowed even ordinary life with a sense of form. Paintings and sculptures often inspired poems, for example, **"Die Narde"** (**"The Nard"**), **"Die Kartäuser"** (**"The Cartusians"**), **"Die gegeisselte Psyche"** (**"Psyche Flagellated"**), **"Der tote Achill"** (**"Dead Achilles"**), and **"Die Jungfrau"** (**"The Virgin"**), in which Meyer presents life in a sort of double stylization. But only in the latter three cases does he succeed in giving the poems the formal ease and significance of their models. His tendency to view life in stylized forms produced the best harvest poem in **"Vor der Ernte"** (**"Before the Harvest"**). Although each of its stanzas is very obviously divided into two equal halves the image of the moon crescent creates an exquisite unity. The crescent of the moon suggests pure beauty, as forms and sounds fuse into a melodious celestial harmony. Below a warm Southern wind—the Föhn—tumultuously agitates the ripe fields symbolizing full, overwhelming life; while the beginning of the harvest indicates activity and tangible richness of the earth. The form of the crescent, repeated everywhere, unites the two contrasting halves. Emil Staiger points out that sky and earth are dissolved in nothing but curved lines and that, thus, the poem captures the moment "when life cools down to art, when nature is transfixed into ornament."[13] This very formal element in the way Meyer views life separates him in yet another respect from the immediacy of *Erlebnisdichtung* and connects him instead with the poets of the turn of the century—Stefan George, Rainer Maria Rilke, and Hugo von Hofmannsthal.

The juxtaposition of life and death in the harvest motif appears in a number of variations. In **"Nach einem Niederländer"** (**"After a Dutch Painting"**) the bedizened bride about to be painted is contrasted with the master's just finished painting of his own young daughter on her deathbed. Again, the discrepancy is heightened by art: on the completed painting the pale beauty of death is accentuated by a flowerbud of deepest color symbolizing a life never to bloom, while the painter's visitors bursting with excitement already project the next work capturing exuberant youth. And the concise image of **"Auf dem Canal Grande"** (**"On the Canal Grande"**) shows how the short span of loud vitality in the glowing sunlight soon fades into the long shadows of extinguished life.

The main variation, however, which becomes a major motif in itself, is the ambivalent figure of Dionysos or

Bacchus. According to Greek mythology, he is the god of spring, of beauty, of orgiastic life, and the conductor of souls to the underworld, the son of Persephone. Other double-faced figures belong to the Dionysian realm: the bacchante described in **"Vor einer Büste"** (**"Looking at a Bust"**) as having a touch of cruelty in her lovely face; Medusa, beautiful but deadly to her beholder (**"Die sterbende Meduse"**—**"Medusa Dying"**); and a winged Eros statue revealed as death extinguishing his torch (**"Der Marmorknabe"**—**"The Marble Youth"**). What in these lyric poems appears as a juxtaposition of extremes is transformed, in the ballads, into dramatic action and sudden change from intense life to death. **"Pentheus"** tells the story of Agave who, abandoning herself to the Dionysian orgy, kills her father Pentheus because he doubts the divinity of Dionysos. Using the name Lyaeus ("loosener") for the god Meyer points to his essential power to release men from all ties, both good and bad, making them express unreservedly their instantaneous desires and feelings. Therefore, he is also a god of art, of full, unrestrained expression which may, however, turn into chaos and destruction. Under the spell of Dionysos men scorn every limit: in **"Der trunkene Gott"** (**"The Drunken God"**) Alexander the Great feels himself an almost divine master of the universe; yet a reminder of his human limitations—shown in his slight physical deformity—sends him into a deadly rage that transforms the rousing celebration into the silence of death. Yet Bacchic scenes and figures are not restricted to ballads with themes from antiquity, they occur in ballads with medieval and Renaissance themes as well (for example, **"König Etzels Schwert"**—**"King Etzel's Sword,"** **"Jung Tirel"**—**"Young Tirel,"** **"Die Seitenwunde"**— **"Wound in the Side,"** **"Cäsar Borgias Ohnmacht"**— **"Cesar Borgia Powerless"**). Clearly, Meyer sees bacchic life as a timeless phenomenon fascinating and frightening at once; and while he might have admired the vitality and daring that nature denied him, he could not help but end all these scenes with death, thus implicitly manifesting his distrust of this life, however brilliant it may be.[14]

In the ballads, Meyer's representation of this bacchic life as well as of historical drama in a more general sense does not always avoid a cramped, mannered style, as the language and the rhymes are forced or too obviously dramatic. Yet in such pieces as **"Der Ritt in den Tod"** (**"Death Ride"**), **"Das Geisterross"** (**"The Phantom Horse"**), **"Bettlerballade"** (**"Beggars' Ballad"**), **"Die Füsse im Feuer"** (**"Feet in the Fire"**) and **"Die Rose von Newport"** (**"The Rose of Newport"**) the poet manifests his craftsmanship. In **"Der Ritt in den Tod"** a bacchic moment is captured most concisely and effectively. Though duels are prohibited by pain of death, a young Roman kills an enemy in a duel; his glorious triumph will be followed by his execution. Choosing the form of a monologue in couplets, Meyer expresses the young man's triumph in a powerful way.

The dactylic meter with its four stresses starting with one or even two unstressed syllables creates a vigorous, almost galloping movement throughout the poem. Terse imperatives and exclamations, often filling only half a line, convey the speaker's boundless pride that prompted him to defy the law. And his feeling of victory coupled with the certainty of imminent death culminates in the grand gesture of raising his head in triumph before submitting to death, the ultimate limitation.

Most popular among the ballads, **"Die Füsse im Feuer"** is an excellent example of Meyer's dramatic art. Avoiding mannerism he here uses the disjunctive style with moderation and to maximum effect. Its irregular rhythm is well suited for the depiction of the storm at the beginning, but more importantly it corresponds to the way in which the King's courier is confronted with shreds of memory that, confirmed by the children's stare, combine to growing terror climaxing in the nightmare. At this point, however, in an ingenious turn, Meyer shifts the dramatic emphasis from the images of crude violence to the subtly indicated agony of the host's internal struggle. The surprise is dramatically complete because the host can enter the guest room through a jib door. The drama ends on a contemplative note contrasting the courier's easy reliance on earthly power and the Huguenot's hard-won acquiescence in divine will. Forgoing rhyme and regular stanzas and even blurring the fixed length of the lines (six iambics) with a varying syntax, Meyer provides the poem with a formal unity by repeating certain words and the image of the feet in the fire. Upon closer examination, the use of the fire marks the dramatic crescendo: first, it signals warmth and hospitality to the courier; then it awakens his memories; finally it spreads in the dream to a fiery sea devouring him, a metaphor for his terror, maybe even his bad conscience; and at the very end, the Huguenot's words "You have devilishly murdered my wife!" associate him with a hellish fire of hatred.

A masterful use of varying images and repetitions is displayed in **"Die Rose von Newport."** King Charles I of England is presented in two mirror scenes that repeat a basic situation—his arrival in Newport, where a girl offers him the city's emblem, a rose. First, he comes as the young prince and future king amid flowers and cheers. The girl offering the rose is his, and the whole world seems to lie at his feet. Many years later he arrives as the king, but as a fugitive in the midst of a snowstorm, unheralded and unheeded. The world, once so welcoming, has turned into a forbidding precipice, the rose is now withered, and the girl offering it is begging. She is an outcast like him, and her face mirrors his own face and misery. Referring to the refrain of the first stanza "Tomorrow the linden trees will tell the tale / Of the defoliated rose of Newport" the reader can see this girl as his own child, but she can also be interpreted as a purely symbolic image of his own withered life devoid of promise and bliss. While the sequence, and even the structure of the images, remain the same in both stanzas, the poet allows for enough deviation in length to preserve an element of natural life within a strict form. The impression of vividness is also rooted in the unrhymed dactylic lines which produce a light rhythm appropriate to the cheerful ride at the beginning as well as to the hasty, aimless flight at the end. Looking back to **"Der Ritt in den Tod,"** the other equestrian poem, we realize what different effects a skillful poet can achieve with the same form.

Meyer's ballads overwhelm the reader with a wealth of historical material, they span history from classical antiquity to the Reformation and the seventeenth century, introducing kings and crusaders, monks, reformers, artists, and lovers. They talk about noble passions, about piety and greed, fulfilled and thwarted love, and about many a death; they present a world built on wide knowledge and reading. This seems to indicate that Meyer is here commanding the rich world which his time expected to be the natural domain of the creative writer. And as the poem **"Fülle" ("Abundance")** at the beginning of the poetry collection shows, he accepted this view and wanted to conform to it. Yet his praise of the world's copious riches is not altogether convincing: the negative expressions—"enough is not enough," "enough will never ever be enough"—suggest that the poet's prime basis is not so much the direct experience of abundance as the lack of it which, in turn, incites a strong desire to reach out for the riches of life. This desire is certainly genuine and produces some excellent ballads, but it is only part of his creative personality. **"Fülle"** must be seen together with the following poem **"Das heilige Feuer" ("The Sacred Fire")** that compares the poet to a priestess watching the sacred fire at the dead of night. Here, the poet is in austere surroundings; lonely and separated from the mainstream of life, he is intently bent on only one purpose: his art. And while neither poem alone can describe Meyer's entire work, **"Das heilige Feuer"** does describe the more fundamental part, for even in depicting the fullness of life he cannot draw on experience, on natural identification, but has to rely on his artistic sense, his intuition, observation, and reading.

V *Architectural Form*

Form is a dominant aspect of Meyer's poetry. In the *Gedichte* of 1882 he uses a much larger variety of meters, rhyme patterns, and stanzas—including forms without rhymes and stanzas—than in his earlier collections. His persistence in recasting and polishing poems, in isolating and developing individual motifs is rooted in a deep concern to find the congenial form for ideas, images, and feelings, many of them alien to the literature of the time. And this working process demonstrates clearly to what an extent form can be improved by aesthetic reflection, and that a good poem is not only inspired but also "made." Or as Mallarmé once put it: "It isn't with ideas but with words that one makes a poem."[15] In contrast to the French symbolists Meyer practiced this conscious way of writing—he often called it "building"—without any theories, without knowing that he was engaged in something new. This very lack of theoretical foundation exacerbated his frequent doubts concerning the validity of his poems in terms of "life" and "truth" which for him were still tantamount to good poetry. In 1881, when he was giving the bulk of his poetry its final, often original and perfect form, the question of whether his poetry had true life still haunted him, as is shown in the poem **"Möwenflug" ("Sea Gulls in Flight")**. The image of sea gulls circling a rock is so clearly reflected in the green water far below them that there is no difference between reality and its mere reflection, "that deceit and truth completely resembled each other." In analogy to this image the poet asks:

> Und du selber? Bist du echt beflügelt?
> Oder nur gemalt und abgespiegelt?
> Gaukelst du im Kreis mit Fabeldingen?
> Oder hast du Blut in deinen Schwingen?

> And you yourself? Are you truly winged?
> Or merely painted and mirrored?
> Are you dallying in a circle with fabled
>   creatures?
> Or do you have blood in your wings?

While ending in a series of questions, the poem itself is the answer, for its unassuming beauty with its light touches of white, green, and grey has the quality of true art that naturally saturates an image with significance transcending intellectual constructs. The image used here is in itself a symbol of Meyer's art: the motifs of the deep water and the free-flying birds represent parts of his poetic world. His art has "blood," not in the sense of an immediate expression of personal feelings but in that of beauty clearly tinged with Meyer's individuality, in the sense of exquisite images that betray, in their elaborate composition, his recondite feelings down to their slightest vibrations. And one must not forget that form, the counterpart of the "blood," has a double function: while mitigating emotions and creating detachment it also provides the protective frame that allows expression of the deepest experiences.

The importance of formal structure also comes to the fore in the organization of the poetry collection as a whole. Meyer divided the poems he selected for the volume into nine cycles, which he entitled "Vorsaal" ("Antechamber"), "Stunde" ("Hour"), "In den Bergen" ("In the Mountains"), "Reise" ("Travel"), "Liebe" ("Love"), "Götter" ("Gods"), "Frech und fromm" ("Impudent and Pious"), "Genie" ("Genius"), and "Männer" ("Men"). As in *Romanzen und Bilder (Ballads and*

Images), there is an obvious division between lyric poems (1-5) and ballads (6-9). Yet upon a closer look this genre distinction becomes blurred, because the lyric cycles contain some ballads, as the ballad cycles contain a number of lyric poems. Moreover, many narrative poems have little or no direct action—**"Das verlorene Schwert"** (**"The Lost Sword"**), **"Die Söhne Haruns"** (**"Harun's Sons"**), and **"Das Auge des Blinden"** (**"The Eye of the Blind"**) to name just a few. An extreme is reached in **"Der Ritt in den Tod"** and **"Die Rose von Newport"** which represent but momentary glimpses of climactic situations. The development of these ballads confirms this: in the course of reworking the long, wordy poems of the 1860s, Meyer made them more compact and expressive and condensed their narrative content ever more into one dramatic situation charged with contrasts. Thus, even the narrative poems assume, over the years, more of the static character typical for Meyer's lyric poems which so often present motionless images, memories transfixed by death, or scenes perpetuated by an artist. This loss of dynamic, and the increasing prevalence of static, forms indicate that elaborate art rather than direct representation of life shapes this poetic world.

The cycles and their arrangement corroborate this, too. The poems of the second through ninth cycles are arranged according to subject matter in the broad sense suggested by the cycles' headings and in the narrower sense of imagery common to several poems within a cycle. Such juxtaposition has implications which are typical for Meyer's poetry. The time when a poem was first written or published is disregarded. The group of the three Venice poems covers a time span of twenty-five years: **"Venedigs erster Tag"** (**"Venice's First Day"**) was published in 1864 in *Zwanzig Balladen;* **"Venedig"** was written in 1881-1882; and **"Auf dem Canal Grande"** was composed in 1889 and added to the fourth edition of the *Gedichte* in 1891. Further, the poems about the dead beloved have no chronological sequence at all, as is shown by their dates of composition: **"Weihgeschenk,"** 1869; **"Der Blutstropfen,"** 1881; **"Stapfen,"** 1865; **"Wetterleuchten,"** 1880; **"Lethe,"** 1860; and **"Einer Toten,"** 1873. Thus Meyer implicitly confirms that his poetry is not to be read in a biographical light. Also, the juxtaposition of poems with common imagery or theme does not necessarily guarantee a common or related significance. The group consisting of **"Die gegeisselte Psyche,"** **"Der tote Achill,"** and **"Der Musensaal"** is put together because they were all inspired by sculptures Meyer had seen in Rome, but they differ widely in their meaning, and only **"Der tote Achill"** refers at all to Meyer's association of death and art; while **"Der Musensaal"** proclaims an opposite attitude by picturing the muses freed from their calm sculptural attitudes and engaged in a passionate dialogue about the segments of life assigned to each of them. In his *Conrad Ferdinand Meyer und das Kunstwerk seiner*

Gedichtsammlung,[16] Walther Brecht establishes meaningful relationships—such as parallels, contrasts, supplements—for the sequence of all poems within a cycle.

Brecht made a very valuable contribution, since he was the first to recognize the formal composition of the nine cycles, the first to call attention to the fact that not only the poetry but also the arrangement of poems is meant as a work of art. In his view, the fifth cycle "Love" is the center, the inner sanctum, so to speak, which is symmetrically surrounded by the cycles 1 to 4 concerned with Meyer's personal life, the world of his own experiences, and the cycles 6 to 9 devoted to the wider realm of European history. The latter four cycles each span a certain period: "Gods," Greek and especially Roman antiquity; "Impudent and Pious," the Middle Ages with their mixture of pious endeavor and earthly passion; while "Genius" focuses on the Renaissance with its extraordinary artists and towering political figures, and "Men" centers on the Reformation period. This historical macrocosm has a counterpart in the first four cycles outlining the microcosm of the poet's own world. For Brecht, "Antechamber" offers an introduction indicating the main themes of the collection, that is, poetry, love, and death, "Hour" concentrates on the poet's immediate surroundings, the lake, the harvest in the fields, the woods—and the moods associated with them; "In the Mountains" and "Travel" show the expansion of Meyer's poetic horizons.

Yet for all of Brecht's insights this interpretation of the volume's structure is not entirely satisfying, because the fifth part does not quite fit into this symmetry of inner and outer world. Moreover, the poems of the first cycle not only lack a common subject matter, but they are also, on the whole, of a somewhat inferior artistic value. For this reason, Henel separates this cycle from the other eight which then evenly represent the personal world (2-5) and the historical world (6-9). Noting that the poems in "Antechamber" focus on unlived lives, frustrations, the "dream hoard" of poetry, Henel convincingly concludes that this part represents the mute stage of Meyer's life when he himself lived in a dream world and was unable to express his experiences.[17] The very difficulty of understanding the main concept for this first cycle shows again to what extent Meyer needed and used impersonal forms as a protective screen for his own world with its formless depths and its visions of extreme forces threatening with chaos. The volume's formal composition—described as "architectural" by Brecht, as a "temple" by Henel—functions very much like the form in a poem: it sets up a visible, clear form for a world that threatens to disintegrate. For Meyer, only form, visible, plastic images, and strict composition made individual expression possible.

The poem **"Schwarzschattende Kastanie"** (**"Dark Shadowing Chestnut Tree"**) encompasses essential elements of Meyer's art in a beautiful picture:

Schwarzschattende Kastanie,
Mein windgeregtes Sommerzelt,
Du senkst zur Flut dein weit Geäst,
Dein Laub, es durstet und es trinkt,
Schwarzschattende Kastanie!
Im Porte badet junge Brut
Mit Hader oder Lustgeschrei,
Und Kinder schwimmen leuchtend weiss
Im Gitter deines Blätterwerks,
Schwarzschattende Kastanie!
Und dämmern See und Ufer ein
Und rauscht vorbei das Abendboot,
So zuckt aus roter Schiffslatern
Ein Blitz und wandert auf dem Schwung
Der Flut, gebrochnen Lettern gleich,
Bis unter deinem Laub erlischt
Die rätselhafte Flammenschrift,
Schwarzschattende Kastanie!

Dark shadowing chestnut tree,
My wind-stirred summer tent,
You lower your far-flung branches to the
     water,
Your foliage thirsts and drinks,
Dark shadowing chestnut tree!
In the harbor cove the young are bathing
Quarreling or shouting in delight,
And children swim gleaming white
In the lattice works of your leaves,
Dark shadowing chestnut tree!
And when lake and shore merge in dusk
And the evening boat murmurs past,
There flashes from the ship's red lantern
A streak of lightning and wanders on the
     surge
Of water, like broken lettering,
Until beneath your foliage vanishes
The mysterious flame-writing,
Dark shadowing chestnut tree!

The refrain "Schwarzschattende Kastanie" builds an architectural frame around the poem with its unrhymed verses. This clear frame separates the poet's own place—close to the water—from the wider world outside. The children swimming in the sunlight, their cries of joy and quarrel suggest a life full of activity and passions. The evening scene with the boat and the red reflections on the dark water suggest that realm where life, light, and emotion flash up once more before vanishing into darkness. The poet tries to capture this bright life in his work but does not quite succeed; life vanishes too fast for him and leaves only the flaming signals on the dark waters; it has become a mysterious text with an elusive meaning.

The image of the broken inscription is significant in a larger context as well. For the later nineteenth century life grew ever more disintegrated and less comprehensible, and philosophers gave up trying to devise a unified system encompassing all of life's phenomena; characteristically, Nietzsche's work offers but parts of a philosophical system and is often structured in short paragraphs. And the individual feels increasingly lost among a growing mass of people and in the face of a fast developing technology. Disintegration of larger meaning into smaller, disconnected parts is reflected in Meyer's writing process that tends more and more to isolate individual motifs which, in addition, are often composed of originally separate elements. In this respect, he is remarkably close to the principle of modern poetry as outlined by Baudelaire: "Imagination decomposes the entire creation and, with the materials thus accumulated and disposed according to rules for which the origin cannot be found but in the deepest depths of the soul, imagination creates a new world, produces the sensation of the new."[18] Against this background of decomposing reality and recomposing it in a new way, the principle of deliberate formal structure is shown in its full importance. For structure, artistic form, endow life with significance that can no longer be derived from a direct, emotional identification with the world, an intuitive understanding. Meyer's poetry opens a door to this new art: he is conventional in his openly professed endeavors—to create true, full life—and in parts of his imagery—abundance, heroic gestures—but at the same time he is an innovator in using new creative processes and in extending the limits of lyric beauty far into the realm of death.

Notes

[1] This estimate is based on the material available in Volumes 2-4 of the historical-critical edition, covering the first seven of the nine cycles in *Gedichte*.

[2] For this reason, there are few manuscripts for poems written after 1879 when Betsy ceased to act as secretary.

[3] (Madison: University of Wisconsin Press, 1954), p. 139; hereafter referred to as *Poetry*.

[4] Meyer's interest in French literature—strongest in the 1840s and 1850s—was always mainly directed toward classical and romantic works.

[5] See Heinrich Henel on "Lethe," "Stapfen," and "Das Seelchen"; Emil Staiger on "Die tote Liebe"; Beatrice Sandberg-Braun on "Liederseelen," "Schwüle," and "Nachtgeräusche"; and Gustav Beckers on "Der verwundete Baum." See also the bibliography.

[6] See "Lyrik der Beschaulichkeit," *Monatshefte* 60 (1968), p. 227.

[7] "Linguistic Patterns, Literary Structure, and the Genesis of 'Der römische Brunnen,'" *Language and Style* 4 (1971), 83-115; the article also contains an extensive bibliography.

[8] For a thorough discussion of the differences between romantic and symbolist poetry see Heinrich Henel, "Erlebnisdichtung und Symbolismus," *Deutsche Vierteljahrsschrift für Literaturwissenschaft und Geistesgeschichte* 32 (1958), especially pp. 82-85, and Emil Staiger, "Das Spätboot," in *Die Kunst der Interpretation* (Zurich: Atlantis, 1955), pp. 254-56.

[9] See above p. 60-61.

[10] See also p. 54. The poem "Tag, schein herein, und Leben, flieh hinaus" is another case in point: in the last version Meyer changes the middle stanza so as to describe his youth when he was "stifled in a dream." This change creates a moving contrast to the hope and brightness expressed in the first and third stanzas (*W*, III, 161-64).

[11] Lena F. Dahme in *Women in the Life and Art of C. F. Meyer* attributes "Weihgeschenk" and "Der Blutstropfen" to Constance von Rodt, "Stapfen," "Wetterleuchten," "Lethe," and "Einer Toten" to Clelia Weydmann. Yet the death motif in "Lethe" is already present in the first version of 1860, years before Clelia died, while the death motif in "Stapfen" is not developed until the very last version of 1881-1882.

[12] See Heinrich Henel, "Conrad Ferdinand Meyer: 'Lethe,'" in Benno von Wiese, ed., *Die deutsche Lyrik*, 2 vols. (Dusseldorf: Bagel 1957), II, 222.

[13] See Emil Staiger, "Das Spätboot," p. 273.

[14] See also Betty Loeffler Fletcher, "The Supreme Moment as a Motif in C. F. Meyer's Poems," *Monatshefte* 42 (1950), 27-32, and my dissertation *C. F. Meyer und die antike Mythologie*, Zürcher Beiträge zur deutschen Literatur- und Geistesgeschichte, vol. 25 (Zurich: Atlantis 1966), especially the chapters "Der trunkene Gott" and "Traumbesitz."

[15] Quoted in Anna Balakian, *The Symbolist Movement* (New York: Random House, 1967), p. 87.

[16] Vienna: W. Braumüller, 1918.

[17] See Henel, *Poetry*, pp. 245-52.

[18] See "Salon de 1859," part III, "La reine des facultés," in *Oeuvres Complètes* (Paris: Gallimard, 1961), pp. 1037-38.

Works Cited

Primary Sources

Gedichte an seine Braut. Edited by Constanze Speyer (Zurich: Oprecht, 1940).

[Beckers, Gustav.] "Der verwundete Baum. Infrastrukturelle Analyse zum genetischen Typus lyrischer Arbeit bei Conrad Ferdinand Meyer." *Colloquia Germanica* (1973), 257-312. . . .

Burkhard, Marianne. *C. F. Meyer und die antike Mythologie*. Zürcher Beiträge zur deutschen Literatur und Geistesgeschichte, vol. 25 (Zurich: Atlantis, 1966). . . .

Dahme, Lena F. *Women in the Life and Art of Conrad Ferdinand Meyer* (New York: Columbia University Press, 1936). . . .

Fletcher, Betty Loeffler. "The 'Supreme Moment' as a Motif in C. F. Meyer's Poems." *Monatshefte* 42 (1950), 27-32. . . .

Henel, Heinrich. "Psyche. Sinn und Werden eines Gedichtes [Das Seelchen] von C. F. Meyer." *Deutsche Vierteljahrsschrift für Literaturwissenschaft und Geistesgeschichte* 27 (1953), 358-86.

———. *The Poetry of Conrad Ferdinand Meyer* (Madison: University of Wisconsin Press, 1954).

———. "Erlebnisdichtung und Symbolismus." *Deutsche Vierteljahrsschrift für Literaturwissenschaft und Geistesgeschichte* 32 (1958), 71-98.

———. *Gedichte Conrad Ferdinand Meyers: Wege ihrer Vollendung*. Deutsche Texte, vol. 8 (Tübingen: Niemeyer, 1962).

———. "Conrad Ferdinand Meyer: 'Lethe' and 'Stapfen,'" In *Die deutsche Lyrik: Von der Spätromantik bis zur Gegenwart*, edited by Benno von Wiese, pp. 217-29, 230-42 (Düsseldorf: Bagel, 1962). . . .

Sandberg-Braun, Beatrice. *Wege zum Symbolismus: Zur Entstehungsgeschichte dreier Gedichte Conrad Ferdinand Meyers*. Zürcher Beiträge zur deutschen Literatur und Geistesgeschichte, vol. 32 (Zürich: Atlantis, 1969). . . .

Staiger, Emil. "Das Spätboot. Zu Conrad Ferdinand Meyers Lyrik." In *Die Kunst der Interpretation*, pp. 237-73 (Zurich: Atlantis, 1955).

Dennis McCort (essay date 1988)

SOURCE: "*Gustav Adolfs Page* as a Tragedy of the Unconscious" in *States of Unconsciousness in Three Tales by C. F. Meyer*, Bucknell University Press, 1988, pp. 33-76.

[*In the following excerpt, McCort considers Meyer's* Gustav Adolfs Page *a psychological "tragic drama" of the repression of femininity that leads to a fundamental distortion of the central character's interpretation of reality.*]

In the late 1870s, Meyer became drawn to the idea of writing a dramatic tragedy about the great Protestant standard-bearer of the Thirty Years War, King Gustavus Adolphus of Sweden. The king's loyal page, August Leubelfing, son of a Nürnberg patrician, was also to figure prominently in the action. However, as time passed a curious reversal of priorities began to occur in Meyer's imagination such that, by the fall of 1881, he was paying almost as much attention to the supporting character as to the protagonist. Thinking now about the royal page, and perhaps already glimpsing the rich narrative vis-à-vis the meager dramatic possibilities of his subject, he writes coyly to his literary mentor, Louise von François: "and Page Leubelfing, . . . yes, what becomes of him is my secret."[1] Of course, Meyer's "secret," revealed in the finished tale, *Gustav Adolfs Page,* was his intention to turn the historical Leubelfing into a girl, "Gustel," who dons the disguise of a male soldier, affects a stentorian baritone, takes her cousin's place in conscription and follows the king she idolizes to a glorious death in battle. The fact that the historical Gustavus Adolphus was known to have been severely nearsighted lent credibility to the improbable premise.

An astonishing footnote to this literary history is that Louise von François actually guessed Meyer's secret plans for a "sex-change operation" on Leubelfing, for in her response to his letter three weeks later, she facetiously envisioned the character of Leubelfing as "a Lutheran Joan of Arc."[2] But even more astonishing, perhaps, than this deft bit of mind-reading was her uncanny settling on none other than Joan of Arc as a point of comparison. In this, von François was positively prophetic, for if one translates the mythical context that, for example, Schiller creates for Joan in his dramatic prologue into psychological terms, it becomes clear that there is a far deeper bond between these two heroines than the enchanting image of the militant maiden. Viewed psychologically, both suffer under the prohibition by the father against feminine experiencing. In *Die Jungfrau von Orleans* Schiller makes God the mythical equivalent of the dictatorial father who forbids his daughter the natural joys of sexual love and motherhood for the sake of a "higher" destiny he holds in store for her.[3] Meyer, on the other hand, penned *Gustav Adolfs Page* at a later time, when an author was as likely to draw inspiration from the philosophical and sociocritical antecedents of modern depth psychology as from mythological conceits in his portrayal of familial conflict. Coming under the sway of these nascent psychological ideas, he weaves his tragic narrative, as I will show, out of an unconscious tension in Gustel between her stifled natural feminity and the masculine persona foisted upon her by an insensitive father and ironically emblematized by her male page's disguise. A further irony is that the change of sex from male to female to which Meyer subjected the historical Leubelfing has its precise mirror-image in the theme of his story: the maiden's unconscious quest to become a man for her father. It is possible, though one cannot be certain, that the idea of the historical liberty sparked the narrative theme in Meyer's mind by reverse association.

The why's and wherefore's of Gustel's unconscious dilemma occupy our attention here, for it is only when read psychologically as a tragedy of the unconscious that the full aesthetic power of Meyer's story is released. Curiously, while some critics have alluded to the interplay of unconscious designs within and between the characters, no one has taken the subliminal dimension of the narrative seriously enough to trace its clear omnipotence over the life and death of the heroine.[4] This is especially puzzling with respect to the critical literature appearing since 1950, when evidence of the role played by *Gustav Adolfs Page* in Freud's formation of the early psychoanalytic concept of deferred action came to light.[5]

More generally, Freud's letters to Fliess reveal an intense preoccupation with Meyer's works during the few years preceding the publication of the historic *Traumdeutung* (1900), critical years for the working-out of such fundamental theories as the family romance and the Oedipus complex.[6] All indications are that, for Freud, Meyer belonged in the heady company of Dostoyevsky, Goethe, Shakespeare, and Sophocles, a pantheon of intuitive psychologists blessed with the genial capacity "to salvage the deepest insights from the maelstrom of their own feelings quite effortlessly, insights towards which the rest of us can only blaze a trail with agonizing uncertainties and tireless groping."[7] One is impressed by the scientist's homage to the poet's intuitive gift; but, as I have suggested, there was more to Meyer's awareness of the hidden motives of the human heart than intuition: confirming and crystallizing this intuition was an intellectual familiarity with certain current proto-Freudian conceptions of the unconscious with which he came into contact through books and acquaintances. My analysis of *Gustav Adolfs Page* as a tragedy of the unconscious will close with a sketch of the confluence of some of these ideas in Meyer's thought. Taken together, textual analysis and intellectual-historical sketch argue for the profound effects of the emerging depth psychology on Meyer's artistic vision. Indeed, one discovers in this oft-slighted tale[8] that the psychological definition of Meyer's characters could at times go far beyond the patented sculpturing of revealing gestures and articulate facial expressions, beyond the plastic qualities of the *Augenmensch* for which he is so well known, to the intricate creation of characters whose entire strategies for living are shaped by motives and conflicts parted from their own normal waking consciousness, as William James so aptly phrased it, "by the filmiest of screens."[9]

My thesis that the unconscious is the locus of all significant action in **Gustav Adolfs Page** rests on four cumulatively persuasive observations. The first of these—negative in character—is simply that, read straightforwardly as the tale of a young girl's patriotic hero-worship, this narrative, originally conceived in epic-heroic terms as "a drama of Schillerian proportions"[10] centering on the Swedish king, suffers from a misplaced focus of attention on a peripheral character, that reduces it to the trivial. This is, in fact, a criticism that has dogged the story from its earliest appearance down to the present day.[11] But it is inconceivable that Meyer's sure aesthetic instincts could have prompted him to abandon a momentous issue for a banal one, that there was nothing more at work in his turning from aristocratic drama to bourgeois novella than a self-indulgent impulse to fashion an amusing companion piece to Goethe's Klärchen. In his remark to Hans Blum linking the two characters,[12] it is clear that Meyer is alluding to Klärchen, not as a model for Gustel, but as a catalyst for the creation of a quite different character, whose "secret love"[13] for the king hints at needs and motives totally alien to the artless quality of Klärchen's love for Egmont. Something about Klärchen's heedless devotion must have suggested to Meyer a psychological possibility intriguing and weighty enough to allow him to drop the cherished idea for a dramatic tragedy of royalty without suffering the artist's grief over an "unborn child." I propose that the only sufficient cause for this would have been a "secret love" in Gustel conceived by the author as "unconscious love," a lifelong unacknowledged yearning for the father who never accepted her and, upon his death, for the king as a father-substitute. This yearning gathers up within its smoldering impotence all the important themes of her personal history and is played out on the always-curtained stage of the unconscious where each individual is his own highborn protagonist.

My second observation concerns the intense anxiety, at times escalating to panic, that plagues Gustel from the moment she arrives in the Swedish camp near Nürnberg in her male page's disguise. Ostensibly, she fears the puritanical king's harsh censure, should he see through her ruse ("Such moments [when the king seemed to sense something] caused the page a sudden fear" [2:41]), and the stain on his honor that exposure by a third party would bring. Reasonable grounds for apprehension, one might assume at first glance, and yet the relentless, almost savage quality of what can only be called her dread ("the page had become extremely worried to the point of distraction about her disguise and her sex" [2:44]) seems decidedly out of proportion to the issue. She has, after all, entered into this deception for the very noblest of motives, to serve and protect her king, if necessary even with her life; indeed,

so bizarre a deception could only be viewed as an indication of the lengths to which she is prepared to go to express her devotion. Subjectively at least, Gustel would have every reason to feel at peace with her own motives. Moreover, late in the story she is assured by her godfather, Colonel Ake Tott, whom she meets in her hysterical flight from camp, that women disguised as soldiers are a common fact of camp life over which no one is raising any eyebrows, and that, in fact, "you weren't exactly risking your neck. If he'd found you out, he [Gustav Adolf] would have scolded you with 'Beat it, you foolish brat!', and a moment later he'd be thinking of something else" (2:57). All of this leads one strongly to suspect that the true and sufficient cause of Gustel's exaggerated fear of exposure is hidden even from herself and is at bottom the threat of self-exposure. It is the threat of intolerable insight into the true meaning of her feelings for the king that feeds her anxiety, a threat consciously symbolized and masked by the, at best, marginally legitimate concern over exposure to others.

Thirdly, one observes a curious ambiguity surrounding the chronology of Gustel's birth and her parents' marriage, background exposition conveyed to us in chapter 1 through repartee between Gustel and her relatives, old Uncle Leubelfing and his son, August. From the old man it is learned that Gustel's father, Rupert, a soldier in the Swedish service, had married her mother at seventeen and been killed in a brawl at thirty. Yet Gustel has previously mentioned that "until I was almost fifteen I was always on horseback with my mother and father and wore just my short riding outfit" (2:36). If one takes Gustel literally here, one cannot avoid the author's possible insinuation that young Rupert assumed the burdens of marriage and parenthood with some reluctance, perhaps yielding to pressure to provide his lover's expected child with a name. This line of speculation is supported by Gustel's enigmatic revelation that her father "fell in defense of my mother's honor" (2:37)—enigmatic, that is, until the reader, having just been alerted to the ambiguous circumstances of Gustel's birth, deduces from the remark that her father was killed attempting to avenge some loose-tongued cohort's slurring allusion to his wife's sexual indiscretion. Taken together, these veiled implications give one pause to question the true nature of the emotional bond between father and daughter.

Interestingly, Burkhard and Stevens, the only critics to have noticed the chronological anomaly, do not even entertain the interpretive implications of a "shotgun marriage" between Gustel's parents, preferring instead to censure Meyer for a "lapse" in "accurate attention to chronology."[14] I suggest, however, that Meyer was too much the "bleeder," the painstaking stylist and careful architect of plots, to have made so significant an error, notwithstanding his description of the genesis of **Page** as "a sudden idea that I carried out without interruption,"[15] and that the chronological ambiguity is a deftly planted clue to the unconscious forces that shape the adult behavior of this unwanted child. What emerges, then, as the dominant theme of Gustel's life is her desperate struggle to win the love of a reluctant father, an impetuous "roughneck" (2:36), as old Leubelfing sees him, who, hardly more than a boy himself, was not nearly ready for the moral and emotional responsibilities of parenthood that were suddenly thrust upon him.

Gustel's struggle to win her father's love ensnares her in a conflict between true and false identities, between the person nature intends her to be and the persona she believes she must become to please her father. This brings me to my fourth observation, which is of a key image that occurs quite subtly in the first chapter while recurring more conspicuously in the second. The image functions as the author's emblematic indication to the reader of the irony implicit in Gustel's unawareness of her identity conflict and of the specifically sexual form which the conflict assumes. In the opening scene Meyer has just introduced Gustel in terms more befitting a virile youth than a modest maiden: "A girl as supple as a poplar tree entered the room. She had laughing eyes, short hair, the figure of a boy, and rather cavalrylike manners" (2:35). After dinner, as she prepares to listen to the Leubelfings' tale of woe concerning August's impending conscription as a royal page, the author says that she "shoved back her chair, and folded her arms. She crossed her slender legs under her blue skirt with its pouch and keyring hanging from the belt" (2:36). The image of the juxtaposed pouch and keys suspended from her belt in the general vicinity of the pelvis would not of itself evoke associations to the male and female genitals, were it not unequivocally reinforced at the beginning of chapter 2 as the queen, in her fussy admonition to the new page not to shrink from the little sartorial tasks that go with the job, "put it [a silver thimble] on a finger [of the page]" (2:39). The king, who has been silently observing Gustel's disgusted reaction to this unexpected "womanish" side of soldiering, "now burst out in hearty laughter as he caught sight of his page with a short sword on his left hip and a thimble in his right hand" (2:39). The image of the keys and pouch in the earlier scene, mentioned only casually by the narrator in a subordinate clause, is here repeated as sword and thimble and is made the ostentatious focus of the reader's attention. The clash of genital emblems is no longer oblique but obvious. Gustel stands poised between them as if in mock-allegorical representation of the battle between the realms of light and darkness for dominion over her soul.

It also becomes clear from the context of the second scene that this configuration of conflicting genital images has less to do with physical sexuality per se than with the larger dimension of sexual identity. The reader's immediate association from sword and thimble to phallic and vaginal does not stop there but moves on to an awareness of a fundamental male-female antagonism within Gustel, a primal struggle between natural and artificial gender identities by which she is unconsciously gripped. One could say here that the ludicrous pairing of genital images underlines an internal conflict that is essentially sexual-political. It is, after all, the amusing way in which Gustel's *tableau vivant* unwittingly violates the code of "separate but equal" sexual *roles* (protector vs. protected, destroyer vs. mender), that tickles the king's funny bone, and not an association to the sexual organs that he would not be likely (consciously) to make. The reader also becomes aware at this point that Gustel's donning of the soldier's uniform, done with the conscious intention of merely *pretending* to become a man, represents an unconscious wish *truly* to become one. The male uniform superimposed on the female body symbolizes the suppression of the feminine principle by the masculine in Gustel.

"The entire complex of feelings and fantasies that have for their content the woman's feeling of being discriminated against, her envy of the male, her wish to be a man and to discard the female role, we call the *masculinity complex of woman*," Karen Horney writes in 1926 (italics hers) and alludes to Schiller's Joan as a literary prototype of the aberration.[16] She could as well have pointed to Meyer's Gustel and to the roots of the complex in Gustel's disturbed relationship with her father, a relationship that appears anything but disturbed until one looks closely at old Leubelfing's and her own casual reminiscences in chapter 1. The implication from these, mentioned above, of a marriage forced upon an adolescent father with many wild oats left to sow and not a thought of parenthood in his head, is the vital clue signaling us to look for trouble in Gustel's self-imagined childhood paradise. How does such a man-child deal with the terrifying trap of involuntary fatherhood? He deals with it by not dealing with it: by psychologically denying its reality. When Gustel mentions that she has never quite gotten used to skirts, that as a child she spent most of her time in riding breeches becoming an expert horseman in the company of her father, and when it is later learned from Ake Tott that Gustel rode with her father's regiment "until she was fourteen and more" (2:56), it becomes apparent that the father escaped the parental trap by turning his daughter into an army crony. To the extent that he was able to mold Gustel in the image of an apprentice comrade-in-arms, effectively making her into the only kind of person to whom he could easily relate—a member of his male regiment—to that extent he managed psychologically to deny the fact that he had a child. Moreover, in having been made by her father into a crony, Gustel was deprived not only of her status as a child, but of her femininity as well. Had Gustel been a son, the damage caused by the father's need to deny parenthood would still have been great; as it is, the damage is incalculable.

Of course, nothing of this twisted scenario is evident to any of the characters, least of all Gustel. On the surface and judged by Gustel's spirited assertions of pride in "my father's good name" (2:37), all had been sweetness and light between father and daughter. It is a measure of Meyer's skill as a psychological writer that he is able to convey the covertly destructive quality of the parent-child relationship without recourse to an omniscient narrator's psychic dissection such as we find, for example, in Keller's close tracing of Vrenchen's mental anguish in *Romeo und Julia auf dem Dorfe* or Mann's detailed anatomy of little Hanno Buddenbrook's creeping despair. The suffering of both children at the hands of brutalizing fathers is made palpable to us primarily through a discursive presentation by the narrator of their mental life. Meyer spins the tangled web of Gustel's emotions with hardly a lapse into such "non-artistic" explanatory modes of characterization. Nor does he allow an especially insightful character to speak for him in calling the reader's attention to Gustel's hidden plight (as he does, for instance, with the sagacious Fagon vis-à-vis Julien Boufflers in ***Das Leiden eines Knaben***), since his artistic purpose is precisely to construct a world in which human beings act out of motives beyond their own or anyone else's immediate awareness or control. (The one possible exception to this— Ake Tott's observations in chapter 4—is discussed below.) Meyer limits himself to purely literary means in evoking the subtle sway of the unconscious: the use of ironic symbol, the gentle nudging of the reader towards inferences based on the characters' offhand remarks, and, most revealingly, the gradual establishment within the heroine of a pattern of behavioral and attitudinal details that points toward a dominant life-directing intention not evident from any single act or attitude by itself.

As we have seen, the chronic dread of exposure that grips Gustel in camp, out of proportion to any realistic threat of reprisal, is part of this pattern. So, too, the contempt she displays in the opening chapter for anything that reinforces her jaded conception of feminity as trivial, weak and pussillanimous. Thus her arrogant spurning of the company of the local women, with whom she had refused to sit during the king's reception, as "limp" and "silly"; her churlish aversion to the encumbrances of a woman's skirts: "women's dresses don't fit me"—pants provide the mobility she needs for the manly activities she prefers; her tongue-in-cheek suggestion to cousin August, who fears conscription, to hide among the giggling girls, "just like young Achilles here in the fancy work on the stove tiles. And when crafty old Ulysses spreads out the weapons in front of them, don't you go leaping for a sword" (2:37).

Toward the end of this scene, as the disguised Gustel is about to leave with the cornet, she performs two acts in quick succession that clearly show how both her fear of exposure and contempt for femininity are inextricably linked to the dominant unconscious craving for her father's love and approval. Upon taking leave of cousin August, "switching suddenly to unconstrained gaity, the 'page' seized young Leubelfing's right hand, pumped it up and down, and cried, 'Farewell, sweet [female] cousin!'" (2:38). This mock-ceremonious exchange of identities is, in the fashion of most jokes, the conscious expression of a profoundly earnest unconscious aim; Gustel symbolically consigns her femininity to the male cousin who needs it. At the same time, in donning her father's uniform, she courts his approval by literally identifying with his rejection of her femininity. In fact, in its most elemental sense, the donning of the uniform becomes a ritual of *total* identification. By "becoming" her father, she attempts, if not to fill, at least with his sartorial effigy to cover over the inner void where his love should be. Rather than incorporating the love-object, she has herself incorporated *by* it, an expression of her passive need to *be* loved.

The farewells completed, Gustel suddenly bristles at the cornet's move to slip his arm into hers to escort her out. Stepping back and reaching for her sword, she shouts: "Friend, hands off! I don't like to be crowded!" (2:38). An inexplicably harsh reaction to a friendly gesture, until one sees it as the first eruption of that dread of exposure that later plagues Gustel in camp. Once committed to masculinity, she must avoid any and all contact with men that could compromise this strategy. Any overtures from men that could evoke even the slightest stirrings of feminine feeling and thus undermine the repression are from now on taboo. Any experiencing of herself as a woman can only alienate her father further. (The fact of her father's death is no deterrent to this aim of her unconscious, where the reality of death is mitigated by the illusion of introjection. The father lives on as a phantom of Gustel's inner world, his death only serving to intensify her strategy.) Both acts, then, the joking farewell to her new *Base* (female cousin) and the repelling of the cornet's gesture of contact, are part of Gustel's monolithic unconscious quest to win her father's love by becoming a man for him.

Gustel's overvaluation of things male and denigration of things female—her masculinity complex in Horney's sense—is not simply a matter of errant pride or eccentric preference, but of psychological survival. Her tragedy is that the conditions for her survival, not to speak of growth and fulfillment, are impossible and condemn her to an existential impasse between gender identities. Neither can she become a man, nor can she as a woman effect a *rapprochement* with her father in reality. His death ensures his survival in her unconscious as an implacable martinet.

Indeed, one may view the circumstances surrounding the father's death as aspects of an event of "critical mass" that irrevocably locks Gustel into her present impasse. As has been seen, the chronology establishes that he was violently struck down when Gustel was about thirteen, that is, near the onset of puberty when all the early unresolved issues of the Oedipus complex reassert themselves with great force. Horney argues that women who display obvious masculinity strivings have passed through a phase of unusually strong father fixation in early life, thus attempting, in the first instance, to resolve the Oedipus complex in the normal way by retaining their original identification with the mother and, like her, taking the father as love object. It is only when this strategy fails, that is, when her love is unrequited, that the daughter abandons the father as love object and shifts to an identification with him.[17] From this perspective, I interpret the death of Gustel's father as proof, in the logic of her unconscious, of the irredeemable failure of her efforts to win his love for herself as a woman and as cement to her conviction that she can only shine in his eyes by recreating herself in his male image. After all, if her womanhood had been acceptable to him, he would not have died. Moreover, if he was in fact killed "in defense of my mother's honor," becoming in the daughter's eyes a blood sacrifice on the altar of Demonic Womanhood, then the daughter would magically assume guilt for his death, to the extent that she had carried into puberty vestiges of that primal identification with the mother of which Horney speaks. She would actually have "learned" from his death that femininity kills and is therefore an evil to be despised and extinguished. She must therefore at all costs extinguish this evil in herself.

In this intricate shaping of Gustel's dilemma, Meyer illustrates beautifully the Byzantine ontological laws by which the unconscious operates. He shows it to be a world in which the protean exchange of identities, either in whole or in part, is routine, and in which life and death wear each other's hats in clownish collusion to dissolve the strict boundary that separates them in consciousness. In this world it is possible for Gustel to feel guilty for her father's death and to regard her own femininity as a murder weapon, while at the same time intensifying out of this very guilt her resolve to achieve the masculinity he has always demanded, as though he were now more alive than ever.

Entering the king's service under the identity of her cousin, Gustel is a veritable transference phenomenon waiting to happen. All the psychic liabilities of her relationship to her father now rivet themselves with demonic force to the Swedish monarch in whose close

presence she commences to pass her days. She rides with him by day in his fruitless sallies against the Hapsburg foe, takes her meals with him by dusk, keeps his makeshift quarters comfortable for him, provides an ear for his complaints and a nodding head for his musing and moralizing. All in the shadow, eerily sensed by both, of imminent death in battle: "Leubelfing sensed it: the king was also on familiar terms with death" (2:44).

This sense of doom that envelops Gustel is enmeshed with an equally potent exhileration over the awareness that, at any moment, a stray bullet could end her impossible adventure. Indeed, in fantasy she challenges the bullet to strike her: "Then her eyes flashed as she joyously rode into a hail of deadly bullets, challenging them to end her uneasy dream" (2:44; the translation used here does not always adhere to Meyer's rule of referring to Gustel with the masculine pronoun, in keeping with her disguise). It is this perverse blend of scorching death-anxiety and an almost erotic daring of sudden death to take her that points to the transference phenomenon. With the reappearance of her father in the form of the king, Gustel has been given a second chance, as it were. By succeeding this time in becoming a man, a comrade-in-arms, she can "undo" the death inflicted on him by her own femininity. But it is at this point that the lethal paradox of Gustel's unconscious strategy traps her. The king is, in reality, not at all like her father. He is a thoughtful, sensitive man, generous with his affection:

> And afterwards, when the king roughed up her hair with a hearty laugh after catching her in some foolishness or at something she didn't know as he relaxed in the evening by the cozy lamplight, she would say to herself, all aquiver with rapturous happiness and fear, "This is the last time!"

> So time passed for her as death's proximity helped her enjoy the greatest moments of her life. (2:44)

Each time he reaches out to her in this way with fatherly affection, he arouses the buried yearning of a daughter ("herzliche Lust"), that most fundamental matrix of feminine feeling that can be repressed but never extinguished. In their surge toward consciousness these daughterly feelings evoke, so to speak, a double-tiered anxiety in Gustel. On the more profound level, they threaten to crumble the repression and confront her with the painful awareness of her unmet need for her father's love. At the same time, they generate, on the level of delusion or magical thought, a concomitant dread for the king's (father's) safety ("herzliche Angst"), lest her femininity kill again. And in unconscious anticipation of this "second murder," Gustel is flooded by feelings of guilt so intense that she all but commands the bullet to strike her down in retribution. Only in this light does the puzzling complex of feelings that grips her in camp make sense: her intense pleasure in the king's company, in apparent contradiction to her fear of his little intimacies, and her anxiety over their mutual imminent death, even as she invites this death for herself. The narrator obliquely confirms this view—but only obliquely, consistent with his eschewing of the omniscient explanatory mode—in summing up Gustel's days with the king as "transports of bliss, . . . everything that only a youthful spirit can absorb and only a carefree heart enjoy before the moment of death from a bullet, or the moment on the brink of humiliating disclosure" (2:40). Through the equation of the "deadly bullet" with the "humiliating disclosure" via grammatical parallelism, the narrator is hinting that Gustel is prepared to accept death in atonement for any manifestation of her lethal femininity.

Meyer uses not only the grammatical voice of the narrator but the emotional reactions of the secondary characters as well in alerting us to Gustel's unconscious experience of the king as a father-imago, that is, an idealized version of the unloving father in reality. In the opening scene, cousin August lashes out at her in reaction to her arrogant scorn of his fear of conscription: " 'I have it!' cried the tormented boy. '*You* go to the king as his page! . . . Go on, go to your idol and worship him! After all,' he continued, 'who knows? Maybe you've had that in mind all along! Don't you dream of him anyway? You went all over the world with him when you were little [at her father's side], awake and asleep' " (2:37). Casting discretion to the winds of rage, August blurts out his private contempt for the obsessive mawkishness that has always characterized Gustel's attitude towards the king. To him she is a lovesick teenager who goes about in a chronic swoon over an airy idol. One notes here Meyer's subtle use of August as unwitting psychologist, who, in his offhand allusion to the inner, developmental structure of Gustel's obsession, says far more than he knows, but, in so doing, communicates to us exactly what Meyer wants us to know of the unconscious roots of that obsession: "who knows? Maybe you've had that in mind all along!" ("wer weiß, ob du das nicht schon lange in dir trägst?"). That August has struck a deeply sensitive nerve in Gustel is clear from her embarrassed reaction: "The girl turned away as a deep blush suffused her cheeks and forehead" (2:37).

This initial embarrassment in Gustel is paralleled near the end of the tale by a similar reaction that she registers to a related psychological thunderbolt, directed at her this time by Ake Tott. Having fled the king and the unbearable anxiety of that close relationship, she now sits in her godfather's tent at a remote outpost of the camp and listens to his recollection of an event from her early infancy. It seems the king had once taken baby Gustel from his arms and showered her with spontaneous affection:

"Well, I've always said, you shouldn't kiss little children. Kisses like that can sleep and then burst into flames when lips are fuller and more ready for them. You know, don't you, that the king took you out of my arms more than once? Cousin, he used to tickle you and kiss you with a great big smacking sound. You were a very lively and pretty baby." The page knew nothing of these kisses, and a deep blush was the only reply. (2:57)

If cousin August's outburst calls Gustel's embarrassed attention to the present-day manifestations of her obsession, Tott's recollection and "analytic" interpretation of the king's kiss give her an uneasy glimpse into its early origins. The obsession is grounded in the kiss of infancy that "sleeps" during the latency period only to "burst into flame" at puberty "when lips are fuller and more ready." Although Gustel cannot specifically recall the kiss, she does reexperience it somatically at this moment ("aber er empfand ihn wild errötend" [*SW,* 11:205]) and, in the extremity of her embarrassment, intuit the overwhelming power with which it has shaped her life. Literally, her fate has been "sealed with a kiss."

We thus learn from Tott that Gustel was indeed predisposed to make the king into a father-imago in place of the father found so wanting in reality. The astuteness of this seventeenth-century soldier's insight into psychodynamic processes borders on the anachronistic and probably reflects Meyer's eagerness to ensure that the reader pick up on the priority of the unconscious level of narrative action. Only here does he come close to indulging, through the mouth of a character, the natural urge of the narrator to explain.

These complementary episodes with cousin and godfather leave no doubt that Gustel's relationship to the king is to be read as an enactment of what Freud would later come to call the *Familienroman* or "family romance." (Indeed, as previously mentioned, Freud did cite Gustel's devotion to the king, in a letter to Fliess of 9 June 1898, as an example of "deferred action" motivated by the kiss in infancy. While ***Gustav Adolfs Page*** thus helped Freud to clarify his earliest speculations on the importance of childhood experiences in adulthood, the larger theory of the family romance was still in its germinal stages and would, in fact, draw heavily in its initial form on another story by Meyer, ***Die Richterin.***)[18] In the family romance, the child, or in this instance, the fixated adolescent, seizes the opportunity to replace the unloving (read: deceased) parent in fantasy with an idealized version who ranks higher, or as here, highest, in the social order. The inference is clear from Tott's words that Gustel had already harbored such fantasies in early infancy and, from August's, that these fantasies had flared up again with enormous virulence during puberty with the traumatic event of her father's death.

In seizing on the king as a father-substitute, Gustel is attempting to use the deeply rooted fantasies of the family romance to provide a new ending to the Oedipal drama that had originally climaxed in what she imagines to be the father's fatal victimization by her own femininity. By becoming a male page ("man") for the king and eradicating every trace of a female sexuality she believes lethal, she hopes to undo the "primal parricide" and absolve herself of guilt. But the repression of one's very sexual matrix is too radical an act of self-alienation to be wholly successful, and one finds veiled expressions of the girl's need to give herself up to the "new father's" manly embrace subverting the ruse on all sides.

These veiled expressions occur mainly as fantasies whose sexual import is quite obvious to the reader but obscure to Gustel. In chapter 2, for example, the king peruses a book of maxims by various historical personages in search of a proper inscription of a signet ring he has in mind for his daughter. In keeping with fashion, the inscription should be some brief but telling expression of the wearer's attitude toward life. When Gustel, peering over the king's shoulder, points to the anonymous *Courte et bonne!* he takes her to task for her most un-Protestant "epicurean" taste. When he then asks her to specify how she thinks the expression is to be taken, she waxes ecstatic: "Solchergestalt, mein gnädiger Herr: Ich wünsche mir alle Strahlen meines Lebens in *ein* Flammenbündel und in den Raum *einer* Stunde vereinigt, daß statt einer blöden Dämmerung ein kurzes, aber blendend helles Licht von Glück entstünde, um dann zu löschen wie ein zuckender Blitz" (*SW*, 11:181). If she could, Gustel would condense all the energies normally dissipated over a lifetime into one hour of flaming passion ("*ein* Flammenbündel") that would "give rise to a brief but blinding flash of happiness," dwindling down, in its turn, "like a quivering spark." The pyrotechnic metaphor is blatantly erotic and, in the expression given it by Gustel, closely parallels the lancet-arched rhythm of the sexual act. Indeed, Gustel envisions the ideal life in terms precisely befitting the climax of coition: "Courte et bonne!" Before the king can cut off this covert confession of desire during her pause for breath, she is again, in the narrator's words, "swept with passion" ("leidenschaftlich hingerissen") and cries out, "Yes, that's how I'd have it! *Courte et bonne!*" (2:42). Suddenly coming to her senses, she instinctively creates a smoke screen around what she has just come close to admitting by diverting attention to the multiplicity of interpretations admitted by the maxim: "Oh, Sire! Perhaps I don't understand it correctly. It has several meanings, just as the others do in your book here" (2:42).

Near the end of chapter 2, Gustel lulls herself to sleep with another, more delicate, but equally transparent sexual fantasy, this time explicitly involving the king. As she lies in her bed that is separated from his by only a thin partition, the reader is told that "It [her state of reverie] had all started from a silly childish realization that her name ended with the same syllable that his started with. Sleep put an end to her thoughts" (2:44). Gustel derives childish pleasure from the thought that their names are linked, in fact, literally fused together, by a common syllable: Au(gust)av. The fantasy of coupled names barely disguises the wish for sexual coupling.[19] One notes the narrator's care in pointing out that the fantasy arises at the threshold of sleep, in that moment of hypnagogic consciousness when psychological defenses are slack.[20] Also, his description of the fantasy as "a silly childish realization" cues us to its Oedipal roots.

Meyer may have an additional, symbolic intent in focusing the reader's attention on the common syllable, "gust," that fuses the two names. "Gust" or "güst" is an old agricultural adjective in the Southwest German dialect familiar to the Swiss Meyer and means "unfruitful," "infertile," or "milkless." It is properly descriptive of mares and cows but, in the earthy metaphor of the farmer, may on occasion be applied to a woman. The other root syllable in Gustel's formal name (Auguste), "Au," means "meadow" or "pasture." When Gustel spins this fantasy of her link to the king by the common element "gust," she may be serving as Meyer's symbolic vehicle for telling us that, with respect to her womanhood, such a link can only be "unfruitful," that she is doomed to remain "a barren meadow" ("eine guste Au"), childless and sexually unfulfilled, as long as she persists in her unconscious game. A poignant irony emerges, then, from the contradiction between the unconscious erotic meaning of *gust* for Gustel with its procreative valence and this symbolic sense of barrenness as privately understood between author and reader.

This symbolism becomes more plausible when one considers it in connection with the event immediately preceding Gustel's fantasy in the same scene. Before drifting into reverie, she had been holding her ear to the partition to eavesdrop on the king, who was preparing for sleep. She could hear

> wie Gustav inbrünstig betete und seinen Gott bestürmte, ihn im Vollwerte hinwegzunehmen, wenn seine Stunde da sei, bevor er ein Unnötiger oder Unmöglicher werde. Zuerst quollen der Lauscherin die Tränen, dann erfüllte sie vom Wirbel zur Zehe eine selbstsüchtige Freude, ein verstohlener Jubel, ein Sieg, ein Triumph über die Ähnlichkeit ihres kleinen mit diesem großen Lose. (*SW*, 11:185)

Gustav prays, almost demands ("bestürmte"), that God take him in the fullness of manhood ("im Vollwerte"), before he should become, as he revealingly phrases it, "a superfluous or disabled man." In secret, Gustel first sheds tears of pity, but, in the dialectical rhythm of emotions, this surface reaction suddenly yields to a deep, selfish joy, a darkly powerful rush of triumph as she senses that their destinies are somehow tragically parallel. Clearly, Gustel's unconscious is momentarily attuned to that of the king. His manifest prayer for deliverance from a potentially disabling injury in battle expresses, even as it conceals, a profound fear of sexual impotence, resulting rather from the ravages of age and worry over war than of war itself. It is from *this* disability that he would be spared, one that would make him, in a way he could not endure, "a superfluous man." Far better to be taken "im Vollwerte." The sinister joy that wells up in Gustel, blotting out the conscious tearful pity, springs from her unconscious identification of the king's sexual anxiety with her own. It is the sad, desperate joy over having found a fellow sufferer, a joy she rationalizes to herself as a kind of devil-may-care attitude towards the physical dangers they face together in battle. This emotion then leads directly into the name-coupling reverie with her drowsy doting on the common *gust.* One sees, then, how the symbolic wordplay functions in the larger context of the scene as a subtle clue to a sexual impasse that king and page suffer in common and that constitutes their common primal destiny.

In matters of the unconscious, it is a short, inevitable step from common to mutual suffering. Buried needs seek each other out. In a story suffused from first word to last with psychological irony, the most elaborate irony of all revolves around this latent fear of impotence on the part of the king. It is a fear that implicates him in a kind of unconscious *folie à deux* with Gustel which entangles her all the more hopelessly in her dilemma. One finds that the king, in compensation for his doubts about his own virility, unwittingly colludes with her in her reenactment of the Oedipal drama by accepting the role she has assigned him—but with a twist: for, whereas she would have him play the misogynous father to her masculinity strivings, his own need is to play the father who reaffirms his virility by seducing the daugher. Of course, this "seduction" never gets beyond frequent pats on the cheek and caresses of hair; but, as we have seen, such affectionate gestures arouse those dormant feminine feelings she longs but dreads to express ("all aquiver with rapturous happiness and fear"), with their attendant guilt, and, in so doing, are enough to drive her to invoke the only release from that guilt of which she can be certain: "This is the last time!" she consoles herself. Death will see to that.

That the king is unconsciously responding to Gustel, not simply as a woman, but specifically in quasi-incestuous terms as a daughter to be seduced is subtly suggested by his reaction of profound dismay to the letter from his daughter's governess. The governess reports that his daughter's tutor in French, ostensibly a Swedish Protestant gentleman of upstanding character, has been exposed as a devious Jesuit who had been secretly proselytizing the girl. While his outrage is certainly justified, still the king's couching of the priest's treachery in curiously carnal terms ("seiner geheimen bösen Lust, das bildsame Gehirn meines Kindes mißhandelt zu haben" [*SW,* 11:183]) prompts the reader's suspicion that he "doth protest too much." For several evenings he paces his quarters, obsessively brooding over—in his own words—"this misfortune, this crime," over this (Jesuit) father's (religious) seduction of his daughter, even after acknowledging that the girl could not have suffered any serious harm: "[The governess] was to make as little fuss as possible with his daughter about the matter; to treat it as just another bit of childish behavior" (2:43). One observes here the workings of a psychological projection: the father by blood disowns his own deeply repressed incestuous fantasies toward his daughter by casting them onto the unscrupulous behavior of this spiritual father. Illicit proselytism, the cunning seduction of a young girl from her belief system, is sufficiently analogous to sexual seduction to make the priest a convenient scapegoat. With this incident Meyer cleverly intimates the psychological basis for the king's unconscious collusion with Gustel. In the absence of his real daughter, Gustel serves as a substitute for the seduction through which he hopes to rejuvenate his flagging potency.

So the king's fatherly affection towards Gustel, at first glance a selfless expression, takes on, after all, its own sinister aspect. It should be noted here that the unconscious collusion masked by this affection is not just a reconstruction of mine based on inferences drawn from the king's behavior, but is explicitly suggested by Meyer in a fascinating passage that has him (the king) virtually "free-associating" to the ulterior erotic basis of his relationship with her. The reader is told that, in that welcome hour of leisure before sleep when he could relax and unwind, he would often tell his page "harmlose Dinge, wie sie eben in seinem Gedächtnisse *obenauf lagen*" (*SW,* 11:179); my emphasis), that is, things told, literally, "off the top of his head" in apparently random sequence. Sometimes the sexual motive in these musings would be only obliquely expressed, as in his anecdote of the "pompous sermon . . . he had heard at the Court Church when he went to Berlin to get married" (2:41), in which, as Freud has observed with respect to dreams,[21] the insignificant image (the sermon) holds the spotlight while the revealing one (the wedding) is relegated to the background. At other times, however, the king's idle chatter would come within a hair's breadth of laying bare his tacit approval—indeed, eager abetting—of Gustel's unconscious designs, as in "the incredible story of how they had told *him,* the King!, after the birth of his child that it was a boy, and he had let himself be deceived for a while" (2:41). One can scarcely imagine a clearer signal to Gustel to continue her transvestite masquerade (thereby making her desired feminine presence permissible) than this "offhand" recollection of having fondly indulged the delusion, at his daughter's birth, that she was really a son, hence, a male heir. At still other times, the narrator continues, he would tell his page tales geared to the fancy rather of a girl than a youth, for instance, "about parties and costume balls," as if

> the hoodwinked king, without being aware of it, felt the effect of the deception his page was practicing; as if the king were unwittingly savoring beneath the façade of a good-natured youth the playful charms of an attentive woman. (2:41)

"Without being aware of it" the king senses the deception; "unwittingly" he savors the charms of the woman. This is the author-narrator's sole direct reference, not only to the king's unconscious collusion, but, by extension, to the primacy throughout *Gustav Adolfs Page* of the unconscious level of narrative action. As expected, Gustel is plunged into panic the instant she senses in turn that he is playing to her hidden sensuality: "Such moments caused the page a sudden fear" (2:41).

The king thus becomes a totally ambiguous father-figure for Gustel. On the one hand, he is made by her into the authoritarian father who esteems only maleness and prohibits the expression of any feminine impulse; on the other, he is disconcertingly perceived by her as the seductive father who subverts his own prohibition. This contradictory bind is reflected in a sequence of punishment dreams that afflict Gustel, the first one occurring, "appropriately,"[22] during the sleep that follows her hypnagogic name-coupling reverie:

> But the page's dreams were not good ones, for her conscience intruded upon them. Images of judgment rose before her dreaming eyes: first the king, with furious eye and damning gesture, driving away from his side the unmasked page; then the queen chasing her out with a broom and with coarse words of anger such as never passed the well-bred lady's lips during the day; indeed, words she probably didn't even know. (2:44)

The roles of the royal parents in this punishment dream dramatize the twofold burden of guilt by which Gustel is crushed. Not only is she banished by the mother for violating the "normal" Oedipal prohibition against a liaison with the father (the queen "sweeps" her out of the family circle with a barrage of uncharacteristic gutter language that aptly expresses the "debased" nature of her desires), but she is ostracized as well by the royal father's "furious eye and damning gesture" for the "sin" of feminine love. She is damned not only for loving but for loving as a woman.

While the king's role in this first dream is unequivocally that of authoritarian misogynist, a subsequent dream illustrates with brilliant succinctness the blurred effect that has crept into Gustel's image of him with the passage of time and the persistence of his subliminal overtures:

> One time the page dreamed her bay mare was running away with her. It galloped toward a chasm across a barren ground made red by an angry sunset. The king was chasing her, but before the eyes of her saviour or pursuer she plunged into the hideous depths to the sound of diabolical laughter. (2:44-45)

The configuration of conflicting forces that make up the relationship is captured in a handful of salient images and actions. Gustel is carried off by her runaway horse through a landscape (read: mindscape) described as "barren" (again, the barrenness theme) and "made red by an angry sunset" (the red condensing the misogynous father's anger and the mutual passion between her and the seductive father). Off in pursuit of her is the king, but the dreamer is uncertain whether his pursuit betokens the intent to stop the horse or spur it on ("saviour or pursuer"). The runaway horse embodies the repressed feminine desires over which Gustel is losing control. Will the king overtake the horse and help her regain control of it (that is, as misogynous father "save" her from being carried away by her "evil" feminine nature) or is his pursuit a sexual chase that is actually causing her to lose the reins of control? While the meaning of the bolting horse is clear, that of the king's pursuit remains pointedly ambiguous. The image of her plunge into the shattering abyss represents the dreamer's unconscious awareness of the psychic havoc being wrought by the paralyzing ambiguity of the relationship. But the resounding satanic laughter of the king that accompanies the plunge reveals her even deeper understanding that a clarification of his role either way would, in the end, resolve nothing. His laughter is a condensed image conveying the message that each of them has, out of his own motives, contributed to Gustel's unconscious transformation of the king into a two-faced demon, *both* of whose faces are lethal: no matter whether as the misogynous father she would have him be or the seductive father he would be himself, he is instrumental in her "fall."

The dream action strikingly anticipates the image of the bolting horse that seizes control from the rider that Freud uses in the *New Introductory Lectures on Psychoanalysis* to describe the ego's abdication to the id, or, as he puts it, "the not precisely ideal situation of the rider being obliged to guide the horse along the path by which it itself wants to go."[23] But Meyer's image has its literary ancestors as well. In Tieck's Romantic fairy tale, *Der blonde Eckbert,* the hero's dawning awareness of his incestuous relationship with his sister occurs on an aimless journey during which he allows his horse to go its own way.[24] And even predating the Romantics with their intense cultivation of psychic processes is the famous chariot metaphor spoken by Goethe's Egmont in which the id-tendencies are mythically projected as "invisible spirits" whose relentless whiplash drives "time's solar horses with our destiny's fragile coach; and for us there remains nothing but to take heart and firmly hold the reins, steering the wheels out of harm's way, now right, now left, from a rock here and a drop there."[25]

Gustel's bolting-horse dream marks the dramatic culmination of the first two chapters, which make up, respectively, the exposition and development sections of the unconscious narrative. Since the unconscious scenario set up in these chapters is so elusive to a casual reading, elaborated as it is with studied subtlety, it demands the bulk of the interpretive work. Once this work is done, however, the final three chapters, ending with the deaths of king and page, easily yield their significance as a kind of "falling action," a series of tragically inevitable consequences decreed by the fatal blindness of each to his own (and their mutual) psychological reality.

Enter at this point the Duke of Lauenburg, a German *Reichsfürst* under the Swedish banner, and General von Wallenstein, leader of the Catholic opposition. Each, in his own way, quickly becomes a pawn in the unconscious, self-victimizing game being played by king and page. The first thing to be observed about Lauenburg is that he poses a real, imminent threat to the king's life. He holds Gustav responsible for the death of his concubine, the fiery Slav Korinna, who had taken her own life at the prospect of being sent by Gustav to a Protestant house of correction in Sweden. Moreover, adding insult to injury, Gustav has just humiliated him in the presence of the other German nobles for leading them in a pillaging raid on a group of defenseless refugees. So the unscrupulous Lauenburg is now hell-bent on employing all his savage cunning to gain revenge.

His significance, however, resides far less in the objective danger he poses than in the distorted unconscious interpretations that king and page place on this danger, which render them helpless to thwart his evil machinations. Gustel's first reaction to Lauenburg is one of shock over the resemblance of his voice to her own feigned baritone. As she listens from behind a curtain to his sarcastic rejoinder to the king's tirade, the reader is told that "at Lauenburg's first words, the page had flinched at the uncanny similarity between this voice and his [her] own. The same sound, the same pitch and timbre" (2:51). Once the king leaves the room, Lauenburg is free to spew out his bilious invective to the captive audience of princes, and the cutting edge of his hate-ridden voice sends waves of horror through Gustel: "Now his [Gustel's] fright became horror . . . [as] Lauenburg forced a laugh and exclaimed sharply, 'He curses like a stable boy, our Swedish farmer! By

damn, we got under his skin today! *Pereat Gustavus!* Long live German liberty!'" (2:51). But the princes have been sobered by the king's anger, and they spurn Lauenburg's overtures of comradery ostensibly based on "German solidarity." As they make their exit one by one, Lauenburg sees himself subjected to the further indignity of ostracism by his peers:

> His expression became a grimace. In his rage the marked man balled his fist, raised it, and threatened either his destiny or the king.

> The page could not understand the muttered words, but the expression on the aristocratic features was so diabolic that the eavesdropper felt very faint. (2:51)

Meyer carefully implies that Gustel's horror is much more than an objective reaction to the implications of Lauenburg's menacing gesture towards the king. For one thing, the reader is told that she could not be sure at that moment just what the object of his seething anger was ("his destiny or the king"), since his muttering was beyond earshot. Then too, she is clearly shown in that instant as transfixed to the point of fainting by Lauenburg's satanic expression, hence beyond any capability of rational deduction. When one traces this spellbound horror back to its origins—her initial shock over the similarity of their voices—it becomes evident that the unconscious scenario is at work here. The extremity of Gustel's reaction to what is, at worst, an annoying coincidence of nature indicates that she is not seeing Lauenburg for what he is, but is transforming him into something else—in truth, into an effigy of her own disavowed feminine nature, or, as she herself recognizes in a later, lucid moment, her "Doppelgänger" (*SW,* 11:202). Her appalled perception of their similar voices is a manifestation in consciousness of a perverse unconscious identification with Lauenburg as a lethal threat to the king. An accident of nature becomes the occasion for an intense flaring-up of Gustel's repressed anxieties about her own "lethal" femininity, a femininity that once killed the father and, now reactivated by this demonic doubleganger with matching voice, threatens to do so again. Thus "the expression on the aristocratic features was so diabolic that the eavesdropper felt very faint." That she "sculpts" her feminine doubleganger out of a *man* is explained by the congruence between Lauenburg as a deceitful male and her own deceitful male's façade. It is precisely the image of Lauenburg as the male who is not what he seems, the male who conceals a threat, that engages the symbolizing power of her unconscious to produce the identification.[26]

In the midst of all this, one notices how Meyer uses a feature of the interior decor to give palpable symbolic shape to these impalpable psychic events. The thick damask curtain that fronts Gustel provides an unobtrusive but unmistakable image for the inner barrier of repression by which she shields herself from full awareness of this crucial act in the unconscious drama. No more than the voice of the doubleganger is able to penetrate the "censuring curtain."

Gustel's re-creation of Lauenburg as the masked feminine self she abhors blinds her to his obvious intention to revenge himself on the king. Since she unconsciously perceives his threat as coming from herself, in effect, as an extension of the very power of her woman's nature to destroy that she has had to keep in check all along, she takes no steps to warn Gustav of the real danger that stalks him. Her gross distortion of reality leaves him exposed to his true enemy's treachery and results, ultimately, in both their tragic deaths.

It remains for Wallenstein inadvertently to set the wheels of psychic destiny in motion. This he does through his visit to Gustav late that same evening to warn him of a possible assassination attempt by one of his own men. Having overheard the suspicious dream-ramblings of the disguised Lauenburg, who had dozed off in his anteroom that noon while waiting to keep a business appointment, the general felt compelled by honor to alert his esteemed opponent.

Wallenstein's warning has momentous unintended effects, not only on the king but also on the page, who eavesdrops on the conversation through a crack in her bedroom wall. Meyer knew the unconscious mind to be the fertile soil of conscious superstition, and he ingeniously uses the image of Wallenstein popularized by Schiller—that of the great strategist obsessed by the occult causes of events, who cannot make a move without first consulting his astrological charts—to ignite in the heroine's unconscious the fateful explosion of magical thinking primed by the doubleganger experience. He virtually announces this intention in the narrator's remark prefacing the Wallenstein interview that "A vague feeling caused him [the page] to associate this visit [from Wallenstein] with his own fate" (2:52). While waiting for the king to appear, Wallenstein had been struck by the resemblance of the page's voice to that of the masked dreamer and had succeeded through a clever ruse in demonstrating a perfect fit between the glove left behind by the suspect and the page's hand. When he connects these clues to Gustel during the interview, the king scoffs: "I am ready to rest my slumbering head in my Leubelfing's lap" (2:54). But the king's assurances cannot pierce the armor of superstition that envelops Wallenstein; even if Gustel is not involved, he suggests, "I still would want no page around me, not even my favorite, whose voice sounds like the voice of the man who hates me and whose hand is the same size as my potential assassin's. That's going too far; it's tempting fate. That could be the end" (2:54). Of course, this irrational condemnation by resemblance plays right into the dynamics of Gustel's

identification with Lauenburg. The entire overheard conversation was "like a ghost which made his [Gustel's] hair stand on end" (2:55). She is incapable of making the obvious association of the clues to Lauenburg because she has unconsciously erased all distinctions between herself and him and is now overwhelmed by the conscious conviction that Wallenstein is, in some dark, unfathomable sense, right about her:

> Then the eavesdropper left his [her] post and staggered out into his room. Collapsing next to his cot, he begged heaven to protect his hero. Leubelfing's very presence—Wallenstein had said it, and now even the page was beginning to believe it—seemed to offer a mysterious threat to the king.

> "No matter what it takes," the page vowed in despair, "I'll tear myself away from him; I'll free him and make it impossible for my evil presence to harm him in any way." (2:55)

For his part, the king is also profoundly affected by Wallenstein's superstitious apprehensions about Gustel, despite his better judgment of their absurdity. When Wallenstein admits that the motives for his warning are not entirely noble, inasmuch as for him their destinies as opposed standard-bearers are interdependent in the same way that night and day can only exist in relation to each other, Gustav is suddenly vexed by the morbid thought that the general has been vouchsafed some astrological revelation of their mutual deaths: "Again the king thought for a moment. It was hard to suppress the assumption that some conjunction in the heavens or a configuration of the planets had shown the duke a common hour of death, one of them following the other with furtive steps and shrouded head. Oddly enough, this feeling suddenly gained authority over him despite his trust in God" (2:54). This reaction parallels Gustel's in its psychodynamic form: the abrupt clouding of the king's Christian belief by an astrological image alien to it, a momentary obliteration of his normal set of mind pointedly described, in the German, as "involuntary" and "forceful," indicates the surge to consciousness, in disguised form, of an unconscious idea: "Now the Christian king felt the atmosphere of superstition that surrounded Wallenstein beginning to infect him" (2:54). What has happened is that the king has come under veiled attack from his own conscience for his quasi-incestuous impulses towards Gustel. A harsh superego, steeled by the piercing Nordic winds of Stockholm and by its role as Defender of a loftily ascetic Prostestantism, has seized the cautioning Wallenstein as a projection screen from which to denounce those nightly flirtatious interludes with the daughter substitute. Since the king, in his self-appointed status as moral exemplar, could never tolerate even the faintest awareness of the drama of seduction, the internal accuser cannot confront him directly in its primary Protestant form but must itself go underground in order to come at him from an oblique angle. This it does by entering his awareness camouflaged as a disquieting sense of having been somehow infected by Wallenstein's superstitious fears regarding Gustel and, as he imagines, his astrological vision of their intertwined deaths.

Thus the uncanny sense of a link between Gustel and his own imminent death presses itself on the king's awareness. He "knows" it is only a temporary succumbing to the morbid idiosyncrasy of his visitor, but still the unwanted thought clings to him. He does not know the unconscious source of the thought's power. Wallenstein's warning, against all logic, that Gustel may be mortally dangerous to him is a projected warning from his own conscience against playing with sexual fire. The illicit erotic relationship with the daughter substitute, entered into to allay fears of impotence, must be renounced; it can only lead to psychological and spiritual death.

In the brief scene that follows Wallenstein's departure, king and page come to an ironic parting of the ways. The scene is a triumph of the awesome ability of the unconscious to ravage true communication by simulating it. Each senses the necessity for Gustel to leave, and each senses that the other senses this. But their unconscious motives for this tacit agreement, although congruent, are totally unrelated: Gustel perceives herself as a dire threat to the king's life; so too he. Moreover, each believes Gustel's covert femininity to be the source of the threat. But, whereas for her the danger of her sex resides in its proven potential for parricide, for him that danger consists in its power to lure him into the forbidden orbit of incest. Thus, under the hidden sway of the incest taboo, which he imagines to be an unaccountable "contagion" of Wallenstein's superstition, the king finds himself behaving as though Gustel were in fact suspect. Feigning nonchalance, "He playfully took the page's left hand and drew the soft leather over his fingers" (2:55). Contrary to all reason, he feels compelled to assemble evidence against Gustel as his would-be assassin. When she realizes he is doing precisely this, she is overcome by the ultimate horror of exposure: unconsciously she perceives the father to whom she would prove her masculinity as having seen through the façade to her noxious feminine core and interprets the glove's perfect fit as the final "proof" of that noxious core to both of them. His pronouncement, "It fits," carrying the weight of a condemnation by its stark simplicity, she reads as her cue to flee:

> . . . the page threw himself down before the king, seized both his hands and covered them with tears. "Farewell," he sobbed, "My lord, my everything! May God and all His Host protect you!"

> Quickly jumping up, he dashed from the room like a man possessed. Gustav rose and called

him back. But the king could already hear the hoofbeats of a galloping horse. (2:55)

What was actually the self-condemning finger of the king's conscience, she has taken to be leveled at herself.

The king's attempt to call Gustel back is merely perfunctory. In truth, her departure is a relief to him, since it will enable him to carry out his unconscious resolve to renounce the seduction. The narrator is certainly alluding to this when he puts tongue in cheek and observes in a tone of mock curiosity that "—seltsam—der König ließ weder in der Nacht noch am folgenden Tage Nachforschungen über die Flucht und das Verbleiben seines Pagen anstellen" (*SW,* 11:202). The emphatic setting-off of "seltsam" by dashes points the reader towards this concealed motive for the king's failure to have his page retrieved. The strategic punctuation is then immediately reinforced by the narrator's offhand suggestion of an obviously false motive: "Of course his hands were already full, for he had decided to give up his camp at Nürnberg" (2:55).[27] Meyer has skillfully placed the narrator's affectation of ignorance in the service of the reader's illumination.

In flight from her waking nightmare Gustel gives free rein to "the horse's headlong gallop" (2:55). This image of the horse that, although galloping at full speed, remains under the rider's control counterbalances that of the bolting horse in Gustel's dream. There the horse, symbolizing the woman's desire, has usurped control from the rider; her passion runs away with her, as it were. Here we observe the contrary: the rider retains (passive) control by consenting to the animal's unrestrained run, each stride echoing her desperate desire to protect the father from herself by putting distance between them.

The horse as an objective image of its rider's emotions is then carried a step further in the rhetorical parallel drawn between the animal's gradual wearying and Gustel's calming down: "Gradually it [the horse] tired by itself at the camp's outermost perimeter. The rider's excited emotions also calmed down" (2:55). With physical distance comes a measure of inner clarity, the glint of a fresh perspective. The dizzying push-and-pull of strange emotions that has plagued Gustel for weeks finally resolves into an ever sharpening focus on Lauenburg as a doubleganger of her own making:

> More sober reflection . . . enabled the page to identify his double. . . . It had to be Lauenburg. Hadn't the page seen the marked man clench his fist and challenge the king's justice? And didn't the object of the king's wrath have a voice that sounded like his own? Wasn't he himself woman enough to have spotted in that one terrifying moment how small the prince's balled fist was? There could be no doubt about it; Lauenburg was planning revenge, was planning to murder the page's beloved idol! (2:55-56)

Through a rare use of *erlebte Rede* Meyer shows the first dawning of insight within Gustel. Although having no notion of how or why, she sees clearly that she has been viewing Lauenburg as a reflection of some unacknowledged aspect of herself and that this reflection has eclipsed the objective reality of his imminent threat to the king. She is oppressed by the irony that her flight, undertaken to ensure the king's safety, has only served to jeopardize that safety even further: "And this moment when the king was being pursued with uncanny stealth was the time he had chosen to banish himself from the threatened man's side" (2:56).

Strangely, however, Gustel's insight does not lead to effective action, for instead of dashing back to the king posthaste to warn him of danger, she can only decide "not to leave the camp. . . . 'I can fall in with some regiment and no one will spot me with all the marching and the fatigue. And then the battle!'" (2:56). For the present she will remain on the periphery of the encampment, neither too near nor too far from the inner circle. This settling on a middle ground, in effect a compromise between leaving and staying, reflects the fragile, tentative quality of her insight, for the compromise is at bottom one between reality and delusion. Although she now sees Lauenburg for the evil he is, she still cannot shake the feeling that that same evil also dwells within herself. To leave would be to abandon the king to the external enemy; to stay would be to expose him to the inner. The separation of identities must remain incomplete as long as the forces of delusion and fantasy remain themselves essentially intact, still lurking beneath the surface of her awareness, twisting that awareness to their own designs.

The most intimate of these fantasies belong to the woman, the "enemy within" whose exposure has driven Gustel away from the king. Relaxing her inner vigilance in the safety of distance and feeling the pain of sudden separation, she fills the leisurely autumn weeks at Ake Tott's station with erotic daydreams of the idealized father. Memories, glided by yearning, drift through her mind of the days when she could enjoy his occasional touch and the nights when she could almost imagine there was no partition separating their beds: "Gustav Adolf was all the page could see in his mind's eye, even if in transfigured and unapproachable form. The days were past when the king would run his hand through the page's hair. Now the page no longer had his master beside him at night, separated only by the thin wall, and audible when he turned over or cleared his throat" (2:58). On one occasion, when she is detained in Naumburg on an errand long enough to witness the king's triumphal procession through the town square, she is brought to tears by a rush of love and hero-worship. But just as suddenly these emotions reveal their shadow side of intense jealousy as she sees the father gesture affectionately to her rival in the royal Oedipal triangle: "Tears welled from the page's eyes.

But when he caught sight of the queen watching from a window across the square and saw the king wave a tender farewell to her, burning jealousy filled his heart" (2:58).

It takes an unequivocally sinister omen to jolt Gustel out of the clouds of fantasy back to reality. One day during maneuvers near Lützen, she notices the persistent circling of a bird of prey over the royal coach and is shocked by the image into renewed apprehension of the stalking Lauenburg. Unable to stay away any longer, she hastens back to the king, slipping into his quarters early the following morning during the bustle of preparations for the major offensive planned for that day. But even at this point not one word of warning issues from her lips. Indeed, one is struck by the fact that Gustel does not speak at all throughout this climactic scene. She is rendered mute by the fear that any utterance against Lauenburg will somehow magically turn straight against herself. Caught in a paralyzing nether zone between approach and avoidance, she is reduced to hovering nervously and unobtrusively at arm's length from the beloved father she would protect: "Now he [Gustel] made himself small in a corner, concealed by the officers' comings and goings" (2:59).

In the king, however, she finds an oddly transformed man who gives the distinct impression of needing nothing, least of all protection: "The king had finally finished issuing his orders. His mood was a peculiar one. . . . Did he already sense the truth and the mercy of the realm he felt himself so near to?" (2:59). Turning to the assembled German princes, "He gestured and spoke very softly, almost as though he were dreaming, more with his ghostlike eyes than through his scarcely moving lips" (2:59). Casting himself as a perceptive observer, the narrator suggests the basis for the king's unnatural serenity on the verge of a crucial battle: he has renounced the things of this world and resigned himself to death. Lützen, he is convinced, will number him among its casualties.

This otherwordly fatalism that has engulfed the king during Gustel's absence must be viewed in the light of his nettled reaction to Wallenstein's warning against her. What began as a seemingly trivial irritation over the general's ludicrous superstition has burgeoned into an irreversible poisoning of the spirit. Such a profound lapse into morbidity can only be accounted for in terms of the unconscious scenario. On this level, the warning was seen to be a projected sting of the king's own conscience, provoked by his seductive overtures towards Gustel as a substitute for his daughter. However, once forced by conscience to renounce the seduction, he is left with those haunting fears of dwindling virility that originally prompted it, and no permissible strategy for counteracting them. The renunciation of Gustel also implies that of the nubile daughter for whom she stands, since the unconscious does not distinguish between real and symbolic love-objects. In blanket fashion the incest taboo prohibits his use of the daughter or any image of her to bolster his sexual confidence.

On the unconscious level, then, I interpret Gustav's resignation to death as a final surrender to the fear of impotence. He announces this surrender in the opening of his last address to the German princes, consciously casting it in terms of a presentiment of disaster in the impending battle: "Gentlemen, friends, I feel that my hour has come" (2:59). One is reminded of that first masked expression of sexual anxiety, voiced in his distraught prayer to be taken "im Vollwerte . . . , wenn seine Stunde da sei, bevor er ein Unnötiger oder Unmöglicher werde." There it was seen how the apparent worry over a disabling injury in battle concealed a dread of the gradual crippling of sexual capacity (his "Vollwert") by wartime pressures. Here the king is shown as having capitulated to that dread; bereft by conscience of his means of combatting it, he has chosen to die rather than subject himself to it any longer. What began as a prayer, a wish, has now become a choice. This most private and intimate of defeats, by virtue of his very unawareness of having suffered it, lends strong pathos to the address which he believes to be his final public "testament": "Gentlemen, friends, I feel that my hour has come. I wish to leave with you my final testament. Not in matters concerning the war— those who go on living will take care of that. But, after my own salvation, in the matter of what you think of me" (2:59).

As he goes on to review the long, epic struggle to secure "the undefiled Word" of Protestantism in Germany, he is moved to reveal an ulterior motive for that struggle:

> "After the victory at Breitenfeld I could have dictated an acceptable peace to the Emperor. And with the Word secure, I could have returned with my booty like some bird of prey to my Swedish cliffs.

> "But I was thinking about German affairs. Not entirely without a desire for your crown, gentlemen! But truly, my concern for the Empire won out over my personal ambition. It must not belong to a Hapsburg any longer because it is now a Protestant empire." (2:59)

Almost by his own admission, the king's altruistic concern for the integrity of the Protestant religion in Germany is a rationalization of a secret "Gelüst" ("desire") for the German crown. In terms of the present discussion, however, the craving for political hegemony in that country must itself be seen as, at best, a partially successful compensation for the diminution of sexual potency. One must assume that the king's initial strategy had been to recoup the loss of sexual through the acquisition of political power. If he could no longer take a woman, he could at least take a country. In the end, however, this shift of interest from the primal sexual to the symbolic political sphere must have been half-hearted, otherwise his incestuous attraction to the maturing daughter and, in her absence, the daughter substitute would not have arisen. Having now been forced by conscience to renounce a girl already once removed from the truly coveted love-object, the king finds he can no longer sustain the much more remote displacement to the sphere of political conquest. If his renunciation of Gustel is a capitulation to conscience, his renunciation in his address of all political ambitions in Germany is a resignation to the complete failure of political power to compensate symbolically for the loss of sexual power: "Yet you are thinking and saying, let's not have a foreign king ruling us! And you are right. For so it is written: a foreigner shall not succeed to the throne" (2:59). The king's last address, delivered in the solemn tones of a Baroque ascetic who has cast off all ties to this den of *vanitas* and humbly awaits entry into the *Jenseits,* is, finally, the testament of a man who has been undone by a most nineteenth-century version of unconscious determinism.

The scene climaxes in a powerful ensemble of psychological co- and cross-purposes. With the dismissal of the princes and the entrance of Lauenburg in the sham attitude of repentant Prodigal Son, king and page come together with the instrument of their destinies to play out their unconscious scripts. All three are like marionettes responding to the hidden movements of some malevolent hand. Each acts on behalf of an intention, whether his own or another's, of which he is unaware. Lauenburg does not realize that his attempt, through feigned repentance, to get close enough to the king to murder him is playing right into the latter's wish for death. While consciously accepting Lauenburg's prostration at face value ("The king raised him from the floor and enfolded him in his arms" [2:60]), on the unconscious level Gustav is well attuned to his true motives. His embrace of the man who is about to assassinate him is a kind of eerie implicit benediction of the deed. He will allow his enemy to become the vehicle of his longed-for departure from this vale of tears.

Gustel, who has been witnessing this strange reconciliation with mounting anxiety, remains trapped in the miasma of delusion, unable to see the obvious. Even in this critical moment with the king's life in the balance, and in spite of her earlier glimpse of the autonomous reality of Lauenburg's threat, she continues to project onto these antagonists aspects of her own inner conflict and is thereby rendered helpless. The king is still the idealized father and Lauenburg the doubleganger embodying the evil feminine self. The father's embrace of the doubleganger touches her deepest need to be loved by him as a woman, and she is thus moved to perceive the apparent reconciliation in these self-referential terms. The sinister motives behind Lauenburg's contrite posture are partially clouded from view as part of her dares to hope that the father is at last accepting her for what she truly is. Aberrant hope and urgent reality compete with each other for a claim on her awareness, keeping her wracked by indecision: "The men embracing seemed to float in a dizzy mist before the page's outraged eyes. *Was* this, *could* this be real? Had the king's own sanctity wrought a miracle in his depraved enemy? Or was it a diabolical trick? Was this wickedest of hypocrites deliberately befouling the purest words known? This was the way the page's doubts tumbled about, senses bewildered, temples throbbing" (2:60).

The final transaction between king and page epitomizes the tragedy of the unconscious scenario. The call to battle sounded, Gustel forces herself at the last instant to approach the king, but her approach and his response could only be described as an exercise in mutual futility. Stepping forward, she wordlessly extends the protective armor to him, which he refuses with the excuse that it is too confining:

> The page . . . started to help the king put it [the bulletproof armor] on. But the king, not at all astonished to see his page, resisted. His glance was kinder than words can describe, and he ran his fingers through Leubelfing's curly hair as was his custom.
>
> "No, Gust," he said. "I don't want it. It pinches. Give me my jacket." (2:60)

What should be an insistent gesture of protection, made with all the persuasion at her command, is rendered mute and feeble by Gustel's delusive hope that protection is no longer necessary, that in having received the doubleganger into his arms the father has, as if in a single act of unconditional love, magically dissolved the threat of her womanhood. The reality, of course, is that in embracing Lauenburg the king had unconditionally embraced death; his refusal of the armor so tentatively offered is that of a man who does not wish to be protected. In a curious sense, the acceptance of death is all the protective armor he needs. Once having taking hold, this psychological attitude provides the one truly invulnerable armor, insulating him from all earthly concerns and filling him with a saintlike serenity that takes all events in stride. Thus, in declining the armor, he shows no surprise whatever at Gustel's sudden reappearance but simply responds to her with the deep kindness born of transcendent detachment, a kindness that she irresistibly mistakes for the long-awaited demonstration of paternal love.

Here, then, is a climactic scene in which lethal decisions—Lauenburg's to murder, the king's to *be* murdered—are put into effect that elude the awareness or control of those victimized. Neither the king, who blesses his own assassin, nor the page, who witnesses the blessing, grasps the significance of what amounts to an unconscious ritual of suicide. Each is predetermined by hidden internal forces to gloss a morbid reality. By his conscious acceptance of Lauenburg as Prodigal Son returned, the king masks from his own obstructive Protestant conscience his unconscious acceptance of Lauenburg as a weapon of suicide, while Gustel, as has been seen, is driven by unmet need to twist the king's embrace of the assassin into the father's embrace of her womanhood. Each is lost to himself and the other, each marooned on his own island of unawareness, shrouded in the opaque mists of self-deception and delusion.

Meyer puts his symbolic signature to this bleak, psychologically deterministic view of the human condition in the single-sentence paragraph with which the chapter ends: "Kurz nachher sprengte der König davon, links und rechts hinter sich den Lauenburger und seinen Pagen Leubelfing" (*SW,* 11:209). Twice before I have observed the use of the rider-horse image to convey the precariousness of the individual's control over the forces of unacknowledged needs and passions. That sense of precariousness is heightened here to a pitch of tragic irony as king, duke and page ride off together in model equestrian formation, to all appearances united in a common cause.

Meyer might well have chosen to end his tale here, for with the departure of the three on horseback the primary psychological narrative is over. Even though the final fifth chapter has Lauenburg actually carrying out his heinous regicide and Gustel taking a fatal bullet while valiantly attempting to deliver the slain king to secluded quarters away from the chaos of battle, these events are nevertheless anticlimactic, the inexorable physical fulfillment of predetermined psychological destinies. That Meyer considers them so is clear from the fact that he does not trouble to narrate them, but allows them to happen between chapters, as it were, thereafter simply to be reported by the secondary characters.

The author has a far more interesting and esthetically appealing purpose in mind for the final chapter, and that is to provide the tale with an ironic epilogue in which the major theme of unconscious self-deception is extended to the motley cast of surrounding characters with the implication that man's inability to face the dark, elemental side of his own nature will continue to curse him. Having brought the king's body to the parsonage of magister Tödanus with the cornet's help, Gustel now becomes the bearer of harsh truths, truths that the various characters, who find their way there one by one, willfully suppress. The brutal reality of the assassination, carried out right before her eyes, has chastened her. "Lauenburg's shot" has had the effect of a violent catharsis, sweeping in a single report the vertiginous fog of fantasy and delusion, forcing her to face, not just an earth-shattering calamity, but the unbearable knowledge that she allowed her own mind-games to prevent her from averting that calamity. One can only assume an authentic ontological guilt, a scathing sense of irredeemable personal failure, to have empowered her herculean effort, partially witnessed by the cornet, to lift the dead king onto her mount and carry him off to seclusion:[28] "The cornet spoke, choosing his words very carefully. 'I found the young man, my comrade, galloping off the battlefield and holding the king in front of him on his horse. He sacrificed his own life for His Majesty!" (2:61). The sacrifice of self indeed, but in a sense the cornet could hardly imagine. The enemy bullet Gustel had formerly wished for herself, out of a delusive guilt over the destructive power of her femininity, but which had eluded her, has finally struck her now that her guilt is legitimate. Deliberately leaving herself an open target as she spirited the victim of her "sin of omission" away, she was not long in experiencing the sudden fulfillment of her desire for atonement.

Now, as life drains from her, a sobered, enlightened Gustel struggles to set the record straight, to make her last act an unflinching testimony to a grim reality: " 'I can't die yet! I have to tell you . . . ' gasped the page. 'The king . . . in the fog . . . Lauenburg's shot—' " (2:62). But death intervenes before she can clearly identify the assassin, enabling the bystanders conveniently to dismiss the obvious implication of her stammerings.

The collusive denial of an unacceptable reality by this cross-section of society—the pastor, the noble officer Ake Tott, the bourgeois merchant August Leubelfing, the cornet, and the pastor's housekeeper—lifts the theme of Gustel's individual self-deception to the level of civilized humanity in general. The individual's falsification of reality is now perpetuated by the group, even in the face of the individual's death-bed attempt to establish the truth for history. The epilogue chapter consists, then, in the tragic-ironic transposition of the deception theme from the intrapsychic to the collective social dimension.

In fact, the two major facets of the intrapsychic theme, Gustel's unconscious denial of her own femininity and her consequent blindness to Lauenburg's objective evil, recur in somber closing variations in the group's conspiracy of silence for reasons of social propriety. When an examination of Gustel's wound finally reveals her female identity, the pastor enjoins all present to secrecy, lest the king's martyrdom be tainted by sexual scandal: "I am a servant of God's Word; you are a man of gray hair, colonel; you, cornet, are an aristocrat. Mr. Laubfinger, it is to your profit and advantage. I will vouch for Mrs. Ida. We will remain silent" (2:62). It is as if the lie of sexual identity, released from Gustel's soul at the moment of death, is now free like some

unchained malevolent spirit to invade the society at large. Through its silence, society will keep her lie alive. "And so I will have it [the name August Leubelfing] on your gravestone" (2:62), the pastor promises her.

A moment later, upon Gustel's passing, it is again the pastor who persuades the company to regard her disjointed but unmistakable accusation of Lauenburg as irrational rambling. The idea of the royal father's murder by one of his most distinguished sons is too repugnant to him: "The pastor, however, still with great presence of mind, was not about to have his patriotic senses [*sic*] besmirched by the thought that the saviour of Germany and the Protestant cause—for him one and the same thing—had fallen by the assassin hands of a German prince. He emphatically admonished them all to let this fragment of a deathbed utterance be buried with the page" (2:63). All comply in this profound dissembling of an unpalatable history, and the evildoer has now been twice protected, before the deed by Gustel's silence, after it by the group's. Once more, as in the matter of Gustel's sex, one sees the movement of the deception theme from the individual intrapsychic to the collective social sphere.

In both spheres, Lauenburg is experienced as a demonic internal force that threatens to disrupt a carefully preserved (but in reality, artificial) self-image, in the one instance of father-placating masculinity, in the other of Pan-Protestant solidarity. No less than the individual is the society driven to cover up rather than confront what it takes to be its own shadow side. Both counterfeit their own histories. The pastor, a self-committed "Diener am Wort," society's exemplar of the truthful word, leads the others in burying that word with its speaker. With this collective burial they could be said to repeat Gustel's individual act of repression on the level of society as a whole.

Gustav Adolfs Page anticipates Freud's famous dictum that repression is the price man has had to pay for civilization. Meyer knew, and helped Freud to discover, that disowned passions take refuge in the abode of the unconscious, from which they sooner or later return as demons to haunt one. The first four chapters of the tale portray this unhappy truth in the lives of the titular characters, who are, in the end, devoured by their own inner demons. The epilogue chapter, in casting a broader spotlight on society's habit of cosmeticizing its own blemishes, ominously implies the continued sovereignty of the dark denizens of the unconscious over the lives of society's future members, commoners and kings alike.

The tale ends in an image of light that is tinged with melancholy irony. The bodies of king and page are laid out together before the church altar, their reposing faces transfigured by a morning sunbeam from a nearby window: "A cloudless blue sky had followed yesterday's gloomy day, and now a ray of morning sunlight slipped through the low church window to transfigure a king's face. A tiny little beam was left over for the curly head of page Leubelfing" (2:63). This light is a deliberate allusion to those shafts of metaphysical illumination that frame the heads of saints and martyrs in the religious painting of earlier centuries. The effect is one of nostalgia for a time when men's earthly destinies, whether joyful or sad, were felt to be sanctioned by a benevolent, purposeful, infinitely wise Providence—in other words, nostalgia for the Christian world view contemporary to the characters in the work. But in symbolically commemorating an idealized world view long since called into question, this beam of light throws into stark relief the menacing darkness of the unconscious contemporary to the author's world, a darkness in which he felt compelled by intellectual and artistic honesty to shroud the destinies of his characters. Perhaps, then, the most poignant irony of all in *Gustav Adolfs Page* emerges from the shadow cast by the world view of the work over that of its characters. . . .

Notes

[1] In a letter of 25 September 1881, in Anton Bettelheim, ed., *Louise von François und Conrad Ferdinand Meyer: Ein Briefwechsel,* 2d ed. (Berlin: VWV, 1920), p. 23.

[2] Von François's letter is dated 16 October 1881. See Bettelheim, *François und Meyer: Briefwechsel,* p. 25. Emil Ermatinger offers persuasive evidence that Meyer derived the idea of a female page from Heinrich Laube's early drama, *Gustav Adolf* ("Eine Quelle zu C. F. Meyers Novelle 'Gustav Adolfs Page,'" *Das literarische Echo* 19 [1916]: 22-26). If von François was likewise familiar with this youthful effort of Laube's, which, although remaining unpublished in the nineteenth century, had been described by the author in detail in his introduction to an 1845 edition of the play *Monaldeschi,* then her guessing of Meyer's "secret" becomes less telepathic.

[3] For an elaboration of this point of view, see Karen Horney, *Feminine Psychology,* ed. Harold Kelman, trans. Edward R. Clemmens, John M. Meth, Edward Schattner, and Gerda F. Willner (New York: Norton, 1973), pp. 80-81.

[4] Even Friedrich Kittler, who brings to the tale many insights of Freudian and Lacanian psychoanalysis, nevertheless does not distinguish between conscious and unconscious narrative levels as such; rather he views the tale within a combined framework of discourse and speech-act theory in terms of the opposition between valid and invalid discourse, or, more precisely, between discourse and its absence, the latter exemplified by such phenomena as dreams (for example, Gustel's *Wunschtraum* of serving under the king) in which "communication" is unilateral, private or interior, there being no real "Hörer" (*Der Traum und die Rede: Eine Analyse der Kommunikationssituation Conrad Ferdinand Meyers* [Bern: Francke, 1977], pp. 7, 24). Thus, notwithstanding Kittler's frequent recourse to depth-psychological ideas, the fact remains that his hybrid conceptual paradigm and the depth-psychological approach employed here result in radically diverse interpretations. My own hinges on the inference, based on a pattern of textual evidence, that Gustel unconsciously and magically believes her own femininity to have been responsible for her father's death and that her attachment to the king as a father-substitute is an attempt to "undo" the imagined parricide and its attendant overwhelming guilt by becoming a man (hence, male page) for him. The ultimate object of Gustel's quest as seen here is the real father's love and acceptance. The strategy of masculinity she adopts in pursuit of these implies the profound repression of the hated feminine self. The narrative is viewed, then, as the portrayal of the heroine's symbolic reenactment of the primal father-daughter relationship or, in Freudian terms, her carrying-out of a repetition compulsion.

Kittler's point of departure, by contrast, is that "Gleichwohl ist der leibliche Vater nicht das Ziel des [von Gustels Traum artikulierten] Wunsches. Denn nur darum tritt die Traumrednerin an dessen Platz, um in der Nähe des Königs zu sein, den sie als 'Abgott' und 'Helden' verehrt. . . . Ein lebender, allmächtiger und idealer Vater tritt an die Leerstelle, die der Tod des leiblichen aufgetan hat. Der vom Traum artikulierte Wunsch kann also artikuliert werden als das Begehren, anstelle des toten Vaters in der Nähe des idealen zu sein" (p. 194). My central thesis, that Gustel holds herself to blame for her father's death, leads me to conclude that the king is for her a father-imago or transference object over against which she plays out the unconscious drama of guilt and yearning for love. Kittler, who prescinds entirely from the issues of imagined parricide and guilt, views the king as having an autonomous paternal status in Gustel's world, that is, he cannot be said to represent for her anyone but himself in his function as ideal father ("'Abgott' und 'Helden'"). These different premises lead to altogether different readings.

More recently, Christian Sand has made some intriguing speculations on Gustel's dilemma as reflective of Meyer's early childhood experience (*Anomie und Identität: Zur Wirklichkeitsproblematik in der Prosa von C. F. Meyer,* Stuttgarter Arbeiten zur Germanistik no. 79, ed. Ulrich Müller, Franz Hundsnurscher, and Cornelius Sommer [Stuttgart: Hans-Dieter Heinz, 1980], pp. 114-18. Using the analytical techniques of depth psychology and the sociology of knowledge (*Wissenssoziologie),* Sand views Gustel as an expression of Meyer's own Oedipal or even pre-Oedipal conflicts.

The inversion of sex, from male author vis-à-vis mother to female protagonist in pursuit of the father-figure, is supposedly intended to defuse the author's own harsh Calvinist ethic which proscribes over filial gestures of love toward the mother. Sand concludes that "vieles dafür spricht, daß der Page Leubelfing in den ödipalen Identifikationsprozessen [Meyers] seinen Ursprung hat" (p. 115). While he foregoes analysis of the text of *Gustav Adolfs Page,* Sand's biographical hypotheses lend external support to the analysis offered here.

In her excellent article, "Conrad Ferdinand Meyer, Gustav Adolfs Page: Versuch einer Interpretation," Claudia Liver analyzes the tale in terms of its dominant Baroque *teatrum mundi* topos, but is well aware of the tale's essentially modern sensibility as conveyed by the narrator's interpolated comments "deren Inhalt nicht in der Gedankenwelt der mitspielenden Figur lokalisiert werden kann und deren [psychologische] Form ihrer Denkweise widerspricht" (*Annali* 19, no. 3 [1976]: 7-36; quotation from p. 18, note 27). While I take issue with parts of Liver's argument (see, for example, note 26 below), I am in complete accord with her general approach—indeed, my own interpretation may be taken as essentially complementary to hers: while she deals with the fundamental theme of determinism as Meyer styles it in the manifest features of the *teatrum mundi* topos, I attempt to disclose its underlying, occasionally explicit but mainly implicit, psychodynamic dimension.

Periodically through the decades, several other critics have referred to this or that element of the tale's unconscious narrative level, either to leave it at that or to proceed in pursuit of other, peripheral lines of interpretation: thus Hertling: "wie ein Märchentraum wird sein [i.e., Gustel's] so 'kindischer' und langgehegter, dem Bewußtsein zunächst verschlossen bleibender Wunsch [to serve under the king] tatsächlich 'Gestalt gewinnen'" (*Conrad Ferdinand Meyers Epik* [: *Traumbeseelung, Traumbesinnung* and *Traumbesitz* (Bern: Francke, 1973)], p. 116). Fehr most likely implies the eruption of unconscious motives in Gustel in describing her flight from camp as "eine Flucht vor sich selbst aus einer für sie unerträglich gewordenen Spannung" (*Conrad Ferdinand Meyer,* p. 69). Brückner suggests Gustel's resistance to the repressed when he writes: "Sie ist sich plötzlich bewusst, dass sie ein unnatürliches Dasein führt und nennt sich selbst 'eine Lügnerin, eine Sophistin'" (*in Prosawerk Conrad Ferdinand Meyers,* Europäische Hochschulschriften: Deutsche Literatur und Germanistik, series 1, 38 (Bern: Herbert Leng, 1970)] *Heldengestaltung,* p. 25). Burkhard and Stevens note the covert workings of the unconscious, but only with respect to the king, and even there dismiss the theme as insignificant: "The portrayal of platonic relations between a young girl and a great hero who is ignorant of her sex is, moreover, not a particularly fruitful or significant problem.

The association has no more than an unconscious effect on the man, and terminates, in Meyer's account, before any important formative or disruptive effects on the women's character ensue" ("[Conrad Ferdinand] Meyer Reveals Himself [: A Critical Examination of 'Gustor Adolfs Page'" *Germanic Review* 15 (1940)]," p. 203). Interpreting Gustel's relationship with the king as anything but platonic, Edgar Krebs argues that her dreams signal her unconscious conflict between sexual wish and conscience ("Das Unbewußte in den Dichtungen Conrad Ferdinand Meyers," *Die psychoanalytische Bewegung* 2 [1930]: 336-37). Felix Emmel observes the king's unconscious sensing of Gustel's femaleness and the latter's "eifersüchtiges, unbewußtes Wünschen" (p. 409) with respect to the queen ("Der Eros und der Tod. Zu Conrad Ferdinand Meyers Pagennovelle," *Preussische Jahrbücher* 179 [1920]: 404-15). For Emmel the tale is part of Meyer's complex response to his "späte Pubertätszeit" (p. 408). It should be noted that none of the critics listed here discerns the link between Gustel's noxious relationship to her father, inferable from remarks of the various characters, and her present-time behavior. As stated above, the interpretation offered here is an elucidation of precisely this link.

Finally, there are still other readers who hold other views, prescinding entirely from considerations of the unconscious. Georges Brunet, for example, in his book, *C. F. Meyer et la nouvelle,* sees as the primary issue in *Gustav Adolfs Page,* as in all of Meyer's fiction, that of "des rapports de l'existence humaine et de l'éthique" [Paris: Didier, 1967], p. 269. Brunet's interpretation focuses on what he takes to be the tragic flaws in the king's character, his lust for power and, as standard-bearer of a "just" religious cause, his presumption of invulnerability. On the other hand, both Lily Hohenstein and von Lerber insist on the supposedly innocent, even spiritual quality of Gustel's love as the tale's dominant theme, the former characterizing it as a true "Einklang der Seelen," the latter as "verhalten, keusch, in Zucht genommen" (Hohenstein, *Conrad Ferdinand Meyer* [Bonn: Athenäum, 1957], p. 240; [Helene] von Lerber, *C. F. Meyer: Der Mensch in der Spannung,* [(Basel: Reinhardt, 1949)], p. 136).

[5] In a letter of 9 June 1898 to Fliess, published posthumously in Sigmund Freud, *Aus den Anfängen der Psychoanalyse* (London: Imago, 1950), this according to Frederick J. Beharriell, "C. F. Meyer and the Origins of Psychoanalysis," *Monatshefte* 47 (1955): 142-43. In the psychoanalytic lexicon, deferred action (*Nachträglichkeit*) refers to that behavior performed by an adult in unconscious reaction to an early childhood experience. In Meyer's story Gustel's godfather, Ake Tott, recalls the king's playful fondling and kissing of the infant Gustel and points to this as the basis of her present blind devotion to him. As Beharriell's article (pp. 140-48) demonstrates, the

Anfänge, a collection of letters and documents written by Freud between 1887 and 1902, contains many references to works by Meyer.

[6] Beharriell, "C. F. Meyer and the Origins of Psychoanalysis," p. 148.

[7] Ibid.

[8] Especially in the older critical literature, *Gustav Adolfs Page* did not fare well. See, for example, Burkhard and Stevens throughout, who find the tale so wanting in virtually every respect that they cannot avoid a concluding admission of having "cruelly analyzed" it ("Meyer Reveals Himself," p. 211); Maync, whose tactful understatement, "Unter seine Meisterwerke ist 'Gustav Adolfs Page' nicht zu rechnen," betrays a similar attitude (*C. F. Meyer und Sein Werk,* p. 212); Emmel, who announces more candidly in his opening sentence, "In der ersten Hälfte des Jahres 1882 schuf Conrad Ferdinand Meyer eine seiner weniger bedeutenden Novellen: 'Gustav Adolfs Page'" ("Der Eros und der Tod," p. 404); and T. de Wyzewa, who throws discretion to the winds in calling the narrative "banale, gauche, puérile" ("Un romancier suisse, Conrad Ferdinand Meyer," *Revue des deux Mondes* 152 [1899]: 938).

At least one current critic agrees with this earlier group. Evans weeds the tale out from those she finds worthy of analysis since "in struktureller Hinsicht ist diese Novelle oft verschwommen und wirkt im Vergleich mit der profilierten Figurenkonstellation im *Heiligen* und der raffinierten Konstruktion verschiedener stofflicher Ebenen und literarischer Anspielungen im *Schuß von der Kanzel* schemenhaft" (*Formen der Ironie,* p. 6). The present interpretation may be said to defend the tale against the bulk of these assertions, and most vigorously with respect to its alleged lack of a "raffinierten Konstruktion verschiedener stofflicher Ebenen."

[9] See [William] James, *Varieties of Religious Experience* [(New York: Mentor, 1958)], p. 298.

[10] As Zeller and Zach put it in [*Conrad Ferdinand Mayer, Sämtliche Werke. Historisch-Kritische Ausgabe,* ed. Hans Zeller and Alfred Zäch (Bern: Benteli, 1959)] 11:279.

[11] See, for example, von François's letter of 4 October 1882, in Bettelheim, *François und Meyer: Briefwechsel,* p. 65, and Alfred Zäch, *Conrad Ferdinand Meyer: Dichtkunst als Befreiung aus Lebenshemmnissen* (Frauenfeld: Huber, 1973), pp. 176-77.

[12] "Ich las Goethes Egmont und vertiefte mich in den Gedanken: es lohnte wohl, ein Weib zu zeichnen, das ohne Hingabe, ja ohne daß der Held nur eine Ahnung von ihrem Geschlecht hat, einem hohen Helden in verschwiegener Liebe folgt und für ihn in den Tod geht." Quoted in *SW,* 11:280.

[13] Ibid.

[14] Burkhard and Stevens, "Meyer Reveals Himself," p. 198.

[15] In a letter of 4 July 1882 to Rodenberg, in August Langmesser, ed., *Conrad Ferdinand Meyer und Julius Rodenberg: Ein Briefwechsel* (Berlin: Paetel, 1918), p. 112.

[16] Horney, *Feminine Psychology,* p. 74. See also note 3.

[17] Ibid., pp. 43-50.

[18] See note 5. Although Freud did not publish his theory of the family romance until 1909, the first statement of its main features is contained in a brief essay on Meyer's *Die Richterin* written for Fliess in June of 1898 and first published in the *Anfänge* of 1950 (see Beharriell, "C. F. Meyer and the Origins of Psychoanalysis," pp. 144-45). This essay is generally considered to be the first explicit application of psychoanalysis to a work of literature.

[19] To be sure, Freud would later note the power, not only of personal names but even of their individual syllabic components, to arouse incestuous desires. In *Totem and Taboo* (1913), which demonstrates the close parallels between individual compulsive-neurotic behavior and the rigidly observed customs of "primitive" peoples, he discusses, for example, the elaborate precautions taken by the natives of Lepers Island in the New Hebrides to prevent any social contact between brothers and sisters that might expose them to the lures of incest. Prohibitions extend even to the brother's speaking the sister's name aloud: "He will not even mention her name and will guard against using any current word if it forms part of her name. This avoidance, which begins with the ceremony of puberty, is strictly observed for life." See *The Basic Writings of Sigmund Freud,* ed. and trans. A. A. Brill (New York: The Modern Library, 1938), p. 814.

[20] The special fascination held by this transitional phase of consciousness for Meyer the lyricist is discussed by [Heinrich] Henel, *The Poetry of C. F. Meyer* [(Madison, Wisconsin: University of Wisconsin Press, 1954)], p. 30. . .

[21] See that section of *The Interpretation of Dreams* entitled, "The Work of Displacement," in *The Basic Writings of Sigmund Freud,* pp. 336-39.

[22] "Appropriately," that is, in the sense of Freud's observation that punishment dreams characteristically

occur "if the thoughts which are day-residues are of a gratifying nature, but express illicit gratifications" (here: the erotic name-coupling reverie immediately preceding sleep). The narrator's remark that Gustel "träumte mit seinem Gewissen" anticipates Freud's singling-out of punishment dreams as a special class in which "it is not the unconscious wish from the repressed material (from the system Ucs. [unconscious]) that is responsible for dream-formation, but the punitive wish reacting against it, a wish pertaining to the ego, even though it is unconscious (i.e., preconscious)." See *The Basic Writings of Sigmund Freud,* p. 504. In a footnote on the same page, added to *The Interpretation of Dreams* in 1930, Freud implies this distinction would have been clearer if he had had at his disposal at the original time of writing "the idea of the super-ego which was later recognized by psychoanalysis."

[23] Sigmund Freud, *New Introductory Lectures on Psychoanalysis,* ed. and trans. James Strachey (New York: Norton, 1965), p. 77.

[24] See Victoria L. Rippere's excellent article, "Ludwig Tieck's 'Der blonde Eckbert': A Psychological Reading," *PMLA* 85 (1970), 473-86, esp. 484.

[25] My translation from the play, in Goethe, *Dramen, Novellen,* vol. 2 of *Goethe Werke* (Frankfurt a. M.: Insel, 1970), p. 202.

[26] Critics have been generally stymied by the apparently gratuitous introduction of this *Doppelgängermotiv:* Marianne Burkhard speaks of "the implausible resemblance between Gustel and the duke of Lauenburg" as responsible in part for the work's being "not fully convincing" (*Conrad Ferdinand Meyer,* Twayne's World Authors Series, no. 480, ed. Ulrich Weisstein [Boston: G. K. Hall, 1978], p. 125). Liver regards the motif as one of a number of "unwahrscheinlich anmutenden Elemente" in the tale that have no explanation beyond the fact that they stand "im Dienst einer irrationalistischen Beleuchtung des Schicksals" ("Gustav Adolfs Page," p. 30, number 61). For Zäch, the motif is an absurd contrivance forced upon Meyer by the exigencies of plot: "Und was für Zufälle müssen mitwirken, damit eine Verwechslung des Lauenburgers mit Leubelfing möglich wird!" (*Dichtkunst als Befreiung,* p. 175). Beharriell stands behind Freud's own criticism of the motif as "'an sich so unwahrscheinlich und gar nicht weiter begründet.' Most critics will agree that this complaint is a just one" ("C. F. Meyer and the Origins of Psychoanalysis," pp. 143-44).

The point is, I think, that the resemblance between Gustel and Lauenburg is indeed completely gratuitous in and of itself and takes on meaning only in the context of Gustel's unconscious perception. It is the psychological identification she forms from the resemblance with its fatal consequences that imbues an otherwise irrelevant "accident of nature" with significance. A few critics have attempted to see past the accidental: Kittler, for instance, observes in semiotic terms that "der Doppelgänger [ist] kein bloßes Spiel der Natur und d.h. willkürlich; was ihn ermöglicht, ist das Spiel der Signifikanten, innerhalb dessen die Spiele der Natur erst zählen" (*Der Traum und die Rede,* p. 208). However, beyond our initial agreement that the meaning of the resemblance resides in its meaning-for-Gustel, we have opposite views on what that meaning is: while Kittler argues that "so präsentiert der Doppelgänger der Lauscherin diejenige familiale Position, die sie einnähme, wenn ihr Betrug die Wahrheit wäre" (p. 209), which he consequently interprets as that of rebellious son, a stance shocking to her daughter's attitude of "Idolatrie" (p. 210), I assert conversely that it is the lethal *daughter,* concealed behind the doubleganger's correspondingly docile male façade, which Gustel unconsciously and symbolically (mis)perceives and to which she reacts with shock by virtue of her identification with it. For Wiesmann the element of recognition so shocking to Gustel is Lauenburg's adulterous liaison with Corinna, an unconscious reminder of her own illicit desires with respect to the king: "Nur läßt der Lauenburger seinen Trieben freien Lauf, während sich der Page keusch zurückhält (*Dichter des Todes,* p. 148). This is seconded by Brückner: "Ihr Doppelgänger, der Lauenburger, führt in seinem Verhältnis zu Corinna das aus, worauf Auguste im Unterbewusstsein hofft" (*Heldengestaltung,* p. 25). The view here, however, is that Gustel is not held back by the fear of violating conventional sanctions against adultery, or at least not primarily by such fear, but rather that she is gripped by the far more primal terror that any feminine overtures might again result in parricide.

[27] The foregoing arguments may serve as a response to Burkhard and Stevens, who consider Gustel's sudden flight and "the King's lack of interest in Gustel's action and whereabouts" to be among "the least convincing elements in the story" ("Meyer Reveals Himself," pp. 195-96). Indeed, if one neglects to take the unconscious dimension of the narrative into account, these elements have little or no comprehensible basis.

[28] The motif of the surge of enormous physical strength resulting from the despair of conscience, enabling a woman to lift a burden far beyond her normal capacity, fascinated Meyer. As Hertling notes, the motif informs the central background legend of the cross-bearing duchess in *Plautus im Nonnenkloster,* the penitent founder of the cloister "deren 'Gewissen . . . Gott . . . gerührt' hatte . . . , ja die infolgedessen das echte Kreuz 'gehoben haben . . . mochte . . . mit den Riesenkräften der Verzweiflung und der Inbrunst' " (*Conrad Ferdinand Meyers Epik,* p. 115). . . .

FURTHER READING

Bridgwater, W. P. "C. F. Meyer and Nietzsche." *The Modern Language Review* 60, No. 4 (October 1965): 568-83.

Examines the elements of convergence between Meyer and Nietzsche's worldviews.

Burkhard, Arthur. *Conrad Ferdinand Meyer: The Style and the Man.* Cambridge: Harvard University Press, 1932, 225 p.

An early study of Meyer's literary style analyzed in connection with biographical details.

Dahme, Lena F. *Women in the Life and Art of Conrad Ferdinand Meyer.* New York: Columbia University Press, 1936, 420 p.

Investigates the characterization of females in Meyer's work and his personal relationships with women.

Grinstein, Alexander. *Conrad Ferdinand Meyer and Freud: The Beginnings of Applied Psychoanalysis.* Madison, Conn.: International University Press, 1922, 399 p.

Amplifies Freud's persisting interest in Meyer's work as proto-psychoanalytic literature.

Jackson, D. A. "Conrad Ferdinand Meyer, *Hutten letzte Tage* and the Liberal Ideal." In *Oxford German Studies 5,* edited by T. J. Reed, pp. 67-89. Oxford: Clarendon Press, 1970.

Traces the veiled literary manifestations of Meyer's political liberalism.

Jennings, Lee B. "The Ambiguous Explosion: C. F. Meyer's *Der Schuß von der Kanzel.*" *The German Quarterly* 43, No. 2 (March 1970): 210-22.

Contends that psychoanalytic insights govern Meyer's portrayals of nineteenth-century bourgeois life.

Komar, Kathleen L. "Fact, Fiction, and Focus: Their Structural Embodiment in C. F. Meyer's *Der Heilige.*" *Colloquia Germanica* 14, No. 3 (1981): 332-41.

Studies Meyer's innovative use of framing in *Der Heilige.*

Laane, Tiiu V. *Imagery in Conrad Ferdinand Meyer's Prose Works: Form, Motifs, and Functions.* Berne: Peter Lang, 1983, 258 p.

A thorough discussion of recurring themes and images in Meyer's novellas.

Lund, Deborah S. *Ambiguity as Narrative: Strategy in the Prose Work of C. F. Meyer.* New York: Peter Lang, 1990, 207 p.

Contends that Meyer's writing is dominated in a variety of respects by the logic of ambiguity.

Plater, Edward M. V. "The Figure of Dante in *Die Hochzeit des Mönchs.*" *Modern Language Notes* 90, No. 5 (October 1975): 678-86.

Examines the complex role of Dante Alighieri as mediator between the frame of the story and its narrative content.

Schimmelpfennig, Paul. "Meyer's Religion of the Heart: A Reevaluation of *Das Amulett.*" *The Germanic Review* 47, No. 3 (May 1972): 181-202.

Disputes the common critical conclusion that the early novella *Das Amulett* lacks the stylistic and psychological sophistication of Meyer's later work.

Tusken, Lewis W. "C. F. Meyer's *Der Heilige:* The Problem of Becket's Conversion." *Seminar: A Journal of Germanic Studies* 7, No. 3 (October 1971): 201-15.

Claims that Meyer subtly maintains the complexity of Thomas à Becket's motivations in his fictional portrayal of the archbishop's "conversion."

Williams, W. D. *The Stories of C. F. Meyer.* Oxford: Clarendon Press, 1962, 221 p.

Charts Meyer's innovations in his prose narratives and includes critical discussions of the major novellas.

Walt Whitman

1819-1892

American poet, essayist, novelist, short story writer, journalist, and editor. For more information on Whitman's life and works, see *NCLC,* Volumes 4 and 31.

INTRODUCTION

Although commonly and critically regarded as one of America's premier poets, Whitman remains in some ways a controversial figure. *Leaves of Grass,* his masterpiece, was revolutionary in both its style and content, praising the divinity of the self, of the common individual. The volume was directed at those Americans who, in Whitman's opinion, had been ignored by their country's literature, a literature which had typically targeted the upper echelons of society. Throughout his life and work, Whitman promoted himself as the poet of American democracy and of the common man. Yet the focus of his poetry on the sanctity and divinity of the self has been criticized as being more egotistical than spiritual, and his exploration and exaltation of sexuality and homosexuality has been both deplored and downplayed. Additionally, critics have analyzed how the Civil War changed Whitman's poetry, and have studied his ambivalent views on the subject of the treatment of Native Americans during his lifetime.

Biographical Information

Born on Long Island and raised and educated on Long Island and in Brooklyn, Whitman was the second of nine children. Leaving school at age eleven, he worked as a law office clerk, and later, as a typesetter's apprentice. After teaching school and starting his own newspaper, he began editing various papers. He also published poems and short stories in periodicals. In 1842, Whitman published a temperance novel entitled *Franklin Evans; or, the Inebriate*; he later dismissed the work as "damned rot." The first edition of *Leaves of Grass* was published in 1855 at Whitman's own expense. Nine editions would eventually be published. During the Civil War, Whitman cared for wounded soldiers in Washington, D.C., beginning in 1862 and later worked as a copyist in the army paymaster's office from 1863 to 1864. After the war, he worked for a short time for the Department of the Interior but was fired when it was discovered that he was the author of the allegedly obscene *Leaves of Grass*. Rehired as a Justice Department clerk, Whitman remained in this position until he suffered a paralytic stroke in 1873, which left him partially disabled. He had recently published a philosophical essay, *Democratic Vistas* (1871) and the fifth edition of *Leaves of Grass*. While he lived for nearly twenty more years, Whitman produced little new work of significance, focusing instead on revising and rearranging *Leaves of Grass*.

Major Works

Leaves of Grass, in its final version, contains poems Whitman wrote between 1855 and 1892. The major themes of the work include democracy, sexuality, death, and immortality; universality and the divine nature of the self are also concepts that thread their way through much of his work. The first edition contained twelve poems, which shocked the public with their realistic imagery and candid discussions of sexuality. The volume received little praise from critics, with Ralph Waldo Emerson being the notable exception. In later editions of *Leaves of Grass,* Whitman created new poems, revised existing ones, added and changed titles, and thematically grouped the poems. In *Drum-Taps* (1865) and *Sequel to Drum-Taps* (1865-66), Whitman recorded many of his war experiences and mourned the loss of nation and lives. *Drum-Taps* was later incorporated into *Leaves of Grass.*

Critical Reception

While many critics concede that Whitman's concept of the self is of major significance in his work, V. K. Chari maintains that it is *the* "organizing principle" of Whitman's poetry. In analyzing Whitman's notion of the self, Chari maintains that to Whitman, the self was the true meaning and center of all existence, and that reality was not separate or different from the self. Chari demonstrates both the influence of Ralph Waldo Emerson's writing on Whitman and identifies the similarities between Whitman's views and Hindu philosophy. Additionally, while many critics observe a duality in Whitman's concept of the self (the body versus the spirit, the individual versus the universal), Chari emphasizes the unified, monistic nature of Whitman's self. E. Fred Carlisle concentrates on the relationship in Whitman's poetry between the self and both death and spirit. Carlisle argues that Whitman portrays death in a variety of ways: as a passage into a new life or into oblivion, as an end to suffering, as a threat, and as completion and fulfillment. Throughout *Leaves of Grass,* Carlisle states, Whitman attempts to comprehend how death serves or links the self and the spirit. Like Chari and Carlisle, David Kuebrich is concerned with Whitman's spirituality and argues that, contrary to the conviction of numerous critics, Whitman intended to begin a "new religion" and promoted his readers' spiritual development by offering them an orderly vision linking religion with contemporary ideas on American culture. Kuebrich outlines the way in which many modern critics address Whitman's spirituality, showing that they dismiss his religious language as "the symbolic manifestation of the distorted desires of the id," and that his spirituality is disregarded as his attempt, later in life, to fashion his earlier work as religious and prophetic. For M. Jimmie Killingsworth, Whitman's notion of the self is one that contains elements of the individual and the universal. Unlike Chari, Killingsworth highlights the duality of Whitman's concept of self, focusing on an apparent tension between singularity and diversity. Similarly, Mitchell Robert Breitwieser identifies in Whitman's poetry two distinct "I's" or "selves," the first "I" being a small, timid, individual, voice and the second "I" being a large, universal, affirming voice.

Just as the nature and significance of Whitman's concept of the self is a battleground for many critics, so is the issue of the centrality and importance of the sexual, and homosexual, themes in his poetry. Kenneth M. Price maintains that sexual themes—such as voyeurism, nonprocreative sexuality, and female sexuality—and the way Whitman treats such topics, influenced writers of narrative fiction. Price analyzes the way in which the approaches to sexual themes in the works of Hamlin Garland, Kate Chopin, and E. M. Forster are indebted to Whitman. Byrne R. S. Fone surveys the manner in which the homoeroticism in Whitman's text has been addressed by early and modern critics. Byrne argues that, in many cases, the homophobia inherent in the discourse of these Whitman scholars has detracted from the quality of textual and biographical analyses. Similarly, Betsy Erkkila notes that there is a critical tradition which has been responsible for "silencing, spiritualizing, heterosexualizing, or marginalizing Whitman's sexual feeling for men." Erkkila states that when critics do recognize the centrality of homosexuality to Whitman's work, often they maintain a distinction between the private Whitman and the public Whitman, as "the poet of democracy." In challenging this distinction, Erkkila contends that Whitman's "sexual love of men" is central to his "democratic vision and experimental poetics" in *Leaves of Grass.*

Whitman's interest in democracy and American political events and issues is revealed in his poetry and is a major focus of criticism. In particular, critics observe how the Civil War and Whitman's experience in it greatly influenced his poetry. James Dougherty investigates this influence, as demonstrated in *Drum-Taps.* Dougherty states that "*Drum-Taps* represents Whitman's bid to be 'absorbed' by America not as a radically democratic visionary but as the inheritor and master of a tradition according to which poems were like pictures." In his analysis of the strong visual images in *Drum-Taps,* Dougherty argues that while at first glance such "photographic" poems seem to be a new element in Whitman's work and seem to characterize *Drum-Taps,* in fact, such poems were presaged by Whitman's earlier work and are not the only type of poem in the volume. Furthermore, Dougherty identifies a conflict in the book between different styles and different points of view. This conflict, Dougherty argues, represents a tension not only between Whitman's pre-war faith in "physical and spiritual regeneration" and his post-war loss of that faith; the conflict also points to Whitman's doubts regarding his "original poetic." Another American political issue to fascinate Whitman was the treatment of Native Americans. Noting that Whitman's professional life was "framed" beginning in the late 1830s by the Great Removal of Native Americans to what would become Oklahoma, and fifty years later by the Wounded Knee massacre, Ed Folsom observes in Whitman's poetry and short stories a deeply ambivalent attitude toward Native Americans. Folsom asserts that "Whitman's plan to absorb the Indian via his poetry was . . . double-edged: his project admitted the inevitable loss of Indian cultures, but it simultaneously argued for the significance of those cultures and for the necessity of preserving them—as a warning, lesson, inspiration—at the heart of our memories, deep in the lines of authentic American poems."

PRINCIPAL WORKS

Franklin Evans; or, the Inebriate (novel) 1842
Leaves of Grass (poetry) 1855, 1856, 1860-61, 1867, 1871, 1876, 1881-82, 1891-92
*Drum-Taps (poetry) 1865
*Sequel to Drum-Taps (poetry) 1865-66
Democratic Vistas (essay) 1871
*Passage to India (poetry) 1871
Specimen Days & Collect (essays and journals) 1882-83
*November Boughs (poetry) 1888
The Wound-Dresser; A Series of Letters Written from Hospitals in Washington during the War of the Rebellion (letters) 1898
An American Primer (essays) 1904
The Half-Breed and Other Stories (short stories) 1927
The Correspondence of Walt Whitman 6 vols. (letters) 1961-77
Prose Works, 1892. 2 vols. (essays) 1963-64
Walt Whitman: Notebooks and Unpublished Prose Manuscripts. 6 vols. (essays and notes) 1984

*These works were incorporated in later editions of *Leaves of Grass.*

CRITICISM

V. K. Chari (essay date 1964)

SOURCE: "Emergent Ego," in *Whitman in the Light of Vedantic Mysticism: An Interpretation,* University of Nebraska Press, 1964, pp. 53-93.

[*In the following essay, Chari stresses the centrality of the notion of the self in Whitman's poetry, demonstrating the parallels between Whitman's conception of the self as the meaning of existence and the totality of reality, and the view of the self offered by Hindu mysticism.*]

> . . . the mystical identity the real I or Me or
> You
> (***Complete Writings,*** Vol. VI, Part I, No. 28)

Any consistent interpretation of Whitman should, in my opinion, be centered around the concept of self, for the self is at once the organizing principle in his poetry and the stuff of the experience that it dramatizes. This unity of theme corresponds to a central identity of experience, which the poet finds in the very nature of consciousness itself. All unity is to be sought within the self, as all consciousness is the consciousness of self. The problem of the poet-mystic is to construct a cosmos out of "this multifarious mad chaos" and achieve inner and outer unity. To Whitman this principle of unity lies in his own self. It is not an outside fact. Here, the native egotism of the man might have induced him to seek unity within his own self, instead of seeking it outside. The "colossal egoism" of **"Song of Myself,"** which has puzzled many of his students and evoked the odium of his critics, is the key to the man and his work. For Whitman the "I" is the very center and meaning of all existence.[1] This egotistical disposition also explains the attraction of idealism for Whitman and his advocacy of it as the proper guide and base of New World metaphysics.[2] Whitman's own spiritual experiences induced him to think that the clue to the world lay in his own self and that reality itself was not different from the self. Idealism gave intellectual sanction to his convictions, as it sought to explain the nature of things by reference to the self of man, and by making him the center of the universe. In **"A Backward Glance"** Whitman writes; "In the center of all, and object of all, stands the human being, towards whose heroic and spiritual evolution poems and everything directly and indirectly tend, Old World or New.[3]

The conception that man is the master and measure of all things, no doubt, goes back to the Greek philosophers; but, as we have seen, it is in the post-Kantian idealistic systems that it emerges as a definite doctrine of self. Fichte, Schelling, and Hegel constructed a metaphysic after the pattern of the self. Fichte saw the ego as the ultimate reality, and the world as its creation. Schelling, too, referred all existence to selfconsciousness. To Hegel the self is the absolute. But, since for all these philosophers dialectic is the vehicle of their thought, their conception of self is also dialectical. The self is a dialectical and antithetical being to which dualism and opposition become a necessary condition of existence. The Fichtean ego conceives itself as opposed by a not-ego in order to realize itself as ego or intelligence, and the world is the product of its self-conscious activity. Schelling's self, too, is thus committed to an internal differentiation, for the self, to be a self-knower, has to determine itself by an object. Its ideal or infinite aspect depends on its real or finite aspect. Hegel made opposition the principle of creation and transcendence. The self subsists by subduing the opposition of the not-self. Nature is an obstacle, a necessary obstacle, or an inferior phase of the spirit, or at best it is an instrument which the absolute exploits for its own needs. Neither is the individual's position assured. Though for these dialecticians self is the principle of their philosophy, this self is not the self of all, but a superarrogant absolute standing above our heads. The individuals are instruments subserving the absolute purpose. Reality is, thus, an external fact existing in superaddition to the individual selves. If, however, the individual fancied that he was the absolute, whole and undivided, it would be, in the opinion of our idealists, an unpardonable presumption.

Whitman's essentially mystical thinking would be opposed to any doctrine that accords to the individual but a dependent and inferior status. Whitman asserts, "And nothing, not God, is greater to one than one's self is."[4] A true doctrine of self is that which holds that the individual is coeval and coeternal with the absolute and accords to every particle of the universe the status of the supreme. This attitude is expressed in the wellknown passage of the Upanishads, "The Whole is all That. The Whole is all This. The Whole is born out of the Whole. When the Whole is absorbed into the Whole the Whole alone remains."[5] It is the Upanishads that develop a supreme doctrine of self. It is true that in the Plotinian system, too, the individual soul is assumed to be the all-soul complete. However, it is in the Upanishads that this emphasis and the approach to reality from the inner principle of the self is most clearly developed. The Upanishadic system conceives reality on the pattern of the inner core or *atman,* the permanent substance which remains immutable and identical amidst the changing panorama of the outer world. This *atman* or soul is the internal *atman* of all created things . . . , and as such the only unifying principle in the world. The opposition of the not-self which confronts the self at every step is not its own wilful creation, nor a necessity—in which case it would be impossible to transcend—but the result of an unreal self-limitation on the part of the self. Unity is established when the self gets to know itself and eradicates the wrong belief in its limitation. Finitude is the outcome of man's limited vision; man can realize the limitlessness of his nature by enlarging his consciousness. The way to attain this vision is by growing into our surroundings, as it were, through an interpenetration of our being into all objects. Nature is not an antithesis of spirit, nor is it an inferior term, but it exists as it is, as the immortal Brahman. "All this universe has sprung from immortal life and is vibrating with life.[6] The Upanishads express the view that nature is not merely "spirit unconscious," as Schelling assumed, but is itself intelligence and immortal Brahman.[7] Since self is the reality and since it is identical with the universe, recognition of its real nature is the ultimate end and fulfilment of life. To be one's own self is to establish unity with the all.

II

Whitman's intense self-awareness might have sprung from the early autoerotic emotions of his boyhood and a primary narcissism. But it manifested itself as a certain habit of mentally returning upon himself, of reflecting upon his own inner processes. Whitman was a dreamy boy, a languid mystical type, with a lazy, contemplative habit of mind. He was exceptionally susceptible to his physical and spiritual environment. His own mystical inclination was aided by the strong religious proclivities of his paternal family, who were followers of Quakerism, and the boy's early training, in the belief in "inner light," made him all the more receptive to "quietism" and predisposed him to a mystical life. The "child" who went forth every day becoming the object he looked upon showed a wonderful capacity for intuitive identification. **"The Sleepers"** describes the poet's habit, going back to his early boyhood, of living in a visionary world, identifying himself with the life and objects around—a habit he continued into his maturity; the poem offers a key to Whitman's poetic genesis. Whitman's boundless love of life together with a natural vigor and fulness of spirit, made him seek warm, living contact with the stuff of life. And his education among the elemental forces of nature, the ocean, the daylight, the woods, increased this tendency to mystical communion. He was to express this later in the lines:

> In me the caresser of life wherever moving,
>   backward as well as forward sluing,
> To niches aside and junior bending, nor a
>   person or object missing,
> Absorbing all to myself and for this song.[8]

Even from his early boyhood Whitman seems to have felt intuitively that nature and the world of objects were in some sense "flowing" or "fluid" and that between himself and the universe there was an intercommunion. The "child" who became part of the objects and of whom the objects became a part felt no barriers between the universe and his soul, each flowed into the other, each interpenetrated the other. In men and nature he saw the same essence or life and spoke of them and contacted them with equal enthusiasm. Whitman's interest in the teeming life of New York on the one hand, and in the natural objects of the seaside, where his birthplace was, continued side by side, and he retained this wholesome balance till his death. This was so because his instincts revealed to him the unity of life everywhere, and his later meditations confirmed this.

For over ten years before 1855, Whitman sauntered about in New York, watching men and things and charmed by the panorama of life in the city, the crowds, the shops, the theaters. Yet, this was no young beast "wallowing in the stream of his sensibilia,"[9] flooded by the phantasmagoria of continuous visions and images, for the youth who appeared so deeply absorbed in the moving world around had no tendency to be obsessed by it. Walking Broadway, riding the omnibus tops, or watching the crowds in the streets, he was watching his own self; he was all the time aware of himself as walking, riding, moving. He had an unusual capacity for standing aloof while in the midst of the crowd, to ponder, to contemplate the seething life. He had a capacity for both intuitive identification and mystical abstraction, "Or withdrawn to muse and meditate in some deep recess, / Far from the clank of crowds intervals passing rapt and happy."[10] It was also this capacity for abstracting from his surroundings that was, as his mind matured, to give him an insight into his own real nature and show it to be different from the outer forms and shows. But this realization was to come to him only by an active responsiveness to the surge of life, by participation and mergence in the great life of the all. "As for me," Whitman said,

> I blessed my lucky stars; for merely to sail—to lie on my back and gaze by the half-hour at the passing clouds overhead—merely to breathe and live in the sweet air and clear sunlight—to hear the musical clatter of girls as they pursued their own glee,—was happiness enough for one day—there is an ecstatic satisfaction in such lazy philosophy, such passive yielding up of one's self to the pure emanation of nature, better than the most exciting pleasures.[11]

This indicates a mind framed at once for passive receptivity and intense self-awareness, a heart alive both to the "influx" and the "efflux," absorbing that which flows from without and that which wells from within.

The years between 1838 and 1855, when Whitman lived in Brooklyn and New York, absorbing the life of the cities with great avidity, were years of unusual activity in Whitman's life, and formed the special gestation period of the *Leaves*.[12] Whitman is reported to have said of his work: "Remember, the book arose out of my life in Brooklyn and New York from 1838 to 1855, absorbing a million people with an intimacy, an eagerness, an abandon, probably never equaled."[13] These were also years of intense spiritual activity, when Whitman, perhaps goaded by the deep emotional needs natural to youth, started upon the path of self-quest, though it was not until about 1847-48, following a long process of spiritual incubation, that he was to attain a true knowledge of himself. Whitman's writings of this period, though as literary compositions they sound banal and amateurish, are of immense significance for his spiritual history because they reveal a mind in turmoil, a torn soul, tormented by

doubts and uncertainties, struggling to free itself from its own cravings. The restlessness and travail that his juvenile poems betray were the signs of the spirit's growth, the birth throes of a new life. Through these conflicts we discover the aspiring soul. Here is a poem published in 1838:

> This breast which now alternate burns
>   With flashing hope and gloomy fear,
> Where beats a heart that knows the hue
>   Which aching bosoms wear;
> This curious frame of human mold,
>   Where craving wants unceasing play
> The troubled heart and wondrous form
>   Must both alike decay.
> The close wet earth will close around
>   Dull senseless limbs and a shy face,
> But where, O Nature! where will be
>   My mind's abiding place?
> Will it even live? For though its light
>   Must shine till from the body torn;
> Then when the oil of life is spent,
>   Still shall the taper burn?
> O, Powerless is this struggling brain
>   To pierce the mighty mystery;
> In dark, uncertain awe it waits,
>   The common doom to die!
> Mortal can thy swelling soul
>   Live with the thought that all its life
> Is centered in this earthly cage
>   Of care, and tears, and life?
> Not so, that sorrowing heart of thine
>   Ere long will find a house of rest;
> Thy form, repurified shall rise,
>   In robes of beauty drest.
> The flickering taper's glow shall change
>   To bright and star-like majesty,
> Radiant with pure and piercing light
>   From the Eternal's eye.[14]

This reveals how seriously the nineteen-year-old boy was pondering on the great mysteries of human life and death. Human mortality presented to him a baffling problem. He was convinced that worldly ambition and fame were vanities of vanities because they were forms of death,[15] and belonged to man's finite existence. The same meditations on death, the vanity of ambition and fame recur in his other poems written during the same period.[16] **"My Departure"** (1839) reveals the poet's spirit struggling to free itself from the trammels of flesh.

> O mighty powers of Destiny!
> When from this coil of flesh I'm free—
> When through my second life I rove,
> Let me but find one heart to love,
> As I would wish to love.
> For vainly through this world below
> We seek affection. Nought but woe

> Is with our earthly journey wove,
> And so the heart must look above,
>   Or die in dull despair.[17]

Earthly love too is perishable; it is a bondage. The poet has, however, a vague intuition of an existence freed from the bondage of matter. Spiritual activity begins with a dissatisfaction with the transient values of the world and a craving for the permanent. The capacity to discriminate between the eternal and the non-eternal is an essential qualification of the seeker of wisdom. Nachiketas in the Katha Upanishad refuses to be tempted by the offer by Yama (the god of the underworld) of worldly wealth and happiness. "Like corn decays the mortal and like corn is born again."[18] "What are these riches to me," asks Maitreyi in the Brihadaranyaka, "If I am not thereby to gain life eternal?"[19] The desire for immortality is the starting point of metaphysics; in the Brihadaranyaka metaphysical inquiry begins with the craving for eternal life. "But where, O Nature! Where will be / My mind's abiding place?" is the cry of Whitman's spirit. The poet had to wait before he could discover the heart of the mystery, but constant meditation seemed for the while to bear fruit. In a paper written in 1840 Whitman recorded a change that had come over him, a new sense and an altered point of view:

> a wondrous and important discovery . . . I have found that it is a very dangerous thing to be rich. For a considerable time past this idea has been pressing upon me and I am now fully and unalterably convinced of its truth. Some years ago when my judgement was in the bud I thought that riches were desirable things. But I have altered my mind. Light had flowed in upon me . . . the mists and clouds have cleared away, and I can now behold things as they really are.[20]

The cosmic sense had begun to grow in upon him. Money symbolizes man's hankering after what is finite and perishable; worldly possessions are limitations set upon the spirit. Because of a wrong identification the poet's soul had been cherishing false values. But now the veil of ignorance had cleared away; he could behold things in their true perspective. Another paper written in the same year shows the eager soul in search of truth. Whitman wrote:

> I reflected on the folly and vanity of those objects with which most men occupy their lives; and the awe and dread with which they approach its close. I remembered the strife for temporary and puerile distinctions—the seeking after useless and cumbersome wealth—the yielding up the diseased mind to be a prey to constant melancholy and discontent; all which may be daily seen by those who have intercourse with the sons of man.[21]

Whitman's experience of the world had convinced him of "the littleness of all earthly achievements."[22] He had realized the true value of renunciation; and true renunciation consists in the rejection of the unstable and a dedication to the eternal. The Katha says,

> The childish go after outward pleasure;
> They walk into the net of widespread death,
> But the wise, knowing immortality,
> Seek not the stable among things, which are
>   unstable here.[23]

Spiritual life starts with a transformation of values. But this, as yet, is the beginning. Renunciation is but a prelude in the life of the aspirant. The supreme sense of fulfilment and peace, which is the goal of the mystic quest, had not yet come to Whitman. The highest truth, namely the self, still remained to be discovered. But this could only be accomplished through an arduous psychological process, entailing the complete remaking of character, a purging of the dross, as it were.[24]

In **"Morbid Appetite for Money"** Whitman wrote, "On no particular matter is the public mind more unhealthy than the appetite for money."[25] More dreadful than poverty was the "poverty of soul," by which the wealthy were afflicted. Really sublime and grand characters were those who loved silent and unknown without the desire for fame. Whitman spoke of "enjoying the treasures of soul inherent within." A new sense of values was impinging on him; and here are clear indications that the poet's gaze was turning more and more inward. Whitman was beginning to see that "self-reliance" might be the clue to the "curious abrupt questionings"[26] that were stirring within him, but the vision was still inchoate and needed greater clarifying. As the editor of the Brooklyn *Daily Eagle*, Whitman was engaged in the political controversies of his time. But though thus seriously employed with politics and social reform, Whitman still had time for inner communings. In the midst of his journalistic activities Whitman would snatch an hour or two for a stroll or a swim. Or he would go into the solitary retreats of nature and sit by a pond-side, brooding. The following lines, though written actually during a later period, give us a glimpse into Whitman's inner life and habits.

> In paths untrodden
> In the growth by margins of pond-waters,
> Escaped from the life that exhibits itself,
> From all the standards hitherto published,
>   from the pleasures, profits, conformities,
> Which too long I was offering to feed my soul,
> Clear to me now standards not yet publish'd . . .
>
>   . . . . .
>
> Here by myself away from the clank of the
>   world . . .

. . . . .

> Strong upon me the life that does not exhibit
>   itself, yet contains all the rest.[27]

His inner life was not, however, growing in opposition to the outer. All the time he was engaged in politics and journalism, Whitman was living intensely, thinking and understanding. The life around him was the very stuff of his contemplation, and he had a genius for turning everything to spiritual account and making it food for his thought. Whitman had learned to appreciate the worthlessness of worldly pursuits and possessions; hence, he was not to be engrossed by them. But he had not won the fight for self-mastery. His nature was torn by an internal dualism; his spirit was restive under the bondage of matter. The senses claimed their toll. The consciousness of human mortality haunted him like a nightmare. In his manuscript notebook dated 1847-48 he noted down:

> I am not glad tonight. Gloom has gathered round me like a mantle tightly folded. Yet I know not why I should be sad. Around me are my brother men merry and jovial. No dear one is in danger. . . . Thus comes that I am not glad tonight. I feel cramped in these coarse walls of flesh. The soul disdains. . . . O mystery of death I pant for the time when I shall solve you.[28]

These notebook jottings give evidences of deep emotional experiences that Whitman might have gone through during these years. But these experiences revealed to him mysterious depths within himself and brought him to a keener consciousness of himself. The floodgates of a sexually passionate nature, the "Pent-up aching rivers"[29] of himself gave way. Whitman later dramatized his fight for self-mastery in these lines of **"Song of Myself"**:

> I am given up by traitors,
> I talk wildly, I have lost my wits, I and
>   nobody else am the greatest traitor,
> I went myself first to the headland, my own
>   hands carried me there.
> You villain touch! What are you doing?. . . .
> Unclench your floodgates, you are too much
>   for me.[30]

Whitman had not yet realized that he had all the while been laboring under a false notion, a wrong identification; all sense of conflict is a mere illusion superimposed on the soul. Whitman was in fact fighting a contrary tendency within his own self. He was in need of some clue, some guidance, or some philosophy which would aid and precipitate the internal activity of his mind. His conflicts and unrest were due to the heterogeneousness of his nature. His personality had to be integrated, his inner self unified. And this would not be achieved so long as the sense of duality continued. The self must get to know its identity and its expansive nature.

During the years before the composition of the first *Leaves* Whitman passed through a phase of self-instruction. He was an indefatigable reader and the range of his knowledge was extraordinary, if judged by his preparatory reading and thought. Whitman read widely, doubtless pursuing some clue for his own inner life. He, like Emerson, "regarded reading as a creative activity."[31] In an article entitled **"Thoughts on Reading"** in the May, 1845, issue of the *American Whig Review,* Whitman underscored, "An author enriches us, not so much by giving us his ideas, as by unfolding in us the same powers that originated them."[32] Reading clarified his own native visions and confirmed his intuitions.

Of all the diverse thought currents and intellectual movements which moulded Whitman's poetic faith during these years, the young America movement and the *Democratic Review,* Epicurean and Stoic ideas,[33] to mention but a few of them, the most influential in the shaping of his mind and art were the "transcendental" ideas of Emerson and *Dial* magazine. Whitman's acquaintance with Emerson's works probably began about 1847, for in that year he reviewed Emerson's "Spiritual Laws." This date is significant because about the same time, probably, Whitman underwent a spiritual "conversion." The growing pressure within compelled him to search for spiritual guidance. He attended "Swedenborg meetings." He was roused to know more and more about the peoples of the world and their thoughts. India, Palestine, and Egypt attracted his imagination, and he seems to have read about their literatures, at least superficially, in magazine articles. Above all was the transcendental philosophy of Emerson which proved of inestimable value to Whitman's spiritual growth. "The same, the same,"[34] Emerson wrote, quoting from the Hindu scriptures, "without identity at base chaos must be forever." The soul is the "one Bottom," the universal ground. Echoing the Upanishads, he said, "For it is only the finite that has wrought and suffered; the infinite lies stretched in smiling repose."[35] He emphasized the importance of self-knowledge. "Trust Thyself," he said, by which he meant "Know thyself and be thyself," for the soul is limitless and free. No laws can circumscribe it; it exists on its own strength. Conflict, unhappiness, and mortality belong to finite existence and are not of the real nature of the self. Man sees the world broken because he is broken within. What a revelation it must have been to the toiling soul of Whitman! Here was a philosophy that answered to his deepest cravings. Here was the solution he had been struggling to find. Emerson's transcendentalism offered him light at a time when he was passing through a crisis of development. Emerson helped him to "find himself." "I was simmering, simmering, simmering," Whitman said; "Emerson brought me to a boil." Emerson's essays provided the needed precipitant. What had been in a state of subconscious incubation was now brought to consciousness. Whitman, had, at last, found the self.

The year 1847/48 marked the new birth. "A remarkable accession of power," an enlargement and clarification of vision had come to Whitman. He recorded this astounding discovery and new spirit in his notebook (No. 1), which contains a clear, though half-articulate, adumbration of **"Song of Myself."** Through his emotional turmoil Whitman had come out spiritually emergent. By constant brooding and meditation and self-mastery, and by the practice of discrimination, Whitman had come to know his real self and realize it in its glory. For the first time in the writings of this period we come across this utterance: "I cannot understand the mystery, but I am always conscious of myself as two—as my soul and I and I reckon it is the same with all men and women."[36] The soul is the transcendental self, the "I," the surface consciousness, or the empirical ego—which is falsely identified with the objects and experiences of the world. Ignorance consists in confounding the one with the other, in the superposition of the object on the subject. . . . Discrimination between the two is the starting point as well as the end of all knowledge. The Gita says: "Those who perceive by their eye of wisdom the distinction between the Field (nature, not-self) and the Knower of the field (transcendental subject, the witness) attain to the Supreme. This knowledge is the true knowledge."[37] And Whitman had gained this. He had also realized that his "soul" is the "universal and fluid soul."[38] The result of this knowledge is the termination of bondage and an unobstructed expansion of the soul and its identification with all existence.

> The soul or spirit transmits itself into all matter, into rocks and can live the life of a rock—into the sea, and can feel itself the sea—into the oak . . . into an animal, and feel itself a horse, a fish or bird, into the earth—into the motions of sun and stars.[39]

With this self-expansion Whitman felt that the ubiquitous soul of man enters into all existence and bestows reality on it. The object is real and interesting only insofar as it is impregnated by the subject:

> A man only is interested in anything when he identifies himself with it—he must himself be whirling and speeding through space like the planet Mercury—he must be driving like a cloud—he must shine like the sun—he must be orbic and balanced in the air, like this earth—he must crawl like the pismire—he must—he would be growing fragrantly in the air, like the locust blossoms—he would rumble and crash like the thunder in the sky—he would spring like a cat on his prey—he would splash like a whale. . . . [40]

There is no doubt that Whitman's poetic fancy caught fire from astronomy and the celestial wonders that it revealed to his imagination. Whitman's interest in astronomy was aroused probably in the year 1847.[41] Astronomy opened out new inner horizons in the poet's mind and suggested the "transcendental" symbols appropriate to his inner growth and even aided that process. The ideas of cosmic flight, of space and time, which became in the **"Song of Myself"** symbols of the soul's dynamism, could have been suggested by the imaginary flights into the stellar spaces that Whitman had read about in astronomical literature. It is this sense of inner expansion suggested by astronomy that Whitman recorded in his notebooks.

> All the vastness of Astronomy—and space—and systems of suns . . . carried in their computation to the farthest that figures are able . . . and then multiplied in geometrical progression ten thousand billion fold do not more than symbolize the reflection of the reflection, of the spark thrown off a spark, from some emanation of God. . . . [42]

and,

> Afar in the sky was a nest,
> And my soul flew thither and squat, and
> looked out
> And saw the journeywork of suns and systems
> of suns. . . . [43]

Astronomical space and time suggest to him the notion of plenitude of being. Whitman speaks of the "Plenty of time and space."[44] And again, in a passage that describes the new mystical elation he had experienced, he says:

> Amelioration is the blood that runs through the body of the universe—I do not lag—I do not hasten . . . I bide my hour over billions of years—I exist in the . . . void that takes uncounted time and coheres to a nebula, and in further time cohering to an orb, marches gladly round, a beautiful tangible creature. . . . My right hand is time, and my left hand is space—both are ample—a few quintillions of cycles, a few sextillions of cubic leagues, are not of importance to me. . . . [45]

The same sense of timeless expansion is recorded in the following lines, which are among the first lines of Whitman's free verse: "I am alive in New York and San Francisco, / Again I tread the streets after two thousand years."[46]

As a result of this new birth Whitman now realizes the fulness and joy of being. He has overcome all the contractile elements of mind that characterized his "sick-soul" phase:

> Poem incarnating the mind of an old man, whose life has been magnificently developed—the wildest

and most exuberant joy—the utterance of hope and floods of anticipation—faith in whatever happens—but all enfolded in joy, joy, joy, which underlies and overtops the whole effusion.[47]

In this state of ecstasy he feels that life is a miracle, a "limitless and delicious wonder," and that body and soul, instead of being in conflict, are one.

> My life is a miracle and my body which lives is a miracle; but of what I can nibble at the edges of the limitless and delicious wonder I know that I cannot separate them, and call one superior and the other inferior, any more than I can say my sight is greater than my eyes.[48]

In another remarkable notebook passage, in which musical, erotic, and astronomical images are mingled, Whitman describes how the ecstasy of physical sensation produced by listening to music causes in him a supreme sense of "dilation" and release, "uncaging" in him unsuspected powers.

> I want the tenor, large and fresh as the creation, the orbed parting of whose mouth shall lift over my head the sluices of all the delight yet discovered for our race. I want the soprano that lithely overleaps the stars, and convulses me like the love-grips of her in whose arms I lay last night. . . . I want the chanted Hymn whose tremendous sentiment shall uncage in my breast a thousand wide-winged strengths and unknown ardors and terrible ecstasies—putting me through the flights of all the passions—dilating me beyond time and air . . . calmly sailing me all day on a bright river with lazy slapping waves . . . and awakening me again to know by that comparison, the most positive wonder in the world, and that's what we call life.[49]

He also feels a certain largeness, a strange capaciousness within himself:

> He drinks up quickly all terms, all languages and meanings. . . . To his curbless and bottomless powers, they be like ponds of rain water to the migrating herds of buffalo, who make the earth miles square look like a creeping spread.—See! he has only passed this way, and they are drained dry.[50]

There is also the urge for limitless expansion characteristic of the dynamic self:

> I think the soul will never stop, or attain to any growth beyond which it shall not go.—When I walked at night by the sea shore and looked up at the countless stars, I asked of my soul whether it would be filled and satisfied when it should become God enfolding all these . . . and the answer was plain to me. . . . No, when I reach there, I shall want to go further still.[51]

Whitman has also known the transcendental character of the soul, its "greatness, immortality, purity."

"Never speak of the soul as anything but intrinsically great."[52] The only evil Whitman now seems to recognize is the metaphysical evil, namely, ignorance. Ignorance is bondage, wisdom release. He emphasizes the distinction between ignorance and wisdom, rather than that between good and evil. "The ignorant man is demented with the mania of owning things. . . . But the wisest soul knows that no object can really be owned."[53] The distinction between good and evil is a false distinction. The soul enfolds both good and evil. There is, in fact, no evil: "I am the poet of sin, / For I do not believe in sin."[54] Hence, the all-inclusive soul encloses within itself the dualities of good and evil: "The universal and fluid soul impounds within itself not only all good characters and heroes, but the distorted characters, murderers, thieves."[55] The Gita makes out that the man of intelligence casts away both good and evil, for the perception of imperfection outside is an indication of imperfection within. And Whitman notes: "Wickedness is most likely the absence of freedom and health in the soul." And "The mean and bandaged spirit is perpetually dissatisfied with itself, and it is too wicked or too poor or too feeble."[56] The meditations of more than a decade and a half of spiritual life had now come to fruition. The poet of the *Leaves of Grass* was born. It now only remained for Whitman to give shape and expression to his thoughts. The years from 1848 to the appearance of the first *Leaves* represented the poet's struggle for self-expression, as the years preceding it marked the struggle for self-discovery. The inner conflicts and tensions of his early life were now at rest; Whitman had achieved inner peace. This sense of poise and self-possession which thus came of the liberating knowledge of the self did not leave him entirely, even in periods of crisis, and sustained him through much stress and turmoil.

III

As Whitman came to realize that the secret of the universe was contained in his own self and that the highest wisdom was the effusion of the soul, he felt that his mission in life as a prophet and bard was "to articulate and faithfully express in literary or poetic form"[57] his own personality. True poetry is an autobiography of the soul. Goethe's "auto-biography" had earlier inspired in him a desire to write such a biographical work rendering the history of his soul's growth.[58] He was now resolved. "I will effuse egotism and show it underlying all, and I will be bard of personality."[59] This vast egotism in Whitman might have been, on a lower level, an abnormal narcissistic tendency rooted in his autoerotic emotions, but it certainly had an important role to play in his spiritual growth. It increased his mystical tendencies and turned him more and more upon himself. It developed in him, at an early period, the habit of communicating with his soul, while his strong homoerotic nature furnished the motive power for the enlargement of sympathies he was later to undergo.[60] As has been noted by scholars, Whitman's poetic personality was to him a powerful instrument for integrating his ego and overcoming original inhibitions and separation anxiety. *Leaves of Grass* was the outcome of a long process of sublimation.[61] His own egotism, moreover, brought him into a consciousness of the material objective universe, the not-me perpetually confronting the me, the mystical identity. He had known the English idealistic thinkers, Coleridge and Carlyle, and absorbed something, though perhaps indirectly, of the idealistic thought of Germany. It was finally, about 1847, when he discovered Emerson, that Whitman's vision attained clarity.

In his *Essays,* First (1841) and Second Series (1844), and in his *Addresses* (1836-38) Emerson, partly under the inspiration of the Hindu scriptures, to which he was early introduced through the Roy literature, developed a conception of self closely resembling the Hindu doctrine of *atman-brahman.* The central preaching of the essay "Self-Reliance" is "be thyself." It is only because man is weak and ignorant that he goes out of himself in search of support; he relies on objects, instruments, and the like. He looks for "foreign support," all the while forgetting his own "self-sufficiency" and "self-reliant soul." He is blind to the hidden pools of resources within himself. The reliance on outside objects is the want of self-reliance, the search for sufficiency outside one's self points to a deplorable sense of insufficiency within. So man ought to live "wholly from within." He should respect the laws of his own nature because his own law is the eternal law. The "inmost" and the "outmost" coincide in the self. Self-existence is the supreme end of life; for only thus can man conquer dualism and achieve "unity in nature and consciousness." In the hour of vision the soul perceives that the world of things, space, light, and time, is not diverse from itself; that the "aboriginal self" in man is the source of all life and all existence, "the foundation of action and of thought." This soul which is the prime mover and the underlying principle of things, is the "immense intelligence"[62] in which we all share. It is the one "universal mind," the "illimitable essence," the principle of identity running through the endless mutations of form.[63] In "Compensation" and "Over-soul" Emerson further develops the idea of a soul which is above the relational existence, of a transcendental self, the soul within man, the vast spiritual background and the substratum of all functions and states of consciousness. It is the self-luminous, self-effulgent light which illuminates the intellect and animates all organs and faculties. "The American Scholar" gives a mandate for knowing one's self. Emerson declares: "The world is nothing, the man is all; in yourself is the law of all nature . . . in yourself slumbers the whole of Reason; it is for you to know all, it is for you to dare all." One

cannot fail to see the striking resemblance between these ideas and the Upanishadic concept of *atman-brahman.* Ideas such as these no doubt helped Whitman gain the new consciousness. They formed the basis of his poetic thought. In this strong emphasis in Emerson's writings upon the soul Whitman could not have failed to recognize a close kinship to the deepest problems of his own nature, though, of course, in Whitman the personal and prophetic elements are to be rendered more conspicuous. This emphasis on the individual soul as the absolute reality belongs exclusively to Hindu mysticism.

> It is your own self that is within all. That which breathes through the Prana, that which pervades through the Vyana, the self that inhabits the earth, the water, the fire, it is your own immortal self. The light that shines yonder is the light within you. The ultimate exists within your own self. That which is the subtle essence, that is the self, that is the true, and That Thou Art.[64]

If Whitman needed confirmation for his egocentric perspective, he could find it here in an ample measure, enough at any rate, to satisfy "the glut" of his soul. For Vedanta, better by far than any system in the West, effuses "egotism" and shows it "underlying all." The *atman*-centric way of Indian philosophy was a close analogy to Whitman's "animated ego style."[65]

Leaves of Grass was born out of a sense of fulness and completion in the poet. It was the expression of a full man and a completed process, the effusion of a soul that had come to itself. "I now thirty-seven years old in perfect health begin, / Hoping to cease not till death."[66] The poet had suddenly grown conscious of unsuspected depths in himself; what had long been maturing now reached fruition. In the exultation of the new discovery he shouts "eureka": "Whoever you are, to you endless announcements."[67] The new discovery that Whitman felt was the emergence of the transcendental self after a prolonged conflict and internal travail. Coming as it did, like a flash, this new sense left him in amazement. "This then is life," the poet exclaims: "Here is what has come to the surface after so many throes and convulsions."[68]

The new consciousness, which in the beginning arose as a passionate, though indistinct, yearning for immortality and a brooding sense of incompleteness and transience, resulted in an intensified spiritual activity and gradually grew into a deeper conviction in a permanent entity—the "soul" within himself. The sense of infinite existence became a realized fact, not a vain longing. This new conversion was marked by a "changed attitude of the ego"[69] and the emergence of a new set of values.

> I bring what you much need yet always have,
> Not money, amours, dress, eating, erudition,
>   but as good,

> I send no agent or medium, offer no
> representative of value, but *offer the value
> itself.*[70]

Maya is the bondage to unreal values. Salvation is the passage into the realm of real values, from a small universe of petty desires into a larger spiritual life. "From the unreal lead me to the real, from darkness lead me to light, from death lead me to immortality"[71] is the prayer of the spirit craving for enlightenment. Men are outgoing in their tendencies and pursue objects of desire; they do not know their own world. It is only the discerning, whose intelligence is not engrossed by external objects, that set themselves to the task of finding "the eternal meanings."[72] The Katha Upanishad says: "The self-existent pierced the openings (of the senses) outward; therefore one looks outward, not within himself. . . . A certain wise man, while seeking immortality . . . turned the eye inward and saw the self."[73] Whitman, the poet of the cosmos, advanced "through all interpositions and coverings and turmoils and stratagems to first principles."[74] It was by such an introspective vision, and a persistent effort not to be engrossed by the passing shows that Whitman was able to penetrate the veil of Maya and gain a knowledge of the essential self deep down within. To him, however, the inner vision and the outer are one and the same. Whether he is looking at the flowing panorama of life, or "meditating in some deep recess," he sees the same truth; beneath the surface of "qualities and things" he apprehends the essence. In intuitive knowledge introspection and extrospection coincide. For that which is outside is inside, that inside is outside. Hence do the Upanishads proclaim: "The self alone is to be meditated upon, the self alone should be realized, for one knows all this through it; this self is dearer than a son, dearer than wealth, dearer than everything else, and is innermost. One should meditate upon the self alone as dear."[75]

Beneath the flood of "ego" phantoms is the true self, the only real existence. . . . Hence "see the self and be the self" say the Vedantists. Whitman's own native tendencies led him to the exploration of his inner self; but it was, however, when he discovered Emerson that his thoughts were given a new drift and an added impetus. The vision of the true self dawned on him at first as a vague awareness of a certain doubleness or duality within himself. "I am always *conscious of myself as two,*" he noted in his manuscript,[76] "as my soul and I," the "I" being the limited ego and "my soul" the universal soul. Spiritual knowledge starts with this self-awareness, this power to discriminate between the finite and the eternal, the apparent and the real. This idea of a permanent and universal self beneath the phenomenal folds is by no means peculiar to Whitman. The Hindu concept of self was gaining currency at the time by the popularization of the Hindu scriptures like the Gita, Vishnupurana, and the Upanishads; and all spiritually aspiring men, the Concordians especially,

seem to have attempted to realize in their personal lives the truths which they had discovered in the Indian books. Curiously enough we come across similar utterances in Emerson and Thoreau, too. Emerson said in a speech in 1833:

> I recognize the distinction of the outer and the inner self; the *double consciousness* that within this erring, passionate, mortal self sits a supreme, calm immortal mind, whose powers I do not know; but it is stronger than I; it is wiser than I; it never approved me in any wrong; I seek counsel of it in my doubts; I repair to it in my dangers; I pray to it in my undertakings. It seems to me the face which the creator uncovers to his child.[77]

Thoreau wrote in *Walden:*

> I only know myself as a human entity; *the scene so to speak, of thoughts and affections,* and am *sensible of a certain doubleness* by which *I can stand as remote from myself as from another.* How intense my experience, I am conscious of the presence of and criticism of a part of me, which, as it were, is not a part of me, *but spectator, sharing no experience,* but taking note of it; and *that is no more I than it is you.* When the play of life is over, the spectator goes his way. It was a kind of fiction, a work of the imagination only, so far as he was concerned. . . . [78]

The idea of the self as the ground of all experience, and the spectator of the scene of the world, and the further conception that this self is the common self of all—is expressed here. Emerson speaks of the inner self or the immortal essence "within this erring, passionate, mortal self." The similarity between these ideas and the utterances of the Gita and the Upanishads is unmistakable; the Indian scriptures might have possibly been the sources for Emerson as well as Thoreau. In the case of Thoreau, it was undeniably so, for Thoreau read the "stupendous and cosmogonal philosophy of the Bhagwat Geeta"[79] during his Walden days and in his book quoted copiously from the Indian scriptures. The conception of the self, as a spectator unattached to actions and their consequences, and standing aloof from the world of events, is strikingly similar to the description of the sovereign self of the knower in the Bhagavad Gita.[80] For Whitman, too, the belief in the existence of a permanent self underlying all content of consciousness, a central identity persisting through all changes, is an unshakable conviction and forms the quintessence of his mystical realization. Whitman wrote in his notes, "He evidently thinks that behind all faculties of the human being, as the sight, the other senses and even the emotions and the intellect stands the real power, the *mystical identity the real I or Me or You.*"[81]

For him the ordinary condition of man is not his ultimate being; he has in him a deeper self. Emerson also expresses the same thought in the "Over-soul" essay. This unique conception that man's surface mentality does not constitute his real self, and that apart from and basic to the mind and its faculties is the spirit, which is the true self of man, and that this self is the universal self of all, is the fundamental thesis of Vedanta.[82] Whitman has, by means of his intuitive vision, penetrated to the spiritual center within himself and discovered the true glory and independence of his self. Early his intuition had led him to believe that his role in the world was more or less that of a detached witness. With the attainment of fuller realization he became convinced that his real self was different from the fettered ego that acts, enjoys, or suffers, that the outward events are not he, that his self is not a doer but a mere spectator, sharing all experience, yet unattached to it, standing apart and watching the masquerade of life:

> Trippers and askers surround me,
> People I meet, the effect upon me of my early
>   life or the ward and city I live in, or the
>   nation,
> The latest dates, discoveries, inventions,
>   societies, authors old and new,
> My dinner, dress, associates, looks,
>   compliments, dues,
> The real or fancied indifference of some man
>   or woman I love,
> The sickness of one of my folks or of myself,
>   or ill-doing or loss or lack of money, or
>   depressions or exaltations,
> Battles, the horrors of fratricidal war, the
>   fever of doubtful news, the fitful events;
> These come to me days and nights and go
>   from me again,
> *But they are not the Me myself.*
>
> *Apart from the pulling and hauling stands
>   what I am,*
> Stands amused, *complacent,* compassionating,
>   idle, unitary,
> Looks down, is erect, or bends an arm on an
>   impalpable certain rest,
> Looking with side-curved head curious what
>   will come next,
> *Both in and out of the game and watching
>   and wondering at it.*[83]

The self which says "they are not the Me myself," which witnesses and waits while the endless spectacle of the world goes by, and which retains its identity in the midst of the shifting processes is the transcendental witness in us, of which the scriptures speak. The poet who wanders all night in his vision, dreaming all the dreams of the other dreamers, who traverses the whole span of the universe, becoming by turns the bride, the bridegroom, the hounded slave, and "the sleepless widow looking out on the winter midnight"

is the self as *sākṣi* or the detached percipience.[84] The Upanishads describe two birds perching on a tree, one of which feeds on the delicious fruit, while the other, not tasting of it looks on.[85] The one is the empirical subject, the other the perpetual percipient which sees but does not enjoy. The Gita speaks of the supreme self in the body which is the witness, permitter, supporter and the experiencer. "He appears to have the qualities of all the senses, and yet is without the senses, *unattached* yet *supporting all, free from the dispositions of Prakriti and yet enjoying them.*"[86] Though participating in the world action this self is unfettered. According to the Upanishads, "After enjoying himself and roaming, and merely seeing good and evil, he [stays] in a state of profound sleep and comes back to his former condition. Whatever he sees there he is untouched by it, for this infinite being is unattached."[87] This consciousness of distinction between his real nature or "soul" and the phenomenal strata of his mind is constant in Whitman.

Critics have recognized a duplex personality in the ***Leaves of Grass,***[88] an objective and a symbolic Whitman. Dr. Bucke considers this phenomenon to be common in men having cosmic consciousness.[89] This dual consciousness, as witnessed in Whitman, is not the pathological condition of the "divided self" that William James describes. James attributes this to a certain discordance or heterogeneity in the natural constitution of the subject. He cites the following case of Alphonse Daudet:

> Homo duplex, homo duplex! The first time that I perceived that I was two was at the death of my brother Henri, when my father cried out so dramatically: "He is dead, he is dead!" While my first self wept, my second self thought, "how truly given was that cry, how fine it would be at the theatre!" I was then fifteen years old.
>
> This horrible duality has often given me matter for reflection. Oh, this terrible second me, always seated whilst the other is on foot, acting, living, suffering, bestirring itself. This second me that I have never been able to intoxicate, to make shed tears, or put to sleep. And how it sees into things, and how it moves![90]

It is likely that this dual consciousness was brought home to Whitman's mind during crises of sensual ecstasies and sharpened by his habit of extricating himself from his own "experience." In some mysterious way, the very ecstasy of erotic sensation seems to release him from "anchors and holds," giving him a strange feeling of freedom and self-sufficiency. "What is it that frees me so in storms?" Through the madness of erotic experience Whitman's "inebriate soul" rises supreme: "To rise thither with my inebriate soul!"[91]

This soul of Whitman is not a pose; nor is it his poetic faculty, that he in old age called "my Fancy," dramatized as a personality.[92] It is his transcendental self. When he says, "I believe in you my soul, the other I am must not abase itself to you / And you must not be abased to the other,"[93] the "soul" with which he communicates is the metaphysical essence, the cosmic consciousness, and the "other I am," the physical self or the ordinary consciousness. The "I" may be the grammatical subject of the speaker, strictly, indistinguishable from the physical self, but spoken of as a separate entity. Again, he thinks of himself as

> Another self, the *duplicate of everyone,*
> skulking and hiding it goes,
> Formless and wordless through the streets of
> the cities, polite and bland in the parlors,
> In the cars of the railroads, in steamboats, in
> the public assembly,
>
>   . . . . .
>
> . . . speaking not a syllable of itself,
> Speaking of any thing else but never of
> itself.[94]

This duplicate self is the perpetual witness in us. Through an assiduous practice of discrimination and by a persistent refusal to be deceived by appearances, Whitman has succeeded in getting at the essential soul in him, the noumenal entity in the center of phenomenal existence.

> Whoever you are, I fear you are walking the
> walks of dreams,
> I fear these *supposed realities* are to melt
> from under your feet and hands,
> Even now your features, joys, speech, house,
> trade, manners, troubles, follies, costume,
> crimes, dissipate away from you,
> Your true soul and body appear before me,
> They stand forth out of affairs, out of
> commerce, shops, works, farms, clothes, the
> house, buying, selling, eating, drinking,
> suffering, dying.
>
>   . . . . .
>
> O I could sing such grandeurs and glories
> about you!
> *You have not known what you are, you have
> slumber'd upon yourself all your life,*
> Your eyelids have been the same as closed
> most of the time,
> *What you have done returns already in
> mockeries,*
> (Your thrift, knowledge, prayers, if they do
> not return in mockeries, what is their
> return?)
>
> *The mockeries are not you,*
> Underneath them and within them I see you lurk,

> I pursue you where no one else has pursued you,
> Silence, the desk, the flippant expression, the
> night, the accustom'd routine, if these
> conceal you from others or from yourself,
> they do not conceal you from me,
>
>   . . . . .
>
> The pert apparel, the deform'd attitude,
> drunkenness, greed, premature death, all
> *these I part aside.*[95]

Because of our false identification with the mind and the organs, we mistake our real nature and think that "I am the body, I am these organs," we feel as it were, think as it were, and move and shake as it were, whereas our real self is far removed from such surface perturbations.[96] We hug shams and cherish illusions, "supposed realities." But when through discriminate knowledge our wrong identification is removed, all illusions melt and dissipate, and the "true soul" emerges in its transcendent glory. "Where is he who tears off the husks for you and me?" Whitman asks, "Where is he that undoes strategems and envelopes for you and me?"[97] It is only when, with the aid of the discriminating intellect, one separates the outer coatings of desires, passions, objects—superimposed on the self by ignorance, that the kernel, the *ātman* is revealed. Only thus can one discover the reality subsisting underneath the mockeries of affairs, commerce, house, trades, joys, follies, etc. The poet strongly feels that it is the self, finally, that survives the dissolution of material objects, the only immutable and identical substance amidst an outer region of change and impermanence.

> Quick sand years that whirl me I know not
> whither,
> Your schemes, politics, fail, lines give way,
> substances mock and elude me,
> Only the theme I sing, *the great and
> strong-possess'd soul eludes not,*
> *One's self must never give way—that is the
> final substance—that out of all is sure,*
> Out of politics, triumphs, battles, life, *what at
> last finally remains?*
> *When shows break up what but One's-self is
> sure?*[98]

To Whitman, the self alone is, in the ultimate analysis, reality; substances are elusive and unreal. The unseen soul governs absolutely at last.[99] The self is the substratum of the changing world of phenomena, which without such a world-ground would all be non-existent, mere apparitions. "The soul, its destinies, the *real real,* / (Purport of all these apparitions of the real)."[100] The Upanishads, too, express the same thought: "Now the designation for him is 'the Real of the Real' (*satyasya satyam*). Verily, breathing creatures are the real. He is their Real."[101] Again Whitman says,

> Thy body permanent,
> The body lurking there within the body,
> The only purport of the form thou art, the real
>   I myself,
>   An image, an eidólon.[102]

The "real I myself" is the self lurking within; the outward form, the material shell, but an apparition. In **"A Song for Occupations,"** Section 5, he declares that the only reality is the soul of persons, not things, and that "you and your soul enclose all things." It is also the self ultimately that confers value on the world and gives it its meaning and vitality.[103] And this self, being the very root, is also the self of all.

This self is not, however, the dialectical being of the Germans, torn by an inner differentiation and caught in an endless web of relationships. It is suprarelational, indeterminate, and transcendental. It is completely independent of external laws, self-subsistent, and complete in itself. It is not the "many in one" of Hegel but an "identity," the soul identified with the infinite *brahman*,[104] the eternal self which remains immutable through the processes of metempsychosis. "To these proud laws of the air, the water and ground, *proving my interior soul impregnable*, / And nothing exterior shall ever take command of me."[105] This thought is very much the same as the Upanishadic conception of the self as the sovereign, the "lord of what has been and what is to be,"[106] as imperishable and unfettered, and transcending the relational existence. Again, the passage,

> *The soul is of itself,*
> All verges to it, all has reference to what
>   ensues,
> All that a person does, says, thinks, is of
>   consequence,[107]

has its source in the thought of Emerson: "There is a deeper fact in the soul than compensation, to wit its own nature. The soul is not a compensation, but a life. The soul is."[108] Whereas the world is governed by the laws of compensation, the soul is independent of such laws and subsists in its own right; "the soul is of itself"; it follows out its own laws and standards and is never the object of an external will. "Whatever satisfies souls is true; / The soul has that measureless pride which revolts from every lesson but its own."[109] It is the lord of a "million universes," bending them to its purposes, "All submit to them, where they sit, *inner, secure, unapproachable to analysis* in the soul."[110] Being pure and self-luminous, it effuses light out of itself. "Dazzling and tremendous how quick the sunrise would kill me / If I could not now and always *send sun-rise out of me*."[111] Being transcendental, it is unapproachable to ordinary imagination. "My final merit I refuse you, I refuse putting from me what I really am, / Encompass worlds, but never try to encompass me."[112]

> As if any man really knew aught of my life,
> Why even I myself I often think how little or
>   nothing of my real life,
> Only a few hints, a few diffused faint clews
>   and indirections
> I seek for my own use to trace out here.[113]

The real life of man is transcendental and eludes the grasp of the empirical mind. It is not possible for the biographer to give a real account of it. Only the soul in moments of insight can catch vaguest glimpses or faint echoes of the inner life. Whitman often feels that it is presumptuous of him to think that he has comprehended his real self, more so to have attempted to express it. It is this consciousness which sometimes gives rise to a sense of frustration in him:

> O baffled, balk'd, bent to the very earth,
> Oppress'd with myself that I have dared to
>   open my mouth,
> Aware now that amid all that blab whose
>   echoes recoil upon me, I have not once had
>   the least idea who or what I am,
> But that before all my arrogant poems the real
>   Me stands yet untouch'd, untold, altogether
>   unreach'd.[114]

But it must not be supposed that to Whitman the self remained finally incomprehensible; for though it is transcendent to thought, it is not "unknowable," but is an experience, an immediate and immanent reality. It is not an inference of the ratiocinating mind but an intuitive certainty.

> Facts, religions, improvements, politics, trades,
>   are as real as before,
> *But the soul is also real, it too is positive and
>   direct,*
> No reasoning, no proof has establish'd it.
> Undeniable growth has establish'd it.[115]

"Will you seek afar off?" asks Whitman, "you surely come back at last, / In things best known to you finding the best."[116] Again,

> It is not far, it is within reach,
> Perhaps you have been on it since you were
>   born and did not know,
> Perhaps it is everywhere on water and on
>   land.[117]

The quest of truth is not an outgoing journey but the realization of something implicit in the universe and the self. Only our eyes must be opened to the reality around us. Whitman declares this reality in **"Starting from Paumanok"** (13) and **"A Song for Occupations"** (2) "Was somebody asking to see the soul? / See your own shape and countenance, persons, substances, beasts, the trees, the running rivers, the rocks and sands." And

"It is for you whoever you are, it is no farther from you than your hearing and sight are from you, / It is hinted by nearest, commonest, readiest, it is ever provoked by them." The Upanishads say, "The Brahman that is immediate and direct, the self that is within all."[118] Reality is known in every object, since it is the absolute core of things. It is not far off but immediate, *aparōksa.* So Whitman sings in **"Song of Myself"** (48), "I hear and behold god in every object." In the faces of men and women he sees god and finds letters from god dropped in the street. Reality to him is an enveloping presence. His mystical realization is not, however, as William James thinks[119] of a sporadic type; it is to him an ever present sense, governing his whole attitude and suffusing his outlook.[120]

From this supreme realization of self is born the mystic who has succeeded in integrating all the forces of his mind and achieved inner unity and peace. It is this knowledge of his true self that has enabled Whitman to shed all inhibitions and complexes and attain harmony and poise. For knowledge of the soul is immortality and strength. According to the Upanishad, with knowledge one wins immortality. The Kena (2.2) says, "The Brahman is known well, when it is known as the witness of every state of consciousness; for by such knowledge one attains immortality. *By this self he attains strength and by knowledge immortality.*" This knowledge came to Whitman. He is now no longer the sick soul torn by contrarieties and crying for light: "O Mystery of Death! I pant for the time when I shall solve you."[121] Now death presents no problem for him. He has realized the immortal essence in him, the eternal and the all-pervading. Immortality is now a certainty.

> I know I am deathless,
> I know this orbit of mine cannot be swept
>   away by a carpenter's compass,
> I know I shall not pass like a child's carlacue
>   cut with a burnt stick at night.[122]

Death is no longer an incubus weighing upon a stricken spirit but is a pathway to a higher and nobler existence; for Whitman has realized that so long as man is not freed from the bonds of material existence, the higher spiritual truths are not exhibited to him.[123] Whitman himself has been released by his spiritual knowledge from the bondage of matter, and has realized that his real self is an essence and its existence immaterial:

> The real life of my senses and flesh
>   transcending my senses and flesh,
> My body done with materials, my sight done
>   with material eyes,
> Proved to me this day beyond Cavil that it is
>   not my material eyes which finally see,
> Nor my material body which finally loves,
>   walks, laughs, shouts, embraces,
>   procreates.[124]

Before this realization came to him, Whitman had been fighting his own tendencies, wrestling, so to say, with his own shadows. The evil outside baffled him, and he saw much evil within. His spirit felt cramped and bandaged in the coils of flesh; he felt the opposition of matter. In "Nature" Emerson said, "The reason why the world lacks unity, and lies broken and in heaps, is, because man is disunited with himself." This might have been revealing to Whitman. The saying of the Gita, "Let a man lift himself by himself; let him not degrade himself; for the self alone is the friend of the self and the self alone is the enemy of the self,"[125] is a theory of "self-reliance" par excellence. Consequently, Whitman was led to search for unity within his own self and found it there. He does not now feel any opposition, for all sense of opposition is false. The world of material objects no longer confronts him, for his own soul has become the soul of all beings.[126] The opposition of the not-self has evaporated in the expansion of the self. Whitman has arrived at the astounding conclusion, "Objects gross and unseen soul are one."[127] Flesh is not evil; the conflict between spirit and matter is an illusion. Even the sense of duality between body and soul is false. Thus, he discovers, "Clear and sweet is my soul, clear and sweet is all that is not my soul."[128] As a result of the attainment of the correct knowledge of self the false notion of the self as opposed by a not-self is removed, and identity, is established. And Whitman's question, "And if the body were not the soul, what is the soul?"[129] is the result of his perception of identity, of a non-dualistic conception of the universe.[130] This sense of the identity of body and soul came to him with his new realization and was certainly not present from the beginning.[131] Whitman's poems are exceptionally free from the spirit of dualism—of matter and spirit, subject and object, the sensible and the suprasensible—which is so prominent in Christian and Platonic mysticism.[132] Whitman, like the Vedantists, does not recognize the division of existence into the sensible and the suprasensible. The sensible resolves itself into the suprasensible, "the unseen is proved by the seen, / Till that becomes unseen and receives proof in its turn."[133]

From concrete life and materialism eventuate "invisible spiritual results" and the world of material objects is engulfed in the all-embracing self of the poet. In the self alone is real unity realized. When man comes to know that his own self is the infinite, universal *brahman,* all dualisms are ended, and all oppositions annulled. In the Upanishad, one sees that "The self alone is to be meditated upon, for all these are unified in it."[134] Real self-integration is possible only through the realization of the universal nature of the self. James's "heterogeneous personality" is the result of an inner schism, a dualism between the actual and the ideal, the ego and the universe. When the soul awakens to the perception of the ideal in the actual, and of the self in the all, equilibrium is achieved. It is thus that Whitman has been able to achieve what William James terms "healthy-mindedness," internal poise, and serenity of mind. Out of this supreme feeling of inward strength and fulness Whitman sings:

> Me imperturbe, standing at ease in Nature,
> Master of all or mistress of all, a-plomb in the
>   midst of irrational things,
> Me wherever my life is lived, O to be
>   *self-balanced for* contingencies.[135]

We find this serene knowledge in **"Song of Myself,"** 48: "I say to any man or woman, Let your soul stand cool and composed, before a million universes." Whitman has experienced "the joy of my soul leaning pois'd on itself."[136] His friends and critics testify to the extraordinary equanimity and self-poise of the man. Edward Carpenter was struck by the absence in him of the fear of death and by the sense of eternal life in which he seemed always to live.[137] We have also Dr. Bucke's testimony:

> Perhaps, indeed, no man who ever lived liked so many things and disliked so few as Walt Whitman. . . . I never knew him to argue or dispute, and he never spoke about money. . . . He appeared to like all the men, women, children, he saw; he seldom expressed a preference for any person, . . . would not allow his tongue to give expression to fretfulness, antipathy, complaint, and remonstrance. He never spoke deprecatingly of any nationality or class of men, or time in the world's history, or against any trades or occupations—not even against any animals, insects, or inanimate things, nor any of the laws of nature, . . . such as illness, deformity, and death. He never complained or grumbled at the weather, pain, illness or anything else. . . . he never spoke in anger and apparently never was angry. *He never exhibited fear, and I do not believe he ever felt it.*[138]

Such a description of the character and mind of Whitman answers to the description of "Yogi" in the Gita as "free from dualities, firmly fixed in purity, possessed of the self," "even of mind," as one who neither loathes nor desires, who has ever the spirit of renunciation, who remains the same in pain and pleasure, who sees with an equal eye, who enjoys his peace from within, and who has conquered his self and attained the calm of self-mastery.[139]

For all his eager interest in the world Whitman was but a detached and passive witness. And through all its vagaries he possessed the same detachment and refused to become absorbed in the milieu of life. He describes himself as one who enjoys so much seeing the busy world move by him, and exhibiting itself for his amusement, while he takes it easy and observes.[140] Again, "After continued personal ambition and effort, as a young fellow to enter with the rest into competition for the usual rewards, business, liter-

ary, political, . . . *I found myself remaining possessed.*"[141] The eternal life is opened to Whitman; and he has now realized that the dualities of pain and pleasure, of fortune and misfortune obtain only in finite existence, while the infinite remains untouched. The truth of the great Upanishads has dawned on him: "The Infinite is bliss. There is no bliss in what is small. The Infinite alone is bliss. But one should understand the Infinite" (Chhandogya, 7.23.1). "The Self alone is immortal; everything else but him is mortal" (Brihadaranyaka, 3.7.23). "The Self is imperceptible for it is never perceived, undecaying for it never decays; unattached, for it is never attached; unfettered, it never feels pains, and never suffers injury" (Brihadaranyaka, 3.9.26). When Whitman understood this, he could sit and look out on the world of misery, evil, and suffering with supreme indifference and detachment. "All these—all the meanness and agony without end I sitting look out upon, / See, hear, and am silent."[142] Emperor Janaka said: "If Mithila is burnt, nothing that is mine is burnt." The *atman* is not tainted by the world's grief.[143]

> Over the mountain-growths disease and
>   sorrow,
> An uncaught bird is ever hovering, hovering,
> High in the purer, happier air.[144]

The "uncaught bird" may be the poet's spirit which, though seated amidst miserable surroundings, stands aloof from them.[145] Knowledge exempts one from good and evil. The knower of the self transcends all ethical distinctions. "Apart from right, apart from the unright, / Apart from both what has been done and what has not been done" (Katha, 2.14). Consequently, Whitman has been freed from all sense of moral good and evil. "What blurt is this about virtue and about vice? / Evil propels me and reform of evil propels me, *I stand indifferent.*"[146]

The presence of contradictions in the world does not disturb his composure.

> Do I contradict myself?
> Very well, then, I contradict myself;
> (I am large—I contain multitudes).[147]

For Whitman has realized the self, the principle of identity underlying all contradictions. Diversities are embraced in the consciousness of oneness; contradictions are finally lost in the identity of the self.

William James has noticed in Whitman "an inability to feel evil"—a tendency he calls "healthy-mindedness." Whitman's optimism is not, however, a facile quality of mind, nor bravado, nor a kind of cannibalism. It is but the natural concomitant of his attainment of metaphysical knowledge, the result of the conviction that evil is an unreality, to be sloughed off, outgrown, and negated. Evil is a lie; it simply does not arise when the soul awakens to its real being. Healthy-mindedness follows on overcoming dualities. Whitman, among modern men, is an outstanding example of such a condition of perfect freedom from dualities. Carlyle, despite his earnestness, remained a "sick-soul," haunted by the spectre of world-destruction.[148] Emerson suffered from congenital low spirits. "I shiver in and out." "My pulse is slow, my blood is cold, my stammering tongue is rudely turned." Emerson lacked the fulness of spirit that Whitman possessed. There was a sickliness and a want of vitality about him. Neither could Emerson achieve the perfect internal harmony that Whitman did. There was still a discord, a duality, lurking in Emerson's personality. He was inhibited by his inherent puritanism. His journals are confessions of this conflict; in him much remained unrealized.[149] Thoreau, too, could not, in spite of his remarkable peace and poise, rise to Whitman's attitude of unqualified approval and universal affirmation. He was a man of denials, as Whitman was a man of affirmations.[150]

Such faith in the supremacy of self could not be shaken from Whitman's mind. Through poverty, degradations, and conflicts, Whitman held his conviction that his real self would come forth triumphant, overmastering all.[151] Critics have expressed the view that the 1860 edition records a spiritual crisis in Whitman's life and that the poet was troubled by some deep perturbations of sexual passion. According to this view, the **"Calamus"** cluster and poems like **"As I Ebb'd with the Ocean of Life"** and **"Out of the Cradle Endlessly Rocking"** reflect such a crisis.[152] However, the fateful character of the **"Calamus"** love is only apparent, for, the saving knowledge of self never deserted Whitman even in his moments of deepest perturbation,[153] and it sustained him through all struggles and turmoils of life. The supreme spirit of detachment and renunciation is preserved in the midst of the deepest passions:

> Whoever you are holding me now in hand,
> Without one thing all will be useless,
> I give you fair warning before you attempt me
> further,
> *I am not what you supposed, but far different.*
>
> . . . . .
>
> But these leaves conning you con at peril,
> For these leaves and me you will not understand,
> They will elude you at first and still more
> afterward,
> *I will certainly elude you.*
>
> . . . . .
>
> For all is useless without that which you may
> guess at many times and not hit, that which
> I hinted at;

> Therefore *release me and depart on your
> way.*[154]

And elsewhere, "What beckonings of love you receive you shall only answer with passionate kisses of parting, / You shall not allow the hold of those who spread their reach'd hands towards you."[155] Whitman, the impassioned lover of comrades, is all the while escaping the bonds of his affections. Each confession of love is followed by a clear recognition that he is untouched by his passions, and each time his comrade is warned that "I am not what you supposed, but far different," that he cannot be entangled in his love because his real self is elusive.[156] Whitman recognizes the binding quality of love and resists strongly the tendency to be enslaved by it. The spirit of inward withdrawal and renunciation never leaves him for a moment. In the office or on the battlefront, nursing in the hospitals or lying ill in bed, the consciousness that "they are not the Me myself" is never absent from his mind.

As a result of this self-realization and the consequent expulsion of all contrary elements, Whitman feels an ineffable sense of fruition and fulness. "I am satisfied, I see, dance, laugh, sing."[157] Eternity is blissful being; it is the state of self-fulfilment. The mystic who has found the supreme self feels no urges and is disturbed by no desires, for the self is eternally realized. The knower of the self is once for all freed from the endless processes of becoming. It is this supreme state that is indicated in the following lines:

> I exist as I am, that is enough,
> If no other in the world be aware I sit
> content,
> And if each and all be aware I sit content.[158]

The Upanishads point out that the man of realization lives in the peace that comes of self-fulfilment. He attains all the objects of desire, since they are but the self to him. To realize the self . . . is to have all desires satisfied . . . and thus to transcend desires. . . . [159] Dissatisfaction is symptomatic of the "bandaged spirit." The poet has vowed to himself: "Wherever I have been I have charged myself with contentment and triumph."[160] The animals bring him tokens of his own attitude. "They do not sweat and whine." Not one is dissatisfied.[161] One's world is nothing but one's own self; he who has gained his self gains the whole world. The Brihadaranyaka (1.4.15) tells us: "One should meditate only upon the world called the Self," and Whitman echoes, "One world is aware and by far the largest to me, and that is myself."[162] The self alone is one's greatest wealth and glory, one's supremest world and bliss.[163] One who has experienced one's self-sufficiency need not look for wealth outside one's self.

> Henceforth I ask not good-fortune, *I myself
> am good-fortune,*

Henceforth I whimper no more, *postpone no
  more, need nothing,*
Done with indoor complaints, libraries,
  querulous criticisms,
Strong and content I travel the open road.[164]

The soul alone will maintain itself: "I will make the
true poem of riches / To earn for the body and the
mind whatever adheres and goes forward, and is not
dropt by death."[165] The true poem of riches is the
"Song of Myself." The scriptures describe the wise
man who has attained his self as one who has delight
in the self . . . , who revels with the self . . . , who
is content with the self . . . , who has intercourse with
the self . . . , and who has bliss in the self. . . . Such
a man becomes autonomous . . . (self-king).[166] Whitman,
too, has attained to his soul's natural and supreme state.
He knows he is "august," and he is content to live in the
ecstasy of self-communion: "O soul thou pleasest me, I
thee."[167] With this sovereignty he can declare, "I dote on
myself, there is that lot of me and all so luscious. / *Each
moment and whatever happens thrills me with joy.*"[168]

His habit of entering into a mystical intercourse with
his soul, which induces in him an ecstatic, even erotic,
feeling—finds a notable expression here:

I believe in you my soul. . . .

. . . . .

Loafe with me on the grass, loose the stop
  from your throat,
Not words, not music or rhyme I want, not
  custom or lecture, not even the best,
Only the lull I like, the hum of your valvèd
  voice,
I mind how once we lay such a transparent
  summer morning,
How you settled your head athwart my hips
  and gently turn'd over upon me,
And parted the shirt from my bosom-bone,
  and plunged your tongue, to my bare-stript
  heart,
And reach'd till you felt my beard, and
  reach'd till you held my feet.[169]

It is through this feeling of fulfilment that Whitman
has gained the sense of eternal "being," the eternal
"now" of the mystic. "This minute that comes to me
over the past decillions, / There is no better than it and
now."[170] The realized self is not a growth or becoming
but a fulfilment and being. A life of ever increasing
aspiration is inconsistent with self-knowledge. It is thus
that Whitman arrives at the conclusion that the real is
perfect and ideal, and that nothing can improve upon
the goodness and completeness of his present existence. In **"A Song for Occupations,"** 6, he tells us,
"Happiness, knowledge, not in another place but this

place, not for another hour but this hour." Perfection is
not to be sought as a distant ideal but is to be known
as already accomplished in the actual and the now. It
is this sense that is suggested in these words of Thoreau:

Men esteem truth remote, in the outskirts of the
system, behind the farthest star, before Adam and
after the last man. In eternity there is indeed
something true and sublime. But all these times
and places and occasions are now and here. God
himself culminates in the present moment, will
never be more divine in the lapse of all the ages.[171]

Notes

[1] Cf. Emerson: "I—this thought which is called I—is
the mould in which the world is poured like melted
wax" ("The Transcendentalist").

[2] See "Democratic Vistas," *Complete Poetry and Selected Prose and Letters,* edited by Emory Holloway
(London: Nonesuch Press, 1938), p. 713.

[3] *Ibid.,* p. 866.

[4] "Song of Myself," 48.

[5] Brihadaranyaka Upanishad, 5.1.

[6] Katha Upanishad, 6.2.

[7] There is no difference even in degree between the
conscious spirit of man and nature. The Upanishads do
not recognize any dualism between matter and intelligence. Matter itself is God.

[8] "Song of Myself," 13.

[9] George Santayana, *Interpretations of Poetry and
Religion* (New York: Charles Scribner's Sons, 1916),
p. 180.

[10] "Starting from Paumanok," 1.

[11] Quoted in Emory Holloway, *Whitman: An Interpretation
in Narrative* (New York: Alfred A. Knopf, 1926), p. 190.

[12] For excellent reconstructions of this period in Whit-
man's biography, see Gay Wilson Allen, *The Solitary
Singer* (New York: Macmillan Co., 1955), H. S. Canby,
Walt Whitman: An American (Boston: Houghton Mifflin
Co., 1943), and Emory Holloway, *Whitman.*

[13] Quoted in the *Complete Writings of Walt Whitman* (New
York: G. P. Putnam's Sons, 1902), VII, Part IV, 103.

[14] "Our Future Lot," *Uncollected Poetry and Prose,*
edited by Emory Holloway (New York: Doubleday,
Doran & Co., 1922), Vol. I.

15 *"mrtyōhrūpāni"*, Brihadaranyaka, 4.3.7.

16 "Fame's Vanity" (1839), "Ambition" (1842), "The Love That Is Hereafter" (1840), "End of All" (1840). See Holloway, *op. cit.,* Vol. I.

17 Holloway, *op. cit.,* Vol. I.

18 Katha, 1.6.

19 Brihadaranyaka, 2.4.3.

20 Sun-Down Papers, No. 7 (1840), Holloway, *op. cit.,* Vol. I.

21 *Ibid.,* No. 8.

22 *Ibid.*

23 Katha, 4.2.

24 See Evelyn Underhill, *Mysticism: A Study in the Nature and Development of Man's Spiritual Consciousness* (London: Methuen & Co., Ltd., 1919). p. 96.

25 Holloway, *op. cit.,* I, 123.

26 "Crossing Brooklyn Ferry," 5.

27 "In Paths Untrodden," in "Calamus."

28 Holloway, *op. cit.,* II, 89.

29 "Children of Adam."

30 "Song of Myself," 28; see also Holloway, *op. cit.,* II, 73.

31 Allen, *The Solitary Singer,* p. 126.

32 Quoted from *The Solitary Singer,* p. 126.

33 For a discussion of the literary influences on Whitman, see *The Solitary Singer,* chap. iv.

34 "Plato" (1850).

35 "Spiritual Laws." Cf., Chhandogya Upanishad, 7.23.1, "The Infinite is bliss; there is no bliss in what is small."

36 Holloway, *op. cit.,* II, 63-76.

37 Gita, 13.2.24.

38 Notebook I, Holloway, *op. cit.,* II, 63-76.

39 *Ibid.*

40 *Ibid.,* p. 64.

41 See Allen, *The Solitary Singer,* p. 123.

42 Notebook II, Holloway, *op. cit.,* II, 86.

43 *Ibid.,* p. 70.

44 *Ibid.*

45 *Ibid.,* p. 79.

46 *Ibid.,* p. 74.

47 *Ibid.,* p. 79.

48 *Ibid.,* p. 66.

49 *Ibid.,* p. 85.

50 *Ibid.,* p. 84.

51 *Ibid.,* p. 66.

52 *Ibid.,* p. 53.

53 *Ibid.,* p. 67.

54 *Ibid.,* p. 71.

55 *Ibid.,* p. 65-66.

56 *Ibid.,* p. 65.

57 "A Backward Glance," Holloway, *Complete Poetry and Selected Prose and Letters,* p. 860.

58 See Holloway, *op. cit.,* I, 140.

59 "Starting from Paumanok," 12.

60 Havelock Ellis thinks that Whitman's inversion plays but a small part in his work. See *Studies in the Psychology of Sex* (Philadelphia: F. A. Davis, 1930), Vol. II (*Sexual Inversion*).

61 See Gustav Bychowski, "Walt Whitman: A Study in Sublimation," *Psychoanalysis and the Social Sciences,* III, 223-61. Muriel Rukeyser says, "I venture to suggest that the inclusive personality which Whitman created from his own conflict is heroic proof of a life in which apparent antagonisms have been reconciled and purified into art" (*The Life of Poetry* [New York: Current Books, 1949], p. 78). That Whitman himself had been trying to understand his own egoistical nature during his formative period is indicated by the fact that he read a magazine article in 1845 on egotism (*Complete Writings,* Vol. VII, Part V, No. 219).

62 Cf., *Prajñūnaghana,* "a mass of consciousness," Mandukya Upanishad, 5; *Vijñūnamūnandam Brahma,*

"Brahman is knowledge and bliss," Brihadaranyaka Upanishad, 3.9.28.

[63] Emerson, "History."

[64] See Brihadaranyaka, 3.4.1, and Chhandogya, 6.5.2 and 6.8[.7].

[65] *Complete Writings,* Vol. VII, Part III, No. 131.

[66] "Song of Myself," I (final version).

[67] "Starting from Paumanok," 14.

[68] *Ibid.,* 2.

[69] "the quite changed attitude of the ego": "A Backward Glance," Holloway, *op. cit.,* p. 861.

[70] "A Song for Occupations," 2. (Italics mine.)

[71] Katha, 4.1. . . .

[72] "A Song for Occupations," I.

[73] Katha, 4.1.

[74] Preface, 1855 Edition, Holloway, *op. cit.,* p. 581.

[75] Brihadaranyaka, 1.4.7-8.

[76] Notebook I, Holloway, *op. cit.,* II, 63-76. (Italics mine.)

[77] Quoted in Richard Garnette, *Life of Ralph Waldo Emerson* (London: Walter Scott Publishing Co., Ltd., 1888). (Italics mine.)

[78] Walden, chap. v, "Solitude." (Italics mine.)

[79] *Ibid.,* chap xvi, "The Pond in Winter."

[80] The Self is no doer; work is done by the modes of nature, Gita, 3.27, 5.14, 13.29. The Self is the transcendental witness, subject and experiencer, 13.12.

[81] *Complete Writings,* Vol. VI, Part I, No. 28. (Italics mine.)

[82] See Mandukya Upanishad. The self is the *turiya* or "transcendental consciousness," the substratum of all other states of consciousness, the original unity beneath thought forms.

[83] "Song of Myself," 4. (Italics mine.)

[84] See Mahendranath Sircar, *Hindu Mysticism According to the Upanishads* (London: Kegan Paul, French, Trubner & Co., Ltd., 1934), p. 282.

[85] Mundaka Upanishad, 3.1.1.

[86] Gita, 13.22; 13.14. (Italics mine.) Cf., "Both in and out of the game," "Song of Myself," 4.

[87] Brihadaranyaka, 4.3.15; also Gita, 13.31-32. The supreme imperishable self neither acts, nor is tainted.

[88] See Clifton Joseph Furness, *Walt Whitman's Workshop* (Cambridge: Harvard University Press, 1928), n. 36, "Creative self as an identity separate from his ordinary self-conscious personality," "division of consciousness," "dual personality."

[89] *Cosmic Consciousness* (14th ed.; New York: E. P. Dutton & Co., 1948), p. 63.

[90] William James, *Varieties of Religious Experience* (New York: Modern Library, 1936), p. 164.

[91] "One Hour to Madness and Joy," in "Children of Adam." Also, "We Two, How Long We Were Fool'd," in "Children of Adam." Love acts as a liberating force and induces cosmic expansion.

[92] See Allen, *Walt Whitman Handbook* (New York: Hendricks House, Inc., 1957), p. 252, "Thus by being conscious of his imaginative faculty as a distinct identity or personality, which he addresses as 'my Soul' . . . he suceeds . . . in composing like 'one divinely possessed.' . . ." See also Gay Wilson Allen and Charles T. Davis, *Walt Whitman's Poems* (Grove Press, Inc., 1959), p. 11 (Introduction). Here Allen and Davis recognize that Whitman's "soul" in "Song of Myself" is not what he later called his Fancy—his poetic faculty.

[93] "Pioneers! O Pioneers!," in "Birds of Passage."

[94] "Song of the Open Road," 13. (Italics mine.)

[95] "To You," in "Birds of Passage." (Italics mine.)

[96] See Brihadaranyaka, 4.3.7 and 4.4.5-6, and Sankara's commentaries.

[97] "Song of the Open Road," 6.

[98] "Quicksand Years," in "Whispers of Heavenly Death." (Italics mine.)

[99] "It was originally my intention after chanting in *Leaves of Grass* the songs of the body and existence, to . . . make the unseen soul govern absolutely at last" (Preface to the Centennial Edition, Holloway, *op. cit.,* p. 729).

[100] "Thou Mother with Thy Equal Brood," 6. (Italics mine.) Also, "real of the real," "Riddle Song," in "From Noon to Starry Night."

[101] Brihadaranyaka, 2.3.6.

[102] "Eidólons," in "Inscriptions."

[103] See Preface to the Centennial Edition, Holloway, *op. cit.,* p. 734, "All serves, helps—but in the centre of all, absorbing all, giving for your purpose the only meaning and vitality to all, master and mistress of all, under the law, stands Yourself."

[104] The "identified soul" (Holloway, *op. cit.,* p. 693) is not the soul "that has received its identity"—the atomic individual; but it is the soul that has realized its potential divinity and universality, and attained selfhood. In other words, it is the self come to its own. Cf. Allen, *Walt Whitman Handbook,* pp. 303-11; Romain Rolland, *Prophets of New India: The Life of Vivekananda* (Almora: Advaita Ashram, 1944), p. 63.

[105] "Song of Joys." (Italics mine.)

[106] Katha, 4.5.

[107] "Song of Prudence," in "Autumn Rivulets." (Italics mine.)

[108] "Compensation."

[109] "Song of Prudence."

[110] "Tests," in "Autumn Rivulets." (Italics mine.) Cf., Katha, 2.12, "ancient, hard to see, lodged in the inmost recess, located in intelligence."

[111] "Song of Myself," 25. (Italics mine.) Also, "of the inherent light greater than the rest," "Thoughts," in "From Noon to Starry Night." Cf. Brihadaranyaka, 4.3.6.

[112] "Song of Myself," 25.

[113] "When I Read the Book," in "Inscription."

[114] "As I Ebb'd with the Ocean of Life," 2, in "Sea-Drift."

[115] "A Song of the Rolling Earth," 3. (Italics mine.)

[116] "A Song for Occupations," 6.

[117] "Song of Myself," 46.

[118] Brihadaranyaka, 3.4.1 . . . and 3.7, "The immortal soul and the inner controller." Katha, 2.20, "in the heart of each living being."

[119] *Op. cit.,* p. 387.

[120] See Underhill, *op. cit.,* pp. 231-32, "Amongst modern men Walt Whitman possessed in a supreme degree the permanent sense of this glory."

[121] Holloway, *op. cit.,* II, 89.

[122] "Song of Myself," 20.

[123] See "Whispers of Heavenly Death."

[124] "A Song of Joys." See Chhandogya, 8.3.4, "after having risen from this body," and Sankara's commentary, "disembodied is the form of the self."

[125] Gita, 6.5.

[126] Cf., "sarvabhūtātmabhūtātmā," Gita, 4.7.

[127] "A Song for Occupations," 5.

[128] "Song of Myself," 3. An extreme school of Vedantists do not recognize the existence even of maya. See Gaudapada, Mandukya Karikas, Chapter 2.32, "There is no dissolution, no birth, none in bondage, none aspiring for wisdom, no seeker of liberation, and none liberated. This is the absolute truth". Even according to Sankara, illusion or maya loses its reality the moment knowledge is attained.

[129] "I Sing the Body Electric," I, in "Children of Adam."

[130] See R. D. O'Leary, "Swift and Whitman as Exponents of Human Nature," *International Journal of Ethics,* Vol. XXIV. The view of the writer that "this implied identification of body and soul represents a monistic conception of human nature" supports this interpretation. To Whitman soul and body are one fact, a single identity. Whitman does not recognize the merely animal and gross anywhere; all is spirit and all is divine.

[131] Note his early verse and manuscript jottings of the "journalistic" period, in which the sense of conflict is ever present.

[132] See Sircar, *op. cit.,* pp. 191-92.

[133] "Song of Myself," 3.

[134] Brihadaranyaka, 1.4.7.

[135] "Me Imperturbe," in "Inscriptions."

[136] "A Song of Joys."

[137] See Edgar Lee Masters, *Whitman* (New York: Charles Scribner's Sons, 1937), p. 84.

[138] *Walt Whitman* (Philadelphia: David McKay, 1883), p. 221. See Isa, 7. With the perception of identity, all fear is expunged.

[139] Gita, 2.15, 2.45, 2.48, 3.18, 3.24, 4.3, 6.7.

[140] *Complete Writings,* Vol. V, Letters of 1868, Letter No. 5.

[141] "A Backward Glance," Holloway, *op. cit.,* p. 860. (Italics mine.)

[142] "I Sit and Look Out," in "By the Roadside."

[143] See Katha, 5.11.

[144] "Song of the Universal," in "Birds of Passage." The optimism expressed in this poem might seem to be of the Hegelian type. Whitman derived much solace from Hegel's philosophy of harmonious becoming in his later days when the disturbing national tragedy of the Civil War and the darkening social outlook had considerably shaken his faith in America's manifest destiny.

[145] See Katha, 2.12, "Seated amidst miserable surroundings the intelligent man renounces joy and grief."

[146] "Song of Myself," 22.

[147] *Ibid.,* 51.

[148] See "Carlyle from American Points of View," Holloway, *op. cit.,* p. 785.

[149] See Holbrook Jackson, *Dreamers of Dreams* (London: Faber & Faber, Ltd., 1948), Chapter on Emerson.

[150] *Ibid.,* p. 256, "Leaves of Grass is a fanfare of affirmations . . . Whitman is Nature's 'yes' man, the personification of the Everlasting Yea." *Walden* is full of criticisms and negations. Contrast Whitman, "My gait is no fault-finder's or rejector's gait," "Song of Myself," 22.

[151] "Ah, Poverties, Wincings," in "From Noon to Starry Night."

[152] See Allen, *Walt Whitman Handbook,* pp. 68, 87, 145. Also, *The Solitary Singer,* chap. vi.

[153] See Holloway, *op. cit.,* II, 94, Notebook 9 (dated 1868-70). Perhaps inspired by Epictetus, Whitman noted down the following self-instruction: "It is imperative that I obviate and remove myself (& my orbit) at all hazards . . . from this incessant & enormous . . . Perturbation."

[154] "Whoever You Are Holding Me Now in Hand," in "Calamus." (Italics mine.)

[155] "Song of the Open Road," 11.

[156] "Even as a lotus leaf is untouched by water," Gita, 5.10.

[157] "Song of Myself," 3.

[158] *Ibid.,* 20.

[159] Brihadaranyaka, 1.3.21.

[160] "Thoughts," in "Songs of Parting."

[161] "Song of Myself," 32.

[162] "Song of Myself," 3.

[163] Brihadaranyaka, 4.3.32. . . .

[164] "Song of the Open Road," 1. (Italics mine.)

[165] "Starting from Paumanok," 12. Also, "The most affluent man is he that confronts all the shows he sees by equivalence out of the stronger wealth of himself" (Holloway, *op. cit.,* p. 578).

[166] See Chhandogya, 7.25.1; Gita, 3.17.

[167] "Passage to India," 8.

[168] "Song of Myself," 24. (Italics mine.)

[169] *Ibid.,* 5.

[170] *Ibid.,* 22.

[171] *Walden,* chap. iii.

Mitchell Robert Breitwieser (essay date 1983)

SOURCE: "Who Speaks in Whitman's Poems?" in *Bucknell Review,* Vol. 28, No. 1, 1983, pp. 121-43.

[In the following essay, Breitwieser suggests that Whitman's usage of multiple voices in Leaves of Grass *has political parallels. Breitwieser emphasizes the conflict in the poems between the voice of the small, individual "I" and that of the large, magnanimous, universal "I."]*

> Why even speak of "I," he dreams, which
> interests me almost not at all?
> —Williams, *Paterson*

> The breadth of the problem is great, for the poet is representative. He stands among partial men for the complete man, and apprises us not of his wealth, but of the common wealth. The young man reveres men of genius, because, to speak truly, they are more himself than he is.
> —Emerson, "The Poet"

I

The word *I* in **Leaves of Grass** seems to be used by two speakers, one timid, gentle, frequently disconsolate, the other large, all-inclusive, affirming. The distinction between these two voices and the implicit dialogue between them may usefully lead us to call them entirely different selves, rather than examples of the variability of mood natural to anyone. This distinction not inadvertently corresponds to the opposition between particular or special interest and general representativeness that was the premier concern of American politics in Whitman's time. We do well to consider the plurality of voice in *Leaves of Grass* as a deliberate image of and commentary on the predicament of political division.

Whitman's variety of transcendentalism and the sense of urgent vocation that accompanied it were "brought to a boil" by his reading of Emerson on the representative man. In the concluding pages of "The Poet," Emerson had contended that America lacked its needed sequel to Plato, Shakespeare, Swedenborg et al., and hence had failed spiritually to coalesce. Franklin, certainly, had transcended factionism and summed up the American character, but his universal representativeness, founded on ingenuity, must have seemed to lack the dense, fusing, spiritual quiddity that Emerson felt was necessary if nineteenth-century division were to be healed.

Whitman took this complaint to be an anticipation of *Leaves of Grass,* though Emerson may have been thinking of Bronson Alcott. The sentences in the preface to the first edition of *Leaves of Grass* borrow from Emerson's loose apothegmatic declarativeness, and from his cadences. Consequently, Whitman's receipt of the letter from Emerson after the first edition was issued made him eager to publish it as an advertisement in the second. He offered it to the public as Emerson's *nunc dimittis.* From 1855 until the 1870s, at least, Whitman was to present himself as a "poetic president." He hoped that, as a poet, he would be able to plunge his "semitic muscle" deep enough into the American populace to find an authentic common characteristic. He would thereby elude the blandness, prevarication, or shortsightedness that comes of being all things to all people, the malaise that afflicted the presidency in the antebellum period as it does in ours. Whitman presented himself as the man who had found the secret, the man in whose person would be resolved all the particular characters of Americans. In him, the general would come into view, but not at the price of neglecting the diverse and particular life of those so represented.

This determination to reveal the general without eliding the particular is the reason for Whitman's gravitation toward Hegel, in *Democratic Vistas* and elsewhere. Though he remained indifferent to the subtleties of Hegel's careful descriptions of logical, self-aware mind,[1] Whitman did pay close attention to the view of contradiction that is the center of Hegel's dialecticism: Hegel makes use of the word *aufheben,* which means both *cancel* and *preserve;* just so, in Whitman's represen-

tativeness, the sharp edge of individuality among American isolates (or "sporades," as he called them)— the drunks, the onanists, the wounded, the poor, the self-preoccupied, the avaricious, the inhibited—would be annulled; at the same time, the native vigor of individuality would be distilled out and preserved to make the universal self firm-fibered and real. Like Hegel, Whitman sought an infinity that was not a simple opposite to what is merely finite.

This copresence of cancellation and preservation is the key to Whitman's "great songs of death." For all of their plangency, for example, **"Out of the Cradle Endlessly Rocking"** and **"When Lilacs Last in the Dooryard Bloom'd"** are not characteristic of the whole of Whitman's verse. The intensity of the grief, the despair and anxiety they express, contradict the affirmation that remained the major note of Whitman's sensibility. But both poems end with affirmation, as if to bring us to the threshold of that major note. The solitary despondency of the speaker is made amenable to reunion with community, at the same time that his circumspections are retained:

> Victorious song, death's outlet song, yet
>   varying ever-altering song,
> As low and wailing, yet clear the notes, rising
>   and falling, flooding the night,
> Sadly sinking and fainting, as warning and
>   warning, and yet bursting with joy.[2]

The modulations in the song from the lamentation of the solitary griever to the informed joy of reunion allow it to contain at once both the cancellation of grief and its memorial preservation as a deepening and realizing element in what might otherwise be banal assent. Whitman, with Hegel, calls attention to tragedy in the local instance, and comedy in the larger unfolding pattern.[3] This is his version of *aufheben:* though there is no corresponding satisfying word in English, Whitman's frequent use of "tally" was a result of his search for such a word. Tallying individuals (himself among them), Whitman explores the contours of their specificity, while directing them on to the passional fusion that is the whole reason for the poem. When the poem is a personal remembrance such as **"Out of the Cradle Endlessly Rocking"** or **"When Lilacs Last in the Dooryard Bloom'd,"** there are two speakers, two "I's," the one who is tallied ("Sadly sinking and fainting, as warning and warning"), and the one who tallies ("and yet bursting with joy").

II

This painful arrival at passional fusion is a political concept. Jefferson's presidential experience led him to concede that the dream of physiocratic consensus he shared with Crèvecoeur might not apply to the nineteenth century, and Whitman's journalistic encounters with virulent controversy and the fracturing of the Democratic Party would have been further confirmation of the obsolescence of the Jeffersonianism his father so much admired. As Justin Kaplan has written, "the time of Whitman's growing up was a long farewell salute to the receding world of the founders, a series of remarkable deaths, days of national mourning, acts of patriotic commemoration."[4]

Though the dream of consensus may have been shown to be impossible as early as the arguments between Jefferson and Hamilton in Washington's cabinet, it remained a regular part of American rhetoric, as Sacvan Bercovitch has shown.[5] Whitman absorbed this rhetoric, but **Leaves of Grass** is not a simple instance of such common-coin ideology. Rather, as Bercovitch hints, it is a "diffusion" or "deflection":[6] in **Leaves of Grass** Whitman relocated the opposition of sect and consensus to a wider frame. What agreement, he asks, could be found that would reveal American solidarity and provide the *locus standi* ("To the perfect shape comes common ground") for a genuinely representative man? Whitman moves this inquiry from politics construed in the orthodox sense to lowest common denominators—the individual's need to believe in the legitimacy of his or her life, sex, death, and the use of the word *I*.

A great number of Whitman's readers have been attracted to his poems by his attention to what Lionel Trilling, in *The Liberal Imagination,* praised in Sherwood Anderson's writing: "The small legitimate existence, so necessary for the majority of men to achieve, is in our age so very hard, so nearly impossible, for them to achieve." Whitman's poems are full of attention to the fragile sanctity of the careful, common lives of plants and animals as well as of men and women. He celebrates the small, stalwart heroism of seemingly undistinguished labor, of the life firmly in place.

But Whitman's accompanying celebration of sex and death go in an opposite direction, one not explored by Sherwood Anderson. Whitman represents sex and death as forces that fracture whatever small, tender security self-protection may have achieved. Sex is the infinite, fusing, equalizing life of the community, as death is, but, like death, it seems to terminate what little a hostile world has let be safe:

> It wrenches such ardors from me I did not
>   know I possess'd them,
> It sails me, I dab with bare feet, they are
>   licked by the indolent waves,
> I am cut by bitter and angry hail, I lose my
>   breath,
> Steep'd amid honey'd morphine, my windpipe
>   throttled in fakes of death.
>
> [*LG* [*Leaves of Grass*] p. 56]

Whitman feels the throat constriction usual with extreme anxiety: contact is peril, an interruption of personal continuities that were at best insecure. This is what led Henry Adams to contend that Whitman was one of the very few American artists "who had ever insisted on the power of sex." Adams cast Whitman as an alternative to his own confessed debility in the face of force. But, as Whitman makes sex deathly, so too he makes death sexy:

> Double yourself and receive me darkness,
> Receive me and my lover too, he will not let
>   me go without him.
>
> I roll myself upon you as upon a bed, I resign
>   myself to the dusk.
> He whom I call answers me and takes the
>   place of my lover,
> He rises with me silently from the bed.
>
> Darkness, you are gentler than my lover, his
>   flesh was sweaty and panting,
> I feel the hot moisture that he left me.
>
> [*LG,* pp. 426-27]

Death is a "strong and delicious word": by affiliating sex and death, Whitman at once makes sex more grave, and death not a termination. Together, virtually indistinguishable songs of love and songs of death oppose what the individual had been or had guarded. They dislocate the familiar, transpose it.

And they preserve as well as cancel, in a finer key. Afterward, in the post-coital, post-holocaust calm that Whitman implies is the best mood, it is revealed that only the crud of the self has been purged, that some part of the self survives that keeps particular at the same time that it emerges onto the common ground on which consensus may begin: "At length let up again to feel the puzzle of puzzles, / And that we call Being" (*LG,* p. 56). Or:

> Swiftly arose and spread around me the peace
>   and knowledge that pass all the argument of
>   the earth,
> And I know that the hand of God is the
>   promise of my own,
> And I know that the spirit of God is the
>   brother of my own,
> And that all men ever born are also my
>   brothers, and the women my sisters and
>   lovers,
> And that a kelson of the creation is love,
> And limitless are leaves stiff and drooping in
>   the fields,
> And brown ants in the little wells beneath them,
> And mossy scabs of the worm fence, heap'd
>   stones, elder, mullein and poke-weed.
>
> [*LG,* p. 33]

This scene is immediately preceded by an allegorical fellation of the body by the soul, a climax whimsically reprised in the poet's serene notice of the two states of turgidity among the leaves. Let up from the grip, the throat loosed, the poet arises and spreads, echoing the Christian benediction ("the peace that passeth all understanding"). He is rid of encumbering self-insistence, available to the thousand beckoning affinities that now offer themselves up to be tallied. But the motion toward the expansive and the liturgically declarative turns away from predication and toward the particular: the poet keeps specific in the triple trochaic mention of the humble weeds. Love, then, is not an antidote to death, or even opposed to it, because both have the power to release from confinement, and to cancel while preserving the best of what is surpassed.

As love or death approach, according to Whitman, one will resist them, sensing their hostility to the uneasy safety his life's work has erected. In the calm that follows the onslaught, however, the resistance will have disappeared, because he will have realized that there is strange preservation, too. He is released from the private hell of the small self in which he was bound: "Smartly attired, countenance smiling, form upright, death under the breast-bones, hell under the skull-bones. . . . " (*LG,* p. 158). Now, his loosed attention is a traveler: distilled from out of the small self, he acquires the unselective because unprejudiced attention to small things—elder, mullein, pokeweed—that contain the secret of places and show "perfect rectitude":

> I believe in those wing'd purposes,
> And acknowledge red, yellow, white, playing
> 　within me,
> And consider green and violet and the tufted
> 　crown intentional,
> And do not call the tortoise unworthy because
> 　she is not something else,
> And the jay in the woods never studied the
> 　gamut, yet trills pretty well to me,
> And the look of the bay mare shames silliness
> 　out of me.
>
> 　　　　　　　　　　　[*LG,* p. 40]

The silliness is shamed out of him, that is, he is released from the predicament that William James describes in a lecture that pays tribute to Whitman:

> We are practical beings, each of us with limited functions and duties to perform. Each is bound to feel intensely the importance of his own duties and the significance of the situations that call these forth. But this feeling is in each of us a vital secret, for sympathy with which we vainly look to others. The others are too much absorbed in their own vital secrets to take an interest in ours. Hence the stupidity and injustice of our opinions, so far as they deal with the significance of alien lives.[7]

For Whitman, sex or death split this narrow stupidity and institute the wider view James describes: "it seems almost as if it were necessary to become worthless as a practical being, if one is to hope to attain to any breadth of insight into the impersonal world of worths as such, to have any perception of life's meaning on a large objective scale."[8] So, at the end of **"When Lilacs Last in the Dooryard Bloom'd,"** his grief tallied by the "knowledge of death," the poet has acquired the large vision that can only follow the seeming extinction of the small man: "While my sight that was bound in my eyes unclosed, / As to long panoramas of vision." Let out from his bondage in stupidity, however, he is not attentive just to abstract generality: rather, his attention to particular things is more perfect because it is not adulterated by an "axis of vision," to borrow from Emerson, that is not "coincident with the axis of things." The release from the confining particular life does not condemn him to a cloudy existence among visions of unformed infinity. Instead, it gives him a more exact bearing toward things, because they are not constantly received and registered with relation to a personal project. He comprehends each thing's unique, unreproducible structure, and also its place in the overarching design. He tallies.

He is, then, at once, a particular man, with a past and a name, and a traveler, an observer who has been wrenched loose from the familiar codes of home and who is consequently able to objectively record the life as it goes on in the places he visits. Consequently, the word *I* as it is used in **Leaves of Grass** varies in its denotation. On the one hand, it is used to amass and represent the whole of Walt Whitman's personal history as a sort of confession. On the other hand, it expresses a picaresque anonymity, not tied to self-protective individuality, a kind of devoided receptacle able to receive and appreciate without constantly puzzling meaning based on personal usefulness. In the first case, "I" gives us Walt Whitman, a "knot intrinsicate," a feeling, wanting individual; in the second, it gives us an attentive traveler who, after the catastrophe that ejected him from comfort (**"Out of the Cradle Endlessly Rocking"**), has left his preoccupied selfhood behind (**"Song of the Open Road"**). The second "I" cancels the first—shames its silliness—but preserves it as one of the countless essential data that are tallied. This second "I" cannot, properly, be called Walt Whitman:

> O take my hand Walt Whitman!
> Such gliding wonders! Such sights and sounds!
> Such join'd unended links, each hook'd to the
> 　next,
> Each answering all, each sharing the earth
> 　with each.

Here, what was "I," Walt Whitman, has become a *you* addressed by the new attentive traveler that has been gestating within him:

What widens within you Walt Whitman?
What waves and soils exuding?
What climes? What persons and cities are
    here?

[*LG,* p. 137]

Whitman, the first "I," mothers the "earth," the second "I," the meeting place of analogies and particulars, of all that could conceivably be known. The awareness of this larger frame—preposterously—says "I" and addresses the bearer of the proper name "Walt Whitman" as "you."

Thus the word *I* shuttles between the small self that Trilling describes, intent on its legitimate claims to safety, and the attentiveness that survives the twin catastrophes of sex and death. This second "I" cancels the first's insistence on its own centrality, but it lovingly preserves respect for that small self's unreproducible placement among its countless companions. Searching for a lowest common denominator on which to base consensus, Whitman found opposed impulses—legitimacy and catastrophe. This is his poetic "deflection" of the political opposition between divisive, self-protecting particularity and magnanimous, representative generality. The small, unsafe "I" of *Leaves of Grass* and the terrestrially large "I" are Whitman's equivalents to the options that guided American political thought.

III

I follow quickly. . . . I ascend to the nest in
    the fissure of the cliff.
                —Whitman, **"Song of Myself"**

    in that cavern, that profound cleft,
                        a flickering green
inspiring terror, watching. . . .
And standing, shrouded there, in that din,
Earth, the chatterer, father of all
speech. . . .
                —Williams, *Paterson*

We should not conflate or confuse these two voices that use the word *I* in *Leaves of Grass.* They are separate entities. Whitman's great poems—**"Song of Myself," "The Sleepers," "This Compost," "Calamus," "Out of the Cradle Endlessly Rocking," "DrumTaps," "When Lilacs Last in the Dooryard Bloom'd"**—are *crisis poems* meant to show Americans how the first, familiar "I" is cruelly cleft to open the way for a terrifying infant, the second "I." This is the importance of terror in Whitman's poems of growth:

Now I am terrified at the Earth, it is that calm
    and patient,
It grows such sweet things out of such
    corruptions,

It turns harmless and stainless on its axis,
    with such endless successions of diseas'd
    corpses,
It distills such exquisite winds out of such
    infused fetor,
It renews with such unwitting looks its
    prodigal, annual, sumptuous crops,
It gives such divine materials to men, and
    accepts such leavings from them at last.
                        [*LG,* pp. 369-70]

"The Earth" is a vitality bank that loans wonder to matter, reclaims it at death, when that wonder is both cancelled and preserved in new forms, such as the lilacs that might grow above Lincoln's "good manure." In the passage above, the speaking "I" fears the awful cleaving, but the reluctant admiration building through dactyls in "prodigal, annual, sumptuous" signals the imminent affirmation, when "I" will be the Earth speaking rather than the man who fears its disdainful "innocence":

I find I incorporate gneiss and coal and
    long-threaded moss and fruits and grains
    and esculent roots,
And am stucco'd with quadrupeds and birds
    all over,
And have distanced what is behind me for
    good reasons,
And call anything close again when I desire it.
                        [*LG,* p. 59]

Here Whitman becomes the ecosphere he elsewhere was terrified by. He is large, prolific, indifferent to instances of life, able to produce satisfactory duplicates if whim so chooses.

These two treatments of the Earth, juxtaposed, show the difference between Whitman's "I's." His crisis poems depict the motion of voice between them, from the timid "I" of the first passage—fixed to special loves, terrified of force—to the "I" of the second passage—cruel, blithe, transcendent. Whitman succeeds as a poet not when he delineates either the first or the second "I," but when he narrates the vertiginous transit from the first to the second, when he dramatically depicts the cancellation of individuality that is also its preservation in a painfully depersonalized wonder.

This is, to repeat, related to Hegel's dialecticism, though Whitman diverges from Hegel when it comes to specifying the consciousness that stands clear at the end of the process. Still, the resemblance exists, as witnessed by this passage where Hegel considers such a mutation within the word *I.*

Nature does not bring its . . . [nous, mind] into consciousness: it is man who first makes himself double so as to be universal for a universal. This first happens when man knows that he is 'I.' By the term 'I' I mean myself, a singular and altogether determinate person. And yet I really utter nothing peculiar to myself, for everyone else is an 'I' or 'ego,' and when I call myself 'I,' though I indubitably mean the single person myself, I express a thorough universal. . . . 'I' is the vacuum or receptacle for anything and everything: for which everything is and which stores everything in itself.[9]

Each makes himself double when he uses the word *I:* that is, he collects his experience, unifies it, and designates himself as a subject or knower, as a *project,* or bundle of intentions, as well as something to be known. In common usage, "I" is the self-designation of each such individual subject, excluding all others. But Hegel notices two things. First, "I" circulates freely among the members of the human conversation, traveling across the continent of human possibility. Second, it signifies anew at each moment of its use, it connotes nothing intrinsic about the person who uses it for self-designation, and it does not refer to any abstract concept. From this, Hegel suggests that we may get a sense of collective mind, the anonymous "vacuum and receptacle of anything and everything," if we imagine that "I" *does* correspond to a concept, that it has a meaning independent of the instances of its use, and that it does convey something intrinsic about what it refers to even without any accompanying reference to the biographical, historical, and geographical circumstances in which it is spoken. Such a universal would be like Whitman's speaking Earth: "And I know I am solid and sound, / To me the converging objects of the universe perpetually flow, / All are written to me, and I must get what the writing means" (*LG*, p. 47). Such an "I" would cancel the exclusiveness it has for each individual speaker—including Walt Whitman, Brooklyn, 1855—and "release" the anonymous knowing subjectivity that is its latent actual content.

This is Whitman's boldest proposition, his second "I" independent of any speaker and any specific conversation in which it might be used. Like "leaf," this second "I" could exist as a potentiality. It floats free, descending into the conversations of Americans, but not captured in those conversations. This would be an "I" for whom all imaginable speakers of the word *I* would be instances, as each leaf is an instance of the concept denoted by the word *leaf.* "I" would be a conceptual term. This "I," giving such "divine materials to men," *identity,* accepting such "leavings from them at last," would be a subjectivity bank (as the earth is a vitality bank), loaning reflecting doubleness to matter at birth, reclaiming it at death.

Emile Benveniste reveals that, from the linguist's position, "I" cannot be classed as a potentiality along with abstract nouns. Calling the word *I* a "unique but mobile sign" (what better description of Whitman's

persona?) he suggests that Hegel's and Whitman's intimations of an objectively constant "I" are linguistic nonsense:

> Each instance of use of a noun is referred to a fixed and "objective" notion, capable of remaining potential or of being actualized in a particular object and always identical with the mental image it awakens. But the instances of the use of *I* do not constitute a class of reference since there is no "object" definable as *I* to which these instances can refer in identical fashion. Each *I* has its own reference and corresponds each time to a unique being who is set up as such. . . . *I* can only be identified by the instance of discourse that contains it, and by that alone. . . . It cannot admit of any potential or "objective" form.[10]

Nevertheless, this is what Whitman proposes to us: an "I" for which complete dependence on specific individuality is cancelled; in which doubleness, or knowing subjectivity, is preserved without exclusive individuality; the "Earth," from which all "I-sayers" draw their life, itself saying "I." As the corpse returns to the earth, so the individual "I" returns to this subjectivity bank, but the large "I" is not silenced, as the concept "leaf" does not perish with every leaf.

This is Whitman's second "I," the survivor of sex or death, let up from exclusive individuality, able to enter and animate all Americans and even the insentient among common things. We should not confuse it with any persona meant to convey the tender historical man Walt Whitman. This is the poetic president who has survived the holocaust that lifted him out of self-interested singularity and made him able to represent all such singularities. A close corollary would be the eerie self-indication of a dead man. But unlike the "I" of Hamlet's ghost or the "I" in a will read out loud by a lawyer to survivors, the dead man's "I" would have to be imagined without any spectral grudge or intention, completely divested of the pursuit of particular interest and released from the need to protect his "small legitimacy": "I am as one disembodied, triumphant, dead." Metaphysically, this may be nonsense: linguistically, it certainly is. At various points, Whitman called *Leaves of Grass* both a "language experiment" and a "new bible." Put them together: these incongruous assertions lead us to wonder whether Whitman's ontology of the self may not have its root in planned linguistic "deflection."

IV

When Benveniste refers to an "instance of discourse," he means a moment of speaking: "*I* signifies 'the person who is uttering the present instance of the discourse containing *I.*'"[11] At this moment, "each speaker takes over all the resources of the language for his own behalf."[12] Benveniste ignores the problems that arise when the word *I* is written, particularly when the partners in the conversation do not share a single geographical and temporal "instance," in favor of a simpler analysis of the word *I* spoken in the shared presence of face-to-face conversation.

Leaves of Grass calls attention to itself as writing at the same time that it mounts the ruse of spoken conversation. Whitman wanted his poems to foster the illusion of conversational intimacy—the sense of a shared moment between Americans. This desire motivated the frequent inclusion of the word *you* to travel with the equally frequent "I." We are to be there with him: "I celebrate myself, and sing myself, / And what I assume you shall assume, / For every atom belonging to me as good belongs to you" (*LG,* p. 28). At the beginning of his poem, Whitman "takes over all the resources of language for his own behalf" and presents himself as a *speaker* and the poem as a shared time and place. He generously anticipates the reply, and the ensuing, swelling conversation in which affectionate interchange will so blur the boundaries between the alternating "I's" and "you's" that separate individuality will grow indistinct, "atoms" that had been private property will fraternize, and, above the hum and buzz of this *concordia discordans,* the second "I" will tally and rise. The conversation will be a "common ground" for the "perfect shape," the poetic president. Whitman describes this dialectical transcendence:

> Urge and urge and urge,
> Always the procreant urge of the world.
>
> Out of the dimness opposite equals advance,
>   always substance and increase, always sex,
> Always a knit of identity, always distinction,
>   always a breed of life.
>   [*LG,* p. 31]

The participants are knitted together (cancellation of individuality), yet remain distinct (preservation of individuality), and from this union the infant second "I" is born. Two lines later, the infant speaks for itself:

> Sure as the most certain sure, plumb in the
>   uprights, well entretied, braced in the
>   beams,
> Stout as a horse, affectionate, haughty,
>   electrical,
> I and this mystery here we stand.
>   [*LG,* p. 31]

Stout as a horse, this representative "I" is not guilty of the gritless representativeness of the antebellum presidents.

In the last of these lines—"I and this mystery here we stand [now]"—"I" is joined by three words—"this," "here," and, implicitly, "now"—that also lack "objec-

tive" independence, and depend instead on an "instance of discourse." They require a hearer's or reader's colloquial participation to give them meaning. As Benveniste writes:

> By simultaneous ostention, *this* will be the object designated in the present instance of discourse and the reference implicit in the form . . . which associates it with *I* and *you.* Outside this class, but on the same plane and associated in the same frame of reference, we find the adverbs *here* and *now.* Their relationship with *I* will be shown by defining them: *here* and *now* delimit the spatial and temporal instance coextensive and contemporary with the present instance of discourse containing *I.*[13]

All of these words—"I," "here," "now," "this"—lack "objective" definition, and can only be relationally defined: "I am he who is here, now, indicating this." And they conspire to enlist our inclusion in the semblance of conversation. In this series of words, "you" is essential: "I am he who is here, now, with you, indicating this." Without a "you" spoken to, and, consequently, a shared time and place, all sense is lost.

But the "you" whom Whitman addresses *reads* this feigning of *speaking.* He or she is not at the same place and time with the fervently uttering poet. Whitman often emphasizes both his ruse of shared colloquial presence and the unknown distance between a writer and a reader. This bifurcation in rhetorical strategy can be seen in poems such as **"Recorders Ages Hence"** or **"Crossing Brooklyn Ferry,"** or lines such as these: "This hour I tell things in confidence, / I might not tell everybody, but I will tell you" (*LG,* p. 47). One cannot select readers, usually, or know their time and place, yet this line pretends an author can do so.

When we encounter the words Benveniste discusses (technically called "deictics") in writing, we require contextual information such as the proper name of the speaker, the proper name or latitude and longitude of the place, the time and date. Given these, we may accede in a suspension of disbelief, an imaginative dismissal of the time and place of our reading the book, and pretend that we are there, then, actually hearing this. We jump over the confusion latent in written deixis, and imaginatively live in a time before our births, in a place we may not have visited, listening to a man who, with Lincoln, may since have pushed up lilacs. Whitman's first literary enthusiasms were Scott and the *Arabian Nights,* so he would have been familiar with such self-projection into lost times and places such as Bagdad or the Highlands "sixty years hence."

But, though his first love was such imaginative literature, Whitman does not mean for us to make this leap with such facility when reading *Leaves of Grass.* True, we do travel with his roaming "I" to past scenes—the

Alamo, or the Bonhomme Richard—and to distant places—the Sierras, for example, which he had not seen. But there is no center for imagined contemporaneity. What would be the real center we imaginatively join him at before beginning these forays? The copyright page suggests New York, 1855. But 1855 is compromised by the present tense in the last line of **"Song of Myself"**:

> I bequeath myself to the dirt to grow from the
>   grass I love,
> If you want me again look for me under your
>   bootsoles.
>
> You will hardly know who I am or what I
>   mean,
> But I shall be good health to you nevertheless,
> And filter and fiber your blood.
>
> Failing to catch me at first keep encouraged,
> Missing me one place search another,
> I stop somewhere waiting for you.
>
> > *[LG,* p. 89]

The temporal center of these lines shuttles between Whitman's time ("I bequeath myself"), his imagination of the reader's time ("You will hardly know"), and the reader's actual time ("I stop somewhere waiting for you"). There is also no spatial center: imagining his future decomposition and dispersion ("For every atom belonging to me as good belongs to you"), Whitman is at no single place, but instead is in the grass and in the blood of countless readers. The amassing and consolidating performed by the spoken "I" is in contradiction with the dispersion of time and place between the written "I" and the reading "you," an ambiguity further exploited in these lines:

> When you read these I that was visible am
>   become invisible,
> Now it is you, compact, visible, realizing my
>   poems, seeking me,
> Fancying how happy you were if I could be
>   with you and become your comrade,
> Be it as if I were with you. (Be not too
>   certain but I am now with you.)
>
> > *[LG,* p. 136]

Though spoken deixis implies at least two people who are both compact and visible at the same time and place, written deixis calls our attention to the fact that either the writer or the reader is discernibly compact and visible, but not both: "Will you speak before I am gone? Will you prove already too late?" (*LG,* p. 89).

Written deixis is an image of spoken presence, split off from it and therefore become uncanny. In this, it is like the *eidola* that Whitman made note of in his reading of Lucretius's *On the Nature of the Universe:*

> Now I will embark on an explanation of a highly relevant fact, the *existence of what we call "images" of things,* a sort of outer skin perpetually peeled off the surface of objects and flying about this way and that through the air. It is these whose impact scares our minds, whether waking or sleeping, on those occasions when we catch a glimpse of strange shapes and the phantoms of the dead.[14]

Written deictic words are eerie images that are peeled off the vitality of conversation that can haunt. They are the presence of an absence, an impossible colloquiality. As the atoms of the body bequeathed to the earth acquire ubiquity and become once more eligible for infinite transformation, so the "I" bequeathed to writing loses the specificity it keeps when spoken in particular present "instances of discourse." When we encounter "I" in writing, unhedged by clear geographical, temporal, and biographical supplements, we do encounter the self-designation of a dead man in the present moment. We witness a perplexing widening of the contradiction latent even in the spoken "I," a "unique *but* mobile sign" (emphasis mine). Feigning conversation, as in the first lines of **"Song of Myself,"** Whitman calls attention to the unique, individual "compactness" of the man who writes; calling attention to the writer's deadness for the reader, he emphasizes the transtemporal and transspatial mobility of "I." The "mobility" of the written "I" cancels the unique exclusiveness of the spoken "I," but preserves perplexing "I-ness."

Thus Whitman's exploration of the fault between speaking and writing enables him to evoke some sense of the meaning of the large "I" postulated in his meditations. "I" and its concomitant "here," "now," and "this" are without particular content in themselves. Unless they appear in an "instance of discourse" or are supplemented by a proper name (Walt Whitman), and an identified time and place (Brooklyn, 1855), they are adrift on a flood of times and places, like the Brooklyn Ferry. They are in such cases uncanny, because they necessarily cause us to contemplate their meaning independent of identifiable instance. Their common use, essential to verbal performance, is "deflected" or "diffused," as will be any rhetoric of consensus that uses such an evasive presence as its foundation. Never contained in a single imaginable person, place, or time, the "mobility" of these words, present even in their verbal use, comes to the fore and mimes the conceptual independence Benveniste calls absurd: they seem to indicate the eidetic bearing (here, now) of the "vacuum or receptacle for anything and everything" (I) toward the world on which it doubles back (this). Though this may be linguistic nonsense, it is a nonsense latent in spoken deixis, and at the front of written deixis not circumscribed by the conventions of reading.

Whitman frequently denies us the ability to avoid this nonsense because it allows some sense of his representative man, the second "I" that speaks in his poems: on the one hand, it is intimate, because the deictics beckon with the close hug of two persons sharing a time and a place and appropriating the whole of the language for their purposes; on the other hand, it is forbidding, because the intimacy turns out to be placeless, time-less, abysmal. The common ground is no ground: "Afar down I see the huge first Nothing." The common ground is not a plain, but a "fissure in a cliff," "a profound cleft," a fissure in spoken being that "inspires terror," a vacancy where Earth speaks.

The writing in a book cancels:

> Come closer to me,
> Push close my lovers and take the best I possess,
> Yield closer and closer and give me the best
>   you possess.
> This is unfinished business with me . . . how
>   is it with you?
> I was chilled with the cold types and cylinder
>   and wet paper between us.
>
> [*LG,* p. 628]

And it preserves, too:

> Or if you will, thrusting me beneath your
>   clothing,
> Where I may feel the throbs of your heart or
>   rest upon your hip,
> Carry me when you go forth over land or sea;
> For thus merely touching you is enough, is best,
> And thus touching you would I silently sleep
>   and be carried eternally.
>
> [*LG,* p. 116]

In the first of these passages, "I" is the particular compact man, Walt Whitman, mindful that writer and reader do not share the intimate "instance of discourse" that can be verified by touch; in the second, "I" is the book speaking, the burial turf of no-longer-live intention, a sublation of the man into personalized anonymity, like the speaking Earth. Impossibly, the printed volume *Leaves of Grass* is said to identify itself and to love the throbs from the person carrying it, as the leaves of grass in section six of **"Song of Myself"** are said to be the "uttering tongues" of those fertilizing corpses buried beneath them. This, like the objectively independent "I," is non-sense, or, better, a planned catachresis meant to upset the reader's settled comfort with conventional notions of a universally representative man.

V

Beginning with the first lines of **"Song of Myself,"** Whitman is constantly attentive to and curious about what his reader must be thinking, as if they were both alive at once and could talk it out. He is eager not to impose a truth or a point of view so much as to elicit a response. Though in those lines he writes that "what I assume you shall assume," he later writes that "he most honors my style who learns under it to destroy the teacher" (*LG,* p. 84). Though he frequently lectures, the object of such bombast is not indoctrination: rather, it is to provoke the reader to quick thought, to being a partner in agile conversation, to "wrestle" with the teacher. To do this, Whitman assaulted the conventions of sense, rectitude, and reading, whether by outraging, offending, seducing, or confusing the reader. His subversion of the conventions that usually circumscribe written deixis is one example of this attempt to upset readerly passivity. Encountering a text that makes a common place and time one of its first premises at the same time that it adamantly emphasizes the impossibility of a common place and time between author and reader, the reader is unable to simply receive. He finds himself in contradictory modes of being toward the poet, and so, like a traveler on a Moebius strip, always finds himself on the reverse side of where he was the last time he was there. Instead, then, of simply receiving, he must either be puzzled or willfully overlook some large part of the poem's push.

By undergoing such puzzlement, the reader is at once abstracted from the particular time and place that seemed to be what Bertrand Russell called the "sharp point" of his "essential privacy,"[15] and apprised of what large nonsense transtemporal and transspatial identity would be. He is deflected from both particularity and generality: he is made conscious both of his own prior "partiality" and of the complexity of the representativeness that, for instance, Daniel Webster so questionably claimed for himself when he announced that he spoke not "as a Massachusetts man, not as a Northern man, but as an American" when declaring his opposition to the Wilmot Proviso in 1850. Webster's declaration reveals that the kind of transcendental egotism explored in *Leaves of Grass* was present, in simple form, in popular American political thought. The opposition between partial, particular interest and general, magnanimous representativeness that is explored in *Leaves of Grass* is the central characteristic of the worsening ideological fracture that led, for example, to Robert E. Lee's famous agonized indecision about whether he should think of himself as a Virginian or as an American. This ideological *agon* is not the invention of Emerson, Thoreau, and Whitman in their meditations on partiality and representativeness: rather, these are abstract renderings of the dilemma convulsing American ideology that transpose or deflect it into a wider frame where its apparent simplicity is dispelled. This is why arguments over whether Whitman did or did not mean for us to take his idea of a poetic president seriously miss the point: his aim in dwelling on partiality and representativeness is to reveal the complexity of an idea present in common thought and to dispel the illusion of simple and merely political choice. The idea of a poetic president implicates a political idea in questions of sex, death, pathos, and identity, all lowest common denominators in a kind of universal politics.

Rather than presenting the reader with propositions that elicit assent, then, Whitman aims at an irresistibly unsettling posing of the problem that will compel an agile, imaginative disposition rather than the complacency of simple opinion:

> A great poem is no finish to a man or woman but rather a beginning. Has anyone fancied he could sit at last under some due authority and rest satisfied with explanations and realize and be content and full? To no such terminus does the great poet bring . . . he brings neither cessation or sheltered fatness and ease. [*LG,* p. 727]

Whitman does not accept the common rendering of the opposition between partiality and representativeness. He "translates" the problem into a new rendering—the wider frame—and leaves us unable to detect a clear and soothing stance. The intent behind widening the question of general representativeness is less to present a general representative than it is, finally, to bring into view the assumptions about general representativeness that are commonly left unexamined; the proposition of a poetic president is made less for its truth than for the expansion of free reflection it will eventually instigate in the confused reader.

This is most clear in Whitman's 1856 poem **"Respondez."** Here, as the title suggests, Whitman demands that the "you" addressed at the beginning of **"Song of Myself"** take up its part and respond. To this end, every sentence in this curious poem is in the imperative mode, like the title, taking the general form "Let X happen." This is a curious sort of imperative because it commands inactivity. Because all of its imperatives take the form "Let X happen" rather than "Do Y," the reader may surmise that the poem is a sarcastic satire of his passivity. The poem depicts the results of neglect, or of a populace that fails to vigorously *respond.* And it does so without any direct use of propositions that could be judged true or false: imperative statements such as "Close the door!" do not assert, and hence do not lie. The poem is entirely performative; none of it is constative.[16]

But imperative statements do imply collateral assertions. "Close the door!" may imply "The hall is noisy," "The noise interferes with our conversation," et cetera. Usually, an implied constative stance can be derived from imperative statements. But not for this poem: the assertions implied in Whitman's imperatives refuse to be brought to the bar of consistency. Some of the recommendations accord with what we expect from Whitman:

> Let the cow, the horse, the camel, the
>   garden-bee—let the mud-fish, the lobster,

the mussel, the eel, the sting-ray, and the grunting pig-fish—let these, and the like of these, be put on a perfect equality with man and woman!

> [*LG,* p. 592]

But, though this proposition resembles some opinions expressed in, for instance, **"Song of Myself,"** the inclusion of the grotesque beasts makes it somehow strange, like this command:

> Let us all, without missing one, be exposed in public, naked, monthly at the peril of our lives! let our bodies be freely handled and examined by whoever chooses!

> [*LG,* p. 592]

Most of the imperatives seem opposed to what might be called familiar Whitman dogma:

> Let a man seek pleasure everywhere except in himself!
> Let a woman seek happiness everywhere except in herself!

> [*LG,* p. 594]

Others seem completely undecidable:

> Let the reformers descend from the stands where they are forever bawling! let an idiot or insane person appear on each of the stands!

> [*LG,* p. 593]

Or:

> Let the she-harlots and he-harlots be prudent! let them dance on, while seeming lasts! (O seeming! seeming! seeming!)

> [*LG,* p. 593]

The speaker is delirious. Any attempt to sort out the straightforward from the ironic, to interpret toward a coherent stance, will fail. Hermeneutic rendering is impossible when confronted by such dislocation: "Play up there! the fit is whirling me fast" (*LG,* p. 426). We cannot simply receive, and then assent to or reject, such a poem.

The poem thus satirizes the reader's usual passivity. It is a refusal to take a coherent stance, it puzzles, it demands an outraged response: "let him who is without my poems be assassinated!" (*LG,* p. 592). This is the most explicit development of Whitman's desire to write a poem that would not bring the reader to a "terminus." The "I" that makes these propositions is certainly a general representative of American humanity, insofar as every reader should be able to find at least one proposition to approve. But the poem's large effect is to complicate and confuse the reader's loyalty to any particular stance (including the one he may have identified as Whitman's) without providing a general substitute position with the coherence that could elicit assent and found consensus. The poem is irreducibly heterotopic. Thus, like the written "I" not clothed by the conventions of reading, **"Respondez"** aims to expel the reader from the settled complacency of partial self-protective particularity (**"Out of the Cradle Endlessly Rocking"**) without providing an abstract and facile substitute such as Daniel Webster's "I Am an American."

The original title of the poem was "Poem of the Propositions of Nakedness," but very few of the propositions are actually concerned with being without clothes. "Nakedness," then, would have to be the reader's unsheltered state:

> O hotcheeked and blushing! O foolish hectic!
> O for pity's sake, no one must see me now!
>   . . . my clothes were stolen while I was
>   abed,
> Now I am thrust forth, where shall I run?
>   [*LG,* p. 626]

VI

In the 1830s and 1840s, Daniel Webster, realizing that the Federalist party could no longer provide a viable base for power, became the spokesman for union, for Americanness free of particular interest. In repudiating Calhoun's doctrine of nullification, he was also implicitly repudiating his own earlier interest in the New England particularism expressed at the Hartford convention. His later opposition to the Wilmot Proviso and his support for the Fugitive Slave Law revealed that his representative Americanness precluded him from taking any particular stance when particular stances seemed to be the only possible ones. His oversight of social questions that would not be ignored seemed to be the only other option for general representativeness beside the noncommittal uncertainty of, for example, William Henry Harrison, who died before trial. Any student of antebellum politics will have come to the conclusion that the political parties of the time were devoid of ideological coherence so that the idea of a representative American transcending party was doubly problematic, complicated by muddy factors such as the vehement anti-Masonic vote.

Before 1850, Carlyle and Emerson had lauded Webster as an instance of the kind of elemental, charismatic hero they felt divided times demanded. This accounts for Emerson's vehement sense of betrayal after Webster supported the Fugitive Slave Law. It showed him how liable his idea of general representativeness was to guile when it was developed in the political sphere, and it may have contributed to trepidations already present in "Politics" and the repudiation of political charisma in "Demonism."

In its political context, then, the transcendentalist idea of a representative man was controversial. Whitman's political awareness developed during the period when the eminence of the early presidents—Washington, Adams, Jefferson, Madison, Monroe, Quincy Adams, Jackson, even Van Buren—was collapsing, leaving puerile successors—Harrison, Tyler, Polk, Taylor, Fillmore, Pierce. The idea of general representativeness was being publicly bowdlerized every four years, and the idea of consensus was being conspicuously cheapened. Whitman concluded he had to lift general representation from political idea to poetical image, exploring deeper coherences and fusions. To do this, he extended the idea of divisive particularity past class and region to its extremity—self-interested and selfprotective individuality—and he extended the idea of general representativeness to its extremity, an "I" that impersonally receives and knows the entirety of being. He took the opposition that was the usual stuff of political rhetoric and resituated it in an imagistic, associative frame where implications are vaster and simple choices are impertinent.

So, five years after Webster claimed to speak "not as a Massachusetts man, not as a Northern man, but as an American," Whitman made an apparently similar claim:

> I am of old and young, of the foolish as much
>   as the wise,
> Regardless of others, ever regardful of others,
> Maternal as well as paternal, a child as well
>   as a man,
> Stuffed with the stuff that is coarse, and
>   stuffed with the stuff that is fine,
> One of the great nations, the nation of many
>   nations—the smallest the same and the
>   largest the same,
> A southerner as soon as a northerner, a planter
>   nonchalant and hospitable,
> A Yankee bound my own way . . . ready for
>   trade . . . my joints the limberest joints on
>   earth and the sternest joints on earth. . . .
>   [*LG,* p. 44]

Whitman's claim resembles Webster's, but is vastly more extensive, stretching what "I" includes so that the personal coherence that "I" connotes seems impossible. Here America says "I": "I am . . . the nation of many nations." Whitman takes Webster's apparently credible claim and stretches it to extremity, implying that such a large objective "I" would have to have surpassed and cancelled the usual identity of personality.

If we see this passage as an exposition of the problem latent in the common idea of general representativeness, rather than as a proposition meant to elicit assent, as a text meant to make us aware that a devastating cancellation of familiar personality would have to lie between the particular and the general "I," we will see the difference between Webster's and Whitman's stances. General representativeness is not opposed or refuted here. Instead, it is made into an image rather than a proposition: as such, it has the power that Gaston Bachelard contends is generally proper to images;[17] it is less a member of an existing structure of thought than it is a fresh vantage on that structure as a whole. Rather than wondering whether Webster or Harrison *is* a general representative, Whitman compels us to probe and contemplate general representativeness itself, and to extricate ourselves from the merely political and facile rendering of democratic humanism. We think about the idea rather than accepting the idea and thinking about specific candidates. Whitman's proposition in this passage—and wherever he proposes the completely inclusive and transcendental poetic president—*is* hyperbolic and outrageous; but the outrageousness of such propositions, which have often been the locus of objections to Whitman's thought, is their motive. The written "I" that is broken out of specific speakers, the delirious "I" implicit in **"Respondez,"** the Earth or America saying "I" as in the passage above—all of these are preposterous assertions of what can amass itself into consensus and then represent itself. But their preposterousness is explicit, unlike Webster's, and, as images, they propose the impossible cosmicity that is latent though unacknowledged in American political rhetoric.

In **"Starting from Paumonok,"** Whitman promises to "make a song for the ears of the president, full of weapons with menacing points." His image seems to be borrowed from Hamlet's desire to expose the corruption underlying Claudius's attempt to consolidate the kingdom under the sun of faked disinterestedness. Whitman's second "I" is such a dagger because it shows how large, transcendent, and cruelly impersonal and innocent a genuinely inclusive "I" would have to be.

VII

In *Leaves of Grass* the opposition between disinterested generality and particular self-interest is taken from being an assumption in popular thought and made into something to be thought about. Hence, we should not follow the opposition by assuming that Whitman's point in problematizing claims to representativeness is to encourage a relapse into the self-satisfaction of either the "planter nonchalant" or the "Yankee bound [his] own way." Whitman would approve of Sherwood Anderson's celebration of the small man's selfinsistence; still, he would conclude that this particularity, like huge representativeness, is unsatisfactory in itself. As the huge claims of the second "I" that speaks in *Leaves of Grass* complicate acquiescence in representativeness, so the terrified resistance to harsh wonder expressed by the speaking

personae of the crisis poems complicates easy identification with the first "I." The second "I" includes so much it no longer seems the personal self-designation of a possible man: the first "I" is convincingly possible, but it includes too little wonder, and warps what it does include to its purposes. Our sense of the humanly possible, based on the first "I," leaves us incredulous toward the second; our sense of the wondrous and diverse, based on the second "I," leaves us dissatisfied with the first.

Neither of the two "I's" that speak in *Leaves of Grass* is left unperturbed by the other. This is why Whitman's great poems, as I have argued above, are crisis poems that concern themselves with being between these possibilities, in what Heidegger calls "the time of the double-Not," the "no-more of the gods that were and the not-yet of the god that will be."[18] The great poems are dynamic fields in which the two "I's" are simultaneously extant, at the instant of violent parturition that hurts both the mother-self and the infant-self. Always already expelled from the Eden of safe and settled legitimacy, the released "I" never reaches the India it tends toward. It remains naked, unclothed by either self-centered particularity or representative inclusion, always a traveler let out of the bias of home, heading in a direction but not arriving, meanwhile curious about the actual glory of "elder, mullein, poke-weed," and the thousand other surrounding things suddenly available to catastrophically freed attention. The word *I* in *Leaves of Grass* is the self-designation of two entities, one a single member of the wide spectrum of American possibility, the other a reverse prism that, after such single members have painfully resigned their warped centrality, collects them and emits the plain friendly light of day: "He judges not as the judge judges but as the sun falling around a helpless thing" (*LG*, p. 713). What we call "Whitman" is always both the blessing sun and one of the naked, helpless things it blesses.

Notes

[1] This point is made by Olive W. Parsons in "Whitman the Non-Hegelian," *PMLA* 58 (December 1943): 1073-93. Parsons contends that, though Whitman refers to Hegel in *Democratic Vistas* and elsewhere, he is not really a "Hegelian" because he does not share Hegel's use of cold analysis. I think she is correct, but her point is limited: Whitman could be called a "non-Hegelian" in the same way that Marx, Nietzsche, and Kierkegaard might be called "non-Hegelians." The comparison, in other words, is extremely useful, despite Parsons's well-argued assertions.

[2] Walt Whitman, *Leaves of Grass: Comprehensive Reader's Edition,* ed. Harold W. Blodgett and Sculley Bradley (New York: New York University Press, 1965) p. 337. Hereafter, all quotations from Whitman will be

from this edition and will be cited as *LG* in the text. The reader should notice that I have for the most part confined myself to quotations from the first two editions of *Leaves of Grass:* my sense is that during the 1870s and after, Whitman rid his poetry of some of the complexity I describe in this essay. But that is beyond the present scope.

[3] See Hayden White, *Metahistory: The Historical Imagination in Nineteenth-Century Europe* (Baltimore, Md.: Johns Hopkins University Press, 1973), pp. 81-133.

[4] Justin Kaplan, *Walt Whitman: A Life* (New York: Simon and Schuster, 1980), p. 66.

[5] Sacvan Bercovitch, *The American Jeremiad* (Madison, Wis.: University of Wisconsin Press, 1978).

[6] Ibid., p. 203.

[7] William James, "On a Certain Blindness in Human Beings," in *Essays on Faith and Morals* (New York: Longmans, Green and Co., 1949), p. 259.

[8] Ibid., p. 272.

[9] Georg Wilhelm Friedrich Hegel, *Logic,* trans. William Wallace (London: Oxford University Press, 1975), p. 38.

[10] Emile Benveniste, *Problems in General Linguistics* (Coral Gables, Fla.: University of Miami Press, 1971), pp. 218 and 220.

[11] Ibid., p. 218.

[12] Ibid., p. 220.

[13] Ibid., p. 219.

[14] Lucretius, *On the Nature of the Universe* (New York: Penguin Books, 1951), p. 131.

[15] Bertrand Russell, "Egocentric Particulars," in *Human Knowledge: Its Scope and Limits* (New York: Simon and Schuster, 1948), p. 90.

[16] See J. L. Austin, *How to Do Things with Words* (Cambridge, Mass.: Harvard University Press, 1975).

[17] See Gaston Bachelard, "Introduction," *The Poetics of Space* (Boston: Beacon Press, 1969), pp. xi-xxxv and 51.

[18] Martin Heidegger, "Hölderlin and the Essence of Poetry," in *Existence and Being,* trans. Douglas Scott (Chicago: Henry Regnery Company, 1949), p. 289.

David Kuebrich (essay date 1989)

SOURCE: "Reconsidering Whitman's Intention," in *Minor Prophecy: Walt Whitman's New American Religion,* Indiana University Press, 1989, pp. 1-11.

[*In the following essay, Kuebrich contends that Whitman intended his poetry to be, in a sense, a "new religion," in that he hoped to encourage the spiritual growth of his readers and offer a vision which would fuse religious experience with contemporary views on science, technology, and the emerging American republic.*]

"A little group are to signalize here on the prairies by the Wabash, the day that gave us the most divine of men."[1] This statement would not be noteworthy as a Christian's declaration of his plans to commemorate the birth of Christ. It is remarkable, however, because its author was not a Christian but a Whitmanite, the day referred to is not December 25 but May 31, and the "most divine of men" is not Christ but Walt Whitman.

Harvard professor Bliss Perry helped establish Whitman's reputation among academic critics by declaring that no American poet seems "more sure to be read, by the fit persons, after one hundred or five hundred years."[2] Horace Traubel, Whitman's close friend and the biographer of his last years, penned a scorching rebuttal. Reviewing Perry's book, he charged that the professor from Cambridge failed to realize that **Leaves of Grass** was "valuable for its religious rather than its esthetic inspiration"; and he condemned Perry's critical weighing of the respective merits of Keats and Whitman: "You might just as well set off Shake-speare against the Bhagavad Gita."[3]

A book that Traubel would have found more to his liking was Will Hayes's extended analogy of Whitman and Christ, *Walt Whitman: The Prophet of the New Era.*[4] The chapter titles indicate how the comparison informs the study; the first is "The Christ of Our Age" and others include "The Carpenter of Brooklyn," "A Friend of Publicans and Sinners," and "The Least of These My Brethren."

These items remind us that many of Whitman's earliest readers and critics hailed him as a religious prophet. For them, the **Leaves** was more than literary art; it was sacred scripture. These disciples created a loose confederation of groups, The Walt Whitman Fellowship: International, committed to the dissemination of the new religion of **Leaves of Grass.** Chapters were established, among other places, in New York, Philadelphia, Boston, Chicago, Atlanta, Knoxville, Toronto, and Bolton, England. But the Whitman cult was never large and in the 1920s it disappeared. The chief disciples had died and their places were taken by more academically oriented scholars. Religious enthusiasm had gradually given way to the more detached perspective of the professional critic.

Today's scholarship, looking back upon the enthusiasts, credits them with providing important biographical materials and with pioneering the effort to collect Whitman's prose and poetry in the ten-volume *Complete Writings* of 1902. However, the disciples' assessment of Whitman is judged naïve or inane, if not insane. Perry dismissed the disciples as "hot little prophets," and both the label and the judgment have endured. In the view of Charles R. Willard, the historian of Whitman's American reputation, the demise of the enthusiasts took the critical discussion out of the hands of rather peculiar individuals and established it on "the plane of sane and traditional literary criticism."[5] More recently, Gay Wilson Allen has asserted that although not all of the disciples were "crackpots," nevertheless they were most likely to be "emotionally unstable, of uncertain sexual psychology, or subliterary minds who applied too literally Whitman's injunctions against literary conventions."[6]

But it seems to me that these early Whitmanites deserve a more sympathetic evaluation. Certainly they made their mistakes. They overvalued Whitman in likening him to such major religious founders as Christ or the Buddha. A more serious shortcoming was their method of proclamation. Their writings, often poignantly confessional and always insistently hagiographic, were insufficiently exegetical. Yet of all Whitman's critics, it is these early enthusiasts who have most clearly perceived the nature and purpose of the poet's labors. Whitman did want to begin a new religion. He wanted his poetry to serve two functions: to promote the spiritual development of his readers and to provide them with a coherent vision which would integrate their religious experience with the dominant modes of modern thought and action—science, technology, and democracy. It was these aspects of Whitman's effort that attracted his early followers. "For me the reading of his poems is truly a new birth of the soul," testified Anne Gilchrist, widow of the Blake biographer Alexander Gilchrist.[7] University of Chicago professor Oscar Lovell Triggs found in *Leaves of Grass* "a new and modernized theology"; it was "the one book of considerable importance . . . that breaks utterly with feudal forms and assumes the processes of democracy, and that is at the same time intentionally religious in basic purpose."[8] And it was Whitman's vision, declared the English scholar John Addington Symonds, that enabled him "to comprehend the harmony between the democratic spirit, science, and that larger religion to which the modern world is being led."[9]

In the process of saving Whitman from the adulation of the early disciples, academic criticism lost sight of the prophetic purpose that constitutes the heart of Whitman's lifelong poetic effort. Rejecting the notion that Whitman's poetry is to be understood as an at-

tempt to create a new religion, modern criticism has developed three (sometimes overlapping) views toward the issue of Whitman's spirituality. One approach, which is most clearly present in the psychoanalytic studies of Whitman, assumes that an author's religious language is really something other: namely, the symbolic manifestation of the distorted desires of the id. Consequently, this criticism denies that there is any important religious dimension in the *Leaves*.[10] Another, which might be termed the "phases" approach, views Whitman's assertion of a fundamental religious purpose and prophetic self-image as the fabrication and posturing of an older, chastened, and complacent poet. This body of criticism, which now dominates Whitman studies, asserts that in the late 1850s Whitman underwent a personal crisis, precipitated by a homosexual affair, which radically altered the tone and content of *Leaves.* Whitman affirmed the emotional liberation and reality of his new sexual identity; but at the same time this new self-understanding forced him to reexamine the Transcendental faith in a unified cosmos, spiritual correspondences, and immortality that was present in his earlier poetry. In the process, the former buoyant optimism gave way to metaphysical doubting and a tragic melancholy which characterizes the poetry of the second stage (lasting from approximately 1859 to 1868). Then in the third and final stage, bowing to the emotional legacy of the war years, physical infirmity, a decline in genius, and a wider public acceptance, an older and more conventional Whitman set about writing new poems and revising the *Leaves.* He deleted some poems, altered others, and rearranged the overall order in an effort to obscure what he now perceived to be the waywardness of his middle years. It was only this later Whitman that tried, in hindsight, to invest his poetry with a religious purpose and to adopt the posture of a prophet of a new democratic faith. The task of the critic became one of saving the genuine Whitman from this later inauthentic poet-prophet and the scholarship that had assisted in perpetuating this image of the poet.[11] The third approach to Whitman acknowledges the presence of a religious theme in the various editions but unwittingly misinterprets it in two important respects. It distorts the character of Whitman's spirituality by treating it as a set of intellectual convictions rather than a special transhistorical mode of consciousness that gives rise to certain recurring religious values and beliefs; it also depreciates the importance of Whitman's religious faith by presenting it as just one of several themes in the *Leaves* rather than seeing it as constituting an emotional substratum that pervades and integrates the various themes into a unified symbolic vision.[12]

My purpose is to engage in a scholarly quarrel with these current views of Whitman and to propose a revisionist interpretation, one that tries to resurrect the earlier prophetic reading of Whitman's intention and to establish it at the center of Whitman studies. But to do this a new approach must be adopted which enables the critic to make a close analysis of Whitman's spirituality. In the present study, I have attempted to do this in three complementary ways. First, I have turned to existing phenomenological studies of religion for initial working definitions of certain key elements of Whitman's religion, for example, his notion of the soul, the basic structure of his religious cosmology, and his theory of religious symbolism. I have also employed a phenomenological approach, as a supplement to a traditional close reading of the text, to interpret what might be termed the epiphanic passages in some of Whitman's major poems because I believe that it is only by analyzing the religious experience underlying these passages that we can understand the poems themselves and see how they are informed by the poet's larger vision. Second, I have tried to relate Whitman's poetry to several currents of religious and political thought in antebellum culture which provided the basis of, and early inspiration for, his belief in a future religious democracy. Finally, rather than viewing the *Leaves* as an anthology of discrete poems or clusters of poems, I feel that the individual poems must be seen as the parts of a coherent religious myth. Perhaps Whitman's new religion was never articulated to the complete satisfaction of either himself or his readers. Nevertheless Whitman did arrive at a unified religious vision during the process of writing the first edition of the *Leaves,* and he continued to elaborate that vision throughout the rest of his life. The individual poems and sections of the *Leaves* are informed by this new religion and they cannot be considered in isolation.

Let me begin to discuss my use of the phenomenology of religion by distinguishing between several stages of religious activity. The primary level is the perception of the sacred in nature and history and the externalization of these experiences in religious symbols. At a secondary level is theology, or the systematic reflection upon the symbols of a particular religious tradition, which gives rise to creeds, doctrines, and moral codes. In addition, there are also the activities of religious institutions which attempt, by means of liturgy and instruction, to preserve and disseminate the experiences and ideas of the first two levels. Whitman was not concerned with—in fact, he was distrustful of—ritual and ecclesiastical institutions, and while his poetry does have moral and theological dimensions, these are subordinate elements. The *Leaves* deals mainly with the primary level of religion; accordingly, the interpreter must begin by investigating the nature and forms of Whitman's religious experience.

In analyzing the experiential dimension of Whitman's spirituality, his natural experience and spiritual beliefs should be viewed as a continuum rather than a dichotomy. For the mystic or profoundly religious personality insists, and Whitman strives to make fresh demonstration of this fact that spiritual experience comes not from avoiding this world but rather through

engaging it more fully. Whitman felt that the natural, if fully experienced, gave off intimations of the supernatural. Practically speaking, this means that a poem in the *Leaves* that seems merely to depict an encounter with nature (e.g., with the sun or stars) or a fellow human (e.g., the love relationships in **"Calamus"**) may be pregnant with religious meaning. Therefore, the interpreter's task is a demanding one: to discern and explain those processes of consciousness whereby Whitman's sensory experience affected deeper layers of his psyche, subtly instilling a sense of supernatural realities. The critic must also disclose the nature and meanings of the various symbols Whitman used to express his spiritual insights and show how he attempted to organize his symbols into a rationally consistent and coherent vision. In short, the interpreter must elucidate Whitman's mental universe. When faced with this difficult undertaking, it is helpful to draw upon the scholarship and methodology of phenomenologists of religion.[13]

One reason for this arises from the novelty of Whitman's world view. In attempting to create a post-Christian myth, Whitman rejected the inherited religious vocabulary. When he does give expression to forms of religious experience that are present in Christianity, as he often does, he clothes them in new symbols and transforms them by adapting them to modern thought. The *Leaves,* with its emphasis upon the religious significance of nature, includes modes of religious experience and expression not present in the Judaeo-Christian tradition, like terrestrial or astral symbolism, which a critic only familiar with Western religion can easily misconstrue or even overlook altogether. One way to develop a broader understanding of religion is through the study of existing phenomenological descriptions of forms of religious experience that occur in other religious traditions. Obviously if the author studied is a Romantic poet like Whitman, it is especially important to be sensitive to the nature of religious symbolism and the essential meanings that various segments of nature have had in humankind's religious history. These descriptions can help the critic recognize and interpret these forms of religious experience when they appear in the *Leaves.*

A second reason for using this scholarship results from Whitman's distinctive method. In 1941, F. O. Matthiessen lamented the lack of an "adequately detailed scrutiny" of even such a major poem as **"When Lilacs Last in the Dooryard Bloom'd."**[14] Matthiessen himself never provided this close analysis of Whitman's achievement; and in the succeeding decades, although the *Leaves* has received more intensive scrutiny, it has continued to prove itself strangely resistant to a close reading. This resistance derives from the large contribution which the *Leaves* expects from the reader. Whitman devised a method in which he intentionally did not give full expression to many of his ideas. Instead he provided only "hints" or "suggestions" (the terms are his), and along with these he made existential demands upon the reader which were to lead to the full realization of what was merely hinted at in the text. This existential element in Whitman's poetic is one of the major reasons he considered the *Leaves* a new experiment in poetry, and the result is that the interpreter is left in a pretty fix. She or he finds that a close analysis of the language is insufficient; one must also somehow bring to the text those meanings which the poet intended but did not express. Phenomenological scholarship can provide some of these meanings, for it rather fully describes many recurring elements of religious life which Whitman merely suggests. Consequently, these descriptions can frequently be used to supplement the interpreter's understanding of the text.[15]

While the major tradition in Whitman studies has repudiated the idea that Whitman wished to limn a myth for a new spiritual era, a small group of critics, notably Malcolm Cowley, James E. Miller, Jr., Thomas Crawley, and more recently George Hutchinson, have emphasized Whitman's spirituality and prophetic intentions. But for the most part these studies have been hampered by too narrow a notion of religion and also by speaking of religion as if it occurred in a historical vacuum. For instance, Malcolm Cowley, in his often cited essay on the mysticism in "Song of Myself," declares that the poem is "hardly at all concerned with American nationalism, political democracy, contemporary progress or other social themes"; and he further de-Americanizes Whitman with the subsequent assertion that most of his doctrines "belong to the mainstream of Indian philosophy."[16] With the introduction of the study of American literature into Indian universities, this judgment has received still further development, finding its best expression in V. K. Chari's *Whitman in the Light of Vedantic Mysticism.*[17] Cowley and Chari are correct in their observation that the *Leaves* and Vedantism both utilize a dynamic of knowing which gives the subject a sense of participating in a more real spiritual order and consequently leads him or her to hold the material world to be less real or illusory. But what both scholars present as a unique parallel is actually a fundamental pattern of religious experience, one found not only in the *Leaves* and Vedantism but also in Christianity and many other religions. Whitman was a mystic who gave expression to modes of experience which, in their essential forms, are transhistorical and therefore have parallels in other traditions, but he was also an antebellum American who subscribed to contemporary ideas about science, religion, and literature and their role in the developing American republic—and these ideas find expression in his poetry.

There is also an implicit ahistoricism in Miller and Crawley which stems in part from an earlier formalistic style of criticism which deemphasized the work's historical context and in part from their ahistorical use of ideal models for interpreting Whitman's religion (Underhill's stages of Christian mysticism and the biblical Christ-figure respectively).[18] Neither of these studies attempted to relate Whitman's spirituality to mid-nineteenth-century American culture. Benefiting from the interdisciplinary and historical nature of current literary studies, Hutchinson employs a much more sophisticated hermeneutic, aptly drawing upon current anthropological and historical-phenomenological studies for an understanding of the nature and function of religion. While accepting the notion of transhistorical or ideal forms of religious experience, Hutchinson is careful to insist that these are always historically conditioned. However, Hutchinson's study is insufficiently historical, ignoring, for instance, the influence of such major historical currents as science and evolutionary thought on Whitman's spirituality; as a consequence, he distorts Whitman by exaggerating his similarities with the shaman of archaic and traditional cultures.[19]

Three bodies of thought are especially important for an understanding of Whitman's spirituality and its relation to contemporary American culture. The first of these, which might be termed the Romantic religious world view (which includes but is not limited to American Transcendentalism), provided Whitman with a poetic and a basic religious cosmology. The second, the newly developing evolutionary thought in geology, astronomy, and biology, not only gave Whitman a process understanding of the natural world but also inspired him to make new formulations of divine immanence and human immortality. Third are the closely paired doctrines of perfectionism and millennialism that in some manner or another, ranging from scholarly theological treatises to more popular expression in the writings of reformers, communitarians and practitioners of various forms of medical and spiritual pseudo-sciences, permeated mid-nineteenth-century American culture and provided the source of Whitman's particular versions of these beliefs: his call for a new superior race of Americans and his dream of a future religious democracy. There are, of course, numerous helpful discussions of Whitman's debts to Emerson, evolutionary science, and the liberal political ideas of his day. I have not tried to trace over these well-charted paths but rather to call attention to the largely overlooked but crucial influence of antebellum Evangelical ideas and some of their more popular derivatives. This sheds new light upon Whitman's use of Emerson and other sources. Furthermore, it provides a better understanding of certain important religious themes in Whitman's poetry and helps to disclose the fundamental structure and unity of his vision.

"No one can know *Leaves of Grass* who judges it piecemeal," Whitman warned (*Camden,* II, 116). He asserted that his poems constituted a "totality" or "ensemble" or "massings" and claimed that they possessed a controlling "atmosphere" or an "orbic" quality.[20] But these words are not very illuminating; furthermore the Whitman scholar learns that unfortunately one cannot always take the poet's word as gospel. Yet Whitman so insistently cautions that his poetry must be read as a whole that these warnings cannot be ignored as yet another example of the "good gray poet's" annoying capacity for the sustained, artful fib. Rather Whitman's search for appropriate terms to suggest the unity of the *Leaves,* along with the novelty of the poems themselves, points to the need to develop an interpretive method that corresponds to the uniqueness of Whitman's text. As Gay Wilson Allen has stated: "The great [unresolved] problem in interpreting the poems . . . is to find a suitable context, some pattern of ideas, philosophy, religion, or psychology in which such terms as 'self,' 'soul,' 'spirit,' 'identity,' 'sex,' 'death,' etc., have interrelated meaning."[21]

Foiled in their efforts to find such a context, most critics have concluded that none exists. For instance, Hyatt H. Waggoner has recently asserted that Whitman's themes are "raw, crude, impure . . . impossible to fit into any coherent system of thought."[22] In a longer and more nuanced discussion of this issue, Roger Asselineau argued that Whitman began with "no idea of the way in which he was to organize this rich material [the themes of the *Leaves*] and compose his book" and that any order "found in the later additions was imposed from the outside; it represents an intervention posterior to the act of creation."[23]

Asselineau is certainly correct in rejecting the claims of Whitman's disciples—claims inspired by Whitman himself—that the *Leaves* has a perfect structural unity, having been planned as carefully as a grand cathedral with each poem "designed and written with reference to its place in an ideal edifice."[24] But Asselineau moves too far in the counter direction, exaggerating the disunity of the *Leaves.* Whitman did begin with a unifying principle and the *Leaves,* from first edition to last, is informed by a coherent world view. This did not provide Whitman with an architectonic structure for his constantly growing book of poems, but it did provide his poetry with intellectual coherence.

In order to disclose the unity of the vision and the relations between its themes, it is crucial, in addition to attending to Whitman's background and the structure of his religious experience, to recognize that he employs a special vocabulary of spiritual terms and symbols to express the intricacies of his spiritual vision. In making this point I am not referring to Whitman's penchant for neologism but to the much more important fact that Whitman subtly invests what seems to be ordinary language with a level of mystical meaning. Such words as "real," "new," "athletic," "touch," "love," "secret," "limitless," (and other *'-less'* words), "aroma," "tally," "whispers," "pulse," "power," "pride," "urge," "want," "yearnings"—the list could be made

much longer—have religious significance. These terms are never explicitly defined, but their meanings are learned by examining their usage throughout the *Leaves.* Similarly, Whitman consistently uses certain natural and historical facts—for example, the waters, the stars, the grass—as symbols of spiritual truths. With each usage the reader is only provided a few hints about the symbol's meaning, and to interpret the symbol it is necessary to accumulate the hints from a variety of passages.

The consistency of Whitman's vocabulary and symbolism arises from his unified vision. In the years between 1848 and 1855, as Whitman went through his metamorphosis from newspaper editor to poet-prophet, he fashioned a new religious world view which consisted of five interrelated parts: a religious cosmology, a religious psychology or theory of the soul, a program or set of existential demands for the soul's development, a millennial interpretation of history, and a coherent set of religious symbols. All of these are, in their essential structures, traditional religious elements, but Whitman modernized them by adapting them to the theories of evolutionary science and contemporary American political and religious thought. By integrating these traditional elements with modern culture, Whitman arrived at a vision in which the evolution of nature and the instinctual and emotional longings of humanity are seen as manifestations of an immanent divinity in its upward ascent toward reunion with its transcendent source, and the course of history is viewed as a movement toward the universal redemption of humankind—a divinely ordained global drama in which the United States, because of its material wealth, democratic institutions, and new Whitmanian religion, would play a decisive role for centuries to come. During the period of his poetic maturity Whitman undoubtedly changed his mind about many things, but the basic structure of his vision, the notion of a deity whose immanent nature courses its way upward through all of creation toward its transcendent source, remained constant.

By not paying sufficient attention to Whitman's religious experience and language, scholarship has failed to perceive how the individual poems combine to elaborate a coherent religious vision. And the practice of analyzing the poems independently of one another as if they were not parts of a larger system but only units in an anthology has compounded that initial error. This has frequently led to interpretations that seriously distort Whitman's intention.

In analyzing the *Leaves,* I have used the final edition, complying with Whitman's own judgment that this was his preferred and authorized text. My purpose is to disclose the unified world view that informs the poetry as Whitman bequeathed it to posterity, but at the same time to show, because it is crucial to an understanding of both the poetry and Whitman's conception of his vocation, how less elaborate forms of this same vision—the same religious psychology, cosmology, and complex of millennial ideas—informed the earlier editions.[25] My examination of the evidence shows that Whitman had developed most of the principal features of his world view before 1855 and that all of them find at least rudimentary expression in the 1855 Preface and **"Song of Myself."** Whitman may or may not have weathered a crisis in the late 1850s, perhaps involving issues of a political, sexual, and vocational nature, but there is no evidence for asserting, as many critics have, that he lost his Transcendental faith and belief in personal immortality in these years. Nor is there any basis for arguing, as some critics have, that Whitman only later, in the years after the Civil War, began to conceive of himself as a religious prophet. It is true that during these later decades Whitman's poetry becomes less concrete, less sensuous, less personal, and is no longer animated by its earlier psychological tension and close engagement with the historical process. As a consequence, it loses much of its earlier vitality, the spirituality is more abstract, and the prophetic intentions more explicit. But this should be seen as a diminution of power and not as an effort to superimpose a newly conceived religious purpose upon the earlier poetry. In sum, there is a good deal more unity both in the *Leaves* and in Whitman's vocation and career than current criticism acknowledges.

The next two chapters [of *Minor Prophecy*] describe the structure of Whitman's religion: how he ordered his religious experience into an evolutionary version of a traditional religious cosmology (chapter 2), and how he integrated this process cosmology with a theology of history that incorporated two of the most pervasive religious themes of antebellum culture, millennialism and perfectionism (chapter 3). Chapter 4, on Whitman's style, elucidates the existential dimensions of his poetic and relates these to his theory and practice of symbolism. Chapters 5, 6, and 7 interpret respectively Whitman's announcement of his new faith and introduction of himself as a poet-prophet in **"Song of Myself"**; his belief in immortality in his two great poems on death, **"Out of the Cradle Endlessly Rocking"** and the **"Lilacs"** elegy; and his purposes for including two sequences of love poetry, **"Children of Adam"** and **"Calamus"** (chapter 7). The closing chapter considers Whitman's utility, assessing the extent to which his aesthetic and the poetry itself provide materials for a school of democratic literature.

Needless to say, this study does not illuminate every jot and tittle of the *Leaves.* Indeed, I argue at places that Whitman's suggestive method and intentionally ambiguous treatment of certain issues make it sometimes impossible to provide objective, fully convincing interpretations. However, if my thesis is correct that Whitman should be read as attempting to begin a modern religion, then my discussion of the structure of his vision does provide a new conceptual framework for the critical study of his poetry. My point is that Whitman's religious views are not just one theme that can be discussed in isolation and arranged alongside discussions of his other themes, for example, his treatment of politics, science, sex, and death, but that his religious ideas constitute a coherent world view that informs the other themes and integrates them with one another. Consequently, the interpreter's first task is to elucidate the structure of Whitman's vision. This in turn allows for a substantially closer reading of the individual poems and a more accurate critical portrait of the poet. The image of Whitman that finally emerges is, like that of the early enthusiasts, the figure of a prophet. But whereas theirs was a major religious founder, mine is that of a mere "would be" founder: a founder who failed in his chief ambition of creating a new religion, but in the process earned himself a lasting place in American poetry and also perhaps should be recognized, as I argue in the final chapter, as a minor prophet of a needed American civil faith.

In addition to providing a revised understanding of the *Leaves* as a religious text, I have also wanted to indicate its possible relevance to several areas of religious studies. For instance, in discussing the poet's symbolism, I have attempted to show how he adapted certain traditional religious symbols to modern culture by investing them with new elements of form and meaning. This aspect of Whitman's achievement perhaps deserves the attention of the historian of religions who is concerned to trace the changes symbols undergo as they appear in new historical contexts. Similarly, scholars in religious studies discuss the nature of myth, its feasibility in a scientific age, and the possible form it might assume. They may, therefore, be interested in Whitman's attempt to create a coherent set of symbols which would wed religion and modern science. Whitman's undertaking is also relevant to the recent interest in American civil religion. The new public faith Whitman presents for the United States rests upon a Transcendental metaphysics that is unacceptable to contemporary Americans, but perhaps there are elements of his poetic and theory of democracy that might provide both inspiration and materials for the creation of a new national vision to promote political and cultural revitalization.

After referring to my differences with the dominant scholarly view of the nature and purpose of Whitman's art, I also want to express my indebtedness to other critics. I have repeatedly drawn upon their work to enrich my understanding of Whitman's biography and poetry. Usually I have explicitly acknowledged my borrowings; where I have not, I trust they are evident to the specialists. My goal has been to make a judicious use of existing studies, combining the findings of earlier analyses with the insights offered by my religious reading in order to provide a comprehensive overview of Whitman as poet-prophet. In writing an interdisciplinary study that attempts to speak to scholars of literature and religion as well as to the interested general reader, I have encountered the unavoidable problem of writing for a diverse audience. I have tried to resolve this difficulty by giving the beginning student of Whitman or the scholar from another discipline a general introduction to Whitman and some of the central issues of Whitman scholarship.

Abbreviations

Camden: Horace L. Traubel, *With Walt Whitman in Camden.* Vol. I, Boston, 1906. Vol. II, New York, 1908. Vol. III, New York, 1914. Vol. IV, Philadelphia, 1953. Vol. V, Carbondale, Ill., 1964.

NPM: Notebooks and Unpublished Prose Manuscripts, 6 vols., ed. Edward F. Grier. *The Collected Writings of Walt Whitman.* New York, 1984.

PW: Prose Works 1892, 2 vols., ed. Floyd Stovall. *The Collected Writings of Walt Whitman.* New York, 1963 and 1964.

Workshop: Walt Whitman's Workshop, ed. Clifton Joseph Furness. Cambridge, 1928.

Unless otherwise indicated, references to Whitman's poetry are from *"Leaves of Grass": Comprehensive Reader's Edition,* ed. Harold W. Blodgett and Sculley Bradley. *The Collected Writings of Walt Whitman.* New York, 1963.

Notes

[1] J. H. Clifford, Letter, *The Conservator* 10 (July 1899), 72; as quoted in Charles B. Willard, *Whitman's American Fame,* (Providence, R.I.: Brown Univ. Press, 1950), p. 72.

[2] *Walt Whitman* (Boston: Houghton Mifflin, 1906), p. 308.

[3] *The Conservator* 18 (November 1906), 139 & 140.

[4] London: C. W. Daniel, 1921.

[5] Willard, *Whitman's American Fame,* p. 32.

[6] Gay Wilson Allen, *Walt Whitman as Man, Poet, and Legend* (Carbondale: Southern Illinois Univ. Press, 1961), pp. 107-108.

[7] "A Woman's Estimate of Walt Whitman," *In Re Walt Whitman,* ed. Richard M. Bucke et al. (Philadelphia: David McKay, 1893), p. 42.

[8] *The Changing Order* (Chicago: Charles H. Kerr, 1906), pp. 264-65.

[9] *Walt Whitman* (London: John C. Nimmo, 1893), p. 159.

[10] The three most important psychoanalytic studies are Edwin Haviland Miller, *Walt Whitman's Poetry: A Psychological Journey* (New York: Houghton Mifflin, 1968); Stephen Black, *Whitman's Journeys into Chaos* (Princeton, N.J.: Princeton University Press, 1975), and David Cavitch, *My Soul and I: The Inner Life of Walt Whitman* (Boston: Beacon Press, 1985). This criticism sees little that is religious in Whitman's personality and poetry and even less evidence of a prophet deeply engaged with his historical environment in an effort to influence the course of American culture. For example, Miller, asserting that he does not hear a "consistently prophetic voice" and that "the external world is of little importance" in Whitman's poetry, argues that the *Leaves* is essentially an inner psychological drama best understood in terms of the "brilliant insights of Freud"; not surprisingly, the product of Whitman's poetic imagination is viewed as "regressive imagery, fantasy, and [the] reactivation of infantile longings," but Whitman, nevertheless, lays claim to our attention by the "profundity" of his "intuitive insights" and his "ability to put into artistic order what remains inarticulate and formless for lesser minds and sensibilities" (pp. 3, 8, & vii-viii). Miller's study has many merits, chief among them being his use of psychoanalytic theory to speculate, often quite cogently, on the psychic roots of Whitman's mature themes and symbols and his insistence upon the importance of Whitman's sexuality to an understanding of both the production and content of his poetry. But psychoanalytic studies such as Miller's suffer from the absence in Freud of an adequate conceptual understanding of the relationship between infantile imagery and the religious personality's subsequent investment of this imagery with mature religious intentions; accordingly Whitman's religious symbols are reduced to little more than obscure expressions of libidinal longing. Also, while an approach such as Miller's rightly claims that to deny "the sexual component in art is to indulge in cultural castration" (p. 4), it is equally true that an exclusive focus on the inner life completely uproots Whitman from his cultural context.

This tendency to de-historicize and secularize Whitman is continued by Black and Cavitch. For instance, the latter's recent study begins by declaring that it takes history seriously (p. xiv), but it soon becomes clear that the interest is largely limited to Whitman's family history; Cavitch quickly shows his lack of interest in Whitman's religious experience and purposes by defining Whitman not as a religious poet but as a poet who uses traditional sacred language to express a modern secular psychology. After describing Whitman's account of a mystical experience in section 5 of "Song of Myself" (which includes lines such as "And I know that the hand of God is the promise of my own, / And I know that the spirit of God is the brother of my own. . . . "), Cavitch acknowledges that the ecstasy "resembles the holy passion of a Christian conversion or the transfiguration of a mystic." But he then goes on to argue that Whitman asserts that this experience "has an *internal* cause; and God does not do anything or play a necessary part in Whitman's explanation." Referring to "the utter naturalness of the experience," Cavitch maintains that Whitman holds "a wholly secular attitude toward the world" (p. 49).

Without denying the value of such psychoanalytic studies or the skill of the practitioners, it must still be argued that their interpretations inevitably lead to partial and distorted views of Whitman. Assuming that it is unnecessary to discover Whitman's own understanding of his religious experience because religion is really something else and ignoring Whitman's social, political, economic, and religious concerns because it is also assumed that the public world is ultimately not important to an understanding of the inner life, this criticism does not provide a picture of the complete Whitman but of the poet who is most amenable to a particular psychoanalytic methodology.

[11] In a 1932 article, Floyd Stovall provided a framework for much subsequent criticism by dividing Whitman's career into three periods: the first Whitman (1855-59) was a "sensualist," "materialist," and "egotist"; the second (1859-65) underwent the experiences of love and death and became "humble, melancholy and perplexed"; the third (1866-death) "retained and expanded" the ideas of the second and emphasized immortality and "thoughts of the spiritual side of life." According to Stovall, Whitman's spiritual interests first emerge in the second phase and only become fully pronounced in the third. Thus Whitman's claim in the 1872 Preface that the underlying principle of *Leaves of Grass* had always been religious ("one deep purpose underlay the others, and has underlain it and its execution ever since—and that has been the religious purpose") is referred to and explicitly denied: "I can find no slightest trace of a religious purpose in these early poems [of the first stage], unless the joyous and sensuous love of life may be called religious" ("Main Drifts in Whitman's Poetry," *American Literature* 4, [March 1932], 8).

In the early 1960s a group of important and frequently reprinted essays by Stephen Whicher, Roy Harvey Pearce, R. W. B. Lewis, and Clark Griffith both built upon and altered Stovall's interpretation to establish the current general conception of Whitman's development which I have stated in the text. Whicher's essay, "Whitman's Awakening to Death: Toward a Biographical Reading of 'Out of the Crade Endlessly Rocking'," was first delivered at the 1960 English Institute and was subsequently published in *Studies in Romanticism*

1 (Autumn 1961), 9-28; *The Presence of Walt Whitman,* ed. R. W. B. Lewis (New York: Columbia Univ. Press, 1962), pp. 1-27; *A Century of Whitman Criticism,* ed. Edwin Haviland Miller (Bloomington: Indiana Univ. Press, 1969), pp. 285-92; *"Out of the Cradle Endlessly Rocking",* ed. Dominick P. Consolo (Columbus, Ohio: Charles E. Merrill, 1971), pp. 85-103; *Critics on Whitman,* ed. Richard H. Rupp (Coral Gables, Fla.: Univ. of Miami Press, 1972), pp. 61-65; and *Walt Whitman: A Collection of Criticism,* ed. Arthur Golden (New York: McGraw-Hill, 1974), pp. 77-96. Pearce's article, "Whitman Justified: The Poet in 1860," was also delivered at the 1960 English Institute and subsequently appeared in *Minnesota Review* 1 (1961), 261-94; *The Presence of Walt Whitman,* pp. 72-109; and *Whitman: A Collection of Critical Essays,* ed. Roy Harvey Pearce (Englewood Cliffs, N. J.: Prentice-Hall, Inc., 1962), pp. 37-59. An altered version of the article was used as the introductory essay to *Leaves of Grass: Facsimile Edition of the 1860 Text* (Ithaca, N.Y.: Cornell Univ. Press, 1961). Lewis's essay first appeared as an introduction to Whitman in *Major Writers of America,* ed. Perry Miller (New York: Harcourt, Brace and World, 1962), vol. I, pp. 969-87; it was reprinted in Lewis, *Trials of the Word: Essays in American Literature and the Humanistic Tradition* (New Haven: Yale Univ. Press, 1965), pp. 3-35; *Major Writers of America: Shorter Edition,* ed. Perry Miller (New York: Harcourt, Brace and World, 1966), pp. 567-83; and *Walt Whitman: Modern Critical Views,* ed. Harold Bloom (New York: Chelsea House Publishers, 1985), pp. 99-125. Griffith's "Sex and Death: The Significance of Whitman's 'Calamus' Themes" appeared in *Philological Quarterly* 39 (January 1960), 18-38; and *"Out of the Cradle Endlessly Rocking,"* pp. 69-76.

While these articles are not completely consistent with one another, their combined effect was to shift the locus of critical attention from the final to the 1860 (and to a lesser extent the 1867) edition of the *Leaves,* to view the stages in Whitman's development not as an orderly, consistent progression (as Stovall had maintained) but rather as radical transformations, and to deemphasize further the religious dimensions of the *Leaves* by viewing them as emendations introduced in the final period of Whitman's career which distorted the earlier, genuine Whitman and the best poetry. For example, Pearce distinguished between the earlier "poetic" and later "prophetic" Whitmans and argued for the superiority of the 1860 *Leaves,* reading it as an archetypal biography of the Romantic poet. Noting Whitman's assertion in "A Backward Glance" of more than literary purposes ("No one will get at my verses who insists upon viewing them as a literary performance, or attempt at such performance, or as aiming mainly toward art or aestheticism"), Pearce dismisses this as a later innovation, arguing that it is not true of "the earlier Whitman, I daresay the authentic Whitman, whose verses did aim mainly toward art and aestheticism, toward a definition of the vocation of the poet in that part of the modern world which was the United States." Acknowledging that Whitman does in fact announce a new religion in "Starting from Paumanok" (1860), Pearce asserts that he really means something different: "he gives no indication that it is to be a religion of anything else but the poet's universalized vocation. (My misuse of the word 'religion' is his.),", *Facsimile Edition,* pp. xvii-xviii and xxviii. This depreciation of Whitman's religious intention as a later imposition upon the earlier poetry has continued in subsequent criticism. For instance, E.H. Miller and Jerome Loving dismiss Whitman's 1872 claim that his poetry had always possessed an underlying religious purpose as "feeble rationalizations" or a "fabrication" (Miller, *Walt Whitman's Poetry,* p. 222; Loving, *Emerson, Whitman, and the American Muse* [Chapel Hill: Univ. of North Carolina Press, 1982], pp. 188-89).

[12] I use this third approach to characterize the treatment of Whitman's spirituality in the two most important studies of the last forty years, Roger Asselineau's *The Evolution of Walt Whitman,* 2 vols. (Cambridge: Harvard Univ. Press, 1960-1962) and Gay Wilson Allen's *The Solitary Singer* (New York: New York Univ. Press, 1955, rev. 1967). In contrast to proponents of the "phases" interpretation, Asselineau and Allen correctly read the *Leaves* as having an important religious dimension from its inception. Also, while both conceive of Whitman as going through an emotional crisis in the late 1850s, neither sees this experience as destroying his earlier optimism to such an extent that the 1860s *Leaves* has a decidedly different philosophical vision.

My reading of Whitman differs from those of Asselineau and Allen in part because they employ a different methodological approach in pursuit of a different objective. Their studies are critical biographies which correlate the content of Whitman's poetry to his personal life and surrounding cultural and intellectual influences. Primarily concerned to elucidate the sources and development of Whitman's ideas, they understandably give less attention to analyzing the meaning of his poems and the unity of his vision. Nevertheless, I would argue that both studies provide a misleading account of the nature and development of Whitman's life and poetry because they present his spirituality as a discrete part of his intellectual belief system (a set of ethical and metaphysical ideas) rather than seeing it as the fundamental dimension of his consciousness that informs his personality and unites all of his experience and poetic themes. Thus Whitman is presented, for instance, as a democratic, scientific, and religious poet rather than as a religious poet whose spirituality permeates and integrates his scientific and political ideas.

[13] I am using the term "phenomenology of religion" to refer to a distinctive method of studying religion and the body of scholarship it has produced. Phenomenologists intentionally ignore the issue of the truth or falsehood of religious propositions and instead use a method of intuition and careful analysis to describe the life world, the inner dynamics and existential values, of the religious consciousness. Some phenomenological studies limit themselves to an examination of the moments of religious experience in a particular religious personality. But a more common form of scholarship describes the essential structure and meanings of an aspect of religious life, e.g., the phenomenon of spiritual rebirth or the experiencing of stars as religious symbols, which recurs in the religions of different cultures and historical periods. The chief phenomenologists of religion are relatively few: Rudolf Otto, Gerardus van der Leeuw, W. Brede Kristensen, Paul Tillich, Paul Ricoeur, and Mircea Eliade. In addition, one might add Evelyn Underhill and William James, whose studies of mysticism, while not consciously employing a phenomenological method, nevertheless provide careful analyses of various recurring structures of religious experience. The work of these scholars is generally recognized as providing the best existing discussion of religious experience and its expression in myth and symbol.

[14] *American Renaissance* (New York: Oxford Univ. Press, 1941), Preface, p. xi.

[15] Of course, this must be done with care to avoid imposing extraneous meanings upon the poetry. Ideas brought to the *Leaves* must help to account for its language and to disclose patterns of imagery and thought which could only exist as a result of the poet's conscious arrangement of his materials. My goal has been to determine the unique characteristics of Whitman's thought and feeling, but it is beneficial if the discussion of a particular religious element in the *Leaves* also indicates its essential or recurring meaning. This discloses what Whitman's spirituality shares with other religious visions, and at the same time it highlights what is distinctive or innovative in the *Leaves,* thus providing a basis for judging the poet's thoughtfulness and creativity.

[16] *Walt Whitman's Leaves of Grass: The First (1855) Edition* (New York: Viking Press, 1959), Introduction, pp. xiv & xxii.

[17] Lincoln: Univ. of Nebraska Press, 1964.

[18] Miller, *A Critical Guide to "Leaves of Grass"* (Chicago: Univ. of Chicago Press, 1957); Crawley, *The Structure of "Leaves of Grass"* (Austin: Univ. of Texas Press, 1970).

[19] Hutchinson, *The Ecstatic Whitman: Literary Shamanism & the Crisis of the Union* (Columbus: Ohio State Univ. Press, 1986).

[20] *Camden,* I, 105 and 271-72; II, 115, 297, 373 and 512; III, 320-21.

[21] *A Reader's Guide to Walt Whitman* (New York: Farrar, Straus & Giroux, 1970), p. 148.

[22] *American Visionary Poetry* (Baton Rouge: Louisiana State Univ. Press, 1982), pp. 28-29.

[23] *Evolution of Walt Whitman,* vol. I, pp. 10 & 12. Elsewhere Asselineau asserts that Whitman's poetry "continually implies a confused and complex metaphysic upon which, at first, it seems impossible to impose an order"; however, "the contradictions are explained and the logic of his position becomes evident if one considers, instead of the present totality of *Leaves of Grass,* the temporal succession of the ideas which Whitman in turn tried to express" (*The Evolution of Walt Whitman,* vol. II, pp. 21-22). These statements imply that there is a unity, or at least a logic, in Whitman's thought, but that it cannot be discerned from the analysis of any single edition, even the final one. Rather it only becomes clear from a longitudinal study of the various editions placed within the context of Whitman's other writings. Asselineau uses this approach skillfully to make exhaustive chronological surveys of selected themes, for instance, "democracy" or "industrialism," which have greatly contributed to an understanding of the evolution of Whitman's thought. However, such an approach does not lend itself to discovering the underlying unity in Whitman's vision or the relationship between various ideas. In addition, it can also lead to misreadings of individual poems or passages by taking them out of the larger context of the *Leaves.*

In addition to disagreeing with Asselineau's judgment about the disunity of the *Leaves,* I also believe his effort to describe Whitman's world view ("The Implicit Metaphysics," *The Evolution of Walt Whitman,* vol. II, pp. 21-77) is wrong or inadequate in several fundamental respects. For instance, it characterizes Whitman's view of God's relationship to the world as pantheistic whereas it should be seen as theistic, and this fundamental misunderstanding leads to distortions of other aspects of Whitman's thought. Asselineau also incorrectly attributes to Whitman a doctrine of metempsychosis rather than seeing that Whitman conceived of the soul as following a course of progressive development toward higher forms of spiritual organization. More important, it may be said as a general statement that Asselineau fails to recognize how Whitman's world view is unified around a belief in progress: the progressive evolution of nature, the millennial movement of history, and the soul's ascent toward divinity.

[24] Oscar L. Triggs, "The Growth of *Leaves of Grass,*" *The Complete Writings of Walt Whitman* (New York, 1902), vol. X, p. 101.

[25] Another reason for choosing the final edition is that it is the only text to which most readers of Whitman have easy access. However, at times it has been necessary to refer to earlier editions either because my argument discusses passages or poems that were later deleted or because I argue that the evidence for my interpretation of a particular poem or aspect of Whitman's vision was present not only in the final edition but also in earlier editions. For instance, in analyzing "Song of Myself" I cite the final edition, but I also argue that the evidence for my religious reading of the poem was already present in the 1855 edition. To demonstrate this point and to deal with possible objections to this part of my argument, I maintain a running commentary on the 1855 text in my footnotes that indicates relevant deletions, additions, and other alterations. Similarly, in my less frequent references to *Prose Works 1892,* I have cited the honored text which is based upon Whitman's *Complete Prose Works* of 1892, but whenever my argument is based upon an earlier edition of the text, I have always checked the editorial notes to ascertain that the material cited was present (without substantive change) in the earlier version.

Kenneth M. Price (essay date 1990)

SOURCE: "Sexual Equality and Marital Ideology: Whitman and the Novel," in *Whitman and Tradition: The Poet in His Century,* Yale University Press, 1990, pp. 96-121.

[*In the following essay, Price examines how prominent sexual themes in Whitman's poetry—such as non-procreative sexuality and female sexuality—influenced later writers of narrative fiction such as Kate Chopin and Hamlin Garland.*]

On March 1, 1882, *Leaves of Grass* was officially classified as obscene literature. Ironically, just when Whitman had asserted his centrality to American literature in *Specimen Days,* just when he was poised to achieve a new degree of recognition through publication by the established house of James R. Osgood, the district attorney of Boston judged his verse to be immoral and the postmaster banned *Leaves* from the mails. Yet notoriety had its advantages: when Osgood refused to contest the matter in court, *Leaves* was reissued by Rees Welsh & Co. of Philadelphia and, predictably, sold briskly, at least for a brief period. Already famous for his sexual themes, Whitman now became an even more powerful symbol and inspiration for various writers chating under the convention of reticence. Until the final decades of the nineteenth century, as Henry James noted, novelists had neglected "whole categories of manners, whole corpuscular classes and provinces." There had been, James perceived, an "immense omission" in English and American fiction, "a mistrust of any but the most guarded treatment of the great relation between men and women, the constant world-renewal."[1] At the turn of the century, however, Whitman's example enlarged the realm of possibility, as a variety of writers—including Hamlin Garland, Kate Chopin, and E. M. Forster—strove to overcome gentility.

Harold Bloom notes that "Whitman has been an inescapable influence not only for most significant poets after him . . . but also for the most gifted writers of narrative fiction. This influence transcends matters of form, and has everything to do with the Whitmanian split between the persona of the rough Walt and the ontological truth of the real me."[2] Whitman fashioned both public and private selves in order to present even the most intimate of experiences, to highlight what genteel culture had evaded, denied, or repressed. Whitman insisted that the gap between what was experienced and what was expressed should be closed, that art—if it was to be serious, honest, and complete—must deal with sex. The famous eleventh section of **"Song of Myself"** provides a fine example of Whitman gaining access to the hidden life of his culture, the life "aft the blinds of the window":

> Twenty-eight young men bathe by the shore,
> Twenty-eight young men and all so friendly;
> Twenty-eight years of womanly life and all so
>   lonesome.
> She owns the fine house by the rise of the bank,
> She hides handsome and richly drest aft the
>   blinds of the window.
> Which of the young men does she like the
>   best?
> Ah the homeliest of them is beautiful to her.
> Where are you off to, lady? for I see you,
> You splash in the water there, yet stay stock
>   still in your room.
> Dancing and laughing along the beach came
>   the twenty-ninth bather,
> The rest did not see her, but she saw them
>   and loved them.
> The beards of the young men glisten'd with
>   wet, it ran from their long hair,
> Little streams pass'd all over their bodies.
> An unseen hand also pass'd over their bodies,
> It descended tremblingly from their temples
>   and ribs.
> The young men float on their backs, their
>   white bellies bulge to the sun, they do not
>   ask who seizes fast to them,
> They do not know who puffs and declines
>   with pendant and bending arch,
> They do not think whom they souse with spray.
>   [*CRE*, pp. 38-39]

For the nineteenth century, this voyeuristic passage was startling: it depicts an independent woman (she "owns the fine house"), acknowledges her sexual yearnings, describes these longings as occurring outside of mar-

riage, accepts nonprocreative sexuality, and suggests that the "lady" crosses boundaries of age and class consciousness in her fantasized life with carefree "young men" rather than a dignified gentleman. Although Whitman was not always consistent in his statements about female sexuality, it was unconventional ideas such as these that most influenced novelists.

Shortly after the Boston suppression controversy, Whitman recorded an important insight, arguing in **"A Memorandum at a Venture"** (June 1882) that the prevailing conventional treatment of sex in literature was the "main formidable obstacle" blocking the "movement for the eligibility and entrance of women amid new spheres of business, politics, and the suffrage" (*PW* 2:494). Several recent critics have come to the same conclusion, contending that the emancipation of women required a greater candor about sexuality.[3] Until the 1890s, marriage was rarely scrutinized in fiction. Instead, writers focused on courtship: it offered suspense and a clearly understood reward, it seemed to possess inherent form, and it dealt more with sexual attraction than with sexual relationships. "Nothing so well marks [the modern] period," according to Carolyn G. Heilbrun, as the "refusal to take marriage for granted or to be content only to hint at its defects." And the shortcomings of marriage could be surveyed only once people had begun to speak candidly about sex and to understand what marriage ought to have in common with friendship.[4] In the closing decades of the nineteenth century, in both England and America, people debated the virtues and failings of the institution of marriage, especially the role of marriage in promoting polarized gender roles and the submission of wives to husbands. Such writers as Garland, Chopin, and Forster, dissatisfied both with the prevailing marital ideology and with the restricted scope of the novel, gained inspiration from Whitman's candor, his self-conscious primitivism, his free love themes, his questioning of gender roles, his democratizing of relationships, and his focus on companionship.

Unfortunately, twentieth-century critics frequently oversimplify Whitman's ideas about women: too often the poet's praise of motherhood is stressed to the exclusion of all else. Granted: motherhood was important to Whitman's thought, and the reproductive power of women is sometimes presented in ways that modern readers find intrinsically limiting. Yet Whitman also was able to envisage women with possibilities beyond "divine maternity," and it was his potentially liberating ideas that influenced Hamlin Garland's *Rose of Dutcher's Coolly* (1895), Kate Chopin's *The Awakening* (1899), and E. M. Forster's *A Room With A View* (1908). Garland, Chopin, and Forster offer important accounts of women's sexuality and depict heroines who yearn to be more than subservient beings. All three authors employ Whitman's ideal of comradeship as a means to highlight the limitations of conventional marriage.

Whereas Garland and Forster endorse Whitman's ideals, Chopin, in her more pessimistic novel, both admires and laments them—admiring their attractiveness and lamenting their near impossibility for a nineteenth-century woman to realize. Chopin faces more squarely than either Garland or Forster the biological factor—the likelihood that sexual awakening might lead to pregnancy—and thus she accounts better for the painful conflict between liberation and reproduction.

Garland's Rose on the Open Road

Hamlin Garland created in *Rose of Dutcher's Coolly* one of the first American novels to depict the developing sexuality of a young girl as she matures into a woman—in this case, into a "new woman" of the 1890s intent on self-development and on establishing a love relationship based on equality rather than hierarchy. Of the many influences on *Rose,* Whitman may have been the most important.[5] Garland had admired Whitman since the mid 1880s, and by the early 1890s, when he began *Rose of Dutcher's Coolly,* he was ready to explore Whitman's theme of "healthy" sex in a full-length novel.[6]

Both the frank treatment of sexuality and the praise of "comrades" in *Rose* owe much to Whitman. Rose's sexuality is an issue throughout the book. In the opening pages, John Dutcher, a Wisconsin farmer, worries about rearing his daughter alone after the death of his wife. An inquisitive child, Rose asks her father how she came to be born. Dutcher feels awkward at even the thought of discussing reproduction with his daughter. Although he lacks intellectual sophistication and conversational skills, Dutcher is the first of four kind and sensitive older men in Rose's life. Father and daughter develop a relationship that will later serve as a model for other alliances: "her comradeship was sweet to John Dutcher" and he found himself "completely . . . companioned by Rose."[7]

In general, Garland is at pains to create in Rose a character free from prescribed gender roles. As a child, she chases gophers and bugs and beetles, leads her schoolmates in building a stove, excels in sports, and thinks nothing of having dirt and warts on her hands. Her "heart rebelled" the few times she encountered "sex distinction," once in winter, when the boys established the right to segregate the room so that they could set nearer the fire, and again in summer, when the boys drove the girls away from the swimming hole. Like Whitman's twenty-ninth bather, "she looked longingly at the naked little savages running about and splashing in the water. There was something so fine and joyous in it." It seemed unfair that the boys could "strip and have a good time, but girls must primp around and try to keep nice and clean."[8]

As if to underscore Rose's freedom from prescribed societal norms, Garland entitles the second chapter "Child-Life, Pagan Free." A type of pastoralism contributes to the depiction of Rose's sexuality. Garland's pastoralism is "less a matter of shepherdesses and sheep than a mode by which the civilized imagination exempts itself from the claims of its own culture."[9] Garland evades many of his culture's assumptions about women by lifting Rose out of time. Occassionally, when Rose was alone, "she slipped off her clothes and ran amid the tall corn-stalks like a wild thing. . . . Some secret, strange delight, drawn from ancestral sources, bubbled over from her pounding heart, and she ran until wearied and sore with the rasping corn leaves, then she sadly put on civilized dress once more." Again, after picking berries one June day, Rose and her friends become "carried out of themselves" as they respond to the "sweet and wild and primeval scene." They play games "centuries old" and enact mock marriage ceremonies. Rose, paired with Carl, has "forgotten home and kindred" as she lives "a strange new-old life, old as history, wild and free once more." When Carl puts his head in Rose's lap, she feels her first surge of passion and yearns "to take his head in her arms and kiss it. Her muscles ached and quivered with something she could not fathom."[10] Garland attempts to gain perspective by placing sex in a primal context, by moving "beyond culture" and the particular mores of time and place.[11] This, of course, was what Garland's contemporaries had seen Whitman accomplish. (Willa Cather wrote in 1896 that Whitman is "sensual . . . in the frank fashion of the old barbarians"; John Burroughs wrote in the same year that "Whitman has the virtues of the primal and savage"; and George Santayana argued in 1900 that Whitman possesses "the innocent style of Adam.")[12] Following Whitman, Garland employed what would become a central strategy of modernism: the revitalizing and reassessing of the present by means of the primitive.

Garland is inconsistent in his treatment of sex, however: sometimes he presents it in the light of primitive purity, but at other times he displays ambivalence about sex and the changing role of women. Garland waxes Whitmanian in his praise of "the healthy, wholesome physical." For example, Garland describes Rose's "fine and pure physical joy" when, in the secrecy of her room, "she walked up and down, feeling the splendid action of her nude limbs." Yet after arguing that the "sweet and terrible attraction of men and women towards each other is as natural and as moral as the law of gravity," Garland goes on to say: "Its perversion produces trouble. Love must be good and fine and according to nature, else why did it give such joy and beauty?" To Garland's way of thinking, Rose does not always act in harmony with "nature" for she experiences an "out-break of premature passion." Rose's experience, before the age of fifteen, of youthful petting with Carl is something she must "live down." The daring introduction of this theme is offset by Garland's brief, vague, and decorous treatment of it. Rose generally controls her passion because of her "organic magnificent inheritance of moral purity." The descendant of "generations of virtuous wives and mothers, [she is] saved . . . from the whirlpool of passion."[13] The quoted passages indicate that, despite Garland's attempt to move "beyond culture" and despite his ostensible acceptance of sexuality and freedom, he remained partly bound by conventional notions of purity and restraint.[14]

Rose moves beyond her physical attraction to Carl when she encounters William de Lisle, one of the circus performers, in the chapter entitled "Her First Ideal." Sexuality and spirituality, the real and the ideal, are not antithetical: these performers have "invested their nakedness with something which exalted them." Rose formulates her first "vast ambitions" when she dreams of being his "companion." William de Lisle does her "immeasurable good" because he moves her to yearn for comparable greatness as a scholar or writer and because he enables her to escape "mere brute passion" and an early marriage.[15]

It may seem incongruous that Garland links lofty aspirations to what is largely an erotic response. Yet for Garland the real and the ideal were not to be separated but united. Genteel writers failed, he believed, because they habitually divided life into exclusive spheres: love, art, and the ideal were opposed to sex and everyday experience. Garland, regarding himself as a "follower" of Whitman, attempted to break down restricting divisions. As he remarked in "The Evolution of American Thought," "the *idealization of the real* . . . underlies the whole theory of Whitman. . . . He is master of the real, nothing daunts him. The mud and slush in the street, the gray and desolate sky, the blackened walls, the rotting timbers of the wharf—the greedy, the ragged, the prostitute—vulgarity, deformity, all—no matter how apparently low and common, his soul receives and transforms."[16] Garland was committed to illustrating that Rose's sexual knowledge, experience, and fantasies produced neither personal nor social catastrophe. Instead, sex contributed to her overall development. No genuine understanding of Rose is possible, Garland implicitly argues, unless one perceives the difficulties and mistakes, the joy and general "healthiness" of her sexual life.

William de Lisle stands alone as Rose's ideal until she encounters Dr. Thatcher. While she attends the University of Wisconsin, Rose lives with the Thatcher family, and Dr. Thatcher becomes an ideal more "substantial" though "less sweet and mythical" than de Lisle. William de Lisle was a vision in the distance; Thatcher, as a married man, is also distanced from Rose, but at least she can regard him as an "uncle and adviser." Though Thatcher struggles with his more than avuncular attraction to Rose, he treats her with concern for her wellbeing, her intellectual development, and her growth as a person. William de Lisle had (unknowingly) helped

her avert an early marriage by the power of his image; Thatcher tells Rose explicitly, "you will do whatever you dream of—*provided* you don't marry." Thanks to these men and Mrs. Spencer (a female role model who recommends marriage only after thirty), Rose leaves Madison alone and eager to embark on the "open road."[17]

Garland's reference to Whitman's **"Song of the Open Road"** is appropriate because the buoyant optimism of that poem matches the hopefulness of Garland's novel. (To reinforce this allusion, Garland entitles a later chapter "Rose Sets Face towards the Open Road.") Like Whitman, Rose has ordained herself "loos'd of limits and imaginary lines"; she goes where she chooses, her "own master total and absolute." When Rose moves to Chicago after college, she impresses nearly everyone with her talents. Only Warren Mason is critical. This brilliant, middle-aged newspaperman and frustrated novelist sees great potential in Rose, but he understands that her poetry thus far is derivative, that it does little more than echo English classics.

Through Mason, Garland expresses many of his own ideas. With regard to marriage, Mason has little faith in "sentiment and love-lore." Moreover, as he tells his friend Sanborn, he is troubled by the "possible woman." He "can't promise any woman to love her till death" because "another might come with a subtler glory, and a better fitting glamour, and then—." As Mason becomes increasingly attracted to Rose, he realizes that marriage might hinder her development. Eventually, by letter, Mason makes a proposal indebted to Whitman's ideals and language:

> I exact nothing from you. I do not require you to cook for me, nor keep house for me. You are mistress of yourself; to come and go as you please, without question and without accounting to me. You are at liberty to cease your association with me at any time, and consider yourself perfectly free to leave me whenever any other man comes with power to make you happier than I.

> I want you as comrade and lover, not as subject or servant, or unwilling wife. . . . You are a human soul like myself, and I shall expect you to be as free and sovereign as I, to follow any profession or to do any work which pleases you.[18]

In describing the Mason-Rose relationship, Garland draws on the spirit of **"Song of the Open Road"**:

> Camerado, I give you my hand!
> I give you my love more precious than money,
> I give you myself before preaching or law;
> Will you give me yourself? will you come
>   travel with me?
> Shall we stick by each other as long as we live?
>   [*CRE,* p. 159]

The speaker in Whitman's poem offers the hope of permanency, whereas Mason promises only a limited loyalty. Nonetheless, Garland informs the reader that Mason's word "comrade" pleased Rose: "It seemed to be wholesome and sweet, and promised intellectual companionship never before possible to her."[19] The concept was far from pleasing to Garland's contemporaries, however, who, because of Mason's stress on personal freedom, feared that he was proposing a free love union or a trial marriage. Garland may indeed have had a marital experiment in mind, but he hastily retreated from any such suggestion when he revised the book in 1899 and ended it with an explicit mention of a civil wedding (never mentioned in the 1895 edition) and a glimpse of domestic bliss.[20]

In *Rose* Garland failed to integrate fully Whitman's themes with his own unconscious assumptions. The idea of comradeship is undermined because Garland too frequently depicts Rose as a follower. We are told that her father functioned as her "hero and guide," that William de Lisle was "a man fit to be her guide," that Dr. Thatcher's "dominion [over Rose] was absolute," and that Mason "always . . . dominated her."[21] Garland seems unaware that he has further weakened his praise of equality by presenting Rose as a character who really seeks another father rather than a comrade. The oedipal warp in her affections is unmistakable: de Lisle, Thatcher, and Mason are all significantly older than she is, and she regards men her own age as dull. Finally, Garland weakens his theme of equality by suggesting that Rose finds fulfillment and identity not in her self but in her union with Mason.

Some of the inconsistencies in *Rose* can be attributed to intellectual failings, but others probably resulted from Garland's own unresolved psychological conflicts. There is a strong autobiographical element in *Rose,* and— although Garland has reversed the sexual roles—one might speculate about the analogies between Rose's strong link to her father, movement to the city, development as a poet, and late marriage and Garland's own strong attachment to his mother, removal to Boston, growth as a writer, and long bachelorhood. Just as Rose's search for a comrade is undermined insofar as she sees men as heroes and guides, so too is Garland's use of Whitman—his literary father—damaging to the extent that he accepts Whitman's ideas uncritically and fails to make them his own. In many places the novel illustrates the accuracy of Henry James's harsh verdict on Garland: he was the "soaked sponge of his air and time."[22] Garland endorsed Whitman's ideas in *Rose,* but because he had not sufficiently internalized these ideas, the novel, for all its power, is at odds with itself.

Whitman's Twenty-Ninth Bather in Forster's Sacred Lake

In his use of Whitman's themes, E. M. Forster resembles Garland, though his treatment of these themes is more subtle. Forster drew inspiration from Whitman's poetry to promote a greater acceptance of sexuality and employed Whitman's idea of comradeship as a model for relationships between men and women. It is important to stress that at least by 1907, and probably earlier, Forster thought Whitman to be homosexual, as one of his diary notes indicates.[23] Some critics have argued that *A Room with a View,* published in 1908, is a crypto-homosexual novel embedded within what appears to be a traditional domestic comedy. What is certainly clear is that Forster had difficulty, throughout his career, in producing believable accounts of heterosexual love and that the single most convincing depiction of passion in this novel occurs during a homoerotic bathing scene reminiscent of section eleven of **"Song of Myself."**[24] Intriguingly, Forster transferred the values he associated with this scene and his insight into these personal relations to his treatment of the love between Lucy Honeychurch and George Emerson, the one fulfilling heterosexual relationship in Forster's fiction.

Whitman's impact on *A Room* has not been sufficiently acknowledged because critics have not appreciated how Forster manipulated names. Forster, as it were, reversed literary history by having his two characters named Emerson express Whitman's values and vision.[25] This transference of Whitman's ideas onto Mr. Emerson and his son George Emerson gave Forster certain advantages: the underpinnings of the novel appear to rest on the values of "a saint who understood" (Mr. Emerson), a saint related in name to the irreproachable sage of Concord. Yet George Emerson takes part in the crucial bathing scene that calls Whitman to mind, and both Mr. Emerson and George share Whitman's faith in sex and use Whitman's language. That Forster's Mr. Emerson and George are closer to Whitman than to Ralph Waldo Emerson is everywhere suggested: like Whitman, Mr. Emerson has been a journalist and is associated with socialistic causes; the Emersons are of the lower class; these Emersons frequently advocate "comradeship"; and the Emersons are convinced of the "holiness of direct desire." In a fine ironic touch, Forster has Mr. Emerson argue that we shall not return to the Garden until we cease to be ashamed of our bodies. Perhaps Forster knew that Ralph Waldo Emerson had feared how the public would respond to Whitman's own return to the Garden in **"Children of Adam."**

To understand Forster's thinking about Whitman is to grasp a central theme of *A Room*—the contrast between a "medieval" and a modern vision. One year before the publication of *A Room,* Forster read a paper on Dante to the Working Men's College Literary Society, arguing there that

> Man consists of body and soul. So the middle ages thought, and so we think today. . . . We believe that a material element and a spiritual element go to make us up. . . . But—and here comes the

difference—the middle ages thought that between the body and the soul one can draw a distinct line, that it is possible to say which of our actions is material, which spiritual. . . .

Now I need hardly point out to you how different our attitude is today. He is a rash man who would assert where the body ends and where the soul begins. . . . Most modern thinkers realize that the barrier eludes definition. . . . It is there, but it is impalpable; and the wisest of our age, Goethe, for example, and Walt Whitman, have not attempted to find it, but have essayed the more human task of harmonizing the realms that it divides.[26]

Forster, in *A Room,* calls for more of the sort of poetry Whitman wrote when he described the union of body and soul in section five of **"Song of Myself."** Forster's character Mr. Emerson speaks for the author himself when he says: "I only wish poets would say this, too: that love is of the body; not the body, but of the body. . . . Ah for a little directness to liberate the soul."[27]

Italian settings and American ideas serve Forster in *A Room* as his means to reach "beyond culture" in his critique of marriage. As he traces the progress of his heroine Lucy, Forster endorses conclusions similar to those of Garland, though Lucy is markedly different from Rose. In *Rose* we witness a gradual increase in the heroine's culture and sophistication; in *A Room* Lucy learns to discard her early notions about gender, relationships, and class. Both Forster and Garland, drawing on Whitman, argue for marriage between equals and indicate that equality can be achieved only once women are recognized as sexual beings.

Early in the novel, in that portion set in Italy, we learn about Lucy's authentic self when we see her at the piano. Here she enters "a more solid world." "Like every true performer," Lucy was "intoxicated by the mere feel of the notes: they were fingers caressing her own; and by touch, not by sound alone, did she come to her desire." When Lucy sits at the piano she need no longer be "either deferential or patronizing; no longer either a rebel or a slave"[28]; like many other late nineteenth-century heroines, she escapes the limits of her role through artistic sensibility. But her instinctual passionate force must fight against training and the social conventions that are enforced, in Italy, by Lucy's chaperone, Charlotte. Charlotte believes in the "medieval lady," though the dragons and knights are gone. Thus Charlotte informs Lucy that most "big things [are] unladylike." She explained that it is "not that ladies were inferior to men; it was that they were different. Their mission was to inspire others to achievement rather than to achieve themselves."[29]

Lucy engages in a quiet, unplanned revolt against the likes of Charlotte when she yearns to do something her well-wishers would disapprove of. Vaguely, hesitantly, Lucy intuits that the yearning she feels (and her sense of "muddle") results from repression of the body. At Santa Croce, she views Giotto's frescoes and hears two rival interpretations of the source of their power. The clergyman, Mr. Eager, contends that the paintings result from spiritual force; Mr. Emerson applauds their "tactile values." Throughout the novel Lucy is called on to balance and reconcile the (apparently) conflicting claims of the body and the soul. A few days after the scene at Santa Croce, Lucy has clearly begun to recognize the claims of the body: it is not accidental that she purchases photographs of "The Birth of Venus" and other nudes. While carrying her nudes, she witnesses a murder. When she falls into George Emerson's arms, love and death are emblematically united. Lucy has crossed a "spiritual boundary" as surely as the dead man. On the return home, George throws her pictures, now splattered with blood, into the river and—instead of "protecting" Lucy— tells her about the blood on them. She does not yet fully appreciate that he is treating her as an equal. But this idea is enforced by the first use of the key term "comrade." As Lucy and George lean together against the parapet of the embankment, the narrator comments: "There is at times a magic in identity of position; it is one of the things that have suggested . . . eternal comradeship." Lucy does not fully realize until much later that she was a "rebel . . . who desired . . . equality beside the man she loved." Italy was offering her "the most priceless of all possessions—her own soul," but she is slow to take it.[30]

One sees how faltering Lucy's progress is when she becomes engaged, shortly after her return to England, to a man who can imagine only one sort of relationship: a "feudal" one. Cecil Vyse thinks in narrow terms of "protector and protected"; he has no understanding of "the comradeship after which the girl's heart yearned." Part of George's appeal, in contrast, has always been that "in him Lucy can see the weakness of men." George accurately analyzes his rival when he remarks that Cecil "daren't let a woman decide. He's the type who's kept Europe back for a thousand years." When Lucy accuses George himself of similar behavior, he does not deny the charge but instead observes that the "desire to govern a woman—it lies very deep, and men and women must fight it together before they shall enter the Garden."[31]

The closest any of Forster's characters come to the Garden—to uniting body and soul, to reconciling animality and spirituality—occurs during the naked bathing scene in the Sacred Lake, a small pond near Windy Corner, where the Honeychurch family lives. Shortly after the Emersons move to Windy Corner, Lucy's brother Freddy suggests to George and Reverend Beebe that they "go for a bathe." As the upper-class Freddy, the lower-class George, and the clergyman strip, they shed restricting social distinctions and ennui. "It had been a call to the blood and to the relaxed will, a passing benediction whose influence did not pass, a holiness, a spell, a momentary chalice for youth."[32] When Cecil, walking through the woods with Lucy and her mother, encounters naked bodies and the clergyman's undergarments floating on the pond, he immediately tries to protect Lucy from this scene. As Bonnie Finkelstein points out, "the freedom of men to bathe naked, which Forster contrasts with the lack of freedom for women to do the same thing, points out [a] central theme of *A Room with a View,* the question of the freedom of women in society."[33] In the past, Lucy had bathed in the Sacred Lake until she was discovered by Charlotte.

In **Leaves of Grass** and *A Room with a View* (and, indeed, in *The Awakening*) outdoor bathing, along with more general references to the values associated with the "open air," represent an alternative approach to life, a life of spontaneity and freedom unbound by conventional indoor limitations. If, in its most extreme form, the Victorian ideal of woman was "the angel *in* the house," the woman outdoors, in immediate contact with nature, represents an anti-ideal which could free women from the restrictions of an artificial purity. It is clear that Lucy is beginning to move beyond indoor restrictions when she informs Cecil that she associates him with a room without a view. He knows enough to want to be associated with the open air. This key expression comes up again later in the novel: Lucy thinks she has overcome her inclinations toward George, but once in the "open air" she pauses, and (fortunately) follows her feelings rather than her socially conditioned thought.[34]

Lucy eventually marries George, a man better suited to her than Cecil. But since Forster has indicated that marriage—at the turn of the century—is generally oppressive and feudal, he makes it clear that she enters not the conventional institution, but rather the highest personal relation between two equal individuals, a relation based on "tenderness . . . comradeship, and . . . poetry"—that is, on "the things that really matter."[35] Appropriately, George and Lucy begin their married life in Italy, back in Mr. Emerson's old room, for they have both accepted his affirmative view of life. But Forster's ending is problematic. Like Garland, Forster offers a radical critique of marriage through much of his novel only to endorse the institution (admittedly revised through Whitman's concept of comradeship) by closing in the conventional way, with the union of the hero and heroine. Neither Forster nor Garland chose the open forms favored by Henry James in his later works. Forster, however, shared James's reservations about such endings, for he believed that it was false, in his time, to end a novel with a happy marriage.[36] Indeed, in an early draft of *A Room* he ends the novel by having George killed in a bicycle accident.[37] Forster

rejected this ending, I believe, because he had invested so much personal hope in the novel, despite the distancing he achieved by transferring his own belief in homosexual comradeship onto his depiction of heterosexual love. As John Colmer notes, this transference produced a "creative tension between a personal ideology only belatedly raised to full consciousness and an alien social ideology enshrined in a literary form [domestic comedy] to which he was strongly attracted on stylistic grounds."[38] Marriage might frequently be corrupt, and heterosexual love hard for him to imagine, but for Forster's own well-being he had to believe in the value and possibility of personal relations based on comradeship.

The Awakening: *The Twenty-Ninth Bather at Sea*

When Kate Chopin wrote her fiction—usually in the family living room and "in the midst of much clatter"—she kept "at hand" copies of both Whitman's prose works and his **Leaves of Grass.**[39] Like Garland and Forster, Chopin was emboldened by Whitman's example. To Chopin, Whitman—almost alone among American writers—dealt frankly and freely with life. Other American writers, she believed, suffered in comparison to French writers because "limitations imposed on their art by their environment hamper a full and spontaneous expression."[40] Whitman's impact on *The Awakening* has been noted by many, including Lewis Leary, who describes the novel as "pervaded" with the spirit of **"Song of Myself,"** and Elizabeth House, who finds numerous connections between the novel and **"Out of the Cradle Endlessly Rocking."** Chopin's biographer, Per Seyersted, goes so far as to label *The Awakening* Chopin's **Leaves of Grass.** Our understanding of this literary relationship can be clarified, however, once we perceive that Chopin did not passively accept the poet's ideas.[41] Instead, *The Awakening* offers a critique of Whitman's visionary ideas by testing them against the hard truths of experience—that is, against one nineteenth-century woman's social, psychological, and physiological circumstances.

Unlike Rose and Lucy, who move toward fulfillment in comradeship with Mason and George, Edna, when we first meet her in *The Awakening,* has already achieved wealth, social status, and marriage with the seemingly worthy Léonce Pontellier. (By shunning the form of the courtship novel, Chopin avoids even the implication that a woman achieves identity through marriage.) *The Awakening* is not "about sex," as some have argued, but is instead a record of Edna's desire to achieve identity after marriage, her struggle to become a full self. Chopin, like Forster, alludes to Whitman's scene with the twenty-nine bathers, though she puts the scene to different uses from the Englishman. We recall that section eleven of **"Song of Myself"** opens with an insistent repetition of the number twenty-eight. Chopin alludes to this scene through her own repetition of this number in a conversation early in the novel between the twenty-eight-year-old Edna Pontellier and her companion Robert Lebrun. Robert asks her,

> . . ."Didn't you know this was the twenty-eighth of August?"
>
> "The twenty-eighth of August?"
>
> "Yes. On the twenty eighth of August . . . a spirit that has haunted these shores for ages rises up from the Gulf. With its own penetrating vision the spirit seeks some one mortal worthy to hold him company, worthy of being exalted for a few hours into realms of the semi-celestials."[42]

Whereas Whitman presented a vignette of the woman "aft the blinds" in section eleven of **"Song of Myself,"** Chopin goes much further, giving the full account of *her* twenty-ninth bather, providing a narrative of struggle, development, and death. Chopin uses Whitman in a tough-minded fashion, revising the poet in a number of ways. Whitman's unencumbered twenty-ninth bather "owned" her house on the hill; Edna Pontellier, in contrast, has a husband and children, and (much more typical for a nineteenth-century woman) owns very little. Her husband Léonce values the furnishings in his house because they are "his" and values Edna as his "possession."

Edna's development is sparked by encounters with contrasting people who nonetheless illuminate facets of Edna's own character. Two encounters are crucial to Edna's growth into an awareness of her own physical nature and her artistic potential: first, she experiences physical intimacy with the "mother woman" Adèle Ratignolle; second, she hears the music of the antisocial artist Mademoiselle Reisz. These experiences help Edna in her attempt to understand "her position in the universe as a human being, and to recognize her relations as an individual to the world within and about her." Like Whitman himself, Edna has always had a dual sense of self, aware of both "the outward existence which conforms" and "the inward life which questions." In her effort to close the gap between the two, Edna eventually will become even more radical than Whitman in her complete rejection of her conventional role. Early in the novel Edna has her first alluring invitation from the sea, promising an ultimate fusion of outer life and consciousness:

> The voice of the sea is seductive; never ceasing, whispering, clamoring, murmuring, inviting the soul to wander for a spell in abysses of solitude; to lose itself in mazes of inward contemplation.
>
> The voice of the sea speaks to the soul. The touch of the sea is sensuous, enfolding the body in its soft, close embrace.[43]

This experience is expressed in Whitmanian terms, as is clear from the abundance of participles, the imagery drawn from **"Out of the Cradle,"** and the key phrase—"inviting the soul"—inspired by section five of **"Song of Myself."** Chopin has intertwined the hopeful sense of fulfillment from **"Song of Myself"** with the most nightmarish aspects of **"Out of the Cradle."** Chopin mentions that Edna's soul is "invited" three times in *The Awakening,* but the invitations carry sinister implications along with promise. There is the possibility of a dangerous "seduction," the enchantment of a "spell" (this play on words is reinforced by later references to Snow White), and the trap of a labyrinthian "maze" of thought.

The immediate results of Whitman's and Edna's vision differ greatly: for Whitman, inviting the soul yields clarification; for Edna, it produces confusion. After the union of body and soul, Whitman exclaims: "Swiftly arose and spread around me the peace and joy and knowledge that pass all the art and argument on earth," and he then proceeds to catalog examples of what he now "knows" (*CRE,* p. 33). Edna experiences no such epiphany. Knowledge comes to her in a more perplexing and gradual fashion: "the beginning of things, of a world especially, is necessarily vague, tangled, chaotic, and exceedingly disturbing. How few of us ever emerge from such beginning! How many souls perish in its tumult!" Edna's difficulty is directly related to her role as a woman. When Edna begins to understand her "position in the universe," the narrator comments that "this may seem like a ponderous weight of wisdom to descend upon the soul of a young woman of twenty-eight—perhaps more wisdom than the Holy Ghost is usually pleased to vouchsafe to any woman."[44] Edna faces a larger task than Whitman, Chopin implicitly argues, for she requires greater transformations to bring into accord her vision and existing conditions.

Whitman had celebrated a country with values of his own imagining. An early notebook passage illustrates his characteristic strategy: "I will not descend among professors and capitalists,—I will turn up the ends of my trowsers around my boots, and my cuffs back from my wrists, and go with drivers and boatmen and men that catch fish or work in the field. I know they are sublime" (*NUPM* 1:67). Whitman reverses social values and accompanying hierarchies in American life: he will not "descend" into the upper class when the "sublime" resides in the common and ordinary. But Whitman did not argue for an alternative society. For him, opposition was not a rejection of society but an attempt to bring America into line with the vision of the founders and the legacy of Jackson. Thus, despite failings all around him, he saw the "perfect fitness and equanimity of things." Edna, on the other hand, rejects even her surroundings: "The street, the children, the fruit vender, the flowers growing there under her eyes, were all part and parcel of an alien world which had suddenly become antagonistic." By the end of the novel, she rejects not only her family and social circumstances: after witnessing Adèle's accouchement—that "scene [of] torture"—she "revolt[s] against the ways of Nature."[45]

Edna's sole hope is negation; she can awaken only through sleep and dreams. (It is thus a misunderstanding to blame Edna, as many critics have done, for being passive, impractical, deluded, and sleepy.) Unable to constitute a new social order, her response is anti-language. Her earliest revolt is as a child, wading through a sea of grass away from the Presbyterian church service: "'I was a little *un*thinking child in those days, just following a *mis*leading impulse without question. . . . Sometimes I feel this summer as if I were walking through the green meadow again; idly, aim*lessly, un*thinking, and *un*guided'" [emphasis added].[46] Whitman may well have been the model for this strong use of negation, for as C. Carroll Hollis points out, Whitman—the most optimistic of American poets—leads them all in the use of negatives. In the first three editions of **Leaves of Grass,** "Whitman, on social, religious, and sexual matters, imagines a world and conduct within that world pointedly contrary to the world presented by other writers in the 1850s."[47] Whereas the poet created his own autonomous world, Chopin creates a realistic novel in which a single character yearns for an isolated world while still held in a life of time and consequences. Whitman sought to purify his culture; Edna requires a separation from culture.

Edna's awakening, appropriately, comes on Grand Isle, a realm separated from patriarchal culture. Islands are poignant realms of possibility for Chopin. (In "A Little Free-Mulatto" she recounts the difficulties of a girl of mixed race who finds a place only on L'Isle des Mulatres, where "everyone is just like herself.")[48] Edna's fantasies with Robert take place on the Baratarian islands, and to some extent Edna and Robert act out their fantasies on Chênière Caminada. These are separate worlds where the dream of a reconstituted order seems possible. Whitman was on the shore in **"Out of the Cradle"** and other poems, on the border between spheres, joining the finite and the infinite. Edna looks for a more radical break: she yearns for an island, self-enclosed, self-sufficient.

Never having seen any precedent for her vision of sexual equality within society, Edna can only imagine utopia elsewhere. She repeatedly envisions an ideal community: she longs to be with Robert at Grande Terre, "watching the slimy lizards writhe in and out among the ruins of the old fort." (Apparently this was a vision of abundant sexual activity—as the imagery suggests—and a vision of the decay of an aggressive, masculine, and militaristic society.) Similarly, when Edna and Robert are in Chênière Caminada they seem to be in a magic land. Robert tells her she has slept one hundred years and she agrees that "the whole

island seems changed. A new race of beings must have sprung up, leaving only you and me as past relics. How many ages ago did Madame Antoine and Tonie die? and when did our people from Grand Isle disappear from the earth?"[49]

Like Whitman's twenty-ninth bather who was drawn to younger men, Edna sees in the youthful Robert potential joy and freedom and companionship. He is not financially secure, but he has the appeal George had for Lucy: in him, Edna can see the weakness of men. What is important is that he is "interested" in Edna's conversation, shares in the care of the children, and takes on domestic duties. Robert and Adèle have helped her reach for freedom, but when Robert returns from Mexico, he adopts many of the traditional masculine roles. He now buys a box of cigars, yearns to possess Edna as his wife, and imagines Léonce giving her up.[50] Edna realizes, however, that she is no longer a possession, no longer dependent on Léonce to set her free.

Edna's difficulties in fusing outer life with consciousness are clear in her relationship with men. She achieves sexual fulfillment without love with Alcée Arobin and achieves love without sexual fulfillment with Robert. Only with the sea does she fuse inner and outer: "But that night she was like the little tottering, stumbling, clutching child, who of a sudden realizes its powers, and walks for the first time alone, boldly and with over-confidence. She could have shouted for joy. She did shout for joy, as with a sweeping stroke or two she lifted her body to the surface of the water."[51] The shift from "could have" to "did," as Paula Treichler points out, "signals real changes in her behavior and understanding."[52] Edna learns that even romantic love is transient; it cannot satisfy her longing for perfection and boundlessness, life's "delirium." As Dr. Mandelet explains, "youth is given up to illusions." Belief in romantic love "seems to be a provision of Nature; a decoy to secure mothers for the race."[53]

Chopin originally entitled her novel "A Solitary Soul." In the closing pages Edna imitates the man in "Solitude" who goes to the shore and stands naked. She has stripped herself of societal conventions, yet the world of New Orleans retains its sharply differentiated gender codes. Edna can find satisfaction neither in the traditional role of "feminine" nor in the possessive power of the masculine world. Thus, as Anne Goodwyn Jones argues, "acting in the best way she has discovered to feel power without harming others, she swims into the sensuous sea."[54] The voice of the sea refrain has been subtly changed in this second use of it. She is no longer called to wander "for a spell" in abysses of solitude. She has now chosen to protect her essential self permanently. Chopin, Forster, and Garland all responded to Whitman's ability to create his own self, to envision a heroic self that was a match for the pressures of social conformity. In doing so, they created heroines whose "capacity to be, or to want to be, themselves, is so great as to be charismatic."[55] These heroines struggle, though, with cultural forms and institutions that threaten to deny their status as authentic, whole persons. Whitman's idea of comradeship was put to work for feminism, even if—as in the case of Kate Chopin—it was a subtle statement that the ideals of Whitman were unrealizable for nineteenth-century women.

Whitman's example was a liberating force for novelists, but they were curiously hampered in carrying through on his sexual ideals. Novelists, for various reasons, are caught up in the theme of marriage—a theme Whitman downplays. Long after the incorporation of sexuality into our literature, the problem remains of tying it to marriage effectively. Each writer discussed above waffles a bit on the matter of marriage and sexuality. The problematics of marriage these novelists identify continue to give difficulties to AngloAmerican artists treating the adult theme of love.

Notes

[1] *Theory of Fiction: Henry James,* ed. James E. Miller, Jr. (Lincoln: University of Nebraska Press, 1972), pp. 342-43.

[2] *New York Review of Books* 26 (April 16, 1984), 6.

[3] See, for example, Joseph Allen Boone, "Wedlock as Deadlock and Beyond: Closure and the Victorian Marriage Ideal," *Mosaic* 17 (1984), 65-81, and Annette Niemtzow, "Marriage and the New Woman in *The Portrait of a Lady,*" *American Literature* 47 (1975), 377-95.

[4] "Marriage Perceived: English Literature, 1873-1941," in *What Manner of Woman: Essays on English and American Life,* ed. Marlene Springer (New York: New York University Press, 1977), pp. 168 and 171.

[5] For an account of other influences on *Rose,* see Robert Bray, "Hamlin Garland's *Rose of Dutcher's Coolly,*" *Great Lakes Review* 3 (1976), 5.

[6] Kenneth M. Price, "Hamlin Garland's 'The Evolution of American Thought': A Missing Link in the History of Whitman Criticism," *Walt Whitman Quarterly Review* 3 (1985), 1-20.

[7] Garland, *Rose of Dutcher's Coolly,* ed. Donald Pizer (1895; reprint, Lincoln: University of Nebraska Press, 1969), p. 25.

[8] Ibid., p. 17.

[9] Linda Dowling, "The Decadent and the New Woman in the 1890's," *Nineteenth-Century Fiction* 33 (1979), 449.

[10] *Rose,* pp. 19 and 29-31.

[11] The quoted phrase is from Dowling, p. 450.

[12] Cather's comment first appeared in the *Nebraska State Journal* for January 19, 1896; it is reprinted in *Critical Essays on Walt Whitman,* ed. James Woodress (Boston: G. K. Hall, 1983), p. 177. For Burroughs, see *Walt Whitman: The Critical Heritage,* ed. Milton Hindus (London: Routledge & Kegan Paul, 1971), p. 251. For Santayana, see "The Poetry of Barbarism," in *Interpretations of Poetry and Religion* (1900; reprint, New York: Harper & Row, 1957), p. 178.

[13] *Rose,* pp. 310, 63, 128, 39, 83, 127, and 120.

[14] Donald Pizer, "Introduction," *Rose,* p. xviii.

[15] *Rose,* pp. 55, 61, and 62.

[16] Price, "Hamlin Garland's 'The Evolution of American Thought,'" p. 14.

[17] *Rose,* pp. 151 and 143.

[18] Ibid., pp. 309, 380.

[19] Ibid., pp. 382-83.

[20] For differing interpretations of what kind of marriage Garland had in mind in the 1895 version, compare Pizer "Introduction," pp. xxxii-xxxiii, and Bray, "Hamlin Garland's *Rose of Dutcher's Coolly,*" p. 14*n*11.

[21] *Rose,* pp. 24, 60, 113, and 303.

[22] The remark by James is quoted in B. R. McElderry, Jr., "Hamlin Garland and Henry James," *American Literature* 23 (1952), 435.

[23] P. N. Furbank, *E. M. Forster: A Life* (London: Secker and Warburg, 1977), 1:159*n,* cites two lists. Robert Martin, "Edward Carpenter and the Double Structure of *Maurice,*" *Journal of Homosexuality* 8 (1983), 35-46, first noted that the second list is made up of artists Forster believed to be homosexual.

[24] Samuel Hynes comments on Forster's habit of writing crypto-homosexual stories: "one feels in so many of Forster's novels a kind of transference at work, as though one were reading a different sort of story, but translated into socially acceptable terms" (*Edwardian Occasions: Essays on English Writing in the Early Twentieth Century* [New York: Oxford University Press, 1972], p. 116). In "Vacant Heart and Hand and Eye': The Homosexual Theme in *A Room with a View,*" Jeffrey Meyers argues that "a fundamental questioning of the value of heterosexual love is recurrent in Forster's works" (*English Literature in Transition* 13 [1970], 185).

25 For a brief but helpful account of the influence of American transcendentalism on *A Room with a View,* see Herbert Howarth, "Whitman and the English Writers" in *Papers on Walt Whitman,* ed. Lester F. Zimmerman and Winston Weathers (Tulsa: University of Tulsa, 1970), p. 9. Howarth discusses effectively the presence of Emerson, Thoreau, and Whitman in *A Room with a View,* but he does not note the irony involved in Forster's giving to his character Mr. Emerson traits of Whitman.

26 Forster, *Albergo Empedocle and Other Writings,* ed. George H. Thomson (New York: Liveright, 1971), pp. 154-55.

27 Forster, *A Room with a View,* ed. Oliver Stallybrass (London: Edward Arnold, 1977), p. 202.

28 Ibid., pp. 29-30.

29 Ibid., p. 39.

30 Ibid., pp. 44 and 110.

31 Ibid., pp. 154 and 166.

32 Ibid., p. 133.

33 Bonnie Blumenthal Finkelstein, *Forster's Women: Eternal Differences* (New York: Columbia University Press, 1975), p. 67.

34 *A Room,* pp. 106 and 168.

35 Ibid., p. 202.

36 Forster, "Pessimism in Literature" (1906), in *Albergo Empedocle and Other Writings,* pp. 129-45.

37 Oliver Stallybrass, "Editor's Introduction," *A Room,* p. xvii.

38 John Colmer, "Marriage and Personal Relations in Forster's Fiction," in *E. M. Forster: Centenary Revaluations,* ed. Judith Scherer Herz and Robert K. Martin (Toronto: University of Toronto Press, 1982), p. 113.

39 See Kate Chopin's letter to Waitman Barbe, October 2, 1894, and [Sue V. Moore?,] "Mrs. Kate Chopin," *St. Louis Life* 10 (June 9, 1894), 11-12. Both items are reproduced in *A Kate Chopin Miscellany,* ed. Per Seyersted and Emily Toth (Oslo and Natchitoches: Universitetsforlaget and Northwestern State University Press, 1979), pp. 120 and 114-15.

40 William Schuyler, "Kate Chopin," *The Writer 7* (August 1894), 115-17; reprinted in *A Kate Chopin Miscellany,* pp. 115-19.

41 See Lewis Leary, "Introduction" to Kate Chopin, *The Awakening and Other Stories* (New York: Holt, Rinehart, and Winston, 1970), p. xiii; Elizabeth House, "*The Awakening:* Kate Chopin's 'Endlessly Rocking' Cycle," *Ball State University Forum* 20 (1979), 53-58; and Per Seyersted, *Kate Chopin: A Critical Biography* (Baton Rouge: Louisiana State University Press, 1969), p. 162. My own thinking about the Chopin-Whitman relationship is perhaps closest to that of Otis Wheeler, who remarks that *The Awakening* involves "a rejection of the pervasive nineteenth-century faith in the individual, in spite of the Whitmanesque imagery. For what we see in Edna's story is a reversal of the Romantic dream of the unlimited outward expansion of the self" ("The Five Awakenings of Edna Pontellier," *The Southern Review* 11 [1975], 118-28). I would differ slightly from Wheeler, however, by arguing that Chopin does not so much reject this ideal as she laments the impossibility of realizing it.

42 *The Awakening,* in *The Complete Works of Kate Chopin,* ed. Per Seyersted (Baton Rouge: Louisiana State University Press, 1969), 2:909-10.

43 Ibid., 2:893.

44 Ibid., 2:893.

45 Ibid., 2:935 and 995.

46 Ibid., 2:896-97.

47 Hollis, *Language and Style in* Leaves of Grass (Baton Rouge: Louisiana State University Press, 1983), p. 134.

48 *The Complete Works of Kate Chopin* 1:202-03.

49 *The Awakening* 2:915 and 919.

50 See Anne Goodwyn Jones, *Tomorrow Is Another Day: The Woman Writer in the South, 1859-1936* (Baton Rouge: Louisiana State University Press, 1981), pp. 157-61, for a helpful discussion of sexual roles in the novel.

51 *The Awakening* 2:908.

52 Paula A. Treichler, "The Construction of Ambiguity in *The Awakening:* A Linguistic Analysis," in *Women and Language in Literature and Society,* ed. Sally McConnell-Ginet et al. (New York: Praeger, 1980), p. 244.

53 *The Awakening* 2:996.

54 Jones, p. 182.

55 Roy Harvey Pearce, *The Continuity of American Poetry* (Princeton: Princeton University Press, 1961), p. 254.

Abbreviations

The following abbreviations are used parenthetically in the text.

C: Walt Whitman: The Correspondence, ed. Edwin Haviland Miller, 6 vols. (New York University Press, 1961-1977).

CRE: Walt Whitman: Leaves of Grass, Comprehensive Reader's Edition, ed. Harold W. Blodgett and Sculley Bradley (New York: New York University Press, 1965).

LG 1855: Leaves of Grass: The First (1855) Edition, ed. Malcolm Cowley (New York: Viking, 1959).

LG 1856: Leaves of Grass, Facsimile of 1856 Edition: By Walt Whitman, intro. Gay Wilson Allen (n.p.: Norwood, 1976).

LG 1860: Leaves of Grass, by Walt Whitman: Facsimile Edition of the 1860 Text, intro. Roy Harvey Pearce (Ithaca, N.Y.: Cornell University Press, 1961).

NUPM: Walt Whitman: Notebooks and Unpublished Prose Manuscripts, ed. Edward F. Grier, 6 vols. (New York: New York University Press, 1984).

James Perrin Warren (essay date 1990)

SOURCE: "The 'Thought of the Ensemble': Whitman's Theory of Language," in *Walt Whitman's Language Experiment,* Pennsylvania State University Press, 1990, pp. 7-33.

[*In the following essay, Warren maintains that, through works such as* Leaves of Grass *and in several essays, Whitman established a theory of language—one directly connected with literature and linguistic development and specifically focused on the significant role of literature in effecting linguistic change and diversity.*]

> *This subject of language interests me—interests me: I never quite get it out of my mind. I sometimes think the Leaves is only a language experiment— that it is an attempt to give the spirit, the body, the man, new words, new potentialities of speech—an American, a cosmopolitan (the best of America is the best cosmopolitanism) range of self-expression. The new world, the new times, the new peoples, the new vista, need a tongue according—yes, what is more, will have such a tongue—will not be satisfied until it is evolved.*[1]

Although Whitman made this statement late in life, it indicates that "this subject of language" is fundamental to his poetic vision of America in the latter half of the nineteenth century. According to the poet, the "new potentialities of speech" embodied in *Leaves of Grass* should somehow meet the needs of "the new world, the new times, the new peoples, the new vista." Whitman's theory of language implies a theory of literature; even more, it implies a way of interpreting humankind's place in the temporal flux of the natural world. By incorporating his vision of "the new vista" into his theory of language, Whitman provides himself with a theoretical basis for conducting the "language experiment" of *Leaves of Grass.*

It is hardly surprising that Whitman's theory of language has not received the attention it warrants, for the poet published only two essays on language during his lifetime. The first, **"America's Mightiest Inheritance,"** appeared in the 12 April 1856 issue of *Life Illustrated,* a "family magazine" owned by Fowler and Wells. The second, **"Slang in America,"** did not appear until November 1885, in the *North American Review.* The only other linguistic work by Whitman to reach the general reading public was *An American Primer,* a series of notes edited by Horace Traubel and published in 1904. Recently, however, several unpublished manuscripts have come to light, the most important of which is the notebook *Words.* Finally, the most coherent expression of Whitman's theory of language is contained in *Rambles Among Words,* a popular book on English etymology, signed by William Swinton and first printed in 1859.[2]

Scholarship of the last ten years indicates that the "subject of language" occupied an important place in the literary culture of nineteenth-century America. The chapter "Language" in Emerson's *Nature* and the entire essay "The Poet" spring immediately to mind. Thoreau's philological extravagances in *Walden,* the linguistic focus on representation in such novels as *The Scarlet Letter* and *Moby Dick,* and poems like Dickinson's "Many a phrase has the English language" (#276) follow quickly.[3] In addition to these canonized texts, we can find numerous articles on language in English and American journals of the period, and the decade 1850-60 saw a host of books published on the "new science" of historial linguistics.[4]

"America's Mightiest Inheritance" suggests the intensity of Whitman's interest in the subject of language. He makes the grandiose claim that the English language "subordinates any perfection of politics, erudition, science, metaphysics, inventions, poems, the judiciary, printing, steam-power, mails, architecture, or what not."[5] By placing language ahead of all the cultural and technological advances of the nineteenth century, Whitman suggests that the "language experiment" of *Leaves of Grass* creates more than simply "new potentialities of speech"—it creates the "cosmopolitan . . . range of self-expression" necessary for "any perfection" of culture whatsoever.

This claim for the all-encompassing nature of the English language is similar to Whitman's view of its history. After giving a retrospective treatment of the Indo-European languages and of the "composite" history of English, Whitman asserts that "the history of language is the most curious and instructive of any history, and embraces the whole of the rest. It is the history of the movements and developments of men and women over the entire earth. In its doings every thing appears to move from east to west as the light does" (p. 57). The westward migrations of prehistoric Indo-European tribes become an analogue for the westward expansion of the United States. This implied argument for the doctrine of Manifest Destiny becomes clear in a later passage of the essay:

> The English language seems curiously to have flowed through the ages, especially toward America, for present use, and for centuries and centuries of future use; it is so composed of all the varieties that preceded it, and so absorbs what is needed by it. (p. 59)

The chronological structure of the sentence takes us from retrospect to prospect, from the history of the English language to the "new vista" of English in America. In addition, Whitman's history emphasizes the active qualities of the English language. Flowing, composing, and absorbing, language takes on the characteristics of a self-directed, purposive entity, while in the earlier passage language is figured as a natural being, one that "appears to move from east to west as the light does."

These passages from **"America's Mightiest Inheritance"** are, like Whitman's view of the history of language, both "curious and instructive." They indicate that language—particularly the English language in America—gives Whitman an enthusiastic and enabling vision of "the new vista."

An early manuscript essay, **"Our Language and Literature,"** originally titled "Our Language, and Future & Literature," shows Whitman's characteristic concern for the "vista" of future linguistic developments, and it couples that concern with the specific role of literature in encouraging "new potentialities of speech."[6] The manuscript begins with terms that strongly echo **"America's Mightiest Inheritance."** Whitman calls the English language "our most precious inheritance—greater than arts, politics, religions or greater than any wealth or any inventions" (p. 809). The catalogue of cultural advances is more general than that of the published essay, suggesting that **"Our Language and Literature"** contains draft material used in **"America's Mightiest Inheritance."**

The remaining pages of the manuscript connect the history and future development of American English with the differences between British and American literary language. And in this regard the manuscript displays

connections with the August 1856 **"Letter"** to Emerson. For example, in the manuscript Whitman asserts that "the life-spirit of These States must be engrafted upon their inherited language:—indeed I see the beginning of this already and enjoy it. As for myself I love to go away from books, and walk amidst the strong coarse talk of men as they give muscle and bone to every word they speak" (p. 811). In the 1856 **"Letter,"** the play among past, present, and future is more fully developed:

> To poets and literats—to every woman and man, today or any day, the conditions of the present . . . are the perfect conditions on which we are here, and the conditions for wording the future with indissuadable words. These States, receivers of the stamina of past ages and lands, initiate the outlines of repayment a thousand fold. . . . Always America will be agitated and turbulent. This day it is taking shape, not to be less so, but to be more so, stormily, capriciously, on native principles, with such vast proportions of parts! As for me, I love screaming, wrestling, boiling-hot days.[7]

The rhetoric of the last sentence, with its "as for me," recalls the "as for myself" of the manuscript passage. More important, the passage from the **"Letter"** develops Whitman's call for an "engrafting" of the American "life-spirit" upon the English language by announcing the "conditions for wording the future with indissuadable words." Whitman portrays America as the perfect "receiver" of the past, possessing in its present the "perfect conditions" for "wording the future" through its literature. In the last three sentences, the sequence of past participles, adverbs, adjectives, and present participles marks those conditions as, above all, dynamic and active. So Whitman's vision of America would seem to call for a dynamic and active language to match the dynamic and active "life-spirit."

This cluster of texts suggests that in 1856 Whitman was preoccupied with the "subject of language," and it argues for a close relationship between the poet's view of American English and his view of American literature. In both general and specific terms, the texts indicate that the "language experiment" of *Leaves of Grass* should reveal Whitman's strategies for unlocking "new potentialities" in the speech and spirit of nineteenth-century America. But they do not present, in any focused argument, the theoretical underpinnings of Whitman's hortatory and polemical assertions. Unless we are willing to allow the poet a large measure of jingoistic bombast, we must examine the theory of language underlying his bravado.

Whitman's theory emerges in three texts dating from 1855 to 1859: the notebooks *Words* and *Primer of Words,* and the last two chapters of *Rambles Among Words,* which Whitman authored.[8] In **"The Growth of Words,"** the penultimate chapter of *Rambles,* Whitman places himself within a specific tradition of language theorists. He takes as his epigraph a quotation from Wilhelm von Humboldt:

> An idiom is an organism subject, like every organism, to the laws of development. One must not consider a language as a product dead and formed but once: it is an animate being and ever creative.[9]

Humboldt is a major figure in the tradition of "organic," or transcendental, language theory. Throughout the early years of the nineteenth century, the transcendentalists attempted to alter the empiricist theory of language as an arbitrary set of conventional signs designed by human beings to further communication.[10] Countering the theory of language as a means of communication, the transcendentalists proposed a theory of language as an expression of the spirit, whether individual or collective. For the transcendental theorists, language is essentially an activity of the spirit, functioning to unify sense-data and concepts. Language is an "organism," in Humboldt's view, in a metaphorical sense. It is the process of spiritual formation through which the subjective and objective poles of being are joined. The "organic" or transcendental theory stresses the "laws of development" inherent in language because these laws reveal the development of the human spirit. As Humboldt phrases the point, "Language is the formative organ of *thought. Intellectual activity,* entirely mental, entirely internal, and to some extent passing without trace, becomes, through *sound,* externalized in speech and perceptible to the senses. Thought and language are therefore one and inseparable from each other" (p. 54).

The organic theory of language relates directly to the rise of historical Indo-European linguistics in the nineteenth century. Faced with a seemingly chaotic welter of unrelated languages, the transcendental theorists were forced to ask whether the truth formulated in Peking was the same as the truth formulated in Bombay, in Berlin, or in ancient Athens or Rome. The aim of comparative philologists like Bopp, the Schlegels, Grimm, Humboldt, and Schleicher was to find the historical "laws of development" that would reveal a unity underlying both the diversity of languages and the temporal changes within any given language. Humboldt makes this point in the first section of the Kawi work: "The *comparative study of languages,* the exact establishment of the manifold ways in which innumerable peoples resolve the same task of language formation that is laid upon them as men, loses all higher interest if it does not cleave to the point at which language is connected with the shaping of the *nation's mental power*" (p. 21).

In the analogies existing between Sanskrit and most of the ancient and modern European languages, the transcendental comparatists were provided with an important first clue to the unity of languages.[11] The similarities among certain languages led to the idea that kinships existed among them and that they were descendants of a single mother tongue, primitive Indo-European. The apparent differences among languages melted away in the light of a common ancestry. But the comparatists were still faced with the problem of relating other families of languages to the Indo-European family. Was Chinese related to Latin, German, or English?

The transcendentalists solved this larger problem of linguistic unity by proposing a typology of languages, classifying them as Isolating, Agglutinating, and Inflecting.[12] The typology is based upon the ways lexical elements (the base, or root) and grammatical elements (inflectional endings, particles, and affixes) relate to one another. The root is the material unit of signification, while the grammatical elements mark the formal relation of roots to one another. Such isolating, or Monosyllabic, languages as Chinese simply employ monosyllabic units for designating objects. Agglutinating languages employ grammatical markers, but these markers bear no direct relation to the internal form of the root. Inflecting, or Organic, languages unify lexical and grammatical elements according to morphological rules.[13]

In the three types of language we see a philological version of Hegel's dialectic. The Monosyllabic languages merely designate the empirical given. In the clash between lexical and grammatical elements, the Agglutinating languages represent the opposition between the empirical given and *a priori* forms. Finally, the Organic languages represent the synthesis of the empirical given and *a priori* forms in the act of thought expressing itself in language. Thus the Organic languages represent the unity of subject and object, and it so happens that the Indo-European languages form that class.[14]

The cultural bias of linguistic typology is immediately apparent. Moreover, the Hegelian dialectic is interpreted by linguists like August Schleicher as a temporal, historical fact, so that the Organic languages are seen as more "developed" or "evolved" than those of the other two classes. And this view eventually leads to the idea that the "organism" of language is like any other natural organism, obeying the Darwinian laws of evolution.[15]

Humboldt's response to the problem of linguistic unity is more complicated, for he never views language as an organism subject to natural laws of evolution. Instead, Humboldt's treatment of the problem leads in the direction of pure spirit. And because the spirit is, like language, a never-ceasing activity, the principle of linguistic unity can never be fully grasped:

> If we are not to forego all discovery of a connection between phenomena in the human race, we still have to come back to some independent and original *cause,* not itself in turn conditioned and transitory

in appearance. But we are thereby most naturally led to an inner life-principle, freely developing in its fullness, whose particular manifestations are not intrinsically unlinked because their outer appearances are presented in isolation. This viewpoint is totally different from that of the purposive theory, since it does not proceed towards a set goal, but from an admittedly unfathomable cause. (p. 26)

The "inner life-principle" is Humboldt's formula for the creative power of the language-making mind, and it functions as a noumenal, *a priori* principle of unity underlying the "outer appearances" of particular languages. The "inner life-principle" also allows Humboldt to distinguish his own theory from a "purposive theory," one which would employ the concept of communication as the primary purpose of language.

The "inner life-principle" recalls Whitman's idea of an American "life-spirit" announced in **"Our Language and Literature,"** but in neither case is the concept as monolithic as it would first appear to be. Humboldt's unifying principle is not necessarily the same in all languages, and each language incarnates the spirit of the nation which speaks the language. The only feature the various languages necessarily have in common is that the inner principle of each is equally mysterious:

> All *becoming* in nature, but especially of the organic and living, escapes our observation. However minutely we may examine the preparatory stages, between the latter and the phenomenon there is always the cleavage that divides the something from the nothing; and this is equally so with the moment of *cessation*. All comprehension of man lies only between the two. In languages, a period of origination, from perfectly accessible historical times, affords us a striking example. We can follow out a multiple series of changes that the *language of the Romans* underwent during its decline and fall, and can add to them the minglings due to invading tribesmen: we get no better explanation thereby of the origin of the living seed which again germinated in various forms into the organism of newly burgeoning languages. An inner principle, newly arisen, rebuilt the collapsing structure, for each in its own fashion, and we, since we always find ourselves situated among its effects only, become aware of its transformations only by the multitude thereof. (p. 43)

Humboldt's solution to the problems of linguistic unity and variety depends upon a radical "cleavage" between spirit and matter, for he bases his interpretation of linguistic change and variety on the unknowable, noumenal origin of an endless unfolding of forms. Moreover, this linguistic idealism entails an optimistic view of language, since Humboldt sees in all languages "the *endeavour* to secure being in reality for the idea of *linguistic completeness*" (p. 27). The "endeavour" can and does take varying forms, but the comparative phi-lologist searches for the constant and uniform structures underlying apparently diverse manifestations of the ideal of "linguistic completeness." The "endeavour" is another term for the "inner life-principle" or "living seed" of language, and each language is the spontaneous, involuntary expression of this noumenal and inexplicable principle.

Humboldt gives the abstract theory of the "inner life-principle" a concrete focus when he considers the three classes of languages. He argues that "all spiritual progress can only proceed from an internal emission of force, and to that extent has always a hidden, and because it is autonomous, an inexplicable basis," and he then proceeds to offer linguistic typology as an example:

> For it now follows at once that where enhanced appearances of the same endeavour are perceivable, we cannot, unless the facts imperatively demand it, presuppose a *gradual progress,* since every significant enhancement appertains, rather, to a peculiar creative force. An example may be drawn from the structure of the Chinese and Sanscrit languages. One might certainly suppose here a gradual progression from the one to the other. But if we truly feel the nature of language as such, and of these two in particular, if we reach the point of fusion between thought and sound in both, we discover there the outgoing creative principle of their differing organization. At that stage, abandoning the possibility of a gradual development of one from the other, we shall accord to each its own basis in the spirit of the race, and only within the general trend of linguistic evolution, and thus ideally only, will regard them as stages in a successful construction of language. By neglecting the careful separation here proposed of the calculable stepwise progress and the unpredictable, immediately creative advance of human mental power, we banish outright from world-history the effects of *genius,* which is no less displayed at particular moments in peoples than it is in individuals. (pp. 31-32)

Here Humboldt attempts to discredit the temporal, evolutionary view of the three types, but he still wishes to preserve an ideal model of "stages in a successful construction of language." Thus he can deny any "stepwise progress" of Monosyllabic languages toward the Organic languages, but he will still argue, in a later chapter on linguistic typology, that the "so-called agglutinating languages do not differ in type from the inflectional ones, as do those which reject all indication by means of inflection; they deviate only to the extent that their obscure endeavour in the same direction is more or less of a failure" (p. 107). This is to say, then, that Humboldt's vision of language as an organism is teleological but not evolutionary.

Humboldt's Kawi introduction marks an important chapter in the history of linguistics, for the transcendental comparatists had arrived at a crossroads in the treatment of language as an organism. In later interpretations of the problem of unity and variety, theorists like August Schleicher treat language as a self-contained entity that develops according to general laws; in their view, language is a natural organism that, prior to the utilitarian concern for communication, evolves in the same ways that plants and animals evolve.[16] Thus theorists like Schleicher employ a diachronic, evolutionary model of language in order to posit a principle of unity underlying linguistic variety and change. In Humboldt's account of language as an organism, on the other hand, the "inner life-principle" is a synchronic, atemporal principle of unity. The influx of spiritual, creative energy into a nation is registered in the unfolding forms of the nation's language, but this "spirit of the race" is not part of a gradual evolution.

The distinction between the synchronic and diachronic approaches to language has been made familiar by the work of Ferdinand de Saussure, but it is a distinction that many nineteenth-century linguists did not recognize. It fits within Saussure's larger purpose of arguing for the arbitrary nature of the linguistic sign, an argument that directly counters the nineteenth-century view of language as an organism. Thus, for instance, Saussure argues against the idea of language as a purposive organism that evolves toward a necessary system of forms, and he insists that language be regarded as form only, not as substance.[17] Perhaps the best way to appreciate Saussure's point is to consider what would happen if a theory were to combine an evolutionary, diachronic account of linguistic change and diversity with Humboldt's idealist, synchronic account. The result could be called a theory of "spiritual and linguistic evolution" or "the evolution of the national spirit." According to such a view, the "spirit of the race" would be temporally revealed in the three stages of language, so that the languages of the more "evolved" races—those of the Indo-European family—would reveal a more highly developed spirit through more highly developed forms.

By invoking Humboldt at the beginning of **"The Growth of Words,"** Whitman confronts the problem of finding unity within linguistic diversity and change. His response is precisely the theory of spiritual evolution that results from giving a diachronic interpretation of Humboldt's synchronic idealism. One reason for the response is that Whitman's knowledge of Humboldt stems from his reading of Christian C. J. Bunsen's *Outlines of the Philosophy of Universal History* and Maxmilian Schele de Vere's *Outlines of Comparative Philology,* both of which present the combination of the two approaches in a fully articulated account of language as an organism.

Bunsen's evolutionary theory of language permeates the text of *Outlines.* In the chapter "Mutual Relation of the three Forms of Language, progressive and retro-

gressive," for example, Bunsen reacts to Humboldt's argument against the idea of "gradual progress" with a combination of consternation and disbelief:

> After this lucid statement of the gradual growth of grammatical forms, it is extraordinary that Humboldt should still have doubted a possible historical transition between the different forms. Professor Boethlingk's words on this point deserve to be quoted together with Humboldt's. "It is inconceivable," he writes, "how, with such a view on the origin of inflection, any one can doubt for a moment about the possibility of two such languages as Chinese and Sanskrit having the same origin."[18]

Bunsen's solution to the problem of unity is precisely the theory of "gradual progress" that Humboldt wishes to avoid. That is, Bunsen views Chinese as simply a less developed version of Sanskrit. Because Sanskrit has already passed through the Monosyllabic and Agglutinative "stages," it reveals a higher development along the scale of spiritual evolution.

Bunsen's account of Humboldt's theory influenced Whitman's view of language considerably, and we can see that influence in two entries Whitman made in the notebook **Words** concerning Humboldt. In the first, Whitman quotes directly from Bunsen's summary of Humboldt's Kawi introduction: "Language is the outward expression of what he calls the spirit or individuality of a nation" (**DBN,** III, 721; cf. **Outlines,** I, 282). In the second note, Whitman summarizes Bunsen's account of Humboldt's three classes of language:

Von Humboldt

"Language expresses originally objects only, and leaves the understanding to supply the connecting form—afterwards facilitating and improving the connections and relations by degrees. (**DBN,** III, 721)

The first part of the passage—from the quotation mark to the dash—is a direct citation of Bunsen's version of Humboldt's discussion of linguistic typology. Humboldt bases his discussion of the three classes of language on the dual function of any word: "For to the act of designating the *concept* itself there is allied also a special operation of the mind which transposes that concept into a particular *category* of thought or speech; and the word's full meaning is the simultaneous outcome of that conceptual expression and this modifying hint" (p. 100). Bunsen simplifies Humboldt's ideas by making designation depend upon the correspondence of word to *object* rather than word to *concept*. More important, Whitman's summary of the passage transforms Humboldt into a diachronic, evolutionary theorist. The adverb "afterwards" shows Whitman's temporal interpretation of Humboldt, while the verbs "facilitating" and "improving" reveal the poet's evolutionary view of changing grammatical forms. And Whitman's first note suggests that this evolution is not merely linguistic, since the language is the "outward expression of . . . the spirit or individuality of a nation."

A second major source for Whitman's theory of spiritual evolution is Maxmilian Schele de Vere's *Outlines of Comparative Philology*.[19] Schele de Vere's admitted purpose is "to state briefly, in a popular manner and with a view to give rather suggestive than complete information, what Comparative Philology is, and what it has done" (*Philology,* p. 3). At numerous points in the book, Schele de Vere shows that he adheres to the transcendental theory of language and that, like other popularizers of the theory, he merges the synchronic and diachronic treatments of language. For example, in the chapter "Methods of Comparative Philology," Schele de Vere repeats the idea of language as a living expression of the national spirit:

> Languages appear, then, no longer mere mechanical structures, but, in their higher vocations, as enveloping and embodying specific national notions. . . . Modern science . . . sees even in the caprices and fancies of an idiom only so many crystallized expressions of that mind of the nation which works unceasingly at the loom of its language, and weaves the fine texture of its idiom. (*Philology,* pp. 212-13)

Schele de Vere clearly follows Humboldt's idea of the "inner life-principle" of language, but the evolutionary interpretation of the "mind of the nation" is not so clear here as it is in Bunsen. In the chapter "The Three Great Classes of Language," however, he seems to agree with Bunsen's evolutionary interpretation of linguistic typology:

> The intimate connection between the mental life and culture of a nation and its language, explains why these most perfect and most highly developed idioms are found to be the work of those nations which have been or are now the best representatives of the progress made by man. The races that have successively ruled the world, have also possessed the languages that show the highest development, in expressing most, and that most best. To this third class of inflectional idioms [i.e., the Organic] belong, therefore, the Indo-European languages. (*Philology,* p. 233)

Schele de Vere's ethnocentrism is obvious enough, and the progressivist assumptions underlying such phrases as "most perfect and most highly developed idioms" and "the best representatives of the progress made by man" do not require clarification. He differs from Bunsen, on the other hand, in his rejection of the idea that "every language had to pass through each of these three classes, as through so many stages of gradual development, progressing from a monosyllabic expres-

sion of the idea only to a mechanical combination of two sounds, in order finally to accomplish the organic union of inflected words" (p. 234). Schele de Vere's view of language, then, appears to be much like Humboldt's: Because languages are created prior to our knowledge of them, we cannot assert that all languages passed through the three stages (p. 235).

Schele de Vere's version of spiritual evolution emerges from his discussion of the so-called decay of modern Indo-European languages, and his treatment of language is as evolutionary as Bunsen's. The idea of linguistic "decay" arose from the observation that highly inflected languages like Sanskrit, Greek, and Latin had developed into analytic languages, which employ word order rather than inflectional endings to signal the grammatical function of a word. To some theorists, this process seemed to signal the reversal of language making, since the Organic languages appeared to be reverting to the stage of the Monosyllabic languages.[20] But Schele de Vere asserts that this "decay" is only apparent, that "it is, in reality, a progress and improvement." To support that assertion, he invokes the principle of least effort:

> Language, being a spiritual manifestation of the mind, tries, like the mind itself, to rise above matter; it has a tendency, ever active and ever progressive, to strip off all forms with which thought is encumbered; it strives to free itself more and more. (*Philology,* pp. 238-39)

In Schele de Vere's view, the process of "leveling," by which synthetic, inflected languages move toward analytic, uninflected languages, is a progressivist process of spiritual evolution. Through leveling, language can cast aside the encumbering "body" of grammatical forms in order to move toward the expressive freedom of pure spirit and thought. Language, as a purposive, evolving organism, "strives to free itself more and more," and the striving is a form of spiritual evolution. Moreover, Schele de Vere calls this "the same law which governs language as well as all organic nature" (p. 240). Thus Schele de Vere shows himself to be a less naive evolutionist than Bunsen, but he is nonetheless an evolutionist. In both of these popular introductions to the new science of comparative philology, Humboldt's synchronic idealism becomes a diachronic, evolutionary account of the linguistic organism.

The shifts I have described in the history of transcendental language theory are reenacted in the last two chapters of *Rambles Among Words.* Whitman begins with the synchronic, philosophical aspect of the organic theory, but he moves to a diachronic treatment of language as a temporally evolving organism. In **"The Growth of Words,"** the poet begins with the idea that language is "begotten of the blended love of spirit and of matter," but he finds that in his search for a unifying principle he must state the idea of unity again and again: "Language is begotten of a lustful longing to express, through the plastic vocal energy, man's secret sense of his unity with nature" (***Rambles,*** p. 266). One reason for this restatement is the persistence of "lustful longing"; another is that the human sense of unity with nature is "secret." Whitman cannot actually prove the unity of spirit and matter; he can only state and restate his "secret sense," which is itself never completely known or completely expressed.

If Whitman's philosophy of language seems close to the transcendental idealism of Humboldt, the parallel is even more striking in the next two paragraphs:

> This vitality of speech manifests itself in a two-fold manifestation: in the possession of a distinctive personality and identity—in material elements and formal laws that stamp it with the stamp of linguistic individuality; and, further, in that other characteristic of every living organism—in the exhibition of growth, progress, decay—in the ongoing processes of absorption, assimilation and elimination—in the inworking and outworking of the creative energy.
>
> And it is in this sense that the English language is alive—as displaying successive processes of growth and development within the limits of its linguistic individuality. (p. 266)

Here Whitman states his two laws of language, which correspond to the twin problems of linguistic diversity and linguistic change. Like Humboldt, Whitman perceives language as a never-ceasing dialectic between the finite forms of linguistic individuality and the formless flux of linguistic change. But unlike Humboldt—and like Bunsen and Schele de Vere—he proposes an evolutionary solution to the opposition. He therefore combines the two signs of linguistic vitality in "successive processes of growth and development." For Humboldt the influx of spiritual energy into a language is inexplicable, a part of the "inner life-principle." For Whitman, on the other hand, the influx is part of the inherent, organic development of a language through time, and it can be understood by grasping the evolution of a language through history. So Whitman responds to the metaphysical problem of the "secret sense" of unity by translating it into progressivist terms of "growth and development."

Whitman's shift from metaphysics to evolution is accompanied by a move from the individual spirit to the national spirit. He hints at the movement by specifying that the *English* language is alive, and he proceeds to direct his attention to the evolution of English as an organism:

> Shooting its deep tap-root into eldest antiquity, drawing from the pith and sap of that grandest of all families of races and tongues—the Indo-European

stock; receiving living grafts from France and Italy and Scandinavia, this divine tree of the English Speech has grown up into its sublime proportions nurtured by the history of a thousand years. (p. 267)

As in **"America's Mightiest Inheritance"** and **"Our Language and Literature,"** Whitman's grandiose claims for the English language are based on an evolutionary interpretation of its history. The Indo-European languages are the "grandest of all families of races and tongues," and English has become a "divine tree" of "sublime proportions" because the spirit of Englishspeaking nations is the most highly evolved in history. As Whitman asserts in the same paragraph, "the History of a Language is measurable only in terms of all the factors that have shaped a people's life" (p. 267). From **"America's Mightiest Inheritance"** we know that those factors would include the "perfection of politics, erudition, science, metaphysics, inventions, poems, the judiciary, printing, steam-power, mails, architecture" (p. 55). We can therefore see that an evolutionary account of language entails an evolutionary account of the national spirit.

In order to support the organic metaphor of English as a "divine tree," Whitman turns to the history of the language, a turn similar to the chronological argument of **"America's Mightiest Inheritance."** And it is here that the "thought of the Ensemble" comes sharply into focus:

> A History of the English Language, rising out of a full appreciation of the Philosophy of Speech (to which must go that large hospitality and impartiality that flows from the thought of the Ensemble), answering the requirements of modern research, and after the broad, free methods America lets down, has yet to come. (***Rambles,*** p. 268)

This involved sentence raises several important points. First, the diachronic "History" of language and the synchronic "Philosophy of Speech" merge in the flow of Whitman's "thought of the Ensemble." Second, while referring to objective concepts like "History," "Philosophy," and "Ensemble," Whitman's language emphasizes the subjective, personal "appreciation," "hospitality and impartiality," and "thought" of an unnamed thinker, a thinker who must also be modern, scholarly but freely methodical, and American. Third, in the main clause of the sentence Whitman denounces the present lack of the "History," but in the three qualifying phrases he defines the formula for its future realization. His rhetoric mixes the present and future in much the same way that his theory mixes the synchronic and diachronic approaches to language.

This threefold merging provides a glimpse into the workshop of Whitman's theory. In the three phrases qualifying **"History of the English Language,"** style overrides logic, emphasizing a progressive, evolutionary "flow" within which the boundaries between opposites blur and very nearly dissolve. That tendency in Whitman's thought is particularly clear in the concept of "Ensemble," which he defines later in **Rambles Among Words:** "The totality as distinguished from the details. A noble word with immense vista" (p. 283). When Whitman thinks the "thought of the Ensemble," he disregards "details" of difference in order to perceive a "totality" underlying linguistic diversity and change.

The concept of the "Ensemble" is, without doubt, what we would now call a totalizing figure. And the etymology of the word, from the late Latin *insimul,* meaning "at the same time," suggests a synchronic, timeless notion of totality. But in defining the word himself, Whitman links this totalizing figure to the figure of "vista." In Whitman's vocabulary, "vista" indicates the temporal flow toward the future. In **"By Blue Ontario's Shore,"** for example, the poet proclaims that "others take finish, but the Republic is ever constructive and ever keeps vista."[21] Similarly, in the dialogue with Traubel concerning **Leaves of Grass** as a "language experiment," the "new vista" corresponds to the progressivist spirit of America that "will not be satisfied" until its "new potentialities of speech" are "evolved." Thus the word "vista" evokes a diachronic, evolutionary view of both language and spirit, while "ensemble" evokes a synchronic, idealist view of totality and unity. And Whitman will keep neither the two ideas nor the two approaches separate from one another. "Ensemble" and "vista" merge in the poet's evolutionary perception of an America that is "ever constructive," both in its language and in its national "life-spirit."

The evolutionary merging of "ensemble" and "vista" develops more fully when Whitman repeats his "appreciation of the organic laws of the English Language in its historic unfolding," an appreciation that is "inseparable from considerations that embrace the ensemble of Languages" (**Rambles,** p. 268). The only "ensemble of Languages" Whitman actually considers is the Indo-European (he also refers to it as the Japhetic, or Iranic, family), for it contains the "noble and highly developed languages" that reflect the IndoEuropean mind, the highest product of the evolutionary process: "Science was born in that mind, the intuition of nature, the instinct for political organization and that direct practical normal conduct of life and affairs" (p. 269). The poet's embrace of the Indo-European "ensemble" leaves no room for any pessimism associated with the "decay" of languages:

> From this mind, too, flowered out the grandest and most spiritual of languages. The Japhetic or Iranic tongues are termed by the master-philologers the Organic Group, to distinguish them from the Agglutinative and Inorganic speech-floors that underlie them in the Geology of Language. They alone have reached the altitude of free intellectual

individuality and organism. To them belongs the splendid plasticity of Sanskrit, Greek, German, English! (pp. 269-70)

This passage registers the combined impact of Bunsen and Schele de Vere. Bunsen provides the evolutionary slant that Whitman gives to the three classes of language, while Schele de Vere provides the emphasis he places on the ever-increasing spirituality and "free intellectual individuality" of the Indo-European languages. Whitman's four examples of "splendid plasticity"—Sanskrit, Greek, German, and English—are arranged in a rough chronological order, from most ancient to most modern. Even more important, however, is the order according to the process of leveling: Sanskrit is the most synthetic of the four languages, while English is the most analytic. In Schele de Vere's terms, English is more spiritually evolved than the earlier languages and modern German because it has freed itself from the encumbering forms of inflectional endings. Once again, therefore, Whitman interprets the "ensemble" of Indo-European languages by their progressive evolution toward the "free intellectual individuality and organism" of English. And the geological metaphor that controls the passage implies that the evolution is ancient, inevitable, and ongoing.

In the remaining pages of **"The Growth of Words,"** Whitman develops the implication that the English language exhibits the world's highest "altitude" of spiritual evolution. Taking the fall of the Roman Empire as his historical locus, he contrasts the "vigorous, individual, egotistic German" to the "decaying Latin." The "Teutonic genius" acts on the Latin language, "breaking up the crystalline structure of the classic mould, freeing the grammatical forms from their absorption in the terminations of nouns and verbs, and erecting them into independent prepositions and auxiliaries" (**Rambles,** p. 271). The poet's example recalls Humboldt's account of the new "living seed" that rebuilt the crumbling structure of late Latin, and his assessment of the phenomenon of leveling, the "passage from synthesis to analysis" (p. 271), is, like Schele de Vere's, overwhelmingly optimistic.

Whitman's optimism extends to the composite character of modern English, which forms an "ensemble" of diverse linguistic sources. Instead of bemoaning the fact that the "Teutonic genius" of Old English has been conquered by linguistic invasions from classical and modern civilizations, Whitman praises "the genius of the English race, which is unequaled in absorption and assimilation, in receptive and applicative power" (p. 272). Once again the historical discussion is cast in evolutionary terms: Anglo-Saxon is the heart and spine of English, but Norman French was needed for the Anglo-Saxon to grow into the English tongue, for without it the Anglo-Saxon could never have freed itself of "those useless and cumbersome forms" of inflection (p. 274). The classical contributions, which Whitman attributes exclusively to the Renaissance, "furnished the spiritual conceptions, and endowed the material body of the English speech with a living soul" (p. 277). The evolution—from Saxon to French to Greek and Latin—is always in the direction of increased spirituality, even though the late "inoculations" of classical words would seem to be more materialistic because of their "cumbersome forms." Moreover, Whitman ignores the process of "elimination" in his treatment of English as an organism. In terms reminiscent of **"America's Mightiest Inheritance,"** he asserts that "every addition to practical civilization, every scientific generalization, commerce in all its branches, foreign literary influence, diplomacy, religion, philosophy, sociology are the perpetual agents of linguistic increase" (p. 280). Because Whitman's concept of "ensemble" is irrevocably tied to the "vista" of future progress, the English "ensemble" is figured as perpetually growing and increasing.

The poet's progressivist vision of the "vista" of American English clearly structures the last two chapters of *Rambles Among Words.* **"The Growth of Words"** moves from the philosophical, synchronic concern for "man's secret sense of his unity with nature" to the "historic unfolding" of language as it evolves into a more and more highly spiritualized organism. From an attempted explanation of the metaphysical origins of language, Whitman moves to a spiritual genealogy of the English language. And in the last chapter, **"English in America,"** the genealogy moves into the present and, inevitably, into the future.

In **"English in America"** Whitman focuses upon the English language as "the speech of the Modern," expressing "the spirit of the modern, breaking up the crystalline structure of the classic mould—the splendid newness, the aspirations of freedom, Individualism, democracy" (p. 286). The American spirit will act in the English language, which "expresses aristocracy and monarchy among the rest" of the spiritual influences shaping it, in exactly the same way that the "Teutonic genius" acted upon late Latin—"breaking up the crystalline structure of the classic mould." American English, then, expresses the "genius of a new age," and it will be subject to specifically American "agents of linguistic increase." The "mind of the ages" has thrown off aristocracy and monarchy, and it is not by accident that English has been transported to the new and vaster arena of America:

> Of course the English Language must take on new powers in America. And here we are favored by the genius of this grand and noble language, which more than all others lends itself plastic and willing to the moulding power of new formative influences. Was it supposed that the English Language was finished? But there is no finality to a Language! The English has vast vista in it—vast vista in America. (*Rambles*, p. 287)

Whitman's progressivist vision is signaled by the single word "vista." Although the English language is an "ensemble" of the past's formative influences, it must take on new powers if it is to express the new democratic spirit of America. For that reason Whitman turns to "future expansions" of American English, expansions that "follow the divine indications" the history of the language provides.

Whitman takes as a "spinal fact" of that history the "composite character of our language" (p. 288) because the composite "ensemble" of the English language is a divine indication of the "spirit of the Language—moulded more and more to a large hospitality and impartiality" (p. 289). Because America is made up of diverse individual spirits from diverse nations and races, American English must express the "immense diversity of race, temperament, character" in "free, rich growths of speech." And America must never be content to crystallize its spirit in one "mould," for then the organism would cease to grow:

> Land of the Ensemble, to her the consenting currents flow, and the ethnology of the States draws the grand outline of that hospitality and reception that must mark the new politics, sociology, literature and religion. (p. 288)

For Whitman, linguistic diversity and linguistic change are mutually supporting processes of spiritual evolution. The "ensemble" must flow into "vista," and the "vista" must contribute to the receptive hospitality of the "ensemble." The poet applies the progressivist theory of spiritual evolution to the special case of English in America, where the English language and American social conditions coincide exactly. Each has absorbed and assimilated diverse elements from diverse lands, and each reflects the union of those elements in the "vista" of a totalized and evolving "ensemble."

Whitman's entire account of language has as its basis the process of spiritual evolution, and the goal of the process is, in his eyes, the "spontaneous expansions" of American English and American "life-spirit." As the poet nears the end of his account, the evolutionary nature of his theory leads him to consider how these future "spontaneous expansions" are to be encouraged. Opposing his own theory of "hospitality and reception" to the "theory of repression" that stresses ethnic and linguistic uniformity, Whitman calls for a new "American literat," a figure whose principal qualities will be "large knowledge of the philosophy of speech" and "rich aesthetic instincts" (pp. 289-90). The first of these qualities recalls Whitman's requirement for a history of the English language (p. 268), and the two qualities taken together raise the question of why the poet's evolutionary theory of spirit and language must imply a theory of literary expression.

One answer would focus upon the poet's inability to distinguish between his theoretical and practical interests, between historical linguistics and *Leaves of Grass.* A second, perhaps better, answer would focus on Whitman's sense of the relationship between language at large and the uses language is put to in literature. The coda to **"English in America"** hits upon that very relationship:

> Over the transformations of a Language the genius of a nation unconsciously presides—the issues of Words represent issues in the national thought. And in the vernal seasons of a nation's life the formative energy puts forth verbal growths opulent as flowers in spring. (p. 291)

The "genius of a nation" and "the formative energy" are virtual synonyms here, and they combine to represent American English as an unconscious and necessary expression of "national thought." The passage recalls Humboldt's view of an "inner life-principle," and it suggests that the "formative energy" of American English will seek expression in vernal/verbal "growths."

The idea of language as an unconscious expression of the national spirit is important for Whitman's theory of literature because he gives the idea his characteristic evolutionary twist. In a passage from *Rambles Among Words* that clearly echoes **"America's Mightiest Inheritance,"** Whitman transfers the "inner life-principle" of language to the lips of the democratic people:

> And the vast billowy tendencies of modern life, too— the new political, social, scientific births—are making new demands on the English idiom. It is for America especially to evoke new realizations from the English speech. Always waiting in a language are untold possibilities. On the lips of the people, in the free rich unconscious utterance of the popular heart are the grand eternal leadings and suggestions.

> Of all the heritages which America receives the English language is beyond all comparison the mightiest. Language of the grand stocks, language of reception, of hospitality, it is above all fitted to be the speech of America. There is nothing fortuitous in language. It is for reasons the English idiom is here. In the English, more than all others, was concentrated the spirit of the modern, breaking up the old crystalline classic mould. No language has, no language ever had, such immense assimilation as the English. Freely it absorbs whatever is of use to it, absorbs and assimilates it to its own fluid and flexible substance. This rich copious hospitable flow is to be encouraged. (p. 12)

The function of literature is to encourage the "rich copious hospitable flow" of both American English and the American "spirit of the modern." The spirit is always present in the "free rich unconscious utterance" of the people, but literature can take the "popular heart" toward "the grand eternal leadings and suggestions." That is, literature encourages the evolution of the "popular heart" toward spiritual fluidity and flexibility. Whitman envisions literature as the expression of "untold possibilities" in the twin realms of language and spirit, for it evokes "new realizations" that match "the new political, social, scientific births," and those realizations carry the "popular heart" from material to spiritual "leadings and suggestions." Literature points the reader in that direction by employing an exemplary "language of reception," a "fluid and flexible substance."

Democratic Vistas shows how fundamental the theory of spiritual evolution is to Whitman's vision of American politics, society, and literature.[22] The theme of "the grand experiment of development," of "the law over all, and law of laws . . . the law of successions" (*PW,* II, 380-81), runs throughout the poet's attempt to reconcile democracy and the individual, but it is crystallized in one particular passage. Faced with the ruptures of the "Secession War" and the corruptions of postwar American government and business, Whitman calls for America to "attain harmony and stability by consulting ensemble and the ethic purports, and faithfully building upon them." His account of the "ensemble" is, as in *Rambles Among Words,* based upon the "vista" of linguistic and spiritual evolution. There are, says Whitman, three stages of development in America:

> The First stage was the planning and putting on record the political foundation rights of immense masses of people. . . .

> The Second stage relates to material prosperity, wealth, produce, laborsaving machines. . . .

> The Third stage, rising out of the previous ones, to make them and all illustrious, I, now, for one, promulge, announcing a native expression-spirit, getting into form, adult, and through mentality, for these States, self-contain'd, different from others, more expansive, more rich and free, to be evidenced by original authors and poets to come, by American personalities, plenty of them, male and female, transversing the States, none excepted—and by native superber tableaux and growths of language, songs, operas, orations, lectures, architecture—and by a sublime and serious Religious Democracy, sternly taking command, dissolving the old, sloughing off surfaces, and from its own interior and vital principles, reconstructing, democratizing society. (*PW,* II, 409-10)

Whitman divides the three stages according to their position in time: The first is referred to in the past tense, the second in the present, and the third in a combination of present and future. Of course, the third stage exists only in Whitman's rhetorical act of "promulging" it. But without it, the first two stages would be incomplete, for the third stage bears the promise that the principles embodied in the Declaration of Independence and the federal Constitution will give rise to more than "laborsaving machines."

The third-stage mixture of present and future tenses recalls Whitman's simultaneous criticism and prophecy concerning the "History of the English Language" (*Rambles,* p. 268), and both passages typify the rhetoric of what Sacvan Bercovitch has called the "American jeremiad," in which the prophetic speaker fixes his eye both on the present failings of his people and on the future promise of their destiny. Modeled on the American Puritan political sermon, the American jeremiad fuses secular and sacred history in the same way that Bunsen, Schele de Vere, and Whitman fuse the diachronic and synchronic approaches to language. As Bercovitch explains, the progressivist theory of spiritual evolution is the basic assumption behind the American jeremiad, just as it is the underpinning of Whitman's theory of language and literature:

> The American Puritan jeremiad was the ritual of a culture on an errand—which is to say, a culture based on a faith in process. Substituting teleology for hierarchy, it discarded the Old World ideal of stasis for a New World vision of the future. Its function was to create a climate of anxiety that helped release the restless "progressivist" energies required for the success of the venture. . . . The future, though divinely assured, was never quite there, and New England's Jeremiahs set out to provide the sense of insecurity that would ensure the outcome. Denouncing or affirming, their vision fed on the distance between promise and fact.[23]

In *Democratic Vistas,* which Bercovitch calls "a work of symbolic interpretation" (p. 198), Whitman uses the theory of spiritual evolution to fill the gap between the ideals of American democracy—the symbol *America* itself—and the material results of democratic society. Whitman's ideal is a "Religious Democracy" in which the same American "growths of language" he called for in *Rambles Among Words* will be realized. His rhetoric does not present the ideal simply as a utopian dream; rather, it places the ideal in an evolving present, so that the ideal is "getting into form" in the act of the prophet's "announcing." By adding the "Third stage, rising out of the previous ones," Whitman returns America to a spiritual dimension he sees immanent in the Declaration and the Constitution. Nor is it an accident that the first and the third stages are characterized by verbal artifacts: In both, words are supposed to embody "interior and vital principles;" in both, matter and spirit, thing and word, are one.

Whitman's symbolic interpretation of America bears a remarkable similarity to the popularized versions of linguistic typology we have seen in Bunsen and Schele de Vere. The first stage represents the primary unity of spirit and matter, thought and word, embodied in the Declaration and the Constitution. The second represents the opposition of spirit and matter, where there are no words or thoughts at all—only "laborsaving machines." The third represents the reunion of spirit and matter in the synthesis of the previous two stages, in which material progress and spiritual progress are mirror images, both reflecting the "native expression-spirit."

For Whitman, literature is the "mightiest original non-subordinated SOUL" (*PW,* II, 413) that will lead America beyond mere material progress, beyond "the growing excess and arrogance of realism" (p. 417). The meaning of literature lies not so much in what it says or does but in what it leads to, and Whitman places his faith in the idea that it contributes to the evolution of a future American "Religious Democracy." For the poet, the promise of both language and literature is the promise of the spirit that "lies sleeping, aside, unrecking itself, in some western idiom, or native Michigan or Tennessee repartee, or stump speech— or in Kentucky or Georgia, or the Carolinas—or in some slang or local song or allusion of the Manhattan, Boston, Philadelphia, or Baltimore mechanic" (pp. 412-13). Literature functions to awaken that spirit, but it can do so only when its language answers to the constantly evolving national spirit:

> Prospecting thus the coming unsped days, and that new order in them—marking the endless train of exercise, development, unwind, in nation as in man, which life is for—we see, fore-indicated, amid these prospects and hopes, new law-forces of spoken and written language—not merely the pedagogue-forms, correct, regular, familiar with precedents, made for matters of outside propriety, fine words, thoughts definitely told out—but a language fann'd by the breath of Nature, which leaps overhead, cares mostly for impetus and effects, and what it plants and invigorates to grow—tallies life and character, and seldomer tells a thing than suggests or necessitates it. In fact, a new theory of literary composition for imaginative works of the very first class, and especially for highest poems, is the sole course open to these States. Books are to be call'd for, and supplied, on the assumption that the process of reading is not a half-sleep, but, in highest sense, an exercise, a gymnast's struggle; that the reader is to do something for himself, must be on the alert, must himself or herself construct indeed the poem, argument, history, metaphysical essay—the text furnishing the hints, the clue, the start or framework. Not the book needs so much to be the complete thing, but the reader of the book does. That were to make a nation of supple and athletic minds, well-train'd, intuitive, used to depend on themselves, and not on a few coteries of writers. (pp. 424-25)

According to Whitman's theory, literature does not provide clear-cut, well-defined forms in which the spirit of the reader can rest. To do so would be to sink into the inactivity of a "crystalline mould." Instead, literature must employ a language that "suggests or necessitates" a direction for the reader's waking spirit. By raising the unconscious power of American English to the level of conscious literary form, Whitman asserts, the "new law-forces of spoken and written language" will ensure the future spiritual progress of American readers. Just as the English language is America's "mightiest inheritance," therefore, so American literature is its "mightiest . . . SOUL," a soul that is as progressivist and evolutionary as Whitman's vistalike "thought of the Ensemble."

Abbreviations

CRE: Leaves of Grass: Comprehensive Reader's Edition, ed. Harold W. Blodgett and Sculley Bradley (New York: New York University Press, 1965).

DBN, III: *Daybooks and Notebooks,* III, ed. William White (New York: New York University Press, 1978).

Outlines: Christian C. J. Bunsen, *Outlines of the Philosophy of Universal History, Applied to Language and Religion* (London: Longmans, 1854).

Philology: Maxmilian Schele de Vere, *Outlines of Comparative Philology* (New York: Putnam's, 1853).

PW: Prose Works 1892 (vols. 1 and 2), ed. Floyd Stovall (New York: New York University Press, 1964).

Rambles: William Swinton, *Rambles Among Words,* rev. ed. (New York: Ivison, Blakeman, Taylor, 1872).

Notes

[1] Walt Whitman, *An American Primer,* ed. Horace Traubel (Boston: Small, Maynard, 1904), pp. viii-ix.

[2] For a useful bibliography of articles on Whitman and language, see Sherry G. Southard, "Whitman and Language: An Annotated Bibliography," *WWQR* 2:2 (1984): 31-49. Three book-length studies deserve special mention here: John E. Bernbrock, S.J., "Walt Whitman and 'Anglo-Saxonism,'" Ph.D. diss., University of North Carolina, 1961; Michael R. Dressman, "Walt Whitman's Study of the English Language," Ph.D. diss., University of North Carolina, 1974; and C. Carroll Hollis, *Language and Style in "Leaves of Grass"* (Baton Rouge: Louisiana State University Press, 1983).

Fowler and Wells published *American Phrenological Journal, Water-Cure Magazine,* and the first two editions of *Leaves of Grass.* "America's Mightiest Inheritance" is reprinted in *New York Dissected,* ed. Emory Holloway and Ralph Adimari (New York: Rufus Rockwell Wilson, 1936), pp. 51-65.

"Slang in America" was reprinted in *November Boughs* (1888) and appears in *PW,* II, 572-77. All references to Whitman's prose works are to this two-volume edition and are cited in my text as *PW,* with volume and page numbers.

[3] The most important study of the subject, though it does not treat Whitman and Dickinson, is Philip Gura's *The Wisdom of Words* (Middletown, Conn.: Wesleyan University Press, 1981).

[4] For a highly readable account of the numerous publications in England, see Hans Aarsleff, *The Study of Language in England, 1780-1860* (Princeton University Press, 1967; reprint University of Minnesota Press, 1983), pp. 162-263.

[5] "America's Mightiest Inheritance," p. 55. All further references to this essay appear in my text, cited by page number.

[6] "Our Language and Literature" appears in *DBN,* III, 809-11; all further references to the manuscript appear in my text.

[7] *CRE,* p. 738.

[8] The *Primer* notes appear in *DBN,* III, 728-57. *Words* appears in *DBN,* III, 664-727. All citations of Whitman's *Primer* and *Words* notebooks refer to *DBN,* III.

For an account of Whitman's role in the writing of *Rambles Among Words,* see my "Whitman as Ghost-Writer: The Case of *Rambles Among Words,*" *WWQR* 2:2 (1984): 22-30. Selections from *Rambles* have been published recently in *Notebooks and Unpublished Prose Manuscripts,* ed. Edward F. Grier (New York: New York University Press, 1984), V, 1624-62. Grier's introduction to the selections is helpful, but it was written before the publication of my essay, and Whitman's authorship is presented as more problematic than it in fact is. All references to Grier's edition appear in my text, cited as *NUPM.*

[9] *Rambles,* p. 265. As Grier points out, all three of the editions of *Rambles* are identical except for prefatory material (*NUPM,* V, 1624). Because I do not always cite material excerpted by Grier, I have chosen to refer to *Rambles Among Words* by short title and original page numbers; this will also serve to distinguish the printed book from Whitman's unpublished manuscript notes and notebooks. In editing *Rambles* for inclusion in *NUPM,* Grier provides the page numbers of the original edition, so in most cases the interested reader can easily find the cited passage.

The quotation from Humboldt is a translation of the second sentence of Section 11, "The Form of Language," in the introduction to the Kawi work. The title of the introduction is "Uber die Verschiedenheit des menschlichen Sprachbaues und ihren Einfluss auf die geistige Entwicklung des Menschengeschlechts" (1830-35). An English translation of the introduction is now available: *On Language,* trans. Stephen Heath (New York: Cambridge University Press, 1988). All quotations from Humboldt refer to this translation.

[10] My discussion of transcendental language theory has been aided by the following works: Oswald Ducrot et al., *Qu'est-ce que le structuralisme?* (Paris: Seuil, 1968), pp. 16-34; Oswald Ducrot and Tzvetan Todorov, *Encyclopedic Dictionary of the Sciences of Language,* trans. Catherine Porter (Baltimore, Md.: Johns Hopkins University Press, 1979), pp. 3-14; Ernst Cassirer, *The Philosophy of Symbolic Forms. Volume One: Language,* trans. Ralph Manheim (New Haven, Conn.: Yale University Press, 1955), pp. 117-67; Holger Pedersen, *The Discovery of Language: Linguistic Science in the Nineteenth Century,* trans. John Webster Spargo (Bloomington: Indiana University Press, 1962); Hans Aarsleff, *The Study of Language in England, 1780-1860,* and *From Locke to Saussure* (Minneapolis: University of Minnesota Press, 1982); and Michel Foucault, *The Order of Things: An Archaeology of the Human Sciences,* trans. Alan Sheridan (New York: Pantheon, 1970).

[11] Sir William Jones's address to the Asiatick Society in Calcutta on 2 February 1786 began the work developed most fully by Franz Bopp in *On the Conjugational System of the Sanskrit Language, in Comparison with that of the Greek, Latin, Persian, and Germanic Languages* (Frankfurt, 1816). See Aarsleff, *Study,* pp. 115-61, and Foucault, *Order,* pp. 280-300.

[12] Many versions of the typology exist in the discourse of nineteenth-century comparative philology. See, for example, Humboldt, *On Language,* pp. 100-108.

[13] See Otto Jespersen, *Progress in Language* (New York: Macmillan, 1894), pp. 1-16.

[14] Ibid.

[15] Schleicher's view is set forth clearly in his introduction to *A Compendium of the Comparative Grammar of the Indo-European, Sanskrit, Greek and Latin Languages,* trans. Herbert Bendall (London: Trübner, 1874), pp. 1-5. For the most extreme statement concerning linguistics as a natural science, see Schleicher, *Die Darwinsche Theorie und die Sprachwissenschaft* (Weimar: Hermann Böhlau, 1863).

[16] In order to make this argument, Schleicher divides human history and physical nature into separate categories. *Philology* is the study of the spiritual being of a people, and it concerns itself with *history* as the sphere within which the human will operates. *Linguistics,* by contrast, is the study of the unconscious necessity of language, and it concerns itself with *nature* as the sphere of immutable (phonetic) laws. See Schleicher, *Die Sprachen Europas* (Bonn: H.B. König, 1850), pp. 1-39. For an analysis of the distinction, see John Arbuckle, "August Schleicher and the Linguistics/Philology Dichotomy: A Chapter in the History of Linguistics," *Word* 26 (1970), 17-31.

[17] Ferdinand de Saussure, *Course in General Linguistics,* trans. Wade Baskin (New York: McGraw-Hill, 1966), pp. 79-100, especially pp. 83-87. For a clear account of Saussure's argument within the context of nineteenth-century linguistics, see Jonathan Culler, *Ferdinand de Saussure* (Harmondsworth, U.K.: Penguin, 1977), pp. 36-63.

[18] *Outlines,* I, 283. All quotations refer to this edition and are cited in my text as *Outlines.*

[19] A copy of *Philology,* with "Wm. Swinton, Greensboro, North Carolina," inscribed on the flyleaf, was part of Whitman's library at the time of his death. See C. Carroll Hollis, "Walt Whitman and William Swinton: A Cooperative Friendship," *American Literature* 30 (1959), 436.

[20] Schleicher affords clear examples of this view throughout his work, while Schele de Vere devotes a chapter to a survey of the problem in *Philology,* pp. 236-41.

[21] Line 19. Unless otherwise noted, all quotations from *Leaves of Grass* refer to *Variorum.* The printed text of the *Variorum* is the same as *CRE,* which follows the 1881 edition.

[22] *Democratic Vistas* (New York: J. S. Redfield, 1871). The eighty-four-page pamphlet combines two previously published essays: "Democracy" and "Personalism," both in *The Galaxy* in 1867 and 1868. See Gay Wilson Allen, *The New Walt Whitman Handbook* (New York: New York University Press, 1975), pp. 128-32.

[23] Sacvan Bercovitch, *The American Jeremiad* (Madison: University of Wisconsin Press, 1978), p. 23.

Byrne R. S. Fone (essay date 1992)

SOURCE: "Words Unsaid," in *Masculine Landscapes: Walt Whitman and the Homoerotic Text,* Southern Illinois University Press, 1992, pp. 10-19.

[*In the following essay, Fone offers an overview of how the homoeroticism in Whitman's work has been interpreted by critics over time. Fone maintains that when Whitman criticism has been centered on the subject of homosexuality, the homophobia inherent in much of the criticism has hampered both textual and biographical study.*]

It is without name . . . it is a word unsaid. . . .
—**"Song of Myself,"** 1855

Among the multitude of identities Walt Whitman claimed to contain, one, his "homosexual identity," has been the continued subject of a vexed questioning raised during his lifetime and pursued ever since. Presumptions were made: that he was homosexual, that he was heterosexual, that he was not sexual at all, that he transcended sexuality entirely, that he was bisexual. Of course, when he wrote *Leaves of Grass* (1855) and during most of his lifetime, these particular terms were specifically unavailable to him, even though the medical models that lie behind them were rapidly coalescing. During the late eighteenth and early nineteenth centuries, old, largely religious proscriptions concerned with sexual object choice—increasingly problematized, laden with anxiety, and historically unstable at best— coexisted in a state of considerable speculative dissonance with new theories—mostly legal and medical. These last posited very different ways of classification, identification, interpretation, and judgment of the social/historical (and hence political) as well as textual/ aesthetic consequences of sexual desire and act. These discourses, so furiously intent on self-revelation, as Foucault has observed and Smith-Rosenberg elaborated, were equally at odds with one another. As Smith-Rosenberg has said, "sexual discourse was just that, a discourse, at times a babel, but never a monologue." These discourses "created disparate fantasies, debated one another, condemned one another—all in the language of sexuality." Running as an obbligato beneath, around, and interpenetratingly through this general sexual discourse—was a hesitant, though incipiently powerful companion discourse engaged with both the theories about and the political actualities of the existence and experiences—in both the generally social and specifically sexual sense—of a discrete sexual minority whose constitution—self-defined not imposed—derived not from act but from the implications and imperatives of homoerotic desire. It is to this last discourse that Whitman most powerfully contributes. He was a major participant in this debate in his journalism, early verse, fiction, and notebooks, and *Leaves of Grass* appeared and was revised and enlarged at the time when that discourse became a monologue, dominated as Smith-Rosenberg says by "the voice of the bourgeois male."[1]

When the giddy formation and reformation of these radical speculations about sexuality (as opposed to sex to borrow Foucault's distinction) began to interpenetrate not only general texts but specific critical discussions, especially Whitman criticism, that dominant male voice was there most often heard. But the substance of these discourses was only hazily appreciated and sometimes even more vaguely appropriated by those writers who addressed what most saw as the "problem" of Whitman's sexuality. More damaging, the discourse was often deliberately misread, especially by those who chose to definitively situate Whitman within one or another spectrum of sexuality. In section 52 of **"Song of Myself,"** Whitman foretold the coming fluctuating ambiguity of critical language when he said about himself *as text:* "I effuse my flesh in eddies and drift it in lacy jags." To most early readers Whitman's sexuality seemed more important than textuality. At one obsessed juncture even Symonds—Whitman's earliest and in many ways still most provocative critic— was more interested in what the text revealed about Whitman's extra-textual activities than what the text revealed about itself.

Many critics who addressed the subject after Whitman's death vehemently denied what many of them clearly felt was a blot on the purity of the legend or attempted to dehomosexualize the undeniable celebrations of the text by forceful denial, by ingenious misreading, or as in the celebrated instance of Emory Holloway's pronomial blindness, by textual tampering.[2] Even if the homoeroticism of the texts was grudgingly admitted, critics recoiled at the possibility that what art implied life might ratify. But just as Foucault said in the larger context, it was through this continued process of constant verbal denial that the discourse was begun. Even if the physical manifestation was doubted, dismissed, or trivialized, the homosexuality thus defused, diffused, or purified as a "psychical" predilection (to use a term from Eduard Bertz, an early commentator who did presume that Whitman was homosexual), the question about Whitman's sexuality rather than about the sexual resonance of the texts became inevitably the paramount subject.[3] For example, in 1906 Bliss Perry, Whitman's earliest scholarly biographer insisted that "as far as I know there has never been the slightest evidence that Whitman practised homo-sexuality." He asserted that in his conversations with those who knew Whitman well—Burroughs, Traubel, and Bucke—"I have never heard the slightest hint of the charge" that Whitman was homosexual.[4] As Robert K. Martin in *The Homosexual Tradition in American Poetry* has shown, such denial and fear of criminalization (note "charge") has dominated Whitman biography until very recently. Martin describes this general "distortion of meaning and the willful misreading" of the poet as a powerful example of the maintenance of "social and moral prejudice." It should be noted, he adds, that "the very few critics who spoke against this tradition of distortion were Europeans, who perhaps did not share American society's total and relentless hostility to the homosexual."[5]

Since Martin wrote, some of the blunt instruments used to threaten the academic homosexual discourse concerned with Whitman's homosexual discourse have been tactfully retired, but much of the hostility is still present, and subtler weapons with sharper edges are still wielded.[6] In 1955, for example, G. W. Allen could assert that the early Calamus emotions were "not yet pathological" and doubted that "actual perversion" was likely between Peter Doyle and Whitman.[7] While three decades later such language is rarely used, and indeed—except in political or religious homophobic discourse—is no longer acceptable, nevertheless, some recent critics have suggested that Whitman's homosexual discourse is not an issue worth talking about. Writing in 1985 about "Whitman in the Eighties," William White—to whom Whitman scholars are so much in debt—mentions that in the 1980s a few scholars have written an "article or two, or a chapter in a book, on the subject of Whitman's homosexuality." Most critics nowadays, he says, are not "sidestepping the issue." But he continues, "for some of us it is simply not an issue since there is no real evidence that Whitman was a practicing homosexual." White seems to feel that without practice there is no homosexuality. Hence it is not a subject worth discussing, since, as he says, even though "writers in gay magazines" feel that Whitman was one of them, most "contributors to the periodicals prefer dealing with other subjects."[8]

Writing in 1988, David S. Reynolds is not willing to come "to a firm conclusion about Whitman's sexual preferences" and instead does seem to sidestep the "issue" by asserting that Whitman "wanted to avoid the deceit and artificiality, the amorality, that he associated with the heterosexual love plot." Reynolds argues that a way of "avoiding the love plot was to emphasize adhesive love," which "in the phrenological terms of the day was not associated with homosexuality." Thus Reynolds seems to imply that Whitman didn't really mean it.[9] It is true that Whitman drew his term *adhesive* from phrenology; it is true that he was appalled by sentimental plots about heterosexual love. But that did not stop him from writing sentimental stories about veiled homoerotic relationships between men and boys, and most of his poems in **"Calamus"** are, after all, love plots dealing with relationships between men. Furthermore, in ***Democratic Vistas*** (1871) Whitman noted that he looked for the presence of "adhesive love" to offset the long reign of "amative love hitherto possessing imaginative literature," making a clear distinction between the two and for good measure adding "love" to phrenology's non-specific terms (***PW*** 414). He insisted in **"Song of the Open Road"** (1856) that his use of the term was new: it was "not previously fashioned." He specifically equates it with the emotions and the acts of homosexual desire.[10] Both White and Reynolds seem eager to disassociate "Whitman" from homosexuality, and despite their evenhandedness their narrative is in that sense homophobic. What White overlooks is that gay scholars—until recently—have been as threatened by the subtle as by the blunt instruments of academic power and that such comments trivialize and affect the viability and visibility of an exchange between scholars—gay or not—about gay writers. The possibility that Reynolds overlooks, more simply, is that it may not have been only the deceit and amorality of the "heterosexual love plot" that Whitman disliked; it may have been the heterosexuality.

Both early and recent discussions of Whitman's sexuality tend to deny the possibility of homosexual acts or the validity of homosexual feelings, employ a language powerfully charged with disapprobation, and dismiss the question as relatively unimportant, as Bliss Perry's early and David Reynolds' and William White's later examples demonstrate. To some writers, homosexual feelings are so repugnant that their presence in a text seems almost to invalidate the text itself. For example, this position, documented by Martin in his observations on the work of several critics, was taken by Mark van Doren in 1942 when he described Whitman's "manly love" as "deficient and abnormal love," and by Edwin Miller (1968), who suggested that Whitman's "deviancy" and "absence of [heterosexual] experience" are barriers to a mature art. This position admits the homosexuality but insists, as Martin observes, that homosexuality contributed to his art in no way "except to flaw it."[11] So John Snyder (1975) speculates that the "lover in **"Calamus"** . . . fails because failure is the given end of homosexuality" and thus implies that because of that double failure the text fails too. David Leverenz (1989) bluntly announces that Whitman's homosexuality and homoeroticism "make me, as a heterosexual male, recoil."[12] Leverenz' comment is only the most recent example of an attitude engaged by the earliest reviewer of ***Leaves of Grass,*** Rufus Griswold, whose angry review in *The New York Criterion* of 10 November 1855 concluded with the warning that these texts dealt with the unspeakable, so unspeakable that he could not name "it" in English. In one of the earliest recognitions of the homoerotic textuality of Whitman's poetry, Griswold asserted his own speechlessness concerning the presumed subject of the text: "In our allusion to this book, we have found it impossible to convey . . . even the most faint idea of its style and contents, and of our disgust and detestation of them, without employing language that cannot be pleasing to ears polite." He relies on Latin to make his point: "Peccatum illud horribile, inter Christianos non nominandum."[13] This same classic description of sodomy was given by a Maryland court in 1810 that described it as the most "horrid and detestable crime, (among Christians not to be named)."[14] The formula has been—and seems occasionally still to be—constantly written: homosexuality is a sin not to be named, repugnant not only to Christians but also to critics.

The Whitman discourse, when centered on homosexuality, has had to carry a heavy baggage of externalized and (surely) internalized homophobia, which freight has encumbered textual and biographical study. But of course, this homophobia is also a useful part of the discourse, since it sets in train fecund speculation about the place of such prohibitive discourses in current thought about Whitman and within the nexus, not only of his own self-evaluation, but of the aesthetic, historical, and political siting of his texts as counterdiscourses. The deep questions are thus implied in Leverenz's word "recoil" or raised by asking why it is, as White says, that critics "prefer dealing with other subjects" than Whitman's homosexuality, with other subjects than that which Whitman himself described as the "pulse" of his life. Indeed, even so careful and intuitive a critic as M. Jimmie Killingsworth, who does deal with the subject in *Whitman's Poetry of the Body* (1989), can speak of "indulging homosexual experiences" as opposed to "engaging" in them, can perhaps unintentionally refer to Whitman's "indirect denial of his perversion," and can also say, somewhat astoundingly given his otherwise careful language throughout the book, that "to charge Whitman with homosexuality, we need to have Whitman in our historical background." The theory is unexceptionable, the diction—that unhappy "charge"—distressing.[15]

It was Whitman himself who first recognized that these are attitudes shared by both the critic and the culture. His recognition is implicit in the very formulations of his text. When he speaks in **"Vigil Strange I Kept on the Field One Night"** about a "boy of responding kisses" for example, implicit therein is the presumption that most boys do not respond to the kisses of men and that boys who do are "men like me," who, like those in **"Calamus"** 4, love "as I am capable of loving." The qualifications of his texts are significant, not the presumed subjects or actions. Here *responding, like,* and *as*—not *kisses* or *loving* or *men*—are the key signs that show the nature of the discourse. Just so the key elements in his statement "Or may-be a stranger will read this who has secretly loved me" (Bowers 94), are *stranger* and *loved*." The specific "stranger" who could be loved in the specifically anonymous though significantly public locale *stranger* suggests, spotlights and defines the nature of the "love", the kind of love that deliberately transgresses against public codes of privacy, intimacy, and decency and has a specific, encoded speech that can be read by those who can understand it, a speech created not through logic but by signified desire, a desire ratified through sexual contact. Whitman was well aware that most people (Smith-Rosenberg's "bourgeois males") would answer no to his questions since a yes answer might well invoke those dangerous concerns Sedgwick has described as "homosexual panic."[16] Those who could say yes to the question would be eligible for admittance into what these few—at least if our own current research is on the right track—were beginning to suspect was most surely a fraternity.

It was also clear to Whitman how both culture and the common reader might respond to his writing, and a good deal of the critical heritage has proved him right.

He enunciates the insight hesitantly in one of his earliest stories, **"The Child's Champion"** (1841), when he observes that "the forms of custom . . . so generally smother" the "wish to love and be loved" (*NUPM* 1:74 n. 23). Whitman emphasises "wish" here, not act. In the rather narrow area of act, Allen is right when he says that unless positive proof of homosexual acts can be obtained, then no biographer can make an assertion that a homosexual act—he calls it "sodomy"—actually took place.[17] As Justin Kaplan also observes, "coherent, honest, and sensitive biographical narrative relies on intimate evidence and . . . evidence of this sort is hard to find when you're dealing with Whitman." Kaplan goes on to suggest that "maybe it doesn't matter" what "Whitman actually 'did' with Peter Doyle and the others." Of course it does matter, and saying that it doesn't is another example of the critical trivialization of homosexual sex and desire. Kaplan is precisely correct, however, when he says that "what does matter is the way Whitman defines himself as homosexual in his poetry, in his letters and journals, in his daily conduct, in his frequently tormented relations with younger men and his evasive relations with women." He further says that it is important how Whitman defines himself as homosexual "in the way he uses democratic political models as a way of emancipating sexuality, in the way he invokes androgyny as a liberating imaginative mode." Kaplan insists that "we have to acknowledge the gulf that exists between the life Whitman lived, to the extent that we can learn it, and the imagined life that appears in his poems."[18]

Kaplan believes that the "cycle of discussion, as far as the sexuality issue is concerned, seems to have completed and maybe exhausted itself."[19] I am not at all sure that this is so, and I am supported by a good deal of the most recent criticism. Indeed the sexuality question—though perhaps in a very different sense than Kaplan means—is still provocatively being explored. The tradition of such current explorations begins of course with J. A. Symonds. Symonds' letters to Whitman (despite the gossipy subtext concerned with who, what, and when) and his *Walt Whitman, A Study* (1893) mark the precise moments wherein the study of the sexual interpenetrations of Whitman's textuality begins. And that process is ratified, perhaps inadvertently and in a prohibitive context (note "diagnosis"), by Eduard Bertz in a letter (1914) to W.C. Rivers, wherein he observes that "for the diagnosis of homosexuality, such deeds are of secondary importance only, it is true; the manner of feeling unveiled in Whitman's works, is primarily evidential."[20] Continued by Edward Carpenter in *Days With Walt Whitman* (1906) and *Some Friends of Walt Whitman: A Study of Sex Psychology* (1924), the gradual process of disentangling Whitman's texts, at least from the rigors of critical homophobia, were best assisted by Frederik Schyberg (1933), Malcolm Cowley (1946), Newton Arvin (1938), and Roger Asselineau (1960/1962), among earlier studies, while the work of Robert K. Martin, *The*

Homosexual Tradition in American Poetry (1979), stands as an original bridge between them and recent books by Betsy Erkkila (1989), M. Jimmie Killingsworth (1989), and Michael Moon (1991), which reflect the new and richly provocative paths that gay and feminist gender studies have begun to open.[21] Martin's book, now a classic study, first fully opened up the possibilities of considering Whitman's texts as homosexual texts rather than as poems by a writer who may have been homosexual. His book is a landmark in gay studies, and though he has been criticized for his unitary articulation of "the" Homosexual Tradition, his conclusions about the homosexual text have anticipated most later studies, and are the foundation upon which they rightfully rest.

Erkilla, in *Whitman: The Political Poet,* is most interested in the structures of Whitman's texts as they are produced by and affect questions of power, race, class, and gender, that is, questions of politics and history. Erkilla's argument that Whitman conflated his own eroticized body and the political body of America is unexceptionable; the book is a carefully and excitingly documented study. Her reading of the homosexual textuality of **"Song of Myself,"** though, is not as extensive, and of **"Calamus"** not as profound, as Martin's or as Killingsworth's in *Whitman's Poetry of the Body: Sexuality, Politics, and the Text.* Killingsworth considers many of the same questions that Erkilla poses but confronts more conclusively and provocatively the question of sexuality and the homosexual text. Erkilla's study derives its force from the dense texture of political text and context, deals with the homosexual textuality largely as a surface manifestation, and is, it seems to me, limited in its observations about the generalized "(homo)sexuality," as she describes it, of the texts. Killingsworth, while solidly attending to the political context, also derives his illuminating conclusions by situating his readings of Whitman within a context that includes sexual advice and health literature and early feminist texts contemporaneous with Whitman. Killingsworth's book addresses the deep homosexual texture of the poetry more extensively and originally than any study since Martin, explores Whitman's sexual politics, and maps, as he says using Sedgwick's word's, "an 'anxious, sharply dichotomised landscape' of social, political, and poetic relationships" within which Whitman "lived and wrote."[22] Michael Moon's *Disseminating Whitman: Revision and Corporeality in "Leaves of Grass"* explores the fascinating and largely unexplored matter of Whitman's revisions of **Leaves of Grass** and foregrounds Whitman's project of representing sexuality and especially sexuality between men. Moon's readings not only firmly situate Whitman within the context of nineteenth-century sexual discourse but also link Whitman's revisionary practice in the text to the poet's own unsettled and increasingly revised position after 1860 concerning the social implications of a politics of male-male sexual desire. These books as well as other works by Gilbert, Martin, Moon, and Sedgwick, have

well begun the siting of Whitman within a fluid—not static—history of sexual and political relations, within what appears to be a destabilized pattern of concepts of male-bonding and gender, and within a cultural frame in which those challenges Foucault has made to received theories of nineteenth-century sexuality can be fully elaborated.

The sexuality issue then, far from being exhausted, will have to be raised in order to explore the matrix of intertextuality that combines to form the textual and imaginative fabric of what has been described (though perhaps with just as much anxiety) as the homosexual imagination, an "imaginative mode," a "sensibility," which—if it exists—is quite different from that which defines itself as heterosexual.[23] I do not think at all that the sexuality issue is exhausted because neither sex nor sexual acts are the precise issue—sexual desire is. Thus, the important homosexual question is not whether Whitman was homosexual. Instead we must ask what homosexuality—whatever its construction—meant to Whitman and what his construction of it was? To what extent if at all did he construct and identify himself and his texts as situated within a homosexual context and as participating in a discourse of desire? And what are the defining textual characteristics—those Bloomian tropes—that he invoked to explain to his readers and to himself why these desires were so powerful that he was impelled to utter them? Actions after all, are the consummation of desire; it is desire that fuels the imagination; it is desire that defines the meaning of an act, especially when that act becomes text.

In 1877, in **"A Backward Glance O'er Travel'd Roads,"** Whitman touched on the sexuality issue in precisely this way:

> It has become in my opinion, imperative to achieve a shifted attitude from superior men and women towards the thought and fact of sexuality, as an element of character, personality, the emotions, and a theme in literature. I am not going to argue the question by itself; it does not stand by itself. The vitality of it is altogether in its relations, bearings, significance. . . . *Leaves of Grass* . . . has mainly been the outcropping of my own emotional and other personal nature—an attempt, from the first to the last, to put a Person, a human being (myself, in the latter half of the Nineteenth Century, in America,) freely, fully, and truly on record." (*PW* 2:728)

In what might be construed to be a breathtaking anticipation of Foucault, Whitman seems pointedly to choose "sexuality" instead of sex, though at other textual crises he habitually "drenched" his songs specifically in sex. The point is that sexuality "does not stand by itself" and it cannot be argued uniquely. Therefore, in these terms—his terms—I am not at all sure that the sexuality issue has been exhausted because I am not sure that it has really been fully explored.[24]

Kaplan asks why "after more than a century of biographical inquiry we still have only the most approximate notion of how and why Walter Whitman, printer, schoolteacher, editor, fiction writer, and building contractor, a shadowy figure in most accounts, untamed, untranslateable, projected his barbaric yawp over the roofs of the world. This of course is the heart of his mystery."[25] The shadowy figure who also inhabits this list is that other Walter Whitman who so early on not only asked why the forms of custom smother the wish to be loved but also observed that the need to be loved "will sometimes burst forth in spite of all obstacles." In Whitman's typical invocation of ejaculative power—"burst forth"—there is inscribed all those tropes he would later engage in **"Song of Myself"** to answer that same, so often repeated question, tropes that would radically transgress all obstacles, (those social, political, and aesthetic forms of custom), tropes that would confront "creeds and schools" and the "grammar of the old cartouches" with "a new identity" and "a new tongue," the translated tongue and mastered writing of the homoerotic text. That is the real heart of his mystery.

Notes

[1] Carroll Smith-Rosenberg, *Disorderly Conduct: Visions of Gender in Victorian America* (New York: Oxford University Press, 1985), 91. See Michael Moon, *Disseminating Whitman: Revision and Corporeality in "Leaves of Grass"* (Cambridge, Mass.: Harvard University Press, 1991), 20-25, for a discussion of the anti-onanist discourse, which Moon sees also as homophobic discourse. Moon's book concerns itself precisely and cogently with the process of Whitman's revisions not only in response to, but as a counterdiscourse within, the spectrum of sexual discourse.

[2] See Martin (*Homosexual Tradition,* 4) on Holloway's willingness to deduce heterosexuality from the later published version of an earlier manuscript that clearly suggests homosexuality.

[3] Eduard Bertz to W.C. Rivers, quoted in Martin Duberman, *About Time: Exploring the Gay Past* (New York: Gay Presses of New York, 1986), 92.

[4] Duberman 87.

[5] Martin, *Homosexual Tradition,* 6. See Moon, *Disseminating Whitman,* 4-25, for commentary on the early origins of American homophobia.

[6] The sad story of Newton Arvin is too familiar, and academic homophobia still sits smugly on promotions committees. After a surface coverage of several gay studies programs, a recent article in *The New York Times* (12/30/90) entitled "Out of the Closet, Into the University," by Felicity Barringer, concludes with a comment by Roger Chace, president of Wesleyan Methodist University, who observes that the study of "particularisms, i.e. gender or ethnic or gay studies will be one of the "driving energies" of higher education. Chace then wonders whether the intellectual questions posed by these studies are "inherently interesting" and ends the piece saying that "some gay studies programs will be founded and fail. At other places they will be founded and succeed. My guess is, that number will be small." The homophobic logic of Professor Chace's opinion, ill-concealed beneath the appearance of evenhanded scrutiny, leads inevitably to the conclusion that they will fail because they are not inherently interesting. This exemplifies a general academic attitude that willingly and uncritically trivializes gay studies in the same way that gay people are often trivialized by pejorative social constructions. The instruments are not blunt here. See Sedgwick (*Epistemology,* 52-53) for a witty and very useful schematization of the kinds of objections routinely raised against the legitimacy of homosexual texts.

[7] Gay Wilson Allen, *The Solitary Singer: A Critical Biography of Walt Whitman* (New York: Macmillan, 1955), 222.

[8] William White, "Walt Whitman in The Eighties: A Bibliographical Essay," in *Walt Whitman Here and Now,* ed. Joann P. Krieg (Westport: Greenwood Press, 1985), 223. He makes what is I hope an unintended comparison between apparently serious heterosexual contributors in serious scholarly journals as opposed to frivolous gay "writers" in even more frivolous gay magazines. One of the "other subjects" he mentions is an article on an unknown Whitman letter recommending an Army Doctor, which addition to primary texts I do not denigrate nor mock when I wonder if this physician while taking a pulse could have detected that more primary pulse as well.

[9] David S. Reynolds, *Beneath the American Renaissance: The Subversive Imagination in the Age of Emerson and Melville* (Cambridge, Mass.: Harvard University Press, 1988), 328. Reynolds' important book has no indexed entry on homosexuality, and the entry for Whitman's "sexual orientation" leads us only to Reynolds' unwillingness to come to any conclusion.

[10] See Martin (*Homosexual Tradition,* 33) on "adhesiveness."

[11] Martin, *Homosexual Tradition,* 6. Martin's book itself sustains that kind of attack in the pages of Edwin H. Miller's *Walt Whitman's "Song of Myself": A Mosaic of Interpretations* (Iowa City: University of Iowa Press, 1989), wherein Miller dismisses some of Martin's comments. For example see notes 37 and 138 in Miller's text.

[12] John Snyder, *The Dear Love of Man: Tragic and Lyric Communion in Walt Whitman* (Boston, 1975). David S. Leverenz, *Manhood in The American Renaissance* (New York, 1989), 30. Robert K. Martin draws attention to this passage also, in his review of the Leverenz book in *Walt Whitman Quarterly Review* 7 (Winter 1990): 143-46. As Martin says, "no one can possibly talk about manhood in the American Renaissance without Whitman or his young men." In fact, Leverenz devotes only a few pages to Whitman.

[13] Milton Hindus, ed., *Walt Whitman: The Critical Heritage* (London: Routledge, 1971), 33.

[14] Quoted in Jonathon Ned Katz, *Gay American History,* (New York: Thomas Y. Crowell, 1976) 26.

[15] See M. Jimmie Killingsworth, *Whitman's Poetry of the Body: Sexuality, Politics, and the Text* (Chapel Hill: University of North Carolina Press, 1989), 36, 164, 97. This is not to accuse Killingsworth of homophobia. His book amply demonstrates the absence of that. It only suggests that even the most wary scholar must tread delicately through the thorny lexical thickets that still surround definition with judgment.

[16] Eve Kosofsky Sedgwick, *Between Men: English Literature and Male Homosocial Desire* (New York: Columbia University Press, 1985), intro., 83.

[17] Duberman 94.

[18] Justin Kaplan, "The Biographer's Problem," in *Walt Whitman, Sex and Gender, The Mickle Street Review* 11 (1989), 87-88.

[19] Kaplan, "Biographer's Problem," 88.

[20] Duberman 92.

[21] See Frederik Schyberg, *Walt Whitman,* trans. Evie Allison Allen (New York: Columbia University Press, 1951); Martin, *Homosexual Tradition;* David Cavitch, *My Soul and I: The Inner Life of Walt Whitman* (Boston: Beacon, 1985); Betsy Erkilla, *Whitman: The Political Poet* (New York: Oxford University Press, 1989); Killingsworth; and Michael Moon (1991). The history of the critical response to Whitman's homosexuality and/or his homoerotic texts and the history of the homosexual response to Whitman's homosexuality and his texts, two somewhat different subjects, have not yet been adequately written. The first subject is indirectly handled in such books as Harold Blodgett's *Walt Whitman in England* (Ithaca: Cornell University Press, 1934), wherein Blodgett discusses Whitman's English reception. But Blodgett did not recognize, nor could he have recognized in 1934, the questions about gay textuality that have now only lately arisen. Similar strictures may be applied to Betsy Erkilla's *Walt Whitman*

Among the French (New Haven: Princeton University Press, 1980) and to a lesser extent, Gay Wilson Allen's *The New Walt Whitman Handbook* (New York: New York University Press, 1985), which does make an attempt to indicate whether critics have dealt with the homosexuality of poet and text. However, in speaking of Symonds' reactions for example, he says that Symonds "recognized symptoms of emotional abnormality in the poet" (12), and he goes on to say that Whitman's incredible letter denying the homosexual content of *Calamus* "allayed Symonds' worst suspicions about the origin of the Calamus emotions" (19). Symonds' suspicions were certainly there, but he was disappointed not mollified by Whitman's letter, and by the time he wrote to Whitman, he certainly held no opinions about homosexuality that described it as an emotional abnormality. Allen's interpretation offers another example of the discomfort that critics seem to feel when confronted with gay people and our texts.

As to the homosexual response to Whitman, that is a book in itself or at least a major article. Obviously, an important chapter in such a book would include the response to Whitman by American gay writers like Taylor and Stoddard. Symonds' interrogations of Whitman and Whitman's response have been so often dealt with that I have not discussed them here. However, those who have discussed this, and this includes every important biographer, have not really looked carefully at Symonds' questions, which are not questions about "sexual orientation" but about the sexual context of texts, precisely my subject here.

Such a discussion both of the critical response to Whitman's homosexuality and the homosexual response to Whitman's "homotextuality" will show that in the former category such comments as White's, Leverenz', and Reynolds' have not changed much in kind from Emory Holloway's sadly duplicitous attempt to rewrite the history of the pronouns of "Once I pass'd through a populous city," in *Whitman: An Interpretation In Narrative* (New York: Knopf, 1926) or even in vehemence from Mark Van Doren's comment in "Walt Whitman, Stranger," in *The Private Reader* (New York, 1942), that Whitman's "manly love is neither more nor less than an abnormal and deficient love" (82). Even Justin Kaplan, *Walt Whitman—A Life* (New York: Simon and Schuster, 1980), who offers a fairly full account of Whitman's relationships with Doyle and Stafford, sees the *Calamus* poems as growing out of self-doubt and renunciation, and one cannot help feeling that Whitman's homosexuality is only partially perceived and perhaps somewhat pitied. Both the myth of a New Orleans romance, created perhaps to disguise the possibility that there were no women at all, and the myth of six children, which Whitman fostered to allay the supposed suspicions of Symonds, have been proven to be folly, yet Paul Zweig in *Walt Whitman—The Making of a Poet* (New York: Basic Books, 1984) can observe: "A century later, Whitman's sexual life is still a a mystery. Was he homosexual? Did he become openly homosexual in the 1850's, his new poetry a celebration of erotic freedom?" Zweig's answers to these questions are offered in an elegant essay, yet at the end of it all, we realize that his question, like so many others, has been aimed at what Whitman did, not at what conception of a homosexual identity his texts supply.

Some sort of comment on the question of homosexuality and Whitman is made by the Whitman contents of one of the most recent major anthologies of American literature, the vast *The American Tradition in Literature,* 6th ed., ed. George Perkins, et. al. (New York: W. W. Norton, 1985). Therein Whitman is represented by a fair number of poems, including "Song of Myself." But for *Calamus* there are only three, "For You O Democracy," "I Saw in Louisiana a Live Oak Growing," and "I Hear It Was Charged Against Me," three poems that are perhaps the most "innocent" of the group. In fact, the central and significant *Calamus* 1 has not been published in any anthologies I possess. In this anthology, a footnote describes the Calamus root as being a symbol of male comradeship, but in the critical and biographical preface to the selections, there is not the first breath of manly love, and no mention of homosexuality at all.

The critical suspicions about Whitman's homosexuality begin early enough with Griswold's sibylline Latin warning in 1855 that Whitman's poetry contained material instinct with that terrible crime that cannot be named among Christians and continue with Thomas Wentworth Higginson's observation in the *Nation* in 1892 that the object of "anything like personal or romantic love" always "turns out to be a man not a woman." The battle moved back and forth between those critics who saw or suspected homosexuality, (Symonds, Carpenter, Donaldson—though he insisted that the *Calamus* emotions were not based on any real experience—Bertz, Schyberg, Canby, Arvin, Asselineau, Cowley) and those who denied it (Bucke, O'Conner, Kennedy, Traubel, Binns, Perry, Bazalgette, De Selincourt, Allen) or didn't mention it at all or considered it to be the product of an unhealthy mood or while admitting it characterized it as morbid or pathological. Later critics, and the number is too vast to summarize in this note, essentially continued to fight the "is he or isn't he?" battle, while some, like White, think it is not an issue. Others have more collateral trouble with the homosexuality than with the person or the text, and many seem to want to separate sexuality and text, subscribing to Havelock Ellis' assertion that Whitman's homosexuality had nothing to do with his work at all: "However important inversion may be as a psychological key to Whitman's personality, it plays but a small part in Whitman's work, and for many who care for that work a negligible part" (Have-

lock Ellis, *Sexual Inversion* [1901], 19.) Richard Chase presumed Whitman's sexuality to be troubled, yet felt that this discord impelled Whitman to write his poem. E. H. Miller, in *Walt Whitman's Poetry: A Psychological Journey* (Boston: Beacon, 1968), took a thoroughly Freudian approach, arriving at conclusions involving emotional immaturity, troubled family relations, and a concept of homosexuality as deficient and deviant. For so many critics, the subtext seemed and seems still to be whether or not they recoil, like Leverenz, from homosexuality and homosexuals.

Symonds, Carpenter, and Xavier Mayne are the earliest critics to espouse, however partially, a theory of homosexual textuality in Whitman's writings; Symonds' readings are very profound and go beyond the question of personal sexuality to questions of textuality. Recent re-evaluations of Whitman's homoerotic texts have begun to be written. See Martin, *Homosexual Tradition* (1979); Byrne R. S. Fone, "This Other Eden: Arcadia and The Homosexual Imagination," in *Literary Visions of Homosexuality,* ed. Stuart Kellogg (New York: Haworth Press, 1983), 13-35; Joseph Cady in various articles, among them "Drum-Taps and Nineteenth-Century Male Homosexual Literature," in Krieg 49-61; Sedgwick, *Between Men,* 201; Sandra Gilbert, "The American Sexual Poetics of Walt Whitman and Emily Dickinson," in *Reconstructing American Literary History,* ed. Sacvan Bercovitch (Cambridge, Mass.: Harvard University Press, 1986), 123-54; Charley Shively, *Calamus Lovers* (San Francisco: Gay Sunshine Press, 1987); Erkilla, *Political Poet;* Killingsworth, *Poetry of the Body;* Michael Moon, *Disseminating Whitman.* Martin's book is of such seminal importance that it holds a place in Whitman and gay criticism comparable in some respects to Foucault's work. I am more than happy to be in his debt, and I believe that I have been able to extend in directions of which I hope he would approve. Many of his conclusions so often anticipate and helped me to arrive at many of my own. As Martin describes this task in a review in *WWQR*5 (Spring 1988), "we must see Whitman . . . in the context of an emerging sense of homosexual identity. . . . we must move from looking at what the text says to how it says it, recognizing that . . . meaning inheres in the text's shape, tensions, and rhythms. . . . we must look at the sexuality of the poems" (47).

[22] Killingsworth, xvi (Sedgwick, *Between Men,* 204).

[23] The introduction here of *sensibility* placed perilously close to *homosexual* inevitably suggests the phrase "homosexual sensibility" and its companion "homosexual imagination." The literature and the debate on whether there are such things is also rich, and a bibliography is too long to include here, but it probably can be said that there are conventions of homosexual texts that can be identified. Whether those conventions mean the same thing to those who interpret them now as they meant to those who engaged them is one

of the questions of homosexual literary study. For early discussions of the concept of a gay sensibility and imagination see Xavier Mayne, *The Intersexes* (Naples, 1908) and John Addington Symonds, *A Problem in Greek Ethics* (Bristol: Ballantyne and Hansen, 1883). For an early collection of essays that presumes there is such a sensibility see Louie Crew and Rictor Norton, eds., *The Homosexual Imagination,* Vol. 36, no. 3 of *College English* (1974), especially the essays by the editors and by Jacob Stockinger. See also Louie Crew, ed., *The Gay Academic* (Palm Springs: ETC Publications, 1978), especially the essays by Byrne R. S. Fone, James W. F. Somerville, and Jacob Stockinger, the source for the term *homotextuality.* A later collection is Stuart Kellogg, ed., *Literary Visions of Homosexuality* (New York: Haworth, 1983), especially the editor's introductions and the essays by Louie Crompton, Byrne R. S. Fone and Robert K. Martin. Katz makes important observations on the topic, and Byrne R. S. Fone, *Hidden Heritage: History and the Gay Imagination* (New York: Avocation, 1979), Robert K. Martin, *Homosexual Tradition,* and Louie Crompton, *Byron and Greek Love: Homophobia in 19th-Century England* (Berkeley and Los Angeles: University of California Press, 1985) all engage in the discussion.

[24] See Moon, "Disseminating Whitman," (in Butters, Clum, and Moon, 238), who has also drawn attention to Whitman's formulation.

[25] Justin Kaplan, "Whitman and the Biographers," in Krieg 14.

Primary References

All references to "Song of Myself" (1855) are from Malcolm Cowley, ed., *"Leaves of Grass": The First (1855) Edition,* New York: Viking, 1959. In all cases references to "Song of Myself" are to the untitled first poem of the first edition. Line citations in the text are indicated when necessary by the abbreviation *SM* and the line number.

Citations from "Calamus" drawn from Fredson Bowers, ed., *Whitman's Manuscripts: Leaves of Grass (1860),* Chicago: Chicago University Press, 1955, are cited in text as Bowers. All other citations from *Calamus* are identified by the numbering of the 1860 edition.

All other citations of Whitman's work are included in the text under the following abbreviations.
Citations from Gay Wilson Allen et al., eds., *The Collected Writings of Walt Whitman,* New York: New York University Press, 1961-84:

NUPM: Edward F. Grier, ed. *Notebooks and Unpublished Manuscripts.* 6 vols. 1984.

PW: Floyd Stovall, ed. *Prose Works 1892.* 2 vols. 1963-64.

Citations from sources other than Allen et al.:

Bradley: Sculley Bradley and Harold W. Blodgett, eds. *Leaves of Grass.* New York: W. W. Norton, 1973.

Cowley: Malcolm Cowley, ed. *"Leaves of Grass": The First (1855) Edition.* New York: Viking, 1959.

Trigg: Oscar Lovell Trigg. "Variorum Readings of Leaves of Grass," in *Leaves of Grass,* ed. Emory Holloway, Inclusive Edition. New York: Doubleday, Doran, 1928.

M. Jimmie Killingsworth (essay date 1992)

SOURCE: "Tropes of Selfhood: Whitman's 'Expressive Individualism,'" in *The Continuing Presence of Walt Whitman: The Life After the Life,* edited by Robert K. Martin, University of Iowa Press, 1992, pp. 39-52.

[*In the following essay, Killingsworth argues that the concept of expressive individualism—a twentieth-century attitude which promotes success as its primary goal and looks to "internal, intuitive measures of achievement" rather than external standards—exemplifies Whitman's beliefs about the nature of selfhood as both individual and universal.*]

> *Power ceases in the instant of repose; it resides in the moment of transition from a past to a new state, in the shooting of the gulf, in the darting to an aim. This one fact the world hates, that the soul becomes . . .*
>
> —Ralph Waldo Emerson

> *The limits of language, as of reality itself, are not rigid but fluid. Only in the mobile and multiform word, which seems to be constantly bursting its own limits, does the fullness of the world forming logos find its counterpart. Language itself must recognize all the distinctions which it necessarily effects as provisional and relative distinctions which it will withdraw when it considers the object in a new perspective.*
>
> —Ernst Cassirer

In *Habits of the Heart: Individualism and Commitment in American Life,* the best-selling study of national character as revealed through hundreds of interviews with contemporary Americans, Robert Bellah and four distinguished coauthors are the latest generation of American social scientists to find in Walt Whitman a representative voice for selfhood in the United States. Like the first generation, which included William

James, these cartographers of the soul are attracted by the poet whose great theme was what he believed to be simultaneously (and ironically) most common and most precious—"myself":

> I resist anything better than my own diversity,
>
>   . . . . .
>
> This is the grass that grows wherever the land
>   is and the water is,
> This is the common air that bathes the globe.
>
> This is the breath of laws and songs and
>   behaviour,
> This is the tasteless water of souls . . .
>   (**"Song of Myself"** [1855], 347, 358-361)

Within himself, Whitman felt "the current and the index" of human life, in the general as well as in the particular. In his first great poems, published in 1855 and inspired by the physical strength of a robust middle age, he put his secret intuitions onto the record of public life in an attempt to live out the Emersonian dictum that, in speaking his inmost thoughts, he would make universal sense. Trusting inner resources, he proclaimed in **"Song of Myself"**: "These are the thoughts of all men in all ages and lands, they are not original with me, / If they are not yours as much as mine they are nothing or next to nothing" (353-354).

The poet's confidence in the sympathy of readers was hardly unflagging, however, even in the early poems. By 1860, **"Calamus"** would record the downward turn of selfhood, the crisis of identity, the alienation of the isolated individual, the anxious homosexual in a predominantly heterosexual culture: "I wonder if other men ever have the like out of the like feelings?" he would ask (see Killingsworth, 102). Throughout his life, through the flow and ebb of extensive sympathy and defensive withdrawal, Whitman would continue to ask the big questions that, despite methodological sophistication and ever-deepening specialization, still haunt the social sciences: "What is a man anyhow? What am I? and what are you?" (**"Song of Myself"** [1855], 390).

Bellah and his colleagues and James before them have, in one sense, rescued Whitman from his isolation. For them, the Whitmanian "I" has come to represent a prototypical relationship between self and society. However, the honor of being a representative person, an Emersonian hero, is compensated negatively by the requirement that the self sacrifice its proud "diversity," the very thing which resists "anything better." Fitting Whitman into a category has meant neglecting the power of his poetic language to transform categories, indeed, to overwhelm them. What Ernst Cassirer has said of dogmatic metaphysical systems may be applied just as well to the categories theorized in the social sciences: "Most of them are nothing other than . . . hypostases of a definite logical, or aesthetic, or religious principle. In shutting themselves up in the abstract universality of this principle, they cut themselves off from particular aspects of cultural life and the concrete totality of its forms" (82). Dealing with what Cassirer calls "the problem of signs"—the question of how a sing like "I" relates to and interpenetrates the multiform realities that it represents—is for social psychology a matter of looking "backward to its ultimate 'foundations'" in mental life; Whitman's poems, on the other hand, engender an attitude of discovery that looks forward, pressing language toward a "concrete unfolding and configuration in . . . diverse cultural spheres" (105). In poetic language, Whitman discovered a fluidity that denied the trivialization of selfhood, that broke through the limits imposed by too tight a system, and that curved back upon its source. Indeed, he found that expression of the self tended to erode and reformulate that which had been expressed. Like Emerson before him, he realized the "one fact the world hates, that the soul becomes."

According to the scheme developed in *Habits of the Heart,* history has produced two distinctively modern attitudes of the self toward society at large, utilitarian individualism and expressive individualism. In contrast to the earlier republican and biblical versions of autonomous selfhood, both utilitarian and expressive individualism are seen as failures, for they undermine the connection between person and community. In the view of Bellah and his coauthors, the utilitarian and the expressivist lose sight of historical tradition and subsequently view community as merely an environment of personhood. This ahistorical psychic isolation produces a chronic lack of social commitment in contemporary American life.

Utilitarian individualism is the characteristic attitude of the "self-made" woman or man. Utilitarians may allow their personal goals to be defined by external standards—better salaries and bigger houses or progress up the social ladder—but they are motivated exclusively by the drive for individual success. The great predecessor of the utilitarian outlook, according to Bellah, is Benjamin Franklin, particularly as he appeared in his own *Autobiography*. The difference between Franklin and modern utilitarian individualists is that he tempered his drive for success with a measure of republican idealism, which his cultural descendants lack altogether. The legacy of his famous list of practical virtues has thus become the cult of professionalism, the sixty-hour workweek, the fast fortune, dressing for success, and, ultimately, conspicuous consumption.

Expressive individualism, like its utilitarian cousin, is preoccupied with success, but the expressivist longs to break even more completely with community, trusting internal, intuitive measures of achievement instead of accepting external standards. Whereas for the utilitarian individualist success is merely a technical matter of finding the right means to a preestablished end, the expressivist tries to extract both means and ends from the inner sources of body, heart, and soul. For Bellah, Whitman is the cultural prototype of expressive individualism. His legacy in our times—which, like Franklin's, has lost its republican moorings—is the therapeutic search for identity and the overthrowing of communities based on kinship and regional or national identity in favor of homogeneous "life-style enclaves," the ubiquitous support groups of our age, gatherings defined by special interests and expressive styles of behavior rather than by shared traditions or political goals. How, Bellah seems to ask, could Whitman's democratic personalism have come to this?

Despite this conservative tendency to valorize figures from the past at the expense of contemporary Americans, however, it is quite possible to argue that Whitman made some progress toward the completed image of modern expressivism quite on his own. At times he reached points where his expressiveness came to threaten not only the basis for community but also the very concept of the individual. Exploring the tensions inherent in expressive individualism, the poet found himself, like many of our contemporary expressivists, on the very brink of selfhood, the place theorized by the sociologist Erving Goffman and by the deconstructionists, for whom there is no foundational self at all but, in Bellah's words, "merely a series of social masks that change with each successive situation," an "absolutely empty, unencumbered and improvisational self" (80).

Bellah argues that Whitman's idea of success "had little to do with material acquisition": "A life rich in experience, open to all kinds of people, luxuriating in the sensual, as well as the intellectual, above all a life of strong feeling, was what he perceived as a successful life" (14). Whitman's homosexuality, in this reading, represents one "way in which he rejected the narrow definition of the male ego dominant in his day" (15). If we extend this line of reasoning, accounting for the rhetorical as well as the expressive aims of the poems, we come to see **"Calamus"** as an encouragement for like-minded men to join him in ignoring the "plaudits in the capital," to follow him down "paths untrodden," bypassing the impositions of class, region, and economic condition—much as he himself had done in choosing his friends from among young intellectuals and working-class men in the late 1850s—and forming an enclave of comrades bound by the sentiment and expression of "manly love."

If we use Bellah's interpretive line as a critical tool, however, we must allow that such an enclave could have but a weak effect on the political life and social com-

mitment of the individual members. Its chief character, the persona of the "tenderest lover," is too malleable, too ephemeral, too promiscuous, too concerned with image and appeal to inspire communal action. In **"Are You the New Person Drawn toward Me?"** the speaker wards off a would-be disciple with this admonition:

> Are you the new person drawn toward me?
> To begin with take warning, I am surely far
>   different from what you suppose;
> Do you suppose you will find in me your
>   ideal?
>
>   . . . . .
>
> Do you suppose yourself advancing on real
>   ground toward a real heroic man?
> Have you no thought O dreamer that it may
>   be all maya, illusion?
>
>   (1-3, 8-9)

In like manner, Whitman would fend off John Addington Symonds, a homosexual who sought a political ally, and he would snub the advances of his female admirer Anne Gilchrist with these words: "Dear friend, let me warn you somewhat about myself—& yourself also. You must not construct such an unauthorized & imaginary ideal Figure, & call it W. W. and so devotedly invest your loving nature in it. The actual W. W. is a very plain personage, & entirely unworthy such devotion" (*Correspondence,* 2:170). Of course, the "actual" Walt Whitman in these biographical instances could well be read as yet another expressive trope, fulfilling within other contexts the need of the self for defense against external social demands.

In the very concept of expressive individualism, then, there is a deep tension which in his poems and public life Whitman freely tested. Individualism favors singularity, but expression favors multiplicity, diversity. Except in its most radically expressive phase, individualism is a foundationalist concept, placing the certain inner self at the center of an uncertain world. Expression tends to dislocate every center, to undermine every foundation, including the self, and to impinge, for example, upon the private self of the **"Calamus"** poet, rooting out either a confession of his true nature or stimulating yet another evasion, yet another mask. As the self is expressed, it is transformed, yielding by turns the "tenderest lover" of the **"Calamus"** poems, the "friendly and flowing savage" of **"Song of Myself,"** or the "very plain personage" of the letters.

In **"O Living Always, Always Dying,"** which was originally grouped in **"Calamus,"** the speaker chants, "O to disengage myself from those corpses of me, which I turn and look at where I cast them, / To pass on, (O living! always living!) and leave the corpses behind" (5-6). Living, in this trope, is a transcenden-

Title page from the first edition of Walt Whitman's Leaves of Grass.

tal act of expression, shedding the old self as the new self emerges. In its final placement in the **"Whispers of Heavenly Death"** cluster, the poem strikes a bold contrast with its companion, **"A Noiseless Patient Spider,"** which in a superb figure relates the soul to an "isolated" spider launching filaments out of itself, seeking among the surrounding spheres a "ductile anchor" for its "gossamer thread." While the spidersoul stands at the center of expressive life, the snake-soul of **"O Living Always, Always Dying"** sheds the self with each new expression, leaving behind an empty and discarded skin, a mere corpse.

Whitman thus demonstrates a division within the category of expressive individualism. The self may remain more or less secure and thereby realize expressions as its products. Or it may with each strong expression utterly refashion its very basis for being. If it is continually re-expressed—or if expression becomes an end in itself—the self loses its status as a substance and becomes the empty cipher "I" that semioticists have described as the sign most clearly disconnected from any stable referential base. "What is the reality to which *I* or *you* refers?" asks Émile Benveniste. "It is solely a 'reality of discourse'" (218-219). Whitman himself

approached this extreme reduction of "myself" to a linguistic reality in a now-famous latter-day reflection on his poems: "I sometimes think the *Leaves* is only a language experiment—that it is an attempt to give the spirit, the body, the man, new words, new potentialities of speech" (***American Primer,*** viii-ix).

In light of the tension between foundationalist individualism and the antifoundationalist tendency of tropic expressiveness, what can we identify as the sources of selfhood for expressive individualism in general and for Walt Whitman in particular? Three possibilities arise in ***Leaves of Grass.*** The first is the body, attention to which brings forth a kind of physical individualism, such as that of the libertine. The second is the soul, the intuition, the unconscious, which produces psychic individualism or egotism. The third is language, the poem, the text, or tropic individualism. In Whitman's poetry, if not in every instance of expressive individualism, all three sources are invoked, often simultaneously. Unlike the deconstructionists, who insist that individuality is always undone in its own making and thereby discharged into a consuming network of intertextuality, Whitman never completely uncouples tropic individuality from physical and psychic sources.

In the 1850s he seems indeed to have generated tropic power by seeking language adequate for expressing the demands of the robust body and the corresponding shapes of soulful fantasy. The tropes of **"Song of Myself"** are especially dazzling as a result of this interior interchange. In section 5, for example, we find the physical self addressing the "other I am," the soul, seducing the unconscious, and liberating an orgasmic flow of language that wraps in ambiguity the conventional gender relations of body and soul: " . . . you settled your head athwart my hips and gently turn'd over upon me, / And parted the shirt from my bosombone, and plunged your tongue to my bare-stript heart" (88-89).

Language provides the negative principle of the poem, playing Shiva the destroyer to the soul's and body's Brahma the creator. The body is erotic and as such demands intercourse with others. The Emersonian soul is republican and seeks communion through the sympathetic imagination. The text obliges with its fluent "I am" but insists as well upon distinction, upon "not." The tropes of selfhood require continual differentiation:

> People I meet, the effect upon me of my early
>   life or the ward and city I live in, or the
>   nation . . .
> These come to me days and nights and go
>   from me again,
> But they are not the Me myself.
>
>   (67, 73-74)

And what is the "Me myself" if not a poem resisting the reading of others?

> Apart from the pulling and hauling stands
>   what I am,
> Stands amused, complacent, compassionating,
>   idle, unitary,
>
>   . . . . .
>
> Looking with side-curved head curious what
>   will come next,
> Both in and out of the game and watching
>   and wondering at it.
>
>   (75-76, 78-79)

Language is the medium that provides distance, the detachment in the attitude of these lines. Writing creates the space wherein the self becomes free from the demands of the body and the power of the soul to overwhelm the senses and to drive loving observation into self-absorbed reverie. In the strongest poems of *Leaves of Grass,* the demands of body and soul merge in images of the fantastic, delightfully recorded by the writer standing "Apart from the pulling and hauling . . . / . . . amused, complacent, compassionating, idle, unitary . . . / Looking with side-curved head curious what will come next."

Not only in the energetic bursts of the 1855 **"Song of Myself"** but also in the later poems, in which the force of physical life is somewhat withdrawn, Whitman celebrates the de-centering and re-creative power of poetic language. **"Passage to India"** (1874) is among the best examples. In his old age Whitman told Horace Traubel, "There's more of me, the essential ultimate me, in that than in any of the poems. There is no philosophy, consistent or inconsistent, in that poem . . . but the burden of it is evolution—the one thing escaping the other—the unfolding of cosmic purposes" (Traubel, 1:156-157). The poem begins with a celebration of the soul's power to set the foundations for material progress. Centuries before the transatlantic cable was laid in 1866—"The seas inlaid with eloquent gentle wires"—the self, here in its guise as the Emersonian oversoul, established its networks of sympathetic union across the seas and over the lands. The actual placing of the cable, like the building of the Suez Canal and the transcontinental railroad—all the spanning accomplishments of Whitman's era—is but a late realization of the connections pioneered by soulful meditation. Even with these realizations, the soul will not rest:

> After the seas are all cross'd, (as they seem
>   already cross'd,)
> After the great captains and engineers have
>   accomplish'd their work,
> After the noble inventors, after the scientists,
>   the chemist, the geologist, ethnologist,
> Finally shall come the poet worthy of that
>   name,
> The true son of God shall come singing his
>   songs.
>
>   (101-105)

Ironically, the soul of this "true son of God" is self-surpassing. The soul that had been the foundation for material progress has come by the poem's conclusion to be the principle by which that progress is discounted, surpassed, erased. In wiping the slate clean, the troping self risks all, even its own status as a foundation for further invention, further realization:

> Sail forth—steer for the deep waters only,
> Reckless O soul, exploring, I with thee, and
>   thou with me,
> For we are bound where mariner has not yet
>   dared to go,
> And we will risk the ship, ourselves and all.
>
>   (248-251)

Bellah's homage to Whitman, the attribution of paternity in the lineage of expressive individualism, fails to do justice to the range and the political value of the Whitmanian self. The sociologist's conservative reading particularly neglects the linguistic root of anti-foundationalist expressivism. In like manner, William

James honored Whitman with metaphysical oversim-plification, finding in the poet the very type of "healthy-mindedness," the tendency toward a radical openness whose mysticism is large and whose democratic em-brace contains multitudes (81-83). But Whitman's po-ems eloquently protest such reduction; even if reduc-tion takes breadth as its theme, its net effect is a conceptual narrowing.

It is not especially surprising that the Whitman of the poems resists the Whitman of the social scientists. To say that they fall short is not to slander James and Bellah—for who could exhaust the meanings of the best poems?—but is instead a comment on the differ-ent politics of poetry and the social sciences. Poems like Whitman's have their own social agenda. They aim to explode just the kind of categories that the social sciences work to build, explanatory frameworks that make life stand still, solid structures in the un-certain sweep of history.

Whitman's expressivism arose in opposition to the flatness and meanness that had overwhelmed the re-publican spirit. Developed in the mood of 1848, the poems of the fifties were no doubt a "language ex-periment," a radical essay in consciousness, whose aim, in Whitman's own words, was "to give the spirit, the body, the man, new words, new potentialities of speech" (**American Primer,** viii-ix). As the philoso-pher Charles Taylor has recently suggested, in the "search to recover a language of commitment to a greater whole," Bellah and his colleagues "write as though there were not really an independent problem of the loss of meaning in our culture, as though the recovery of a Tocquevillian commitment would some-how also fully resolve our problems of meaning, of expressive unity, of the loss of substance and reso-nance in our man-made environment, of a disenchanted universe" (509). The so-called human potential move-ment—which, like Bellah, Taylor traces to Emerson and Whitman—and all other forms of sentimental, therapeutic expressivism aim to create a haven of selfhood away from the demands of commitment. In contrast to this weak strand of expressivism stands a strong form of expression that challenges the indi-vidual to test external demands against the needs of the body and to experiment with the tropes of a new life, as Whitman did in all of his best poems, perhaps most clearly in **"I Sing the Body Electric"** (see Killingsworth, 1-15).

Bellah gives no criteria for distinguishing between weak and strong versions of expressive individualism. Nor, for that matter, does he provide criteria for distinguish-ing between weak and strong republican individual-ism. He appears to suggest that republicanism is inher-ently stronger than expressivism and thus ignores the historical development of republicanism toward the aggressive and domineering practices of male, middle-

class, middle-aged, heterosexual, white, and industrial-ist individuals. It was no doubt the emergence of this hegemony within the bosom of republican individual-ism that urged Whitman and other strong expressivists to look within themselves for alternatives.

In this light, life-style enclaves, which Bellah views as necessarily degenerate, take on a different aspect as well; they arise when traditional communities fail to meet the needs of certain groups. The one example discussed at any length in *Habits of the Heart* is retirement commu-nities, which clearly fill the gap left when families no longer can or will care for their oldest members. Pre-sumably for rhetorical reasons, Bellah waffles on the exact status of certain other groups, notably the gay and lesbian communities. Though fitting rather well the definition of a lifestyle enclave, these groups and oth-ers like them may represent rising forces of life-style expression that try out a political will that is destined eventually to alter the current of a more general community's mainstream. Just as there are strong and weak versions of expressivism, there are strong and weak life-style enclaves. While the weak enclave discovers its ultimate goal in adjustment to the status quo, the strong enclave is at the very least protopolitical. Like the strong poem, it encourages the individual to hold fast against contrary social demands and to remake social life ac-cording to a new image.

In his poems and in his life, Whitman embodied the waverings of the expressivist spirit, with full pendu-lum swings from strong to weak and back again. In moments of personal doubt and in periods of dryness he withdrew his faith from the text, leaving the poems mere vehicles for asserting a conventional soul, an I'm-ok-you're-ok therapeutic crutch. This trend is par-ticularly noticeable in **Drum-Taps** and in certain po-ems of the early 1870s, when the Civil War and physi-cal hardship had numbed the poet's body and stifled his confidence in tropic individuality—a condition chronicled in this war-struck poem:

> Quicksand years that whirl me I know not
>   whither,
> Your schemes, politics, fail, lines give way,
>   substances mock and elude me,
> Only the theme I sing, the great and
>   strong-possess'd soul, eludes not,
> One's-self must never give way—that is the
>   final substance—that out of all is sure,
> Out of politics, triumphs, battles, life, what at
>   last finally remains?
> When shows break up what but One's-Self is
>   sure?
>
> **("Quicksand Years")**

The considerable beauty of this poem depends upon the reader's identification of the expressed soul as the center of the poet's pain. The pain comes partly from grief over republican individualism, the hopes of which, for Whitman as for many others, had died in the Civil War (see Killingsworth). And the pain comes partly from the thought that the poet of **"Song of Myself"** and **"Calamus"** could stand for this reduction of expressive individualism to such an empty cipher abstractly expressed—"the theme," "One's-self," "the final substance," "the soul."

In the hundred years since Whitman's death, American social sciences have used the poet's tropes of selfhood as mere emblems for social categories—healthymindedness, expressive individualism. The suggestiveness of this work cannot be denied; the concept of expressivism, if not definitive, has a great deal of heuristic power. Moreover, through the attention of readers as prominent as James and Bellah, Whitman's place in American culture is affirmed. In many ways, the homage of social scientists is the realization of all the poet longed for—a form of canonization (in both the literary and the religious senses). "The proof of a poet is that his country absorbs him as affectionately as he has absorbed it," he wrote in 1855 in the preface to *Leaves of Grass.*

And yet *Leaves of Grass,* when read not as the product of a talkative ego but rather as a "language experiment," may seem to challenge the social theorists of the next hundred years to value the specific instance or experience in the face of the abstract category, to treat with suspicion the label, the system, the class, all that narrows, confines, or brutalizes by denying singularity, to recognize in language a creative medium that will not remain a slave to the world of referents, and to regard the ambiguity of poetic language as a means of social revitalization.

> All truths wait in all things,
> They neither hasten their own delivery nor
>   resist it,
> They do not need the obstetric forceps of the
>   surgeon,
> The insignificant is as big to me as any,
> What is less or more than a touch?
>
> Logic and sermons never convince,
> The damp of the night drives deeper into my soul.
>
> Only what proves itself to every man and
>   woman is so,
> Only what nobody denies is so.
>   ("**Song of Myself**" [1855], 647-655)

James Dougherty (essay date 1993)

SOURCE: "Satan, Wound-Dresser, Witness," in *Walt Whitman and the Citizen's Eye,* Louisiana State University Press, 1993, pp. 76-107.

[*In the following essay, Dougherty assesses Whitman's Drum-Taps, maintaining that while the poetry in the volume is similar in some ways to Whitman's pre-Civil War poetry, Drum-Taps also represents a sense of loss—not only a loss of faith in "physical and spiritual regeneration," but also the poet's loss of faith in his "original poetic."*]

"Cavalry Crossing a Ford," from *Drum-Taps,* offers just such a visual image:

> A line in long array where they wind betwixt
>   green islands,
> They take a serpentine course, their arms
>   flash in the sun—hark to the musical
>   clank,
> Behold the silvery river, in it the splashing
>   horses loitering stop to drink,
> Behold the brown-faced men, each group,
>   each person, a picture, the negligent rest on
>   the saddles,
> Some emerge on the opposite bank, others are
>   just entering the ford—while,
> Scarlet and blue and snowy white,
> The guidon flags flutter gayly in the wind.
>   (*V,* II, 457)

This is the kind of poem (presented here in its familiar, post-1871 version) that we suppose is typical of *Drum-Taps.* Describing it, writers on Whitman have resorted inevitably to pictorial metaphors, such as "realist," "photographic," or "imagist." But if these metaphors imply an artless and unmediated seeing, they are not accurate. Also, this is not the only kind of poem in Whitman's book about the Civil War. There is a war going on in *Drum-Taps,* a *duellum intestinum* in which several different poets contend, each armed with his own style and point of view. The spare, direct visual poem, which represents *Drum-Taps* to us today, is the medium of one of those poets, but he is a minority presence in the book. And though his style seems innovative because his coming is unforecasted by Whitman's earlier work, there is much in that style that conforms to earlier pictorial conventions; for *Drum-Taps* represents Whitman's bid to be "absorbed" by America not as a radically democratic visionary but as the inheritor and master of a tradition according to which poems were like pictures.

Drum-Taps often speaks with the voice of 1855 and 1856, as though nothing had happened, as though the doubts hinted at in those years had never broken forth in the *Calamus* poems. Whitman had been writing throughout the war, but he had published no book since 1860. With the war winding down, he was eager to reassert his claims as a national poet.[1] The familiar bardic voice of **"Our Old Feuillage"** and **"Salut au Monde!"** speaks first in the book that Whitman published in May of 1865:

First, O songs, for a prelude,
Lightly strike on the stretch'd tympanum,
   pride and joy in my city,
How she led the rest to arms—how she gave
   the cue,
How at once with lithe limbs, unwaiting a
   moment, she sprang;
(O superb! O Manhattan, my own, my
   peerless! [. . .]

                              (*V*, II, 453)

This prelude begins the war as Whitman did, in New York City. Throughout **Drum-Taps** appear other poems from Manhattan's point of view: encamped recruits, parades, wagons of supplies rolling down to the wharves. And most of all, we hear the rhetoric of newspapers and public speakers proclaiming the eagle's-eye view of war:

Long for my soul, hungering gymnastic, I
   devour'd what the earth gave me;
Long I roam'd the woods of the north—long I
   watch'd Niagara pouring;
I travel'd the prairies over, and slept on their
   breast—I cross'd the Nevadas, I cross'd the
   plateaus;
I ascended the towering rocks along the
   Pacific, I sail'd out to sea;
I sail'd through the storm, I was refresh'd by
   the storm;
I watch'd with joy the threatening maws of
   the waves;
[. . .]
—These, and such as these, I, elate, saw—saw
   with wonder, yet pensive and masterful;
All the menacing might of the globe uprisen
   around me;
Yet there with my soul I fed—I fed content,
   supercilious.
   ("Rise O Days from Your Fathomless Deeps,"
                              § 1, *V*, II, 483-84)

And together with his continent-encompassing vision, he takes up also the rhetorical devices that support that vision. Like **"Song of Myself"** and **"By Blue Ontario's Shore,"** these poems are sustained by the poet's declamatory tone and by the strength of a will that can compel disparate things into one poetic line. Whitman asserts once more the power of consciousness to assimilate and unify a discordant nation. His grasp of those things is quick and light: sketchy epithets and a ballon-view perspective are enough to make his claim on Niagara, the rockbound Pacific, and the mountaintop at Chattanooga. An even more glorious future is foreseen:

Over the carnage rose prophetic a voice,
Be not dishearten'd—Affection shall solve the
   problems of Freedom yet;

Those who love each other shall become
   invincible—they shall yet make Columbia
   victorious.
("Over the Carnage Rose Prophetic a Voice,"
                              V, II, 373)

The expansive, spread-eagle posture of national consciousness has not changed. **Drum-Taps** includes **"A Broadway Pageant,"** that hymn to Manifest Destiny, which Whitman had written five years earlier, with its chant of the "new empire" and its brief descriptive tags for the continents and archipelagoes soon to be united with America. Closer at hand, the Canadians are served notice that the American poet-nation will "absorb Kanada in myself" (**"From Paumanok Starting I Fly like a Bird,"** *V*, II, 468).[2] And the poet declares again his self-conscious delight in consciousness. A short lyric early in the book confesses frankly the pleasure of being the connoisseur of one's own experience:

Beginning my studies, the first step pleas'd
   me so much,
The mere fact, consciousness—these forms—
   the power of motion,
The least insect or animal—the senses—eyesight;
The first step, I saw, aw'd me and pleas'd me
   so much,
I have never gone, and never wish'd to go,
   any farther,
But stop and loiter all my life, to sing it in
   extatic songs.
          ("Beginning My Studies," *V*, II, 468)

Nor does **Drum-Taps** have the kind of dramatic structure in which the old posture is finally replaced by a new. In the book's finale, the poet, as a just-discharged soldier "forth from my tent emerging for good," resumes the songs that bind together the Alleghenian hills, the tireless Mississippi, the prairie spreading wide, Northern ice and rain, and the hot sun of the South (**"To the Leaven'd Soil They Trod,"** *V*, II, 556). Repeatedly throughout **Drum-Taps,** Whitman proclaims anew the bardic vision of 1855.

But still things were not as they had been in 1855. The nation had been torn apart, and every rank of society riddled with losses. Whitman's faith in his absorbing consciousness and in the rhetoric that gave national utterance to that consciousness had been rebuked. Other styles interrupt and contradict the bard. Whitman made plain the losses and the broken confidence when, reissuing **Drum-Taps** as part of the 1871 **Leaves of Grass,** he set as its epigraph a few lines he later added to **"The Wound-Dresser":**

Aroused and angry,
I thought to beat the alarum, and urge
   relentless war;

But soon my fingers fail'd me, my face
    droop'd, and I resign'd myself,
To sit by the wounded and soothe them, or
    silently watch the dead.

                    (*V*, III, 630)

These lines, though, simplify the conflict evident in the ensemble of poems comprising the original *Drum-Taps.* Of course, his glimpse of the reality of war, his plentiful experience of death in the military hospitals that surrounded Washington, and the recent break in his own health had made it impossible to renew absolutely his faith in physical and spiritual regeneration, or to entrust his poetic vision altogether to the declamatory style of the original *Leaves of Grass,* or to adapt it to the nation's insatiate demand for patriotic poetry. But the problem was older than that. The 1855 Preface had spoken of infidelity and of the poet's need to keep faith. But the flaws within his original poetic had led him to confess his doubts in **"There was a Child Went Forth,"** in **"Song of the Open Road,"** and in several of the *Calamus* poems. Remember:

May-be the things I perceive—the animals,
    plants, men, hills, shining and flowing
    waters,
The skies of day and night—colors, densities,
    forms—May-be these are, (as doubtless they
    are,) only apparitions, and the real
    something has yet to be known,
(How often they dart out of themselves, as if
    to confound me and mock me!
How often I think neither I know, nor any
    man knows, aught of them;)
May-be they only seem to me what they are,
    (as doubtless they indeed but seem,) as from
    my present point of view—And might
    prove, (as of course they would,) naught of
    what they appear, or naught any how, from
    entirely changed points of view.

    ("Of the Terrible Doubt of Appearances,"
                    V, II, 377)

Words (as we have seen) may fail to render experience accurately or to express the Self truthfully. Experience may prove phantasmal, a flicker of dots and specks; and the Soul may dissolve in self-doubt and in the recognition of one's own hypocrisy.[3]

Many of the poems of *Drum-Taps* renew these doubts, questioning the reality of the Not-Me, confessing the bad faith of the I and its inability to speak frankly to You. Near the center of the book stands **"Give Me the Splendid Silent Sun,"** in which Whitman rededicates himself to the prosecution of the war, by embracing Manhattan with its munitions, its shipping, its military parades—and its illusory "shows" and "pageants": "give me these phantoms incessant and endless along the trottoirs!" (§2, *V*, II, 498). To endorse the Union cause

is to turn one's back on the "primal sanities" of Nature and to accept an urban world that seemed as unembraceable as a specter. Again in one of *Drum-Taps'* concluding poems, **"How Solemn as One by One,"** as one of the disbanding regiments marches by him, Whitman observes the soldiers' masklike faces:

[. . . T]he faces, the masks appear as I glance
    at the faces, studying the masks;
(As I glance upward out of this page, studying
    you, dear friend, whoever you are;)
How solemn the thought of my whispering
    soul, to each in the ranks, and to you.

                    (*V*, II, 554)

So even near the book's end, a street experience in Washington tells him again what the streets had always told him: that identity is a mask draped on an indeterminacy of dreams and dots; that there is forever a mask, or a quarrel, or a book between I and You. Much of the patriotic poetry in *Drum-Taps,* which to modern readers seems illuded or dishonest, the strutting and preening of the spring of 1861 (though doubtless sincerely meant), can be read as a city vision of the Civil War, limited to parades, publicity, and speechmaking—displays of emotion and rhetoric that never dilate into an extended contemplation of the actuality of war. That would come later, in hospital interiors and in the fields.

In *Drum-Taps,* the voice of doubt and of bad faith is not always contained within parentheses nor used to set a question that the rest of the poem will resolve, as it was in the *Calamus* poems. Often it speaks out unchallenged. **"Chanting the Square Deific"** identifies this skeptic voice as that of Satan—not the malignant one of *Paradise Lost* but the Satan of Job, of Blake's Milton, and of Byron—a spiritual power for dissent, self-criticism, and rebellion against constraint, here apotheosized as the fourth person of the Godhead: "Aloof, dissatisfied, plotting revolt, / Comrade of criminals, brother of slaves, / Crafty, despised [. . .], brooding, with many wiles" (§3, *V*, II, 544-45). Ever and again in *Drum-Taps,* Satan speaks forth as the voice of subversion, the accents of one who will never be absorbed by America's citizens:

Did you ask dulcet rhymes from me?
Did you find what I sang erewhile so hard to
    follow, to understand?
Why I was not singing erewhile for you to
    follow, to understand—nor am I now;
—What to such as you, anyhow, such a poet
    as I?—therefore leave my works,
And go lull yourself with what you can
    understand;
For I lull nobody—and you will never
    understand me.

    ("To a Certain Civilian," *V*, II, 500)

"**Song of Myself**" had spoken on behalf of slaves and criminals, to draw them back within the spiritual commonwealth from which they had been excluded. Now Whitman speaks as an outsider himself: a citizen whose democratic anarchism was affronted by the Union's suppression of political dissent and by the elitism of its military leadership, and whose humane impulses were enraged by the suffering and human wastage he saw in the hospitals;[4] a bard whose book had been denied publication, whose poems had caused him to be dismissed from his job, whose volumes would find the library doors closed against them;[5] a homosexual whose secret could never be frankly avowed.[6] He begins to speak not as the president of regulation (as he had called himself in the 1855 Preface), but as the perpetual revolutionary:

> I know I am restless, and make others so;
> I know my words are weapons, full of danger,
>   full of death;
> [. . .]
> For I confront peace, security, and all the
>   settled laws, to unsettle them;
> I am more resolute because all have denied
>   me, than I could ever have been had all
>   accepted me.
>
>   ("**As I Lay with my Head in Your Lap
>   Camerado**," *V*, II, 549)

In the early volumes, Whitman had addressed an idealized reader, an undiscriminating democratic consciousness like his own or one that with some instruction and example could become like his own. As early as the open letter to Emerson, he had recognized that actual readers did not prove so readily sympathetic. Now acknowledging the warfare between the public and himself, he enfranchises "Satan" as his general and spokesman. Mingled with the hymns of national triumph that conclude ***Drum-Taps*** are poems—some sullen, some filled with bravado—that tell of an "old, incessant war" conducted on two fronts. One front is within the Self:

> You degradations—you tussle with passions
>   and appetites;
> You smarts from dissatisfied friendships, (ah
>   wounds, the sharpest of all;)
> You toil of painful and choked articulations—
>   you meannesses;
> You shallow tongue-talks at tables, (my
>   tongue the shallowest of any;)
>
> ("**Ah Poverties, Wincings, and Sulky Retreats**,"
>   *V*, II, 548)

And the other front is against the American people, both as his subject and as his readers:

> Of the endless trains of the faithless—of cities
>   fill'd with the foolish;

> Of myself forever reproaching myself, (for
>   who more foolish than I, and who more
>   faithless?)
> Of eyes that vainly crave the light—of the
>   objects mean—of the struggle ever renew'd;
> Of the poor results of all—of the plodding
>   and sordid crowds I see around me;
> [. . .]
> The question, O me! so sad, recurring—What
>   good amid these, O me, O life?
>
>   ("**O Me! O Life!**" *V*, II, 547)

Both of these poems conclude as did the earlier poem about the doubt of appearances, with a brief, forced reconciliation; but the burden of these pages is Whitman's acknowledgment of an interminable civil war between the poet and his fickle nation, between the poet and the falseness of his own personae. One concluding poem manages to be about both wars: "**Spirit whose Work is Done**" begins as a patriotic invocation to the American Bellona, celebrating and honorably discharging the spirit of relentless belligerence with which the Civil War had been prosecuted; but it ends by transferring this spirit to Whitman himself:

> Touch my mouth, ere you depart—press my
>   lips close!
> Leave me your pulses of rage! bequeath them
>   to me! fill me with currents convulsive!
> Let them scorch and blister out of my chants,
>   when you are gone;
> Let them identify you to the future in these
>   songs.
>
>   (*V*, II, 542-43)

But ***Drum-Taps*** does not introduce a phase of Whitman's work devoted to shocking the bourgeois or excoriating the hypocritical reader; and though Satan's voice issues from many of the lyrics of this volume, Whitman does not adopt him as exclusive spokesman. For while this book was being written and published, Whitman had acquired another, actual spokesman, in character quite the opposite of his Satan—William Douglas O'Connor, in whose house he boarded during his years in Washington and who defended him when he was turned out of his position in the Department of the Interior. O'Connor's apologia for him, *The Good Gray Poet*, creates an image of the poet somewhat like that proposed early in the 1855 Preface—the bard as curator of a national gallery of attitudes and images, the keeper of the Matter of America. "The nation is in it!" O'Connor wrote of ***Leaves of Grass***—probably with Whitman at his elbow. "In form a series of chants, in substance it is an epic of America." There follows one of those patented panoramic catalogs: "the prairie solitudes, the vast pastoral plateaus; the Mississippi; the land dense with villages and farms . . . the august figure of Washington . . . the Federal Mother, seated with more than antique majesty in the midst of her many children." Although O'Connor seems more concerned with defending the benignity of the person than with the wholesomeness of the poetry, nevertheless his Whitman is a poet who could be affectionately absorbed by his people. *Leaves of Grass,* he writes, has a "national character and national purpose": namely, a "vigorous re-enforcement and service to all that we hold most precious."[7] Cooperating—or collaborating—with O'Connor, Whitman in *Drum-Taps* made many concessions to popular literary taste. Roger Asselineau has noted the appearance of poetic archaisms for the first time in this book, and the overtures into regular stanza structure and rhyme, which were to issue in two of his most popular poems: the unrhymed but regular trochaics of **"Pioneers! O Pioneers!"** and the singsong stanzas of **"O Captain! My Captain!"**[8] Justin Kaplan speaks of a "Tennysonian sonority and sweetness of diction" even in the Lincoln elegy—evidence of a "retreat from the idiomatic boldness and emotional directness of Whitman's earlier work."[9]

More was involved than matters of diction. Whitman began to create other identities, other points of view. As Richard Chase once put it, "The brash, egotistic Whitman and the troubled, doubting Whitman both give way to the self-sacrificing, even self-annihilating hospital visitor."[10] The former Whitman, the nationalistic bard of 1855 and 1856, had founded his poems on a moment of unmediated vision on a transparent summer morning. So authorized, that poet had detached his Self from all mediating points of view, all merely local or partial ways of seeing and saying. The latter Whitman, for whom Satan speaks in *Drum-Taps,* sets himself in explicit defiance of all the mediators of his country's culture—librarians, reviewers, bureaucrats, priests. As we have seen, this professedly unmediated vision is recontextualized in consciousness and in tacit allusions to the conventions of popular visual media, so that the visionary I could communicate his ecstasy to the unenlightened You. In *Drum-Taps,* there are other viewpoints, such as the hospital visitor's, through whom Whitman seeks more frankly to join his readers within a mediating context.

The wound-dresser and mourner sees the war not from Manhattan but from Washington, where Whitman first came in December of 1862. This city was not only the capital and center of military command, but also a fortress at the eastern salient of the Union battle line. It was filled not with the metonymies of war, like New York, but with its actual stuff: troops, convalescents, prisoners, politicians, civil servants, office seekers. What he saw there burst into life in *Specimen Days.* There he would write of a city swarming with convalescent and furloughed soldiers ("Their blue pants and overcoats are everywhere. The clump of crutches is heard up the stairs of the paymasters' offices" [*PW,* I, 85]). There, prowling the city at night, he would come on the "strange scene" of Congress still in session at dawn: "The gas-light, mix'd with the dingy day-break, produced an unearthly effect. The poor little sleepy, stumbling pages, the smell of the hall, the members with heads leaning on their desks, the sounds of the voices speaking, with unusual intonations . . . —the grandeur of the hall itself, with its effect of vast shadows up toward the panels and spaces over the galleries—all made a mark'd combination" (*PW,* I, 96). Whitman made himself a citizen of Washington, absorbing it as he had New York, wandering its streets day and night and frequenting its public buildings and saloons as well as the military hospitals that lay on the hills all around it.

But the city experiences of those years were consigned to the anecdotal prose of *Specimen Days.*[11] When he looked at the Civil War with the eye of a poet, his actual citizenship in Washington gave him no ground on which to address the American people. For all its experiential substance, it could not provide him with a mediating context for his own "songs, / Fit for war" (**"Not Youth Pertains to Me,"** *V,* II, 528). It may be that he found the pose of the *flâneur* and saunterer, even in Washington, too remote to acknowledge the reality of awe and of mourning. These required instead his fictive membership in the army, the mostly invisible context of the hospital ward—and an implicit reference to pictorial conventions in popular art and in landscape poetry.

The two mediating groups for Whitman's war book are the army and the hospital. In some of the poems, he speaks in the person of a soldier—in combat, musing by his campfire, or reminiscing after the war's end. In others, what is depicted requires experience available only to a soldier: a troop of cavalry, a bivouac. Adopting this viewpoint allows him to speak directly for the common soldier, eliminating secondary interpreters such as the *flâneur,* the journalist, or the speechmaker. Although these poems are in a way extensions of the feats of empathy found in **"Song of Myself,"** where Whitman spoke for hounded slaves and crushed firemen, now he emphasizes not the poet's power of assimilation but the undistinguished dignity, suffering, and heroism of the soldiers. These poems have the quality of testimonies, experiences retold not for their personal value to the speaker but for what they might contribute to sustaining the faith of a community—the people of America whose soldiers and kin these were; whose poet Whitman desired to be.

Although Whitman's friends from O'Connor's time till today have pressed the claim of his devoted hospital service, relatively few of the poems make explicit use of that setting. Nevertheless, it is implicitly a powerful mediating context, as a liminal place between life and death, military and civilian. In *Specimen Days,* his prose memoranda of the war, he said that "the marrow of the tragedy [was] concentrated in those Army Hospitals—(it seem'd sometimes as if the whole interest of the land, North and South, was one vast central hospital, and all the rest of the affair but flanges)" (*PW*, I, 117). The hospital epitomized the interminable misery and losses of the war, as well as Whitman's doubts about whether the struggle could be justified, and his respect and love for the young men who suffered its wounds in their flesh. Also, it was the context from which Whitman launched his first efforts to mediate between the war and a readership, as he wrote family letters on behalf of the soldiers he nursed, and then as he sought a way to raise funds for their comfort.

Soon after the 1860 *Leaves of Grass* appeared, his publishers announced a sequel, *Banner at Day-Break.* The proposed title, drawn from a poem that eventually appeared in *Drum-Taps,* suggests that Whitman was planning a directly patriotic campaign for recognition by America's readers. By 1863, however, his instinct for self-promotion had been complicated by his need to raise money to buy gifts and treats for the wounded soldiers whom he was visiting. That year he wrote to the Boston publisher James Redpath, who was soliciting funds for this cause: "Do you want to print a little 30 or 50ct book about the scenes, war, camp, hospitals &c (especially the &c)."[12] (Redpath had recently published a popular book of hospital sketches by Louisa May Alcott, contributing part of his profit to the care of children orphaned by the war.[13]) Nine days later he wrote again, proposing more than just a fund-raising pamphlet: "My idea is a book of the time, worthy the time—something considerably beyond mere hospital sketches—a book for sale perhaps in a larger American market—the premises of skeleton memoranda of incidents, persons, places, sights, the past year [. . .] a book full enough of mosaic, but all fused to one comprehensive thing."[14] This project was eventually to be realized as his prose books *War Memoranda* (1873) and *Specimen Days* (1882).

These letters show that as Whitman thought of ways to reach a "larger American market," he thought also about recording his experience of the war in a pictorial way, as "scenes" or "sketches," whether in prose or in poetry. In 1864 he told William Douglas O'Connor he was writing "thumb-nail sketches" of the war for a volume of poems he now called *"Drum-Taps."*[15] At the end of that year, he wrote that his poems had "photographed" the war (*N*, IV, 1449). No longer restricting himself to his experiences in the hospital, Whitman was now planning to respond to the war comprehensively—and pictorially.

There were other, competing books of war "sketches" in print. In 1863, as another fund raiser for orphans, John Henry Hayward had compiled *Poetical Pen-Pictures of the War;* and in 1864 Ledyard Bill issued a similar collection of poems and of journalists' eye-witness reports, *Pen-Pictures of the War.*[16] Perhaps the public was hungry for more vivid descriptions of a war that was daily chronicled in the newspapers and

whose scenes and combatants were so close to them. However, readers seeking in Hayward or Bill for any specific news of battle, hospital, or camp would have been disappointed by the vagueness of the stock imagery of almost all their poems:

> The march was o'er—the toilsome march,
>   Through forest dark, and tangled wild—
> Each soldier sought his couch of leaves,
>   And slumbered like a wearied child.
> The swift Potomac coursed along
>   Beside them, like a silver thread,
> And mingling with its rushing tide
>   Came echoes of the sentry's tread.[17]

The chief merit of Alcott's *Sketches* was her Dickensian sketches of wounded or dying soldiers. In proposing a book of "sketches" or "photographs," Whitman was marketing his considerable descriptive talents to a reading public that had responded to Alcott, eager for details and feelings, and accustomed to visualizing events through the medium of words. As he urged Redpath to publish his "sketches" in time to catch the Christmastime gift trade, he was preparing to accommodate his bardic role to readers as he took them to be and to their taste for the visual, rather than waiting for the appearance of the idealized disciples whom he had sought to create in the 1855 and 1856 editions of *Leaves of Grass.*

Because *Drum-Taps* is a book divided between several voices and several poetics, not all the visualist poetry in it is of the same sort. Descriptive and narrative poems like **"Song of the Banner at Day-break"** and **"The Centenarian's Story"** consort perfectly with those declamatory poems, quoted above, that spoke with the rhetorical confidence of 1855, to beat the alarum and urge relentless war. Most, though, take a humbler perspective. In a prose passage probably drafted around the time he was completing *Drum-Taps,* he wrote that

> future years will never know the seething hell and the black infernal background of countless minor scenes and interiors, (not the official surface-courteousness of the Generals, not the few great battles) of the Secession war; and it is best they should not—the real war will never get in the books. . . . Its interior history will not only never be written—its practicality, minutiae of deeds and passions, will never be even suggested. The actual soldier of 1862-65, North and South, with all his ways, his incredible dauntlessness, habits, practices, tastes, language, his fierce friendship, his appetite, rankness, his superb strength and animality, lawless gait, and a hundred unnamed lights and shades of camp, I say, will never be written—perhaps must not and should not be. (*Specimen Days, PW,* I, 116-17)

Here Whitman sets the course that he would follow in those poems that have proven the most important and enduring part of *Drum-Taps.* Disaffiliated, like his Satan, from the war's grand gestures—from the courtly generals and the great battles—Whitman was nevertheless eager to serve as bard for the new, proven America emerging from its struggle. The subversive tones of Satan, heard so clearly in some of the poems of *Drum-Taps,* could modulate into the more acquiescent voice of a citizen who remembers the cost of victory; who stands aside from the triumph to sing dirges for the fallen. In one of the book's last poems, he says that he brings "No poem proud [. . .] nor mastery's rapturous verse," but rather "a little book, containing night's darkness, and blood-dripping wounds,/And psalms of the dead" (**"Lo, Victress on the Peaks,"** *V,* II, 555). Despite this phrase about darkness and wounds, few of the poems would look directly into the seething hell of battlefield death and mutilation; and his hospital sketches, though more candid about delirium and agony than Alcott's sketches, would not tell the worst that he had known.[18] Rather, he would redeem from oblivion the best that the war had produced—the unremarkable virtues and courage of the common soldier in his daily life.

And the mode for this muted commemoration would be pictorial description. The lines from *Specimen Days* emphasize the "background" of "minor scenes and interiors" and of the "lights and shades of camp." He would "sketch" for his readers the "interior" war, the unofficial war of the private soldier in the camps and hospitals that he knew from their own words. Through him the wounded had told their stories to their families. He had attempted to pass along the soldiers' war to the readers of the New York *Times,* as he had heard it from them during his sojourn with the 51st New York Regiment:

> [September] 18 [1862] lay in the neighborhood, (no grub for two days,) expecting an attack from Secesh but they now retired for scores and hundreds and hundreds of miles—all this through mud, rain, heat, snow, cold, woods, bog, fording rivers, slipping down steep descents, climbing upright & hills, . . . amidst an active enemy, in secretiveness, the inhabitants full of treachery and venom, our men often marching without food, often worse, no water, the muddiest water sometimes a precious luxury, dragging their limbs, deadly tiresome, carrying heavy burdens, . . . shoes worn out, feet bleeding, clothing torn, dirty, not only sleeping on the ground in the open air, (that was nothing), sometimes having to scrape away the snow to make a place to lie down.[19]

But the *Times* did not print this. It offered a journalistic translation:

> They were on the march, fighting, advancing or retreating, for nearly four months, with seldom any intermission. It was life on the bivouac in earnest, sleeping on the ground where night overtook them, and up and on again the next day, with battle or pursuit every week, and often men falling by the road from utter exhaustion. Thus they promenaded by rapid marches, through heat, dust, rain or snow, crossing mountains, fording rivers, etc., often without food to eat or water to drink.[20]

The real war did not even get into the newspapers.

Encountering these soldiers' stories in camps and hospitals, Whitman lent them his powers for empathetic participation and intense visual detail, to throw a democratic light on the commonplace heroism of this war. Thus he would subvert those canons of cultural taste that had rendered "actual soldiers" and their deeds invisible. That was what he had done in the indecorous juxtapositions of **"Song of Myself"** and the other long poems of 1855 and 1856. And he would present them as he had in **"Song of Myself"**—in ways that invoked the popular artistic styles with which his readers were familiar.

Those artistic styles were not, of themselves, styles of subversion. *Drum-Taps* contains several poems depicting an altogether "official" war. And despite the epigraph lines claiming that he early abandoned writing verses that urged relentless war, graphic images of bellicose patriotism appear throughout the book. No fewer than four of its poems invoke the Union's iconic image, the Stars and Stripes. Despite his disclaimer in the poem quoted earlier, Whitman was well practiced in the declamatory mode appropriate for rapturous verse proclaiming "mastery."

> Flag of stars! thick-sprinkled bunting!
> Long yet your road, fateful flag!—long yet
>   your road, and lined with bloody death!
> For the prize I see at issue, at last is the
>   world!
> All its ships and shores I see, interwoven with
>   your threads, greedy banner!
>   (**"Thick-Sprinkled Bunting,"** *V,* II, 518)

The cause of democracy now vindicated in war, America is called to extend her virtues to all nations. The flag appears in *Drum-Taps* as it did in the battle tactics, the political cultus, and the songs and the popular art of that time: a visual reference point in combat, a symbol of divinely ratified principles, and an emblem of national hegemony. Sight passes into vision, physical description to prophetic interpretation of the banner's meaning and America's character or future.

One of these poems invokes it as "flag like a beautiful woman!" (**"Bathed in War's Perfume,"** *V,* II, 493). *Drum-Taps* abounds with such personifications. In the 1855 *Leaves of Grass,* Whitman's search for a You often had led him to the rhetorical device of apostrophe.

By 1860 the apostrophe was beginning to take visual, personal shape: "Democracy! / Near at hand to you a throat is now inflating itself and joyfully singing. / Ma femme!" ("**Starting from Paumanok**," §12, *V*, II, 282). In *Drum-Taps,* when Whitman invokes "Democracy" and other muses of American heroic poetry, they assume fully pictorial form as the female figures that had become part of the national iconography displayed in public statuary, on governmental seals and on the national coinage, and in printed media such as editorial cartoons and engraved or lithographed prints. The most famous of these figures, Luigi Bartholdi's Liberty, had not yet arisen on Bedloe's Island off Manhattan, but Thomas Crawford's statue of Freedom was mounted on the Capitol dome in 1863 . . . ; and Brumidi's mural on the interior of that dome, completed two years later, displayed many allegorical female figures, among them *Armed Freedom.* In *Drum-Taps,* Whitman addresses a bevy of personifications: Manhattan ("Lady of this teeming and turbulent city"), Democracy, Freedom, Ireland ("at her feet fallen an unused royal harp"), "Libertad" ("be not alarmed—turn your undying face"), Columbia (unnamed), Death ("Dark Mother, always gliding near, with soft feet"), the belligerent "Spirit" quoted some pages earlier, and, most fully set forth in the iconography of popular illustration, victorious America:

> [. . .] Victress on the peaks!
> Where thou standest, with mighty brow,
>   regarding the world,
> [. . .]
> Where thou, dominant, with the dazzling sun
>   around thee,
> Towerest now unharm'd, in immortal
>   soundness and bloom[.][21]

In later years, as his energies withered, Whitman would turn more and more frequently to recording the proclamations of Columbia, Freedom, the Star of France, America, Columbus, and other symbolic figures from the nation's scrapbook.[22] But never did he draw so explicitly on a popular pictorial idiom, with such a wealth of visual detail, as in the apostrophes of the *Drum-Taps* years.

Also, *Drum-Taps* affords one direct glimpse of the official war, as it might have appeared in a lithograph commemorating the valor of some commander:

> I saw old General at bay;
> (Old as he was, his grey eyes yet shone out in
>   battle like stars;)
> His small force was now completely hemmed
>   in, in his works;
> He call'd for volunteers to run the enemy's
>   lines—a desperate emergency;
> I saw a hundred and more step forth from the ranks
> [. . .].
>   ("**I Saw Old General at Bay**," *V*, II, 521)

Although the poem's ending, a few lines later, dwells on the courage of the volunteers making the sortie, nevertheless it implies that the general's example has summoned up or even created this bravery. And so the poem commemorates the official, chivalric Civil War, invoking those illustrations that employed the conventions of historical painting in which the general commands not only the field but the canvas, where he is given foreground space of his own, individualized modeling, and a conventionally heroic stance. . . . Theodore Davis, one of the artists of the war, remarked that conventional military painting implied "that all battlefields have some elevated spot upon which the general is located, and that from this spot the commander can see his troops, direct all their maneuvers and courteously furnish special artists an opportunity of sketching the scene."[23]

However, most of the pictorial poetry in *Drum-Taps* takes a different approach than this, though it still invokes the schemata of popular art. Some of the most successful poems in *Drum-Taps* represent a compromise between Whitman's original poetic and the conventions of nineteenth-century poetry—not a capitulation, as in "**Pioneers! O Pioneers**" and "**O Captain! My Captain!,**" but a compromise in which Whitman's rhythm and sensibility are mated with the emotions and situations of popular poetry. The intention is to paint a picture or to tell a story—not a picture confined to the brain-gallery, or a story that has been absorbed by the omnivorous Self, but objects and events presented as objectively real and as the occasion of true and widely accepted emotions. In these poems, invoking poetic and pictorial conventions and often framed in a more traditional poetic idiom, the Good Gray Poet was exploring yet another path between dumb real objects and the souls of common folk, a highway far less challenging than the endless reversals of field, I and Not-Me, in "**Song of Myself.**"

There are several narrative poems in *Drum-Taps,* and they are usually cast in the form of dramatic monologs. In "**Song of Myself**," Whitman had entered sympathetically the experience of a hounded slave or a dying fireman, but he had done so to demonstrate the expanse and power of the democratic imagination. When the slave spoke, or the sailor, it was from within the protean, encompassing Soul that was the real subject of Whitman's inaugural poem, just as the fishermen in "**A Paumanok Picture**" began their labors as an image within "**Salut au Monde!**" Narrative, or sustained description, appeared only as a momentary dilation in the poem's current of catalog or rhetorical invocation. In *Drum--aps,* the motive is more naïvely mimetic; it is an account told by a defined character. The poet is describing a world, just as real as himself, in which he takes a place. When Whitman thought about Chancellorsville, he did not ask whether it was all flashes and specks.

This transition is yet incomplete in **"The Centenarian's Story,"** one of the early poems in ***Drum-Taps.*** In it a veteran of the Revolutionary War recounts the battle of Brooklyn Heights, a story Whitman had told in **"The Sleepers"** (1855). What was five lines in the earlier poem has now become seventy, reviewing the events of several days and developing several visually striking scenes:

> As I talk, I remember all—I remember the
>   Declaration:
> It was read here—the whole army paraded—it
>   was read to us here;
> By his staff surrounded, the general stood in
>   the middle—he held up his unsheath'd
>   sword,
> It glitter'd in the sun in full sight of the army.
> [. . .]
> [. . . D]ull and damp and another day;
> But the night of that, mist lifting, rain
>   ceasing,
> Silent as a ghost, while they thought they
>   were sure of him, my General retreated.
> I saw him at the river-side,
> Down by the ferry, lit by torches, hastening
>   the embarcation.

However, at the end of the old soldier's reminiscence, Whitman self-consciously resumes his encompassing bardic role:

> Enough—the Centenarian's story ends;
> The two, the past and present, have
>   interchanged;
> I myself, as connector, as chansonnier of a
>   great future, am now speaking.
>
> (*V,* II, 471, 473)

The poem is bound together by its repeated references to the Brooklyn landscape and by the theatrical pictures of Washington, but Whitman is still the presiding consciousness.

In **"The Wound-Dresser,"** Whitman becomes himself the centenarian, an old man reminiscing on his hospital service during the Civil War, now long in the past. Dramatizing the fluid transitions of memory, it is another poem of ego-consciousness. But here the I does not just absorb the Not-Me. Consciousness is set in a specific, double context: one established by the old man talking with young people about the bygone war; the other by the wartime hospital, recalled "in silence, in dream's projections." The dresser's memories flood back in tableaux of great visual power:

> From the stump of the arm, the amputated
>   hand,
> I undo the clotted lint, remove the slough,
>   wash off the matter and blood;

> Back on his pillow the soldier bends, with
>   curv'd neck, and side-falling head;
> His eyes are closed, his face is pale, he dares
>   not look on the bloody stump,
> And has not yet looked on it.
>
> (§3, *V,* II, 480-82)

The memories are contained within and selected by the schema of "hospital sketches"—the subject he had proposed to Redpath in 1863; and the poem's *mise en scène* binds them, as a "past," with a specific "present." The poem's dramatic movement is that of an old man's memories, not the unfettered caprice of the democratic imagination depicted in **"Song of Myself"** or **"Salut au Monde!"**[24] As the wound-dresser moves from ward to ward, from one vivid scene to another, the "doors of time" through which he passes separate each memory from the others and yet unite them as the experiences of a specific place and time.

The hospital is a schema within which these personal reflections can be shared with others—not only the "young men and maidens" around him, but also the reader, You, whom the dresser invites to enter that mediating context, both book and hospital: "[. . .] I enter the doors—(while for you up there, / Whoever you are, follow me without noise, and be of strong heart.)" (§2, *V,* II, 480). That context unites both poet and reader with all other Americans, through their common devotion toward those who had suffered in the war.[25] Such emotions aroused by the war offered Whitman a bond of shared faith by which he might be united with his readers, and he entered some of the common situations of war poetry in order to evoke those emotions and to invoke that faith.

One of those genres plumbed the anxiety and grief of the soldier's loved ones. Because the war's poems were mainly written for civilians, it was a very popular genre. **"Come Up from the Fields Father"** is Whitman's essay into sentimental narrative. Both in and out of the story, he speaks for the members of an Ohio family as they read a letter, just arrived, about their soldier son Pete; and he sets them in a conventional pastoral setting intended to make their experience representative:

> Lo, 'tis autumn;
> Lo, where the trees, deeper green, yellower
>   and redder,
> Cool and sweeten Ohio's villages, with leaves
>   fluttering in the moderate wind;
> Where apples ripe in the orchards hang, and
>   grapes on the trellis'd vines;
> [. . .]
> Above all, lo, the sky, so calm, so transparent
>   after the rain, and with wondrous clouds;
> Below, too, all calm, all vital and beautiful—
>   and the farm prospers well.
>
> (*V,* II, 488)

The scene is one of peace and plenty: it evokes the title of an Inness painting and the implicit subtitle of many a lithograph of Summer or The American Farm. Here calm is invoked as a conventionally ironic prelude to catastrophe. The poem shifts into dramatic utterance:

> Open the envelope quickly;
> O this is not our son's writing, yet his name
>   is sign'd;
> O a strange hand writes for our dear son—O
>   stricken mother's soul!
> All swims before her eyes—flashes with
>   black—she catches the main words only:
> Sentences broken—*gun-shot wound in the*
>   *breast, cavalry skirmish, taken to hospital,*
> *At present low, but will soon be better.*

Then the poet interrupts, with an insight sharpened by his experience as letter writer for wounded soldiers:

> Alas, poor boy, he will never be better, (nor
>   may-be needs to be better, that brave and
>   simple soul;)
> While they stand at home at the door, he is
>   dead already;
> The only son is dead.

The poem ends, though, not with this irony but with a sentimental anticipation of Pete's mother's untempered grief, her wish to "withdraw unnoticed—silent from life, escape and withdraw, / To follow, to seek, to be with her dear dead son." Although the rhythms of the final stanza are Whitman's own, its events and emotions are entirely conventional, like those of **"O Captain!"** They preempt the poet's obligation either to respond for his Self, as mediator, or to acknowledge the actions and feelings of the stricken family.

In another poem, **"Vigil Strange I Kept on the Field One Night,"** Whitman depicts another of the conventional situations of the war's poetry—the battlefield at night, littered with the slain. But he does not stop with the convention. He invests himself completely in the person of the soldier who keeps watch beside his dead son:

> Long there and then in vigil I stood, dimly
>   around me the battle-field spreading;
> Vigil wondrous and vigil sweet, there in the
>   fragrant silent night;
> But not a tear fell, not even a long-drawn
>   sigh—Long, long I gazed;
> Then on the earth partially reclining, sat by
>   your side, leaning my chin in my hands;
> Passing sweet hours, immortal and mystic
>   hours with you, dearest comrade—Not a
>   tear, not a word;
> [. . .]

> Till at latest lingering of the night, indeed just
>   as the dawn appear'd,
> My comrade I wrapt in his blanket, envelop'd
>   well his form,
> Folded the blanket well, tucking it carefully
>   over head, and carefully under feet;
> And there and then, and bathed by the rising
>   sun, my son in his grave, in his rude-dug
>   grave I deposited.
>
>   (*V*, II, 492)

The poem has a double subject: the formulaic situation of a soldier's body discovered on the battlefield by a relative or lover and a more individualized evocation of the father's mental quietude during his "vigil." Although less explicitly about memory than **"The Wound Dresser,"** it is still a poem of reminiscence, promising that the dying and the vigil will not be forgotten. Its implicit context is the camp or the hospital, places where memories are exchanged. The setting of the vigil itself remains unrealized, but the soldier gives a clear sense of his featureless, nightlong meditation, in its mixture of exhaustion, shock, and genuine peace; and so the dearth of visual details supports Whitman's reluctance to violate this inward stillness by setting names to it. Whereas **"Come Up from the Fields"** clogged its situation with stock figures and stock attitudes in a conventional landscape, **"Vigil Strange"** enters a space in which the reader can create for himself the soldier's emptiness of mind. That space is, first, the army, which provides both a context for comradeship and also an unsayable explanation for his lassitude. Second, it is the hospital, where the wound-dresser sits, beside men like this, building poems out of silences like his.

In the midst of so many poems that are quick to impose their emotions and opinions on the events of the war, **"Vigil Strange"** is striking for the reticence of its soldier-persona. His I stands mute and passive in the presence of a Not-Me that exceeds his capacity to respond; and Whitman's imagination embraces that emptiness, not filling its void as he did at the end of **"Come Up from the Fields."** In *Drum-Taps,* there are about ten poems in which the struggle between the Soul and the World ceases, opening a brief glimpse of an intensely visualized experience. Most of these are the minor scenes of the war's "interior," genre pictures of the commonplaces of march and bivouac. These events had not got into the books: for these "unnamed lights and shades" there was no vocabulary of conventional phrases and emotions. Many of them assume the viewpoint of an eyewitness like the soldier in **"Vigil Strange,"** speaking in the character of that mourner into which "Satan" had modulated. It is for these poems that *Drum-Taps* is known today.

Probably the most powerful poem in *Drum-Taps* is **"A March in the Ranks Hard-Prest, and the Road Un-**

known." In this poem, Whitman unites the visual scene painting of **"The Wound-Dresser"** with the dramatic realization of an eyewitness point of view like that in **"Vigil Strange"** or **"The Artilleryman's Vision."** Whitman developed it from a wounded soldier's story set down in one of his notebooks.[26] Its subject is one unfamiliar in the anthology poetry: defeat and death, not on the field but in the unpoetic wretchedness of a hospital.

> A march in the ranks hard-prest, and the road
>   unknown;
> A route through a heavy wood, with muffled
>   steps in the darkness;
> Our army foil'd with loss severe, and the
>   sullen remnant retreating;
> Till after midnight glimmer upon us, the lights
>   of a dim-lighted building;
> We come to an open space in the woods, and
>   halt by the dim-lighted building;
> 'Tis a large old church, at the crossing
>   roads—'tis now an impromptu hospital;
> —Entering but for a minute, I see a sight
>   beyond all the pictures and poems ever
>   made:
> Shadows of deepest, deepest black, just lit by
>   moving candles and lamps,
> And by one great pitchy torch, stationary, with
>   wild red flame, and clouds of smoke;
> By these, crowds, groups of forms, vaguely I
>   see, on the floor, some in the pews laid
>   down;
> At my feet more distinctly, a soldier, a mere
>   lad, in danger of bleeding to death, (he is
>   shot in the abdomen;)
> I staunch the blood temporarily, (the
>   youngster's face is white as a lily;)
> Then before I depart I sweep my eyes o'er the
>   scene, fain to absorb it all;
> Faces, varieties, postures beyond description,
>   most in obscurity, some of them dead;
> Surgeons operating, attendants holding lights,
>   the smell of ether, the odor of blood;
> The crowd, O the crowd of the bloody
>   forms of soldiers—the yard outside also
>   fill'd;
> Some on the bare ground, some on planks or
>   stretchers, some in the death-spasm
>   sweating;
> An occasional scream or cry, the doctor's
>   shouted orders or calls;
> The glisten of the little steel instruments
>   catching the glint of the torches;
> These I resume as I chant—I see again the
>   forms, I smell the odor;
> Then hear outside the orders given, *Fall in,*
>   *my men, Fall in;*
> But first I bend to the dying lad—his eyes
>   open—a half-smile gives he me;

> Then the eyes close, calmly close, and I speed
>   forth to the darkness,
> Resuming, marching, ever in darkness
>   marching, on in the ranks,
> The unknown road still marching.
>
>   (*V,* II, 493-94)

Bursting upon the reader in three lines of urgent phrases that never cohere into a sentence, and then in collecting into syntactic unity, the poem speaks from the midst of firsthand experience. "I am the man. . . . I suffered. . . . I was there," Whitman had said in **"Song of Myself"**; but here the verbs are present tense and the sympathetic immediacy almost complete. ("Almost," because in one parenthetic line, "These I resume as I chant—I see again the forms, I smell the odor," he reveals to his readers that this is a soldier's reminiscence, like **"The Artilleryman's Vision"**— and that the soldier, with Whitman's aid, is making his memories into a poem.)

The poem is not arranged to imitate the flux of reminiscence, as was **"The Wound-Dresser."** Rather, it recreates a sequence of physical movements and visual discoveries. Whitman's earlier poems sometimes had dilated into an "experiential" mode, as when **"Song of the Broad-Axe"** paused to contemplate the motions of the housebuilders, and **"A Song for Occupations,"** the rhythms of the mill and the slaughterhouse. Here the entire poem is set in the experiential mode. It begins and ends with the army's huggermugger retreat, a compelled movement down the road (and through the poem's lines) where nothing is foreknown and expected. Words repeat themselves without plan or provision: *march, dim-lighted building, marching, unknown road, darkness.* Objects appear as the soldier approaches them, then disappear. The poem's motion is the movement of his hard-pressed striding body, his incurious eyes.

Then this motion is arrested. We have entered the church. The viewpoint stands still as the soldier first takes in "a sight beyond all the pictures and poems ever made." As a "sight," it is a lurid impression of light—he has just come in from the night road—contrasted with darkness. Lamps and torch flicker against shadows and smoke, and in the foreground there is the white face of a dying soldier. Two simple planes of attention, with a dramatic contrast in illumination, it is the kind of view that could have been managed very effectively in the wood engravings that newspapers were just beginning to employ in the 1860s. Yet it is beyond pictures and poems. He has opened the door of a church and found hell inside. Here are the unnamed lights and shades and the black infernal background of that "interior" war that Whitman knew would never get into the books. A hundred or two of the "Dying Soldier" poems in Hayward's *Poetical Pen-Pictures* would not make anything in this room intelligible.

The boy at his feet is not his son, not his comrade, but a stranger, like everything he sees. Nevertheless, the soldier's attention focuses on him, for he can be seen distinctly; and as he is seen ("a mere lad, in danger of bleeding to death, . . . shot in the abdomen"), he becomes something on which the poem likewise can focus its attention, as the appropriate subject of a customary emotion. But no emotion is named. As the soldier attends to his hemorrhaging would, the poem utters its only metaphor: "the youngster's face is white as a lily"—a conventional comparison for pallor, but just as right, in this situation, as the soldier's automatic and ineffectual aid for the boy.

Now the visitor looks again at the church's interior. It resolves into a "scene," and its occupants assume "postures." Not only its lighting but its composition is, for the moment, resolved into tableau.[27] He identifies the middle-ground figures as surgeons and attendants; he connects the crowd inside with the crowd outside awaiting attention; he hears the soldiers' screams and the doctors' calls, and smells the ether and the blood. The officer outside shouts; he focuses again on the foreground; the boy loses consciousness. The "scene" is over. Its sequence of impressions, directed by the visitor's darting eye, gives way to a renewal of the dogged succession of *march . . . darkness . . . road.*

Whitman's imagination has achieved something like the passivity of the father keeping vigil by his son—perhaps the passivity he had attained beside many hospital beds—in which it is not necessary for the Soul to vaunt its powers of absorption or to dominate the experience with its own rhetorical patterning. Rather, the actions of the participants have set the rhythm for the entire poem. This graphic series of movements and glimpses, presented both as mediated reminiscence and as the immediate experience of an *eye*witness, provide for the reader an imaginative path between the war's realities and his own soul. The power of sympathy has allowed Whitman temporarily to forsake his own I for a stranger's point of view and to acknowledge the Not-Me as reality rather than as the phenomena of an omnivorous consciousness. The mystery of the eyesight has brought poet and reader together as ministrants to the young soldier, whose brief glance up at you (whoever you are) is the glance of recognition.

Closest in technique to **"A March in the Ranks"** is **"A Sight in Camp in the Day-Break Gray and Dim,"** where the succession of images again matches the unfolding physical and visual experience of the speaker—though the sequence is less complex than in the former poem. In this case, it appears that the memory is Whitman's own:[28]

> A sight in camp in the day-break grey and
> dim,
> As from my tent I emerge so early, sleepless,

> As slow I walk in the cool fresh air, the path
> near by the hospital-tent,
> Three forms I see on stretchers lying, brought
> out there, untended lying,
> Over each the blanket spread, ample brownish
> woolen blanket,
> Grey and heavy blanket, folding, covering
> all.

> Curious, I halt, and silent stand;
> Then with light fingers I from the face of the
> nearest, the first, just lift the blanket:
> Who are you, elderly man so gaunt and grim,
> with well-grey'd hair, and flesh all sunken
> about the eyes?
> Who are you, my dear comrade?

> Then to the second I step—And who are you,
> my child and darling?
> Who are you, sweet boy, with cheeks yet
> blooming?
> Then to the third—a face nor child, nor old,
> very calm, as of beautiful yellow-white
> ivory:
> Young man, I think I know you—I think this
> face of yours is the face of the Christ
> himself;
> Dead and divine, and brother of all, and here
> again he lies.
>
> 　　　　　　　　　　　　*(V, II, 495-96)*

Here too the poem means to make you *see*, introducing a visually "dim" setting and then providing a series of disclosures suspended within an account of the speaker's movements. Promised "a sight" in its first words, we are led through several lines of circumstantial motion until the three shrouded bodies appear; and, after a detailed scrutiny of the blankets, we must participate in the discovery of one stranger's face, then another's, knowing that the third will be no stranger and that it will fulfill the promise of the poem's opening. So it does: "brother" (or perhaps "lover") is added to "father" and "son," so that every reader may find his, or her, worst fear embodied here. Sight culminates in recognition, though not of the soldier's individual identity. As in **"A March in the Ranks,"** the pale face suggests a metaphor—this time a reference to art (a crucifix, an ivory diptych), and through art to the story of Christ. Sight culminates in vision, assimilating the soldier's death into a communally accepted story of sacrificial death and of apotheosis. In this poem, Whitman dresses the wounds of his readers, affirming through a series of intensely visual descriptions the spiritual identity of "soldier" with "brother" and "Christ." This process of discovery bonds Whitman with his reader, and the readers with one another. The mystery of the eyesight foreruns the identities of the spiritual world.

Notes

[1] Whitman hurried *Drum-Taps* into print, anticipating a boom in patriotic poetry at the war's end. "Nothing else meant so much to him as to be accepted by the American people as a poet" (Gay Wilson Allen, *The Solitary Singer* [Rev. ed.; New York, 1967], 357).

[2] The Canadians at that moment were federating themselves into a more formidable political entity. Although they may have been unaware of Whitman's poetic expansiveness, they were alert to its political equivalent in the United States.

[3] Richard Chase writes that "by 1859 . . . Whitman's personal troubles and doubts led him to question whether the self really had any dependable psychological or metaphysical status at all, and at the same time the confusion and aimlessness of a nation on the brink of the war gave little assurance that it would continue to be a source of strength and an object of admiration" (*Walt Whitman Reconsidered,* 149).

[4] George M. Fredrickson, *The Inner Civil War: Northern Intellectuals and the Crisis of the Union* (New York, 1965), 94-95, 148-49.

[5] Denise Askin has described *Drum-Taps* as a struggle between a grandiloquent "prophetic" voice, public and assured, and a "private" voice, doubting, "demonic," which sits by the wounded and counts the dead ("Retrievements Out of the Night: Prophetic and Private Voices in Whitman's *Drum-Taps,*" *ATQ,* LI [1981], 211-23). Daniel Aaron also describes the split between public and private in *Drum-Taps,* tracing it to the poet's doubts about the war, his inner divisions, and his deepening alienation from his hoped-for readership (*The Unwritten War: American Writers and the Civil War* [New York, 1973], 68). As we will see, there are more than two speakers in *Drum-Taps.*

[6] See Joseph Cady, "*Drum-Taps* and Nineteenth-Century Male Homosexual Literature," in *Walt Whitman Here and Now,* ed. Krieg, 56-57.

[7] William Douglas O'Connor, *The Good Gray Poet* [1866]; rpr. in Richard Maurice Bucke, *Walt Whitman* (Philadelphia, 1883), 117-18.

[8] Roger Asselineau, *The Evolution of Walt Whitman* (Cambridge, Mass., 1960), II, 226, 249-50. Arthur Golden refers to Whitman's assuming, after 1866, a "public personality," though he seems to include *Drum-Taps* within the decade when Whitman was not "assuming postures of one kind or another but concentrating his efforts on writing a number of his most important poems" (Introduction to *Walt Whitman's Blue Book* [New York, 1968], II, xix). James Perrin Warren dates the change later still, from 1871: Whitman's theory of the evolution of language, he says, led him to introduce "archaic, formal, abstract diction" so that *Leaves of Grass* "enacts the cumulative quality of American English, blending the ancient and the modern to form a linguistic 'ensemble'" (*Walt Whitman's Language Experiment,* 138).

[9] Justin Kaplan, *Walt Whitman: A Life* (New York, 1980), 309-10.

[10] Chase, *Walt Whitman Reconsidered,* 150.

[11] M. Wynn Thomas has traced through *Specimen Days* the process by which Whitman passed from hostility toward the capital, seen as an epitome of "that other civil war between the people and their estranged officers and institutions," to a recognition of how Lincoln and the common soldiers had made it "a truly American city and a genuine national capital" (*Lunar Light,* 185-90).

[12] Edwin Haviland Miller, ed., *The Correspondence of Walt Whitman (1842-1867)* (New York, 1961), I 164.

[13] Louisa May Alcott, *Hospital Sketches* (1863; rpr. Cambridge, Mass., 1960); Kaplan, *Walt Whitman,* 278.

[14] Miller, ed., *Correspondence of Walt Whitman,* I, 171.

[15] *Ibid.,* 239.

[16] John Henry Hayward, ed., *Poetical Pen-Pictures of the War* (1863; rpr. Louisville, 1975).

[17] George F. Bourne, "The Night Guard," in Hayward, *Poetical Pen-Pictures,* 214.

[18] Fredrickson has questioned Whitman's reticence about the extremes of suffering: "It is possible that raw descriptions of the hospital life and battlefield carnage were too jarring and sensational to be suitable material for poetry. . . . He could give no formal expression to his sense of the war as an anonymous 'slaughterhouse,' not only because his readers could not assimilate such an insight, but because, ultimately, he could not accept it himself" (*The Inner Civil War,* 95). Timothy Sweet says more harshly that Whitman was obeying "the ideology of Union," which dictated that deaths and wounds be represented only typically, as sacrifice, or through the conventions of elegy or pastoral (*Poetry, Photography, and the Crisis of the Union* [Baltimore, 1990], 11-77). Sweet, however, does not acknowledge the other voices in *Drum-Taps* that gainsay the Unionist bard.

[19] Charles I. Glicksberg, ed., *Walt Whitman and the Civil War* (Philadelphia, 1933), 76-77.

[20] New York *Times,* October 29, 1864, p. 2. The translator of Whitman the poet may, of course, have been Whitman the journalist.

[21] These figures appear in "First O Songs for a Prelude" (*V,* II, 453), "Rise O Days from Your Fathomless Deeps" (II, 485), "Years of the Modern" (II, 504), "Old Ireland" (II, 518), "Turn O Libertad" (II, 525), "Pensive on Her Dead Gazing" (II, 526-27), "When Lilacs Last in the Dooryard Bloom'd" §14 (II, 536), "Spirit whose Work is Done" (II, 542-43), and "Lo, Victress on the Peaks" (II, 555).

[22] In 1867 he revised "By Blue Ontario's Shore," which had begun its life as the brashly self-confident Preface to the 1855 *Leaves of Grass,* so that it became a dream vision inspired by the muse-mother Democracy:

> Democracy! while weapons were everywhere
>   aim'd at your breast,
> I saw you serenely give birth to children—saw
>   in dreams your dilating form;
> Saw you with spreading mantle covering the
>   world.
>
>   (§17, *V,* I, 208)

Betsy Erkkila provides a historical background for these feminine personifications in "Whitman as Revolutionary Son," *Prospects,* X (1985), 421-41. Timothy Sweet interprets them as ideologically manipulable substitutes for the actual bodies of soldiers (*Poetry, Photography,* 16-23).

[23] Quoted in Stephen W. Sears, ed., *The American Heritage Century Collection of Civil War Art* (New York, 1974), 125. For this quotation I am indebted to M. Wynn Thomas, "Whitman and the American Democratic Identity Before and During the Civil War," *Journal of American Studies,* XV (1981), 93.

[24] In 1866, a year after *Drum-Taps,* John Greenleaf Whittier was to publish *Snow-Bound.* Though his poem has more narrative structure and the pictorial scenes are longer sustained, Whittier's structural principle, like Whitman's, is the dramatizing of the behavior of memory. Mark Twain's career shows that the Gilded Age found reminiscence more palatable than prevision.

[25] The nation responded to the war's death toll through a rhetoric of quasi-religious sacrifice that subsumed personal grief in a bond of national piety. Lincoln's address at Gettysburg is only the most familiar expression of a pervasive communal piety. See Sweet, *Poetry, Photography,* 11-43.

[26] "Scene in the woods on the peninsula—told me by Milton Roberts, ward G, (Maine)" (Glicksberg, ed., *Walt Whitman and the Civil War,* 123-24). Whitman identifies the battle as that of White Oaks Church, actually White Oak Swamp (June 30, 1862).

[27] Thomas, noting the "somber use of the picturesque," attributes it to a wish to escape guilt for having sur-

vived, so "mastering" the unmanageable pain and suffering of the war (*Lunar Light,* 209-13). The tableau, however, lasts only a moment before dissolving into the shifting immediacy of the experience.

[28] Glicksberg, ed., *Walt Whitman and the Civil War,* 73-74.

Abbreviations

N: Walt Whitman. *Notebooks and Unpublished Prose Manuscripts.* Edited by Edward F. Grier. 6 vols. New York, 1984.

PW: Walt Whitman. *Prose Works, 1892.* Edited by Floyd Stovall. 2 vols. New York, 1963-64.

Betsy Erkkila (essay date 1994)

SOURCE: "Whitman and the Homosexual Republic," in *Walt Whitman: The Centennial Essays,* edited by Ed Folsom, University of Iowa Press, 1994, pp. 153-71.

[*In the following essay, Erkkila maintains that critics who focus on the centrality of sexuality, and particularly homosexuality, in Whitman's work typically distinguish between the private and public Whitman, and between the themes of homosexuality and democracy. Erkkila argues against this reading, stressing instead the relationship, rather than the distinction, between homosexuality and democracy in Whitman's poetry.*]

In a letter dated March 13, 1946, Malcolm Cowley wrote to Kenneth Burke: "I'm working on Whitman, the old cocksucker. Very strange amalgam he made between cocksucking and democracy."[1] The letter itself seems strange coming from Malcolm Cowley, who in his famous 1959 introduction to the Viking edition of the 1855 *Leaves of Grass* became instrumental in the critical construction of Whitman as neither cocksucker nor democratic poet but as an essentially spiritual poet who had been miraculously transformed from hack political journalist to prophetic poet by a "mystical experience."[2] But Cowley's private and public comments are characteristic of a critical tradition that has insisted on silencing, spiritualizing, heterosexualizing, or marginalizing Whitman's sexual feeling for men.[3] Recent works on Whitman by gay critics and others have sought to name the sexual love of men that earlier critics insisted on silencing, but while these approaches have emphasized the centrality of Whitman's sexuality and homosexuality to his work, they have also tended to maintain a distinction between Whitman the private poet and Whitman the public poet, Whitman the homosexual poet and Whitman the poet of democracy, that unduly privatizes and totalizes Whitman's sexual feeling for men.[4] It is this distinction between private and public, homosexuality and democracy, that

I would like to question and problematize in this essay by exploring what Cowley very aptly called the "very strange amalgam" of "cocksucking and democracy" in Whitman's work.

I would like to begin by describing a brief public service announcement produced by the Philadelphia Lesbian and Gay Task Force as a means of reflecting on the uses to which Whitman may and may not be put in contemporary American culture. A young man stands at the Delaware River's edge, with the Walt Whitman Bridge in the background, and says:

> Hey, I just found out Walt Whitman was gay . . . you know the guy they named the bridge after. I wish I had known that when I was in high school. Back then, I got hassled all the time by the other kids, 'cause I'm gay—and the teachers—they didn't say anything. Why didn't they tell me Walt Whitman was gay?

All six television stations in the Philadelphia market refused to air this public service announcement, arguing that it was too "controversial" and that it "advocated a particular lifestyle." When two of the stations called the Walt Whitman Poetry Center, the director said that to tell the world that Whitman was gay "would really be detrimental to the Center. A lot of our programming is geared to teens. Kids don't need a lot to scare them off."[5] At issue in this controversy was not the question of whether Whitman was gay; there seemed to be widespread if covert agreement that he was. At issue was the idea that Whitman's gayness must not be aired publicly and the belief that such public airing would be detrimental to the American public and "scare" young kids. What the controversy suggests, finally, is the extent to which Whitman as the poet of the people, the poet of democracy, and the American poet, has also become an American public property whose image is bound up with the maintenance of American public health and American national policy. It is not only the academic and critical establishment but those in positions of social and cultural power and, I would add, the national government itself, that are heavily invested in keeping Whitman's sexuality, and specifically his sexual love for men, out of any discussion of his role as the poet of democracy, and the American poet.[6] In other words, if we can control Whitman's sexuality, we can also control the sexuality of the nation.

Against those who insist on separating Whitman's work into an either/or proposition—either Whitman the private poet or Whitman the public poet, Whitman the poet of gay men or Whitman the democratic poet, Whitman the homosexual or Whitman the poet of the American republic—I would like to argue that we take Whitman seriously when, in the preface to the 1876 centennial edition of *Leaves of Grass,* he says of the

"ever new-interchange of adhesiveness, so fitly emblematic of America" that "the special meaning of the 'Calamus' cluster of *Leaves of Grass* (and *more or less running through the book,* and cropping out in 'Drum-Taps,')* mainly resides in its *political significance.*" "It is," Whitman goes on to say, "by a fervent, accepted development of comradeship, the beautiful and sane affection of man for man, latent in all the young fellows, north and south, east and west—it is by this, I say, and by what goes directly and indirectly along with it, that the United States of the future, (I cannot too often repeat,) are to be most effectually welded together, intercalated, anneal'd into a living union" (*PW,* 2:471, emphasis added).

In arguing for the political significance of adhesiveness as a fervent passion among and between men in the **"Calamus"** poems, *Drum-Taps,* and throughout *Leaves of Grass,* I do not mean to return to older interpretations of Whitman's love poems to men as allegories of American democracy. Rather, I mean to argue the centrality of Whitman's sexual love of men to the democratic vision and experimental poetics of *Leaves of Grass* and to Whitman's hopes for welding the American republic into a "living union," especially in the post-Civil War period. In making this argument, I want to explore the ways the discourse of democracy intersects with material transformations in labor, industry, and social relations in the nineteenth century in the United States to construct homosexuality as a type and a pathology.[7] But in exploring the emergence of homosexuality as a modern type and sensibility in nineteenth-century America, and in Whitman's work in particular, I want to try to avoid the tendency among recent critics, despite their distinction between what Jeffrey Weeks calls "homosexual behavior, which is universal, and a homosexual identity, which is historically specific," to construct both homosexual behavior and homosexual identity as transhistorical and monolithic categories.[8] I want to insist, that is, on the fact that the word and the category *homosexual* did not exist when Whitman began writing. As he himself put it in *An American Primer:* "The lack of any words . . . is as historical as the existence of words. As for me, I feel a hundred realities, clearly determined in me, that words are not yet formed to represent" (*AP,* 21). The words Whitman did use to articulate and name his erotic feeling for men were the words of democracy—of comradeship, brotherhood, equality, social union, and the glories of the laborer and the common people. But Whitman also used other languages. And thus, against those who tend to treat homosexuality as an a priori or monolithic given in Whitman's work, I want to argue the fluidity of Whitman's articulation of same-sex love among men as the language of democracy intersects with other languages, including the languages of temperance, sexual reform, artisan republicanism, labor radicalism, phrenology, heterosexual love, familial and specifically father-son relationships, and spirituality in Whitman's attempt, as he says, to express "a hundred realities, clearly determined in me, that words are not yet formed to represent."

In past approaches to Whitman's work, there has been a tendency to discuss the arc of Whitman's poetic development as if he emerged miraculously as a "homosexual poet" in the 1860 *Leaves of Grass* and then disappeared or was sublimated just as miraculously during the Civil War and in the post-Civil War period. As Charley Shively and Michael Moon have pointed out, however, Whitman's desire to name his erotic attraction to men is already evident in his early story **"The Child's Champion"** (1841, later entitled **"The Child and the Profligate"**) and in his temperance novel ***Franklin Evans; or the Inebriate*** (1842), both published by the *New World,* a popular and widely circulated workingman's magazine.[9] But while these stories name a kind of sexual cruising among men in the city, to which youths newly arrived from the country are particularly prone, they also locate physical relations among men under the sign of intemperance, thus rendering them potentially dangerous to the healthy and virtuous personal relationships and republican body the stories advocate. While the profligate is transformed into a provider by his erotic attraction to the child, and while he sleeps that night with the young boy folded in his arms, the narrator makes it clear that this is not a totally "unsullied affection": "Fair were those two creatures in their unconscious beauty—glorious, but yet how differently glorious! One of them was innocent and sinless of all wrong: the other—O to that other, what evil had not been present, either in action or to his desires!" (*EPF*, 76).

Similarly, while ***Franklin Evans*** seems driven by a narrative urge to kill off women and heterosexual marriage in the interest of affirming the primacy of social and erotic bonding among men, these relationships are associated with intemperance as a sign of drinking, carousing, and other forms of bodily excess and therefore ultimately at odds with the temperance and virtue necessary for a healthy republican body politic. When Franklin Evans is transformed from inebriate into advocate of temperance, the transformation is figured in the political language of republican regeneration and manifest destiny: "Now man is free! He walks upon the earth, worthy the name of one whose prototype is God! We hear the mighty victory chorus sounding loud and long. Regenerated! Regenerated! . . . Victory! Victory! The Last Slave of Appetite is free, and the people are regenerated!" (*EPF*, 223).

Sometime in the 1840s this apparent antithesis between unhealthy sexuality among men and a healthy republican body politic begins to shift in Whitman's work, as he begins to articulate a position different from but often expressed in the same language as such popular male purity and antimasturbation tracts as Sylvester Graham's *Lecture to Young Men on Chastity* (1834) and Orson Fowler's *Amativeness: Or Evils and Remedies of Excessive and Perverted Sexuality* (1844), in which masturbation and sexual play among men are presented as destructive to the physical and moral health of a productive, reproductive, and ultimately heterosexual American republic.[10] In Whitman's notebook dated 1847, in which he begins working toward the experimental language and form of *Leaves of Grass,* he insists on locating the soul and vision in the body and matter. And in an early version of the famous touch sequence in **"Song of Myself,"** he represents masturbation, which also doubled in the nineteenth century as a code word for sexuality among and between men, as a source at once of sexual ecstasy, mystical vision, and poetic utterance.

> I do not wonder that one feeling now does so much for me,
> He is free of all the rest,—and swiftly begets offspring of them, better than the dams.
> A touch now reads me a library of knowledge in an instant.
> It smells for me the fragrance of wine and lemon-blows.
> It tastes for me ripe strawberries and melons,—
> It talks for me with a tongue of its own,
> It finds an ear wherever it rests or taps.
>
> (*UPP,* 2:72)

Just as in **"Song of Myself,"** where the pleasures of touching, either oneself or "what is hardly different from myself," and the orgasmic spilling of male seed give rise to the nationalist vision of "Landscapes projected masculine full-sized and golden" (*LG* 55, 53, 54), so in his notebook entry Whitman reverses the nonreproductive figurations of masturbation and same-sex touching in the male purity tracts, associating the sexual pleasure of "He" who "is free of all the rest" and "better than the dams" with the "offspring" of vision, voice, poetic utterance, and a gloriously reproductive image of nature and nation.

This figuration of the body, sexuality, and same-sex love among men as the site of ecstasy, vision, and poetic utterance becomes even more emphatic in the first edition of *Leaves of Grass.* In his long opening poem, later entitled **"Song of Myself,"** the poet describes the "sexual experience" that is at the origins of his democratic voice and vision.

> I believe in you my soul. . . . the other I am must not abase itself to you,
> And you must not be abased to the other.
> Loafe with me on the grass. . . . loose the stop from your throat,
> Not words, not music or rhyme I want. . . . not custom or lecture, not even the best,

Only the lull I like, the hum of your valved
    voice.
I mind how we lay in June, such a transparent
    summer morning;
You settled your head athwart my hips and
    gently turned over upon me,
And parted the shirt from my bosom-bone,
    and plunged your tongue to my barestript
    heart,
And reached till you felt my beard, and
    reached till you held my feet.

                              (*LG* 55, 28-29)

"Isn't this cocksucking plain and simple?" Charley
Shively asks, arguing that in this passage "Whitman
demonstrates part of his Americanness by placing cocksucking at the center of *Leaves of Grass*."[11] But before
we completely literalize this passage as a direct transcription of cocksucking among men, it is important to
recognize that the "I" and "you" are unspecified and
ungendered in the passage and that the passage has
also been read as the transcription of what James E.
Miller calls an "inverted mystical experience."[12]

Rather than posing cocksucking and mysticism as antithetical readings, however, or arguing that Whitman
seeks consciously to disguise his homosexuality through
the language of the soul, I would like to suggest that
this passage is paradigmatic of the ways the languages
of sexuality and spirituality, same-sex love and love
between men and women, private and public, intersect
and flow into each other in Whitman's work. It is
unclear finally whether Whitman is describing sexuality in the language of spiritual ecstasy or a mystical
experience in the language of sexual ecstasy, for he
seems to be doing both at once. What is clear is that
the democratic knowledge the poet receives of an entire universe bathed in an erotic force that links men,
women, God, and the natural world in a vision of mystic
unity is associated with sexual and bodily ecstasy, an
ecstasy that includes but is not limited to the pleasures
of cocksucking between men. In other words, here we
have precisely Malcolm Cowley's strange amalgam
"between cocksucking and democracy" in Whitman's
work. Giving tongue is associated at once with sexuality, including sexuality between men, democracy,
spiritual vision, and poetic utterance.

This amalgam between men loving men and democracy would become even more emphatic in Whitman's
work as the actual political union—on which Whitman
had staked his identity and faith as a democratic poet—
began to dissolve. In traditional readings of Whitman's
life and work, it is argued that at some time in the
late 1850s Whitman had a love affair that caused him
to turn away from his public role as the poet of democracy toward the privacy of love. To disguise the
real "homosexual" content of his "Calamus" poems
in the 1860 edition of *Leaves of Grass,* it is argued,

Whitman interspersed more public poems of democracy,
such as "For You O Democracy," with more private
and personal poems of homosexual love. Joseph Cady
argues that Whitman's attempt to invent a "new order
based on his private experience as a homosexual" was
only partially successful because in the "least satisfying" strain of "Calamus," Whitman does not sustain his
separation and conflict but seeks to "translate" his experience into the language of common culture.[13]

But this notion of a neat division between the more
revolutionary impulses of the private poet of homosexual love and the more conventional impulses of the
public poet of democracy is not born out by a close
reading of the "Live Oak with Moss" sequence, the
original sheaf of twelve love poems of "manly love"
out of which the "Calamus" poems emerged. In this
sequence, it is precisely in and through rather than
against the more conventional language of democratic
comradeship, phrenological adhesiveness, and brotherly love that the poet articulates his feelings for men.[14]
"I dreamed in a dream of a city where all men were
like brothers," Whitman writes in the poem that would
later become "Calamus" 34:

O I saw them tenderly love each other—I
    often saw them, in numbers, walking hand
    in hand;
I dreamed that was the city of robust
    friends—Nothing was greater there than
    manly love—it led the rest,
It was seen every hour in the actions of the
    men of that city, and in all their looks and
    words.

                             (*MLG*, 114)

What this poem suggests is that, in its most visionary
realization, the dream of democracy will give rise to a
city—and ultimately an American republic—in which
men loving men can live and love and touch openly—
a dream city, I might add, that we are still very far from
achieving despite the fact that the first lines of "Calamus" 34 ("I dreamed in a dream, I saw a city invincible," *LG* 60, 373) are now inscribed on the Camden
city hall. Although the "Live Oak With Moss" sequence
and the "Calamus" sequence bear the traces of a rather
appealing crisis of representation in which Whitman
realizes that he may not speak for everybody, there is no
distinct separation between the poet of democracy and
the poet of "manly love." Like other poems in the "Live
Oak" sequence and in the "Calamus" sequence, "I
Dream'd in a Dream" marks not so much a conflict
between Whitman the democratic poet and Whitman the
lover of men but a shift in Whitman's conceptualization
of his role as democratic poet that locates his personal
and sexual love for men at the very center of his vision,
role, and faith as the poet of democracy. Thus, in the
opening poem of "Calamus," "In Paths Untrodden,"
the poet avows his desire "To tell the secret of my

nights and days, / To celebrate the need of comrades" (342). While these lines might be read as a sign of the separation and conflict between private and public poet, they might also be read paratactically as an example of the ways Whitman's "secret" love of men is articulated together with, in the same language as and as the very condition of, his celebration of democratic comrades in the **"Calamus"** poems.

"Ah lover and perfect equal," Whitman writes in **"Calamus"** 41 (**"Among the Multitude"**), suggesting the ways the proliferation of the eighteenth-century natural law philosophies of equality and natural rights come to underwrite and in some sense produce the emergence of homosexuality simultaneously with the emergence and spread of democracy in the United States. It is no coincidence that the proliferation of the rhetoric (if not the reality) of democratic equality during the Age of Jackson corresponded with the emergence of the temperance movement, the male purity crusade, and an increasing cultural anxiety about drinking, masturbation, same-sex sexuality, and other forms of bodily excess and indulgence among and between men. In other words, democracy, particularly in its more egalitarian and fraternal forms, might be said to have simultaneously produced, affirmed, and demonized the modern homosexual as a distinct identity and role.

In *Whitman the Political Poet,* I argued that the **"Calamus"** sequence was Whitman's most radical sequence of poems both personally and politically.[15] But in this essay, I would like to revise that reading to suggest that the **"Children of Adam"** poems (originally entitled **"Enfans d'Adam"**) may indeed be the more sexually radical sequence that Emerson and the censors who banned *Leaves of Grass* in Boston in 1882 always believed it to be. In traditional accounts of Whitman's poetic development, **"Children of Adam"** is represented as an afterthought, a sequence of poems that Whitman added to the 1860 edition of *Leaves of Grass* in order to provide a legitimizing heterosexual context for the actually more radical personal love poems to men in the **"Calamus"** sequence. A notebook entry suggests that Whitman initially conceptualized **"Children of Adam"** as a companion piece to his **"Calamus"** poems: "A string of Poems (short etc.), embodying the amative love of woman—the same as Live Oak Leaves do the passion of friendship for man" (*NF,* 169). But whatever Whitman's initial intentions, the **"Children of Adam"** poems do not read as a neatly heterosexual counterpart to his poems of passion for men in the **"Calamus"** sequence. (And here it is perhaps important to remember that the term *heterosexual* actually came later than the term *homosexual* in the construction of modern sexuality.) While the **"Children of Adam"** poem **"A Woman Waits for Me"** consistently provoked nineteenth-century censorship for its representation of an athletic, sexually charged, and desiring female body, the poem is in fact atypical in its emphasis on the amative, and ultimately procreative and eugenically productive, love between men and women.

"Singing the phallus" and the "bedfellow's song," many of the **"Children of Adam"** poems are not about women or procreation or progeny at all but about amativeness as a burning, aching, "resistless," emphatically physical "yearning" for young men (see **"From Pent-Up Aching Rivers"**). Whereas in the **"Calamus"** poems physical love among men is limited to touching and kissing, in the **"Children of Adam"** poems Whitman, in the figure of a "lusty," "tremulous," and insistently "phallic" Adam, names and bathes his songs in an active, orgiastic, and physical sexuality among men. "Give me now libidinous joys only!" the poet exclaims in **"Enfans d'Adam"** 8 (**"Native Moments"**), evoking scenes of nonreproductive sexual play and pleasure among men:

> I am for those who believe in loose delights—
>   I share the midnight orgies of young men,
> I dance with the dancers, and drink with the
>   drinkers,
> The echoes ring with our indecent calls,
> I take for my love some prostitute—I pick out
>   some low person for my dearest friend,
> He shall be lawless, rude, illiterate—he shall
>   be one condemned by others for deeds
>   done;
> I will play a part no longer—Why should I
>   exile myself from my companions?
>   (*LG* 60, 311)

Even the poem **"A Woman Waits for Me"** is as much a celebration of a deliciously phallic male sexuality as it is a celebration of sexual love between men and women. Associating the "woman" of the title with traditionally masculine activities, the language of the poem slips ambiguously between a celebration of same-sex and opposite-sex love. Moreover, in later revisions of the **"Enfans d'Adam"** poems, Whitman actually edited out several of the more explicit "heterosexual" references while retaining the emphasis on an insistently phallic and physical male sexuality. Thus, Whitman's later deletion of the phrase "I take for my love some prostitute" in the above passage from **"Native Moments"** ends up underscoring the "libidinous joys" and "loose delights" of an explicitly same-sexuality among and between men.[16]

Whereas in the 1860 *Leaves of Grass* the **"Enfans d'Adam"** poems are immediately followed by **"Poem of the Road"** (**"Song of the Open Road"**), **"To the Sayers of Words"** (**"A Song of the Rolling Earth"**), **"A Boston Ballad,"** and then the **"Calamus"** sequence, in the final edition of *Leaves of Grass,* the **"Calamus"** poems immediately follow the **"Children of Adam"** poems. Rather than suggesting a neatly "heterosexual" and "homosexual" pairing, however, this final arrangement further underscores the fluid relationship between the "lusty, phallic" and ultimately nonreproductive and nonmonogamous sexual play and pleasure among men in the **"Children of Adam"** poems and the less insistently phallic but nonetheless explicitly physical lover and democrat of the **"Calamus"** poems. "Touch me, touch the palm of your hand to my body as I pass, / Be not afraid of my body," says the naked Adamic speaker in the final poem of the **"Children of Adam"** sequence, as he passes and steps quite imperceptibly into the "paths untrodden" and more emphatically (but not exclusively) male contexts of the **"Calamus"** poems (*LG*, 111).

Against popular associations of masturbation and excessive adhesiveness among men with solitude, impotence, and emasculation, it was Whitman's invention not only to extend the meaning of adhesiveness, the phrenological term for friendship, to same-sex love among men as a virile and socially productive force for urban, national, and international community, but also to extend amativeness, the phrenological term for procreative love between men and women, to include physical and procreative love among men. Implicit in the sexual and social vision of **"Children of Adam"** is a new world garden and a new American republic ordered not by the marital, procreative, familial, and monogamous bonds between men and women but by the sexually and socially productive and nonmonogamous relations among men. While the **"Children of Adam"** appear to refer to *all* the children produced presumably by Adam and Eve, as the exclusive emphasis on Adam in the title suggests, these children are also the male children produced and "prepared for" by the "act divine" and "stalwart loins" of a phallic and virile Adam, whose sexual union with men bears the creative and procreative seeds of both his poetry and the ultimate realization of the American republic and the American race.

In his important article "'Here is Adhesiveness': From Friendship to Homosexuality," Michael Lynch argues that when in the 1856 edition of *Leaves of Grass* Whitman wrote "Here is adhesiveness, it is not previously fashioned—it is apropos" in reference to exclusively same-sex relationships among men, his words marked an important shift toward a definition of the homosexual and heterosexual as distinct types. "Whitman's restriction of Adhesiveness to male-male relationships opened the way for an understanding of same-sex expression of a sexual instinct that was polar to an opposite-sex expression of it." Rather than representing the emergence of what Lynch calls "a distinct 'homosexual identity' and 'homosexual role,'"[17] I would argue that Whitman's **"Calamus"** and **"Children of Adam"** poems imply just the opposite. By conceptualizing and articulating his love for men in the language of democratic comradeship and by celebrating physical pleasure among men in the context

of male and female amativeness and procreation, Whitman in fact suggests the extent to which the bounds between private and public, male and female, heterosexual and homosexual, are still indistinct, permeable, and fluid in his work.

In most critical discussions of Whitman's life and work, it has become almost axiomatic to argue that Whitman's "homosexual" love crisis of the late 1850s was sublimated in the figure of the "wound-dresser" during the Civil War and ultimately silenced and suppressed in the "good gray" politics and poetics of the post-Civil War period. Here, again, however, a close reading of Whitman's Civil War writings suggests that just the opposite may be the case: that in fact the discourses of desire among men and the occasions and contexts for their expression in Whitman's work actually proliferated during the Civil War.[18] "How I love them! how I could hug them, with their brown faces, and their clothes and knapsacks cover'd with dust!" Whitman exclaims in the opening poem of *Drum-Taps,* **"First O Songs for a Prelude,"** as the fire of his passion for men bursts forth along with and in the same language as the "torrents of men" and "the pent fire" of the Civil War (**"Rise O Days from Your Fathomless Deeps,"** (*DT,* 6, 37). Rather than sublimating his feelings for men, the historical role Whitman played in visiting thousands of soldiers in the Washington hospitals and the poetic role he played as the "wound-dresser" actually enabled a range of socially prohibited physical contacts and emotional exchanges among men. Soothing, touching, hugging, and kissing the sick and dying soldiers, the private poet merges with the public, female with male, "wound-dresser" with soldier, lover with democratic patriot, in Whitman's poems of the Civil War. "Many a soldier's loving arms about this neck have cross'd and rested, / Many a soldier's kiss dwells on these bearded lips" (**"The Dresser,"** 34).

The intensity of Whitman's passion for men, released and allowed by the "manly" context of war, is particularly evident in **"Vigil Strange I Kept on the Field One Night,"** which along with **"When I Heard at the Close of the Day"** is perhaps Whitman's most intense and lyrically moving expression of same-sex love. But having said this, it is also important to recognize the ways the languages of manly love, paternity, military comradeship, and maternal care intermix and mingle in the poem.

> Vigil strange I kept on the field one night,
> When you, my son and my comrade, dropt at
>   my side that day,
> One look I but gave, which your dear eyes
>   return'd, with a look I shall never forget;
> One touch of your hand to mine, O boy,
>   reach'd up as you lay on the ground;
> Then onward I sped in the battle, the
>   even-contested battle;

Till late in the night reliev'd, to the place at
    last again I made my way;
Found you in death so cold, dear comrade—
    found your body, son of responding kisses,
    (never again on earth responding).

                  (***DT***, 42)[19]

As the poet carefully envelopes his "dearest comrade,"
his "son" and "soldier," and his "boy of responding
kisses" in a blanket and buries him "where he fell," he,
in effect, prepares the ground which, as in **"A March in
the Ranks Hard-Prest, and the Road Unknown," "A
Sight in Camp in the Daybreak Gray and Dim,"** and
"As I Toilsome Wander'd Virginia's Woods," will
enable him to carry on amid what he called the "malig-
nancy," butchery, and surrounding darkness of the war.

The centrality of the Civil War in testing and affirming not only the American union but a range of physical and emotional bonds of affection and intimacy
among men as the foundation of the future American
republic is most explicitly expressed in **"Over the
Carnage Rose Prophetic a Voice,"** which, with the
exception of the opening and closing lines, was transferred from the **"Calamus"** sequence into ***Drum-Taps
and Sequel*** (1865):

Over the carnage rose prophetic a voice,
Be not dishearten'd—Affection shall solve the
    problems of Freedom yet;
Those who love each other shall become
    invincible—they shall yet make Columbia
    victorious.

As in **"I Dream'd in a Dream,"** the poet affirms the
relation between "manly affection," physical touching
among men across state and class bounds, and the
dreams of democracy:

It shall be customary in the houses and streets
    to see manly affection;
The most dauntless and rude shall touch face
    to face lightly;
The dependence of Liberty shall be lovers,
The continuance of Equality shall be
    comrades.
These shall tie you and band you stronger
    than hoops of iron;
I, extatic, O partners! O lands! with the love
    of lovers tie you.

                  (***DT***, 50)

Rather than representing a retreat from the privacy of
same-sex love, in Whitman's writings of the post-Civil
War period this love actually proliferates, even in the
most public context of Whitman's famous wartime
elegy for Abraham Lincoln, **"When Lilacs Last in
the Dooryard Bloom'd,"** where the poet mourns the
death of Lincoln as "lustrous" comrade and lover.

The Civil War not only affirmed "manly affection" as
the ground of a new democratic order, it also gave
Whitman a more militant and combative language in
which to affirm his commitment to the ongoing struggle
for this order in the post-Civil War period. "I know my
words are weapons, full of danger, full of death," the
poet declares in **"As I Lay with My Head in Your
Lap, Camerado,"** urging his readers to join him in the
democratic struggle:

For I confront peace, security, and all the
    settled laws, to unsettle them;
I am more resolute because all have denied
    me, than I could ever have been had all
    accepted me;
I heed not, and have never heeded, either
    experience, cautions, majorities, nor ridicule;
And the threat of what is call'd hell is little
    or nothing to me;
And the lure of what is call'd heaven is little
    or nothing to me;
. . . Dear camerado! I confess I have urged
    you onward with me, and still urge you,
    without the least idea what is our
    destination,
Or whether we shall be victorious, or utterly
    quell'd and defeated.

                (***Sequel, DT***, 19)

Ironically, it was in the fields and hospitals of the Civil
War that Whitman came closest to realizing his democratic and homosexual dream of a "new City of Friends."
Included among the poems of demobilization, **"As I
Lay with My Head in Your Lap, Camerado"** registers uneasiness as the poet moves away from the true
democracy of wartime comradeship toward the potentially oppressive structures of a peacetime—and heterosexual—economy. Addressing a "you" who is, as
in **"Calamus,"** both personal lover and democratic
comrade, the poet expresses renewed dedication to a
boundless democratic "destination" that will include
and indeed be grounded in same-sex love among men.[20]

It is ironic that the iconography of the good gray poet
came to dominate Whitman's public image and later
critical treatments of his life and work at the very time
that we have the most specific historical documenta-
tion in Whitman's notebooks and in his correspondence
with Peter Doyle and Harry Stafford of his emotional
and loving attachments to young working-class men.[21]
In a notebook entry that apparently refers to the "*enormous* PERTURBATION" of his "FEVERISH, FLUCTUATING"
emotional attachment to Peter Doyle, Whitman writes:

Depress the adhesive nature
It is in excess—making life a torment
All this diseased, feverish disproportionate
    adhesiveness.

                (***UPP***, 2:96)

In Whitman criticism, this entry is usually cited as an instance of the poet's attempt to suppress his sexual desire for men in order to transform himself into the safer and more publicly acceptable image of the good gray poet. But at no place in his notebooks does Whitman suggest that "adhesiveness" is itself "diseased." Rather, like the male purity tracts, what Whitman suggests is that it is "adhesiveness" in excess that makes "life a torment" and must be brought under control. "PURSUE HER NO MORE," Whitman writes, coyly changing the object of his passion from him to her. But the change once again suggests the extent to which the languages of male and female love and male/male love intersect and are articulated together in Whitman's work. What is important for my point is the fact that the poet's perception of his "adhesiveness" as "diseased" and "disproportionate" and in excess does not change even if the object of his excessive attachment is a woman.

In support of the idea of the increasing split between private and public in Whitman's works in the postwar years, as Whitman the lover of men gives way to the iconography of the good gray poet, many emphasize the changes that Whitman made in his **"Calamus"** poems after he was fired from his job at the Department of the Interior for moral turpitude.[22] But here again, a close study of the changes that Whitman made in future editions of *Leaves of Grass* reveals no clear pattern of suppressing or even toning down his love poems to men. In fact, Whitman's decision to delete three poems from **"Calamus"**—**"Who Is Now Reading This?," "I Thought That Knowledge Alone Would Suffice,"** and **"Hours Continuing Long"**—suggests that he sought not to tone down or suppress his expression of "manly love" but rather to suppress the more negative dimensions of his love for men and to blur the distinction between public poet and private lover he set forth in **"I Thought That Knowledge Alone Would Suffice."** Moreover, in **"The Base of All Metaphysics,"** the one poem he added to the **"Calamus"** sequence in 1871, Whitman represents "The dear love of man for his comrade, the attraction of friend to friend" as the "base and finale too for all metaphysics," underlying the philosophies of Plato, Socrates, and Christ and the systems of German philosophy represented by Fichte, Schelling, and Hegel (*LG*, 121).

This representation of same-sex love between men as the base of a new social order underlies the visionary democracy of *Democratic Vistas* (1871). In this important and wide-ranging attempt to come to terms with the problems of democracy in America, Whitman concludes that "intense and loving comradeship, the personal and passionate attachment of man to man," represents "the most substantial hope and safety of the future of these States." "It is to the development, identification, and general prevalence of that fervid comradeship, (the adhesive love, at least rivaling

amative love hitherto possessing imaginative literature, if not going beyond it)," Whitman explains in a footnote, "that I look for the counterbalance and offset of our materialistic and vulgar American democracy, and for the spiritualization thereof." Amid what he called the aggressive selfism, vulgar materialism, and widespread corruption of the Gilded Age, Whitman looked not to marriage or to the traditional family but to "the personal and passionate attachment of man to man" as the social base and future hope of the American republic. "I say democracy infers such loving comradeship as its most inevitable twin or counterpart, without which it will be incomplete, in vain, and incapable of perpetuating itself" (*PW*, 2:414-415).[23]

So, if what I have been arguing is correct, why did Whitman not just come out with it in his famous exchange with John Addington Symonds in 1890, when Symonds asked him outright if his "conception of Comradeship" included the possibility of "semi-sexual emotions & actions" between men? Whitman could have said, "Yes, John, *Leaves of Grass* is, indeed, about cocksucking and democracy. You found me out." Instead, he disavowed Symonds's "morbid inferences" about the **"Calamus"** poems as "undream'd," "unreck'd," and "damnable" and cautioned him about the necessity of construing "all parts & pages" of *Leaves of Grass* "by their own ensemble, spirit & atmosphere" (*CORR*, 5:72-73). Although Whitman's response is coy, it also seems right to me for all the reasons I have been trying to suggest. Whitman and Symonds were speaking two different, not entirely separable languages. Whereas Havelock Ellis and John Addington Symonds were central in the process of medicalizing and singling out the homosexual as abnormal and pathological,[24] Whitman was talking about physical and emotional love between men as the basis for a new social and religious order. Given his representation of male sexual love as the source of spiritual and poetic vision and the ground for a new democratic social order and given Ellis's and Symonds's medicalization of physical love between men as "sexual inversion" and "abnormal instinct," it makes sense that Whitman would disavow Symonds's attempt to medicalize and sexually categorize the **"Calamus"** poems as "morbid inferences" contrary to the "ensemble, spirit & atmosphere" of *Leaves of Grass* (73).

Whitman's famous assertion, in this same letter to Symonds, that he had fathered six children is, to say the least, disingenuous. But it is not wholly at odds with the amative, reproductive, and familial languages and contexts in which he expressed the loving relationships among and between men. In fact, given the languages of paternal, maternal, and familial affection in which Whitman carried on his relationships and correspondence with Peter Doyle, Harry Stafford, and some of the soldiers he met during the war, one might argue that Whitman was thinking of some of the "illegitimate sons" he adopted, fathered, and mothered over the course of his life.

In his attempt to give Whitman's conception of comradeship and his **"Calamus"** poems only one reading, Symonds in some sense anticipates the tendency among recent Whitman critics to treat Whitman's homosexuality as a single, transhistorical monolith. Against those who see in Whitman's work an instance of what Symonds would have called "sexual inversion" or what Michael Lynch has recently called "a distinct 'homosexual identity' or 'homosexual role,'"[25] I have been arguing that we read Whitman's expression of sexual, emotional, and social intimacy among men not as a monolithic homosexual presence but as the complex, multiply located, and historically embedded sexual, social, and discursive phenomenon it was. To those who insist on dividing Whitman the private poet and Whitman the public poet, Whitman the lover of men and Whitman the poet of democracy, or in Malcolm Cowley's apt phrase, "cocksucking and democracy," I have been trying to suggest that read within what Whitman calls the "ensemble, spirit & atmosphere" of his work the homosexual poet and the American republic refuse any neat division; they intersect, flow into each other, and continually break bounds. "Who need be afraid of the merge?" Whitman asked in **"Song of Myself."** The answer to that question is still, in this centennial year, we all are.

Notes

[1] Paul Jay, ed., *Selected Correspondence of Kenneth Burke and Malcolm Cowley* (New York: Viking, 1988), 273.

[2] Cowley, "Introduction," LG55, xii.

[3] In letters to his lover, Russell Cheyney, F. O. Matthiessen had also drawn sympathetic attention to Whitman's erotic attachments to men, but in his influential book *American Renaissance: Art and Expression in the Age of Emerson and Whitman* (New York: Oxford University Press, 1941), he dismissed the "vaguely pathological and homosexual" quality of Whitman's work and sought to reclaim him for serious national and international attention by an insistently formalist approach to *Leaves of Grass* as a "language experiment" with analogues in oratory, opera, the ocean, and the visual arts (517-625). For a review of Whitman criticism and homosexuality, see Robert K. Martin, *The Homosexual Tradition in American Poetry* (Austin: University of Texas Press, 1979), 3-8; Scott Giantvalley, "Recent Whitman Studies and Homosexuality," *Cabirion and Gay Books Bulletin* 12 (Spring/Summer 1985): 14-16. Justin Kaplan, in "The Biographer's Problem," *Mickle Street Review* II (1989): 80-88, begins by observing that "the history of over a century of Whitman biography is

to a large extent the history of a pussyfooting accommodation to the issue of sexuality, more specifically, homosexuality. One sees biography being skewed in the interests of literary public relations" (83-84). But he concludes by reconsigning the "issue" of Whitman's homosexuality to the margins when he notes that "perhaps it's time to move on to a broader focus" (88).

[4] Robert K. Martin pioneered in the field of gay studies and in the study of Whitman and homosexuality in his groundbreaking article "Whitman's *Song of Myself:* Homosexual Dream and Vision," *Partisan Review* 42 (1975): 80-96. See also Martin's chapter on Whitman in *The Homosexual Tradition,* 3-89; Joseph Cady, "Not Happy in the Capitol: Homosexuality and the Calamus Poems," *American Studies* 19 (Fall 1978): 5-22; Cady, "*Drum-Taps* and Nineteenth-Century Male Homosexual Literature," in Joann P. Krieg, ed., *Walt Whitman: Here and Now* (Westport, Conn.: Greenwood Press, 1985), 49-60; Charley Shively, ed., *Calamus Lovers: Walt Whitman's Working Class Camerados* (San Francisco: Gay Sunshine Press, 1987). M. Jimmie Killingsworth, *Whitman's Poetry of the Body: Sexuality, Politics, and the Text* (Chapel Hill: University of North Carolina Press, 1989), and Michael Moon, *Disseminating Whitman: Revision and Corporeality in Leaves of Grass* (Cambridge: Harvard University Press, 1991), both focus on Whitman's "sexual politics," but in emphasizing the split between the corporeal and the social self in Whitman's work, they tend to maintain the bounds between private and public, sexuality and politics, homosexuality and democracy, as separate and relatively distinct realms. Killingsworth, for example, notes: "Two voices predominate in Whitman's poetry of the body. One is private—confessional, inward, at times self-indulgent and sentimental. The other is public—the voice of the orator and journalist" (46). For a recent attempt to problematize the private/public binary in critical interpretations of Whitman's work, see Jay Grossman, "'The Evangel-Poem of Comrades and of Love': Revising Whitman's Republicanism," *American Transcendental Quarterly* 4 (September 1990): 201-218. See also Betsy Erkkila, "Democracy and (Homo)Sexual Desire," in *Whitman the Political Poet* (New York: Oxford University Press, 1989), 155-189.

[5] David Warner, "The Good G(r)ay Poet," *Philadelphia City Paper,* January 12-19, 1990.

[6] Given the controversy surrounding the National Endowment for the Arts and homosexuality, it cannot be entirely coincidental that the Library of Congress, which holds the largest and most substantial collection of Whitman materials in the world, sponsored no exhibit or other series of events in commemoration of the centennial of the poet's death.

[7] For a study of the relation between between capitalist transformation and the male purity movement, see

Carroll Smith-Rosenberg, "Sex as Symbol in Victorian Purity: An Ethnohistorical Analysis of Jacksonian America," *American Journal of Sociology* 84 (Supplement 1978): 5,212-5,247.

[8] Jeffrey Weeks, *Sexuality and Its Discontents: Meanings, Myths, and Modern Sexualities* (London: Routledge & Kegan Paul, 1985), 6. See also Michel Foucault's comment on the emergence of the homosexual as a distinct personage in the nineteenth century: "The sodomite had been a temporary aberration; the homosexual was now a species" in *The History of Sexuality: An Introduction,* trans. Robert Hurley (New York: Random House, 1978), 43.

[9] Shively; Moon.

[10] Sylvester Graham, *Lecture to Young Men on Chastity* (Boston: Light and Stearns, 1834); Oscar Fowler, *Amativeness: Or Evils and Remedies of Excessive and Perverted Sexuality Including Warning and Advice to the Married and Single* (New York: Fowler and Wells, 1844).

[11] Shively, 21.

[12] James E. Miller, Jr., "'Song of Myself' as Inverted Mystical Experience," *PMLA* 70 (September 1955): 636-661.

[13] Cady, "Not Happy," 15; Killingsworth (99) makes a similar distinction between sentimental rhetoric and homoerotic love in Whitman's *Calamus* poems.

[14] For studies of Whitman and phrenology, see Edward Hungerford, "Walt Whitman and His Chart of Bumps," *American Literature* 2 (1931): 350-384; Harold Aspiz, *Walt Whitman and the Body Beautiful* (Urbana: University of Illinois Press, 1980); Michael Lynch, "'Here is Adhesiveness': From Friendship to Homosexuality," *Victorian Studies* 29 (Autumn 1985): 67-96.

[15] Erkkila, 183.

[16] See also Whitman's deletion of the reference to "the perfect girl" in "Enfans" 2 ("From Pent-Up Aching Rivers") and the explicit references to the female in "Enfans" 6 ("One Hour to Madness and Joy").

[17] Lynch, 91, 67.

[18] Cady makes a similar point in "Male Homosexual Literature," but he continues to insist on a neat division between the private poet of homosexual love and the more public figure of the soldier-comrade through whom Whitman self-protectively masks his homosexual desire. What I want to stress is the inseparability of the private discourses of male homosexual desire from the more public discourses of combat and democratic nationalism in Whitman's poems of the Civil War.

[19] The language of paternal and familiar care is so marked in "Vigil Strange I Kept on the Field One Night" that M. Wynn Thomas, in *The Lunar Light of Whitman's Poetry* (Cambridge: Harvard University Press, 1987), actually reads the poem as literally about a father mourning the loss of his son during the war (208).

[20] As I argue in *Whitman the Political Poet,* this representation of same-sex love between men as the ground of democracy is accompanied by an increased emphasis on the feminine and the maternal in Whitman's post-Civil War writings (261-262).

[21] For a study of the erotic bonds Whitman formed with soldiers during the Civil War, see Charley Shively, ed., *Drum-Beats: Walt Whitman's Civil War Boy Lovers* (San Francisco: Gay Sunshine Press, 1989). Killingsworth and Moon both argue for a clear division between what Moon (11) calls the "visionary and utopian project" of the pre-Civil War Whitman and the Whitman of the post-Civil War years.

[22] For a recent version of this argument, see Killingsworth: "Propriety had become a central tenet for the postwar Whitman" (148).

[23] See also *Specimen Days* (1882), where Whitman finds among the workers and crowded city streets of "Human and Heroic New York" "a palpable outcropping of that personal comradeship I look forward to as the subtlest, strongest future hold of this many-item'd Union" (PW, 1:172).

[24] See Havelock Ellis and John Addington Symonds, *Sexual Inversion* (London: Wilson and Macmillan, 1897).

[25] Lynch, 67.

Abbreviations

AP: Horace Traubel, ed., *An American Primer* (1904; rpt., Stevens Point, Wis.: Holy Cow! Press, 1987). . . .

CORR: Edwin Haviland Miller, ed., *Walt Whitman: The Correspondence* (New York: New York University Press, 1961-1977), 6 vols. . . .

DT: F. DeWolfe Miller, ed., *Drum-Taps (1865) and Sequel to Drum-Taps (1865-66): A Facsimile Reproduction* (Gainesville, Fla.: Scholars' Facsimiles and Reprints, 1959).

EPF: Thomas L. Brasher, ed., *Early Poetry and Fiction* (New York: New York University Press, 1963). . . .

LG: Sculley Bradley and Harold W. Blodgett, eds., *Leaves of Grass: Comprehensive Reader's Edition* (New York: New York University Press, 1965).

LG55: Malcolm Cowley, ed., *Leaves of Grass: The First (1855) Edition* (New York: Viking, 1959).

LG60: Roy Harvey Pearce, ed., *Leaves of Grass, 1860 Facsimile Text* (Ithaca: Cornell University Press, 1961).

MLG: Fredson Bowers, ed., *Whitman's Manuscripts, Leaves of Grass (1860): A Parallel Text* (Chicago: University of Chicago Press, 1955).

NF: Richard Maurice Bucke, ed., *Notes and Fragments* (Ontario, Canada: A. Talbot, 1899). . . .

PW: Floyd Stovall, ed., *Prose Works, 1892* (New York: New York University Press, 1963-1964), 2 vols. . . .

UPP: Emory Holloway, ed., *The Uncollected Poetry and Prose of Walt Whitman* (Garden City, N.Y.: Doubleday, Page, 1921), 2 vols.

Ed Folsom (essay date 1994)

SOURCE: "Whitman and American Indians," in *Walt Whitman's Native Representations,* Cambridge University Press, 1994, pp. 55-98.

[*In the following essay, Folsom contends that, through-out Whitman's life and work, the poet maintained an ambivalent attitude toward Native Americans. Folsom notes that American "aborigines," as Whitman referred to Native Americans, were often described in his poetry with a mixture of disdain and admiration.*]

> (Have I forgotten any part? any thing in the
>   past?
> Come to me whoever and whatever, till I give
>   you recognition.)
>   Whitman, **"With Antecedents"** (*LG* 241)

Whitman was always on the lookout for cultural activities that signaled some emerging autochthonous form. If baseball was an enterprise that endorsed his hope for truly native patterns of shared experience, America's bloody encounters with the Indians undermined those hopes, for much of nineteenth-century American history had come to seem an outright attack on the aboriginal, an attempt to erase the autochthonous from our cultural memory. By the end of the century, it sometimes seemed that all that remained of the truly native was a parody.

A revealing icon of this parodic transformation appeared in baseball. In the 1890s, just a few years after Whitman's death, Lou "Chief" Sockalexis, a Penobscot Indian, actually played in the National League, the first native American to make it to the majors; though a talented hitter, runner, and fielder, he lasted only a couple of seasons, and his presence in the league prompted some

of the first real crowd maliciousness. Every time the "Chief" would come to bat, fans would shout war whoops and yell threats. Sockalexis was ultimately suspended for drunkenness: only a few years after the Wounded Knee massacre, he was reduced to another cultural symbol of the stereotyped drunken Indian as he was ridiculed out of the national sport, which by National League edict had begun in the 1890s to be literally a white man's domain. (Black players were excluded from league play in 1889, and Sockalexis's presence in the league after that ban simply intensified the ambiguity of the red race's perceived position in relation to the white race—no longer seen as a cultural threat, Indians could be tolerated and ridiculed in the white man's game.) Like the earlier endless Indian delegations to Washington, D.C., Sockalexis found himself in an alien uniform, playing an alien game, one he learned to play very well in a culture he adapted himself to skillfully. (He attended Holy Cross and Notre Dame.) Like those Indian delegations, and like the "civilized tribes" of the Southeast, he had played by all the rules, had taken on all the necessary beliefs and attitudes that should have merged him into the white man's culture, only to find that at best he would be incorporated into that culture as a token gesture and would eventually be betrayed by an ugly mass reaction that insisted on his difference.

There are two accounts of Sockalexis's postbaseball years: in one, he ends up a drunken beggar on the streets, a late casualty of the white man's traditional weapon against the Indian—whiskey; in the other (more reliable) account, he returns to the Penobscot reservation, works as a woodcutter, and dies in the woods at age forty-two. Either version of his demise turns his life into a symbolic tale of the commonly perceived plight of American Indians; they were corrupted by civilization if they tried to blend in, or they were doomed to be lonely hunters, unfit for civilized life and tragically destined to die in the disappearing forests. American Indians would never embrace baseball in any significant way, but American baseball would continue to use the Indian in coercive ways, naming its teams such things as the Mohicans (a nineteenth-century New York club); even today, the major leagues contain the Braves and the Indians, whose controversial club emblem—a grotesque, grinning, red-faced, feathered caricature of a native American—is a cartoonish nod back to Lou Sockalexis, who played his one year of major-league baseball in Cleveland. That emblem serves as a twentieth-century counterpart to the derisive war whoops that, a century ago, mocked the Indian in the white man's uniform.

I. "Native States of Rudeness"

By the time Whitman was born in 1819, all the major battles between whites and Indians east of the Mississippi had been fought; Whitman grew up knowing this region as the secure United States. But during his adult years, a series of explosive battles west of the Mississippi occurred, from the Pueblo uprising in 1847 to the Grattan fight in 1854 and the Rains fight in 1855 (when *Leaves of Grass* first appeared), on through the countless battles and massacres of the 1860s and 1870s (when names like Birch Coulee, Canyon de Chelly, Rosebud, and Warbonnet Creek entered the American common vocabulary), culminating in the Wounded Knee massacre at the end of 1890, a little over a year before Whitman's death. These were the troubling battles that America fought to take back what early explorers had dismissed as the great American Desert, the land west of the Mississippi that, it then seemed, only the Indians could ever want. Three days before Whitman's eleventh birthday, the Indian Removal Bill was passed by Congress, and Andrew Jackson, the former Indian fighter turned president, got what he wanted: the power to take away Indian lands east of the Mississippi by giving tribes western lands in exchange. The so-called civilized tribes of the Southeast, many of whom owned homes and farms, were moved out to what would become Oklahoma. The various skirmishes, court battles, and presidential orders that accompanied the removal continued over the next ten years, through Whitman's teenage years into his early adulthood, as the Choctaws, then the Creeks, then the Chickasaws, then—in the infamous "Trail of Tears" in 1838 and 1839, as Whitman turned twenty—the Cherokees; finally the Seminoles in 1842 surrendered and were marched west. By the time he had reached his majority, Whitman knew an America where the natives had been brutally separated and removed, an America where they had been promised western lands forever, and an America that was already hungry to make something out of the very lands it had just given up. His adult years, then, were framed by the Great Removal when he was twenty and the Wounded Knee massacre when he was seventy, and like many Americans who lived through this period, Whitman never stopped struggling with the insoluble "Indian problem." By 1890, he was comparing it to the Irish struggle for independence from Britain, where there were "two interests conflicting—strings pulling two ways—the one all Ireland, all for Irishman, who know nothing but Ireland—the other for the British Empire—that compact of vaster interests touching all parts of the globe":

> Indeed, it is our Indian question repeated—which has interests purely for the Indian, interests then of the whole body of states, leading to the largest results. In the meantime the poor aboriginals, so to call them, suffer, go down, are wiped out. (*WWC* 6:423)

The Indians, Whitman knew, had been abused and treated unjustly, but he also subscribed to the notion of progress and social evolution and believed that it was inevitable and ultimately valuable that America extend itself from sea to sea, in service of the "largest result" of the "whole body of the states." As always with Whitman, union was the overriding good; the only clear thing was the certainty that the Indians themselves would be "wiped out." So commonplace had the removal and betrayal of the Indians become during Whitman's life that by the time of the 1889 Oklahoma land rush—what Whitman called "the Oklahoma land grab"—which undid another sacred treaty with the Indians, he took little notice of it, dismissing it simply as a "funny affair altogether" (*WWC* 5:91).

When Whitman asks in the 1855 *Leaves* about "The friendly and flowing savage. . . . Who is he?" he embodies a key cultural question:

> The friendly and flowing savage. . . . Who is he?
> Is he waiting for civilization or past it and mastering it?
>
> Is he some southwesterner raised outdoors? Is he Canadian?
> Is he from the Mississippi country? or from Iowa, Oregon or California? or from the mountains? or prairie life or bush-life? or from the sea?
>
>   . . . . .
>
> Behavior lawless as snow-flakes. . . . words simple as grass. . . . uncombed head and laughter and naivete;
> Slowstepping feet and the common features, and the common modes and emanations,
> They descend in new forms from the tips of his fingers,
> They are wafted with the odor of his body or breath. . . . they fly out of the glance of his eyes.
>
>   (*LGV* 61)

If the "savage" is truly (as the roots of the word suggest) the sylvan occupant, the dweller in American woods and forests—with his simple words, lawless behavior, uncombed head, and common manner—then is he a white backwoodsman or a red native? Whitman's description could apply to either one, and his ambiguity underscores the cultural tension about who holds rightful possession of the American wilderness: "Is he waiting for civilization or past it and mastering it?" When Whitman asks about this emerging new American figure—"Is he from the Mississippi country? or from Iowa, Oregon, or California?"—he is asking a question that echoes much of the history of his own day, recalling perhaps Black Hawk's brave stand at Rock Island, Illinois, in 1832 as he refused to be moved across the Mississippi into the Iowa territory, or recalling perhaps the much more recent Whitman Mission murders in 1847, when his white namesakes were murdered in an episode that led to a decade of battles between white settlers and Indians in the Oregon country. Mississippi and Iowa in the 1830s and Oregon in the 1840s and 1850s were major stages on which the "Indian problem" was being most vividly acted out; the "savages" in Mississippi, Iowa, and Oregon were no longer "friendly," and as Whitman's emerging new white American savage came to replace the native savage, a half-century of unfriendly encounters would mark the transition: all that would be "flowing" would be blood. Whitman's haunting lines in **"Song of Myself,"** then, capture the cultural ambivalence of a country that was at once destroying and honoring the "savage," that was denigrating "savagery" in the Indians while celebrating it in whites.

When Frederick Jackson Turner described the closing of the frontier in 1893, he created a memorable image of how the white frontiersman went through a process of deevolution back to the "savage," absorbing the natives' strength, cunning, energy, and independence, qualities that he would retain even as he once again regained his "civilized" status: that, in fact, is what made the distinctive American character, said Turner, a mixture of savage and civilized traits. Turner, who was a great admirer of and often quoted Whitman's Western poems to his university history classes, no doubt gathered some of his crucial insights from the poet. For Turner, as for Whitman, the individual who was uniquely American was a "friendly and flowing savage."

In Webster's 1847 *American Dictionary,* Whitman would have found the ambivalence about "savagery" embodied in the very definition: while Webster traced the etymology of the word to the Latin *silvicola,* "an inhabitant of a wood," he went on to offer a rambling description that embodied the very paradoxes that Whitman was working with in his "friendly and flowing savage":

> A human being in his native state of rudeness; one who is untaught, uncivilized, or without cultivation of mind or manners. The *savages* of America, when uncorrupted by the vices of civilized men, are remarkable for their hospitality to strangers, and for their truth, fidelity, and gratitude to their friends, but implacably cruel and revengeful toward their enemies. From this last trait of the savage character, the word came to signify, (2) A man of extreme, unfeeling, brutal cruelty; a barbarian.

Webster's definition underscores the association of sylvan existence with brutal behavior by offering the example of the American Indian (an example that, significantly, was removed by Chauncey Goodrich and Noah Porter when they revised the *American Dictionary* in 1864). American Indians, Webster posits, are models of virtue "when uncorrupted by the vices of civilized men," but they are "cruel and revengeful toward their enemies," and thus they are people of no

feelings, of "brutal cruelty." This definitional slippage from innocent virtue to unbridled vice tracks the response of the culture toward its natives. Whitman and others would come to see the irony in taking the natives to task for their cruelty toward their enemies: Birch Coulee, Sand Creek, Rosebud, Wounded Knee, and countless other massacres during Whitman's adult life would demonstrate beyond doubt that Webster's second definition of "savage" applied at least as effectively to the white man as to the Indian.

While the savage, by this definition, can be very human, his gentle naive humanity is woven into a pattern that includes his dangerously uncivil behavior: he is hopelessly inconsistent and unpredictable, like a wild animal, by turns gentle and brutal. So, for Webster, "civilization" is "the state of being refined in manners from the grossness of savage life," and "savagism" is "the state of rude, uncivilized men"; each concept simply defines the other by opposition, and "savage" becomes precisely that behavior that "civilized" humans, by definition, do not engage in.

Roy Harvey Pearce used Webster's 1828 definitions of "savage," "savagism," and "civilization" (definitions that remained unchanged in the 1847 Webster's) as the epigraph for his *Savagism and Civilization,* a book that can be read as an extended meditation on the implications of how the American culture defined those words. For Pearce, Webster's definitions embodied the "American theorizing about the Indian" that led to the culture's belief in "the savage's essential inferiority, the final inferiority of even his savage virtues" (76, 95). While Pearce does not quote Webster's definitions of the adjectival form of "savage," that entry contains in many ways the most revealing meanings: Webster begins by tracing the etymology of the word to French, Armenian, Italian, Spanish, and Latin words meaning "a wood," then goes on to give a series of definitions that cumulatively sharpen the particular edge the word had gained in the American experience:

> 1. Pertaining to the forest; wild; remote from human residence and improvements; uncultivated; as, a *savage* wilderness. . . .

> 2. Wild; untamed; as *savage* beasts of prey.

> 3. Uncivilized; untaught; unpolished; rude; as, *savage* life; *savage* manners. . . .

> 4. Cruel; barbarous; fierce; ferocious; inhuman; brutal; as a *savage* spirit.

The series reads as if it is a developing set of circumstances moving inexorably to a particular condition—as if remoteness from "human residence and improvements" in an "uncultivated" place leads to "wild," "untamed" behavior because one has never been properly polished or taught the virtues of civilization, and this lack of polish, this rudeness, perversely blossoms as cruelty, barbarity, and brutality: remoteness from human residence, in other words, leads inevitably to inhumanity.

At times Whitman used "savage" very much in line with Webster's definitions: saluting the world, looking into "vapors exhaling from unexplored countries," he says he can "see the savage types, the bow and arrow, the poison'd splint" (*LG* 144). But most of the time when Whitman employs the word in his poetry, he does so in ways that undermine Webster's sure dichotomy between "savagery" and "civilization." We have already seen how Whitman's call for the "friendly and flowing savage" resonates with the culture's growing ambivalence about the loss of the "savage" side of life, the side of life that civilization seemed to repress. He uses the word continually as a kind of linguistic lure, to draw the "savage" close to him, to see the savage within himself; as he looks to the "Unnamed Lands" of the distant past, he sees how some of the people stand "naked and savage": "Afar they stand, yet near to me they stand" (*LG* 372). In **"Song of Prudence,"** Whitman proposes that wisdom and moral virtue do not reside only or even necessarily with the refined and well-taught, and he collapses the "savage" into the full spectrum of human experience and action:

> Who has been wise receives interest,
> Savage, felon, President, judge, farmer, sailor,
>   mechanic, literat, young, old, it is the same.
>
> (*LG* 374)

And while in the Platte Canyon, on his 1879 journey to the West, Whitman sensed the same wild "Spirit that form'd this scene" at work within his own soul: "I know thee, savage spirit—we have communed together" (*LG* 486). In the poem he chose as the conclusion to the body of *Leaves* (**"So Long!"**), Whitman offers a long series of announcements of what will eventually emerge in America; the poem culminates with the line: "I announce a race of splendid and savage old men" (*LG* 504): part of the emerging new Union would be a new "adhesiveness," and the "splendid and savage old men" will be a key part of the compact, vital and alive and challenging the notion that authority and power reside with the cultivated and the mannered. Whitman was aware that a civilization that repressed the savage or that pretended the savage did not exist within its boundaries was an artificial and self-blinding nation. So he would call his own poetry "my savage song" (*LG* 355) and would recognize "my wilful and savage soul's volition" (*LG* 119), always looking for ways to break down the barriers between savage and civilized, to achieve the wholeness that the culture seemed bent on dividing in half, to see within himself, a savage old man, rudeness and insolence and even brutality ("To taste the savage taste of blood—to be so

devilish!" [*LG* 180]), for he knew that the real savagery was not external to civilization, but rather was buried at its heart:

> The devilish and the dark, the dying and
>   diseas'd,
> The countless (nineteen-twentieths) low and
>   evil, crude and savage.
>
> (*LG* 554)

Through his subtle weaving of the word "savage" into the fabric of his poetry, then, Whitman created a text that embodied qualities of the Indian that the culture at large defined in negative ways, and then he shifted the meaning: the "savage" came to be not the brutal native out there, but the wild vitality within the soul. And it was the savage sould of white America, after all, that imposed the word and concept of savagism on the native peoples of this continent.

II. "Custer's Last Rally"

In August 1881, Whitman sat for an hour in front of a massive new painting by John Mulvany entitled *Custer's Last Rally* and wrote a long meditation on it, which he published the next year in **Specimen Days;** he had never described any painting in such detail before. The giant (twenty by eleven feet) canvas was on a national tour, beginning a decade's travel that would make it one of the most familiar and popular paintings in nineteenth-century America. Whitman was transfixed by this haunting image that captured the history of the American West as it had been lived during his adult life; it was a summarizing emblem: "Altogether a western, autochthonic phase of America, the frontiers, culminating, typical, deadly, heroic to the uttermost." Whitman saw the painting as distinctively American, noting "an almost entire absence of the stock traits of European war pictures." But for all of its power and native artistry, the painting did not make for easy viewing: one needed, Whitman said, "good nerves to look at it." And seeing it only once would not suffice: "It needs to be seen many times—needs to be studied over and over again." Like the event it portrayed—the violent tableau of white man against Indian, of the new westward-flowing savage claiming nativity on this land against the original native savage (*this* was the "autochthonic phase of America," the violent seeking of sanction to the title "native")—this painting needed to be replicated to be understood, to settle into a pattern: "I could look on such a work at brief intervals all my life without tiring," Whitman notes, and of course he *had* looked in on such events (the endless battles between whites and Indians) at regular intervals from his childhood throughout his life. What made the painting "grim and sublime," "very tonic to me," with a bracing "ethic purpose below all" was the fact that it incorporated the repeated encounters of white and red and cast them in a condensed image onto a huge canvas in all their tangled ambiguity: the scene struck Whitman as "dreadful, yet with an attraction and beauty that will remain in my memory." The painting also struck Whitman as intensely realistic, with "no tricks": "It is all at first painfully real, overwhelming. . . . The physiognomy of the work is realistic and Western" (*PW* 275-76). But what was "real" in the artificial and highly composed image was not its physical accuracy (there were, of course, no white survivors to assess the accuracy of any image of *that* battle), but its tensed ambivalence about the two groups it portrayed, an ambivalence that Whitman shared and struggled with his whole life.

The white men in the painting are a "great lot of muscular, tan-faced men," reminding Whitman of his own image of post-Civil War pioneers, those "tan-faced children" of "the youthful sinewy races" in his 1865 **"Pioneers! O Pioneers!"** In Whitman's poem, these pioneers are pursued by "those swarms upon our rear . . . ghostly millions frowning there behind us urging"; in this case swarms of white people from the past, urging the pioneers on to greater accomplishments, or swarms of the recent Civil War dead, urging the survivors on to deeds worthy of the sacrifices made for them (*LG* 229-30). In the painting, the pioneers face a different swarm: "swarms upon swarms of savage Sioux, in their war-bonnets, frantic . . . like a hurricane of demons." Wherever in art there are "swarms" of people, humans turned into undifferentiated vast force (a hurricane), there are individuals to stand up against and be defined by their difference from the swarm. In the painting, a number of individuals emerge in contradistinction to the swarm; the primary one, of course, is Custer himself, even given an uncharacteristic haircut (Mulvany had altered Custer's image at the last minute, shortening his "long yellow locks") to emphasize his civilized resistance: "Custer (his hair cut short) stands in the middle, with dilated eye and extended arm, aiming a huge cavalry pistol." Around him are individuated men—"death ahold of them, yet every man undaunted, not one losing his head"—singled out by the "every" and the "one," facing the swarm (*PW* 275-76).

But the ambiguities enter in when we examine Whitman's reactions to the Indians in Mulvany's painting, for they are of two types: on the one hand, savage, massed, and undifferentiated, as we have seen, but on the other hand, individual, large, heroic. In the background are the "swarms upon swarms of savage Sioux," but in the foreground are "two dead Indians, herculean, . . . very characteristic." For Whitman, Indians—when they were alive and in large groups—were worthy of extinction; isolated, alone, dead, or dying, they were noble and worthy of preservation. Other early commentators on the painting found these two dead Indians to have a "hideous countenance" and "features . . . horribly savage, even in death" (Taft 370). But Whitman sees no hideous savagery in the giant figures, only a kind of mythic largeness (*PW* 275-76).

In 1876, within days of the news of the Battle of Little Big Horn, Whitman had written a poem about Custer's last stand, a poem that has often been read as a jingoistic endorsement of Custer's bravery. It is instructive to compare Whitman's poetic visualization of the battle with Mulvany's painting that would so transfix him five years later. Whitman's Custer, with his "tawny flowing hair in battle," is clearly a different figure from Mulvany's shorn, controlled figure; he carries "a bright sword in [his] hand" rather than a "huge cavalry pistol" (many early romantic representations of the battle portrayed sabers as the main weapons [Taft 365, 367n, 382]), and unlike Mulvany's more realistic soldier, Whitman's Custer is portrayed as a hero straight out of romantic legend, is addressed as "thee," is in fact part of a historic chain of heroism, one who "Continues yet the old, old legend of our race." Whitman pictures the "little circle" of men, "with their slaughter'd horses for breast-works," something quite different from the "great lot" of men in Mulvany's painting (though Mulvany, too, portrays "The slaughter'd or halfslaughter'd horses, for breastworks," something that Whitman ironically finds a "peculiar feature" of the painting, even though it is one of the few things that Mulvany's portrayal shares with his [*PW* 276]). But in Whitman's poem, the Indians are virtually absent; the battle takes place in the lands of "the dusky Sioux," but the landscape is described only as "wild" and "lonesome" and silent, a "fatal environment" in which there is a mere mention of an "Indian ambuscade" but no real signs of actual Indians. The poem is finally more about Whitman's own "dark days," his reduced life in a reduced materialistic America, searching desperately for any signs of vital American ideas and ideals—"Lone, sulky, through the time's thick murk looking in vain for light, for hope"; the poet is looking west for a glimmer of a heroic democratic individual, some sort of reborn Civil War hero who could stir up the old fires of hope. Custer was the best that current events could offer. So, for Whitman, Custer ends up aptly described as "Desperate and glorious," and there is clearly some desperation on Whitman's part in having to cast up Custer as the model of American glory (*LG* 483-84).

The absence of the Indians in Whitman's poem tells us much about his conflicted and conflicting response to the American natives, for at first glance Indians seem absent not only in this poem but in all his poetry. Certainly we don't think of Whitman as a writer who dealt in depth with the problems of American Indians or devoted himself to telling their stories. But a more careful look at his work reveals a surprising frequency of Indian imagery. And that imagery reveals a tortured ambivalence about the role America's natives would play in the development of the country's character; it is an ambivalence so deep that by the time of Custer's last stand, the only way Whitman could deal with it was to leave the Indians out of the picture.

III. "Whitman Thought They Were His Own"

In 1849, after Whitman had resigned as editor of the *Brooklyn Freeman,* a rival editor bid him a facetious farewell: Whitman, "hot-headed" and "full of egotism," is, said the editor, "what you call a civilized but not a polished *Aborigine.* And, by the way, it has been asserted by one of his brother Editors that he is a lineal descendent from some Indian tribe, with what truth we will not venture to say" (quoted in Rubin 223). There is no truth at all, of course: this sarcastic portrait of Whitman as the American primitive is the only recorded suggestion that Whitman actually had Indian blood in him. He did once point with pride, though, at the fact that one of the early Whitmans was "a great linguist, and sometimes acted in the courts as interpreter with the Indians" (*PW* 353), and there have even been several suggestions that Whitman was a spiritual compatriot of Indians. Maurice Mendelsohn has investigated what he calls a "kinship between Whitman's poetry and the folklore of . . . the Indians" and concludes that many of his poems "resemble American Indian folklore both in form and spirit" (25, 28). Norma Wilson claims that no "Ameropean" before Whitman had ever "approximated so closely the Native Americans' conception of the spiritual and commonplace as one"; she does not see Whitman's perspective as Native American but believes "that the important source and intention of his art were essentially the same as those of Native American writers," and she points out parallels between Whitman's thought and that of Lame Deer (14, 15). William Least Heat Moon, a contemporary Osage writer, endorses the resemblance and fuses Whitman's ways and native ways in his book *Blue Highways,* a record of his journey on what is left of the "open road" in America, driving his van named Ghost Dancing, carrying two guidebooks: Whitman's **Leaves of Grass** and John Neihardt's *Black Elk Speaks* (8). Joseph Bruchac, a contemporary American Indian poet, senses the kinship too; he finds "Whitman's spirit" in the works of recent Native American writers like Leslie Silko and claims that "Whitman's celebration of the earth and natural things, his precise namings, are very much like Native American song" (**"Song of Myself"** echoes, he says, the Navajo Night Chant) (Perlman 276).

The problem with finding "Whitman's spirit" in Native American works is that his spirit is many-sided and changeable. There is a Whitman spirit that is imperial and dominating, a spirit that can chant "we the virgin soil upheaving, / Pioneers! O Pioneers!," that can sing the song of the broadax, that can imagine the last redwoods gladly giving themselves up to the axes of "the superber race" (*LG* 230, 207). But there is also a Whitman spirit that absorbs and caresses, that catalogs and celebrates difference, that extols a self that embodies diversity: "Of every hue and caste am I, of every rank and religion, / . . . I resist any thing better than my own diversity" (*LG* 45). So, while we may agree with Bruchac that Whitman's spirit can be found in the works of recent American Indian writers, we need to be careful about clarifying just which Whitmanian spirit manifests itself where.

The dominating and imperialistic side of Whitman's spirit, in fact, has led some contemporary Native American writers to view Whitman in purely negative terms: Maurice Kenny, a Mohawk poet, mourns Whitman's "indifference" to the Indian and believes Whitman's heroes are the Custer-like scouts, frontiersmen, and Indian fighters: "Whitman, apparently, was a proponent of the *manifest destiny* bilge" (108), and he "closed his ears and shut his eyes to the Indians' death cries" (113). The contemporary American poet W. S. Merwin, who has long identified himself with American Indian causes, voices similar concerns: "It makes me extremely uneasy when [Whitman] talks about the American expansion and the feeling of manifest destiny in a voice of wonder. I keep thinking about the buffalo, about the Indians, and about the species that are being rendered extinct." The most extended condemnation of Whitman's attitude toward American Indians is Leadie M. Clark's 1955 study in which he charges that "Whitman might be construed as advocating genocide in the United States." In Clark's reading, Whitman believed "the Indians were not to be allowed to exist as an independent race of people," and "the Indian was marked as the man who must vanish": "The Indian was to be allowed no place in the developing society, and his contribution could only be the bequeathal of his past to the conquerors of his land" (68, 48, 51, 53, 56). There is some truth to Clark's portrayal of Whitman, of course, but it is an incomplete picture, a simplistic analysis of a highly complex mesh of attitudes.

Simon Ortiz, a poet from Acoma Pueblo, in his book-length poem *From Sand Creek,* records a growing ambivalence toward Whitman that helps illuminate Whitman's ambivalence about Indians. In a prose gloss to his poem, Ortiz inscribes his growing uncertainty: "When I was younger—and America was young too in the 19th century—Whitman was a poet I loved, and I grew older. And Whitman was dead" (80). Whitman remains for Ortiz a mystery, at once both the spiritual leader of America's destructive urgings of manifest destiny and the leader of the resistance to those destructive impulses, the poet of love and nature. In *From Sand Creek,* he raises the vexing question of how the poet would have reacted to the news of the Sand Creek massacre of Cheyennes in 1864 when the U.S. commanding officer ordered his troops to "kill and scalp all, big and little; nits make lice" (quoted in Drinnon 502); over a hundred Cheyenne and Arapaho women and children and twenty-eight men were slaughtered by more than seven hundred U.S. troops. Ortiz can imagine Whitman reacting with sorrow to America's bloody westering process, but he can also imagine him reacting with joy, and—the most troubling possibility of all—he can imagine him not reacting at all:

> They wasted
> their sons and uncles
> as they came westward,
> sullenly insisting
> that perhaps, O Whitman,
> O Whitman, he was wrong
> and had mis-read the goal
> of mankind.
>   And Whitman
> who thought they were his own—
> did he sorrow?
> did he laugh?
> Did he, did he?
>
>   (81)

We recall Whitman's response to the 1889 Oklahoma betrayal of the Indians, how he found it a "funny affair altogether." Ortiz sees the failure of Americans to absorb the Indian, to manifest the friendly and flowing savage, as leading to the construing of the Native American as alien and other, as savage and primitive, as worthy of extermination. If the Whitman of 1855 articulated the dream of amalgamation, of absorption and open embrace, by the time of the Sand Creek massacre this Whitman and his dream had died:

> O Whitman
> spoke for them,
> of course,
>   but he died.
> That shed their sorrow
> and shame
> and cultured their anxiety.
> They spoke an cloquent arrogance
> by which they thought
> they would be freed.
>
>   (81)

Once the sorrow and the shame were shed, once white anxiety was channeled into cultural activity, Ortiz suggests, Native Americans became mere hindrances to be wiped out. Sand Creek can be read as a symptom of white America's cultured anxiety.

The conflicting reactions of critics as well as of American Indian writers to Whitman's attitudes are understandable, for Whitman's association with the American Indian is a deep and tangled one, and it has never been more than superficially investigated. He had a lifelong fascination with Indians, and he expressed that fascination in many forms, in many moods, on a myriad of occasions. His attitudes toward the Indians—a contradictory but characteristically American mix of disdain and admiration, of desires to absorb natives and find his antecedents in them fused with desires to dis-

tance himself from them—help to define a central problem in our culture's troubled relationship with its native people and let us see how Whitman was bound by the biases and preconceptions of his time, as well as how he occasionally and remarkably transcended them.

IV. The Trapper and the Red Girl

A fascination with Indians was, of course, not uncommon for a writer living during the years of the closing of the American frontier; Whitman was planning his own life work, ***Leaves of Grass,*** just as the ethnologist Henry Rowe Schoolcraft was issuing his massive study *History, Condition, and Prospects of the Indian Tribes of the United States* (1851-57) and just as the anthropologist Lewis Henry Morgan was publishing the first of his pioneering accounts of Indian tribes. ***Leaves*** appeared the same year as Longfellow's *Hiawatha,* a poem that cashed in on the national fascination with Indians; even Whitman liked *Hiawatha,* admiring its "Indian process of thought" (***NUPM*** 5:1730). Whitman knew George Catlin, the painter of Indians and chronicler of tribal customs, and was a supporter of the movement to have the United States buy Catlin's gallery as the foundation for a national museum; as noted, his final years were presided over by a Catlin painting of the Seminole chief Osceola, given him by the artist, which hung on a wall in his Camden home (***NUPM*** 241; Rubin 121; ***WWC*** 6:400). In Washington, he enjoyed visiting the Smithsonian to view John Mix Stanley's Indian paintings (***NUPM*** 2:530). Whitman encountered actual Indians as a boy on Long Island and as a young editor in New Orleans (***PW*** 606). He saw Indian troops who fought in the Civil War (***C*** 212) and admired General Grant's military secretary, Colonel E. S. Parker, a Seneca Indian whose "squa mother," in a gesture Whitman approved of, refused to succumb to Anglo convention by choosing never to wear a bonnet (***NUPM*** 347). Whitman was the only major American poet actually to work in the Indian Bureau of the Department of the Interior, and for the half-year he was there in 1865, he met several impressive Indian delegations and had "quite animated and significant conversations with them" (***PW*** 579); on his western trip in the 1870s, he saw a "squad of Indians at Topeka" (***NUPM*** 3:1039), and he visited a Chippewa settlement during a trip to Canada in 1880. Indians were a major part of Whitman's actual and imaginative life, and as he developed his distinctive American aesthetic, Indians became a crucial part of his ongoing poetic project. Setting out to absorb America, to open his lines democratically and indiscriminately to the world around him, Whitman was aware that American Indians would need to be part of the song of himself, but he also realized that his celebration of America's progressive expansion undermined any easy celebration of the natives that that expansion was displacing. In a manuscript notebook from the late 1850s, Whitman noted plans for a *"poem of the aborigines,"* one that would embody "every principal aboriginal trait, and name" (*NUPM* 1:275). He never wrote that poem, but, from the beginning, *Leaves of Grass* was more dedicated to that project than is generally recognized. (One early reviewer of *Leaves* actually noted the central importance of Whitman's concern with the Indian, though the insight was quickly lost; Whitman's style, said this reviewer, is "a fitting measure for the first distinctive American bard who speaks for our large scaled nature, for the red men who are gone, for our vigorous young population" [C.P.P., "Walt Whitman's New Volume," *Saturday Press* (June 23, 1860), 1:5]).

In his 1855 preface, as Whitman cataloged the ways "a bard is to be commensurate with a people," he noted, "To him enter the essences of real things and past and present events—of the enormous diversity of temperature and agriculture and mines—the tribes of red aborigines." The aborigines were to be an essential part of "the great psalm of the republic" (*LG* 711-12). In 1856, Whitman would portray this new American bard, "His spirit surrounding his country's spirit, unclosed to good and evil . . . / Surrounding just found shores, islands, tribes of red aborigines" (*LG* 344). And in **"Pictures,"** the manuscript poem that anticipates the 1855 *Leaves of Grass,* Whitman catalogs the "many pictures" of his world, of his fantasies, and of history—the pictures that compose his imagination—and again Indians have their place: "A string of my Iroquois, aborigines—see you, where they march in single file, without noise, very cautious, through passages in the old woods" (*LG* 647). In his drafts for the poem, he celebrates the exotic domestic center of the Chippewas: "And here a tent and domestic utensils of the primitive Chippewa, the red-faced aborigines, / See you, the tann'd buffalo hides, the wooden dish, the drinking vessels of horn" (*LG* 649).

The first edition of *Leaves* (1855) contains twelve poems; five of them explicitly embody Indians. In his catalog of human faces (in the poem later entitled **"Faces"**), Whitman demonstrates that all people "show their descent from the Master himself": "I except not one . . . red white or black, all are deific. . . . " (He affirms this antidiscriminatory stance in **"I Sing the Body Electric"**: "Examine these limbs, red, black, or white, they are cunning in tendon and nerve" [*LG* 126, 98].) And in the 1855 poem that would become **"To Think of Time,"** Whitman again makes an effort, somewhat strained with double negatives, not to exclude the Indians from those he "shall go with," those who are part of the universal soul: "The common people of Europe are not nothing . . . the American aborigines are not nothing, / A Zambo or a foreheadless Crowfoot or a Camanche is not nothing" (*LGV* 106). "I see not merely that you are polite or whitefaced," says Whitman in the poem that would later become **"A Song for Occupations,"** as he looks to absorb life beyond the genteel surface: "Iroquois eating the warflesh—fish-

tearer in his lair of rocks and sand . . . Esquimaux in the dark cold snowhouse" (*LGV* 86). In the poem later titled **"The Sleepers,"** Whitman records a haunting dream/memory of a "red squaw" who visits his mother for an afternoon and then disappears forever (*LGV* 115-16). And in **"Song of Myself,"** the Indian enters the long catalog of America in Section 15, where, surrounded by the "Wolverine" setting his trap on a creek near the Huron and a "connoisseur peer[ing] along the exhibition gallery," appears "The squaw wrapt in her yellow-hemm'd cloth . . . offering moccasins and bead-bags for sale" (*LG* 42). In other catalogs in **"Song of Myself,"** Indians add essential ingredients: as Whitman absorbs Jehovah, Kronos, Zeus, Brahma, Buddha, and other deities into his universal religion, he places "Manito," the nature god of the Algonquian Indians, in his "portfolio," and as he encloses "worship ancient and modern and all between ancient and modern," dancing in "phallic processions," "minding the Koran," he also walks "the teokallis, spotted with gore from the stone and knife, beating the serpent-skin drum," thus admitting Aztec sacrifice worship into his all-absorbing faith.

The one extended image of the Indian in **"Song of Myself"** is the well-known passage in which Whitman imagines himself (with the help of an Alfred Jacob Miller painting) "far in the wilds and mountains" (*LGV* 11):

> I saw the marriage of the trapper in the open
>   air in the far-west. . . . the bride was a red
>   girl,
> Her father and his friends sat near by
>   crosslegged and dumbly smoking. . . . they
>   had moccasins to their feet and large thick
>   blankets hanging from their shoulders;
> On a bank lounged the trapper. . . . he was
>   dressed mostly in skins. . . . his luxuriant
>   beard and curls protected his neck,
> One hand rested on his rifle. . . . the other
>   hand held firmly the wrist of the red girl,
> She had long eyelashes. . . . her head was
>   bare. . . . her coarse straight locks
>   descended upon her voluptuous limbs and
>   reached to her feet.

Here, this marriage on the frontier between the East and the West, the civilized and the savage, anticipates the birth of Whitman's new American character, emerging from the encounter of Europe and the New World, the refined civilization of the past penetrating the raw topography of the future: it is Whitman's first attempt to resolve the paradox of celebrating both the American Indian and the expansion of the United States. As he so often does, Whitman resolves irreconcilable opposites by marrying them, by constructing a unity that is large enough to embody both; the marriage of the Indian girl and the white man suggests that America cannot achieve fulfillment without absorbing the native it displaces, and that the native cannot achieve a fullness of meaning until absorbed into the expanding and inevitable creation of the white man. Thus, as we have seen, Whitman's suggestion of "The friendly and flowing savage" (*LG* 73) is cast in such a way that it portrays a person who is simultaneously both Whitman himself and a stereotypical Indian. As his early rival editor said, Whitman was a "civilized but not a polished *Aborigine*," straddling the frontier, looking for a formless form, trying to make himself the issue of the marriage of the trapper and the red girl, looking to join what he saw as the dumb natural eloquence of the Indian to the vocalized expression of the English language.

For Whitman, the Indian was synonymous with authenticity, a raw and unmediated experience of this land, the natural embodiment and expression of the topography. As such, the Indians' images, attitudes, words, all would become crucial elements in Whitman's poetry. Whitman once criticized Emerson's work because it was, he said, "always a *make*, never an unconscious *growth*." Emerson's writings were like "the procelain figure" of the "Indian hunter"—"a very choice statuette too—appropriate for the rosewood or marble bracket of parlor or library." But, Whitman added, "The least suspicion of such actual . . . Indian, or of Nature carrying out itself would put all those good people to instant terror and flight" (*PW* 515-16). Whitman was out to smash the statuette, to haul the actual Indian into his poetry, to make words that didn't cushion experience but *became* experience.

V. "Poison-Tipped Arrows"

Whitman's fascination with the Indian extends long before the beginning of *Leaves of Grass*. One of his earliest poems, in fact, is about an Indian. **"The Inca's Daughter,"** a newspaper verse written when Whitman was twenty, tells the story, in conventional ballad rhyme and meter, of a "captive Indian maiden" preferring death over living "ingloriously" as "the white lord's slave." She stabs herself with a poisoned arrow and gives the Spaniards a lesson in pride:

> "Now, paleface see! the Indian girl
>   Can teach thee how to bravely die:
> Hail! spirits of my kindred slain,
>   A sister ghost is nigh!"
>
> **(EPF 6-7)**

Whitman is a long way yet from any marriage of the Indian and white man, any resolution of racial and experiential opposites.

Two years later, in 1842, he published a temperance novel, *Franklin Evans*, and chapter 2 is an Indian tale, later reprinted separately as a story, **"The Death of Wind-Foot."** It is a revenge tale about a chief named

"The Unrelenting" whose only living son, Wind-Foot, is killed by a Kansi after the Unrelenting had killed the Kansi's father to avenge his older son's death: the cycle of death and grief is unbreakable. There is a "poison-tipped arrow" in this story, too, and the bathos is just as deadly as in **"The Inca's Daughter."** But Whitman's method of framing this tale in *Franklin Evans* anticipates a deepening of his concern for the Indian. A group of characters are on the journey from Long Island to New York City, and one of the journeyers tells the tale; he is a Whitman-like figure, a "sportsman" with a "fondness for prying into the olden history of this, his native island; a sort of antiquarian taste for the stories and incidents connected with the early settlers, and with the several tribes of Indians who lived in it before the whites came." He sounds, in fact, much like the Whitman of 1861, who would himself write a long series of articles called **"Brooklyniana,"** in which he would indulge in exactly this antiquarian taste, telling of the first settlers and aboriginal inhabitants of Long Island. The sportsman of the novel dwells "with much eloquence upon the treatment the hapless red men had received from those who, after dispossessing them of land and home, now occupied their territory, and were still crowding them from the face of their old hunting-grounds," again sounding much like Whitman, who in an 1850 newspaper piece wrote:

> Alas! that was a bad day for the red man—that day, nearly two centuries and a half ago, when the Half-moon sailed up these waters, with the first civilized visitors . . . to the island of Manhattan, and its long brother nearby. Poets have sucked all the juice so completely, however, out of this sort of reflection that I may as well forebear,—though to tell the truth, I feel powerfully like adding to the heap. (*PR* 34)

Later, in **"Brooklyniana,"** Whitman, touring Montauk, would take pride in the fact that

> the long peninsula contains many thousands [of] acres, lying comparatively waste. And it makes one think better of humanity when he doth discover such a fact as I did in my travels, that the valuable tract of land is kept thus unseized and unsold by the town of Easthampton, principally because the few remaining Indians hold in it a usufructuary interest, or right of enjoying and using it. (*UPP* 2:316-17).

The sportsman goes on to point to rum as "the greatest curse ever introduced" among the Indians: "A whole people—the inhabitants of a mighty continent—are crushed by it, and debased into a condition lower than the beasts of the field." The Indians "drink this fatal poison"—rum is the vengeful poisoned arrow that the white man uses to murder the Indian—and find themselves "deprived not only of their lands and what property they hitherto owned, but of everything that made them noble and grand as a nation!" The listeners on the journey are literally, though only temporarily, sobered by this horrifying tale: "We could not but feel the justice of his remarks" (*EPF* 133). The temperance moral is clear: like the endless revenge cycle of the warring Indian tribes, the poison of rum will come back to destroy the white man who used it as a weapon to destroy the Indian.

Whitman wrote another Indian tale in the 1840s, called **Arrow-Tip,** later revised as **The Half-Breed: A Tale of the Western Frontier.** This novella is set on "one of the upper branches of the Mississippi" in a new settlement that only recently had been "a tangled forest, roamed by the savage in pursuit of game." If Whitman's idealized "friendly and flowing savage" in **"Song of Myself"** was the unifying and noble offspring of "the marriage of the trapper" and "a red girl," the main character of this story is the fragmented, dark other side of such Indian-white coupling: here the half-breed is Boddo, a deformed and deceitful amalgam of the worst qualities of both races, a "monstrous abortion." Boddo's father is a white hunter-adventurer who repents of his "wild and wayward course of life" and becomes a monk; Boddo's mother is presented to us only as an "Indian girl." Arrow-Tip and his brother, the Deer, are purebred Indians, and so they, of course, are noble and doomed. Boddo lies and tricks his way into having Arrow-Tip hanged for a murder that never took place, and the Deer vanishes into the sunset: "Many hundred miles distant, an Indian leader, the remnant of his family, led his tribe still farther into the west, to grounds where they never would be annoyed, in their generation at least, by the presence of the white intruders" (*EPF* 272, 291).

VI. "Unlimn'd They Disappear"

We can see that, to this point, most of Whitman's attitudes toward the Indian finally amount to little more than a melange of savagist stereotypes—what Roy Harvey Pearce and others have defined as savagism, a cultural construct that portrays Indians as generally of a lower order than white Americans, as childlike hunters, innocents whose every encounter with civilization corrupted them. Indians, in the savagist view, were incapable of adaptation and improvement, bound to arcane traditions, and superstitious and lazy. Alone, solitary, they could be admirable noble vestiges, like the Inca's daughter or Arrow-Tip; but as tribes, in groups, they were dangerous, cunning, cruel, like the Unrelenting's tribe in perpetual combat with the Kansi tribe, or, as Whitman said in 1850, like "the aboriginals of Long Island"—a "tolerably war-like people . . . frequently involved in disputes and hostilities, accompanied by all the savage cruelty known to be practiced among them toward enemies" (*PR* 33). Given all of these qualities, Indians were doomed to extinction, doomed to evaporate before the inexorable progress of civilization, to which they could

never accommodate themselves. White Americans might be saddened or moved by this inevitable loss, but they would acquiesce to it nonetheless. (It was a widespread attitude in nineteenth-century American culture and one that Whitman could well have picked up in cleverly articulated form from Frances Wright, whose works he studied and admired.) Frederick Jackson Turner, in his influential frontier thesis, endorsed the idea that it was "the universal disposition of Americans to emigrate to the Western wilderness, in order to enlarge their dominion over inanimate nature," and felt that the Indians were devalued by being identified with that "inanimate nature," victims of "an expansive power . . . inherent" in Americans, so that "long before the pioneer farmer appeared on the scene, primitive Indian life had passed away" (Turner 36). In Turner's scheme, Indians were not decimated as America manifested itself on the continent, but rather they magically "evolved" into the hunter or trapper, who in turn evolved into the rancher, who evolved into the farmer, who evolved into the townsman, who evolved into the city-dweller. Whitman was fond of portraying a similar almost instant evolution among the "war-like" Long Island Indians once they were absorbed into the white man's ways: "That the Indians of Long Island . . . have the germs of a good intellectual development in them, has been proved through the cases of several native children, brought up in white families and educated thoroughly" (*PR* 32). But for Whitman such cases were always the exception; late in his life, he would still be recalling the failure of Indians to be "informed" by white institutions of education; he recalls his conversations with early authorities on Indian life:

> When I was a young man, these men were interested with others in educating Indians. They reasoned: we will select samples out of the tribes, put them in the schools, colleges,—inform them—use them to our ways—then send them forth among their people, to enlighten, to reform them. And so they persevered—sent out many men in this way—with the usual result: one out of a dozen would come to a little something, the others almost totally relapse. (*WWC* 6:56)

The easy assumptions here—that "our ways" are superior, that "inform[ing]" the Indians will lead to their "reform[ing]" other Indians—are instructive, for the concept of "form" is for Whitman the key: if white ways can be injected into the natives so that they are formed into "us" from within—"inform[ed]"—then they will be "use[d]" to our ways just as we "use them" to endorse our ways. Then, fully "inform[ed]," they will be ready for the larger effort of "reform[ing]" their people, "us[ing]" them all to our ways. But the effort at in-formation and re-formation failed, ended in collapse and "relapse": the native material was too rigidly formed to old ways, could not be reformed even when informed of the new and superior ways. The superior natives become, then, by definition, those rare few who re-form themselves into us, who leap evolutionary generations in their desire to be used by our ways. So Whitman celebrated Indians who had in effect evolved into white men, like the Reverend Samuel Occum, "the glory of the Indian nation," who, after he became a Presbyterian minister, "taught . . . the little red children" and left descendents who carried on the evolutionary disappearance act as they "intermarried with the whites." Another "very pious" Indian preacher was Paul Cuffee, whom Whitman admired because he "labored earnestly to restrain his countrymen from their vices and degrading habits," one of which was no doubt the rum curse; even the good Reverend Occum "had one failing . . . being a little too much addicted to drinking." For Whitman, even the most advanced Indians still had vestigial vice trailing from them as a result of their lower evolutionary status (*PR* 32-33). Such thinking allowed the destruction of the Indians to be disguised behind an evolutionary model that saw them as somehow absorbed in us, thus absolving us of guilt.

This absorption of the Indians into the American as Indians themselves vanished from the land was a crucial concern of Whitman's. He sang of an America that was to be a "Union holding all, fusing, absorbing . . ." (*LG* 203). We have seen that he set out to assure that his song absorbed the Indians, fused them into the unifying song of himself and his country. We have also seen that he saw the Indians as inevitably vanishing—the Deer leading his people endlessly westward until there was no more West and they vanished. It is consequently not surprising that the most extended poems that Whitman wrote about Indians were of them dying. From his very early **"Inca's Daughter"** to his very late **"Red Jacket (from Aloft)"** (1884) and **"Osceola"** (1890), the focus was on noble death. Red Jacket, the great Iroquois leader, is pictured as "a towering human form" aloft in the clouds, watching bemused, "a half-ironical smile curving [his] phantom lips," as the puny people who displaced him and his people erect a monument to him (*LG* 519-20). And Osceola, a Seminole chief, is pictured "When his hour for death had come" as a prisoner of U.S. troops at Fort Moultrie; he puts on war paint, puts "the scalp-knife carefully in his belt," then smiles and sinks "faintly low to the floor (tightly grasping the tomahawk handle)," dying as stoically as the Inca's daughter. This poem was written, Whitman said, "almost word for word out of conversations I had with Catlin: Catlin, the great Indian man." Whitman, we have noted, lived his final years—what he called "the Indian Summer of my life" (*NUPM* 1092, 1109)—in Camden with a Catlin lithograph of Osceola hanging on his wall (*WWC* 6:400). (It is as if Whitman sensed that the demise of the Indians was analogous to his own physical decline, with his latter years truly an Indian summer—a final, brief flourish before disappearance.) The chief was a

lingering presence in Whitman's life, and the final line of his poem for Osceola is quiet, parenthetical: "(And here a line in memory of his name and death.)" With the poem about Osceola, Whitman seems to be making a late acknowledgment of white betrayal of Indians, incorporating at the end of *Leaves* an oblique recognition of white racism, even while he would elsewhere ascribe Osceola's virtue to his "dash" of white blood: "Osceola was like a great many of the niggers—like Douglass—in being of mixed blood, having a dash of white, not pure Indian" (*WWC* 6:400). Osceola, a brave leader during the so-called Second Seminole War (the First Seminole War was that in which Andrew Jackson had made his reputation fighting Seminoles, Creeks, and runaway slaves in what he called "this savage and negro War" [Drinnon, 106]), led the Seminole resistance using remarkably modern guerrilla tactics; he was captured finally only by an act of treachery, when U.S. troops promised to meet him under a flag of truce and then incarcerated him—his wife was sold as a slave and he died in prison. Whitman's note to his poem ignores these facts, focusing instead on how the U.S. physicians and officers "made every allowance and kindness possible" for the chief, but then again Whitman claims to have heard the story firsthand from "one of the return'd U.S. Marines from Fort Moultrie, S.C.," where Osceola was imprisoned (*LG* 550-51). What does come through in Whitman's poem is a sense of honor betrayed and a quiet gesture toward righting the wrong by offering "a line" in *Leaves* to the Indian's bravery.

To give Indians a *line* in the song of America seemed to be Whitman's continual motivation, to absorb them into the American song before they vanished forever, to preserve them in English words. So Whitman's most successful late poem about Indians, **"Yonnondio"** (1887), dwells on this desire:

> A song, a poem of itself—the word itself a
>   dirge,
> Amid the wilds, the rocks, the storm and
>   wintry night,
> To me such misty, strange tableaux the
>   syllables calling up;
> Yonnondio—I see, far in the west or north, a
>   limitless ravine, with plains and mountains
>   dark,
> I see swarms of stalwart chieftains,
>   medicine-men, and warriors,
> As flitting by like clouds of ghosts, they pass
>   and are gone in the twilight,
> (Race of the woods, the landscapes free, and
>   the falls!
> No picture, poem, statement, passing them to
>   the future:)
> Yonnondio! Yonnondio!—unlimn'd they
>   disappear;
> To-day gives place, and fades—the cities,
>   farms, factories fade;

A muffled sonorous sound, a wailing word is
  borne through the air for a moment,
Then blank and gone and still, and utterly
  lost.

                       (*LG* 524)

Whitman includes a note, telling us that the title is an "Iroquois term," the sense of which is "lament for the aborigines" (*LG* 524), though he reveals through his uncertainty about the meaning of the word just how distant he really was from any true understanding of native languages. In 1888, talking to Horace Traubel, he recounted his problems with the word:

> Yonnondio: you notice that name? They printed it in The Critic first, and the Critic fellows objected to it that my use of the word was not correct, not justified. You remember, see . . . I make it mean *lament* and so forth: they say, no, that is not it: Yonnondio signifies governor—was an Indian name given to the French governors sent over to this continent in colonial times. No doubt there's considerable to warrant their argument, but . . . I had already committed myself to my own meaning— written the poem: so here it stands, for right or wrong.

Whitman goes on to tell Traubel that he picked up his meaning of the word from "an old man—a wise, reticent old man—much learned in Injun tongues, lore— in Injun habits and the history of them so far as known," and he concludes that finally the argument would be "inconclusive" anyway and would remain "always as wide open at the end as at the start" (*WWC* 2:269). The word was one more sign of the unbridgeable differences between the cultures, of the essential mystery of Indians to the white man.

But what Whitman insisted on was not so much the meaning of the word as the way in which the word itself functioned as a poem, calling up the vanished wilderness and its inhabitants, reversing Turner's progressive frontier evolution as "cities, farms, factories fade" and "stalwart chieftains" appear in their place. And what Whitman laments here is not so much the loss of the Indians as the fact that there is "No picture, poem, statement, passing them to the future"—no mechanism by which they are absorbed into America: "*unlimn'd* they disappear." If only they were limned, drawn, portrayed in words, illuminated in the poet's manuscript: thus, this poem gives them words, includes them in *Leaves of Grass,* utters them as part of the American poem. Otherwise they are "blank and gone and still, and utterly lost" (*LG* 524). Without the act of absorbing them, giving them a *line,* the page that should contain them is blank, the words that should evoke them still, unuttered, "utterly lost." In the 1880s, echoing his expressed desire of thirty years earlier to write a long *"poem of the aborigines"* complete with "every principal aboriginal trait, and name," Whitman laid out

plans to write a poem of "some length to be called *Yonnondio*" and vowed to do research: "get Indian acct's & books" (*NUPM* 1211); he may have been inspired by William Howe Cuyler Hosmer's lengthy and popular narrative poem called *Yonnondio, or Warriors of the Genesee.* Allen Ginsberg has gone so far as to see Whitman's brief "Yonnondio" as a remarkably deep and compact prophecy ("It's an odd little political poem at the end, warning us of Black Mesa, of the Four Corners, of the civilization's destruction of the land and the original natives there" [Perlman 251]), but clearly the poem is far less than Whitman had originally conceived. Whitman's vast plans diminished, and what began as a major project ended up imitating in its compact final form the reduced but still powerful presence of Native Americans in Whitman's overall vision. They indeed ended up limned, given only a few lines in the vast poem of *Leaves of Grass.*

But it was a line, an utterance, nevertheless, and to give the Indian voice in *Leaves* was vital. As early as 1846, Whitman had announced this concern in an editorial in the *Brooklyn Daily Eagle;* he lamented that people would flock to lectures about ancient Egypt, while programs dealing with "Indian life and past history"—the "graphic and authentic narrative of aboriginal matters"—would draw "a baker's dozen only." Whitman expresses a desire to find "some itinerant author," who, "willing to travel through wood and forest, over prairie and swamp, . . . in short, amid any and every part of what is now the margin of our cultivated American territory," could "gather up the stories of the settlers, and the remnants of Indian legends which abound among them." Then, Whitman says, we would have "the true and legitimate romance of this continent." The Indians were disappearing, utterance of them lost:

> Have we no memories of a race, the like of which never was seen on any other part of the earth— whose existence was freedom—whose language sonorous beauty? Far, far in the darkness of times past, we may turn our fancy—and bring up the spectres of the Brown Men, with their stately forms, and their flashing eyes, and their calm demeanor— and say, Are *these* not the proper subjects for the bard or the novelist? Who can produce better? (*GF* 2:136-37)

And the need for the American bard to capture the native American was urgent, for the Indian stock was weakening quickly:

> In the course of events, it is but reasonable to suppose that not many seasons will recede, before every tangible representative of true Indian character will have passed from sight. Indeed it is almost so now. The weakened, degraded, and effeminate beings who prowl our frontier towns, make the name of their forefathers synonymous with disgrace. (*GF* 2:138-39)

This would often be the attitude Whitman took when he actually saw Indians: in 1880, visiting the Chippewa reservation in Canada, he found "nothing at all of aboriginal life or personality" (*DBN* 617). And when, around the same time, Whitman wrote his autobiographical reminiscences, he gauged the accelerating disappearance of the native; he recalls seeing "the few remaining Indians, or half-breeds" on Montauk as a young man, "but now I believe [they are] altogether extinct" (*PW* 11). The quick native vanishing act seemed to be going on all around Whitman; his notes on his 1877 journey to the New Jersey Pine Barrens record the loss: "60 years ago the Indians were quite plenty (a fragment of the Delaware tribe used to come round & work among the farmers . . .)." Whitman fondly records that "there used to be an old Indian called Joe" who "used to work around"; Joe still had a few descendants scattered about, but Whitman's incessant past tense undermines any notion of a real remaining native presence: "They were good basket makers" (*NUPM* 991).

VII. "All Aboriginal Names Sound Good"

So what could the bard do to absorb the Indian before it was too late? "We may love the traditions of the hapless Indians—and cherish their names—and bestow those names on rivers, lakes, or States, more enduring than towering monuments of brass" (*GF* 2:138). Here Whitman announces a lifelong passion: absorbing into the muscular and malleable English language the exotic rich words of the Native Americans. He was part of a revival of interest in native names, a movement in the 1840s to absorb Indian words into the language by restoring their names to the geography of the land. Webster himself was a part of the group urging native names (though he argued that they needed to be "accommodated to a civilized people" by having pronunciation "softened" and spelling normalized [quoted in Simpson, 211]). The popular poet Lydia Sigourney had summed up the argument for the preservative effect of Indian names in a poem written in the early 1840s: "Ye say, they have all passed away, / That noble race and brave, / . . . That mid the forest where they roamed / There rings no hunter's shout; / But their name is on your waters, / Ye may not wash it out" (258).

Whitman's own notions of the power of native languages may have been prompted by his study of the chapter "Language" of Emerson's "Nature" (1836), an essay that influenced much of Whitman's work. In that essay, Emerson observed:

> Because of this radical correspondence between visible things and human thoughts, savages, who have only what is necessary, converse in figures. As we go back in history, language becomes more picturesque, until in its infancy, when it is all poetry; or all spiritual facts are represented by natural symbols. (199)

But Whitman's admiration of native words went beyond Emerson's love of their symbolic power; for Whitman there was a physical power as well. He loved the feel of their words in his mouth—**"Yonnondio"** was a "song, a poem of itself . . . a dirge." And part of Whitman's campaign was to realign the English tongue, tune it American, by absorbing the Indian nomenclature, the native names for this land, "Making its rivers, lakes, bays, embouchure in him, / Mississippi with yearly freshets and changing chutes . . ." (*LG* 344). Whitman's friend Richard Maurice Bucke once called "those lines of Indian names . . . one of the choice bits" in *Leaves of Grass,* and Whitman agreed (*WWC* 4:324). In his *American Primer* from the 1850s, Whitman explained,

> What name a city has—What name a State, river, sea, mountain, wood, prairie, has—is no indifferent matter.—All aboriginal names sound good. I was asking for something savage and luxuriant, and behold here are the aboriginal names. I see how they are being preserved. They are honest words— they give the true length, breadth, depth. They all fit. Mississippi!—the word winds with chutes—it rolls a stream three thousand miles long. Ohio, Connecticut, Ottawa, Monongehela, all fit. *Names are magic.*—One word can pour such a flood through the soul. (*AP* 19-20)

The sportsman who tells the Wind-Foot story in *Franklin Evans* introduces it by pointing out a lake and calling it by "a long and unpronounceable word, which he said was the Indian name for it" (*EPF* 133). Those long and unpronounceable words needed to enter into English, Whitman felt, to replace European name-impositions, to come to sound familiar, *American:*

> *Names of cities, islands, rivers, new settlements, &c.* These should/must assimilate in sentiment and in sound, to something organic in the place, or identical with it.—It is far better to call a new inhabited island by the native word, than by its first discoverer, or to call it New anything.— Aboriginal names always tell finely. . . . All classic names are objectionable. How much better Ohio, Oregon, Missouri, Milwaukee &c. Iowa than New York, Ithaca, Naples, &c. (*DBN* 705)

Whitman's belief was that *"All lies folded in names,"* and he knew that "real names never come . . . easily" (*AP* 33), so it would be necessary to undo the hasty European naming of this continent: "California is sown thick with the names of all the little and big saints. Chase them away and substitute aboriginal names" (*AP* 29-30). He expressed disappointment when the state of Washington was admitted bearing a non-Indian name, preferring "Tacoma! how fine that would have been for one of the new States!" (*WWC* 4:324). He was attracted to the proposition in the late 1880s to rename West Virginia "Kanawtha" (though he felt Virginia had "its own old long reasons for being what it is," and he could see already the imposed names taking on their own tradition) (*WWC* 4:324). He praised the name "Dakota," finding it the "right" name for the territory where "the proud & vengeful Dakota warriors had lived," and he argued that, in a similar fashion, "'Chippewa' is the best name for the new n.w. Territory" (*NUPM* 5:1672, 1707). He admired the Indian names of towns he passed through or near on his Western trip in 1879: "Tongahocksa . . . Eagle Trail after a chief" (*NUPM* 3:1040). He felt relief that Indian names had "saved" many American rivers with their "Majestic & musical names—Monongahela, Alabama," but he advised, "some one should authoritatively re-name the mountains," even if it would take "an act of Congress" (*NUPM* 5:1672). Whitman's necessary American alignment of names was not a project that would deal only with *places:* "In These States, there must be new Names for all the Months of the year— They must be characteristic of America— . . . What is the name January to us?" (*DBN* 3:700-701).

Late in his life, Whitman lost hope that Indian names would become as widespread as he had hoped or that they would replace European-imposed names, but he never gave up his fervid desire to have American topography keyed to the names native to it. Occasionally Whitman resolutely resisted the classically imposed names because they were so foreign to the continent; Horace Traubel records in 1889 a moment when Whitman

> tried to name one of the Western rivers—a Greek name—but it "failed" him. He laughed—"It was a terrible one." I put in—"Named by the drunken pedagogue who gave names to the New York towns?" He laughed—"Probably a relative: you mean the Ithaca, Utica, Troy man?"

Whitman went on to lament city names like "Memphis," "a fearful name—with no smack of the soil whatever—yet hundreds, thousands, like it!" "The great Indian names," mourned Whitman, "'lost like so many opportunities!'" (*WWC* 5:358).

Whitman came to think of his poetry, his own new speech tuned to conversational rhythms, away from European conventions, as aboriginal. His early notes on oratory show that he derived his characteristic emphasis on the first person, his disarming familiarity with his readers, from Indian models: "Why not mention myself by name, Walt Whitman . . . aboriginal fashion?—as in the speech of Logan [Tah-gah-jute, a Cayuga chief]? or that of Boh'ongahelas [Delaware Indian chief]?" (*NUPM* 2233). Indian names, he said, "are totally genuine—we could say of them what [Richard W.] Gilder said of my poetry—that they stand specifically alone—are not to be imitated—not to be manufactured" (*WWC* 5:488). He enjoyed sitting with

friends and reciting Indian place names; "No one," he said, "has better reason for believing [in the beauty of Indian names] than I" (*WWC* 5:487). Whitman claimed he "often threatened . . . to make a collection" of Indian names—perhaps as part of his often-projected but never-realized "poem of the aborigines"; for "nothing in all language, ancient or modern" was "so significant—so individual—so of a class—as these names" (*WWC* 5:488). While Whitman says that he never actually did make such lists, some of his early notebooks do contain catalogs of Indian words (see *DBN* 670, 726); he at least initiated the project. He even toyed once with the idea of writing a play "embodying character of strength savage wildness Indian" (*DBN* 822).

The word "Indian" itself demonstrated to Whitman the problem of European naming, of losing verbal touch with the native land. Indians were the native people of the land for whom English had only awkward terms, dispossessing names. "Indian" was a European-imposed word, meaningful only from the perspective of European history, misrepresenting, grossly misnaming, even displacing the natives of a land that the original European explorers could not see for what it was and thus named for what it wasn't. "Of course the word 'Indian' does not apply to the American aborigines," Whitman chastised in a notebook; "An Indian is a man or woman of the southern and eastern half of Asia. It confuses and vexes language to have such synonyms with contra-meanings" (*DBN* 3:709). This practice of "calling the American aborigines *Indians*," he said, is a lesson in how "names or terms get helplessly misapplied & wrench'd from their meanings," clouding the language by allowing "a great mistake [to be] perpetuated in a word," so that even if "the mistake is rectified . . . the word remains" (*NUPM* 5:1664). Whitman, then, generally avoided the term, preferring "aborigines," with its root emphasis on "origin"; his own emerging sensitivity to the issue can be traced in his manuscripts, in which he often crosses out "Indian" in favor of "aborigine" (*NUPM* 275). The word "aborigine" actually has no clear etymology, only dim origins; it relates to "original," suggesting people that were there *ab origine,* from the beginning. But Whitman, given his fascination with etymologies, no doubt knew that there were problems with this word too— it probably derives from a botched Latin echo of the native name of some now-forgotten European tribe, the word itself doing what Western cultures seem so proficient at doing to cultures they label primitive: misnaming them, burying them in a misnomer and preserving them in wrong words so that they always seem, both topographically and linguistically, out of place. In *Rambles Among Words,* the book that Whitman may well have coauthored with the linguist William Swinton, we find a long discussion about how words of abuse and misrepresentation evolve, how the word "barbarians," for example, may be nothing but "a general imitation of a (to the Greeks) foreign tongue," thus revealing much more about the Greeks and their "infinite contempt" for "foreign nations" than about the people the word referred to. We must remember, **Rambles** tells us, that many words that appear to have "some inherent virtue and valor of their own" are in fact "poverty-stricken and impotent" (Swinton 126). Clearly "Indians" was such a word for Whitman, while "aboriginal" at least retained a satisfying echo of "original."

In the 1847 Webster's, "Indian" is defined as a "general name of any native of the Indies; as, an East *Indian* or a West *Indian*. It is particularly applied to any native of the American continent." The adjectival form of the word, said Webster, had to do with "pertaining to either of the Indies, . . . or to the aborigines of America." In this definition, Webster seems to agree with Whitman that "aborigine" is the accurate word for American natives; he defines "aborigine" as a "word not regularly formed, but [one] that has become generally prevalent" for referring to the "first inhabitants of a country," and an "aboriginal" according to Webster is any "original inhabitant," as the "Indians in America." "Native," on the other hand, is not associated by Webster with Indians (except for the one moment when he uses it in his definition of "Indian"); it is a word reserved for "one born in any place" who becomes "a native of that place, whether country, city, or town." Clearly "country, city, or town" suggests a "civilized" person. By definition, then, an Indian who had been exiled from the United States would never become a "native American." By 1864, Webster's dictionary had added to the definition of "Indian" an acknowledgment of the inaccuracy of the word: "One of the aboriginal inhabitants of America;—so called originally from the idea, on the part of Columbus and the early navigators, of the identity of America with India." Succeeding dictionaries would continue to note the error, but it wouldn't be until a century later that a general uneasiness with the word would bring about attempts at new coinages ("Amerindian," "Native Americans").

These aboriginal inhabitants, Whitman knew, formed the origin of human contact with this land; the words, legends, rituals, and stories that evolved out of their long contact with this land were therefore vital for Euro-Americans to absorb, to learn, if they were to make the land their own. But Whitman, like Webster, would never grant the Indians the word "natives." That was a word he reserved for what "real" Americans would come to be when they fully and democratically absorbed the world around them: "As for native American individuality, though certain to come . . . it has not yet appear'd" (*LG* 571; see *NUPM* 1588). In 1860 Whitman entitled his group of poems that celebrated an emerging distinctive American character **Chants Democratic and Native**
American. He wanted to "promulge Native American models" so that "foreign models" would be reduced to "the second class" (*NUPM* 1588). Whitman's concern with the term "Native American" seemed calculated to wrest the name away from those who were tainting it—it was the name of a vehemently antiimmigrant, anti-Catholic, and generally antiabsorptive political party, better known as the Know-Nothings, that flourished from the 1840s until about 1860. Whitman sought to associate the quality of being native American with the qualities of absorption and democratic inclusiveness; in this sense, Indians could at best *become* a part of the native Americans, but were themselves *pre*-Americans, native to the land but not native to the country that in Whitman's view brought that land to life.

But the Indians' nativity on the land was for Whitman a vital quality. Probing his native ground for authentic origins, Whitman made an attempt to rename his own locales with aboriginal accents, calling Long Island "Paumanok" and referring to New York City as "Mannahatta." He admired the accurate name of Jamaica—a town he lived and taught in—which derived, he believed, from the Yeniachah Indians (*NUPM* 456). He insisted on the accuracy and vitality of such names, affirming that he got "Mannahatta" from two of the country's best philologists ("knowers of Indian tongues"): "How this word clung and clung!" (*WWC* 5:470). In the 1850s, he lashed out against the absurdity of naming his great democratic city after "the meanest and feeblest tyrant that ever press'd the English throne, the Duke of York, duly James the Second—the burner of women and torturer of men, for the least freedom in thought or words." Whitman was rankled that "every time the hitherto name of this city is written with the pen or spoken with the mouth it celebrates that man." "Mannahatta," then, was a far superior name for "the grandest freest and most beautiful city of the world" (*NUPM* 407-408). In 1878, Whitman records his exhilaration at seeing New York for the first time from the top of a skyscraper—"Up, up, up, in the elevator some eight nine or ten stories, to the top of the tall tower" where his "thoughts of the beauty and amplitude of these bay & river surroundings [are] confirmed" and where his conviction of "a fitter name" was "also confirmed": "*Mannahatta*—'the place around which there are hurried and joyous waters continually'—(that's the sense of the old aboriginal word)" (*NUPM* 1010-11). And late in his life, he was still explaining how "the Indians use the word to indicate a plot of ground, an island, about which the waters flow—keep up a devil of a swirl. . . . To me it is all meaning and music!" (*WWC* 5:470). In his 1860 poem "Mannahatta," he recorded his initial joy at finding the word:

> I was asking for something specific and
>   perfect for my city,
> Whereupon lo! upsprang the aboriginal name.

Now I see what there is in a name, a word,
    liquid, sane, unruly, musical, self-sufficient,
I see that the word of my city is that word
    from of old,
Because I see that word nested in nests of
    water-bays, superb.

                        (*LG* 474)

And in an 1888 poem, he was still praising the "fit and noble name": "Choice aboriginal name, with marvellous beauty, meaning" (*LG* 507). Near the end of his life, even when his friend Dr. Daniel G. Brinton, a well-known anthropologist, tried to correct Whitman about the meaning of "Mannahatta" (Brinton had been told by Indians that the word meant "the place where bows are bought"), Whitman clung to his original notion: "That seems to me improbable: according to the definition I got of it, it meant some center point about which the waters whirl and storm with great vehemence . . . a point of land surrounded by rushing, tempestuous, demonic waters: it is so I have used it—and shall continue" (*WWC* 6:56). Whitman's turbulent definition was vital to him, for it allowed him to connect his place, his city, with his view of the self as a still point in the ceaseless whirl of experience:

Trippers and askers surround me,
. . . Battles, the horrors of fratricidal war, the
    fever of doubtful news, the fitful events;
These come to me days and nights and go
    from me again,
But they are not the Me myself.
Apart from the pulling and hauling stands
    what I am.

                        (*LG* 32)

Like Mannahatta, Whitman would be the native quiet center, formed by but apart from the unstoppable wash of life that crashed on his shores.

Magical, too, was the name of Paumanok, where Whitman started from. He often signed his early poems and newspaper essays with the pen name "Paumanok," thus associating himself with the native view of his home ground. In his "Brooklyniana" articles, he argued for the new/old name for his island:

We have heard it suggested, (and we think the idea worth serious consideration), that the original name of this island ought on many accounts to be resumed, and made the legal and customary name again. That original name was PAUMANOK, the sense of which is . . ." the island with its breast long drawn out, and laid against the sea." This is a beautiful and appropriate signification, as the word itself is a pleasant one to the ear. (*UPP* 2:274)

Again, the native definition of place essentially characterized the position of the poet *of* that place; Whitman,

like Paumanok, would stretch out on the ground, lean and loaf at his ease, absorbing the sea that surrounded him. Whitman referred to the restoration of the name as "poetic justice" for the vanished Delaware tribes: "Now that they have all forever departed, it seems as if their shades deserve at least the poor recompense of the compliment connected in preserving the old name by which they themselves designated and knew this territory" (*UPP* 2:275). The contemporary poet James Schevill, in his poem called "A Changing Inventory for Walt Whitman," turns such comments by Whitman—his love of the word "Paumanok" and its Indian associations—into a biting irony:

Once Paumanok, what is it about your name,
    your thing, Walt? we know Long Island and
    its commuter-luxuries, Paumanok has a
    wistful Indian tone of memory . . . We killed
    most of them good, Walt, the Redskins, why
    should a commuter long for a Redskin?

                        (30)

But if today we can see the dark and hypocritical underside to Whitman's affectionate use of the Indian word for his home place, for Whitman himself the utterance still seemed to work magic.

In **"By Blue Ontario's Shore,"** Whitman refers to his poetry as a "savage song"; the title of that poem, situating Whitman's ruminations beside a lake that carries its Iroquois name, is another instance of his love of native place-names. During Whitman's adult life, of course, the new states entering the Union often carried native names, as did an increasing number of the rivers, lakes, mountains, and other named features within the landscapes of those states. So Whitman's hopes that Indian words and names would enter into the American dictionary were slowly realized. *Rambles Among Words* in 1859 had celebrated the fact that there was "scarce a tongue on the planet which the all-absorbing Saxon genius has not laid under contribution to enrich the exchequer of its conquering speech" (Swinton 279), and it goes on to list words that have entered the lexicon from "aboriginal American dialects," words like "tobacco," "wigwam," "Yankee," and "potato." As early as 1800, when Samuel Johnson, Jr., and John Elliott published their *Selected, Pronouncing and Accented Dictionary* (the rudimentary forerunner of Webster's work), American lexicographers had seen the potential for identifying the emerging American language through inclusion of Americanisms, including Indian-based words; Johnson and Elliott included such things as "tomahawk" and "wampum" (Friend 12). Webster increased the number of Americanisms and included several dozen words of Indian origin; Whitman used a good many of these words in *Leaves:* in fact, it is almost as if Whitman scoured the 1847 Webster's to find the native words that had already worked their way into the language, then included them in *Leaves* so that his book would have a noticeably strong native American accent. Whitman's Indian-based lexicon includes "hickory," "moccasin," "opossum," "pecan," "moose," "persimmon," "poke-weed," "powwow," "quahaug," "raccoon," "sachem," "squaw," and "wigwam"; all of these words were available to him in the 1847 Webster's, identified there as "derived from the natives." But the overall impact of native languages on English would remain modest, far less than Whitman imagined and hoped for; today's dictionaries do not carry noticeably more Indian-based words than did the dictionaries of Whitman's time.

VIII. "See, In Arriere, the Wigwam"

It was on Paumanok that Whitman first saw Indians, learned of their aboriginal money (quahog shells, among other things) and way of life, even saw "the cave of an old Indian hermit" who "must have been a pretty fair counterpart of Chingachgook" (*UPP* 2:316). In **"The Sleepers,"** he tells what may be a true story of an Indian woman visiting the "old homestead" of the Whitmans on Paumanok and spending a day with his mother: "Her step was free and elastic. . . . her voice sounded exquisitely as she spoke." Whitman's mother is delighted and amazed at the woman's beauty, "her tallborne face and full and pliant limbs." We feel the mother's love of this native woman, and we feel Whitman's own desire for her as he recreates her in words: "The more she looked upon her she loved her." When the squaw leaves in the afternoon, the sense of loss is palpable:

> O my mother was loth to have her go away,
> All the week she thought of her. . . . she
>   watched for her many a month,
> She remembered her many a winter and many
>   a summer,
> But the red squaw never came nor was heard
>   of there again.
>
>   (*LGV* 116)

It is a cultural loss seen through the filter of a family memory; this squaw with her natural beauty vanishes from the real world and evanesces into a legend, enacting the imminent disappearance of an entire race. Whitman's sensitive portrayal of a maternal love for the "red squaw" stands as a quiet and uncharacteristic counterpoint to the violent decimation of the native race that America's cultural fathers would be engaging in during the very years this poem kept appearing in edition after edition of *Leaves* (1855-92).

Generally, then, by Whitman's time, the noble Indians seemed few, and his usual encounters with the natives were far different from his dream/memory of the beautiful squaw's visit; the real Indians around him did not lift his spirits, even seemed anathema to poetry: "Several specimens of men, women and children whom I saw were quite enough to take the poetry out of one's aboriginal ideas. They are degraded, shiftless, and intemperate—very much after the lowest classes of blacks" (*UPP* 313).

This racist side of Whitman's attitude coexisted with his admiration for the Indian; the paradox seems more pronounced for us today certainly than it did in the nineteenth century. The degradation that he found in modern-day Indians seemed to justify their "elimination" in the name of evolution and progress: "The nigger, like the Injun, will be eliminated: it is the law of races, history, what-not: always so far inexorable—always to be. Someone proves that a superior grade of rats comes and then all the minor rats are cleared out." (When Horace Traubel hears Whitman say this, he tells the poet, "That sounds like Darwin," and Whitman replies, "Does it? It sounds like me, too" [*WWC* 2:283].) In moods like this, Whitman felt that "amalgamation" of the races was not possible, would result only in human debilitation, in monsters like Boddo, his demented halfbreed character. Thus, the Indians often appeared in his catalogs of the "Encircling . . . American Soul," but only in "arriere," in the back of the parade of progress and evolution. "After all," wrote Whitman in the 1850s, "are not the Rocky Mountain and California aborigines quite as bestial a type of humanity as any?" (*NUPM*, 1976). To such "backward races," Whitman would offer only the comfort that "I do not say one word against you away back there where you stand, / (You will come forward in due time to my side.)" (*LG* 148). But by the time these backward races came forward to him, they would have been, of course, magically transformed into whites as they themselves disappeared. So as the American soul lunged into the future, it would absorb but leave behind the vanishing native: "In arriere the peace-talk with the Iroquois the aborigines, the calumet, the pipe of good-will, arbitration, and indorsement, . . . / The drama of the scalp dance" (*LG* 174).

That terrifying drama was an all too realistic one for Whitman, and late Indian uprisings prompted his most sweeping condemnation of the aborigines. For a while he dismissed them all as regressive savages and found the idea of the noble savage nothing but sentimental rubbish. After hearing Jane Grey Swisshelm's account in 1863 of the 1862 Sioux uprising, Whitman wrote:

> It was enough to harrow one's soul. The poetical Indian is all lollypop. The real reds of our northern frontiers, of the present day, have propensities, monstrous and treacherous, that make them unfit to be left in white neighborhood. The details of their murders, mutilations, last fall in Minnesota and the violations of women and children, make as bloody and heart-rending an episode as there is in American history. (*NUPM* 565)

As people from myriad countries came to the shores of America to forge a new amalgam of identities, then these "real reds" had to make way, fade out: "See, in my poems immigrants continually coming and landing, / See, in arriere, the wigwam, the trail, the hunter's hut . . . and the backwoods village" (*LG* 27). As the frontier vanishes, transformed into civilization, the Indians disappear with it. It is this attitude that leads Leadie Clark to conclude that, for Whitman, "that the Indian was disappearing was regrettable but right, for it was a circumstance that could not be prevented. The Indian was to be allowed no place in the developing society." Clark avers that "Whitman generally excluded the Indian from his catalogs because he could find no place for the only truly native American man" (56-57).

But this is only part of the story. Whitman, as we have seen, did not exclude the Indian from the catalog of his writings; quite the opposite. While he was usually disappointed in current manifestations of the Indian, such was not always the case. Even at the time of his most sweeping condemnation of the Indians, Whitman was working his way beyond the easy route of simplistic stereotyping. Watching an army brigade on drill near the end of 1862, Whitman records in a notebook that "the drill closed with a spirited charge, the men shouting like wild Indians." Then, as if he suddenly realized the absurdity of this easy characterization, he corrects himself. He crosses out "Indians" and writes in "Comanches," at least narrowing the scope of his abuse and pulling back from outrageous generalizations. But then he goes even further: "This is an error," he writes to himself, and goes on to observe that while the men "do cry loudly," this does not reflect on the behavior of Comanches so much as it reflects on the behavior of any warriors of whatever color entering battle: "Our troops generally go in with loud cries" (*NUPM* 515). A few months later he jotted down his admiration of the First Kansas Colored Volunteers: "a fine reg't," with several companies "of Indian breed." This regiment was sent West to fight in the Indian territory, and now Whitman admires what at other times he condemned: "They fight like demons, use the knife, scalp the dead, &c. They are real warriors in every respect, nothing to take them back" (*NUPM* 637). In the 1860s, then, Whitman is clearly struggling (as were many Euro-Americans) with his attitudes toward the Indians, attitudes that had developed an uneasy mixture of fear and respect, horror and fascination.

In 1865, while working at the Indian Bureau at a job that he initially seemed most pleased with for its light work load, he actually encountered Indians, and they began to break through his biases, overwhelm him with the force of their personality and strength, restore some of the "poetry" to his aboriginal ideas. At times for Whitman, these "aborigines, left by time and events upon our hands" were "strange and impressive," but they were also quite human (*NUPM* 2:785). Once he told a delegation of "these Natural Kings" that "we are all really the same men and brethren together, at last, however different our places, and dress and language" (*NUPM* 2:881). But the Indians' response, an "approv-

ing chorus of guttural 'Ugh's,'" serves to undercut Whitman's affirmation of oneness and sameness. Years earlier, Whitman had noticed "one peculiarity about the Indians, under all circumstances—they are hard to be on thee-and-thou terms with." He was confused, in effect, by their refusal to be backslapping, embracing American camerados: "They will not readily talk and tell all about themselves, and where they came from, and where they are going to, to a stranger. All my attempts to 'draw them out' in this way have been met with a cool indifference" (*PR* 32-33). In fact, Whitman usually was more struck by Indians' difference from, rather than their similarity to, white Americans, but occasionally that difference made them seem superior:

> There is something about these aboriginal Americans, in their highest characteristic representations, essential traits, and the ensemble of their physique and physiognomy—something very remote, very lofty, arousing comparisons with our own civilized ideals— something that our literature, portrait painting, etc., have never caught, and that will almost certainly never be transmitted to the future, even as a reminiscence. No biographer, no historian, no artist, has grasp'd it—perhaps could not grasp it. It is so different, so far outside our standards of eminent humanity. (*PW* 2:579)

Here again is Whitman's obsession with trying to capture the Indian in words, to absorb Indians into "our" art in order to transmit them to the future. These Indians he saw in front of him could not be dismissed as mere primitives, savages: "I should not apply the word savage (at any rate, in the usual sense) as a leading word in the description of those great aboriginal specimens." Indeed, by contrast, *white Americans* at times seemed the diminished race, the evolutionary falling off from a finer form: "There were moments, as I look'd at them or studied them, when our own exemplification of personality, dignity, heroic representation anyhow (as in the conventions of society, or even in the accepted poems and plays,) seem'd sickly, puny, inferior" (*PW* 2:579). These Indians were "real American Red Men," their "savage and hardy Nature" standing in proud contrast to "the cities of the pale face" (*NUPM* 2:881).

This revelation of American society's "inferior" status is not a usual one for Whitman, but it does play into the complex of his attitudes toward the Indians. In order to reach this realization, Whitman carefully frames his statement: he is looking at "specimens" of the aborigine, and he is "certainly" seeing "many of the best"; they are "the most wonderful proofs of what nature can produce," but unlike the "degraded, shiftless and intemperate" vestigial specimens of Indians and half-breeds he had seen on Paumanok, these "aboriginal visitors" represent the other end of Darwinian law— "the survival of the fittest, no doubt—all the frailer samples dropt, sorted out by death" (*PW* 2:577). As the fit survivors of a race they are "indeed *chiefs, in heroic massiveness, imperturbability, muscle, and that last and highest beauty consisting of strength—the full exploration and fruitage of human identity."* These Indians were the culmination not of "'culture' and artificial civilization," but of *nature,* "tallying our race, as it were, with grand, vital, gnarl'd, enduring trees, . . . humanity holding its own with the best of said trees . . . and outdoing them" (*PW* 2:577). These Indians were indeed model representatives of Whitman's "friendly and flowing savage" with "Behavior lawless as snow-flakes, words simple as grass" (*LG* 73). They were the hearty embodiments of a rugged life lived in consonance with nature, not a life artificially constructed in false and modest recoil from the "fleshy sensual, eating, drinking and breeding" (*LG* 552) that constitutes life in this world, that constitutes the life Whitman celebrated in his poetry, the life that America would have to embrace, Whitman believed, in order to fully realize its democratic potential.

IX. *"Leaving Such to the States They Melt"*

So, for Whitman, depending on his moods and motivations, Indians could be the debris of evolutionary progress, the primitive versions of American selves that were left far behind, in "arriere," on the road to what the culture became, or they could be the advance guard, the model fit survivors, embodying qualities that Americans had to move *toward.* In either case, though, the Indians were doomed to extinction; if they were degraded and primitive, they would die out by the Darwinian law of the survival of the fittest; if they were themselves the fittest, they would die a noble and poignant death in the name of civilization—they were simply too good, too pure, to exist in the still unperfected present. Whitman sometimes contorts to make it all work: in the Indian Bureau, the heroic people he saw, he noted, were generally old; the best specimens were "the old or elderly chiefs, and the wise men." It's as if the Indian tribes had been thinned out, winnowed down to these few fit, heroic, and ancient samples, blazing forth in one final moment of greatness and leaving only degenerate and unfit heirs, who would soon of necessity disappear. Their fate clearly was now out of their own hands, these "five hundred? thousand . . . American aborigines, left by time & events upon our hands" (*NUPM* 786).

It might help here to recall Whitman's description of John Mulvany's painting of Custer's Last Stand, in which Whitman perceived that the Indians were of two types: on the one hand, savage, massed, and undifferentiated; on the other, individual, large, heroic. In the background are "swarms upon swarms of savage Sioux, in their war-bonnets, frantic, . . . like a hurricane of demons"; but in the foreground are "two dead Indians, herculean, . . . very characteristic." As usual for Whitman, alive and in large groups,

Indians were worthy of extinction; isolated, alone, dead or dying, they were noble and worthy of preservation.

It was the heroic and noble side of the natives, their healthy attachment to American landscape, that Whitman believed he could absorb into the American consciousness via native words, stories, sounds. As the natives died out, the bard had to lead the way in ensuring that, in departing, they left us their words embodying their wisdom, buried deep in the sounds that they attached to this continent over thousands of years. So, in **"Starting from Paumanok,"** a poem of origins, Whitman pauses "a moment . . . for America," celebrating the present and future. (This section of the poem was a late insertion; originally Whitman had conceived of the section as a separate poem, entitled **"Aborigines,"** and as such it may represent another of his failed attempts to compose a long poem about native Americans [see *WM* lii-liii, 30-31].)

> And for the past I pronounce what the air
>   holds of the red aborigines.
>
> The red aborigines,
> Leaving natural breaths, sounds of rain and
>   winds, calls as of birds and animals in the
>   woods, syllabled to us for names,
> Okonee, Koosa, Ottawa, Monongahela, Sauk,
>   Natchez, Chattahoochee, Kaqueta, Oronoco,
> Wabash, Miami, Saginaw, Chippewa, Oshkosh,
>   Walla-Walla,
> Leaving such to the States they melt, they
>   depart, charging the water and the land with
>   names.
>
> (*LG* 26)

The Indians "melt" into their words, which flow into American language, nomenclature, and poems; thus the Indians are "leaving" (it's the central pun of *Leaves of Grass*)—leaving in three ways: as they "depart," vanish, *leave;* as they put forth leaf in us, *leaving* in a new spring cycle of birth; and as they are absorbed in our language and our works, charging our *leaves,* our pages, as we absorb their words that are literally their breaths, the sounds in which they breathed out their inspiration of this land. It was an old dream of Whitman's, expressed first in an 1856 article he wrote for *Life Illustrated,* in which he noted that "of all that nations help to build, nothing endures but their language, when it is real and worthy." The Indians have been left to their words and live there:

> There are, doubtless, now in use every hour along
> the banks of the Hudson, the St. Lawrence, the
> Sacramento, and the Colorado . . . words but little
> modified, or not modified at all, from the same use
> and sound and meaning they had twenty thousand
> years ago, in empires whose names have long been
> rubbed out from the memories of the earth. . . .
> The American aborigines, of whom a few more years

shall see the last physical expiration, will live in the names of Nantucket, Montauk, Omaha, Natchez, Sauk, Walla-Walla, Chattahoochee, Anahuac, Mexico, Nicaragua, Peru, Orinoco, Ohio, Saginaw, and the like. (*NYD* 58)

The poet's job was to fight to preserve these names, for he came to discover that the words do not always persist on their own.

X. "The Palimpsest On Which Every Page Is Written"

And so Whitman embarked on a life-long poetic archaeological expedition; in 1888, he was still concerned with digging up and preserving America's autochthonous past: "I think now is the time for archaeology to be exploited here anyhow—especially American archacology." He was stung by British poet Monckton Milnes's remark that "your people don't think enough of themselves . . . they do not realize that they not only have a present but a past, the traces of which are rapidly slipping away from them" (*WWC* 1:128-29). In early notebooks, Whitman had sketched out his poetics of archaeology: he believed there "were busy, populous and powerful nations" on the American continent thousands of years ago, but "no one can now tell the names of those nations." There is a "total vacuity of our letters about them, their places blank upon the map, not a mark nor a figure that is demonstrably so." Whitman was haunted by the sense of loss, by the absence of words for these original inhabitants:

> The Ruins in North America—the copper mines of Lake Superior which have been worked many centuries since—probably more than a thousand years ago, perhaps two or three thousand—the mounds in the valley of the Mississippi—the vast ruins of Central America, Mexico and South America—grand temple walls &c., now overgrown with old trees—all prove beyond cavil the existence, ages since, in the Western World, of powerful, populous and probably civilized nations, whose names, histories, and even traditions had been lost long before the discovery of Columbus and Vespuccius. (*NF* 76-77)

The vanishing Indians, then, were the last vestiges of Atlantis-like "civilized nations" that had long since disappeared beneath the wilderness growth of America. (Such a belief was commonplace in the mid-1800s; William Cullen Bryant's "The Prairie" is built on the conceit that the aboriginal native race on this continent was noble but was displaced by the ignoble red man.) There is always, Whitman said, "the palimpsest on which every page is written" (*BG* 21), and he recommended that we should keep that in mind in reading *Leaves.* He called the United States the "greatest poem" (*LG* 709), but it was a poem written over other texts, scratched over a palimpsest of past cultures. Part of his purpose was to

illuminate the subtexts, the dim lower layers of the palimpsest, those "Nations ten thousand years before these States, and many times ten thousand years before these States," those nations of which "Not a mark, not a record remains—and yet all remains." His faith was that those "billions of men" lived on in some "unseen world," but that the way they really lived on was by our poets giving them voice, reaching back, imagining them into our present and giving them room (a line) there: "Afar they stand, yet near to me they stand" (*LG* 372). For Whitman, nothing vanished, but rather all was absorbed in the widening and voracious American soul, which expands without discarding, carves out the future while giving voice to the past. So the broadax, tool of the American frontier, also "Served the mound-raiser on the Mississippi, served those whose relics remain in Central America" (*LG* 191). Americans are joined in mystical and yet palpable ways to their aboriginal past, which stands at the center of what they have become.

In 1883, Whitman still did not feel that his poetic archaeology had had the necessary effect on the country: "We Americans have yet to really learn our own antecedents, and sort them, to unify them" (*PW* 2:552). We need something to "counterbalance" (*PW* 2:553) the notion that the United States was fashioned on European models. One place to search for the necessary native antecedents, Whitman affirmed, was in "American ethnology":

> As to our aboriginal or Indian population—the Aztec in the South, and many a tribe in the North and West—I know it seems to be agreed that they must gradually dwindle as time rolls on, and in a few generations more leave only a reminiscence, a blank. But I am not at all clear about that. As America from its many far-back sources and current supplies, develops, adapts, entwines, faithfully identifies its own—are we to see it cheerfully accepting and using all the contributions of foreign lands from the whole outside globe—and then rejecting the only ones distinctively its own—the autochthonic ones? (*PW* 2:553-54)

Whitman often argued for the value of these autochthonic sources, associating Indian song and poetry with the "florid, rich, first phases of poetry" that produced the Greek and Hebrew epics (*NUPM* 1555), and in notes for **"Song of Myself,"** he searches for a primitive authenticity—"Something that presents the sentiment of the Druid walking in the woods . . . of the Indian pow-wow . . . of the Sacramental supper . . . of the Grecian religious rites" (*NUPM* 1312). He even saw the native singers as models for the new American poet to emulate; Whitman speaks with some envy of the "audiences for the singers and poets of those rude races, . . . [that] made the bards who spoke to them sacred and beloved" (*NUPM* 1559).

XI. Welding the Present to the Past

Whitman, starting from Paumanok, wandering Mannahatta, chanting the Indian names, looking for the aboriginal words, seeking the "friendly and flowing savage," did his best to begin to accept aboriginal sources for the American character. He tried to trace out "arriere-threads to all pre-history" and demonstrate how those seemingly fragile threads are actually stronger than "steel and iron" and "weld the inhabitants of New York, Chicago, San Francisco and New Orleans to the vanished peoples retrospects of the past—to a hundred unknown nations" (*NUPM* 5:1684). It would be up to "Poets to Come" to "prove and define" what Whitman began. We can see William Carlos Williams's *In the American Grain* as one attempt to "justify" Whitman with an imaginative history that guides us back to the native and the land as the ground of our being, that allows us to trace our genealogy in such a way that our origins root us "Here, not there" (74). And Gary Snyder's *Turtle Island,* with its resurrection of "the old/new name for the continent, based on many creation myths of the people who have been living here for millennia," is an intensification of Whitman's poetic archaeology: "The 'U.S.A.' and its states and countries are arbitrary and inaccurate impositions on what is really here." In an essay echoing Whitman in many ways, appropriately called "Passage to More Than India," Snyder puts forth the idea of "White Indians," of white Americans who absorb the legends, rituals, chants, and "old ways" of the Indians and live by them, becoming "literally hunters and gatherers, playfully studying the old techniques of acorn flour, seaweed-gathering, yucca-fiber, rabbit snaring and bow hunting." When the haunting memory of the American Indian eventually is so fully absorbed in the American mind that it can "claim the next generation as its own," then "citizens of the USA will at last begin to be Americans, truly at home on the continent, in love with their land" (Snyder 1969, 110-12). Snyder sees the fulfillment of Whitman's democratic vistas in a growing reemergence of Indians and Indian ways: "When [Whitman] says there should be more democracy, I go along with that. We all see what more democracy means, too. It means that the Navajo should get their own nation, that Rosebud and Pine Ridge maybe should be a separate nation, that the Indians of Puget Sound should have fishing rights" (Snyder 1980, 74).

Absorption of the Indian words, tales, rituals into the English language and the subsequent creation of "White Indians" has its negative side, too, of course. The dilemma of many Indian writers and visionaries has been whether they should allow their tribe's tales and visions to be absorbed into and conquered by the white man's language. The poet and translator W. S. Merwin, speaking of the translations of indigenous American works, notes the hopeless and sad irony of how "our knowledge of these words out of the past of the America in which we were born and learned to speak depends (entirely, in most cases) on their representations in languages brought from Europe by the same conquest that overran the American natives." And Merwin, too, sees the double-edged nature of this linguistic conquering of native cultures:

> One thing that troubles us in their presence is the growing certainty that what has been lost was rightfully ours, a part of ourselves not only in so far as we are Americans—but in so far as we are a people—or people—at all.

He notes:

> We are drawn with a peculiar insistence by these works to the recognition that what of America has been lost to us was ours like our own forgotten dreams, and that it had something to impart to us about ourselves, which we may now have to grope for in nameless bewilderment, before we can truly awaken. (Merwin 277-78)

It is the American dilemma: as the old ways of various tribes die out, is it better to have the visions die with the tribes, or to twist them into translations, freeze ever-changing oral tales into a single written form in the language of those who destroyed the cultures that produced the tales? There are no easy answers. Black Elk tells the story of his vision, through an interpreter, to John G. Neihardt, who tells it in English. Black Elk knows that his vision, handed over to the white man's culture, has lost its power and purity, but his hope is that nevertheless it might alter the white man's mind-set, make him see, even if only indistinctly, a possibility for a different and better relationship to the natural world. So he takes the risk. Whitman's plan to absorb the Indian via his poetry was similarly double-edged: his project admitted the inevitable loss of Indian cultures, but it simultaneously argued for the significance of those cultures and for the necessity of preserving them—as a warning, lesson, inspiration—at the heart of our memories, deep in the lines of authentic American poems.

Texts Cited

Allen, Gay Wilson. *The Solitary Singer* (New York: New York University Press, 1955).

Clark, Leadic M. *Walt Whitman's Concept of the American Common Man* (New York: Philosophical Library, 1955).

Drinnon, Richard. *Facing West: The Metaphysics of Indian-Hating and Empire-Building* (New York: Meridian, 1980).

Emerson, Ralph Waldo. *Selected Writings of Ralph Waldo Emerson,* ed. William H. Gilman (New York: Signet, 1965).

Friend, Joseph H. *The Development of American Lexicography, 1798-1864* (The Hague: Mouton, 1967).

Kenny, Maurice. "Whitman's Indifference to Indians." *Greenfield Review* 14 (Summer-Fall 1987), 99-113.

Lane, Margaret. *Frances Wright and the "Great Experiment"* (Totowa, NJ: Rowman & Littlefield, 1972).

Least Heat Moon, William. *Blue Highways* (Boston: Little, Brown, 1982).

Mendelsohn, Maurice. "Whitman and the Oral Indian Tradition," *American Dialog* 7 (Summer 1972), 25-28.

Merwin, W. S. *Regions of Memory,* ed. Ed Folsom and Cary Nelson (Champaign: University of Illinois Press, 1987).

Neihardt, John G. *Black Elk Speaks* (New York: Pocket Books, 1972).

Ortiz, Simon J. *From Sand Creek* (Oak Park, NY: Thunder's Mouth Press, 1981).

Pearce, Roy Harvey. *Savagism and Civilization: A Study of the Indian and the American Mind* (1953; rev. Berkeley: University of California Press, 1988).

Perlman, Jim, Ed Folsom, and Dan Campion, eds. *Walt Whitman: The Measure of His Song* (Minneapolis, MN: Holy Cow!, 1981).

Rubin, Joseph Jay. *The Historic Whitman* (University Park: Pennsylvania State University Press, 1973).

Schevill, James. "A Changing Inventory: For Walt Whitman," *American Dialog* 5 (Spring-Summer 1969), 30-31.

Sigourney, L[ydia]. H. *Select Poems* (Philadelphia: U. Hunt & Son, 1843).

Simpson, David. *The Politics of American English, 1776-1850* (New York: Oxford University Press, 1986).

Snyder, Gary. *Earth House Hold* (New York: New Directions, 1969).

Turtle Island (New York: New Directions, 1974).

The Real Work: Interviews and Talks, 1964-1979 (New York: New Directions, 1980).

Swinton, William. *Rambles Among Words: Their Poetry, History and Wisdom* (New York: Charles Scribner, 1859).

Taft, Robert. "The Pictorial Record of the Old West: IV. Custer's Last Stand—John Mulvany, Cassilly Adams and Otto Becker," *Kansas Historical Quarterly* 14 (November 1946), 361-90.

Turner, Frederick Jackson. *The Significance of the Frontier in American History* (1893; rpt. New York: Ungar, 1963).

Williams, William Carlos. *In the American Grain* (1925; rpt. New York: New Directions, 1956).

Wilson, Norma. "Heartbeat: Within the Visionary Tradition," *Mickle Street Review,* no. 7 (1985), 14-23.

A Note on Sources Concerning Whitman and the Indians

Two books that have fundamentally shifted assumed Western cultural perspectives about the relationship of Euro-Americans to native tribes are Richard Drinnon, *Facing West: The Metaphysics of Indian-Hating and Empire-Building* (New York: Meridian, 1980); and Richard Slotkin, *Regeneration Through Violence: The Mythology of the American Frontier, 1600—1860* (Middletown, CT: Wesleyan University Press, 1973); I am deeply indebted to both. Robert F. Sayre, *Thoreau and the American Indians* (Princeton, NJ: Princeton University Press, 1977), demonstrates the centrality to Thoreau's thought of questions concerning the Indians and suggests directions for realigning our study of "classic" American authors. These books have all built on Roy Harvey Pearce's seminal study *Savagism and Civilization: A Study of the Indian and the American Mind* (1953; rev. Berkeley: University of California Press, 1988).

Slotkin does mention Whitman, but only in passing; at one point, he loosely associates Whitman with the Indians:

> Chanticleer Whitman's "barbaric yawp" sounding like Indian war cries full of bloodlust and sexual threat over the rooftops of the assaulted town, was perhaps more dramatically effectual [than *Walden*] as a statement of identification with the Indian character and spirit of the wilderness and the erotic impulses of the subconscious mind. (534)

And Asebrit Sundquist glances at Whitman's use of Indian women in *Pocahontas & Co.: The Fictional American Indian Woman in Nineteenth-Century Literature* (Atlantic Highlands, NJ: Humanities Press International, 1987). In the major studies of the relationship of American Indians to Anglo-American writers and to Anglo-American literature, however, Whitman is virtually ignored. See Ray Allen Billington, *Land of Savagery, Land of Promise* (New York: Norton, 1981); Albert Keiser, *The Indian in American Literature* (1933;

rpt. New York: Octagon, 1970); Elemire Zolla, *The Writer and the Shaman: A Morphology of the American Indian* (New York: Harcourt, Brace, Jovanovich, 1973); Louise K. Barnett, *The Ignoble Savage: American Literary Racism, 1790-1890* (Westport, CT: Greenwood, 1975); and Pearce, where Whitman is never mentioned, and Drinnon, where "Facing West from California's Shores" serves as cpigraph and furnishes the title, but where Whitman's own views of Indians are never explored. Donald D. Kummings, in his bibliography of work done on Whitman since 1940 (*Walt Whitman, 1940-1975: A Reference Guide* [Detroit: Gale, 1983], x), notes the strange paucity of comment on Whitman's attitudes toward Indians, and he views the failure to deal with the subject as one of the major oversights of Whitman criticism.

As I note in this chapter, Whitman's view of the American Indian in some ways never progressed much beyond that of Frances Wright, the freethinking author of *A Few Days in Athens* (1822), whom Whitman heard speak and whose work he absorbed; he called her "one of the best in history" and recalled how he "fell down before her": "I never felt so glowingly toward any other woman" (quoted in Allen 30). In her *Views of Society and Manners in America* (1821), which Whitman no doubt knew well, she offers the usual equivocation of early-nineteenth-century white liberal attitudes: a sadness about the inevitable loss of the native, "the wasting remnant that must soon disappear with the receding forest," but a recognition of—even an enthusiasm for—the necessity of that loss:

> The falling greatness of this people, disappearing from the face of their native soil, at first strikes mournfully on the imagination; but such regrets are scarcely rational. The savage, with all his virtues, and he has some virtues, is still a sayage. . . . The increase and spread of the white population at the expense of the red, is, as it were, the triumph of peace over violence. (quoted in Lane 11).

On her travels, she came upon an Indian sitting, pensive, on the shores of Lake Erie. She was surprised to find his "countenance had much in it of dignity and savage grandcur" as he seemed to muse "upon the fallen strength of his tribe." Wright feels a momentary regret "that even this conquest of the peaceful over the savage arts, should have been made at the expense of this wild race," but the feeling passes as she recalls that it is all for the best: "for the well-being of man, how glorious the change, which has turned these vast haunts of panthers, wolves and savages, into the abode of industry, and the sure asylum of the oppressed." Wright's own utopian scheme, her community of Nashoba, set up to free slaves and educate them, as well as to test out her advanced theories of free love and affection, was itself carved out of cheap land in Tennessee from which the Chickasaw Indians had recently been cleared. Whitman's similar progressive ideals dominate his writing, and he

was usually comfortable celebrating how America was "enacting to-day the grandest arts, poems, &c., by beating up the wilderness into fertile farms" (*PW* 369).

Abbreviations

AP: Horace Traubel, ed., *An American Primer by Walt Whitman* (1904; rpt. Stevens Point, WI: Holy Cow!, 1987).

BG: Sculley Bradley and John Stevenson, eds., *Walt Whitman's Backward Glances* (Philadelphia: University of Pennsylvania Press, 1949).

C: Edwin Haviland Miller, ed., *The Correspondence*, 6 vols. (New York: New York University Press, 1961-77).

DBN: William White, ed., *Daybooks and Notebooks*, 3 vols. (New York: New York University Press, 1978).

EPF: Thomas L. Brasher, ed., *The Early Poems and Fiction* (New York: New York University Press, 1963).

GF: Cleveland Rodgers and John Black, eds., *The Gathering of the Forces*, 2 vols. (New York: Putnam, 1920).

LG: Sculley Bradley and Harold W. Blodgett, eds., *Leaves of Grass*. Norton Critical Edition (New York: Norton, 1973).

LGV: Sculley Bradley, Harold W. Blodgett, Arthur Golden, William White, eds., *Leaves of Grass: A Textual Variorum of the Printed Poems*, 3 vols. (New York: New York University Press, 1980).

NF: Richard Maurice Bucke, ed., *Notes and Fragments Left by Walt Whitman* (London: Talbot, 1899).

NUPM: Edward F. Grier, ed., *Notebooks and Unpublished Prose Manuscripts*, 6 vols. (New York: New York University Press, 1984).

NYD: Emory Holloway and Ralph Adimari, eds., *New York Dissected* (New York: Rufus Rockwell Wilson, 1936).

PR: William White, "Walt Whitman: An Unknown Piece by 'Paumanok,'" in Vince Clemente and Graham Everett, eds., *Paumanok Rising* (Port Jefferson, NY: Street Press, 1981).

PW: Floyd Stovall, ed., *Prose Works, 1892*, 2 vols. (New York: New York University Press, 1963).

UPP: Emory Holloway, ed., *The Uncollected Poetry and Prose of Walt Whitman*, 2 vols. (1921; rpt. Gloucester: Peter Smith, 1972).

WM: Fredson Bowers, ed., *Whitman's Manuscripts: Leaves of Grass (1860)* (Chicago: University of Chicago Press, 1955).

WWC: Horace Traubel, *With Walt Whitman in Camden,* 7 vols. Vols. 1-3 (1906-14; rpt. New York: Rowman & Littlefield, 1961); Vol. 4, ed. Sculley Bradley (Philadelphia: University of Pennsylvania Press, 1953); Vol. 5, ed. Gertrude Traubel (Carbondale: University of Southern Illinois Press, 1964); Vol. 6, ed. Gertrude Traubel and William White (Carbondale: University of Southern Illinois Press, 1982); Vol. 7, ed. Jeanne Chapman and Robert MacIsaac (Carbondale: University of Southern Illinois Press, 1992). The notes for the last few years of Whitman's life remain unpublished and are in manuscript in the Whitman/Feinberg collection in the Library of Congress; quotations from this collection are abbreviated "*WWC* MS."

WWCW: Charles I. Glicksberg, ed., *Walt Whitman and the Civil War* (1933; rpt. New York: Barnes, 1963).

Kerry McSweeney (essay date 1998)

SOURCE: "Whitman: The Feeling of Health," in *The Language of the Senses: Sensory-Perceptual Dynamics in Wordsworth, Coleridge, Thoreau, Whitman, and Dickinson,* McGill-Queen's University Press, 1998, pp. 117-43.

[*In the following essay, McSweeney studies the relationship between physical health and imaginative power in Whitman's poetry, arguing that the differences in energy and tone between the poems of the 1855 and 1856 editions of* Leaves of Grass *and those poems added for the 1860 edition can at least in part be attributed to a shift in Whitman's emotional and physical health.*]

"In health," Thoreau notes in his journal, "all the senses are indulged and each seeks its own gratification.—it is a pleasure to see, and to walk, and to hear—&c" (**J* i 204). Walt Whitman agreed: in health, "the whole body is elevated to a state by others unknown—inwardly and outwardly illuminated, purified, made solid, strong, yet bouyant . . . there is no more borrowing trouble in advance. A man realizes the venerable myth—he is a god walking the earth, he sees new eligibilities, powers and beauties everywhere; he himself has a new eyesight and hearing . . . Merely *to move* is then a happiness, a pleasure" (1272-3). With Whitman, as with Coleridge and Thoreau, physical health and imaginative power are closely connected. At the beginning of **"Song of Myself"** (post-1855 version), he describes himself as "now thirty-seven years old in perfect health." In section 50 of the same poem he is at a loss for words to describe

the "something" that he feels working within himself that "is not chaos or death . . . it is eternal life . . . it is happiness." Whatever the something is, it is clear that its enabling condition is physical health.[1]

One could even argue that the sprawling shapelessness of **"Song of Myself"** is itself the result of the poet's robust physical health. An entry in Thoreau's journal for 1841 uncannily anticipates both the content of Whitman's poem and the way it conducts itself: "there are times when we feel a vigor in our limbs—and our thoughtas are like a flowing morning light . . . And if we were to sing at such an hour, There would be no catastrophe contemplated in our verse—no tragic element in it . . . It is epic without beginning or end—an eternal interlude without plot.—not subordinate one part to another, but supreme as a whole—at once—leaf and flower—and fruit" (**J* i 331).

The "feeling of health" (#2) is not only a presupposition of **"Song of Myself;"** it is also a principal subject of the poem. In a notebook entry from the time, Whitman jotted down the idea for a "poem in which is minutely described the whole particulars and ensemble of a *first-rate healthy Human Body*—it looked into and through, as if it were transparent and of pure glass" (**Notebooks** 304). He does not seem to have composed such a poem; but **"Song of Myself"** has elements of it, as does another 1855 poem, **"I Sing the Body Electric."** In **"Song of Myself,"** the principal indicator of good health is sensory acuity. The notation of visual images is as sharp as in **"There Was a Child Went Forth."** Acute aural registrations range from natural sounds ("the katydid work[ing] her chromatic reed on the walnut-tree over the well" [#33]), through natural cum domestic ("the bravuras of birds. . . . the bustle of growing wheat. . . . gossip of flames. . . . clack of sticks cooking my meals" [#26]); to urban noise ("The blab of the pave. . . . the tires of carts and sluff of bootsoles. . . . the clank of the shod horses on the granite floor" [#8]).

There is also abundant evidence that Whitman had a sharp and discriminating sense of smell, which remained acute even into later life. The natural descriptions in **Specimen Days** (1882), for example, often include olfactory notations. In one of them Whitman notes that "there is a scent to everything, even the snow, if you can only detect it—no two places, hardly any two hours, anywhere, exactly alike. How different the odor of noon from midnight, or winter from summer, or a windy spell from a still one" (876). In **"Song of Myself,"** as later, it is predominantly natural scents in which Whitman delights: "The sniff of green leaves and dry leaves, and of the shore and darkcolored sea-rocks, and of the hay in the barn" (#2); "the white roses sweet-scented and growing" (#49); "Delicate sniffs of the seabreeze. . . . smells of sedgy grass and fields by the shore" (#36); even "The scent of these arm-pits," which is pronounced "aroma finer than prayer" (#24).

The few discrete images of taste are in the main a function of touch, the most conspicuously indulged sense in the poems of 1855-6. In a draft section of **"Song of Myself,"** the other senses are described as "emulous" to become as intensely feeling as touch: "Every one must be a touch.—/Or else she will . . . nibble only at the edges of feeling . . . Each brings the best she has,/For each is in love with touch." Touch is not only the most intense and immediate of the senses; it is even said to subsume the others:

> A touch now reads me a library of knowledge
>   in an instant,
> It smells for me the fragrance of wine and
>   lemon-blows,
> It tastes for me ripe strawberries and
>   melons.—
> It talks for me with a tongue of its own,
> It finds an ear wherever it rests or taps,
> It brings the rest around it . . .
>
> *(Notebooks* 75-6)

The sense of touch was not present in **"There Was a Child,"** for reasons explained in chapter 1; but it is overwhelmingly present in the central 1855 poem, **"Song of Myself."** Whitman is here "the caresser of life wherever moving" (#13): "the press of my foot to the earth springs a hundred affections" (#14); "Divine am I inside and out, and I make holy whatever I touch or am touched from" (#24). "Mine is no callous shell," he boasts in what has been called the "outstanding understatement in American poetry" (Rosenthal and Gall 37):

> I have instant conductors all over me whether
>   I pass or stop,
> They seize every object and lead it harmlessly
>   through me.
>
> I merely stir, press, feel with my fingers, and
>   am happy,
> To touch my person to some one else's is
>   about as much as I can stand.
>
> (#27)

In trying to account for this extraordinary degree of haptic sensitivity, Roger Asselineau suggests that Whitman had "a hyperesthesia of all the sense, particularly that of touch . . . which is perhaps connected with the repression of his sexual instincts. He appears constantly to feel the need of rubbing himself, in his imagination, against things and against people, probably because he could not satisfy his desires otherwise"; the fable of the woman and the twenty-eight bathers in section 11 of **"Song of Myself"** is "a case of repression which probably was a mere transposition of his own" (13,

277n). Asselineau has a point—if it is qualified by noting that some passages celebrate the satisfaction (at least the auto-erotic satisfaction) of his desires, and that touch is presented more than once as a redemptive force. Such speculation, however, is ultimately reductive and detracts attention from the great haptic delicacy and comprehensiveness of **"Song of Myself."**

In his **Notebooks**, Coleridge distinguishes several gradations in the intensity of this sensory mode. The last three in ascending order are: (*a*) "retentive power extinguishing the sense of touch, or making it mere feeling"; for example, "The Hand grasping firmly an inanimate Body—that is the one extreme of this." (*b*) touch with "retentive power"; for example, the "Lips, or the thumb and forefinger in a slight pressure." (*c*) "Touch with the sense of immediate power"; for example, "mem. vi/Riley. in acts of Es*sex*"; that is, the *membrum virile*—the phallus (i #2399). Another notebook entry elaborates on this: the erect penis is "the mutually assimilant Junction" of "*Love* & Lust"; "the vital & personal linked to & combined with the external." The passage continues (the reference seems clearly to be to the phallus): "an organ acting with what intensity of personal Life/compare it with the Eye & Ear/then at a less distance with the Smell, still less with the Taste/less still with the diffused or concentered Touch/yet at what a distance from all these" (i #1822). In other entries Coleridge speaks of "the influence of bodily vigor and strong Grasp of Touch in facilitating the passion of Hope" (ii #2398), and of the "coadunation [unifying] of Feeling & Sensation [as] the specific character of the sexual Pleasure: and that which renders this particular mode of bodily intercourse the apt outward Sign, Symbol, & sensuous Language of the union desired & commenced by the *Souls* of sincere Lovers" (ii #3605).[2]

Loosely using Coleridge's framework, one can sketch a qualitative typology of touch in **"Song of Myself."** (*a*) *Mere feeling:* "each man and each woman of you I lead upon a knoll,/My left hand hooks you round the waist . . . If you tire . . . rest the chuff of your hand on my hip" (#46); the hand of the *accoucheur* "pressing receiving supporting" the woman during childbirth (#49). (*b*) *Touch with retentive power:* "A few light kisses. . . . a few embraces. . . . a reaching around of arms" (#2); "the press of a bashful hand . . . the touch of my lips to yours" (#19); feeling the arms of young men "on my neck as I stood, or the negligent leaning of their flesh against me as I sat" (**"Crossing Brooklyn Ferry"**); "to be surrounded by beautiful curious breathing laughing flesh is enough,/To pass among them. .to touch any one. . . . to rest my arm ever so lightly round his or her neck for a moment . . . I do not ask any more delight" (**"I Sing the Body Electric"**).

(*c*) *Touch with immediate power:* this category divides into two parts. In the first, the *erotic,* most of the examples are instances of passive touch, of being touched rather than touching. They include "The souse upon me of my lover the sea, as I lie willing and naked" (**"Bunch Poem"**); lovers "Crowding my lips, and thick on the pores of my skin . . . Bussing my body with soft and balsamic busses" (#45); or the "curious roamer, the hand, roaming all over the body—the bashful withdrawing of flesh where the fingers soothingly pause and edge themselves"—one place of this haptic reconnaissance being "The sensitive, orbic, underlapped brothers, that only privileged feelers may be intimate where they are" (**"Bunch Poem"**).

The second is the *phallic*. The *membrum virile* or "phallic thumb of love" (**"Bunch Poem"**) is the dominant organ in the most extraordinary passage in **"Song of Myself"** (#26-29). Section 27 emphasizes the speaker's extreme haptic sensitivity and the primacy of touch in his sensorium, and stresses the importance of tactile interaction in breaking down the barriers between subject and object, self and external world: "To be in any form, what is that?/If nothing lay more developed the quahaug [a large clam] and his callous shell were enough." In the preceding section, Whitman began by announcing that he would do nothing but listen. The ensuing aural catalogue commenced with natural and domestic sounds; then came urban sounds that grew louder; and finally musical sounds with strong emotional, then erotic, pulls: "the trained soprano . . . convulses me like the climax of my love-grip"; the orchestra "wrenches unnamable ardors from my breast." The vocal and orchestral music intensifies tactile sensitivity until their sounds transmogrify into an engulfing oceanic feeling: "It sails me. . . . I dab with bare feet. . . . they are licked by the indolent waves" (as in sections 21-22, immersion in the sea is a figure for the dominance of touch). Finally, the immersion is total: "I am . . . Steeped amid honeyed morphine. . . . my windpipe squeezed in the fakes [coils of a rope] of death." "Is it then a touch," section 28 begins,

> quivering me to a new identity,
> Flames and ether making a rush for my veins,
> Treacherous tip of me reaching and crowding
>   to help them.
> My flesh and blood playing out lightning, to
>   strike what is hardly different from myself.
> On all sides prurient provokers stiffening my
>   limbs,
> Straining the udder of my heart for its
>   withheld drip,
> Behaving licentious toward me, taking no
>   denial,
> Depriving me of my best as for a purpose,
> Unbuttoning my clothes and holding me by
>   the bare waist,
> Deluding my confusion with the calm of the
>   sunlight and pasture fields.

There follows an extraordinary sequence full of obscure associations and displacements as inner and outer merge and consciousness becomes tactile. The "fellow-senses," having initially acted as "prurient provokers" of quivering arousal, become recessive; they are "bribed to swap off with touch, and go and graze at the edges of me." In a manuscript reading, they have "left me helpless to the torrent of touch" (*Notebooks* 76). The torrent is clearly sexual and culminates in orgasm. But what exactly is going on? Is it consensual sodomy, as Robert K. Martin seems to think? Is it anal rape, as Karl Keller conjectures? Or fellatio, as manuscript readings perhaps suggest? Or is it masturbation, as most commentators think? A reading of the figures in sensory terms is helpful. The grazing herd, the sentries who have deserted "every other part of me," and "the traitors" are all figurations of the other senses. Flames and ether rushing into the body while lightning is "playing out" from the flesh and blood suggests the conflation or merging of active and passive touch. The phallus is the "headland" by metaphor; by metonomy, it is the "red marauder" (it is engorged with blood). "I went myself first to the headland. . . . my own hands carried me there": this surely suggests an auto-erotic act.

The passage reaches its orgasmic climax when "villain touch"—"Blind loving wrestling touch"—unclenches its floodgates. Section 29 beautifully adumbrates the orgasmic expansion of consciousness:

> Parting tracked by arriving. . . . perpetual
>   payment of the perpetual loan,
> Rich showering rain, and recompense richer
>   afterward.
>
> Sprouts take and accumulate. . . . stand by
>   the curb prolific and vital,
> Landscapes projected masculine full-sized and
>   golden.

The compensatory ebb-and-flow figures in the first distich suggest in the first instance the tumescent-detumescent rhythm of phallic touch; but they also recall the "respiration and inspiration" of the poet's lungs and the systole and diastole of the beating of his heart celebrated in section 2. These are all synecdochal figurations of the poet's indefatigably curious self— "Partaker of influx and efflux" (#22)—whose subject matter is "the thrust and withdrawal, the heightening and declining, the flowing and ebbing of his psychic and creative energy" (Lewis 5) as well as of his sexual energy. The second distich associates this rhythm with the natural cycle—harvest abundance after germinating rain. The urban herbage at the curbside metonymically evokes a rural landscape of fully ripened wheat; and the masculine thrust of its stalks in turn recalls the orgasmic bounty—the semen or seed—just poured out. In short, section 29 offers a condensed epitome of what Emerson called that "great principle of Undulation in nature, that shows itself in the inspiring and expiring of the breath; in desire and satiety; in the ebb and flow of the sea; in day and night . . ." (62).

Sections 26-9 are one of two places in **"Song of Myself"** in which an allusively described sexual act triggers visionary experience. The other is found in the fifth section, but here the experience is sweetly transporting, not roughly destabilizing. In Coleridge's terms, it is more loving than lustful and thus meta-phallic: touch facilitating the passion of hope—an outward sign of spiritual union.

> Loafe with me on the grass. . . . loose the
>   stop from your throat,
> Not words, not music or rhyme I want. . . .
>   not custom or lecture, not even the best,
> Only the lull I like, only the hum of your
>   valved voice.
> I mind how we lay in June, such a transparent
>   summer morning;
> You settled your head athwart my hips and
>   gently turned over upon me,
> And parted my shirt from my bosom-bone,
>   and plunged your tongue to my barestript
>   heart,
> And reached till you felt my beard, and
>   reached till you held my feet.
>
> Swiftly arose and spread around me the peace
>   and joy and knowledge that pass all the art
>   and argument of the earth;
> And I know that the hand of God is the
>   elderhand of my own,
> And I know that the spirit of God is the
>   eldest brother of my own,
> And that all the men ever born are also my
>   brothers. . . . and the women my sisters
>   and lovers,
> And that a kelson of the creation is love;
> And limitless are leaves stiff or drooping in
>   the fields,
> And brown ants in the little wells beneath them,
> And mossy scabs by the wormfence, and
>   heaped stones, and elder and mullen and
>   pokeweed.

As in sections 26-9, rhythmic sounds—here a lulling hum like "the murmur of yearning" in section 19—initiate a shift in sensory dominance. Lying on the ground diminishes the power of the eye and in other ways leads to a loosening of the sensory stays; as the other senses recede, touch becomes dominant. It is unclear what precisely transpires when the tongue and the hands of the "you" take over. Fellatio would be not a bad guess; for one thing, "orality links vocal and sexual activity" (Nathanson 132). But the important point is that this is an instance of what Allen Ginsberg

calls "friendly touch" (238). Section 5 has nothing convulsive, prurient, marauding, or predatory.

The expansion of consciousness experienced on this transparent summer morning has been compared to Emerson's "transparent eyeball" experience. But Whitman's is grounded in touch rather than in sight. The part or particle of God that he becomes is figured by his hand, not his eyeball; and it is not the visual organ that is reflected in the "leaves stiff or drooping in the fields." The onset of transparency—the fusion of inner and outer—is signalled by the shift from the past to the present tense ("And I know . . ."). The speaker enters a visionary, trans-temporal and trans-spatial *now* in which inner and outer perfectly mirror each other: "This is the far-off depth and height reflecting my own face," as Whitman puts it in a later section, "This is the thoughtful merge of myself and the outlet again" (#19). The last three lines describe the outlet. As visionary expansion begins to contract, sight once again becomes dominant: "limitless" is succeeded by the visual limit of what the recumbent speaker can see. What is visible is the opposite of cosmic: tiny ants and their miniature craters, mossy scabs, stones, and common weeds. But in the afterglow of his visionary experience of cosmic love, nothing is marginalized; even the weeds by the fence are lovingly particularized. They are not the phallic "sprouts . . . prolific and vital" of section 29, but both are woven out of the same "hopeful green stuff" as the grass that the questioning child brings the poet in the following section.

. . . . .

In his preface to the first edition of *Leaves of Grass,* Whitman observes that "folks expect of the poet to indicate more than the beauty and dignity which always attach to dumb real objects. . . . they expect him to indicate the path between reality and their souls." In discovering this path, the dominant organ of perception is not touch but sight: the "greatest poet . . . is a seer . . . the other senses corroborate themselves, but [eyesight] is removed from any proof but its own and foreruns the identities of the spiritual world" (10). Put more simply in **"Song of Myself,"** the unseen is proved by the seen" (#3).

At the center of the concern with the unseen spiritual world was the question of life after death. One poem in the 1855 edition is entirely devoted to the subject. **"To Think of Time"** is a meditation on temporality—on what de Man calls an authentically human destiny:

> To think of today . . and the ages continued
>   henceforward.
> Have you guessed you yourself would not
>   continue? Have you dreaded those
>   earth-beetles?
> Have you feared the future would be nothing
>   to you?

The poem is unsatisfactory both formally and conceptually because it breaks in two. The felt awareness of mortality is powerfully evoked in the first five sections, especially in the description of the December funeral of a stage driver. But in the sixth stanza, somber meditation abruptly gives way to assertive optimism: "What will be will be well—for what is is well . . . You are not thrown to the winds . . . you gather certainly and safely around yourself,/ Yourself! Yourself! Yourself forever and ever." You were not born to be diffused but to receive identity and having received it you are "henceforth secure, whatever comes or goes"; the pattern or law is "systematic" and "eternal."

What gives rise to these assertions is simply that it is too awful to think otherwise: "We cannot be stopped at a given point. . . . that is no satisfaction . . . We must have the indestructible breed of the best, regardless of time." Once uttered, Whitman attempts to bolster these assertions by circular reasoning: if he were to "suspect death I should die now,/Do you think I could walk pleasantly and well-suited toward annihilation?" But he does walk pleasantly and well-suited and therefore, although he cannot define his destination, he knows that it must be good.

That Whitman was himself dissatisfied with these formulations is suggested by his return to the subject the next year in the masterpiece of the 1856 edition, **"Crossing Brooklyn Ferry."** In this poem, he adapted to his particular concern with future existence the form that M. H. Abrams denominated the greater Romantic lyric.[3] As in a number of earlier poems of this type, coleridge's "This Lime-Tree Bower" and "Frost at Midnight" for example, symbolic perception (the relation of natural facts to spiritual facts) is the *sine qua non of* **"Crossing Brooklyn Ferry."** The natural facts are the particulars of the physical setting—what is seen while crossing by ferry from Brooklyn to Manhattan. These are evoked in the third section's composite panorama: the December seagulls high in the air, seeming to float with motionless wings; the reflection of the summer sky; "the fine centrifugal spokes of light round the shape of my head in the sunlit water"; the schooners, sloops, barges, steamers, lighters, steam-tugs, and hay-boats; the scalloped-edged waves in the twilight; "the fires from the foundry chimneys burning high and glaringly into the night."

The other subject is spiritual facts: "The impalpable sustenence of me from all things . . . the well-join'd scheme, myself disintegrated, every one disintegrated yet part of the scheme . . . The others that are to follow me, the ties between me and them." The goal of **"Crossing Brooklyn Ferry"** is to establish a connection between the two sets of facts. The poem's principal strategy is to address a "you"—not a "you" living in present time as in **"To Think of Time"** and **"Song of Myself,"** but a "you" living in the future—"Fifty years hence . . . A hundred years hence, or ever so many hundred years hence"—who in crossing from Brooklyn to Manhattan will enjoy the very same perceptual experiences, "The glories strung like beads on my smallest sights and hearings," that Whitman did in 1856.

In the course of the poem intimacy between the present "I" and future "you" increases. In the third section, the speaker softly assures his auditor that time and space are of no avail in separating them: "I am with you" in the sense that, in looking at river and sky, in being part of a living crowd, "you" are experiencing exactly what "I" experienced. The word used to describe this degree of analogical intimacy is "similitudes"—"Just as you feel . . . so I felt"; "just as you are refresh'd . . . I was refresh'd." In sections 5 and 6, a more intimate connection is suggested: both "I" and "you" have felt "the curious abrupt questionings stir within." These curious feelings or "dark patches" include doubts about achievement ("The best I had done seem'd to me blank and suspicious"); "the old knot of contrariety" (a variety of moral and emotional failings); and erotic longings. In the next section, recognition of these shared intimate feelings is said to have brought speaker and addressee "closer yet."

In section 8, the speaker briefly recapitulates the perceptual similitudes of the natural setting, using the grasping of hands and being called by his "nighest name" as figures for the inner congruences. Then—it is the poem's climactic moment in more ways than one—the object of the loving embrace becomes the future "you": "What is more subtle than this," the speaker asks, "Which fuses me into you now, and pours my meaning into you?" Now there is no more "I" and "you"; there is "we":

> We understand then do we not?
> What I promis'd without mentioning it, have
>   you not accepted?
> What the study could not teach—what the
>   preaching could not accomplish is
>   accomplish'd, is it not?

What exactly had been promised? and what is it that can be said to have been accomplished? One key to understanding the speaker's assertion is the shift in addressee in the poem's closing section. Here the "you" is no longer the future reader of the poem: "you" are the natural facts of the physical scene— the "dumb beautiful ministers" whom "we" directly address. The section opens with a second panoramic description of the physical scene—only this time a celebratory imperative present replaces the earlier past indicative. As in Coleridge's "This Lime-Tree Bower," the change marks the shift from ordinary to visionary perception—from outlooker to participatory consciousness. What is celebrated is the fluid merging of inner and outer. The visual particulars of the scene are no longer individual glories hung on the speaker's higher senses; they are now figured as a "necessary film . . . envelop[ing] the soul." In another image registering the same supersession of sight by feeling/touch, the whole of the spatiotemporal continuum of **"Crossing Brooklyn Ferry"** is figured as an "eternal float of solution." This trope refers back to the cryptic last lines of the fifth section:

> I too had been struck from the float forever
>   held in solution,
> I too had receiv'd identity by my body,
> That I was I knew was of my body, and what
>   I should be I knew I should be of my body.

To be struck from the float is to be born, to assume individual human form and substance. To die is to become "disintegrated"; this happens to "every one," yet every one remains "part of the scheme." Thus, there can be contact between present "I" and future "you"; indeed, such felt contact is the evidence of the existence of the "float."

Thus, by the final section the speaker has in some psychologically satisfying way come to affirm his continued future existence by means of the natural facts, the "dumb beautiful ministers" that "furnish your parts toward eternity." What is said is beautifully expressed, but what precisely is being affirmed is far from clear. The asserted relationship of natural facts to spiritual facts is not the similitude of tenor and vehicle as in simile, metaphor, and the Swedenborgian system of correspondences in which the visible is the dial-plate of the invisible. Nor is the relationship metonymic—the graduated contiguity of part to whole as with a Coleridgean symbol in which the temporal shows forth the eternal. Neither of these kinds of symbolizing would be adequate to Whitman's purpose, which is to affirm not an eternal supernatural world but rather an endless trans-natural world of perpetual floating or "crossing."

It is important to note that while the continuum—the film or float—is "impalpable," it is not wholly imperceptible. In the final stanza of **"Crossing Brooklyn Ferry,"** what is said to be hung "About my body for me, and your body for you" are not sights and sounds but "our divinest aromas." This is not the scent of armpits but some quintessential olfactory distillation. "Unlike sight," writes F. Gonzalez-Crussi, "olfaction deals with the airy, the insubstantial, and the formless . . . smells often defy localization in space. Sight has regard to the actualities of space, but olfaction lives in time . . . Of all our senses, this is the one most closely related to time: to the past, because, better than the others, it evokes memory; to the future, because, more effectively than the others, it elicits anticipation and awakens our deepest yearnings" (71).

Bluntly put, the assertion at the end of **"Crossing Brooklyn Ferry"** is that natural facts *are* spiritual facts. The riddling couplet later added by Whitman to one of the 1855 poems might have been better deployed as the epigraph for **"Crossing Brooklyn Ferry"**: "Strange and hard that paradox true I give,/Objects gross and the unseen soul are one" (**"A Song for Occupations"**). Anagogy is the name for the kind of symbolizing in which the duality of tenor and vehicle, signifier and signified, is overcome. Anagogic symbolism, says Northrop Frye, "is the conceivable or imaginative limit of desire, which is infinite, eternal, and hence apocalyptic. By an apocalypse I mean primarily the imaginative conception of the whole of nature as the content of an infinite and eternal living body which, if not human, is closer to being human than to being inanimate" (*Anatomy* 119).

But there is nothing apocalyptic in the biblical or Blakean sense about **"Crossing Brooklyn Ferry,"** which is not a prophetic book but an intimate lyric communication specifically addressed to a singular "you" living in the future, on union or fusion with whom everything in the poem depends. From the point of view of "you" the reader living a hundred or hundreds of years hence, surely the only achieved "eternity" is aesthetic—the perfected verbal artwork that represents for later readers what Whitman felt at what he saw and what still is the look of things (to paraphrase Wallace Stevens' "A Postcard from the Volcano"). Despite the poem's canny assertions of the continuing existence of the "soul," it is very hard to think of **"Crossing Brooklyn Ferry"** as offering anything other than what Thomas Hardy called an "Idealism of Fancy: that is . . . an imaginative solace in the lack of any substantial solace to be found in life" (333). Certainly this was how the matter came to appear to Whitman only four years later in **"Of the Terrible Doubt of Appearance"**:

> Of the uncertainty after all, that we may be
>   deluded,
>
>   . . . . .
>
> That may-be identity beyond the grave is a
>   beautiful fable only,
> May-be the things I perceive . . . are (as
>   doubtless they are) only apparitions.
>
>   . . . . .

The extraordinary differences between the poems in the 1855 and 1856 editions of *Leaves of Grass* and those added for the edition of 1860 have been variously explained. There can be little doubt that the unhappy aftermath of a homosexual love relationship was a contributing factor: "Was it I who walked the earth disclaiming all except what I had in myself?" Whitman wonders in a manuscript poem: "Was it I boasting how complete I was in myself?/O little I counted the comrade indispensable to me!" (*Manuscripts* 68). This is also the subject of one of Whitman's best-known lyrics, **"I Saw in Louisiana a Live-Oak Growing,"** one of the twelve poems of the **"Live Oak with Moss"** sequence (copied into a notebook in the spring of 1859) that alludes to the love affair more directly than the forty-five **"Calamus"** poems of the 1860 *Leaves of Grass,* of which after reordering they became part.

> I saw in Louisiana a live-oak growing,
> All alone stood it and the moss hung down
>   from the branches,
> Without any companion it grew there uttering
>   joyous leaves of dark green,
> And its look, rude, unbending, lusty, made me
>   think of myself,
> But I wonder'd how it could utter joyous
>   leaves standing alone there without its
>   friend near, for I knew I could not,
> And I broke off a twig with a certain number
>   of leaves upon it, and twined around it a
>   little moss,
> And brought it away, and I have placed it in
>   sight in my room,
> It is not needed to remind me as of my own
>   dear friends,
> (For I believe lately I think of little else than
>   of them,)
> Yet it remains to me a curious token, it makes
>   me think of manly love;
> For all that, and though the live-oak glistens there
>   in Louisiana solitary in a wide flat space,
> Uttering joyous leaves all its life without a
>   friend a lover near,
> I know very well I could not.

At one level, "manly love" may be taken to refer to the love of same-sex comrades or to love of a particular man. But the context of Whitman's poetic development presents another, more suggestive and resonant meaning: self-confident, independent love as opposed to unmanly love which is sentimentally dependent on another or others. The declension in meaning of the adjective in "a curious token" as compared to its deployment in **"There Was a Child Went Forth"** or **"Crossing Brooklyn Ferry"** is telling. Here "curious" means something quirky or arbitrary rather than something inciting wonder (the difference is similar to that between unmanly and manly). In **"Song of Myself,"** natural objects had a rich symbolic suggestiveness; but now we have a token of a token. The twig is a synecdoche for the oak, which is a metaphor for the independent and joyous poet Whitman once was. But the poet of 1860 can no longer generate (utter) joyous leaves of himself; he can only collect tokens. As such, he bears only a token resemblance to the poet of 1855-6.

Other evidence suggests that the determining factor in the change from 1855-6 to 1860 was Whitman's physical health: he simply did not feel as good at the beginning of the 1860s as he had only a few years before. In **"A Hand-Mirror"** (1860), for example, the speaker takes stock of his physical being: "No more a flashing eye, no more a sonorous voice or springy step"; instead, "Words babble, hearing and touch callous,/No brain, no heart left, no magnetism of sex." The flashing eye and sexual magnetism are facets of what in another poem of 1860 Whitman calls his "electric self out of the pride of which I utter poems." The reference is in part to his extraordinary tactile sensitivity. The skin "is an especially good electrical conductor"; there are those "who when they touch another feel 'a sort of electrical current' passing between them." But while some individuals "retain this sensitivity into old age, others tend to lose it in middle age" (Montagu 148). For Whitman, the diminution of this current may be considered the equivalent of Wordsworth's loss of the visual acuity that had made the natural world seem "apparelled in celestial light,/The glory and the freshness of a dream" and left him toiling "In darkness lost, the darkness of the grave" (Intimations Ode).

The onset of middle age is the life-cycle term for this change. The degree of destabilization and desolation recorded in Whitman's poems of 1860 suggest that one should go a step further and apply the concept of mid-life crisis. A number of other nineteenth- and twentieth-century writers experienced a mid-life crisis that formed a divide in their careers. Its precipitates and/or symptoms include the feeling that, perceptually and creatively, something has fled—a loss that makes earlier works seem like fantastications and fresh creative achievement impossible. Wordsworth's Intimations Ode, Coleridge's Dejection Ode, and Emerson's "Experience" are all important points of comparison for the Whitman of 1860. So is Tolstoy's *Confession,* which relates the great watershed in his creative and spiritual life to irreversible bodily changes. Tolstoy recalled a time when, like the poet of **"Song of Myself,"** he believed that "Everything develops, differentiates, moving towards complexity and refinement and there are laws governing its progress. You are part of a whole." During this period he was developing physically and intellectually and it was "natural for me to believe that there was a law governing the world, in which I could find the answers to the questions of my life." But the time came when he stopped growing: "I felt that I was . . . drying up, my muscles were growing weaker, my teeth falling out." He realized that "I had taken for a law something which I had discovered in myself at a certain time of my life . . . it became clear to me that there could be no law of perpetual development" (35-6).

In **"As I Ebb'd with the Ocean of Life"** Whitman's crisis is unflinchingly faced. The poem opens with the poet musing late in the autumn day as he walks along the seashore, which since boyhood had been a special place for him because of its analogical suggestiveness. It was the "dividing line, contact, junction, the solid marrying the liquid—that curious, lurking something, (as doubtless every objective form finally becomes to the subjective spirit,) which means far more than its mere first sight, grand as that is—blending the real and ideal, and each made portion of the other" (796). Not surprisingly, then, as he wends his way along the shore Whitman is thinking the "old thought of likenesses." He is self-consciously the poet of **"Song of Myself"** the "electric self seeking types."

As he walks, he is "gazing off southward"—that is, looking out from the Atlantic coast of Long Island into the limitless expanse of sky and ocean. But he is also hearing the continual "hoarse and sibilant" sounds of the waves hitting the shore, which seem to be expressing the timelessness of human suffering and isolation: "the fierce old mother [the sea] endlessly cries for her castaways." The visual correlative of these natural sounds is not the distant line of the horizon, the place where Emerson said in *Nature* a man could behold something "as beautiful as his own nature" (10). It is the harshly and sibilantly described particulars on the shore that come to compel the attention of this seeker of types. He is

> . . . seiz'd by the spirit that trails in the lines
>   underfoot,
> The rim, the sediment that stands for all the
>   water and all the land of the globe.
>
> Fascinated, my eyes . . . dropt, to follow those
>   slender windrows,
> Chaff, straw, splinters of wood, weeds, and
>   the sea-gluten,
> Scum, scales from shining rocks, leaves of
>   salt-lettuce, left by the tide . . .
>
> . . . . .
>
> I too but signify at the utmost a little
>   wash'd-up drift,
> A few sands and dead leaves to gather,
> Gather, and merge myself as part of the sands
>   and drift.
>
> . . . . .
>
> I too have bubbled up, floated the measureless
>   float, and been wash'd on your shores,
> I too am but a trail of drift and debris,
> I too leave little wrecks upon you, you
>   fish-shaped island.

These extraordinary statements demand to be read against the background of Whitman's earlier self-

proclamations. The symbolic plenitude of the grass in section 6 of **"Song of Myself,"** for example, against the "few sands and dead leaves to gather"; the measureless float of **"Crossing Brooklyn Ferry"** against merging with the sands and drift; the undulating but always outwardly expanding movement of **"Song of Myself"** against the monotonous linearity of the miles-long trail of debris along the shore—a difference enacted in the lines of the poem, which are linear rather than undulating, prosaic rather than poetic; and the claims of the poet of **"Song of Myself"** to be in intimate creative contact with the "Me myself" against the energetic recantation of this presumption:

> Aware now that amid all that blab whose
>   echoes recoil upon me I have not once had
>   the least idea who or what I am,
> But that before all my arrogant poems the real
>   Me stands yet untouch'd untold, altogether
>   unreach'd,
> Withdrawn far, mocking me with
>   mock-congratulatory signs and bows,
> With peals of distant ironical laughter at every
>   word I have written,
> Pointing in silence to these songs, and then to
>   the sand beneath.

In section 22 of **"Song of Myself,"** Whitman had importuned the sea to "rock me in billowy drowse,/ Dash me with amorous wet. . . . I can repay you"; and elsewhere in the poem the earth and sea were figured as lovers. But in **"As I Ebb'd,"** Whitman has nothing to offer anything or anyone; and there is nothing erotic about the coming together of land and sea. In the poem's third section they are figured as parents from whom the poet desperately seeks revelation. The paternal shore is beseeched to "Breathe to me while I hold you close the secret of the murmuring I envy," for (to cite the later excised line that followed in the 1860 edition) "I fear I shall become crazed, if I cannot emulate it, and utter myself as well as it" (1860: 198). But the longing for haptic intensity, the clinging to the shore/father and asking to be touched "with your lips as I touch those I love," together with the continual maternal murmuring of the sea, also suggests the desire to "merge myself as part of the sands and drift"—that is, to be steeped in a numbing substance, to return to the oceanic state of hearing/touch.

The former plea may be said to be answered in the sense that, like Wordsworth in the Intimations Ode and Coleridge in the Dejection Ode, Whitman does powerfully utter himself in his poem about no longer being a poet. But there is no engulfment, no merging. There is white space and then the poem's fourth and final section. It opens on a distinctly false note. "Ebb, ocean of life, (the flow will return)" recapitulates the opening of the poem which found Whitman held by his prideful self-conception as an electric self. This momentary regression to the imperative, affirmative mode of the end of **"Crossing Brooklyn Ferry"** suggests a nostalgia for the "the old thought of likenesses" and the float forever held in solution. But the plenitude of 1855-6 has been superseded by the perceptual realities of the 1860 shoreline, by which in the closing lines the poet's attention is once again seized:

> I mean tenderly by you and all,
> I gather for myself and for this phantom
>   looking down where we lead, and following
>   me and mine.
>
> Me and mine, loose windrows, little corpses,
> Froth, snowy white, and bubbles,
> (See, from my dead lips the ooze exuding at
>   last,
> See, the prismatic colors glistening and
>   rolling,)
> Tufts of straw, sands, fragments,
> Bouy'd hither from many moods, one
>   contradicting another,
> From the storm, the long calm, the darkness,
>   the swell,
> Musing, pondering, a breath, a briny tear, a
>   dab of liquid or soil,
> Up just as much out of fathomless workings
>   fermented and thrown,
> A limp blossom or two, torn, just as much
>   over waves floating, drifted at random,
> Just as much for us that sobbing dirge of
>   Nature,
> Just as much whence we came that blare of
>   the cloud-trumpets,
> We, capricious, brought hither we know not
>   whence, spread out before you,
> You up there walking or sitting,
> Whoever you are, we too lie in drifts at your
>   feet.

Who is the phantom? There are two different but not mutually exclusive possibilities. The first is "the real Me" now recognized as chimerical. Its defining feature is that it is the part of Whitman "not wholly involved in Nature"—to quote from another text of Thoreau's that seems uncannily anticipatory of a Whitman poem. "I may be either the drift-wood in the stream, or Indra in the sky looking down on it," Thoreau reflects in the "Solitude" chapter of *Walden:* "However intense my experience, I am conscious of the presence and criticism of a part of me, which, as it were, is not a part of me, but spectator, sharing no experience, but taking note of it; and that is no more I than it is you" (135). The other possibility is that the "you" is the future reader, union with whom in **"Crossing Brooklyn Ferry"** gave Whitman the assurance that he was not doomed to extinction. Taking the "Whoever you are" of the last line to be the reader allows for a final contrast between

Whitman in 1855-6 and in 1860. In **"Song of Myself"** and **"Crossing Brooklyn Ferry,"** the poet was fully in control of the poem's addressee. Here the situation is very different; the poet has as little knowledge of "you" as of "the real Me." At the end of **"As I Ebb'd,"** the "you" is an unknown being at the feet of whom the speaker and his seashore types "lie in drifts." As Whitman reads the lines on the shore, "you" the reader read the "lines" on his page, in the words of which his failure and weakness are inscribed.

But something else is inscribed in these lines. The spiritual facts suggested by the natural facts of the shore have the same symbolic suggestiveness that they possessed in the poem's second section: randomness; contradiction; mortality; continual lament; and the shriving contrast between past plenitude and present emptiness. There is a difference, however. In the closing lines we have not terse prosaic cataloguing but copious rhythmic enumeration. For one critic, the length and tone of the passage suggest "a biding of time, a wish to prolong the lull between storms" (Larson 203). But I hear something stronger, a commitment to the natural facts. It is, to be sure, a commitment *faute de mieux*. The void has not grown luminous; but the chastened, no longer proud poet has found in the debris of the shore sufficient symbolic suggestiveness to allow him to utter himself. How impressive this effort is, and how difficult to sustain, can be gauged by comparing the end of **"As I Ebb'd"** to those of two other major Whitman poems, in both of which the sea or its figural equivalent does reveal "the secret of the murmuring I envy."

．．．．．

In **"Out of the Cradle Endlessly Rocking"** and **"When Lilacs Last in the Dooryard Bloom'd,"** Whitman moves away from the silent paternal shore toward a liquid mother who communicates a saving message. At the climax of both poems, the sense of touch, or rather Whitman's distinctive amalgam of hearing/touch, resumes its dominance. We have already noted this collocation in the key expansion of consciousness experiences in **"Song of Myself,"** in which rhythmic or musical sounds, what Tenney Nathanson nicely calls an "archaic fluidity activated by voice" (132), trigger visionary ecstasy.

In **"Out of the Cradle,"** engulfment in operatic sound begins with the pyrotechnics of the poem's overture, which shows how a curious boy absorbs and vicariously participates in experiences. The mature poet's imaginative act—adumbrated in the overture—recapitulates the child's imaginative act. Like **"As I Ebb'd,"** the opening of this poem includes an explicit back reference to 1855-6: "I, chanter of pains and joys, uniter of here and hereafter." The chanter is the poet of **"Song of Myself;"** the uniter is the visionary of **"Crossing**

Brooklyn Ferry." But in 1860 the subject is not "now" or "forever"; it is a reminiscence. The implications of this difference are most sharply seen in the contrasting accounts of how the person becomes the poet. In **"Song of Myself,"** the figuring of poetic incarnation emphasized fulfillment and plenitude: the fusion of the ordinary self with "the real Me" or "my soul," with sexual climax as the trigger of expanded consciousness and heightened perception. In contrast, the fable of poetic incarnation in **"Out of the Cradle"** offers a loss-based explanation. Listening both to the unmanly crooning of the lovelorn he-bird, and to its undertone, the incessant moaning of the sea, the boy experiences a tremendous emotional release. In a moment of empathetic identification, he becomes "the outsetting bard": "now in a moment I know what I am for, I awake/ . . . Never more the cries of unsatisfied love be absent from me." The boy becomes the poet the moment he recognizes that loss and unfulfillment are both his subject matter and his fate: his awakened songs will be fueled by "the fire, the sweet hell within,/ The unknown want, the destiny of me."

At the climax of **"Out of the Cradle,"** the boy/poet wonders if "the sweet hell within" will burn forever unquenched and if so whether he will be able to bear it. "O give me the clew!" he cries, "O if I am to have so much, let me have more!" In the **"Clef Poem"** of 1856, the clew (or clef) was that "A vast similitude interlocks all"—including "All identities that have existed or may exist on this globe." In **"Out of the Cradle"** the clew is a musical clef or key: the "low and delicious word death" whispered by the sea in mantric repetition. It offers a merging and engulfing in which the fire will be quenched and identity obliterated:

> . . . edging near as privately for me rustling at
>   my feet,
> Creeping thence steadily up to my ears and
>   laving me softly all over,
> Death, death, death, death, death.

In sensory terms, both he-bird and boy/poet are suffering from touch-deprivation, a need that originates in infancy. In the womb the fetus is surrounded by, is steeped in, amniotic fluid; it also feels the systole and diastole of the maternal heartbeat and experiences the mother's motions as a gentle rocking. After birth, this condition is replicated outside the womb: swaddling increases tactile stimulation and engulfing; lulling, humming sounds recall the maternal heartbeat, which is often mimed in an infant's first sounds (mama, papa); and cradle-rocking approximates the floating sensation. Against this sensory background, the appositeness of the later-added, often-lamented, penultimate line of the poem becomes clear:

> That strong and delicious word which,
>   creeping to my feet,

> (Or like some old crone rocking the cradle,
>   swathed in sweet garments, bending aside,)
> The sea whisper'd me.

In the climactic revelation of **"When Lilacs Last in the Dooryard Bloom'd,"** death is once again imaged as a maternal liquidity in which the synesthetic richness of infantile feeling/touch is recovered. But the Lincoln elegy conducts itself in a manner very different from that of **"Out of the Cradle"** and offers a much richer orchestration of its themes. Three natural objects dominate the poem: star, lilac, and bird. The "great star early droop'd in the western sky in the night" is Hesper, the evening star (the planet Venus when seen in the western sky). It is an elegiac trope of long standing (see, for example, the four-line Greek lyric attributed to Plato that Shelley used as the epigraph for *Adonais*). But the star also has a personal meaning for the American elegist. The drooping star with the countenance full of woe that Whitman saw in Washington in March 1865 came to be associated by him with the death the following month of President Lincoln, "the sweetest, wisest soul of all my days and lands." At the limit of visual perception, the star functions as a determine symbol (or in de Man's sense an allegory) of the dead leader.

The lilac, blooming in April, has "heart-shaped leaves of rich green, [and] many a pointed blossom rising delicate." A sprig from it, ritually bestowed in section 6, is the funereal offering (another elegiac convention), the token of the poet's grief. In perceptual terms, the lilac is proximate sight plus scent ("the perfume strong I love," the "mastering odor"). Figurally, as the poem opens out geographically from "the dooryard fronting an old farm-house near the white-wash'd palings" to the continental expanse of America, "the varied and ample land," the lilac "blooming perennial" becomes a synecdochal symbol of natural process and cyclic renewal ("ever-returning spring"). The third of the poem's trio of natural facts is the solitary hermit-thrush, whose song comes from "the swamp in the dimness." Here, the sensory mode is first hearing then hearing/touch. Since the bird speaks for himself, it is perhaps best considered not as a figure of speech, but as a character in a psychodrama representing an awareness in the dark depths of the speaker's being—of the "knowledge of death" that finally supersedes "the thought of death."

The sensory and perceptual movement of **"Lilacs"** is, then, from distanced sight, through proximate sight and scent, to hearing and hearing/touch, and finally (as we shall see) to non-perceptual insight; from star to lilac to bird's song to vision. The movement from the dominance of the lilac to the dominance of the thrush also recapitulates Whitman's development from 1855 to 1865. As the lilac "With every leaf a miracle" recalls the natural supernaturalism of **"Song of Myself,"** so the solitary singing bird recalls the he-bird of **"Out of** the Cradle"—the "singer solitary, projecting me." As in that poem, the turning point of **"Lilacs"** comes when "the voice of my spirit tallied the song of the bird." It is in its climactic vision of a Civil War battlefield that **"Lilacs"** finally goes beyond **"Out of the Cradle."**

On the thematic level, the star is the "thought of death" (the death of Lincoln); it is associated with "black murk" and "the long black trail" of the funeral journey of the murdered President's corpse through the cities draped in black. This awareness is internalized as "the harsh surrounding cloud that will not free my soul" that keeps Whitman from tallying with the song of the bird. Because of its consolatory and renovative potential, the lilac and what it symbolizes also detains the speaker. The description of the diurnal movement of the sun in section 12 invites an analogy between the phases of a human life and the phases of the day. Each part of the non-linear pattern is welcome and fulfilling, including the inevitable arrival of "the welcome night and the stars," while something more than acceptance is offered by the repeatedly emphasized timelessness of natural process: the "ever-returning spring"; "the endless grass"; "the trees prolific"; the growing wheat, "every grain from its shroud in the dark-brown fields uprisen," with its nearly explicit suggestion of a corresponding human triumph over the temporal. And in section 11, to adorn the walls of "the burial-house of him I love" the poet selects "Pictures of growing spring and farms and homes . . . With the fresh herbage under foot." Implicit here is what **"Crossing Brooklyn Ferry"** made explicit: natural wonders furnish their parts for eternity, for the soul.

In 1865, however, this is not the last word. The "beautiful fable" of 1856 is alluded to, but it is not believed. In **"Lilacs,"** Whitman does not succumb to the temptation (in de Man's words) "for the self to borrow . . . the temporal stability that it lacks from nature" (197). The pill of an authentically human destiny is swallowed—but it is heavily coated with sugar. Whitman finally hears the bird's song, "liquid and free and tender," after he has "fled forth to the hiding receiving night . . . Down to the shores of the water, the path by the swamp in the dimness." As Helen Vendler has noted, while in the periodic stanzas of the rest of the poem long lines and long sentences that drop to a conclusion are "the embedded syntactic figure for the temporality of all life and action," the rhythm of the death carol is "not periodic. Rather, like the waves of the ocean . . . it is recursive, recurrent, undulant, self-reflexive, self-perpetuating"; it expands "into oceanic and cosmic space" ("Reading" 145-46).

The drooping star in the sky, the burgeoning land and swelling sun are all apprehended visually; the dark swamp is not seen but heard and felt. There is no perception of objects by a subject, but a merging, an engulfment. In the death carol, all is soothing and soft: "Lost in the loving floating ocean of thee,/Laved in the flood of thy bliss O Death." This is haptic absorption, a "nestling close" in the "sureenwinding arms of cool-enfolding death." It is a version of being steeped amid honeyed morphine and squeezed in the fakes of death. This black hole absorbs into it the sunlit world celebrated in the earlier sections of the poem: "the sights of the open landscape and the high-spread sky . . . And life and the fields . . . the myriad fields and the prairies wide." It also sucks in earlier texts of Whitman: the "objects and knowledge curious" of **"There Was a Child"**; the "life and joy" and "the dense-pack'd cities" of **"Song of Myself;"** the teeming wharves and ways" of **"Crossing Brooklyn Ferry"**; "The ocean shore and the husky whispering wave" of **"Out of the Cradle."**

As in **"Song of Myself,"** immersion in touch brings an expansion of consciousness: "the sight that was bound in my eyes unclosed,/ As to long panoramas of visions." But the vision of section 15 is very different from that of section 5 and 29 of **"Song of Myself."** There is no sense of experiential immortality or of sprouts prolific and vital; and the other senses are not heightened, but curtailed—sight is blinkered and hearing entirely suppressed:

> And I saw askant the armies,
> I saw as in noiseless dreams hundreds of battle-flags,
> Borne through the smoke of the battles and pierc'd with missiles I saw them,
> And carried hither and you through the smoke, and torn and bloody,
> And at last but a few shreds left on the staffs, (and all in silence,)
> And the staffs all splinter'd and broken.
> I saw battle-corpses, myriads of them,
> And the white skeletons of young men, I saw them,
> I saw the debris and debris of all the slain soldiers of the war,
> But I saw they were not as was thought,
> They themselves were fully at rest, they suffer'd not,
> The living remain'd and suffer'd, the mother suffer'd,
> And the wife and the child and the musing comrade suffer'd,
> And the armies that remained suffer'd.

In the first stanza, seeing "askant" means not seeing soldiers pierced with missiles and torn and bloody; one sees only the battle flags and their staffs. It is these, not the limbs and bones of the soldiers, that are "all splinter'd and broken." Seeing "askant" also means seeing from a great distance. The second stanza cuts from the shredded flags and splintered staffs to corpses "fully at rest" and white skeletons, not a few but "myriads," including in this temporal as well as spatial panorama "all the slain soldiers of the war." This increase in visual distance has a blurring and numbing effect. At the distance necessary for panoramic vision, nothing hurts or disturbs. Moreover, to continue the cinematic analogy, the scene is filmed without sound; it is a noiseless battle. In the account of the naval battle in **"Song of Myself"** aural imagery was used to give a powerful sense of the suffering of the wounded and dying: "The hiss of the surgeon's knife and the gnawing teeth of his saw, / The wheeze, the cluck, the swash of falling blood. . . . the short wild scream, the long dull tapering groan" (#36). The suppression of sound here has exactly the opposite effect. It acts as a *cordon sanitaire* between the viewer and the horror of war.

Vendler has called attention to Whitman's "profound de-Christianizing" of the elegiac form in **"Lilacs,"** the plot of which she describes as the attempt "to find, in the language of perception, an equivalent for transcendence" ("Reading" 145, 136). But the poem's plot can be described another way—a preferable way for readers like myself who consider **"Lilacs"** a magnificent poem but find the death carol and the vision it evokes unwholesome—who prefer the Whitman of **"As I Ebb'd,"** compelled to recognize himself in the debris on the shore, to the anaesthetized vision of seeing "the debris of all the slain soldiers of the war." In Charles Feidelson's formulation, the symbolic objects in the poem "behave like characters in a drama, the plot of which is the achievement of a poetic utterance" (22). This self-reflexive aspect of the elegy is conspicuous in section 4, 10 and 16, which make explicit the poem's re-enactment of the problem explored in both **"Out of the Cradle"** and **"As I Ebb'd":** the problem of how to utter oneself, how to turn pain and suffering into poetry. At the end of the elegy, the completed utterance is foregrounded. A farewell to the poem's symbols is followed by the assurance that each and all of them have nonetheless been kept, and then by the offering of the completed poem to the memory of its subject:

> and this for his dear sake,
> Lilac and star and bird twined with the chant
>   of my soul,
> There in the fragrant pines and the cedars
>   dusk and dim.

The poem is not only the funereal offering of the poet Whitman (as the lilac sprig was of the grieving Whitman within the poem); it is also his version of the crucial substitution—not that but this—which is the turning point in the movement of elegy from loss to recompense. To say this is virtually to say that the ultimate consolation in **"Lilacs"** is the creative activity of the mind—the making of metaphors and other figures. The completed poem, and not simply the two most extraordinary of its component parts,

is the principal consolation for the loss that initially held the poet powerless and inarticulate.

. . . . .

In Whitman's later poetry, as has often been noted, the Romantic visionary was largely superseded by the public bard programmatically celebrating democracy, America and the spiritual evolution of mankind.[4] The shift from private to public was already marked by 1873, when at the age of fifty-three Whitman suffered a paralytic stroke and left Washington an invalid, moving to Camden, New Jersey, to live with one of his brothers. The stroke was the beginning of two decades of sharply curtailed physical activity and failing physical health—subjects to which he often referred in his letters, his prefaces and afterwords to editions of *Leaves of Grass,* and sometimes in his poems.

When Richard Maurice Bucke visited Whitman in 1880, however, he noted that the senses of the sixty-one-year-old poet remained "exceptionally acute, his hearing especially so," and that his "favorite occupation seemed to be strolling or sauntering about outdoors by himself, looking at the grass, the trees, the flowers, the vistas of light, the varying aspects of the sky, and listening to . . . all the hundreds of natural sounds. It was evident that these things gave him a feeling of pleasure far beyond what they give to ordinary people" (216, 220). The literary result of these saunterings were the **"Nature-notes 1877-'81"** (collected in *Specimen Days*), which consist of numberous passages of "spontaneous" natural description written "on the spot" (690, 807). In these notes, "all the senses, [that is] sight, sound, smell, [are] delicately gratified" (876).[5]

In two self-reflexive passages of the **"Nature-notes,"** Whitman made extremely interesting observations on his new way of perceiving the external world:

> The *emotional* aspects and influences of Nature! I, too, like the rest, feel these modern tendencies (from all the prevailing intellections, literature and poems,) to turn everything to pathos, ennui, morbidity, dissatisfaction, death. Yet how clear it is to me that those are not the born results, influences of Nature at all, but of one's own distorted, sick or silly soul. Here, amid this wild, free scene, how healthy, how joyous, how clean and vigorous and sweet! (813-14)

> [Even in the presence of a magnificent July dawn, he felt] not the weight of sentiment or mystery, or passion's ecstasy indefinable—not the religious sense, the varied All, distill'd and sublimated into one, of the night just described. Every star now clear-cut, showing for just what it is, there in the colorless ether. The character of the heralded morning, ineffably sweet and fresh and limpid, but for the esthetic sense alone, and for purity without sentiment. (826)

The "modern tendencies" described in the first passage are the dark side of the common nineteenth-century assumption that (in Francis Jeffrey's formulation) "the very essence of poetry . . . consists in the fine perception and vivid expression of that subtle and mysterious Analogy which exists between the physical and the moral world" (474). The second passage rejects the other *raison d'être* of symbolic perception: the sense sublime of natural phenomena symbolizing the transcendent. Instead, the older Whitman looks at nature without subjective projection. Looking naively rather than sentimentally, he finds a tonic freshness and health and a purity without sentiment.

"**Nature-notes,**" then, records Whitman's partial recovery of the aesthetic mode of perception of the child who went forth every day. But unlike the child, the older Whitman is self-conscious and reflective and thus aware of the symbiotic bond between himself and what he perceives:

> there comes a time . . . when one feels through his whole being, and pronouncedly the emotional part, that identity between himself subjectively and Nature objectively which Schelling and Fichte are so fond of pressing. How it is I know not, but I often realize a presence here—in clear moods I am certain of it, and neither chemistry nor reasoning nor esthetics will give the least explanation. All the past two summers it has been strengthening and nourishing my sick body and soul, as never before. (809)

Friedrich Schelling and Johann Fichte were proponents of *Naturphilosophie,* the doctrine that all phenomena, including the human self, are organically related and maintained in being by a force energized by the opposition of polar powers. The doctrine may be regarded as a philosophical cum scientific amplification of the Romantic sense of the one life within and abroad. The weeds mentioned at the end of the passage recall the elder and mullen and pokeweed enumerated at the end of the representation of expanded consciousness in section 5 of "**Song of Myself.**" But the differences between the two passages are more telling than the similarities. In the latter, the "delicious medicine" (809) is not the elixir of touch but the less intoxicating objects of the senses of sight, sound and smell. As a result, there is reciprocity but not merging, invigoration but not ecstasy.

One July evening, however ("the night just described" referred to in a passage above), Whitman had an experience different in kind from those described in the other "**Nature-notes**":

> from a little after 9 till 11 the atmosphere and the whole show above were in [a] state of exceptional clearness and glory . . . A large part of the sky seem'd just laid in great splashes of phosphorous.

You could look deeper in, farther through, than usual; the orbs thick as heads of wheat in a field. [There was] a curious general luminousness throughout to sight, sense, and soul . . . There, in abstraction and stillness . . . the copiousness, the removedness, vitally, loose-clear-crowdedness, of that stellar concave spreading overhead, softly absorb'd into me, rising so free, interminably high, stretching east, west, north, south—and I, though but a point in the center below, embodying all.

> As if for the first time, indeed, creation noiselessly sank into and through me its placid and untellable lesson . . . the visible suggestion of God in space and time—now once definitely indicated, if never again. The untold pointed at—the heavens all paved with it. (825)

The elemental Wordsworthian grandeur of the sky, particularly its unusual depth, perceived by a combination of sight and feeling/touch (here called "sense"), triggers an expansion of consciousness experience. In Whitman's terminology it is "the religious sense [of] the varied All, distill'd and sublimated into one" (826); in the cognate terms used elsewhere in this study, it is the sublime sense of the infinite symbolized by the finite—"the visible suggestion of God in space and time."

Was the one-life medicine, which on one extraordinary occasion rose to definite transcendent intimations, sufficient to reconcile the aging poet to his temporal destiny, which had been his antagonist in 1855-6 and his suffocating savior in "**Out of the Cradle**" and "**Lilacs**"? Two short poems of natural description, written a few years before Whitman's death in 1892 at the age of seventy-two, suggest that the correct answer is *yes* and *no*. In "**Twilight,**" the recognition of mortality is explicit:

> The soft voluptuous opiate shades,
> The sun just gone, the eager light dispell'd—
>   (I too will soon be gone, dispell'd,)
> A haze—nirwana—rest and night—oblivion.

This is Whitman's last poetic registration of longing to be merged, steeped, squeezed, floated, laved, enwound, enfolded in some numbing oceanic continuum. In the other poem, "**A Prairie Sunset,**" the recognition of mortality (here implicit) prompts a different reaction:

> Shot gold, maroon and violet, dazzling silver,
>   emerald, fawn,
> The earth's whole amplitude and Nature's
>   multiform power consign'd for once to
>   colors;
> The light, the general air possess'd by them—
>   colors till now unknown,

No limit, confine—not the Western sky
    alone—the high meridian—North, South,
    all,
Pure luminous color fighting the silent
    shadows to the last.

In **"Song of Myself,"** Whitman had described his response to a spectacular daybreak: "The air tastes good to my palate . . . / Something I cannot see puts upward libidinous prongs, / Seas of bright juice suffuse heaven." The "dazzling and tremendous" sunrise would "kill" him, he says, if he could not meet it as an equal, "could not now and always send sunrise out of me" (#24-25). But this abounding egotism and figural exuberance, an epitome of the alpha point of his poetic career, was now four decades in the past. **"A Prairie Sunset"** is an epitome of the omega point. The aged poet is not competing with the spectacular sunset, as the younger poet did with the dawn; in tandem with the setting sun, he is fighting the silent shadows to the last.

Notes

[1] In referring to the speaker of "Song of Myself" as Whitman, I do not mean to suggest that in every physical particular the "I" of the poem is identical with its author. The difference between the physical health of the "mythic Whitman persona" and that of "Whitman's flesh-and-blood self" (3) is discussed in Harold Aspiz' *Walt Whitman and the Body Beautiful*. Aspiz also shows that Whitman's interest in the body and the physiological and medical lore of his time informs the first editions of *Leaves of Grass*. In another cultural study, *Healing the Republic: The Language of Health and the Culture of Nationalism in Nineteenth-Century America*, Joan Burbick discusses the "biodemocracy" of the early editions of *Leaves of Grass*, in which "the healthy body [is] the perfect 'natural symbol' for the nation"—a figuration that presupposes Whitman's "ability to represent the felt sensations of the healthy body in poetic language" (116-30). In a note (322-3n), Burbick usefully summarizes other recent work on Whitman and the body.

[2] Coleridge's typology anticipates the discoveries of modern neurological science. For example, (*a*) "retentive power extinguishing the sense of touch" describes the loss of salience that is the result of sustained contact between animate and inanimate objects. When neurons are in a constant state of stimulation from the same identifiable source, after a short interval they will stop transmitting the 'on' message. An everyday example is the rapidity with which one forgets about the clothes one is wearing. Their touch becomes a "mere feeling" of presence. Concerning (*b*), "touch with retentive power": areas like the lips and fingertips are exceptionally receptive and contain a much greater density of highly specialized touch neurons than a less sensitive area like the back. There are surface receptors and subcutaneous receptors; in each case some of the receptors are quickly adapting and some slowly adapting. Their co-presence accounts for the "retentive" quality of tactile impressions in these areas.

[3] "Crossing Brooklyn Ferry" closely approximates Abrams' paradigm of poems that "present a determinate speaker in a particularized, and usually a localized, outdoor setting, whom we overhear as he carries on, in a fluent vernacular which rises easily to more formal speech, a sustained colloquy, sometimes with himself or with the outer scene, but more frequently with a silent human auditor, present or absent. The speaker begins with a description of the landscape . . . [a meditative movement of mind is evoked] which remains closely intervolved with the outer scene. [At the poem's climax, the speaker has an insight or realization.] Often the poem rounds upon itself to end where it began, at the outer scene, but with an altered mood and deepened understanding which is the result of the intervening meditation" (*Breeze* 76-7).

[4] The qualitative implications for Whitman's poetry were summarized by Wallace Stevens: "It is useless to treat everything in Whitman as of equal merit. A great deal of it exhibits little or none of his specific power. He seems often to have driven himself to write like himself. The good things, the superbly beautiful and moving things, are those that he wrote naturally, with an extemporaneous and irrepressible vehemence of emotion" (*Letters* 871).

[5] Here are two examples:

> *June 19th, 4 to 6[:30] p.m.*—Sitting alone by the creek . . . the wild flageolet-note of a quail near by—the just-heard fretting of some hylas down there in the pond—crows cawing in the distance—a drove of young hogs rooting in soft ground near the oak under which I sit—some come sniffing near me, and then scamper away, with grunts. And still the clear notes of the quail—the quiver of leaf-shadows over the paper as I write . . . the swift darting of many sand-swallows coming and going, their homes in the neighboring marl-bank—the odor of the cedar and oak, so palpable, as evening approaches—perfume, color, the bronze-and-gold of nearly ripen'd wheat—clover-fields, with honey-scent—the well-up maize, with long and rustling leaves—the great patches of thriving potatoes, dusky green, fleck'd all over with white blossoms—the old, warty, venerable oak above me—and ever, mix'd with the dual notes of the quail, the soughing of the wind through some near-by pines. (787)

> . . . *9th [March]*.—A snowstorm in the morning, and continuing most of the day. But I took a walk over two hours . . . amid the falling flakes. No wind, yet the musical low murmur through the pines, quite pronounced, curious, like waterfalls,

now still'd, now pouring again . . . Every snowflake lay where it fell on the evergreens, hollytrees, laurels, &c., the multitudinous leaves and branches piled, bulging-white, defined by edge-lines of emerald— the tall straight columns of the plentiful bronze-topt pines—a slight resinous odor blending with that of the snow. (876)

Note on Texts and Citations

COLERIDGE In quoting from Coleridge, I have used wherever possible the editions in the *Collected Works,* general editor Kathleen Coburn. The text for quotations from the poems is Ernest Hartley Coleridge's edition of the *Complete Poetical Works.* . . .

EMERSON Unless otherwise noted, the text for quotations from Emerson is the Library of America edition of *Essays and Lectures,* edited by Joel Porte. . . .

THOREAU Wherever possible, the texts for quotations from Thoreau's works are those in the Princeton University Press edition of his works. For later entries from the *Journal* I have used the fourteen-volume Torrey and Allen edition of 1906.

WHITMAN Unless otherwise indicated, the text of all quotations from Whitman's poetry and prose is the Library of America edition of the *Complete Poetry and Collected Prose,* edited by Justin Kaplan. This edition includes the text of the 1855 edition of *Leaves of Grass,* which is cited for the poems that first appeared in it (e.g., "Song of Myself" and "There Was a Child Went Forth"). But quotations from "Song of Myself" are identified by the section divisions Whitman later added to the poem.

WORDSWORTH Unless otherwise noted, the text for all quotations from Wordsworth's poetry (except the *Prelude*) and prose is the *Poetical Works,* edited by E. de Selincourt and Helen Darbishire. For the *Prelude* I have used *The Prelude 1799, 1805, 1850,* edited by Jonathan Wordsworth, M.H. Abrams, and Stephen Gill. Unless otherwise indicated, the 1805 version is the text cited. Line numbers are parenthetically supplied for quotations from the *Prelude.* Similar information is supplied for other poems only when its absence would make a passage difficult to find.

In addition to shortened forms of titles, the following abbreviations are used in citations:

PW: Wordsworth's *Poetical Works*

J: Thoreau's *Journal* (Torrey and Allen edition)

*J: Thoreau's *Journal* (Princeton edition)

SM: Coleridge's *Statesman's Manual*

FURTHER READING

Allen, Gay Wilson. *Walt Whitman as Man, Poet, and Legend.* Carbondale: Southern Illinois University Press, 1961, 260 p.

　　Includes biographical information, discussion and analysis of Whitman's poetry, a survey of the twentieth-century critical assessment of Whitman, and a bibliography.

Aspiz, Harold. *Walt Whitman and the Body Beautiful.* Urbana: University of Illinois Press, 1980, 290 p.

　　Studies Whitman's views on the human body within the context of the scientific knowledge and morality of the time.

Clarke, Graham. *Walt Whitman: The Poem as Private History.* London: Vision Press, 1991, 176 p.

　　Examines Whitman's poetry as a proclamation of an "ideal American self" which includes both a light, ideal side as well as Whitman's dark, neurotic, ambiguous side.

Erkkila, Betsy. *Whitman the Political Poet.* New York: Oxford University Press, 1989, 360 p.

　　Explores Whitman's overt politics as well as "the more subtle and less conscious" political undertones in his poetry.

Greenspan, Ezra. *Walt Whitman and the American Reader.* Cambridge: Cambridge University Press, 1990, 267 p.

　　Reviews Whitman's biography within the context of the nature of American literary culture from 1820 to 1850, and studies Whitman's poetry and its reception throughout the nineteenth century.

————, ed. *The Cambridge Companion to Walt Whitman.* Cambridge: Cambridge University Press, 1995, 234 p.

　　Collection of essays concerned with such themes as the treatment of the Civil War, politics, and the nature of selfhood in Whitman's poetry, as well as with topics such as Whitman's poetics and the response to his work among nineteenth-century women readers.

Hunt, Russell A. "Whitman's Poetics and the Unity of 'Calamus.'" *American Literature* 46, No. 1 (March 1974): 482-94.

　　Argues that each poem in the "Calamus" section of *Leaves of Grass* should be read as part of "an organic whole," and that the entire section is more rich and complex than a simple expression of homoeroticism.

Kaplan, Justin. *Walt Whitman: A Life.* New York: Simon and Schuster, 1980, 429 p.

　　Critical biography of Whitman.

Killingsworth, Myrth Jimmie. "Whitman and Motherhood: A Historical View." *American Literature* 54, No. 1 (March 1982): 28-43.

>   Maintains that Whitman's views on women's rights and motherhood should be read within the context of nineteenth-century thought, and suggests that Whitman's poetry on this subject is "notoriously bad" due to both cultural and personal confusion regarding the role of women in society.

Loving, Jerome. "Emerson and Whitman in the 1850s." In *Emerson, Whitman, and the American Muse,* pp. 83-108. Chapel Hill: University of North Carolina Press, 1982.

>   Traces the influence Emerson and Whitman had on one another's work.

Perlman, Jim, Ed Folsom, and Dan Campion, eds. *Walt Whitman: The Measure of His Song.* Minneapolis: Holy Cow! Press, 1981, 394 p.

>   Collection of reprinted poems and essays by poets and writers who have recorded their responses to Whitman and his work.

Pollak, Vivian R. "'In Loftiest Spheres': Whitman's Visionary Feminism." In *Breaking Bounds: Whitman and American Cultural Studies,* ed. by Betsy Erkkila and Jay Grossman, pp. 92-111. New York: Oxford University Press, 1996.

>   Analyzes Whitman's feminism and antifeminism, arguing that while Whitman resisted "linguistically totalizing norms" he nevertheless embraced the cult of motherhood of the time.

Reynolds, David S. *Walt Whitman's America: A Cultural Biography.* New York: Alfred A. Knopf, 1995, 671 p.

>   A critical biography studying Whitman's life within the context of nineteenth-century American culture and history.

Thomas, M. Wynn. *The Lunar Light of Whitman's Poetry.* Cambridge, Mass.: Harvard University Press, 1987, 313 p.

>   Explores Whitman's poetry as a product of and response to the historical circumstances of the poet's time, which the critic describes as a "Period of Social Crisis."

For additional coverage of Whitman's life and career, see the following sources published by The Gale Group: *Poetry Criticism,* Vol. 3; *World Literature Criticism, 1500 to the Present;* **and** *Dictionary of Literary Biography,* **Vols. 3 and 64.**

Nineteenth-Century Literature Criticism

Cumulative Indexes
Volumes 1-81

How to Use This Index

The main references

Calvino, Italo
1923–1985 .... CLC 5, 8, 11, 22, 33, 39,
73; SSC 3

list all author entries in the following Gale Literary Criticism series:

BLC = *Black Literature Criticism*
CLC = *Contemporary Literary Criticism*
CLR = *Children's Literature Review*
CMLC = *Classical and Medieval Literature Criticism*
DA = *DISCovering Authors*
DAB = *DISCovering Authors: British*
DAC = *DISCovering Authors: Canadian*
DAM = *DISCovering Authors: Modules*
    DRAM: *Dramatists Module;* *MST*: *Most-Studied Authors Module;*
    MULT: *Multicultural Authors Module;* *NOV*: *Novelists Module;*
    POET: *Poets Module;* *POP*: *Popular Fiction and Genre Authors Module*
DC = *Drama Criticism*
HLC = *Hispanic Literature Criticism*
LC = *Literature Criticism from 1400 to 1800*
NCLC = *Nineteenth-Century Literature Criticism*
PC = *Poetry Criticism*
SSC = *Short Story Criticism*
TCLC = *Twentieth-Century Literary Criticism*
WLC = *World Literature Criticism, 1500 to the Present*

The cross-references

See also CANR 23; CA 85-88;
obituary CA116

list all author entries in the following Gale biographical and literary sources:

AAYA = *Authors & Artists for Young Adults*
AITN = *Authors in the News*
BEST = *Bestsellers*
BW = *Black Writers*
CA = *Contemporary Authors*
CAAS = *Contemporary Authors Autobiography Series*
CABS = *Contemporary Authors Bibliographical Series*
CANR = *Contemporary Authors New Revision Series*
CAP = *Contemporary Authors Permanent Series*
CDALB = *Concise Dictionary of American Literary Biography*
CDBLB = *Concise Dictionary of British Literary Biography*
DLB = *Dictionary of Literary Biography*
DLBD = *Dictionary of Literary Biography Documentary Series*
DLBY = *Dictionary of Literary Biography Yearbook*
HW = *Hispanic Writers*
JRDA = *Junior DISCovering Authors*
MAICYA = *Major Authors and Illustrators for Children and Young Adults*
MTCW = *Major 20th-Century Writers*
NNAL = *Native North American Literature*
SAAS = *Something about the Author Autobiography Series*
SATA = *Something about the Author*
YABC = *Yesterday's Authors of Books for Children*

Literary Criticism Series
Cumulative Author Index

Alberti, Rafael 1902- **CLC 7**
See also CA 85-88; CANR 81; DLB 108; HW
2
Albert the Great 1200(?)-1280 **CMLC 16**
See also DLB 115
Alcala-Galiano, Juan Valera y
See Valera y Alcala-Galiano, Juan
Alcott, Amos Bronson 1799-1888 **NCLC 1**
See also DLB 1
Alcott, Louisa May 1832-1888 **NCLC 6, 58;
DA; DAB; DAC; DAM MST, NOV; SSC
27; WLC**
See also AAYA 20; CDALB 1865-1917; CLR
1, 38; DA3; DLB 1, 42, 79; DLBD 14; JRDA;
MAICYA; SATA 100; YABC 1
Aldanov, M. A.
See Aldanov, Mark (Alexandrovich)
Aldanov, Mark (Alexandrovich) 1886(?)-1957
TCLC 23
See also CA 118
Aldington, Richard 1892-1962 **CLC 49**
See also CA 85-88; CANR 45; DLB 20, 36, 100,
149
Aldiss, Brian W(ilson) 1925- **CLC 5, 14, 40;
DAM NOV; SSC 36**
See also CA 5-8R; CAAS 2; CANR 5, 28, 64;
DLB 14; MTCW 1, 2; SATA 34
Alegria, Claribel 1924-**CLC 75; DAM MULT;
HLCS 1; PC 26**
See also CA 131; CAAS 15; CANR 66; DLB
145; HW 1; MTCW 1
Alegria, Fernando 1918- **CLC 57**
See also CA 9-12R; CANR 5, 32, 72; HW 1, 2
Aleichem, Sholom **TCLC 1, 35; SSC 33**
See also Rabinovitch, Sholem
Aleixandre, Vicente 1898-1984
See also CANR 81; HLCS 1; HW 2
Alepoudelis, Odysseus
See Elytis, Odysseus
Aleshkovsky, Joseph 1929-
See Aleshkovsky, Yuz
See also CA 121; 128
Aleshkovsky, Yuz **CLC 44**
See also Aleshkovsky, Joseph
Alexander, Lloyd (Chudley) 1924- **CLC 35**
See also AAYA 1, 27; CA 1-4R; CANR 1, 24,
38, 55; CLR 1, 5, 48; DLB 52; JRDA;
MAICYA; MTCW 1; SAAS 19; SATA 3, 49,
81
Alexander, Meena 1951- **CLC 121**
See also CA 115; CANR 38, 70
Alexander, Samuel 1859-1938 **TCLC 77**
Alexie, Sherman (Joseph, Jr.) 1966- **CLC 96;
DAM MULT**
See also AAYA 28; CA 138; CANR 65; DA3;
DLB 175, 206; MTCW 1; NNAL
Alfau, Felipe 1902- **CLC 66**
See also CA 137
Alger, Horatio, Jr. 1832-1899 **NCLC 8**
See also DLB 42; SATA 16
Algren, Nelson 1909-1981**CLC 4, 10, 33; SSC
33**
See also CA 13-16R; 103; CANR 20, 61;
CDALB 1941-1968; DLB 9; DLBY 81, 82;
MTCW 1, 2
Ali, Ahmed 1910- **CLC 69**
See also CA 25-28R; CANR 15, 34
Alighieri, Dante
See Dante
Allan, John B.
See Westlake, Donald E(dwin)
Allan, Sidney
See Hartmann, Sadakichi

Allan, Sydney
See Hartmann, Sadakichi
Allen, Edward 1948- **CLC 59**
Allen, Fred 1894-1956 **TCLC 87**
Allen, Paula Gunn 1939- **CLC 84; DAM
MULT**
See also CA 112; 143; CANR 63; DA3; DLB
175; MTCW 1; NNAL
Allen, Roland
See Ayckbourn, Alan
Allen, Sarah A.
See Hopkins, Pauline Elizabeth
Allen, Sidney H.
See Hartmann, Sadakichi
Allen, Woody 1935- **CLC 16, 52; DAM POP**
See also AAYA 10; CA 33-36R; CANR 27, 38,
63; DLB 44; MTCW 1
Allende, Isabel 1942- **CLC 39, 57, 97; DAM
MULT, NOV; HLC 1; WLCS**
See also AAYA 18; CA 125; 130; CANR 51,
74; DA3; DLB 145; HW 1, 2; INT 130;
MTCW 1, 2
Alleyn, Ellen
See Rossetti, Christina (Georgina)
Allingham, Margery (Louise) 1904-1966**CLC
19**
See also CA 5-8R; 25-28R; CANR 4, 58; DLB
77; MTCW 1, 2
Allingham, William 1824-1889 **NCLC 25**
See also DLB 35
Allison, Dorothy E. 1949- **CLC 78**
See also CA 140; CANR 66; DA3; MTCW 1
Allston, Washington 1779-1843 **NCLC 2**
See also DLB 1
Almedingen, E. M. **CLC 12**
See also Almedingen, Martha Edith von
See also SATA 3
Almedingen, Martha Edith von 1898-1971
See Almedingen, E. M.
See also CA 1-4R; CANR 1
Almodovar, Pedro 1949(?)-**CLC 114; HLCS 1**
See also CA 133; CANR 72; HW 2
Almqvist, Carl Jonas Love 1793-1866 **N C L C
42**
Alonso, Damaso 1898-1990 **CLC 14**
See also CA 110; 131; 130; CANR 72; DLB
108; HW 1, 2
Alov
See Gogol, Nikolai (Vasilyevich)
Alta 1942- **CLC 19**
See also CA 57-60
Alter, Robert B(ernard) 1935- **CLC 34**
See also CA 49-52; CANR 1, 47
Alther, Lisa 1944- **CLC 7, 41**
See also CA 65-68; CAAS 30; CANR 12, 30,
51; MTCW 1
Althusser, L.
See Althusser, Louis
Althusser, Louis 1918-1990 **CLC 106**
See also CA 131; 132
Altman, Robert 1925- **CLC 16, 116**
See also CA 73-76; CANR 43
Alurista 1949-
See Urista, Alberto H.
See also DLB 82; HLCS 1
Alvarez, A(lfred) 1929- **CLC 5, 13**
See also CA 1-4R; CANR 3, 33, 63; DLB 14,
40
Alvarez, Alejandro Rodriguez 1903-1965
See Casona, Alejandro
See also CA 131; 93-96; HW 1
Alvarez, Julia 1950- **CLC 93; HLCS 1**
See also AAYA 25; CA 147; CANR 69; DA3;

MTCW 1
Alvaro, Corrado 1896-1956 **TCLC 60**
See also CA 163
Amado, Jorge 1912- CLC 13, 40, 106; DAM
MULT, NOV; HLC 1
See also CA 77-80; CANR 35, 74; DLB 113;
HW 2; MTCW 1, 2
Ambler, Eric 1909-1998 **CLC 4, 6, 9**
See also CA 9-12R; 171; CANR 7, 38, 74; DLB
77; MTCW 1, 2
Amichai, Yehuda 1924- **CLC 9, 22, 57, 116**
See also CA 85-88; CANR 46, 60; MTCW 1
Amichai, Yehudah
See Amichai, Yehuda
Amiel, Henri Frederic 1821-1881 **NCLC 4**
Amis, Kingsley (William) 1922-1995**CLC 1, 2,
3, 5, 8, 13, 40, 44; DA; DAB; DAC; DAM
MST, NOV**
See also AITN 2; CA 9-12R; 150; CANR 8, 28,
54; CDBLB 1945-1960; DA3; DLB 15, 27,
100, 139; DLBY 96; INT CANR-8; MTCW
1, 2
Amis, Martin (Louis) 1949-**CLC 4, 9, 38, 62,
101**
See also BEST 90:3; CA 65-68; CANR 8, 27,
54, 73; DA3; DLB 14, 194; INT CANR-27;
MTCW 1
Ammons, A(rchie) R(andolph) 1926-**CLC 2, 3,
5, 8, 9, 25, 57, 108; DAM POET; PC 16**
See also AITN 1; CA 9-12R; CANR 6, 36, 51,
73; DLB 5, 165; MTCW 1, 2
Amo, Tauraatua i
See Adams, Henry (Brooks)
Amory, Thomas 1691(?)-1788 **LC 48**
Anand, Mulk Raj 1905- **CLC 23, 93; DAM
NOV**
See also CA 65-68; CANR 32, 64; MTCW 1, 2
Anatol
See Schnitzler, Arthur
Anaximander c. 610B.C.-c. 546B.C.**CMLC 22**
Anaya, Rudolfo A(lfonso) 1937- **CLC 23;
DAM MULT, NOV; HLC 1**
See also AAYA 20; CA 45-48; CAAS 4; CANR
1, 32, 51; DLB 82, 206; HW 1; MTCW 1, 2
Andersen, Hans Christian 1805-1875**NCLC 7,
79; DA; DAB; DAC; DAM MST, POP;
SSC 6; WLC**
See also CLR 6; DA3; MAICYA; SATA 100;
YABC 1
Anderson, C. Farley
See Mencken, H(enry) L(ouis); Nathan, George
Jean
Anderson, Jessica (Margaret) Queale 1916-
CLC 37
See also CA 9-12R; CANR 4, 62
Anderson, Jon (Victor) 1940- **CLC 9; DAM
POET**
See also CA 25-28R; CANR 20
Anderson, Lindsay (Gordon) 1923-1994**C L C
20**
See also CA 125; 128; 146; CANR 77
Anderson, Maxwell 1888-1959**TCLC 2; DAM
DRAM**
See also CA 105; 152; DLB 7; MTCW 2
Anderson, Poul (William) 1926- **CLC 15**
See also AAYA 5; CA 1-4R; CAAS 2; CANR
2, 15, 34, 64; CLR 58; DLB 8; INT CANR-
15; MTCW 1, 2; SATA 90; SATA-Brief 39;
SATA-Essay 106
Anderson, Robert (Woodruff) 1917-**CLC 23;
DAM DRAM**
See also AITN 1; CA 21-24R; CANR 32; DLB
7

Anderson, Sherwood 1876-1941 **TCLC 1, 10, 24; DA; DAB; DAC; DAM MST, NOV; SSC 1; WLC**
See also AAYA 30; CA 104; 121; CANR 61; CDALB 1917-1929; DA3; DLB 4, 9, 86; DLBD 1; MTCW 1, 2

Andier, Pierre
See Desnos, Robert

Andouard
See Giraudoux, (Hippolyte) Jean

Andrade, Carlos Drummond de   **CLC 18**
See also Drummond de Andrade, Carlos

Andrade, Mario de 1893-1945   **TCLC 43**

Andreae, Johann V(alentin) 1586-1654 **LC 32**
See also DLB 164

Andreas-Salome, Lou 1861-1937   **TCLC 56**
See also CA 178; DLB 66

Andress, Lesley
See Sanders, Lawrence

Andrewes, Lancelot 1555-1626   **LC 5**
See also DLB 151, 172

Andrews, Cicily Fairfield
See West, Rebecca

Andrews, Elton V.
See Pohl, Frederik

Andreyev, Leonid (Nikolaevich) 1871-1919 **TCLC 3**
See also CA 104

Andric, Ivo 1892-1975   **CLC 8; SSC 36**
See also CA 81-84; 57-60; CANR 43, 60; DLB 147; MTCW 1

Androvar
See Prado (Calvo), Pedro

Angelique, Pierre
See Bataille, Georges

Angell, Roger 1920-   **CLC 26**
See also CA 57-60; CANR 13, 44, 70; DLB 171, 185

Angelou, Maya 1928- **CLC 12, 35, 64, 77; BLC 1; DA; DAB; DAC; DAM MST, MULT, POET, POP; WLCS**
See also AAYA 7, 20; BW 2, 3; CA 65-68; CANR 19, 42, 65; CDALBS; CLR 53; DA3; DLB 38; MTCW 1, 2; SATA 49

Anna Comnena 1083-1153   **CMLC 25**

Annensky, Innokenty (Fyodorovich) 1856-1909 **TCLC 14**
See also CA 110; 155

Annunzio, Gabriele d'
See D'Annunzio, Gabriele

Anodos
See Coleridge, Mary E(lizabeth)

Anon, Charles Robert
See Pessoa, Fernando (Antonio Nogueira)

Anouilh, Jean (Marie Lucien Pierre) 1910-1987 **CLC 1, 3, 8, 13, 40, 50; DAM DRAM; DC 8**
See also CA 17-20R; 123; CANR 32; MTCW 1, 2

Anthony, Florence
See Ai

Anthony, John
See Ciardi, John (Anthony)

Anthony, Peter
See Shaffer, Anthony (Joshua); Shaffer, Peter (Levin)

Anthony, Piers 1934-   **CLC 35; DAM POP**
See also AAYA 11; CA 21-24R; CANR 28, 56, 73; DLB 8; MTCW 1, 2; SAAS 22; SATA 84

Anthony, Susan B(rownell) 1916-1991 **TCLC 84**
See also CA 89-92; 134

Antoine, Marc

See Proust, (Valentin-Louis-George-Eugene-) Marcel

Antoninus, Brother
See Everson, William (Oliver)

Antonioni, Michelangelo 1912-   **CLC 20**
See also CA 73-76; CANR 45, 77

Antschel, Paul 1920-1970
See Celan, Paul
See also CA 85-88; CANR 33, 61; MTCW 1

Anwar, Chairil 1922-1949   **TCLC 22**
See also CA 121

Anzaldua, Gloria 1942-
See also CA 175; DLB 122; HLCS 1

Apess, William 1798-1839(?) **NCLC 73; DAM MULT**
See also DLB 175; NNAL

Apollinaire, Guillaume 1880-1918 **TCLC 3, 8, 51; DAM POET; PC 7**
See also Kostrowitzki, Wilhelm Apollinaris de
See also CA 152; MTCW 1

Appelfeld, Aharon 1932-   **CLC 23, 47**
See also CA 112; 133

Apple, Max (Isaac) 1941-   **CLC 9, 33**
See also CA 81-84; CANR 19, 54; DLB 130

Appleman, Philip (Dean) 1926-   **CLC 51**
See also CA 13-16R; CAAS 18; CANR 6, 29, 56

Appleton, Lawrence
See Lovecraft, H(oward) P(hillips)

Apteryx
See Eliot, T(homas) S(tearns)

Apuleius, (Lucius Madaurensis) 125(?)-175(?) **CMLC 1**
See also DLB 211

Aquin, Hubert 1929-1977   **CLC 15**
See also CA 105; DLB 53

Aquinas, Thomas 1224(?)-1274   **CMLC 33**
See also DLB 115

Aragon, Louis 1897-1982   **CLC 3, 22; DAM NOV, POET**
See also CA 69-72; 108; CANR 28, 71; DLB 72; MTCW 1, 2

Arany, Janos 1817-1882   **NCLC 34**

Aranyos, Kakay
See Mikszath, Kalman

Arbuthnot, John 1667-1735   **LC 1**
See also DLB 101

Archer, Herbert Winslow
See Mencken, H(enry) L(ouis)

Archer, Jeffrey (Howard) 1940-   **CLC 28; DAM POP**
See also AAYA 16; BEST 89:3; CA 77-80; CANR 22, 52; DA3; INT CANR-22

Archer, Jules 1915-   **CLC 12**
See also CA 9-12R; CANR 6, 69; SAAS 5; SATA 4, 85

Archer, Lee
See Ellison, Harlan (Jay)

Arden, John 1930- **CLC 6, 13, 15; DAM DRAM**
See also CA 13-16R; CAAS 4; CANR 31, 65, 67; DLB 13; MTCW 1

Arenas, Reinaldo 1943-1990 **CLC 41; DAM MULT; HLC 1**
See also CA 124; 128; 133; CANR 73; DLB 145; HW 1; MTCW 1

Arendt, Hannah 1906-1975   **CLC 66, 98**
See also CA 17-20R; 61-64; CANR 26, 60; MTCW 1, 2

Aretino, Pietro 1492-1556   **LC 12**

Arghezi, Tudor 1880-1967   **CLC 80**
See also Theodorescu, Ion N.
See also CA 167

Arguedas, Jose Maria 1911-1969 **CLC 10, 18;**

HLCS 1
See also CA 89-92; CANR 73; DLB 113; HW 1

Argueta, Manlio 1936-   **CLC 31**
See also CA 131; CANR 73; DLB 145; HW 1

Arias, Ron(ald Francis) 1941-
See also CA 131; CANR 81; DAM MULT; DLB 82; HLC 1; HW 1, 2; MTCW 2

Ariosto, Ludovico 1474-1533   **LC 6**

Aristides
See Epstein, Joseph

Aristophanes 450B.C.-385B.C. **CMLC 4; DA; DAB; DAC; DAM DRAM, MST; DC 2; WLCS**
See also DA3; DLB 176

Aristotle 384B.C.-322B.C.   **CMLC 31; DA; DAB; DAC; DAM MST; WLCS**
See also DA3; DLB 176

Arlt, Roberto (Godofredo Christophersen) 1900-1942 **TCLC 29; DAM MULT; HLC 1**
See also CA 123; 131; CANR 67; HW 1, 2

Armah, Ayi Kwei 1939- **CLC 5, 33; BLC 1; DAM MULT, POET**
See also BW 1; CA 61-64; CANR 21, 64; DLB 117; MTCW 1

Armatrading, Joan 1950-   **CLC 17**
See also CA 114

Arnette, Robert
See Silverberg, Robert

Arnim, Achim von (Ludwig Joachim von Arnim) 1781-1831   **NCLC 5; SSC 29**
See also DLB 90

Arnim, Bettina von 1785-1859   **NCLC 38**
See also DLB 90

Arnold, Matthew 1822-1888 **NCLC 6, 29; DA; DAB; DAC; DAM MST, POET; PC 5; WLC**
See also CDBLB 1832-1890; DLB 32, 57

Arnold, Thomas 1795-1842   **NCLC 18**
See also DLB 55

Arnow, Harriette (Louisa) Simpson 1908-1986 **CLC 2, 7, 18**
See also CA 9-12R; 118; CANR 14; DLB 6; MTCW 1, 2; SATA 42; SATA-Obit 47

Arouet, Francois-Marie
See Voltaire

Arp, Hans
See Arp, Jean

Arp, Jean 1887-1966   **CLC 5**
See also CA 81-84; 25-28R; CANR 42, 77

Arrabal
See Arrabal, Fernando

Arrabal, Fernando 1932-   **CLC 2, 9, 18, 58**
See also CA 9-12R; CANR 15

Arreola, Juan Jose 1918-
See also CA 113; 131; CANR 81; DAM MULT; DLB 113; HLC 1; HW 1, 2

Arrick, Fran   **CLC 30**
See also Gaberman, Judie Angell

Artaud, Antonin (Marie Joseph) 1896-1948 **TCLC 3, 36; DAM DRAM**
See also CA 104; 149; DA3; MTCW 1

Arthur, Ruth M(abel) 1905-1979   **CLC 12**
See also CA 9-12R; 85-88; CANR 4; SATA 7, 26

Artsybashev, Mikhail (Petrovich) 1878-1927 **TCLC 31**
See also CA 170

Arundel, Honor (Morfydd) 1919-1973 **CLC 17**
See also CA 21-22; 41-44R; CAP 2; CLR 35; SATA 4; SATA-Obit 24

Arzner, Dorothy 1897-1979   **CLC 98**

Asch, Sholem 1880-1957   **TCLC 3**
See also CA 105

Ash, Shalom
  See Asch, Sholem
Ashbery, John (Lawrence) 1927-**CLC 2, 3, 4,**
    6, 9, 13, 15, 25, 41, 77; DAM POET; PC 26
  See also CA 5-8R; CANR 9, 37, 66; DA3; DLB
    5, 165; DLBY 81; INT CANR-9; MTCW 1,
    2
Ashdown, Clifford
  See Freeman, R(ichard) Austin
Ashe, Gordon
  See Creasey, John
Ashton-Warner, Sylvia (Constance) 1908-1984
    CLC 19
  See also CA 69-72; 112; CANR 29; MTCW 1,
    2
Asimov, Isaac 1920-1992 **CLC 1, 3, 9, 19, 26,**
    76, 92; DAM POP
  See also AAYA 13; BEST 90:2; CA 1-4R; 137;
    CANR 2, 19, 36, 60; CLR 12; DA3; DLB 8;
    DLBY 92; INT CANR-19; JRDA; MAICYA;
    MTCW 1, 2; SATA 1, 26, 74
Assis, Joaquim Maria Machado de
  See Machado de Assis, Joaquim Maria
Astley, Thea (Beatrice May) 1925- **CLC 41**
  See also CA 65-68; CANR 11, 43, 78
Aston, James
  See White, T(erence) H(anbury)
Asturias, Miguel Angel 1899-1974 **CLC 3, 8,**
    13; DAM MULT, NOV; HLC 1
  See also CA 25-28; 49-52; CANR 32; CAP 2;
    DA3; DLB 113; HW 1; MTCW 1, 2
Atares, Carlos Saura
  See Saura (Atares), Carlos
Atheling, William
  See Pound, Ezra (Weston Loomis)
Atheling, William, Jr.
  See Blish, James (Benjamin)
Atherton, Gertrude (Franklin Horn) 1857-1948
    TCLC 2
  See also CA 104; 155; DLB 9, 78, 186
Atherton, Lucius
  See Masters, Edgar Lee
Atkins, Jack
  See Harris, Mark
Atkinson, Kate   **CLC 99**
  See also CA 166
Attaway, William (Alexander) 1911-1986**CLC**
    92; BLC 1; DAM MULT
  See also BW 2, 3; CA 143; CANR 82; DLB 76
Atticus
  See Fleming, Ian (Lancaster); Wilson, (Thomas)
    Woodrow
Atwood, Margaret (Eleanor) 1939-**CLC 2, 3,**
    4, 8, 13, 15, 25, 44, 84; DA; DAB; DAC;
    DAM MST, NOV, POET; PC 8; SSC 2;
    WLC
  See also AAYA 12; BEST 89:2; CA 49-52;
    CANR 3, 24, 33, 59; DA3; DLB 53; INT
    CANR-24; MTCW 1, 2; SATA 50
Aubigny, Pierre d'
  See Mencken, H(enry) L(ouis)
Aubin, Penelope 1685-1731(?)   **LC 9**
  See also DLB 39
Auchincloss, Louis (Stanton) 1917-**CLC 4, 6,**
    9, 18, 45; DAM NOV; SSC 22
  See also CA 1-4R; CANR 6, 29, 55; DLB 2;
    DLBY 80; INT CANR-29; MTCW 1
Auden, W(ystan) H(ugh) 1907-1973**CLC 1, 2,**
    3, 4, 6, 9, 11, 14, 43; DA; DAB; DAC; DAM
    DRAM, MST, POET; PC 1; WLC
  See also AAYA 18; CA 9-12R; 45-48; CANR
    5, 61; CDBLB 1914-1945; DA3; DLB 10,
    20; MTCW 1, 2

Audiberti, Jacques 1900-1965 **CLC 38; DAM**
    DRAM
  See also CA 25-28R
Audubon, John James 1785-1851   **NCLC 47**
Auel, Jean M(arie) 1936- **CLC 31, 107; DAM**
    POP
  See also AAYA 7; BEST 90:4; CA 103; CANR
    21, 64; DA3; INT CANR-21; SATA 91
Auerbach, Erich 1892-1957   **TCLC 43**
  See also CA 118; 155
Augier, Emile 1820-1889   **NCLC 31**
  See also DLB 192
August, John
  See De Voto, Bernard (Augustine)
Augustine 354-430**CMLC 6; DA; DAB; DAC;**
    DAM MST; WLCS
  See also DA3; DLB 115
Aurelius
  See Bourne, Randolph S(illiman)
Aurobindo, Sri
  See Ghose, Aurabinda
Austen, Jane 1775-1817**NCLC 1, 13, 19, 33, 51,**
    81; DA; DAB; DAC; DAM MST, NOV;
    WLC
  See also AAYA 19; CDBLB 1789-1832; DA3;
    DLB 116
Auster, Paul 1947-   **CLC 47**
  See also CA 69-72; CANR 23, 52, 75; DA3;
    MTCW 1
Austin, Frank
  See Faust, Frederick (Schiller)
Austin, Mary (Hunter) 1868-1934 **TCLC 25**
  See also CA 109; 178; DLB 9, 78, 206
Averroes 1126-1198   **CMLC 7**
  See also DLB 115
Avicenna 980-1037   **CMLC 16**
  See also DLB 115
Avison, Margaret 1918- **CLC 2, 4, 97; DAC;**
    DAM POET
  See also CA 17-20R; DLB 53; MTCW 1
Axton, David
  See Koontz, Dean R(ay)
Ayckbourn, Alan 1939- **CLC 5, 8, 18, 33, 74;**
    DAB; DAM DRAM
  See also CA 21-24R; CANR 31, 59; DLB 13;
    MTCW 1, 2
Aydy, Catherine
  See Tennant, Emma (Christina)
Ayme, Marcel (Andre) 1902-1967   **CLC 11**
  See also CA 89-92; CANR 67; CLR 25; DLB
    72; SATA 91
Ayrton, Michael 1921-1975   **CLC 7**
  See also CA 5-8R; 61-64; CANR 9, 21
Azorin   **CLC 11**
  See also Martinez Ruiz, Jose
Azuela, Mariano 1873-1952 **TCLC 3; DAM**
    MULT; HLC 1
  See also CA 104; 131; CANR 81; HW 1, 2;
    MTCW 1, 2
Baastad, Babbis Friis
  See Friis-Baastad, Babbis Ellinor
Bab
  See Gilbert, W(illiam) S(chwenck)
Babbis, Eleanor
  See Friis-Baastad, Babbis Ellinor
Babel, Isaac
  See Babel, Isaak (Emmanuilovich)
Babel, Isaak (Emmanuilovich) 1894-1941(?)
    TCLC 2, 13; SSC 16
  See also CA 104; 155; MTCW 1
Babits, Mihaly 1883-1941   **TCLC 14**
  See also CA 114
Babur 1483-1530   **LC 18**

Baca, Jimmy Santiago 1952-
  See also CA 131; CANR 81; DAM MULT; DLB
    122; HLC 1; HW 1, 2
Bacchelli, Riccardo 1891-1985   **CLC 19**
  See also CA 29-32R; 117
Bach, Richard (David) 1936- **CLC 14; DAM**
    NOV, POP
  See also AITN 1; BEST 89:2; CA 9-12R; CANR
    18; MTCW 1; SATA 13
Bachman, Richard
  See King, Stephen (Edwin)
Bachmann, Ingeborg 1926-1973   **CLC 69**
  See also CA 93-96; 45-48; CANR 69; DLB 85
Bacon, Francis 1561-1626   **LC 18, 32**
  See also CDBLB Before 1660; DLB 151
Bacon, Roger 1214(?)-1292   **CMLC 14**
  See also DLB 115
Bacovia, George   **TCLC 24**
  See also Vasiliu, Gheorghe
Badanes, Jerome 1937-   **CLC 59**
Bagehot, Walter 1826-1877   **NCLC 10**
  See also DLB 55
Bagnold, Enid 1889-1981   **CLC 25; DAM**
    DRAM
  See also CA 5-8R; 103; CANR 5, 40; DLB 13,
    160, 191; MAICYA; SATA 1, 25
Bagritsky, Eduard 1895-1934   **TCLC 60**
Bagrjana, Elisaveta
  See Belcheva, Elisaveta
Bagryana, Elisaveta 1893-1991   **CLC 10**
  See also Belcheva, Elisaveta
  See also CA 178; DLB 147
Bailey, Paul 1937-   **CLC 45**
  See also CA 21-24R; CANR 16, 62; DLB 14
Baillie, Joanna 1762-1851   **NCLC 71**
  See also DLB 93
Bainbridge, Beryl (Margaret) 1933-**CLC 4, 5,**
    8, 10, 14, 18, 22, 62; DAM NOV
  See also CA 21-24R; CANR 24, 55, 75; DLB
    14; MTCW 1, 2
Baker, Elliott 1922-   **CLC 8**
  See also CA 45-48; CANR 2, 63
Baker, Jean H.   **TCLC 3, 10**
  See also Russell, George William
Baker, Nicholson 1957- **CLC 61; DAM POP**
  See also CA 135; CANR 63; DA3
Baker, Ray Stannard 1870-1946   **TCLC 47**
  See also CA 118
Baker, Russell (Wayne) 1925-   **CLC 31**
  See also BEST 89:4; CA 57-60; CANR 11, 41,
    59; MTCW 1, 2
Bakhtin, M.
  See Bakhtin, Mikhail Mikhailovich
Bakhtin, M. M.
  See Bakhtin, Mikhail Mikhailovich
Bakhtin, Mikhail
  See Bakhtin, Mikhail Mikhailovich
Bakhtin, Mikhail Mikhailovich 1895-1975
    CLC 83
  See also CA 128; 113
Bakshi, Ralph 1938(?)-   **CLC 26**
  See also CA 112; 138
Bakunin, Mikhail (Alexandrovich) 1814-1876
    NCLC 25, 58
Baldwin, James (Arthur) 1924-1987**CLC 1, 2,**
    3, 4, 5, 8, 13, 15, 17, 42, 50, 67, 90; BLC 1;
    DA; DAB; DAC; DAM MST, MULT, NOV,
    POP; DC 1; SSC 10, 33; WLC
  See also AAYA 4; BW 1; CA 1-4R; 124; CABS
    1; CANR 3, 24; CDALB 1941-1968; DA3;
    DLB 2, 7, 33; DLBY 87; MTCW 1, 2; SATA
    9; SATA-Obit 54
Ballard, J(ames) G(raham) 1930-**CLC 3, 6, 14,**

36; **DAM NOV, POP; SSC 1**
See also AAYA 3; CA 5-8R; CANR 15, 39, 65;
DA3; DLB 14, 207; MTCW 1, 2; SATA 93
Balmont, Konstantin (Dmitriyevich) 1867-1943
TCLC 11
See also CA 109; 155
Baltausis, Vincas
See Mikszath, Kalman
Balzac, Honore de 1799-1850**NCLC 5, 35, 53;
DA; DAB; DAC; DAM MST, NOV; SSC
5; WLC**
See also DA3; DLB 119
Bambara, Toni Cade 1939-1995 **CLC 19, 88;
BLC 1; DA; DAC; DAM MST, MULT;
SSC 35; WLCS**
See also AAYA 5; BW 2, 3; CA 29-32R; 150;
CANR 24, 49, 81; CDALBS; DA3; DLB 38;
MTCW 1, 2
Bamdad, A.
See Shamlu, Ahmad
Banat, D. R.
See Bradbury, Ray (Douglas)
Bancroft, Laura
See Baum, L(yman) Frank
Banim, John 1798-1842   **NCLC 13**
See also DLB 116, 158, 159
Banim, Michael 1796-1874   **NCLC 13**
See also DLB 158, 159
Banjo, The
See Paterson, A(ndrew) B(arton)
Banks, Iain
See Banks, Iain M(enzies)
Banks, Iain M(enzies) 1954-   **CLC 34**
See also CA 123; 128; CANR 61; DLB 194;
INT 128
Banks, Lynne Reid   **CLC 23**
See also Reid Banks, Lynne
See also AAYA 6
Banks, Russell 1940-   **CLC 37, 72**
See also CA 65-68; CAAS 15; CANR 19, 52,
73; DLB 130
Banville, John 1945-   **CLC 46, 118**
See also CA 117; 128; DLB 14; INT 128
Banville, Theodore (Faullain) de 1832-1891
NCLC 9
Baraka, Amiri 1934-CLC 1, 2, 3, 5, 10, 14, 33,
115; BLC 1; DA; DAC; DAM MST, MULT,
POET, POP; DC 6; PC 4; WLCS**
See Jones, LeRoi
See also BW 2, 3; CA 21-24R; CABS 3; CANR
27, 38, 61; CDALB 1941-1968; DA3; DLB
5, 7, 16, 38; DLBD 8; MTCW 1, 2
Barbauld, Anna Laetitia 1743-1825**NCLC 50**
See also DLB 107, 109, 142, 158
Barbellion, W. N. P.   **TCLC 24**
See also Cummings, Bruce F(rederick)
Barbera, Jack (Vincent) 1945-   **CLC 44**
See also CA 110; CANR 45
Barbey d'Aurevilly, Jules Amedee 1808-1889
NCLC 1; SSC 17
See also DLB 119
Barbour, John c. 1316-1395   **CMLC 33**
See also DLB 146
Barbusse, Henri 1873-1935   **TCLC 5**
See also CA 105; 154; DLB 65
Barclay, Bill
See Moorcock, Michael (John)
Barclay, William Ewert
See Moorcock, Michael (John)
Barea, Arturo 1897-1957   **TCLC 14**
See also CA 111
Barfoot, Joan 1946-   **CLC 18**
See also CA 105

Barham, Richard Harris 1788-1845**NCLC 77**
See also DLB 159
Baring, Maurice 1874-1945   **TCLC 8**
See also CA 105; 168; DLB 34
Baring-Gould, Sabine 1834-1924   **TCLC 88**
See also DLB 156, 190
Barker, Clive 1952-   **CLC 52; DAM POP**
See also AAYA 10; BEST 90:3; CA 121; 129;
CANR 71; DA3; INT 129; MTCW 1, 2
Barker, George Granville 1913-1991 **CLC 8,
48; DAM POET**
See also CA 9-12R; 135; CANR 7, 38; DLB
20; MTCW 1
Barker, Harley Granville
See Granville-Barker, Harley
See also DLB 10
Barker, Howard 1946-   **CLC 37**
See also CA 102; DLB 13
Barker, Jane 1652-1732   **LC 42**
Barker, Pat(ricia) 1943-   **CLC 32, 94**
See also CA 117; 122; CANR 50; INT 122
Barlach, Ernst 1870-1938   **TCLC 84**
See also CA 178; DLB 56, 118
Barlow, Joel 1754-1812   **NCLC 23**
See also DLB 37
Barnard, Mary (Ethel) 1909-   **CLC 48**
See also CA 21-22; CAP 2
Barnes, Djuna 1892-1982**CLC 3, 4, 8, 11, 29;
SSC 3**
See also CA 9-12R; 107; CANR 16, 55; DLB
4, 9, 45; MTCW 1, 2
Barnes, Julian (Patrick) 1946- **CLC 42; DAB**
See also CA 102; CANR 19, 54; DLB 194;
DLBY 93; MTCW 1
Barnes, Peter 1931-   **CLC 5, 56**
See also CA 65-68; CAAS 12; CANR 33, 34,
64; DLB 13; MTCW 1
Barnes, William 1801-1886   **NCLC 75**
See also DLB 32
Baroja (y Nessi), Pio 1872-1956**TCLC 8; HLC
1**
See also CA 104
Baron, David
See Pinter, Harold
Baron Corvo
See Rolfe, Frederick (William Serafino Austin
Lewis Mary)
Barondess, Sue K(aufman) 1926-1977 **CLC 8**
See also Kaufman, Sue
See also CA 1-4R; 69-72; CANR 1
Baron de Teive
See Pessoa, Fernando (Antonio Nogueira)
Baroness Von S.
See Zangwill, Israel
Barres, (Auguste-) Maurice 1862-1923**TCLC
47**
See also CA 164; DLB 123
Barreto, Afonso Henrique de Lima
See Lima Barreto, Afonso Henrique de
Barrett, (Roger) Syd 1946-   **CLC 35**
Barrett, William (Christopher) 1913-1992
CLC 27
See also CA 13-16R; 139; CANR 11, 67; INT
CANR-11
Barrie, J(ames) M(atthew) 1860-1937 **TCLC
2; DAB; DAM DRAM**
See also CA 104; 136; CANR 77; CDBLB
1890-1914; CLR 16; DA3; DLB 10, 141,
156; MAICYA; MTCW 1; SATA 100; YABC
1
Barrington, Michael
See Moorcock, Michael (John)
Barrol, Grady

See Bograd, Larry
Barry, Mike
See Malzberg, Barry N(athaniel)
Barry, Philip 1896-1949   **TCLC 11**
See also CA 109; DLB 7
Bart, Andre Schwarz
See Schwarz-Bart, Andre
Barth, John (Simmons) 1930-CLC 1, 2, 3, 5, 7,
9, 10, 14, 27, 51, 89; DAM NOV; SSC 10**
See also AITN 1, 2; CA 1-4R; CABS 1; CANR
5, 23, 49, 64; DLB 2; MTCW 1
Barthelme, Donald 1931-1989**CLC 1, 2, 3, 5, 6,
8, 13, 23, 46, 59, 115; DAM NOV; SSC 2**
See also CA 21-24R; 129; CANR 20, 58; DA3;
DLB 2; DLBY 80, 89; MTCW 1, 2; SATA 7;
SATA-Obit 62
Barthelme, Frederick 1943-   **CLC 36, 117**
See also CA 114; 122; CANR 77; DLBY 85;
INT 122
Barthes, Roland (Gerard) 1915-1980**CLC 24,
83**
See also CA 130; 97-100; CANR 66; MTCW
1, 2
Barzun, Jacques (Martin) 1907-   **CLC 51**
See also CA 61-64; CANR 22
Bashevis, Isaac
See Singer, Isaac Bashevis
Bashkirtseff, Marie 1859-1884   **NCLC 27**
Basho
See Matsuo Basho
Basil of Caesaria c. 330-379   **CMLC 35**
Bass, Kingsley B., Jr.
See Bullins, Ed
Bass, Rick 1958-   **CLC 79**
See also CA 126; CANR 53; DLB 212
Bassani, Giorgio 1916-   **CLC 9**
See also CA 65-68; CANR 33; DLB 128, 177;
MTCW 1
Bastos, Augusto (Antonio) Roa
See Roa Bastos, Augusto (Antonio)
Bataille, Georges 1897-1962   **CLC 29**
See also CA 101; 89-92
Bates, H(erbert) E(rnest) 1905-1974**CLC 46;
DAB; DAM POP; SSC 10**
See also CA 93-96; 45-48; CANR 34; DA3;
DLB 162, 191; MTCW 1, 2
Bauchart
See Camus, Albert
Baudelaire, Charles 1821-1867 **NCLC 6, 29,
55; DA; DAB; DAC; DAM MST, POET;
PC 1; SSC 18; WLC**
See also DA3
Baudrillard, Jean 1929-   **CLC 60**
Baum, L(yman) Frank 1856-1919   **TCLC 7**
See also CA 108; 133; CLR 15; DLB 22; JRDA;
MAICYA; MTCW 1, 2; SATA 18, 100
Baum, Louis F.
See Baum, L(yman) Frank
Baumbach, Jonathan 1933-   **CLC 6, 23**
See also CA 13-16R; CAAS 5; CANR 12, 66;
DLBY 80; INT CANR-12; MTCW 1
Bausch, Richard (Carl) 1945-   **CLC 51**
See also CA 101; CAAS 14; CANR 43, 61; DLB
130
Baxter, Charles (Morley) 1947- **CLC 45, 78;
DAM POP**
See also CA 57-60; CANR 40, 64; DLB 130;
MTCW 2
Baxter, George Owen
See Faust, Frederick (Schiller)
Baxter, James K(eir) 1926-1972   **CLC 14**
See also CA 77-80
Baxter, John

Brief 27

Bennett, Louise (Simone) 1919-**CLC 28; BLC
    1; DAM MULT**
    See also BW 2, 3; CA 151; DLB 117
Benson, E(dward) F(rederic) 1867-1940
    TCLC 27
    See also CA 114; 157; DLB 135, 153
Benson, Jackson J. 1930-   **CLC 34**
    See also CA 25-28R; DLB 111
Benson, Sally 1900-1972   **CLC 17**
    See also CA 19-20; 37-40R; CAP 1; SATA 1,
    35; SATA-Obit 27
Benson, Stella 1892-1933   **TCLC 17**
    See also CA 117; 155; DLB 36, 162
Bentham, Jeremy 1748-1832   **NCLC 38**
    See also DLB 107, 158
Bentley, E(dmund) C(lerihew) 1875-1956
    TCLC 12
    See also CA 108; DLB 70
Bentley, Eric (Russell) 1916-   **CLC 24**
    See also CA 5-8R; CANR 6, 67; INT CANR-6
Beranger, Pierre Jean de 1780-1857**NCLC 34**
Berdyaev, Nicolas
    See Berdyaev, Nikolai (Aleksandrovich)
Berdyaev, Nikolai (Aleksandrovich) 1874-1948
    TCLC 67
    See also CA 120; 157
Berdyayev, Nikolai (Aleksandrovich)
    See Berdyaev, Nikolai (Aleksandrovich)
Berendt, John (Lawrence) 1939-   **CLC 86**
    See also CA 146; CANR 75; DA3; MTCW 1
Beresford, J(ohn) D(avys) 1873-1947 **TCLC
    81**
    See also CA 112; 155; DLB 162, 178, 197
Bergelson, David 1884-1952   **TCLC 81**
Berger, Colonel
    See Malraux, (Georges-)Andre
Berger, John (Peter) 1926-   **CLC 2, 19**
    See also CA 81-84; CANR 51, 78; DLB 14, 207
Berger, Melvin H. 1927-   **CLC 12**
    See also CA 5-8R; CANR 4; CLR 32; SAAS 2;
    SATA 5, 88
Berger, Thomas (Louis) 1924-**CLC 3, 5, 8, 11,
    18, 38; DAM NOV**
    See also CA 1-4R; CANR 5, 28, 51; DLB 2;
    DLBY 80; INT CANR-28; MTCW 1, 2
Bergman, (Ernst) Ingmar 1918- **CLC 16, 72**
    See also CA 81-84; CANR 33, 70; MTCW 2
Bergson, Henri(-Louis) 1859-1941 **TCLC 32**
    See also CA 164
Bergstein, Eleanor 1938-   **CLC 4**
    See also CA 53-56; CANR 5
Berkoff, Steven 1937-   **CLC 56**
    See also CA 104; CANR 72
Bermant, Chaim (Icyk) 1929-   **CLC 40**
    See also CA 57-60; CANR 6, 31, 57
Bern, Victoria
    See Fisher, M(ary) F(rances) K(ennedy)
Bernanos, (Paul Louis) Georges 1888-1948
    TCLC 3
    See also CA 104; 130; DLB 72
Bernard, April 1956-   **CLC 59**
    See also CA 131
Berne, Victoria
    See Fisher, M(ary) F(rances) K(ennedy)
Bernhard, Thomas 1931-1989 **CLC 3, 32, 61**
    See also CA 85-88; 127; CANR 32, 57; DLB
    85, 124; MTCW 1
Bernhardt, Sarah (Henriette Rosine) 1844-1923
    TCLC 75
    See also CA 157
Berriault, Gina 1926- **CLC 54, 109; SSC 30**
    See also CA 116; 129; CANR 66; DLB 130

Berrigan, Daniel 1921-   **CLC 4**
    See also CA 33-36R; CAAS 1; CANR 11, 43,
    78; DLB 5
Berrigan, Edmund Joseph Michael, Jr. 1934-
    1983
    See Berrigan, Ted
    See also CA 61-64; 110; CANR 14
Berrigan, Ted   **CLC 37**
    See also Berrigan, Edmund Joseph Michael, Jr.
    See also DLB 5, 169
Berry, Charles Edward Anderson 1931-
    See Berry, Chuck
    See also CA 115
Berry, Chuck   **CLC 17**
    See also Berry, Charles Edward Anderson
Berry, Jonas
    See Ashbery, John (Lawrence)
Berry, Wendell (Erdman) 1934- **CLC 4, 6, 8,
    27, 46; DAM POET; PC 28**
    See also AITN 1; CA 73-76; CANR 50, 73; DLB
    5, 6; MTCW 1
Berryman, John 1914-1972**CLC 1, 2, 3, 4, 6, 8,
    10, 13, 25, 62; DAM POET**
    See also CA 13-16; 33-36R; CABS 2; CANR
    35; CAP 1; CDALB 1941-1968; DLB 48;
    MTCW 1, 2
Bertolucci, Bernardo 1940-   **CLC 16**
    See also CA 106
Berton, Pierre (Francis Demarigny) 1920-
    CLC 104
    See also CA 1-4R; CANR 2, 56; DLB 68; SATA
    99
Bertrand, Aloysius 1807-1841   **NCLC 31**
Bertran de Born c. 1140-1215   **CMLC 5**
Besant, Annie (Wood) 1847-1933   **TCLC 9**
    See also CA 105
Bessie, Alvah 1904-1985   **CLC 23**
    See also CA 5-8R; 116; CANR 2, 80; DLB 26
Bethlen, T. D.
    See Silverberg, Robert
Beti, Mongo   CLC 27; BLC 1; DAM MULT
    See also Biyidi, Alexandre
    See also CANR 79
Betjeman, John 1906-1984 **CLC 2, 6, 10, 34,
    43; DAB; DAM MST, POET**
    See also CA 9-12R; 112; CANR 33, 56; CDBLB
    1945-1960; DA3; DLB 20; DLBY 84;
    MTCW 1, 2
Bettelheim, Bruno 1903-1990   **CLC 79**
    See also CA 81-84; 131; CANR 23, 61; DA3;
    MTCW 1, 2
Betti, Ugo 1892-1953   **TCLC 5**
    See also CA 104; 155
Betts, Doris (Waugh) 1932-   **CLC 3, 6, 28**
    See also CA 13-16R; CANR 9, 66, 77; DLBY
    82; INT CANR-9
Bevan, Alistair
    See Roberts, Keith (John Kingston)
Bey, Pilaff
    See Douglas, (George) Norman
Bialik, Chaim Nachman 1873-1934 **TCLC 25**
    See also CA 170
Bickerstaff, Isaac
    See Swift, Jonathan
Bidart, Frank 1939-   **CLC 33**
    See also CA 140
Bienek, Horst 1930-   **CLC 7, 11**
    See also CA 73-76; DLB 75
Bierce, Ambrose (Gwinett) 1842-1914(?)
    **TCLC 1, 7, 44; DA; DAC; DAM MST; SSC
    9; WLC**
    See also CA 104; 139; CANR 78; CDALB
    1865-1917; DA3; DLB 11, 12, 23, 71, 74,

186
Biggers, Earl Derr 1884-1933   **TCLC 65**
    See also CA 108; 153
Billings, Josh
    See Shaw, Henry Wheeler
Billington, (Lady) Rachel (Mary) 1942- **C L C
    43**
    See also AITN 2; CA 33-36R; CANR 44
Binyon, T(imothy) J(ohn) 1936-   **CLC 34**
    See also CA 111; CANR 28
Bioy Casares, Adolfo 1914-1999**CLC 4, 8, 13,
    88; DAM MULT; HLC 1; SSC 17**
    See also CA 29-32R; 177; CANR 19, 43, 66;
    DLB 113; HW 1, 2; MTCW 1, 2
Bird, Cordwainer
    See Ellison, Harlan (Jay)
Bird, Robert Montgomery 1806-1854**NCLC 1**
    See also DLB 202
Birkerts, Sven 1951-   **CLC 116**
    See also CA 128; 133; 176; CAAE 176; CAAS
    29; INT 133
Birney, (Alfred) Earle 1904-1995**CLC 1, 4, 6,
    11; DAC; DAM MST, POET**
    See also CA 1-4R; CANR 5, 20; DLB 88;
    MTCW 1
Biruni, al 973-1048(?)   **CMLC 28**
Bishop, Elizabeth 1911-1979 **CLC 1, 4, 9, 13,
    15, 32; DA; DAC; DAM MST, POET; PC
    3**
    See also CA 5-8R; 89-92; CABS 2; CANR 26,
    61; CDALB 1968-1988; DA3; DLB 5, 169;
    MTCW 1, 2; SATA-Obit 24
Bishop, John 1935-   **CLC 10**
    See also CA 105
Bissett, Bill 1939-   **CLC 18; PC 14**
    See also CA 69-72; CAAS 19; CANR 15; DLB
    53; MTCW 1
Bissoondath, Neil (Devindra) 1955-**CLC 120;
    DAC**
    See also CA 136
Bitov, Andrei (Georgievich) 1937-   **CLC 57**
    See also CA 142
Biyidi, Alexandre 1932-
    See Beti, Mongo
    See also BW 1, 3; CA 114; 124; CANR 81;
    DA3; MTCW 1, 2
Bjarme, Brynjolf
    See Ibsen, Henrik (Johan)
Bjoernson, Bjoernstjerne (Martinius) 1832-
    1910   **TCLC 7, 37**
    See also CA 104
Black, Robert
    See Holdstock, Robert P.
Blackburn, Paul 1926-1971   **CLC 9, 43**
    See also CA 81-84; 33-36R; CANR 34; DLB
    16; DLBY 81
Black Elk 1863-1950 **TCLC 33; DAM MULT**
    See also CA 144; MTCW 1; NNAL
Black Hobart
    See Sanders, (James) Ed(ward)
Blacklin, Malcolm
    See Chambers, Aidan
Blackmore, R(ichard) D(oddridge) 1825-1900
    TCLC 27
    See also CA 120; DLB 18
Blackmur, R(ichard) P(almer) 1904-1965
    CLC 2, 24
    See also CA 11-12; 25-28R; CANR 71; CAP 1;
    DLB 63
Black Tarantula
    See Acker, Kathy
Blackwood, Algernon (Henry) 1869-1951
    TCLC 5

See also CA 21-24R; CAAS 16; CANR 10; DLB 53

Bowering, Marilyn R(uthe) 1949- **CLC 32**
See also CA 101; CANR 49

Bowers, Edgar 1924- **CLC 9**
See also CA 5-8R; CANR 24; DLB 5

Bowie, David **CLC 17**
See also Jones, David Robert

Bowles, Jane (Sydney) 1917-1973 **CLC 3, 68**
See also CA 19-20; 41-44R; CAP 2

Bowles, Paul (Frederick) 1910- **CLC 1, 2, 19, 53; SSC 3**
See also CA 1-4R; CAAS 1; CANR 1, 19, 50, 75; DA3; DLB 5, 6; MTCW 1, 2

Box, Edgar
See Vidal, Gore

Boyd, Nancy
See Millay, Edna St. Vincent

Boyd, William 1952- **CLC 28, 53, 70**
See also CA 114; 120; CANR 51, 71

Boyle, Kay 1902-1992 **CLC 1, 5, 19, 58, 121; SSC 5**
See also CA 13-16R; 140; CAAS 1; CANR 29, 61; DLB 4, 9, 48, 86; DLBY 93; MTCW 1, 2

Boyle, Mark
See Kienzle, William X(avier)

Boyle, Patrick 1905-1982 **CLC 19**
See also CA 127

Boyle, T. C. 1948-
See Boyle, T(homas) Coraghessan

Boyle, T(homas) Coraghessan 1948- **CLC 36, 55, 90; DAM POP; SSC 16**
See also BEST 90:4; CA 120; CANR 44, 76; DA3; DLBY 86; MTCW 2

Boz
See Dickens, Charles (John Huffam)

Brackenridge, Hugh Henry 1748-1816 **NCLC 7**
See also DLB 11, 37

Bradbury, Edward P.
See Moorcock, Michael (John)
See also MTCW 2

Bradbury, Malcolm (Stanley) 1932- **CLC 32, 61; DAM NOV**
See also CA 1-4R; CANR 1, 33; DA3; DLB 14, 207; MTCW 1, 2

Bradbury, Ray (Douglas) 1920- **CLC 1, 3, 10, 15, 42, 98; DA; DAB; DAC; DAM MST, NOV, POP; SSC 29; WLC**
See also AAYA 15; AITN 1, 2; CA 1-4R; CANR 2, 30, 75; CDALB 1968-1988; DA3; DLB 2, 8; MTCW 1, 2; SATA 11, 64

Bradford, Gamaliel 1863-1932 **TCLC 36**
See also CA 160; DLB 17

Bradley, David (Henry), Jr. 1950- **CLC 23, 118; BLC 1; DAM MULT**
See also BW 1, 3; CA 104; CANR 26, 81; DLB 33

Bradley, John Ed(mund, Jr.) 1958- **CLC 55**
See also CA 139

Bradley, Marion Zimmer 1930- **CLC 30; DAM POP**
See also AAYA 9; CA 57-60; CAAS 10; CANR 7, 31, 51, 75; DA3; DLB 8; MTCW 1, 2; SATA 90

Bradstreet, Anne 1612(?)-1672 **LC 4, 30; DA; DAC; DAM MST, POET; PC 10**
See also CDALB 1640-1865; DA3; DLB 24

Brady, Joan 1939- **CLC 86**
See also CA 141

Bragg, Melvyn 1939- **CLC 10**
See also BEST 89:3; CA 57-60; CANR 10, 48;

DLB 14

Brahe, Tycho 1546-1601 **LC 45**

Braine, John (Gerard) 1922-1986 **CLC 1, 3, 41**
See also CA 1-4R; 120; CANR 1, 33; CDBLB 1945-1960; DLB 15; DLBY 86; MTCW 1

Bramah, Ernest 1868-1942 **TCLC 72**
See also CA 156; DLB 70

Brammer, William 1930(?)-1978 **CLC 31**
See also CA 77-80

Brancati, Vitaliano 1907-1954 **TCLC 12**
See also CA 109

Brancato, Robin F(idler) 1936- **CLC 35**
See also AAYA 9; CA 69-72; CANR 11, 45; CLR 32; JRDA; SAAS 9; SATA 97

Brand, Max
See Faust, Frederick (Schiller)

Brand, Millen 1906-1980 **CLC 7**
See also CA 21-24R; 97-100; CANR 72

Branden, Barbara **CLC 44**
See also CA 148

Brandes, Georg (Morris Cohen) 1842-1927 **TCLC 10**
See also CA 105

Brandys, Kazimierz 1916- **CLC 62**

Branley, Franklyn M(ansfield) 1915- **CLC 21**
See also CA 33-36R; CANR 14, 39; CLR 13; MAICYA; SAAS 16; SATA 4, 68

Brathwaite, Edward (Kamau) 1930- **CLC 11; BLCS; DAM POET**
See also BW 2, 3; CA 25-28R; CANR 11, 26, 47; DLB 125

Brautigan, Richard (Gary) 1935-1984 **CLC 1, 3, 5, 9, 12, 34, 42; DAM NOV**
See also CA 53-56; 113; CANR 34; DA3; DLB 2, 5, 206; DLBY 80, 84; MTCW 1; SATA 56

Brave Bird, Mary 1953-
See Crow Dog, Mary (Ellen)
See also NNAL

Braverman, Kate 1950- **CLC 67**
See also CA 89-92

Brecht, (Eugen) Bertolt (Friedrich) 1898-1956 **TCLC 1, 6, 13, 35; DA; DAB; DAC; DAM DRAM, MST; DC 3; WLC**
See also CA 104; 133; CANR 62; DA3; DLB 56, 124; MTCW 1, 2

Brecht, Eugen Berthold Friedrich
See Brecht, (Eugen) Bertolt (Friedrich)

Bremer, Fredrika 1801-1865 **NCLC 11**

Brennan, Christopher John 1870-1932 **TCLC 17**
See also CA 117

Brennan, Maeve 1917-1993 **CLC 5**
See also CA 81-84; CANR 72

Brent, Linda
See Jacobs, Harriet A(nn)

Brentano, Clemens (Maria) 1778-1842 **NCLC 1**
See also DLB 90

Brent of Bin Bin
See Franklin, (Stella Maria Sarah) Miles (Lampe)

Brenton, Howard 1942- **CLC 31**
See also CA 69-72; CANR 33, 67; DLB 13; MTCW 1

Breslin, James 1930-1996
See Breslin, Jimmy
See also CA 73-76; CANR 31, 75; DAM NOV; MTCW 1, 2

Breslin, Jimmy **CLC 4, 43**
See also Breslin, James
See also AITN 1; DLB 185; MTCW 2

Bresson, Robert 1901- **CLC 16**
See also CA 110; CANR 49

Breton, Andre 1896-1966 **CLC 2, 9, 15, 54; PC 15**
See also CA 19-20; 25-28R; CANR 40, 60; CAP 2; DLB 65; MTCW 1, 2

Breytenbach, Breyten 1939(?)- **CLC 23, 37; DAM POET**
See also CA 113; 129; CANR 61

Bridgers, Sue Ellen 1942- **CLC 26**
See also AAYA 8; CA 65-68; CANR 11, 36; CLR 18; DLB 52; JRDA; MAICYA; SAAS 1; SATA 22, 90; SATA-Essay 109

Bridges, Robert (Seymour) 1844-1930 **TCLC 1; DAM POET; PC 28**
See also CA 104; 152; CDBLB 1890-1914; DLB 19, 98

Bridie, James **TCLC 3**
See also Mavor, Osborne Henry
See also DLB 10

Brin, David 1950- **CLC 34**
See also AAYA 21; CA 102; CANR 24, 70; INT CANR-24; SATA 65

Brink, Andre (Philippus) 1935- **CLC 18, 36, 106**
See also CA 104; CANR 39, 62; INT 103; MTCW 1, 2

Brinsmead, H(esba) F(ay) 1922- **CLC 21**
See also CA 21-24R; CANR 10; CLR 47; MAICYA; SAAS 5; SATA 18, 78

Brittain, Vera (Mary) 1893(?)-1970 **CLC 23**
See also CA 13-16; 25-28R; CANR 58; CAP 1; DLB 191; MTCW 1, 2

Broch, Hermann 1886-1951 **TCLC 20**
See also CA 117; DLB 85, 124

Brock, Rose
See Hansen, Joseph

Brodkey, Harold (Roy) 1930-1996 **CLC 56**
See also CA 111; 151; CANR 71; DLB 130

Brodskii, Iosif
See Brodsky, Joseph

Brodsky, Iosif Alexandrovich 1940-1996
See Brodsky, Joseph
See also AITN 1; CA 41-44R; 151; CANR 37; DAM POET; DA3; MTCW 1, 2

Brodsky, Joseph 1940-1996 **CLC 4, 6, 13, 36, 100; PC 9**
See also Brodskii, Iosif; Brodsky, Iosif Alexandrovich
See also MTCW 1

Brodsky, Michael (Mark) 1948- **CLC 19**
See also CA 102; CANR 18, 41, 58

Bromell, Henry 1947- **CLC 5**
See also CA 53-56; CANR 9

Bromfield, Louis (Brucker) 1896-1956 **TCLC 11**
See also CA 107; 155; DLB 4, 9, 86

Broner, E(sther) M(asserman) 1930- **CLC 19**
See also CA 17-20R; CANR 8, 25, 72; DLB 28

Bronk, William (M.) 1918-1999 **CLC 10**
See also CA 89-92; 177; CANR 23; DLB 165

Bronstein, Lev Davidovich
See Trotsky, Leon

Bronte, Anne 1820-1849 **NCLC 71**
See also DA3; DLB 21, 199

Bronte, Charlotte 1816-1855 **NCLC 3, 8, 33, 58; DA; DAB; DAC; DAM MST, NOV; WLC**
See also AAYA 17; CDBLB 1832-1890; DA3; DLB 21, 159, 199

Bronte, Emily (Jane) 1818-1848 **NCLC 16, 35; DA; DAB; DAC; DAM MST, NOV, POET; PC 8; WLC**
See also AAYA 17; CDBLB 1832-1890; DA3; DLB 21, 32, 199

Brooke, Frances 1724-1789 **LC 6, 48**
See also DLB 39, 99
Brooke, Henry 1703(?)-1783 **LC 1**
See also DLB 39
Brooke, Rupert (Chawner) 1887-1915 **TCLC 2, 7; DA; DAB; DAC; DAM MST, POET; PC 24; WLC**
See also CA 104; 132; CANR 61; CDBLB 1914-1945; DLB 19; MTCW 1, 2
Brooke-Haven, P.
See Wodehouse, P(elham) G(renville)
Brooke-Rose, Christine 1926(?)- **CLC 40**
See also CA 13-16R; CANR 58; DLB 14
Brookner, Anita 1928- **CLC 32, 34, 51; DAB; DAM POP**
See also CA 114; 120; CANR 37, 56; DA3; DLB 194; DLBY 87; MTCW 1, 2
Brooks, Cleanth 1906-1994 **CLC 24, 86, 110**
See also CA 17-20R; 145; CANR 33, 35; DLB 63; DLBY 94; INT CANR-35; MTCW 1, 2
Brooks, George
See Baum, L(yman) Frank
Brooks, Gwendolyn 1917- **CLC 1, 2, 4, 5, 15, 49; BLC 1; DA; DAC; DAM MST, MULT, POET; PC 7; WLC**
See also AAYA 20; AITN 1; BW 2, 3; CA 1-4R; CANR 1, 27, 52, 75; CDALB 1941-1968; CLR 27; DA3; DLB 5, 76, 165; MTCW 1, 2; SATA 6
Brooks, Mel **CLC 12**
See also Kaminsky, Melvin
See also AAYA 13; DLB 26
Brooks, Peter 1938- **CLC 34**
See also CA 45-48; CANR 1
Brooks, Van Wyck 1886-1963 **CLC 29**
See also CA 1-4R; CANR 6; DLB 45, 63, 103
Brophy, Brigid (Antonia) 1929-1995 **CLC 6, 11, 29, 105**
See also CA 5-8R; 149; CAAS 4; CANR 25, 53; DA3; DLB 14; MTCW 1, 2
Brosman, Catharine Savage 1934- **CLC 9**
See also CA 61-64; CANR 21, 46
Brossard, Nicole 1943- **CLC 115**
See also CA 122; CAAS 16; DLB 53
Brother Antoninus
See Everson, William (Oliver)
The Brothers Quay
See Quay, Stephen; Quay, Timothy
Broughton, T(homas) Alan 1936- **CLC 19**
See also CA 45-48; CANR 2, 23, 48
Broumas, Olga 1949- **CLC 10, 73**
See also CA 85-88; CANR 20, 69
Brown, Alan 1950- **CLC 99**
See also CA 156
Brown, Charles Brockden 1771-1810 **NCLC 22, 74**
See also CDALB 1640-1865; DLB 37, 59, 73
Brown, Christy 1932-1981 **CLC 63**
See also CA 105; 104; CANR 72; DLB 14
Brown, Claude 1937- **CLC 30; BLC 1; DAM MULT**
See also AAYA 7; BW 1, 3; CA 73-76; CANR 81
Brown, Dee (Alexander) 1908- **CLC 18, 47; DAM POP**
See also AAYA 30; CA 13-16R; CAAS 6; CANR 11, 45, 60; DA3; DLBY 80; MTCW 1, 2; SATA 5, 110
Brown, George
See Wertmueller, Lina
Brown, George Douglas 1869-1902 **TCLC 28**
See also CA 162
Brown, George Mackay 1921-1996 **CLC 5, 48, 100**
See also CA 21-24R; 151; CAAS 6; CANR 12, 37, 67; DLB 14, 27, 139; MTCW 1; SATA 35
Brown, (William) Larry 1951- **CLC 73**
See also CA 130; 134; INT 133
Brown, Moses
See Barrett, William (Christopher)
Brown, Rita Mae 1944- **CLC 18, 43, 79; DAM NOV, POP**
See also CA 45-48; CANR 2, 11, 35, 62; DA3; INT CANR-11; MTCW 1, 2
Brown, Roderick (Langmere) Haig-
See Haig-Brown, Roderick (Langmere)
Brown, Rosellen 1939- **CLC 32**
See also CA 77-80; CAAS 10; CANR 14, 44
Brown, Sterling Allen 1901-1989 **CLC 1, 23, 59; BLC 1; DAM MULT, POET**
See also BW 1, 3; CA 85-88; 127; CANR 26; DA3; DLB 48, 51, 63; MTCW 1, 2
Brown, Will
See Ainsworth, William Harrison
Brown, William Wells 1813-1884 **NCLC 2; BLC 1; DAM MULT; DC 1**
See also DLB 3, 50
Browne, (Clyde) Jackson 1948(?)- **CLC 21**
See also CA 120
Browning, Elizabeth Barrett 1806-1861 **NCLC 1, 16, 61, 66; DA; DAB; DAC; DAM MST, POET; PC 6; WLC**
See also CDBLB 1832-1890; DA3; DLB 32, 199
Browning, Robert 1812-1889 **NCLC 19, 79; DA; DAB; DAC; DAM MST, POET; PC 2; WLCS**
See also CDBLB 1832-1890; DA3; DLB 32, 163; YABC 1
Browning, Tod 1882-1962 **CLC 16**
See also CA 141; 117
Brownson, Orestes Augustus 1803-1876 **NCLC 50**
See also DLB 1, 59, 73
Bruccoli, Matthew J(oseph) 1931- **CLC 34**
See also CA 9-12R; CANR 7; DLB 103
Bruce, Lenny **CLC 21**
See also Schneider, Leonard Alfred
Bruin, John
See Brutus, Dennis
Brulard, Henri
See Stendhal
Brulls, Christian
See Simenon, Georges (Jacques Christian)
Brunner, John (Kilian Houston) 1934-1995 **CLC 8, 10; DAM POP**
See also CA 1-4R; 149; CAAS 8; CANR 2, 37; MTCW 1, 2
Bruno, Giordano 1548-1600 **LC 27**
Brutus, Dennis 1924- **CLC 43; BLC 1; DAM MULT, POET; PC 24**
See also BW 2, 3; CA 49-52; CAAS 14; CANR 2, 27, 42, 81; DLB 117
Bryan, C(ourtlandt) D(ixon) B(arnes) 1936- **CLC 29**
See also CA 73-76; CANR 13, 68; DLB 185; INT CANR-13
Bryan, Michael
See Moore, Brian
Bryant, William Cullen 1794-1878 **NCLC 6, 46; DA; DAB; DAC; DAM MST, POET; PC 20**
See also CDALB 1640-1865; DLB 3, 43, 59, 189
Bryusov, Valery Yakovlevich 1873-1924 **TCLC 10**
See also CA 107; 155
Buchan, John 1875-1940 **TCLC 41; DAB; DAM POP**
See also CA 108; 145; DLB 34, 70, 156; MTCW 1; YABC 2
Buchanan, George 1506-1582 **LC 4**
See also DLB 152
Buchheim, Lothar-Guenther 1918- **CLC 6**
See also CA 85-88
Buchner, (Karl) Georg 1813-1837 **NCLC 26**
Buchwald, Art(hur) 1925- **CLC 33**
See also AITN 1; CA 5-8R; CANR 21, 67; MTCW 1, 2; SATA 10
Buck, Pearl S(ydenstricker) 1892-1973 **CLC 7, 11, 18; DA; DAB; DAC; DAM MST, NOV**
See also AITN 1; CA 1-4R; 41-44R; CANR 1, 34; CDALBS; DA3; DLB 9, 102; MTCW 1, 2; SATA 1, 25
Buckler, Ernest 1908-1984 **CLC 13; DAC; DAM MST**
See also CA 11-12; 114; CAP 1; DLB 68; SATA 47
Buckley, Vincent (Thomas) 1925-1988 **CLC 57**
See also CA 101
Buckley, William F(rank), Jr. 1925- **CLC 7, 18, 37; DAM POP**
See also AITN 1; CA 1-4R; CANR 1, 24, 53; DA3; DLB 137; DLBY 80; INT CANR-24; MTCW 1, 2
Buechner, (Carl) Frederick 1926- **CLC 2, 4, 6, 9; DAM NOV**
See also CA 13-16R; CANR 11, 39, 64; DLBY 80; INT CANR-11; MTCW 1, 2
Buell, John (Edward) 1927- **CLC 10**
See also CA 1-4R; CANR 71; DLB 53
Buero Vallejo, Antonio 1916- **CLC 15, 46**
See also CA 106; CANR 24, 49, 75; HW 1; MTCW 1, 2
Bufalino, Gesualdo 1920(?)- **CLC 74**
See also DLB 196
Bugayev, Boris Nikolayevich 1880-1934 **TCLC 7; PC 11**
See also Bely, Andrey
See also CA 104; 165; MTCW 1
Bukowski, Charles 1920-1994 **CLC 2, 5, 9, 41, 82, 108; DAM NOV, POET; PC 18**
See also CA 17-20R; 144; CANR 40, 62; DA3; DLB 5, 130, 169; MTCW 1, 2
Bulgakov, Mikhail (Afanas'evich) 1891-1940 **TCLC 2, 16; DAM DRAM, NOV; SSC 18**
See also CA 105; 152
Bulgya, Alexander Alexandrovich 1901-1956 **TCLC 53**
See also Fadeyev, Alexander
See also CA 117
Bullins, Ed 1935- **CLC 1, 5, 7; BLC 1; DAM DRAM, MULT; DC 6**
See also BW 2, 3; CA 49-52; CAAS 16; CANR 24, 46, 73; DLB 7, 38; MTCW 1, 2
Bulwer-Lytton, Edward (George Earle Lytton) 1803-1873 **NCLC 1, 45**
See also DLB 21
Bunin, Ivan Alexeyevich 1870-1953 **TCLC 6; SSC 5**
See also CA 104
Bunting, Basil 1900-1985 **CLC 10, 39, 47; DAM POET**
See also CA 53-56; 115; CANR 7; DLB 20
Bunuel, Luis 1900-1983 **CLC 16, 80; DAM MULT; HLC 1**
See also CA 101; 110; CANR 32, 77; HW 1
Bunyan, John 1628-1688 **LC 4; DA; DAB;**

DAC; DAM MST; WLC
See also CDBLB 1660-1789; DLB 39

Burckhardt, Jacob (Christoph) 1818-1897
NCLC 49

Burford, Eleanor
See Hibbert, Eleanor Alice Burford

Burgess, AnthonyCLC **1, 2, 4, 5, 8, 10, 13, 15, 22, 40, 62, 81, 94; DAB**
See also Wilson, John (Anthony) Burgess
See also AAYA 25; AITN 1; CDBLB 1960 to Present; DLB 14, 194; DLBY 98; MTCW 1

Burke, Edmund 1729(?)-1797 **LC 7, 36; DA; DAB; DAC; DAM MST; WLC**
See also CA DA3; DLB 104

Burke, Kenneth (Duva) 1897-1993 CLC **2, 24**
See also CA 5-8R; 143; CANR 39, 74; DLB 45, 63; MTCW 1, 2

Burke, Leda
See Garnett, David

Burke, Ralph
See Silverberg, Robert

Burke, Thomas 1886-1945 **TCLC 63**
See also CA 113; 155; DLB 197

Burney, Fanny 1752-1840 **NCLC 12, 54**
See also DLB 39

Burns, Robert 1759-1796 **LC 3, 29, 40; DA; DAB; DAC; DAM MST, POET; PC 6; WLC**
See also CDBLB 1789-1832; DA3; DLB 109

Burns, Tex
See L'Amour, Louis (Dearborn)

Burnshaw, Stanley 1906- **CLC 3, 13, 44**
See also CA 9-12R; DLB 48; DLBY 97

Burr, Anne 1937- **CLC 6**
See also CA 25-28R

Burroughs, Edgar Rice 1875-1950 **TCLC 2, 32; DAM NOV**
See also AAYA 11; CA 104; 132; DA3; DLB 8; MTCW 1, 2; SATA 41

Burroughs, William S(eward) 1914-1997CLC **1, 2, 5, 15, 22, 42, 75, 109; DA; DAB; DAC; DAM MST, NOV, POP; WLC**
See also AITN 2; CA 9-12R; 160; CANR 20, 52; DA3; DLB 2, 8, 16, 152; DLBY 81, 97; MTCW 1, 2

Burton, Sir Richard F(rancis) 1821-1890
NCLC 42
See also DLB 55, 166, 184

Busch, Frederick 1941- **CLC 7, 10, 18, 47**
See also CA 33-36R; CAAS 1; CANR 45, 73; DLB 6

Bush, Ronald 1946- **CLC 34**
See also CA 136

Bustos, F(rancisco)
See Borges, Jorge Luis

Bustos Domecq, H(onorio)
See Bioy Casares, Adolfo; Borges, Jorge Luis

Butler, Octavia E(stelle) 1947- **CLC 38, 121; BLCS; DAM MULT, POP**
See also AAYA 18; BW 2, 3; CA 73-76; CANR 12, 24, 38, 73; DA3; DLB 33; MTCW 1, 2; SATA 84

Butler, Robert Olen (Jr.) 1945-CLC **81; DAM POP**
See also CA 112; CANR 66; DLB 173; INT 112; MTCW 1

Butler, Samuel 1612-1680 **LC 16, 43**
See also DLB 101, 126

Butler, Samuel 1835-1902 **TCLC 1, 33; DA; DAB; DAC; DAM MST, NOV; WLC**
See also CA 143; CDBLB 1890-1914; DA3; DLB 18, 57, 174

Butler, Walter C.

See Faust, Frederick (Schiller)

Butor, Michel (Marie Francois) 1926-CLC **1, 3, 8, 11, 15**
See also CA 9-12R; CANR 33, 66; DLB 83; MTCW 1, 2

Butts, Mary 1892(?)-1937 **TCLC 77**
See also CA 148

Buzo, Alexander (John) 1944- **CLC 61**
See also CA 97-100; CANR 17, 39, 69

Buzzati, Dino 1906-1972 **CLC 36**
See also CA 160; 33-36R; DLB 177

Byars, Betsy (Cromer) 1928- **CLC 35**
See also AAYA 19; CA 33-36R; CANR 18, 36, 57; CLR 1, 16; DLB 52; INT CANR-18; JRDA; MAICYA; MTCW 1; SAAS 1; SATA 4, 46, 80; SATA-Essay 108

Byatt, A(ntonia) S(usan Drabble) 1936- **C L C 19, 65; DAM NOV, POP**
See also CA 13-16R; CANR 13, 33, 50, 75; DA3; DLB 14, 194; MTCW 1, 2

Byrne, David 1952- **CLC 26**
See also CA 127

Byrne, John Keyes 1926-
See Leonard, Hugh
See also CA 102; CANR 78; INT 102

Byron, George Gordon (Noel) 1788-1824
NCLC 2, 12; DA; DAB; DAC; DAM MST, POET; PC 16; WLC
See also CDBLB 1789-1832; DA3; DLB 96, 110

Byron, Robert 1905-1941 **TCLC 67**
See also CA 160; DLB 195

C. 3. 3.
See Wilde, Oscar

Caballero, Fernan 1796-1877 **NCLC 10**

Cabell, Branch
See Cabell, James Branch

Cabell, James Branch 1879-1958 **TCLC 6**
See also CA 105; 152; DLB 9, 78; MTCW 1

Cable, George Washington 1844-1925 **T C L C 4; SSC 4**
See also CA 104; 155; DLB 12, 74; DLBD 13

Cabral de Melo Neto, Joao 1920- **CLC 76; DAM MULT**
See also CA 151

Cabrera Infante, G(uillermo) 1929-CLC **5, 25, 45, 120; DAM MULT; HLC 1**
See also CA 85-88; CANR 29, 65; DA3; DLB 113; HW 1, 2; MTCW 1, 2

Cade, Toni
See Bambara, Toni Cade

Cadmus and Harmonia
See Buchan, John

Caedmon fl. 658-680 **CMLC 7**
See also DLB 146

Caeiro, Alberto
See Pessoa, Fernando (Antonio Nogueira)

Cage, John (Milton, Jr.) 1912-1992 **CLC 41**
See also CA 13-16R; 169; CANR 9, 78; DLB 193; INT CANR-9

Cahan, Abraham 1860-1951 **TCLC 71**
See also CA 108; 154; DLB 9, 25, 28

Cain, G.
See Cabrera Infante, G(uillermo)

Cain, Guillermo
See Cabrera Infante, G(uillermo)

Cain, James M(allahan) 1892-1977CLC **3, 11, 28**
See also AITN 1; CA 17-20R; 73-76; CANR 8, 34, 61; MTCW 1

Caine, Mark
See Raphael, Frederic (Michael)

Calasso, Roberto 1941- **CLC 81**

See also CA 143

Calderon de la Barca, Pedro 1600-1681 **L C 23; DC 3; HLCS 1**

Caldwell, Erskine (Preston) 1903-1987CLC **1, 8, 14, 50, 60; DAM NOV; SSC 19**
See also AITN 1; CA 1-4R; 121; CAAS 1; CANR 2, 33; DA3; DLB 9, 86; MTCW 1, 2

Caldwell, (Janet Miriam) Taylor (Holland) 1900-1985CLC **2, 28, 39; DAM NOV, POP**
See also CA 5-8R; 116; CANR 5; DA3; DLBD 17

Calhoun, John Caldwell 1782-1850NCLC **15**
See also DLB 3

Calisher, Hortense 1911-CLC **2, 4, 8, 38; DAM NOV; SSC 15**
See also CA 1-4R; CANR 1, 22, 67; DA3; DLB 2; INT CANR-22; MTCW 1, 2

Callaghan, Morley Edward 1903-1990CLC **3, 14, 41, 65; DAC; DAM MST**
See also CA 9-12R; 132; CANR 33, 73; DLB 68; MTCW 1, 2

Callimachus c. 305B.C.-c. 240B.C. **CMLC 18**
See also DLB 176

Calvin, John 1509-1564 **LC 37**

Calvino, Italo 1923-1985CLC **5, 8, 11, 22, 33, 39, 73; DAM NOV; SSC 3**
See also CA 85-88; 116; CANR 23, 61; DLB 196; MTCW 1, 2

Cameron, Carey 1952- **CLC 59**
See also CA 135

Cameron, Peter 1959- **CLC 44**
See also CA 125; CANR 50

Camoens, Luis Vaz de 1524(?)-1580
See also HLCS 1

Camoes, Luis de 1524(?)-1580
See also HLCS 1

Campana, Dino 1885-1932 **TCLC 20**
See also CA 117; DLB 114

Campanella, Tommaso 1568-1639 **LC 32**

Campbell, John W(ood, Jr.) 1910-1971 **C L C 32**
See also CA 21-22; 29-32R; CANR 34; CAP 2; DLB 8; MTCW 1

Campbell, Joseph 1904-1987 **CLC 69**
See also AAYA 3; BEST 89:2; CA 1-4R; 124; CANR 3, 28, 61; DA3; MTCW 1, 2

Campbell, Maria 1940- **CLC 85; DAC**
See also CA 102; CANR 54; NNAL

Campbell, (John) Ramsey 1946-CLC **42; SSC 19**
See also CA 57-60; CANR 7; INT CANR-7

Campbell, (Ignatius) Roy (Dunnachie) 1901-1957 **TCLC 5**
See also CA 104; 155; DLB 20; MTCW 2

Campbell, Thomas 1777-1844 **NCLC 19**
See also DLB 93; 144

Campbell, Wilfred **TCLC 9**
See also Campbell, William

Campbell, William 1858(?)-1918
See Campbell, Wilfred
See also CA 106; DLB 92

Campion, Jane **CLC 95**
See also CA 138

Campos, Alvaro de
See Pessoa, Fernando (Antonio Nogueira)

Camus, Albert 1913-1960CLC **1, 2, 4, 9, 11, 14, 32, 63, 69, 124; DA; DAB; DAC; DAM DRAM, MST, NOV; DC 2; SSC 9; WLC**
See also CA 89-92; DA3; DLB 72; MTCW 1, 2

Canby, Vincent 1924- **CLC 13**
See also CA 81-84

Cancale
See Desnos, Robert

See also Hinde, Thomas
See also CA 5-8R
Chivers, Thomas Holley 1809-1858 **NCLC 49**
See also DLB 3
Choi, Susan   **CLC 119**
Chomette, Rene Lucien 1898-1981
See Clair, Rene
See also CA 103
Chopin, Kate TCLC 5, 14; DA; DAB; SSC 8;
WLCS
See also Chopin, Katherine
See also CDALB 1865-1917; DLB 12, 78
Chopin, Katherine 1851-1904
See Chopin, Kate
See also CA 104; 122; DAC; DAM MST, NOV;
DA3
Chretien de Troyes c. 12th cent. - **CMLC 10**
See also DLB 208
Christie
See Ichikawa, Kon
Christie, Agatha (Mary Clarissa) 1890-1976
CLC 1, 6, 8, 12, 39, 48, 110; DAB; DAC;
DAM NOV
See also AAYA 9; AITN 1, 2; CA 17-20R; 61-
64; CANR 10, 37; CDBLB 1914-1945; DA3;
DLB 13, 77; MTCW 1, 2; SATA 36
Christie, (Ann) Philippa
See Pearce, Philippa
See also CA 5-8R; CANR 4
Christine de Pizan 1365(?)-1431(?)   **LC 9**
See also DLB 208
Chubb, Elmer
See Masters, Edgar Lee
Chulkov, Mikhail Dmitrievich 1743-1792**LC 2**
See also DLB 150
Churchill, Caryl 1938-   **CLC 31, 55; DC 5**
See also CA 102; CANR 22, 46; DLB 13;
MTCW 1
Churchill, Charles 1731-1764   **LC 3**
See also DLB 109
Chute, Carolyn 1947-   **CLC 39**
See also CA 123
Ciardi, John (Anthony) 1916-1986 **CLC 10,**
40, 44; DAM POET
See also CA 5-8R; 118; CAAS 2; CANR 5, 33;
CLR 19; DLB 5; DLBY 86; INT CANR-5;
MAICYA; MTCW 1, 2; SAAS 26; SATA 1,
65; SATA-Obit 46
Cicero, Marcus Tullius 106B.C.-43B.C.
CMLC 3
See also DLB 211
Cimino, Michael 1943-   **CLC 16**
See also CA 105
Cioran, E(mil) M. 1911-1995   **CLC 64**
See also CA 25-28R; 149
Cisneros, Sandra 1954- **CLC 69, 118; DAM**
MULT; HLC 1; SSC 32
See also AAYA 9; CA 131; CANR 64; DA3;
DLB 122, 152; HW 1, 2; MTCW 2
Cixous, Helene 1937-   **CLC 92**
See also CA 126; CANR 55; DLB 83; MTCW
1, 2
Clair, Rene   **CLC 20**
See also Chomette, Rene Lucien
Clampitt, Amy 1920-1994   **CLC 32; PC 19**
See also CA 110; 146; CANR 29, 79; DLB 105
Clancy, Thomas L., Jr. 1947-
See Clancy, Tom
See also CA 125; 131; CANR 62; DA3; INT
131; MTCW 1, 2
Clancy, Tom CLC 45, 112; DAM NOV, POP
See also Clancy, Thomas L., Jr.
See also AAYA 9; BEST 89:1, 90:1; MTCW 2

Clare, John 1793-1864 **NCLC 9; DAB; DAM**
POET; PC 23
See also DLB 55, 96
Clarin
See Alas (y Urena), Leopoldo (Enrique Garcia)
Clark, Al C.
See Goines, Donald
Clark, (Robert) Brian 1932-   **CLC 29**
See also CA 41-44R; CANR 67
Clark, Curt
See Westlake, Donald E(dwin)
Clark, Eleanor 1913-1996   **CLC 5, 19**
See also CA 9-12R; 151; CANR 41; DLB 6
Clark, J. P.
See Clark, John Pepper
See also DLB 117
Clark, John Pepper 1935- **CLC 38; BLC 1;**
DAM DRAM, MULT; DC 5
See also Clark, J. P.
See also BW 1; CA 65-68; CANR 16, 72;
MTCW 1
Clark, M. R.
See Clark, Mavis Thorpe
Clark, Mavis Thorpe 1909-   **CLC 12**
See also CA 57-60; CANR 8, 37; CLR 30;
MAICYA; SAAS 5; SATA 8, 74
Clark, Walter Van Tilburg 1909-1971**CLC 28**
See also CA 9-12R; 33-36R; CANR 63; DLB
9, 206; SATA 8
Clark Bekederemo, J(ohnson) P(epper)
See Clark, John Pepper
Clarke, Arthur C(harles) 1917-**CLC 1, 4, 13,**
18, 35; DAM POP; SSC 3
See also AAYA 4; CA 1-4R; CANR 2, 28, 55,
74; DA3; JRDA; MAICYA; MTCW 1, 2;
SATA 13, 70
Clarke, Austin 1896-1974   **CLC 6, 9; DAM**
POET
See also CA 29-32; 49-52; CAP 2; DLB 10, 20
Clarke, Austin C(hesterfield) 1934-**CLC 8, 53;**
BLC 1; DAC; DAM MULT
See also BW 1; CA 25-28R; CAAS 16; CANR
14, 32, 68; DLB 53, 125
Clarke, Gillian 1937-   **CLC 61**
See also CA 106; DLB 40
Clarke, Marcus (Andrew Hislop) 1846-1881
NCLC 19
Clarke, Shirley 1925-   **CLC 16**
Clash, The
See Headon, (Nicky) Topper; Jones, Mick;
Simonon, Paul; Strummer, Joe
Claudel, Paul (Louis Charles Marie) 1868-1955
TCLC 2, 10
See also CA 104; 165; DLB 192
Claudius, Matthias 1740-1815   **NCLC 75**
See also DLB 97
Clavell, James (duMaresq) 1925-1994**CLC 6,**
25, 87; DAM NOV, POP
See also CA 25-28R; 146; CANR 26, 48; DA3;
MTCW 1, 2
Cleaver, (Leroy) Eldridge 1935-1998**CLC 30,**
119; BLC 1; DAM MULT
See also BW 1, 3; CA 21-24R; 167; CANR 16,
75; DA3; MTCW 2
Cleese, John (Marwood) 1939-   **CLC 21**
See also Monty Python
See also CA 112; 116; CANR 35; MTCW 1
Cleishbotham, Jebediah
See Scott, Walter
Cleland, John 1710-1789   **LC 2, 48**
See also DLB 39
Clemens, Samuel Langhorne 1835-1910
See Twain, Mark

See also CA 104; 135; CDALB 1865-1917; DA;
DAB; DAC; DAM MST, NOV; DA3; DLB
11, 12, 23, 64, 74, 186, 189; JRDA;
MAICYA; SATA 100; YABC 2
Cleophil
See Congreve, William
Clerihew, E.
See Bentley, E(dmund) C(lerihew)
Clerk, N. W.
See Lewis, C(live) S(taples)
Cliff, Jimmy   **CLC 21**
See also Chambers, James
Cliff, Michelle 1946-   **CLC 120; BLCS**
See also BW 2; CA 116; CANR 39, 72; DLB
157
Clifton, (Thelma) Lucille 1936- **CLC 19, 66;**
BLC 1; DAM MULT, POET; PC 17
See also BW 2, 3; CA 49-52; CANR 2, 24, 42,
76; CLR 5; DA3; DLB 5, 41; MAICYA;
MTCW 1, 2; SATA 20, 69
Clinton, Dirk
See Silverberg, Robert
Clough, Arthur Hugh 1819-1861   **NCLC 27**
See also DLB 32
Clutha, Janet Paterson Frame 1924-
See Frame, Janet
See also CA 1-4R; CANR 2, 36, 76; MTCW 1,
2
Clyne, Terence
See Blatty, William Peter
Cobalt, Martin
See Mayne, William (James Carter)
Cobb, Irvin S(hrewsbury) 1876-1944 **T C L C**
77
See also CA 175; DLB 11, 25, 86
Cobbett, William 1763-1835   **NCLC 49**
See also DLB 43, 107, 158
Coburn, D(onald) L(ee) 1938-   **CLC 10**
See also CA 89-92
Cocteau, Jean (Maurice Eugene Clement) 1889-
1963**CLC 1, 8, 15, 16, 43; DA; DAB; DAC;**
DAM DRAM, MST, NOV; WLC
See also CA 25-28; CANR 40; CAP 2; DA3;
DLB 65; MTCW 1, 2
Codrescu, Andrei 1946- **CLC 46, 121; DAM**
POET
See also CA 33-36R; CAAS 19; CANR 13, 34,
53, 76; DA3; MTCW 2
Coe, Max
See Bourne, Randolph S(illiman)
Coe, Tucker
See Westlake, Donald E(dwin)
Coen, Ethan 1958-   **CLC 108**
See also CA 126
Coen, Joel 1955-   **CLC 108**
See also CA 126
The Coen Brothers
See Coen, Ethan; Coen, Joel
Coetzee, J(ohn) M(ichael) 1940- **CLC 23, 33,**
66, 117; DAM NOV
See also CA 77-80; CANR 41, 54, 74; DA3;
MTCW 1, 2
Coffey, Brian
See Koontz, Dean R(ay)
Coffin, Robert P(eter) Tristram 1892-1955
TCLC 95
See also CA 123; 169; DLB 45
Cohan, George M(ichael) 1878-1942**TCLC 60**
See also CA 157
Cohen, Arthur A(llen) 1928-1986 **CLC 7, 31**
See also CA 1-4R; 120; CANR 1, 17, 42; DLB
28
Cohen, Leonard (Norman) 1934- **CLC 3, 38;**

Dickinson, Emily (Elizabeth) 1830-1886
  **NCLC 21, 77; DA; DAB; DAC; DAM
  MST, POET; PC 1; WLC**
    See also AAYA 22; CDALB 1865-1917; DA3;
    DLB 1; SATA 29
Dickinson, Peter (Malcolm) 1927-**CLC 12, 35**
    See also AAYA 9; CA 41-44R; CANR 31, 58;
    CLR 29; DLB 87, 161; JRDA; MAICYA;
    SATA 5, 62, 95
Dickson, Carr
    See Carr, John Dickson
Dickson, Carter
    See Carr, John Dickson
Diderot, Denis 1713-1784   **LC 26**
Didion, Joan 1934-**CLC 1, 3, 8, 14, 32; DAM
  NOV**
    See also AITN 1; CA 5-8R; CANR 14, 52, 76;
    CDALB 1968-1988; DA3; DLB 2, 173, 185;
    DLBY 81, 86; MTCW 1, 2
Dietrich, Robert
    See Hunt, E(verette) Howard, (Jr.)
Difusa, Pati
    See Almodovar, Pedro
Dillard, Annie 1945- **CLC 9, 60, 115; DAM
  NOV**
    See also AAYA 6; CA 49-52; CANR 3, 43, 62;
    DA3; DLBY 80; MTCW 1, 2; SATA 10
Dillard, R(ichard) H(enry) W(ilde) 1937-
  CLC 5
    See also CA 21-24R; CAAS 7; CANR 10; DLB
    5
Dillon, Eilis 1920-1994   **CLC 17**
    See also CA 9-12R; 147; CAAS 3; CANR 4,
    38, 78; CLR 26; MAICYA; SATA 2, 74;
    SATA-Essay 105; SATA-Obit 83
Dimont, Penelope
    See Mortimer, Penelope (Ruth)
Dinesen, Isak   **CLC 10, 29, 95; SSC 7**
    See also Blixen, Karen (Christentze Dinesen)
    See also MTCW 1
Ding Ling   **CLC 68**
    See also Chiang, Pin-chin
Diphusa, Patty
    See Almodovar, Pedro
Disch, Thomas M(ichael) 1940-   **CLC 7, 36**
    See also AAYA 17; CA 21-24R; CAAS 4;
    CANR 17, 36, 54; CLR 18; DA3; DLB 8;
    MAICYA; MTCW 1, 2; SAAS 15; SATA 92
Disch, Tom
    See Disch, Thomas M(ichael)
d'Isly, Georges
    See Simenon, Georges (Jacques Christian)
Disraeli, Benjamin 1804-1881**NCLC 2, 39, 79**
    See also DLB 21, 55
Ditcum, Steve
    See Crumb, R(obert)
Dixon, Paige
    See Corcoran, Barbara
Dixon, Stephen 1936-   **CLC 52; SSC 16**
    See also CA 89-92; CANR 17, 40, 54; DLB 130
Doak, Annie
    See Dillard, Annie
Dobell, Sydney Thompson 1824-1874 **NCLC
  43**
    See also DLB 32
Doblin, Alfred   **TCLC 13**
    See also Doeblin, Alfred
Dobrolyubov, Nikolai Alexandrovich 1836-1861
  NCLC 5
Dobson, Austin 1840-1921   **TCLC 79**
    See also DLB 35; 144
Dobyns, Stephen 1941-   **CLC 37**
    See also CA 45-48; CANR 2, 18

Doctorow, E(dgar) L(aurence) 1931- **CLC 6,
  11, 15, 18, 37, 44, 65, 113; DAM NOV, POP**
    See also AAYA 22; AITN 2; BEST 89:3; CA
    45-48; CANR 2, 33, 51, 76; CDALB 1968-
    1988; DA3; DLB 2, 28, 173; DLBY 80;
    MTCW 1, 2
Dodgson, Charles Lutwidge 1832-1898
    See Carroll, Lewis
    See also CLR 2; DA; DAB; DAC; DAM MST,
    NOV, POET; DA3; MAICYA; SATA 100;
    YABC 2
Dodson, Owen (Vincent) 1914-1983 **CLC 79;
  BLC 1; DAM MULT**
    See also BW 1; CA 65-68; 110; CANR 24; DLB
    76
Doeblin, Alfred 1878-1957   **TCLC 13**
    See also Doblin, Alfred
    See also CA 110; 141; DLB 66
Doerr, Harriet 1910-   **CLC 34**
    See also CA 117; 122; CANR 47; INT 122
Domecq, H(onorio Bustos)
    See Bioy Casares, Adolfo
Domecq, H(onorio) Bustos
    See Bioy Casares, Adolfo; Borges, Jorge Luis
Domini, Rey
    See Lorde, Audre (Geraldine)
Dominique
    See Proust, (Valentin-Louis-George-Eugene-)
    Marcel
Don, A
    See Stephen, SirLeslie
Donaldson, Stephen R. 1947- **CLC 46; DAM
  POP**
    See also CA 89-92; CANR 13, 55; INT CANR-
    13
Donleavy, J(ames) P(atrick) 1926-**CLC 1, 4, 6,
  10, 45**
    See also AITN 2; CA 9-12R; CANR 24, 49, 62,
    80; DLB 6, 173; INT CANR-24; MTCW 1,
    2
Donne, John 1572-1631**LC 10, 24; DA; DAB;
  DAC; DAM MST, POET; PC 1; WLC**
    See also CDBLB Before 1660; DLB 121, 151
Donnell, David 1939(?)-   **CLC 34**
Donoghue, P. S.
    See Hunt, E(verette) Howard, (Jr.)
Donoso (Yanez), Jose 1924-1996**CLC 4, 8, 11,
  32, 99; DAM MULT; HLC 1; SSC 34**
    See also CA 81-84; 155; CANR 32, 73; DLB
    113; HW 1, 2; MTCW 1, 2
Donovan, John 1928-1992   **CLC 35**
    See also AAYA 20; CA 97-100; 137; CLR 3;
    MAICYA; SATA 72; SATA-Brief 29
Don Roberto
    See Cunninghame Graham, R(obert) B(ontine)
Doolittle, Hilda 1886-1961**CLC 3, 8, 14, 31, 34,
  73; DA; DAC; DAM MST, POET; PC 5;
  WLC**
    See also H. D.
    See also CA 97-100; CANR 35; DLB 4, 45;
    MTCW 1, 2
Dorfman, Ariel 1942-   **CLC 48, 77; DAM
  MULT; HLC 1**
    See also CA 124; 130; CANR 67, 70; HW 1, 2;
    INT 130
Dorn, Edward (Merton) 1929-   **CLC 10, 18**
    See also CA 93-96; CANR 42, 79; DLB 5; INT
    93-96
Dorris, Michael (Anthony) 1945-1997 **CLC
  109; DAM MULT, NOV**
    See also AAYA 20; BEST 90:1; CA 102; 157;
    CANR 19, 46, 75; CLR 58; DA3; DLB 175;
    MTCW 2; NNAL; SATA 75; SATA-Obit 94

Dorris, Michael A.
    See Dorris, Michael (Anthony)
Dorsan, Luc
    See Simenon, Georges (Jacques Christian)
Dorsange, Jean
    See Simenon, Georges (Jacques Christian)
Dos Passos, John (Roderigo) 1896-1970 **C L C
  1, 4, 8, 11, 15, 25, 34, 82; DA; DAB; DAC;
  DAM MST, NOV; WLC**
    See also CA 1-4R; 29-32R; CANR 3; CDALB
    1929-1941; DA3; DLB 4, 9; DLBD 1, 15;
    DLBY 96; MTCW 1, 2
Dossage, Jean
    See Simenon, Georges (Jacques Christian)
Dostoevsky, Fedor Mikhailovich 1821-1881
  **NCLC 2, 7, 21, 33, 43; DA; DAB; DAC;
  DAM MST, NOV; SSC 2, 33; WLC**
    See also DA3
Doughty, Charles M(ontagu) 1843-1926
  TCLC 27
    See also CA 115; 178; DLB 19, 57, 174
Douglas, Ellen   **CLC 73**
    See also Haxton, Josephine Ayres; Williamson,
    Ellen Douglas
Douglas, Gavin 1475(?)-1522   **LC 20**
    See also DLB 132
Douglas, George
    See Brown, George Douglas
Douglas, Keith (Castellain) 1920-1944 **T C L C
  40**
    See also CA 160; DLB 27
Douglas, Leonard
    See Bradbury, Ray (Douglas)
Douglas, Michael
    See Crichton, (John) Michael
Douglas, (George) Norman 1868-1952 **T C L C
  68**
    See also CA 119; 157; DLB 34, 195
Douglas, William
    See Brown, George Douglas
Douglass, Frederick 1817(?)-1895**NCLC 7, 55;
  BLC 1; DA; DAC; DAM MST, MULT;
  WLC**
    See also CDALB 1640-1865; DA3; DLB 1, 43,
    50, 79; SATA 29
Dourado, (Waldomiro Freitas) Autran 1926-
  CLC 23, 60
    See also CA 25-28R; 179; CANR 34, 81; DLB
    145; HW 2
Dourado, Waldomiro Autran 1926-
    See Dourado, (Waldomiro Freitas) Autran
    See also CA 179
Dove, Rita (Frances) 1952-**CLC 50, 81; BLCS;
  DAM MULT, POET; PC 6**
    See also BW 2; CA 109; CAAS 19; CANR 27,
    42, 68, 76; CDALBS; DA3; DLB 120;
    MTCW 1
Doveglion
    See Villa, Jose Garcia
Dowell, Coleman 1925-1985   **CLC 60**
    See also CA 25-28R; 117; CANR 10; DLB 130
Dowson, Ernest (Christopher) 1867-1900
  TCLC 4
    See also CA 105; 150; DLB 19, 135
Doyle, A. Conan
    See Doyle, Arthur Conan
Doyle, Arthur Conan 1859-1930**TCLC 7; DA;
  DAB; DAC; DAM MST, NOV; SSC 12;
  WLC**
    See also AAYA 14; CA 104; 122; CDBLB 1890-
    1914; DA3; DLB 18, 70, 156, 178; MTCW
    1, 2; SATA 24
Doyle, Conan

See also CA 5-8R; 158; CAAS 1; CANR 5, 63; DLB 6, 206; INT CANR-5

Eastman, Charles A(lexander) 1858-1939 **TCLC 55; DAM MULT**
See also CA 179; DLB 175; NNAL; YABC 1

Eberhart, Richard (Ghormley) 1904- **CLC 3, 11, 19, 56; DAM POET**
See also CA 1-4R; CANR 2; CDALB 1941-1968; DLB 48; MTCW 1

Eberstadt, Fernanda 1960- **CLC 39**
See also CA 136; CANR 69

Echegaray (y Eizaguirre), Jose (Maria Waldo) 1832-1916 **TCLC 4; HLCS 1**
See also CA 104; CANR 32; HW 1; MTCW 1

Echeverria, (Jose) Esteban (Antonino) 1805-1851 **NCLC 18**

Echo
See Proust, (Valentin-Louis-George-Eugene-) Marcel

Eckert, Allan W. 1931- **CLC 17**
See also AAYA 18; CA 13-16R; CANR 14, 45; INT CANR-14; SAAS 21; SATA 29, 91; SATA-Brief 27

Eckhart, Meister 1260(?)-1328(?) **CMLC 9**
See also DLB 115

Eckmar, F. R.
See de Hartog, Jan

Eco, Umberto 1932- **CLC 28, 60; DAM NOV, POP**
See also BEST 90:1; CA 77-80; CANR 12, 33, 55; DA3; DLB 196; MTCW 1, 2

Eddison, E(ric) R(ucker) 1882-1945 **TCLC 15**
See also CA 109; 156

Eddy, Mary (Ann Morse) Baker 1821-1910 **TCLC 71**
See also CA 113; 174

Edel, (Joseph) Leon 1907-1997 **CLC 29, 34**
See also CA 1-4R; 161; CANR 1, 22; DLB 103; INT CANR-22

Eden, Emily 1797-1869 **NCLC 10**

Edgar, David 1948- **CLC 42; DAM DRAM**
See also CA 57-60; CANR 12, 61; DLB 13; MTCW 1

Edgerton, Clyde (Carlyle) 1944- **CLC 39**
See also AAYA 17; CA 118; 134; CANR 64; INT 134

Edgeworth, Maria 1768-1849 **NCLC 1, 51**
See also DLB 116, 159, 163; SATA 21

Edison, Thomas 1847-1931 **TCLC 96**

Edmonds, Paul
See Kuttner, Henry

Edmonds, Walter D(umaux) 1903-1998 **C L C 35**
See also CA 5-8R; CANR 2; DLB 9; MAICYA; SAAS 4; SATA 1, 27; SATA-Obit 99

Edmondson, Wallace
See Ellison, Harlan (Jay)

Edson, Russell **CLC 13**
See also CA 33-36R

Edwards, Bronwen Elizabeth
See Rose, Wendy

Edwards, G(erald) B(asil) 1899-1976 **CLC 25**
See also CA 110

Edwards, Gus 1939- **CLC 43**
See also CA 108; INT 108

Edwards, Jonathan 1703-1758 **LC 7; DA; DAC; DAM MST**
See also DLB 24

Efron, Marina Ivanovna Tsvetaeva
See Tsvetaeva (Efron), Marina (Ivanovna)

Ehle, John (Marsden, Jr.) 1925- **CLC 27**
See also CA 9-12R

Ehrenbourg, Ilya (Grigoryevich)

See Ehrenburg, Ilya (Grigoryevich)

Ehrenburg, Ilya (Grigoryevich) 1891-1967 **CLC 18, 34, 62**
See also CA 102; 25-28R

Ehrenburg, Ilyo (Grigoryevich)
See Ehrenburg, Ilya (Grigoryevich)

Ehrenreich, Barbara 1941- **CLC 110**
See also BEST 90:4; CA 73-76; CANR 16, 37, 62; MTCW 1, 2

Eich, Guenter 1907-1972 **CLC 15**
See also CA 111; 93-96; DLB 69, 124

Eichendorff, Joseph Freiherr von 1788-1857 **NCLC 8**
See also DLB 90

Eigner, Larry **CLC 9**
See also Eigner, Laurence (Joel)
See also CAAS 23; DLB 5

Eigner, Laurence (Joel) 1927-1996
See Eigner, Larry
See also CA 9-12R; 151; CANR 6, 84; DLB 193

Einstein, Albert 1879-1955 **TCLC 65**
See also CA 121; 133; MTCW 1, 2

Eiseley, Loren Corey 1907-1977 **CLC 7**
See also AAYA 5; CA 1-4R; 73-76; CANR 6; DLBD 17

Eisenstadt, Jill 1963- **CLC 50**
See also CA 140

Eisenstein, Sergei (Mikhailovich) 1898-1948 **TCLC 57**
See also CA 114; 149

Eisner, Simon
See Kornbluth, C(yril) M.

Ekeloef, (Bengt) Gunnar 1907-1968 **CLC 27; DAM POET; PC 23**
See also CA 123; 25-28R

Ekelof, (Bengt) Gunnar
See Ekeloef, (Bengt) Gunnar

Ekelund, Vilhelm 1880-1949 **TCLC 75**

Ekwensi, C. O. D.
See Ekwensi, Cyprian (Odiatu Duaka)

Ekwensi, Cyprian (Odiatu Duaka) 1921- **CLC 4; BLC 1; DAM MULT**
See also BW 2, 3; CA 29-32R; CANR 18, 42, 74; DLB 117; MTCW 1, 2; SATA 66

Elaine **TCLC 18**
See also Leverson, Ada

El Crummo
See Crumb, R(obert)

Elder, Lonne III 1931-1996 **DC 8**
See also BLC 1; BW 1, 3; CA 81-84; 152; CANR 25; DAM MULT; DLB 7, 38, 44

Elia
See Lamb, Charles

Eliade, Mircea 1907-1986 **CLC 19**
See also CA 65-68; 119; CANR 30, 62; MTCW 1

Eliot, A. D.
See Jewett, (Theodora) Sarah Orne

Eliot, Alice
See Jewett, (Theodora) Sarah Orne

Eliot, Dan
See Silverberg, Robert

Eliot, George 1819-1880 **NCLC 4, 13, 23, 41, 49; DA; DAB; DAC; DAM MST, NOV; PC 20; WLC**
See also CDBLB 1832-1890; DA3; DLB 21, 35, 55

Eliot, John 1604-1690 **LC 5**
See also DLB 24

Eliot, T(homas) S(tearns) 1888-1965 **CLC 1, 2, 3, 6, 9, 10, 13, 15, 24, 34, 41, 55, 57, 113; DA; DAB; DAC; DAM DRAM, MST,** **POET; PC 5; WLC**
See also AAYA 28; CA 5-8R; 25-28R; CANR 41; CDALB 1929-1941; DA3; DLB 7, 10, 45, 63; DLBY 88; MTCW 1, 2

Elizabeth 1866-1941 **TCLC 41**

Elkin, Stanley L(awrence) 1930-1995 **CLC 4, 6, 9, 14, 27, 51, 91; DAM NOV, POP; SSC 12**
See also CA 9-12R; 148; CANR 8, 46; DLB 2, 28; DLBY 80; INT CANR-8; MTCW 1, 2

Elledge, Scott **CLC 34**

Elliot, Don
See Silverberg, Robert

Elliott, Don
See Silverberg, Robert

Elliott, George P(aul) 1918-1980 **CLC 2**
See also CA 1-4R; 97-100; CANR 2

Elliott, Janice 1931- **CLC 47**
See also CA 13-16R; CANR 8, 29, 84; DLB 14

Elliott, Sumner Locke 1917-1991 **CLC 38**
See also CA 5-8R; 134; CANR 2, 21

Elliott, William
See Bradbury, Ray (Douglas)

Ellis, A. E. **CLC 7**

Ellis, Alice Thomas **CLC 40**
See also Haycraft, Anna
See also DLB 194; MTCW 1

Ellis, Bret Easton 1964- **CLC 39, 71, 117; DAM POP**
See also AAYA 2; CA 118; 123; CANR 51, 74; DA3; INT 123; MTCW 1

Ellis, (Henry) Havelock 1859-1939 **TCLC 14**
See also CA 109; 169; DLB 190

Ellis, Landon
See Ellison, Harlan (Jay)

Ellis, Trey 1962- **CLC 55**
See also CA 146

Ellison, Harlan (Jay) 1934- **CLC 1, 13, 42; DAM POP; SSC 14**
See also AAYA 29; CA 5-8R; CANR 5, 46; DLB 8; INT CANR-5; MTCW 1, 2

Ellison, Ralph (Waldo) 1914-1994 **CLC 1, 3, 11, 54, 86, 114; BLC 1; DA; DAB; DAC; DAM MST, MULT, NOV; SSC 26; WLC**
See also AAYA 19; BW 1, 3; CA 9-12R; 145; CANR 24, 53; CDALB 1941-1968; DA3; DLB 2, 76; DLBY 94; MTCW 1, 2

Ellmann, Lucy (Elizabeth) 1956- **CLC 61**
See also CA 128

Ellmann, Richard (David) 1918-1987 **CLC 50**
See also BEST 89:2; CA 1-4R; 122; CANR 2, 28, 61; DLB 103; DLBY 87; MTCW 1, 2

Elman, Richard (Martin) 1934-1997 **CLC 19**
See also CA 17-20R; 163; CAAS 3; CANR 47

Elron
See Hubbard, L(afayette) Ron(ald)

Eluard, Paul **TCLC 7, 41**
See also Grindel, Eugene

Elyot, Sir Thomas 1490(?)-1546 **LC 11**

Elytis, Odysseus 1911-1996 **CLC 15, 49, 100; DAM POET; PC 21**
See also CA 102; 151; MTCW 1, 2

Emecheta, (Florence Onye) Buchi 1944- **C L C 14, 48; BLC 2; DAM MULT**
See also BW 2, 3; CA 81-84; CANR 27, 81; DA3; DLB 117; MTCW 1, 2; SATA 66

Emerson, Mary Moody 1774-1863 **NCLC 66**

Emerson, Ralph Waldo 1803-1882 **NCLC 1, 38; DA; DAB; DAC; DAM MST, POET; PC 18; WLC**
See also CDALB 1640-1865; DA3; DLB 1, 59, 73

Eminescu, Mihail 1850-1889 **NCLC 33**

Gasset, Jose Ortega y
See Ortega y Gasset, Jose
Gates, Henry Louis, Jr. 1950-**CLC 65; BLCS; DAM MULT**
See also BW 2, 3; CA 109; CANR 25, 53, 75; DA3; DLB 67; MTCW 1
Gautier, Theophile 1811-1872 **NCLC 1, 59; DAM POET; PC 18; SSC 20**
See also DLB 119
Gawsworth, John
See Bates, H(erbert) E(rnest)
Gay, John 1685-1732 **LC 49; DAM DRAM**
See also DLB 84, 95
Gay, Oliver
See Gogarty, Oliver St. John
Gaye, Marvin (Penze) 1939-1984 **CLC 26**
See also CA 112
Gebler, Carlo (Ernest) 1954- **CLC 39**
See also CA 119; 133
Gee, Maggie (Mary) 1948- **CLC 57**
See also CA 130; DLB 207
Gee, Maurice (Gough) 1931- **CLC 29**
See also CA 97-100; CANR 67; CLR 56; SATA 46, 101
Gelbart, Larry (Simon) 1923- **CLC 21, 61**
See also CA 73-76; CANR 45
Gelber, Jack 1932- **CLC 1, 6, 14, 79**
See also CA 1-4R; CANR 2; DLB 7
Gellhorn, Martha (Ellis) 1908-1998 **CLC 14, 60**
See also CA 77-80; 164; CANR 44; DLBY 82, 98
Genet, Jean 1910-1986**CLC 1, 2, 5, 10, 14, 44, 46; DAM DRAM**
See also CA 13-16R; CANR 18; DA3; DLB 72; DLBY 86; MTCW 1, 2
Gent, Peter 1942- **CLC 29**
See also AITN 1; CA 89-92; DLBY 82
Gentile, Giovanni 1875-1944 **TCLC 96**
See also CA 119
Gentlewoman in New England, A
See Bradstreet, Anne
Gentlewoman in Those Parts, A
See Bradstreet, Anne
George, Jean Craighead 1919- **CLC 35**
See also AAYA 8; CA 5-8R; CANR 25; CLR 1; DLB 52; JRDA; MAICYA; SATA 2, 68
George, Stefan (Anton) 1868-1933**TCLC 2, 14**
See also CA 104
Georges, Georges Martin
See Simenon, Georges (Jacques Christian)
Gerhardi, William Alexander
See Gerhardie, William Alexander
Gerhardie, William Alexander 1895-1977 **CLC 5**
See also CA 25-28R; 73-76; CANR 18; DLB 36
Gerstler, Amy 1956- **CLC 70**
See also CA 146
Gertler, T. **CLC 34**
See also CA 116; 121; INT 121
Ghalib **NCLC 39, 78**
See also Ghalib, Hsadullah Khan
Ghalib, Hsadullah Khan 1797-1869
See Ghalib
See also DAM POET
Ghelderode, Michel de 1898-1962 **CLC 6, 11; DAM DRAM**
See also CA 85-88; CANR 40, 77
Ghiselin, Brewster 1903- **CLC 23**
See also CA 13-16R; CAAS 10; CANR 13
Ghose, Aurabinda 1872-1950 **TCLC 63**
See also CA 163

Ghose, Zulfikar 1935- **CLC 42**
See also CA 65-68; CANR 67
Ghosh, Amitav 1956- **CLC 44**
See also CA 147; CANR 80
Giacosa, Giuseppe 1847-1906 **TCLC 7**
See also CA 104
Gibb, Lee
See Waterhouse, Keith (Spencer)
Gibbon, Lewis Grassic **TCLC 4**
See also Mitchell, James Leslie
Gibbons, Kaye 1960-**CLC 50, 88; DAM POP**
See also CA 151; CANR 75; DA3; MTCW 1
Gibran, Kahlil 1883-1931 **TCLC 1, 9; DAM POET, POP; PC 9**
See also CA 104; 150; DA3; MTCW 2
Gibran, Khalil
See Gibran, Kahlil
Gibson, William 1914- **CLC 23; DA; DAB; DAC; DAM DRAM, MST**
See also CA 9-12R; CANR 9, 42, 75; DLB 7; MTCW 1; SATA 66
Gibson, William (Ford) 1948- **CLC 39, 63; DAM POP**
See also AAYA 12; CA 126; 133; CANR 52; DA3; MTCW 1
Gide, Andre (Paul Guillaume) 1869-1951 **TCLC 5, 12, 36; DA; DAB; DAC; DAM MST, NOV; SSC 13; WLC**
See also CA 104; 124; DA3; DLB 65; MTCW 1, 2
Gifford, Barry (Colby) 1946- **CLC 34**
See also CA 65-68; CANR 9, 30, 40
Gilbert, Frank
See De Voto, Bernard (Augustine)
Gilbert, W(illiam) S(chwenck) 1836-1911 **TCLC 3; DAM DRAM, POET**
See also CA 104; 173; SATA 36
Gilbreth, Frank B., Jr. 1911- **CLC 17**
See also CA 9-12R; SATA 2
Gilchrist, Ellen 1935-**CLC 34, 48; DAM POP; SSC 14**
See also CA 113; 116; CANR 41, 61; DLB 130; MTCW 1, 2
Giles, Molly 1942- **CLC 39**
See also CA 126
Gill, Eric 1882-1940 **TCLC 85**
Gill, Patrick
See Creasey, John
Gilliam, Terry (Vance) 1940- **CLC 21**
See also Monty Python
See also AAYA 19; CA 108; 113; CANR 35; INT 113
Gillian, Jerry
See Gilliam, Terry (Vance)
Gilliatt, Penelope (Ann Douglass) 1932-1993 **CLC 2, 10, 13, 53**
See also AITN 2; CA 13-16R; 141; CANR 49; DLB 14
Gilman, Charlotte (Anna) Perkins (Stetson) 1860-1935 **TCLC 9, 37; SSC 13**
See also CA 106; 150; MTCW 1
Gilmour, David 1949- **CLC 35**
See also CA 138, 147
Gilpin, William 1724-1804 **NCLC 30**
Gilray, J. D.
See Mencken, H(enry) L(ouis)
Gilroy, Frank D(aniel) 1925- **CLC 2**
See also CA 81-84; CANR 32, 64; DLB 7
Gilstrap, John 1957(?)- **CLC 99**
See also CA 160
Ginsberg, Allen 1926-1997**CLC 1, 2, 3, 4, 6, 13, 36, 69, 109; DA; DAB; DAC; DAM MST, POET; PC 4; WLC**

See also AITN 1; CA 1-4R; 157; CANR 2, 41, 63; CDALB 1941-1968; DA3; DLB 5, 16, 169; MTCW 1, 2
Ginzburg, Natalia 1916-1991**CLC 5, 11, 54, 70**
See also CA 85-88; 135; CANR 33; DLB 177; MTCW 1, 2
Giono, Jean 1895-1970 **CLC 4, 11**
See also CA 45-48; 29-32R; CANR 2, 35; DLB 72; MTCW 1
Giovanni, Nikki 1943- **CLC 2, 4, 19, 64, 117; BLC 2; DA; DAB; DAC; DAM MST, MULT, POET; PC 19; WLCS**
See also AAYA 22; AITN 1; BW 2, 3; CA 29-32R; CAAS 6; CANR 18, 41, 60; CDALBS; CLR 6; DA3; DLB 5, 41; INT CANR-18; MAICYA; MTCW 1, 2; SATA 24, 107
Giovene, Andrea 1904- **CLC 7**
See also CA 85-88
Gippius, Zinaida (Nikolayevna) 1869-1945
See Hippius, Zinaida
See also CA 106
Giraudoux, (Hippolyte) Jean 1882-1944 **TCLC 2, 7; DAM DRAM**
See also CA 104; DLB 65
Gironella, Jose Maria 1917- **CLC 11**
See also CA 101
Gissing, George (Robert) 1857-1903**TCLC 3, 24, 47**
See also CA 105; 167; DLB 18, 135, 184
Giurlani, Aldo
See Palazzeschi, Aldo
Gladkov, Fyodor (Vasilyevich) 1883-1958 **TCLC 27**
See also CA 170
Glanville, Brian (Lester) 1931- **CLC 6**
See also CA 5-8R; CAAS 9; CANR 3, 70; DLB 15, 139; SATA 42
Glasgow, Ellen (Anderson Gholson) 1873-1945 **TCLC 2, 7; SSC 34**
See also CA 104; 164; DLB 9, 12; MTCW 2
Glaspell, Susan 1882(?)-1948**TCLC 55; DC 10**
See also CA 110; 154; DLB 7, 9, 78; YABC 2
Glassco, John 1909-1981 **CLC 9**
See also CA 13-16R; 102; CANR 15; DLB 68
Glasscock, Amnesia
See Steinbeck, John (Ernst)
Glasser, Ronald J. 1940(?)- **CLC 37**
Glassman, Joyce
See Johnson, Joyce
Glendinning, Victoria 1937- **CLC 50**
See also CA 120; 127; CANR 59; DLB 155
Glissant, Edouard 1928- **CLC 10, 68; DAM MULT**
See also CA 153
Gloag, Julian 1930- **CLC 40**
See also AITN 1; CA 65-68; CANR 10, 70
Glowacki, Aleksander
See Prus, Boleslaw
Gluck, Louise (Elisabeth) 1943-**CLC 7, 22, 44, 81; DAM POET; PC 16**
See also CA 33-36R; CANR 40, 69; DA3; DLB 5; MTCW 2
Glyn, Elinor 1864-1943 **TCLC 72**
See also DLB 153
Gobineau, Joseph Arthur (Comte) de 1816-1882 **NCLC 17**
See also DLB 123
Godard, Jean-Luc 1930- **CLC 20**
See also CA 93-96
Godden, (Margaret) Rumer 1907-1998 **CLC 53**
See also AAYA 6; CA 5-8R; 172; CANR 4, 27, 36, 55, 80; CLR 20; DLB 161; MAICYA;

SAAS 12; SATA 3, 36; SATA-Obit 109
Godoy Alcayaga, Lucila 1889-1957
See Mistral, Gabriela
See also BW 2; CA 104; 131; CANR 81; DAM
MULT; HW 1, 2; MTCW 1, 2
Godwin, Gail (Kathleen) 1937- **CLC 5, 8, 22,**
31, 69; DAM POP
See also CA 29-32R; CANR 15, 43, 69; DA3;
DLB 6; INT CANR-15; MTCW 1, 2
Godwin, William 1756-1836 **NCLC 14**
See also CDBLB 1789-1832; DLB 39, 104, 142,
158, 163
Goebbels, Josef
See Goebbels, (Paul) Joseph
Goebbels, (Paul) Joseph 1897-1945 **TCLC 68**
See also CA 115; 148
Goebbels, Joseph Paul
See Goebbels, (Paul) Joseph
Goethe, Johann Wolfgang von 1749-1832
NCLC 4, 22, 34; DA; DAB; DAC; DAM
DRAM, MST, POET; PC 5; WLC
See also DA3; DLB 94
Gogarty, Oliver St. John 1878-1957**TCLC 15**
See also CA 109; 150; DLB 15, 19
Gogol, Nikolai (Vasilyevich) 1809-1852**NCLC**
5, 15, 31; DA; DAB; DAC; DAM DRAM,
MST; DC 1; SSC 4, 29; WLC
See also DLB 198
Goines, Donald 1937(?)-1974**CLC 80; BLC 2;**
DAM MULT, POP
See also AITN 1; BW 1, 3; CA 124; 114; CANR
82; DA3; DLB 33
Gold, Herbert 1924- **CLC 4, 7, 14, 42**
See also CA 9-12R; CANR 17, 45; DLB 2;
DLBY 81
Goldbarth, Albert 1948- **CLC 5, 38**
See also CA 53-56; CANR 6, 40; DLB 120
Goldberg, Anatol 1910-1982 **CLC 34**
See also CA 131; 117
Goldemberg, Isaac 1945- **CLC 52**
See also CA 69-72; CAAS 12; CANR 11, 32;
HW 1
Golding, William (Gerald) 1911-1993**CLC 1,**
2, 3, 8, 10, 17, 27, 58, 81; DA; DAB; DAC;
DAM MST, NOV; WLC
See also AAYA 5; CA 5-8R; 141; CANR 13,
33, 54; CDBLB 1945-1960; DA3; DLB 15,
100; MTCW 1, 2
Goldman, Emma 1869-1940 **TCLC 13**
See also CA 110; 150
Goldman, Francisco 1954- **CLC 76**
See also CA 162
Goldman, William (W.) 1931- **CLC 1, 48**
See also CA 9-12R; CANR 29, 69; DLB 44
Goldmann, Lucien 1913-1970 **CLC 24**
See also CA 25-28; CAP 2
Goldoni, Carlo 1707-1793**LC 4; DAM DRAM**
Goldsberry, Steven 1949- **CLC 34**
See also CA 131
Goldsmith, Oliver 1728-1774 **LC 2, 48; DA;**
DAB; DAC; DAM DRAM, MST, NOV,
POET; DC 8; WLC
See also CDBLB 1660-1789; DLB 39, 89, 104,
109, 142; SATA 26
Goldsmith, Peter
See Priestley, J(ohn) B(oynton)
Gombrowicz, Witold 1904-1969**CLC 4, 7, 11,**
49; DAM DRAM
See also CA 19-20; 25-28R; CAP 2
Gomez de la Serna, Ramon 1888-1963**CLC 9**
See also CA 153; 116; CANR 79; HW 1, 2
Goncharov, Ivan Alexandrovich 1812-1891
NCLC 1, 63

Goncourt, Edmond (Louis Antoine Huot) de
1822-1896 **NCLC 7**
See also DLB 123
Goncourt, Jules (Alfred Huot) de 1830-1870
NCLC 7
See also DLB 123
Gontier, Fernande 19(?)- **CLC 50**
Gonzalez Martinez, Enrique 1871-1952
TCLC 72
See also CA 166; CANR 81; HW 1, 2
Goodman, Paul 1911-1972 **CLC 1, 2, 4, 7**
See also CA 19-20; 37-40R; CANR 34; CAP 2;
DLB 130; MTCW 1
Gordimer, Nadine 1923-**CLC 3, 5, 7, 10, 18, 33,**
51, 70; DA; DAB; DAC; DAM MST, NOV;
SSC 17; WLCS
See also CA 5-8R; CANR 3, 28, 56; DA3; INT
CANR-28; MTCW 1, 2
Gordon, Adam Lindsay 1833-1870 **NCLC 21**
Gordon, Caroline 1895-1981**CLC 6, 13, 29, 83;**
SSC 15
See also CA 11-12; 103; CANR 36; CAP 1;
DLB 4, 9, 102; DLBD 17; DLBY 81; MTCW
1, 2
Gordon, Charles William 1860-1937
See Connor, Ralph
See also CA 109
Gordon, Mary (Catherine) 1949- **CLC 13, 22**
See also CA 102; CANR 44; DLB 6; DLBY
81; INT 102; MTCW 1
Gordon, N. J.
See Bosman, Herman Charles
Gordon, Sol 1923- **CLC 26**
See also CA 53-56; CANR 4; SATA 11
Gordone, Charles 1925-1995**CLC 1, 4; DAM**
DRAM; DC 8
See also BW 1, 3; CA 93-96; 180; 150; CAAE
180; CANR 55; DLB 7; INT 93-96; MTCW
1
Gore, Catherine 1800-1861 **NCLC 65**
See also DLB 116
Gorenko, Anna Andreevna
See Akhmatova, Anna
Gorky, Maxim 1868-1936**TCLC 8; DAB; SSC**
28; WLC
See also Peshkov, Alexei Maximovich
See also MTCW 2
Goryan, Sirak
See Saroyan, William
Gosse, Edmund (William) 1849-1928**TCLC 28**
See also CA 117; DLB 57, 144, 184
Gotlieb, Phyllis Fay (Bloom) 1926- **CLC 18**
See also CA 13-16R; CANR 7; DLB 88
Gottesman, S. D.
See Kornbluth, C(yril) M.; Pohl, Frederik
Gottfried von Strassburg fl. c. 1210- **CMLC**
10
See also DLB 138
Gould, Lois **CLC 4, 10**
See also CA 77-80; CANR 29; MTCW 1
Gourmont, Remy (-Marie-Charles) de 1858-
1915 **TCLC 17**
See also CA 109; 150; MTCW 2
Govier, Katherine 1948- **CLC 51**
See also CA 101; CANR 18, 40
Goyen, (Charles) William 1915-1983**CLC 5, 8,**
14, 40
See also AITN 2; CA 5-8R; 110; CANR 6, 71;
DLB 2; DLBY 83; INT CANR-6
Goytisolo, Juan 1931- **CLC 5, 10, 23; DAM**
MULT; HLC 1
See also CA 85-88; CANR 32, 61; HW 1, 2;
MTCW 1, 2

Gozzano, Guido 1883-1916 **PC 10**
See also CA 154; DLB 114
Gozzi, (Conte) Carlo 1720-1806 **NCLC 23**
Grabbe, Christian Dietrich 1801-1836**NCLC**
2
See also DLB 133
Grace, Patricia Frances 1937- **CLC 56**
See also CA 176
Gracian y Morales, Baltasar 1601-1658**LC 15**
Gracq, Julien **CLC 11, 48**
See also Poirier, Louis
See also DLB 83
Grade, Chaim 1910-1982 **CLC 10**
See also CA 93-96; 107
Graduate of Oxford, A
See Ruskin, John
Grafton, Garth
See Duncan, Sara Jeannette
Graham, John
See Phillips, David Graham
Graham, Jorie 1951- **CLC 48, 118**
See also CA 111; CANR 63; DLB 120
Graham, R(obert) B(ontine) Cunninghame
See Cunninghame Graham, R(obert) B(ontine)
See also DLB 98, 135, 174
Graham, Robert
See Haldeman, Joe (William)
Graham, Tom
See Lewis, (Harry) Sinclair
Graham, W(illiam) S(ydney) 1918-1986 **C L C**
29
See also CA 73-76; 118; DLB 20
Graham, Winston (Mawdsley) 1910- **CLC 23**
See also CA 49-52; CANR 2, 22, 45, 66; DLB
77
Grahame, Kenneth 1859-1932**TCLC 64; DAB**
See also CA 108; 136; CANR 80; CLR 5; DA3;
DLB 34, 141, 178; MAICYA; MTCW 2;
SATA 100; YABC 1
Granovsky, Timofei Nikolaevich 1813-1855
NCLC 75
See also DLB 198
Grant, Skeeter
See Spiegelman, Art
Granville-Barker, Harley 1877-1946**TCLC 2;**
DAM DRAM
See also Barker, Harley Granville
See also CA 104
Grass, Guenter (Wilhelm) 1927-**CLC 1, 2, 4, 6,**
11, 15, 22, 32, 49, 88; DA; DAB; DAC;
DAM MST, NOV; WLC
See also CA 13-16R; CANR 20, 75; DA3; DLB
75, 124; MTCW 1, 2
Gratton, Thomas
See Hulme, T(homas) E(rnest)
Grau, Shirley Ann 1929- **CLC 4, 9; SSC 15**
See also CA 89-92; CANR 22, 69; DLB 2; INT
CANR-22; MTCW 1
Gravel, Fern
See Hall, James Norman
Graver, Elizabeth 1964- **CLC 70**
See also CA 135; CANR 71
Graves, Richard Perceval 1945- **CLC 44**
See also CA 65-68; CANR 9, 26, 51
Graves, Robert (von Ranke) 1895-1985 **C L C**
1, 2, 6, 11, 39, 44, 45; DAB; DAC; DAM
MST, POET; PC 6
See also CA 5-8R; 117; CANR 5, 36; CDBLB
1914-1945; DA3; DLB 20, 100, 191; DLBD
18; DLBY 85; MTCW 1, 2; SATA 45
Graves, Valerie
See Bradley, Marion Zimmer
Gray, Alasdair (James) 1934- **CLC 41**

See also CA 126; CANR 47, 69; DLB 194; INT 126; MTCW 1, 2

Gray, Amlin 1946-   **CLC 29**
See also CA 138

Gray, Francine du Plessix 1930-   **CLC 22; DAM NOV**
See also BEST 90:3; CA 61-64; CAAS 2; CANR 11, 33, 75, 81; INT CANR-11; MTCW 1, 2

Gray, John (Henry) 1866-1934   **TCLC 19**
See also CA 119; 162

Gray, Simon (James Holliday) 1936- **CLC 9, 14, 36**
See also AITN 1; CA 21-24R; CAAS 3; CANR 32, 69; DLB 13; MTCW 1

Gray, Spalding 1941-**CLC 49, 112; DAM POP; DC 7**
See also CA 128; CANR 74; MTCW 2

Gray, Thomas 1716-1771**LC 4, 40; DA; DAB; DAC; DAM MST; PC 2; WLC**
See also CDBLB 1660-1789; DA3; DLB 109

Grayson, David
See Baker, Ray Stannard

Grayson, Richard (A.) 1951-   **CLC 38**
See also CA 85-88; CANR 14, 31, 57

Greeley, Andrew M(oran) 1928-   **CLC 28; DAM POP**
See also CA 5-8R; CAAS 7; CANR 7, 43, 69; DA3; MTCW 1, 2

Green, Anna Katharine 1846-1935 **TCLC 63**
See also CA 112; 159; DLB 202

Green, Brian
See Card, Orson Scott

Green, Hannah
See Greenberg, Joanne (Goldenberg)

Green, Hannah 1927(?)-1996   **CLC 3**
See also CA 73-76; CANR 59

Green, Henry 1905-1973   **CLC 2, 13, 97**
See Yorke, Henry Vincent
See also CA 175; DLB 15

Green, Julian (Hartridge) 1900-1998
See Green, Julien
See also CA 21-24R; 169; CANR 33; DLB 4, 72; MTCW 1

Green, Julien   **CLC 3, 11, 77**
See Green, Julian (Hartridge)
See also MTCW 2

Green, Paul (Eliot) 1894-1981**CLC 25; DAM DRAM**
See also AITN 1; CA 5-8R; 103; CANR 3; DLB 7, 9; DLBY 81

Greenberg, Ivan 1908-1973
See Rahv, Philip
See also CA 85-88

Greenberg, Joanne (Goldenberg) 1932- **C L C 7, 30**
See also AAYA 12; CA 5-8R; CANR 14, 32, 69; SATA 25

Greenberg, Richard 1959(?)-   **CLC 57**
See also CA 138

Greene, Bette 1934-   **CLC 30**
See also AAYA 7; CA 53-56; CANR 4; CLR 2; JRDA; MAICYA; SAAS 16; SATA 8, 102

Greene, Gael   **CLC 8**
See also CA 13-16R; CANR 10

Greene, Graham (Henry) 1904-1991**CLC 1, 3, 6, 9, 14, 18, 27, 37, 70, 72; DA; DAB; DAC; DAM MST, NOV; SSC 29; WLC**
See also AITN 2; CA 13-16R; 133; CANR 35, 61; CDBLB 1945-1960; DA3; DLB 13, 15, 77, 100, 162, 201, 204; DLBY 91; MTCW 1, 2; SATA 20

Greene, Robert 1558-1592   **LC 41**

See also DLB 62, 167

Greer, Richard
See Silverberg, Robert

Gregor, Arthur 1923-   **CLC 9**
See also CA 25-28R; CAAS 10; CANR 11; SATA 36

Gregor, Lee
See Pohl, Frederik

Gregory, Isabella Augusta (Persse) 1852-1932 **TCLC 1**
See also CA 104; DLB 10

Gregory, J. Dennis
See Williams, John A(lfred)

Grendon, Stephen
See Derleth, August (William)

Grenville, Kate 1950-   **CLC 61**
See also CA 118; CANR 53

Grenville, Pelham
See Wodehouse, P(elham) G(renville)

Greve, Felix Paul (Berthold Friedrich) 1879-1948
See Grove, Frederick Philip
See also CA 104; 141; 175; CANR 79; DAC; DAM MST

Grey, Zane 1872-1939   **TCLC 6; DAM POP**
See also CA 104; 132; DA3; DLB 212; MTCW 1, 2

Grieg, (Johan) Nordahl (Brun) 1902-1943 **TCLC 10**
See also CA 107

Grieve, C(hristopher) M(urray) 1892-1978 **CLC 11, 19; DAM POET**
See also MacDiarmid, Hugh; Pteleon
See also CA 5-8R; 85-88; CANR 33; MTCW 1

Griffin, Gerald 1803-1840   **NCLC 7**
See also DLB 159

Griffin, John Howard 1920-1980   **CLC 68**
See also AITN 1; CA 1-4R; 101; CANR 2

Griffin, Peter 1942-   **CLC 39**
See also CA 136

Griffith, D(avid Lewelyn) W(ark) 1875(?)-1948 **TCLC 68**
See also CA 119; 150; CANR 80

Griffith, Lawrence
See Griffith, D(avid Lewelyn) W(ark)

Griffiths, Trevor 1935-   **CLC 13, 52**
See also CA 97-100; CANR 45; DLB 13

Griggs, Sutton Elbert 1872-1930(?)**TCLC 77**
See also CA 123; DLB 50

Grigson, Geoffrey (Edward Harvey) 1905-1985 **CLC 7, 39**
See also CA 25-28R; 118; CANR 20, 33; DLB 27; MTCW 1, 2

Grillparzer, Franz 1791-1872   **NCLC 1**
See also DLB 133

Grimble, Reverend Charles James
See Eliot, T(homas) S(tearns)

Grimke, Charlotte L(ottie) Forten 1837(?)-1914
See Forten, Charlotte L.
See also BW 1; CA 117; 124; DAM MULT, POET

Grimm, Jacob Ludwig Karl 1785-1863**NCLC 3, 77; SSC 36**
See also DLB 90; MAICYA; SATA 22

Grimm, Wilhelm Karl 1786-1859**NCLC 3, 77; SSC 36**
See also DLB 90; MAICYA; SATA 22

Grimmelshausen, Johann Jakob Christoffel von 1621-1676   **LC 6**
See also DLB 168

Grindel, Eugene 1895-1952
See Eluard, Paul
See also CA 104

Grisham, John 1955-   **CLC 84; DAM POP**
See also AAYA 14; CA 138; CANR 47, 69; DA3; MTCW 2

Grossman, David 1954-   **CLC 67**
See also CA 138

Grossman, Vasily (Semenovich) 1905-1964 **CLC 41**
See also CA 124; 130; MTCW 1

Grove, Frederick Philip   **TCLC 4**
See also Greve, Felix Paul (Berthold Friedrich)
See also DLB 92

Grubb
See Crumb, R(obert)

Grumbach, Doris (Isaac) 1918-**CLC 13, 22, 64**
See also CA 5-8R; CAAS 2; CANR 9, 42, 70; INT CANR-9; MTCW 2

Grundtvig, Nicolai Frederik Severin 1783-1872 **NCLC 1**

Grunge
See Crumb, R(obert)

Grunwald, Lisa 1959-   **CLC 44**
See also CA 120

Guare, John 1938- **CLC 8, 14, 29, 67; DAM DRAM**
See also CA 73-76; CANR 21, 69; DLB 7; MTCW 1, 2

Gudjonsson, Halldor Kiljan 1902-1998
See Laxness, Halldor
See also CA 103; 164

Guenter, Erich
See Eich, Guenter

Guest, Barbara 1920-   **CLC 34**
See also CA 25-28R; CANR 11, 44, 84; DLB 5, 193

Guest, Edgar A(lbert) 1881-1959 **TCLC 95**
See also CA 112; 168

Guest, Judith (Ann) 1936- **CLC 8, 30; DAM NOV, POP**
See also AAYA 7; CA 77-80; CANR 15, 75; DA3; INT CANR-15; MTCW 1, 2

Guevara, Che   **CLC 87; HLC 1**
See also Guevara (Serna), Ernesto

Guevara (Serna), Ernesto 1928-1967**CLC 87; DAM MULT; HLC 1**
See also Guevara, Che
See also CA 127; 111; CANR 56; HW 1

Guicciardini, Francesco 1483-1540   **LC 49**

Guild, Nicholas M. 1944-   **CLC 33**
See also CA 93-96

Guillemin, Jacques
See Sartre, Jean-Paul

Guillen, Jorge 1893-1984   **CLC 11; DAM MULT, POET; HLCS 1**
See also CA 89-92; 112; DLB 108; HW 1

Guillen, Nicolas (Cristobal) 1902-1989 **C L C 48, 79; BLC 2; DAM MST, MULT, POET; HLC 1; PC 23**
See also BW 2; CA 116; 125; 129; CANR 84; HW 1

Guillevic, (Eugene) 1907-   **CLC 33**
See also CA 93-96

Guillois
See Desnos, Robert

Guillois, Valentin
See Desnos, Robert

Guimaraes Rosa, Joao 1908-1967
See also CA 175; HLCS 2

Guiney, Louise Imogen 1861-1920 **TCLC 41**
See also CA 160; DLB 54

Guiraldes, Ricardo (Guillermo) 1886-1927 **TCLC 39**
See also CA 131; HW 1; MTCW 1

Gumilev, Nikolai (Stepanovich) 1886-1921

NOV, POET; PC 8; SSC 2; WLC
See also CA 104; 123; CDBLB 1890-1914;
DA3; DLB 18, 19, 135; MTCW 1, 2
Hare, David 1947-   **CLC 29, 58**
See also CA 97-100; CANR 39; DLB 13;
MTCW 1
Harewood, John
See Van Druten, John (William)
Harford, Henry
See Hudson, W(illiam) H(enry)
Hargrave, Leonie
See Disch, Thomas M(ichael)
Harjo, Joy 1951-**CLC 83; DAM MULT; PC 27**
See also CA 114; CANR 35, 67; DLB 120, 175;
MTCW 2; NNAL
Harlan, Louis R(udolph) 1922-   **CLC 34**
See also CA 21-24R; CANR 25, 55, 80
Harling, Robert 1951(?)-   **CLC 53**
See also CA 147
Harmon, William (Ruth) 1938-   **CLC 38**
See also CA 33-36R; CANR 14, 32, 35; SATA
65
Harper, F. E. W.
See Harper, Frances Ellen Watkins
Harper, Frances E. W.
See Harper, Frances Ellen Watkins
Harper, Frances E. Watkins
See Harper, Frances Ellen Watkins
Harper, Frances Ellen
See Harper, Frances Ellen Watkins
Harper, Frances Ellen Watkins 1825-1911
**TCLC 14; BLC 2; DAM MULT, POET;
PC 21**
See also BW 1, 3; CA 111; 125; CANR 79; DLB
50
Harper, Michael S(teven) 1938-   **CLC 7, 22**
See also BW 1; CA 33-36R; CANR 24; DLB
41
Harper, Mrs. F. E. W.
See Harper, Frances Ellen Watkins
Harris, Christie (Lucy) Irwin 1907- **CLC 12**
See also CA 5-8R; CANR 6, 83; CLR 47; DLB
88; JRDA; MAICYA; SAAS 10; SATA 6, 74
Harris, Frank 1856-1931   **TCLC 24**
See also CA 109; 150; CANR 80; DLB 156,
197
Harris, George Washington 1814-1869**NCLC
23**
See also DLB 3, 11
Harris, Joel Chandler 1848-1908   **TCLC 2;
SSC 19**
See also CA 104; 137; CANR 80; CLR 49; DLB
11, 23, 42, 78, 91; MAICYA; SATA 100;
YABC 1
Harris, John (Wyndham Parkes Lucas) Beynon
1903-1969
See Wyndham, John
See also CA 102; 89-92; CANR 84
Harris, MacDonald   **CLC 9**
See also Heiney, Donald (William)
Harris, Mark 1922-   **CLC 19**
See also CA 5-8R; CAAS 3; CANR 2, 55, 83;
DLB 2; DLBY 80
Harris, (Theodore) Wilson 1921-   **CLC 25**
See also BW 2, 3; CA 65-68; CAAS 16; CANR
11, 27, 69; DLB 117; MTCW 1
Harrison, Elizabeth Cavanna 1909-
See Cavanna, Betty
See also CA 9-12R; CANR 6, 27
Harrison, Harry (Max) 1925-   **CLC 42**
See also CA 1-4R; CANR 5, 21, 84; DLB 8;
SATA 4
Harrison, James (Thomas) 1937- **CLC 6, 14,**

33, 66; SSC 19
See also CA 13-16R; CANR 8, 51, 79; DLBY
82; INT CANR-8
Harrison, Jim
See Harrison, James (Thomas)
Harrison, Kathryn 1961-   **CLC 70**
See also CA 144; CANR 68
Harrison, Tony 1937-   **CLC 43**
See also CA 65-68; CANR 44; DLB 40; MTCW
1
Harriss, Will(ard Irvin) 1922-   **CLC 34**
See also CA 111
Harson, Sley
See Ellison, Harlan (Jay)
Hart, Ellis
See Ellison, Harlan (Jay)
Hart, Josephine 1942(?)-**CLC 70; DAM POP**
See also CA 138; CANR 70
Hart, Moss 1904-1961 **CLC 66; DAM DRAM**
See also CA 109; 89-92; CANR 84; DLB 7
Harte, (Francis) Bret(t) 1836(?)-1902**TCLC 1,
25; DA; DAC; DAM MST; SSC 8; WLC**
See also CA 104; 140; CANR 80; CDALB
1865-1917; DA3; DLB 12, 64, 74, 79, 186;
SATA 26
Hartley, L(eslie) P(oles) 1895-1972**CLC 2, 22**
See also CA 45-48; 37-40R; CANR 33; DLB
15, 139; MTCW 1, 2
Hartman, Geoffrey H. 1929-   **CLC 27**
See also CA 117; 125; CANR 79; DLB 67
Hartmann, Eduard von 1842-1906   **TCLC 97**
Hartmann, Sadakichi 1867-1944   **TCLC 73**
See also CA 157; DLB 54
Hartmann von Aue c. 1160-c. 1205**CMLC 15**
See also DLB 138
Hartmann von Aue 1170-1210   **CMLC 15**
Haruf, Kent 1943-   **CLC 34**
See also CA 149
Harwood, Ronald 1934-   **CLC 32; DAM
DRAM, MST**
See also CA 1-4R; CANR 4, 55; DLB 13
Hasegawa Tatsunosuke
See Futabatei, Shimei
Hasek, Jaroslav (Matej Frantisek) 1883-1923
TCLC 4
See also CA 104; 129; MTCW 1, 2
Hass, Robert 1941-   **CLC 18, 39, 99; PC 16**
See also CA 111; CANR 30, 50, 71; DLB 105,
206; SATA 94
Hastings, Hudson
See Kuttner, Henry
Hastings, Selina   **CLC 44**
Hathorne, John 1641-1717   **LC 38**
Hatteras, Amelia
See Mencken, H(enry) L(ouis)
Hatteras, Owen   **TCLC 18**
See also Mencken, H(enry) L(ouis); Nathan,
George Jean
Hauptmann, Gerhart (Johann Robert) 1862-
1946   **TCLC 4; DAM DRAM**
See also CA 104; 153; DLB 66, 118
Havel, Vaclav 1936-   **CLC 25, 58, 65; DAM
DRAM; DC 6**
See also CA 104; CANR 36, 63; DA3; MTCW
1, 2
Haviaras, Stratis   **CLC 33**
See also Chaviaras, Strates
Hawes, Stephen 1475(?)-1523(?)   **LC 17**
See also DLB 132
Hawkes, John (Clendennin Burne, Jr.) 1925-
1998   **CLC 1, 2, 3, 4, 7, 9, 14, 15, 27, 49**
See also CA 1-4R; 167; CANR 2, 47, 64; DLB
2, 7; DLBY 80, 98; MTCW 1, 2

Hawking, S. W.
See Hawking, Stephen W(illiam)
Hawking, Stephen W(illiam) 1942- **CLC 63,
105**
See also AAYA 13; BEST 89:1; CA 126; 129;
CANR 48; DA3; MTCW 2
Hawkins, Anthony Hope
See Hope, Anthony
Hawthorne, Julian 1846-1934   **TCLC 25**
See also CA 165
Hawthorne, Nathaniel 1804-1864 **NCLC 39;
DA; DAB; DAC; DAM MST, NOV; SSC
3, 29; WLC**
See also AAYA 18; CDALB 1640-1865; DA3;
DLB 1, 74; YABC 2
Haxton, Josephine Ayres 1921-
See Douglas, Ellen
See also CA 115; CANR 41, 83
Hayaseca y Eizaguirre, Jorge
See Echegaray (y Eizaguirre), Jose (Maria
Waldo)
Hayashi, Fumiko 1904-1951   **TCLC 27**
See also CA 161; DLB 180
Haycraft, Anna
See Ellis, Alice Thomas
See also CA 122; MTCW 2
Hayden, Robert E(arl) 1913-1980 **CLC 5, 9,
14, 37; BLC 2; DA; DAC; DAM MST,
MULT, POET; PC 6**
See also BW 1, 3; CA 69-72; 97-100; CABS 2;
CANR 24, 75, 82; CDALB 1941-1968; DLB
5, 76; MTCW 1, 2; SATA 19; SATA-Obit 26
Hayford, J(oseph) E(phraim) Casely
See Casely-Hayford, J(oseph) E(phraim)
Hayman, Ronald 1932-   **CLC 44**
See also CA 25-28R; CANR 18, 50; DLB 155
Haywood, Eliza (Fowler) 1693(?)-1756 **LC 1,
44**
See also DLB 39
Hazlitt, William 1778-1830   **NCLC 29**
See also DLB 110, 158
Hazzard, Shirley 1931-   **CLC 18**
See also CA 9-12R; CANR 4, 70; DLBY 82;
MTCW 1
Head, Bessie 1937-1986 **CLC 25, 67; BLC 2;
DAM MULT**
See also BW 2, 3; CA 29-32R; 119; CANR 25,
82; DA3; DLB 117; MTCW 1, 2
Headon, (Nicky) Topper 1956(?)-   **CLC 30**
Heaney, Seamus (Justin) 1939- **CLC 5, 7, 14,
25, 37, 74, 91; DAB; DAM POET; PC 18;
WLCS**
See also CA 85-88; CANR 25, 48, 75; CDBLB
1960 to Present; DA3; DLB 40; DLBY 95;
MTCW 1, 2
Hearn, (Patricio) Lafcadio (Tessima Carlos)
1850-1904   **TCLC 9**
See also CA 105; 166; DLB 12, 78, 189
Hearne, Vicki 1946-   **CLC 56**
See also CA 139
Hearon, Shelby 1931-   **CLC 63**
See also AITN 2; CA 25-28R; CANR 18, 48
Heat-Moon, William Least   **CLC 29**
See also Trogdon, William (Lewis)
See also AAYA 9
Hebbel, Friedrich 1813-1863**NCLC 43; DAM
DRAM**
See also DLB 129
Hebert, Anne 1916-**CLC 4, 13, 29; DAC; DAM
MST, POET**
See also CA 85-88; CANR 69; DA3; DLB 68;
MTCW 1, 2
Hecht, Anthony (Evan) 1923- **CLC 8, 13, 19;**

DAM POET
See also CA 9-12R; CANR 6; DLB 5, 169

Hecht, Ben 1894-1964 **CLC 8**
See also CA 85-88; DLB 7, 9, 25, 26, 28, 86

Hedayat, Sadeq 1903-1951 **TCLC 21**
See also CA 120

Hegel, Georg Wilhelm Friedrich 1770-1831
NCLC 46
See also DLB 90

Heidegger, Martin 1889-1976 **CLC 24**
See also CA 81-84; 65-68; CANR 34; MTCW
1, 2

Heidenstam, (Carl Gustaf) Verner von 1859-
1940 **TCLC 5**
See also CA 104

Heifner, Jack 1946- **CLC 11**
See also CA 105; CANR 47

Heijermans, Herman 1864-1924 **TCLC 24**
See also CA 123

Heilbrun, Carolyn G(old) 1926- **CLC 25**
See also CA 45-48; CANR 1, 28, 58

Heine, Heinrich 1797-1856**NCLC 4, 54; PC 25**
See also DLB 90

Heinemann, Larry (Curtiss) 1944- **CLC 50**
See also CA 110; CAAS 21; CANR 31, 81;
DLBD 9; INT CANR-31

Heiney, Donald (William) 1921-1993
See Harris, MacDonald
See also CA 1-4R; 142; CANR 3, 58

Heinlein, Robert A(nson) 1907-1988**CLC 1, 3,
8, 14, 26, 55; DAM POP**
See also AAYA 17; CA 1-4R; 125; CANR 1,
20, 53; DA3; DLB 8; JRDA; MAICYA;
MTCW 1, 2; SATA 9, 69; SATA-Obit 56

Helforth, John
See Doolittle, Hilda

Hellenhofferu, Vojtech Kapristian z
See Hasek, Jaroslav (Matej Frantisek)

Heller, Joseph 1923-**CLC 1, 3, 5, 8, 11, 36, 63;
DA; DAB; DAC; DAM MST, NOV, POP;
WLC**
See also AAYA 24; AITN 1; CA 5-8R; CABS
1; CANR 8, 42, 66; DA3; DLB 2, 28; DLBY
80; INT CANR-8; MTCW 1, 2

Hellman, Lillian (Florence) 1906-1984**CLC 2,
4, 8, 14, 18, 34, 44, 52; DAM DRAM; DC 1**
See also AITN 1, 2; CA 13-16R; 112; CANR
33; DA3; DLB 7; DLBY 84; MTCW 1, 2

Helprin, Mark 1947-**CLC 7, 10, 22, 32; DAM
NOV, POP**
See also CA 81-84; CANR 47, 64; CDALBS;
DA3; DLBY 85; MTCW 1, 2

Helvetius, Claude-Adrien 1715-1771 **LC 26**

Helyar, Jane Penelope Josephine 1933-
See Poole, Josephine
See also CA 21-24R; CANR 10, 26; SATA 82

Hemans, Felicia 1793-1835 **NCLC 71**
See also DLB 96

Hemingway, Ernest (Miller) 1899-1961 **C L C
1, 3, 6, 8, 10, 13, 19, 30, 34, 39, 41, 44, 50,
61, 80; DA; DAB; DAC; DAM MST, NOV;
SSC 1, 25, 36; WLC**
See also AAYA 19; CA 77-80; CANR 34;
CDALB 1917-1929; DA3; DLB 4, 9, 102,
210; DLBD 1, 15, 16; DLBY 81, 87, 96, 98;
MTCW 1, 2

Hempel, Amy 1951- **CLC 39**
See also CA 118; 137; CANR 70; DA3; MTCW
2

Henderson, F. C.
See Mencken, H(enry) L(ouis)

Henderson, Sylvia
See Ashton-Warner, Sylvia (Constance)

Henderson, Zenna (Chlarson) 1917-1983**SSC
29**
See also CA 1-4R; 133; CANR 1, 84; DLB 8;
SATA 5

Henkin, Joshua **CLC 119**
See also CA 161

Henley, Beth **CLC 23; DC 6**
See also Henley, Elizabeth Becker
See also CABS 3; DLBY 86

Henley, Elizabeth Becker 1952-
See Henley, Beth
See also CA 107; CANR 32, 73; DAM DRAM,
MST; DA3; MTCW 1, 2

Henley, William Ernest 1849-1903 **TCLC 8**
See also CA 105; DLB 19

Hennissart, Martha
See Lathen, Emma
See also CA 85-88; CANR 64

Henry, O. **TCLC 1, 19; SSC 5; WLC**
See also Porter, William Sydney

Henry, Patrick 1736-1799 **LC 25**

Henryson, Robert 1430(?)-1506(?) **LC 20**
See also DLB 146

Henry VIII 1491-1547 **LC 10**
See also DLB 132

Henschke, Alfred
See Klabund

Hentoff, Nat(han Irving) 1925- **CLC 26**
See also AAYA 4; CA 1-4R; CAAS 6; CANR
5, 25, 77; CLR 1, 52; INT CANR-25; JRDA;
MAICYA; SATA 42, 69; SATA-Brief 27

Heppenstall, (John) Rayner 1911-1981 **C L C
10**
See also CA 1-4R; 103; CANR 29

Heraclitus c. 540B.C.-c. 450B.C. **CMLC 22**
See also DLB 176

Herbert, Frank (Patrick) 1920-1986 **CLC 12,
23, 35, 44, 85; DAM POP**
See also AAYA 21; CA 53-56; 118; CANR 5,
43; CDALBS; DLB 8; INT CANR-5; MTCW
1, 2; SATA 9, 37; SATA-Obit 47

Herbert, George 1593-1633 **LC 24; DAB;
DAM POET; PC 4**
See also CDBLB Before 1660; DLB 126

Herbert, Zbigniew 1924-1998 **CLC 9, 43;
DAM POET**
See also CA 89-92; 169; CANR 36, 74; MTCW
1

Herbst, Josephine (Frey) 1897-1969 **CLC 34**
See also CA 5-8R; 25-28R; DLB 9

Heredia, Jose Maria 1803-1839
See also HLCS 2

Hergesheimer, Joseph 1880-1954 **TCLC 11**
See also CA 109; DLB 102, 9

Herlihy, James Leo 1927-1993 **CLC 6**
See also CA 1-4R; 143; CANR 2

Hermogenes fl. c. 175- **CMLC 6**

Hernandez, Jose 1834-1886 **NCLC 17**

Herodotus c. 484B.C.-429B.C. **CMLC 17**
See also DLB 176

Herrick, Robert 1591-1674**LC 13; DA; DAB;
DAC; DAM MST, POP; PC 9**
See also DLB 126

Herring, Guilles
See Somerville, Edith

Herriot, James 1916-1995**CLC 12; DAM POP**
See also Wight, James Alfred
See also AAYA 1; CA 148; CANR 40; MTCW
2; SATA 86

Herrmann, Dorothy 1941- **CLC 44**
See also CA 107

Herrmann, Taffy
See Herrmann, Dorothy

Hersey, John (Richard) 1914-1993**CLC 1, 2, 7,
9, 40, 81, 97; DAM POP**
See also AAYA 29; CA 17-20R; 140; CANR
33; CDALBS; DLB 6, 185; MTCW 1, 2;
SATA 25; SATA-Obit 76

Herzen, Aleksandr Ivanovich 1812-1870
NCLC 10, 61

Herzl, Theodor 1860-1904 **TCLC 36**
See also CA 168

Herzog, Werner 1942- **CLC 16**
See also CA 89-92

Hesiod c. 8th cent. B.C.- **CMLC 5**
See also DLB 176

Hesse, Hermann 1877-1962**CLC 1, 2, 3, 6, 11,
17, 25, 69; DA; DAB; DAC; DAM MST,
NOV; SSC 9; WLC**
See also CA 17-18; CAP 2; DA3; DLB 66;
MTCW 1, 2; SATA 50

Hewes, Cady
See De Voto, Bernard (Augustine)

Heyen, William 1940- **CLC 13, 18**
See also CA 33-36R; CAAS 9; DLB 5

Heyerdahl, Thor 1914- **CLC 26**
See also CA 5-8R; CANR 5, 22, 66, 73; MTCW
1, 2; SATA 2, 52

Heym, Georg (Theodor Franz Arthur) 1887-
1912 **TCLC 9**
See also CA 106

Heym, Stefan 1913- **CLC 41**
See also CA 9-12R; CANR 4; DLB 69

Heyse, Paul (Johann Ludwig von) 1830-1914
TCLC 8
See also CA 104; DLB 129

Heyward, (Edwin) DuBose 1885-1940 **T C L C
59**
See also CA 108; 157; DLB 7, 9, 45; SATA 21

Hibbert, Eleanor Alice Burford 1906-1993
CLC 7; DAM POP
See also BEST 90:4; CA 17-20R; 140; CANR
9, 28, 59; MTCW 2; SATA 2; SATA-Obit 74

Hichens, Robert (Smythe) 1864-1950 **T C L C
64**
See also CA 162; DLB 153

Higgins, George V(incent) 1939-**CLC 4, 7, 10,
18**
See also CA 77-80; CAAS 5; CANR 17, 51;
DLB 2; DLBY 81, 98; INT CANR-17;
MTCW 1

Higginson, Thomas Wentworth 1823-1911
TCLC 36
See also CA 162; DLB 1, 64

Highet, Helen
See MacInnes, Helen (Clark)

Highsmith, (Mary) Patricia 1921-1995**CLC 2,
4, 14, 42, 102; DAM NOV, POP**
See also CA 1-4R; 147; CANR 1, 20, 48, 62;
DA3; MTCW 1, 2

Highwater, Jamake (Mamake) 1942(?)- **C L C
12**
See also AAYA 7; CA 65-68; CAAS 7; CANR
10, 34, 84; CLR 17; DLB 52; DLBY 85;
JRDA; MAICYA; SATA 32, 69; SATA-Brief
30

Highway, Tomson 1951-**CLC 92; DAC; DAM
MULT**
See also CA 151; CANR 75; MTCW 2; NNAL

Higuchi, Ichiyo 1872-1896 **NCLC 49**

Hijuelos, Oscar 1951- **CLC 65; DAM MULT,
POP; HLC 1**
See also AAYA 25; BEST 90:1; CA 123; CANR
50, 75; DA3; DLB 145; HW 1, 2; MTCW 2

Hikmet, Nazim 1902(?)-1963 **CLC 40**
See also CA 141; 93-96

See also CA 13-14; CANR 58; CAP 1; MTCW 2

Horatio
See Proust, (Valentin-Louis-George-Eugene-) Marcel

Horgan, Paul (George Vincent O'Shaughnessy) 1903-1995 **CLC 9, 53; DAM NOV**
See also CA 13-16R; 147; CANR 9, 35; DLB 212; DLBY 85; INT CANR-9; MTCW 1, 2; SATA 13; SATA-Obit 84

Horn, Peter
See Kuttner, Henry

Hornem, Horace Esq.
See Byron, George Gordon (Noel)

Horney, Karen (Clementine Theodore Danielsen) 1885-1952 **TCLC 71**
See also CA 114; 165

Hornung, E(rnest) W(illiam) 1866-1921 **TCLC 59**
See also CA 108; 160; DLB 70

Horovitz, Israel (Arthur) 1939-**CLC 56; DAM DRAM**
See also CA 33-36R; CANR 46, 59; DLB 7

Horvath, Odon von
See Horvath, Oedoen von
See also DLB 85, 124

Horvath, Oedoen von 1901-1938 **TCLC 45**
See also Horvath, Odon von
See also CA 118

Horwitz, Julius 1920-1986 **CLC 14**
See also CA 9-12R; 119; CANR 12

Hospital, Janette Turner 1942- **CLC 42**
See also CA 108; CANR 48

Hostos, E. M. de
See Hostos (y Bonilla), Eugenio Maria de

Hostos, Eugenio M. de
See Hostos (y Bonilla), Eugenio Maria de

Hostos, Eugenio Maria
See Hostos (y Bonilla), Eugenio Maria de

Hostos (y Bonilla), Eugenio Maria de 1839-1903 **TCLC 24**
See also CA 123; 131; HW 1

Houdini
See Lovecraft, H(oward) P(hillips)

Hougan, Carolyn 1943- **CLC 34**
See also CA 139

Household, Geoffrey (Edward West) 1900-1988 **CLC 11**
See also CA 77-80; 126; CANR 58; DLB 87; SATA 14; SATA-Obit 59

Housman, A(lfred) E(dward) 1859-1936 **TCLC 1, 10; DA; DAB; DAC; DAM MST, POET; PC 2; WLCS**
See also CA 104; 125; DA3; DLB 19; MTCW 1, 2

Housman, Laurence 1865-1959 **TCLC 7**
See also CA 106; 155; DLB 10; SATA 25

Howard, Elizabeth Jane 1923- **CLC 7, 29**
See also CA 5-8R; CANR 8, 62

Howard, Maureen 1930- **CLC 5, 14, 46**
See also CA 53-56; CANR 31, 75; DLBY 83; INT CANR-31; MTCW 1, 2

Howard, Richard 1929- **CLC 7, 10, 47**
See also AITN 1; CA 85-88; CANR 25, 80; DLB 5; INT CANR-25

Howard, Robert E(rvin) 1906-1936 **TCLC 8**
See also CA 105; 157

Howard, Warren F.
See Pohl, Frederik

Howe, Fanny (Quincy) 1940- **CLC 47**
See also CA 117; CAAS 27; CANR 70; SATA-Brief 52

Howe, Irving 1920-1993 **CLC 85**

See also CA 9-12R; 141; CANR 21, 50; DLB 67; MTCW 1, 2

Howe, Julia Ward 1819-1910 **TCLC 21**
See also CA 117; DLB 1, 189

Howe, Susan 1937- **CLC 72**
See also CA 160; DLB 120

Howe, Tina 1937- **CLC 48**
See also CA 109

Howell, James 1594(?)-1666 **LC 13**
See also DLB 151

Howells, W. D.
See Howells, William Dean

Howells, William D.
See Howells, William Dean

Howells, William Dean 1837-1920**TCLC 7, 17, 41; SSC 36**
See also CA 104; 134; CDALB 1865-1917; DLB 12, 64, 74, 79, 189; MTCW 2

Howes, Barbara 1914-1996 **CLC 15**
See also CA 9-12R; 151; CAAS 3; CANR 53; SATA 5

Hrabal, Bohumil 1914-1997 **CLC 13, 67**
See also CA 106; 156; CAAS 12; CANR 57

Hroswitha of Gandersheim c. 935-c. 1002 **CMLC 29**
See also DLB 148

Hsun, Lu
See Lu Hsun

Hubbard, L(afayette) Ron(ald) 1911-1986 **CLC 43; DAM POP**
See also CA 77-80; 118; CANR 52; DA3; MTCW 2

Huch, Ricarda (Octavia) 1864-1947**TCLC 13**
See also CA 111; DLB 66

Huddle, David 1942- **CLC 49**
See also CA 57-60; CAAS 20; DLB 130

Hudson, Jeffrey
See Crichton, (John) Michael

Hudson, W(illiam) H(enry) 1841-1922 **TCLC 29**
See also CA 115; DLB 98, 153, 174; SATA 35

Hueffer, Ford Madox
See Ford, Ford Madox

Hughart, Barry 1934- **CLC 39**
See also CA 137

Hughes, Colin
See Creasey, John

Hughes, David (John) 1930- **CLC 48**
See also CA 116; 129; DLB 14

Hughes, Edward James
See Hughes, Ted
See also DAM MST, POET; DA3

Hughes, (James) Langston 1902-1967**CLC 1, 5, 10, 15, 35, 44, 108; BLC 2; DA; DAB; DAC; DAM DRAM, MST, MULT, POET; DC 3; PC 1; SSC 6; WLC**
See also AAYA 12; BW 1, 3; CA 1-4R; 25-28R; CANR 1, 34, 82; CDALB 1929-1941; CLR 17; DA3; DLB 4, 7, 48, 51, 86; JRDA; MAICYA; MTCW 1, 2; SATA 4, 33

Hughes, Richard (Arthur Warren) 1900-1976 **CLC 1, 11; DAM NOV**
See also CA 5-8R; 65-68; CANR 4; DLB 15, 161; MTCW 1; SATA 8; SATA-Obit 25

Hughes, Ted 1930-1998 **CLC 2, 4, 9, 14, 37, 119; DAB; DAC; PC 7**
See also Hughes, Edward James
See also CA 1-4R; 171; CANR 1, 33, 66; CLR 3; DLB 40, 161; MAICYA; MTCW 1, 2; SATA 49; SATA-Brief 27; SATA-Obit 107

Hugo, Richard F(ranklin) 1923-1982 **CLC 6, 18, 32; DAM POET**
See also CA 49-52; 108; CANR 3; DLB 5, 206

Hugo, Victor (Marie) 1802-1885**NCLC 3, 10, 21; DA; DAB; DAC; DAM DRAM, MST, NOV, POET; PC 17; WLC**
See also AAYA 28; DA3; DLB 119, 192; SATA 47

Huidobro, Vicente
See Huidobro Fernandez, Vicente Garcia

Huidobro Fernandez, Vicente Garcia 1893-1948 **TCLC 31**
See also CA 131; HW 1

Hulme, Keri 1947- **CLC 39**
See also CA 125; CANR 69; INT 125

Hulme, T(homas) E(rnest) 1883-1917 **TCLC 21**
See also CA 117; DLB 19

Hume, David 1711-1776 **LC 7**
See also DLB 104

Humphrey, William 1924-1997 **CLC 45**
See also CA 77-80; 160; CANR 68; DLB 212

Humphreys, Emyr Owen 1919- **CLC 47**
See also CA 5-8R; CANR 3, 24; DLB 15

Humphreys, Josephine 1945- **CLC 34, 57**
See also CA 121; 127; INT 127

Huneker, James Gibbons 1857-1921**TCLC 65**
See also DLB 71

Hungerford, Pixie
See Brinsmead, H(esba) F(ay)

Hunt, E(verette) Howard, (Jr.) 1918- **CLC 3**
See also AITN 1; CA 45-48; CANR 2, 47

Hunt, Kyle
See Creasey, John

Hunt, (James Henry) Leigh 1784-1859**NCLC 1, 70; DAM POET**
See also DLB 96, 110, 144

Hunt, Marsha 1946- **CLC 70**
See also BW 2, 3; CA 143; CANR 79

Hunt, Violet 1866(?)-1942 **TCLC 53**
See also DLB 162, 197

Hunter, E. Waldo
See Sturgeon, Theodore (Hamilton)

Hunter, Evan 1926- **CLC 11, 31; DAM POP**
See also CA 5-8R; CANR 5, 38, 62; DLBY 82; INT CANR-5; MTCW 1; SATA 25

Hunter, Kristin (Eggleston) 1931- **CLC 35**
See also AITN 1; BW 1; CA 13-16R; CANR 13; CLR 3; DLB 33; INT CANR-13; MAICYA; SAAS 10; SATA 12

Hunter, Mary
See Austin, Mary (Hunter)

Hunter, Mollie 1922- **CLC 21**
See also McIlwraith, Maureen Mollie Hunter
See also AAYA 13; CANR 37, 78; CLR 25; DLB 161; JRDA; MAICYA; SAAS 7; SATA 54, 106

Hunter, Robert (?)-1734 **LC 7**

Hurston, Zora Neale 1903-1960**CLC 7, 30, 61; BLC 2; DA; DAC; DAM MST, MULT, NOV; SSC 4; WLCS**
See also AAYA 15; BW 1, 3; CA 85-88; CANR 61; CDALBS; DA3; DLB 51, 86; MTCW 1, 2

Huston, John (Marcellus) 1906-1987 **CLC 20**
See also CA 73-76; 123; CANR 34; DLB 26

Hustvedt, Siri 1955- **CLC 76**
See also CA 137

Hutten, Ulrich von 1488-1523 **LC 16**
See also DLB 179

Huxley, Aldous (Leonard) 1894-1963 **CLC 1, 3, 4, 5, 8, 11, 18, 35, 79; DA; DAB; DAC; DAM MST, NOV; WLC**
See also AAYA 11; CA 85-88; CANR 44; CDBLB 1914-1945; DA3; DLB 36, 100, 162, 195; MTCW 1, 2; SATA 63

82; DLB 41; MTCW 2

Knight, Sarah Kemble 1666-1727   **LC 7**
See also DLB 24, 200

Knister, Raymond 1899-1932   **TCLC 56**
See also DLB 68

Knowles, John 1926-   **CLC 1, 4, 10, 26; DA;**
  DAC; DAM MST, NOV
See also AAYA 10; CA 17-20R; CANR 40, 74,
76; CDALB 1968-1988; DLB 6; MTCW 1,
2; SATA 8, 89

Knox, Calvin M.
See Silverberg, Robert

Knox, John c. 1505-1572   **LC 37**
See also DLB 132

Knye, Cassandra
See Disch, Thomas M(ichael)

Koch, C(hristopher) J(ohn) 1932-   **CLC 42**
See also CA 127; CANR 84

Koch, Christopher
See Koch, C(hristopher) J(ohn)

Koch, Kenneth 1925-   **CLC 5, 8, 44; DAM**
  POET
See also CA 1-4R; CANR 6, 36, 57; DLB 5;
INT CANR-36; MTCW 2; SATA 65

Kochanowski, Jan 1530-1584   **LC 10**

Kock, Charles Paul de 1794-1871   **NCLC 16**

Koda Shigeyuki 1867-1947
See Rohan, Koda
See also CA 121

Koestler, Arthur 1905-1983 **CLC 1, 3, 6, 8, 15,**
33
See also CA 1-4R; 109; CANR 1, 33; CDBLB
1945-1960; DLBY 83; MTCW 1, 2

Kogawa, Joy Nozomi 1935-   **CLC 78; DAC;**
  DAM MST, MULT
See also CA 101; CANR 19, 62; MTCW 2;
SATA 99

Kohout, Pavel 1928-   **CLC 13**
See also CA 45-48; CANR 3

Koizumi, Yakumo
See Hearn, (Patricio) Lafcadio (Tessima Carlos)

Kolmar, Gertrud 1894-1943   **TCLC 40**
See also CA 167

Komunyakaa, Yusef 1947-**CLC 86, 94; BLCS**
See also CA 147; CANR 83; DLB 120

Konrad, George
See Konrad, Gyoergy

Konrad, Gyoergy 1933-   **CLC 4, 10, 73**
See also CA 85-88

Konwicki, Tadeusz 1926- **CLC 8, 28, 54, 117**
See also CA 101; CAAS 9; CANR 39, 59;
MTCW 1

Koontz, Dean R(ay) 1945-   **CLC 78; DAM**
  NOV, POP
See also AAYA 9, 31; BEST 89:3, 90:2; CA 108;
CANR 19, 36, 52; DA3; MTCW 1; SATA 92

Kopernik, Mikolaj
See Copernicus, Nicolaus

Kopit, Arthur (Lee) 1937-**CLC 1, 18, 33; DAM**
  DRAM
See also AITN 1; CA 81-84; CABS 3; DLB 7;
MTCW 1

Kops, Bernard 1926-   **CLC 4**
See also CA 5-8R; CANR 84; DLB 13

Kornbluth, C(yril) M. 1923-1958   **TCLC 8**
See also CA 105; 160; DLB 8

Korolenko, V. G.
See Korolenko, Vladimir Galaktionovich

Korolenko, Vladimir
See Korolenko, Vladimir Galaktionovich

Korolenko, Vladimir G.
See Korolenko, Vladimir Galaktionovich

Korolenko, Vladimir Galaktionovich 1853-
1921   **TCLC 22**
See also CA 121

Korzybski, Alfred (Habdank Skarbek) 1879-
1950   **TCLC 61**
See also CA 123; 160

Kosinski, Jerzy (Nikodem) 1933-1991**CLC 1,**
2, 3, 6, 10, 15, 53, 70; DAM NOV
See also CA 17-20R; 134; CANR 9, 46; DA3;
DLB 2; DLBY 82; MTCW 1, 2

Kostelanetz, Richard (Cory) 1940-   **CLC 28**
See also CA 13-16R; CAAS 8; CANR 38, 77

Kostrowitzki, Wilhelm Apollinaris de 1880-
1918
See Apollinaire, Guillaume
See also CA 104

Kotlowitz, Robert 1924-   **CLC 4**
See also CA 33-36R; CANR 36

Kotzebue, August (Friedrich Ferdinand) von
1761-1819   **NCLC 25**
See also DLB 94

Kotzwinkle, William 1938-   **CLC 5, 14, 35**
See also CA 45-48; CANR 3, 44, 84; CLR 6;
DLB 173; MAICYA; SATA 24, 70

Kowna, Stancy
See Szymborska, Wislawa

Kozol, Jonathan 1936-   **CLC 17**
See also CA 61-64; CANR 16, 45

Kozoll, Michael 1940(?)-   **CLC 35**

Kramer, Kathryn 19(?)-   **CLC 34**

Kramer, Larry 1935-**CLC 42; DAM POP; DC**
8
See also CA 124; 126; CANR 60

Krasicki, Ignacy 1735-1801   **NCLC 8**

Krasinski, Zygmunt 1812-1859   **NCLC 4**

Kraus, Karl 1874-1936   **TCLC 5**
See also CA 104; DLB 118

Kreve (Mickevicius), Vincas 1882-1954**TCLC**
27
See also CA 170

Kristeva, Julia 1941-   **CLC 77**
See also CA 154

Kristofferson, Kris 1936-   **CLC 26**
See also CA 104

Krizanc, John 1956-   **CLC 57**

Krleza, Miroslav 1893-1981   **CLC 8, 114**
See also CA 97-100; 105; CANR 50; DLB 147

Kroetsch, Robert 1927- **CLC 5, 23, 57; DAC;**
  DAM POET
See also CA 17-20R; CANR 8, 38; DLB 53;
MTCW 1

Kroetz, Franz
See Kroetz, Franz Xaver

Kroetz, Franz Xaver 1946-   **CLC 41**
See also CA 130

Kroker, Arthur (W.) 1945-   **CLC 77**
See also CA 161

Kropotkin, Peter (Alekseievich) 1842-1921
  TCLC 36
See also CA 119

Krotkov, Yuri 1917-   **CLC 19**
See also CA 102

Krumb
See Crumb, R(obert)

Krumgold, Joseph (Quincy) 1908-1980 **C L C**
12
See also CA 9-12R; 101; CANR 7; MAICYA;
SATA 1, 48; SATA-Obit 23

Krumwitz
See Crumb, R(obert)

Krutch, Joseph Wood 1893-1970   **CLC 24**
See also CA 1-4R; 25-28R; CANR 4; DLB 63,
206

Krutzch, Gus

See Eliot, T(homas) S(tearns)

Krylov, Ivan Andreevich 1768(?)-1844**N C L C**
1
See also DLB 150

Kubin, Alfred (Leopold Isidor) 1877-1959
  TCLC 23
See also CA 112; 149; DLB 81

Kubrick, Stanley 1928-1999   **CLC 16**
See also AAYA 30; CA 81-84; 177; CANR 33;
DLB 26

Kumin, Maxine (Winokur) 1925- **CLC 5, 13,**
28; DAM POET; PC 15
See also AITN 2; CA 1-4R; CAAS 8; CANR 1,
21, 69; DA3; DLB 5; MTCW 1, 2; SATA 12

Kundera, Milan 1929- **CLC 4, 9, 19, 32, 68,**
115; DAM NOV; SSC 24
See also AAYA 2; CA 85-88; CANR 19, 52,
74; DA3; MTCW 1, 2

Kunene, Mazisi (Raymond) 1930-   **CLC 85**
See also BW 1, 3; CA 125; CANR 81; DLB
117

Kunitz, Stanley (Jasspon) 1905-**CLC 6, 11, 14;**
PC 19
See also CA 41-44R; CANR 26, 57; DA3; DLB
48; INT CANR-26; MTCW 1, 2

Kunze, Reiner 1933-   **CLC 10**
See also CA 93-96; DLB 75

Kuprin, Aleksandr Ivanovich 1870-1938
  TCLC 5
See also CA 104

Kureishi, Hanif 1954(?)-   **CLC 64**
See also CA 139; DLB 194

Kurosawa, Akira 1910-1998   **CLC 16, 119;**
  DAM MULT
See also AAYA 11; CA 101; 170; CANR 46

Kushner, Tony 1957(?)-**CLC 81; DAM DRAM;**
  DC 10
See also CA 144; CANR 74; DA3; MTCW 2

Kuttner, Henry 1915-1958   **TCLC 10**
See also Vance, Jack
See also CA 107; 157; DLB 8

Kuzma, Greg 1944-   **CLC 7**
See also CA 33-36R; CANR 70

Kuzmin, Mikhail 1872(?)-1936   **TCLC 40**
See also CA 170

Kyd, Thomas 1558-1594**LC 22; DAM DRAM;**
  DC 3
See also DLB 62

Kyprianos, Iossif
See Samarakis, Antonis

La Bruyere, Jean de 1645-1696   **LC 17**

Lacan, Jacques (Marie Emile) 1901-1981
  CLC 75
See also CA 121; 104

Laclos, Pierre Ambroise Francois Choderlos de
1741-1803   **NCLC 4**

La Colere, Francois
See Aragon, Louis

Lacolere, Francois
See Aragon, Louis

La Deshabilleuse
See Simenon, Georges (Jacques Christian)

Lady Gregory
See Gregory, Isabella Augusta (Persse)

Lady of Quality, A
See Bagnold, Enid

La Fayette, Marie (Madelaine Pioche de la
  Vergne Comtes 1634-1693   **LC 2**

Lafayette, Rene
See Hubbard, L(afayette) Ron(ald)

Laforgue, Jules 1860-1887**NCLC 5, 53; PC 14;**
  SSC 20

Lagerkvist, Paer (Fabian) 1891-1974 **CLC 7,**

10, 13, 54; **DAM DRAM, NOV**
 See also Lagerkvist, Par
 See also CA 85-88; 49-52; DA3; MTCW 1, 2
Lagerkvist, Par   **SSC 12**
 See also Lagerkvist, Paer (Fabian)
 See also MTCW 2
Lagerloef, Selma (Ottiliana Lovisa) 1858-1940
 TCLC 4, 36
 See also Lagerlof, Selma (Ottiliana Lovisa)
 See also CA 108; MTCW 2; SATA 15
Lagerlof, Selma (Ottiliana Lovisa)
 See Lagerloef, Selma (Ottiliana Lovisa)
 See also CLR 7; SATA 15
La Guma, (Justin) Alex(ander) 1925-1985
 CLC 19; BLCS; DAM NOV
 See also BW 1, 3; CA 49-52; 118; CANR 25,
 81; DLB 117; MTCW 1, 2
Laidlaw, A. K.
 See Grieve, C(hristopher) M(urray)
Lainez, Manuel Mujica
 See Mujica Lainez, Manuel
 See also HW 1
Laing, R(onald) D(avid) 1927-1989 **CLC 95**
 See also CA 107; 129; CANR 34; MTCW 1
Lamartine, Alphonse (Marie Louis Prat) de
 1790-1869NCLC 11; **DAM POET; PC 16**
Lamb, Charles 1775-1834 **NCLC 10; DA;**
 DAB; DAC; DAM MST; WLC
 See also CDBLB 1789-1832; DLB 93, 107, 163;
 SATA 17
Lamb, Lady Caroline 1785-1828 **NCLC 38**
 See also DLB 116
Lamming, George (William) 1927- **CLC 2, 4,**
 66; BLC 2; DAM MULT
 See also BW 2, 3; CA 85-88; CANR 26, 76;
 DLB 125; MTCW 1, 2
L'Amour, Louis (Dearborn) 1908-1988 **C L C**
 25, 55; DAM NOV, POP
 See also AAYA 16; AITN 2; BEST 89:2; CA 1-
 4R; 125; CANR 3, 25, 40; DA3; DLB 206;
 DLBY 80; MTCW 1, 2
Lampedusa, Giuseppe (Tomasi) di 1896-1957
 TCLC 13
 See also Tomasi di Lampedusa, Giuseppe
 See also CA 164; DLB 177; MTCW 2
Lampman, Archibald 1861-1899 **NCLC 25**
 See also DLB 92
Lancaster, Bruce 1896-1963 **CLC 36**
 See also CA 9-10; CANR 70; CAP 1; SATA 9
Lanchester, John   **CLC 99**
Landau, Mark Alexandrovich
 See Aldanov, Mark (Alexandrovich)
Landau-Aldanov, Mark Alexandrovich
 See Aldanov, Mark (Alexandrovich)
Landis, Jerry
 See Simon, Paul (Frederick)
Landis, John 1950-   **CLC 26**
 See also CA 112; 122
Landolfi, Tommaso 1908-1979 **CLC 11, 49**
 See also CA 127; 117; DLB 177
Landon, Letitia Elizabeth 1802-1838 **N C L C**
 15
 See also DLB 96
Landor, Walter Savage 1775-1864 **NCLC 14**
 See also DLB 93, 107
Landwirth, Heinz 1927-
 See Lind, Jakov
 See also CA 9-12R; CANR 7
Lane, Patrick 1939- **CLC 25; DAM POET**
 See also CA 97-100; CANR 54; DLB 53; INT
 97-100
Lang, Andrew 1844-1912 **TCLC 16**
 See also CA 114; 137; DLB 98, 141, 184;

 MAICYA; SATA 16
Lang, Fritz 1890-1976 **CLC 20, 103**
 See also CA 77-80; 69-72; CANR 30
Lange, John
 See Crichton, (John) Michael
Langer, Elinor 1939-   **CLC 34**
 See also CA 121
Langland, William 1330(?)-1400(?) **LC 19;**
 DA; DAB; DAC; DAM MST, POET
 See also DLB 146
Langstaff, Launcelot
 See Irving, Washington
Lanier, Sidney 1842-1881 **NCLC 6; DAM**
 POET
 See also DLB 64; DLBD 13; MAICYA; SATA
 18
Lanyer, Aemilia 1569-1645 **LC 10, 30**
 See also DLB 121
Lao-Tzu
 See Lao Tzu
Lao Tzu fl. 6th cent. B.C.- **CMLC 7**
Lapine, James (Elliot) 1949- **CLC 39**
 See also CA 123; 130; CANR 54; INT 130
Larbaud, Valery (Nicolas) 1881-1957TCLC 9
 See also CA 106; 152
Lardner, Ring
 See Lardner, Ring(gold) W(ilmer)
Lardner, Ring W., Jr.
 See Lardner, Ring(gold) W(ilmer)
Lardner, Ring(gold) W(ilmer) 1885-1933
 TCLC 2, 14; SSC 32
 See also CA 104; 131; CDALB 1917-1929;
 DLB 11, 25, 86; DLBD 16; MTCW 1, 2
Laredo, Betty
 See Codrescu, Andrei
Larkin, Maia
 See Wojciechowska, Maia (Teresa)
Larkin, Philip (Arthur) 1922-1985CLC 3, 5, 8,
 9, 13, 18, 33, 39, 64; DAB; DAM MST,
 POET; PC 21
 See also CA 5-8R; 117; CANR 24, 62; CDBLB
 1960 to Present; DA3; DLB 27; MTCW 1, 2
Larra (y Sanchez de Castro), Mariano Jose de
 1809-1837   **NCLC 17**
Larsen, Eric 1941-   **CLC 55**
 See also CA 132
Larsen, Nella 1891-1964 **CLC 37; BLC 2;**
 DAM MULT
 See also BW 1; CA 125; CANR 83; DLB 51
Larson, Charles R(aymond) 1938- **CLC 31**
 See also CA 53-56; CANR 4
Larson, Jonathan 1961-1996 **CLC 99**
 See also AAYA 28; CA 156
Las Casas, Bartolome de 1474-1566 **LC 31**
Lasch, Christopher 1932-1994 **CLC 102**
 See also CA 73-76; 144; CANR 25; MTCW 1,
 2
Lasker-Schueler, Else 1869-1945 **TCLC 57**
 See also DLB 66, 124
Laski, Harold 1893-1950 **TCLC 79**
Latham, Jean Lee 1902-1995 **CLC 12**
 See also AITN 1; CA 5-8R; CANR 7, 84; CLR
 50; MAICYA; SATA 2, 68
Latham, Mavis
 See Clark, Mavis Thorpe
Lathen, Emma   **CLC 2**
 See also Hennissart, Martha; Latsis, Mary J(ane)
Lathrop, Francis
 See Leiber, Fritz (Reuter, Jr.)
Latsis, Mary J(ane) 1927(?)-1997
 See Lathen, Emma
 See also CA 85-88; 162
Lattimore, Richmond (Alexander) 1906-1984

CLC 3
 See also CA 1-4R; 112; CANR 1
Laughlin, James 1914-1997 **CLC 49**
 See also CA 21-24R; 162; CAAS 22; CANR 9,
 47; DLB 48; DLBY 96, 97
Laurence, (Jean) Margaret (Wemyss) 1926-
 1987 **CLC 3, 6, 13, 50, 62; DAC; DAM**
 MST; SSC 7
 See also CA 5-8R; 121; CANR 33; DLB 53;
 MTCW 1, 2; SATA-Obit 50
Laurent, Antoine 1952- **CLC 50**
Lauscher, Hermann
 See Hesse, Hermann
Lautreamont, Comte de 1846-1870NCLC 12;
 SSC 14
Laverty, Donald
 See Blish, James (Benjamin)
Lavin, Mary 1912-1996CLC 4, 18, 99; **SSC 4**
 See also CA 9-12R; 151; CANR 33; DLB 15;
 MTCW 1
Lavond, Paul Dennis
 See Kornbluth, C(yril) M.; Pohl, Frederik
Lawler, Raymond Evenor 1922- **CLC 58**
 See also CA 103
Lawrence, D(avid) H(erbert Richards) 1885-
 1930 **TCLC 2, 9, 16, 33, 48, 61, 93; DA;**
 DAB; DAC; DAM MST, NOV, POET; SSC
 4, 19; WLC
 See also CA 104; 121; CDBLB 1914-1945;
 DA3; DLB 10, 19, 36, 98, 162, 195; MTCW
 1, 2
Lawrence, T(homas) E(dward) 1888-1935
 TCLC 18
 See also Dale, Colin
 See also CA 115; 167; DLB 195
Lawrence of Arabia
 See Lawrence, T(homas) E(dward)
Lawson, Henry (Archibald Hertzberg) 1867-
 1922   **TCLC 27; SSC 18**
 See also CA 120
Lawton, Dennis
 See Faust, Frederick (Schiller)
Laxness, Halldor   **CLC 25**
 See also Gudjonsson, Halldor Kiljan
Layamon fl. c. 1200- **CMLC 10**
 See also DLB 146
Laye, Camara 1928-1980 CLC 4, 38; **BLC 2;**
 DAM MULT
 See also BW 1; CA 85-88; 97-100; CANR 25;
 MTCW 1, 2
Layton, Irving (Peter) 1912-CLC 2, 15; **DAC;**
 DAM MST, POET
 See also CA 1-4R; CANR 2, 33, 43, 66; DLB
 88; MTCW 1, 2
Lazarus, Emma 1849-1887 **NCLC 8**
Lazarus, Felix
 See Cable, George Washington
Lazarus, Henry
 See Slavitt, David R(ytman)
Lea, Joan
 See Neufeld, John (Arthur)
Leacock, Stephen (Butler) 1869-1944TCLC 2;
 DAC; DAM MST
 See also CA 104; 141; CANR 80; DLB 92;
 MTCW 2
Lear, Edward 1812-1888 **NCLC 3**
 See also CLR 1; DLB 32, 163, 166; MAICYA;
 SATA 18, 100
Lear, Norman (Milton) 1922- **CLC 12**
 See also CA 73-76
Leautaud, Paul 1872-1956 **TCLC 83**
 See also DLB 65
Leavis, F(rank) R(aymond) 1895-1978CLC 24

See also CA 21-24R; 77-80; CANR 44; MTCW
1, 2

Leavitt, David 1961-   **CLC 34; DAM POP**
See also CA 116; 122; CANR 50, 62; DA3; DLB
130; INT 122; MTCW 2

Leblanc, Maurice (Marie Emile) 1864-1941
TCLC 49
See also CA 110

Lebowitz, Fran(ces Ann) 1951(?)-CLC 11, 36
See also CA 81-84; CANR 14, 60, 70; INT
CANR-14; MTCW 1

Lebrecht, Peter
See Tieck, (Johann) Ludwig

le Carre, John   **CLC 3, 5, 9, 15, 28**
See also Cornwell, David (John Moore)
See also BEST 89:4; CDBLB 1960 to Present;
DLB 87; MTCW 2

Le Clezio, J(ean) M(arie) G(ustave) 1940-
CLC 31
See also CA 116; 128; DLB 83

Leconte de Lisle, Charles-Marie-Rene 1818-
1894   **NCLC 29**

Le Coq, Monsieur
See Simenon, Georges (Jacques Christian)

Leduc, Violette 1907-1972   **CLC 22**
See also CA 13-14; 33-36R; CANR 69; CAP 1

Ledwidge, Francis 1887(?)-1917   **TCLC 23**
See also CA 123; DLB 20

Lee, Andrea 1953-   **CLC 36; BLC 2; DAM
MULT**
See also BW 1, 3; CA 125; CANR 82

Lee, Andrew
See Auchincloss, Louis (Stanton)

Lee, Chang-rae 1965-   **CLC 91**
See also CA 148

Lee, Don L.   **CLC 2**
See also Madhubuti, Haki R.

Lee, George W(ashington) 1894-1976CLC 52;
BLC 2; DAM MULT
See also BW 1; CA 125; CANR 83; DLB 51

Lee, (Nelle) Harper 1926-   **CLC 12, 60; DA;
DAB; DAC; DAM MST, NOV; WLC**
See also AAYA 13; CA 13-16R; CANR 51;
CDALB 1941-1968; DA3; DLB 6; MTCW
1, 2; SATA 11

Lee, Helen Elaine 1959(?)-   **CLC 86**
See also CA 148

Lee, Julian
See Latham, Jean Lee

Lee, Larry
See Lee, Lawrence

Lee, Laurie 1914-1997 **CLC 90; DAB; DAM
POP**
See also CA 77-80; 158; CANR 33, 73; DLB
27; MTCW 1

Lee, Lawrence 1941-1990   **CLC 34**
See also CA 131; CANR 43

Lee, Li-Young 1957-   **PC 24**
See also CA 153; DLB 165

Lee, Manfred B(ennington) 1905-1971CLC 11
See also Queen, Ellery
See also CA 1-4R; 29-32R; CANR 2; DLB 137

Lee, Shelton Jackson 1957(?)-   **CLC 105;
BLCS; DAM MULT**
See also Lee, Spike
See also BW 2, 3; CA 125; CANR 42

Lee, Spike
See Lee, Shelton Jackson
See also AAYA 4, 29

Lee, Stan 1922-   **CLC 17**
See also AAYA 5; CA 108; 111; INT 111

Lee, Tanith 1947-   **CLC 46**
See also AAYA 15; CA 37-40R; CANR 53;

SATA 8, 88

Lee, Vernon   **TCLC 5; SSC 33**
See also Paget, Violet
See also DLB 57, 153, 156, 174, 178

Lee, William
See Burroughs, William S(eward)

Lee, Willy
See Burroughs, William S(eward)

Lee-Hamilton, Eugene (Jacob) 1845-1907
TCLC 22
See also CA 117

Leet, Judith 1935-   **CLC 11**

Le Fanu, Joseph Sheridan 1814-1873NCLC 9,
58; **DAM POP; SSC 14**
See also DA3; DLB 21, 70, 159, 178

Leffland, Ella 1931-   **CLC 19**
See also CA 29-32R; CANR 35, 78, 82; DLBY
84; INT CANR-35; SATA 65

Leger, Alexis
See Leger, (Marie-Rene Auguste) Alexis Saint-
Leger

**Leger, (Marie-Rene Auguste) Alexis Saint-
Leger** 1887-1975   **CLC 4, 11, 46; DAM
POET; PC 23**
See also CA 13-16R; 61-64; CANR 43; MTCW
1

Leger, Saintleger
See Leger, (Marie-Rene Auguste) Alexis Saint-
Leger

Le Guin, Ursula K(roeber) 1929- CLC 8, 13,
22, 45, 71; **DAB; DAC; DAM MST, POP;
SSC 12**
See also AAYA 9, 27; AITN 1; CA 21-24R;
CANR 9, 32, 52, 74; CDALB 1968-1988;
CLR 3, 28; DA3; DLB 8, 52; INT CANR-
32; JRDA; MAICYA; MTCW 1, 2; SATA 4,
52, 99

Lehmann, Rosamond (Nina) 1901-1990CLC 5
See also CA 77-80; 131; CANR 8, 73; DLB 15;
MTCW 2

Leiber, Fritz (Reuter, Jr.) 1910-1992 **CLC 25**
See also CA 45-48; 139; CANR 2, 40; DLB 8;
MTCW 1, 2; SATA 45; SATA-Obit 73

Leibniz, Gottfried Wilhelm von 1646-1716LC
35
See also DLB 168

Leimbach, Martha 1963-
See Leimbach, Marti
See also CA 130

Leimbach, Marti   **CLC 65**
See also Leimbach, Martha

Leino, Eino   **TCLC 24**
See also Loennbohm, Armas Eino Leopold

Leiris, Michel (Julien) 1901-1990   **CLC 61**
See also CA 119; 128; 132

Leithauser, Brad 1953-   **CLC 27**
See also CA 107; CANR 27, 81; DLB 120

Lelchuk, Alan 1938-   **CLC 5**
See also CA 45-48; CAAS 20; CANR 1, 70

Lem, Stanislaw 1921-   **CLC 8, 15, 40**
See also CA 105; CAAS 1; CANR 32; MTCW
1

Lemann, Nancy 1956-   **CLC 39**
See also CA 118; 136

Lemonnier, (Antoine Louis) Camille 1844-1913
TCLC 22
See also CA 121

Lenau, Nikolaus 1802-1850   **NCLC 16**

L'Engle, Madeleine (Camp Franklin) 1918-
CLC 12; DAM POP
See also AAYA 28; AITN 2; CA 1-4R; CANR
3, 21, 39, 66; CLR 1, 14, 57; DA3; DLB 52;
JRDA; MAICYA; MTCW 1, 2; SAAS 15;

SATA 1, 27, 75

Lengyel, Jozsef 1896-1975   **CLC 7**
See also CA 85-88; 57-60; CANR 71

Lenin 1870-1924
See Lenin, V. I.
See also CA 121; 168

Lenin, V. I.   **TCLC 67**
See also Lenin

Lennon, John (Ono) 1940-1980 **CLC 12, 35**
See also CA 102

Lennox, Charlotte Ramsay 1729(?)-1804
NCLC 23
See also DLB 39

Lentricchia, Frank (Jr.) 1940-   **CLC 34**
See also CA 25-28R; CANR 19

Lenz, Siegfried 1926-   **CLC 27; SSC 33**
See also CA 89-92; CANR 80; DLB 75

Leonard, Elmore (John, Jr.) 1925-CLC 28, 34,
71, 120; **DAM POP**
See also AAYA 22; AITN 1; BEST 89:1, 90:4;
CA 81-84; CANR 12, 28, 53, 76; DA3; DLB
173; INT CANR-28; MTCW 1, 2

Leonard, Hugh   **CLC 19**
See Byrne, John Keyes
See also DLB 13

Leonov, Leonid (Maximovich) 1899-1994
CLC 92; DAM NOV
See also CA 129; CANR 74, 76; MTCW 1, 2

Leopardi, (Conte) Giacomo 1798-1837NCLC
22

Le Reveler
See Artaud, Antonin (Marie Joseph)

Lerman, Eleanor 1952-   **CLC 9**
See also CA 85-88; CANR 69

Lerman, Rhoda 1936-   **CLC 56**
See also CA 49-52; CANR 70

Lermontov, Mikhail Yuryevich 1814-1841
NCLC 47; PC 18
See also DLB 205

Leroux, Gaston 1868-1927   **TCLC 25**
See also CA 108; 136; CANR 69; SATA 65

Lesage, Alain-Rene 1668-1747   **LC 2, 28**

Leskov, Nikolai (Semyonovich) 1831-1895
NCLC 25; SSC 34

Lessing, Doris (May) 1919-CLC 1, 2, 3, 6, 10,
15, 22, 40, 94; **DA; DAB; DAC; DAM MST,
NOV; SSC 6; WLCS**
See also CA 9-12R; CAAS 14; CANR 33, 54,
76; CDBLB 1960 to Present; DA3; DLB 15,
139; DLBY 85; MTCW 1, 2

Lessing, Gotthold Ephraim 1729-1781 **LC 8**
See also DLB 97

Lester, Richard 1932-   **CLC 20**

Lever, Charles (James) 1806-1872 **NCLC 23**
See also DLB 21

Leverson, Ada 1865(?)-1936(?)   **TCLC 18**
See also Elaine
See also CA 117; DLB 153

Levertov, Denise 1923-1997 **CLC 1, 2, 3, 5, 8,
15, 28, 66; DAM POET; PC 11**
See also CA 1-4R; 178; 163; CAAE 178; CAAS
19; CANR 3, 29, 50; CDALBS; DLB 5, 165;
INT CANR-29; MTCW 1, 2

Levi, Jonathan   **CLC 76**

Levi, Peter (Chad Tigar) 1931-   **CLC 41**
See also CA 5-8R; CANR 34, 80; DLB 40

Levi, Primo 1919-1987 **CLC 37, 50; SSC 12**
See also CA 13-16R; 122; CANR 12, 33, 61,
70; DLB 177; MTCW 1, 2

Levin, Ira 1929-   **CLC 3, 6; DAM POP**
See also CA 21-24R; CANR 17, 44, 74; DA3;
MTCW 1, 2; SATA 66

Levin, Meyer 1905-1981 **CLC 7; DAM POP**

See also AITN 1; CA 9-12R; 104; CANR 15; DLB 9, 28; DLBY 81; SATA 21; SATA-Obit 27

Levine, Norman 1924- **CLC 54**
See also CA 73-76; CAAS 23; CANR 14, 70; DLB 88

Levine, Philip 1928-**CLC 2, 4, 5, 9, 14, 33, 118; DAM POET; PC 22**
See also CA 9-12R; CANR 9, 37, 52; DLB 5

Levinson, Deirdre 1931- **CLC 49**
See also CA 73-76; CANR 70

Levi-Strauss, Claude 1908- **CLC 38**
See also CA 1-4R; CANR 6, 32, 57; MTCW 1, 2

Levitin, Sonia (Wolff) 1934- **CLC 17**
See also AAYA 13; CA 29-32R; CANR 14, 32, 79; CLR 53; JRDA; MAICYA; SAAS 2; SATA 4, 68

Levon, O. U.
See Kesey, Ken (Elton)

Levy, Amy 1861-1889 **NCLC 59**
See also DLB 156

Lewes, George Henry 1817-1878 **NCLC 25**
See also DLB 55, 144

Lewis, Alun 1915-1944 **TCLC 3**
See also CA 104; DLB 20, 162

Lewis, C. Day
See Day Lewis, C(ecil)

Lewis, C(live) S(taples) 1898-1963**CLC 1, 3, 6, 14, 27, 124; DA; DAB; DAC; DAM MST, NOV, POP; WLC**
See also AAYA 3; CA 81-84; CANR 33, 71; CDBLB 1945-1960; CLR 3, 27; DA3; DLB 15, 100, 160; JRDA; MAICYA; MTCW 1, 2; SATA 13, 100

Lewis, Janet 1899-1998 **CLC 41**
See also Winters, Janet Lewis
See also CA 9-12R; 172; CANR 29, 63; CAP 1; DLBY 87

Lewis, Matthew Gregory 1775-1818**NCLC 11, 62**
See also DLB 39, 158, 178

Lewis, (Harry) Sinclair 1885-1951 **TCLC 4, 13, 23, 39; DA; DAB; DAC; DAM MST, NOV; WLC**
See also CA 104; 133; CDALB 1917-1929; DA3; DLB 9, 102; DLBD 1; MTCW 1, 2

Lewis, (Percy) Wyndham 1882(?)-1957**TCLC 2, 9; SSC 34**
See also CA 104; 157; DLB 15; MTCW 2

Lewisohn, Ludwig 1883-1955 **TCLC 19**
See also CA 107; DLB 4, 9, 28, 102

Lewton, Val 1904-1951 **TCLC 76**

Leyner, Mark 1956- **CLC 92**
See also CA 110; CANR 28, 53; DA3; MTCW 2

Lezama Lima, Jose 1910-1976**CLC 4, 10, 101; DAM MULT; HLCS 2**
See also CA 77-80; CANR 71; DLB 113; HW 1, 2

L'Heureux, John (Clarke) 1934- **CLC 52**
See also CA 13-16R; CANR 23, 45

Liddell, C. H.
See Kuttner, Henry

Lie, Jonas (Lauritz Idemil) 1833-1908(?) **TCLC 5**
See also CA 115

Lieber, Joel 1937-1971 **CLC 6**
See also CA 73-76; 29-32R

Lieber, Stanley Martin
See Lee, Stan

Lieberman, Laurence (James) 1935- **CLC 4, 36**

See also CA 17-20R; CANR 8, 36

Lieh Tzu fl. 7th cent. B.C.-5th cent. B.C. **CMLC 27**

Lieksman, Anders
See Haavikko, Paavo Juhani

Li Fei-kan 1904-
See Pa Chin
See also CA 105

Lifton, Robert Jay 1926- **CLC 67**
See also CA 17-20R; CANR 27, 78; INT CANR-27; SATA 66

Lightfoot, Gordon 1938- **CLC 26**
See also CA 109

Lightman, Alan P(aige) 1948- **CLC 81**
See also CA 141; CANR 63

Ligotti, Thomas (Robert) 1953-**CLC 44; SSC 16**
See also CA 123; CANR 49

Li Ho 791-817 **PC 13**

Liliencron, (Friedrich Adolf Axel) Detlev von 1844-1909 **TCLC 18**
See also CA 117

Lilly, William 1602-1681 **LC 27**

Lima, Jose Lezama
See Lezama Lima, Jose

Lima Barreto, Afonso Henrique de 1881-1922 **TCLC 23**
See also CA 117

Limonov, Edward 1944- **CLC 67**
See also CA 137

Lin, Frank
See Atherton, Gertrude (Franklin Horn)

Lincoln, Abraham 1809-1865 **NCLC 18**

Lind, Jakov **CLC 1, 2, 4, 27, 82**
See also Landwirth, Heinz
See also CAAS 4

Lindbergh, Anne (Spencer) Morrow 1906- **CLC 82; DAM NOV**
See also CA 17-20R; CANR 16, 73; MTCW 1, 2; SATA 33

Lindsay, David 1878-1945 **TCLC 15**
See also CA 113

Lindsay, (Nicholas) Vachel 1879-1931 **TCLC 17; DA; DAC; DAM MST, POET; PC 23; WLC**
See also CA 114; 135; CANR 79; CDALB 1865-1917; DA3; DLB 54; SATA 40

Linke-Poot
See Doeblin, Alfred

Linney, Romulus 1930- **CLC 51**
See also CA 1-4R; CANR 40, 44, 79

Linton, Eliza Lynn 1822-1898 **NCLC 41**
See also DLB 18

Li Po 701-763 **CMLC 2**

Lipsius, Justus 1547-1606 **LC 16**

Lipsyte, Robert (Michael) 1938-**CLC 21; DA; DAC; DAM MST, NOV**
See also AAYA 7; CA 17-20R; CANR 8, 57; CLR 23; JRDA; MAICYA; SATA 5, 68

Lish, Gordon (Jay) 1934- **CLC 45; SSC 18**
See also CA 113; 117; CANR 79; DLB 130; INT 117

Lispector, Clarice 1925(?)-1977 **CLC 43; HLCS 2; SSC 34**
See also CA 139; 116; CANR 71; DLB 113; HW 2

Littell, Robert 1935(?)- **CLC 42**
See also CA 109; 112; CANR 64

Little, Malcolm 1925-1965
See Malcolm X
See also BW 1, 3; CA 125; 111; CANR 82; DA; DAB; DAC; DAM MST, MULT; DA3; MTCW 1, 2

Littlewit, Humphrey Gent.
See Lovecraft, H(oward) P(hillips)

Litwos
See Sienkiewicz, Henryk (Adam Alexander Pius)

Liu, E 1857-1909 **TCLC 15**
See also CA 115

Lively, Penelope (Margaret) 1933- **CLC 32, 50; DAM NOV**
See also CA 41-44R; CANR 29, 67, 79; CLR 7; DLB 14, 161, 207; JRDA; MAICYA; MTCW 1, 2; SATA 7, 60, 101

Livesay, Dorothy (Kathleen) 1909-**CLC 4, 15, 79; DAC; DAM MST, POET**
See also AITN 2; CA 25-28R; CAAS 8; CANR 36, 67; DLB 68; MTCW 1

Livy c. 59B.C.-c. 17 **CMLC 11**
See also DLB 211

Lizardi, Jose Joaquin Fernandez de 1776-1827 **NCLC 30**

Llewellyn, Richard
See Llewellyn Lloyd, Richard Dafydd Vivian
See also DLB 15

Llewellyn Lloyd, Richard Dafydd Vivian 1906-1983 **CLC 7, 80**
See also Llewellyn, Richard
See also CA 53-56; 111; CANR 7, 71; SATA 11; SATA-Obit 37

Llosa, (Jorge) Mario (Pedro) Vargas
See Vargas Llosa, (Jorge) Mario (Pedro)

Lloyd, Manda
See Mander, (Mary) Jane

Lloyd Webber, Andrew 1948-
See Webber, Andrew Lloyd
See also AAYA 1; CA 116; 149; DAM DRAM; SATA 56

Llull, Ramon c. 1235-c. 1316 **CMLC 12**

Lobb, Ebenezer
See Upward, Allen

Locke, Alain (Le Roy) 1886-1954 **TCLC 43; BLCS**
See also BW 1, 3; CA 106; 124; CANR 79; DLB 51

Locke, John 1632-1704 **LC 7, 35**
See also DLB 101

Locke-Elliott, Sumner
See Elliott, Sumner Locke

Lockhart, John Gibson 1794-1854 **NCLC 6**
See also DLB 110, 116, 144

Lodge, David (John) 1935-**CLC 36; DAM POP**
See also BEST 90:1; CA 17-20R; CANR 19, 53; DLB 14, 194; INT CANR-19; MTCW 1, 2

Lodge, Thomas 1558-1625 **LC 41**

Lodge, Thomas 1558-1625 **LC 41**
See also DLB 172

Loennbohm, Armas Eino Leopold 1878-1926
See Leino, Eino
See also CA 123

Loewinsohn, Ron(ald William) 1937-**CLC 52**
See also CA 25-28R; CANR 71

Logan, Jake
See Smith, Martin Cruz

Logan, John (Burton) 1923-1987 **CLC 5**
See also CA 77-80; 124; CANR 45; DLB 5

Lo Kuan-chung 1330(?)-1400(?) **LC 12**

Lombard, Nap
See Johnson, Pamela Hansford

London, Jack **TCLC 9, 15, 39; SSC 4; WLC**
See also London, John Griffith
See also AAYA 13; AITN 2; CDALB 1865-1917; DLB 8, 12, 78, 212; SATA 18

London, John Griffith 1876-1916

See London, Jack
See also CA 110; 119; CANR 73; DA; DAB; DAC; DAM MST, NOV; DA3; JRDA; MAICYA; MTCW 1, 2
Long, Emmett
See Leonard, Elmore (John, Jr.)
Longbaugh, Harry
See Goldman, William (W.)
Longfellow, Henry Wadsworth 1807-1882
NCLC 2, 45; DA; DAB; DAC; DAM MST, POET; WLCS
See also CDALB 1640-1865; DA3; DLB 1, 59; SATA 19
Longinus c. 1st cent. - **CMLC 27**
See also DLB 176
Longley, Michael 1939- **CLC 29**
See also CA 102; DLB 40
Longus fl. c. 2nd cent. - **CMLC 7**
Longway, A. Hugh
See Lang, Andrew
Lonnrot, Elias 1802-1884 **NCLC 53**
Lopate, Phillip 1943- **CLC 29**
See also CA 97-100; DLBY 80; INT 97-100
Lopez Portillo (y Pacheco), Jose 1920-**CLC 46**
See also CA 129; HW 1
Lopez y Fuentes, Gregorio 1897(?)-1966**C L C 32**
See also CA 131; HW 1
Lorca, Federico Garcia
See Garcia Lorca, Federico
Lord, Bette Bao 1938- **CLC 23**
See also BEST 90:3; CA 107; CANR 41, 79; INT 107; SATA 58
Lord Auch
See Bataille, Georges
Lord Byron
See Byron, George Gordon (Noel)
Lorde, Audre (Geraldine) 1934-1992**CLC 18, 71; BLC 2; DAM MULT, POET; PC 12**
See also BW 1, 3; CA 25-28R; 142; CANR 16, 26, 46, 82; DA3; DLB 41; MTCW 1, 2
Lord Houghton
See Milnes, Richard Monckton
Lord Jeffrey
See Jeffrey, Francis
Lorenzini, Carlo 1826-1890
See Collodi, Carlo
See also MAICYA; SATA 29, 100
Lorenzo, Heberto Padilla
See Padilla (Lorenzo), Heberto
Loris
See Hofmannsthal, Hugo von
Loti, Pierre **TCLC 11**
See also Viaud, (Louis Marie) Julien
See also DLB 123
Lou, Henri
See Andreas-Salome, Lou
Louie, David Wong 1954- **CLC 70**
See also CA 139
Louis, Father M.
See Merton, Thomas
Lovecraft, H(oward) P(hillips) 1890-1937
TCLC 4, 22; DAM POP; SSC 3
See also AAYA 14; CA 104; 133; DA3; MTCW 1, 2
Lovelace, Earl 1935- **CLC 51**
See also BW 2; CA 77-80; CANR 41, 72; DLB 125; MTCW 1
Lovelace, Richard 1618-1657 **LC 24**
See also DLB 131
Lowell, Amy 1874-1925 **TCLC 1, 8; DAM POET; PC 13**
See also CA 104; 151; DLB 54, 140; MTCW 2

Lowell, James Russell 1819-1891 **NCLC 2**
See also CDALB 1640-1865; DLB 1, 11, 64, 79, 189
Lowell, Robert (Traill Spence, Jr.) 1917-1977
CLC 1, 2, 3, 4, 5, 8, 9, 11, 15, 37, 124; DA; DAB; DAC; DAM MST, NOV; PC 3; WLC
See also CA 9-12R; 73-76; CABS 2; CANR 26, 60; CDALBS; DA3; DLB 5, 169; MTCW 1, 2
Lowenthal, Michael (Francis) 1969-**CLC 119**
See also CA 150
Lowndes, Marie Adelaide (Belloc) 1868-1947
TCLC 12
See also CA 107; DLB 70
Lowry, (Clarence) Malcolm 1909-1957**T C L C 6, 40; SSC 31**
See also CA 105; 131; CANR 62; CDBLB 1945-1960; DLB 15; MTCW 1, 2
Lowry, Mina Gertrude 1882-1966
See Loy, Mina
See also CA 113
Loxsmith, John
See Brunner, John (Kilian Houston)
Loy, Mina **CLC 28; DAM POET; PC 16**
See also Lowry, Mina Gertrude
See also DLB 4, 54
Loyson-Bridet
See Schwob, Marcel (Mayer Andre)
Lucan 39-65 **CMLC 33**
See also DLB 211
Lucas, Craig 1951- **CLC 64**
See also CA 137; CANR 71
Lucas, E(dward) V(errall) 1868-1938 **T C L C 73**
See also CA 176; DLB 98, 149, 153; SATA 20
Lucas, George 1944- **CLC 16**
See also AAYA 1, 23; CA 77-80; CANR 30; SATA 56
Lucas, Hans
See Godard, Jean-Luc
Lucas, Victoria
See Plath, Sylvia
Lucian c. 120-c. 180 **CMLC 32**
See also DLB 176
Ludlam, Charles 1943-1987 **CLC 46, 50**
See also CA 85-88; 122; CANR 72
Ludlum, Robert 1927-**CLC 22, 43; DAM NOV, POP**
See also AAYA 10; BEST 89:1, 90:3; CA 33-36R; CANR 25, 41, 68; DA3; DLBY 82; MTCW 1, 2
Ludwig, Ken **CLC 60**
Ludwig, Otto 1813-1865 **NCLC 4**
See also DLB 129
Lugones, Leopoldo 1874-1938 **TCLC 15; HLCS 2**
See also CA 116; 131; HW 1
Lu Hsun 1881-1936 **TCLC 3; SSC 20**
See also Shu-Jen, Chou
Lukacs, George **CLC 24**
See also Lukacs, Gyorgy (Szegeny von)
Lukacs, Gyorgy (Szegeny von) 1885-1971
See Lukacs, George
See also CA 101; 29-32R; CANR 62; MTCW 2
Luke, Peter (Ambrose Cyprian) 1919-1995
CLC 38
See also CA 81-84; 147; CANR 72; DLB 13
Lunar, Dennis
See Mungo, Raymond
Lurie, Alison 1926- **CLC 4, 5, 18, 39**
See also CA 1-4R; CANR 2, 17, 50; DLB 2; MTCW 1; SATA 46
Lustig, Arnost 1926- **CLC 56**

See also AAYA 3; CA 69-72; CANR 47; SATA 56
Luther, Martin 1483-1546 **LC 9, 37**
See also DLB 179
Luxemburg, Rosa 1870(?)-1919 **TCLC 63**
See also CA 118
Luzi, Mario 1914- **CLC 13**
See also CA 61-64; CANR 9, 70; DLB 128
Lyly, John 1554(?)-1606**LC 41; DAM DRAM; DC 7**
See also DLB 62, 167
L'Ymagier
See Gourmont, Remy (-Marie-Charles) de
Lynch, B. Suarez
See Bioy Casares, Adolfo; Borges, Jorge Luis
Lynch, B. Suarez
See Bioy Casares, Adolfo
Lynch, David (K.) 1946- **CLC 66**
See also CA 124; 129
Lynch, James
See Andreyev, Leonid (Nikolaevich)
Lynch Davis, B.
See Bioy Casares, Adolfo; Borges, Jorge Luis
Lyndsay, Sir David 1490-1555 **LC 20**
Lynn, Kenneth S(chuyler) 1923- **CLC 50**
See also CA 1-4R; CANR 3, 27, 65
Lynx
See West, Rebecca
Lyons, Marcus
See Blish, James (Benjamin)
Lyre, Pinchbeck
See Sassoon, Siegfried (Lorraine)
Lytle, Andrew (Nelson) 1902-1995 **CLC 22**
See also CA 9-12R; 150; CANR 70; DLB 6; DLBY 95
Lyttelton, George 1709-1773 **LC 10**
Maas, Peter 1929- **CLC 29**
See also CA 93-96; INT 93-96; MTCW 2
Macaulay, Rose 1881-1958 **TCLC 7, 44**
See also CA 104; DLB 36
Macaulay, Thomas Babington 1800-1859
NCLC 42
See also CDBLB 1832-1890; DLB 32, 55
MacBeth, George (Mann) 1932-1992**CLC 2, 5, 9**
See also CA 25-28R; 136; CANR 61, 66; DLB 40; MTCW 1; SATA 4; SATA-Obit 70
MacCaig, Norman (Alexander) 1910-**CLC 36; DAM POET**
See also CA 9-12R; CANR 3, 34; DLB 27
MacCarthy, Sir(Charles Otto) Desmond 1877-1952 **TCLC 36**
See also CA 167
MacDiarmid, Hugh**CLC 2, 4, 11, 19, 63; PC 9**
See also Grieve, C(hristopher) M(urray)
See also CDBLB 1945-1960; DLB 20
MacDonald, Anson
See Heinlein, Robert A(nson)
Macdonald, Cynthia 1928- **CLC 13, 19**
See also CA 49-52; CANR 4, 44; DLB 105
MacDonald, George 1824-1905 **TCLC 9**
See also CA 106; 137; CANR 80; DLB 18, 163, 178; MAICYA; SATA 33, 100
Macdonald, John
See Millar, Kenneth
MacDonald, John D(ann) 1916-1986 **CLC 3, 27, 44; DAM NOV, POP**
See also CA 1-4R; 121; CANR 1, 19, 60; DLB 8; DLBY 86; MTCW 1, 2
Macdonald, John Ross
See Millar, Kenneth
Macdonald, Ross **CLC 1, 2, 3, 14, 34, 41**
See also Millar, Kenneth

1, 2

Mannheim, Karl 1893-1947   **TCLC 65**
Manning, David
   See Faust, Frederick (Schiller)
Manning, Frederic 1887(?)-1935   **TCLC 25**
   See also CA 124
Manning, Olivia 1915-1980   **CLC 5, 19**
   See also CA 5-8R; 101; CANR 29; MTCW 1
Mano, D. Keith 1942-   **CLC 2, 10**
   See also CA 25-28R; CAAS 6; CANR 26, 57;
   DLB 6
Mansfield, KatherineTCLC 2, 8, 39; DAB; SSC
   9, 23; WLC
   See also Beauchamp, Kathleen Mansfield
   See also DLB 162
Manso, Peter 1940-   **CLC 39**
   See also CA 29-32R; CANR 44
Mantecon, Juan Jimenez
   See Jimenez (Mantecon), Juan Ramon
Manton, Peter
   See Creasey, John
Man Without a Spleen, A
   See Chekhov, Anton (Pavlovich)
Manzoni, Alessandro 1785-1873   **NCLC 29**
Map, Walter 1140-1209   **CMLC 32**
Mapu, Abraham (ben Jekutiel) 1808-1867
   NCLC 18
Mara, Sally
   See Queneau, Raymond
Marat, Jean Paul 1743-1793   **LC 10**
Marcel, Gabriel Honore 1889-1973 **CLC 15**
   See also CA 102; 45-48; MTCW 1, 2
March, William 1893-1954   **TCLC 96**
Marchbanks, Samuel
   See Davies, (William) Robertson
Marchi, Giacomo
   See Bassani, Giorgio
Margulies, Donald   **CLC 76**
Marie de France c. 12th cent. - **CMLC 8; PC**
   22
   See also DLB 208
Marie de l'Incarnation 1599-1672   **LC 10**
Marier, Captain Victor
   See Griffith, D(avid Lewelyn) W(ark)
Mariner, Scott
   See Pohl, Frederik
Marinetti, Filippo Tommaso 1876-1944TCLC
   10
   See also CA 107; DLB 114
Marivaux, Pierre Carlet de Chamblain de 1688-
   1763   **LC 4; DC 7**
Markandaya, Kamala   **CLC 8, 38**
   See also Taylor, Kamala (Purnaiya)
Markfield, Wallace 1926-   **CLC 8**
   See also CA 69-72; CAAS 3; DLB 2, 28
Markham, Edwin 1852-1940   **TCLC 47**
   See also CA 160; DLB 54, 186
Markham, Robert
   See Amis, Kingsley (William)
Marks, J
   See Highwater, Jamake (Mamake)
Marks-Highwater, J
   See Highwater, Jamake (Mamake)
Markson, David M(errill) 1927-   **CLC 67**
   See also CA 49-52; CANR 1
Marley, Bob   **CLC 17**
   See also Marley, Robert Nesta
Marley, Robert Nesta 1945-1981
   See Marley, Bob
   See also CA 107; 103
Marlowe, Christopher 1564-1593 **LC 22, 47;**
   DA; DAB; DAC; DAM DRAM, MST; DC
   1; WLC

See also CDBLB Before 1660; DA3; DLB 62
Marlowe, Stephen 1928-
   See Queen, Ellery
   See also CA 13-16R; CANR 6, 55
Marmontel, Jean-Francois 1723-1799   **LC 2**
Marquand, John P(hillips) 1893-1960CLC 2,
   10
   See also CA 85-88; CANR 73; DLB 9, 102;
   MTCW 2
Marques, Rene 1919-1979   **CLC 96; DAM**
   MULT; HLC 2
   See also CA 97-100; 85-88; CANR 78; DLB
   113; HW 1, 2
Marquez, Gabriel (Jose) Garcia
   See Garcia Marquez, Gabriel (Jose)
Marquis, Don(ald Robert Perry) 1878-1937
   TCLC 7
   See also CA 104; 166; DLB 11, 25
Marric, J. J.
   See Creasey, John
Marryat, Frederick 1792-1848   **NCLC 3**
   See also DLB 21, 163
Marsden, James
   See Creasey, John
Marsh, (Edith) Ngaio 1899-1982 **CLC 7, 53;**
   DAM POP
   See also CA 9-12R; CANR 6, 58; DLB 77;
   MTCW 1, 2
Marshall, Garry 1934-   **CLC 17**
   See also AAYA 3; CA 111; SATA 60
Marshall, Paule 1929-   **CLC 27, 72; BLC 3;**
   DAM MULT; SSC 3
   See also BW 2, 3; CA 77-80; CANR 25, 73;
   DA3; DLB 157; MTCW 1, 2
Marshallik
   See Zangwill, Israel
Marsten, Richard
   See Hunter, Evan
Marston, John 1576-1634LC 33; DAM DRAM
   See also DLB 58, 172
Martha, Henry
   See Harris, Mark
Marti (y Perez), Jose (Julian) 1853-1895
   NCLC 63; DAM MULT; HLC 2
   See also HW 2
Martial c. 40-c. 104   **CMLC 35; PC 10**
   See also DLB 211
Martin, Ken
   See Hubbard, L(afayette) Ron(ald)
Martin, Richard
   See Creasey, John
Martin, Steve 1945-   **CLC 30**
   See also CA 97-100; CANR 30; MTCW 1
Martin, Valerie 1948-   **CLC 89**
   See also BEST 90:2; CA 85-88; CANR 49
Martin, Violet Florence 1862-1915 **TCLC 51**
Martin, Webber
   See Silverberg, Robert
Martindale, Patrick Victor
   See White, Patrick (Victor Martindale)
Martin du Gard, Roger 1881-1958 **TCLC 24**
   See also CA 118; DLB 65
Martineau, Harriet 1802-1876   **NCLC 26**
   See also DLB 21, 55, 159, 163, 166, 190; YABC
   2
Martines, Julia
   See O'Faolain, Julia
Martinez, Enrique Gonzalez
   See Gonzalez Martinez, Enrique
Martinez, Jacinto Benavente y
   See Benavente (y Martinez), Jacinto
Martinez Ruiz, Jose 1873-1967
   See Azorin; Ruiz, Jose Martinez

See also CA 93-96; HW 1
Martinez Sierra, Gregorio 1881-1947TCLC 6
   See also CA 115
Martinez Sierra, Maria (de la O'LeJarraga)
   1874-1974   **TCLC 6**
   See also CA 115
Martinsen, Martin
   See Follett, Ken(neth Martin)
Martinson, Harry (Edmund) 1904-1978 C L C
   14
   See also CA 77-80; CANR 34
Marut, Ret
   See Traven, B.
Marut, Robert
   See Traven, B.
Marvell, Andrew 1621-1678   **LC 4, 43; DA;**
   DAB; DAC; DAM MST, POET; PC 10;
   WLC
   See also CDBLB 1660-1789; DLB 131
Marx, Karl (Heinrich) 1818-1883   **NCLC 17**
   See also DLB 129
Masaoka Shiki   **TCLC 18**
   See also Masaoka Tsunenori
Masaoka Tsunenori 1867-1902
   See Masaoka Shiki
   See also CA 117
Masefield, John (Edward) 1878-1967CLC 11,
   47; DAM POET
   See also CA 19-20; 25-28R; CANR 33; CAP 2;
   CDBLB 1890-1914; DLB 10, 19, 153, 160;
   MTCW 1, 2; SATA 19
Maso, Carole 19(?)-   **CLC 44**
   See also CA 170
Mason, Bobbie Ann 1940-CLC 28, 43, 82; SSC
   4
   See also AAYA 5; CA 53-56; CANR 11, 31,
   58, 83; CDALBS; DA3; DLB 173; DLBY
   87; INT CANR-31; MTCW 1, 2
Mason, Ernst
   See Pohl, Frederik
Mason, Lee W.
   See Malzberg, Barry N(athaniel)
Mason, Nick 1945-   **CLC 35**
Mason, Tally
   See Derleth, August (William)
Mass, William
   See Gibson, William
Master Lao
   See Lao Tzu
Masters, Edgar Lee 1868-1950   **TCLC 2, 25;**
   DA; DAC; DAM MST, POET; PC 1;
   WLCS
   See also CA 104; 133; CDALB 1865-1917;
   DLB 54; MTCW 1, 2
Masters, Hilary 1928-   **CLC 48**
   See also CA 25-28R; CANR 13, 47
Mastrosimone, William 19(?)-   **CLC 36**
Mathe, Albert
   See Camus, Albert
Mather, Cotton 1663-1728   **LC 38**
   See also CDALB 1640-1865; DLB 24, 30, 140
Mather, Increase 1639-1723   **LC 38**
   See also DLB 24
Matheson, Richard Burton 1926-   **CLC 37**
   See also AAYA 31; CA 97-100; DLB 8, 44; INT
   97-100
Mathews, Harry 1930-   **CLC 6, 52**
   See also CA 21-24R; CAAS 6; CANR 18, 40
Mathews, John Joseph 1894-1979 **CLC 84;**
   DAM MULT
   See also CA 19-20; 142; CANR 45; CAP 2;
   DLB 175; NNAL
Mathias, Roland (Glyn) 1915-   **CLC 45**

See also CA 97-100; CANR 19, 41; DLB 27
Matsuo Basho 1644-1694   **PC 3**
  See also DAM POET
Mattheson, Rodney
  See Creasey, John
Matthews, Brander 1852-1929   **TCLC 95**
  See also DLB 71, 78; DLBD 13
Matthews, Greg 1949-   **CLC 45**
  See also CA 135
Matthews, William (Procter, III) 1942-1997
  CLC 40
  See also CA 29-32R; 162; CAAS 18; CANR
  12, 57; DLB 5 .
Matthias, John (Edward) 1941-   **CLC 9**
  See also CA 33-36R; CANR 56
Matthiessen, Peter 1927-**CLC 5, 7, 11, 32, 64;**
  DAM NOV
  See also AAYA 6; BEST 90:4; CA 9-12R;
  CANR 21, 50, 73; DA3; DLB 6, 173; MTCW
  1, 2; SATA 27
Maturin, Charles Robert 1780(?)-1824**NCLC
6**
  See also DLB 178
Matute (Ausejo), Ana Maria 1925-   **CLC 11**
  See also CA 89-92; MTCW 1
Maugham, W. S.
  See Maugham, W(illiam) Somerset
Maugham, W(illiam) Somerset 1874-1965
  CLC 1, 11, 15, 67, 93; DA; DAB; DAC;
  DAM DRAM, MST, NOV; SSC 8; WLC
  See also CA 5-8R; 25-28R; CANR 40; CDBLB
  1914-1945; DA3; DLB 10, 36, 77, 100, 162,
  195; MTCW 1, 2; SATA 54
Maugham, William Somerset
  See Maugham, W(illiam) Somerset
Maupassant, (Henri Rene Albert) Guy de 1850-
  1893**NCLC 1, 42; DA; DAB; DAC; DAM**
  MST; SSC 1; WLC
  See also DA3; DLB 123
Maupin, Armistead 1944-**CLC 95; DAM POP**
  See also CA 125; 130; CANR 58; DA3; INT
  130; MTCW 2
Maurhut, Richard
  See Traven, B.
Mauriac, Claude 1914-1996   **CLC 9**
  See also CA 89-92; 152; DLB 83
Mauriac, Francois (Charles) 1885-1970 **C L C**
  4, 9, 56; SSC 24
  See also CA 25-28; CAP 2; DLB 65; MTCW 1,
  2
Mavor, Osborne Henry 1888-1951
  See Bridie, James
  See also CA 104
Maxwell, William (Keepers, Jr.) 1908-**CLC 19**
  See also CA 93-96; CANR 54; DLBY 80; INT
  93-96
May, Elaine 1932-   **CLC 16**
  See also CA 124; 142; DLB 44
Mayakovski, Vladimir (Vladimirovich) 1893-
  1930   **TCLC 4, 18**
  See also CA 104; 158; MTCW 2
Mayhew, Henry 1812-1887   **NCLC 31**
  See also DLB 18, 55, 190
Mayle, Peter 1939(?)-   **CLC 89**
  See also CA 139; CANR 64
Maynard, Joyce 1953-   **CLC 23**
  See also CA 111; 129; CANR 64
Mayne, William (James Carter) 1928-**CLC 12**
  See also AAYA 20; CA 9-12R; CANR 37, 80;
  CLR 25; JRDA; MAICYA; SAAS 11; SATA
  6, 68
Mayo, Jim
  See L'Amour, Louis (Dearborn)

Maysles, Albert 1926-   **CLC 16**
  See also CA 29-32R
Maysles, David 1932-   **CLC 16**
Mazer, Norma Fox 1931-   **CLC 26**
  See also AAYA 5; CA 69-72; CANR 12, 32,
  66; CLR 23; JRDA; MAICYA; SAAS 1;
  SATA 24, 67, 105
Mazzini, Guiseppe 1805-1872   **NCLC 34**
McAlmon, Robert (Menzies) 1895-1956**TCLC
97**
  See also CA 107; 168; DLB 4, 45; DLBD 15
McAuley, James Phillip 1917-1976   **CLC 45**
  See also CA 97-100
McBain, Ed
  See Hunter, Evan
McBrien, William Augustine 1930-   **CLC 44**
  See also CA 107
McCaffrey, Anne (Inez) 1926-**CLC 17; DAM
NOV, POP**
  See also AAYA 6; AITN 2; BEST 89:2; CA 25-
  28R; CANR 15, 35, 55; CLR 49; DA3; DLB
  8; JRDA; MAICYA; MTCW 1, 2; SAAS 11;
  SATA 8, 70
McCall, Nathan 1955(?)-   **CLC 86**
  See also BW 3; CA 146
McCann, Arthur
  See Campbell, John W(ood, Jr.)
McCann, Edson
  See Pohl, Frederik
McCarthy, Charles, Jr. 1933-
  See McCarthy, Cormac
  See also CANR 42, 69; DAM POP; DA3;
  MTCW 2
McCarthy, Cormac 1933- **CLC 4, 57, 59, 101**
  See also McCarthy, Charles, Jr.
  See also DLB 6, 143; MTCW 2
McCarthy, Mary (Therese) 1912-1989**CLC 1,
3, 5, 14, 24, 39, 59; SSC 24**
  See also CA 5-8R; 129; CANR 16, 50, 64; DA3;
  DLB 2; DLBY 81; INT CANR-16; MTCW
  1, 2
McCartney, (James) Paul 1942-   **CLC 12, 35**
  See also CA 146
McCauley, Stephen (D.) 1955-   **CLC 50**
  See also CA 141
McClure, Michael (Thomas) 1932-**CLC 6, 10**
  See also CA 21-24R; CANR 17, 46, 77; DLB
  16
McCorkle, Jill (Collins) 1958-   **CLC 51**
  See also CA 121; DLBY 87
McCourt, Frank 1930-   **CLC 109**
  See also CA 157
McCourt, James 1941-   **CLC 5**
  See also CA 57-60
McCourt, Malachy 1932-   **CLC 119**
McCoy, Horace (Stanley) 1897-1955**TCLC 28**
  See also CA 108; 155; DLB 9
McCrae, John 1872-1918   **TCLC 12**
  See also CA 109; DLB 92
McCreigh, James
  See Pohl, Frederik
McCullers, (Lula) Carson (Smith) 1917-1967
  CLC 1, 4, 10, 12, 48, 100; DA; DAB; DAC;
  DAM MST, NOV; SSC 9, 24; WLC
  See also AAYA 21; CA 5-8R; 25-28R; CABS
  1, 3; CANR 18; CDALB 1941-1968; DA3;
  DLB 2, 7, 173; MTCW 1, 2; SATA 27
McCulloch, John Tyler
  See Burroughs, Edgar Rice
McCullough, Colleen 1938(?)-   **CLC 27, 107;**
  DAM NOV, POP
  See also CA 81-84; CANR 17, 46, 67; DA3;
  MTCW 1, 2

McDermott, Alice 1953-   **CLC 90**
  See also CA 109; CANR 40
McElroy, Joseph 1930-   **CLC 5, 47**
  See also CA 17-20R
McEwan, Ian (Russell) 1948-   **CLC 13, 66;**
  DAM NOV
  See also BEST 90:4; CA 61-64; CANR 14, 41,
  69; DLB 14, 194; MTCW 1, 2
McFadden, David 1940-   **CLC 48**
  See also CA 104; DLB 60; INT 104
McFarland, Dennis 1950-   **CLC 65**
  See also CA 165
McGahern, John 1934-**CLC 5, 9, 48; SSC 17**
  See also CA 17-20R; CANR 29, 68; DLB 14;
  MTCW 1
McGinley, Patrick (Anthony) 1937- **CLC 41**
  See also CA 120; 127; CANR 56; INT 127
McGinley, Phyllis 1905-1978   **CLC 14**
  See also CA 9-12R; 77-80; CANR 19; DLB 11,
  48; SATA 2, 44; SATA-Obit 24
McGinniss, Joe 1942-   **CLC 32**
  See also AITN 2; BEST 89:2; CA 25-28R;
  CANR 26, 70; DLB 185; INT CANR-26
McGivern, Maureen Daly
  See Daly, Maureen
McGrath, Patrick 1950-   **CLC 55**
  See also CA 136; CANR 65
McGrath, Thomas (Matthew) 1916-1990**CLC
28, 59; DAM POET**
  See also CA 9-12R; 132; CANR 6, 33; MTCW
  1; SATA 41; SATA-Obit 66
McGuane, Thomas (Francis III) 1939-**CLC 3,
7, 18, 45**
  See also AITN 2; CA 49-52; CANR 5, 24, 49;
  DLB 2, 212; DLBY 80; INT CANR-24;
  MTCW 1
McGuckian, Medbh 1950-   **CLC 48; DAM
POET; PC 27**
  See also CA 143; DLB 40
McHale, Tom 1942(?)-1982   **CLC 3, 5**
  See also AITN 1; CA 77-80; 106
McIlvanney, William 1936-   **CLC 42**
  See also CA 25-28R; CANR 61; DLB 14, 207
McIlwraith, Maureen Mollie Hunter
  See Hunter, Mollie
  See also SATA 2
McInerney, Jay 1955-**CLC 34, 112; DAM POP**
  See also AAYA 18; CA 116; 123; CANR 45,
  68; DA3; INT 123; MTCW 2
McIntyre, Vonda N(eel) 1948-   **CLC 18**
  See also CA 81-84; CANR 17, 34, 69; MTCW
  1
McKay, Claude **TCLC 7, 41; BLC 3; DAB; PC
2**
  See also McKay, Festus Claudius
  See also DLB 4, 45, 51, 117
McKay, Festus Claudius 1889-1948
  See McKay, Claude
  See also BW 1, 3; CA 104; 124; CANR 73; DA;
  DAC; DAM MST, MULT, NOV, POET;
  MTCW 1, 2; WLC
McKuen, Rod 1933-   **CLC 1, 3**
  See also AITN 1; CA 41-44R; CANR 40
McLoughlin, R. B.
  See Mencken, H(enry) L(ouis)
McLuhan, (Herbert) Marshall 1911-1980
  CLC 37, 83
  See also CA 9-12R; 102; CANR 12, 34, 61;
  DLB 88; INT CANR-12; MTCW 1, 2
McMillan, Terry (L.) 1951- **CLC 50, 61, 112;
BLCS; DAM MULT, NOV, POP**
  See also AAYA 21; BW 2, 3; CA 140; CANR
  60; DA3; MTCW 2

Millett, Kate 1934-   **CLC 67**
See also AITN 1; CA 73-76; CANR 32, 53, 76;
DA3; MTCW 1, 2
Millhauser, Steven (Lewis) 1943-**CLC 21, 54,
109**
See also CA 110; 111; CANR 63; DA3; DLB 2;
INT 111; MTCW 2
Millin, Sarah Gertrude 1889-1968   **CLC 49**
See also CA 102; 93-96
Milne, A(lan) A(lexander) 1882-1956**TCLC 6,
88; DAB; DAC; DAM MST**
See also CA 104; 133; CLR 1, 26; DA3; DLB
10, 77, 100, 160; MAICYA; MTCW 1, 2;
SATA 100; YABC 1
Milner, Ron(ald) 1938-**CLC 56; BLC 3; DAM
MULT**
See also AITN 1; BW 1; CA 73-76; CANR 24,
81; DLB 38; MTCW 1
Milnes, Richard Monckton 1809-1885 **N C L C
61**
See also DLB 32, 184
Milosz, Czeslaw 1911- **CLC 5, 11, 22, 31, 56,
82; DAM MST, POET; PC 8; WLCS**
See also CA 81-84; CANR 23, 51; DA3; MTCW
1, 2
Milton, John 1608-1674 **LC 9, 43; DA; DAB;
DAC; DAM MST, POET; PC 19; WLC**
See also CDBLB 1660-1789; DA3; DLB 131,
151
Min, Anchee 1957-   **CLC 86**
See also CA 146
Minehaha, Cornelius
See Wedekind, (Benjamin) Frank(lin)
Miner, Valerie 1947-   **CLC 40**
See also CA 97-100; CANR 59
Minimo, Duca
See D'Annunzio, Gabriele
Minot, Susan 1956-   **CLC 44**
See also CA 134
Minus, Ed 1938-   **CLC 39**
Miranda, Javier
See Bioy Casares, Adolfo
Miranda, Javier
See Bioy Casares, Adolfo
Mirbeau, Octave 1848-1917   **TCLC 55**
See also DLB 123, 192
Miro (Ferrer), Gabriel (Francisco Victor) 1879-
1930   **TCLC 5**
See also CA 104
Mishima, Yukio 1925-1970**CLC 2, 4, 6, 9, 27;
DC 1; SSC 4**
See also Hiraoka, Kimitake
See also DLB 182; MTCW 2
Mistral, Frederic 1830-1914   **TCLC 51**
See also CA 122
Mistral, Gabriela   **TCLC 2; HLC 2**
See Godoy Alcayaga, Lucila
See also MTCW 2
Mistry, Rohinton 1952-   **CLC 71; DAC**
See also CA 141
Mitchell, Clyde
See Ellison, Harlan (Jay); Silverberg, Robert
Mitchell, James Leslie 1901-1935
See Gibbon, Lewis Grassic
See also CA 104; DLB 15
Mitchell, Joni 1943-   **CLC 12**
See also CA 112
Mitchell, Joseph (Quincy) 1908-1996**CLC 98**
See also CA 77-80; 152; CANR 69; DLB 185;
DLBY 96
Mitchell, Margaret (Munnerlyn) 1900-1949
TCLC 11; DAM NOV, POP
See also AAYA 23; CA 109; 125; CANR 55;

CDALBS; DA3; DLB 9; MTCW 1, 2
Mitchell, Peggy
See Mitchell, Margaret (Munnerlyn)
Mitchell, S(ilas) Weir 1829-1914   **TCLC 36**
See also CA 165; DLB 202
Mitchell, W(illiam) O(rmond) 1914-1998**CLC
25; DAC; DAM MST**
See also CA 77-80; 165; CANR 15, 43; DLB
88
Mitchell, William 1879-1936   **TCLC 81**
Mitford, Mary Russell 1787-1855   **NCLC 4**
See also DLB 110, 116
Mitford, Nancy 1904-1973   **CLC 44**
See also CA 9-12R; DLB 191
Miyamoto, (Chujo) Yuriko 1899-1951 **T C L C
37**
See also CA 170, 174; DLB 180
Miyazawa, Kenji 1896-1933   **TCLC 76**
See also CA 157
Mizoguchi, Kenji 1898-1956   **TCLC 72**
See also CA 167
Mo, Timothy (Peter) 1950(?)-   **CLC 46**
See also CA 117; DLB 194; MTCW 1
Modarressi, Taghi (M.) 1931-   **CLC 44**
See also CA 121; 134; INT 134
Modiano, Patrick (Jean) 1945-   **CLC 18**
See also CA 85-88; CANR 17, 40; DLB 83
Moerck, Paal
See Roelvaag, O(le) E(dvart)
Mofolo, Thomas (Mokopu) 1875(?)-1948
TCLC 22; BLC 3; DAM MULT
See also CA 121; 153; CANR 83; MTCW 2
Mohr, Nicholasa 1938-**CLC 12; DAM MULT;
HLC 2**
See also AAYA 8; CA 49-52; CANR 1, 32, 64;
CLR 22; DLB 145; HW 1, 2; JRDA; SAAS
8; SATA 8, 97
Mojtabai, A(nn) G(race) 1938- **CLC 5, 9, 15,
29**
See also CA 85-88
Moliere 1622-1673**LC 10, 28; DA; DAB; DAC;
DAM DRAM, MST; WLC**
See also DA3
Molin, Charles
See Mayne, William (James Carter)
Molnar, Ferenc 1878-1952   **TCLC 20; DAM
DRAM**
See also CA 109; 153; CANR 83
Momaday, N(avarre) Scott 1934- **CLC 2, 19,
85, 95; DA; DAB; DAC; DAM MST,
MULT, NOV, POP; PC 25; WLCS**
See also AAYA 11; CA 25-28R; CANR 14, 34,
68; CDALBS; DA3; DLB 143, 175; INT
CANR-14; MTCW 1, 2; NNAL; SATA 48;
SATA-Brief 30
Monette, Paul 1945-1995   **CLC 82**
See also CA 139; 147
Monroe, Harriet 1860-1936   **TCLC 12**
See also CA 109; DLB 54, 91
Monroe, Lyle
See Heinlein, Robert A(nson)
Montagu, Elizabeth 1720-1800   **NCLC 7**
Montagu, Mary (Pierrepont) Wortley 1689-
1762   **LC 9; PC 16**
See also DLB 95, 101
Montagu, W. H.
See Coleridge, Samuel Taylor
Montague, John (Patrick) 1929- **CLC 13, 46**
See also CA 9-12R; CANR 9, 69; DLB 40;
MTCW 1
Montaigne, Michel (Eyquem) de 1533-1592
LC 8; DA; DAB; DAC; DAM MST; WLC
Montale, Eugenio 1896-1981**CLC 7, 9, 18; PC

13**
See also CA 17-20R; 104; CANR 30; DLB 114;
MTCW 1
Montesquieu, Charles-Louis de Secondat 1689-
1755   **LC 7**
Montgomery, (Robert) Bruce 1921(?)-1978
See Crispin, Edmund
See also CA 179; 104
Montgomery, L(ucy) M(aud) 1874-1942
TCLC 51; DAC; DAM MST
See also AAYA 12; CA 108; 137; CLR 8; DA3;
DLB 92; DLBD 14; JRDA; MAICYA;
MTCW 2; SATA 100; YABC 1
Montgomery, Marion H., Jr. 1925-   **CLC 7**
See also AITN 1; CA 1-4R; CANR 3, 48; DLB
6
Montgomery, Max
See Davenport, Guy (Mattison, Jr.)
Montherlant, Henry (Milon) de 1896-1972
CLC 8, 19; DAM DRAM
See also CA 85-88; 37-40R; DLB 72; MTCW
1
Monty Python
See Chapman, Graham; Cleese, John
(Marwood); Gilliam, Terry (Vance); Idle,
Eric; Jones, Terence Graham Parry; Palin,
Michael (Edward)
See also AAYA 7
Moodie, Susanna (Strickland) 1803-1885
NCLC 14
See also DLB 99
Mooney, Edward 1951-
See Mooney, Ted
See also CA 130
Mooney, Ted   **CLC 25**
See also Mooney, Edward
Moorcock, Michael (John) 1939-**CLC 5, 27, 58**
See also Bradbury, Edward P.
See also AAYA 26; CA 45-48; CAAS 5; CANR
2, 17, 38, 64; DLB 14; MTCW 1, 2; SATA
93
Moore, Brian 1921-1999**CLC 1, 3, 5, 7, 8, 19,
32, 90; DAB; DAC; DAM MST**
See also CA 1-4R; 174; CANR 1, 25, 42, 63;
MTCW 1, 2
Moore, Edward
See Muir, Edwin
Moore, G. E. 1873-1958   **TCLC 89**
Moore, George Augustus 1852-1933**TCLC 7;
SSC 19**
See also CA 104; 177; DLB 10, 18, 57, 135
Moore, Lorrie   **CLC 39, 45, 68**
See also Moore, Marie Lorena
Moore, Marianne (Craig) 1887-1972**CLC 1, 2,
4, 8, 10, 13, 19, 47; DA; DAB; DAC; DAM
MST, POET; PC 4; WLCS**
See also CA 1-4R; 33-36R; CANR 3, 61;
CDALB 1929-1941; DA3; DLB 45; DLBD
7; MTCW 1, 2; SATA 20
Moore, Marie Lorena 1957-
See Moore, Lorrie
See also CA 116; CANR 39, 83
Moore, Thomas 1779-1852   **NCLC 6**
See also DLB 96, 144
Mora, Pat(ricia) 1942-
See also CA 129; CANR 57, 81; CLR 58; DAM
MULT; DLB 209; HLC 2; HW 1, 2; SATA
92
Morand, Paul 1888-1976   **CLC 41; SSC 22**
See also CA 69-72; DLB 65
Morante, Elsa 1918-1985   **CLC 8, 47**
See also CA 85-88; 117; CANR 35; DLB 177;
MTCW 1, 2

Moravia, Alberto 1907-1990 **CLC 2, 7, 11, 27, 46; SSC 26**
See also Pincherle, Alberto
See also DLB 177; MTCW 2

More, Hannah 1745-1833   **NCLC 27**
See also DLB 107, 109, 116, 158

More, Henry 1614-1687   **LC 9**
See also DLB 126

More, Sir Thomas 1478-1535   **LC 10, 32**

Moreas, Jean   **TCLC 18**
See also Papadiamantopoulos, Johannes

Morgan, Berry 1919-   **CLC 6**
See also CA 49-52; DLB 6

Morgan, Claire
See Highsmith, (Mary) Patricia

Morgan, Edwin (George) 1920-   **CLC 31**
See also CA 5-8R; CANR 3, 43; DLB 27

Morgan, (George) Frederick 1922- **CLC 23**
See also CA 17-20R; CANR 21

Morgan, Harriet
See Mencken, H(enry) L(ouis)

Morgan, Jane
See Cooper, James Fenimore

Morgan, Janet 1945-   **CLC 39**
See also CA 65-68

Morgan, Lady 1776(?)-1859   **NCLC 29**
See also DLB 116, 158

Morgan, Robin (Evonne) 1941-   **CLC 2**
See also CA 69-72; CANR 29, 68; MTCW 1; SATA 80

Morgan, Scott
See Kuttner, Henry

Morgan, Seth 1949(?)-1990   **CLC 65**
See also CA 132

Morgenstern, Christian 1871-1914 **TCLC 8**
See also CA 105

Morgenstern, S.
See Goldman, William (W.)

Moricz, Zsigmond 1879-1942   **TCLC 33**
See also CA 165

Morike, Eduard (Friedrich) 1804-1875 **NCLC 10**
See also DLB 133

Moritz, Karl Philipp 1756-1793   **LC 2**
See also DLB 94

Morland, Peter Henry
See Faust, Frederick (Schiller)

Morley, Christopher (Darlington) 1890-1957 **TCLC 87**
See also CA 112; DLB 9

Morren, Theophil
See Hofmannsthal, Hugo von

Morris, Bill 1952-   **CLC 76**

Morris, Julian
See West, Morris L(anglo)

Morris, Steveland Judkins 1950(?)-
See Wonder, Stevie
See also CA 111

Morris, William 1834-1896   **NCLC 4**
See also CDBLB 1832-1890; DLB 18, 35, 57, 156, 178, 184

Morris, Wright 1910-1998 **CLC 1, 3, 7, 18, 37**
See also CA 9-12R; 167; CANR 21, 81; DLB 2, 206; DLBY 81; MTCW 1, 2

Morrison, Arthur 1863-1945   **TCLC 72**
See also CA 120; 157; DLB 70, 135, 197

Morrison, Chloe Anthony Wofford
See Morrison, Toni

Morrison, James Douglas 1943-1971
See Morrison, Jim
See also CA 73-76; CANR 40

Morrison, Jim   **CLC 17**
See also Morrison, James Douglas

Morrison, Toni 1931- **CLC 4, 10, 22, 55, 81, 87; BLC 3; DA; DAB; DAC; DAM MST, MULT, NOV, POP**
See also AAYA 1, 22; BW 2, 3; CA 29-32R; CANR 27, 42, 67; CDALB 1968-1988; DA3; DLB 6, 33, 143; DLBY 81; MTCW 1, 2; SATA 57

Morrison, Van 1945-   **CLC 21**
See also CA 116; 168

Morrissy, Mary 1958-   **CLC 99**

Mortimer, John (Clifford) 1923- **CLC 28, 43; DAM DRAM, POP**
See also CA 13-16R; CANR 21, 69; CDBLB 1960 to Present; DA3; DLB 13; INT CANR-21; MTCW 1, 2

Mortimer, Penelope (Ruth) 1918-   **CLC 5**
See also CA 57-60; CANR 45

Morton, Anthony
See Creasey, John

Mosca, Gaetano 1858-1941   **TCLC 75**

Mosher, Howard Frank 1943-   **CLC 62**
See also CA 139; CANR 65

Mosley, Nicholas 1923-   **CLC 43, 70**
See also CA 69-72; CANR 41, 60; DLB 14, 207

Mosley, Walter 1952- **CLC 97; BLCS; DAM MULT, POP**
See also AAYA 17; BW 2; CA 142; CANR 57; DA3; MTCW 2

Moss, Howard 1922-1987 **CLC 7, 14, 45, 50; DAM POET**
See also CA 1-4R; 123; CANR 1, 44; DLB 5

Mossgiel, Rab
See Burns, Robert

Motion, Andrew (Peter) 1952-   **CLC 47**
See also CA 146; DLB 40

Motley, Willard (Francis) 1909-1965 **CLC 18**
See also BW 1; CA 117; 106; DLB 76, 143

Motoori, Norinaga 1730-1801   **NCLC 45**

Mott, Michael (Charles Alston) 1930- **CLC 15, 34**
See also CA 5-8R; CAAS 7; CANR 7, 29

Mountain Wolf Woman 1884-1960   **CLC 92**
See also CA 144; NNAL

Moure, Erin 1955-   **CLC 88**
See also CA 113; DLB 60

Mowat, Farley (McGill) 1921- **CLC 26; DAC; DAM MST**
See also AAYA 1; CA 1-4R; CANR 4, 24, 42, 68; CLR 20; DLB 68; INT CANR-24; JRDA; MAICYA; MTCW 1, 2; SATA 3, 55

Mowatt, Anna Cora 1819-1870   **NCLC 74**

Moyers, Bill 1934-   **CLC 74**
See also AITN 2; CA 61-64; CANR 31, 52

Mphahlele, Es'kia
See Mphahlele, Ezekiel
See also DLB 125

Mphahlele, Ezekiel 1919-   **CLC 25; BLC 3; DAM MULT**
See also Mphahlele, Es'kia
See also BW 2, 3; CA 81-84; CANR 26, 76; DA3; MTCW 2

Mqhayi, S(amuel) E(dward) K(rune Loliwe) 1875-1945 **TCLC 25; BLC 3; DAM MULT**
See also CA 153

Mrozek, Slawomir 1930-   **CLC 3, 13**
See also CA 13-16R; CAAS 10; CANR 29; MTCW 1

Mrs. Belloc-Lowndes
See Lowndes, Marie Adelaide (Belloc)

Mtwa, Percy (?)-   **CLC 47**

Mueller, Lisel 1924-   **CLC 13, 51**
See also CA 93-96; DLB 105

Muir, Edwin 1887-1959   **TCLC 2, 87**

See also CA 104; DLB 20, 100, 191

Muir, John 1838-1914   **TCLC 28**
See also CA 165; DLB 186

Mujica Lainez, Manuel 1910-1984   **CLC 31**
See also Lainez, Manuel Mujica
See also CA 81-84; 112; CANR 32; HW 1

Mukherjee, Bharati 1940- **CLC 53, 115; DAM NOV**
See also BEST 89:2; CA 107; CANR 45, 72; DLB 60; MTCW 1, 2

Muldoon, Paul 1951- **CLC 32, 72; DAM POET**
See also CA 113; 129; CANR 52; DLB 40; INT 129

Mulisch, Harry 1927-   **CLC 42**
See also CA 9-12R; CANR 6, 26, 56

Mull, Martin 1943-   **CLC 17**
See also CA 105

Muller, Wilhelm   **NCLC 73**

Mulock, Dinah Maria
See Craik, Dinah Maria (Mulock)

Munford, Robert 1737(?)-1783   **LC 5**
See also DLB 31

Mungo, Raymond 1946-   **CLC 72**
See also CA 49-52; CANR 2

Munro, Alice 1931- **CLC 6, 10, 19, 50, 95; DAC; DAM MST, NOV; SSC 3; WLCS**
See also AITN 2; CA 33-36R; CANR 33, 53, 75; DA3; DLB 53; MTCW 1, 2; SATA 29

Munro, H(ector) H(ugh) 1870-1916
See Saki
See also CA 104; 130; CDBLB 1890-1914; DA; DAB; DAC; DAM MST, NOV; DA3; DLB 34, 162; MTCW 1, 2; WLC

Murdoch, (Jean) Iris 1919-1999 **CLC 1, 2, 3, 4, 6, 8, 11, 15, 22, 31, 51; DAB; DAC; DAM MST, NOV**
See also CA 13-16R; 179; CANR 8, 43, 68; CDBLB 1960 to Present; DA3; DLB 14, 194; INT CANR-8; MTCW 1, 2

Murfree, Mary Noailles 1850-1922   **SSC 22**
See also CA 122; 176; DLB 12, 74

Murnau, Friedrich Wilhelm
See Plumpe, Friedrich Wilhelm

Murphy, Richard 1927-   **CLC 41**
See also CA 29-32R; DLB 40

Murphy, Sylvia 1937-   **CLC 34**
See also CA 121

Murphy, Thomas (Bernard) 1935-   **CLC 51**
See also CA 101

Murray, Albert L. 1916-   **CLC 73**
See also BW 2; CA 49-52; CANR 26, 52, 78; DLB 38

Murray, Judith Sargent 1751-1820 **NCLC 63**
See also DLB 37, 200

Murray, Les(lie) A(llan) 1938- **CLC 40; DAM POET**
See also CA 21-24R; CANR 11, 27, 56

Murry, J. Middleton
See Murry, John Middleton

Murry, John Middleton 1889-1957 **TCLC 16**
See also CA 118; DLB 149

Musgrave, Susan 1951-   **CLC 13, 54**
See also CA 69-72; CANR 45, 84

Musil, Robert (Edler von) 1880-1942 **TCLC 12, 68; SSC 18**
See also CA 109; CANR 55, 84; DLB 81, 124; MTCW 2

Muske, Carol 1945-   **CLC 90**
See also Muske-Dukes, Carol (Anne)

Muske-Dukes, Carol (Anne) 1945-
See Muske, Carol
See also CA 65-68; CANR 32, 70

Musset, (Louis Charles) Alfred de 1810-1857

NCLC 7
See also DLB 192
Mussolini, Benito (Amilcare Andrea) 1883-1945
TCLC 96
See also CA 116
My Brother's Brother
See Chekhov, Anton (Pavlovich)
Myers, L(eopold) H(amilton) 1881-1944
TCLC 59
See also CA 157; DLB 15
Myers, Walter Dean 1937- **CLC 35; BLC 3;**
DAM MULT, NOV
See also AAYA 4, 23; BW 2; CA 33-36R;
CANR 20, 42, 67; CLR 4, 16, 35; DLB 33;
INT CANR-20; JRDA; MAICYA; MTCW 2;
SAAS 2; SATA 41, 71, 109; SATA-Brief 27
Myers, Walter M.
See Myers, Walter Dean
Myles, Symon
See Follett, Ken(neth Martin)
Nabokov, Vladimir (Vladimirovich) 1899-1977
CLC 1, 2, 3, 6, 8, 11, 15, 23, 44, 46, 64;
DA; DAB; DAC; DAM MST, NOV; SSC
11; WLC
See also CA 5-8R; 69-72; CANR 20; CDALB
1941-1968; DA3; DLB 2; DLBD 3; DLBY
80, 91; MTCW 1, 2
Nagai Kafu 1879-1959 **TCLC 51**
See also Nagai Sokichi
See also DLB 180
Nagai Sokichi 1879-1959
See Nagai Kafu
See also CA 117
Nagy, Laszlo 1925-1978 **CLC 7**
See also CA 129; 112
Naidu, Sarojini 1879-1943 **TCLC 80**
Naipaul, Shiva(dhar Srinivasa) 1945-1985
CLC 32, 39; DAM NOV
See also CA 110; 112; 116; CANR 33; DA3;
DLB 157; DLBY 85; MTCW 1, 2
Naipaul, V(idiadhar) S(urajprasad) 1932-
CLC 4, 7, 9, 13, 18, 37, 105; DAB; DAC;
DAM MST, NOV
See also CA 1-4R; CANR 1, 33, 51; CDBLB
1960 to Present; DA3; DLB 125, 204, 206;
DLBY 85; MTCW 1, 2
Nakos, Lilika 1899(?)- **CLC 29**
Narayan, R(asipuram) K(rishnaswami) 1906-
CLC 7, 28, 47, 121; DAM NOV; SSC 25
See also CA 81-84; CANR 33, 61; DA3; MTCW
1, 2; SATA 62
Nash, (Frediric) Ogden 1902-1971 **CLC 23;**
DAM POET; PC 21
See also CA 13-14; 29-32R; CANR 34, 61; CAP
1; DLB 11; MAICYA; MTCW 1, 2; SATA 2,
46
Nashe, Thomas 1567-1601(?) **LC 41**
See also DLB 167
Nashe, Thomas 1567-1601 **LC 41**
Nathan, Daniel
See Dannay, Frederic
Nathan, George Jean 1882-1958 **TCLC 18**
See also Hatteras, Owen
See also CA 114; 169; DLB 137
Natsume, Kinnosuke 1867-1916
See Natsume, Soseki
See also CA 104
Natsume, Soseki 1867-1916 **TCLC 2, 10**
See also Natsume, Kinnosuke
See also DLB 180
Natti, (Mary) Lee 1919-
See Kingman, Lee
See also CA 5-8R; CANR 2

Naylor, Gloria 1950-**CLC 28, 52; BLC 3; DA;**
DAC; DAM MST, MULT, NOV, POP;
WLCS
See also AAYA 6; BW 2, 3; CA 107; CANR 27,
51, 74; DA3; DLB 173; MTCW 1, 2
Neihardt, John Gneisenau 1881-1973**CLC 32**
See also CA 13-14; CANR 65; CAP 1; DLB 9,
54
Nekrasov, Nikolai Alekseevich 1821-1878
NCLC 11
Nelligan, Emile 1879-1941 **TCLC 14**
See also CA 114; DLB 92
Nelson, Willie 1933- **CLC 17**
See also CA 107
Nemerov, Howard (Stanley) 1920-1991**CLC 2,**
6, 9, 36; DAM POET; PC 24
See also CA 1-4R; 134; CABS 2; CANR 1, 27,
53; DLB 5, 6; DLBY 83; INT CANR-27;
MTCW 1, 2
Neruda, Pablo 1904-1973**CLC 1, 2, 5, 7, 9, 28,**
62; DA; DAB; DAC; DAM MST, MULT,
POET; HLC 2; PC 4; WLC
See also CA 19-20; 45-48; CAP 2; DA3; HW
1; MTCW 1, 2
Nerval, Gerard de 1808-1855**NCLC 1, 67; PC**
13; SSC 18
Nervo, (Jose) Amado (Ruiz de) 1870-1919
TCLC 11; HLCS 2
See also CA 109; 131; HW 1
Nessi, Pio Baroja y
See Baroja (y Nessi), Pio
Nestroy, Johann 1801-1862 **NCLC 42**
See also DLB 133
Netterville, Luke
See O'Grady, Standish (James)
Neufeld, John (Arthur) 1938- **CLC 17**
See also AAYA 11; CA 25-28R; CANR 11, 37,
56; CLR 52; MAICYA; SAAS 3; SATA 6,
81
Neville, Emily Cheney 1919- **CLC 12**
See also CA 5-8R; CANR 3, 37; JRDA;
MAICYA; SAAS 2; SATA 1
Newbound, Bernard Slade 1930-
See Slade, Bernard
See also CA 81-84; CANR 49; DAM DRAM
Newby, P(ercy) H(oward) 1918-1997 **CLC 2,**
13; DAM NOV
See also CA 5-8R; 161; CANR 32, 67; DLB
15; MTCW 1
Newlove, Donald 1928- **CLC 6**
See also CA 29-32R; CANR 25
Newlove, John (Herbert) 1938- **CLC 14**
See also CA 21-24R; CANR 9, 25
Newman, Charles 1938- **CLC 2, 8**
See also CA 21-24R; CANR 84
Newman, Edwin (Harold) 1919- **CLC 14**
See also AITN 1; CA 69-72; CANR 5
Newman, John Henry 1801-1890 **NCLC 38**
See also DLB 18, 32, 55
Newton, (Sir)Isaac 1642-1727 **LC 35, 52**
Newton, Suzanne 1936- **CLC 35**
See also CA 41-44R; CANR 14; JRDA; SATA
5, 77
Nexo, Martin Andersen 1869-1954 **TCLC 43**
Nezval, Vitezslav 1900-1958 **TCLC 44**
See also CA 123
Ng, Fae Myenne 1957(?)- **CLC 81**
See also CA 146
Ngema, Mbongeni 1955- **CLC 57**
See also BW 2; CA 143; CANR 84
Ngugi, James T(hiong'o) **CLC 3, 7, 13**
See also Ngugi wa Thiong'o
Ngugi wa Thiong'o 1938- **CLC 36; BLC 3;**

DAM MULT, NOV
See also Ngugi, James T(hiong'o)
See also BW 2; CA 81-84; CANR 27, 58; DLB
125; MTCW 1, 2
Nichol, B(arrie) P(hillip) 1944-1988 **CLC 18**
See also CA 53-56; DLB 53; SATA 66
Nichols, John (Treadwell) 1940- **CLC 38**
See also CA 9-12R; CAAS 2; CANR 6, 70;
DLBY 82
Nichols, Leigh
See Koontz, Dean R(ay)
Nichols, Peter (Richard) 1927- CLC 5, 36, 65
See also CA 104; CANR 33; DLB 13; MTCW
1
Nicolas, F. R. E.
See Freeling, Nicolas
Niedecker, Lorine 1903-1970 **CLC 10, 42;**
DAM POET
See also CA 25-28; CAP 2; DLB 48
Nietzsche, Friedrich (Wilhelm) 1844-1900
TCLC 10, 18, 55
See also CA 107; 121; DLB 129
Nievo, Ippolito 1831-1861 **NCLC 22**
Nightingale, Anne Redmon 1943-
See Redmon, Anne
See also CA 103
Nightingale, Florence 1820-1910 **TCLC 85**
See also DLB 166
Nik. T. O.
See Annensky, Innokenty (Fyodorovich)
Nin, Anais 1903-1977 **CLC 1, 4, 8, 11, 14, 60;**
DAM NOV, POP; SSC 10
See also AITN 2; CA 13-16R; 69-72; CANR
22, 53; DLB 2, 4, 152; MTCW 1, 2
Nishida, Kitaro 1870-1945 **TCLC 83**
Nishiwaki, Junzaburo 1894-1982 **PC 15**
See also CA 107
Nissenson, Hugh 1933- **CLC 4, 9**
See also CA 17-20R; CANR 27; DLB 28
Niven, Larry **CLC 8**
See also Niven, Laurence Van Cott
See also AAYA 27; DLB 8
Niven, Laurence Van Cott 1938-
See Niven, Larry
See also CA 21-24R; CAAS 12; CANR 14, 44,
66; DAM POP; MTCW 1, 2; SATA 95
Nixon, Agnes Eckhardt 1927- **CLC 21**
See also CA 110
Nizan, Paul 1905-1940 **TCLC 40**
See also CA 161; DLB 72
Nkosi, Lewis 1936- **CLC 45; BLC 3; DAM**
MULT
See also BW 1, 3; CA 65-68; CANR 27, 81;
DLB 157
Nodier, (Jean) Charles (Emmanuel) 1780-1844
NCLC 19
See also DLB 119
Noguchi, Yone 1875-1947 **TCLC 80**
Nolan, Christopher 1965- **CLC 58**
See also CA 111
Noon, Jeff 1957- **CLC 91**
See also CA 148; CANR 83
Norden, Charles
See Durrell, Lawrence (George)
Nordhoff, Charles (Bernard) 1887-1947
TCLC 23
See also CA 108; DLB 9; SATA 23
Norfolk, Lawrence 1963- **CLC 76**
See also CA 144
Norman, Marsha 1947-**CLC 28; DAM DRAM;**
DC 8
See also CA 105; CABS 3; CANR 41; DLBY
84

See also CA 85-88; 145; CANR 32, 63; DLB 113; HW 1, 2; MTCW 1, 2

O Nuallain, Brian 1911-1966
See O'Brien, Flann
See also CA 21-22; 25-28R; CAP 2

Ophuls, Max 1902-1957   **TCLC 79**
See also CA 113

Opie, Amelia 1769-1853   **NCLC 65**
See also DLB 116, 159

Oppen, George 1908-1984   **CLC 7, 13, 34**
See also CA 13-16R; 113; CANR 8, 82; DLB 5, 165

Oppenheim, E(dward) Phillips 1866-1946
    TCLC 45
See also CA 111; DLB 70

Opuls, Max
See Ophuls, Max

Origen c. 185-c. 254   **CMLC 19**

Orlovitz, Gil 1918-1973   **CLC 22**
See also CA 77-80; 45-48; DLB 2, 5

Orris
See Ingelow, Jean

Ortega y Gasset, Jose 1883-1955   **TCLC 9; DAM MULT; HLC 2**
See also CA 106; 130; HW 1, 2; MTCW 1, 2

Ortese, Anna Maria 1914-   **CLC 89**
See also DLB 177

Ortiz, Simon J(oseph) 1941-   **CLC 45; DAM MULT, POET; PC 17**
See also CA 134; CANR 69; DLB 120, 175; NNAL

Orton, Joe   **CLC 4, 13, 43; DC 3**
See also Orton, John Kingsley
See also CDBLB 1960 to Present; DLB 13; MTCW 2

Orton, John Kingsley 1933-1967
See Orton, Joe
See also CA 85-88; CANR 35, 66; DAM DRAM; MTCW 1, 2

Orwell, George   **TCLC 2, 6, 15, 31, 51; DAB; WLC**
See also Blair, Eric (Arthur)
See also CDBLB 1945-1960; DLB 15, 98, 195

Osborne, David
See Silverberg, Robert

Osborne, George
See Silverberg, Robert

Osborne, John (James) 1929-1994 **CLC 1, 2, 5, 11, 45; DA; DAB; DAC; DAM DRAM, MST; WLC**
See also CA 13-16R; 147; CANR 21, 56; CDBLB 1945-1960; DLB 13; MTCW 1, 2

Osborne, Lawrence 1958-   **CLC 50**

Osbourne, Lloyd 1868-1947   **TCLC 93**

Oshima, Nagisa 1932-   **CLC 20**
See also CA 116; 121; CANR 78

Oskison, John Milton 1874-1947   **TCLC 35; DAM MULT**
See also CA 144; CANR 84; DLB 175; NNAL

Ossian c. 3rd cent. -   **CMLC 28**
See also Macpherson, James

Ossoli, Sarah Margaret (Fuller marchesa d') 1810-1850
See Fuller, Margaret
See also SATA 25

Ostrovsky, Alexander 1823-1886 **NCLC 30, 57**

Otero, Blas de 1916-1979   **CLC 11**
See also CA 89-92; DLB 134

Otto, Rudolf 1869-1937   **TCLC 85**

Otto, Whitney 1955-   **CLC 70**
See also CA 140

Ouida   **TCLC 43**
See also De La Ramee, (Marie) Louise

See also DLB 18, 156

Ousmane, Sembene 1923-   **CLC 66; BLC 3**
See also BW 1, 3; CA 117; 125; CANR 81; MTCW 1

Ovid 43B.C.-17 **CMLC 7; DAM POET; PC 2**
See also DA3; DLB 211

Owen, Hugh
See Faust, Frederick (Schiller)

Owen, Wilfred (Edward Salter) 1893-1918
TCLC 5, 27; DA; DAB; DAC; DAM MST, POET; PC 19; WLC
See also CA 104; 141; CDBLB 1914-1945; DLB 20; MTCW 2

Owens, Rochelle 1936-   **CLC 8**
See also CA 17-20R; CAAS 2; CANR 39

Oz, Amos 1939- **CLC 5, 8, 11, 27, 33, 54; DAM NOV**
See also CA 53-56; CANR 27, 47, 65; MTCW 1, 2

Ozick, Cynthia 1928- **CLC 3, 7, 28, 62; DAM NOV, POP; SSC 15**
See also BEST 90:1; CA 17-20R; CANR 23, 58; DA3; DLB 28, 152; DLBY 82; INT CANR-23; MTCW 1, 2

Ozu, Yasujiro 1903-1963   **CLC 16**
See also CA 112

Pacheco, C.
See Pessoa, Fernando (Antonio Nogueira)

Pacheco, Jose Emilio 1939-
See also CA 111; 131; CANR 65; DAM MULT; HLC 2; HW 1, 2

Pa Chin   **CLC 18**
See also Li Fei-kan

Pack, Robert 1929-   **CLC 13**
See also CA 1-4R; CANR 3, 44, 82; DLB 5

Padgett, Lewis
See Kuttner, Henry

Padilla (Lorenzo), Heberto 1932-   **CLC 38**
See also AITN 1; CA 123; 131; HW 1

Page, Jimmy 1944-   **CLC 12**

Page, Louise 1955-   **CLC 40**
See also CA 140; CANR 76

Page, P(atricia) K(athleen) 1916- **CLC 7, 18; DAC; DAM MST; PC 12**
See also CA 53-56; CANR 4, 22, 65; DLB 68; MTCW 1

Page, Thomas Nelson 1853-1922   **SSC 23**
See also CA 118; 177; DLB 12, 78; DLBD 13

Pagels, Elaine Hiesey 1943-   **CLC 104**
See also CA 45-48; CANR 2, 24, 51

Paget, Violet 1856-1935
See Lee, Vernon
See also CA 104; 166

Paget-Lowe, Henry
See Lovecraft, H(oward) P(hillips)

Paglia, Camille (Anna) 1947-   **CLC 68**
See also CA 140; CANR 72; MTCW 2

Paige, Richard
See Koontz, Dean R(ay)

Paine, Thomas 1737-1809   **NCLC 62**
See also CDALB 1640-1865; DLB 31, 43, 73, 158

Pakenham, Antonia
See Fraser, (Lady) Antonia (Pakenham)

Palamas, Kostes 1859-1943   **TCLC 5**
See also CA 105

Palazzeschi, Aldo 1885-1974   **CLC 11**
See also CA 89-92; 53-56; DLB 114

Pales Matos, Luis 1898-1959
See also HLCS 2; HW 1

Paley, Grace 1922- **CLC 4, 6, 37; DAM POP; SSC 8**
See also CA 25-28R; CANR 13, 46, 74; DA3;

DLB 28; INT CANR-13; MTCW 1, 2

Palin, Michael (Edward) 1943-   **CLC 21**
See also Monty Python
See also CA 107; CANR 35; SATA 67

Palliser, Charles 1947-   **CLC 65**
See also CA 136; CANR 76

Palma, Ricardo 1833-1919   **TCLC 29**
See also CA 168

Pancake, Breece Dexter 1952-1979
See Pancake, Breece D'J
See also CA 123; 109

Pancake, Breece D'J   **CLC 29**
See also Pancake, Breece Dexter
See also DLB 130

Panko, Rudy
See Gogol, Nikolai (Vasilyevich)

Papadiamantis, Alexandros 1851-1911 **TCLC 29**
See also CA 168

Papadiamantopoulos, Johannes 1856-1910
See Moreas, Jean
See also CA 117

Papini, Giovanni 1881-1956   **TCLC 22**
See also CA 121; 180

Paracelsus 1493-1541   **LC 14**
See also DLB 179

Parasol, Peter
See Stevens, Wallace

Pardo Bazan, Emilia 1851-1921   **SSC 30**

Pareto, Vilfredo 1848-1923   **TCLC 69**
See also CA 175

Parfenie, Maria
See Codrescu, Andrei

Parini, Jay (Lee) 1948-   **CLC 54**
See also CA 97-100; CAAS 16; CANR 32

Park, Jordan
See Kornbluth, C(yril) M.; Pohl, Frederik

Park, Robert E(zra) 1864-1944   **TCLC 73**
See also CA 122; 165

Parker, Bert
See Ellison, Harlan (Jay)

Parker, Dorothy (Rothschild) 1893-1967 **CLC 15, 68; DAM POET; PC 28; SSC 2**
See also CA 19-20; 25-28R; CAP 2; DA3; DLB 11, 45, 86; MTCW 1, 2

Parker, Robert B(rown) 1932- **CLC 27; DAM NOV, POP**
See also AAYA 28; BEST 89:4; CA 49-52; CANR 1, 26, 52; INT CANR-26; MTCW 1

Parkin, Frank 1940-   **CLC 43**
See also CA 147

Parkman, Francis, Jr. 1823-1893   **NCLC 12**
See also DLB 1, 30, 186

Parks, Gordon (Alexander Buchanan) 1912-
CLC 1, 16; BLC 3; DAM MULT
See also AITN 2; BW 2, 3; CA 41-44R; CANR 26, 66; DA3; DLB 33; MTCW 2; SATA 8, 108

Parmenides c. 515B.C.-c. 450B.C. **CMLC 22**
See also DLB 176

Parnell, Thomas 1679-1718   **LC 3**
See also DLB 94

Parra, Nicanor 1914- **CLC 2, 102; DAM MULT; HLC 2**
See also CA 85-88; CANR 32; HW 1; MTCW 1

Parra Sanojo, Ana Teresa de la 1890-1936
See also HLCS 2

Parrish, Mary Frances
See Fisher, M(ary) F(rances) K(ennedy)

Parson
See Coleridge, Samuel Taylor

Parson Lot

See also CA 9-12R; 45-48; DLB 14

Quinn, Martin
See Smith, Martin Cruz

Quinn, Peter 1947- **CLC 91**

Quinn, Simon
See Smith, Martin Cruz

Quintana, Leroy V. 1944-
See also CA 131; CANR 65; DAM MULT; DLB 82; HLC 2; HW 1, 2

Quiroga, Horacio (Sylvestre) 1878-1937 **TCLC 20; DAM MULT; HLC 2**
See also CA 117; 131; HW 1; MTCW 1

Quoirez, Francoise 1935- **CLC 9**
See also Sagan, Francoise
See also CA 49-52; CANR 6, 39, 73; MTCW 1, 2

Raabe, Wilhelm (Karl) 1831-1910 **TCLC 45**
See also CA 167; DLB 129

Rabe, David (William) 1940- **CLC 4, 8, 33; DAM DRAM**
See also CA 85-88; CABS 3; CANR 59; DLB 7

Rabelais, Francois 1483-1553 **LC 5; DA; DAB; DAC; DAM MST; WLC**

Rabinovitch, Sholem 1859-1916
See Aleichem, Sholom
See also CA 104

Rabinyan, Dorit 1972- **CLC 119**
See also CA 170

Rachilde 1860-1953 **TCLC 67**
See also DLB 123, 192

Racine, Jean 1639-1699 **LC 28; DAB; DAM MST**
See also DA3

Radcliffe, Ann (Ward) 1764-1823 **NCLC 6, 55**
See also DLB 39, 178

Radiguet, Raymond 1903-1923 **TCLC 29**
See also CA 162; DLB 65

Radnoti, Miklos 1909-1944 **TCLC 16**
See also CA 118

Rado, James 1939- **CLC 17**
See also CA 105

Radvanyi, Netty 1900-1983
See Seghers, Anna
See also CA 85-88; 110; CANR 82

Rae, Ben
See Griffiths, Trevor

Raeburn, John (Hay) 1941- **CLC 34**
See also CA 57-60

Ragni, Gerome 1942-1991 **CLC 17**
See also CA 105; 134

Rahv, Philip 1908-1973 **CLC 24**
See also Greenberg, Ivan
See also DLB 137

Raimund, Ferdinand Jakob 1790-1836 **NCLC 69**
See also DLB 90

Raine, Craig 1944- **CLC 32, 103**
See also CA 108; CANR 29, 51; DLB 40

Raine, Kathleen (Jessie) 1908- **CLC 7, 45**
See also CA 85-88; CANR 46; DLB 20; MTCW 1

Rainis, Janis 1865-1929 **TCLC 29**
See also CA 170

Rakosi, Carl 1903- **CLC 47**
See also Rawley, Callman
See also CAAS 5; DLB 193

Raleigh, Richard
See Lovecraft, H(oward) P(hillips)

Raleigh, Sir Walter 1554(?)-1618 **LC 31, 39**
See also CDBLB Before 1660; DLB 172

Rallentando, H. P.
See Sayers, Dorothy L(eigh)

Ramal, Walter

See de la Mare, Walter (John)

Ramana Maharshi 1879-1950 **TCLC 84**

Ramoacn y Cajal, Santiago 1852-1934 **TCLC 93**

Ramon, Juan
See Jimenez (Mantecon), Juan Ramon

Ramos, Graciliano 1892-1953 **TCLC 32**
See also CA 167; HW 2

Rampersad, Arnold 1941- **CLC 44**
See also BW 2, 3; CA 127; 133; CANR 81; DLB 111; INT 133

Rampling, Anne
See Rice, Anne

Ramsay, Allan 1684(?)-1758 **LC 29**
See also DLB 95

Ramuz, Charles-Ferdinand 1878-1947 **TCLC 33**
See also CA 165

Rand, Ayn 1905-1982 **CLC 3, 30, 44, 79; DA; DAC; DAM MST, NOV, POP; WLC**
See also AAYA 10; CA 13-16R; 105; CANR 27, 73; CDALBS; DA3; MTCW 1, 2

Randall, Dudley (Felker) 1914- **CLC 1; BLC 3; DAM MULT**
See also BW 1, 3; CA 25-28R; CANR 23, 82; DLB 41

Randall, Robert
See Silverberg, Robert

Ranger, Ken
See Creasey, John

Ransom, John Crowe 1888-1974 **CLC 2, 4, 5, 11, 24; DAM POET**
See also CA 5-8R; 49-52; CANR 6, 34; CDALBS; DA3; DLB 45, 63; MTCW 1, 2

Rao, Raja 1909- **CLC 25, 56; DAM NOV**
See also CA 73-76; CANR 51; MTCW 1, 2

Raphael, Frederic (Michael) 1931- **CLC 2, 14**
See also CA 1-4R; CANR 1; DLB 14

Ratcliffe, James P.
See Mencken, H(enry) L(ouis)

Rathbone, Julian 1935- **CLC 41**
See also CA 101; CANR 34, 73

Rattigan, Terence (Mervyn) 1911-1977 **CLC 7; DAM DRAM**
See also CA 85-88; 73-76; CDBLB 1945-1960; DLB 13; MTCW 1, 2

Ratushinskaya, Irina 1954- **CLC 54**
See also CA 129; CANR 68

Raven, Simon (Arthur Noel) 1927- **CLC 14**
See also CA 81-84

Ravenna, Michael
See Welty, Eudora

Rawley, Callman 1903-
See Rakosi, Carl
See also CA 21-24R; CANR 12, 32

Rawlings, Marjorie Kinnan 1896-1953 **TCLC 4**
See also AAYA 20; CA 104; 137; CANR 74; DLB 9, 22, 102; DLBD 17; JRDA; MAICYA; MTCW 2; SATA 100; YABC 1

Ray, Satyajit 1921-1992 **CLC 16, 76; DAM MULT**
See also CA 114; 137

Read, Herbert Edward 1893-1968 **CLC 4**
See also CA 85-88; 25-28R; DLB 20, 149

Read, Piers Paul 1941- **CLC 4, 10, 25**
See also CA 21-24R; CANR 38; DLB 14; SATA 21

Reade, Charles 1814-1884 **NCLC 2, 74**
See also DLB 21

Reade, Hamish
See Gray, Simon (James Holliday)

Reading, Peter 1946- **CLC 47**

See also CA 103; CANR 46; DLB 40

Reaney, James 1926- **CLC 13; DAC; DAM MST**
See also CA 41-44R; CAAS 15; CANR 42; DLB 68; SATA 43

Rebreanu, Liviu 1885-1944 **TCLC 28**
See also CA 165

Rechy, John (Francisco) 1934- **CLC 1, 7, 14, 18, 107; DAM MULT; HLC 2**
See also CA 5-8R; CAAS 4; CANR 6, 32, 64; DLB 122; DLBY 82; HW 1, 2; INT CANR-6

Redcam, Tom 1870-1933 **TCLC 25**

Reddin, Keith **CLC 67**

Redgrove, Peter (William) 1932- **CLC 6, 41**
See also CA 1-4R; CANR 3, 39, 77; DLB 40

Redmon, Anne **CLC 22**
See also Nightingale, Anne Redmon
See also DLBY 86

Reed, Eliot
See Ambler, Eric

Reed, Ishmael 1938- **CLC 2, 3, 5, 6, 13, 32, 60; BLC 3; DAM MULT**
See also BW 2, 3; CA 21-24R; CANR 25, 48, 74; DA3; DLB 2, 5, 33, 169; DLBD 8; MTCW 1, 2

Reed, John (Silas) 1887-1920 **TCLC 9**
See also CA 106

Reed, Lou **CLC 21**
See also Firbank, Louis

Reeve, Clara 1729-1807 **NCLC 19**
See also DLB 39

Reich, Wilhelm 1897-1957 **TCLC 57**

Reid, Christopher (John) 1949- **CLC 33**
See also CA 140; DLB 40

Reid, Desmond
See Moorcock, Michael (John)

Reid Banks, Lynne 1929-
See Banks, Lynne Reid
See also CA 1-4R; CANR 6, 22, 38; CLR 24; JRDA; MAICYA; SATA 22, 75, 111

Reilly, William K.
See Creasey, John

Reiner, Max
See Caldwell, (Janet Miriam) Taylor (Holland)

Reis, Ricardo
See Pessoa, Fernando (Antonio Nogueira)

Remarque, Erich Maria 1898-1970 **CLC 21; DA; DAB; DAC; DAM MST, NOV**
See also AAYA 27; CA 77-80; 29-32R; DA3; DLB 56; MTCW 1, 2

Remington, Frederic 1861-1909 **TCLC 89**
See also CA 108; 169; DLB 12, 186, 188; SATA 41

Remizov, A.
See Remizov, Aleksei (Mikhailovich)

Remizov, A. M.
See Remizov, Aleksei (Mikhailovich)

Remizov, Aleksei (Mikhailovich) 1877-1957 **TCLC 27**
See also CA 125; 133

Renan, Joseph Ernest 1823-1892 **NCLC 26**

Renard, Jules 1864-1910 **TCLC 17**
See also CA 117

Renault, Mary **CLC 3, 11, 17**
See also Challans, Mary
See also DLBY 83; MTCW 2

Rendell, Ruth (Barbara) 1930- **CLC 28, 48; DAM POP**
See also Vine, Barbara
See also CA 109; CANR 32, 52, 74; DLB 87; INT CANR-32; MTCW 1, 2

Renoir, Jean 1894-1979 **CLC 20**

See also CA 129; 85-88

Resnais, Alain 1922-   **CLC 16**

Reverdy, Pierre 1889-1960   **CLC 53**
  See also CA 97-100; 89-92

Rexroth, Kenneth 1905-1982 **CLC 1, 2, 6, 11, 22, 49, 112; DAM POET; PC 20**
  See also CA 5-8R; 107; CANR 14, 34, 63; CDALB 1941-1968; DLB 16, 48, 165, 212; DLBY 82; INT CANR-14; MTCW 1, 2

Reyes, Alfonso 1889-1959 **TCLC 33; HLCS 2**
  See also CA 131; HW 1

Reyes y Basoalto, Ricardo Eliecer Neftali
  See Neruda, Pablo

Reymont, Wladyslaw (Stanislaw) 1868(?)-1925 **TCLC 5**
  See also CA 104

Reynolds, Jonathan 1942-   **CLC 6, 38**
  See also CA 65-68; CANR 28

Reynolds, Joshua 1723-1792   **LC 15**
  See also DLB 104

Reynolds, Michael Shane 1937-   **CLC 44**
  See also CA 65-68; CANR 9

Reznikoff, Charles 1894-1976   **CLC 9**
  See also CA 33-36; 61-64; CAP 2; DLB 28, 45

Rezzori (d'Arezzo), Gregor von 1914-1998 **CLC 25**
  See also CA 122; 136; 167

Rhine, Richard
  See Silverstein, Alvin

Rhodes, Eugene Manlove 1869-1934 **TCLC 53**

Rhodius, Apollonius c. 3rd cent. B.C.- **CMLC 28**
  See also DLB 176

R'hoone
  See Balzac, Honore de

Rhys, Jean 1890(?)-1979 **CLC 2, 4, 6, 14, 19, 51, 124; DAM NOV; SSC 21**
  See also CA 25-28R; 85-88; CANR 35, 62; CDBLB 1945-1960; DA3; DLB 36, 117, 162; MTCW 1, 2

Ribeiro, Darcy 1922-1997   **CLC 34**
  See also CA 33-36R; 156

Ribeiro, Joao Ubaldo (Osorio Pimentel) 1941- **CLC 10, 67**
  See also CA 81-84

Ribman, Ronald (Burt) 1932-   **CLC 7**
  See also CA 21-24R; CANR 46, 80

Ricci, Nino 1959-   **CLC 70**
  See also CA 137

Rice, Anne 1941-   **CLC 41; DAM POP**
  See also AAYA 9; BEST 89:2; CA 65-68; CANR 12, 36, 53, 74; DA3; MTCW 2

Rice, Elmer (Leopold) 1892-1967 **CLC 7, 49; DAM DRAM**
  See also CA 21-22; 25-28R; CAP 2; DLB 4, 7; MTCW 1, 2

Rice, Tim(othy Miles Bindon) 1944- **CLC 21**
  See also CA 103; CANR 46

Rich, Adrienne (Cecile) 1929- **CLC 3, 6, 7, 11, 18, 36, 73, 76; DAM POET; PC 5**
  See also CA 9-12R; CANR 20, 53, 74; CDALBS; DA3; DLB 5, 67; MTCW 1, 2

Rich, Barbara
  See Graves, Robert (von Ranke)

Rich, Robert
  See Trumbo, Dalton

Richard, Keith   **CLC 17**
  See also Richards, Keith

Richards, David Adams 1950- **CLC 59; DAC**
  See also CA 93-96; CANR 60; DLB 53

Richards, I(vor) A(rmstrong) 1893-1979 **CLC 14, 24**
  See also CA 41-44R; 89-92; CANR 34, 74; DLB

27; MTCW 2

Richards, Keith 1943-
  See Richard, Keith
  See also CA 107; CANR 77

Richardson, Anne
  See Roiphe, Anne (Richardson)

Richardson, Dorothy Miller 1873-1957 **TCLC 3**
  See also CA 104; DLB 36

Richardson, Ethel Florence (Lindesay) 1870-1946
  See Richardson, Henry Handel
  See also CA 105

Richardson, Henry Handel   **TCLC 4**
  See also Richardson, Ethel Florence (Lindesay)
  See also DLB 197

Richardson, John 1796-1852 **NCLC 55; DAC**
  See also DLB 99

Richardson, Samuel 1689-1761 **LC 1, 44; DA; DAB; DAC; DAM MST, NOV; WLC**
  See also CDBLB 1660-1789; DLB 39

Richler, Mordecai 1931- **CLC 3, 5, 9, 13, 18, 46, 70; DAC; DAM MST, NOV**
  See also AITN 1; CA 65-68; CANR 31, 62; CLR 17; DLB 53; MAICYA; MTCW 1, 2; SATA 44, 98; SATA-Brief 27

Richter, Conrad (Michael) 1890-1968 **CLC 30**
  See also AAYA 21; CA 5-8R; 25-28R; CANR 23; DLB 9, 212; MTCW 1, 2; SATA 3

Ricostranza, Tom
  See Ellis, Trey

Riddell, Charlotte 1832-1906   **TCLC 40**
  See also CA 165; DLB 156

Ridgway, Keith 1965-   **CLC 119**
  See also CA 172

Riding, Laura   **CLC 3, 7**
  See also Jackson, Laura (Riding)

Riefenstahl, Berta Helene Amalia 1902-
  See Riefenstahl, Leni
  See also CA 108

Riefenstahl, Leni   **CLC 16**
  See also Riefenstahl, Berta Helene Amalia

Riffe, Ernest
  See Bergman, (Ernst) Ingmar

Riggs, (Rolla) Lynn 1899-1954 **TCLC 56; DAM MULT**
  See also CA 144; DLB 175; NNAL

Riis, Jacob A(ugust) 1849-1914   **TCLC 80**
  See also CA 113; 168; DLB 23

Riley, James Whitcomb 1849-1916 **TCLC 51; DAM POET**
  See also CA 118; 137; MAICYA; SATA 17

Riley, Tex
  See Creasey, John

Rilke, Rainer Maria 1875-1926 **TCLC 1, 6, 19; DAM POET; PC 2**
  See also CA 104; 132; CANR 62; DA3; DLB 81; MTCW 1, 2

Rimbaud, (Jean Nicolas) Arthur 1854-1891 **NCLC 4, 35; DA; DAB; DAC; DAM MST, POET; PC 3; WLC**
  See also DA3

Rinehart, Mary Roberts 1876-1958 **TCLC 52**
  See also CA 108; 166

Ringmaster, The
  See Mencken, H(enry) L(ouis)

Ringwood, Gwen(dolyn Margaret) Pharis 1910-1984   **CLC 48**
  See also CA 148; 112; DLB 88

Rio, Michel 19(?)-   **CLC 43**

Ritsos, Giannes
  See Ritsos, Yannis

Ritsos, Yannis 1909-1990   **CLC 6, 13, 31**

See also CA 77-80; 133; CANR 39, 61; MTCW 1

Ritter, Erika 1948(?)-   **CLC 52**

Rivera, Jose Eustasio 1889-1928   **TCLC 35**
  See also CA 162; HW 1, 2

Rivera, Tomas 1935-1984
  See also CA 49-52; CANR 32; DLB 82; HLCS 2; HW 1

Rivers, Conrad Kent 1933-1968   **CLC 1**
  See also BW 1; CA 85-88; DLB 41

Rivers, Elfrida
  See Bradley, Marion Zimmer

Riverside, John
  See Heinlein, Robert A(nson)

Rizal, Jose 1861-1896   **NCLC 27**

Roa Bastos, Augusto (Antonio) 1917- **CLC 45; DAM MULT; HLC 2**
  See also CA 131; DLB 113; HW 1

Robbe-Grillet, Alain 1922- **CLC 1, 2, 4, 6, 8, 10, 14, 43**
  See also CA 9-12R; CANR 33, 65; DLB 83; MTCW 1, 2

Robbins, Harold 1916-1997 **CLC 5; DAM NOV**
  See also CA 73-76; 162; CANR 26, 54; DA3; MTCW 1, 2

Robbins, Thomas Eugene 1936-
  See Robbins, Tom
  See also CA 81-84; CANR 29, 59; DAM NOV, POP; DA3; MTCW 1, 2

Robbins, Tom   **CLC 9, 32, 64**
  See also Robbins, Thomas Eugene
  See also AAYA 32; BEST 90:3; DLBY 80; MTCW 2

Robbins, Trina 1938-   **CLC 21**
  See also CA 128

Roberts, Charles G(eorge) D(ouglas) 1860-1943 **TCLC 8**
  See also CA 105; CLR 33; DLB 92; SATA 88; SATA-Brief 29

Roberts, Elizabeth Madox 1886-1941 **TCLC 68**
  See also CA 111; 166; DLB 9, 54, 102; SATA 33; SATA-Brief 27

Roberts, Kate 1891-1985   **CLC 15**
  See also CA 107; 116

Roberts, Keith (John Kingston) 1935- **CLC 14**
  See also CA 25-28R; CANR 46

Roberts, Kenneth (Lewis) 1885-1957 **TCLC 23**
  See also CA 109; DLB 9

Roberts, Michele (B.) 1949-   **CLC 48**
  See also CA 115; CANR 58

Robertson, Ellis
  See Ellison, Harlan (Jay); Silverberg, Robert

Robertson, Thomas William 1829-1871 **NCLC 35; DAM DRAM**

Robeson, Kenneth
  See Dent, Lester

Robinson, Edwin Arlington 1869-1935 **TCLC 5; DA; DAC; DAM MST, POET; PC 1**
  See also CA 104; 133; CDALB 1865-1917; DLB 54; MTCW 1, 2

Robinson, Henry Crabb 1775-1867 **NCLC 15**
  See also DLB 107

Robinson, Jill 1936-   **CLC 10**
  See also CA 102; INT 102

Robinson, Kim Stanley 1952-   **CLC 34**
  See also AAYA 26; CA 126; SATA 109

Robinson, Lloyd
  See Silverberg, Robert

Robinson, Marilynne 1944-   **CLC 25**
  See also CA 116; CANR 80; DLB 206

Robinson, Smokey   **CLC 21**

See also Robinson, William, Jr.
Robinson, William, Jr. 1940-
See Robinson, Smokey
See also CA 116
Robison, Mary 1949- **CLC 42, 98**
See also CA 113; 116; DLB 130; INT 116
Rod, Edouard 1857-1910 **TCLC 52**
Roddenberry, Eugene Wesley 1921-1991
See Roddenberry, Gene
See also CA 110; 135; CANR 37; SATA 45;
SATA-Obit 69
Roddenberry, Gene **CLC 17**
See also Roddenberry, Eugene Wesley
See also AAYA 5; SATA-Obit 69
Rodgers, Mary 1931- **CLC 12**
See also CA 49-52; CANR 8, 55; CLR 20; INT
CANR-8; JRDA; MAICYA; SATA 8
Rodgers, W(illiam) R(obert) 1909-1969**CLC 7**
See also CA 85-88; DLB 20
Rodman, Eric
See Silverberg, Robert
Rodman, Howard 1920(?)-1985 **CLC 65**
See also CA 118
Rodman, Maia
See Wojciechowska, Maia (Teresa)
Rodo, Jose Enrique 1872(?)-1917
See also CA 178; HLCS 2; HW 2
Rodriguez, Claudio 1934- **CLC 10**
See also DLB 134
Rodriguez, Richard 1944-
See also CA 110; CANR 66; DAM MULT; DLB
82; HLC 2; HW 1, 2
Roelvaag, O(le) E(dvart) 1876-1931**TCLC 17**
See also CA 117; 171; DLB 9
Roethke, Theodore (Huebner) 1908-1963**CLC
1, 3, 8, 11, 19, 46, 101; DAM POET; PC 15**
See also CA 81-84; CABS 2; CDALB 1941-
1968; DA3; DLB 5, 206; MTCW 1, 2
Rogers, Samuel 1763-1855 **NCLC 69**
See also DLB 93
Rogers, Thomas Hunton 1927- **CLC 57**
See also CA 89-92; INT 89-92
Rogers, Will(iam Penn Adair) 1879-1935
TCLC 8, 71; DAM MULT
See also CA 105; 144; DA3; DLB 11; MTCW
2; NNAL
Rogin, Gilbert 1929- **CLC 18**
See also CA 65-68; CANR 15
Rohan, Koda **TCLC 22**
See also Koda Shigeyuki
Rohlfs, Anna Katharine Green
See Green, Anna Katharine
Rohmer, Eric **CLC 16**
See also Scherer, Jean-Marie Maurice
Rohmer, Sax **TCLC 28**
See also Ward, Arthur Henry Sarsfield
See also DLB 70
Roiphe, Anne (Richardson) 1935- **CLC 3, 9**
See also CA 89-92; CANR 45, 73; DLBY 80;
INT 89-92
Rojas, Fernando de 1465-1541**LC 23; HLCS 1**
Rojas, Gonzalo 1917-
See also HLCS 2; HW 2
Rojas, Gonzalo 1917-
See also CA 178; HLCS 2
**Rolfe, Frederick (William Serafino Austin
Lewis Mary)** 1860-1913 **TCLC 12**
See also CA 107; DLB 34, 156
Rolland, Romain 1866-1944 **TCLC 23**
See also CA 118; DLB 65
Rolle, Richard c. 1300-c. 1349 **CMLC 21**
See also DLB 146
Rolvaag, O(le) E(dvart)

See Roelvaag, O(le) E(dvart)
Romain Arnaud, Saint
See Aragon, Louis
Romains, Jules 1885-1972 **CLC 7**
See also CA 85-88; CANR 34; DLB 65; MTCW
1
Romero, Jose Ruben 1890-1952 **TCLC 14**
See also CA 114; 131; HW 1
Ronsard, Pierre de 1524-1585 **LC 6; PC 11**
Rooke, Leon 1934- **CLC 25, 34; DAM POP**
See also CA 25-28R; CANR 23, 53
Roosevelt, Franklin Delano 1882-1945**TCLC
93**
See also CA 116; 173
Roosevelt, Theodore 1858-1919 **TCLC 69**
See also CA 115; 170; DLB 47, 186
Roper, William 1498-1578 **LC 10**
Roquelaure, A. N.
See Rice, Anne
Rosa, Joao Guimaraes 1908-1967 **CLC 23;
HLCS 1**
See also CA 89-92; DLB 113
Rose, Wendy 1948-**CLC 85; DAM MULT; PC
13**
See also CA 53-56; CANR 5, 51; DLB 175;
NNAL; SATA 12
Rosen, R. D.
See Rosen, Richard (Dean)
Rosen, Richard (Dean) 1949- **CLC 39**
See also CA 77-80; CANR 62; INT CANR-30
Rosenberg, Isaac 1890-1918 **TCLC 12**
See also CA 107; DLB 20
Rosenblatt, Joe **CLC 15**
See also Rosenblatt, Joseph
Rosenblatt, Joseph 1933-
See Rosenblatt, Joe
See also CA 89-92; INT 89-92
Rosenfeld, Samuel
See Tzara, Tristan
Rosenstock, Sami
See Tzara, Tristan
Rosenstock, Samuel
See Tzara, Tristan
Rosenthal, M(acha) L(ouis) 1917-1996 **C L C
28**
See also CA 1-4R; 152; CAAS 6; CANR 4, 51;
DLB 5; SATA 59
Ross, Barnaby
See Dannay, Frederic
Ross, Bernard L.
See Follett, Ken(neth Martin)
Ross, J. H.
See Lawrence, T(homas) E(dward)
Ross, John Hume
See Lawrence, T(homas) E(dward)
Ross, Martin
See Martin, Violet Florence
See also DLB 135
Ross, (James) Sinclair 1908-1996 **CLC 13;
DAC; DAM MST; SSC 24**
See also CA 73-76; CANR 81; DLB 88
Rossetti, Christina (Georgina) 1830-1894
**NCLC 2, 50, 66; DA; DAB; DAC; DAM
MST, POET; PC 7; WLC**
See also DA3; DLB 35, 163; MAICYA; SATA
20
Rossetti, Dante Gabriel 1828-1882 **NCLC 4,
77; DA; DAB; DAC; DAM MST, POET;
WLC**
See also CDBLB 1832-1890; DLB 35
Rossner, Judith (Perelman) 1935-**CLC 6, 9, 29**
See also AITN 2; BEST 90:3; CA 17-20R;
CANR 18, 51, 73; DLB 6; INT CANR-18;

MTCW 1, 2
Rostand, Edmond (Eugene Alexis) 1868-1918
**TCLC 6, 37; DA; DAB; DAC; DAM
DRAM, MST; DC 10**
See also CA 104; 126; DA3; DLB 192; MTCW
1
Roth, Henry 1906-1995 **CLC 2, 6, 11, 104**
See also CA 11-12; 149; CANR 38, 63; CAP 1;
DA3; DLB 28; MTCW 1, 2
Roth, Philip (Milton) 1933-**CLC 1, 2, 3, 4, 6, 9,
15, 22, 31, 47, 66, 86, 119; DA; DAB; DAC;
DAM MST, NOV, POP; SSC 26; WLC**
See also BEST 90:3; CA 1-4R; CANR 1, 22,
36, 55; CDALB 1968-1988; DA3; DLB 2,
28, 173; DLBY 82; MTCW 1, 2
Rothenberg, Jerome 1931- **CLC 6, 57**
See also CA 45-48; CANR 1; DLB 5, 193
Roumain, Jacques (Jean Baptiste) 1907-1944
TCLC 19; BLC 3; DAM MULT
See also BW 1; CA 117; 125
Rourke, Constance (Mayfield) 1885-1941
TCLC 12
See also CA 107; YABC 1
Rousseau, Jean-Baptiste 1671-1741 **LC 9**
Rousseau, Jean-Jacques 1712-1778**LC 14, 36;
DA; DAB; DAC; DAM MST; WLC**
See also DA3
Roussel, Raymond 1877-1933 **TCLC 20**
See also CA 117
Rovit, Earl (Herbert) 1927- **CLC 7**
See also CA 5-8R; CANR 12
Rowe, Elizabeth Singer 1674-1737 **LC 44**
See also DLB 39, 95
Rowe, Nicholas 1674-1718 **LC 8**
See also DLB 84
Rowley, Ames Dorrance
See Lovecraft, H(oward) P(hillips)
Rowson, Susanna Haswell 1762(?)-1824
NCLC 5, 69
See also DLB 37, 200
Roy, Arundhati 1960(?)- **CLC 109**
See also CA 163; DLBY 97
Roy, Gabrielle 1909-1983 **CLC 10, 14; DAB;
DAC; DAM MST**
See also CA 53-56; 110; CANR 5, 61; DLB 68;
MTCW 1; SATA 104
Royko, Mike 1932-1997 **CLC 109**
See also CA 89-92; 157; CANR 26
Rozewicz, Tadeusz 1921- **CLC 9, 23; DAM
POET**
See also CA 108; CANR 36, 66; DA3; MTCW
1, 2
Ruark, Gibbons 1941- **CLC 3**
See also CA 33-36R; CAAS 23; CANR 14, 31,
57; DLB 120
Rubens, Bernice (Ruth) 1923- **CLC 19, 31**
See also CA 25-28R; CANR 33, 65; DLB 14,
207; MTCW 1
Rubin, Harold
See Robbins, Harold
Rudkin, (James) David 1936- **CLC 14**
See also CA 89-92; DLB 13
Rudnik, Raphael 1933- **CLC 7**
See also CA 29-32R
Ruffian, M.
See Hasek, Jaroslav (Matej Frantisek)
Ruiz, Jose Martinez **CLC 11**
See also Martinez Ruiz, Jose
Rukeyser, Muriel 1913-1980**CLC 6, 10, 15, 27;
DAM POET; PC 12**
See also CA 5-8R; 93-96; CANR 26, 60; DA3;
DLB 48; MTCW 1, 2; SATA-Obit 22
Rule, Jane (Vance) 1931- **CLC 27**

See also CA 25-28R; CAAS 18; CANR 12; DLB
60

Rulfo, Juan 1918-1986   **CLC 8, 80; DAM
    MULT; HLC 2; SSC 25**
    See also CA 85-88; 118; CANR 26; DLB 113;
    HW 1, 2; MTCW 1, 2

Rumi, Jalal al-Din 1297-1373   **CMLC 20**

Runeberg, Johan 1804-1877   **NCLC 41**

Runyon, (Alfred) Damon 1884(?)-1946 T C L C
    10
    See also CA 107; 165; DLB 11, 86, 171; MTCW
    2

Rush, Norman 1933-   **CLC 44**
    See also CA 121; 126; INT 126

Rushdie, (Ahmed) Salman 1947- **CLC 23, 31,
    55, 100; DAB; DAC; DAM MST, NOV,
    POP; WLCS**
    See also BEST 89:3; CA 108; 111; CANR 33,
    56; DA3; DLB 194; INT 111; MTCW 1, 2

Rushforth, Peter (Scott) 1945-   **CLC 19**
    See also CA 101

Ruskin, John 1819-1900   **TCLC 63**
    See also CA 114; 129; CDBLB 1832-1890;
    DLB 55, 163, 190; SATA 24

Russ, Joanna 1937-   **CLC 15**
    See also CANR 11, 31, 65; DLB 8; MTCW 1

Russell, George William 1867-1935
    See Baker, Jean H.
    See also CA 104; 153; CDBLB 1890-1914;
    DAM POET

Russell, (Henry) Ken(neth Alfred) 1927-C L C
    16
    See also CA 105

Russell, William Martin 1947-   **CLC 60**
    See also CA 164

Rutherford, Mark   **TCLC 25**
    See also White, William Hale
    See also DLB 18

Ruyslinck, Ward 1929-   **CLC 14**
    See also Belser, Reimond Karel Maria de

Ryan, Cornelius (John) 1920-1974   **CLC 7**
    See also CA 69-72; 53-56; CANR 38

Ryan, Michael 1946-   **CLC 65**
    See also CA 49-52; DLBY 82

Ryan, Tim
    See Dent, Lester

Rybakov, Anatoli (Naumovich) 1911-1998
    CLC 23, 53
    See also CA 126; 135; 172; SATA 79; SATA-
    Obit 108

Ryder, Jonathan
    See Ludlum, Robert

Ryga, George 1932-1987 **CLC 14; DAC; DAM
    MST**
    See also CA 101; 124; CANR 43; DLB 60

S. H.
    See Hartmann, Sadakichi

S. S.
    See Sassoon, Siegfried (Lorraine)

Saba, Umberto 1883-1957   **TCLC 33**
    See also CA 144; CANR 79; DLB 114

Sabatini, Rafael 1875-1950   **TCLC 47**
    See also CA 162

Sabato, Ernesto (R.) 1911-**CLC 10, 23; DAM
    MULT; HLC 2**
    See also CA 97-100; CANR 32, 65; DLB 145;
    HW 1, 2; MTCW 1, 2

Sa-Carniero, Mario de 1890-1916   **TCLC 83**

Sacastru, Martin
    See Bioy Casares, Adolfo

Sacastru, Martin
    See Bioy Casares, Adolfo

Sacher-Masoch, Leopold von 1836(?)-1895

NCLC 31

Sachs, Marilyn (Stickle) 1927-   **CLC 35**
    See also AAYA 2; CA 17-20R; CANR 13, 47;
    CLR 2; JRDA; MAICYA; SAAS 2; SATA 3,
    68; SATA-Essay 110

Sachs, Nelly 1891-1970   **CLC 14, 98**
    See also CA 17-18; 25-28R; CAP 2; MTCW 2

Sackler, Howard (Oliver) 1929-1982 **CLC 14**
    See also CA 61-64; 108; CANR 30; DLB 7

Sacks, Oliver (Wolf) 1933-   **CLC 67**
    See also CA 53-56; CANR 28, 50, 76; DA3;
    INT CANR-28; MTCW 1, 2

Sadakichi
    See Hartmann, Sadakichi

Sade, Donatien Alphonse Francois, Comte de
    1740-1814   **NCLC 47**

Sadoff, Ira 1945-   **CLC 9**
    See also CA 53-56; CANR 5, 21; DLB 120

Saetone
    See Camus, Albert

Safire, William 1929-   **CLC 10**
    See also CA 17-20R; CANR 31, 54

Sagan, Carl (Edward) 1934-1996**CLC 30, 112**
    See also AAYA 2; CA 25-28R; 155; CANR 11,
    36, 74; DA3; MTCW 1, 2; SATA 58; SATA-
    Obit 94

Sagan, Francoise   **CLC 3, 6, 9, 17, 36**
    See also Quoirez, Francoise
    See also DLB 83; MTCW 2

Sahgal, Nayantara (Pandit) 1927-   **CLC 41**
    See also CA 9-12R; CANR 11

Saint, H(arry) F. 1941-   **CLC 50**
    See also CA 127

St. Aubin de Teran, Lisa 1953-
    See Teran, Lisa St. Aubin de
    See also CA 118; 126; INT 126

Saint Birgitta of Sweden c. 1303-1373 C M L C
    24

Sainte-Beuve, Charles Augustin 1804-1869
    NCLC 5

**Saint-Exupery, Antoine (Jean Baptiste Marie
    Roger) de** 1900-1944 **TCLC 2, 56; DAM
    NOV; WLC**
    See also CA 108; 132; CLR 10; DA3; DLB 72;
    MAICYA; MTCW 1, 2; SATA 20

St. John, David
    See Hunt, E(verette) Howard, (Jr.)

Saint-John Perse
    See Leger, (Marie-Rene Auguste) Alexis Saint-
    Leger

Saintsbury, George (Edward Bateman) 1845-
    1933   **TCLC 31**
    See also CA 160; DLB 57, 149

Sait Faik   **TCLC 23**
    See also Abasiyanik, Sait Faik

Saki   **TCLC 3; SSC 12**
    See also Munro, H(ector) H(ugh)
    See also MTCW 2

Sala, George Augustus   **NCLC 46**

Salama, Hannu 1936-   **CLC 18**

Salamanca, J(ack) R(ichard) 1922-**CLC 4, 15**
    See also CA 25-28R

Salas, Floyd Francis 1931-
    See also CA 119; CAAS 27; CANR 44, 75;
    DAM MULT; DLB 82; HLC 2; HW 1, 2;
    MTCW 2

Sale, J. Kirkpatrick
    See Sale, Kirkpatrick

Sale, Kirkpatrick 1937-   **CLC 68**
    See also CA 13-16R; CANR 10

Salinas, Luis Omar 1937-   **CLC 90; DAM
    MULT; HLC 2**
    See also CA 131; CANR 81; DLB 82; HW 1, 2

Salinas (y Serrano), Pedro 1891(?)-1951
    TCLC 17
    See also CA 117; DLB 134

Salinger, J(erome) D(avid) 1919-**CLC 1, 3, 8,
    12, 55, 56; DA; DAB; DAC; DAM MST,
    NOV, POP; SSC 2, 28; WLC**
    See also AAYA 2; CA 5-8R; CANR 39; CDALB
    1941-1968; CLR 18; DA3; DLB 2, 102, 173;
    MAICYA; MTCW 1, 2; SATA 67

Salisbury, John
    See Caute, (John) David

Salter, James 1925-   **CLC 7, 52, 59**
    See also CA 73-76; DLB 130

Saltus, Edgar (Everton) 1855-1921   **TCLC 8**
    See also CA 105; DLB 202

Saltykov, Mikhail Evgrafovich 1826-1889
    NCLC 16

Samarakis, Antonis 1919-   **CLC 5**
    See also CA 25-28R; CAAS 16; CANR 36

Sanchez, Florencio 1875-1910   **TCLC 37**
    See also CA 153; HW 1

Sanchez, Luis Rafael 1936-   **CLC 23**
    See also CA 128; DLB 145; HW 1

Sanchez, Sonia 1934-   **CLC 5, 116; BLC 3;
    DAM MULT; PC 9**
    See also BW 2, 3; CA 33-36R; CANR 24, 49,
    74; CLR 18; DA3; DLB 41; DLBD 8;
    MAICYA; MTCW 1, 2; SATA 22

Sand, George 1804-1876**NCLC 2, 42, 57; DA;
    DAB; DAC; DAM MST, NOV; WLC**
    See also DA3; DLB 119, 192

Sandburg, Carl (August) 1878-1967**CLC 1, 4,
    10, 15, 35; DA; DAB; DAC; DAM MST,
    POET; PC 2; WLC**
    See also AAYA 24; CA 5-8R; 25-28R; CANR
    35; CDALB 1865-1917; DA3; DLB 17, 54;
    MAICYA; MTCW 1, 2; SATA 8

Sandburg, Charles
    See Sandburg, Carl (August)

Sandburg, Charles A.
    See Sandburg, Carl (August)

Sanders, (James) Ed(ward) 1939-   **CLC 53;
    DAM POET**
    See also CA 13-16R; CAAS 21; CANR 13, 44,
    78; DLB 16

Sanders, Lawrence 1920-1998**CLC 41; DAM
    POP**
    See also BEST 89:4; CA 81-84; 165; CANR
    33, 62; DA3; MTCW 1

Sanders, Noah
    See Blount, Roy (Alton), Jr.

Sanders, Winston P.
    See Anderson, Poul (William)

Sandoz, Mari(e Susette) 1896-1966   **CLC 28**
    See also CA 1-4R; 25-28R; CANR 17, 64; DLB
    9, 212; MTCW 1, 2; SATA 5

Saner, Reg(inald Anthony) 1931-   **CLC 9**
    See also CA 65-68

Sankara 788-820   **CMLC 32**

Sannazaro, Jacopo 1456(?)-1530   **LC 8**

Sansom, William 1912-1976 **CLC 2, 6; DAM
    NOV; SSC 21**
    See also CA 5-8R; 65-68; CANR 42; DLB 139;
    MTCW 1

Santayana, George 1863-1952   **TCLC 40**
    See also CA 115; DLB 54, 71; DLBD 13

Santiago, Danny   **CLC 33**
    See also James, Daniel (Lewis)
    See also DLB 122

Santmyer, Helen Hoover 1895-1986 **CLC 33**
    See also CA 1-4R; 118; CANR 15, 33; DLBY
    84; MTCW 1

Santoka, Taneda 1882-1940   **TCLC 72**

Santos, Bienvenido N(uqui) 1911-1996 **C L C 22; DAM MULT**
See also CA 101; 151; CANR 19, 46
Sapper **TCLC 44**
See also McNeile, Herman Cyril
Sapphire
See Sapphire, Brenda
Sapphire, Brenda 1950- **CLC 99**
Sappho fl. 6th cent. B.C.- **CMLC 3; DAM POET; PC 5**
See also DA3; DLB 176
Saramago, Jose 1922- **CLC 119; HLCS 1**
See also CA 153
Sarduy, Severo 1937-1993 **CLC 6, 97; HLCS 1**
See also CA 89-92; 142; CANR 58, 81; DLB 113; HW 1, 2
Sargeson, Frank 1903-1982 **CLC 31**
See also CA 25-28R; 106; CANR 38, 79
Sarmiento, Domingo Faustino 1811-1888
See also HLCS 2
Sarmiento, Felix Ruben Garcia
See Dario, Ruben
Saro-Wiwa, Ken(ule Beeson) 1941-1995 **C L C 114**
See also BW 2; CA 142; 150; CANR 60; DLB 157
Saroyan, William 1908-1981 **CLC 1, 8, 10, 29, 34, 56; DA; DAB; DAC; DAM DRAM, MST, NOV; SSC 21; WLC**
See also CA 5-8R; 103; CANR 30; CDALBS; DA3; DLB 7, 9, 86; DLBY 81; MTCW 1, 2; SATA 23; SATA-Obit 24
Sarraute, Nathalie 1900- **CLC 1, 2, 4, 8, 10, 31, 80**
See also CA 9-12R; CANR 23, 66; DLB 83; MTCW 1, 2
Sarton, (Eleanor) May 1912-1995 **CLC 4, 14, 49, 91; DAM POET**
See also CA 1-4R; 149; CANR 1, 34, 55; DLB 48; DLBY 81; INT CANR-34; MTCW 1, 2; SATA 36; SATA-Obit 86
Sartre, Jean-Paul 1905-1980 **CLC 1, 4, 7, 9, 13, 18, 24, 44, 50, 52; DA; DAB; DAC; DAM DRAM, MST, NOV; DC 3; SSC 32; WLC**
See also CA 9-12R; 97-100; CANR 21; DA3; DLB 72; MTCW 1, 2
Sassoon, Siegfried (Lorraine) 1886-1967 **C L C 36; DAB; DAM MST, NOV, POET; PC 12**
See also CA 104; 25-28R; CANR 36; DLB 20, 191; DLBD 18; MTCW 1, 2
Satterfield, Charles
See Pohl, Frederik
Saul, John (W. III) 1942- **CLC 46; DAM NOV, POP**
See also AAYA 10; BEST 90:4; CA 81-84; CANR 16, 40, 81; SATA 98
Saunders, Caleb
See Heinlein, Robert A(nson)
Saura (Atares), Carlos 1932- **CLC 20**
See also CA 114; 131; CANR 79; HW 1
Sauser-Hall, Frederic 1887-1961 **CLC 18**
See also Cendrars, Blaise
See also CA 102; 93-96; CANR 36, 62; MTCW 1
Saussure, Ferdinand de 1857-1913 **TCLC 49**
Savage, Catharine
See Brosman, Catharine Savage
Savage, Thomas 1915- **CLC 40**
See also CA 126; 132; CAAS 15; INT 132
Savan, Glenn 19(?)- **CLC 50**
Sayers, Dorothy L(eigh) 1893-1957 **TCLC 2, 15; DAM POP**
See also CA 104; 119; CANR 60; CDBLB 1914-

1945; DLB 10, 36, 77, 100; MTCW 1, 2
Sayers, Valerie 1952- **CLC 50, 122**
See also CA 134; CANR 61
Sayles, John (Thomas) 1950- **CLC 7, 10, 14**
See also CA 57-60; CANR 41, 84; DLB 44
Scammell, Michael 1935- **CLC 34**
See also CA 156
Scannell, Vernon 1922- **CLC 49**
See also CA 5-8R; CANR 8, 24, 57; DLB 27; SATA 59
Scarlett, Susan
See Streatfeild, (Mary) Noel
Scarron
See Mikszath, Kalman
Schaeffer, Susan Fromberg 1941- **CLC 6, 11, 22**
See also CA 49-52; CANR 18, 65; DLB 28; MTCW 1, 2; SATA 22
Schary, Jill
See Robinson, Jill
Schell, Jonathan 1943- **CLC 35**
See also CA 73-76; CANR 12
Schelling, Friedrich Wilhelm Joseph von 1775-1854 **NCLC 30**
See also DLB 90
Schendel, Arthur van 1874-1946 **TCLC 56**
Scherer, Jean-Marie Maurice 1920-
See Rohmer, Eric
See also CA 110
Schevill, James (Erwin) 1920- **CLC 7**
See also CA 5-8R; CAAS 12
Schiller, Friedrich 1759-1805 **NCLC 39, 69; DAM DRAM**
See also DLB 94
Schisgal, Murray (Joseph) 1926- **CLC 6**
See also CA 21-24R; CANR 48
Schlee, Ann 1934- **CLC 35**
See also CA 101; CANR 29; SATA 44; SATA-Brief 36
Schlegel, August Wilhelm von 1767-1845 **NCLC 15**
See also DLB 94
Schlegel, Friedrich 1772-1829 **NCLC 45**
See also DLB 90
Schlegel, Johann Elias (von) 1719(?)-1749 **L C 5**
Schlesinger, Arthur M(eier), Jr. 1917- **CLC 84**
See also AITN 1; CA 1-4R; CANR 1, 28, 58; DLB 17; INT CANR-28; MTCW 1, 2; SATA 61
Schmidt, Arno (Otto) 1914-1979 **CLC 56**
See also CA 128; 109; DLB 69
Schmitz, Aron Hector 1861-1928
See Svevo, Italo
See also CA 104; 122; MTCW 1
Schnackenberg, Gjertrud 1953- **CLC 40**
See also CA 116; DLB 120
Schneider, Leonard Alfred 1925-1966
See Bruce, Lenny
See also CA 89-92
Schnitzler, Arthur 1862-1931 **TCLC 4; SSC 15**
See also CA 104; DLB 81, 118
Schoenberg, Arnold 1874-1951 **TCLC 75**
See also CA 109
Schonberg, Arnold
See Schoenberg, Arnold
Schopenhauer, Arthur 1788-1860 **NCLC 51**
See also DLB 90
Schor, Sandra (M.) 1932(?)-1990 **CLC 65**
See also CA 132
Schorer, Mark 1908-1977 **CLC 9**
See also CA 5-8R; 73-76; CANR 7; DLB 103
Schrader, Paul (Joseph) 1946- **CLC 26**

See also CA 37-40R; CANR 41; DLB 44
Schreiner, Olive (Emilie Albertina) 1855-1920 **TCLC 9**
See also CA 105; 154; DLB 18, 156, 190
Schulberg, Budd (Wilson) 1914- **CLC 7, 48**
See also CA 25-28R; CANR 19; DLB 6, 26, 28; DLBY 81
Schulz, Bruno 1892-1942 **TCLC 5, 51; SSC 13**
See also CA 115; 123; MTCW 2
Schulz, Charles M(onroe) 1922- **CLC 12**
See also CA 9-12R; CANR 6; INT CANR-6; SATA 10
Schumacher, E(rnst) F(riedrich) 1911-1977 **CLC 80**
See also CA 81-84; 73-76; CANR 34
Schuyler, James Marcus 1923-1991 **CLC 5, 23; DAM POET**
See also CA 101; 134; DLB 5, 169; INT 101
Schwartz, Delmore (David) 1913-1966 **CLC 2, 4, 10, 45, 87; PC 8**
See also CA 17-18; 25-28R; CANR 35; CAP 2; DLB 28, 48; MTCW 1, 2
Schwartz, Ernst
See Ozu, Yasujiro
Schwartz, John Burnham 1965- **CLC 59**
See also CA 132
Schwartz, Lynne Sharon 1939- **CLC 31**
See also CA 103; CANR 44; MTCW 2
Schwartz, Muriel A.
See Eliot, T(homas) S(tearns)
Schwarz-Bart, Andre 1928- **CLC 2, 4**
See also CA 89-92
Schwarz-Bart, Simone 1938- **CLC 7; BLCS**
See also BW 2; CA 97-100
Schwitters, Kurt (Hermann Edward Karl Julius) 1887-1948 **TCLC 95**
See also CA 158
Schwob, Marcel (Mayer Andre) 1867-1905 **TCLC 20**
See also CA 117; 168; DLB 123
Sciascia, Leonardo 1921-1989 **CLC 8, 9, 41**
See also CA 85-88; 130; CANR 35; DLB 177; MTCW 1
Scoppettone, Sandra 1936- **CLC 26**
See also AAYA 11; CA 5-8R; CANR 41, 73; SATA 9, 92
Scorsese, Martin 1942- **CLC 20, 89**
See also CA 110; 114; CANR 46
Scotland, Jay
See Jakes, John (William)
Scott, Duncan Campbell 1862-1947 **TCLC 6; DAC**
See also CA 104; 153; DLB 92
Scott, Evelyn 1893-1963 **CLC 43**
See also CA 104; 112; CANR 64; DLB 9, 48
Scott, F(rancis) R(eginald) 1899-1985 **CLC 22**
See also CA 101; 114; DLB 88; INT 101
Scott, Frank
See Scott, F(rancis) R(eginald)
Scott, Joanna 1960- **CLC 50**
See also CA 126; CANR 53
Scott, Paul (Mark) 1920-1978 **CLC 9, 60**
See also CA 81-84; 77-80; CANR 33; DLB 14, 207; MTCW 1
Scott, Sarah 1723-1795 **LC 44**
See also DLB 39
Scott, Walter 1771-1832 **NCLC 15, 69; DA; DAB; DAC; DAM MST, NOV, POET; PC 13; SSC 32; WLC**
See also AAYA 22; CDBLB 1789-1832; DLB 93, 107, 116, 144, 159; YABC 2
Scribe, (Augustin) Eugene 1791-1861 **N C L C 16; DAM DRAM; DC 5**

Author Index

Shepherd, Michael
See Ludlum, Robert
Sherburne, Zoa (Lillian Morin) 1912-1995
CLC 30
See also AAYA 13; CA 1-4R; 176; CANR 3, 37; MAICYA; SAAS 18; SATA 3
Sheridan, Frances 1724-1766 **LC 7**
See also DLB 39, 84
Sheridan, Richard Brinsley 1751-1816**N C L C 5; DA; DAB; DAC; DAM DRAM, MST; DC 1; WLC**
See also CDBLB 1660-1789; DLB 89
Sherman, Jonathan Marc **CLC 55**
Sherman, Martin 1941(?)- **CLC 19**
See also CA 116; 123
Sherwin, Judith Johnson
See Johnson, Judith (Emlyn)
Sherwood, Frances 1940- **CLC 81**
See also CA 146
Sherwood, Robert E(mmet) 1896-1955**T C L C 3; DAM DRAM**
See also CA 104; 153; DLB 7, 26
Shestov, Lev 1866-1938 **TCLC 56**
Shevchenko, Taras 1814-1861 **NCLC 54**
Shiel, M(atthew) P(hipps) 1865-1947**TCLC 8**
See also Holmes, Gordon
See also CA 106; 160; DLB 153; MTCW 2
Shields, Carol 1935- **CLC 91, 113; DAC**
See also CA 81-84; CANR 51, 74; DA3; MTCW 2
Shields, David 1956- **CLC 97**
See also CA 124; CANR 48
Shiga, Naoya 1883-1971 **CLC 33; SSC 23**
See also CA 101; 33-36R; DLB 180
Shikibu, Murasaki c. 978-c. 1014 **CMLC 1**
Shilts, Randy 1951-1994 **CLC 85**
See also AAYA 19; CA 115; 127; 144; CANR 45; DA3; INT 127; MTCW 2
Shimazaki, Haruki 1872-1943
See Shimazaki Toson
See also CA 105; 134; CANR 84
Shimazaki Toson 1872-1943 **TCLC 5**
See also Shimazaki, Haruki
See also DLB 180
Sholokhov, Mikhail (Aleksandrovich) 1905-1984 **CLC 7, 15**
See also CA 101; 112; MTCW 1, 2; SATA-Obit 36
Shone, Patric
See Hanley, James
Shreve, Susan Richards 1939- **CLC 23**
See also CA 49-52; CAAS 5; CANR 5, 38, 69; MAICYA; SATA 46, 95; SATA-Brief 41
Shue, Larry 1946-1985**CLC 52; DAM DRAM**
See also CA 145; 117
Shu-Jen, Chou 1881-1936
See Lu Hsun
See also CA 104
Shulman, Alix Kates 1932- **CLC 2, 10**
See also CA 29-32R; CANR 43; SATA 7
Shuster, Joe 1914- **CLC 21**
Shute, Nevil **CLC 30**
See also Norway, Nevil Shute
See also MTCW 2
Shuttle, Penelope (Diane) 1947- **CLC 7**
See also CA 93-96; CANR 39, 84; DLB 14, 40
Sidney, Mary 1561-1621 **LC 19, 39**
Sidney, Sir Philip 1554-1586 **LC 19, 39; DA; DAB; DAC; DAM MST, POET**
See also CDBLB Before 1660; DA3; DLB 167
Siegel, Jerome 1914-1996 **CLC 21**
See also CA 116; 169; 151
Siegel, Jerry

See Siegel, Jerome
Sienkiewicz, Henryk (Adam Alexander Pius) 1846-1916 **TCLC 3**
See also CA 104; 134; CANR 84
Sierra, Gregorio Martinez
See Martinez Sierra, Gregorio
Sierra, Maria (de la O'LeJarraga) Martinez
See Martinez Sierra, Maria (de la O'LeJarraga)
Sigal, Clancy 1926- **CLC 7**
See also CA 1-4R
Sigourney, Lydia Howard (Huntley) 1791-1865 **NCLC 21**
See also DLB 1, 42, 73
Siguenza y Gongora, Carlos de 1645-1700**L C 8; HLCS 2**
Sigurjonsson, Johann 1880-1919 **TCLC 27**
See also CA 170
Sikelianos, Angelos 1884-1951 **TCLC 39**
Silkin, Jon 1930- **CLC 2, 6, 43**
See also CA 5-8R; CAAS 5; DLB 27
Silko, Leslie (Marmon) 1948-**CLC 23, 74, 114; DA; DAC; DAM MST, MULT, POP; WLCS**
See also AAYA 14; CA 115; 122; CANR 45, 65; DA3; DLB 143, 175; MTCW 2; NNAL
Sillanpaa, Frans Eemil 1888-1964 **CLC 19**
See also CA 129; 93-96; MTCW 1
Sillitoe, Alan 1928- **CLC 1, 3, 6, 10, 19, 57**
See also AITN 1; CA 9-12R; CAAS 2; CANR 8, 26, 55; CDBLB 1960 to Present; DLB 14, 139; MTCW 1, 2; SATA 61
Silone, Ignazio 1900-1978 **CLC 4**
See also CA 25-28; 81-84; CANR 34; CAP 2; MTCW 1
Silver, Joan Micklin 1935- **CLC 20**
See also CA 114; 121; INT 121
Silver, Nicholas
See Faust, Frederick (Schiller)
Silverberg, Robert 1935- **CLC 7; DAM POP**
See also AAYA 24; CA 1-4R; CAAS 3; CANR 1, 20, 36; CLR 59; DLB 8; INT CANR-20; MAICYA; MTCW 1, 2; SATA 13, 91; SATA-Essay 104
Silverstein, Alvin 1933- **CLC 17**
See also CA 49-52; CANR 2; CLR 25; JRDA; MAICYA; SATA 8, 69
Silverstein, Virginia B(arbara Opshelor) 1937-**CLC 17**
See also CA 49-52; CANR 2; CLR 25; JRDA; MAICYA; SATA 8, 69
Sim, Georges
See Simenon, Georges (Jacques Christian)
Simak, Clifford D(onald) 1904-1988**CLC 1, 55**
See also CA 1-4R; 125; CANR 1, 35; DLB 8; MTCW 1; SATA-Obit 56
Simenon, Georges (Jacques Christian) 1903-1989 **CLC 1, 2, 3, 8, 18, 47; DAM POP**
See also CA 85-88; 129; CANR 35; DA3; DLB 72; DLBY 89; MTCW 1, 2
Simic, Charles 1938- **CLC 6, 9, 22, 49, 68; DAM POET**
See also CA 29-32R; CAAS 4; CANR 12, 33, 52, 61; DA3; DLB 105; MTCW 2
Simmel, Georg 1858-1918 **TCLC 64**
See also CA 157
Simmons, Charles (Paul) 1924- **CLC 57**
See also CA 89-92; INT 89-92
Simmons, Dan 1948- **CLC 44; DAM POP**
See also AAYA 16; CA 138; CANR 53, 81
Simmons, James (Stewart Alexander) 1933-**CLC 43**
See also CA 105; CAAS 21; DLB 40
Simms, William Gilmore 1806-1870 **NCLC 3**

See also DLB 3, 30, 59, 73
Simon, Carly 1945- **CLC 26**
See also CA 105
Simon, Claude 1913-1984 **CLC 4, 9, 15, 39; DAM NOV**
See also CA 89-92; CANR 33; DLB 83; MTCW 1
Simon, (Marvin) Neil 1927-**CLC 6, 11, 31, 39, 70; DAM DRAM**
See also AAYA 32; AITN 1; CA 21-24R; CANR 26, 54; DA3; DLB 7; MTCW 1, 2
Simon, Paul (Frederick) 1941(?)- **CLC 17**
See also CA 116; 153
Simonon, Paul 1956(?)- **CLC 30**
Simpson, Harriette
See Arnow, Harriette (Louisa) Simpson
Simpson, Louis (Aston Marantz) 1923-**CLC 4, 7, 9, 32; DAM POET**
See also CA 1-4R; CAAS 4; CANR 1, 61; DLB 5; MTCW 1, 2
Simpson, Mona (Elizabeth) 1957- **CLC 44**
See also CA 122; 135; CANR 68
Simpson, N(orman) F(rederick) 1919-**CLC 29**
See also CA 13-16R; DLB 13
Sinclair, Andrew (Annandale) 1935- **CLC 2, 14**
See also CA 9-12R; CAAS 5; CANR 14, 38; DLB 14; MTCW 1
Sinclair, Emil
See Hesse, Hermann
Sinclair, Iain 1943- **CLC 76**
See also CA 132; CANR 81
Sinclair, Iain MacGregor
See Sinclair, Iain
Sinclair, Irene
See Griffith, D(avid Lewelyn) W(ark)
Sinclair, Mary Amelia St. Clair 1865(?)-1946
See Sinclair, May
See also CA 104
Sinclair, May 1863-1946 **TCLC 3, 11**
See also Sinclair, Mary Amelia St. Clair
See also CA 166; DLB 36, 135
Sinclair, Roy
See Griffith, D(avid Lewelyn) W(ark)
Sinclair, Upton (Beall) 1878-1968 **CLC 1, 11, 15, 63; DA; DAB; DAC; DAM MST, NOV; WLC**
See also CA 5-8R; 25-28R; CANR 7; CDALB 1929-1941; DA3; DLB 9; INT CANR-7; MTCW 1, 2; SATA 9
Singer, Isaac
See Singer, Isaac Bashevis
Singer, Isaac Bashevis 1904-1991**CLC 1, 3, 6, 9, 11, 15, 23, 38, 69, 111; DA; DAB; DAC; DAM MST, NOV; SSC 3; WLC**
See also AAYA 32; AITN 1, 2; CA 1-4R; 134; CANR 1, 39; CDALB 1941-1968; CLR 1; DA3; DLB 6, 28, 52; DLBY 91; JRDA; MAICYA; MTCW 1, 2; SATA 3, 27; SATA-Obit 68
Singer, Israel Joshua 1893-1944 **TCLC 33**
See also CA 169
Singh, Khushwant 1915- **CLC 11**
See also CA 9-12R; CAAS 9; CANR 6, 84
Singleton, Ann
See Benedict, Ruth (Fulton)
Sinjohn, John
See Galsworthy, John
Sinyavsky, Andrei (Donatevich) 1925-1997
CLC 8
See also CA 85-88; 159
Sirin, V.
See Nabokov, Vladimir (Vladimirovich)

See also CA 85-88; 147; CAAS 3; CANR 47; MTCW 1, 2

Stewart, Mary (Florence Elinor) 1916-**CLC 7, 35, 117; DAB**
See also AAYA 29; CA 1-4R; CANR 1, 59; SATA 12

Stewart, Mary Rainbow
See Stewart, Mary (Florence Elinor)

Stifle, June
See Campbell, Maria

Stifter, Adalbert 1805-1868**NCLC 41; SSC 28**
See also DLB 133

Still, James 1906- **CLC 49**
See also CA 65-68; CAAS 17; CANR 10, 26; DLB 9; SATA 29

Sting 1951-
See Sumner, Gordon Matthew
See also CA 167

Stirling, Arthur
See Sinclair, Upton (Beall)

Stitt, Milan 1941- **CLC 29**
See also CA 69-72

Stockton, Francis Richard 1834-1902
See Stockton, Frank R.
See also CA 108; 137; MAICYA; SATA 44

Stockton, Frank R. **TCLC 47**
See also Stockton, Francis Richard
See also DLB 42, 74; DLBD 13; SATA-Brief 32

Stoddard, Charles
See Kuttner, Henry

Stoker, Abraham 1847-1912
See Stoker, Bram
See also CA 105; 150; DA; DAC; DAM MST, NOV; DA3; SATA 29

Stoker, Bram 1847-1912**TCLC 8; DAB; WLC**
See also Stoker, Abraham
See also AAYA 23; CDBLB 1890-1914; DLB 36, 70, 178

Stolz, Mary (Slattery) 1920- **CLC 12**
See also AAYA 8; AITN 1; CA 5-8R; CANR 13, 41; JRDA; MAICYA; SAAS 3; SATA 10, 71

Stone, Irving 1903-1989 **CLC 7; DAM POP**
See also AITN 1; CA 1-4R; 129; CAAS 3; CANR 1, 23; DA3; INT CANR-23; MTCW 1, 2; SATA 3; SATA-Obit 64

Stone, Oliver (William) 1946- **CLC 73**
See also AAYA 15; CA 110; CANR 55

Stone, Robert (Anthony) 1937-**CLC 5, 23, 42**
See also CA 85-88; CANR 23, 66; DLB 152; INT CANR-23; MTCW 1

Stone, Zachary
See Follett, Ken(neth Martin)

Stoppard, Tom 1937-**CLC 1, 3, 4, 5, 8, 15, 29, 34, 63, 91; DA; DAB; DAC; DAM DRAM, MST; DC 6; WLC**
See also CA 81-84; CANR 39, 67; CDBLB 1960 to Present; DA3; DLB 13; DLBY 85; MTCW 1, 2

Storey, David (Malcolm) 1933-**CLC 2, 4, 5, 8; DAM DRAM**
See also CA 81-84; CANR 36; DLB 13, 14, 207; MTCW 1

Storm, Hyemeyohsts 1935- **CLC 3; DAM MULT**
See also CA 81-84; CANR 45; NNAL

Storm, Theodor 1817-1888 **SSC 27**

Storm, (Hans) Theodor (Woldsen) 1817-1888 **NCLC 1; SSC 27**
See also DLB 129

Storni, Alfonsina 1892-1938 **TCLC 5; DAM MULT; HLC 2**

See also CA 104; 131; HW 1

Stoughton, William 1631-1701 **LC 38**
See also DLB 24

Stout, Rex (Todhunter) 1886-1975 **CLC 3**
See also AITN 2; CA 61-64; CANR 71

Stow, (Julian) Randolph 1935- **CLC 23, 48**
See also CA 13-16R; CANR 33; MTCW 1

Stowe, Harriet (Elizabeth) Beecher 1811-1896 **NCLC 3, 50; DA; DAB; DAC; DAM MST, NOV; WLC**
See also CDALB 1865-1917; DA3; DLB 1, 12, 42, 74, 189; JRDA; MAICYA; YABC 1

Strachey, (Giles) Lytton 1880-1932 **TCLC 12**
See also CA 110; 178; DLB 149; DLBD 10; MTCW 2

Strand, Mark 1934-**CLC 6, 18, 41, 71; DAM POET**
See also CA 21-24R; CANR 40, 65; DLB 5; SATA 41

Straub, Peter (Francis) 1943- **CLC 28, 107; DAM POP**
See also BEST 89:1; CA 85-88; CANR 28, 65; DLBY 84; MTCW 1, 2

Strauss, Botho 1944- **CLC 22**
See also CA 157; DLB 124

Streatfeild, (Mary) Noel 1895(?)-1986**CLC 21**
See also CA 81-84; 120; CANR 31; CLR 17; DLB 160; MAICYA; SATA 20; SATA-Obit 48

Stribling, T(homas) S(igismund) 1881-1965 **CLC 23**
See also CA 107; DLB 9

Strindberg, (Johan) August 1849-1912**TCLC 1, 8, 21, 47; DA; DAB; DAC; DAM DRAM, MST; WLC**
See also CA 104; 135; DA3; MTCW 2

Stringer, Arthur 1874-1950 **TCLC 37**
See also CA 161; DLB 92

Stringer, David
See Roberts, Keith (John Kingston)

Stroheim, Erich von 1885-1957 **TCLC 71**

Strugatskii, Arkadii (Natanovich) 1925-1991 **CLC 27**
See also CA 106; 135

Strugatskii, Boris (Natanovich) 1933-**CLC 27**
See also CA 106

Strummer, Joe 1953(?)- **CLC 30**

Strunk, William, Jr. 1869-1946 **TCLC 92**
See also CA 118; 164

Stryk, Lucien 1924- **PC 27**
See also CA 13-16R; CANR 10, 28, 55

Stuart, Don A.
See Campbell, John W(ood, Jr.)

Stuart, Ian
See MacLean, Alistair (Stuart)

Stuart, Jesse (Hilton) 1906-1984**CLC 1, 8, 11, 14, 34; SSC 31**
See also CA 5-8R; 112; CANR 31; DLB 9, 48, 102; DLBY 84; SATA 2; SATA-Obit 36

Sturgeon, Theodore (Hamilton) 1918-1985 **CLC 22, 39**
See also Queen, Ellery
See also CA 81-84; 116; CANR 32; DLB 8; DLBY 85; MTCW 1, 2

Sturges, Preston 1898-1959 **TCLC 48**
See also CA 114; 149; DLB 26

Styron, William 1925-**CLC 1, 3, 5, 11, 15, 60; DAM NOV, POP; SSC 25**
See also BEST 90:4; CA 5-8R; CANR 6, 33, 74; CDALB 1968-1988; DA3; DLB 2, 143; DLBY 80; INT CANR-6; MTCW 1, 2

Su, Chien 1884-1918
See Su Man-shu

See also CA 123

Suarez Lynch, B.
See Bioy Casares, Adolfo; Borges, Jorge Luis

Suassuna, Ariano Vilar 1927-
See also CA 178; HLCS 1; HW 2

Suckow, Ruth 1892-1960 **SSC 18**
See also CA 113; DLB 9, 102

Sudermann, Hermann 1857-1928 **TCLC 15**
See also CA 107; DLB 118

Sue, Eugene 1804-1857 **NCLC 1**
See also DLB 119

Sueskind, Patrick 1949- **CLC 44**
See also Suskind, Patrick

Sukenick, Ronald 1932- **CLC 3, 4, 6, 48**
See also CA 25-28R; CAAS 8; CANR 32; DLB 173; DLBY 81

Suknaski, Andrew 1942- **CLC 19**
See also CA 101; DLB 53

Sullivan, Vernon
See Vian, Boris

Sully Prudhomme 1839-1907 **TCLC 31**

Su Man-shu **TCLC 24**
See also Su, Chien

Summerforest, Ivy B.
See Kirkup, James

Summers, Andrew James 1942- **CLC 26**

Summers, Andy
See Summers, Andrew James

Summers, Hollis (Spurgeon, Jr.) 1916-**CLC 10**
See also CA 5-8R; CANR 3; DLB 6

Summers, (Alphonsus Joseph-Mary Augustus) Montague 1880-1948 **TCLC 16**
See also CA 118; 163

Sumner, Gordon Matthew **CLC 26**
See also Sting

Surtees, Robert Smith 1803-1864 **NCLC 14**
See also DLB 21

Susann, Jacqueline 1921-1974 **CLC 3**
See also AITN 1; CA 65-68; 53-56; MTCW 1, 2

Su Shih 1036-1101 **CMLC 15**

Suskind, Patrick
See Sueskind, Patrick
See also CA 145

Sutcliff, Rosemary 1920-1992 **CLC 26; DAB; DAC; DAM MST, POP**
See also AAYA 10; CA 5-8R; 139; CANR 37; CLR 1, 37; JRDA; MAICYA; SATA 6, 44, 78; SATA-Obit 73

Sutro, Alfred 1863-1933 **TCLC 6**
See also CA 105; DLB 10

Sutton, Henry
See Slavitt, David R(ytman)

Svevo, Italo 1861-1928 **TCLC 2, 35; SSC 25**
See also Schmitz, Aron Hector

Swados, Elizabeth (A.) 1951- **CLC 12**
See also CA 97-100; CANR 49; INT 97-100

Swados, Harvey 1920-1972 **CLC 5**
See also CA 5-8R; 37-40R; CANR 6; DLB 2

Swan, Gladys 1934- **CLC 69**
See also CA 101; CANR 17, 39

Swarthout, Glendon (Fred) 1918-1992**CLC 35**
See also CA 1-4R; 139; CANR 1, 47; SATA 26

Sweet, Sarah C.
See Jewett, (Theodora) Sarah Orne

Swenson, May 1919-1989**CLC 4, 14, 61, 106; DA; DAB; DAC; DAM MST, POET; PC 14**
See also CA 5-8R; 130; CANR 36, 61; DLB 5; MTCW 1, 2; SATA 15

Swift, Augustus
See Lovecraft, H(oward) P(hillips)

Swift, Graham (Colin) 1949- **CLC 41, 88**

See also CA 117; 122; CANR 46, 71; DLB 194;
MTCW 2

Swift, Jonathan 1667-1745   **LC 1, 42; DA;
DAB; DAC; DAM MST, NOV, POET; PC
9; WLC**
See also CDBLB 1660-1789; CLR 53; DA3;
DLB 39, 95, 101; SATA 19

Swinburne, Algernon Charles 1837-1909
**TCLC 8, 36; DA; DAB; DAC; DAM MST,
POET; PC 24; WLC**
See also CA 105; 140; CDBLB 1832-1890;
DA3; DLB 35, 57

Swinfen, Ann   **CLC 34**

Swinnerton, Frank Arthur 1884-1982**CLC 31**
See also CA 108; DLB 34

Swithen, John
See King, Stephen (Edwin)

Sylvia
See Ashton-Warner, Sylvia (Constance)

Symmes, Robert Edward
See Duncan, Robert (Edward)

Symonds, John Addington 1840-1893 **N C L C
34**
See also DLB 57, 144

Symons, Arthur 1865-1945   **TCLC 11**
See also CA 107; DLB 19, 57, 149

Symons, Julian (Gustave) 1912-1994 **CLC 2,
14, 32**
See also CA 49-52; 147; CAAS 3; CANR 3,
33, 59; DLB 87, 155; DLBY 92; MTCW 1

Synge, (Edmund) J(ohn) M(illington) 1871-
1909   **TCLC 6, 37; DAM DRAM; DC 2**
See also CA 104; 141; CDBLB 1890-1914;
DLB 10, 19

Syruc, J.
See Milosz, Czeslaw

Szirtes, George 1948-   **CLC 46**
See also CA 109; CANR 27, 61

Szymborska, Wislawa 1923-   **CLC 99**
See also CA 154; DA3; DLBY 96; MTCW 2

T. O., Nik
See Annensky, Innokenty (Fyodorovich)

Tabori, George 1914-   **CLC 19**
See also CA 49-52; CANR 4, 69

Tagore, Rabindranath 1861-1941**TCLC 3, 53;
DAM DRAM, POET; PC 8**
See also CA 104; 120; DA3; MTCW 1, 2

Taine, Hippolyte Adolphe 1828-1893 **N C L C
15**

Talese, Gay 1932-   **CLC 37**
See also AITN 1; CA 1-4R; CANR 9, 58; DLB
185; INT CANR-9; MTCW 1, 2

Tallent, Elizabeth (Ann) 1954-   **CLC 45**
See also CA 117; CANR 72; DLB 130

Tally, Ted 1952-   **CLC 42**
See also CA 120; 124; INT 124

Talvik, Heiti 1904-1947   **TCLC 87**

Tamayo y Baus, Manuel 1829-1898 **NCLC 1**

Tammsaare, A(nton) H(ansen) 1878-1940
TCLC 27
See also CA 164

Tam'si, Tchicaya U
See Tchicaya, Gerald Felix

Tan, Amy (Ruth) 1952- **CLC 59, 120; DAM
MULT, NOV, POP**
See also AAYA 9; BEST 89:3; CA 136; CANR
54; CDALBS; DA3; DLB 173; MTCW 2;
SATA 75

Tandem, Felix
See Spitteler, Carl (Friedrich Georg)

Tanizaki, Jun'ichiro 1886-1965**CLC 8, 14, 28;
SSC 21**
See also CA 93-96; 25-28R; DLB 180; MTCW

2

Tanner, William
See Amis, Kingsley (William)

Tao Lao
See Storni, Alfonsina

Tarassoff, Lev
See Troyat, Henri

Tarbell, Ida M(inerva) 1857-1944   **TCLC 40**
See also CA 122; DLB 47

Tarkington, (Newton) Booth 1869-1946**TCLC
9**
See also CA 110; 143; DLB 9, 102; MTCW 2;
SATA 17

Tarkovsky, Andrei (Arsenyevich) 1932-1986
CLC 75
See also CA 127

Tartt, Donna 1964(?)-   **CLC 76**
See also CA 142

Tasso, Torquato 1544-1595   **LC 5**

Tate, (John Orley) Allen 1899-1979**CLC 2, 4,
6, 9, 11, 14, 24**
See also CA 5-8R; 85-88; CANR 32; DLB 4,
45, 63; DLBD 17; MTCW 1, 2

Tate, Ellalice
See Hibbert, Eleanor Alice Burford

Tate, James (Vincent) 1943-   **CLC 2, 6, 25**
See also CA 21-24R; CANR 29, 57; DLB 5,
169

Tavel, Ronald 1940-   **CLC 6**
See also CA 21-24R; CANR 33

Taylor, C(ecil) P(hilip) 1929-1981   **CLC 27**
See also CA 25-28R; 105; CANR 47

Taylor, Edward 1642(?)-1729   **LC 11; DA;
DAB; DAC; DAM MST, POET**
See also DLB 24

Taylor, Eleanor Ross 1920-   **CLC 5**
See also CA 81-84; CANR 70

Taylor, Elizabeth 1912-1975   **CLC 2, 4, 29**
See also CA 13-16R; CANR 9, 70; DLB 139;
MTCW 1; SATA 13

Taylor, Frederick Winslow 1856-1915 **T C L C
76**

Taylor, Henry (Splawn) 1942-   **CLC 44**
See also CA 33-36R; CAAS 7; CANR 31; DLB
5

Taylor, Kamala (Purnaiya) 1924-
See Markandaya, Kamala
See also CA 77-80

Taylor, Mildred D.   **CLC 21**
See also AAYA 10; BW 1; CA 85-88; CANR
25; CLR 9, 59; DLB 52; JRDA; MAICYA;
SAAS 5; SATA 15, 70

Taylor, Peter (Hillsman) 1917-1994**CLC 1, 4,
18, 37, 44, 50, 71; SSC 10**
See also CA 13-16R; 147; CANR 9, 50; DLBY
81, 94; INT CANR-9; MTCW 1, 2

Taylor, Robert Lewis 1912-1998   **CLC 14**
See also CA 1-4R; 170; CANR 3, 64; SATA 10

Tchekhov, Anton
See Chekhov, Anton (Pavlovich)

Tchicaya, Gerald Felix 1931-1988   **CLC 101**
See also CA 129; 125; CANR 81

Tchicaya U Tam'si
See Tchicaya, Gerald Felix

Teasdale, Sara 1884-1933   **TCLC 4**
See also CA 104; 163; DLB 45; SATA 32

Tegner, Esaias 1782-1846   **NCLC 2**

Teilhard de Chardin, (Marie Joseph) Pierre
1881-1955   **TCLC 9**
See also CA 105

Temple, Ann
See Mortimer, Penelope (Ruth)

Tennant, Emma (Christina) 1937-**CLC 13, 52**

See also CA 65-68; CAAS 9; CANR 10, 38,
59; DLB 14

Tenneshaw, S. M.
See Silverberg, Robert

Tennyson, Alfred 1809-1892   **NCLC 30, 65;
DA; DAB; DAC; DAM MST, POET; PC
6; WLC**
See also CDBLB 1832-1890; DA3; DLB 32

Teran, Lisa St. Aubin de   **CLC 36**
See St. Aubin de Teran, Lisa

Terence c. 184B.C.-c. 159B.C.**CMLC 14; DC 7**
See also DLB 211

Teresa de Jesus, St. 1515-1582   **LC 18**

Terkel, Louis 1912-
See Terkel, Studs
See also CA 57-60; CANR 18, 45, 67; DA3;
MTCW 1, 2

Terkel, Studs   **CLC 38**
See also Terkel, Louis
See also AAYA 32; AITN 1; MTCW 2

Terry, C. V.
See Slaughter, Frank G(ill)

Terry, Megan 1932-   **CLC 19**
See also CA 77-80; CABS 3; CANR 43; DLB 7

Tertullian c. 155-c. 245   **CMLC 29**

Tertz, Abram
See Sinyavsky, Andrei (Donatevich)

Tesich, Steve 1943(?)-1996   **CLC 40, 69**
See also CA 105; 152; DLBY 83

Tesla, Nikola 1856-1943   **TCLC 88**

Teternikov, Fyodor Kuzmich 1863-1927
See Sologub, Fyodor
See also CA 104

Tevis, Walter 1928-1984   **CLC 42**
See also CA 113

Tey, Josephine   **TCLC 14**
See also Mackintosh, Elizabeth
See also DLB 77

Thackeray, William Makepeace 1811-1863
**NCLC 5, 14, 22, 43; DA; DAB; DAC; DAM
MST, NOV; WLC**
See also CDBLB 1832-1890; DA3; DLB 21,
55, 159, 163; SATA 23

Thakura, Ravindranatha
See Tagore, Rabindranath

Tharoor, Shashi 1956-   **CLC 70**
See also CA 141

Thelwell, Michael Miles 1939-   **CLC 22**
See also BW 2; CA 101

Theobald, Lewis, Jr.
See Lovecraft, H(oward) P(hillips)

Theodorescu, Ion N. 1880-1967
See Arghezi, Tudor
See also CA 116

Theriault, Yves 1915-1983   **CLC 79; DAC;
DAM MST**
See also CA 102; DLB 88

Theroux, Alexander (Louis) 1939- **CLC 2, 25**
See also CA 85-88; CANR 20, 63

Theroux, Paul (Edward) 1941- **CLC 5, 8, 11,
15, 28, 46; DAM POP**
See also AAYA 28; BEST 89:4; CA 33-36R;
CANR 20, 45, 74; CDALBS; DA3; DLB 2;
MTCW 1, 2; SATA 44, 109

Thesen, Sharon 1946-   **CLC 56**
See also CA 163

Thevenin, Denis
See Duhamel, Georges

Thibault, Jacques Anatole Francois 1844-1924
See France, Anatole
See also CA 106; 127; DAM NOV; DA3;
MTCW 1, 2

Thiele, Colin (Milton) 1920-   **CLC 17**

See also CA 29-32R; CANR 12, 28, 53; CLR 27; MAICYA; SAAS 2; SATA 14, 72

Thomas, Audrey (Callahan) 1935-**CLC 7, 13, 37, 107; SSC 20**
See also AITN 2; CA 21-24R; CAAS 19; CANR 36, 58; DLB 60; MTCW 1

Thomas, Augustus 1857-1934   **TCLC 97**

Thomas, D(onald) M(ichael) 1935- **CLC 13, 22, 31**
See also CA 61-64; CAAS 11; CANR 17, 45, 75; CDBLB 1960 to Present; DA3; DLB 40, 207; INT CANR-17; MTCW 1, 2

Thomas, Dylan (Marlais) 1914-1953**TCLC 1, 8, 45; DA; DAB; DAC; DAM DRAM, MST, POET; PC 2; SSC 3; WLC**
See also CA 104; 120; CANR 65; CDBLB 1945-1960; DA3; DLB 13, 20, 139; MTCW 1, 2; SATA 60

Thomas, (Philip) Edward 1878-1917 **TCLC 10; DAM POET**
See also CA 106; 153; DLB 98

Thomas, Joyce Carol 1938-   **CLC 35**
See also AAYA 12; BW 2, 3; CA 113; 116; CANR 48; CLR 19; DLB 33; INT 116; JRDA; MAICYA; MTCW 1, 2; SAAS 7; SATA 40, 78

Thomas, Lewis 1913-1993   **CLC 35**
See also CA 85-88; 143; CANR 38, 60; MTCW 1, 2

Thomas, M. Carey 1857-1935   **TCLC 89**

Thomas, Paul
See Mann, (Paul) Thomas

Thomas, Piri 1928-   **CLC 17; HLCS 2**
See also CA 73-76; HW 1

Thomas, R(onald) S(tuart) 1913- **CLC 6, 13, 48; DAB; DAM POET**
See also CA 89-92; CAAS 4; CANR 30; CDBLB 1960 to Present; DLB 27; MTCW 1

Thomas, Ross (Elmore) 1926-1995   **CLC 39**
See also CA 33-36R; 150; CANR 22, 63

Thompson, Francis Clegg
See Mencken, H(enry) L(ouis)

Thompson, Francis Joseph 1859-1907**TCLC 4**
See also CA 104; CDBLB 1890-1914; DLB 19

Thompson, Hunter S(tockton) 1939- **CLC 9, 17, 40, 104; DAM POP**
See also BEST 89:1; CA 17-20R; CANR 23, 46, 74, 77; DA3; DLB 185; MTCW 1, 2

Thompson, James Myers
See Thompson, Jim (Myers)

Thompson, Jim (Myers) 1906-1977(?)**CLC 69**
See also CA 140

Thompson, Judith   **CLC 39**

Thomson, James 1700-1748   **LC 16, 29, 40; DAM POET**
See also DLB 95

Thomson, James 1834-1882 **NCLC 18; DAM POET**
See also DLB 35

Thoreau, Henry David 1817-1862**NCLC 7, 21, 61; DA; DAB; DAC; DAM MST; WLC**
See also CDALB 1640-1865; DA3; DLB 1

Thornton, Hall
See Silverberg, Robert

Thucydides c. 455B.C.-399B.C.   **CMLC 17**
See also DLB 176

Thurber, James (Grover) 1894-1961 **CLC 5, 11, 25; DA; DAB; DAC; DAM DRAM, MST, NOV; SSC 1**
See also CA 73-76; CANR 17, 39; CDALB 1929-1941; DA3; DLB 4, 11, 22, 102; MAICYA; MTCW 1, 2; SATA 13

Thurman, Wallace (Henry) 1902-1934**T C L C**

6; BLC 3; DAM MULT
See also BW 1, 3; CA 104; 124; CANR 81; DLB 51

Ticheburn, Cheviot
See Ainsworth, William Harrison

Tieck, (Johann) Ludwig 1773-1853 **NCLC 5, 46; SSC 31**
See also DLB 90

Tiger, Derry
See Ellison, Harlan (Jay)

Tilghman, Christopher 1948(?)-   **CLC 65**
See also CA 159

Tillinghast, Richard (Williford) 1940-**CLC 29**
See also CA 29-32R; CAAS 23; CANR 26, 51

Timrod, Henry 1828-1867   **NCLC 25**
See also DLB 3

Tindall, Gillian (Elizabeth) 1938-   **CLC 7**
See also CA 21-24R; CANR 11, 65

Tiptree, James, Jr.   **CLC 48, 50**
See also Sheldon, Alice Hastings Bradley
See also DLB 8

Titmarsh, Michael Angelo
See Thackeray, William Makepeace

Tocqueville, Alexis (Charles Henri Maurice Clerel, Comte) de 1805-1859**NCLC 7, 63**

Tolkien, J(ohn) R(onald) R(euel) 1892-1973 **CLC 1, 2, 3, 8, 12, 38; DA; DAB; DAC; DAM MST, NOV, POP; WLC**
See also AAYA 10; AITN 1; CA 17-18; 45-48; CANR 36; CAP 2; CDBLB 1914-1945; CLR 56; DA3; DLB 15, 160; JRDA; MAICYA; MTCW 1, 2; SATA 2, 32, 100; SATA-Obit 24

Toller, Ernst 1893-1939   **TCLC 10**
See also CA 107; DLB 124

Tolson, M. B.
See Tolson, Melvin B(eaunorus)

Tolson, Melvin B(eaunorus) 1898(?)-1966 **CLC 36, 105; BLC 3; DAM MULT, POET**
See also BW 1, 3; CA 124; 89-92; CANR 80; DLB 48, 76

Tolstoi, Aleksei Nikolaevich
See Tolstoy, Alexey Nikolaevich

Tolstoy, Alexey Nikolaevich 1882-1945**T C L C 18**
See also CA 107; 158

Tolstoy, Count Leo
See Tolstoy, Leo (Nikolaevich)

Tolstoy, Leo (Nikolaevich) 1828-1910**TCLC 4, 11, 17, 28, 44, 79; DA; DAB; DAC; DAM MST, NOV; SSC 9, 30; WLC**
See also CA 104; 123; DA3; SATA 26

Tomasi di Lampedusa, Giuseppe 1896-1957
See Lampedusa, Giuseppe (Tomasi) di
See also CA 111

Tomlin, Lily   **CLC 17**
See also Tomlin, Mary Jean

Tomlin, Mary Jean 1939(?)-
See Tomlin, Lily
See also CA 117

Tomlinson, (Alfred) Charles 1927-**CLC 2, 4, 6, 13, 45; DAM POET; PC 17**
See also CA 5-8R; CANR 33; DLB 40

Tomlinson, H(enry) M(ajor) 1873-1958**TCLC 71**
See also CA 118; 161; DLB 36, 100, 195

Tonson, Jacob
See Bennett, (Enoch) Arnold

Toole, John Kennedy 1937-1969 **CLC 19, 64**
See also CA 104; DLBY 81; MTCW 2

Toomer, Jean 1894-1967**CLC 1, 4, 13, 22; BLC 3; DAM MULT; PC 7; SSC 1; WLCS**
See also BW 1; CA 85-88; CDALB 1917-1929;

DA3; DLB 45, 51; MTCW 1, 2

Torley, Luke
See Blish, James (Benjamin)

Tornimparte, Alessandra
See Ginzburg, Natalia

Torre, Raoul della
See Mencken, H(enry) L(ouis)

Torrence, Ridgely 1874-1950   **TCLC 97**
See also DLB 54

Torrey, E(dwin) Fuller 1937-   **CLC 34**
See also CA 119; CANR 71

Torsvan, Ben Traven
See Traven, B.

Torsvan, Benno Traven
See Traven, B.

Torsvan, Berick Traven
See Traven, B.

Torsvan, Berwick Traven
See Traven, B.

Torsvan, Bruno Traven
See Traven, B.

Torsvan, Traven
See Traven, B.

Tournier, Michel (Edouard) 1924-**CLC 6, 23, 36, 95**
See also CA 49-52; CANR 3, 36, 74; DLB 83; MTCW 1, 2; SATA 23

Tournimparte, Alessandra
See Ginzburg, Natalia

Towers, Ivar
See Kornbluth, C(yril) M.

Towne, Robert (Burton) 1936(?)-   **CLC 87**
See also CA 108; DLB 44

Townsend, Sue   **CLC 61**
See also Townsend, Susan Elaine
See also AAYA 28; SATA 55, 93; SATA-Brief 48

Townsend, Susan Elaine 1946-
See Townsend, Sue
See also CA 119; 127; CANR 65; DAB; DAC; DAM MST

Townshend, Peter (Dennis Blandford) 1945-**CLC 17, 42**
See also CA 107

Tozzi, Federigo 1883-1920   **TCLC 31**
See also CA 160

Traill, Catharine Parr 1802-1899 **NCLC 31**
See also DLB 99

Trakl, Georg 1887-1914   **TCLC 5; PC 20**
See also CA 104; 165; MTCW 2

Transtroemer, Tomas (Goesta) 1931-**CLC 52, 65; DAM POET**
See also CA 117; 129; CAAS 17

Transtromer, Tomas Gosta
See Transtroemer, Tomas (Goesta)

Traven, B. (?)-1969   **CLC 8, 11**
See also CA 19-20; 25-28R; CAP 2; DLB 9, 56; MTCW 1

Treitel, Jonathan 1959-   **CLC 70**

Tremain, Rose 1943-   **CLC 42**
See also CA 97-100; CANR 44; DLB 14

Tremblay, Michel 1942- **CLC 29, 102; DAC; DAM MST**
See also CA 116; 128; DLB 60; MTCW 1, 2

Trevanian   **CLC 29**
See also Whitaker, Rod(ney)

Trevor, Glen
See Hilton, James

Trevor, William 1928-**CLC 7, 9, 14, 25, 71, 116; SSC 21**
See also Cox, William Trevor
See also DLB 14, 139; MTCW 2

Trifonov, Yuri (Valentinovich) 1925-1981

CLC 45
See also CA 126; 103; MTCW 1

Trilling, Lionel 1905-1975　　**CLC 9, 11, 24**
See also CA 9-12R; 61-64; CANR 10; DLB 28, 63; INT CANR-10; MTCW 1, 2

Trimball, W. H.
See Mencken, H(enry) L(ouis)

Tristan
See Gomez de la Serna, Ramon

Tristram
See Housman, A(lfred) E(dward)

Trogdon, William (Lewis) 1939-
See Heat-Moon, William Least
See also CA 115; 119; CANR 47; INT 119

Trollope, Anthony 1815-1882**NCLC 6, 33; DA; DAB; DAC; DAM MST, NOV; SSC 28; WLC**
See also CDBLB 1832-1890; DA3; DLB 21, 57, 159; SATA 22

Trollope, Frances 1779-1863　　**NCLC 30**
See also DLB 21, 166

Trotsky, Leon 1879-1940　　**TCLC 22**
See also CA 118; 167

Trotter (Cockburn), Catharine 1679-1749**LC 8**
See also DLB 84

Trout, Kilgore
See Farmer, Philip Jose

Trow, George W. S. 1943-　　**CLC 52**
See also CA 126

Troyat, Henri 1911-　　**CLC 23**
See also CA 45-48; CANR 2, 33, 67; MTCW 1

Trudeau, G(arretson) B(eekman) 1948-
See Trudeau, Garry B.
See also CA 81-84; CANR 31; SATA 35

Trudeau, Garry B.　　**CLC 12**
See also Trudeau, G(arretson) B(eekman)
See also AAYA 10; AITN 2

Truffaut, Francois 1932-1984　　**CLC 20, 101**
See also CA 81-84; 113; CANR 34

Trumbo, Dalton 1905-1976　　**CLC 19**
See also CA 21-24R; 69-72; CANR 10; DLB 26

Trumbull, John 1750-1831　　**NCLC 30**
See also DLB 31

Trundlett, Helen B.
See Eliot, T(homas) S(tearns)

Tryon, Thomas 1926-1991　**CLC 3, 11; DAM POP**
See also AITN 1; CA 29-32R; 135; CANR 32, 77; DA3; MTCW 1

Tryon, Tom
See Tryon, Thomas

Ts'ao Hsueh-ch'in 1715(?)-1763　　**LC 1**

Tsushima, Shuji 1909-1948
See Dazai Osamu
See also CA 107

Tsvetaeva (Efron), Marina (Ivanovna) 1892-1941　　**TCLC 7, 35; PC 14**
See also CA 104; 128; CANR 73; MTCW 1, 2

Tuck, Lily 1938-　　**CLC 70**
See also CA 139

Tu Fu 712-770　　**PC 9**
See also DAM MULT

Tunis, John R(oberts) 1889-1975　　**CLC 12**
See also CA 61-64; CANR 62; DLB 22, 171; JRDA; MAICYA; SATA 37; SATA-Brief 30

Tuohy, Frank　　**CLC 37**
See also Tuohy, John Francis
See also DLB 14, 139

Tuohy, John Francis 1925-1999
See Tuohy, Frank
See also CA 5-8R; 178; CANR 3, 47

Turco, Lewis (Putnam) 1934-　　**CLC 11, 63**
See also CA 13-16R; CAAS 22; CANR 24, 51; DLBY 84

Turgenev, Ivan 1818-1883　　**NCLC 21; DA; DAB; DAC; DAM MST, NOV; DC 7; SSC 7; WLC**

Turgot, Anne-Robert-Jacques 1727-1781　**LC 26**

Turner, Frederick 1943-　　**CLC 48**
See also CA 73-76; CAAS 10; CANR 12, 30, 56; DLB 40

Tutu, Desmond M(pilo) 1931-**CLC 80; BLC 3; DAM MULT**
See also BW 1, 3; CA 125; CANR 67, 81

Tutuola, Amos 1920-1997**CLC 5, 14, 29; BLC 3; DAM MULT**
See also BW 2, 3; CA 9-12R; 159; CANR 27, 66; DA3; DLB 125; MTCW 1, 2

Twain, Mark **TCLC 6, 12, 19, 36, 48, 59; SSC 34; WLC**
See also Clemens, Samuel Langhorne
See also AAYA 20; CLR 58, 60; DLB 11, 12, 23, 64, 74

Tyler, Anne 1941-　**CLC 7, 11, 18, 28, 44, 59, 103; DAM NOV, POP**
See also AAYA 18; BEST 89:1; CA 9-12R; CANR 11, 33, 53; CDALBS; DLB 6, 143; DLBY 82; MTCW 1, 2; SATA 7, 90

Tyler, Royall 1757-1826　　**NCLC 3**
See also DLB 37

Tynan, Katharine 1861-1931　　**TCLC 3**
See also CA 104; 167; DLB 153

Tyutchev, Fyodor 1803-1873　　**NCLC 34**

Tzara, Tristan 1896-1963　　**CLC 47; DAM POET; PC 27**
See also CA 153; 89-92; MTCW 2

Uhry, Alfred 1936-　**CLC 55; DAM DRAM, POP**
See also CA 127; 133; DA3; INT 133

Ulf, Haerved
See Strindberg, (Johan) August

Ulf, Harved
See Strindberg, (Johan) August

Ulibarri, Sabine R(eyes) 1919-**CLC 83; DAM MULT; HLCS 2**
See also CA 131; CANR 81; DLB 82; HW 1, 2

Unamuno (y Jugo), Miguel de 1864-1936　**TCLC 2, 9; DAM MULT, NOV; HLC 2; SSC 11**
See also CA 104; 131; CANR 81; DLB 108; HW 1, 2; MTCW 1, 2

Undercliffe, Errol
See Campbell, (John) Ramsey

Underwood, Miles
See Glassco, John

Undset, Sigrid 1882-1949**TCLC 3; DA; DAB; DAC; DAM MST, NOV; WLC**
See also CA 104; 129; DA3; MTCW 1, 2

Ungaretti, Giuseppe 1888-1970**CLC 7, 11, 15**
See also CA 19-20; 25-28R; CAP 2; DLB 114

Unger, Douglas 1952-　　**CLC 34**
See also CA 130

Unsworth, Barry (Forster) 1930-　　**CLC 76**
See also CA 25-28R; CANR 30, 54; DLB 194

Updike, John (Hoyer) 1932-**CLC 1, 2, 3, 5, 7, 9, 13, 15, 23, 34, 43, 70; DA; DAB; DAC; DAM MST, NOV, POET, POP; SSC 13, 27; WLC**
See also CA 1-4R; CABS 1; CANR 4, 33, 51; CDALB 1968-1988; DA3; DLB 2, 5, 143; DLBD 3; DLBY 80, 82, 97; MTCW 1, 2

Upshaw, Margaret Mitchell
See Mitchell, Margaret (Munnerlyn)

Upton, Mark
See Sanders, Lawrence

Upward, Allen 1863-1926　　**TCLC 85**
See also CA 117; DLB 36

Urdang, Constance (Henriette) 1922-**CLC 47**
See also CA 21-24R; CANR 9, 24

Uriel, Henry
See Faust, Frederick (Schiller)

Uris, Leon (Marcus) 1924-　**CLC 7, 32; DAM NOV, POP**
See also AITN 1, 2; BEST 89:2; CA 1-4R; CANR 1, 40, 65; DA3; MTCW 1, 2; SATA 49

Urista, Alberto H. 1947-
See Alurista
See also CA 45-48; CANR 2, 32; HLCS 1; HW 1

Urmuz
See Codrescu, Andrei

Urquhart, Guy
See McAlmon, Robert (Menzies)

Urquhart, Jane 1949-　　**CLC 90; DAC**
See also CA 113; CANR 32, 68

Usigli, Rodolfo 1905-1979
See also CA 131; HLCS 1; HW 1

Ustinov, Peter (Alexander) 1921-　　**CLC 1**
See also AITN 1; CA 13-16R; CANR 25, 51; DLB 13; MTCW 2

U Tam'si, Gerald Felix Tchicaya
See Tchicaya, Gerald Felix

U Tam'si, Tchicaya
See Tchicaya, Gerald Felix

Vachss, Andrew (Henry) 1942-　　**CLC 106**
See also CA 118; CANR 44

Vachss, Andrew H.
See Vachss, Andrew (Henry)

Vaculik, Ludvik 1926-　　**CLC 7**
See also CA 53-56; CANR 72

Vaihinger, Hans 1852-1933　　**TCLC 71**
See also CA 116; 166

Valdez, Luis (Miguel) 1940-　**CLC 84; DAM MULT; DC 10; HLC 2**
See also CA 101; CANR 32, 81; DLB 122; HW 1

Valenzuela, Luisa 1938-　**CLC 31, 104; DAM MULT; HLCS 2; SSC 14**
See also CA 101; CANR 32, 65; DLB 113; HW 1, 2

Valera y Alcala-Galiano, Juan 1824-1905　　**TCLC 10**
See also CA 106

Valery, (Ambroise) Paul (Toussaint Jules) 1871-1945　　**TCLC 4, 15; DAM POET; PC 9**
See also CA 104; 122; DA3; MTCW 1, 2

Valle-Inclan, Ramon (Maria) del 1866-1936　**TCLC 5; DAM MULT; HLC 2**
See also CA 106; 153; CANR 80; DLB 134; HW 2

Vallejo, Antonio Buero
See Buero Vallejo, Antonio

Vallejo, Cesar (Abraham) 1892-1938**TCLC 3, 56; DAM MULT; HLC 2**
See also CA 105; 153; HW 1

Valles, Jules 1832-1885　　**NCLC 71**
See also DLB 123

Vallette, Marguerite Eymery
See Rachilde

Valle Y Pena, Ramon del
See Valle-Inclan, Ramon (Maria) del

Van Ash, Cay 1918-　　**CLC 34**

Vanbrugh, Sir John 1664-1726　**LC 21; DAM DRAM**
See also DLB 80

von Sternberg, Josef
  See Sternberg, Josef von
Vorster, Gordon 1924-   **CLC 34**
  See also CA 133
Vosce, Trudie
  See Ozick, Cynthia
Voznesensky, Andrei (Andreievich) 1933-
     CLC 1, 15, 57; DAM POET
  See also CA 89-92; CANR 37; MTCW 1
Waddington, Miriam 1917-   **CLC 28**
  See also CA 21-24R; CANR 12, 30; DLB 68
Wagman, Fredrica 1937-   **CLC 7**
  See also CA 97-100; INT 97-100
Wagner, Linda W.
  See Wagner-Martin, Linda (C.)
Wagner, Linda Welshimer
  See Wagner-Martin, Linda (C.)
Wagner, Richard 1813-1883   **NCLC 9**
  See also DLB 129
Wagner-Martin, Linda (C.) 1936- **CLC 50**
  See also CA 159
Wagoner, David (Russell) 1926- **CLC 3, 5, 15**
  See also CA 1-4R; CAAS 3; CANR 2, 71; DLB 5; SATA 14
Wah, Fred(erick James) 1939-   **CLC 44**
  See also CA 107; 141; DLB 60
Wahloo, Per 1926-1975   **CLC 7**
  See also CA 61-64; CANR 73
Wahloo, Peter
  See Wahloo, Per
Wain, John (Barrington) 1925-1994 **CLC 2, 11, 15, 46**
  See also CA 5-8R; 145; CAAS 4; CANR 23, 54; CDBLB 1960 to Present; DLB 15, 27, 139, 155; MTCW 1, 2
Wajda, Andrzej 1926-   **CLC 16**
  See also CA 102
Wakefield, Dan 1932-   **CLC 7**
  See also CA 21-24R; CAAS 7
Wakoski, Diane 1937- **CLC 2, 4, 7, 9, 11, 40; DAM POET; PC 15**
  See also CA 13-16R; CAAS 1; CANR 9, 60; DLB 5; INT CANR-9; MTCW 2
Wakoski-Sherbell, Diane
  See Wakoski, Diane
Walcott, Derek (Alton) 1930- **CLC 2, 4, 9, 14, 25, 42, 67, 76; BLC 3; DAB; DAC; DAM MST, MULT, POET; DC 7**
  See also BW 2; CA 89-92; CANR 26, 47, 75, 80; DA3; DLB 117; DLBY 81; MTCW 1, 2
Waldman, Anne (Lesley) 1945-   **CLC 7**
  See also CA 37-40R; CAAS 17; CANR 34, 69; DLB 16
Waldo, E. Hunter
  See Sturgeon, Theodore (Hamilton)
Waldo, Edward Hamilton
  See Sturgeon, Theodore (Hamilton)
Walker, Alice (Malsenior) 1944- **CLC 5, 6, 9, 19, 27, 46, 58, 103; BLC 3; DA; DAB; DAC; DAM MST, MULT, NOV, POET, POP; SSC 5; WLCS**
  See also AAYA 3; BEST 89:4; BW 2, 3; CA 37-40R; CANR 9, 27, 49, 66, 82; CDALB 1968-1988; DA3; DLB 6, 33, 143; INT CANR-27; MTCW 1, 2; SATA 31
Walker, David Harry 1911-1992 **CLC 14**
  See also CA 1-4R; 137; CANR 1; SATA 8; SATA-Obit 71
Walker, Edward Joseph 1934-
  See Walker, Ted
  See also CA 21-24R; CANR 12, 28, 53
Walker, George F. 1947- **CLC 44, 61; DAB; DAC; DAM MST**

See also CA 103; CANR 21, 43, 59; DLB 60
Walker, Joseph A. 1935-   **CLC 19; DAM DRAM, MST**
  See also BW 1, 3; CA 89-92; CANR 26; DLB 38
Walker, Margaret (Abigail) 1915-1998 **CLC 1, 6; BLC; DAM MULT; PC 20**
  See also BW 2, 3; CA 73-76; 172; CANR 26, 54, 76; DLB 76, 152; MTCW 1, 2
Walker, Ted   **CLC 13**
  See also Walker, Edward Joseph
  See also DLB 40
Wallace, David Foster 1962- **CLC 50, 114**
  See also CA 132; CANR 59; DA3; MTCW 2
Wallace, Dexter
  See Masters, Edgar Lee
Wallace, (Richard Horatio) Edgar 1875-1932 **TCLC 57**
  See also CA 115; DLB 70
Wallace, Irving 1916-1990 **CLC 7, 13; DAM NOV, POP**
  See also AITN 1; CA 1-4R; 132; CAAS 1; CANR 1, 27; INT CANR-27; MTCW 1, 2
Wallant, Edward Lewis 1926-1962 **CLC 5, 10**
  See also CA 1-4R; CANR 22; DLB 2, 28, 143; MTCW 1, 2
Wallas, Graham 1858-1932   **TCLC 91**
Walley, Byron
  See Card, Orson Scott
Walpole, Horace 1717-1797   **LC 49**
  See also DLB 39, 104
Walpole, Hugh (Seymour) 1884-1941 **TCLC 5**
  See also CA 104; 165; DLB 34; MTCW 2
Walser, Martin 1927-   **CLC 27**
  See also CA 57-60; CANR 8, 46; DLB 75, 124
Walser, Robert 1878-1956 **TCLC 18; SSC 20**
  See also CA 118; 165; DLB 66
Walsh, Jill Paton   **CLC 35**
  See also Paton Walsh, Gillian
  See also AAYA 11; CLR 2; DLB 161; SAAS 3
Walter, Villiam Christian
  See Andersen, Hans Christian
Wambaugh, Joseph (Aloysius, Jr.) 1937- **CLC 3, 18; DAM NOV, POP**
  See also AITN 1; BEST 89:3; CA 33-36R; CANR 42, 65; DA3; DLB 6; DLBY 83; MTCW 1, 2
Wang Wei 699(?)-761(?)   **PC 18**
Ward, Arthur Henry Sarsfield 1883-1959
  See Rohmer, Sax
  See also CA 108; 173
Ward, Douglas Turner 1930-   **CLC 19**
  See also BW 1; CA 81-84; CANR 27; DLB 7, 38
Ward, E. D.
  See Lucas, E(dward) V(errall)
Ward, Mary Augusta
  See Ward, Mrs. Humphry
Ward, Mrs. Humphry 1851-1920 **TCLC 55**
  See also DLB 18
Ward, Peter
  See Faust, Frederick (Schiller)
Warhol, Andy 1928(?)-1987   **CLC 20**
  See also AAYA 12; BEST 89:4; CA 89-92; 121; CANR 34
Warner, Francis (Robert le Plastrier) 1937- **CLC 14**
  See also CA 53-56; CANR 11
Warner, Marina 1946-   **CLC 59**
  See also CA 65-68; CANR 21, 55; DLB 194
Warner, Rex (Ernest) 1905-1986 **CLC 45**
  See also CA 89-92; 119; DLB 15
Warner, Susan (Bogert) 1819-1885 **NCLC 31**

See also DLB 3, 42
Warner, Sylvia (Constance) Ashton
  See Ashton-Warner, Sylvia (Constance)
Warner, Sylvia Townsend 1893-1978 **CLC 7, 19; SSC 23**
  See also CA 61-64; 77-80; CANR 16, 60; DLB 34, 139; MTCW 1, 2
Warren, Mercy Otis 1728-1814 **NCLC 13**
  See also DLB 31, 200
Warren, Robert Penn 1905-1989 **CLC 1, 4, 6, 8, 10, 13, 18, 39, 53, 59; DA; DAB; DAC; DAM MST, NOV, POET; SSC 4; WLC**
  See also AITN 1; CA 13-16R; 129; CANR 10, 47; CDALB 1968-1988; DA3; DLB 2, 48, 152; DLBY 80, 89; INT CANR-10; MTCW 1, 2; SATA 46; SATA-Obit 63
Warshofsky, Isaac
  See Singer, Isaac Bashevis
Warton, Thomas 1728-1790 **LC 15; DAM POET**
  See also DLB 104, 109
Waruk, Kona
  See Harris, (Theodore) Wilson
Warung, Price 1855-1911   **TCLC 45**
Warwick, Jarvis
  See Garner, Hugh
Washington, Alex
  See Harris, Mark
Washington, Booker T(aliaferro) 1856-1915 **TCLC 10; BLC 3; DAM MULT**
  See also BW 1; CA 114; 125; DA3; SATA 28
Washington, George 1732-1799 **LC 25**
  See also DLB 31
Wassermann, (Karl) Jakob 1873-1934 **TCLC 6**
  See also CA 104; 163; DLB 66
Wasserstein, Wendy 1950- **CLC 32, 59, 90; DAM DRAM; DC 4**
  See also CA 121; 129; CABS 3; CANR 53, 75; DA3; INT 129; MTCW 2; SATA 94
Waterhouse, Keith (Spencer) 1929- **CLC 47**
  See also CA 5-8R; CANR 38, 67; DLB 13, 15; MTCW 1, 2
Waters, Frank (Joseph) 1902-1995 **CLC 88**
  See also CA 5-8R; 149; CAAS 13; CANR 3, 18, 63; DLB 212; DLBY 86
Waters, Roger 1944-   **CLC 35**
Watkins, Frances Ellen
  See Harper, Frances Ellen Watkins
Watkins, Gerrold
  See Malzberg, Barry N(athaniel)
Watkins, Gloria 1955(?)-
  See hooks, bell
  See also BW 2; CA 143; MTCW 2
Watkins, Paul 1964-   **CLC 55**
  See also CA 132; CANR 62
Watkins, Vernon Phillips 1906-1967 **CLC 43**
  See also CA 9-10; 25-28R; CAP 1; DLB 20
Watson, Irving S.
  See Mencken, H(enry) L(ouis)
Watson, John H.
  See Farmer, Philip Jose
Watson, Richard F.
  See Silverberg, Robert
Waugh, Auberon (Alexander) 1939- **CLC 7**
  See also CA 45-48; CANR 6, 22; DLB 14, 194
Waugh, Evelyn (Arthur St. John) 1903-1966 **CLC 1, 3, 8, 13, 19, 27, 44, 107; DA; DAB; DAC; DAM MST, NOV, POP; WLC**
  See also CA 85-88; 25-28R; CANR 22; CDBLB 1914-1945; DA3; DLB 15, 162, 195; MTCW 1, 2
Waugh, Harriet 1944-   **CLC 6**

See also BW 1; CA 115; 124; DLB 51
White, William Hale 1831-1913
See Rutherford, Mark
See also CA 121
Whitehead, Alfred North 1861-1947**TCLC 97**
See also CA 117; 165; DLB 100
Whitehead, E(dward) A(nthony) 1933-**CLC 5**
See also CA 65-68; CANR 58
Whitemore, Hugh (John) 1936-   **CLC 37**
See also CA 132; CANR 77; INT 132
Whitman, Sarah Helen (Power) 1803-1878
   NCLC 19
See also DLB 1
Whitman, Walt(er) 1819-1892**NCLC 4, 31, 81;**
   DA; DAB; DAC; DAM MST, POET; PC
   3; WLC
See also CDALB 1640-1865; DA3; DLB 3, 64;
   SATA 20
Whitney, Phyllis A(yame) 1903-   **CLC 42;**
   DAM POP
See also AITN 2; BEST 90:3; CA 1-4R; CANR
   3, 25, 38, 60; CLR 59; DA3; JRDA;
   MAICYA; MTCW 2; SATA 1, 30
Whittemore, (Edward) Reed (Jr.) 1919-**CLC 4**
See also CA 9-12R; CAAS 8; CANR 4; DLB 5
Whittier, John Greenleaf 1807-1892**NCLC 8,**
   59
See also DLB 1
Whittlebot, Hernia
See Coward, Noel (Peirce)
Wicker, Thomas Grey 1926-
See Wicker, Tom
See also CA 65-68; CANR 21, 46
Wicker, Tom   **CLC 7**
See also Wicker, Thomas Grey
Wideman, John Edgar 1941-**CLC 5, 34, 36, 67,**
   122; BLC 3; DAM MULT
See also BW 2, 3; CA 85-88; CANR 14, 42,
   67; DLB 33, 143; MTCW 2
Wiebe, Rudy (Henry) 1934-   **CLC 6, 11, 14;**
   DAC; DAM MST
See also CA 37-40R; CANR 42, 67; DLB 60
Wieland, Christoph Martin 1733-1813**N C L C**
   17
See also DLB 97
Wiene, Robert 1881-1938   **TCLC 56**
Wieners, John 1934-   **CLC 7**
See also CA 13-16R; DLB 16
Wiesel, Elie(zer) 1928- **CLC 3, 5, 11, 37; DA;**
   DAB; DAC; DAM MST, NOV; WLCS
See also AAYA 7; AITN 1; CA 5-8R; CAAS 4;
   CANR 8, 40, 65; CDALBS; DA3; DLB 83;
   DLBY 87; INT CANR-8; MTCW 1, 2; SATA
   56
Wiggins, Marianne 1947-   **CLC 57**
See also BEST 89:3; CA 130; CANR 60
Wight, James Alfred 1916-1995
See Herriot, James
See also CA 77-80; SATA 55; SATA-Brief 44
Wilbur, Richard (Purdy) 1921-**CLC 3, 6, 9, 14,**
   53, 110; DA; DAB; DAC; DAM MST,
   POET
See also CA 1-4R; CABS 2; CANR 2, 29, 76;
   CDALBS; DLB 5, 169; INT CANR-29;
   MTCW 1, 2; SATA 9, 108
Wild, Peter 1940-   **CLC 14**
See also CA 37-40R; DLB 5
Wilde, Oscar 1854(?)-1900**TCLC 1, 8, 23, 41;**
   DA; DAB; DAC; DAM DRAM, MST,
   NOV; SSC 11; WLC
See also CA 104; 119; CDBLB 1890-1914;
   DA3; DLB 10, 19, 34, 57, 141, 156, 190;
   SATA 24

Wilder, Billy   **CLC 20**
See also Wilder, Samuel
See also DLB 26
Wilder, Samuel 1906-
See Wilder, Billy
See also CA 89-92
Wilder, Thornton (Niven) 1897-1975**CLC 1, 5,**
   6, 10, 15, 35, 82; DA; DAB; DAC; DAM
   DRAM, MST, NOV; DC 1; WLC
See also AAYA 29; AITN 2; CA 13-16R; 61-
   64; CANR 40; CDALBS; DA3; DLB 4, 7, 9;
   DLBY 97; MTCW 1, 2
Wilding, Michael 1942-   **CLC 73**
See also CA 104; CANR 24, 49
Wiley, Richard 1944-   **CLC 44**
See also CA 121; 129; CANR 71
Wilhelm, Kate   **CLC 7**
See also Wilhelm, Katie Gertrude
See also AAYA 20; CAAS 5; DLB 8; INT
   CANR-17
Wilhelm, Katie Gertrude 1928-
See Wilhelm, Kate
See also CA 37-40R; CANR 17, 36, 60; MTCW
   1
Wilkins, Mary
See Freeman, Mary Eleanor Wilkins
Willard, Nancy 1936-   **CLC 7, 37**
See also CA 89-92; CANR 10, 39, 68; CLR 5;
   DLB 5, 52; MAICYA; MTCW 1; SATA 37,
   71; SATA-Brief 30
William of Ockham 1285-1347   **CMLC 32**
Williams, Ben Ames 1889-1953   **TCLC 89**
See also DLB 102
Williams, C(harles) K(enneth) 1936-**CLC 33,**
   56; DAM POET
See also CA 37-40R; CAAS 26; CANR 57; DLB
   5
Williams, Charles
See Collier, James L(incoln)
Williams, Charles (Walter Stansby) 1886-1945
   TCLC 1, 11
See also CA 104; 163; DLB 100, 153
Williams, (George) Emlyn 1905-1987**CLC 15;**
   DAM DRAM
See also CA 104; 123; CANR 36; DLB 10, 77;
   MTCW 1
Williams, Hank 1923-1953   **TCLC 81**
Williams, Hugo 1942-   **CLC 42**
See also CA 17-20R; CANR 45; DLB 40
Williams, J. Walker
See Wodehouse, P(elham) G(renville)
Williams, John A(lfred) 1925-**CLC 5, 13; BLC**
   3; DAM MULT
See also BW 2, 3; CA 53-56; CAAS 3; CANR
   6, 26, 51; DLB 2, 33; INT CANR-6
Williams, Jonathan (Chamberlain) 1929-
   CLC 13
See also CA 9-12R; CAAS 12; CANR 8; DLB
   5
Williams, Joy 1944-   **CLC 31**
See also CA 41-44R; CANR 22, 48
Williams, Norman 1952-   **CLC 39**
See also CA 118
Williams, Sherley Anne 1944-**CLC 89; BLC 3;**
   DAM MULT, POET
See also BW 2, 3; CA 73-76; CANR 25, 82;
   DLB 41; INT CANR-25; SATA 78
Williams, Shirley
See Williams, Sherley Anne
Williams, Tennessee 1911-1983**CLC 1, 2, 5, 7,**
   8, 11, 15, 19, 30, 39, 45, 71, 111; DA; DAB;
   DAC; DAM DRAM, MST; DC 4; WLC
See also AAYA 31; AITN 1, 2; CA 5-8R; 108;

CABS 3; CANR 31; CDALB 1941-1968;
   DA3; DLB 7; DLBD 4; DLBY 83; MTCW
   1, 2
Williams, Thomas (Alonzo) 1926-1990**CLC 14**
See also CA 1-4R; 132; CANR 2
Williams, William C.
See Williams, William Carlos
Williams, William Carlos 1883-1963**CLC 1, 2,**
   5, 9, 13, 22, 42, 67; DA; DAB; DAC; DAM
   MST, POET; PC 7; SSC 31
See also CA 89-92; CANR 34; CDALB 1917-
   1929; DA3; DLB 4, 16, 54, 86; MTCW 1, 2
Williamson, David (Keith) 1942-   **CLC 56**
See also CA 103; CANR 41
Williamson, Ellen Douglas 1905-1984
See Douglas, Ellen
See also CA 17-20R; 114; CANR 39
Williamson, Jack   **CLC 29**
See also Williamson, John Stewart
See also CAAS 8; DLB 8
Williamson, John Stewart 1908-
See Williamson, Jack
See also CA 17-20R; CANR 23, 70
Willie, Frederick
See Lovecraft, H(oward) P(hillips)
Willingham, Calder (Baynard, Jr.) 1922-1995
   CLC 5, 51
See also CA 5-8R; 147; CANR 3; DLB 2, 44;
   MTCW 1
Willis, Charles
See Clarke, Arthur C(harles)
Willis, Fingal O'Flahertie
See Wilde, Oscar
Willy
See Colette, (Sidonie-Gabrielle)
Willy, Colette
See Colette, (Sidonie-Gabrielle)
Wilson, A(ndrew) N(orman) 1950-   **CLC 33**
See also CA 112; 122; DLB 14, 155, 194;
   MTCW 2
Wilson, Angus (Frank Johnstone) 1913-1991
   CLC 2, 3, 5, 25, 34; SSC 21
See also CA 5-8R; 134; CANR 21; DLB 15,
   139, 155; MTCW 1, 2
Wilson, August 1945-   **CLC 39, 50, 63, 118;**
   BLC 3; DA; DAB; DAC; DAM DRAM,
   MST, MULT; DC 2; WLCS
See also AAYA 16; BW 2, 3; CA 115; 122;
   CANR 42, 54, 76; DA3; MTCW 1, 2
Wilson, Brian 1942-   **CLC 12**
Wilson, Colin 1931-   **CLC 3, 14**
See also CA 1-4R; CAAS 5; CANR 1, 22, 33,
   77; DLB 14, 194; MTCW 1
Wilson, Dirk
See Pohl, Frederik
Wilson, Edmund 1895-1972**CLC 1, 2, 3, 8, 24**
See also CA 1-4R; 37-40R; CANR 1, 46; DLB
   63; MTCW 1, 2
Wilson, Ethel Davis (Bryant) 1888(?)-1980
   CLC 13; DAC; DAM POET
See also CA 102; DLB 68; MTCW 1
Wilson, John 1785-1854   **NCLC 5**
Wilson, John (Anthony) Burgess 1917-1993
See Burgess, Anthony
See also CA 1-4R; 143; CANR 2, 46; DAC;
   DAM NOV; DA3; MTCW 1, 2
Wilson, Lanford 1937- **CLC 7, 14, 36; DAM**
   DRAM
See also CA 17-20R; CABS 3; CANR 45; DLB
   7
Wilson, Robert M. 1944-   **CLC 7, 9**
See also CA 49-52; CANR 2, 41; MTCW 1
Wilson, Robert McLiam 1964-   **CLC 59**

See also CA 132

Wilson, Sloan 1920-   **CLC 32**
See also CA 1-4R; CANR 1, 44

Wilson, Snoo 1948-   **CLC 33**
See also CA 69-72

Wilson, William S(mith) 1932-   **CLC 49**
See also CA 81-84

Wilson, (Thomas) Woodrow 1856-1924 **TCLC 79**
See also CA 166; DLB 47

Winchilsea, Anne (Kingsmill) Finch Counte 1661-1720
See Finch, Anne

Windham, Basil
See Wodehouse, P(elham) G(renville)

Wingrove, David (John) 1954-   **CLC 68**
See also CA 133

Winnemucca, Sarah 1844-1891   **NCLC 79**

Winstanley, Gerrard 1609-1676   **LC 52**

Wintergreen, Jane
See Duncan, Sara Jeannette

Winters, Janet Lewis   **CLC 41**
See Lewis, Janet
See also DLBY 87

Winters, (Arthur) Yvor 1900-1968 **CLC 4, 8, 32**
See also CA 11-12; 25-28R; CAP 1; DLB 48; MTCW 1

Winterson, Jeanette 1959- **CLC 64; DAM POP**
See also CA 136; CANR 58; DA3; DLB 207; MTCW 2

Winthrop, John 1588-1649   **LC 31**
See also DLB 24, 30

Wirth, Louis 1897-1952   **TCLC 92**

Wiseman, Frederick 1930-   **CLC 20**
See also CA 159

Wister, Owen 1860-1938   **TCLC 21**
See also CA 108; 162; DLB 9, 78, 186; SATA 62

Witkacy
See Witkiewicz, Stanislaw Ignacy

Witkiewicz, Stanislaw Ignacy 1885-1939 **TCLC 8**
See also CA 105; 162

Wittgenstein, Ludwig (Josef Johann) 1889-1951 **TCLC 59**
See also CA 113; 164; MTCW 2

Wittig, Monique 1935(?)-   **CLC 22**
See also CA 116; 135; DLB 83

Wittlin, Jozef 1896-1976   **CLC 25**
See also CA 49-52; 65-68; CANR 3

Wodehouse, P(elham) G(renville) 1881-1975 **CLC 1, 2, 5, 10, 22; DAB; DAC; DAM NOV; SSC 2**
See also AITN 2; CA 45-48; 57-60; CANR 3, 33; CDBLB 1914-1945; DA3; DLB 34, 162; MTCW 1, 2; SATA 22

Woiwode, L.
See Woiwode, Larry (Alfred)

Woiwode, Larry (Alfred) 1941-   **CLC 6, 10**
See also CA 73-76; CANR 16; DLB 6; INT CANR-16

Wojciechowska, Maia (Teresa) 1927- **CLC 26**
See also AAYA 8; CA 9-12R; CANR 4, 41; CLR 1; JRDA; MAICYA; SAAS 1; SATA 1, 28, 83; SATA-Essay 104

Wolf, Christa 1929-   **CLC 14, 29, 58**
See also CA 85-88; CANR 45; DLB 75; MTCW 1

Wolfe, Gene (Rodman) 1931- **CLC 25; DAM POP**
See also CA 57-60; CAAS 9; CANR 6, 32, 60; DLB 8; MTCW 2

Wolfe, George C. 1954-   **CLC 49; BLCS**
See also CA 149

Wolfe, Thomas (Clayton) 1900-1938 **TCLC 4, 13, 29, 61; DA; DAB; DAC; DAM MST, NOV; SSC 33; WLC**
See also CA 104; 132; CDALB 1929-1941; DA3; DLB 9, 102; DLBD 2, 16; DLBY 85, 97; MTCW 1, 2

Wolfe, Thomas Kennerly, Jr. 1930-
See Wolfe, Tom
See also CA 13-16R; CANR 9, 33, 70; DAM POP; DA3; DLB 185; INT CANR-9; MTCW 1, 2

Wolfe, Tom   **CLC 1, 2, 9, 15, 35, 51**
See also Wolfe, Thomas Kennerly, Jr.
See also AAYA 8; AITN 2; BEST 89:1; DLB 152

Wolff, Geoffrey (Ansell) 1937-   **CLC 41**
See also CA 29-32R; CANR 29, 43, 78

Wolff, Sonia
See Levitin, Sonia (Wolff)

Wolff, Tobias (Jonathan Ansell) 1945- **CLC 39, 64**
See also AAYA 16; BEST 90:2; CA 114; 117; CAAS 22; CANR 54, 76; DA3; DLB 130; INT 117; MTCW 2

Wolfram von Eschenbach c. 1170-c. 1220 **CMLC 5**
See also DLB 138

Wolitzer, Hilma 1930-   **CLC 17**
See also CA 65-68; CANR 18, 40; INT CANR-18; SATA 31

Wollstonecraft, Mary 1759-1797   **LC 5, 50**
See also CDBLB 1789-1832; DLB 39, 104, 158

Wonder, Stevie   **CLC 12**
See also Morris, Steveland Judkins

Wong, Jade Snow 1922-   **CLC 17**
See also CA 109

Woodberry, George Edward 1855-1930 **TCLC 73**
See also CA 165; DLB 71, 103

Woodcott, Keith
See Brunner, John (Kilian Houston)

Woodruff, Robert W.
See Mencken, H(enry) L(ouis)

Woolf, (Adeline) Virginia 1882-1941 **TCLC 1, 5, 20, 43, 56; DA; DAB; DAC; DAM MST, NOV; SSC 7; WLC**
See also Woolf, Virginia Adeline
See also CA 104; 130; CANR 64; CDBLB 1914-1945; DA3; DLB 36, 100, 162; DLBD 10; MTCW 1

Woolf, Virginia Adeline
See Woolf, (Adeline) Virginia
See also MTCW 2

Woollcott, Alexander (Humphreys) 1887-1943 **TCLC 5**
See also CA 105; 161; DLB 29

Woolrich, Cornell 1903-1968   **CLC 77**
See also Hopley-Woolrich, Cornell George

Wordsworth, Dorothy 1771-1855   **NCLC 25**
See also DLB 107

Wordsworth, William 1770-1850 **NCLC 12, 38; DA; DAB; DAC; DAM MST, POET; PC 4; WLC**
See also CDBLB 1789-1832; DA3; DLB 93, 107

Wouk, Herman 1915- **CLC 1, 9, 38; DAM NOV, POP**
See also CA 5-8R; CANR 6, 33, 67; CDALBS; DA3; DLBY 82; INT CANR-6; MTCW 1, 2

Wright, Charles (Penzel, Jr.) 1935- **CLC 6, 13, 28, 119**

See also CA 29-32R; CAAS 7; CANR 23, 36, 62; DLB 165; DLBY 82; MTCW 1, 2

Wright, Charles Stevenson 1932-   **CLC 49; BLC 3; DAM MULT, POET**
See also BW 1; CA 9-12R; CANR 26; DLB 33

Wright, Frances 1795-1852   **NCLC 74**
See also DLB 73

Wright, Frank Lloyd 1867-1959   **TCLC 95**
See also CA 174

Wright, Jack R.
See Harris, Mark

Wright, James (Arlington) 1927-1980 **CLC 3, 5, 10, 28; DAM POET**
See also AITN 2; CA 49-52; 97-100; CANR 4, 34, 64; CDALBS; DLB 5, 169; MTCW 1, 2

Wright, Judith (Arandell) 1915- **CLC 11, 53; PC 14**
See also CA 13-16R; CANR 31, 76; MTCW 1, 2; SATA 14

Wright, L(aurali) R. 1939-   **CLC 44**
See also CA 138

Wright, Richard (Nathaniel) 1908-1960 **CLC 1, 3, 4, 9, 14, 21, 48, 74; BLC 3; DA; DAB; DAC; DAM MST, MULT, NOV; SSC 2; WLC**
See also AAYA 5; BW 1; CA 108; CANR 64; CDALB 1929-1941; DA3; DLB 76, 102; DLBD 2; MTCW 1, 2

Wright, Richard B(ruce) 1937-   **CLC 6**
See also CA 85-88; DLB 53

Wright, Rick 1945-   **CLC 35**

Wright, Rowland
See Wells, Carolyn

Wright, Stephen 1946-   **CLC 33**

Wright, Willard Huntington 1888-1939
See Van Dine, S. S.
See also CA 115; DLBD 16

Wright, William 1930-   **CLC 44**
See also CA 53-56; CANR 7, 23

Wroth, LadyMary 1587-1653(?)   **LC 30**
See also DLB 121

Wu Ch'eng-en 1500(?)-1582(?)   **LC 7**

Wu Ching-tzu 1701-1754   **LC 2**

Wurlitzer, Rudolph 1938(?)-   **CLC 2, 4, 15**
See also CA 85-88; DLB 173

Wyatt, Thomas c. 1503-1542   **PC 27**
See also DLB 132

Wycherley, William 1641-1715 **LC 8, 21; DAM DRAM**
See also CDBLB 1660-1789; DLB 80

Wylie, Elinor (Morton Hoyt) 1885-1928 **TCLC 8; PC 23**
See also CA 105; 162; DLB 9, 45

Wylie, Philip (Gordon) 1902-1971   **CLC 43**
See also CA 21-22; 33-36R; CAP 2; DLB 9

Wyndham, John   **CLC 19**
See also Harris, John (Wyndham Parkes Lucas) Beynon

Wyss, Johann David Von 1743-1818 **NCLC 10**
See also JRDA; MAICYA; SATA 29; SATA-Brief 27

Xenophon c. 430B.C.-c. 354B.C.   **CMLC 17**
See also DLB 176

Yakumo Koizumi
See Hearn, (Patricio) Lafcadio (Tessima Carlos)

Yamamoto, Hisaye 1921- **SSC 34; DAM MULT**

Yanez, Jose Donoso
See Donoso (Yanez), Jose

Yanovsky, Basile S.
See Yanovsky, V(assily) S(emenovich)

Yanovsky, V(assily) S(emenovich) 1906-1989 **CLC 2, 18**
See also CA 97-100; 129

Author Index

Literary Criticism Series
Cumulative Topic Index

This index lists all topic entries in Gale's *Classical and Medieval Literature Criticism, Contemporary Literary Criticism, Literature Criticism from 1400 to 1800, Nineteenth-Century Literature Criticism,* and *Twentieth-Century Literary Criticism.*

Topic Index

Topic Index

Young Playwrights Festival

NCLC Cumulative Nationality Index

AMERICAN

Alcott, Amos Bronson **1**
Alcott, Louisa May **6, 58**
Alger, Horatio **8**
Allston, Washington **2**
Apess, William **73**
Audubon, John James **47**
Barlow, Joel **23**
Beecher, Catharine Esther **30**
Bellamy, Edward **4**
Bird, Robert Montgomery **1**
Brackenridge, Hugh Henry **7**
Brentano, Clemens (Maria) **1**
Brown, Charles Brockden **22, 74**
Brown, William Wells **2**
Brownson, Orestes **50**
Bryant, William Cullen **6, 46**
Calhoun, John Caldwell **15**
Channing, William Ellery **17**
Child, Lydia Maria **6, 73**
Chivers, Thomas Holley **49**
Cooke, John Esten **5**
Cooper, James Fenimore **1, 27, 54**
Crockett, David **8**
Dana, Richard Henry, Sr. **53**
Dickinson, Emily (Elizabeth) **21, 77**
Douglass, Frederick **7, 55**
Dunlap, William **2**
Dwight, Timothy **13**
Emerson, Mary Moody **66**
Emerson, Ralph Waldo **1, 38**
Field, Eugene **3**
Foster, Stephen Collins **26**
Frederic, Harold **10**
Freneau, Philip Morin **1**
Fuller, Margaret **5, 50**
Hale, Sarah Josepha **75**
Halleck, Fitz-Greene **47**

Hamilton, Alexander **49**
Hammon, Jupiter **5**
Harris, George Washington **23**
Hawthorne, Nathaniel **2, 10, 17, 23, 39, 79**
Holmes, Oliver Wendell **14, 81**
Irving, Washington **2, 19**
Jacobs, Harriet **67**
James, Henry, Sr. **53**
Jefferson, Thomas **11**
Kennedy, John Pendleton **2**
Lanier, Sidney **6**
Lazarus, Emma **8**
Lincoln, Abraham **18**
Longfellow, Henry Wadsworth **2, 45**
Lowell, James Russell **2**
Melville, Herman **3, 12, 29, 45, 49**
Mowatt, Anna Cora **74**
Murray, Judith Sargent **63**
Parkman, Francis **12**
Paulding, James Kirke **2**
Pinkney, Edward **31**
Poe, Edgar Allan **1, 16, 55, 78**
Rowson, Susanna Haswell **5, 69**
Sand, George **57**
Sedgwick, Catharine Maria **19**
Shaw, Henry Wheeler **15**
Sheridan, Richard Brinsley **5**
Signourney, Lydia Howard (Huntley) **21**
Simms, William Gilmore **3**
Smith, Joseph, Jr. **53**
Southworth, Emma Dorothy Eliza Nevitte **26**
Stowe, Harriet (Elizabeth) Beecher **3, 50**
Thoreau, Henry David **7, 21**
Timrod, Henry **25**
Trumbull, John **30**
Tyler, Royall **3**
Very, Jones **9**

Warner, Susan (Bogert) **31**
Warren, Mercy Otis **13**
Webster, Noah **30**
Whitman, Sarah Helen (Power) **19**
Whitman, Walt(er) **4, 31, 81**
Whittier, John Greenleaf **8**
Wilson, Harriet E. **78**
Winnemucca, Sarah **79**

ARGENTINIAN

Echeverria, (Jose) Esteban (Antonino) **18**
Hernandez, Jose **17**

AUSTRALIAN

Adams, Francis **33**
Clarke, Marcus (Andrew Hislop) **19**
Gordon, Adam Lindsay **21**
Kendall, Henry **12**

AUSTRIAN

Grillparzer, Franz **1**
Lenau, Nikolaus **16**
Nestroy, Johann **42**
Raimund, Ferdinand Jakob **69**
Sacher-Masoch, Leopold von **31**
Stifter, Adalbert **41**

CANADIAN

Crawford, Isabella Valancy **12**
Haliburton, Thomas Chandler **15**
Lampman, Archibald **25**
Moodie, Susanna (Strickland) **14**
Richardson, John **55**
Traill, Catharine Parr **31**

COLUMBIAN

Isaacs, Jorge Ricardo **70**

Nationality Index

NCLC-81 Title Index

ISBN 0-7876-3152-3

9 780787 631529

90000